THE WINES *of the* NORTHERN RHÔNE

THE WINES
of the
NORTHERN RHÔNE

John Livingstone-Learmonth

UNIVERSITY OF CALIFORNIA PRESS
Berkeley   Los Angeles   London

The publisher gratefully acknowledges the generous
contribution provided by Inter-Rhône for color photographs and maps in this book.

University of California Press, one of the most distinguished university presses in the United States, enriches lives around the world by
advancing scholarship in the humanities, social sciences, and natural
sciences. Its activities are supported by the UC Press Foundation and
by philanthropic contributions from individuals and institutions. For
more information, visit www.ucpress.edu.

University of California Press
Berkeley and Los Angeles, California
University of California Press, Ltd.
London, England
© 2005 by the Regents of the University of California

Library of Congress Cataloging-in-Publication Data

Livingstone-Learmonth, John.
    The wines of the Northern Rhône / John Livingstone-Learmonth :
with a foreword by Kermit Lynch.
        p.   cm.
    Includes index.
    ISBN 978-0-520-24433-7 (cloth : alk. paper)
    1. Wine and wine making—France—Côtes du Rhône (Region)
2. Wine and wine making—France—Côtes du Rhône (Region)—
Guidebooks.   I. Title.
TP553.L55   2005
641.2'20944—dc22   2006295705

10
10 9 8 7 6 5 4 3

Cover: Clusel-Roch Syrah vines on *Les Grandes Places*, Côte-Rôtie.
Photograph copyright Tim Johnston.

TO EDWARD AND MARINA
Never Stop Seeking the End of the Rainbow

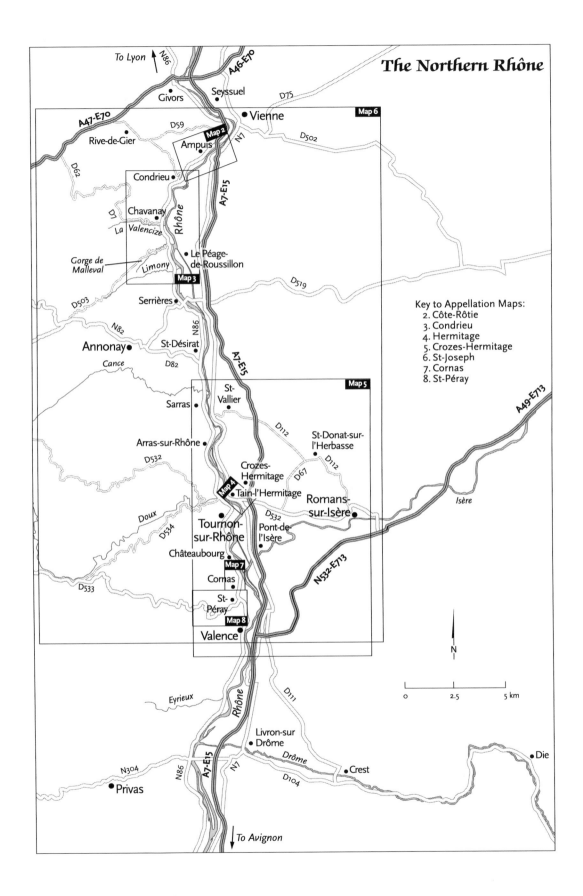

The Northern Rhône

To Lyon
N86
A46-E70
Givors
Seyssuel
D75
A47-E70
Vienne
Map 6
Rive-de-Gier
D59
Map 2
Ampuis
N7
D502
D62
Condrieu
Rhône
A7-E15
D1
Chavanay
La Valencize
Gorge de Malleval
Limony
Le Péage-de-Roussillon
Map 3
D503
Serrières
D519
N82
St-Désirat
N86
Annonay
D82
A7-E15
Cance
St-Vallier
Map 5
Sarras
D112
St-Donat-sur-l'Herbasse
A49-E713
Arras-sur-Rhône
D112
D532
Crozes-Hermitage
D67
Isère
Map 4
Tain-l'Hermitage
Romans-sur-Isère
Doux
D532
D534
Tournon-sur-Rhône
Pont-de-l'Isère
Châteaubourg
Map 7
N532-E713
D533
Cornas
St-Péray
Map 8
Valence

Key to Appellation Maps:
2. Côte-Rôtie
3. Condrieu
4. Hermitage
5. Crozes-Hermitage
6. St-Joseph
7. Cornas
8. St-Péray

Eyrieux
Rhône
D111
Livron-sur-Drôme
Drôme
Die
N304
A7-E15
N7
Crest
D104
Privas
N86

N

0   2.5   5 km

To Avignon

CONTENTS

ACKNOWLEDGMENTS

Excuses first: gasping into the final furlong of a long book is the moment when the previous two years seem to stretch out a lot further into the distance, and the hands that have helped, aided, and coaxed along the way do not necessarily spring straightaway to mind.

The cast of characters resides mostly in the Rhône Valley, as one would expect. The *vignerons* and *vigneronnes* have been uniformly helpful, constructive and above all, patient. Flurries of questions have been handsomely dealt with, even when they have involved plots of land to which several names are attached by local habit.

Of constant help and support, I would highlight the Clape family at Cornas. Auguste, Henriette, Pierre-Marie, and Geneviève have worked hard to specify the delineation of this wonderful vineyard, so that the book now contains a fair first attempt at a precise outline of all its *climats*. The same applies for the map of St-Péray, where the local tiger Stéphan Chaboud contributed fully as well. To the Clapes for their inspiration over the four decades, the simple *merci* is all that is needed.

At Hermitage, the Chave family—Gérard, Monique, and Jean-Louis—have also been constant supporters of the project, with ideas, comments, and suggestions. To Jean-Louis the thanks for the patient surveys of the vineyards—

as fascinating an exercise as one can undertake. Gérard and Monique's hospitality and generosity have also been supreme over the past decades.

Hospitality, good chat, and lovely wines have also been the order of the day chez Guigal, where the work rhythm still amazes me. While Mark Knopfler has gone from Swinging Sultans to Paraguayan postcards, Marcel and Bernadette have established an empire of success. With Philippe, droll as ever, now beside them, I say many thanks and Bravo!

Alain and Elisabeth Graillot's open door, open dining room policy has been another source of great entertainment and pleasure, and it is excellent to see how Maxime has truly caught the wine bug. A flourishing second generation must give profound satisfaction to Alain and Elisabeth.

At Condrieu the arrival of Christine Vernay and Paul Amsellem has considerably brightened matters social: excellent company, plenty of broad thinking, and deliciously refined wines. With father Georges the pillar of Condrieu, his mind so full of sharp memories and anecdotes, this is a friendship of which I am proud. Paul's piano playing these days lightens many an evening, even if the same cannot be said for his 1970s cult rock group in Paris.

At Côte-Rôtie, Gilbert Clusel and Brigitte Roch have always been very informative on the wider aspects of their work—vineyard practices, vineyard sites, and historical features. A sincere thanks to them.

The search at Côte-Rôtie for precise vineyard layout and characteristics was given great impetus by Gilles Barge, who has always offered large amounts of time with good humour and a changing set of hats. Thank you, Gilles.

Great has also been the generosity of the Jasmin family, led by Josette. The tradition of gourmet outings has continued after the sad passing of Robert, and it is good to see Patrick so well established now.

At Tain, many thanks must go to Michel Chapoutier and to his lieutenant Albéric Mazoyer; again, the many questions and verifications have all been dealt with in detail, with the extra sparks provided by Michel, as lively as ever, in the best family tradition. The work of the tasting team led by Yann Pinot and Olivier has also been much appreciated.

I would also thank the Jaboulet family, the three generations led by the twinkling-eyed Louis, who was surely a Musketeer in a former existence.

At Delas, Jacques Grange deserves fulsome thanks for his unerringly accurate answers and his ceding of time for the many enquiries put to him. His hard work and inspiration have yielded excellent results.

At St-Joseph the Coursodon family have been friends for four generations now, and I take my hat off to the late Gustave, who sadly passed away in July 2005, for all his hard work and impish humour over the years. It was an honour to be able to meet all four generations together at the same time in 2004.

Among the hostelries of the region, best wishes must go to Marc and Dominique Grillon at the Chaudron Restaurant in Tournon. Marc's sense of humour is probably worth a small admission fee, but the wine selection is worth much more, and this has to be the centre of operations for anyone seeking good atmosphere with local colour and an array of the finest wines of the northern Rhône. *Trois bises* for Marc and Dominique.

Salutations, too, to Gérald, Françoise, and the team at La Source high above Côte-Rôtie—another fine example of local food in an unpretentious and welcoming setting. Don't let the night lights go out, Gérald!

Fabien Louis in Tain with his wine bar, Les Terrasses du Rhône au Sommelier, has also been a good friend and supporter of the book, including with his camera lens. Brave enough to mount this business with its wine education side, I wish him all future prosperity.

Two of Tain's other characters have to be the doughty Françoise at the Terminus, where lunch is cooked *à l'ancienne*, hearty, filling, and convivial. Would the person who borrowed her asparagus saucepan please return it, by the way?

Georges Lelektsoglou, alias the Greek, has also been enterprising with his Compagnie de l'Hermitage wineshop on the Place du Taurobole. Thank you for hospitality, Georges.

More recently arrived at Tain, M. et Mme. Billon run the Deux Coteaux with great care and commitment. I wish them success. With its wonderful view of the river, the Deux Coteaux has been my *auberge* since 1973.

Plentiful thanks must go as well to the more hidden workers who help the northern Rhône; at the Northern Rhône Institute in Tournon, Jean Gabert and Isabelle Lallemand have been alert and supportive about tastings and information, and very many thanks are due to them for that. Down in Avignon, a big bouquet is due to Emmanuel Drion and Philippe Verdier, with thanks also to their ex-colleague the expressive Thiérry Mellenotte, and François Drouneau. The support of Inter-Rhône has been central to helping the book emerge in a well-produced, well-illustrated way.

The Brigadier, Tim Johnston, rode to the rescue when the photographs needed completion, and happily resumed some of his old friendships with the growers. Being away from the zinc of Juveniles was good for the Old Boy, *il faut dire. Un très grand merci*, Tom, as well as to Steph for all her delicious meals in Paris, with the backdrop of an Auguste Clape Cornas to keep us all on our toes.

In Britain, Jason Yapp and Tom Ashworth have taken up Robin and Judith's mantle at Yapp Brothers with great energy, and thanks go to them for the access to fine and rare bottles from the exceptional domaines that they represent. Robin and Judith's hospitality has been legendary over thirty years, and thoroughly appreciated, in Mere or at Twickenham.

From the independent trade here, I would also highlight the support and conviviality of the boys at O. W. Loeb, the finest set of sportsmen in the trade—thank you, Chris, Brough, Jason, and Francis. The Loeb Magic Bus around the vineyards has been an excellent idea.

I would also thank Marcel Orford-Williams of the Wine Society, for his generosity and humour, as well as Gary Boom of Bordeaux Index, a true Rhône man—if that is not a juxtaposition. Jeremy Hunt, Jonathan Kinns, and John Gauntley have also opened bottles and been ready to help—Jeremy one of the unsung pioneers of the Rhône since we first met in Aix-en-Provence in 1974.

Also appearing on the scene with a strong dedication to detail and authentic wines has come Nick Brookes of Vine Trail, with commemorative dinners likely to encompass hope, triumph, or disaster at Cheltenham as well as the latest fine Gonon wine. Nick's brother-in-law Dan Bosence should also be complimented for his steer on geological dates and correct usage from that arcane but fascinating world.

The maestro of wine writers, Gerald Asher, must step forward into the limelight for his role in connecting me with the University of California Press. With prose that floats across the page, his work in *Gourmet* magazine has always been an inspiration—meticulously researched and elegantly readable. Thank you *mille fois*, Gerald.

My warm thanks go, too, to Kermit Lynch for consenting to write a foreword. Kermit's outlook is one I have always respected, and his humour on paper is enviable. If I am capable of having given him his first hangover since 7 February 1989, on 8 November 2003, Chez Panisse, I must feel honoured! *Allez*, Kermit!

Growers and producers whom I would also single out for their help and illumination are Thiérry Allemand, Isabelle Baratin of Château-Grillet (*chapeau* for its defence, Isabelle), Bernard Burgaud, Julie Campos of the Cave de Tain, Maurice Courbis (he of the unsurpassable *mégot*) and sons Laurent and Dominique, Joël and Éric Durand, Bernard Faurie, Philippe Faury, Bernard and Fabrice Gripa, Laurent Habrard, Jean-Michel Gérin (and wit), Pierre and Jean Gonon, Jean-Louis Grippat, Jean Lionnet, Stéphane Ogier, André Perret, the incomparable Raymond Trollat, and Alain Voge.

I also wish good luck to Richard Dommerc in Ampuis with his new venture the Cercle des Vignerons, and to Jacky and Catherine Rivoire at Le Port in Ampuis, a marvellous *chambre d'hôte*. Nearby at Condrieu, Philippe Gérin and Olivier Leteinturier deserve success for their wine store La Bouteillerie, expanded and more complete than in its old premises—if they have time to work between coffee breaks with Paul Amsellem!

Here in England, I would also say thanks to Stephen Browett of Farr Vintners and Andrew Jefford for their comments and bottles, if not for their support of the Eagles of Crystal Palace. Come on, Fulham!

From the Old Gang, I say thanks for bottles and wisdom shared, and a big *Salut* to Steven Spurrier and Mark Williamson, and I am so glad that we could all get together in Lyon with the man who had the idea for the first book, Melvyn Master. Melvyn: *Oh mais!*

Away in California, my thanks to Blake Edgar, the wine series editor whose patience quota is to be admired, and who with his production team shares the commitment to quality that I was seeking all along. A book with maps, photos, and clean lines—I think I am going to swoon! Thank you, Scott Norton, and also Steven Baker in Oklahoma, for your application in the copy edit.

Last of all, the love and support of a good woman, my wife, Fiona, who has just about prevented my insanity during the writing of the book. It's only every 10 years, darling!

AUTHOR'S NOTE

WINES

With many tasting notes included, a system of stars has been raised to act as a quick reference on top of the words. The words are more important than the stars, naturally. The scale runs from zero to six stars.

> *Cherchez le vin!* Such wines are not usually present. If they are, the note is intended to shed light on a domaine's style.

★ Adequate, drinkable, not inspiring, and for a lesser category like *a vin de pays*, quite good.

★★ Sound wine, has some character; I would consider buying it if the price were right. Very good if a *vin de pays*.

★★★ Good wine, some outright interest; certainly a wine I would buy without hesitation. Would also have potential to develop.

★★★★ Very good wine. Should be balanced, should have correct tannins and ageing potential. From *appellations* like Crozes, St-Joseph, or St-Péray, a firm recommendation to buy.

★★★★★ Excellent wine, a wine of pedigree, balance, and interest. Should have harmony, excellent length, and plenty of potential. If from a senior *appellation* like Hermitage, Côte-Rôtie, Condrieu, or Cornas, a definite buy.

★★★★★★ Outstanding, the cat's whiskers. Grand Vin—sumptuous, majestic, seductive—a wine to make even the veteran drinker stop, pause, and reflect. Bank loans permissible to purchase these wines.

Tasting notes for the wines mentioned in the book are available on my website, www.drink rhone.com, and are fed in on a running basis for future vintages. This site also includes the southern Rhône wines and domaines, as well as interviews and growers' recipes.

Within the tasting notes, the years placed at the end of each note indicate the "drink by" date. The earlier date shows from when the wine should be blooming and starting to show its full array of flavours.

Lastly, the export percentages for each domaine indicate the proportion of the production that is exported and the three principal countries where it is sent.

DOMAINES

Turning to the domaines, there is a group whose wines reflect what I consider to be the beauty of the vineyard and the cellar in one bottle. I call this group the STGT—the Soil to Glass Transfer group. Their wines reflect a sense of place, or *terroir*, the expression of their sector. Simplicity of approach and purity of flavour are features, and the *vigneron*'s hand is present with the lightest of touches.

Some years the wines dance with the magical connection of place and climate—I think of the Cornas Clape 1995 as an example, a wine that was decried by the French press early on for being too tannic. Yet its tannins, heightened by the climate of that year, were true reflections of Cornas Syrah, their mineral or flinty energy always beckoning a long, interesting life ahead.

The wine had started to embrace its different elements by 2004, and its wonderfully clear-cut taste carries a souvenir of the Cornas wines I have drunk and loved for over thirty years—a true embodiment of the place and how its Syrah will never be as copious as that of Hermitage, nor as scented and mellow as that of Côte-Rôtie.

The above gives the clue to the domaine that I consider to be the president of the STGT Club—namely the domaine of Auguste and Pierre-Marie Clape at Cornas. For years, their wines have quietly brought forth the truth about their vineyard and have also carried the vintage style very faithfully. They are made with little fuss or intervention, and show character even in less notable vintages.

This is a numerically small group, one that has survived the onslaught of marketing campaigns, press hype, fashions in winemaking, and wine school orthodoxies. There are a few other domaines that occasionally turn out unfettered wines in the STGT vein, but without the consistency. A sincere wish, of course, is that this group should grow in the coming years.

STGT domaines also frequently turn out wines that do not achieve five- or six-star status—they do not aspire to place demands on the drinkers, or to parade a temple to their high opinion of themselves. Even disasters can occur, with wines askew and out of kilter. So much the better for such transparency.

By *appellation*, the domaines that I rate STGT Club members are

CONDRIEU: Delas Clos Boucher, F. Merlin, A. Perret Chanson and Chéry, C. Pichon, Domaine Georges Vernay Coteau de Vernon.

CORNAS: R. & F. Balthazar, A. Clape, R. Michel La Geynale.

CÔTE-RÔTIE: G. Barge, Clusel-Roch, B. Levet.

CROZES-HERMITAGE: R-J Dard et F. Ribo, O. Dumaine, L. Habrard inc. Hermitage *blanc*.

HERMITAGE: J-L Chave, Chapoutier L'Ermite *blanc*, Delas Les Bessards, B. Faurie, M. Sorrel Les Rocoules *blanc*.

ST-JOSEPH: É. Becheras, P. Faury, La Ferme des Sept Lunes, Domaine Florentin St-Joseph *blanc*, Domaine de Gouye, Domaine Marsanne, P. & J. Gonon, J-P Monier.

FOREWORD

Fe fi fo fum, I did not smell the blood of an Englishman, or even a Scot, when I began exploring the northern Rhône in the mid-1970s. I must have been too focused on what was in my glass, because John Livingstone-Learmonth was sniffing around there, too, thankfully, and I cannot imagine how we missed each other. Many think paradise is to be found on the bleached sand of a Tahitian bay, but some of us feel in our element in the damp underground, slurping and spitting around a barrel of fermented Syrah juice. John and I would have found a lot of wines and winemakers to talk about. When his 1978 book on Rhône wines came out, I loved the way he turned the spotlight on the personalities of the various winemakers. I'm not sure, but his may have been the first book to take such an approach. As Jonathan Nossiter, director of the film *Mondovino,* says, "Only in the wine world have I met so many people with temperaments so like the great actors. They are complex people who show strong emotions."

Back in the seventies, however, most growers had never experienced the visit of a wine importer or wine writer, much less a filmmaker. In fact, there were far fewer domaines to visit then than there are today, because the majority of growers sold to *négociants* or to their local *cave cooperative* instead of bottling their production. I wonder if the current economy combined with the French government's disdain for small farmers might return us to those days.

John Livingstone-Learmonth and I met much later, in the nineties, totally by chance, at the Rhône-friendly Willi's Wine Bar in Paris. With the immediate warmth and generosity of an old Châteauneuf-du-Pape, Mr. Livingstone-Learmonth allowed me to call him John, which left us considerably more time to talk wine. I observed firsthand that Rhône wines make John happy. Might that not interest the medical establishment as it searches for an alternative to all of today's antidepressants that seem to make people suicidal instead?

But let's get back to those early days, only 30 years ago, when some growers of Côte-Rôtie did not know (or care) that their grape variety, which some of them called the Serrine, was the same as the grape grown some 70 or so kilometers south at Hermitage, back before the Syrah vine invaded almost every wine country in the world, before the Rhône Rangers blew wide open the California wine scene. Oh yes, how things have changed. By 1978 I had grown friendly with Gérard Chave, from whom I was purchasing an excellent red and white Hermitage. After yet another glorious tasting through his various cuvées, I told him that I was heading north to taste in Burgundy, and invited him along. He told me that it was his first time tasting in Burgundy, a mere two-hour drive from his home in Mauves! Today that same Chave has traveled to more countries around the globe than I ever want to see, has an international reputation, and has seen older vintages of his wine sell at auction for hundreds if not thousands of dollars.

During the seventies, perhaps only Marcel Guigal in the region had a dream of such an evolution. Otherwise, everything seemed small, rustic, and quaint. The cellars for making wine were usually dug right under the family dwelling. Within the quiet, fragrant, mold-covered walls, the twentieth century seemed not to exist. I remember one funky cellar full of both barrels and rabbit hutches. Yet just minutes away was the crowded *route nationale*, the rapid A7 autoroute, the Paris-to-Marseille railway line, and the increasingly busy air traffic above. How could such cellars, which felt almost prehistoric, exist unspoiled in the midst of so much modern transit, so many vehicles carrying so many people? And then, of course, when one thinks of the objects of great beauty being produced there underground, the juxtaposition seems even more incongruous.

There have been changes, but as you will see in this book, the old world and old-fashioned wines still exist, alongside a lot of modernization. Economic success during the nineties has meant plenty of investments in technology and new oak barrels. For better or worse, seeing a new barrel in the old days was about as likely as seeing a spittoon. There were barrels, but not new barrels. And there was a lot of spitting going on, but directly onto the gravel and earthen cellar floors.

John's big new book seems appropriately weighty. But is there more than a consumer needs to know? You won't be able to answer that question for years, because that is how long you will be digging into it. In its depth and marvelous detail, illuminations abound and your enjoyment of wine (not only Rhône wine) will be enlarged. Each page both satisfies and increases our fascination with wine. Highlights include the finest descriptions you will find about how specific soils can influence the taste of wine. Why does the plot near the creek give a wine round and supple on the palate, while the wine from the parcel next to the oak at the top of the ravine packs a tannic wallop and takes years to show its stuff? The answer is most often found not in the cellar, but out at the vineyard site.

And, dutiful to my métier of wine importer, already I have jotted down a list of interesting northern Rhône cellars to check out—one, for example, that dates from the fifteenth century with the vats "hewn into the rock." Incredible!

KERMIT LYNCH
Berkeley, February 2005

INTRODUCTION

The northern Rhône faces the twenty-first century with its tail apparently up. For so long the poor cousin of the grandee regions of Bordeaux, Burgundy, and Champagne, it is now an established source of fine wine, its dominant Syrah and Viognier varieties much in demand around the world. Vineyards are being revived from the ghosts of the past on its hillsides, often after many decades of abandonment. Prices for the wines are high, the sturdy economics of the area visible through tidied-up towns, restored houses, and smart cellar complexes.

Since the early 1970s, the transformation has been enormous—those were days when so few people bottled their own domaine wine that a sleuthing visit to the Post Office was obligatory to find out who those growers might be. There was no official information office, there were no maps, no signposts. There wasn't much export, and no press coverage apart from lyrical accounts of the annual wine fair opened by His Honour the Mayor.

This was also the period when vineyard care stood on the cusp between the ancient time-intensive practices of a generation that had lived through the Second World War and all its deprivations, and the new "cure in a sachet" methods proposed by ministries and chemical companies alike. It was also an age of innocence compared to today. Growers were happy to spend half a day explaining and talking to a young investigator. The veterans and the wise were modest and viewed their work as nothing specially elevated, their reasoning entrenched in the context of the long-term.

The 1980s were the decade spent indoors. Scales had started to fall off eyes, and with the vineyard safely under control from magic potions, attention could be turned to whizzy new machinery that made vinification easier. *Easier*, note, not better. The years 1982–85 forced growers' hands, anyway. The first of the hot late summer seasons in 1982 led to tearaway fermentations and the immediate risk of volatile wines—previously a humming background factor, not a front-row one. Cooling equipment that was more than a hose pipe of lukewarm water was required. Then new vats, then new techniques, and so on.

Some of these changes were advances. Destemming when stalks were not fully ripened, even though that judgment was more empyrical then than it is today, became more common, and so greatly helped the quality of many an uninspired *vigneron*. The outright cooling of cellars and a severe clampdown on temperature extremes developed from the practice of cooling individual vats. Old casks lined thick with tartrates were thrown out by the sensible. Chestnut gave way to oak.

But somewhere a line had to be drawn, and life became a touch too easy for some growers, who allowed a restlessness of spirit to sink into the cosy comfort of a cruise control sofa. Consequently, there are now only a few sages still present in the northern Rhône, and while there never were many, their number diminishes rather than grows.

The crossroads facing this region now is how to produce good-quality wine that is authentic and acceptable to a better- and better-informed public, one that is also bombarded with choice. The wine's price must therefore be competitive, even though its origins—noble as they may be—denote difficulty and obstruction. Scrabbling around an incline of 60° to produce a bottle of wine that sells for under 20 dollars is not likely to keep body and soul together for long.

While hillsides in 2004–05 were dotted with yellow machines clearing, digging, and opening up old sites, down in the cellars on the plains there is a collective apprehension about how to sell the wine if two or three bountiful vintages in a row came along. Only a few are spared such thoughts—the best names in the best places, a roster that includes Hermitage, Côte-Rôtie, and Cornas, and that excludes St-Joseph, Crozes-Hermitage, St-Péray, and even Condrieu.

Communication is likely to be one of the elements that allows the region to at least confirm its new footing in the world of wine. The northern Rhône is so different from the southern Rhône that its closest proxy in many ways is Burgundy. Its *terroir* is superb, the geology of millions of years ago providing a fascinating complex underlay for most of the vineyards. Indeed, its geology is more diverse than that of Burgundy—the clash of the Massif Central with the Alps and the presence of its powerful river in past and present shape bringing a wonderful array of shifts and surprises within a single hillside.

The hillsides themselves are proper slopes, not gently rolling ones. Stiff ledges that require *bon oeil, bon pied, bon dos*—good eye, good foot, good back—form the men and women who work them, and sculpt their outlooks into a gritty realism. It's easier to sit on a tractor than spend the day puffing up and sliding down the schist.

There is a single variety, too. As Burgundy has the Pinot Noir at the northern limit of its ripening, so the northern Rhône has the Syrah at the northern limit of its ripening.

Like Burgundy, plots are tiny. Men return to Cornas from successful careers elsewhere when they can take over the family's sole hectare of vines. Holding an *are* or two—100 or 200 square metres—at Hermitage is announced with pride and jealously guarded. A grower like Jean-Paul Jamet at Côte-Rôtie can talk of his eight hectares being made up of 25 plots on 17 different *lieux-dits,* or sites.

There is therefore much to explore, a world of charting and logging the realities and characteristics of the land, land that has held vineyards since Roman times. Still, local usage and description vary from person to the next. A stream has two or three different names, a vineyard a couple of sobriquets; some cartographers' names for places are not even known to the people who live and work there.

But back to the land and the people who work it. That is where the truth lies. In the corner of every bottle of wine there resides a piece of the maker's soul. That is what this book seeks to unravel.

THE NORTHERN RHÔNE IN HISTORY

In ancient times the northern Rhône vineyards of Côte-Rôtie and Hermitage were inextricably linked with the fortunes of Lyon and Vienne. The former, founded in 43 BC as Lugdunum, is where the Rhône meets the Saône, two important rivers forming a natural junction for the transport of goods towards Paris, the Alps, or the Mediterranean. For the Romans, Lyon was the hub of their road network in Transalpine Gaul, and a two-metre-wide road lined by walls ran from Lyon to the Narbonne region, tracking along the Rhône's right bank. Traces of this road exist between Cornas and Guilherand today.

Lyon and Vienne were rival cities in Roman times, with much of the local wealth and power centred at first on Vienne. The latter, the locus of the Allobroges people, became a full Roman colony under Caligula before AD 41 and was a flourishing base for Roman soldiers. In those days, its local wine, the *vinum picatum*, gained the attention of venerable Roman writers like Pliny the Elder. *Picatum* means "pitch," the wine holding tarry flavours according to scribes of the time. It was said to have been taken to Rome and appreciated there; whether the appreciation was purely for flavour is not certain, since wines were also critiqued for their potential medicinal powers in Roman times.

One assumes that the grapes for the *picatum* were grown on the hillsides around Vienne: as a colony, Vienne's seven hills were a natural good omen, and the cone of the Rhône valley heading south meant there were sun-filled hillsides for growing plants and vines.

Vienne stands on the east bank of the Rhône, and south of the town the eastern valley broadens out. The west side, however, is marked by steep hillsides, the granite outriders of the Massif Central. These press up against the river and are where today's Côte-Rôtie is situated. Sufficient Roman relics, including amphorae, mosaics, and vessels, have been found in this area to make it certain that there was a thriving local wine culture. This lasted until the feared disciplinarian Emperor Probus halted Lyon's monopoly on the sale of wine in Gaul in AD 280. By this time, the Roman grip on the region was in decline, with invasions from the Rhine and interventions between local tribes.

The legacy of the Roman age stands tall in the inspiring architecture of some of Vienne's buildings and monuments. As a lover of fine food, wine, and horse racing, I salute the Pyramide each time I am in Vienne. This pale stone obelisk stands as the reminder of the finish of furious chariot races gone by, just beyond the front door of Fernand Point's establishment, still a restaurant today, that was itself a temple for gastronomes in the 1950s and 1960s.

The Temple of Augustus and Livia, similar in style to the Maison Carrée in Nîmes, and the amphitheatre, not excavated until 1930 and holding up to 13,000 spectators, are other reminders of this belle époque. Across the river at St-Romain-en-Gal has been excavated since the 1970s a Gallo-Roman site that is thought to have been the working area of a town, with villas, workshops, and thermal baths. The recently established museum there has a thorough display of artefacts of the time, including mosaics.

Further down the river, at a beguiling curl in its course south, is the hill of Hermitage, its town of Tain known in Roman times as Tegna. The "Hermitage" tag on Tain is of course a clever piece of marketing frippery that is only around one hundred years old. Tegna's wine was mentioned in writing by Pliny the Elder in his *Natural History* and by Martial in his *Epigrams*, and while there is no Pyramide or theatre, there is a Taurobolium as the town's most authentic Roman relic.

The Taurobolium is a small, butty statue or altar that was used in the worship ceremonies to the god Mithras and that dates from AD 180. Mithraism was an active cult thought to have involved at most 2 per cent of the population, a male-only gathering of soldiers and minor functionaries who were placed in a hierarchy of seven grades, each one under the protection of the planets—Raven representing Mercury,

Nymphus for Venus, and Soldier for Mars, for instance (*The Oxford Classical Dictionary*, 3rd ed., Oxford University Press, Oxford, 1996). Whether bulls were ritually sacrificed on this very altar is debatable, but local legend has it that way. The Taurobolium's recent spring clean and move to the fore of the *place* in Tain is saluted.

The role of wine after the Roman era becomes less easy to track, with chroniclers only occasionally mentioning land units as apt for vines. It is unlikely that there was much transport and drinking of these wines outside the immediate region in the intervening centuries, until the emergence of the Church as the next powerful force around the ninth century AD.

With ecclesiastical and trade uses, wine production is thought to have become more organised from those times, with monasteries and religious orders cultivating specific plots. Taxes were in part levied in wine, and it became more integrated into local economies. By the sixteenth century, for instance, ownership had widened to include the monarchy with its vineyard at the Clos de Tournon, while the College at Tournon was another, slightly later example of an establishment vineyard owner in the region.

The religious combats of the sixteenth century weakened the Church's hold on local wine production and ownership, and gradually an aristocratic class started to own the most prestigious sites. The most precise records of this relate to the Hermitage hill, where noble families, several of them from the Ardèche, across the river, were present well before the Revolution of 1789.

The most potent influence on the northern Rhône emerged towards the end of the seventeenth century and came in the shape of the port of Bordeaux. As winemaking there developed, growers started to ship casks overseas to a variety of destinations—all to the north. It became evident to some that the addition of a robust wine like Hermitage to the sometimes reedy, thin wines of the Gironde would benefit *tout le monde*, and gradually an active trade in wine travelling from east to west sprang up.

For years, the history of this trade has been largely recounted from the Bordelais perspective. Ideally, one assumes, it was thought better not to make too much noise about this practice, although some labels are thought to have borne the word "Hermitagé" at a time in the nineteenth century when that brought some kudos to the château. Records from a cellar book and local Rhône archives have now come to light that shed much more light on just how extensive and regular was this connection. Only annoying kerfuffles like war with England got in the way of it, indeed.

The northern Rhône beneficiary was Hermitage. That was the sun, the other vineyards its satellites. Even Côte-Rôtie, with its gentler, more perfumed wine, was a subsidiary in this business, its economic progress correspondingly weaker. Hermitage also had a confirmed following of its own in countries like Britain and Russia, whose aristocrats were importing casks by the late seventeenth century.

The cellar book of the Tain vineyard owner and merchant Balthazar Macker records the sale of wines not just from Hermitage and Côte-Rôtie, but from Cornas, St-Péray, Mauves, Croze, Gervans, and Mercurol as well—the latter trio all part of the Crozes-Hermitage *appellation*. Starting in 1760, this record sets down the date of harvests and their quantities. Even the years 1845 to 1880 are quantified, and with an average yield of under 20 hectolitres per hectare, show that for most people, vine growing was only one option in making ends meet. Hence the prevalence of polyculture in all the areas beyond Hermitage—there wasn't similar, regular demand for their wines, production was uncertain, and money was needed through the year. Raising animals and growing cereal or fruit allowed a family to at least subsist.

The Rhône was the natural conduit for the transport of the wine, with routes south and north established; the southern route involved the Mediterranean port of Sète and also the Canal du Languedoc on the way to Bordeaux, a 40-to-60-day journey. The northern route encompassed the Saône, a brief trip along the

Canal du Centre and then the Loire, and out into the Atlantic—another near-two-month operation. A different version of this route was to ship the wine to Condrieu, then cart it by mule across Mont Pilat to St-Rambert-sur-Loire, just northwest of St-Étienne. Water transport was preferred over land because the land taxes were usually double, as each province picked up a share on the way through.

The classic system of transport was a barge towed alongside the river, and it is worth reflecting on just how complicated and costly an operation this was: the goods had to be valuable to justify any long-distance transport. Before steam, the average journey time from Arles to Lyon was six weeks. A large barge required 48 horses, 12 men to direct them, seven mariners, and two lads. Many of the mariners were drawn from Condrieu and the village opposite, Roches-de-Condrieu.

In 1829 a veritable revolution occurred, with the first steam-powered vessel, *Le Pionnier*, taking just three and a half days to travel from Arles to Lyon. By 1855 a further important step forward came with the opening of the Lyon-Avignon-Marseille railway line. By 1856 the railway ran through Lyon, allowing goods to stay on the same train rather than be transshipped if travelling by water. It is said that the Ampuis growers of Côte-Rôtie, however, stuck to water during the nineteenth century—mindful of their pennies, no doubt (C. Montez, *Le Monde du Négoce du Vin*, Université de Lyon, 1993).

Outside Hermitage, a few specific vineyards gained a following, led by enterprising owners in the nineteenth century. The *vin de Mure* was a Crozes-Hermitage made by the counts of Mure, owners at Hermitage as well; the Mercurol *blanc* of Charles Tardy, also a Crozes-Hermitage, was subtitled *Coteau des Pends* on its label at least as early as 1875. The *vin de Mauves* was recognised in literature as well, although domaine names did not accompany it. As Crozes was close to Hermitage, and Mauves was more distant—across the river and a little way south in the Ardèche—there may have been a natural, logistical reason for this lack of precise identity.

Most wine remained sold in cask, with local cafés the principal outlets. Working towns like Valence, Le Puy, and St-Étienne were large buyers, with only a few wines sent up to Lyon. St-Étienne was home to coal miners, and there was steady trade with them, the wine shipped by train as a rule. For Cornas, Valence was a natural customer, the journey flat and simple for a horse and cart.

Bottling was patchy outside Hermitage, Château-Grillet, and Côte-Rôtie until after the Second World War, and the lesser *appellations* depended on nearby merchants, the *négoce* trade, to spread the word and sell further afield. A village like St-Péray was always home to a collection of *négociants* who would buy the wine young from small cultivators. Condrieu lacked enough wine after the two world wars to justify a local merchant, and growers sold the year's wine to local restaurants and private customers by Christmas. It would then be recognised as the chef Fernand Point Condrieu or Viognier ahead of the grower's name.

Wine fairs open to the public also started up. More ceremonial events like Paris, London, and Brussels exhibitions, where medals and diplomas were awarded, had been attended by Rhône growers from the mid-nineteenth century onwards. The Wine Tasting Fair of Tournon and Tain l'Hermitage started in 1928, a three-day December event that included fruits, honey, and the sale of vineyard products. One of the last named paraded under the ominous title of *produits insecticides arsenicaux*—no translation needed. Wine families showing at the 1930 edition included Coursodon and Gonon from Mauves, Michel from Cornas, and Delas and Paul Jaboulet Aîné. Antonin Coursodon and François Michel were both mayors of their villages, incidentally.

The first *appellations* in the Côtes du Rhône of 1940 were divided into three groups. There was a northern group, consisting of Côte-Rôtie, Château-Grillet, and Condrieu; a middle group, consisting of Cornas, St-Péray, Hermitage, and Crozes-Hermitage; and finally a southern Rhône group, made up of Tavel and

Châteauneuf-du-Pape. St-Joseph was added in 1956.

The dual attacks of phylloxera in the 1870s and two world wars that cost many young men their lives meant that the northern Rhône's hillside vineyards were progressively abandoned during the twentieth century. The only solid outpost was Hermitage, its area restricted by law as well as by geography. Côte-Rôtie, Cornas, and Condrieu all lived a precarious existence during the 1950s and 1960s, with the added pressure of land being sold to build houses, since little future could be seen in running a vineyard.

In the early 1970s unexpected sources lent a helping hand. First, Burgundy became very expensive, the growers pushing up prices after the mighty vintages of 1969 and 1971. But quality across Burgundy was bleakly uneven from one domaine to the next; the 1972s started life very high in acidity (only to blossom much later), and 1973, 1974, and 1975 were all pretty hopeless.

The other natural source for important red wines, Bordeaux, experienced the disastrous and much speculated vintage of 1972, when crop was bought by merchants before the wine had even been made. The subsequent washout brought down brokers in London and Bordeaux, and the modest 1973 vintage did little to haul the area out of its mess.

The Rhône was the next stop on the trail for susbstantial red wines, and the early 1970s saw demand rise across both the northern and southern Rhône, with even areas like Gigondas coming to the fore. From a modest base—less than Burgundy and four times less than Bordeaux—exports for the whole Rhône region jumped by over 52 per cent between 1971 and 1973. Britain's imports more than tripled, for instance; Germany's rose by more than 50 per cent. Switzerland, for long the main buyer of Rhône, also rose by 65 per cent.

Naturally, the rush petered out until resuming in 1979, fuelled by the wonderful 1978 vintage. It's worth noting that the United States never really participated in the Rhône's 1970s growth: the USA 1980 figure was 11 per cent below that of 1970, as against the four-times rise for Britain, two and a half times for Germany, and twelve times for the Netherlands, for instance.

With a commercial toehold of sorts established, and a cracking vintage to sell, the late 1970s heralded a more sustained advance by the region. Specialist importers like Robin Yapp in Britain and Kermit Lynch in the United States developed their businesses, and word started to filter out. The first edition of this book appeared in 1978 and was commented on by many importers as guiding them to domaines. More growers bottled some of their wine, and even domaine signposts and *appellation* pamphlets appeared—little details, but the area had been the Wild West before.

Two remaining influences awaited the area to secure its renown for our times. From the United States, Robert Parker started to applaud the wines of the Rhône in his *Wine Advocate* letter. One of the men he most applauded, calling him one of the best winemakers on the planet, was Marcel Guigal, whose family ran a mainly *négoce* business at Ampuis. Both Parker and Guigal are now known the world over, with Guigal the focus of attention on the northern Rhône wines. The Guigals—Marcel; his wife, Bernadette; and their son, Philippe—have become the largest vineyard owners at Côte-Rôtie, while one of Marcel Guigal's less known successes is the amount of white Rhône wine he sells. This represents over 20 per cent of all his wines, and the *appellation* of Condrieu has been a notable beneficiary, with Guigal buying small growers' wines for distribution under the house label.

Côte-Rôtie's advance since the 1980s can be traced back to Guigal and his international effect. Even in 1982, friends of Guigal could buy the select *La Mouline* and *La Landonne* wines by the case or more—the 1978s sold for under 90 francs a bottle at the time. Nowadays, single bottles of these wines have to be prised out, with other wines included in an order; prices are regularly £100 to £200 (US$175–US$350) a bottle according to the vintage. Meanwhile, small-domaine Côte-Rôties are distributed far and wide, even if their prices are nearer £20 (US$35) or more.

Spurred by the demand, Côte-Rôtie grew from 102 hectares in 1982 to 231 hectares in 2005. Not all the new plantings are on full, well-exposed slopes, but the figures show the scale of the advance. Condrieu is another *appellation* that has grown enormously—14 to 135 hectares between 1982 and 2005. Even more so there, quality has not followed hand in hand, but the changed economics have clearly been the prompt for such expansion.

With such a modest past, there never has been much grandeur about the Rhône. This is a region of hands-on workers, not delegators. The northern Rhône also breeds a singular tenacity of spirit and observation—people who are used to being on their own up a hillside, physically contending with the latest set of challenges posed by the nature around them. Their cellars add to this sense of intimacy and ruggedness; they have traditionally been small, cramped affairs, where the litres of wine taken from the hillside are personally handled.

The proximity of the *vigneron* to his or her land is a thread that I have witnessed weaken over the past thirty years. As the wines have sold better, the noble art of the *vigneron* has become more an act of commerce and less one of dedicated intuition that I encountered when I made my first visits in June 1973. This is no surprise, but it is cause for lament. The retirement of growers who know their soil and express no fashionable, explicitly articulated philosophy means that one more genuine link in the chain between human and planet has gone. The door opens to more victims of tech-nology and wine school blight than it does to children of an earlier, more natural, less impos-ing time.

The men of the soil who have most inspired this region in the past 40 years have been Auguste Clape, Gérard Chave, and Georges Vernay. They are all now mostly retired. Their understanding of the vineyards and their boun-teous common sense have meant that they never fell prey to whim. Nor did they stand rooted in an age gone by—they modified prac-tices through a mix of observation, good listen-ing, and accumulated experience. Never, though, did they chase extra yields for commercial rea-sons, never did their belief in the quality and integrity of their vineyards waver, even when housing developers were waving fat cheques at them and their few hillside colleagues. It is thanks to them that today the region's reputa-tion is so solid.

THE NORTHERN RHÔNE TOWARDS 2015

The balancing act for the northern Rhône in the coming decade will be to ensure that prices do not outstrip quality, and so alienate a well-dis-posed clientele. The slump in Burgundy of the 1970s, when quantity got away from quality, and even in parts of the Rhône in the early 1980s, remind one that overcharging remains the great faux pas.

Of course, the debate acquires a wilful turn when one takes into account the provenance of the wines—high slopes that often demand man-ual labour. If one respects the principles of cor-rect practice, and if methods even approach organic status, the costs escalate fast. In the words of Chapoutier's Albéric Mazoyer: "You should calculate 1,200 to 1,400 hours of work a year per hectare on a hillside vineyard. The product's price starts from there; if we can't sell it at that price, then we're in trouble, and of course it goes without saying that the wine must be good."

Planting a vineyard from scratch is no light-weight enterprise, and is another way of showing the stark realities surrounding the price of a hillside wine. Jean-Michel Gérin of Côte-Rôtie estimates the cost of clearing and planting one hectare to be Euros 70,000 (£46,000/ US$80,000). "And then it's four years before that hectare can make any Côte-Rôtie," he adds. As for the cost of buying a hectare of mature vineyard, that goes towards £150,000/ US$270,000.

Some *appellations* can handle the economic balancing act better than others. Hermitage is obviously the first contender. Production there rests in a tight circle of hands, and the wine's reputation is well established. Demand is steady, even though the white can be sadly difficult to sell, and prices are able to reflect the cost realities.

Even within Hermitage, though, a hierarchy of places clearly exists. The muscle and natural depth of the wine comes from the west end of the hill and tapers away the more one moves east. The rocky majesty of *Bessards* and the sun-filled sweep of *Méal* stand in contrast with the more regular slopes of *La Croix* or *Torras et les Garennes*, the last two set in with fruit trees and richer soil. Expect more *climat* identity to be associated by the keen drinkers of this great wine: a Hermitage from the western sites—meaning from the longest-established names like Chapoutier, Delas, and Chave—will always be the "truth" of the place. Were Paul Jaboulet Aîné to restrict their ambition to produce so much *La Chapelle* from sources all over the *appellation*, it too would be a faithful emblem of the heart of the hill.

Côte-Rôtie is more difficult. It's harder to identify a certainty of place among the growers there. There is a diversity of cuvées and styles and, tellingly, a diversity in the quality of the locations across the hills and the plateau. There are some very modernist wines as well, where technique dominates over *terroir*. Modernists would themselves argue that this makes the place a stimulating one, a sort of cultural cross-roads. The consumer would reply that it is hard to know what to expect from different sources,

> "To achieve *grand vin*, you mustn't count—neither the efforts nor the work. You must keep your attention on the end oeuvre, and be patient."
>
> Marcel Guigal, Côte-Rôtie

and also that the quality is not always a given, with the final sting that prices are high by any international standard.

The Côte-Rôtie growers have taken sensible steps to plant a cuttings vineyard derived from the best old Serine woodstock, and as a group, most are no longer spraying insecticides from the helicopter hired to cover the vineyards. But a blind tasting of a large number of domaine wines often brings mixed results, a frustrating number of the wines having been created more in the cellar than in the vineyard.

High-quality sources like Gilles Barge, Clusel-Roch, Jean-Michel Gérin, the Jamet brothers, Patrick Jasmin, René Rostaing, and of course the omnipotent Marcel Guigal all fly the flag high and handsome, even though styles like Gérin and Guigal come from the more oaked school. Other growers are good in some years, less certain in others. If you do not work the best locations, you are always chasing the game, but there is also work to be done here.

Hope at Côte-Rôtie stems from a number of committed young growers who are gradually finding the sort of quality that will ensure the *appellation*'s well-being in the future. What has to follow is the consistency from one year to the next, above all in the wine that most matters—the classic or regular cuvée. It will not be good enough to produce 3,000 bottles of a full-bodied special wine, and sell a diluted regular Côte-Rôtie beside it.

Names to watch here include the Bernard brothers, the Bonnefond brothers, Duclaux (elder brother David from 2004 is sharing the presidency of the Syndicat des Vignerons with Christophe Bonnefond), the questing, talented

Jean-Michel Stéphan, and Stéphane Ogier, especially if he can relax his enthusiasm for extraction and new oak.

Vineyard sites that will become better known in the future, beyond the "regulars" like *Brune, Blonde,* and *Landonne,* are *Les Grandes Places* and *Côte Rozier,* with potential to come, running north to south, from *Montmain, Les Rochains, Moutonnes, Chavaroche, Lancement, Mollard,* and *Maison Rouge.*

An *appellation* with a greater question mark surrounding it is St-Joseph. It is said that St-Joseph sells well in France but is hard to shift outside. A few of the leading domaines sell correctly abroad, but the wine lacks an easy drinking profile such as that possessed by Crozes-Hermitage. It has become too expensive compared to Crozes, but a good part is hillside wine, while a good amount of Crozes comes from an easy-to-cultivate plain.

The likelihood is therefore that there will be two categories of St-Joseph: higher-priced wines from meticulous, high-profile domaines, and a low-priced category with little fancy cask ageing that will be aimed at supermarkets. For any young grower who lacks profile and experience, this is not the time to be the owner of a large Crédit Agricole loan—and an ordinary vineyard at St-Joseph.

Jean-Louis Chave of Hermitage and St-Joseph sees potential buying activity concerning the hills of St-Joseph in the coming years. "The next ten years will see the Drôme *vignerons* investing in St-Joseph," he states, "because they have more money than the Ardechois; they also understand that *terroir* means a lot more in St-Joseph than somewhere like the plain of *Les Chassis* at Crozes-Hermitage. They will come over here for the hillside locations."

This is echoed by Jacques Grange of Delas: "In the next 10 years, people will want to go more deeply into things. Demand for the wine from the best vineyards will be strong. It will be those with the best exposures, and the truth of some of the *lieux-dits* will come through. That will mean sorting out an area like the Hermitage hill, and so the tail end of an *appellation*—the east end of the Hermitage hill, for instance—will not be a popular source."

At St-Joseph the leading vineyard names for the future will include *Les Oliviers, Dardouille, St-Joseph, Vigne de l'Hospice, Ste-Épine,* and *Les Royes.* Both *Oliviers* and *Royes* are good *climats* for white wine, as well. All these lie in the southern zone of the *appellation.*

St-Joseph's other potential development in the coming years is the number and the quality of organic or biodynamic domaines. Already there are two former Co-opérateurs who have set up biodynamically, both of them providing accomplished wines—the Ferme des Sept Lunes and Domaine Monier. There are also growers who fall into the STGT category, whose cuvées retain the simplicity of appeal of good country wines.

Crozes-Hermitage is also an *appellation* where there is enormous room for a greater hierarchy of sites to be recognised. The granite areas of the northern sector are an immediate starting point, but pricing power will always be constrained by the mass market appeal of the fleshy, fruit-forward wines of the low-cost plain in the south. Even though the north possesses greater pedigree, the dilemma for growers there is how far they can push *terroir* while charging a fair, higher price for their wine as compared with the southern area.

The sites exist already. At Gervans, there has always been the sunny hillside of *Les Picaudières,* worked with a sometimes forgetful but willing hand by Raymond Roure in the 1970s. This is now split between Paul Jaboulet Aîné and M. Roure's cousin Robert Rousset. The site's Syrah is rich and wholesome, a wine of true dimension. Along the patchwork vineyards of the northern Crozes area are other sites for both Syrah and Marsanne in waiting, ironically not singled out by their growers as small gems. Around the corner of the Hermitage hill, the white wine site of the *Coteau des Pends,* a south-facing ridge at Mercurol, is likely to become better recognised.

Condrieu's name has been revived since the 1970s as the Viognier has become known and accepted around the world, but it is still an *appellation* of varied quality. Viognier is capricious, and judging the correct moment to harvest it is a fine art: too late, and the wine becomes highly alcoholic, clumsy, and low in acidity; too early, and there is a fake freshness, indeed an austerity embedded in the wine.

The other *cause* surrounding Condrieu is cask use. The trend has become to use new oak with late-harvested crop to make sweet versions of the wine. The reality is that this "formula" suits anyone with young vines; the high levels of residual sugar can mask any lack of matter on the palate. There is a boudoir opulence to the wines, but also a lack of genuine length and grip.

With the polyculture mentality still ingrained in several domaines—fruit production leading the way—and with incomers from other trades, there is certainly some uneven vineyard care and winemaking at Condrieu. The rapid expansion of the vineyard—14 hectares in 1982, up to 135 hectares by 2005—has naturally led to inconsistencies in the wines. Nor are they straightforward to sell in today's competitive market. Expect consolidation of domaines at Condrieu—its price ensures that it's a struggle for smaller growers to place the wine once buyers become cautious or simply drink less.

For the following decade, the hope here must be that growers at Condrieu possess enough confidence to let the soil do the talking. More hands-off vinifications will allow the wine's innate complexity to be better expressed, with more nuance between one site and another. While the sanded granite known locally as *arzelle* remains a common theme, there are variations—harder rock, outcrops of clay and limestone, clear distinctions between exposure and altitude. The result should be crisper, less confected wines, providing growers hold their nerve and do not pander to the sweet 'n' easy market.

Cornas continues on its steady way. Plantation is occurring, with some of the very steep slopes levered back into production after lying overgrown since the wars of the twentieth century. There is a healthy mix of young and veteran, and tremendous respect for the patrimony

> "*Terroir* is above all what counts; after it, the vinification just gives a little helping hand."
>
> Georges Vernay, Condrieu

of the place. Cornas is a village with the utmost wine heritage, and that breeds natural hope for the future.

I would single out Cornas as the northern Rhône *appellation* where winemaking has most improved in the past 20 years. There is much greater clarity of fruit and flavour than in the past, and in a vintage like 2000, Cornas stands well alongside the top two of Hermitage and Côte-Rôtie, at clearly inferior prices.

Issues exist, though. Density of plantation is one. The latest plantings in the northern zone of the *appellation* are a lot less than the old, 10,000-plants-per-hectare rule of thumb. At around 4,000 to 5,000 per hectare, the production of each plant is therefore increased to make up the permitted output, and this is not beneficial for the quality of the juice. A trend that has continued for 30 years at Cornas is therefore that growth in production intensity has outstripped growth of the vineyard area.

Another feature of Cornas, a mathematical one, is that the vineyard has become much younger in the past few years. In the 1970s, plenty of the plots had been planted postphylloxera or between the wars; many of these have now disappeared, and with old sites re-exploited, one-third of the total vineyard by 2005 was under 15 years old.

Down the road, St-Péray, the last of the main northern Rhône *appellations,* has been struggling to rejuvenate itself since the mid-1990s. Initiatives have been taken to broaden the sales network, with the Co-opérative de Tain, Paul Jaboulet Aîné, Chapoutier, and other merchants—even Tardieu-Laurent—intervening. The pity is that this is good white wine *terroir,* with mixes of clay and granite suited to the Marsanne and the Roussanne, too. There is an agreeable nerve in the wines that imparts good definition to them, with the ability to age into greater variety and complexity of flavour and aroma.

And as for the tiniest name of all, Château-Grillet, well, welcome signs of life have emerged since the late 1990s. The wines possess greater core matter and show greater poise than they have done for some years. Despite rumours during the 1990s that the property might be sold, the Neyret-Gachet family has stayed the course, and one can salute its continued independence.

THE NORTHERN RHÔNE VINEYARDS

The prevailing influence on the northern Rhône is the granite rock of the Massif Central, a vast ridge whose eastern flank runs close to the appropriately rugged industrial towns of Roanne and St-Étienne in central France, and extends all the way west towards Cognac. In a vinous sense, the Massif influences both Beaujolais and the northern Rhône, stretching from north of Villefranche-sur-Saône down to south of Valence.

The Massif Central is extremely old, dating from Paleozoic times that started 545 million years ago. Attaching a precise date is very difficult, but some geologists veer towards the end of this Primary Era as it entered the next geological phase, called the Mesozoic—anything from 220 to 350 million years ago. The Massif Central's core granite has weathered and fissured over time, with the change of climate as France has moved north and moved between hot and cold seasons, encouraging the disintegration of rock towards soil over long periods of time.

Granite is composed of many minerals, some of which break down over time more easily than others. Mica, for instance, is more susceptible to chemical weathering than quartz, as are feldspars—compounds that contain potassium, sodium, and calcium. Across the northern Rhône lies this granite mass in its varying degrees of decomposition or rot (technical terms, thanks to the very instructive James E. Wilson, *Terroir*, Mitchell Beazley, London 1998).

On the west side of the Rhône from Côte-Rôtie, down to Cornas and St-Péray, the granite and its associated rocks have weathered at dif-

ferent speeds and under different local influences. Even within the *appellation* of Côte-Rôtie, there are two marked influences. The northern zone is schist—a layered, recrystallised rock with sometimes grey-blue tinges; it contains both white and black mica. Crisp and liable to splinter if firmly impacted, schist is the prevailing element running down to the *Côte Brune* at the centre of the *appellation*. The northern zone holds more slow-weathering iron oxide than the southern Côte-Rôtie areas, and this seems to bring more tension and nerve to the texture of the wines from here.

The southern zone of Côte-Rôtie, broadly starting at the *climat* called the *Côte Blonde*, is more decomposed, grainy, often sandy granite, with traces of the schist present but in much lesser quantity. Here there is gneiss, a rock of very similar composition to granite that weathers to form a light-coloured soil with quartz, weathered feldspars, and white mica present: hence the *blonde* description. The northern soil is darker to the eye, its air more rugged than the softer brown, seemingly warmer southern stone.

The south of Côte-Rôtie at Tupin and Semons marks the start of the development of the *arzelle* topsoil of Condrieu, the next *appellation* south, where the white vine Viognier is grown. The Viognier also performs better in the southern area of Côte-Rôtie than the northern.

As the Rhône runs down towards the Mediterranean, the theme of hillsides lining the west bank continues. One of the variables is how close or how far they stand from the river, with marked changes in shelter and wind flow. High plateau areas at spots like Chavanay, in the north of the St-Joseph *appellation*, are very windy, for instance, whereas some plots like *Montmain* at Côte-Rôtie and *Les Oliviers* at St-Joseph are veritable sun traps, their hill flanks running due west towards the Massif Central landmass.

The broad rule for hill vineyards applies here—namely, that the central slope is the best site, since it gathers the influence of the underlying rock, more naked higher up, with the effects of long-term erosion and mineral-rich soils. It also receives the full effects of the sun. Lower down the slopes come the richer soils, the aggregation of many years of downward drift with the intrinsically richer soil of the plain near the river. That is why one can see flourishing vegetables like cardoons, tomatoes, and beans growing in a little private garden at the foot of the prime granite hill of *Bessards* at Hermitage.

The Massif also provides the natural siting for many a good vineyard because of the mass of rivulets and streams running off it and feeding the Rhône. This creates the underwritten theme of all the west bank *appellations*. Cornas is three kilometres (just under two miles) north to south yet has 11 streams running through it. They are all full after heavy rain, with just one or two providing year-round moisture. Nevertheless, they create a series of brief valleys and inlets, every one of which has a southward-facing slope, ideal for cultivation.

While Côte-Rôtie is a pretty compact *appellation*, Condrieu is more straggling. It runs over sixteen kilometres or ten miles north to south, so there are changes in the nature of the granite along that course. Around the small town of Condrieu, there are a couple of important, broad and steep slopes called *Vernon* and *Chéry*. These are marked by the *arzelle* top soil, about 40 cm (centimetres; 16 inches) deep, constituted of decomposed rock, mica, and some schist, with at times some clay underneath, as can be found at Georges Vernay's *Vernon* plot. These two hills rise quite close above the Rhône.

Further south at Malleval—still part of the Condrieu *appellation*, although outside the first decree of 1940—the granite is harder and younger. There are spots that lose the sun early here, too, in this windy inlet set back from the Rhône. This area accords the wine more mineral features than does the central Condrieu zone, where the flavours are usually rich and opulent.

Across Condrieu, there are shifts in the degree of warmth in the wine—the divide running alone fruit-floral lines on the bouquets, and rich white fruit versus dried fruit–nut flavours

on the palate. Textures are warm and oily or can be more mineral, with a decisive edge, as well.

Like Côte-Rôtie, St-Joseph falls into a north-south divide. The northern area—Chavanay and Serrières, for instance—holds granite that is harder and younger than that of the southern area—villages like St-Jean-de-Muzols and Mauves. The midpoint comes on a line around Arras, where the climate becomes more markedly Mediterranean and signs of southern life like crickets and green oaks appear.

Syrah wines from the north of St-Joseph have a different feel and aspect than the southern Syrahs, as well. The former are often darker —black more than red in colour—and their flavours are marked by peppery black fruit. The southern areas provide more rounded wines, with often less strident tannins. The vineyards in the northern area were also incorporated later into the *appellation*, and their vines are generally younger than the southern spots, where specific sites have become more readily recognised over years of experience.

In the original southern area of St-Joseph, the granite changes between the hill behind the small town of Tournon and St-Jean-de-Muzols, the next *commune* north of the Doux River. The Tournon hill is firmer rock than the St-Jean slopes, while at the next main *commune* of Mauves, there are clear rock differences just one hundred metres apart. There, *Montagnon* has loess mixed in with its granite—what the locals can call *terres mortes* because it is so dusty, while *Paradis,* close by, is firm granite with alluvial stones.

Further south, the one main seam of limestone present at St-Joseph bears fruit in the notable white wines of the Domaine Courbis at Châteaubourg. For their Syrah the Courbis find that more spice and assertive tannins come from the limestone than from their more granite source at the next village of Glun.

The most important wine of the Ardèche, Cornas, comes from a compact zone of a little over one hundred hectares just two miles long. Here the soil differences include some limestone—the extension of the seam running up from St-Péray and on to Châteaubourg—in the northern and northeastern spots. Indeed, there was a conscious decision to exclude the overtly limestone parts of the northern site of *Les Arlettes* from the *appellation* zone, while including those that held more granite. The limestone of *Les Arlettes* produces Syrah Côtes du Rhône, the granite Cornas.

Cornas wines show quite marked tannins and a wild side, or what can be termed rusticity or rawness, when young—in contrast with the savoury richness of the best central slopes, where the decomposed granite or gneiss can be tinged with spots of clay lower down the slopes. The gneiss of the central strip around the famed *Reynards climat* is seemingly less evolved than the sandy granite of the southern sector of Cornas, where the fast-draining soil brings the *appellation*'s most supple wines.

The granite disperses more across the straggly *appellation* of St-Péray, the end of the line for the northern Rhône. With a lot of intruding housing these days, some plots have disappeared altogether, while others amount to one man's small folly. There is a limestone theme from the hill of Crussol that dominates the town, while away to the west the granite incidence revives in the few sites cultivated along the road towards Le Puy. The westerly granite is less weathered than the sanded granite that runs along the boundary with Cornas.

By now, the reader will have granite emerging from his or her temples, but help is at hand. Ah, the Alps, those young intruders! This is where the meeting point of Hermitage and Crozes-Hermitage, the two *appellations* on the east bank of the Rhône, brings forward the variety of rock and soil influences that is compelling when investigating the origins of any wine.

The clash between the shifts of the Alps, with their shedding of amounts of alluvial deposits—rolled glacier stones, dusty debris—and the sturdy righteousness of the Massif Central's granite is at the heart of these two wines. In the Mesozoic age, between 65 million and 245 million years ago, the Alps were still a sea, but what is today Italy was a landmass drifting towards northwest Europe. This is the period when limestones of the northern and southern Rhône were formed. By the Cenozoic age, up to 65 million years ago, the plate movement from Italy was halted by the Massif Central. Around 30 to 35 million years ago, in the Late Eocene to the Early Oligocene age, there sprang up the Alps, composed of great sedimentary deposits. Weathering and erosion followed, including the glacier formations starting from 1.64 million years ago.

Today's southern reaches near the Mediterranean were ocean, that legacy being the marine deposits found in the southern Rhône vineyards near the river. Subsequently in the Quaternary age, the time of the Great Ice Age, the definition of the rivers started to take more final shape in today's terms. The Ice Age was in fact several periods of alternating cold and warm periods, the latter bringing the conditions for man, plants, and animals to grow and develop. As the glaciers melted and rivers eroded the rock faces, great amounts of rock were removed and literally rolled down the young mountainsides, crumbling as they went. But as anyone who has played with stones on a beach knows, the ones there longest are the smoothest, the unceasing friction bringing them to a sleek, near-shiny patina.

That is why there are lots of rolled and rounded stones across the plain of *Les Chassis* at Crozes-Hermitage and also in places along the eastern stretches of the Hermitage *appellation*. These alluvial stones, or *galets*, are the residue of these former rivers eroding into the newly formed Alpine mountains. One of the main conduits was the Isère River. This flows from the direction of the Alps, through Grenoble, and into the Rhône immediately to the south of *Les Chassis*, the meeting of two important fluvial sources. (Reference and further reading recommended from the excellent *Atlas of French Wines and Vineyards,* Hachette 2000.)

The Rhône has another surprise in store, namely that it changed course at some undefined moment a very long time ago. Once upon a time it flowed behind the main hill of Hermitage, whose strong granite rock is linked to that of Tournon opposite across the river. It is rare for such firm granite to be found on this eastern side of the Rhône—witness to the fact that the river subsequently eked out a turn in its route around the west end of the hill, not the east.

With a set of fixed differentials stemming from the geology and siting of the vineyards, the hand of man is another important annual variable. Vineyards can be set on a prime south-facing site, but in clambering around these hillsides, it's clear that some *vignerons* take their responsibilities more seriously than others. Alongside serious dry stone retaining walls, their ledges containing two or three plants across, are shambolic, roughly cast slopes, the vines gripping the loose soil and prone to erosion at the onset of any serious rain. The steady, experienced men raise their eyes heavenwards at such "plantation fever" practices, which can be found at Condrieu as well as on the hill of Hermitage, if you please—not just at the lesser *appellations*.

This sense of Klondyke brings a foreboding of what may afflict the Rhône in the future—too much wine that is sloppily produced from the start to the end of the process. Can one expect a poorly created vineyard to sequel into a natural, handcrafted wine? I think not.

On the surface, vineyard practices have moved along in an encouraging way since the 1980s. Indeed, vineyards are less ignored than they were in those days when technology gripped most domaines. The constraint is the hillside setting, of course. The steeper the slope, the harder and riskier it is to work the soil, with erosion a constant threat. At Côte-Rôtie, Vincent Gasse calculates over 1,000 hours are required to work a hectare during the year, set alongside tasks like spraying weedkiller, which would take 10 hours.

So soil can be worked between rows of vines, and grasses planted as well. Vineyard practices like growing grass between the rows get a lot of attention and sound ecologically correct, but as Jean-Louis Chave points out, "it's often there to restrict abundance and excess growth that is coming from clones in the first place!"

"Green harvesting has become very mediatised," he continues. "The first step to low yields is how you prune—if you prune short and you still have a lot of grapes, it means something's wrong with the vine—be it the woodstock and/or the clone. The other point about green harvesting is that it's very difficult to find the right moment to do it, and you're going against the vintage."

Spraying is less frequent in a lot of cases: the young are generally geared to thoughtful rather than mass prevention. A dry, windy spring can mean a reduction in treatments, rather than doing the same as usual. The Bordeaux copper mixture is applied, but the worst excesses of pesticides and insecticides have been banned at compact *appellations* like Côte-Rôtie, where some of them have been applied by helicopter in the past, involving groups of *vignerons* at a time.

Canopy management has also become much more widespread, although overproduction has forced growers' hands as well. Such is the bounty from many clonal varieties that an unbridled yield would come in with at least 60 to 70 hl/ha (hectolitres per hectare) instead of the 40 hl/ha or so most commonly permitted. Green harvesting and bunch dropping in August are now common practices, but much of this matter could be solved through more responsible pruning in the first place.

The issue of clones reappears when one also considers the creeping trend of lower-density plantation on many vineyards. The old hillside custom was for 8,000 to 10,000 plants per hectare. Now many growers seek at all costs to limit the labour input on their vineyards, and prefer wire rather than wooden stake training and a density of maybe half. Some mechanical tilling is possible if the hill can be converted from ledges into a slope, and each plant has to carry more bunches to make up the maximum yield. A gain in margins, providing the wine is "good enough," is then assured.

THE NORTHERN RHÔNE VINES

SYRAH

The Syrah lies at the heart of the northern Rhône, a variety that finds a natural habitat in the temperate climes of this region. As with Pinot Noir in Burgundy, it grows here towards the northern extremes of its ripening, and it is a misconception to consider this as a hot-weather variety. Finesse, integration of flavours, and complexity are achievable if the wine is not subjected to excess heat day and night.

The Syrah's origins were the subject of lively and meandering debate in the 1970s, when the first edition of this book was written. Etymology brought forth reasoning that sources for the vine could range from Syracuse to Shiraz, the capital of Fars, in Iran.

The Iranian theory needed the answer of how the vine reached the Rhône Valley, and this came in the form of the Greeks of Phocaea, the founders of Marseille. Phocaea was on the west coast of Asia Minor, about 50 kilometres south of the Aegean island of Lesbos. According to Herodotus, the Phocaeans were the first Greeks to undertake distant sea journeys, and around 600 BC opened up the coasts of the Adriatic, France, and Spain: Marseille had been founded by them in 600 BC under the name of Massalia. Their arrival with vine cuttings was thought to have been after the year 546 BC, by when the Phocaeans were under Persian rule.

Massaliote coins, dating from 500–450 BC, have been found along the Rhône as far as the

From the second edition of *The Wines of the Rhône*, 1982

The belief is that the Syrah came originally from around Shiraz, which is today the capital of the state of Fars in Iran. About 850 kilometres (530 miles) from Tehran, and 50 kilometres (30 miles) from the ruins of Persepolis, Shiraz was, until recent Islamic developments, the wine-growing centre of Iran. At Persepolis, founded circa 518 BC, stone tablets have been found bearing inscriptions that mention wine and vintners. Such evidence would seem to suggest that the wine of Shiraz was already quite famous around that time. (William Culican, *The Medes and Persians*, Thames & Hudson, London 1965.). Furthermore, the likeness between the words "Syrah" and "Shiraz" is evident, and M. Paul Gauthier of Hermitage, a leading *négociant*, once found in a book published in 1860 six different spellings of the word "Syrah": Syra, Sirrah, Syras, Chira, Sirac, and Syrac. Their common denominator would appear to be the word "Shiraz."

Alps, near the river's source in Switzerland. At that time wine was a fairly major element of trade, and old Greek amphorae have been found in both Marseille and Tain-l'Hermitage, about 240 kilometres (150 miles) further north.

Of course, the scientific work of Carole Meredith, former professor of viticulture and enology at the University of California, Davis, appears to have blown away such fanciful notions. Research she presented at the American Society of Oenology and Viticulture in 2001 indicated that the Syrah DNA pointed to a northern Rhône origin in less purely ancient times.

In conjunction with the Montpellier Agronomic and Wine School, Dr. Meredith pointed to the likely parents of the Syrah being the Dureza, which originated from the Ardèche region on the west bank of the Rhône, and the Mondeuse from Savoie, away to the east towards the Alps. The Dureza N is the father, the Mondeuse *blanche* B the mother.

The Dureza is said to come from the north of the Ardèche, perhaps around Annonay; it is also called Petit Duret in parts of the Isère and the Drôme on the east side of the Rhône. It was much planted around St. Vallier, just north of Hermitage, in the vineyard reconstruction after phylloxera (P. Viala and V. Vermorel, Ampelographie of 1910, ed. Jeanne Laffitte).

Nevertheless, a question remains about the identity of the vine that made the *vinum picatum,* or tarry pitch wine of Vienne of Roman times, and potentially, about how the vine arrived in this part of France.

The Syrah performs well in the granite outcrops of the northern Rhône and is a hardy vine. Since the 1970s and the introduction of the first clones, its nature has changed. The *héritage,* or legacy, Syrah of olden times was known at Côte-Rôtie as the Sérine, at Hermitage the Petite Syrah. This of course is the vine of reference, the true local resident, but it now represents barely 10 per cent of all northern Rhône Syrah. In decades gone by, there was a diversity of old vines from this source in the vineyards, with minor nuances possible derived from each specific plant from which the cutting had been taken.

The traditional Syrah's leaf is well indented, the bunches are small, their berries small and egg-shaped. Its main blight is fruit failure or *coulure* after flowering, and growers in the old days would prune the plants long to try to ensure greater production. Oïdium and mildew are the most frequent problems requiring treatment.

Since the 1970s the advance of the clones has changed the nature of the plants and the wines of this region. The first steps came around 1970–71 with the development of the Grosse Syrah "of Gervans," named after the village within the Crozes-Hermitage *appellation.* As a productive source, this was taken forward.

With a thick, heavy leaf, large berries that had shoulder pads, more juice, and higher yields, the Grosse Syrah of Gervans set the standard for clones to come. Looking back, one can

In the early 2000s, dark skies have gathered over the Syrah in the Rhône Valley. A degradation of the vine is occurring, a disease stemming from the southern Rhône or Languedoc—no one is really sure. This *dépérissement*—again, there is no formal name—is thought to have started around 1996–97 in the dry areas of the south.

The symptoms are the vine leaves turning red and the vine wood failing to mature. Within two or three years, the plant is dead.

At Côte-Rôtie, the first symptoms appeared in 2001, and the problem has grown each year since then. "It attacks vines around ten to twenty years old," says Gilbert Clusel. "At times, it can mean taking out half a plot at a time."

Jean-Louis Chave at Hermitage observes that it is the clone vines that have been hit. "Studies are being conducted to see if some clones are more prone than others, but it hasn't hit the old vines. Nor is there a confirmed link with the rootstock, the general 3309."

One of the problems is that growers do not know how the bug is transmitted or whether it spreads precisely from one plant to its neighbour. Because of the age of vine being attacked, the vineyards of St-Joseph and Crozes-Hermitage, heavily expanded in the past twenty years, are most at threat within the northern Rhône.

see that the popular 1970s clones of 99 and 100 dented quality: less sugar in the grapes, less colour and concentration, less spice and nuance of flavour—less *terroir.*

The clones developed in the 1980s were not much better. One was the 174, whose bunches were very tight, with rot a consequence. Its wines carried a homogenous black-currant aroma.

In the 1990s the fashionable clones were 747, 525, and 300; it is too early to say just how they will pan out, but the feature of large berries and less natural concentration within the berries continues. This means that ripening has to proceed to extremes if the grower wants to achieve "full ripeness" on these expansive grapes. The cycle that leads to homogeneity in the wines is once more set in motion.

Besides the classic problems of oïdium and mildew, the modern Syrah faces occasional intrusions from pests like the red spider and l'esca, a fungus that attacks and eats the vine wood. Work that must be done regularly, however, is the tying and attachment of the Syrah, for it is fragile and can break in any strong wind. For pruning, the Guyot system as traditionally found at Côte-Rôtie is mostly used on the hillsides, although more Gobelet, with three spurs to the vine, is being seen because of lower labour intensity. When Guyot is practised, the vines are led in pairs, each vine having its stake crossed to form an X with its neighbour.

The Syrah is not water dependent as a rule; it can keep going in dry weather, but clearly benefits from worked soil to allow water access and from rain at suitable moments. Excavated vineyards show its roots can penetrate several metres down, the more so when the granite is decomposed as it is at the southern end of Côte-Rôtie or in western parts of Hermitage. In these instances, a good root spread that can access different soil patches is thought to bring a more varied bounty of minerals to the vine.

Granite is of course the constant across the northern Rhône, but it is not homogenous. There are different stages of decomposition apparent—the north and south of Côte-Rôtie with schist and sanded granite, for instance. Jean-Louis Chave accentuates the role of differing acidity in the granite, as well. "My St-Joseph vineyards include two very separate acidities: at Lemps, on the old family vineyard, the soil is neutral, like Bessards at Hermitage, with a pH of around 7. But at Mauves, the soil is much more acid, the pH nearer 5."

"For me, the extra acidity supplies wines that lack roundness, power, fruit, richness, and voluptuousness," he continues. "Of course, they have to be blended. It's the extremes that the Syrah needs to avoid, the same as if it were grown in largely limestone soil. There are veins of limestone at Bessards, and they serve as a helpful moderation to the granite." Similarly, the best climat at Cornas, Reynards, has its granite interspersed with pockets of clay and limestone.

The granite wines of northern Crozes-Hermitage also lend insight. One of the best sites, Les Picaudières, faces due south; it contains old vines that grow on steep slopes of gore or rotted, oxidised granite. Here the wines can have an animal side in the hottest years, but their richness levels are such as to make the wine warm and wholehearted. From the breezy areas of nearby granite slopes, the Syrahs can show taut, tense tannins when young—wines that are not so rich and full blooded and that require cellar ageing to settle and integrate into a measured harmony. Here the combination of granite that has potentially varying levels of acidity and different exposure means the wines emerge in different ways.

Another of the immediate contrasts between sites in the northern Rhône also comes at Crozes-Hermitage. The sand-clay of the southern plain, the old fruit-growing region, brings gummy, black-fruited wines of immediate appeal. Tannins are discreet.

Meanwhile, the northern zone, where the hills contain granite and are exposed to fresher weather and cooler nights, produces wines that are less intensely coloured—red rather than black—and much more sinewed. Their fruit is stone and pebbly in texture, their tannins more upright and raw at the outset. Pepper tones are drier and more evident than those of the more gourmand southern plain wines.

One of the only domaines in the area with a high incidence of limestone is the Domaine Courbis at Châteaubourg. Its St-Joseph Syrah has its own set of characteristics, according to Laurent Courbis: "We find that more spiced wine with greater acidity comes off the limestone, as well as a more assertive, tannic side than the Syrah off the granite," states Laurent. "The aromas from the limestone are also more garrigue, or herbal Mediterranean; and the colour tends to be more purple from the granite, more dark cherry from the limestone."

One other soil that is not considered apt for the Syrah is loess, the cool, compact dirt residues of sand and silt that can be found in pockets of the northern Rhône, notably on *L'Hermite* at Hermitage. There the white-grape Marsanne is favoured.

The Syrah has become dangerously fashionable around the world, the hot grape in town. Its fleshy fruit and alleged regular spiciness make it easy to like, even if drinkers are not really receiving the vine's wine in anything like a pure form. Supermarkets in California can carry 30 Syrahs from US$5 to US$30 these days, a result of the vine's plantation not often being targeted to the most propitious sites.

The spread of Syrah in California has taken the vine from 2,206 acres (893 hectares) before 1995 to 10,800 acres (4,372 ha) in 2001 and 16,100 acres (6,519 ha) in 2003—an ever accelerating trend. Beside Cabernet Sauvignon's 74,800 acres (30,280 ha), it is still small, but the rush to plant will continue. The most planted regions are San Luis Obispo, south of San Francisco, and Sonoma to the north, as well as San Joaquin, the Central Valley area of fertile land and ordinary quality for wine grapes.

With the Rhône movement now in its third decade in California, and the best Australian estate growers becoming choosier about precise vineyard sites and even *terroir,* more care is being taken about Syrah's planting in these important areas. These are the two leading bases for Syrah or Shiraz outside the Rhône, and it is vital that they show the world what the vine can really do: I'm not thinking commercial, oppressive fruit here, I'm talking quality through finesse, balance, and nuance.

Cooler sites are now being planted, as growers seek not so much to replicate a Rhône style as to fuse the variety with a suitable *terroir* that does it natural justice. In the United States, Washington State, as epitomised by the early leading light of Red Willow, is becoming more sought for Syrah, with valleys like Walla Walla, near the Oregon boundary, attracting talented growers like Christophe Baron. The weather there is pretty tough and very windy, and the mix of alluvial stones and silt is a geological plus, bringing a good marriage between vine and place.

Bruce Neyers is another of the second-wave growers, having started with Syrah in 1994. Neyers Estate makes a leading example of California Syrah, one based on finesse rather than raw power. He regards his best Syrah to be that from Los Carneros, south of the Sonoma Valley, where it receives cool air from the San Pablo Bay.

North and south of the Russian River along the Sonoma Coast is another growing region for California Syrah, where sea breezes play a role. Other twists to the plot come via elevation, with Sierra foothills vineyards at around 2,800 feet (846 metres) in eastern California near Nevada being chosen for Syrah from El Dorado County: again, extra freshness and cool nights can bring more measured ripening.

The Neyers winemaker Aaron Jordan worked for two years with Jean-Luc Colombo at Cornas and is one of the new guard who seek authenticity of place in their wines. To this end, the fermenting vats are open topped, and whole-bunch fermentation, with foot punching, is practised. "This helps to achieve spice and meatiness in the wine," comments Mr. Neyers.

Other California wineries producing restrained, interesting Syrah include Limerick Lane, Havens, and the classics of Edmunds St John, John Alban, Qupé, Ojai, Jim Clendenen, and Randall Grahm at Bonny Doon, although the last named often pursues a blended, true southern path, with other varieties included.

In Australia the Eden Valley—home to the peerless, old-vineyard wines of Stephen and Prue Henschke, Hill of Grace and Mount Edelstone—has for long flown the flag for complex, long-lived Syrahs. Their sense of place has always been more marked than the mighty Grange of Penfolds, the latter always cut with some Cabernet Sauvignon and drawn from crop across Barossa, Clare, and McLaren Vale sources.

Now areas like Western Australia's Margaret River, with its coastal climate; Frankland River (also in western Australia); and the Grampians and Pyrenees, two areas in central western Victoria with their own cooler climate, have sprung to the fore as homes for measured Shiraz with varied flavours. In Victoria another region to provide finely styled Shiraz is Great Western, with wineries like Seppelt St. Peters consciously working towards local imprint in their wines—which means nothing exaggerated or overblown. As a trend, the blockbuster-only group of wines is gradually being accompanied by wines with greater reserve and subtlety.

As well as climate refinements, soil research is stepping up, just as it is in the United States. Michel Chapoutier's joint venture in Mount Benson has targeted vineyards low in clay, with the objective of securing increased elegance in the Syrah. Likewise, the decision to dry farm and not irrigate the red clay at Chapoutier's Heathcote vineyard, where the plantation is formed half from Rhône Syrah, half from Australian Shiraz.

Syrah plantation is growing apace in all other mainstream wine countries—notably Chile and South Africa. There is every reason to believe that Chile has the climate and soil structures to provide first-class fruit, with the elegance that should be present in the best Syrah wines, and I back this country to become a leading high-quality Syrah source in the next 20 years. In Europe, there are already sound Italian and Swiss Syrahs, as well, and providing that growers are dedicated to finding compatible environs for the vine, there is no doubt that it can flourish and upstage Cabernet through its more varied palette of flavours.

VIOGNIER

The northern Rhône's leading white variety is Viognier, the vine that came back from the dead in the early 1970s. In 1971 precisely 13.7 hectares (34 acres) were growing in the northern Rhône at Condrieu and Château-Grillet. That was it—all around the world. The vine's natural caprice and the laborious hillside work required to cultivate it had reduced the number of supporters to a handful.

"A wine should be capable of ageing, and for that it must have balance and structure—those are the words that count."

Gérard Chave, Hermitage

The variety's rise to prominence started in 1981, when Californian enthusiasts Richard Minor (a dentist by profession) of Ritchie Creek and Bill Smith at La Jota both planted some Viognier on hillsides running off the Napa Valley. In Australia a Viognier clone imported from Montpellier was propagated into the eventual 1980 planting of 1.2 ha by Yalumba in the Eden Valley.

In 2003 California alone was home to 2,089 acres (846 ha) of Viognier—four times the amount in 1995. One caution is the quantity being planted in the agricultural areas of San Joaquin in the Central Valley—437 acres, or one-fifth of the total, in fertile, fruit-growing areas that will not provide wines of elegance—just sweet, heavy, and high-alcohol offerings.

The search for the most suitable sites has been active for years now, since Viognier has the effect of seizing rational people and inducing them to fevered quests. One such is John Alban, who grows his own fruit in the Edna Valley on a limestone site, similar to that of Josh Jensen, whose Calera Viognier is also in some of the rare pockets of limestone in California. Alban is also consulting viticulturalist to Steve Edmunds of Edmunds St John.

"What I like about the limestone is that it gives wines more nerve and iron under the flesh, not something traceable from other soils," comments Edmunds. Morgan Clendenen works in similar vein; she makes four Viogniers, led by the acclaimed Cold Heaven from Santa Barbara County. "Our intention is for cool-climate, higher-acidity wines and to avoid excess richness on the palate, what I would call a sensory overload," she states. "The idea is then to ferment the wines dry, even though sometimes the malo can be very slow to occur, as it was in 1998."

Limestone is another feature of most of the Viognier planted in the southwest Swiss cantons of Valais, Vaud, and Geneva. With twenty or so producers now in Switzerland, there is firm commitment to the vine, with poor soil and high elevation a feature of the vineyards.

One of the first two Swiss growers to plant Viognier, Benoît Dorsaz, works with gneiss, a decomposed granite, as his subsoil. This is similar to the vineyards of Condrieu, a rare non-Rhône overlap. His limestone element is only 6 per cent, but with clonal vines, he finds that the crop needs thinning and green harvesting every year.

Traditionally, the Viognier—in its preclone form—was recognised as an awkward vine. Georges Vernay, the top man at Condrieu for fifty harvests, points to its difficulty in adapting away from its curious local topsoil. This *arzelle* is often 40 cm (16 in.) deep, a mix of decomposed rock, mica, and schist, under which there can be some clay, as is found on the prime *climat* of *Vernon*.

At Côte-Rôtie, the Viognier performs better in the southern, sanded granite-mica zones that run into Condrieu than it does in the more schist-slate northern reaches of the *appellation*. Certainly clay soils are not ideal, a loss of finesse resulting: loose granite is very much the dish.

Viognier also has an unpredictable growth pattern. A successful flowering does not guarantee a healthy crop, even with fine weather. The grapes can remain shrivelled. Ripeness can also suddenly take off, with gains of up to 1° in just four days: the baked 2003 vintage was an example, when Condrieu growers had to rush home from holiday to pick their crop.

The Viognier is a rambling vine, its foliage spreading easily, and therefore needing trimming in the summer. In the Rhône only the Guyot method is allowed for its pruning, the shoots led along sticks. Its training can be along wires or against stakes, the latter the traditional method, while overseas growers run the vine along wires.

Viognier at Condrieu suffers mostly from oïdium, with bouts of mildew and black rot possible. The other problem is the failure of the fruit to set after flowering. Even when fully ripe, its grapes remain small. Timing its cropping is an art form: pick too soon and you lose the fatness, the heady, part-floral, part–dried fruit aromas. Pick too late and you have a dull gold, blowsy, low-acidity drink that falls away markedly after the initial palate.

For good fruit quality, Georges Vernay states that the vine must be at least ten years old before it can bring depth in the wine. The Viognier's best fruit is borne between the ages of 25 and 55, although growers continue with the vine beyond then. Vernay still crops around 30 hl/ha from some 1936 Viognier. He also avers that past a yield of 30 hl/ha, quality cannot be assured.

These observations come from the heart of the Viognier's home, and refer also to the old, preclone vine, which was said to be synonymous with the Galopine of the Isère *département,* across the Rhône. But the strains were not numerous, and the twentieth century saw a narrowing in the sources for new stock.

Now production levels are higher and the vine's behaviour less unruly thanks to disease-resistant strains of Viognier being planted. During the 1980s the clone taken up was called 642, but this has its drawbacks. "Clone 642 is very productive," states Philippe Faury, former President of the Growers Union of Condrieu, "and its wines are not greatly aromatic; its grapes are larger than our Viognier here, and in France it's mainly been planted in Languedoc."

While some USA growers talk of the one official 642 clone, they seem sure that others are using different, more productive ones. In Australia a heat-treated clone has been found to have a lower virus index and may come on stream.

Research on the Viognier in the 1960s and 1970s centred on increasing its productivity, for the understandable reason that so little was planted anywhere. Now the ground has shifted towards quality—with two clones developed in 2004 and 2005, numbered 1042 and 1058. Growers wait to see whether these can bring back extra quality.

Meanwhile, the growers at Condrieu have scoured the vineyards to create their own vineyard grown from healthy old vine cuttings. Under M. Faury, this will allow them to work with old *massale* selected stock—and to perhaps lower their yields.

Away from the Rhône, California will continue to fly an important flag for Viognier in the years to come, given the number of committed enthusiasts. Viogniers that appeal from there are Morgan Clendenen's Cold Heaven (crop from Alban), Calera, Seth Kunin, Frick Winery, Copain from Wells Guthrie, Eberle, Garretson, McDowell, Ojai (Ventura), and Qupé (Santa Barbara). Way up north in the more temperate Washington State, Cayuse, run by Frenchman Christophe Baron, and McCrea Cellars have shown up well.

In Australia, Yalumba now has 28 hectares and a nursery propagating Viognier for others. Arch Rhône enthusiasts D'Arenberg also make a Last Ditch Viognier from their McLaren Vale vineyard; Mitchelton have developed Viognier from a total of 2.6 ha (6.5 acres); and Gary Farr's Victoria By Farr Viognier from Bannockburn is another grown on a limestone-clay bedrock.

MARSANNE

The Marsanne is a variety that should be more appreciated. It brings white wine of glorious richness and long life, as personified by the best white Hermitage. The richness is deep-seated, not cellar concocted, and I agree with Jean-Louis Chave when he comments that Hermitage owes a debt to Michel Chapoutier for keeping his commitment to the variety: he could replace his Marsanne with Syrah and sell the wine more easily and more expensively.

The topsoils of predilection in the northern Rhône for the Marsanne are clay-chalk and also loess, with a granite base. Too much granite renders the wine hard and also alcoholic, and takes away the wine's inherent richness. For Jean-Louis Chave, with both clay-chalk and loess topsoils on his *L'Hermite* site at Hermitage, the loess releases floral aromas, while the clay-chalk brings more honey.

At Larnage, one of Crozes-Hermitage's 11 villages, the Marsanne also does well on the kaolin, its compact white-clay soil that is used to produce pizza ovens. Off limestone, as can be found at St-Péray and Châteaubourg within St-Joseph, there is more of a gunflint side to the wine, distinct from the supple, broad white fruits and almond or hazelnut flavours typical elsewhere.

When young, the vine grows a lot of vegetation, and this vigour means its first signs of quality fruit do not come until eight to 10 years of age. It is a vine with extreme longevity possible: some of the oldest plants in the area are those on the ex–Jean-Louis Grippat vineyard on *Les Murets* at Hermitage, said to be postphylloxera and now comfortably over one hundred years old. The Marsanne enthusiasts speak as one on allowing the vine as long a life as possible, in pursuit of its rich juice.

The Marsanne has quite a thick, dark-green leaf that bears several indents. Its habit is also to produce a lot of buds on any shoot; growers have to carefully select the best buds, and also bear in mind that the wind may later snap shoots. When ripe, the grapes are quite small, but the bunches are decently aired. This brings a uniform acceleration towards the end of ripening when the weather is fine. The ripe berries carry a golden, partly brown hue. Their picking must be carefully timed, since waiting too long can mean the wine becomes flat, rather than naturally oily and full of glycerol.

Root growth can extend several metres down, especially if the rock couch is fissured or degraded. The Marsanne therefore handles dry weather passably well, with a requirement for rain at the classic times—spring, mid-July, and mid-August. Away from the high granite of the hills, it is often found in or near clay patches, where the retained moisture suits it well.

It is also observed that the Marsanne's yield can drop in the vintage following a notably abundant year. The principal blight is oïdium; if June is rainy, then mildew can be a problem, while Hermitage can receive attacks from grape worm, or *vers de la grappe*.

The above refers to the traditional Marsanne. The clone story is that the ripe grapes are greener or more yellow—not golden—and are bigger and more tightly packed than the traditional vine. Their fruit is found to give wines that are heavier than the traditional, and low in acidity. Jean Gonon at St-Joseph talks of extra minerality being present on the traditional Marsanne wines, a freshness on the taste that above all shows up towards the finish.

Marsanne is not widely grown around the world, perhaps because it doesn't bear the fashionable sweet opulence of the Viognier. California's surface remains tiny—39 acres (16 ha) in 1995 struggled up to 68 acres (27 ha) in 2003. Qupé Winery has for some years made a respectable Marsanne, but its profile is low. The slight bitterness of young Marsanne on the palate may be a turnoff.

Australia's leading exponent of Marsanne for some years has been Château Tahbilk, in the Goulburn Valley, central Victoria. Its neighbour Mitchelton also works with Marsanne in its white blends that include Viognier and Roussanne. In Switzerland, Marsanne is known as Ermitage Blanc, and is successfully produced in the southwest of the Valais.

ROUSSANNE

Roussanne is the low-profile variety of the northern Rhône but enjoys a secure following elsewhere in the wine-producing world. It is a part contributor to the Marsanne-based wines of Hermitage, St-Joseph, Crozes-Hermitage, and St-Péray, and is usually included for reasons of increased acidity and liveliness in the wines. The Marsanne gives powerful and rich wines; the Roussanne is more aromatic and more elegant.

Its spread has never been great since it is a confirmed sufferer from oïdium, with yields consequently affected, as well as sometimes being hit by poor flowering. At Hermitage, it thrives in the loess areas of the hill—notably the east end of the *L'Hermite climat*—while it is also considered suitable for higher slopes where soils are poor: this helps to restrain its vigour and to preserve the acidity in the grapes.

At times in the past, it was more fashionable. The Sorrel plot at Crozes-Hermitage is half Roussanne, planted in 1945, when the vine's aromatic side was much appreciated. At St-Péray, Roussanne had a following since it was regarded as the natural grape for the sparkling wine, with greater acidity and a higher degree at an earlier stage of ripening in the Marsanne. Even today, up to 30 per cent of the St-Péray vineyard contains Roussanne, but only domaines Chaboud and Tunnel make a pure Roussanne.

The term "Roussanne" has for many years been a confusing one in the northern Rhône. In the early 1970s, growers would talk of two Roussannes—the second being called Roussette. For Jean-François Chaboud at St-Péray, his Roussanne's leaves carry a series of jagged insets—much more than the Marsanne—and also have many more veins on them than the Marsanne. This tallies with the description by St-Joseph's Jean Gonon of the family domaine's Roussanne planted by father, Pierre, in 1974—a ridged leaf with a bud that is slightly red. This is the Bergeron or Roussette de Savoie, according to Jean Gonon, a grape whose wine fears air and that does not age well.

The more regular Roussanne found at Hermitage has more rounded leaves, small berries, and small, compact bunches. This brings the problem of rot, which can spread swiftly from one grape to the next. When ripe, the grapes have a rusted, coppery colour.

There are a couple of Roussanne clones, but so productive are they that, as is so often the case, they demand grape dropping during the summer cycle.

Roussanne has become a big hit in the southern Rhône, led by the fantastic, mature vineyard at the Château de Beaucastel, but some growers in the northern Rhône find the wine can skip on the midpalate when produced on its own. It certainly steps off with a live, direct attack, so adding Marsanne can extend its length and aid its richness.

CLIMATE

The northern Rhône is temperate, and its weather in its northern half is more allied to the Beaujolais–north of Lyon axis than it is to the southern Rhône, where the Provençal and Mediterranean influences come through. The southern area around Hermitage and Cornas is slightly warmer, and presages the higher summer heat experienced to the south.

One of the consistent factors down the Rhône Valley French section, however, is the wind. The prevailing wind blows from the north, its local name here La Bise (the term "Mistral" is reserved for the southern Rhône). Between 1972 and 2001, for instance, a north-northeast wind occurred 43 per cent of the time, the south-southwest wind 22 per cent of the time.

The north wind brings cleansing air currents and is hoped for after rain, whereas the south wind is the precursor of rain and, potentially, rot. Likewise, tasting under the low pressure of the south wind is often harmed, with the lees stirred up and wines tasting subdued and off colour.

Côte-Rôtie experiences consistently cooler temperatures than Hermitage, which may explain why the Viognier has always been incorporated with the Syrah there—to add richness. On any given day Ampuis is often at least 1°C (degree Celsius) cooler than Tain. On the windy areas around the plateau, the freshness is greater still. The climate of Côte-Rôtie seeps into growers' beings, too. Patrick Jasmin of Ampuis says that he regards Tournon as "the south"—the cafés and their tables spread along the main road, the signs of life lived outdoors there.

A shift in climate zones appears around the level of the village of Sarras. Local growers point to the absence of crickets there, whereas they are found at Arras, just three miles south. Nor are there green oaks, southern trees, at Sarras, although they too are present at Arras. In terms of ripening, the Tournon area would usually precede Chavanay at the north of St-Joseph by a week or so.

The two vineyards with an exceptional *microclimat* in the northern Rhône are Hermitage and Cornas. The shape of the Hermitage hill means that much of the north wind is directed towards the westerly extremity, around the low-key site of *Varogne*. Tucked into the lee, sites like *Le Méal* are veritable sun traps and form the heart of noble wines like Jaboulet's *La Chapelle*.

Cornas is set back from the main Rhône corridor, the jutting limestone hill of Châteaubourg giving it protection from the main sweep of northerly weather. Its ripening pattern is very consistent and early, a factor that helped it out in poor vintages like 1993 and 2002.

Statistically, the Marsaz weather station, at 160 metres five miles northeast of Crozes-Hermitage, shows the average temperatures for that region to be as follows for the years 1972–2001 (Gaudriot study of the Ilots Vitrines du Crozes-Hermitage, Feb. 2003). The average monthly maximum was 16.8°C, the monthly average was 11.9°C, and the average monthly minimum was 7°C. July and August were the two hottest months, averaging 27.5°C and 27.2°C for the period, while the coldest months were January and December—6.7°C and 7.3°C, respectively. There was an average of 57 days of frost over the three months December to February—another indicator of how the northern Rhône is more closely linked to the wine regions north of Lyon than to the southern Rhône.

Rainfall patterns ran as follows: the yearly average over 1972–2001 was 840.8 millimetres (mm; 33.6 inches), the months of greatest precipitation being October and September, with 112.1 mm (4.5 in.) and 106.6 mm (4.25 in.), respectively. The driest months were February and January—46 mm (1.84 in.) and 51.3 mm (2.05 in.).

The average number of days per annum with more than 1 mm of rain was 93.6; with more than 10 mm it was 24.8.

WINEMAKING

The northern Rhône has internationalised its winemaking since the early 1990s. This has resulted in cleaner standards, and some more acceptable lower-level wines. At a local fair like that of Cornas or Chavanay, one of the main surprises is the very occasional encounter with a rustic wine, a throwback to the 1970s. In the main *appellations* of Hermitage, Côte-Rôtie, and Cornas, such wines are now extinct.

However, technology brings responsibility with it, and in *appellations* like St-Joseph and Condrieu, where there has been fast vineyard expansion, there are still too many wines made on autopilot. These are overextracted and frequently overoaked and have a nasty habit of drying and then dying in the second or third glass.

Everywhere I would regard tannins as on the defensive. Noble tannins from the grape have become swamped by oaked tannins that grate the palate. Young drinkers and wine tasters alike have never really known proper tannins and so take against the harshness of the wines. As has been happening in Bordeaux with Châteaux like Pavie, tannin is out, thick, heavy fruit overlay is in.

The northern Rhône must therefore be careful to defend its *héritage* of tannin: the Syrah carries tannin naturally, with levels enhanced according to provenance. No better example is the Syrah from *Bessards*, the granite west end of the Hermitage hill, with its moody black-fruit and peppered tannins. From the sunnier, more

stony next-door *climat* of *Le Méal*, the tannins absorb easily into a more oily, savoury wine.

Some commentators would point to better understanding of phenolic ripening these days, and that is certainly true: growers are more conscious of the need to ensure that the tannic ripening is not far behind the sugars at the time of harvesting. Indeed, the underripe stalkiness of wines I tasted in the 1970s has been banished, but the pendulum has swung too far. The dictates of a market like the United States, where the taste is for sweetness in food and drink, should not be allowed to run the show and push growers towards a sellout in the structure of their wines. Syrah is not a Merlot wannabee, after all.

Whole-bunch fermentation is now extremely rare, certainly because of the lack of confidence by growers in working this way: life is easier without the added risk or complication of any excess firmness in the wine. Robert Michel, a classic, old-fashioned *vigneron* of Cornas, is one of the few with a rationale about destalking. He destalks his crop with one exception: the *appellation*'s best site of *Reynards*, where the nobility of the place and its ability to produce balanced, ripe grapes justifies the inclusion of whole bunches. The Clape family is another Cornas domaine that has not yielded to the dictates of fashion, regarding whole-bunch fermentation of Cornas Syrah as the natural *héritage* of the place and its wine.

The northern Rhône is generally well tuned in to the debate on the use of cultured or natural yeasts to provoke fermentation. There is a marked body of growers who eschew outside additions, for the simple reasons of avoiding a diminution of local character in their wines. While it is true that the cellars carry their own yeasts and can distort the vineyard's imprint, it seems contrary to logic to buy a centralised product after much of the year has been spent accentuating local influences in each vineyard plot. Any "organic" grower who then uses cultured yeasts in the vinification strikes me as a trader in double standards.

Fermentation and maceration times have increased since the 1980s, as growers have sought ever darker and more extracted wines. The Syrah gives naturally well coloured wine, but there are plenty of black wines nowadays: a genuinely pretty dark-red *robe* is a fairly rare sight.

Techniques to help extraction have been the usual ones: pumping overs (*remontages*), cap punching (*pigeages*), and doing more *délestages* than previously—the last named being the process whereby a vat is partly emptied for anything up to three hours, then refilled. The fear of reduction, the stinky smell that stems from a lack of access to oxygen, is one that accompanies all workers of Syrah. It is very much part of the Syrah's makeup, and can turn up in the final wine if care is not taken.

> "I look at Graves, for instance, and wonder what is going on—reverse osmosis wines that I call *Monsieur Muscle*—nothing in the head, everything in the arms. It's noise, not music to me."
>
> Michel Chapoutier, Hermitage

Some growers are also pursuing a policy of vinification with no use of sulphur dioxide (SO_2) to counter bacteria. This is moving from a state of conviction to a modish status, counselled by some *oenologues*. Growers like Jean-Michel Stéphan at Côte-Rôtie and Thiérry Allemand at Cornas practise this on some of their cuvées; the inherent risk for the consumer is that some bottles taste great, while others are off, especially if storage or transport have been poor. The goal of reducing SO_2 use is of course praiseworthy, but as usual, balance in its execution is required.

For the extremists, there are games to play with techniques like reverse osmosis, an elimination of water within the wine in order to concentrate colour and matter. This is an act of thuggery on nature's fruit, and outbreaks of it have been reported at certain supposedly progressive domaines, in Crozes-Hermitage and St-Joseph. The result turns up in the glass, since new oak is often an attached condition. Hence these wines lack a relaxed centre and are taut and uneasy, their flavour stretched.

> "You can make concentrated wine without using new oak. Indeed, I find new oak vexes me considerably."
>
> Gérard Villano, Côte-Rôtie and St-Joseph

Acidification was allowed by the authorities for the 2003 vintage, when sugar and alcohol levels were so high. Again, moderation was necessary. Ironically, it was the previous vintage of 2002 that had rustled up the old practice of chaptalisation; so diluted were the musts from the incessant rains that it was a rare year when sugar had to be added.

The march of new oak was a theme during the 1990s and early 2000s in the northern Rhône. It continues to dominate in the wilder zones of St-Joseph, in places at Crozes-Hermitage, and even among some loose domaines at Côte-Rôtie. Imagine such fine *terroir* in the last named being abused by dollops of oak that varies in style from cask to cask and is administered with an excessive, heavy hand in the worst cases. Those who really master its use—the Guigals, Tardieu-Laurent, possibly Pierre Gaillard—fit comfortably on the fingers of a hand or two.

Micro-bullage also came on stream to make life easier for growers: the bubbling into casks of small amounts of oxygen serves ultimately to freshen the wine and to ease its tannins, a technique developed at Madiran, in southwest France, to cope with the Tannat grape's tendency to reduce. Hence the amount of racking, or transferring of wine from one cask to another, can be cut back, and the wine can nourish itself more from the lees of its regular cask.

St-Joseph is the *appellation* where winemaking is most hit-and-miss, and new oak casks are also the lazy or ignorant grower's panacea for unbalanced grapes and a lack of precise technical cellar knowledge. There are many wines that deceive at St-Joseph, techno and charmless, and the incipient wine surplus is certain to sort out some of these domaines in the future.

There is also interest in refining the size of casks serving for ageing the Syrah, and the *demi-muid*, the 550-to-600-litre cask that was popular in the 1960s and 1970s, is making a reappearance. Growers regard its volume as allowing a more gentle oxidation and ageing process for the wine, resulting in softer textures. Only a few of the traditional domaines, like Levet at Côte-Rôtie and Clape at Cornas, use larger barrels of 12 hectolitres or more.

> "There's no really bad wine anymore, but a lot less very good wine. Things are becoming normalised—the rules swamp expression."
>
> Gérard Chave, Hermitage

In-house cask production is starting to appear as de rigueur for some high-profile producers, notably Guigal and Tardieu-Laurent. The aim is to be in control of the oak supply, and above all its seasoning, before the casks are pressed into service.

More growers now produce specific site wines—one thinks of Les Grandes Places and La Landonne at Côte-Rôtie and Le Méal and Bessards at Hermitage, with young pretenders like Les Picaudières and the white Coteau des Pends at Crozes-Hermitage. For growers like Clape at Cornas and J-L Chave at Hermitage, however, blending remains the quintessential cellar challenge. Here the task is to meld together the wines of different soils, from vines of different ages.

"It's much more challenging to blend the white wines than the reds," observes Jean-Louis Chave. "Reds have tannin, colour, and their texture is softer and tighter. With the whites, you have to balance things out with some freshness at the end—white is a continuing challenge. Blending whites, you get one shot and no second chance. With reds you can come back to them."

Fining and filtration of the Syrah reds are now rare among most domaines, while the old practice of multiple bottlings of one vintage is dying out.

White Rhônes remain marginal, with importers reporting them hard to sell. This is a poor state of affairs, since they are often wonderful wines, a natural richness making them excellent food companions. White wine vinification has certainly improved since the early 1990s, away from just a few talented hands like Chave or Jean-Louis Grippat at Hermitage.

The desire to work with very ripe crop has brought these wines back to their more natural harmony, one where rich musts are fermented at natural cellar temperatures, not at excessively low levels like 15°C. The acceptance that the malolactic fermentation should be completed, even if the wine carries lower acidity, has also taken hold once more.

As a result, cask fermentation is more common, with a usually smaller proportion of the crop also fermented in steel. This applies for all three white varieties, Viognier, Marsanne, and Roussanne, although the Viognier and the Roussanne are often exposed to new oak. The new oak proportion applied to the Viognier has shrunk, however, at certain mature domaines like Jean-Michel Gérin and Philippe Faury.

A pre-fermentation skin contact is used successfully by leading Condrieu men like André Perret and Marcel Guigal. At Hermitage this is also practised by Paul Jaboulet and Chapoutier. Most of the northern Rhône whites are then fermented through until they are dry, although the Viognier has attracted a series of late-picked cuvées.

As found with the Syrah, the desire to produce sweet and succulent-tasting wine, whatever the natural style, has edged into white wine–making in the northern Rhône, its most common feature being the practice of lees stirring, or *bâtonnage,* during the wine's raising. A technique to enrich the Chardonnays of Burgundy to the north is therefore employed in the warmer Rhône.

> "I achieve the glycerol in my white wine from ripe Marsanne in the vineyard, not in the cellar afterwards with *bâtonnage."*
>
> Pascal Fayolle, Domaine des Martinelles, Hermitage

The series of Paul Jaboulet Aîné whites of the mid-1990s, when the wines from different *appellations* all carried similar textures, was an example of this warped outlook. The natural ripeness of white varieties in the Rhône should suffice to infuse the wines with richness—the vineyard must talk, surely. For senior growers, *bâtonnage* brings a loss of carbon dioxide and finesse in the wine—all deplorable.

The fashion for sweetening white wines by leaving residual sugar in them—a scourge of Alsace and also the Loire these days—has a veteran like Gérard Chave fuming: "If you leave sugar in white wines, you give the impression they are rich," he states. He describes the following process as totally anti-nature:

1. Harvest early for acidity
2. Chaptalise
3. Block the malolactic fermentation for freshness

For Chave, the main advances in winemaking in the past few years have been better tem-

perature control and understanding, so there are fewer accidents during vinification.

The best whites made from Marsanne-Roussanne are aged over anything up to 18 months. Crozes-Hermitage *blanc,* frequently a wine of low acidity and plain fruit flavour, is often bottled in the spring after the harvest, while St-Joseph and St-Péray, wines of greater structure, are usually bottled within a year. White Hermitage is mostly bottled after eight to 12 months, although J-L Chave, Tardieu-Laurent, and Guigal run between two and three years. The Viogniers are usually bottled earlier, from six months on, with the top wines like Vernay's *Coteau de Vernon* an exception at 12 to 16 months.

Just before bottling, a fining is often required: the Viognier, for instance, generates a lot of vegetal protein and can need clearing of this.

The Viognier used to be made in the 1940s and 1950s in *demi-sec* form, aimed at Christmas sales. Just three growers—Yves Lafoy, the Domaine du Chêne, and Dézormeaux—still make this, their clients all local, and it was the fully sweet version that was taken up in 1990 by Yves Cuilleron and André Perret. With the description *vendange tardive* reserved for Alsace wines, the terms for the sweet Condrieu cover *moelleux, passerillage,* autumnal picking, and all allusions to ripe crop.

The last of the late-harvest crop can be picked in early November if the autumn has been stable—in this instance, the grower may work with a mix of noble rot and grapes that are *passerillé,* or shrivelled. There are also sweet wines made in the *vin de paille* vein, whereby the grapes are laid out on straw racks for a quiet Christmas-onwards fermentation. In both cases, new or young oak is used for the fermentation, with the *passerillage* wine receiving some lees stirring. Residual sugar levels run at about 200+ gm per litre.

For some years André Perret would include a little overripe crop in his *Chéry* wine, to give it more flesh and warmth. François Villard is another grower who relies on marked amounts of overripe crop in his regular Condrieus, seeking the overriding lush textures that are therefore brought to the wine. When vines are young and their grape juice not yet naturally deep, these tactics help out.

COMMERCE

The number of domaines bottling their own wine has shot up since the early 1990s. Forty-nine producers of St-Joseph, including the Co-opératives and vineyard-owning *négociants* like Chapoutier, were listed in the 1992 edition of this book. That figure has more than doubled. At Condrieu, 35 names have become more than 60.

> "The choice is to do things to make money and be the richest man in the cemetery, or to do things well, have some money, and be master of your operations."
>
> Gérard Chave, Hermitage

The trend towards autonomy has hit Co-opérative subscriber numbers, with the Tain Co-opérative losing young growers who have set up in Crozes-Hermitage and St-Joseph. Between 1991 and 2003 the Cave's membership fell from 420 to 390 *adhérents*. Even the Cave de Saint-Désirat has seen some departures, notably two growers wishing to pursue purely organic cultivation.

The Tain Co-opérative is the dominant force in the quantity of wine produced at Crozes-Hermitage, and its decision to greatly increase the amount of wine sold in bottle has squeezed supplies of this popular wine to the wider merchant trade. Prices have therefore been firm for bulk supplies, and lesser-known growers have encountered increased difficulty in selling their domaine wine in the face of the cut-price amounts sold by the Co-opérative.

There has also been an increase in the number of growers offering selected wines as part of a *négociant* business—wines they buy from outside sources. Usually, these domaines are high profile, their *négociant* wines carefully chosen in small batches from a network of small growers. Jean-Louis Chave sells good, genuine St-Joseph, a little Crozes-Hermitage and some Côtes du Rhône in this way, and Stéphane Ogier at Côte-Rôtie also has a *négoce* selection. Louis Barruol at Château de St-Cosme in Gigondas also offers a full northern Rhône range: his Condrieu and Côte-Rôtie are thoroughbred wines.

Emphasis is placed on cask ageing, the quality of the oak high, its age usually young. Such oak-emphasized raising also gives other practitioners, who are not vineyard owners, the chance to buy young wine from a respected source, then to double or triple its price after a year or two's *élevage*.

Some of the old, established *négociants* now complain that it has become harder to source good wines or grapes for their house wines. This is always an issue in most of the northern Rhône *appellations* because they are so small.

Among the newcomer *négociants* are Tardieu-Laurent and, more recently, Patrick Lesec and Eric Texier. Michel Tardieu is the southerner in partnership with Dominique Laurent from Burgundy. They have built up a strong fan base, and now place their top-quality wines in their own Tronçais wood casks. With access to good sources, the wines are genuine, well-polished, and expensive.

Patrick Lesec, a Parisian who has been a psychologist, economist, chef, and painter, started dealing in the Rhône in 1994 on return from Santa Barbara, where he ran the Restaurant du Marché. Prompted by admiration for Dominique Laurent's methods, he sells overtly oaked wines, notably from domaines like Coursodon at St-Joseph and Remizières at Crozes-Hermitage. Commerce rather than *terroir* is the face of this operation, the wines made in the cellar rather than the vineyard—just like the *négoce* of yore.

Eric Texier is a Bordelais who in 1998 started selling Rhônes he had aged in cask. He vinifies some of his wines himself and offers the unusual Brézème Côtes du Rhône from the hinterland between northern and southern Rhône at Livron-sur-Drôme, which lies equidistant between Valence and Montélimar.

The 2002 and 2003 vintages were small across the northern Rhône, which may have been a blessing in disguise for low-profile growers facing the threat of a stock pileup. Prices for the top names have been firm, with Hermitage 2002 sold in bulk at £8/US$14.40 a litre and Côte-Rôtie 2002 in bulk at £7/US$12.60. Alarmingly, the price of St-Joseph 2002 in bulk was relatively dear—at £3/US$5.40 a litre—compared both with Hermitage and Crozes-Hermitage, the latter's 2002 on offer at £2/US$3.60 a litre.

Bulk prices for the 2003 Côte-Rôtie rose by 40 per cent—the small vintage the main factor. The top Syrah wines will find buyers at these levels as long as the vintage's reputation is high and the quantity restrained, but the long, slow fall in the dollar has put off demand from the United States.

The fault lines come in *appellations* like St-Joseph, Condrieu, and to an extent, Crozes-Hermitage. If their prices move too far away from quality, then growers will not see returns on the plentiful investments they made in the 1990s. The particular problem at St-Joseph is that costs remain the same as those at Condrieu but the price is one-third or half that of Condrieu.

EXCERPTS FROM THE 1975 INTRODUCTION

The Rhône Valley possesses some of France's most remarkable and distinguished wines, and its vineyards are probably the oldest in France. It is therefore quite amazing that even today it should still be a comparatively unexplored, little-noticed wine region.

Magnificent wines like Côte-Rotie and Hermitage have been made for over 2,000 years but have strangely never become widely known as two of their country's best red wines. There can be little doubt that *marques* such as Côte-Rôtie's La Mouline and Hermitage's La Chapelle are some of the best red wines in the world.

In the northern part of the Rhône Valley, the growth of factories has brought problems for the owners of vineyards. Young men derive considerably greater financial benefit from entering their local industry than from continuing to work the land. Where all vineyard cultivation must by necessity be manual, the fall in the total size of the vineyards has been most marked: this is the case for nearly all the *appellations* that lie between Vienne and Valence.

A personal list of those wines considered to be the very finest in the Côtes du Rhône, and by logical extension, among the greatest in France is

Côte-Rôtie La Mouline, E. Guigal

Condrieu, G. Vernay

Château-Grillet, Neyret-Gachet

Hermitage La Chapelle, P. Jaboulet Aîné

Hermitage, J-L Chave

Cornas, A. Clape

EXCERPTS FROM THE 1982 INTRODUCTION

In the seven years since 1975, some changes have obviously occurred in an area that, although old by origin, is young and relatively unsophisticated in practice. Many *appellations* are now better known; several are at a crossroads in their development; and some are teetering on the edge of a sorry decline. New influences, particularly on cellar work and vinification, have filtered into the more avant-garde domaines, and attitudes towards wine-making have certainly become less parochial.

Many of the progressive influences have reached the open-minded growers through visits to California rather than through encouragement from within France. In the northern Rhône, the best *vignerons*, such as Guigal and Chave, are also the ones who show most interest in seeing how other people make their wine. Marcel Guigal keeps some of Joseph Phelps's Syrah wine in his cellar at Ampuis to remind himself how the cuttings taken from the vines at Côte-Rôtie and transplanted to California are performing.

Contrast their enthusiasm with the state of affairs in one of the most famous *appellations*, Côte-Rôtie. Here the good name is being upheld by no more than four or five growers; the vineyards are being inexorably expanded, off the slopes and up on to the mediocre soil of the ill-exposed plateau above them. The maximum permitted yield per hectare has been increased from 35 to 40 hectolitres, while the growers seem to be as becalmed as the Ancient Mariner's boat on its painted ocean: very few have modernized any of their cellar equipment but feel the need, derived partly from fashion and partly from economic necessity, to make a lighter wine.

The result is evident in some cuvées of Côte-Rôtie that are disgracefully pale and wishy-washy. There is no zest in the *appellation*, no firm leadership, and the resulting inertia is a bitter pill to swallow for those such as the author, who is a confirmed addict of good Syrah wines. May the growers of Côte-Rôtie remember that quality will always sell, that their wine is undoubtedly better known today than it was ten years ago, and that they are in danger of slipping out of the top bracket.

This view about Côte-Rotie is reinforced when one sees the depth of good-quality wines that exist at Hermitage, for instance. There the name of the wine is not founded on just one or two outstanding cuvées; several growers are making quite exceptional wine without any recourse to lowering their standards or to enlarging the vineyard.

Elsewhere in the Rhône there are areas of hope and pockets of gloom. Hope at Crozes-Hermitage, where the number of private domaines bottling their own wine has risen substantially; the general quality of their wine is not yet irreproachable, but standards are rising and the future looks good.

Some gloom exists, however. Growers at St-Péray and Cornas are depressed about the future of their vineyards, as few young men are showing an interest in looking after these steep hillside vines. At thirty-five, Robert Michel is the youngest *vigneron* at Cornas, and there are no enthusiastic teenagers in sight—they have all gone to seek work in the neighbouring towns.

Overall a tendency has arisen to try to make lighter wines that carry less overriding tannin; in some ways this strips the area of one of its main characteristics, but in others it is a positive development—especially for wines that previously suffered from overextensive ageing. Often those growers who use casks for really prolonged periods of ageing seem unsure about just why it is wood that should be ageing their wine. They fall into the trap of acting on blind instinct, on customs handed down from father to son, and fail to realize that casks need just as much treatment, just as much maintenance and cleanliness, as do concrete or stainless steel vats.

The contradiction is that while many growers in the New World are turning to the use of wood but ensuring that their casks are replaced with great regularity, some growers in the Rhône are tending to move away from it, without grasping that well-cared-for casks can make a valuable contribution to a wine's development.

Lighter wines are also resulting from the move away from crushing and destalking the grapes prior to fermentation. The *raisin entier* technique leaves the grapes to macerate and subsequently commence fermentation mostly within their skins. The process extracts the fruitiness from the grapes without all the accompanying tannins and is proving very beneficial when well applied. It does not involve the use of carbonic gas and should not be confused with the *macération carbonique* process, which strips many wines of their intrinsic character.

The role played by the Côtes du Rhône in the French wine export field is a story of constant development. In 1965 Rhône exports, in bottle and cask, came to 122,278 hectolitres; in 1970, 191,416 hectolitres; in 1975, 418,025 hectolitres, in 1980, 516,282 hectolitres, and in 1981, 602,182 hectolitres. The Rhône is now exporting more wine than Burgundy, having overtaken that area for the first time in 1979, and more than Beaujolais, which it overtook in 1976. It is now second only to Bordeaux in volume of exports, and while the world feels the effects of a steady, uncompromising recession, that is a fortunate position to be in.

Apart from its wine, the Rhône Valley is an important industrial and commercial artery for the rest of France. The River Rhône runs for 808 kilometres (505 miles) altogether, from its torrential source in the east of the Swiss canton of the Valais all the way down to the Mediterranean, west of Marseille. South of Lyon it extends for 370 kilometres (231 miles) and is joined by several fair-sized rivers, all of which help to boost its imposing flow. These rivers include the Isère, the Drôme, the Ardèche, the Aigues, the Ouvèze, and the Durance.

The area is therefore naturally suitable for hydroelectric projects, which have brought an influx of both money and skilled labour into the surrounding countryside. Important schemes exist at Pierre-Benite, near Lyon, at Donzère, and at Valence, for instance. Along the river other heavy industries have sprung up during the last 50 years, including some of the country's leading metallurgical industries at Givors, near Vienne.

The Rhône Valley is extremely fertile, however, and its agriculture, although diminished, has broadly remained on a sound level. North of Montélimar the main fruits are peaches, pears, apricots, and cherries.

In addition to these staple fruits and vegetables, the surrounds of the Rhône produce other fine local specialities. The *département* of the Isère is rich in walnuts, while the *département* of the Ardèche grows plentiful raspberries, bilberries, black currants, and chestnuts. On either side of the river between Lyon and Montélimar, a variety of local goat and cow cheeses are made—notably the Rigottes of Condrieu and the St-Marcellin of the Isère.

The countryside around the river is also rich in poultry and game, and the regional cooking is shaped accordingly. Favourite dishes are the *poulet aux écrevisses* (chicken cooked in a crayfish sauce), *quenelles de brochet* (individual rolls of pike soufflé), *agneau grillé aux herbes* (lamb roasted in herbs), *perdrix aux choux* (partridge cooked in cabbage) and *charcuterie*, or selected pork meats. The *gratin dauphinois* (creamed potato gratin) and the *lièvre en pouvrade* (hare cooked in pepper sauce) are other favourites.

EXCERPTS FROM THE 1991 INTRODUCTION

The 1980s were a good decade for the Rhône. Prosperity came to the region. Its best wines became equated in price and quality with the best French and international wines. Vineyards of the steep terraces of the northern Rhône were reclaimed and replanted. Growers modernized and completely rebuilt their cellars. Young faces appeared, eager to put into practice theories learned at wine school. The value of exports grew remarkably, while the quantity of exports increased only slightly, confirming the Rhône's position as the third French quality region, now only a touch behind Bordeaux and Burgundy, and some would say carrying more potential than the other two for the future. The challenge for the 1990s is to maintain prosperity and quality.

Individual *appellations* have flourished, and the northern Rhône is now humming with activity and ideas. Côte-Rôtie has a new lease of life, the words written in 1982 appearing to come from another epoch. The *vignerons* have slowed down the advance of plateau plantations in poorer locations. Marcel Guigal has burst on the world stage as the maker of highly intense, top-class wines which have captured people's imaginations at a time of some doubt as to how good Bordeaux wines really are.

There is a tight group of young winemakers who have either taken over family vineyards or set up from scratch on their own. They differ from the previous generation in their seriousness: for them, winemaking is more of a science than an art, and they are meticulous in their attention to detail, both in the vineyards and in the cellars. Their presence has raised the quality of many of the wines, and it is to be hoped that in the coming years they will gain increased confidence to express themselves more freely in their winemaking, away from the edicts of wine school and the advocacy of *oenologues*, whose hovering presence sometimes seems to parallel the role of the shrink in modern society.

Condrieu has taken a turn for the better. One only has to drive along the N86 on the west bank of the Rhône to spot fresh plantations on formerly abstract-looking hillsides. But a word of caution here—there are plenty of fruit cultivators or small *agriculteurs* ready to "try their hand" with a spot of Viognier, and the quality of some of the wine that now sells for nearly £12 or US$20 out of the cellars is poor.

The cornerstone of the northern Rhône remains Hermitage, where top-quality red wine is produced every year by some of the growers. Gérard Chave remains utterly committed to quality and is a shining example for many of the region's *vignerons*, especially the younger ones, who understandably hold him in some reverence.

Great progress has been made with the reds at Crozes-Hermitage, where more elegant, better-balanced, and just plain classier wines are now being made. A bold new star here is Alain Graillot, whose reds are superbly succulent and serve to set a yardstick, along with Jaboulet's irreproachable Domaine de Thalabert.

Cornas has recovered from a pervading gloom apparent in the late 1970s. While there are several growers on the threshold of retirement, there are also younger *vignerons* coming through, either to maintain family tradition, as with the excellent Auguste Clape vineyard, or to revise their winemaking methods completely, as in the case of Jean Lionnet, whose great success has been to bring greater finesse to his Cornas without sacrificing its robust nature.

Also on the west bank of the Rhône, St-Joseph has to a certain extent fallen prey to the legislators, whose decision radically to extend the vineyard has brought forth a lot of moderate wine, the quality of which is far removed from that of the main villages such as Mauves and the main producers such as Grippat. At least measures are now being taken to halt this, although

as it is the reversal of vineyard plantations that we are talking about, thirty years have been set aside for their accomplishment.

The climate was a major theme of the 1980s in the Rhône. It was a decade when harvesting dates fell earlier and earlier. First notes for this book made around 1973 show the growers quoting the end of September or early October as the normal date for the *vendanges*. By the late 1980s, the first week of September was a regular occurrence. In 1982 few growers were equipped to cope with the intense day and night temperatures at harvesttime, which is why many of that year's wines tasted stewed and jammy. Cellar equipment, with touch-of-a-button temperature control, has been vastly updated and is now ready to work alongside the crop that nature delivers.

Vineyard care also edged away from the unquestioning use of herbicides, pesticides, and fertilizers produced by large multinational chemical companies. These are topics about which one hears *vignerons* talking and reflecting more now, but marching in the opposite direction is the issue from most local nurseries or *pepiniéristes* of clonally grafted vinestock, with prolific results on yields. A few growers still take their young vine cuttings from old stock in their vineyards, but this is a time-consuming task and requires both dedication and numbers of people—which is why the three members of the Marsanne family of St-Joseph can still manage to do their own grafting.

The main evolution in the style of red wines during the 1980s has been towards greater elegance and more sophistication of taste. Harsh tannins are strictly out; long ageing in old casks is yesterday's game. Less fining is done, and fewer growers filter their wine. Colour extraction is more pronounced through temperature-controlled macerations; intracellular fermentations have been used to encourage greater fruitiness. And something of an obsession with new oak has developed in certain quarters—a lot of it, one cannot help but feel, fuelled by whizz-kid wine journalists who have taken it on as their international cause célèbre. Fashions come and go in winemaking as much as they do with hemlines, and wry amusement is sometimes afforded by the sight of a *vigneron* grappling with offers of oak casks from different origins that have received different degrees of prior smoking. I wonder where their enthusiasm for this new product will be in 10 years' time?

Overseas, the Rhône has caught the imagination of winemakers keen to experiment and to stretch their skills. This is nowhere more apparent than in California, where it is now estimated that 8 per cent of the vines under plantation (those not attacked by phylloxera) are Rhône varieties. Such interest and enthusiasm, personified by the exotic Randall Grahm of Bonny Doon, are a great compliment to the Rhône and its newfound stature.

For the wine drinker, the Rhône still presents uncertainties that reflect the relative innocence of the area. Growers often still like to do several bottlings of any given vintage. There may be an interval of 15 months between the first and last bottling, so one wine can have spent markedly longer, for instance, in cask, or another wine can drink with markedly greater freshness. No indication is given on the labels about this.

In matters of marketing, a certain naïvety is shown by some producers, who tag their wines with all sorts of descriptions about foot of the slopes, high hills, young vines, or very aged, old-gentlemen vines, all of which detract from getting across the *appellation* name and yardstick quality in a clear, easy way.

But these are minor quibbles beside the satisfaction of reading words recorded in 1975 and thinking how irrelevant they are today. The Rhône has reached a level of recognition in keeping with the quality of its wines and the talents of its growers, and while it may be absurd to pay £283 or US$500 for a bottle of Guigal's La Turque, it is most certainly not absurd to pay just £8.50 or US$15 for a Domaine de Thalabert Crozes-Hermitage red—this is one of the great-value buys in French wine today.

1

Côte-Rôtie

THE RHÔNE WINE whose repute has most grown in the past 50 years is Côte-Rôtie. In the northern Rhône, Hermitage bagged the limelight in the post–Second World War years; in the southern Rhône, it was Châteauneuf-du-Pape.

That left Côte-Rôtie, the bridge between Burgundy and the Rhône, somewhere out on a limb. There was no big wine *négociant* structure to spread the word, just the good but sleepy house of Vidal-Fleury. Even Beaujolais was much better known—the fun wine of Lyon from the 1950s to the 1970s.

There are several reasons for the low-profile past. The name is one. "The Roasted Slope" is true and evocative, but which slope, where? When even French visitors arrive in its main village, Ampuis, they are surprised to learn that it is the home of the wine of Côte-Rôtie. The burghers of Tain were shrewd enough to add the Hermitage in the 1920s, just like the inhabitants of Puligny with their Montrachet.

Then the holdings were always small. Hermitage benefited from the Bordeaux connection in the 1800s, grandiose merchant houses and cellars were built, and families built up important collections of plots. Jaboulet and Chapoutier, both founded in the early 1800s, have long possessed large tracts of the vineyard there—respectively about 25 and 30 hectares of the 125 hectares. These are amounts that confer natural advantages of distribution, reputation, and renown. By 2005 a little over 20 hectares was the largest Côte-Rôtie vineyard holding under one name, that of Marcel Guigal, even after all his fast expansion since the 1980s.

The system is different at Côte-Rôtie. The *appellation* lies south of Lyon, in an area used by the Lyonnais for leisure, for second homes rather than business investment. The city of Lyon looked north for its economic growth. The only real *vinicole* grandeur in the northern Rhône region was Château-Grillet, an estate on its own making often-exported white wine. Even it was best known through its rarity.

The land near the river Rhône, with its natural irrigation, also lent itself to vegetable and fruit growing. The hills rising off the plain were craggy and sweltering, so if the wine price didn't compare well with that of the fruit and veg, it wasn't worth the effort.

Côte-Rôtie

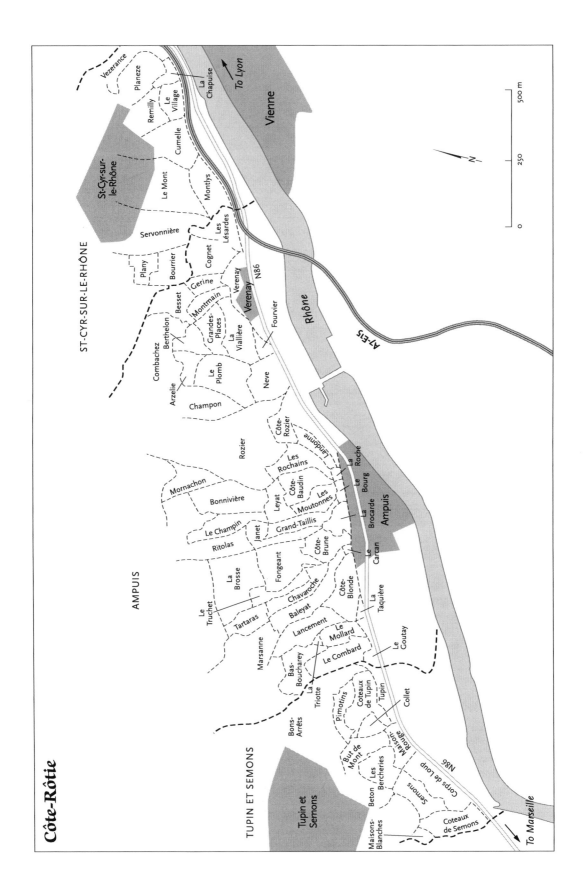

ST-CYR-SUR-LE-RHÔNE

Vezerance
Planeze
Remilly
Le Village
La Chapuise
To Lyon
Cumelle
Le Mont
Montlys
St-Cyr-sur-le-Rhône
Servonnière
Les Lésardes
Plany
Bourrier
Cognet
Gerine
Verenay
Verenay
N86
Besset
Montmain
Berthelon
Grandes-Places
La Viallière
Fourvier
Combachez
Arzelie
Le Plomb
Neve
Champon
Rhône
A7-E15

Côte-Rozier
Rozier
Les Rochains
La Roche
Landonne
Mornachon
Bonnivière
Leyat
Côte-Baudin
Les Moutonnes
Le Bourg
Le Champin
Janet
Grand-Taillis
La Brocarde
Ampuis
Ritolas
Côte-Brune
Le Carcan
La Brosse
Fongeant
AMPUIS
Le Truchet
Chavaroche
Côte-Blonde
La Taquière
Tartaras
Baleyat
Lancement
Le Mollard
Le Goutay
Marsanne
Bas-Boucharey
Le Combard
La Triotte
Pirmotins
Coteaux de Tupin
Tupin
Collet
Bons-Arrêts
But de Mont
Beton
Les Bercheries
Maison Rouge
Corps de Loup
Tupin et Semons
Semons
N86
Maisons-Blanches
Coteaux de Semons
To Marseille

TUPIN ET SEMONS

Vienne

N

500 m
250
0

TABLE 1
Prices from the House of Macker Cellar Book (francs per cask)

	CÔTE-RÔTIE	HERMITAGE	CORNAS	CROZE
1811	240	300	90	125
1815	300	550	120	160
1817	300	350	130	
1822	240	700	72	
1825	500	850	200	
1827	150	400–600	60–72	100
1836	125	200–350	55–60	70

A perspective on where Côte-Rôtie stood against its Rhône wine neighbours comes from the cellar book of the House of Macker, a merchant of the eighteenth and nineteenth centuries based in Tain-l'Hermitage. Part of this ledger gives the cask prices for the period 1811 to 1836 (see table 1). The majority of the years with quoted prices for a full range of northern Rhône wines were those when the merchants of Bordeaux were buyers. Prices are francs per cask.

Côte-Rôtie was rarely considered close to Hermitage in standing and therefore price. No doubt its relative finesse and lack of the vaunted Hermitage "manliness" counted against it when the buyer was seeking a medicine wine to strengthen his weedy, hard offerings from the Gironde. It may not also have been considered a good traveller for export, and this would also have quietened demand for it. Regional fame rather than foreign renown was its lot.

The vineyard chronicler André Jullien wrote in 1816 that the red and white wines of Côte-Rôtie were of less standing than the Hermitage reds and its few whites; the Hermitages were in the first class, the Côte-Rôties were just *vins rouges* (M-L Marcelou, *Vins, Vignes et Vignerons de l'Hermitage 1806–1936*, University Lumière-Lyon 2, 2003).

The timing of phylloxera was another unfortunate blow; it first hit Côte-Rôtie in 1872, and by 1878 the whole vineyard had been knocked out. Rebuilding it took from 1883 to around 1905; the loss of many thousands of young men in the First World War meant that by the 1920s, the vineyard was again slipping back into abandonment. The long lists of Great War fallen in the local churches and village squares serve to emphasize this.

The 1907 figure for the *commune* of Ampuis, as stated in Claudius Roux's *Monographie du Vignoble de Côte-Rôtie* of that year, was 420 hectares of vines, which compares with today's 231 hectares. But crucially, he writes of the general view that the heart of the vineyard amounted to 25 to 38 hectares, not much to go round. At the Concours Agricole of Paris in 1909, the wine of Côte-Rôtie was presented by nine intrepid growers, the only two names still active today being Jasmin and Vidal-Fleury.

Meagre prices during the Depression further compounded Côte-Rôtie's difficulties, and during the Second World War the wine was sold mainly as *vin ordinaire*, even though it had been promoted to full *appellation* status in 1940. That decree, incidentally, covered the area from Tupin in the south to the areas around the *Rozier* vineyards. Verenay—home of *Viallière* and *Grandes Places*, for instance—and St Cyr, further north, were only admitted into the *appellation* in 1965. This didn't stop the intrepid René Clusel, owner of vineyards in Verenay, from selling his wine as "Côte-Rôtie" before then!

Propping up the local economy before the Second World War were the crops of the plain near the river. The most notable fruit was apricot, including a jam variety called the Ampuisais. During harvest time, up to 200 tonnes a day would leave the village to be sold across Europe.

By 1949 Côte-Rôtie was fetching only about one franc a litre—a ridiculous price in view of the work involved, the risks from blight, and the quality of the finished wine. In those pre–industrial weedkiller days, when the soils were purely hand worked and access roads were few, the calculation was one man for one hectare. In a blighted year this would mean he had maybe just 2,600 bottles or less to sell.

Ampuis remained known for its fruit, and for its nuts—*noyeaux*. Many of the growers led fruit and vegetable lives in the 1950s and 1960s; the Bernard family at Tupin grew cardoons, the winter vegetable, and the locally respected Blette d'Ampuis, which would be made into a *gratin*. The wine would be sold away from the region, shipped on trains in casks for *bistrot* drinking.

Appointed Mayor of the village in 1959, before going on to the stage of national politics, Alfred Gérin was an important figure in the 1960s because he was also a winegrower. "The vineyard hadn't changed one iota since the nineteenth century in some respects," he recalls. "Access was often along tracks for mules, and in 1968 we started work on creating roads and proper access routes—10 kilometres (over six miles) of these. Our objective was to fight erosion and to prevent the village flooding. Life was tough then for a *vigneron*, and in 1960, the crop was only 700 hectolitres."

Times remained lean for the winegrowers through the 1960s and early 1970s. In those days it was still uncommon for a small producer to bottle much of his wine: the market for it was too localized and the task was made easier by the existence of merchants who could distribute the grower's lesser cuvées further afield. In my first experiences of the Ampuis Wine Fair, in 1973–74, I saw a handful of old men who bottled a little and found meeting a foreigner a novel experience. There weren't more than six or eight of them, and the event was really an excuse for a local party.

The 1970s also brought other sources of employment. Factories sprang up along the Rhône corridor; France was prosperous, with its manufacturing base moving ahead, leaving seemingly decadent, strike-ridden countries like Britain behind in a wake of smart cars, Chanel and other designer clothes, and secondary residences. Prosperity and the prospect of an enhanced lifestyle filtered into the rural communities. Only the most dedicated were prepared to sweat it out on the hillsides while their contemporaries went for the easy wage in a factory, with extra social cachet and shorter, less strenuous hours. Local industry in Vienne and Lyon served as a big counterattraction to winemaking at this time.

Further threat to the vineyards during the 1960s and early 1970s came from land speculation. Villas were allowed to be built in the vineyards, which explains the apparent anomaly of such houses on the slope at Verenay, as well as half a dozen at the foot of the *Côte Brune* and one beside the Vidal-Fleury sign on the *Côte Blonde*. Then Mayor and *vigneron* Albert Gérin triggered a plan to defend the occupation of the soil, and from the second half of the 1970s this extra menace had been headed off.

Only in the late 1970s and early 1980s did Côte-Rôtie firmly catch the eye of foreign importers rather than pioneers, people who felt confident they could sell the wine to a wider audience. Then the Parisian market woke up to the wine as well, and even Lyonnais restaurants started to lean southwards in their wine lists. Nowadays it is hard to find Beaujolais in Lyon, so fully Rhône-stocked is the city.

Likewise, the January Ampuis Wine Fair is no longer a cosy, local celebration of the new vintage, a time for the growers to take a quiet peep sideways at their neighbours' work in between drinks. The hall is overwhelmed by visitors from all over France and the outside world. The Rhône is popular in Japan, Asia, and the Americas now.

The real filtering down of the new prosperity occurred only in the 1990s, however, after early troubles. After good years from 1988 to 1991, the modest 1992 and 1993 came along. Small growers found their cellars stocked high. Deals were done with merchants at Châteauneuf-du-Pape to offload the wine, and even supermarkets stocked some of the unknown domaines.

The run of good vintages from 1995 to 2001, with just the uneasy 1996 during that time, accelerated the process and made it more democratic. A small crop in 2003 resumed the price pressure. Now there are new porches, new cellars, smart plastering, holidays taken, cars that are shiny. Children are more likely to speak English, and to have travelled around the world. Wine is often sold on allocation, such is the demand. As a sign of rapid price inflation, a hectolitre of bulk Côte-Rôtie 2002 sold for Euros 1,000 (£670/US$1,200), while the admittedly superior 2003 jumped straight to Euros 1,400 (£837/US$1,680).

There are still ways to go on the quality front, however. You can't increase the size of the vineyard by over three times (1973: 72 hectares) in 30 years and expect nothing but high-quality venues to be cultivated. Too many sites that run deep into the farmland of the plateau were permitted as Côte-Rôtie in the 1980s. There are also local people entering wine because it seems to pay well, and yet they have no fundamental grasp of working the land or making wine from it. These are often old family lands that are being revived. They would be much too expensive to buy for the average wallet.

Onward, Côte-Rôtie, please. This is a wine of such wonderfully full elegance, one that has never strayed too far from its earthy roots, that it deserves the continuation of the efforts to revitalise its vineyards that occurred in the 1990s. It deserves to be served at the finest of tables and to be associated with the most accomplished wines anywhere. For the young generation here, there is now everything to play for.

HISTORY

All around these old vineyards, there are no really fancy views or bucolic gems, just a working backdrop. They lie just south of the old Roman town of Vienne, lodged among five wholly inconspicuous hamlets and villages on the west side of the river Rhône. There is a hard, no-frills aspect about the Rhône and its surrounds here. The river flows with sheer power, its semi-industrial backdrop giving it a masculinity that city rivers like the Seine and the Thames do not possess: more New York with an abrasive edge than London plus charm. Its river traffic is also large and menacing—hundreds of yards of dark, low working barges rather than brief, angular pleasure craft.

The centre of Côte-Rôtie is at Ampuis. Entering from the north on a rainy day, mist and urban smog can brood oppressively over the valley, which is dark and dank and even looks smelly. The tough urban tone carries itself down here—the view is of metal, solid textures, pylons, electrical power lines, warehouses, concrete river constructions.

Sitting on the main N86 road from Lyon to Nîmes, Ampuis has become neater since the 1990s, but it's still easily forgotten. For a start, there's no real central hostelry where the visitor and local congregate. The church dominates the square beside the road, and opposite is a line of shops and a few modest eateries. The baker is a maestro, especially when he makes his bread soaked in lees for the Wine Fair, but he stands out. There is a wine bar run by a man who used to work on a wine domaine that is making efforts to raise the quality level. But a cold, wet Tuesday evening in February here is not a barrel of gastronomic delights or laughs.

The busiest moments are Wednesday mornings, when a small market is set up, and on Sunday mornings, there are flurries of activity here as locals meet to chat and drink and the Ampuis rugby bus collects its players. For the rest of the time the sense of a community at work prevails, with the backstreets given up to ferociously barking dogs that howl at the occasional passerby. "I don't feel we're really a southern community," says Patrick Jasmin; "I look at all the cafés and outdoor tables at Tournon, and feel that I have reached the south only when I get there."

During the 1990s the outstanding event for the standing of the village was the redevelopment of the fifteenth-century Château d'Ampuis, down by the river. With its shiny tiled Ardoise roof, it literally gleams under the sun. The masonry is pale brown and newly smoothed, and the park and gardens are also being revived by the Guigal family.

Around Ampuis, one veers back to anonymity. The vineyard area also includes the hamlets of Verenay (officially part of the *commune* of Ampuis) and St-Cyr-sur-le-Rhône at the northern end nearest Vienne. Verenay is home to some noted growers like Clusel-Roch and Jean-Michel Gérin, but there is little there, except for a fruit and vegetable seller in a warehouse by the road.

St-Cyr-sur-le-Rhône is a tiny place with little obvious wine connection—no signs, no cellars. It has fast become a dormitory village for Vienne and Lyon, and the plateau area just above it is full of new housing. A couple of growers, Christophe Semaska at the Château de Montlys and Daniel Vernay, work from here.

The southern end, cheek by jowl with Condrieu, comprises Tupin and, high above it, its twin, Semons. Tupin is a "blink and miss it" hamlet on the N86, but is home to a gathering group of quality seekers, mostly young and motivated—David and Benjamin Duclaux, the Bernard brothers, Jean-Michel Stéphan, and Martin Daubrée. Semons is home to the one great value restaurant *dans le coin*, the Auberge de la Source, with spectacular views over the Rhône.

The heart of Côte-Rôtie remains the hillsides right beside Ampuis. These are what were described in Roman times, when winemaking started here. The Romans had moved in after defeating the local Allobroges tribe at Bollène, to the south in 121 BC. This opened up the region, and Vienne was chosen as a divisional depot for Julius Caesar's army in 58 BC.

Thereafter Lyon and Vienne vied for favour from Rome, and Vienne's early golden period occurred during the reign of Augustus, from 27 BC, when it was the chief commercial centre for the trade in flax and hemp supplying the western Roman Empire. It was then that many of its lasting monuments were built—theatre, temple, circus with its pyramid obelisk. So rich in Roman relics are Vienne and its neighbourhood that a quite varied Roman museum was set up just across the river in the late 1990s.

By the early years after Christ, Vienne was the thriving capital of mid-Gaul, and its wine, the *vinum picatum*, had become famous as the first Gallic wine to reach Rome. According to the writings of Roman authors of the time, such as Lucius Columella in his *De re rustica* (c. AD 60), the *picatum* seems to have been a deeply coloured wine with a certain "pitchy" taste. Helping to spread the word about it was the presence of a serious number of legions, all based in Vienne. Vienne's rivalry with Lyon intensified at this time, and in AD 68, 20,000 men were sent to besiege Lyon (Lugdunum) when its Governor, Julius Vindex, revolted against Nero in what turned out to be the last months of the Emperor's life.

In the following year, Vienne narrowly escaped destruction by the soon-to-be-crowned Emperor Aulus Vitellius, whose army was described as "ill-disciplined." He had been set up for an assault on Vienne by Lyon, but was more interested in heading south to stake his imperial claims in Rome. Vitellius is said to have tried the pitch wine on his way through, and ordered some sent without delay back to Rome (*Histoire de la ville de Vienne*, Mermet Aîné, publ Firmin-Didot, 1828, Paris). Vitellius was tortured and killed in December AD 69—in Rome.

Both Pliny the Elder, who was born in AD 23 and died because he got too close to the eruption of Vesuvius in AD 79, and Martial (c. AD 40–103) had encountered the *picatum*, which was apparently quite a snob drink in their day. In his *Epigrams* (XIII, 107), Martial boasted to his doubting friends that he had been sent the wine from the vine-growing area of Vienne by a friend of his called Romulus. Martial appears to have visited Vienne and seen the vineyards himself, since he had a circle of friends living there.

Pliny (*Natural History* XIV, 26 and 57) discussed the wine with more reverence, as befits probably the world's first wine chronicler. In the 37 books that comprise his *Natural History*, he refers to more than 40 different wines with an expertise undoubtedly acquired from frequent tasting. Pliny was drawn by the very "pitchiness," or coarseness, of the wine from Vienne and found it to be a good example of a country wine—one that was better appreciated in its native place than overseas. Pliny solemnly concluded that one could not know what real *picatum* was like unless it had been drunk in Vienne itself: a handy let-out for a host in Rome if his *picatum* was found to be disappointing!

Vienne started to decline in importance around the second century AD, when the philosopher Emperor Marcus Aurelius (AD 121–180) showed his preference for Lyon. From 250, the whole area's importance to Rome started to decline as the outlying power shifted to places like Trier. Replacing Rome's influence came that of the Church, with both Vienne and Lyon housing important bishoprics. News of the *picatum* goes cold at this juncture.

The region of Côte-Rôtie was therefore rich in Roman remains and traces, although the Saracen attacks of the eighth century destroyed many of these Roman artefacts. Ampuis is not mentioned in despatches at this time, but by the Middle Ages the village was dominated by the Seigneurs of Ampuis—various families who lived at different times in a château raised on the site of a Roman camp.

Today's château by the river was called the Low Château by the year 1339. It became more important than the hillside version, whose ruins are on a rather ghostly little grassy tor on part of the *Côte Blonde* called *La Garde*. From 1380 until 1755 this riverside château was the home of the Maugiron family, its central part built in the mid-fifteenth century. This period marks a quiet time in Ampuis' history, the only claim of some note being that in 1553 the first turkeys ever eaten in France were served at the château!

At the same time the Viennois wine disappears from all chroniclers' records and does not reemerge until the mid-nineteenth century, when the French authors Jules Janin and Cochard praised it under the name of Côte-Rôtie.

CÔTE-RÔTIE VINEYARDS

The most underestimated aspect of Côte-Rôtie is how steep its hills are. Now that they are much covered with vines, the car traveller can whizz past on the Autoroute to the east and look across at a series of green-clad slopes that roll gently south, one after another. The green is dappled, often sunny, and looks all rather pleasant.

Take that comfortable traveller and place him on *Rozier* or *La Viallère* in the north, or *Combard* in the south, under the midday sun, pickaxe in hand, soil sliding underfoot, nothing to hold on to, and he would—if a reasonable person—ask to be let off work, offer respect, and go and sit down and have a glass of the wine, for which he would be happy to pay more.

These hills are tough going—in places like *Combard* their incline is as much as 60°—and their heritage is supreme. Vines are grown here because countless generations have discovered that it works—put in the plants, look after them, and you can bring forth a mighty wine. It's a wonderful, proven location.

There is one rule of thumb when looking at the vineyards and wondering what effect their soil has on the wine. The northern part, from the *Côte Brune* up to Verenay and St-Cyr-sur-le-Rhône is largely composed of schist, with mica bits in it. At times, the rock is grey-blue; underfoot it is sleek and slippery. This gives wines with bone, a more upright, tannin-marked, black fruited, and long-lived version of Côte-Rôtie.

The granite element with more quartz, weathered feldspars, and white mica in it increases markedly in the southern stretches, meaning from the *Reynard* ravine that separates the *Côte Brune* from the *Côte Blonde* on south towards Tupin and Semons and over the *Bassenon* stream into Condrieu. This soft granite is in a very loose, decomposed state, often referred to as *arzelle*. It is very poor quality, low in nutrients, and gives more floral, red fruit wines that don't have the tannic structure to allow long keeping. Their colour is also lighter than the northern-sector wines, and it is no surprise that just a shade further south at Condrieu, on similar soil, it is Viognier that is planted.

The vineyards are made up of a mix of slope, steep hills, and flatter promontories that near the plateau become genuine level ground that can be worked by machine. Terraces make up the prime areas on the granite areas of the south; so crumbling is the soil there that walls are vital to stop constant slippage. These dried stone walls, such as those proclaiming the *Côte Blonde* near the N86, have not changed substantially since the days of the Romans and are still generally held together without the aid of cement. Under the joint attack of wind and rain, they require annual maintenance, which is often done after the harvest and before the winter cold; they are often higher than a man, and many man-hours are spent on them.

In a move to get away from such labour-intensive methods, some growers like Guigal have started to take out the walls on the more solid schist vineyards in the northern sector like *Côte Rozier*. The harder rock face reduces the incidence of soil slippage, and a slope allows more mechanised working. It is not aesthetic, but it is practical.

"The gain can be 10 per cent more vines," comments Jean-Michel Stéphan, "and that's a lot of money if you translate that into the end price of the wine. But of course, you pray there will be no big storms."

Côte-Rôtie is 95 per cent planted with Syrah, with the white grape Viognier also allowed, up to a maximum of 20 per cent in any finished wine. "The limit is set to respect the fact that Côte-Rôtie is a red wine," comments Gilles Barge, "but the reality is that most people work around 3 to 5 per cent, with just a few at 10 per cent or over." Much of the Viognier is grown in the southern area, where the loose granite is similar to the soil found around Condrieu itself, on sites like *Chéry* and *Vernon*.

In recent times, the Syrah's original local name, "Sérine," has taken on a sharper significance, used as it is to denote vines selected from old rootstock rather than clonal produce. Gilbert Clusel has been a prime mover to defend the old genetic heritage of the Syrah from these slopes, and has worked hard to revive the practice of *massale* planting and also to collect a store of older vines in a special programme. This has led to a conservatory vineyard being created for Côte-Rôtie as a whole.

"You get less crop from the Sérine or *massale* selection vines," he comments, "so there is a gain from not having to go round dropping grapes. A lot of the clonal varieties were developed for places like the southern Rhône or California more than here, and because density elsewhere is often around 5,000 to 6,000 plants per hectare, the vines had to be abundant. But here we're at 10,000 plants, so we risk being overrun with volume.

"In wine terms, I find the clonal varieties bring out fresh, pleasant, low-tannin wines; that's not Côte-Rôtie at all—the context is different here," he adds.

The search for the best generating plants started with three guiding criteria:

1. The vine should be producing little.
2. Its grapes should be aromatic when tasted.
3. The berries should be small, with the bunches loosely formed to lessen the risk of rot.

The ideal was a better rapport between juice and skin, since the clones overdid the juice and so lessened the tannic content. Having collected over 100 samples from a series of 60-year-old vines, the growers had to check that there was no virus in any vine's wood. This cut the field to 80. And it is these that are planted in the Conservatory vineyard chez Martin Daubrée at Domaine du Corps de Loup and that form the basis of any new *massale* cuttings. All growers who are members of the Syndicat, which brings in the vast majority of people, are allowed access to these cuttings.

Underlying these moves is an unspoken acceptance that the 1970s and 1980s were largely bad for the vineyards. The chemical companies held sway in people's actions; while young men went off to factories to gain a cushier wage, those left behind on the hot slopes were likely to accept wonder solutions to blight and so lighten their workload. It was a shortsightedness that of course takes a lot longer to unwind than it does to install, but now the voices are being heard, and *appellations* are taking steps from the centre, not just from the fringes.

Not everyone is convinced by the properties of the Sérine, however. After much planting of both Sérine and clones as he expanded his vineyard, Jean-Paul Jamet says that "if I replanted today, I'd use clones only. We use the Viala rootstock, which my grandparents worked with and which is suited to soil with acidity, and also does well in drought conditions; it's also a small producer. We then graft on to the Viala clones that resist rot and ripen earlier for a high-up site like *Mornachon*, and they do us well. We hardly have to thin the vegetation, so we also gain on that front."

"It's too simple to make war on clones," he adds. "When you graft the Sérine on to the Viala, it produces more crop than a clone, for instance. The most crucial point in this whole debate is mastery of yields. A clone's berry may be bigger, but the skin is very thick, meaning there's a good rapport between juice and skin. The Sérine's skin is thin, which leaves it more prone to rot."

The most commonly used rootstock at Côte-Rôtie is the 3309, across an estimated 80 per cent of the vineyard. This is well suited to the rocky areas and any acid soils. Sites like *Lancement*, next to the *Blonde* and *Mornachon*, high up are very acid, while the S04 rootstock adapts better in the more limestone-tinged soils of sites like *Moutonnes*, *Truchet*, and to some extent *Chavaroche*, the last two sharing the same slope.

Another rootstock for the Sérine has been the 101-14. This needs deeper, thicker soil, so is often planted high up, on or near the plateaus. Its drawback is its weakness in drought, which is much more marked than that of the 3309.

Since the late 1990s, a third rootstock has come to the fore, the Fercal. It is not suited to the acid soils, and gives, according to Jean-Paul Jamet, "better-quality grapes." "On our new plantation on *Gerine*, for instance," he continues, "we have three rootstocks, all adapted to the soil changes. We have Viala on the acid soil, 3309 in the middle, and lower down, on the richer limestone soil, we have the Fercal."

A final word on this debate must come via the tasting glass. In 2000 Clusel-Roch made two wines from *La Viallière*, one with clone grapes, the other with *massale* Sérine. The clone vines had to be cut back to stay at 40 hl/ha (hectolitres per hectare); the *massale* bore the same yield without cutback.

Tasting notes ran as follows:

2000 (CLONE WINE) ★ Delicate, quite piercing fruit nose; very delicate, easy wine, some end tannin. Bit light.

2000 (MASSALE WINE) ★★★ Darker nose, bit more profound, less piercing; pretty fruit, lasts nicely, more complete matter.

Analysis showed that the acidity was 0.5 milligrams (mg) higher on the *massale* than on the clone wine. The polyphenols were the same, but their composition was largely from coloured matter on the clone, and more from tannin on the *massale*.

The Viognier is a much less consistent producer than the Syrah and does not adapt to any heavier soils at Côte-Rôtie. The now retired Marius Gentaz-Dervieux was one of the only growers who persisted with it on the prime *Côte Brune*, where the soil contains some clay. But his vines dated from the 1920s. A supporter of the Viognier, with sizeable plantations on the northern sites of *Fongeant* and *La Viallère*, is Pierre Gaillard. "It acts to soften the Syrah," he comments simply.

Bernard Burgaud is not a fan, however: "I planted Viognier in the beginning, but I don't use it in my red wine any more. I don't think it adds anything special—it may well have come into Côte-Rôtie because it produces wines of a degree or two more alcohol than the Syrah if grown in the same conditions. But once it has been vinified in the same vat as the Syrah, at a high temperature of 30°C or more, you've probably rid it of most of its aromas anyway."

A heartland for the Viognier here is the *Côte Blonde*, where the lighter, looser ground suits it well. There are pockets of what the growers call *terres blanches* that contain some limestone in the middle part of the *Blonde*, and its wines can often contain at least 10 per cent Viognier.

Viognier fears oïdium, like the Syrah, which also suffers from black rot. "Since 1988 the vineyard is more crowded, and there is less diversity in the ecosystem," observes Jean-Michel Stéphan, a man dedicated to pure forms of work in the vineyard and the cellar.

Up on the plateau the vines are planted 2.5 metres apart to allow tractor working, but on the steep slopes, there is only half the distance between the vines, space being so precious and one worker requiring so little room for manoeuvre. The rule of thumb for the slopes is one man to work two hectares. This falls to one hectare per man when all work is manual and the soil is worked by hand for pure organic methods.

The traditional form of pruning the vines has been by the Guyot method. To optimise this, each vine has two stakes hammered into the ground around the foot of the plant, and its shoots are led outward along the sticks so as to achieve the greatest possible exposure. The job of hammering these sticks into the rocky ground is arduous; the hammer and the pickaxe used to be the only tools for this operation, but now minicaterpillar bulldozers, angled precariously on the inclines, do some of the clearance.

The 1990s saw increased training along wires, as opposed to the *échalas*, or wood stake system. On the very steep slopes, the stakes serve better to allow the grower to work up and down and sideways across the hillside, which is impossible if there are wires. But labour times are high. Tying the vines in May before the young shoots are broken by the wind takes three times as long for stakes as it is for the same area along wires. Most of the old vines, situated in the best, often steepest areas, are staked.

The most proven attachment for the vines is willow, and the winter is when this is cut and prepared. The completeness of the cycle is apparent, with the willow trees grown near the bottom of the vineyards. Skilled old-timers like René Clusel have a technique to bite the willow attachments, and he swears that they are much more solid than any plastic equivalent.

The Royet system along wires also allows greater aereation, so it has advantages. There is some Gobelet pruning, where the vine stands alone, and the younger vines are pruned right back for this.

Since 1990 the hillside vines have been sprayed for basic treatments from the air, by helicopter. "One man can spray just 0.7 hectare in a day, with the machine on his back," states Jean-Michel Gérin, "whereas the helicopter can treat 17 hectares per hour at three times less the price. At first, we had to have guided tours to Hermitage to see what Philippe Jaboulet had achieved there with the helicopter, to overcome the doubters, though." Now 80 per cent of the growers subscribe to this service, which since 2004 has worked only with organic materials. The helicopter is used around May and June, when the vine's vegetation is growing fast. A refinement from the late 1990s has been the elimination of insecticide spraying, so the focus is on dealing with oïdium, mildew, and black rot.

According to the approach, work times can vary wildly in the vineyards. Brigitte Roch of the excellent Domaine Clusel-Roch estimates them as follows: "On foot, it's a day to spray chemical weedkillers on half a hectare; with a pickaxe, it takes a day to work and weed 0.05 of a hectare, or one-tenth of the sprayed area; and it's a whole day using a winch to till 0.15 to 0.2 hectare." So any *bio*domaine like theirs or Vincent Gasse's has an in-built cost disadvantage compared to many of the others.

The vineyard has more than tripled in plantation since the early 1970s; in 1973 there were 72 hectares, in 1982 102 hectares, in 1991 140 hectares; and by 2005 the vineyard had risen to 231 hectares. But it's still small compared to other famous regions. In Bordeaux, for instance, all *cru classé* wine from St-Julien proceeds from around 910 hectares; the whole Graves *appellation* area runs to around 3,350 hectares for the reds and whites.

Self-control has improved since the feverish days of the mid-1980s. Then a rise in wine prices on the back of vintages like 1983 and 1985 provoked a stampede of requests for new plantations: 16 new hectares were allowed in 1984 and 1985, for instance. The INAO, the national ruling body, was being governed by the growers' wishes, so it was up to them to draw back.

The expansion led to the development of less central locations—previously untilled ground on the plateau above the top slopes, overgrown patches on the high slopes, and the nooks and gulleys leading away from the front hillsides towards the plateau. "This meant that in the early 1980s a lot of young vine fruit was in the wines, which led to a knock on our reputation," recalls Gilles Barge, President of the Growers Union during the early 1990s.

The base yield is now 40 hl/ha (2,153 bottles per acre). There is a maximum 10 per cent top-up on this, which was moved down from 15 per cent by the union in 1989. So in an abundant year of sound quality, a total of 44 hl/ha is allowed—2,370 bottles per acre. Conversely, nature can throw all these figures out of the window and allow just 23 hl/ha, or 1,238 bottles per acre, in a drought-hit vintage like 2003.

However, large-scale new planting remained an issue for some years: in 1993, there were around 20 hectares of plants under four years old waiting to come on stream—on top of a then total area of only 160 hectares. Moderate vintages like 1992, 1993, and 1996 showed up these imbalances.

The growers confirm that the maximum available land for vineyards at Côte-Rôtie is 320 hectares. In active production in 2004 were 216 hectares, with 15 hectares of young vines, and an annual increase of 6 hectares of new vines per year—spread among 50 growers, remember. A general estimate is that another 50 hectares of

sound sites could be planted; "we'll be just about full up by 2013 or so," says Jean-Michel Gérin, former President of the Growers Union.

Most of the untaken area is overgrown and on the steep slopes, and quite apart from the issue of clearing it, there is the extra hassle of making access tracks or roads. Jean-Michel Gérin estimates the cost of clearing and planting one hectare to be Euros 70,000 (GB£45,000/US$70,000). "And then it's four years before that hectare can make any Côte-Rôtie," he adds.

Getting hold of a vineyard is pretty theoretical, since the incipient demand is so high, and no one just launches a large, mature plot on to the open market. Gilles Barge comments that the theoretical price of a planted hectare in a central location might be 1.5 million francs (£150,000/US$225,000).

"The acceleration in prices came after the very good 1989, 1990, and 1991 vintages. These alerted people to the possibilities, especially as the wines sold quickly and in some domaines there was a shortage of wine," he comments. But I can remember lesser domaines than his hawking off their 1993 vintage to Châteauneuf-du-Pape merchants, facing a cash flow squeeze with the poor 1992 and 1993 and uneven 1994 on their hands. The real Klondyke has occurred high and low since the mid-1990s.

The new restraint obliges growers to be patient. Martin Daubrée owns five hectares of unplanted slopes—which he reckons is about one-fifth of the available slope sites—but his annual allowance is just 0.13 of a hectare per year. New plantation rights are designed to favour two groups—growers who already work some vineyards and those under 35 years old, who are allowed double the quantity. Martin, ahem, is not in the second group.

Hanging over the vineyards since the mid-1990s has been a much more serious spectre than any passing blight: the fact that Lyon needs an outer ring road. When it was announced that this would take a westerly route and reconnect with the southern Autoroute du Soleil at Côte-Rôtie, the outcry was predictably raucous. Yes, there were the plans—a tunnel emerging somewhere close to the *Landonne* vineyard, between Verenay and Ampuis.

While the French have excelled in forward-looking transport projects, this was not their Fonctionnaires' finest hour. There has been a hullabaloo, but the plan is stalled at present since the government has run out of funds. "We remain vigilant," states Jean-Michel Gérin. "The head of the Rhône region seems to have turned against the idea, and there could be a delay of 10 to 15 years." Only a delay? Sharpen your pens and e-mail techniques, readers!

The justifiably most famous sites or *climats* are the *Côtes Brune* and *Blonde*, the two adjacent hillsides above Ampuis. Indeed, in a 1909 showcard made for the Paris Concours Agricole, the *Brune* and the *Blonde* were stated to give "the *premiers grands crus*," while "the various other slopes give the *grands crus classés*, the *crus classés* and the *crus bourgeois*"—terminology which is very rarely used today, although Guigal's *La Mouline* used to be called a *premier cru de la Côte Blonde*, a self-styled epithet.

The 1907 study of the vineyard by Claudius Roux supports the contention that the heart of Côte-Rôtie lies across these two slopes. The then estimated value of one hectare on different sites ran as shown in table 2.

It's worth noting that in those days, fruit and vegetable zones near the river were more highly valued for their income potential than all but the very best vine sites, and also that the higher sites up around the plateau, such as *Champin* and *Tartaras*, were poorly regarded, as was the top of the *Blonde*, three times less valuable than its centre. Nothing has changed—the hierarchy has stood the most simple test of time: the best-quality wine comes from the most central places.

CÔTE-RÔTIE TERROIR

The *Reynard* stream that separates the two main slope faces of *Brune* and *Blonde* runs through the centre of Ampuis near the church and

TABLE 2
Côte-Rôtie Estimated Site Value (francs per hectare)

Centre of the *Brune* and the *Blonde*	18,000
Borders of the Rhône	12,000
La Roche	12,000
The *Coteaux* of Verenay	
(*Grandes Places–Viallière* today)	9,000
Mollard, opposite the *Blonde*	9,000
Top of *Blonde*, towards *Boucharey*	6,000
Champin	4,000
Tartaras	3,000

marks the divide between two distinct geological breakdowns. The Tertiary Era movements of the Alps served to fracture the granite masses running across to the Pilat region of the Massif Central; Pilat, now a regional park, is the mountain to the west of Condrieu across the Rozay plateau. The Alpine shift left rock debris of different types in its wake.

To the north of *Reynard*, comprising the *Brune* onwards, lies schist that contains both black and white mica and quartz. The rock can be a blue, steel grey and even black, and is said to contain more iron and manganese. To the south, from the *Blonde* onwards, the incidence of granite increases, starting out with layers of gneiss, described in James E. Wilson's study *Terroir* (Mitchell Beazley, London 1998) as a "granitic-like, metamorphic rock." This runs through the hands and has a pale brown, sandy, loose texture. Here the rock hue is paler, more cream or white or even pink—as it weathers, its colour lightens. The top soil rarely goes much deeper than half a metre.

Beyond these broad delineations are precise localised changes within sites. For instance the *Côte Brune* under the *Pavillon Rouge* was found to contain just 0.06 per cent of limestone, whereas just up the hill from there, on *Truchet*, the level rose to 52 per cent (C. Roux, 1907 *Monographie*). Most growers would tell you that they prefer not to have limestone, which doesn't bring out the true power of the Syrah.

The areas of greatest clay are those high up near the plateau—sites like *Brosse* and

Boucharey contained over 14 per cent in the 1907 study. This brings coarse flavours, and such wines need blending with better-structured wines holding clearer fruit and tannin. In the past, fruit, vegetables, cereals, and rape seed would be widely grown here, in areas where the high cool wind factor leads to later ripening.

At the northern end of the *appellation* is St-Cyr-sur-le-Rhône. This is a peripheral area, where the soil, still largely underpinned by schist and rock, can be heavier than at Verenay. The outskirts of Vienne have intruded here, and several of the listed vineyard sites like *La Chapuise* are now built on. *Chapuise* also has a little château on it.

Montlys, the vineyard above the rather gaunt château, accounts for most of the St-Cyr vineyard nowadays, with around three hectares planted between the Château de Montlys and Daniel Vernay. This enjoys a mix of east and southeast exposures, profiting more from the early than the late sun. North of it, separated by a stream, is *Cumelle*, a fully south-facing site where Christophe Semaska of Château de Montlys has a small plot and Stéphane Montez is clearing and planting. At its bottom now are small factories.

The wines from St-Cyr are correct but lack the resounding structure of the central locations. Their relative finesse requires careful cellar work, and a finely calculated harvesttime at full maturity to ensure the wines contain good juicy matter. The flavour sensation is largely black fruits. Growers in this area include the GAEC Daniel Vernay and Christophe Semaska.

Just south of *Montlys*, which can be a windy spot, is *Les Lésardes*. This is quite a precocious site, its wine more aromatic than the heavyweights of the *commune* of Verenay, Les Grandes Places and Viallière. *Lésardes* is unusual, for it has some small caves, or *grottes*, in the relief of the slope, low down the hillside. Its soil is compacted alluvions, so there are a lot of pale *galet* pebbles on it. Some of it has been recently planted, but it used to be known as a spot for good new potatoes and peas, ripening two weeks ahead of the plain, and also for long-

shaped radishes, called *flamboyants* by the locals, that grew well in its sandy patches. Jean-Michel Gérin, Patrick Jasmin, Stéphane Pichat, and Michel Bonnefond work vines here, the last named selling the fruit to the *négoce* trade.

Up the hill from it is *Cognet*, where Gilles Remiller has a holding among a lot of overgrown ground, and beyond it *Gerine*. The latter also still has two strips of uncultivated land running down it. The Jamet brothers and André François work land higher up, and Jean-Michel Gérin and the Jamet brothers further down on *Gerine*, on which there has been recent planting.

One of the features of the hill above Verenay is the series of streams that create good south-facing flanks for sets of vineyards. The rated *lieu-dit* Montmain lies across the *Montmain* stream north of *Grandes Places* and *Viallière* and enjoys just such a fine exposure, along with its neighbour *Gerine*, which lies a little nearer the Rhône. *Montmain* is partly terraced, partly a slope and is a principal holding for Cédric Papette, while Gilles Remiller also has a small plot there. Both *Montmain* and *Gerine* are well protected from the north wind.

Below it, at the bottom of the flank, is *Verenay*. Here the schist contains some flint, as well as sand because this site is low down the slope. There is also small glacier stone debris. Free draining, this soil helps its few vine plants to ripen quickly.

Above the hamlet of Verenay, the two top spots are *La Viallière* and *Les Grandes Places*. They are split by the *route du Lacat*, which curls steeply up to the plateau, with vines pressing hard up to the roadside. *La Viallière*'s soil is decomposed schist, the schist often found 50 cm (20 in.) down. It is fissured, so the roots can burrow a way through. Rainwater may rush through the topsoil, but it can at least gather around the vine roots. To the eye, lots of small, chiselled sharp stones lie on the light grainy brown topsoil. *Viallière* is one of the largest sites at Côte-Rôtie, thought to be a little under 10 hectares by the growers. It is also very steep, and Brigitte Roch jokes that they quite often start their harvest there, while the team is still energetic!

Viallière lies in two portions, split by a small rocky ravine, and has a mix of southerly and easterly exposure. The northern part is worked by J-M Gérin, Gaillard, and Clusel-Roch. The bottom, southern part of *Viallière*, opposite the Ampuis rugby ground, differs a little, with a finer, less stony soil. In midslope, *Viallière* is very steep—an incline of around 50 to 60 per cent. The southern part is worked by Bonserine, Romain Champet, François Gérard, Rostaing, Clusel-Roch again, and Robert Niéro.

Tucked into the bottom end of *La Viallère* and sharing the same hill flank and soil style is a small slope site called *Fourvier*; this too is schist with stones, in the form of a small east-facing triangle. Part of it was reclaimed in the mid-1990s by Philippe Faury after it had lain abandoned for some decades. J-M Gérin and Romain Champet also have plots here. It is separated from *Viallière* by the *chemin de la Victoire* road.

South of *Fourvier* on the same hill is *Nève*, a very small site of under one hectare. The high part touches the plateau of Verenay, and is split from the low part by a strip of overgrown land. Chapoutier works the high part and Didier Côte, who sells mostly to the merchant trade, the bottom strip, near the N86 road beside the Buffin rock works. The soil being similar to *Viallière*, the wine from *Nève* is based more on power than subtlety. There is also a stream here, the Nève, but it is often dry.

Verenay's other big name is *Les Grandes Places*. This lies above *Viallière* and is a mix of flat areas with very steep outcrops; it is quite rocky and also windy. It is mica-schist with iron elements in the soil. There are three wines bearing this name—those of Jean-Michel Gérin, Clusel-Roch, and Stéphane Montez. The fruit from here is minted and flinty, according to Jean-Michel Gérin. The GAEC Vernay works two plots on *Grandes Places*—one higher than the other—and there are a couple of growers who sell their crop to Guigal.

Both *Grandes Places* and *Viallière* face southeast and provide some of the most slowly developing wines of the *appellation*. The *Grandes Places* vineyard is younger than that of *Viallière*, and I would expect its wines to make progress in years to come. They carry a little more scope for finesse and the tannins are more deep-seated and refined than the overtly sturdy wines of *Viallière*.

Discussing his own wines, Gilbert Clusel explains the difference almost the other way round: "For me, Viallière is a more tender wine to drink young, with all its roundness, while Grandes Places is more robust and complex. Whether that is a function of the age of the vines or the effect of the different *lieux-dits*, I don't know."

Right above *Les Grandes Places* on the same slope is a small *lieu-dit* called *Bertholon*; this is less stony, deeper soil and the top of it is quite flat. Pierre Gaillard and a *viticulteur* who sells crop locally are present here.

The next decisive contour in the vineyard arrives with the Murinand valley. The *Murinand* stream marked the northern limit of the *appellation* until 1965. The soil remains largely schist, but the valley creates a north-south–facing divide. Along the northern border is the site of *Champon*, up near the plateau and separated from the next plateau *lieu-dit* of *Le Plomb* by a dip in the hill. Clusel-Roch, Stéphane Ogier, and Stéphane Pichat all work plots on *Champon*. The south-facing *Le Plomb*—across the winding *route du Lacat* from *Les Grandes Places*—contains plots worked by Clusel-Roch, Philippe Faury, Cédric Papette, Stéphane Pichat, René Rostaing, and Les Vins de Vienne among others.

There is more excitement from the cluster of sites south of the break in the hills caused by the Murinand stream, which is opposite the Vaugris dam over the Rhône. Here names like *Côte Rozier* and, just beyond it on the same hill flank, that of *La Landonne*, start to stir the pulse.

Côte Rozier is an east-south–facing site, helped by another stream-created inlet on the southern side, this time called *La Felodière*. These stream gulleys are a vital part of Côte-Rôtie's makeup, creating small shifts in soil, exposure, and temperature. *Côte Rozier* lies just above the big Vaugris dam across the Rhône; like *La Viallière* and *La Landonne*, part of it is skewed east, giving rise to the old-timers' saying, "Facing east is what makes *le bon vin*."

Côte Rozier can be very steep, with the occasional roughly hewn wooden ladder dropping straight down into the vineyard, a sailor's delight! Here the rock is a dark rust colour with steely blue outcrops and is very close to the surface. Just one 100 metres further on, it can become more covered in loose stones, with granite outcrops.

Côte Rozier is the sort of wine, like Viallière, that is sturdy and often provides a couch and tannic backbone to a blended wine. Until bottling most of it on its own from 1995 as Rose Pourpre, Pierre Gaillard used all his *Côte Rozier* to support his assembled wine called simply "Côte-Rôtie." Growers who are making their mark from this site are Stéphane Ogier, with his Belle Hélène, and Yves Gangloff, who uses its crop in his La Sereine Noire. Christophe Billon, the Bonnefond brothers, Otheguy, and Jamet are others with plots on *Côte Rozier*.

Côte Rozier is also worked by Guigal; here Marcel has created a new slope out of the old uneven terraces. Planting his rows at a spacing of 1 by 1.20 metres, he achieves greater density than the 1 by 1.5 metres needed for a small caterpillar to pass. The pulley, or *treuil*, is used here, the site chosen for this because its rocky composition allows less slippage and erosion than looser granite plots further south around the *Blonde*.

The extension of *Côte Rozier* towards the plateau is *Rozier*. Part of it is southwest facing and flat. There its pale-brown soil is deeper, with pockets of clay and little rock visible. Elsewhere there is decomposed granite. *Rozier*'s wine is less nuanced and more direct than the *Côte Rozier* wine. The Drevons of Domaine de Rosiers work three hectares here, with the Bonnefond brothers their neighbours, as well as Gangloff and Otheguy.

Beyond *Côte Rozier* on the same hill flank lies the well-known *La Landonne*. This has two parts, established by a ruling of 1974. The core

older part is a little more south facing than its more easterly-turned area, which until 1974 was half overgrown and in fact formed part of *Côte Rozier*. The Ampuis water supply tower in those days marked the end of *La Landonne*, with a strip of vineyard beyond it in the middle of *Côte Rozier*; this amounted to two to three hectares cultivated by growers like François Gérard and Vidal-Fleury.

By decree, this strip was doubled in size and allowed to be called *La Landonne*. Now a La Landonne wine is produced in single-vineyard form by Guigal, Rostaing, Delas, and Jean-Michel Gérin. Other growers like Levet, Jamet, and François Gérard include their grapes in assembled wines. The schist contains a lot of iron oxide here, which gives a black *cassis*, overtly warm fruit, along with regular suggestions of smokiness in the bouquet, mocha in Philippe Guigal's words, and plenty of solid tannins.

These areas have grown in stature since the 1970s, and there is little mention of them in old archives. Their wines are often very dark and long-lived, unyielding at first, and take around seven years to loosen. You have only to look at the soil and the hard rock underneath it to understand how far these plots are from the lighter-coloured sandy granite around the *Blonde* and Tupin. These northern plots give dark, brooding wines, while the granite yields the strawberry, red fruit, and florally inspired wines.

Below *Rozier* is a hewn-out dip in the hill and the *lieu-dit* of Les Rochains. This is a bit less than three hectares, and is extremely steep, the incline running to at least 60 degrees. South of the vineyards are several hectares of woods that are unsuitable for vine planting, as they face north. They will provide shelter for the vines, though. *Rochains* is a name that will be promoted by the Garon family, who intend to use this northern schist site for a single-vineyard wine. Other growers here are the Jamets, the Bonnefond brothers, and André François; the Bonneford Rochains cuvée shows real promise.

A wooded gulley (local word *combe*) with the Felodière stream running through it separates the *Rozier* vineyards from the next flank south. At the top, running onto the plateau, lies *Leyat*, across the gulley from *Rozier*. *Leyat* stretches a long way back off the Rhône corridor, and some of it faces northwest. It is not a prime site; its soil is quite deep, with some clay, as would be expected up here. In the past, this was land noted for its fruit production, notably apples, with some pear and apricot trees as well.

Growers on *Leyat* include Bonserine, Burgaud, Otheguy, and Jamet. Its planting was stepped up in the early 1970s at the moment when the surface area was enlarged. It is a site some of whose crop is sold by the growers to the *négoce* trade.

Below *Leyat* the slope starts with the *Côte Baudin*, which is quite east facing and has a little cabin at its top. Growers here include André Blanc, Jamet, Drevon's Domaine de Rosiers, J-M Gérin, and Rostaing. Like *Leyat*, this is the sort of wine suitable for blending; *Leyat*'s wine is a little fresher since it comes from a higher, windier site.

The top name on this hill is probably *Moutonnes*, an early-ripening spot that faces southeast and lies beside and below *Côte Baudin*. *Moutonnes* is a popular site with some limestone in it. Its loose soil is fine, with about 50 cm (20 in.) of it on top of hard rock, so it can suffer in a drought year like 2003. It runs from the middle level of the slope down to the village near the HLM housing blocks.

The wine of *Moutonnes* is meaty and in some years can be reductive (stinky, animal smells) and rustic, so the Jamet brothers choose to raise it in new oak. Although full, it is less elegant than *Landonne*, just beyond it to the north, for instance. Bonserine, Gérard Bonnefond, Burgaud, Bernard Chambeyron, Bernard David, and Jasmin are other growers on *Moutonnes*.

High sites at this level of the vineyard, around the 300-metre (1,000-foot) mark, are *Champin*, near Bernard Burgaud; *Ritolas*; *Mornachon*; and *Bonnivière*, the last named east facing. *Mornachon* is far from the Rhône, set out on its own, with plenty of schist and high up at about 350 metres. The other sites contain more

clay and are subject to a lot of wind. They are all late ripeners.

The next turn in the hill conformation brings in the heart of the action, as the mighty *Côte Brune* approaches. *La Brocarde* runs at midslope height into the *Brune*—in effect the more easterly version of it. It is opposite the petrol station in the village, and is an early-ripening southeast-facing spot where any snow melts early. Two specific-name wines come from here, made by Christophe Billon and François Villard. These carry raspberry flavours and a *Brune*-style earthiness but are also overtly oaked when young, which obscures some of their detail.

Other cultivators on *La Brocarde* are Delas, Rostaing, and the reticent Blanc family, André and Joseph. The Blancs took over Henri Minot's vineyard here. Climbing up the *route de la Côte Brune*, the *Brune* lies on the left-hand side and *Brocarde* on the right.

The climax of Côte-Rôtie's schist area is reached on the *Côte Brune*, a compact 10-hectare *climat*. This lies opposite the Church of Ampuis and, beyond, the château—a fitting duo indeed. It mostly faces full south, an essential part of its character. It contains outcrops of clay within the schist, as well as some gravelly elements. To the eye, the soil's hue is dark brown, at times a little blue, denoting the iron oxide and manganese content; the crisp stones on the topsoil are often grey or blue-flecked. The name is therefore logical.

The *Brune* is a hill that cuts into the granite running west. Down it runs a drainage channel that has been installed in recent years to counteract erosion. Near the ravine at its western end, inside the valley, is the Jamet vineyard; below, near the Reynard River, is Rostaing, with above that Gilles Barge and at the top, highest of all, the Bernard brothers' plot. Guigal's *La Turque* plot stands inside the valley, with Bernard Levet below Guigal towards the ravine.

Bonserine, Chambeyron of the Manin branch of the family, and Chapoutier are all close together, the first two a little more easterly pointing, the last near the Barge cellars. Gilles Barge calls his plot *Pichat*, after the old owner, and recalls that his own grandfather used to refer not to the *Côte Brune* but to *Taramond* as the vineyard here. Gilles grows about 3 per cent Viognier on the *Brune*, and comments, "Viognier does well here—we have vines from the 1950s and they're in good condition."

Guigal also grows Viognier on his *Brune* holding, one that gives his top-grade *La Turque* wine, with a 7 per cent Viognier content. The *Turque* subset of the *Brune* follows the habit of the best sites, being subdivided by the growers into even smaller local spots, others including *Pavillon Rouge* (the site of the varnished red tile roof hut), *Le Moulin,* and *La Pommière.* Guigal's *La Turque* vineyard is identifiable by the pink Vidal-Fleury cabin, which bears the letters *V F* painted in white.

Pierre Gaillard, then an employee of Guigal, recalls the work to replant the *Turque* in 1982: "It's very steep there, around 65°, so we took out the terraces to make a regular slope so we could work a winch on it afterwards." Guigal has one of his advertising signs on *La Turque* now; the *Brune* stretches above it.

The *Côte Brune* gives fantastic wine, wine with the earthy, stewed-fruits aspects of traditional Côte-Rôtie. The tannins are less prominent than *La Landonne*'s or *Grandes Places*', for instance, but give a marked structure around the wonderful enveloping density in the wine. While Joseph Jamet and Marius Gentaz-Dervieux flew the flag for this site in the 1960s and 1970s, it is also very well represented by Gilles Barge's excellent Brune, made since 1994, and by Guigal's La Turque, which in recent years has gained ground on his other top two wines, La Landonne and La Mouline.

Other growers who produce wine off the *Brune* are Rostaing (who has replanted a lot of the old Marius Gentaz-Dervieux site) and Vidal-Fleury.

Touching the east end and then running above the *Côte Brune* is *Janet,* a very gentle slope where Gilles Barge, Martin Daubrée, Drevon, and Rostaing work holdings. It is north of the *lieu-dit* made known by Albert Dervieux as *Font-gent* in days gone by, namely *Fongeant,* and at the plateau level, these two sites are split by the road. The northern stretch of *Fongeant* is flatter than the southern part, which faces the Fongeant stream and is turned southwest. The Fongeant stream feeds into the main Reynard miniriver that splits the *Brune* from the *Blonde.*

Fongeant's wine is lighter than that from the main slopes, reflecting its plateau positioning. It is not especially subtle but is interesting in dry years like 2003, since its soil, with clay in parts, is deeper than the hill areas. Hence it works well within a blended wine. Growers on *Fongeant* include Burgaud, Bonserine, Clusel-Roch, Gaillard, Gallet, François Gérard, and Rostaing.

Separated from the *Brune* by a wooded ravine is a site that sits on an outcrop of its own, *Chavaroche.* On its east side runs the little Fongeant stream that joins the principal Reynard water flow at the foot of the *Côte Brune.* On *Chavaroche*'s other side, there are more woods before the next *lieu-dit* south, *Baleyat.*

Chavaroche is a schist, very hard rock vineyard that faces broadly southwest; there is just a little clay near the top and more sand at the bottom, but the overall effect is of acid soil. The schist dominance means that in drought the vines suffer. Sheltered from the north wind, this rugged walled vineyard, whose terraces are called *cheys* by the locals, can get very hot. *Chavaroche* shares the same brown soil of the *Brune* flank, and its wine is fine and upright, with refined tannins. The Levets, Jamets, and Bernard Chambeyron work plots here, and Levet has to apply lime in the winter to rebalance the soil's pH.

Also part of this hill is *Le Truchet,* which has a more east-northeast frontage. But by contrast with *Chavaroche,* on *Truchet* there are zones of *terres blanches*—limestone mixed in with loess.

Baleyat has clay-chalk at the top, where it moves on to the plateau. This ground is also generically termed *terres blanches* by the locals— and there is plenty of it, a good two metres (seven feet) before hitting the rock. This long top-to-bottom site contains more schist lower down. *Baleyat* is opposite the south of the village, and the Jasmin family had to clear an old apple orchard when planting their holding, which is high up and exposed to the north wind. Other growers on this site are Bernard Levet and Gilles Barge.

The boundary between the *Brune* and the *Blonde* is marked by a wooded area at the top of the slopes, and then by the Reynard stream. As an indication of the extreme heat and drought of 2003, *Reynard* actually dried up near the village, an extremely rare event. It rises about 10 kilometres (six miles) away and in its higher reaches is also called *Le Moulin*.

The *Blonde* is larger than the *Brune*—14 versus 10 hectares. Optically it is different as well, giving the impression of breadth across the hill. Even on this revered site there is the odd residence with vines above and below it—housing put up in the uncertain days of the early 1970s. With its gourmand outlook, the *Blonde* runs all the way down to the N86 as it heads south of Ampuis, and makes an immediate impression due to the masses of bare granite, dry stone walls running across it in crazy lateral patterns.

At its southern extremity, there is a *clos* iron gate leading towards it on the small walled site of *La Taquière*, where the vines grow on a brief stretch of flat ground. Then the granite ledges rise abruptly, the first *Blonde* subset there called *Le Clos*, with on its north side *La Grande Plantée* under the Guigal sign. Both these vineyards are elements of Guigal's Château d'Ampuis wine. Even well into the twentieth century, *vignerons* would refer not to the *Blonde* but to subsets of it—*Le Clos*, *La Garde*, *Chatillonne*, for instance.

Here the soil contains the first loose granite signs that develop going south to Condrieu; it is pale and thin on the surface, a rosé colour, and very skiddy to walk on. Because it is so soft and crumbly, retaining walls are essential to prevent slippage. Technically, there is less iron oxide in the soil than on the *Brune*, and more silica and limestone content.

The *Blonde* flank enjoys a prime southeast, then south exposure, and ripening here is always precocious—this is the heartland of the original vineyard. Past glamour is evoked by the little, shiny Ardoise tile–roofed pavilion belong-ing to René Rostaing on *La Garde*, while Guigal has his other main sign here on the *Mouline* part of the *Blonde*. The first Château d'Ampuis was situated on *La Garde*, above the Vidal-Fleury vineyard sign.

Above Rostaing, Gilles Barge has a plot, their neighbours high up being Jasmin, Gaillard, Chapoutier, and Guigal. Further down, Bonserine, Burgaud, and Didier Chol have plots, the last bottling a Côte Blonde cuvée. The bottom of the *Blonde* almost reaches Gilles Barge's cellars. Other growers with holdings on the *Blonde* are Vidal-Fleury, which continues to produce its excellent Chatillonne directly from here; Jamet; Levet; and Thiérry Villard.

The presence of Viognier is marked here—Vidal-Fleury's Chatillonne contains 12 per cent, Guigal's La Mouline 11 per cent—and the wines bring out the lovely floral, gentle garden fruit side of Côte-Rôtie, the nearest it comes to fine, svelt Burgundy from Volnay, for instance. Tannins are always rounded and compact and the fruits are red, with wild strawberries often coming to mind. These wines often show well early on but do not generally live as long as those from the schist.

The *Brune* and the *Blonde* are the subject of Côte-Rôtie's most often repeated legend, which runs as follows. One of the Maugiron family during their residence in the château they had built had two daughters, both ravishing beauties. One possessed fair, golden hair, the other long, dark tresses. Maugiron decided to bequeath the two slopes to his daughters and to christen them according to the colour of the girls' hair. Such are the bare bones of a story that appears in some form or other in most textbooks on wine. Sometimes it is the similarity between the girls' characters and the wines of the two slopes that is said to have prompted the choice of names: the Blonde being bright and lively when young but fading quickly, the Brune starting off quiet and reserved but growing into a splendid eminence. Certainly, the Maugiron coat of arms is composed of black and white chevrons, now on show in the restored château.

Much Côte-Rôtie has often been subtitled "Brune et Blonde," but this usage is fading as more precise cuvées are produced. The leading example remains Guigal, but his outside suppliers are placed all over the *appellation*, not just from these two sites.

Above the *Blonde* is *Lancement*, largely south facing, and well regarded. It contains a rocky area that cannot be planted with vines, and its drop is very steep. It is mostly terraced, except for the top areas up on the plateau and a site where Jamet has created a slope. Its soil is similar to the *Blonde*, and it offers wines with generous aromas and a fine, elegant texture. Gilles Barge uses his *Lancement* for his Du Plessy wine, its more refined style in contrast to his beefier *Brune* cuvée. Other growers here are Bonserine, Bernard Chambeyron, Gallet, Garon, Levet, and Domaine Georges Vernay. Stéphane Ogier's plot starts on the slope and ends on the flat plateau, forming a vineyard that his father developed to get the domaine going.

Another breezy spot high up across the road from *Baleyat* and also touching *Lancement* is *Boucharey*. This south-southeast–facing *lieu-dit* has varied soils—limestone and mica schist, with also clay patches on the high spots. Its wine can be fresh, a facet that is mitigated if the vines are mature—Patrick Jasmin's 1960s vineyard here is an example. Other growers on *Boucharey* are Barge and Levet. Its crop was useful in 2003 to aid the acidity levels of grapes taken from the hotter central sites.

Split from *Lancement* by a ravine to the south is *Le Mollard*, a well-regarded site with an easterly turn on it. An established name like Patrick Jasmin exploits a small vineyard here, as well as Émile Champet, Gangloff, Garon, and François Gérard. Its soil is varied, with white soil and limestone at the bottom, more flint at the top, and mica and decomposed granite similar to the *Côte Blonde* in the middle. The emphasis here is on red fruits in its wines, with clear, well-defined tannins in a vintage like 2004.

On the Ampuis-Tupin border round the corner from *Mollard*, on the same hill and not far from the site of the new Vidal-Fleury ageing cellars, is *Le Combard*, a steep, multiwalled hill that gives quite tannic, powerful wine, a little more pointed than that of the *Blonde*.

This is the most southerly *lieu-dit* of the *commune* of Ampuis, with L'Aulin, a stream usually in water, marking the border with Tupin at the base of *Combard*. It is also one of the most inset and sheltered south-facing crags of the *appellation*. Here the trio of Gilles Barge, Yves Gangloff, and Stéphane Montez are restoring a vineyard abandoned due first to phylloxera in the 1880s, then to the First World War. Gangloff's plot of vines planted in the first part of the 1990s is on the eastern, Rhône river end, the Barge and Montez sites further into the valley.

The three growers have got together to revive a three-hectare site, the younger men renting from an industrialist's son, M. Chardon, who bought it in the late 1960s. While restoring eight-to-10-foot-high walls, they have also put in a monorail, allowing all three the same access to each person's hectare. This will allow easier transporting of the harvest and all tools, an innovation for Côte-Rôtie.

The soil is poor, quite acid, and, like so often on these old hills, changes a little according to the height of the slope. The top is partly sand with small, round glacier stones, and the middle part is drier rock and sandstone, what is called *grès*. The lowest areas contain a lot of chiselled granite stones. The wine from here mixes the expected finesse with a marked tannic presence. Gangloff's plot contains 8 per cent Viognier, so its wine is aromatic as a rule.

Gilles Barge is chuffed like anything with his monorail, and can't wait to show it off. It runs for 180 metres and takes just three or four minutes to reach the top. It was designed by a Swiss company better known for winter sports ski lifts and equipment, but it had installed a similar system in the Moselle already. It can carry three people or up to 250 kilograms (550 pounds) of goods. Looking around, he says, "It's a lesson in humility up here; a lot of people today think they're the best on the planet, but you come here and see what the old-timers did 100 years ago with no equipment except their hands. The walls are also very old—more than 150 years."

The southern spur of the *appellation* lies beyond the Aulin stream and some woods in the *commune* of Tupin. This brings affinity with Condrieu; the soil is severely slippery, loose granite, with clear-coloured sandy elements, and the wines revolve around finesse rather than power. *Maison Rouge*'s name comes from the bishop of Vienne's house on the site in the 1500s. It is a mix of granite with some clay and delivers a highly aromatic, stylish wine in the hands of the Georges Vernay domaine. David Duclaux has two hectares here and comments that its wine is usually longer and has more soul than his *Coteaux de Tupin* source.

Parts of the *Coteaux de Tupin* are very steep, and its soil can be acid. Even so, here and there can be found strips of clay of 15 to 20 metres (16.5 to 22 yards) across. These are where Bernard David grows his Viognier. Above the *Coteaux du Tupin* is *Pimontins*, up on the flat-land, a breezy spot where ripening can be at least 10 days behind the central *Brune* sites.

Also high up at Tupin is *Bercheries*; like *Pimontins*, this has a wide mixture of soils—clay-chalk and mica schist. It too is flat, and Patrick Jasmin observes that wine from its clay-chalk holds 10.5 to 11° alcohol as a rule, compared to the 12° of wine taken from the mica-schist of the same site. He works a 0.6 ha plot on *Bercheries* and finds the wine more acid and rustic than that from his mainstream areas. Other growers here are the Bernard brothers, Stéphane Montez, Thiérry Villard, and Jean-Michel Stéphan.

A curiosity from Tupin is the earthiness found in some of the wines, something like moist earth. In French this is a *goût de terre*, which can be detected in the wines of Duclaux and Gangloff. The stones around Semons are *galets*, smooth and round rather than the pointed, chiselled stones of the other end of the *appellation*. There are glints of mica in the pale brown, loose soil, and some wire training.

The Rhône runs close to the southern Semons vineyards, and the opposite bank from the Château d'Ampuis along is densely wooded, with a funnel formed from the hills that rise and then taper away opposite Condrieu. This is where a long curling S starts in the Rhône, with the village of Condrieu sitting on the last curl.

In the Semons sector, *Corps de Loup* has been given a boost by Martin Daubrée; a small plot dates from the 1960s, but a lot of new planting on old terraces was done in the early 1990s. Pierre Benetière's holding on *Corps de Loup* also dates form this time. The other top name here is what the growers call *Bassenon*, named on the map as the *Coteaux de Semons*: this is the heart of the Domaine Bernard *Vieilles Vignes*, with 1920s Syrah present, and is also worked by Yves Cuilleron.

Given the high pedigree of many of Côte-Rôtie's sites, especially those around the central *Brune-Blonde* and the *Landonne–Grandes Places* areas, it is gratifying that the 1990s marked a return of interest to the vineyards, which are now better managed than at any time in the past 30 years.

All the responsible growers thin out the vegetation now and drop bunches. The year 1996 was a prime case for this exercise. "It was a generous year, and we were finding 18 to 20 bunches per plant, not six to nine," recalls Gilles Barge. "So I left a row alone to compare later; the thinned row came in at 11.2°, the other one gave just 9.8°: no contest."

Growers are also applying manure more carefully than in the past—all part of the more reasoned approach of the current generation. The Jamet brothers are pure countrymen; neither their father, Joseph, nor they went to wine school. For a long time, they have put down fresh manure on some of their vineyards in early March, repeating the process only every five to six years. The soil is then worked to incorporate the manure properly.

"The vine roots have got lower down, and it allows the younger vines especially to handle drought weather," says Jean-Paul Jamet. "We haven't used any artifical fertilizers since 2000."

Jean-Michel Gérin can top that; he hasn't used any chemical aids since 1990. He sees the synthesis between soil and subsoil as crucial, so that there is life and exchange between them. "These days the vigour of the vines must be controlled," he says, "which takes around 15 years. Without the chemicals, the roots do indeed go deeper and so circulate the soil's minerals better. That shows through in the grapes."

Jean-Michel Gérin was president of the Growers' Union until 2004, at a time when the current crop of growers is more closely tuned in to the needs of the environment than for several generations. "Our great challenge," he states, "is how we do or do not use weedkillers given that our vineyards are on hillsides. Erosion is always just around the corner because of the potential for heavy thunderstorms in July and August here. We must limit the speed of the water, not its volume—our main concern is to slow it down." He observes that getting slope water drained off is now fixed in the growers' minds as a vital challenge.

As with many places, rain at Côte-Rôtie has become more intense when it falls, and hail has occurred more often as well. "1999 was indeed an unusual year," recalls Jean-Paul Jamet; "we hadn't had hail for 30 or 35 years. It hit the higher sites like *Champon* and *Les Grandes Places*, and Clusel-Roch lost nearly all their *Grandes Places* grapes." The GAEC Vernay in the northern *commune* of St-Cyr was also hit by hail in 2003.

Harvest dates at Côte-Rôtie also reflect what is happening with the world's climate. In the early 1970s the *vendanges* started around the end of September, but during the 1980s there was a significant advance in date. Gilles Barge has kept his own records since 1980 for the start of his harvesting, while Clusel-Roch have tracked their harvesting on their vineyard of *Les Grandes Places* in the northern sector for even longer (see table 3).

Before 2003 the earliest harvest that growers could remember was 1947, which started on 7 September. "Spring is hotter earlier, the flower

TABLE 3
Harvest Date Records of Two Côte-Rôtie Vineyards

	CLUSEL-ROCH	BARGE
1964	28 September	
1965	27 September	
1966	28 September	
1967	07 October	
1968	07 October	
1969	06 October	
1970	10 October	
1971	09 October	
1972	13 October	
1973	29 September	
1974	04 October	
1975	11 October	
1976	23 September	
1977	10 October	
1978	10 October	
1979	01 October	
1980	14 October	15 October
1981	01 October	01 October
1982	19 September	22 September
1983	02 October	30 September
1984	03 October	10 October
1985	06 October	01 October
1986	03 October	02 October
1987	08 October	05 October
1988	28 September	26 September
1989	17 September	19 September
1990	29 September	24 September
1991	02 October	30 September
1992	24 September	24 September
1993	26 September	27 September
1994	20 September	21 September
1995	23 September	21 September
1996	27 September	28 September
1997	18 September	16 September
1998	25 September	22 September
1999	24 September	21 September
2000	18 September	19 September
2001	28 September	26 September
2002	18 September	17 September
2003	27 August	26 August
2004	26 September	23 September
2005	15 September	15 September

comes out earlier, so we have less *coulure,* or fruit malformation," states Jean-Michel Gérin. "We're at least 10 days ahead of 15 years ago now for the harvest date."

July is marked by the south wind's dominance. It is even termed the Vent d'Abricots because it helps to ripen the apricots in two or three days in mid-July. Its drawback is the likelihood of rain, often severe, which can lead to mildew in the vineyards. Such was the case in 1991, with some preliminary rain on 29 September and then two days of ferocious rain on 6–7 October.

One danger specific to Côte-Rôtie comes from growers deciding to harvest too early, so as to cut the risk of spoilt crop, and then compensating for their 11°-to-11.5° crop with chaptalisation to hoist the degree. Ripening here is more precarious than in the other northern Rhône *appellations,* and there are years when the depth of the wines here is more fleeting than it is at Hermitage, for instance.

CÔTE-RÔTIE VINIFICATION

Technology has brought vinification methods here closer together. There are not many outsiders to the central system of destalking and then conducting a three-odd–week fermentation and maceration.

The destalking trend started in the second part of the 1980s, Burgaud being one of the first in 1987. His comment was both succinct and provocative: "All that is interesting in the wine comes from the skin."

Now very few growers work with whole bunches—Yves Cuilleron if he can and Champet, while the Jamets, Rostaing, and Levet do not destem more than half the crop. The Guigal policy is to retain the stems if they are ripe.

Gilles Barge's old defence of keeping the stalks would run like this: "The stalks provide a tannic advantage; they also prevent the pips sticking together and so help the circulation in the fermenting vat—the result being a better distribution of the good elements and a better extraction."

In 2002—a very tricky vintage—even Gilles had to destalk, and he has committed to investigating it further. "It's too simple to say the tannins in stalks are bad news," he still says, so it will be interesting to watch for an outcome at this domaine.

There is a different evolution for the wines once destalking enters the process. Jean-Paul Jamet comments that the "destalked" wines suffer more from reduction (a lack of oxygen that the Syrah is prone to, bringing a stinky aroma) and so need more and earlier rackings from one cask to another.

Stainless steel vats abound, although concrete is still used by around 15 per cent of the growers, the most notable names being Burgaud, Duclaux, Jasmin, and Clusel-Roch. The last named mixes it with steel.

A small observation here is that the *appellation* rules dictate that the Viognier must be fermented with the Syrah rather than added to the wine afterwards. This ruling derives from the haphazard planting of the vineyards in previous generations, which meant that the varieties tended to be mixed up together on the narrow terraces. The benefit of cofermentation between Syrah and Viognier was not lost on the growers of yore, and indeed the method is much practiced in California and Australia today. Such wine contains more richness and is plumper, with a kick given to its alcohol level.

Cool crop pre-fermentation has become more common, notably used by Barge, Duclaux, Gaillard, Gasse, Christophe Pichon, and Jean-Michel Stéphan: temperatures run between 5°C (Stéphan) and a more common 10°C. Clusel-Roch tried cooling in 2001 but felt that it made the wine too sleek and short on desirable local quality.

External yeasts and enzymes are used, but there are definite adherents to the patient use of only indigenous yeasts: Burgaud, Gangloff, Garon, Gasse (now Otheguy), Rostaing, and Stéphan are notable growers who are laissez-faire on this.

A recent development to achieve greater colour extraction has been the use of *saignée* methods to bleed off unwanted juice from the newly crushed grapes. Two main figures in the lighter, southern reaches of the *appellation* at Tupin, the Bernard brothers and Duclaux, do this, as well as Jasmin, Stéphan Ogier, and François Villard.

Pumping over of the vats (*remontages*) and cap punching (*pigeages*) are widespread, with just a few growers practising *délestages*, where part of the vat is emptied and refilled to gain increased extraction—Daubrée, Gaillard, and Gangloff do this.

Jean-Michel Stéphan is the lone applicant of overt carbonic maceration methods for his *Coteaux de Tupin* wine, aiming to achieve fruit purity; Gilles Barge immerses his crop with planks to allow a carbonic gas buildup, and so does no pumping or punching.

In pursuit of extreme extraction, some growers heat their vats more than used to be the case. Before the 1990s, a high level was 32–34°C for Guigal and Burgaud, for instance. Now a final flourish can run towards 40°C for Burgaud, who since 1999 finds this brings a gain in the quality and aroma of his fruit. Pierre Gaillard is happy to work between 35° and 40°C, and Jean-Michel Gérin around 35° to 37°C. Others who can be in the high echelons of vat heating are Gangloff, Rostaing, and François Villard.

More cellars are strictly temperature controlled now—Gaillard, Guigal, and Jean-Michel Gérin have been prominent in smart upgrades. A first wave of successful growers had started to cool their cellars after the heat of 1982 and 1983. A second wave, including Louis Drevon, did the same in the late 1980s and early 1990s. This has allowed longer, steadier extraction times and is also vital if the heat effects of summers like 2003 are to be evened out.

For most growers, cask ageing spans 18 months to two years, with a reduced number of rackings now the norm. Guigal is the longest ager, with 42 months for his Big Three of La Mouline, La Landonne, and Turque. Two modernists, Stéphane Montez and Stéphan Ogier, favour 32 months and 30 months in new casks for their special cuvées.

A few growers deviate from the norm of using 225- or 228-litre casks. The *demi-muid* size of 550 to 600 litres has its devotees, because it is less imposing on the young wine. Gilles Barge, who uses casks, *demi-muids*, and 12-to-25-hl (hectolitre) barrels, is upping the proportion of *demi-muids*. Others who use this size are Duclaux, Jamet, Jasmin, Levet, Rostaing, and Daniel Vernay. Cellars with barrels that run between 10 and 40 hl include Barge, Brotte, Joël Champet, Levet, Vidal-Fleury, and Drevon's Domaine de Rosiers.

The age of the wood is the most contentious issue. All over the Rhône there is too much indiscriminate use of new oak, often when the grape matter lacks sufficient depth to absorb it. The result gives wines that are unpleasant or even impossible to drink when young, their true character heavily overridden.

So what about Côte-Rôtie? This, after all, is the place where Marcel Guigal has used new oak on his Big Three wines since their launches well over 25 years ago—La Mouline from 1971, for instance, although large barrels were also used in those days. Jean-Michel Gérin also went straight to new oak casks for his Grandes Places when first issuing it in 1988, adding the twist of American oak, to boot.

Now new oak is well applied by classical growers in quiet proportions, often up to one-fifth of the total. The Bernard brothers, Burgaud, Clusel-Roch (classic wine), Daubrée, Jamet (classic wine), and Rostaing all do this. David Duclaux has started to use new oak for his press wine, and that, too, is a very reasoned approach.

Most special cuvées, be they based on old vines or particular plots, are subjected to overt new-oak ageing. The Bonnefond brothers, Bonserine, Cuilleron, Gaillard, Jean-Michel Gérin, Montez, Ogier, François Villard, and the Vins de Vienne spring to mind here—never less than 80 per cent new casks.

The trouble is, not everyone is as skilled in their oak handling as Marcel Guigal. The head of Vidal-Fleury, Jean-Pierre Rochias, has worked in wine for over 30 years and admits that if he were younger, he would want to study oak—how to master its complex role in helping wines to develop. He sees understanding oak as the most important challenge in winemaking today.

Clumsy oak use is a problem, therefore. When it is applied on grapes that are not properly ripened, one hits formulaic winemaking big-time. The vintage 2002 is a real test showing which growers remain vigilant and are ready to adapt their thinking and their processes to the needs of a harvest that was beset by problems of rot.

In such a year, principles of *terroir* have to be sacrificed to an extent, so one looks to the fine vintages to find its true expression. And, yes, signs are encouraging, if growers remember that Côte-Rôtie is not a monster wine in the modern idiom—it's not a bruiser, but is founded more on steady depth, beguiling aroma, a degree of elegance, and the flowering of puckered tannins as it finishes.

In opening their new cooperage, or *tonnellerie,* in the Château d'Ampuis in 2003, the Guigals have continued to set high standards. Philippe Guigal comments that "above all, we can be more sure about quality here." They need 500 to 600 casks a year, and prefer to allow them to dry out for three years, as used to be the case. Nowadays many casks are dried for only 18 months or less. The heating can also be better monitored, with the Guigal policy one of a light toasting.

While Allier oak is often used, there are those who aim to increase the use of the deluxe Tronçais oak, which is about 30 per cent more expensive. Michel Tardieu of Tardieu-Laurent is raising the proportion of Tronçais above the current 25 per cent and is also relying on casks from his and Dominique Laurent's own cooperage as well.

American oak casks are a lot cheaper than French, and find some favour. The original pioneer, Jean-Michel Gérin, uses up to 20 per cent on his Champin le Seigneur, and those with around 10 per cent include the Bonnefond brothers and Bonserine.

In the meantime, growers like Patrick Jasmin, Gilles Barge, the Jamet brothers, and Vidal-Fleury have stuck to the use of largely aged oak.

There is a hard core of quality growers who express *terroir.* The Jamet brothers, Patrick Jasmin, Bernard and Nicole Levet, Clusel-Roch, and Gilles Barge all make wines that exemplify a truly local feel.

Nowadays there is little filtration, and just a handful of growers do a prebottling fining of their wine to clear it.

CÔTE-RÔTIE

It's important to note that this *appellation's* split between the schist of the northern sector, over half the surface, and the crumbly granite of the southern area is decisive in important ways. I see the wistful longing for the north etched on the faces of the southerners, those whose vineyards are exclusively set on the granite that, once a small stream in Tupin has been crossed, ushers in the Viognier paradise of Condrieu.

Martin Daubrée of Domaine Corps de Loup has vines in both areas. He comments that "there is a big difference between my main location at Tupin-Semons in the south and my holding on *Janet* next to the *Côte Brune.* The wines are much darker from *Janet,* and there's a lot more stuffing in the wine, too."

In the northern sector, *Viallière* at Verenay is an interesting site. Wine from this hill used to be bottled on its own by Albert Dervieux back in the 1960s. The soil is right in the mica-schist zone and extends to the *Grandes Places* above it. Clusel-Roch chooses to bottle Grandes Places on its own, largely because its vines date from the 1930s.

The *La Viallière* vineyard, where the vines average 25 years old, is used as the couch for their classic cuvée. "It's always austere at the outset," comments Brigitte Roch; "you need ripe years if you want to help that grip to loosen." But it performs a fundamental role in providing the wine with a solid base, rather as *Les Bessards* does for the Chaves at Hermitage.

It's left to *Fongeant*, above the more central *Côte Brune* to provide the juicy, elegant fruit topping.

So a rule of thumb is that the northern wines are darkly coloured and their aromas accentuate black, brewed, sometimes bosky scents. Prunes, cedars, leather spring to mind. Their flavours are those of black fruits—berries and stone fruits, with some heat and chewy tannins. The most robust call to mind the *vinum picatum*— the pitch wine of old Vienne. Notably, their tannins can be evident but in good vintages are never over-imposing.

The southern wines are softer, plusher and more immediately wholesome. Their aromas convey gentle red fruit, garden-grown sources, with the occasional floral touch perhaps prompted by the Viognier presence. Their flavours lean more naturally towards *confit*, a word that implies smooth textures and the warm, compact tastes of ripe fruits. At times, these flavours can be supremely seductive, so lingering and prolonged are they, seemingly with no outer edge. The French term *sphérique*, denoting spherical in shape, is perfect for the best wines from the central *Blonde* area, for instance.

These descriptions stand up if the growers have allowed full maturity to occur. The years 2000 and 1997 have been notable for accentuating the charm side of Côte-Rôtie, with 1999 a vintage of superb ripeness but plenty of heat, too—a most unusually potent year. The year 2003 has also been heady, with plenty of stuffing in the wines—warm, ripe, brewed fruit, with less neat balance than the 1999s. Vintages like 1998, 2001, and 2004 contain more assertive tannins, and these years lean more towards the slow-burn northern model. 2001 has in a short time moved from early edginess to the potential to be a very accomplished, expressive year.

The cooler vintages, the likes of 2002, 1996, 1994, and 1993, show marked spice, cinnamon, and clove touches as they age, the more so if the stalks were left on. Here a peppery side comes through as a sequel to the simple garden fruit flavours of their first few years. Finishes are tight and mineral in these less ripe years.

Côte-Rôtie is always softer, more floral and rounded than its neighbour Hermitage. The greatest difference between the two areas probably comes from the local climate, which provides Hermitage with a Mediterranean-type average temperature in the vineyards of nearly 14°C.

When discussing the harvest with growers from the two *appellations*, more often than not it is the Hermitage faction that is more content with the year's weather. To achieve healthy, well-ripened grapes is more straightforward at Hermitage than at Côte-Rôtie. The extra miles north bring that extra slice of freshness, as could be detected in a vintage like 1998.

On an average crop of 8,500 hectolitres (hl), around 60 per cent is now domaine-bottled and 40 per cent sold through the *négociant* channels. The number of bottling domaines has risen from around 35 in the early 1990s to nearer 55 now. Very little wine is handled by merchants based outside the Rhône, and the main makers who buy in crop or wine are Guigal and Vidal-Fleury in Ampuis, Delas at Tournon, Chapoutier and Jaboulet at Hermitage, and small newcomers like Tardieu-Laurent and Les Vins de Vienne.

As the wine has risen in price, it has also suited well-known domaines to run some of their own *négociant* affairs. Stéphan Ogier is one, and in the southern Rhône, Louis Barruol of Château de St-Cosme at Gigondas is another. They involve themselves in advice on vineyard care and vinification, their policy deliberately active to ensure high quality.

In coming years we are likely to see more site-specific wines, produced in small quantities at high prices. Ironically, these are likely to be vinified in similar fashion, with new oak ageing a prerequisite—meaning that most of them will taste of—well, new oak, at first! The coming sites beyond *Brune, Blonde*, and *La Landonne* are, from north to south, *Montmain, Les Grandes Places, Viallière, Rozier, Côte Rozier, Les Rochains, Moutonnes, Lancement*, and possibly *Mollard* and *Combard*.

Beyond the specific vineyard site names come *les marques*—the brand names that are registered and allow the grower or merchant to use grapes from different areas within the *appellation*. Examples here are Jaboulet's Les Jumelles, Guigal's La Mouline and Château d'Ampuis, the Delas Seigneur de Maugiron, and Chapoutier's La Mordorée, which is a blend from plots on the *Côtes Brune* and *Blonde*.

IDEAL FOODS TO ACCOMPANY CÔTE-RÔTIE

Young Côte-Rôtie brings an interesting series of suggestions and combinations. Some growers favour fish—monkfish braised in bacon for Yves Gangloff, and Jean-François Garon talking of a fillet of John Dory (St-Pierre) with a pepper sauce when drinking the sunny wine of 1997.

Other companions for the wine within its first three or four years are game birds—partridge, pheasant (plain roast, lightly cooked)—which are popular with David Duclaux and Marcel Guigal (when the wine is older), while Bernard Burgaud suggests spiced dishes at this early stage. Jean-Paul Jamet favours a grilled beef for the wine when it is three to five years old, profiting from the fruit and freshness of it.

I find that when drinking an aged wine of seven years or so from a cooler vintage—like 1996 or even 1993—the increased graininess works well with partridge and grouse, for instance. These more mineral vintages definitely show best in autumn and spring. A wonderful match came between the Jamet 1983 and roast grouse, when consumed together in the autumn of 1998.

Nicole Levet favours seasoned or marinaded guinea fowl and meats to match the wine's fruit and aromas, and also makes the case for a Côte-Rôtie in the company of truffled dishes. Brigitte Roch also likes guinea fowl, and duck with turnips. "We also have an annual dish of a chamois that is brought by an old hunter in the mountains; we marinade it, then cook it in the oven." Brigitte also suggests wild mushrooms like girolles that can be fricaséed and eaten with mashed potatoes.

Classic accompaniments are red meats, comprising beef and lamb, and firm-flavoured venison or reindeer. Beef is favoured ahead of lamb by Bernard Burgaud; jugged hare and pigeon are other favourites of his, while he holds sweet memories of a saddle of rabbit presented by Troigros in Roanne and eaten in 2003 with a soft 1997 Côte-Rôtie.

Gilles Barge's family have an annual ritual with a hare. "I am a chasseur, but of course that can clash with the harvest," he recounts. "What we have done over the years is try to kill the hare on the Sunday, leave it to hang until the Wednesday, then marinade it. My grandmother would simmer it on the Saturday, and the family would eat it on the Sunday, with Côte-Rôtie that would be about 10 years old."

Marcel Guigal is another supporter of roast or rib of beef, while Daniel Vernay and his niece Gisèle like to drink their wine at around five years old with such classics, as well as roast beef, *boeuf bourguignon,* and wild boar.

Gigot of lamb is enjoyed by Émile Champet when his wine is 10 years old, a dish also singled out by David Duclaux. A more tender pairing is suggested by Martin Daubrée with his casseroled pork and prunes dish.

Among more exotic fish marriages come a lobster in red wine, and the eel stew of yesteryear. The lobster works best in the soft years like 1997. Patrick Jasmin says he is happy to eat fish with his wine, providing it is full flavoured.

The cheese most talked about is the local Rigottes de Condrieu, goat cheese, although the specific Rigottes d'Ampuis, made from cow's milk, is also a great combination when both the cheese and the wine are young. Bernard Chambeyron especially recommends the Rigottes d'Ampuis that his sister makes, but when they are matured. More unusually, Roquefort is spoken of as a fair companion, but not Gruyère, which is too acid. For Brigitte Roch, Camambert is "a disaster" with Côte-Rôtie.

THE PRODUCERS

DOMAINE GILLES BARGE

8 Blvrd des Allées 69420 Ampuis +33(0)474 561390

See also Condrieu, St-Joseph.

Here is one of the central men of Côte-Rôtie; Gilles has been in the thick of events at Ampuis for several decades now. His cellars are a short walk from the main square, his wife, Alice, lets out bed-and-breakfast rooms at the top of their house on the N86, and he was President of the Syndicat des Vignerons, the union, from 1989 to 2001.

Consistently he has worn hats of various exotic styles and shapes, even when rehearsing his opening lines for a Grande Fête; often an Alpine green is favoured, only to be upstaged after an Australian tour in 2003 by a Crocodile Dundee headpiece. Inconsistently, his Zapata moustache has come and gone. He has an expressive face, and a wide, gambolling walk, a man now just past 50 and used to check shirts and work boots rather than smart urban clothes.

He took over from his father, Pierre, officially in 1994, but he had vinified every vintage since 1978. He has kept going despite two heart attacks before the age of 45. His brother Jean-Pierre, 17 years younger, has helped with special attention on the vineyards, and Gilles' son Julien is also starting to appear, so some welcome support exists.

The family started in viticulture in 1860. Gilles' great-grandfather worked for a Lyonnais doctor and looked after his vineyard for him. A family record states that a cask of the 1861 sold in those days for 450 FF (very old francs), which actually works out to more than the bulk price would be today.

The domaine first bottled its wine in 1929, Gilles' grandfather Jules bottling around 900 bottles, or three casks' worth. In the mid-1960s the proportion increased, the very good 1967 acting as a spur, and since 1974 all the wine has been bottled. In those days, around two hectares were worked—a large vineyard for the time,

when the whole *appellation* was only around 75 hectares.

Not surprising given his family's long wine-making pedigree, Gilles' instincts are to make wine along traditional lines. "I have never had a push-button mentality, and once I started to use stainless steel, the challenge was to see how I could regain the texture of before, while profiting from the extra cleanliness and temperature control, which I never like to see exceed 32°C."

So in 1989 Gilles started to immerse the cap, placing planks inside the steel vats. "The gain is aromatic, bringing more refined perfumes," he explains; "*remontage* and *pigeage* stir up the wine too much for me. I don't like violence, whether it's heating the vat too much or stressing the juice. Our way allows a couch of carbonic gas to remain in the vat, and over three to four weeks we achieve a gradual and continuing extraction."

He sees supposedly new techniques like cool crop maceration before fermentation as nothing unusual. "If you put the grapes in the vat at 8 to 10°C in the morning, you have the same effect," he states simply.

The Barge vineyards cover 6.5 hectares, an increase since his new venture on *Le Combard*. There Gilles excavated and planted a very steep three-hectare site with Yves Gangloff and Stéphane Montez. Each grower works part of this.

His core site is his 1.4 ha on the *Côte Brune* above his cellars. There are never more than 5,000 bottles of celebrated Côte Brune wine, which contains 2 to 3 per cent Viognier. It is aged mostly in 550-litre casks, with a little in 228-litre casks. Some of the *Brune* vineyard was planted in 1952–53, with the largest plot in 1976. First produced in 1994, it is a mighty wine, always possessing tannic force and structure, wrapped around the typical earthy, brambly flavours of this core schist vineyard.

His Du Plessy wine is a commercial name, first used in 1994, and is largely from the *Blonde* area, including wine from *Lancement* (1987), above the *Blonde*. Twenty-five thousand bottles are made, and the wine contains about 5 per cent Viognier. Before then, there was just one wine, combining *Blonde* and *Brune* crop.

Combard's original 0.8 ha is a mix of Syrah from the 1950s and 1980s; its grapes and the recent fruit also go into Du Plessy, which is the name of the owner of the *Blonde* vines, a man now in his nineties.

Gilles also works *Janet* (1984–85), across the road from the *Brune*, and *Baleyat*, above the *Blonde*. "I'm lucky to be so centrally located," he states. Overall, he reckons half his vineyard is between 40 and 60 years old, with one-quarter dating from the early 1970s, the other from the early 1980s.

His wood ageing has always lasted two years, in three sizes, 228 litres, 550-litre *demi-muids*, and barrels of 12 to 25 hl. Since the mid-1990s he has been increasing the percentage of *demi-muids*. "Casks alone can tire the wine; anyway, I like to round off my *élevage* with four to five months in the barrels," he states. New oak is used for renewal, not as a matter of policy. There has been no fining nor filtration since 1978.

Encouragement for the future comes from his tall, slim son, Julien, born in 1981, who serves an ideal purpose of translating on Gilles' periodic trips to England. He has studied wine at Belleville and is set to travel and see other vineyards and learn commerce as well.

CÔTE-RÔTIE DU PLESSY

2003 (CASK) ★★ Big black fruit/meaty, dense aroma. The south on palate! Black fruits, curled at the edge. Some freshness, avoids cloy/heaviness. From 2008–09; 2016–19.

2002 (CASKS) ★ Cherry, light grilled aroma. Quiet red berry fruit, some definition, a low-key year. A few end tannins, but lacks core. From 2006; 2012–13.

2001 (CASK) ★★★ Grilled, black fruit/violets nose; clear-cut berry fruit with stuffing. A full year. Tannins need some time. 2012–14.

2000 ★★★ Funky, game and tea notes on bouquet; nicely weighted, fine, grows and delivers pretty fruit aftertaste; cool black fruit texture,

touch end tar. Sound length. Quite complex for the year. 2010–12.

1999 ★★★★ Red fruits/violets, broad, deep nose; aromatic red fruit flavour; very tarry, smoky length and tannins. Good core matter. Very good length. More bite and alcohol than usual. 2013–17.

1998 ★★★ Typical nose, some advance, generous black jam; squeezy fruit start, plump middle. Pretty, quite open wine with some tannic content. 2009–11.

1997 ★★ 2006–08
1996 ★★ 2008–09

CÔTE-RÔTIE CÔTE BRUNE

2003 (CASK) ★★★ Touch farmyard on aroma —earthy. Solid, chocolate-style flavour. Tight tannins woven into its chunkiness. Cooked black fruit/prune on end, chewy finish, with game aspects. Ends cleanly. 2018–21.

2002 (CASK) ★★ Red-plus *robe*; light fruit/licorice/earthy bouquet. Red fruit gums flavour, some dimension on palate. Tannins quietly present. Some acidity. Raspberry fruit late on, quite agreeable. From 2007–08; 2015–17.

2001 (CASK) ★★★★★ Dense, brambly/tarry fruit aroma, plenty to come; very clear flavour, black fruit sinew through it. Good length, classic wine, very persistent, great tannins. 2016–19.

2000 ★★★ Quite intense, stewed fruits, earthy tones; earthy rather than fruity wine, brown, stewed fruit with truffles almost. Well-sewn tannins, chocolate on end, mineral. Good length. From 2007. 2012–14.

1999 (CASK) ★★★★★ Smoky, meat barbecue aromas, a mixed bag; good, square wine with *gras* on second half. Nicely lasting, dry-toned as yet. Licorice finale. Slow-burn wine. 2013–15.

1998 ★★★★★ Smoky red fruits, tar and ripe aspects, good bouquet; tasty wine, has good flesh inside the tannins. Genuine density, burst of blackberry fruit at end. 2011–14.

1997 ★★ 2009–11
1996 ★★ Drink up.
1994 ★★★★ 2014–15

Export 35 per cent (1) Great Britain, (2) USA, (3) Belgium

MARIE AND PIERRE BÉNETIÈRE

42 Grand Rue 69420 Condrieu +33(0)474 861893

See also Condrieu.

Pierre Bénetière works 1.16 hectares. He has just 0.08 ha, a mere smudge on the *Côte Brune* (1991), but it is a useful complement to his lighter, more elegant holding of just over a hectare at *Corps de Loup* (1990, 1999), in Tupin-Semons.

He ferments whole bunches, without crushing and *pigeage*, in his fibreglass vats. Pumping-over is done daily, and a major punching down, at the end of the alcoholic fermentation. The wine is raised for 18 months in casks, 20 per cent new, the rest up to four years old. He fines with eggs from home, but doesn't filter.

In 1999 he made a one-off cuvée for a restaurant friend, called "Le Dolium." This received three years in cask, and just 240 bottles were made.

CÔTE-RÔTIE

2001 (PREBOTTLE EXAMPLE) ★★ Some violet aroma; works on elegance and purity, nice Syrah expression, decent length. Likely to be *joli*.

1999 *Côte-Rôtie Le Dolium* ★★★ Brooding, dark, leathery bouquet, southern; intense, tarry wine, brewed texture, licorice, minty end.

DOMAINE BERNARD

RN86 69420 Tupin et Semons +33(0)474 595404

See also Condrieu.

Risurgimento may be an imposing word for events at Tupin, the southern outpost of Côte-Rôtie, but there is marked change and development in the air. A young generation of winegrowers has moved centre stage here since the late 1990s.

The Bernard brothers Frédéric and Stéphane are either side of 30, and took over from father, Guy, when he retired at 60 in 2000. Across the road the Duclaux brothers are getting into their stride; nearby there is the innovative, laissez-faire winemaking of Jean-Michel Stéphan; while down the road Martin Daubrée is restoring the amphitheatre of vines around the Domaine du Corps de Loup.

The hamlet of Tupin marks the boundary with Condrieu, its twin at the top of the hill, Semons, lending its name to some precipitous crumbly granite slopes. This is the home of some of the finest wine in the *appellation*, the style deriving largely from the presence of *arzelle* in the soil—the very filtering, loose-grained sandy granite that increases south of the *Côte Blonde*.

It pays to have lived here for generations, since this increases the chances of having a spread of holdings further up the *appellation*, where the wines are firmer and darker. In these days of turbopowered wines, the growers of Tupin-Semons can be seen casting reflective glances towards the schist at the other end of the vineyard.

The Bernard brothers are fourth generation, so their spread runs beyond Tupin. They now work 4.5 ha, all planted with Syrah. "Our fief, our core, is what we locals call *Coteau de Bassenon*, but the map calls the *Coteaux de Semons*," explains Frédéric. "We've nearly 1.7 ha there in four plots, one of them a 0.7-hectare plot planted in the 1950s, which goes into our Vieilles Vignes wine."

The other contributor to their Vieilles Vignes is their half hectare of 1920s Syrah on *Rozier*, where the soil is schist, while they also work a precious 0.55 ha on the *Côte Brune*. The family also work *Les Bercheries* (1968, 1970) and a recent plantation on *Coteaux de Tupin*, high above Tupin. *Bassenon* is the stream that separates Côte-Rôtie from Condrieu, and they rent a 0.7-ha vineyard of Viognier just across it.

Frédéric studied for four years at Beaune, whereas Guy, a craggy-faced, wiry man, learnt on the job starting at age 14. He called the wine from his original 0.7 ha site "Côte-Rôtie Cru de Bassenon," and this was sold as a *vin de bistrot*, not to Lyon, but further afield. "It was very tough to sell the wine in the 1960s," he recalls, "and we would sell it up in Nantes in the north-west, despatching it on the train from Ampuis station."

Vineyard practices have evolved. In the mid-1990s, they moved to less intensive planting of 1.2-by-1 metre, instead of the old 0.9-by-0.8 metre, to encourage better ripening. The brothers have also cut back the amount of weed-killers: "In the 1970s our father started a very expensive cure for weeds, but growers didn't know all about them in those days" is how Stéphane puts it. But working the soil remains an elusive goal, due to the immense amount of slippage after any rain.

Jean-Luc Colombo used to be their winemaking adviser, and in 1995 they started to destalk half the crop. Since 2000, the year Guy retired, it has all been destalked. They are also moving away from concrete vats to steel: "Once the concrete gets hot, it's very hard to lower the temperature," says Stéphane, a free and easy, open and likeable man, who studied electronics until he got the wine bug—"like Yves Cuilleron," he adds.

Vinification lasts three weeks, with pumping-over followed by manual punching of the cap. Cask ageing lasts 18 to 24 months, the proportion of 15 to 20 per cent new casks up a little from the mid-1990s. Casks of 10 years or more are also used, so the accent is not heavily one of new oak. There has been no fining since 1997, no filtration since 1999.

All the wine has been bottled since the early 1980s, and now there is just one bottling run. There are two pure Syrah wines, the regular and the Vieilles Vignes, first made in 1994, but not in 2002.

The cellars were revamped in 2000, and this is a domaine on the move, the sons working purposefully and also being open to visitors and the market-related aspects of the winemaker's life.

"We're in a low acidity area at Tupin, which makes our ace card here one of supple, fruited wines," explains Stéphane. "Our slope here faces full south and so the harvest date is a big decision: we can have the sugars ready, but we must also retain some freshness."

CÔTE-RÔTIE

2003 (CASK) ★★ Bosky, stewed, ripe red fruit, raisiny bouquet. Full on palate but stretched, wild berry flavour gives way to obvious tannins. Not fresh, hope won't become oxidative. From 2006; 2013–14.

2002 (CASK) ★★ Seems a firm year, good to drink around 2005–06. They had to bleed early juice off the grapes by the *saignée* method to achieve deeper colour. The wine is modern and will be bottled six months early.

2001 (CASK) ★★ Prominent, smoky black fruit aroma; peppery, bouncy *cassis* fruit with a chewy undertow. Some *souplesse*. Live acidity, can meld. 2011–13.

2000 ★ Light stewed fruit aroma; easy blackberry fruit, bit sweet. Some end licorice. More interesting around 2005–06. Bit ordinary.

1999 ★★★★ Robust dark red, pretty *robe*; varied, interesting bouquet—floral, violet—with depth. Delicious attack, clear-cut fruit, grows in weight towards finish. Discreet power with very good finesse. Some new oak on finale. 2012–16.

CÔTE-RÔTIE VIEILLES VIGNES

2001 (CASK) ★★★★ Violet, seductive bouquet; grand harmony, pretty, chewy fruit. Very stylish, rolls along. Tasty, good width. 2013–14.

2000 ★★★ Blackberry jam aroma; just enough matter here, a round, plump year. Better second half with earthy/truffled notes. Tarry touches at end. From 2006. 2012–13.

1999 ★★★★★ Dark, spice and ripe berry nose, quite heady; long opening brings a floral side. Really clean fruit, lovely cool texture. Very good pure wine, some pepper and tar with the blackberry. Good balance, striking. 2011–14.

Export 40 per cent (1) USA, (2) Great Britain, (3) Switzerland

LOUIS BERNARD

Route de Sérignan 84100 Orange +33(0)490 118686

See also Cornas, Crozes-Hermitage, Hermitage, St-Joseph, St-Péray.

Based at Orange in the southern Rhône, the Louis Bernard *négociant* business produces a Côte-Rôtie in partnership with a local grower. It is 90 per cent Syrah, 10 per cent Viognier and is vinified on the spot for four weeks, before despatch to Orange for an eight-month cask ageing.

DOMAINE BILLON

Rozier 69420 Ampuis +33(0)474 561775

It takes fortitude to do two physically challenging jobs at once, and Christophe Billon is the man for that. He is a strong-framed, stout chap with bronzed, open features. He stands squarely on the ground and imparts a firm sense of forthright hard work.

He works half his week in the Guigal vineyard, and then comes home to look after his own 1.7 hectares. To judge from the new cellar building, he is making progress. He sells half his crop to Guigal and vinifies the rest himself.

"My grandfather was a mixed fruit and vegetable man, with a small plot of 0.17 ha on *Côte Rozier*. I took over my father's vineyard in 1986, planted half a hectare and rented the rest. I started to do some bottles in 1991." He states in the most matter of fact way that his half hectare took 10 years to clear and plant.

His plots are on *Côte Rozier* (1942) and *Côte Baudin* (1950s); *La Brocarde* (1986) on the *Brune* hillside (0.3 ha); *Mollard* and *Le Goutay* (late 1990s) on the *Blonde*; and *La Roche* just below *Landonne*. Several of these *lieux-dits* are on the low areas of the slopes.

He produces two wines, a straight Côte-Rôtie and La Brocarde, an average of 1,400 bottles taken from the plot of the same name. This vineyard is an early ripening slope.

Since 2001 he has destemmed all the crop, but would leave any very ripe grapes entire. He has started to try a 10°C cool premaceration, which is followed by stainless steel fermentation towards a top heat of 32°C. The regular wine receives 18 months' ageing, half in new casks, half in casks one to three years old. The

Brocarde is all new oak raised, with 20 per cent of the oak American, for 26 months. He fines and filters.

Christophe is finding his way, trying new cellar methods, looking for what works best for him. The Brocarde is a good, promising wine, some way ahead of the regular. Both wines show very clear, decisive aromas.

CÔTE-RÔTIE

2002 (CASK) ★ Easy, overt wine, for restaurants. Rounded aromas. Should not leave this in cask for 18 months.

2001 (CASK) Well scented, mix of damp earth/red berry. Firms up after fruit start, bit tight, touch burnt on finish.

CÔTE-RÔTIE LA BROCARDE

2002 (CASK) ★ Even, stewed fruit aroma; tasty, easy palate, some flesh, tender stone, plum fruit. Fair length.

2001 (CASK) ★★★ Sleek raspberry, iris bouquet, fair depth; clear-cut, pure flavour, elegant plus a quiet kick. Raspberries. Length good, oak works fine at end. 2012–14.

2000 ★★ Nose shows some advance, game/violet with raspberry. Palate starts quietly; earthy, chewy texture. Red fruit, but bit stern on end. From 2005 so oak lessens; 2010–13.

JOSEPH AND ANDRÉ BLANC

18 rte de la Brocarde 69420 Ampuis +33(0)474 561358

Growers of vegetables and makers of wine, this family prefers to be out of the spotlight. Part of their holding is on *La Brocarde*.

DOMAINE PATRICK AND CHRISTOPHE BONNEFOND

Mornas 69420 Ampuis +33(0)474 561230

See also Condrieu.

High on the plateau above Ampuis, beyond Bernard Burgaud's domaine, the countryside opens up and gives hawks and buzzards some juicy feeding options. The last domaine set in this windy environment is that of the Bonnefond brothers, Patrick and Christophe, who have worked mightily in the past 10 years to build up their family property. Over recent years, they have been the two toiling shapes frequently spotted among the slopes, with evident signs of full-scale construction beside them.

Their father, Charles, worked 2.5 hectares, whose crop he sold to local merchants. Between 1985 and 1995 the family grew their vineyards up to 5.5 ha of Côte-Rôtie, one hectare of Condrieu, and half a hectare of Syrah *vin de pays des Collines Rhodaniennes*. I call them "the builders." A concrete mixer is still never far away, as they repair crumbled walls when the weather is dry.

The elder, Patrick, a big, broad-beamed man, looks after the vineyards now, while Christophe, tall, dark, and sturdy, works in the cellar and on sales, and in 2004 became Co-President of the Growers Union. They are both active, physical people—Christophe relaxes with motocross, Patrick in a rugby scrum. They got the bottled side of the business going in a small way in 1990, when they set out together, Patrick 23 and Christophe just 21. From 1997 all their wine has been bottled.

There are scatterings of Bonnefonds around the area, several of them in wine and not all of them cousins or indeed chums with each other. These two are making marked progress, their wine vinified in an active, modern way, with well-defined fruit present.

They now produce around 25,000 bottles of all wines per year, with three Côte-Rôties—a classic, with no special name (15,000 bottles), a Côte Rozier (1,500 bottles), and Les Rochains (3,500 bottles), the last two close to La Landonne.

Their original 1 ha vineyard was on *Rochains* (1955), with an overtly schist/mica-schist soil. There are 3.5 ha on *Rozier* and *Côte Rozier,* the vines aged between 30 and 35 years and five to 15 years. There the soil is schist, with the rock around 40cm below the surface. The final hectare is on the loose granite and gneiss of *Semons* (1993) in the south. A tiny 0.06 ha here

is planted with Viognier; since 2000 this has formed 8 to 10 per cent of their Côte Rozier wine and is vinified on its own.

The brothers grow grass between the vines in about half their six plots. This is planted in erosion-prone spots and where the vine vegetation is especially abundant, so the grass can compete.

They like to harvest as late as possible and, since 1993, have destemmed the whole crop. Fermentation lasts 25 days, with *remontages* and *pigeages* in steel vats. Top temperature is 28° to 30°C.

Wood ageing emphasizes new oak; the Rochains and Rozier wines receive up to 24 months in 90 per cent French, 10 per cent new US oak; the classic spends 18 months in 30 per cent new, 70 per cent one-year-old oak casks. There is a light egg-white fining, but no filtration.

The top wine, Rochains, has good weight, handles the new oak well, and shows a nice character of interesting, full, stewed fruits and a touch of earthiness. It is capable of complexity if aged for five years or so. This is a wine of growing stature, one to note for the future.

The Côte Rozier is given to a more streamlined texture, emphasizing the all-important fruitiness that the brothers want. "We want to make fresh, fruited wines that aren't too heavy," explains Christophe. "We work a lot with the restaurant trade, and that's also the style of wine they want." The classic wine, nice and direct, is made from three plots—*Semons, Rozier,* and *Côte Rozier.*

The Syrah *vin de pays* comes from a good location high above the northern end of the *appellation,* near the *lieux-dits Besset* and *Bourrier.* The vines were planted in 1988. This good wine receives a year in casks that are two to three years old.

In the spring of 2003 the brothers fell prey to a break-in and robbery of their bottled stock in the new cellar. This building is set apart from their house, and they joined a growing list of growers who have suffered in this way in recent years.

CÔTE-RÔTIE

2003 (CASKS) ★★★ Sappy, raspberry/oak bouquet, some charm. Suave cherry fruit, with a core of correct tannin. Length OK, oak work sound. From 2007; 2017–19.

2002 ★ Bouquet has life, potential, can soften. Clean berry fruit attack, straight, direct. No great character, needs its acidity to settle. Can roll on. From 2006; 2013–14.

2001 ★★★ Smoky, oaked/floral/berry aroma; open, fruited attack, rocks off the bat. Clear raspberry flavour, some tannin at end. Decisive wine, fruit is very good. From 2005–06; 2011–12.

2000 ★★★ Earthy aromas, dark black fruit/house polish; *cassis* with spice/vanilla topping on attack. Interesting length, gets truffly, the Pinot Noir farmyard touch. Nicely profound at end. 2009–11.

CÔTE-RÔTIE CÔTE ROZIER

2003 (CASK) ★ Minted, upright bouquet, bit sweaty. Dripping fruit start, then stops a little; bit burnt, rather vacant towards finish, runs out of road. From 2006; 2013–14.

2002 (CASK) ★★ Fair berry aroma; good fruit, some end richness, too.

2001 ★★★★ Black cherry *robe*; bacon/*cassis* smoky nose; well-cut, pebbly black fruit. Some richness here, full, silky texture. Peppery aftertaste, nice, live, interesting wine. 2011–13.

2000 ★★★

CÔTE-RÔTIE LES ROCHAINS

2003 (CASK) ★★★ Bland, bit stewed, soaked berry aroma. Coffee, black fruit flavours, meaty wine with width. Broad and a well-set fullness. Decent poise, promise. From 2007; 2018–19.

2002 ★★★ Quiet, dark fruit/mineral bouquet—more in 2006. Decent matter, with structure, correct tannins. Cool, northern style, some richness. Will be elegant, pretty; persists well. From 2007; 2014–16.

2001 ★★★★ Brewed dark red fruit/some violet bouquet; full wine, but clear-cut. Very clear *cassis* fruit on second half, with some acid-

ity to help it. Quite rich, live finish, length sound. 2011–14.

2000 ★★★ Truffly/raspberry, charged aroma; rounded, stewed flavour, earthy, with stone black fruit at end. Nicely dark and dank. 2011–13.

Export 45 per cent (1) USA/Canada, (2) Great Britain

DOMAINE DE BONSERINE

2 chemin de Viallière Verenay 69420 Ampuis
+33(0)474 561427

See also Condrieu, St-Joseph.

This domaine was Franco-American, but in March 2006 it was bought by the Guigal family. It was started in 1972 by the then Mayor of Ampuis, Alfred Gérin, who became a Senator in Lyon. There are 10 hectares of vineyards, one of the largest ownerships at Côte-Rôtie.

M. Gérin had set things rolling in the 1960s, as he explained: "In 1961 I was confident about Côte-Rôtie's future and also anxious to see more wine produced here. So I approached a number of local friends with the idea of buying some of the then many untilled plots of land, with a view to putting them to the vine. We started absolutely from scratch and regrouped many of the plots into better-sized, more workable units."

"Once we had begun to produce and sell our wine in France and abroad, some Americans from New York expressed a desire to import more Côte-Rôtie than we were able to give them. We decided therefore to go straight to the source of the problem and to expand our holding. Some of them, including a chocolate merchant and a lawyer, entered the concern in 1971 and we created the Domaine de Bonserine from the old Domaine Alfred Gérin in 1972." M. Gérin separated from the Americans in 1989, and started what is today his son Jean-Michel Gérin's domaine.

The focus is on the northern end of the *appellation*, with 11 *lieux-dits* there. The main northern sites are their original 2 ha at *Champin*, 2 ha (including a 2003 plantation) at *Fongeant*, and a hectare each on *La Viallière* (1996) and *Moutonnes*, the latter giving its own wine. There is under 1 ha on the *Côte Brune*, and just 0.4 ha on *La Garde*, which is the summit of the *Côte Blonde*. The vineyard averages around 25 years old. Their small southern sites are *Lancement, Baleyat,* and the *Côte Blonde*.

Three wines are made, although in 1997, 1998, and 1999 a single issue called "Côte Brune" was also made: this now enters the workhorse wine of 35,000 bottles, called "La Sarrasine" since 1999. Previously it was called plain "Domaine de Bonserine." This is 97 per cent Syrah and 3 per cent Viognier and comes from several of their plots. Its crop is destemmed, then vinified in steel vats over three weeks, with daily cap punching. The malolactic fermentation occurs in cask (one-third new), where the wine stays for 18 months.

Next up are two special reserve wines produced since 1997, the *Moutonnes*—from its own plot, vines aged between 15 and 40 years old—and *La Garde*, where the vines average 35 years old. *La Garde* has been absorbed into the *Côte Blonde* on the new vineyard map, and this wine is a brand, its final makeup chosen by tasting just before bottling. *La Garde* is marked by its own Roman tower, although it is thought to be getting smaller as growers remove stones from it to rebuild their walls!

Both wines are pure Syrah and receive 22 months in new oak after the same vinification as the *Sarrasine*. Around 10 per cent of the oak is American: former boss Richard Dommerc commented that "we find the American casks are good for a year, but tend to dry in their second year of use." While all three wines are fined, none is filtered. The house style is for elegant wines, with more of a Burgundian than a southern feel to them.

CÔTE-RÔTIE LA SARRASINE

2004 (CASK) ★★ Live, slightly spiced aroma, fair content. Fruit is fresh, with a chocolate, prune side. Three-quarter-weight wine, has matter and freshness. Harmonious around 2008–09. 2017–20.

2003 (CASK) ★★(★) Cooked tone to bouquet —slightly meaty, with chocolate/coffee backdrop. Attractive red fruit start, rounded with pretty, quite sleek feel. Can drink well young. Has developed and settled since Nov. 2004. Esp from 2008; 2016–18. Last tasted March 2005.

2002 ★ Mild, raspberry nose, some breadth. Red berry fruit, some kick; acidity that can settle. Don't expect long life, bit innocuous. Hasn't progressed. From 2008–09. This is the only wine in 2002.

2001 (CASK) ★★ Warm, smoky, floral aromas; red fruits, mix of cooked red fruit/chewiness. Tannins present. From 2006; 2012–14.

2000 ★★ Fair width on bouquet—licorice/pepper/raspberry; upright, cool texture, tannic/fungal aftertaste. Can flesh out. Elegant but lacks oomph. 2011–13.

CÔTE-RÔTIE LA GARDE

2003 (CASK) ★★★ Complete, full bouquet, with expressive black fruits, promising. Stylish, well-formed fruit on palate, long and elegant. Suave texture, with grip on finish. Nicely upright now. Esp from 2008; 2017–19. Last tasted March 2005.

2001 ★★★★ Solid, balanced nose, chocolate aspects; nice matter here, has *gras*, discreet still. From 2007–08; 2015–17.

2000 ★★★ Wide berry fruit aroma, some floral also; refined black juice/raspberry flavour, olives too. Ripe grapes, has restraint. From 2006; 2012–13.

CÔTE-RÔTIE MOUTONNES

2001 ★★★ Refined, floral nose; elegant throughout, nice tannic poise at end. Fair weight, red fruit, oak tinges. From 2006; 2012–14.

2000 ★★ Elegant, berried fruit, smoky, oak, and heat; red fruit, almost jam. *Gras* comes along halfway. From 2005–06; 2011–12.

Export 45 per cent (1) USA, (2) Switzerland, (3) Belgium

DOMAINE BOUCHAREY

Boucharey 69420 Ampuis +33(0)474 561951

Next to Bernard Chambeyron on the windy plateau of Boucharey, his cousin Bruno produces wine, fruit, and vegetables in the time-honoured way of mixed cultivation.

The wine is bottled and sold through an intermediary. It is soft and approachable from an early age.

CÔTE-RÔTIE

2001 ⋆ Cooked jam bouquet, some floral and reduced aromas. Easy-textured wine, red fruits with a spice border. Length OK. No real tannic structure. Drinks fine at three years; by 2008–09.

LAURENT CHARLES BROTTE

rte d'Avignon 84230 Châteauneuf-du-Pape
+33(0)490 837007

See also Condrieu, Cornas, Crozes-Hermitage, Hermitage, St-Joseph
The Châteauneuf-du-Pape house of Brotte produces a 95 per cent Syrah, 5 per cent Viognier. The crop is destalked, and vinification lasts around three weeks in steel, with a maximum temperature of 28° to 30°C. Ageing lasts 12 to 14 months in 40-to-50-hl barrels.

CÔTE-RÔTIE

2002 Modest, bistrot wine, lacks stuffing.

2001 ⋆⋆ Warm, quite smooth red fruit/smoky nose; plump, sappy start, then warm tannins. Viognier helps end sweetness. From 2004–05; 2009–10.

DOMAINE BERNARD BURGAUD

Le Champin 69420 Ampuis +33(0)474 561186

I always reckon you can depend on Bernard Burgaud in a crisis. Maybe it's because he lives independently, away from the other growers, up on the plateau at Le Champin: there's no traffic noise, no miniroundabouts, just a few hens tinkering. A sense of self-reliance hangs over his domaine.

Maybe it's because he never overtalks, just lets out a reef of conversation once he has decided you are OK. Then there's his adoption of two children from Madagascar, something done and only later talked about, even though it was clearly an event of great emotion and strain at the same time.

His winemaking is also marked by this independence and resilience of spirit. He has never joined in the rush to new fashions, and works solidly away on his own, following his own beliefs. In the social gatherings of the village, such as the Gallo-Roman Confrerie, there he is, smiling quietly at the back, taking it all in but keeping a low profile.

He's a man of dark, solid features, a harmonious voice, and a dry sense of humour. He joined his father, Roger, in 1980, Bernard's presence spurring him on to vinifying, then bottling, around 1,500 bottles by 1984. When his father died aged just 62 in 1985, Bernard worked on, his feet well on the ground, his countryman's antennae observing and pondering. I'm sure he has never been near a white coat or a laboratory in his life.

Maybe his father's dilemma motivated him. Grandfather Burgaud had grown cereal and vines, but father Roger went off to work in a factory in the 1950s, as was the order of the day. So when his father became nostalgic for working again in agriculture, he had to buy a plot and gradually plant it, starting again from his bootstraps.

Now in his mid-forties, Bernard walks with a slight dip, his back damaged by the hard hillside work of the past 25 years. He also played rugby for eight years, and one senses that hard graft is part and parcel of his outlook.

He has always sought to make long-lived wines, and states that his reds tend to close up around five years old, until coming back to life from 10 years on. He admits to never having caught the multicuvée fever: just the one wine is made per vintage.

FIGURE 1 Bernard Burgaud in his courtyard. He lives on the often windy plateau high above Ampuis. (Tim Johnston)

His personal liking is for the tougher vintages that demand patience, the Awkward Squad rather than the Sunny Brigade. "1988, 1996, and 2001 are my sort of vintages," he says; "in 1996, there was generally too much crop, and at 38 hl/ha I was unusual in my low cropping, but the year is like 1988—there's lots of matter in the wines, good acidity, and the wines can keep well." Rigour, not comfort, is his style.

His purely Syrah vineyard runs to 4 ha, and the six sites represent the heart of the *appellation*, often high up on the hillside. They are led by two plots on the very steep *Moutonnes* (oldest 75 years, average 30), the flatter *Le Champin* (1980s) near his cellars, *Fongeant* (35 years), *La Brosse* (35 years), *Leyat* (30 years), and the *Côte Blonde* (20 years).

Because the vineyards are spread by altitude, he harvests over a two-week span so he can be precise with different maturity levels; usually *Moutonnes* is the first to ripen, although in the very tough vintage of 2002, it was much later. The plateau vines around *Le Champin* contribute well, he feels, since in a very hot year like 1989, 2003, or even 2001, their grapes bring extra and needed acidity to the rest of the harvest taken from the hot high slopes.

Bernard is also happy to state that he uses weedkillers to keep the vineyards in shape—aware that if he worked the soil, he would have big erosion problems on his hands. "I also recall the summer of 1976, when the vines that had been worked by hand suffered from the drought a lot worse than those that had been sprayed," he says.

He was one of the first to systematically destalk at Côte-Rôtie—75 per cent of the crop in 1987, the whole lot by 1990. The only year when he retained some stalks was the exceptional 1999. "You reach a moment during vinification when the stalks start to take back colour and content elements," he says.

Fermentation is in concrete vats, no external yeasts are used, and because he doesn't like to pump and stir up the wine, he does no *remontages*. Instead he relies on cap punchings. Since 1999 he has allowed the postfermentation temperature to rise to as much as 40°C, which he considers brings a gain in the quality and aromas of the fruit.

Bernard was also a front-runner in the use of new oak, and for 15 years 20 per cent of his wine has been new-oak raised. "I think that wood and *terroir* must go arm in arm," he states emphatically. "I have always used it in a very controlled way—rotation of 20 per cent a year and a very fine heating of my Allier casks before I get them in—so that above all I obtain the presence of the finest tannins possible." Just before bottling, he blends the new oak wine with the rest that has been in oak of up to five years old.

A prime aim is to make a wine that is as tight-knit as possible, one of full integration of both elements and flavour. He assembles the wines from their different locations once the malolactic has finished, then leaves them in the wood for 15 months.

Bottling in January continues this theme. "I find the character of the vintage is present at the end of the year, but by the spring-summertime, it has disappeared," he says. "I want to capture that, so I bottle then to preserve the fruit and keep the wine together." He has never fined nor filtered.

Bernard has always been happy to talk very realistically about his wines. He admits to having used enzymes between 1990 and 1993 to achieve more colour, tannin, and content in his wine. "They were sold to us without real thought from the supplier, and I don't think they served my wines well," he states openly.

The Burgaud wines have, like the man, always been a little apart from the mass. They need working at—they never offer up a fleshy, facile ride and are always quite locked up when young. The occasional vintage like 1999 is drinkable when young, but the style is always a lot more rigorous than a Jasmin, for instance, where the pleasures are usually soft and tender from the start. Patience pays ample dividends, though.

CÔTE-RÔTIE

2003 (CASK) ★★ Full, mineral-tinged black fruit bouquet, floral also. Stewed black fruit palate—violets and an earthy side. Quite rich, bit flat. Fair length. Some typicity near finish. Esp 2008–11. 2013–15.

2002 ★★(★) Well-brewed black fruit aroma, smoky/peppery edges. Fruit has grip, clear-cut black brambly juice. Not esp packed, but is charming, has nice fresh length. From 2007; 2013–16.

2001 ★★★★ Oily, sappy wood/polish aromas; nice ripe matter, olives/blackberries; generous, good potential. Some end tannins. Great until 2005–06, then returns from 2010; 2018–20.

2000 ★★★ Light spice/black fruit aroma, oily/gamey; expressive, round fruit. Truffle touch, violets/black fruit. Full. More complex from 2008; 2015–16.

1999 ★★★★★ Not really typical, but great bouquet: deep, stewed aroma, southern, chocolate style; cherries, packed flavour; *gras* texture grows on second half. No chinks. Violets/olives, variety. 2020–22.

1998 ★★★ Slight fungal aroma, dry edges; cool, black cherry/mineral; dried raisin with air. Restrained cooked black fruit, widens well on palate. Coolness runs through it. Touch short. Fine now (June 2004); 2011–14.

1997 ★★★ 2010–12
1996 ★★★★ 2014–16
1993 ★ 2008–09
1992 ★★ 2007
1991 ★★★ 2010–11
1990 ★★★ 2006–07
1989 ★★★★ 2008–10
1988 ★★★★ 2010

Export 50 per cent (1) Switzerland, (2) Great Britain, (3) USA

BERNARD CHAMBEYRON

69420 Ampuis +33(0)474 561505

See also Condrieu.

Bernard Chambeyron has combined cultivation of "Nick Teen" and "Al K. Hall" in his time. A former tobacco grower, he makes a sound-quality Côte-Rôtie with a thorough Condrieu in support.

His is a low-profile name, although the Chambeyrons have long been a wine family at Ampuis.

Bernard's great-grandfather, one of seven children, came here to work as a stone mason from Rive de Gier. "My grandfather made and sold his wine in bulk, wine from hybrid grapes that would supply the cafés, plus just a little Côte-Rôtie," he comments. "He would be off at six in the morning with his oxen to Rive de Gier to deliver 100-litre and 50-litre casks, the latter we would call *quarterons*."

Bernard's uncle Marius was a large local wine figure in the 1970s. One of the few to bottle some wine, he was always present at the wine fair, a cheery smile emerging from under a tilted tweed flat cap. Meanwhile his own father, Maurice, went ahead growing apricots, a fruit that was very expensive in the 1950s. Ampuis had its own fruit market in those days, with apples and cherries also grown by the Chambeyron family.

Bernard's domaine is high on the windy plateau of Boucharey, and the rolling land led him to grow tobacco between 1972 and 1982, all of it bought by the state company SEITA. "There were 20 producers around about," he recalls. "The advantage was of course a guaranteed purchase, as well as insurance against hail and poor production." There are still some tobacco growers in the Isère near St-Marcellin.

Having started to plant vines to make Côtes du Rhône in 1977, Bernard moved on to Côte-Rôtie in 1981, with a small plot planted on *Chavaroche* the next year, just above his cousin Bernard Levet.

Now he works 1.8 ha, part owned and part rented. Of this, 1.3 ha is on *Chavaroche* (1982, 1984), the rest on *Moutonnes* (1993) and on *Lancement* (1967, planted by Marius Chambeyron, the father of Madame Levet). There is 5 per cent Viognier. Bernard finds *Moutonnes* is the first plot to ripen, about five days ahead of the others, with a drier terrain there.

This is an orderly domaine stepping up a gear. The wines, including the successful Condrieu, are honestly made, and the commitment to detail seems sound. There are times when the fruit content could be more clear-cut, with an earthy down-home presence detectable. All the production has been bottled since 1999, and even the apricots were abandoned in 1998. The crop has all been destemmed since the tricky 1996 vintage, and receives up to three weeks' vatting. Yeasts are added, and pumping-over is done by a *turbo-pigeur* machine; the top temperature is 33°C.

Cask ageing lasts 18 months in 20 per cent new oak, the other 80 per cent up to six years old. There is filtration, but no fining. Around 10,000 bottles are produced.

The agreeable Syrah Côtes du Rhône is also cask aged and shows soft red fruits and some ability to develop over half a dozen years or more. The well-made Viognier *vin de pays* is all vat fermented and raised, and bottled with its malo done in the spring. There is plenty of typical pear flavour in it. Both wines come from the clay plateau near the domaine.

CÔTE-RÔTIE

2004 ★★ Spice, violet mix on bouquet, heightened fruit aroma, some reduction. Soft start, fruit has sound style, some weight. Pretty finish, harmonious, good future ahead. Tannins need till 2008. 2017–18. Last tasted March 2005.

2003 (CASK) ★★ Brewed, chocolate aroma, with rather rustic, farmyard side. Brewed theme continues on palate, red fruit with an earthy tinge. Sound core matter, but could be more decisive, cleaner. Traditional style. 2016–17.

2002 ★ Quite fresh bouquet, though has core, a degree of depth. Broad palate for the year, likeable. Brewed grapes, the fruit could be clearer, but has some local feel. 2010–11.

2001 ★★ Some violet aroma, cooked fruits —quite authentic. Rounded style, pretty tasty. Cooked fruits finish, not especially fresh. Fair length, trace end tannin. Genuine. 2012–13.

CHRISTIANE CHAMBEYRON-MANIN

29 rte de la Taquière +33(0)474 560420

Mikael and Caroline Manin are grandchildren of Marius Chambeyron, and when the domaine was divided up for inheritance purposes, this side of the family received 0.4 ha on the *Côte Brune*. The plot is around their hand-painted sign on the lower reaches of the hill. Its Syrah is a mix of mid-1960s and 1930s.

The wines are traditionally vinified in concrete vats with whole bunches, then aged for two years in used oak casks. These are earthy, sometimes rustic wines, where stewed fruits and brewed flavours abound. One might expect more stuffing in the wines given that their crop is taken from the *Côte Brune*.

The family is better known for its thriving vegetable emporium on the southern outskirts of Ampuis. They grow their own seasonal vegetables, notably *blettes* (a form of Chinese cabbage with dark green leaves and pale stalks), cardoons, cauliflower, carrots and radish, and lettuces. Beside the Rhône they have some apricot trees.

ÉMILE CHAMPET

Le Port 69420 Ampuis

Mimile, as he is affectionately known, cannot stop working. Born in 1925, he still looks after 0.4 ha on *Le Mollard*, with a tiny strip on *La Taquière*, below it, as well as maintaining an exceptional courtyard of flowers and an immaculately tended vegetable plot down beside the old port of Ampuis.

He was 10 years old when his father bought the *Mollard* plot, where the vines run up to 100 years old and around 6 per cent is Viognier. He started out growing flowers and vegetables for a living and gradually developed the wine until doing only that in the 1960s, when it was sold to Chapoutier.

The first bottling was in 1967, and along came a surprise with his 1971, which he was asked to export to Britain. "This man arrived, speaking almost no French, and kept saying the words 'medal, Paris, wine,'" he recalls. "Well, we had submitted the wine to the Paris Wine Fair, but no one had told us the outcome, until this man, who turned out to be Robin Yapp, arrived. He had sped down the motorway straight from Paris and even though his French

was muddy, we managed to send off an order of 30 cases." Yapp Brothers, for long Britain's leading Rhône house, still does business with son Joël and grandson Romain.

At most, Émile barely cultivated more than two hectares, but was a regular presence at the intimate Wine Fairs of the early 1970s, when there were under 10 men bottling wine on any scale. He has always worked in a near-frantic way, finding time to be a mason as well, the skill for which he has passed on to his son. Friends comment that he needs to be tied down if he is to stay in one place for longer than a minute or two.

His cellar has never changed, a tiny spot at Le Port right beside the river. Helped by Joël and Romain, he sticks to no destalking, ferments in concrete for 15 to 17 days, and then raises the wine himself in casks of two to 12 years during 18 months. He fines, does not filter, and sells to his regular locals.

His wife, Paulette, hangs in there with this whirlwind. Gesturing a lot, his pale blue eyes intent, Émile explains that he still sprays his vines himself: "I have the usual 25 kg machine on my back—it drives me rather than the other way around!"

His drinking habits are singular, too. "When I rack a cask full of a new year's wine, there are about eight litres of *vin troublé* left behind—all sorts of little bits in the juice. I put this to one side, let it settle, and then drink it with my sugar lump at midday." Paulette nods. "We've been married 53 years, and he hasn't missed a day of putting a sugar lump in his glass for lunch," she sighs.

His well-knit, typical wines reflect the true simplicity of an age gone by, when the cellar work was largely laissez-faire; he is a remarkable man, his hospitality and enthusiasm endearing, and I'm sure locals are proud to say they know him and buy from him.

CÔTE-RÔTIE

2001 ★★★ Nicely earthy nose, minted black fruit; thorough black fruit/violet flavour, genuine harmony and finesse. Touch end raspberry and tannin. Gains length with air, classic. 2012–13.

2000 ★★★ Tarry, grapey, red fruit/floral nose, very typical; wild strawberry fruit with fresh edge. Tannic/fungal ending. Sound length. From 2007–08; 2013–15.

1999 ★★★★ Oily, cooked red berries/truffle aroma; good interior, lovely depth; has southern tones—cooked black fruit/leather/olives. Broad towards finish, can blossom around 2009; 2019–20.

JOËL AND ROMAIN CHAMPET

12 chemin de la Viallière Verenay 69420 Ampuis
+33(0)474 561486

Joël Champet possesses his father's propensity to keep busy, and not just to stick to wine. He is proud of having built a house for each of his two children. Fast-talking, he declares himself to be both a *vigneron* and a mason.

His three-hectare vineyard is all around his house, set slap-bang on the hillside of *La Viallière*, one of the two top names at Verenay in the north of the *appellation*, next to *Les Grandes Places*. The *Viallière* vineyard took over 35 years to be cleared and fully planted until completed in 1999, with the only original plot of note that of Albert Dervieux just a bit higher up the slope. The rest was wooded.

One of the essential words in French is *bricolage*, which the dictionary solemnly defines as "tinkering about." DIY, or "messing about with bits and pieces" is what *bricolage* is all about, and Joël is an expert. "I work on lorries and do them up, old cars, too; drive them for a bit and then sell them," he says. "Now I'm not clearing vineyards to replant them. I have extra time on my hands, and I like to keep busy."

Just 50, he works traditionally. There is no destalking, and vinification lasts two to three weeks in concrete vats, with some *remontage*, or pumping-over. The wine is raised for 18 months in 550-litre *demi-muids*, with a little in a 22 hl barrel. Fining stopped in 2001, and he does not filter. There are several bottlings.

Joël does all the selling himself, which means around 10,000 bottles, the rest going in bulk to Marcel Guigal.

On the label the wine is called "La Viallière," the old local spelling. It contains around 5 per cent Viognier, although the schist soil here does not really suit the white vine.

A man with tousled dark hair, he has inherited the busy gestures and fast movements of his father. He also went through a serious illness in the early 2000s, and must be pleased that his son Romain, in his early twenties, has studied wine at Belleville. The future lies before this young man to keep the family tradition going.

CÔTE-RÔTIE LA VIALLIÈRE

2002 (CASK) ★★ Quite warm, sweet cooked fruit, violet; very correct, cooked fruits, then some acidity as it tightens. Eight-to-nine-year wine.

2001 ★★★ Full, traditional bouquet—black jam/raspberry/earth; violet and stewed fruits start, nice gras, round blackberry fruit. Degree end tannin/mineral. Full, tasty, from 2005; 2011–13.

Export 10 per cent (1) Great Britain, (2) USA

M. CHAPOUTIER

18 ave Dr Paul Durand BP38 26601 Tain l'Hermitage
+33(0)475 082865

See also Condrieu, Cornas, Crozes-Hermitage, Hermitage, St-Joseph, St-Péray.
A longstanding owner at Côte-Rôtie, Chapoutier works 5 ha and produces two wines, the straightforward Bécasses, a wine of reliable quality, and the more sophisticated, deeper La Mordorée.

The vineyard is split between 3.2 ha of old vines, and 1.8 ha of recent plantings. The prime plots are 1.4 ha on the *Côte Brune* (1940s) and 1.3 ha on the *Côte Blonde* (1940s–1970s). The remaining two sites are juxtaposed—on the northern schist there is 0.8 ha at *Nève*

(2001) next to *La Viallière;* and on the southern sandy granite there is 1.5 ha on *Les Bercheries* above *Maison Rouge,* 0.6 ha of it dating from the 1940s and earlier, the rest planted in 1998.

The staple Côte-Rôtie, called "Les Bécasses" since 1998, is largely the purchase of grapes, mixed in with some of their own crop. It is 97 per cent Syrah, 3 per cent Viognier. Exceptionally in 2002, this came very largely from their own vineyards because of the indifferent quality elsewhere on the open market. "I went up there with my own sorting machine, to discard much of the crop," says Michel Chapoutier, never afraid of stating it as he sees it; "it wasn't an especially popular move," he admits.

Its vinification and maceration lasts four weeks, the temperature held between 25° and 31°C, to seek the most likely extraction. Cap punching is done in open wood fermenting vats. Bécasses then receives 12 to 13 months in cask in smaller years like 1997, 16 to 20 months in bigger vintages like 1999 and 2001. The casks are one-third each new, one year, and two years old.

Bécasses is midrange Côte-Rôtie, marked by soft fruit that can tire in the less structured vintages. In years like 1999 and 2001, when there is greater tannic content, it is more interesting and varied and can live for 15 years or so.

The special wine is La Mordorée, a registered name for a wine made from vineyards beside the large Chapoutier sign on the hillside—a combination of the vineyard's oldest and best vines on the *Brune* and *Blonde.*

Its crop is destemmed and open wood–fermented in the same way as the Bécasses, then aged for 15 to 20 months in half new, half one-to-two-year-old casks. It is bottled unfined and unfiltered.

La Mordorée's pedigree derives from its prime location. It is a wine with genuinely founded red fruit and carries a thorough, warm Côte-Rôtie texture. It shows well if left for six years or so.

CÔTE-RÔTIE LES BÉCASSES

2002 ★★ Overt, juicy *cassis* nose; oak at start, bit taut, brief. Olives flavour. Window to drink around 2006–08.

2001 ★★★ Wide bouquet, potential, soft fruit, will turn gamey. Dark blackberry fruit/oil, quite rich; skips then returns. Upright now, has frame. From 2006; 2012–15.

2000 ★★ Quite soft nose, with red fruits/soil/mushroom; medium-weight, touch plain, but some *gras* near end. Bit dumb, more in 2005; has improved in last year. Lacks true core. 2010–11.

1999 ★★ Extreme ripe grape aroma, truffled, potent; soupy texture, round, chocolate style. Raspberry aftertaste. Air clarifies, helps it. 2014–15.

1998 ★★★ Mushroom, damp leaf, almost Pinot nose, some mineral; quite solid, open wine. Round style; chewy, minty end. Warm wine. Esp from 2004; 2010–11.

1997 ★ Drink now.

1996 ★ 2005

1994 ★★★★ 2008–10

CÔTE-RÔTIE LA MORDORÉE

2003 (CASK) ★★(★) Dark, reserved chocolate/preserved cherries bouquet. Cellar-made wine, oak residue around it. Correct enough. Fruit is clean, but oak must go. From 2007; 2017–20.

2002 (CASK) ★★★ Reduced, broad black fruit nose, earthy. Palate also quite solid. Stewed fruit, dryish end. Peep of end fruit. Esp from 2007; 2012–13.

2001 (CASK) ★★★★ Discreet, fine nose, clear fruit, good *grain*; stylish but reserved substance. Matter in it seems well founded. Live raspberry finish. Quite pure. From 2007; 2012–15.

2000 ★★★ Toasted/grilled aromas, bit tight; medium-weight wine, bit plain. Reserved, fair red fruit, some depth. Length OK. Not sure if elements will combine. More firm than usual. From 2007; 2015–16.

1999 ★★★★★ Tightly packed bouquet, lot of density, some oak; its fullness is gentle, lots of lovely *gras*; rich, juicy, with a chewy, lasting finish. 2015–17.

1998 ★★★ Square, smoky, bit resiny bouquet; fair amount of raspberry fruit, bit dumb. Very chewy, oak-related finish. From 2004; 2012–14.

1997 ★★★★ 2010–12

1994 ★★★★★ 2012–14

LOUIS CLERC

1638-1658 route de Gerbey 38121 Chonas l'Amballan
+33(0)474 563164

See also Condrieu.

"I was much more a fisherman than a schoolboy," comments Louis Clerc, reminiscing about his days seeking carp, tench, and bream from the local waters. Born in 1943, this countryman took the bold step of producing his own wine in 2003, having sold crop and wine to the merchant trade for many years before.

His son Martin, 14, hovers in the background, no doubt the reason for such a late switch of direction. Louis' grandfather was from Savoie, his father from the Beaujolais, where Louis' godson is the noted Jean-Paul Brun, a man who makes wines with an unbridled passion.

"I wanted to be a *vigneron* when I was young, but my parents said we must run a mixed farm, especially growing vegetables—but I don't like vegetables!" he recalls.

Now there are 1.6 hectares of Côte-Rôtie, although there is land for another six hectares of vineyards over time. The domaine is southern, on the *Coteau de Bassenon* and the *Coteaux de Tupin*, the former officially known as *Coteaux de Semons*, the last site before Condrieu. Both vineyards were planted in 1990.

The crop is destemmed, cool macerated for four days, and vinified over three weeks, the final vat temperature 34°C. The malos are done in cask, the oak ranging from 20 per cent new to three years old. Cask raising lasts 12 months, and the wine is filtered.

The 2003 shows signs of STGT characteristics, a true representative of the southern area

with a silky, warm texture. The Condrieu is also honestly made, and the range is completed by 0.5 ha of Syrah and 1.5 ha of Viognier *vins de pays*. This is a domaine to keep an eye on.

CÔTE-RÔTIE PONT DE TUPIN

2003 ★★★ Dark *robe*; full, toffee hints on bouquet, nicely fundamental, big for the southern sector. Palate is elegant, warm, has a lovely silky feel. Abundant wine, with charm. Length good and suave. STGT wine. Can be drunk now, also later. 2016–17. Last tasted March 2005.

DOMAINE CLUSEL-ROCH

15 route du Lacat Verenay 69420 Ampuis
+33(0)474 561595

See also Condrieu.

It pays to have principles. It's fashionable to knock people who act from belief rather than convenience, to accuse them of "not being flexible" enough—they should lighten up. Well, Gilbert Clusel and Brigitte Roch have never lightened up, and now their domaine makes supremely elegant wines, with the magic word "purity" in them.

It was a struggle at first. Gilbert inherited a few vines from his father, René, but the pair's early days were marked by a lot of toil and very little cash to allow them to move swiftly ahead. Their income in those early years came mostly from their vegetables.

Throughout they sought to do the best they could, with the clear rider that they were not going to take a lot of shortcuts to get there. That meant a lot of manual work in the vineyard, respect for the quality of the vines they were planting—which therefore needed hand grafting from the best old stock—and a gradual adoption in the cellar of methods that brought the best out of their grapes.

Early vineyard practices included leaving their cuttings to rot on the soil, and a stop to all chemical products. It was a surprise, therefore, to discover that they were working with modernist *oenologue* Jean-Luc Colombo, who may respect the vineyards but is not averse to full-on extraction and the latest interventionist vinification techniques. But then Colombo was moved off the roster after a couple of years: in their usual discreet way the couple had tried out the goods, assessed them, spotted any positives, and moved on.

Gilbert, a slight, tenacious man whose air of diffidence masks a steely determination, considers their main evolution during the 1990s to have been their work in the vineyards. It is a message echoed by several around the *appellation*. He has an acute mind, is a good listener, and comes across as a quiet Questor.

"As a community, our access to *massale* selection vine cuttings is important for keeping our inheritance intact," he says. "We've only worked with Côte-Rôtie Syrah—a St-Joseph project would use different plants, for instance. Here on the domaine we've purely used *massale* since 1991." "Gilbert had to get out all his books from school when we bought the grafting machine," adds Brigitte, a dark-haired, broad woman with weather in her face. A sidelong smile creeps forth.

In so doing, they are recapturing ground lost in the fallow period of the 1980s. Their pre-1975 plants are all *massale*, so their vineyard now runs at around 95 per cent Sérine, 5 per cent clone. Their disappointment with clones was such that in 1999 they went to the trouble of regrafting their clonal plot on *Viallière*, planted in 1984, with their own *massale* vines. Others following their lead are growers Martin Daubrée, Jean-Michel Stéphan, Vincent Gasse, David Duclaux, and Jean-Michel Gérin, to name a few principal movers and shakers.

Gilbert has also suppressed the use of weedkillers for his Côte-Rôtie vineyards, although some are still used on their Condrieu vines. The domaine was officially declared *en production bio* from 2002. His answer to the question "How do you describe the work of the last 10 years?" comes in an unassuming, countryman's form: "I'm relatively content."

Their Côte-Rôtie area covers nearly 4 ha. The largest *lieu-dit* is the 1.3 ha on *La Viallière*, 1 ha dating from the mid-1980s, the rest from 1958. On *Champon*, also in the northern area of Verenay, they work 0.75 ha (1986–87) and 0.25 ha (1960s)—part on the upper slope, part on the flatter ground at the top.

The rest of the vineyard is composed of 0.6 ha on *Le Plomb* (1998–2000), a small 0.11 ha on *Fongeant* (1993), and their prized 0.7 ha on *Les Grandes Places* (1935). On the last, the soil is mica-schist with iron traces in it.

Like Joseph Jamet's *Brune* vineyard or the Jasmin *Chevalière* vineyard, the *Grandes Places* carries a significance far beyond its raw data. Today's successes can be traced back to these small plots of land, always sited on the most exposed, baking parts of the slopes, always full of the hopes, worries, footprints, and sweat of their forefathers. There must be many a reflection of times gone by and the debt owed when Gilbert and Brigitte are up there under the hot sun.

This vineyard was planted by Gilbert's grandfather Baptiste before the Second World War but was not enough for Gilbert to work on with his father when he finished his wine studies in 1977. So he helped out on the fruit and vegetable side as well, until setting up in 1980 with a tiny, rented 0.25 hectare on *La Viallière*.

Gilbert gradually increased his portion to 2.5 hectares, and when René retired in 1987, aged 66, the two vineyards joined up, and *Grandes Places* became a wine in its own right. Brigitte, who is from the Île de France, in the north, left her job as a teacher in 1989, and the domaine Clusel-Roch was formally started.

The cellar equipment was modernised very gradually. Just one new cask was introduced in 1984, and it took five years to renew and sort out the whole cask lineup. The vats came next. Money never flowed. But by 1992 a system of working with gravity when vinifying had come to fruition, with the cellar done up and burrowed into the side of the *Viallière* hill.

The duo make two wines, a classic (4 per cent Viognier, 12,000 bottles) and their special *Grandes Places* (pure Syrah, 2,500 bottles), taken from the old vines there. The classic wine is composed of fruit from three sets of ages, vines of 10 years or less, 10 to 30 years, and over 30 years. For each vintage 20 to 30 per cent of the crop is destemmed, notably plots where there are clone vines, but so tricky were 2002 and 2003 that 80 per cent was destemmed in each very different vintage.

Vinification is in a mix of concrete and steel vats, there are two *pigeages* and *remontages* a day, and the maximum temperature is a restrained 28° to 31°C. The vertical wooden press is wheeled out, and after pressing, the classic wine is aged for two years in cask, one-fifth new and the rest running up to five years old. The new oak proportion can rise to half if the crop is small and the wine intense, as it was in 2003.

Les Grandes Places spends two years in casks that are half new, half one year old. Until 1993 the wines received 18 months in cask, but the extra time has brought more integration. There is no fining nor filtration.

Some experiments with destemming and a cool premaceration were done in 2001; tasting the wines blind, the new technique produced down-the-line, more international flavours, while the old method with only 20 per cent destemming and no cooling produced a wine with more local tannins and more chewy nuances in the wine. One was sleek, the other more homely. Work continues on these techniques, however.

CÔTE-RÔTIE

2003 ★★★ Purple/mauve *robe*. Lovely round aroma, expressive; good cut, bounds along. Very appealing fruit on attack, excellent definition alongside many 2003s. Chocolate, brewed fruit finale. Well made—not too big. 2016–18. Last tasted March 2005. "Only the old vines on *La Viallière* showed the hot side of the vintage" (B. Roch).

2002 ★★ Cooked, smoked, tarry red fruit bouquet. Berry fruit start. Fresh end with marked, bit severe tannins, needs time. Cool-texture wine as usual from here. From 2006–07; can live given its acidity; 2012–15.

2001 (CASKS) ★★★ Live fruit aromas, some pepper; good firm fruit underlay, has core. Tannins lend support, ends well. Promising. From 2006–07; 2014–16.

2000 ★★★ Black fruits, some earth on bouquet; black fruits, elegant style, good sinew near end, live tannins come along. Cool, persistent fruit, well done. Esp from 2007–08; Burgundian right now; 2013–15.

1999 ★★★ Tight bouquet, smoky black fruit; bits of black fruit, a chewy end, tannins are well woven. Tight, clean finish. There is decent *gras* here. 2014–16.

1998 ★★★ Orderly bouquet, some ripe fruit, spice, dry tones; quite taut start, low-key black fruit. Clean-cut, upright style, flavours are cool. Stylish. Guidance from end tannins. 2010–12.

1997 ★★★ 2007–08
1996 ★★★ 2008–10
1995 ★★★★ 2009–11
1994 ★★★★ 2006–07

CÔTE-RÔTIE LES GRANDES PLACES

2003 ★★★★ Well-cut, full but direct aroma—hints of ripe fruit, smoky bacon. Tight-knit palate, good, full wine with definite elegance, not over potent. STGT from the northern zone, with a tension; clear mineral presence in it. From 2008–09; 2019–22.

2002 Not made.

2001 ★★★★ Hint of fruit, nose dumb as yet; suave, compact black fruits, well-packed. Good length, licorice finale. Tannins are ripe and silky. From 2007; 2017–19.

2000 ★★★★ Full, elegant bouquet, spiced red fruits. Tasty start on palate, a lot of finesse, pure wine. Quietly ripe raspberry fruit, acacia/floral side. Nice length. 2014–16.

1999 ★★★★★ Lot of pretty content, promising nose. Streamlined, decisive flavour, earthy side. Full, orderly matter; restraint works well. Persistent, good length. Tannin/oak end. 2014–16.

1998 ★★★★ Mixed aromas, fruit/spice/soil, smoky, very clear-cut; nice roll of flavour, black fruit/olives, oak on finale. Dry, bit square finish. Good integrity. Only 600 bottles because of the hail. 2013–15.

1997 (CASK) ★★★ 2007–10
1996 ★★★ 2009–11
1995 ★★★ 2010–13
1994 ★★★★ 2008–12

Export 45 per cent (1) Japan, (2) USA, (3) Great Britain/ Switzerland

DOMAINE DE CORPS DE LOUP

69420 Tupin et Semons
+33(0)474 568464

This is a new domaine surrounded by hope and by tragedy. It was bought by Bruno and Martin Daubrée in 1992. Bruno was the man trained in agriculture; Martin was finance director of an advertising agency in Lyon.

The domaine stands just outside Ampuis, with its own drive up through some imposing gates beside the N86. The brothers did not buy the main house, the château that had been a convent before the Revolution. This and the park below it still belong to their neighbour. Instead they purchased the *régisseur*'s farm-house and the wonderful amphitheatre of vines behind it. This old vineyard had been revived in the 1880s after phylloxera, then had fallen fallow again after the First World War. So there was plenty of work to be done to clear the walled terraces and to plant afresh.

The place is called *Le Corps de Loup*, with rumour that here was killed the last wolf in France. A quarter of a hectare was first planted on its very crumbly granite in 1992. In 1994 two older vine *parcelles* were secured, one of 0.55 ha on *Corps de Loup* (1960s), the other of 0.42 ha near the plateau on *Janet* (1960s), in the *commune* of Ampuis with a more *Brune*-style schist soil. So a balance had been obtained between young plantations and some constructive, older vine sources.

The Daubrées were of course outsiders, and as usual there was a degree of local caution towards them as they set up. Martin had been born in Italy, where his parents still live. His father worked for Michelin, and their seven years in Turin was the longest spell the family spent anywhere during his youth.

Plans were running smoothly until the 1995 vintage, when Bruno died in a cellar accident. Martin had to take over, which meant juggling his job in Lyon with looking after the domaine along with his wife, Lucette. Of course he was not the person with the wine knowledge, so life was difficult, to say the least. He recalls support from the domaines of Burgaud, Clusel-Roch, and Duclaux in particular.

Now he is full-time on the wine, a restless man, clearly driven for all sorts of reasons. He explains items with great exactness, and one hopes that he has allowed himself to start to enjoy some moments in his job. The domaine is moving in the right direction, the wine is authentic, and a degree of self-confidence should be present now, the sort that allows hope to flourish. But what a sad story.

Uplifting it is, though, to see the almost one hectare of vineyard beside the cellar building and the family home. It is a craggy and steep stone-terraced curve of vines, an indelible image of the northern Rhône and its formidable origins. There are three hectares around it that can be planted in the future, but with an annual planting allowance of just 0.13 ha, that may be some way off.

"I'm tempted to have a year off the planting," sighs Martin, a tall man who wears light-framed glasses, "just to have a quieter time." For he is busy, also on behalf of the *appellation*. He has contributed to the anti-autoroute campaign by serving on its committee and is also providing the vineyard for the Conservatory of Syrah plants for Côte-Rôtie, a project driven along notably by Gilbert Clusel.

"This is 0.065 hectare of 80 different Syrah varieties, half planted in 2003, half in 2004. There are 10 plants for each variety, making 800 vines in total," he explains. "Gilbert has taken the cuttings for this Conservatory, which is intended to preserve and propogate our vine heritage. I will look after the vineyard, and the Chamber of Agriculture of the Rhône is involved, too, through Magali Deblieux, their technician. As it's a project done by the Growers Union, it will be their members—most of the growers here—who will be first in line to receive plants for future use."

The Sérine, the old preclonal variety of Syrah, will therefore be safeguarded, and it is this that Martin will plant in his own vineyard henceforth. He works 2.25 ha, with all plantation from 1992 up until 2004 having been with clonal plants.

The artistic Lucette is also busy; she prunes most of the vineyard, grows vegetables such as artichokes, courgettes, potatoes, and tomatoes, melons too, and her honeybees provide around 20 kilos a year. She also designs the labels, and their jereboam bottles. Four of the six children they have between them, the eldest 16, live at home. They had been used to Lyonnais life on the weekends, and have had to find their way with much quieter local surroundings.

The vineyard is treated if necessary, but the clear tendency is laissez-faire. Much time is spent on shoring up walls, the main source of worry after heavy rain. Martin estimates that he and a mason do up 30 to 40 square metres of wall a year, his own masonry skills picked up through friends in the Ardèche. There are also new water drains. All this is work that the typical drinker would barely consider when sipping the wine.

Two to three percent of the vineyard is Viognier, which is vinified with the Syrah for their Marions-Les! cuvée. The crop is brought in by friends and family, who are kept in touch with the vineyard's year through a series of newsletters. Since 2002 a destalking machine has been used for years of difficult maturity, and the grapes are crushed on arrival, prior to a three-week vinfication. Two to three daily *remontages* are done for the first two weeks, while *pigeage* is not necessary since the cap is immersed with planks of wood at the top of the fibreglass vats.

The year 2002 also marked the first *délestage* process to increase freshness and extraction. Martin restricts the top temperature to around 30°C, so is careful not to be too full-on in his process.

Ageing lasts around 22 months and takes place in 225-litre casks, 20 per cent of them new, the rest up to 12 years old. For his *Paradis* wine, which is bigger and more backward by nature, he would like to use the larger *demi-muid* of 550 litres in the future and leave the wine another six months in wood. There is neither fining nor filtration.

Until 2000 there was just the one wine; from 2001 he has made three different cuvées. The *Paradis* (1,500 bottles) is from *Janet*, which touches the *Côte Brune*. The *Corps de Loup* (5,000 bottles) is from vineyards near the domaine, as is the *Marions-Les!* (1,200 bottles), which holds 20 per cent Viognier. Its first vintage in 2001 was sold as a *vin de pays*, and since then it has been a full Côte-Rôtie.

The sense of hard work, often performed under pressure, is palpable here. So what would be Martin's dreams and future projects? "I would like to clear out and tidy up the vaulted cellar that goes with the château, except it doesn't belong to me! I would also love to pass over to be a fully biodynamic domaine in years to come. One day, a course of oenology, as well."

In 2003 he planted a dabble of 0.06 ha on *Côte Bonnette*, above Condrieu, where his neighbours are Gangloff, Rostaing, and Gilles Barge. "I like white wine," he says simply. He also sells small amounts of St-Joseph bought from Chavanay and a *vin de table* Viognier from the south of the Ardèche.

CÔTE-RÔTIE MARIONS-LES!

2004 (CASK) (★) Smoky, red fruit aroma. Light, peppered palate, rather green. Lacks core at this stage, plain. Last tasted March 2005.

2003 ★★ Raisin, brewed fruit aroma. Fruit taste is mature, as if later picked. Some width on palate, but is uneven, has a tartness towards finish, not well-knit. Esp from 2007.

2002 (CASK) (⋆) Light fruit, rather stern nose; fair fruit, on a simple level, peppery end, some width. Five-year wine.

CÔTE-RÔTIE CORPS DE LOUP

2004 ⋆⋆ Soft wild red berry jam aroma. Low-key red fruit on palate, some tar with it. Can move along OK, is refined. Fair length. Needs to be left till 2008. 2012–13. Last tasted March 2005.

2003 ⋆⋆ Ripe bouquet, quite compact, stylish, and persists quietly. Good southern-sector feel, mixes soft black fruits, licorice, and is round all way through. Attractive, understated wine. Esp from 2006; 2011–12.

2002 ⋆ Mature fruit aroma—cautious jam scent, also fruit gum, spice. Fine, rather light palate, a slight floral flourish towards finish. Easy drinking, some sinew here. 2007.

2001 (CASK) ⋆⋆ Discreet, strawberry aroma; alert, forward attack, fruit expresses well. Gets peppery, and firm. Fair width, sound length. 2009–10.

CÔTE-RÔTIE PARADIS

2003 ⋆⋆ Smoked, black fruit aroma, licorice/tar combo also. Decent substance, more stuffing than the Corps de Loup cuvée, also more evident tannins, which are ripe. Edgy on finish. From 2007; 2013–14.

2002 (CASK) ⋆⋆ Fair *robe*; raspberry, fair weight of bouquet; nicely grounded wine; decent middle extract, earthy touches. Fine, and good length. 2011–12.

2001 (CASK) ⋆⋆⋆ Black currant/mint/raspberry aromas; upright texture, black currant again; can run on well. Crunchy fruit here. Esp 2006–07; 2011–12.

CÔTE-RÔTIE

2000 ⋆⋆⋆ Ripe, red fruits bouquet; very tasty attack, elegant with stuffing in it. True wine, nice sinew and length. Esp from 2005–06; 2011–12.

1999 ⋆⋆⋆ Ripe, full, quite smoky/oily bouquet. Damp, oily black-fruit flavour, leathery finish. Ripe grapes taste, nicely full with good style. Moving along well, a very consistent evolution due to its good balance. 2009–11.

1998 ⋆ Earthy/violet, some reduction on nose; quite full, plump wine, with farmyard aspects as it ages. Fair dark plum flesh. 2004–06.

1995 ⋆⋆⋆ 2005–07

Export 50 per cent (1) Great Britain, (2) USA, (3) Belgium

YVES CUILLERON

58 RN86 Verlieu 42410 Chavanay +33(0)474 870237

See also Condrieu, St-Joseph.

Along with his greatly increased St-Joseph and Condrieu vineyards, Yves Cuilleron has built up his presence in Côte-Rôtie. He works 5 ha, and makes three wines—Terres Sombres and Madinière, both pure Syrah from the northern schist of the *appellation*; and Bassenon, including 10 per cent Viognier, from the southern, crumbled granite areas of Semons.

His precise holdings are 1 ha on *Bassenon*, official name *Coteaux de Semons* (most 1989–90, plus some 1965); 1 ha on *Rochains,* next to *Landonne* (late 1980s, a little 1974); 0.43 ha on *Rozier* (mid-1990s); and a spread across *Viallière, Mornachon, Le Plomb, Bonnivière, Janet, Grand Taillis,* and *Gerine*. These have mostly been planted from the 1990s onwards, so the essence of his wine comes from mainly young vineyards.

Terres Sombres is largely from *Rochains,* plus *Viallière* and *Rozier*. These three complement each other well; *Rochains* is the more open, the other two more solid, *Rozier* the more elegant of them. Bassenon is from *Coteaux de Semons* and is therefore less long-lived. The two wines are vinified in open steel vats that allow *pigeages* and *remontages* over three to four weeks. Yves only destalks if necessary, since he likes wines that are robust and capable of long life. The malolactic fermentation is done in cask; both wines are aged for 18 to 20 months, Terres Sombres entirely in new oak, Bassenon and

Madinière in half new, half one-year oak. They are fined, but not filtered.

Bassenon seems to struggle with its oak overlay; given its more tender natural style, that is not a complete surprise. Terres Sombres' *terroir* means it is more suited to the oak it receives. Madinière's first vintage in 2004 showed a brewed flavour, with oak in evidence, but enough fruit to suggest a sound life over ten years or more.

CÔTE-RÔTIE BASSENON

2002 ★★★ Smoked red fruit bouquet, fair harmony/potential. Stewed fruit with some style, nicely knit. Black fruit, earthy side to it. Length OK. 2005 on. 2012–13.

2001 (CASK) Smoky, violet, stewed fruit nose; stretched palate, taut attack. Dries towards finish, wow! Second half is all oak. Maybe some day in the future.

2000 ★ Spicy, black stone fruit nose; ripe grape attack, Viognier *gras* in mid-palate. Prune flavour, bit taut; uneasy, rather vacant end.

CÔTE-RÔTIE TERRES SOMBRES

2003 (CASK SAMPLE) (★) Prune/alcohol mix— dripping bouquet. Brewed southern wine; reduced, also an oxidative tendency at this stage. Some raspberry aftertaste. Review later. From 2006; 2011–13. Last tasted Dec. 2004.

2002 ★★ Dark, tarry, brewed bouquet. Good life, berried fruit, vigorous though a bit raw. Parts need till mid-2006 to pull together. Fresh finish. 2012–13.

2001 (cask) ★★★ Suave, floral, squeezed cassis aroma; plump, cooked-fruits attack, straight blackberry flavour. Good fruit theme. 2011–12.

2000 ★★★ Good wide, meaty nose, forest/spice/smoke; chunky start, cooked black fruit middle. Big, charged modern wine. Tannic/oak end. Dark, soaking flavour. Waste to drink before 2007. 2015–16.

BERNARD DAVID

Le Giraud 69420 Ampuis +33(0)474 561483

For a low-profile domaine, Bernard David has built up a sizeable vineyard that runs to 4.5 hectares. A mechanic when a young man in the early 1970s, he started his vineyard work in 1982 while renting a plot of 1940s Syrah on the high site of *Le Champin*. This produced just four or five casks a year, until he took the plunge in 1987 and bought 1.8 hectares on the *Coteaux de Tupin* from a single owner. This was an easy purchase—a later one within the *commune* of Ampuis involved nine different owners for one hectare.

He is the fifth generation to live on the plateau above Ampuis, but any wine made by the family was always drunk at home; most of the crop would be sold to local merchants. For 17 years Bernard worked at a heavy truck factory at St. Priest, nearby, and his project of developing the domaine continued unabated until he suffered a severe stroke in 2001. This caused him paralysis of his right arm, and he admits, "Life is different now. Before that, my aim was to bottle half my wine and sell the rest as crop. That's been delayed, but I'm sticking at having a go."

A short man with streaks of grey in his dark hair, Bernard tucks himself away and appears to like working away from the glare of the *vigneron* community. His practical leaning shows through with his commitment to the careful execution of his wall building, where he uses the pyramid technique of placing 200 to 300 kg (440 to 660 lbs.) stones at the base and gradually smaller ones upwards. His 1.5 hectares of steep slope on the *Coteaux de Tupin* requires 300 metres (330 yards) of walls, for instance.

"I have the possibility of working nine hectares," he comments, "half owned, half rented." His is largely a southern-sector domaine, now with three hectares on the *Coteaux de Tupin* and a hectare on *Pimotins* above it on flat ground. There is also a hectare on *Moutonnes* in the *Brune* sector. Viognier amounts to 8 to 10 per cent, mostly planted on the clay patches of the *Coteaux de Tupin*—"spots that don't suit the Syrah," comments Bernard. In 2003 the Viognier was so ripe—some at 17°—

that Bernard sold it to the *négoce* trade and relied on 100 per cent Syrah.

Around 4,000 bottles—one-third of his harvest—are produced, with the rest of the crop sold to the local merchant trade. Eighty-five per cent of the domaine crop is destalked and undergoes a two-week vatting, with pumping-over and a manual punching down of the cap. Ageing lasts 12 to 15 months, half in vat, half in oak—20 per cent of it new, the rest one to three years old. There is light fining and filtration.

"I want fruited wines," declares Bernard. "That's why I restrict the vat temperature to 30°C or below, and aromas are more refined as a result." He achieves this—his wines are refined and tidy, with gentle fruit and pretty textures present. He is a man of detail and system—his notebook records all his daily vineyard tasks; his explanations are very precise. His wines, likewise, seem to take nothing for granted and do not seek to put on a show. *Tant mieux.*

CÔTE-RÔTIE

2002 None bottled.

2001 ★★ Pretty dark cherry *robe*; light spice/lard aroma, black stone fruit, can develop. Assured, soft texture, some quiet energy within. Rounded black jam, touch of tannin/oak on finale. 2011–12.

2000 ★★ Floral/rose aroma with ripe fruit underlay—pretty bouquet. Supple start on palate, soft middle but skips a touch; red berry/raspberry at end. Fair length. Drink now, or no later than 2008–09.

1999 ★★★ Quite full *robe*. Reserved, light vanilla bouquet with potential. Classic style, *beau vin*. Has local character and ageing potential. Pretty red fruit flavour and aftertaste, correct tannins, balance sound. Not exaggerated. 2014/16.

DOMAINE DE BOISSEYT-CHOL

178 RN86 42410 Chavanay +33(0)474 872345

See also Condrieu, St-Joseph.

Didier Chol likes to make honest, traditional, generally elegant wines. His *Côte Blonde* Côte-Rôtie carries a high, 15-per-cent proportion of Viognier that acts as a softening agent in the wine.

The 0.75-ha vineyard was bought in 1977, when prices were still reasonable. The single plot dates from 1940 and is on the classic sanded, loose granite of this prime site.

The crop is vinified, with a part destalked, in stainless steel over three weeks. Ageing in cask—20 per cent new, 80 per cent four to five years old—lasts two years, there is no fining nor filtration, and on average 3,000 bottles are produced.

CÔTE-RÔTIE CÔTE BLONDE

2002 (CASK) ★ Quite tight-knit, black berries nose; some red fruit, then rather narrow. Some length gives encouragement. Small scale. 2010–11.

2001 ★★★ True bouquet—floral/nuts, some fruit; floral influence at start, then black fruit tightens it, almost like "dry jam." Fair length, broadly tannic. From 2009; 2014–17.

MAISON DELAS

ZA de l'Olivet 07300 Saint-Jean-de-Muzols +33(0)475 086030

See also Condrieu, Cornas, Crozes-Hermitage, Hermitage, St-Joseph, St-Péray.

Delas make two Côte-Rôties. Over many years its regular wine, the Seigneur de Maugiron, has been a steady but never really pulse-quickening offering. Indeed, the Delas relationship with Côte-Rôtie has seemed equivocal since the 1970s, when there was direct family ownership under the late Michel Delas.

Now the Seigneur de Maugiron is 60 per cent crop bought in and 40 per cent sourced from the ex-Delas vineyard, which has continued via M. Maurice Bruyère, the son-in-law of the late Michel Delas. This vineyard dates partly from 1994, partly from the 1950s and earlier.

ALBERT DERVIEUX

One of the central Côte-Rôtie figures—the Italian word *figura* does the job well—during the 1960s and 1970s was Albert Dervieux. He is the father-in-law of René Rostaing and held the Presidency of the Syndicat des Vignerons for over 35 years from 1953. He retired in 1991 and now lives quietly in Verenay.

Born in 1920, M. Dervieux, a small, wiry man always on the move, was one of the first growers to produce different wines, often titled by their vineyard place name. His trio of wines, last made in 1989, was La Garde, the finest, most floral wine taken from the *Blonde* end of the *appellation*; the Fontgent (the map now spells this *Fongeant*) from above the *Brune*—firm, berry-fruited wine; and La Viallère, dark, concentrated, and closed when young, from above Verenay. This would be bottled around two years after the harvest, the others about 15 months after it.

In M. Dervieux's time, the expansion of planting appellation vines on the plateau was a hot issue, as well as the rise in the permitted yield to 40 hl, with a 15 per cent extension on top. Moves have been taken to restrict both these events in the past few years.

Another concern of the day was that newly planted areas of the vineyard, particularly around the area of *Le Mollard*, to the south of the village, were not being built with retaining walls. This left their mainly sandy topsoil prey to being swept away by heavy rains. Neat mechanical excavators just 1.3 metres wide could work the vineyards here, but there was a clear risk.

M. Dervieux was always one of the few people at Côte-Rôtie to have an anciently stocked personal cellar, so he was able to pass views on the top vintages. He rated the 1929 his "year of the century" and considered the best vintages since then to be 1945, 1947, 1955, 1961, 1969, 1971, 1978, and 1999.

"I drank one of my 1929s in 1969, and it was still in marvellous condition," he recalls. "The colour had turned almost brown, I grant you, but the wine had kept much of its strength and all its character. Normally I would say a Côte-Rôtie can live between 20 and 30 years, but they should be good to drink after 10 or 12 years."

The Maugiron comes 70 per cent from the *Brune* sector and 30 per cent from the *Blonde* sector, covering seven different *lieux-dits*, including *Taramond*, a subset name straddling the *Brune* and *Brocarde* on the former hill flank. The wine is pure Syrah, and around 20,000 bottles are made in a normal year.

Since 1997 a top *parcellaire* wine, La Landonne, has been made, except for 2000 and 2002, when the standard was not high enough. Delas buys the crop for this from the Bruyère holding on *La Landonne*, meaning the original core south-southeast–facing site before it was expanded in 1974. The vines are at least 50 years old. Around 2,500 bottles are produced.

The crop for both wines is destemmed and, after a three-day pre-fermentation cold maceration, spends around 20 days in open concrete vats. The top temperature runs between 28° and 30°C, and for 12 days there are daily *pigeages* and *remontages*. Both wines complete their malolactics in cask; the Seigneur de Maugiron receives 16 to 18 months in up to 15 per cent new oak, the rest one year old. The Landonne stays for the same time, with a half new-oak, half one-year-old cask mix.

As an illustration of just how mighty was the 1999 vintage, the Seigneur de Maugiron that year stayed for 25 months in cask, and the Landonne for 26 months, the same as Delas' top Bessards Hermitage.

CÔTE-RÔTIE SEIGNEUR DE MAUGIRON

2003 (CASK) ★★ Brewed black fruit, coffee bouquet, some width. Black berries, tar start, lacks some middle. Sweet tenor. Licorice/pepper finale, fair length. Big, not so succulent as 1999. From 2007; 2017–19.

2002 ★★ Some cooked fruits, smoke/floral touches. Supple vanilla/red fruit flavour, soft wine. Starts gently, fleshes, spices a little, then some tannins. Low-key, but agreeably knit. Drink now to 2010–12.

2001 (CASK) ★★★ Quite full, sappy nose, game aspects; finesse wine, fairly full; tannins sit outside as yet. Can become varied, integrated. From 2007; 2015–17.

2000 ★★ Plain, light cooked fruit nose; some raspberry, bit dumb. Gentle cooked fruit flavour, lacks nuance. 2011–12.

1999 ★★★★★ Cooked garden fruit, truffle aromas, potential; solid wine, more than usual. Latent richness; chewy, masculine. Tannins at end, with raspberry. Powerful, but no excess. 2017–20.

1998 ★★★ Smoky, swirly dark fruits aroma, upright; dry outset, then plenty of matter, fleshy end. More the inky *Brune* style. Chewy finale, length OK. 2009–11

1997 ★★ 2008–10

CÔTE-RÔTIE LA LANDONNE

2003 (CASK) ★★★★ Full, compact bouquet, which has a north-zone mineral glint. Well-knit, structured black fruit; good lines, agreeable breadth. Good fruit, tarry oaked end, is rich. Tannins ripe. From 2008; 2020–22.

2001 ★★★★ Good density on bouquet, gently smoked black fruit, suave; tight-knit fruit, *confit* with raspberry aftertaste. Juicy; has grilled notes, stewed side on end. From 2008; 2018–20.

1999 ★★★★★ Well-defined, pure nose; smoky black aromas, very typical, *vinum picatum*. Smoothly textured, wonderful, oily wine. Berried fruits lead to white truffle finish. Delicious, great promise. From 2006–07; 2020–22.

1998 ★★★★ Wide aroma, some damp tones, mineral, olives, varied. Good warmth, then tannins pounce. Restrained, just starting to evolve. Decant to work round the tannins. 2011–13.

1997 ★★★★ 2013–16

RICHARD DESBORDES

Tartaras 69420 Ampuis +33(0)474 561756

Richard Desbordes set off on the wine trail in 2002, leaving his job with Citroën in Vienne to return to the family holding on the plateau above Ampuis. His father, André, has worked the farm as a mixed enterprise, growing vines and cereals like wheat and barley, as well as raising cattle. Richard is now making his Côte-Rôtie from the Syrah vineyard planted on *Tartaras* by his father in 1989.

The size is small—just 0.4 hectare on this plateau site that contains loose sanded granite with some depth of subsoil. This is supplemented by the *vin de pays* vineyard at Échalas, southwest of Givors, and a site with the *gore*-granite and breakable stones of the outlying Massif Central zones. Here there are Syrah, Chardonnay, and Aligoté grown for the red and white *vins de pays des Collines Rhodaniennes*.

The Côte-Rôtie, called *Tartaras*, is fermented for up to four weeks in a sound year like 2004, with manual cap punching and pumping-over. It is raised for 14 months in two-year-old casks. It is bottled unfined and unfiltered. "I want the wine to hold a silky attack with a tannic follow-through," states Richard, a youthful looking, dark-haired man; "that means the wine can give the drinker several impressions, and not just be monotone."

The correct Syrah *vin de pays* is aged for a year in used casks.

CÔTE-RÔTIE

2003 ★★(★) Lightly brewed, floral bouquet with good core. Gentle fruit, good clarity, has promise. Style and character here. Esp from 2006; 2014–15.

DOMAINE DUCLAUX

RN86 69420 Tupin et Semons +33(0)474 595630

Two new pairs of hands are adding energy to this traditional domaine in the southern part of the *appellation*. Edmond Duclaux reached 60 in

2003, and his sons David and Benjamin, early-30s and mid-20s, respectively, are taking up his baton with evident determination and enthusiasm. Both have studied wine formally, unlike their father, with Benjamin joining in 2001 after a six-month stint in California.

David, a slim, dark, good-looking southerner, is bright, with a sharp sense of humour and his mother Monique's will power. She is very precise, while Edmond is more the gentle countryman, a fisherman who likes to be outdoors. In 2004 David became joint President of the Growers Union with Christope Bonnefond—young blood at the helm.

The Duclaux family have been busily planting recently, and now have a potential six hectares; their 5.15 ha of producing vines may be supplemented from overgrown land that will need clearing in the years to come.

The two largest plots are over two hectares on *Coteaux de Tupin* and another two hectares on *Maison Rouge*—both marked by the decomposed granite of the Tupin area. There is also 0.5 ha on *Coteau de Bassenon*, formally known as the *Coteaux de Semons*.

Edmond estimates that the vineyard is on average 30 years old; the oldest plants date from 1924, with 0.8 ha planted in 1943 and another portion in the 1960s. These older vines make up about a quarter of the total and are Sérine; 5 per cent Viognier is mixed in.

"We are working on *massale* planting, taking cuttings from our best old stock," comments Edmond, who has the wind- and sun-swept features of a man happy to be in his vineyard. "We're up to 1.5 ha of *massale*, which we started around 1997."

The Duclaux moved to Tupin from the Ardèche in 1928 and started out as mixed fruit, vine, and vegetable growers. Edmond, a good friend of the late Robert Jasmin, started to bottle some of his wine in 1976, and by 1979 was bottling everything. In those days there were some successes, some less fine years. Now an all-important consistency has begun to show in their wine, which has not yet succumbed to multicuvée fever. "The wine's there to be drunk and enjoyed," is David's reassuringly sound comment.

Since 1996 the crop has been destalked: "A year when ripeness was poor, so we bought a destemmer with Robert Jasmin," states David. "We have increased the duration of the total maceration, up to 30 days, to gain more body."

Open concrete vats are used, with the plots handled separately: "We want fruit from the young vines, extraction and depth from the old vines," says David. There is a week of cool, 10°C premaceration, to obtain fruit and colour; external yeast was needed in 2002, but is not a fixed item. *Remontages* and *pigeages* are done during the vinification, which by the end of the process may reach a temperature of 33°C for the older vines' crop.

Cask ageing runs almost two years. All the press wine goes into new oak, but the free-run wine does not. The latter is aged in a mix of 600- and 228-litre wood for a year, then all the wine spends 10 months in 228-litre casks. The oak ranges from one to 10 years old. There has been no fining nor filtration since 1997. Two bottlings occur, in September and December, so the second lot receives around three months' more cask ageing.

These wines reflect their southern Côte-Rôtie origins: a lot of fruit and finesse, plenty of floral tones. Up to 98 per cent of their vines stand at between 150 and 250 metres up, an ideal exposure for their ripening. And touches like using new oak for the press wine—maybe 15 per cent of the final drink—show a degree of detail that is encouraging. David first did this in 1999, and finds that it makes the wine more robust and helps to round and refine the tannins.

He and Benjamin, a brown-haired chap with the freckles of youth, make the most of their place and their resources. Benjamin is precise, like his mother, and puts the knowledge of his studies to good, sensible use. Even so, there is a hint of the wistful in David's voice when he says he wouldn't mind a patch on the *Brune* to make a different wine someday—one with bigger shoulders, more longevity.

The brothers already show very good *assemblage* skills here, which bring an authentic house style in tune with the vintage in question. This is one of the great unsung challenges facing a grower producing just the one wine, and it's a tribute to their natural connection with the vineyard that they achieve this.

CÔTE-RÔTIE

2003 (CASK) ★★★ Good oily, soaked bouquet, not overdone. Rich and genuine matter—broad black fruits, length sound. Good *gras*, harmony. Herbal influences on finish. Merit is its definition. Will show early, from 2008; 2017–18.

2002 ★★ Damp, *sous-bois*, prune bouquet. Some richness, length OK. Tasty now, Viognier does a service. Lacks freshness. Drink now to 2009–10.

2001 (CASK) ★★★ Clear red/black fruits, damp earth on nose; chewy, brewed black fruit; violets, truffles bring depth. Quite solid, length OK. Has potential. Fruit will emerge. From 2006; 2012–14.

2000 ★★★ Pretty red fruits, jam aromas; open, more obvious charm than 2001. Chewy, ripe fruit flavour, raspberry, earthy tones. It's almost moist earth, this local touch. Rounded wine, fair length. 2011–12.

1999 ★★★★★ Lovely balance on bouquet; mixes red fruit, with warm, full underlay, chocolate even; wide variety of flavours—prunes, black fruits, very generous. Raspberry essence on finish. Delicious, rich texture. Has never had a hidden moment in its life. 2015–17.

1998 ★★ Quite grainy, leathery bouquet—the dry leaning of the vintage. Wine with sound grip, quite "dark"—contains chewy matter. Tends to be upright. Some tea leaf flavour at end. Moving along quite fast, not holding as well as expected. 2008–09.

Export 30 per cent (1) USA, (2) Canada, (3) Belgium/Brazil

DOMAINE DUMAZET

RN86 07340 Limony +33(0)475 340301

See also Condrieu, Cornas.

Pierre Dumazet, maker of full-flavoured Condrieu at Limony, vinifies the crop of a grower who tills 0.75 ha on the *Côte Brune* (1982). The mix is 95 per cent Syrah, 5 per cent Viognier, and his first wine was in 1989.

There is no destemming, and the wine receives 15 to 16 months ageing in 600-litre barrels; it is lightly fined, but not filtered.

CÔTE-RÔTIE

2000 (CASK) ★★ Gentle bouquet, smoky/spiced raspberry. Discreet fruit cut, sinewy, quite upright. Darker, tarry tones at end. Purity rather than fat. Could surprise nicely by 2009 or so; 2014–16.

1999 ★★★★ Gamey, ripe grape, harmonious bouquet; soaked dark fruit attack, leather/pine traces at end. Upright, minty wine, has good matter. Persistent. From 2007; 2014–16.

DOMAINE PHILIPPE FAURY

La Ribaudy 42410 Chavanay
+33(0)474 872600

See also Condrieu, St-Joseph.
In 2005 Philippe Faury's coverage reached a full hectare on *Fourvier* (1996) and half a hectare on *Le Plomb*, the latter planted by him between 1995 and 1999. They are both on the schist, with some clay, of the northern end of the *appellation*. There is a high, 15 per cent proportion of Viognier in the wine, no doubt inspired by his knowledge of the vine at Condrieu; 4,000 bottles are made.

The crop is 60 to 80 per cent destalked, and vinified over 18 to 20 days in concrete, with *pigeages*. It is raised for 12 to 18 months in casks, 25 per cent of them new. There is neither fining nor filtration.

CÔTE-RÔTIE

2003 (CASK) ★★ Macerated raspberry aroma, florality also, some sweetness. Soaking cassis with sweet texture, olives and southern instincts. Full style, bit ponderous. Sipping, not drinking wine. From 2007; 2014–17.

2002 (CASK) ★ Floral aroma; straight, *cassis* fruit; frank, direct wine. Viognier and young vines effect here.

2001 (CASK) ★ Soft garden fruit nose; soft start; middle gains some breadth; gentle, easy wine. Minted end, fair tannin, length OK.

FERRATON PÈRE ET FILS

13 rue de la Sizeranne 26600 Tain l'Hermitage
+33(0)475 085951

See also Condrieu, Crozes-Hermitage, Hermitage, St-Joseph.

The Ferraton family's joint venture with Chapoutier provides a Côte-Rôtie that is bought in as young wine and aged by them for 16 to 18 months.

Its crop is destemmed and fermented in open wood vats, with twice-daily cap punching, up to a maximum temperature of 32°C. The total maceration runs for 20 to 25 days.

DOMAINE ANDRÉ FRANÇOIS

Mornas 69420 Ampuis +33(0)474 561380

André François changed his career in 1992. "I worked in industry, with packaging machinery," he states, "but as my father had the farm, I thought I would give wine a go." Like several around them, the François family worked the land in different ways—fruit, vegetables, and a few vines. Now it is all wine.

The first bottling was in 1987, and all the production is sold in bottle. There are three hectares, the main plots being *Gerine* and *Les Rochains*, along with 0.35 ha of Syrah *vin de pays*. On average the vines date from the late 1970s. There can be 5 per cent Viognier present.

A slight man, with dark-brown hair and an air of reserve, M. François is not seeking to make showy wines or be too forceful in his approach. "The less you do, the better things go," he says about the vineyard. He is no doubt content that one of his daughters, Nancy, is studying winemaking.

The bunches are vinified whole, with a three-week fermentation in concrete vats, including *pigeages* and *remontages*. No external yeasts are used. Cask raising lasts two years—15 per cent new, the rest up to 10 years old. There is no fining or filtration.

CÔTE-RÔTIE

2003 (CASK) ★★ *Cassis*-jam, coffee bouquet, some life in it. Fair harmony—oily, minted black fruit. Tasty texture, good honest brew. Olives/tapenade aftertaste. From 2006 on. Some risk will dry; 2013–17.

2002 ★★ Smoky, pine scent bouquet; minted, floral dark fruit flavour, has some kick and character. Semisweet end from the chaptalisation. Viognier presence helps. From 2006; 2012–14.

2001 (CASK) (★) Quiet, touch floral aroma; suave, nice fruit that tightens and becomes tarry. Bit rustic, dry end. Core matter is OK.

2000 ★ Quite ripe, earthy/woody and cooked fruit aromas; chewy, stewed texture; traditional, earthy style. Could be fresher. 2009–11.

JEAN-MICHEL AND MICHELLE FRANÇOIS

Mornas 69420 Ampuis +33(0)474 561551

Up on the pastoral plateau at Mornas, this family makes wine and cheese. Buzzards, with their pointed calls, and keen-eyed hawks drift on the winds, the landscape is fringed by woods and fields, and it's not surprising to find a herd of well-bred Holstein cows here, away from the craggy slopes.

Michelle is the sister of Edmond Duclaux's wife, and their brother is Bernard Chambeyron. The couple work closely together. Jean-Michel has enlarged the herd from half a dozen to 28 cows; he grows cereals to feed them, plus some apricots, and looks after the 1.7-hectare vineyards. Michelle, whose short-cropped fair hair adds to the impression of determination that runs through her family, makes the cheese and takes the refrigerated trailer around the local markets, notably Ampuis on Wednesdays and Vienne on Saturdays.

She is continuing a market tradition extending back two or three generations; she sets up at 7 AM on market days, and admits to knowing the stories of the village, serving ladies in their 80s who have known her family all their lives.

Most local cheese, notably the Rigottes of Condrieu, is goat, but theirs is purely a cow's cheese. Michelle's mother-in-law taught her the cheese making, and all ages of Rigotte d'Ampuis are offered, from the very young, soft cheese eaten with a spoon, to the oldest, firmest cheeses that are three to four months old. "Most people buy the cheeses around 10 to 15 days old, when they have just a bit of blue in them," she says.

All their sales are done directly from home, with no shop distribution. Michelle likes olive oil and herbs with her Rigottes and is clearly content that son Yoann is studying wine at Mâcon and is interested by both wine and the cheese.

The Mornas hamlet is full of François family members; just hitting 50, Jean-Michel is André's older brother and has developed the wine side from their father's day, when the crop was all sold to merchants. He has plots on *Ritolas* (1970s) and *Les Rochains* (1988) in the *Brune* sector, part owned, part rented. Both needed clearing before plantation.

The crop is fermented for two to three weeks in concrete vats without destemming, and contains 5 per cent Viognier. There is some pumping over, and wood ageing lasts at least two years in old casks. Around 4,000 bottles are made and sold to private customers, the rest of the crop going to Marcel Guigal.

CÔTE-RÔTIE

2000 ★★ Open, fragrant strawberry nose; nicely natural, gentle red fruit flavours. Pretty wine. 2007–08.

1999 ★ Floral, red fruits/tar, charming nose; fair weight of red fruit, outbreak of tar at end. Straightforward local wine. 2007–08.

1998 ★★

PIERRE GAILLARD

Chez Favier 42520 Malleval +33(0)474 871310

See also Condrieu, St-Joseph.

From a start of just 0.25 hectare in 1986, Pierre Gaillard has worked his way towards exploiting a little over three hectares at Côte-Rôtie. He had been involved in the clearing, wall building, and planting of *La Turque* when he worked for Guigal in 1981–82, so he knew the vineyard there well. There is a hectare at *La Viallière* (1988), above the Champet vineyard; a hectare at *Côte Rozier* (1983); 0.75 ha on *Fongeant* towards the plateau above the *Brune*; and a small plot on the *Côte Blonde* itself. His weighting is therefore towards the sturdy wines of the schist.

His classic wine used to be called "Brune et Blonde," but these days it is labelled plain Côte-Rôtie. He is keen on Viognier in his Côte-Rôtie, so it can contain up to 10 to 15 per cent of the white grape, and is drawn largely from *Fongeant*, the *Côte Blonde*, and *Viallière*. His special cuvée, Rose Pourpre, first made in 1995, comes from the *Côte Rozier*, the northern flank of the *Landonne* site. This is pure Syrah, chosen from the best casks tasted a month before bottling.

The crop is partly destalked and receives a week's cooling at 6° to 8°C before heating, and an alcoholic fermentation also lasting a week. There are thrice-daily automatic *pigeages* and *remontages*, and the end temperature is allowed to run to 35° to 40°C for more extraction. Pierre likes to do a final *délestage*, or partial vat decantation, at the end to reactivate the yeasts and help finish any remaining sugars.

The process continues with a further two to three weeks of maceration at 30°C—"to round out the tannins and so bring more charm," as he puts it. The malolactic fermentation is done in cask. The classic is aged for 18 to 20 months in 30 to 50 per cent new oak, 70 per cent one to three years old; *Rose Pourpre* also receives 18 to 20 months in cask, all of them new. Instead of racking, Pierre uses the system of injecting oxygen into the casks—micro-oxygenation; "I started this around 2000, and find that it tires the wine less and helps to fight reduction on the Syrah, its stale smell," he explains. Finally, there is a fining, but no filtration.

These wines have busy early lives, therefore. For the American market, Pierre sends around 900 bottles of a wine called "Les Viallères," and 300 to 600 bottles of a Côte Blonde, for which the shipper likes an early bottling. The former contains 20 per cent Viognier, and the 2002 in cask ★★ showed decent quality, and a fair depth.

CÔTE-RÔTIE

2003 (CASKS) ★★ Oily, ripe, unusual nose—soaked black fruit, a little leather. Some floral, local presence in the fruit—is black berries. Ripe tannins and a more southern garrigue aspect. Touch stretched on the finish, balance is fair, not totally assured. Licorice aftertaste. From 2008; 2014–16. Last tasted March 2005.

2002 ★★★ Smoky, black fruits/floral aroma. Brewed prune fruit, some richness; compact, midweight; some tannin. Length correct. Safe and sound wine. More variety from 2006; 2012–13.

2001 ★★ Nose mixes floral, light meat, ripe crop, some fungal tones; cooked-up black fruits, prune flavour at end, tannins too. Some *gras*, but seems a bit stretched, and dry at end. Esp 2005; 2011–12.

CÔTE-RÔTIE ROSE POURPRE

2003 (CASK) ★★★ Brewed, dense chocolate style bouquet. Ripe crop and richness, then a firm side from oak; rich, full wine. Mocha, dark fruit finale. A bit stretched, a modern wine. From 2007; 2017–19.

2002 *Côte Rozier* Mixed into classic.

2001 ★★★ Some floral topping, good depth below—red berries; quite ripe, cooked berries, nicely full. Expands well at end; light toast, good punch; stylish. From 2006–07; 2012–15.

2000 ★★ Quite intense stewed berries/oaked aroma, some floral; fair fruit, with *typicité*, holds off the oak; bit dry at end. 2011–13.

DOMAINE GALLET

Boucharey 69420 Ampuis +33(0)474 561222

Set on the wide, panoramic plateau of Boucharey is this 3.5-hectare domaine. Henri and Marie-Thérèse Gallet met in the romantic setting of viewing each other's hamlet across the brief valley. Her family were vine growers; his family had moved to Boucharey in 1807 from Vienne. They grew barley and wheat, raised animals, and had some vines. Casks of the wine would be taken on their two-horse cart to the cafés of Lyon and St-Étienne.

There are overt rural tones up here on this windswept landscape: tractors in fields; warming tunnels for vegetables; peach, apple, and pear trees dotted around. Their neighbour Bernard Chambeyron for some years grew tobacco.

They own three hectares and rent half a hectare at Côte-Rôtie, plus another half hectare for Syrah *vin de pays*. The main plot is the 2.5 ha on *Lancement* (1993) next to the *Côte Blonde* site. Further south, right on the cusp between Ampuis and Tupin, they have a half hectare on *Le Combard*. So the prevailing influence is *Blonde*, meaning finesse and gentle flavours. Indeed, there is 6 per cent Viognier overall.

Just above the *Côte Brune* site, they have 0.2 ha on *Fongeant* and 0.15 ha on *Chavaroche*, the latter planted in the 1920s. Apart from *Lancement*, the rest of the vineyard dates from at least 1978.

In 1991 their son Philippe left the army and came to work on the domaine. He is now in his early 30s and is adding extra momentum.

Half the crop is destalked, although 2002 was so tricky that only 20 per cent was left with stalks on. Vinification runs over three weeks in stainless steel, and the Gallets yeast if they have to. The wine is raised for 18 to 24 months in 40 per cent *demi-muids* and 60 per cent casks, about 15 per cent of them new. There is just the one wine, but several bottlings between April (after 18 months) and September. The wine is fined but not filtered.

Since 1988 just one ton of crop has been sold to Guigal; the rest is vinified and bottled at the domaine. Expect the Gallets to become better known in the coming years.

CÔTE-RÔTIE

2002 (CASK) (★) Light red fruit, some content. 2008.

2001 (CASK) ★ Fair warmth, floral aroma; red currant/cherry fruit, quite upright texture. A peek of roundness, fair tannins. 2010.

2000 ★★ Floral, light red berry jam bouquet, deepens with air; supple wine, gently done, elegant fruit. Some spice at end. 2010–12.

1997 ★★ 2006–07

Export 20 per cent (1) USA, (2) Japan, (3) Switzerland

DOMAINE MATHILDE AND YVES GANGLOFF

2 rue de la Garenne 69420 Condrieu +33(0)474 595704

See also Condrieu.

Yves Gangloff's 2.4 hectares lie mostly on the southern end of Côte-Rôtie, a mixture of old and young vines. His oldest plots, on average dating from the 1950s, are 0.8 ha on *Combard-Mollard* and 0.2 ha on *Côte Rozier*. His 1.4 ha of young vines are half on *Coteaux de Tupin* (10 per cent Viognier), half on *Combard-Mollard* (an overlap between the two plots).

He makes two wines: *Barbarine* dates from 1997, is 10 per cent Viognier and is mainly young vine fruit from *Coteaux de Tupin*, plus some from *Combard-Mollard*. *La Sereine Noire*, pure Syrah, is made from the 50-plus-year vines of *Combard-Mollard* and *Côte Rozier*. There are 6,000 and 5,000 bottles of each wine.

Since 1996 more of the crop has been destemmed—the young vine *Barbarine* entirely, the older *La Sereine Noire* 50 to 70 per cent. "In 1996, quite a lot of the stems were not ripe, so had a vegetal influence," recalls Yves; "but now that I drink my 1996 at seven years old, I know that destemming isn't the only solution. This wine would not be nearly as alive and well if I had destemmed the whole crop."

Fermentation is in steel vats, and Yves prefers not to do *pigeages* on his must: "I do a lot of *remontages* and some *délestages*. My aim is to energise the cap." No external yeasts are used. The temperature can rise to 28° to 35°C.

Both wines are aged for 23 months in oak, the *Barbarine* in casks of two to six years; the *Sereine Noire* in 30 per cent (2001) to 50 per cent (1999) new oak, the rest two to four years old. "You have to leave the wine for nearly two years if you are to allow it to go through several openings-up and closings-down in that period," observes Yves. He neither fines nor filters.

In 2002, 40 per cent of the crop was lost, and there was just one wine. No new oak was used, and cask ageing lasted only 18 months, both sensible decisions. Gangloff's Côte-Rôties carry the trademark finesse and stylish fruit of the domaine, with the Sereine Noire carrying enough weight to age over at least a dozen years.

CÔTE-RÔTIE

2002 ★★ Cool berry, firm aroma. Fair fruit, restrained wine, fresh, early drinking. Small amount of richness—slight gain in last year. 2008–09. Last tasted Nov. 2004.

CÔTE-RÔTIE BARBARINE

2001 (CASK) ★★ Elegant, medium-weight wine, tar and tidy richness on end, some pepper on aroma. Will show well esp 2006–07.

2000 ★★ Fair blackberry/pepper in a reduced bouquet; suave, juicy wine; berried fruit floats along well. Fruit is ripe, quite long, some end tar. Friendly drinking, good in restaurants. 2008–10.

CÔTE-RÔTIE LA SEREINE NOIRE

2001 (CASK) ★★★ Some *cassis* aroma; very closed, a glint of stylish flavour beyond the oak. *Côte Rozier* brings extra juice and width. 2012–14.

2000 ★★★ Sultry bouquet, compact, black fruit, animal touch. Blackberry attack, oily texture, silky tannins appear. *Gras*, chocolatey. Esp from 2006; 2013–15.

JEAN-FRANÇOIS AND CARMEN GARON

58 Le Goutay 69420 Ampuis +33(0)474 561411

I would back this family to do well. They work as a team, and the two sons—good, strong lads—are quietly motivated and attentive. Crucially, they have a strong sense of the importance of their vineyard. One sees growers who assume when it comes to the vineyard—it's just there; then you see the Garons, who listen and observe, and try to understand it better. If they know which pockets ripen better or which ones are more disease prone under different weathers, they will make better wine.

Jean-François could only be French, unless he had a Mexican cousin who once encouraged him to grow a luxuriant moustache. He is dark-haired, steady, and has a firm hand on the tiller. His eyebrows are bushy and signal a strong look. His wife, Carmen, is fair, with warm almond eyes and a hearty laugh; their sons, Kevin and Fabien, born in the late 1970s, have both studied at wine school in Burgundy and the Beaujolais.

There has been a 20-year project to sort out and build up the vineyard. History plays a part here. The Garon family has owned vineyard land since 1836, but it wasn't until 1982 that they started to transform it. The work was from zero, since previous generations had preferred to be wine agents and to raise animals.

"We both always had great passion for wine," Jean-François explains. "Carmen's brother is the third generation of her family to run the Restaurant Berut on the square in Condrieu. And I remember as a young boy burning the old casks here; we had no use for them, but little did I know. So you can see that we wanted to restore things."

"It wasn't bad for the vineyards to rest for a hundred years between plantings," observes Jean-François, "but of course the site was com-pletely overgrown with oak trees, wild roses, and so on; you could hardly see the old terraces."

"We had planted a fair amount by 1985–86. First we sold grapes to Guigal, then wine, which we started to make from 1992. Now we bottle 90 per cent of our wine, the rest going to Guigal."

The planting continues today. There are now 4 ha of vines, over 1 of them dating from the early 2000s. It is all Syrah; as they are based on the *Blonde* area, with its supple wines, no Viognier was required. The most recent plot is on *Le Combard*, dating from 2003.

The core vineyard rises behind the house and cellars on *Le Goutay* and dates from the mid-1980s. This is essentially slippery granite, with a couch of siliceous chalk. We are in full *Blonde* territory here, with further plots on *Lancement, La Triotte,* and *Le Mollard*, all dating from the mid- to late 1980s.

In 1999 the Garons moved on to the more schist, brown-clay soil of *Les Rochains*, a little to the north, near *La Landonne*. This 1980s Syrah vineyard has supplied its own wine since 2003.

Jean-François has an eagle eye in the vineyard, and he is lowering the use of copper treatments. They hand weed, but also have to do some herbicide spraying. Heavy rains in 2000 caused a lot of slippage, a problem that is aggravated once the soil has been turned. The vineyard is sheltered from the north wind, which is good for ripening and as protection against some hail, like the 1998 storm.

"You must never allow distance to come between you and the vine," he says as he walks around the old family vineyard, without doubt overjoyed to see it back in working order. "To harvest a good crop, it's not just a question of a laboratory analysis. You have to walk in the vineyards and see what is going on. I'm aware how far removed I am from the electronic world when I'm here redoing a wall, for instance. But I reckon the true *vignerons* in years to come will be those who are able to say yes or no to intervention in their vineyard because they understand it properly."

The winemaking is traditional, with whole bunches crushed and a two-to-three-week vinification in concrete vats. They work on a plot-by-plot basis to have a better idea of each place's qualities. The only year that outside yeasts were used was 1996. The cap is submerged with planks twice a day. Wood ageing lasts 18 to 24 months, in casks, 30 per cent of them new, the rest one to five years old. They fine, but do not filter.

The wines show marked promise and a pleasing respect for the vintage's character. They reflect the good, clear thought that has gone into them, and stylistically would indeed be termed "traditional."

See also St-Joseph.

CÔTE-RÔTIE

2003 (CASKS) ★★ Floral, gamey mix on quite heavy bouquet. Big-scale wine, has oak to contend with also. Rather straight, with dry finale now. Has richness, can pull together. Wait and hope. From 2006; 2012–14.

2002 ★★ Bosky, mint/tar nose—southern-zone softness within. Tarry wine, some warmth, is reduced, but has some local character. Oak here, though 10 per cent less new oak this year. From 2006; 2011–13.

2001 (CASK) ★★ Soft, violet/pepper/earthy nose; reserved on palate, with quiet richness. Leather/chewy finish, some spice. Sinewy. 2012.

2000 ★★ Quiet pepper/floral bouquet; steady blackberry fruits, in a quiet phase just now; spice towards end. Esp from 2004–06; 2011–12.

1999 ★★★★★ Dense bouquet, chocolate with violet/light licorice top edge; delicious attack, very direct red fruit appeal. Some tannin, well bundled within. Good length. Real charm and *terroir*. 2010–11.

1998 ★★★ Solid bouquet, nice dark fruit; black lissom fruit, soft and rather Pinot style. Overt wine, with jam fruit textures. 2007–09.

1997 ★★★ 2010–11

Export 40 per cent (1) Great Britain, (2) Japan, (3) USA

DOMAINE GASSE LAFOY

16 route de la Roche 69420 Ampuis +33(0)474 561789

See also St-Joseph.

If you were to paint a likely portrait of the Philosopher Grower, Vincent Gasse would conform in picture and words. Appropriately, he lives just outside the main village of Ampuis, in the northern hamlet of Verenay. From here he conducts his private campaign—to solve the conflict of making truly organic wine off slopes that crumble when you hand work their soil.

Reticent at first to meet, he clearly likes to remain out of the limelight. At 60 he is professorial, with a beard and what could be called wild hair, prominent bushy eyebrows, and glasses. His voice is soft and reflective. "I am the son of a grower from Vouvray, in the Loire, while my wife was born here and her family are vineyard owners. We met quite late in life, when I was 45, after I had been a teacher of agriculture for 25 years."

In 2004 he decided to hang up his boots, and made just four casks of Côte-Rôtie from his plot on *Le Goutay*. His 1.3 hectares of vineyards, spread across five plots—*Côte Rozier, Leyat,* and *Le Goutay* on the full slopes and *Bonnivière* and *Ritolas* nearer the plateau—have been rented out to his fellow worker of the past seven years, Stéphane Otheguy. The oldest are *Leyat* and *Bonnivière*—both around 1945–55 and planted by Marie Lafoy's father, Pierre. The rest vary between 1985 and 1999.

M. Gasse feels strongly that the world's resources are being rapidly depleted, so his intention is to make wine in the most constructive way possible. This means covering all the angles, from choice of vinestock and care of the vineyard to the winemaking itself.

"When I started around 1988, I didn't know the possibilities, so I used clones—everyone spoke about them then. But since 1998, I have used only homegrown rootstock, working with cuttings from old Sérine vines. That particular part of the sequence can be mastered," he states.

GENTAZ-DERVIEUX

One of the most unassuming of men, Marius Gentaz-Dervieux has been a wonderful presence at Côte-Rôtie. Born in 1922, he worked all his life in the vines until stopping with the 1993 vintage. His holding was a manfully worked 1.2 ha, an amount that seems insignificant until you remember that there were no winches, no spray helicopters, and not really much market for the wines when he was at his busiest.

But stick at it he did, letting the wine do the talking. And we are left with some of his treasures, glorious wines like his exceptional 1978, his robust, initially backward 1989, his smooth-as-silk 1985, his potent 1990. Carrying the sobriquet Côte Brune, these were wines with great expression of terroir, their earthiness well in keeping with their origins. As a counterpoint to the more tender, floral Côte Blondes, they were unsurpassable.

Marius still lives in a little house above his tiny cellar room not far from the Château d'Ampuis. There is a tiny, dusted-over window just above road level in the cellar; it's like the conduit to his vineyards, so close to them was his wine.

The wine was vinified with an immersed chapeau in concrete vats and then stored in regular old wood for 15 months or so.

M. Gentaz considered his 1989 as his top wine of the 1980s, followed by the 1985 and 1988. And as for the 1978, well, that was a Trésor d'Ampuis. His son-in-law René Rostaing now works his vineyard.

"It's when you want to work in pure *bio* here that the crunch comes. I knew all about the pesticides and intensive farming methods from my teaching. But if you want to be *éco-biologique* here, there are enormous extra costs. The one big problem is how to work the soil—the rest of the issues can be solved."

"On slopes, manual weeding and working will take 1,000-plus hours, versus just 10 hours if you spray weedkiller," he continues. "Say the weather is bad, you go up to 1,500 hours. And where are you going to find the people prepared to do this hard work? The challenge lies in the very word 'Côte-Rôtie'—which the next generation is going to have to find an answer to if they want to make true organic farming here economically sound."

"It's different for other organic producers," he adds. "I can't double the price of my wine, whereas the organic vegetable grower can. By the time I finish, I'd like to have proved that biodynamic wine can be made in extreme conditions, like these hillsides."

His bronzed face in early spring indicates his commitment to his vineyard, and M. Gasse admits that he loves completing the transfer from outside into the cellar. What he has made have been stealthy wines, which creep along quietly before going "boom." They are wines to get into as they enter their second phase, and will rarely be zappy and impressive when young.

The first destalking was in the early 1990s, and vinification was in one open wood and one open concrete vat. No cultured yeasts have ever been used, and after a cool maceration, vinification would last over three weeks. There would be two to three *pigeages* a day for two weeks, with a final maceration temperature rising to a maximum of 33°C.

The two-year ageing was done in used 228-litre casks, all three years and above. All the wine was bottled, without fining or filtration. The first bottling was in 1988, and there was a Cuvée Sophia made from under 20-year Syrah off *Côte Rozier* and *Ritolas*, and a Vieilles Vignes from old vines that are purely *massale* selection, without any clonal presence.

CÔTE-RÔTIE CUVÉE SOPHIA

2002 (CASK) ★ Pepper/floral aromas; good tight fruit, quite mineral, decisive and discreet wine, lacks some richness. 2010.

2001 (CASK) ★★ Pure *cassis* aroma; cherry style fruit, peppered end, quietly tasty. Straight wine, some stuffing. Natural tannins. 2011–13.

2000 ★★★ Quite ripe, dark cherry, toast, and earthy aromas; very good cut on palate, black fruit with earthy touches on end. Fruit is very pure and deeply founded. From 2008; 2014–16.

CÔTE-RÔTIE VIEILLES VIGNES

2001 (CASK) ★★★ Black cherry, tight fruit bouquet, not yet open. Decent weight with a chunky second half, showing *cassis* and light pepper. Chewy end. Pure, upright wine, needs patience. Will flesh out with age. 2014–17.

1999 ★★★ Shiny *robe*; hints of cooked, quite tight black fruit, some vanilla and spice. Nicely textured, good fruit integrity, lot of crushed blackberry fruit that runs well. Dry, more tannic tones on end, wee bit short. 2011–15.

Export 35 per cent (1) USA, (2) Great Britain, (3) Luxembourg

FRANÇOIS GÉRARD

Côte Châtillon 69420 Condrieu +33(0)474 878864

See also Condrieu.

François Gérard was an early example of "going back to the land." His father worked in a factory at Givors, on the west bank of the Rhône above Vienne, but had a few hybrid vines up there. He made a little wine that would be sold to his workmates, and "that got me tempted," confesses François.

Off he went to Beaune to study, and the domaine was set up in Côte-Rôtie in 1980, when he was 29. A very tall man with a friendly, quite grizzled look, he now works three hectares, two of them that he planted on *Mollard* (1980, including 10 per cent Viognier); the remaining hectare is rented, split between *La Viallère* (1920s), *La Landonne* (1981), and *Fongeant* (average 32 years). The total Viognier share is 5 per cent.

Just the one Côte-Rôtie is made, with a little of the wine sold in bulk. A new cellar in 2003 allowed temperature control, a help also for his Condrieu. The crop is destalked, and during the fermentation, which lasts around 16 days, there are automatic cap punchings. Yeasts are added. Cask ageing runs over 20 months, 10 to 15 per cent of the oak new, the rest up to eight years old. The wine is fined and filtered and mostly sold to private customers who come to the door. It reflects the southern area of the *appellation* via its straightforward, light fruit style.

A modest man, whose preference is to be in the vineyards, François is encouraged that his son Xavier has done Mâcon studies: "The fact there's a succession here is what pleases me most of all when I look back," he comments.

CÔTE-RÔTIE

2001 ★ Light raspberry aroma, woods/tar also. Midweight, not especially deep. Has some style, and tannic thread. Fresh—softer by 2005.

DOMAINE JEAN-MICHEL GÉRIN

19 rue Montmain Verenay 69420 Ampuis
+33(0)474 561656

See also Condrieu.

It's always a good sign when the Growers elect a noted Party Animal to be the President of their union. In Jean-Michel Gérin's case, he knows how to celebrate, but also how to work hard and exude a notably energetic outlook. He served as President of the Growers Union until 2004.

He's a sporty man, a doer who likes things physical, and to be busy and involved. Having just hit 40 in 2001, he continued his rugby run-out with the lads: whether the tackles softened is not recounted. "Give me any good sport," he declares; "football, rugby, basketball." His two teenage sons obviously keep him on his toes.

He is married to Gilles Barge's sister Monique and made his first wine, Champin le Seigneur, in 1987. His father is Alfred Gérin, notable for introducing American investors to Côte-Rôtie in the 1960s and later for an eminent career in politics.

Jean-Michel works seven hectares, largely situated in the northern areas of schist with iron-oxide patches. His largest *lieux-dits* are 1.3 ha on *Les Grandes Places* (1940s, 1960s) and 1.2 ha on

La Viallière (late 1970s). His other main sites are 0.8 ha on *Les Lésardes* and on *Fourvier* (1983, 2000), 0.6 ha on *Côte Baudin*, 0.5 ha on *Taquière* (a rare granite-based *Blonde* site), and 0.4 ha on *La Landonne* (1987), which has provided a single-vineyard wine since 1996. Other tiny dabs of vineyards complete the Côte-Rôtie line-up, while he also has a vineyard at Condrieu.

He set to work first on a cellar, and by 1991 had a fully modern one. Then he turned to the vineyards and, since the early 1990s, has applied no chemical fertilizers. "The vineyard is where the difference lies now—we've all got our cellars and equipment," he says. "In 2001 we spent 900 hours on the harvest, and longer—1,100 hours—on the green harvest before it, which is why none of the crop came in at under 12°."

Three wines are made—since the Champin, he has added Les Grandes Places in 1988 and La Landonne in 1996. The Champin (30,000 bottles) is made from all his sites and contains 10 per cent Viognier. Les Grandes Places (6,500 bottles) and La Landonne (2,000 bottles) are both pure Syrah.

The main aspect of the domaine's style is the overt use of oak. His early adviser was Jean-Luc Colombo from Cornas, with other ideas from Michel Rolland of Bordeaux. "Modern ways" was never a phrase to be afraid of here. Jean-Michel was one of the first growers to use American oak in 1993, and Champin now receives about 20 per cent US oak, half the casks new, half one to two years old. The two top wines are purely French oak raised, all in new wood. Cask ageing lasts two years. The wine is left alone for the last year, with no racking. There is no fining, no filtration.

The vinification has been changed a little since 1996, with two high-temperature phases spread over a longer period. After destemming, the crop spends a month or even 33 days in steel at up to 35°C for its alcoholic fermentation and then a maceration, when it is held between 30° and 37°C. "The objective is to bring finesse and elegance, which sounds paradoxical, but that's

FIGURE 2 Dolce Vita! Jean-Michel Gérin sets father, Alfred, to work on the year's harvest. (Author's collection)

what it achieves—rounder tannins, notably," comments Jean-Michel.

Jean-Michel points to a difference in fruit between the big two wines: "There is a lot more iron oxide on *La Landonne* than *Grandes Places*. This translates into a more rounded black fruit style for Landonne, whereas the Places is more minted, with laurel and gunflint tones."

Jean-Michel made three excellent, indeed grandiose 1999s. "It's one of the four best vintages of the last century, along with 1929, 1947, and 1961," he says. "We gained 2.5° of alcohol in the last week—just 1° would be normal; but the acidity also concentrated and didn't dilute, so we had the two sides."

Since 1999 there has been a pretty good Syrah *vin de pays des Collines Rhodaniennes*. This is made from young Côte-Rôtie vines and plateau Syrah aged between three and 50 years growing outside the *appellation*. It is aged for a year in two-to-three-year casks. In 2001 he also set up a venture in Priorat on the northeast coast of Spain with Laurent Combier and Peter Fischer. Its first wine is stylish and threaded with welcome elegance.

CÔTE-RÔTIE CHAMPIN LE SEIGNEUR

2004 (CASK) ★★ Latent bouquet, fruit present, also flowers. Pretty palate, well-weighted middle, elegant. Fruit is cherries. Fair length, hint of oak at this young stage. Esp from 2009; 2019–22. Last tasted March 2005.

2002 (CASK) ★ Soft, bit floral nose; quite juicy, then tightens. Fair fruit. Not very big, peppery edges. 2008–10.

2001 (CASK) ★★ Soft, floral, light fruit nose, some spice; supple, agreeable wine. Floral-style fruit, quite long, soft licorice end. 2010–12.

2000 ★★★ Pebbly, minty fruit, game side on nose; red fruits, some *gras*, good clear Syrah expression; length sound. 2010–12.

1999 ★★★★★ Lot of oil/black fruit on nose, lissom and rich; works well on *gras* and a soaking texture; rich plum flavour. Sweet, animal touches, striking richness. Has power to keep it going. 2018–22.

CÔTE-RÔTIE LA LANDONNE

2004 (CASK) ★★★★ Brewed, quite beefy nose. Plenty of richness on palate, also spice and pepper here. Grilled from the oak, holds good texture. Licorice finale, length is good. To bottle Sept. 2006. 18-year wine. Last tasted March 2005.

2002 (CASK) ★ Reserved, light black fruit/ pepper aroma; mid-plus weight; quite suave *cassis*, bit stretched, oak end.

2001 (CASK) ★★ Quiet oily aroma, lightly smoked black fruit; suave, directed *cassis* fruit. Dry, clear end, oak there. 2013–14.

2000 ★★★ Some animal, mineral aromas; measured *confit*, good and refined texture. Quite sunny wine, fair length, good direction. 2011–13.

1999 ★★★★★★ Quite ripe, tight nose, meat/smoke/olives; strong flavour, but always harmonious. Lasting black fruit extract, cooked and dense. *Gras*, with tannins in step. From 2007; 2023–26.

CÔTE-RÔTIE LES GRANDES PLACES

2002 (CASK) ★★ Lithe, smoky black fruit aroma; fair black fruit content, taut but can run on. Eight-to-10-year wine.

2001 (CASK) ★★★ Tightly packed fruit, some spice/peat; varied flavours, wild blackberry/ mulberry, hedgerows. Dry finish at present. Elegant year. 2013–16.

2000 ★★★★★ Very sleek, assured dark aroma, some oak; delightful, well-cut fruit, tasty, good definition. Tannins well wrapped, good length. Very classy, pretty. From 2005–06; 2016–18.

1999 ★★★★★ Big, ripe crop aroma, minty/prunes, leathery; very intense palate, fruit warms up well, great dimension. Tannins still tight, oak needs time to fill in. From 2006; 2021–25.

Export 40 per cent (1) USA, (2) Great Britain/Belgium/ Switzerland

E. GUIGAL

Château d'Ampuis 69420 Ampuis +33(0)474 561022

See also Condrieu, Crozes-Hermitage, Hermitage, St-Joseph.

Every year at harvest time there is a collective holding of breath around Ampuis as people wait to see what Marcel Guigal will do with both crop and prices. He is the pivot of the *appellation*, recently through vineyard ownership, but for many years through his influence in the open grape market. Both owner and *négociant*, he vinifies over 40 per cent of all Côte-Rôtie. Across the villages, his regular grower sources, sometimes families with just a modest patch of hand-me-down, lovingly tilled vines, are instructed to wait until he gives the green light for the harvest. This is usually late, since the Guigals like to wait.

Many of the noble French wine companies and dynasties were set up in the nineteenth century. Here is one that has moved into the mainstream in just the last 60 years. Étienne Guigal, Marcel's father, started out very humbly in the St-Étienne region, like his future wife, Marcelle.

His own father had died when he was a child, and Étienne had to set to work when only eight years old.

He started out in a modest way, employed by the local Ampuis grandee Vidal-Fleury and rising to become their cellar master and then their head *vigneron*. After 15 years of work chez Vidal-Fleury he left in 1946 to set up his own company, Ets (short for Établissements) Guigal.

Meanwhile Marcelle had been obliged to start work at 16, as a housemaid for the Roche des Breux family, leading lights in the St-Étienne silk industry. Their summer residence in July and August was the Château d'Ampuis, and in her odd moments of free time she would take a quick dip in the Rhône that ran past the gardens.

One fine day she spotted another swimmer as she took time off on the verandah. Such was the impression he made, she picked off many of the geraniums in her excited, timid state, causing Madame to comment later on how poorly the geraniums were doing that year. Étienne and Marcelle married in 1936, two years later.

Their son Marcel was born in 1943, and joined the firm in 1961, earlier than anticipated because his father had been struck by temporary blindness. He set forth on a path of enormous industry and commitment, based on long workdays that start at 5:30 AM and bold, forward-looking decisions that grew in dimension once the firm's foundations had been laid.

One of the first of these was Étienne and Marcel's 1984 coup, the deal that heralded many more moves into vineyard ownership, in buying the House of Vidal-Fleury, beating off potential foreign buyers and multinationals and so gaining control of around 35 per cent of the Côte-Rôtie harvest. So 38 years after leaving as an employee, Étienne had bought his old employer's business, which had fallen on rocky times after Joseph Vidal-Fleury's death.

Much of the appeal of Vidal-Fleury undoubtedly lay in its seven hectares of prime-site vineyards, which brought Guigal's total holding at that time to 12 hectares, with another three hectares that came on stream by 1995. The latter

three hectares are at the summit of *La Viria*, on the north side of *La Landonne*. Looking back, Philippe Guigal considers that Vidal-Fleury move as one of the star moments for the family since the 1970s: "Each time we make a *vin de cru*, a lot of that is due to Vidal-Fleury," he comments.

Both Marcelle and Étienne died in 1988, the latter aged 79, a man who worked on 65 harvests. Marcel recalls him as an expert in the vineyards and a great listener—"He would pick up all possible tips and information." Étienne was rarely parted from his cloth cap, a trait continued by the next two generations. Marcel sports a classic wool version that is usually tilted towards his left ear, making him look younger. Philippe's prefers American-style baseball hats, which carry a variety of logos—sports, banks, and cars most often sighted—and which are also tilted in a jaunty way.

A further example of Guigal's ability to turn history around came in 1995, when he bought the Château d'Ampuis, where his mother and father had met. Its condition had slid downhill under the previous owners, and it had been abandoned for five years. "It was a ruin," comments Marcel simply. "I didn't want this piece of local heritage to be lost."

Now the whole house has been restored with great care and attention to detail; the roof has been completely renovated using the traditional Burgundian varnished tiles that are actually made at Loire-sur-Rhône. Work continues on the formal gardens. In time there is likely to be a smart landing stage on the Rhône at the bottom of the garden.

Built by the Maugiron family, the château has two remaining towers that date from the twelfth century, while the central part of the building is sixteenth century. The most gripping feature is the *oubliettes*, where prisoners were left to rot; except that here there were spikes at the bottom, and the Rhône to wash away any unwanted traces.

This is also the home of the Guigal's own cooperage, set up in buildings dating from the fifteenth and sixteenth century. Their previous suppliers were mainly Seguin-Moreau and François Frères, and this new business is a partnership with Seguin-Moreau. "A cooper can assemble two to three casks a day," says Philippe Guigal, "and so can easily make the up to 600 we need each year. There is a cost saving, but more than anything it's because my father, who's always loved casks, wants to make sure the heating process is right. Our policy is for a light toasting over 45 minutes, but we're also keen to allow the casks to dry for a full three years, not the 18 months or less that you find today."

Philippe shows he has caught his father's bug when he states, "I adore projects—we like to have something on the go all the time." The building of new facilities for winemaking and stockage is the next step, started in 2006 in the *Blonde* area of the *appellation*. A new cellar is also being constructed.

Philippe was born in 1975 and is the only child; he has always been a good, bright student possessed of a sharp, wry sense of humour: "droll" is a word not much heard these days. His dress can be deliberately unstructured, such as a sporty, pinstriped waistcoat topped off by a tweed jacket. On other days, he is more metropolitan—black shirt, black coat—as if ready to hit a Tokyo cocktail bar. He has thick black hair, dark eyes, and a very mobile face, and his eyebrows complete the effect of an amusing raconteur—impersonations, gestures, and all.

His higher education was in biochemistry at Lyon, and he took his baccalaureat early, at 17. In 1996 he spent six months at Château Cheval-Blanc and then went on to receive his oenology degree from Dijon after a two-year course.

Philippe's dissertation for his doctorate was on the Grey Market of Wine in Europe—where wine is traded in parallel, outside country accords —something that the top Guigal wines can experience. For this he visited 17 countries in 10 months to study the management and marketing of wine—stints included four weeks at Davis University, and visits to China and Bulgaria.

There were also two one-month visits to Australia, the first covering the Swan Valley and Margaret River, the second McClaren Vale and Coonawarra. He joined the family firm full-time in February 1999, the year that his father calls "the best wine I've ever made."

Philippe is more chatty than his father, a trait he acquires from his mother, Bernadette, who has run the office and the two men in her life with great tempo and dedication since marrying Marcel in the 1970s. Marcel admits that he is introverted, a word I would replace with "shy." "My work and my family especially take my time and interest," he states in his quiet tones. As he speaks, so he moves—a gliding presence around the *cave* and the office.

When pressed, a little more definition comes forth: "I'm glad to have worked to help the *appellations* to defend themselves," he reflects. "In the future, I would expect there to be four or five excellent *appellations* in the Rhône." The formal line is stated before the more personal one, to wit: "the important thing is that the work of my father is perpetuated, and I'm also very glad that Philippe is so well recognised by others in the wine trade."

Marcel has been honoured by the French state with the award of the Légion d'Honneur, the highest civil decoration in the land. He is also courted by politicians and industrialists from Lyon, with often a troupe of suited men present in the cellars—a sight more expected in Bordeaux than in the Rhône. He is quite definitely a Big Presence, but you wouldn't guess it from his personality.

Things never stand still chez Guigal. In the vineyards, structural work continues apace. In two separate operations three years apart, the *Moulin* site within the *Brune* had its terraces removed and was replanted in sloping rows. The work took 18 months altogether, ending in 2003. Low-yield clones were used for this operation. *Moulin* forms one of the seven components of the Château d'Ampuis wine.

On the *Côte Rozier*, the shape of the hill has been changed, with the terraces taken out and replaced by one single slope, a wall at the top, a wall at the bottom. The plantation density has increased, while the labour needed has reduced.

In 2001 the Guigal vineyard holding at Côte-Rôtie leapt forward through the acquisition of the eight hectares of de Vallouit vines. The most prominent sites are on the *Côte Blonde* next to Guigal's own vineyard, while on the schist area of the north end, there is a large area on *Rozier*, as well as a plot on *Verenay* and on *Viallière*.

The vineyard team has increased now that the Guigals are owners at Hermitage, Crozes-Hermitage, Saint-Joseph, and Condrieu.

Life is even busier than usual at harvest time. Two teams of 50 pickers each work across the vineyards to pick the Guigal crop; they include the Viognier with the Syrah as they go, placing the grapes in small 50 kg (110 lb.) boxes. The harvesters are all locals, so can be on standby to work at short notice, as was needed in 2003.

At the cellars, the crop is launched along two moving carpets, with eight inspectors per carpet. One of the key tasks is to ensure an across-the-board reading of the must, so as to avoid putting in 14° and 11° bunches, for instance—some suppliers have been known to load the grapes rather knowingly.

They operate what they call a Pessimist's System for refusing unhealthy or low-degree crop. "On big-scale operations like this, it's often too late to get the crop back once it's gone down into the reception area, so we have a system of reversing the screw," says Philippe, as he sits side by side with his father while the crop rolls in. The two generations work with their favourite tools, keyboard for Philippe, folder for Marcel. The operation around them reflects their outlooks—it's large and electronic and contains a lot of thought to cover eventualities. "Everyone makes mistakes, but you have to make fewer mistakes," comments Marcel.

The stalks are retained if they are ripe, on what Philippe calls a *"haute couture"* basis—plot by plot. Philippe Guigal contrasts two vintages: "In the poor year of 1993, we harvested late, and the stalks were by then ripe. 1995 was meant to be much better, but many stalks weren't ripe and had to be taken off."

There is no formal crush, with the piping process serving to break the grapes only lightly.

The Guigals work solely with indigenous yeasts. They have also cut their sulphur dioxide use. "Everyone uses it, but no one talks about it," says Philippe. "As it is an anti-oxidant, we apply it immediately on the fresh harvest—doses are injected into the pipes. The result is that we use a lot less than before, around two to three grams per hectolitre instead of five for the reds, and five to six instead of seven to eight for the whites."

Their work in the 50 steel fermenting vats of 100 hl is now split according to the origin of the grapes. Punching down of the cap is split by soil type. The *Blonde* sector wines are pumped over (*remontages*) in pursuit of elegance and finesse. The more robust *Brune* wines, with greater keeping potential, are pumped and punched down (*pigeages*).

Guigal does about two *pigeages* a day, to compress the top matter within the vat in much the way that certain coffee-making machines punch down the grains in the water to gain full extract. "For me," comments Guigal, "the *pigeage* brings a gain of about six-tenths of a degree against an open vat, and provides more bouquet plus colour and tannin through more polyphenols [anthocycans and tannins mainly]. I find this can also help to obtain a lower pH level, taking about 0.2 or 0.3 off the acidity level to drop it to around 3.5."

The two *pigeages* a day run for three to four weeks, during the active phase, then the Guigals taste and decide if more are needed. Together, the alcoholic fermentation and maceration last for three to four weeks. "We are not interventionist," says Philippe Guigal, "and the reds can rise to 33°C, which hasn't changed in many years."

"We work in reverse to the majority," continues Philippe. "In the lighter vintages, our *cuvaisons* are actually shorter—we don't try to make up for the year through more extraction. No, we go with the vintage, which means that in big years we work even more on the matter in the crop."

The cellar was completely redone in 1993–94 on an area of 0.4 hectare (1 acre), with features including anti-vibration cladding due to the nearby railway and anti-seismic insulation as well. The battery of steel vats on the first floor brings a pressure of five tons per square metre. The walls are 70 cm (over two feet) thick. A further 0.5 hectare (1.2 acres) was built on in 1999, giving the space to move into the buying and ageing of Crozes-Hermitage. The cellar temperature is held at 12°C and 87 per cent humidity. The casks are all 228-litre Burgundian.

There are 4,000 casks (up from 3,000 in 2001!) and about ten 60 hl barrels. The barrels are used for all their southern Rhône reds. These barrels are made like a small cask, with no inner curve, which demands more wood and is more expensive than usual. "We would like these casks to last 50 years," comments Philippe. Their bottom doors are steel, not wood, for hygiene, and any residue—pips, stalks—can also be emptied via a central bottom steel tap.

There is also a purely commercial consideration at work here; a much cheaper wine like the Guigal Côtes du Rhône red is put in barrel, where most of the crop spends six to 18 months, because it is economic to do so. Small casks would price it out of its market.

There are two rackings in the first year, and then one per annum, with the Brune et Blonde receiving 36 months' ageing, the Château d'Ampuis 38 months, and the top cuvées 42 months, meaning that trio is always bottled at the end of January. For the first two, the wine from each site is left to develop its own qualities, so there is no blending until just before bottling. The Côte-Rôties are neither fined nor filtered.

The 42-month formula for the top wines has been cross-checked in the past. Étienne Guigal raised one cask of the 1976 Mouline for two and a half years, on the grounds that a friend had suggested it might be better with less oak. The experiment was not repeated. "We compared the two wines sometime later, and markedly preferred the 42 months' wine," says Marcel.

In Rhône terms, Marcel was an early "clean oak" practitioner. He first used 100 per cent new oak for La Mouline in 1971, after starting the wine in 1966 with a little new oak. So much time spent with casks: Marcel maintains that the use of a 228-litre *pièce* develops the wine's bouquet more than a large *foudre*. An experiment in 1970 with raising in a 45 hl barrel was not deemed a success, and only casks have been used since then, piled into high rows. Philippe chips in with his observation that the casks stacked on the second, third, or sometimes fourth level finish their sugars and their malolactics well ahead of the bottom row.

Despite all the air and space of the new cellars, the Guigals still raise wine in what was an old Vidal-Fleury cellar built before the French Revolution across the N86 road from Guigal's building. The Vidal-Fleury family kept 400 barrels there, which used to be looked after by Étienne Guigal, until he left the House of Vidal-Fleury in 1946. Apparently the key to the cellar was lost in 1974, so no one properly used it until Étienne and Marcel put their then new vattery there in 1986. And with Marcel doing nothing by halves in his search for perfection, he had a tunnel bored out underneath the N86 main road to connect the two cellars. The work took five months and was supervised by an engineer who had worked on high-profile projects like the TGV fast train and the Ariane rocket launcher. The tunnel is one metre beneath a road that nowadays has 15,000 vehicles using it per day, and there is not a trace of vibration from the traffic.

All the while, there is tasting. Georges Duboeuf is a legendary taster in the Beaujolais, but Marcel Guigal is not far behind and is also handling much bigger wines. His cramped little tasting cellar is unchanged in 30 years: a few dim lights, lots of samples, minibottles—a workroom, not a showroom. A blender would love to be let loose here.

After the early start in the office—Philippe and Bernadette are also there by 6:30 AM—they move on to the tasting room at midday, when most growers are settling down to lunch, to taste together. This can involve 40 wines, sometimes more, sometimes less. Through the day, it is often Bernadette herself who answers the telephone: there is no pretentious hiding behind ranks of assistants.

Meanwhile, down in the cellars, Gare de Lyon conditions have been known to prevail, although Philippe's arrival has eased the situation—except when he twists his pelvis in the first 25 minutes of a two-day ski-ing holiday! His father may be involved trying to take round visitors—I have counted four of five groups at a time—with Marcel appearing like the prophet giving his sermon as he addresses them all; in the meantime he is also lining up a tasting for a restaurateur and his friends, answering questions over the tannoy about which wine should be drunk with a local fish, and keeping an eye on dispatches out of the cellars.

Marcel confesses to being allergic to computers—there isn't one on his desk—and the slack is taken up by Philippe, in a corner of their crowded inner sanctum family office. I have always considered that much of Marcel's success is due to hard work and, above all, method. But it has consistently been preceded by very lucid strategic thought. He might have given Wellington a fright on the battlefield!

Many habits remain unchanged. Marcel has appeared somewhat scholarly, with his slight figure, wire glasses, and short haircut, since I have known him. He also loves to wear ties; "you can find him sitting on his own in the office on a Saturday morning, yes, wearing a tie," comments Philippe in his laconic way.

His manner remains unpretentious. At an overseas event, he will always seek out a long-known face, as if to touch the old, secure realities. I have never known him to make loud, imposing statements. A smile and a darted look are the usual companions to his softly spoken observations.

The office work often ends between 9 and 9:30 PM, and a simple supper is taken in their home across the gravel courtyard. *En famille*, Marcel is very modest. It's the backseat—often reclining—for him, usually because he is whacked after yet another hard day's work. But his sense of humour, dry in the main, can perk up when it comes to the more fanciful side

effects of his success. A couple of films have featured his wines—nothing set up by him—*The Shooter*, an American film featuring an opening dining scene where La Turque 1988 and La Mouline 1985 are drunk, and then *Une Histoire de Goût*, a French film including La Mouline. Marcel shakes his head self-deprecatingly as Philippe shows the cassettes and everyone has a good old tease.

It's a moment to ask Marcel about his star followers: "Well, Céline Dion buys our wines in Canada and has them shipped to Florida—it's a lot more expensive, but she is a faithful customer," he says. The French acting community are also keen—Gérard Depardieu, Lino Ventura, Carole Bouquet (also a face of Chanel), and Catherine Deneuve, who likes her white Hermitage.

Sales boom along. In 1994–95 the Guigal label sold about 2.15 million bottles, the Vidal-Fleury name 450,000. By 2004–05, Guigal sales had risen to a little under 6 million bottles, Vidal-Fleury to 800,000. A surprising fact is that almost 25 per cent of the wine sold is white. Ask any British wine merchant about white Rhône, for instance, and he'll complain about how hard it is to sell.

The bottling line is state-of-the-art—not surprising with a stockage nowadays of 1.5 million bottles. This can fill 8,000 bottles an hour, and means more single bottlings for their largest-volume wines. A single bottling run of the popular Côtes du Rhône *rouge* can cover 200,000 to 300,000 bottles. There is a monster bottling hall, with, in true Guigal style, just two people working on the line. In all there are only 22 people working in the cellars and the offices. This is indeed a tight ship.

Guigal makes five styles of Côte-Rôtie. The workhorse wine is the Brune et Blonde (250,000 bottles); the upper echelon starts with the Château d'Ampuis (25,000 bottles), made from seven small sites in the centre of the *appellation*, and rises to the top level of the Big Three, made up of La Mouline (5,000–6,000 bottles), La Landonne (12,000 bottles) and La Turque (5,000 bottles).

None of these is typical Côte-Rôtie—they are Guigal Côte-Rôties. Their prolonged exposure to new oak and the use of grapes allowed to ripen to a near extreme mean they are heavily soaked in oily, cooked flavours. Their depth is solid, their breadth secure, their finishes long and richly textured. They carry a brewed tone and are chunky youngsters in the deepest vintages.

This contrasts with the simple, tender fruit of the low-key blends of Côte-Rôtie—wines like Clusel-Roch and Jasmin—that run along Burgundian lines of finesse and clear fruit purity. A shimmer of tannin accompanies these wines, and the bouquets conjure pretty garden-fruit images. The "darker" wines from growers like Jamet and Barge are also less corpulent than Guigal's wines. None of the above domaines uses large amounts of new oak, by the way.

The Big Three are the wines that have propelled Marcel Guigal into international fame. Sold in small quantities at dizzy prices, these are what unite in admiration the rich, the famous, and the genuinely enthusiastic wine lover. But they now form part of the regular and dreaded Wine Collector lexicon, with accessibility severely limited to most mortals. In June 2004 the London auction prices for a case each of the 1985 Big Three were £4,840 (US$8,700) for La Turque, £4,620 (US$8,300) for La Landonne, and £4,400 (US$7,920) for La Mouline.

CÔTE-RÔTIE BRUNE ET BLONDE

This was the wine that first marked out a Guigal style—plenty of wood and a very long, almost forefather-style ageing process. There are two sources. Guigal buys grapes from around 45 small cultivators, the largest of whom tends 2.5 hectares, and in part uses the crop from his 23 hectares of choicely sited vineyards. Only the vineyards for the La Mouline, La Landonne, La Turque, and Château d'Ampuis are excluded from the mix.

Like all the Côte-Rôties, this is aged for a long time in wood—a mix of 80 to 90 per cent casks and the rest barrels that are 15 to 20 years old. From 1988, 25 per cent new oak was used

for the casks, rising to 30 per cent in 1994 and up to 35 per cent now. The remaining casks have held two to three wines. The Brune et Blonde's wood ageing lasts around 36 months in total. It contains around 5 per cent Viognier.

Brune et Blonde is a solid, square style of Côte-Rôtie, in the house vein. There is always padding about its shoulders, placing it well apart from the gentle, floral school of Côte-Rôtie. The quality in the 1970s was extremely good, but there was a wobble in the early 1980s. Form revived in the late 1980s, but the wines traversed a dull period during the 1990s until 1998, when steps were taken to raise quality, notably a cutback to 250,000 bottles.

In the biggest vintages, the wine can live for around 20 years, although well-kept bottles of vintages like 1995 and 1999 will carry on for longer.

2002 (CASKS) ★★(★) Black fruits, stone fruit aroma; chewy flavours, olives; quite direct style, some dry-toned fruit. From 2008; 2015–17.

2000 ★★★ *Confit*/charm, smoky Nordic berries on fair-weighted nose; quite sylish, black flavour. Some *gras*, concerted berried end. Gradually opening. 2015–17.

1999 ★★★★ Chocolatey/cedar full bouquet, still closed; nicely rooted berries—raspberry/bilberry; runs on well, promises long life. Core of the *appellation* in taste. Nice length. 2018–21.

1998 ★★★★ Overt, spiced bouquet, smoky dark jam; well-packed flavour, sustained red fruits, quite solid. Good weight. Back to the 1980s levels. Chewy finale. From 2005–06; 2013–15.

1997 ★ Quite warm, *confit* aroma, pepper hints; straight, easy to drink, lacks core. Light tannins, rather dry end. 2007–08.

1996 ★ Pale strawberry fruit aroma, also fungal, slight licorice; red berry garden fruit, white pepper end. Fine, no great body. Just OK still. 2007.

1995 ★★★ Fairly weighted bouquet, closed for now; red fruits, berries all tightly packed. Discreet depth here, tannins are OK. Power on finish, quite a lot in here. 2011–14.

1994 ★

1993
1992
1991 ★★ 2003–05
1990
1989 ★★★ 2007–09

CÔTE-RÔTIE LE CHÂTEAU D'AMPUIS

First made in 1995, this came from six of the Guigal *lieux-dits* until 2005, when crop from the *Brune's Viria* site was added. From the *Blonde* area the sources are *Le Clos*, where extra planting has been done; *La Grande Plantée*; and *La Garde*, on the top of the *Blonde* itself. The wine's 7 per cent Viognier comes from these three *Blonde* sites.

From the *Brune*, the original trio was *La Pommière*, *Le Pavillon Rouge*, and *Le Moulin*. On average the vines whose fruit is used for the Château d'Ampuis are 40 to 50 years old. Because of the difficulties of the crop that year, the 2002 was made from only four sites, with two contributors, the Grande Plantée from the *Blonde* and the Moulin from the *Brune*, added to the Brune et Blonde wine.

"The National Archives showed us that these vineyards were part of the Château d'Ampuis, and their wines would be sold with that name," explains Marcel. "So we are relinking them once more." About 25,000 bottles are produced.

As usual, the grapes from the different plots are vinified and raised separately in new casks over the course of 38 months. Bottling is in November, three-plus years after the harvest.

Since its first issue, this has been a wine of assured elegance, perhaps closer in texture to Mouline than Landonne and Turque. Its flavours are darker than Mouline's, and I would expect there to be a little more density in the future with the addition of the Viria from the *Côte Brune*. Château d'Ampuis can show well over more than 20 years.

2001 ★★★★ Black fruit, white pepper bouquet, damp side, floral too. Scented fruit attack, then is stylish; rounded texture, live tannins within. Pretty richness, well styled. From 2005–06; 2018–20.

1999 ★★★★★ Compact, stylish black fruit/pine aromas; good silky, streamlined red fruit, then darkens, gets punchy. Quite full end, persists, with sound tannic structure. Esp from 2009; 2019–22.

1998 ★★★★ Refined, white pepper aroma, touch of game; suave black flavour, nicely oily, getting juicy, good mix of cooked fruit/ripe tannins. Mineral/prune end. Nice character, good autumn wine. 2015–17.

1997 ★★★★★ Quite dark; pretty, delicate, minty nose; palate floats nicely—elegant, suave black fruit; nudge of oak at end, with chicory/tar. Tasty, very good. 2016–19.

1995 ★★★ Dark red; ripe fruit nose, pepper/heat, tight; cool texture of fruit, flourishes, then dries a bit with air. Should slowly flesh out, from 2005 or so. Was more lissom. 2012–15.

CÔTE-RÔTIE LA POMMIÈRE

This wine was made just once, in 1989, after the death of Étienne, because it was the first vineyard that he worked when he was 14 years old. It is a subset of the *Côte Brune*. Its wine now goes into the Château d'Ampuis.

1989 ★★★★★★ Good brilliant *robe*; alcohol/pine oil, big aroma, red berry fruits; complex, broad flavour, well measured. Very suave, almost Pomerol texture; dried leaf/tobacco on the warm end. 2010–13.

The Big Three

La Mouline is the softest, plumpest wine of Guigal's elite trio. Its bouquet is always more round and tender than Landonne's and always more open at the same age. Its fruits are red in style rather than Landonne's mix of black fruits and earthiness. The Landonne bouquet is more peppery and upright and expresses blackberry compared to the stewed red fruits of Mouline. Marcel explains that the acidity of La Mouline is usually the lowest of the three, while La Landonne contains the most tannin and the darkest colour.

Reasons for this are various. Mouline comes from an old vineyard averaging 60 years, older than the others—*La Turque* dates from 1980, while *La Landonne* has been planted several times since 1974, the latest portion dating from 2003. The Guigals offer an average age of 20 years for it.

The presence of a high, 11 per cent Viognier plays a strong role in softening the texture and broadening the Mouline aromas. La Turque runs at around 7 per cent Viognier, while the Landonne is pure Syrah. Mouline is also from the siliceous, loose soil of the central hill, Landonne from the schist of the slightly breezier latter's site, its soil heavier. The Mouline crop is harvested first, followed at a few days' interval by both the *Landonne* and *Turque* crop.

There are also differences in the vinification. The Mouline is pumped over, but the cap is not punched, "to leave finesse" in Marcel's words. The Landonne is vinified with the cap submerged, and the pumping-over is done by natural pressure. La Turque has its cap punched down twice daily during the three to four weeks' vatting. The crop is never usually destemmed, although the 1996 and the 2002 Landonnes were because of the uncertain ripening in those years; "it's not something I like to do," says Marcel.

Powerful vintages of Mouline—therefore atypical years—include 2001, 1999, and 1998 in recent times. Old-timers in this vein were 1983, 1978, and 1969. The 1999 was a rare example of more overt tannins in the wine, requiring a 10-year wait. In the more live, refined style of vintage that suits Mouline well comes a year like 1996. An unusual year for Landonne was 1997—the wine much more open and accessible than usual.

The Mouline can usually be drunk earlier and more effortlessly than notably the Landonne, which always has comings and goings—dark, hidden phases as the tannins control the palate.

La Turque I always find lies between Mouline and Landonne, borrowing some features from both of them. Overall, I would place it nearer

Mouline than Landonne. Its flavours when young are straighter and less varied than the other wines. La Turque does not carry the plunging depth or grip of Landonne, but ends more flatteringly and softly. Its aroma can have a touch of damp soil and can be more refined at times than Landonne.

The Turque fruit is often rounded and savoury, without the plumpness of Mouline's. In tannic terms, Turque's tannins are usually less assertive and more integrated from the start than those of La Landonne. Marcel comments that the iron oxide soil of La Turque helps bring *grillotes* (soaked cherries) into the wine. He also considers La Turque to be the freshest of the three wines.

Taking the exceptional vintage of 1999, Marcel and Philippe's favourite is La Turque: "It was a year of very high extract in everything," comments Philippe—"acids, tannins, degree."

For his part, Philippe says that if drinking the wines young, he goes for the Mouline for its flattering charm. "La Turque is the perfect compromise of elegance and matter," he adds. "La Landonne is the most Australian of all—because of its content," he says somewhat mischievously. His preferred 2001 is the Turque, Marcel's is the Mouline. In 2002 both lean towards La Turque, while Philippe's favoured 2003 is La Mouline.

CÔTE-RÔTIE LA MOULINE
5,000–6,000 bottles

89 per cent Syrah, 11 per cent Viognier
Guigal launched his famous Côte Blonde wine, La Mouline, in 1966. It had been the property of Joannes Dervieux and already held a high reputation, selling for double the price of other Côte-Rôties. Dervieux had cherry trees growing within the vineyard, but Guigal took his time to replant, working in half ledges of new vines little by little. Most notably, he brought the amount of Viognier up to about 10 per cent.

The vineyard area for this wine is one hectare, up from the 0.9 hectare of its first 20 years. The average age is said by the Guigals to be 60 years, with plants replaced on a rolling basis; the oldest vines—just a few plants—are centenarian and date from after phylloxera.

With its cellophane-and-wire wrapping, La Mouline was the first of Guigal's specially packaged wines, and early on, its sale was directed at the good restaurants of Lyon and Vienne. Always very full and opulent, this is a fantastically elegant wine whose harmony in vintages like 1989, 1997, and 1998 is breathtaking. Possessing a powerful berries and fruit-extract bouquet even when only four years old, the La Mouline style has continued much the same over its first 40 years or so.

Tasting notes consistently refer to a sustained, red-black colour that moves towards ruby after six to eight years, an intense raspberry and highly scented nose, and always supremely classy, well-rounded flavours on the palate. The wine softens and shows its poise generally from seven years on, and only the most packed years like 1999 or the more tannic ones like 1995 need greater initial patience.

"I find the Mouline starts quietly, with finesse," comments Marcel, "then after three or four years, gains dimension."

The wine is not a real long-liver in the Landonne vein, however; even a memorable vintage like La Mouline 1969 started to move off the summit of its development after 20 years, while the 1978—tremendously round and long on the palate—is now a mature wine. Of recent years, the 1999, a 35-year-plus wine, will be the longest-lived, followed by the 1998 and 2001.

Marcel suggests eating a game bird like partridge, or a simply cooked piece of beef, with his Mouline. He signals out the 1994 as a typical example of a lesser vintage that drinks very well after 10 years and accompanies plainly cooked food well.

Marcel's favourite Moulines are the 1999 and 1976. The former he rates capable of living for over 40 years. Mouline is also his preferred 2001.

2003 (CASK) ★★★★★ Very sustained *robe*. Compact, smoky black fruit/olives bouquet. Dense, homogeneous wine—black fruit/chocolate, length good. Very rich at its heart. Rasp-

berry aftertaste. Adequate tannins, has structure. Was softer, more red fruited. From 2010; 2026–28. Last tasted Dec 2004.

2002 (CASK) ★★★★ Clear fruit, touch floral bouquet, elegant, some earthiness. Likeable black fruit on palate; wends its way, is clear-cut, with some stuffing. Restrained, esp drink from 2008. 2019–23. Last tasted Dec 2004.

2001 (CASK) ★★★★★ Broad, generous, striking ripe red fruit bouquet; tasty attack, stewed plum, fresh with the weight. Nice clean end, fine tannins. Great promise, will blossom. Esp from 2009–10. 2023–27.

2000 (CASK) ★★★★ Gentle floral aroma, discreet oak; quite weighted, some cooked black fruit, not esp intense. Cool texture on fruit, oak tightens it at end, fair length. Charming, without grandeur. 2016–19.

1999 ★★★★★★ Oily black fruit, bosky/pepper tones, much promise; start of sleek fruit, then gets full and prolonged. Still on the tar, bouncy black juice, more tannin than usual. Texture is a delight, a toe caresser. Great length. From 2009; 2028–34.

1998 ★★★★★★ Lovely scented nose, classic Mouline—strawberry, flowers, jam with some edge. Cool fruit, delicious, bit more robust than usual. Lovely extract. Wow! *Beau Vin.* 2019–24.

1997 ★★★★★ Reserved, harmonious smoked black fruit nose; red fruits attack, quite dense, streamlined oak at end, restrains the flesh. Bit hidden; nice oily, plump *gras* at end. 2014–18.

1996 ★★★★ Red fruits nose, quite live; very persistent fruit on palate, good sinew. Has life, character. 2014–18.

1995 ★★★★★★ Spiced black, tapenade, berried nose; very discreet power, good frame, the usual juiciness restrained for once. Good structure, plenty to come. From 2006; 2018–21.

1994 ★★★ 2008–10
1993 ★★★★ 2007–08
1992 ★★★★ 2008–10
1991 ★★★★★★ 2012–15
1990 ★★★★★ 2011–14
1989 ★★★★★★ 2012–14
1988 ★★★★ 2011–13

CÔTE-RÔTIE LA LANDONNE
10,000–12,000 bottles

100 per cent Syrah

Étienne and Marcel launched La Landonne in 1978. "You can't imagine the trouble we went to in order to buy up the *Landonne* vineyard," recalls Marcel. "The first vineyard then was 1.8 hectares, which involved the ownership of 17 smallholders, and I'm sure I shall never have to be so patient again when it comes to buying a single vineyard. It took more than 10 years, buying each small plot individually, but it has proved well worthwhile." The vineyard now covers 2.1 hectares and averages 20 years old.

This is the black, most meaty Côte-Rôtie made by the Guigals. The northern schist runs through its veins and propels a firm, black and tarry texture into the heart of the wine. It always carries an intense colour centred on deep purple and black with some dark red at the top, while its young bouquet has a firm, wild berry fruit combined with new cask aromas, licorice, spice, and mocha-coffee tones.

Flavours run across black berry fruits that are dark and brooding when young, tinted by their tannic surround. The finish can be earthy or truffly. The wine is tightly packed and really clamps the palate when young.

This is a wine to which Marcel accords great longevity. Of the early vintages, the 1978, 1983, and 1988 are all considered capable of a life span of up to 35 years; Marcel views the 1983 to be the longest-lived of the three. Since then, the mightiest vintage has been the 1999, capable of 40 years or more. Other years likely to show well towards 30 years are the 1995, 1998, and 2001.

2003 (CASK) ★★★★★★ Lovely, full bouquet, energy in it—compact, interesting black fruit, coffee/mocha. Wholesome, restrained black fruit, blackberry/prune, then chocolate, tar/licorice on palate. Broad and well done, plenty of tannins abound. Good, live length. From 2010–11; 2031–34. Last tasted Dec. 2004.

2002 (CASK) ★★★★ Second time it was destemmed. Toffee/brewed bouquet, has roasted, meaty side. Quite austere, peppery black fruit—upright, needs time. Barely formed as yet. Some richness within, Bordeaux style, acidity present on end. Will be interesting. From 2010; 2023–26. Last tasted Dec. 2004.

2001 (CASK) ★★★★★ Chocolate and earth, ripe/oily bouquet; dense, prolonged black flavour, good core. Full, good definition. Correct structure, good clear-cut wine. Dry end now. From 2008–09; 2023–26.

2000 (CASK) ★★★★★ Overt grilled, mocha, some pepper aromas; sappy, damp-leaves texture, then freshens. Calmer, truffly end, nice flavour. Fair flesh, shows good *terroir*—that dark earthiness. 2021–25.

1999 ★★★★★★ Bouquet almost has a pretty side, cocoa, oily touches, deep. Very full palate, imposing, shows quality at end—great chew/persistence. Blackberry fruit, this is big. One of most powerful Landonnes I've ever known, a southern beauty. From 2012; 2036–40.

1998 ★★★★★ Dense, black oily fruit, truffly aroma; really good clean extract, well sustained. Balance creates the elegance. Black fruit pastilles/mineral end. 2020–24.

1997 ★★★★★★ Dark; oily, smoky, closely packed bouquet; stones, leather; convincing black fruit, really good tannic structure, fresh also. More finesse than 1998–99 Landonne. Multiflavoured ripe cooked fruit. 2017–20.

1996 ★★★★ Leather/woods/blackberry aromas, still quite fresh; softening fruit attack, working in the acidity now, still ways to go. More gentle than usual. Truffle aftertaste. Esp from 2006–07; 2015–17.

1995 ★★★★★★ Firm, spiced chocolate/mocha, some cooked plum in behind; great density and amounts of compact flavour. Tannins assert, but smoothly. Great oiliness, flavours will unlock slowly. 2020–24.

1993	★★★★	2012–14
1992	★★★★★	2012–14
1991	★★★★★	2013–15
1990	★★★★★	2012–16
1989	★★★★★★	2013–17
1988	★★★★★	2020–25
1986	★★★★★	2011–14

CÔTE-RÔTIE LA TURQUE
5,000 bottles

93 per cent Syrah, 7 per cent Viognier
Started in 1985 with 2,200 bottles from a novice vineyard on a fine central *Côte Brune* site, La Turque burst on the scene to give Guigal its third Big Wine.

This prompted immediate attention from the "Wine Collector" community. The consumerism of the 1980s was in full cry when this wine was launched, and Marcel Guigal tells the story of a Canadian offering him the use of his helicopter, his water-ski powerboat, and his Ferrari if Guigal came to Canada—with one mixed case of the top three Guigal wines for him.

This is a true single vineyard site, at first 0.95 hectare, now a little larger. The slope on *La Turque* is extremely steep, 60° to 70°, and its vines were cultivated until the early 1960s by a smallholder who was regarded by the locals as "*un peu fou.*" For 20 years it had remained an overgrown patch, next to holdings of Marius Gentaz-Dervieux and Vidal-Fleury. M. Gentaz did not wish to take it over, so it became part of the Vidal-Fleury holding that was subsequently bought by Guigal. It was planted in 1980.

La Turque has been remarkably consistent through the 1990s, perhaps even more so than the *Mouline*. I feel it is beginning to move up a gear as the vines mature, with greater complexity present in the young wine than was the case previously. It is more aromatic than the *Landonne*, and expresses mixed tones on the bouquet that can range from flowers to leather and chocolate. Flavours show black fruits that are softer and float more than the profound collection found on the *Landonne*. In scale, it is more muscular than the *Mouline*. It is a wine that is likely to appeal to lovers of refined Bordeaux from the best *Grand Cru* châteaux of St-Julien.

With its tannins usually well integrated from early on, *La Turque* drinks well enough when young, with its savoury side prominent. For a more rewarding set of flavours and subtleties, the wine is better drunk when left for seven or eight years. The very well balanced 1985 is the

oldest example, but a life of up to 30 years is certainly possible for the strongest vintages.

CÔTE-RÔTIE LA TURQUE

2003 (CASK) ★★★★★★ Warm bouquet—closely packed berries, just before they simmer, so some freshness. Smoked black fruit, has richness but under control, broadens well. Light mint side, oak touch. Balance good, is very appealing. From 2009–10; 2028–30. Last tasted Dec. 2004.

2002 (CASK) ★★★★ Soaked cherries, light chocolate on a tight bouquet. Glint of mineral on attack, a pointed, directed wine from the schist. Cool, black stone fruit, licorice after. Grainy, prune finish. Length sound, clear-cut, pretty refined wine. Esp from 2009; 2020–23. Last tasted Dec. 2004.

2001 (CASK) ★★★★★ Pretty dense, floral, persistent ripe fruit/nuts nose; violets, a *perfumato* palate here; good berry flavour, black and squeezy. Tannins well within it, nice fresh length. 2022–24.

2000 (CASK) ★★★★★ Chocolate, quite compact/charming nose, some earth/red berries. Nicely open palate, generous suave wine, good length, chocolate again, *gras* at end. Easy to underestimate its complexity later on. Pretty. 2021–23.

1999 ★★★★★★ Core of black fruit aroma—oak/woody/leathery, heady; firm enough black fruit, lots of matter, oily with good *gras*. Well-worked tannins, more than usual, great length, persistence. 2025–29.

1998 ★★★★★ Tight, grilled bread nose, dark fruits; even black fruit flavour with fresh side. Bit more dark than Mouline, tannins stand out more. Lot of end *gras*. 2018–21.

1997 ★★★★ Quite square aroma, violets/herbs/smoky heat; black fruit, strong density. Violets, then lot of oak/licorice on a chewy end. 2016–20.

1996 ★★★★★ Dark fruit, harmonious, quite full nose; lot of nicely packed flavour, good sinew. Elegant; touch of oak at end. Promising. 2018–20.

1995 ★★★★★★ Oily, leather/cedar, charming nose; very woven black fruit, tannins come out punchy and peppery at end. More grainy texture than Mouline, good *gras* though. From 2007; 2020–23.

    1993 ★★★★★ 2011–14
    1992 ★★★★★ 2010–13
    1991 ★★★★★ 2011–14
    1990 ★★★★★ 2010–14
    1989 ★★★★ 2008–12
    1988 ★★★★★ 2018–22

Export 55 per cent (1) USA, (2) Japan, (3) Canada/ Germany

PAUL JABOULET AÎNÉ

Les Jalets RN7 26600 La Roche-de-Glun
+33(0)475 846893

See also Condrieu, Cornas, Crozes-Hermitage, Hermitage, St-Joseph, St-Péray.
Paul Jaboulet Aîné have long produced a Côte-Rôtie, but it has never been a wine that one feels forms part of their soul. The men from Hermitage rely more on wine than grape purchases for their Les Jumelles, which occasionally has hit the heights—the 1967 and the 1997 spring to mind. The latter is highlighted by Jacques Jaboulet as the best since 1961. Other good vintages were 1983, 1991, and 1995.

Until 1993 the wine came purely from purchased crop. The number of sources varies, and the wine is vinified within Côte-Rôtie. It can contain around 5 per cent Viognier. Its ageing has been cut back to nine to 12 months, in casks that range from two to five years old. Production can run between 12,000 and 15,000 bottles.

CÔTE-RÔTIE LES JUMELLES

2001 ★★★ Some floral/stewed red fruit aromas; fair weight, raspberry, chocolate; leathery, touch dry, bit dumb, can run on. Acidity needs to settle, final heat here. From 2006–07; 2015–16.

2000 ★ Big, open bouquet, quite ripe, dark/leathery side; live fruit attack, but bit stretched, fades. Not a wine to lay down. From 2003–04; 2008–09.

1999 ★★★ Purple/black colour; true, typical bouquet—floral, some depth; good, full palate, lot of flavour, harmonious. Some spice end. Open already. 2011–13.

1998 ★★ Colour evolving, also nose—cooked jam, bosky notes, OK. Sweet, tightly packaged flavour, ends bit dry. 2101–12.

1997 ★★★★★ Heated, varied nose, plenty of fruit/spice, quite *confit;* very rich attack, lots of warm garden fruit jam. Good core richness. Will show well and openly all along. Length sound. 2011–14.

1996 Some bottles past it.

1995 ★★★★ 2010–12

DOMAINE JAMET

Le Vallin 69420 Ampuis +33(0)474 561257

A lot of people would give their right arms to possess even a fraction of this family's vineyards. Theirs is a regal cast of *lieux-dits,* spread across the *appellation's* finest central sites. If you want to taste a wine that sums up the heartlands of Côte-Rôtie, the classic cuvée here should be it.

Jean-Paul is the front man, his brother Jean-Luc a rarer and more silent sighting as he labours away on vineyard tasks. Jean-Paul, now in his mid-40s, pale blue eyes set in a chiselled, strong face, has a close, instinctive knowledge of their vineyards. "We have 25 plots spread across 17 *lieux-dits,*" he almost confesses. Put that in the context of 7.2 hectares of productive vineyards, rising to eight hectares by 2006, and that's a lot of moving around from spot to spot.

Here is someone who can provide a sensible perspective on these ancient vineyards. "For me, the exposure of the slopes is not the most important factor. We have ideal south-facing sites on the *Côte Blonde, Lancement,* and *Leyat,* for instance; we have southwest-facing sites on the *Côte Brune, Fongeant,* and *Rochains,* while *Truchet* is east.

"No, it's the nature of the soil that matters most for maturity. The difference between the

FIGURE 3 Jean-Paul (left) and Jean-Luc Jamet's accomplished Côte-Rôtie is drawn from 25 different vineyards. (Tim Johnston)

schist and the granite is the key. The second factor is the altitude, meaning that there are some years when it's hard to get fully ripe crop high up. In 2002 the high spots were high in acidity, while in 2001 they were the spots that brought the greatest freshness to the wine. They are more windy, so in effect you can get good balance in the wine if you have a spread." As he says this, the wind buffets around his smart new cellar building high on the plateau of Champin.

This leads him on to the nature of blending so many different wines. "We don't put all these wines in our *assemblage*," he says. "The key is to find the best balance in the conditions of the vintage—it's the best compromise that counts. We're lucky enough to have so many different plots that we can keep relearning and understanding what each place means at Côte-Rôtie. That's a passion in our work."

Jean-Paul admits that their planting is more precise these days than 20 years ago. "Soil studies have moved things along. Experience counts a lot, and now that we're planting at *Gerine*, for instance, I can imagine what its wine will be like." So much for textbooks, and fat chequebooks.

The Jamet brothers have been great planters since taking over from father, Joseph, and his four hectares in 1991; he set out in 1950 with just 0.35 hectare on the *Côte Brune* and did his first bottling only in 1976. A wily, friendly man, his clear blue eyes used for darting looks, Joseph is now in his mid-70s and continues to help with the pruning. "In those days, we grew peaches, apricots, and nectarines because the wine didn't pay enough," he recalls. Joseph is the uncle of Gilbert Clusel, demonstrating again the close links that bind many of these wine families.

The sites that always form the backbone of their classic wine are from the core area above Ampuis—*Chavaroche* (1983), *Fongeant* (1991), *Côte-Baudin* (1993, 1997), *Moutonnes* (1978), plus *Landonne* (1987) a little apart. They have just two granite sites, the *Côte Blonde* (1943) and *Lancement* (1989), while the rest are on the brown soil–schist of the middle to north. These are *Côte Rozier* (1943), *Truchet*, *Bonnivière* (both 1968), *Leyat* (1968, 1999), *Le Plomb* (1973, 1993), *Rochains* and *Mornachon* (both 1988), *Tartaras* (1991), and *La Gerine* (2000).

The single-vineyard wine of about 2,000 bottles comes from just under 0.5 ha on the *Côte Brune*, two-thirds 1940s, one-third 1993. This little plot tells the story of hard labour on these hot slopes. Joseph inherited 0.35 ha and cleared and planted another 0.05 ha on his own, and the sons cleared another 0.08 ha or so. It is a precious site.

In 1996, 1997, and 2000 there was also a Cuvée Elegance made for the French market, from sites on the granite of the *Blonde* area, and sold in 50 cl (centilitre) bottles.

The brothers also make a Syrah Côtes du Rhône from a plot just above *Tartaras*, which will be over one hectare by 2005. This is sound, a wine to drink on its fruit within around six years. Near the cellars on the plateau, they work 1.37 ha of Syrah *vin de pays des Collines Rhodaniennes;* some of the vines date from the 1970s, and this wine can be beefed up by fruit from underage Côte-Rôtie vines. These two wines can receive oak and are bottled in June.

Vinification is a joint effort in their cellar, which was revamped in 2001, and is largely traditional. There is usually only 10 to 30 per cent destemming, except in a dodgy year like 2002, when 60 per cent of the crop needed it, and in drought-afflicted 2003, when all the crop was destemmed. Fermentation lasts 18 to 20 days in steel and includes cap punching on the destemmed vats and pumping-over for the whole-bunch vats.

Wood ageing lasts 22 months, in a mix of 228- and 550-litre casks. Twenty per cent of these are new, 80 per cent three to 10 years old. There has been no fining since 1997, and there is no filtration.

The top-grade *Côte Brune* also receives 22 months in cask, 35 per cent of them new. The *Brune* is consistently one of the best wines made at Côte-Rôtie, a satisfying wine, too, for it represents the early toil of Joseph Jamet when he started with a tiny vineyard. It brings out the true notion of unfettered *terroir,* without heavy cellar intervention. In style it resembles another of the great Rôties of the past, the *Côte Brune* of Marius Gentaz-Dervieux. This is where Côte-Rôtie crosses over to top Burgundy in style. There may not be a *Brune* in 2002 due to the poor ripening.

CÔTE-RÔTIE

2003 (CASKS) ★★(★) Tarmac, floral bouquet, compact. Stewed red berries, bit reduced. Soft, jammy fruit gum style; is homogeneous, touch of the south, *garrigue* herbs on finish. From 2007; 2016–18.

2002 ★★ Earthy side, with floral trimming on bouquet. Tasty, straight fruit, clear-cut and pretty, some pepper. Fair length, cool finale. Good, drinkable wine, chaptalised texture. From 2006; 2011–13.

2001 (CASK) ★★★ Elements show brewed fruit, spice, and some game aspects, typical; structure good, crushed fruit, nicely dark, with tannic potential. 2014–17.

2000 ★★★ Open nose, earthy, very ripe black fruits/olives, southern; typical Syrah of yore—black fruit/spice/pepper. Brewed wine, hearty, best when older, esp 2007–08. Not that clear-cut. 2014–15.

1999 ★★★★★ Ripe, sunny, varied berry aromas, potential; rich, stewed fruits attack, sappy, *confit;* delicious raspberry, tasty wine. Still very young. More complexity around 2010; 2018–21.

1998 ★★★★ Floral/earthy mix, stewed fruit bouquet; blackberry, juicy touches, well clad with tar/licorice, oiliness. Pepper, camphor/tar end as tannins of the year take over. Esp from 2006–07; 2012–15.

1997 ★★★ 2011–14
1996 ★★ 2012–15
1995 ★★★ 2012–16
1994 ★

CÔTE-RÔTIE CÔTE BRUNE

2001 (CASK) ★★★★★ Dark fruit/game, quietly solid nose; elegant, then broadens. Serious wine. Full, *gras,* has good cut, fruit persists. Classy, very well wrapped, stylish. From 2008–09; 2021–23.

2000 ★★★★ Dark, compact nose—olives/smoked meat; very tight, rolled-up black flavour. Quite firm, has *gras.* Oak notes on end, tannins OK. Esp 2008–09, when round and persistent; 2014–17.

1999 ★★★★★★ Great bouquet, lightly spiced, nicely ripe fruit/flowers; plenty of matter—olives/black fruits, great richness on second half. Clean, spiced finish. From 2009; 2017–22.

1998 (cask) ★★★ Good depth of aroma, chocolate/dark; well-knit flavour, broadens through the palate. Sustained length. 2014–17.

1997 ★★★★★★ Fantastic bouquet, black cherries/oils, mighty amount; great fruit attack, explosive. Great length, lots of squeezed fruit. Tannins well enrobed. *Grand Vin*. 2015–19.

1994 ★★ 2007–09

Export 40 per cent (1) Belgium, (2) USA, (3) Great Britain

DOMAINE JASMIN

14 rue des Maraîchers 69420 Ampuis +33(0)474 561604

How do you follow Jean Gabin? That was the question playing in people's minds at Côte-Rôtie and abroad after the tragic, accidental death in February 1999 of Robert Jasmin when he was knocked over by a car when out shooting in the foothills of Die. For a Big Man was Robert —strikingly strong, outgoing, a larger-than-life figure in the community, a man of passion and tough principle.

Yet I can recall chatting with Robert in his cellar and watching him cut his slice of baguette with his pruning knife, as if he were trimming one of his vines, peeling off just a small slither. It was a delicate, neat action from such a big, strong man. Off would come a slim length of fresh bread, precisely done.

He was an instinctive winemaker, and seemed most completely at ease in his vineyards. I remember asking Robert the age of a cask when tasting his 1990; his answer was to feel underneath it and mutter that "somewhere here there's an indication."

The family had come to Côte-Rôtie from Champagne through the arrival of Robert Jasmin's grandfather Alexandre to work as chef at the Château d'Ampuis. Developing an eager interest in the village's principal activity, he bought the vineyard that went with the château: this is well situated at one end of the *Côte Brune*,

on what the map today terms *Moutonnes*. The family wine was bottled before 1909 and would be presented at the Foire de Paris in those days.

A prized photograph in the Jasmin home, which sits modestly beside the local railway and is shaded on one side by a generous cherry tree, shows the three generations together in the vineyards—Georges, Robert, and Patrick. Georges died in 1987 aged 83, but his hardiness was salutary. He no doubt exercised the fine twinkle in his eye to great effect with the local demoiselles and, even after suffering from hepatitis when he was 76, carried on the strong-man approach to life by continuing to hop up the hillside until the year before he died. He used to bottle his wine for the famous chef Fernand Point at La Pyramide in Vienne, but the bottles were a random assortment found lying around—no doubt to some diners' consternation.

Many were the gastronomic escapades enjoyed by Robert and his lively, ebullient wife, Josette. They were game for any good venture. They were great friends with Pierre Gagnard in his heyday at St-Étienne, and a visit there used to be a cross-country journey undertaken in sometimes hair-raising circumstances, as was the occasional foray down to Guy Julien's black-truffle empire at Restaurant Beaugravière in Mondragon, near Orange. Robert rarely slept where he ate.

So his son Patrick, another well-built, sturdy man, quieter than his dad, had a big act to follow when he suddenly had to take over the reins of this top-flight family domaine in 1999. Born in 1961, he is now in his early 40s and has started to impress with his quiet determination and low-key approach. He even gave up his motocross racing in 2002, having been champion of France in 2000 at what is called Kart-Cross.

This sport entailed a camper van existence, the whole family on board, for weekends away. "Plenty of *vignerons* did it," says Patrick, "and we would always end up swapping Côte-Rôtie with St-Emilion, for instance. Some people would take their wine along to sell it, as well!"

FIGURE 4 Arlette and Patrick Jasmin, forces of air and earth in one domaine, a generous welcome always assured. (Tim Johnston)

He's a tough man, with short-cropped brown hair, and a broad, expressive face. He's someone who whistles as he moves around the cellar, where he is just making small updates, settling himself in. He is not going to change the wine's roots, just polish it up given the new methods and equipment that exist these days; he admits that his taste is to drink his wine between five and 10 years old, so these will not become block-busters, and are set to remain largely faithful to the deft, enjoyable elegance of their previous decades.

This is a much visited cellar, and Patrick's wife, Arlette, slim and vivacious, plays an important role in organising her family, visitors to the cellar, and paperwork connected to the wines. She has risen to the task of being the Madame of the winemaking house at short notice, and some of her chatty style has spread to Patrick, who speaks more clearly and fluently about his ideas and thoughts than he used to. Certainly Robert was not the sort of father to spend much time going through how to make wine step-by-step, so Patrick's knowledge was a patchwork affair. Indeed, it was Patrick's friend Yves Lafoy who learnt more from Robert—and duly relayed that knowledge of vinification to Patrick with the help of a small notebook.

The confidential cellar is under the house and lies below a trap door and down a set of wooden steps. It's long been a sociable meeting point, the Jasmins always ready to pour and talk with open generosity. It's no surprise that Robert's memorial service was marked by both a full church and an enormous amount of people standing outside in the *place* of Ampuis.

Patrick works about 5.3 ha, of which the 1.2 ha on *Boucharey* above the *Blonde* is a legacy from his grandfather Georges and was planted in three gos in the 1960s. With 11 plots spread across eight *lieux-dits*, he enjoys a great north-south spread across his vineyards, one of the lucky few to have such a well-balanced exposure between the granite and the schist.

Some were planted from scratch. At *Le Baleyat*, facing the south of the village, an apple orchard had grown up; the spot is high up and also exposed to the Vent du Nord. Here the Jasmins had to blast the overgrown rock face to carve out a short approach track to the site, across slopes with a 20 to 30 per cent incline.

The other sites are led by a rented 0.88 ha on the *Côte Blonde* (1966); this they call *La Vigne de Birot*, after its owner, who also rented it to Robert. It contains a little Viognier. Another rented 0.66 ha is on *Les Bercheries* (1981) at Semons, 0.38 ha each on *Le Mollard* (1973) and

Le Truchet (1998), the latter near the *Brune*. The rest of the line-up is all on the schist-based soil—their old Chevalière vineyard of 0.34 ha on *Les Moutonnes*, replanted in 1996–97, 0.6 ha on *Côte Baudin* (1978, 1993), and 0.34 ha on *La Brocarde* with an extra 0.4 ha planted between 2001 and 2004 on *Cognet*. Taken all together, Patrick estimates his domaine's vineyard to bear an average age of 20 to 25 years.

The most precocious sites are classic, centrally located names—the *Côte Blonde*, *Mollard*, and *Moutonnes*, with the *Côte Baudin* next to it. They can ripen a week ahead of the others. This is where the grapes from a breezy, high location like *Boucharey* play a role—their acidity offsetting the intrinsic ripe, sometimes jam textures of the early spots.

"The *Blonde* with its mica-schist and granite mix gives great finesse," says Patrick. "The soil is more structured on *Moutonnes* and *Baudin*, the rock is further down than on the *Blonde*, so the roots can run deeper. These wines are firmer than the *Blonde*'s."

Since 1996 the crop has been wholly destalked; there is 4 to 5 per cent Viognier, which is vinified with the Syrah in concrete vats. The cap is submerged with planks, and Patrick is doing more punching down by foot than in the past. In 2003 he installed a temperature control system in the cellar, which will help to cool the crop.

He has also used a *saignée,* or bleeding, of the crop since taking over. This involves taking out the light-coloured juice at the start of the process. "The old-timers would have looked on in amazement that I would be prepared to throw away 500 litres from around 40 hl," he observes, "but the gain is obvious—the berries are more concentrated, you get colour and better structure. In rainy years, you also get rid of unwanted rain water," he adds.

Vinification lasts 20 to 22 days, with a few days less in the testing vintages of 2002 to preserve its fruit and in 2003 to avoid the risk of volatile acidity. "With the cooling system, I can increase the duration," says Patrick, "but the last thing I want is to make technical wines." Each

lieu-dit's grapes are vinified separately until the first racking around the end of December.

After assemblage in steel, half the wine is aged in 228-litre casks, half in 590-litre *demimuids*. There is no studied emphasis on new oak, with the 30 per cent in 2001 a one-off because 15 new casks were bought that year. Twenty per cent would be nearer the mark. Patrick prepares an early lot of 3,000 bottles for the Ampuis Wine Fair in January, after 14 months' oak.

The first main bottling in April comes after 18 months' ageing, the second in early September after nearly two years. About 23,000 bottles are made. There is no fining, but a light filtration. Patrick suggests that the first bottling wine starts off with more overt fruit than the second, but that the wines approach one another after eight to 10 years.

Patrick's first vintage on his own was 1999, which he will remember for the rest of his life. "I tried a grape before the harvest and it tasted like a prune, or plum jam; because it didn't taste like a grape, I was worried and asked the veteran Marius Gentaz-Dervieux to try one. He just said it reminded him of 1947!"

Along with other top names like Jamet and Ogier, Patrick Jasmin also makes a very good Syrah *vin de pays*, called "La Chevalière," when he has Côte-Rôtie vines that have not reached their fourth leaf. This is a mix of half a hectare of vines dating from the early to mid-1990s on the plain beside the N86 road and any young Côte-Rôtie vines; around 2,000 bottles can be made.

CÔTE-RÔTIE

2003 (CASK) ★★★★ Healthy *robe*; full, complete bouquet, violet/chocolate mix. Full palate—cooked, not excessive flavours—red fruits. Broad, solid wine, lot of content. Well filled, fair end freshness. Esp 2008–09; 2019–21.

2002 (CASK) Broad but not very deep bouquet; fruit on palate runs easily, some richness towards end. Chocolate, brewed style flavour. Hint of oak. Leave till 2007 to let acidity integrate; 2011–13.

2001 ★★★★ Restrained floral/soft red jam bouquet; gentle, stewed black fruits, lots of finesse. Fruit is clean, has tightened up. Has a chunky side, decent tannins fan out at end. Gaining scale as it evolves. From 2005–06; 2013–17.

2000 ★★★ Bouquet gains weight with air, has gentle, sleek black fruit; easy textured, live hedge fruit, blackberries, gets more stylish with air. *En finesse*, quite *confit*. Esp from 2006; 2011–14.

1999 ★★★★★ Warm strawberry aromas, balanced, potential complexity; chocolate/prune style flavour, lot of warmth. Plenty of ripeness, touch burnt, leathery. Rich, full, heated finish. Top-notch. 2017–21.

1998 ★★★ Light spiced jam, licorice aromas, meaty side; plump start, then restrains; discreet tannic edging and length. Some raspberry fruit, quite upright but will be expressive. Bit of tar. 2011–14.

1997 ★★★ 2008–10
1996 ★★ 2006–08
1995 ★★★ 2011–14
1994 ★★★ 2005–08

Export 50 per cent (1) USA, (2) Great Britain, (3) Belgium/Switzerland

JOCELYNE AND YVES LAFOY

8 rue du Vagnot 69420 Ampuis +33(0)474 561926

See also Condrieu.

"Not the best year to start," recalls Yves Lafoy in his gravelly tones. He made his first wine in 1993, cobbling together small vineyards on his and his wife Jocelyne's side so he could move beyond the vegetable and fruit growing.

A short, active man, very much salt of the earth, Yves started with his own 0.22 ha on *Rozier* (1966) and 0.28 ha on a plot called *Gaumont* on the *Brune* (1934). He had worked for his mother-in-law for five years, looking after the mainly cardoon and *blette* production of her vegetable affair.

His father-in-law also held 1.2 ha on *Truchet* (1988) near the *Côte Brune*, so Yves was able to

get going, converting the old storage room for the vegetables into a cosy stone underground cellar.

He now works around two hectares, rising to 2.5 ha by 2006. He also makes a little Condrieu, mainly the semisweet style for locals, and some Syrah *vin de pays* from a hectare of vines planted in 1995.

His tutor in winemaking between 1993 and 1996 was the late Robert Jasmin. "He was a Great Professor; after his father's accident, Patrick came along asking me what were the essentials that I had been taught. As I have no memory, I had written everything down in a notebook, so was able to show him in detail, which of course gave me a lot of satisfaction."

The style is therefore relaxed, without too much heavy intervention. "When you drink wine, you eat grapes, and new oak hides that taste. So I like fruited wines," he comments.

The crop is destalked except for the old vines' fruit and receives a 15-to-18-day vinification in concrete, with two pumping-overs a day, the temperature at a maximum of 30°C. Yeasts are used if necessary.

He makes two wines, both pure Syrah; the special cuvée RG is drawn from the old vines on *Rozier* and *Gaumont*, and was first made in 1999. There are around 2,200 bottles.

Wood ageing lasts 14 months for the classic and 18 months for the RG cuvée, the three-year-old casks coming from Jean-Michel Gérin after they have done their first service *chez lui*. Yves neither fines nor filters.

Something of a party man, Yves' most noted local client has to be the Boules Club of Ampuis. He is a *pointeur*, a lead man who rolls the ball, in a team there. "There are big prizes at times—up to €1,500/US$2,000, or €200/US$260 for local events, when 64 teams may take part," he says. His wine and his convivial spirit no doubt both go down well.

CÔTE-RÔTIE

2004 (CASK) ★★ Clear fruit aroma, lively, mineral. Expressive flavour, quite wide and stylish. Fruit quality good. No pretentions, sound wine. Will drink well esp from 2008. Last tasted March 2005.

2003 ★★★ Really full, blackberry, brambly fruit bouquet—abundant, wholesome, has southern hints. Very bonny wine—palate is broad, well-fruited, and round. Chocolate-style finish, tannins come through well. Oily, bosky wine. 2017–19.

2002 (CASK) ★ Gently stewed black fruit aroma, clear enough; rather sharp start, fair matter, chewy, may move on with time. May live to 2010.

2001 ★★★ Quite scented, floral/black fruit nose, fair depth; tasty start, quiet warmth—licorice/black flavour. Violets all along it, nice length. Good purity, softer in 2005. 2009–11.

CÔTE-RÔTIE CUVÉE RG

2004 (CASK) ★★★ Dark, intense nose, meaty core, hedgerow fruits. Brisk attack, contains very good dark fruit, plenty of matter, and good tannic structure. Good and local, is STGT wine. Esp from 2009–10 onwards. Last tasted March 2005.

2002 (CASK) ★★ Stylish, quietly full bouquet; tasty start, stewed black fruits, gentle flavour. Will live 10 years or so.

2000 ★★★ Truffly, damp earth aromas; good stewed fruits, broad wine, chewy end, tannins still going. Sound *terroir*—dark berry/damp earth effect. Esp from 2006–07; 2012–14.

Export 20 per cent (1) Belgium, (2) Switzerland

DOMAINE BERNARD LEVET

26 Blvd des Allées 69420 Ampuis +33(0)474 561539

Some wines reflect inspiration, others love and care. The Levet wines fall into the second category. Watching Nicole Levet—a *vigneron's* daughter who, with all due deference, is no longer a spring chicken—scamper up ladders and strain to open the bungs on large old barrels, just to give a drop or two to the visitor, brings large amounts of respect.

This couple live a very low-key existence, making their wine without fanfare and running

a spotless cellar, the only one right in the middle of the village, under the Boulevard des Allées. Their vineyard is all old Sérine, with no Viognier, and there is a curl of distaste in Nicole's voice when she has to utter the word "clone."

Nicole's father was Marius Chambeyron, a well-known figure in the 1970s, recognisable for his permanently tilted *casquette* and a weatherbeaten face. He worked three hectares, one of them on *Chavaroche* right in line with the church, the others on *Brune, Blonde, Mollard,* and *Landonne.* "We replace odd plants when they need it, but this is a good, mature vineyard, largely planted in 1946 by my father," states Nicole.

Her husband, Bernard, a local man who worked in commerce before marrying Nicole, brought along half a hectare planted in 1981. The most recent plantation is half a hectare on the *Brune* dating from 1990. As a sign of how recent is the success of Côte-Rôtie, this plot actually lay abandoned until then.

Marius left his vineyard to his daughter in 1983, but their plans were tragically upset when Nicole and Bernard's son was killed with two other Ampuis boys in a vehicle accident in 1986, an accident that is still not properly explained, it seems.

Since 1990 they have made 3,000 bottles of a special wine from *Chavaroche* that they call *La Péroline*; this was not made in the difficult years of 1992 and 1993. The regular wine, just Côte-Rôtie on the label (except for the United States, where the subtitle "La Chavaroche" is added), is made with fruit from all their plots and averages 15,000 bottles a year. The *Péroline* back label is different each year, and is composed by their daughter Agnès. On the regular wine, the back label carries a poem, not hard facts, which contains the French verse:

Il faut cinq ans pour faire une vigne
   productrice
Douze ans pour la rendre intelligente
Cinquante ans pour qu'elle se réalise

It takes five years to make a vine produce
Twelve years to render it intelligent
Fifty years before it comes into its own

FIGURE 5 Modest people, understated wines—Bernard and Nicole Levet were joined by their daughter Agnès in 2004. (Tim Johnston)

The cellar was upgraded in 1992, and there appears to be great attention to detail, all tasks conducted with the most scrupulous care. Uncluttered dedication is a strong presence here.

Between climbing ladders up 33 hl barrels (these are high), Nicole, a small woman with short, red hair, explains their outlook: "Our aim is to improve our quality rather than enlarge our domaine. If we had 10 hectares, the quality wouldn't be the same, we wouldn't run a family business. We have one part-time helper."

"So what do you do?" "Well, I am versatile," she replies, "pruning, the cellar, administration, the shop here in the middle of Ampuis"—spoken like a true *vigneron*'s daughter! With the full-time presence on the domaine of her daughter Agnès from 2004, this doughty tradition will continue, much to Bernard and Nicole's pleasure. Born in 1974, Agnès worked in Co-opératives in the Aude *département* handling their environmental waste before returning home.

The wines improved during the 1990s. They were always carefully made but now appear to show greater consistency and a true sense of place. Some may call them "traditional," but such *terroir* in the drink is one of the joys of wine, the reason the search continues.

Harvesting takes four days with family and friends, and the crop is half destemmed before vinification for two to three weeks in enamel-lined vats. The cap is submerged with planks, rather than being punched down. I must own up to a quiet voice that whispers to me that cap punching would freshen these wines, without loss of local imprint.

For ageing, the Levets use three wood sizes—casks, *demi-muids* of 600 litres, and old Alsatian barrels of 26 to 33 hl. There is 30 per cent new oak each year, and the whole process lasts two years, or three if it is a very big vintage. There is fining, but no filtration.

CÔTE-RÔTIE

2004 (CASK) ★★★ Fair amount on bouquet, a little reduced now. Crisp, elegant fruit, rolls along stylishly. STGT in the making. About 16-year wine. Last tasted March 2005.

2003 (CASK) ★★★ Floral-tinged bouquet, is bulky, with black fruits, too. Brewed fruit in the house style on palate, tarry aftertaste, meaty wine. Earthy, tannins a little dry at finish, but is rich at its core. Length good. Esp from 2008–09 on. To bottle Oct. 2005. 2018–20. Last tasted March 2005.

2002 ★ Brewed, "dark" aroma, farmyard connotations. Palate not esp clean; brewed, earthy fruit, then dries towards finish. Drink only in winter with game meals—has become rustic since last tasted, but may emerge and settle. 2011–13. Last tasted March 2005.

2001 ? A bottle tasted March 2005 was disappointingly dry, with sharp acidity and a lack of balance. Previously, it had been: ★★★ (CASK) Spiced, red stone fruit aroma; good content, tight red fruit with a menthol side; gathers spice, pebbly texture, interesting. Good mix of matter and freshness. Good length. 2010–13.

2000 ★★★ Floral, spiced bouquet; easy, open spiced flavour; very pure, ends with more guts than at the start. Open wine. 2009–11.

1999 ★★★★ Good, brewed nose, oily and rich; full, very round palate. Well-defined taste, suave black fruit, rich all way along, and wide. Oily texture is very 1999, tannins, licorice still there. 2016–18.

CÔTE-RÔTIE LA PÉROLINE

2002 ★★★ Scented, black fruit bouquet with potential. Round attack, more complex towards end, mixes red berry fruit/spice. Refined. Lasts nicely. Esp from 2007 on; has evolved consistently. 2015–17.

2001 (CASK) ★★★ Tight nose, tarry, potential; compact red fruits, more spice than 2002, grows towards a chewy, mineral finish. Very clean. 2014–16.

2000 ★★★ Reserved, plum fruit, light spice nose; tight-knit, well-wrapped flavour with good depth of matter inside. Stone fruit, tannins arrive at end. Will become very round. From 2006; 2015–17.

Export 20 per cent (1) USA, (2) Great Britain, (3) Belgium/Netherlands

JEAN-PIERRE LEZIN

Verlieu 42410 Chavanay +33(0)474 872297

M. Lezin rents a plot above the *Côte Blonde* and bottles a little of his wine, which he sells on the N86 road at Verlieu.

GABRIEL MEFFRE

84190 Gigondas +33(0)490 123021

See also Condrieu, Cornas, Crozes-Hermitage, Hermitage, St-Joseph.
The Gigondas *négociant* serves a Côte-Rôtie Laurus from a mix of schist-clay–loose granite sources: *La Viallière* and *Leyat*, plus the plateau sites of *La Brosse* and *Le Champin*, and *Semons* in the southern zone. It is pure Syrah.

The crop is destemmed and receives a three-week maceration-fermentation. Ageing is in 275-litre new oak casks and lasts 18 months.

CÔTE-RÔTIE LAURUS

2003 (CASKS) ★★(★) Some floral aroma, gentle for the vintage. Refined flavour, quite rich interior. Herb tea, chocolate aftertaste. *En finesse* wine, can be drunk soon. 2012–14.

2001 ★★ Quite dense, sustained bouquet—cooked fruits, light pepper. Pretty, oily texture, black berry fruits, black currant near finish. Ripe fruit use, so some jam fruit. Length pretty good. 2010–11.

DOMAINE DU MONTEILLET, STÉPHANE MONTEZ

Le Montelier 42410 Chavanay +33(0)474 872457

See also Condrieu, St-Joseph.
The energetic Stéphane Montez makes three Côte-Rôties. He is spreading his wings through joint ventures and has a tripartite arrangement with Gilles Barge and Yves Gangloff on the steep hill of *Le Combard* (2001–02) down on the loose granite of the southern end of the *commune* of Ampuis. He is also clearing a half hectare on the schist of *Cumelle* in the northern *commune* of St-Cyr-sur-le-Rhône.

After destalking, the crop is vinified in steel, the alcoholic fermentation held at 23°C for five days, then heated to 30°C. The process lasts three weeks, with cap punching.

His Fortis cuvée is drawn from *Montmain* (1989) and *Les Bercheries* (1998); it is aged for two years, mostly in 580-litre *demi-muids*, the oak all new. It contains around 5 per cent Viognier. La Pèlerine comes from the southern zone—*Bons-Arrêts, Combard,* and a little *Bercheries.* It is aged mostly in new oak and, in Stéphane's words, is intended to be a wine of finesse.

The top wine, Les Grandes Places, is taken from the oldest vines on that site, dating from 1979. It is raised in all new oak casks for up to 33 months. It contains 3 per cent Viognier. From the northern schist, its style is the opposite of La Pèlerine—a firmer, more accentuated wine.

Stéphane is an overt new oak supporter; "I find the *demi-muids* don't render the wine as dry as the 225-litre casks," he comments. He doesn't fine, and filters only if absolutely necessary.

CÔTE-RÔTIE LA PÈLERINE

2002 ★★ Promising bouquet, some floral aromas, with black fruits, is quite warm. Prune, violet flavour, quietly rounded. Finishes with a soft scented side. 2011–12.

CÔTE-RÔTIE FORTIS

2003 (CASK) ★★★ Oily, almost pure southern bouquet, olives and flowers mixed. Round, rich, soaked fruits, has plenty of *gras;* warmly textured. Likeable floral underlay, tasty, ripe tannins. Esp from 2007; 2014–15.

2002 ★★(★) Prolonged prune, black fruit aroma, fairly elegant. Mineral-edged wine, black fruits, violets with an earthy, almost truffled presence. Shows acidity, but can settle. Promising. From 2007; 2013–15.

CÔTE-RÔTIE LES GRANDES PLACES

2003 (CASK) ★★★★ Pretty, floral-edged bouquet, will amplify. Stylish fruit on palate, lot of broad matter, then a tannic thrust. Good structure, chewy finale. Esp from 2009–10; 2018–20.

2002 Not produced.

2001 (CASK) ★★★ Quite earthy, berried/mint nose; some rich early fruit, nicely full. Has *gras,* ends drily. Can come together. 2014–17.

2000 (CASK) ★★★ Ripe black fruit, overt oak; dark-tasting wine, subdued fruit, some raspberry. Quite tight. Licorice, then violets aftertaste. From 2006–07; 2011–13.

CHÂTEAU DE MONTLYS

69560 Saint-Cyr-sur-le-Rhône +33(0)474 781073

The least known of the five *communes* that make up the *appellation* is the most northerly, St-Cyr-sur-le-Rhône. From the road towards Vienne, it's not easy to make out a serious number of vineyards here. But regeneration is in the air.

Christophe Semaska is of Lithuanian origin, his family having arrived in France in 1900. They have always lived at St-Cyr, but did not work in viticulture—his father was an engineer. He rents the farm buildings and much of the vineyard around the château, which was abandoned after the First World War. Its oldest part dates from the late 1500s and, it used to belong to a Parisian family.

As a result, its wine was sold to Parisian restaurants, with the vineyard thought to have been around 1.5 hectares. But the *vigneron* employed by the family was killed in the First World War, and 1920 was the last vintage for many decades.

Christophe set to work to revive the vineyard in 1987, clearing dense woods and growth and repairing terraces and walls. The house is backed against a steep hill, and by 2005 he had over three hectares in production, with a further four hectares possible. At St-Cyr, 2.5 hectares are on *Montlys* (late 1980s) and 0.4 ha on *Cumelle* (1990–91), and there is 0.3 ha on *Cognet* (2002–03), just south in Verenay. These are all rocky, schist sites.

"I was an accountant by education," he explains, "but from 15 I had been keen on wine and loved drinking the good stuff. It was a help that my cousin Gilles Remiller was also a wine man, and we started together. He had studied oenology, so could tell me what to do."

The first bottled wine appeared in 1990. By 1995 the two cousins had gone their separate ways, and Christophe moved on to making two wines from 2003—a top cuvée from the best sites called "La Fleur de Montlys" added in that year.

He first destalked in 2002, out of necessity. Fermentation is in oak vats, and he does manual *pigeages* and *remontages*. Ageing for the classic Château de Montlys wine lasts 18 months in cask, the new-oak proportion rose from 30 per cent in 2004 to 50 percent, the rest being one-to-two-year-old casks. This wine contains 6 per cent Viognier, and around 6,000 bottles are produced.

The Fleur de Montlys is high on Viognier—10 to 15 per cent—and also receives two years in new oak. There are 1,500 bottles of this. Both wines are fined but not filtered. The young vine crop is sold to the local merchant trade, houses like Guigal, Bonserine, and Vins de Vienne.

A man of fair features and short-cropped greying hair, Christophe is feeling his way. He works on his own—his wife is an accountant—and is open to advice, but also to some indecision. His wine is fairly pure, and yet he feels the pressure of the media and noise merchants who shout loudly about the merits of dark, big wines. The Fleur de Montlys to some extent reflects this; its lees are stirred twice a month until the end of March, and there is the new oak overlay as well.

"Maybe I should buy a *turbo-pigeur*," Christophe ruminates out loud (as the name implies, a machine for a more forced extraction). With such a heritage of terraced granite vineyards, it would of course be a crying shame if he put distance between their fruit and the final wine.

CÔTE-RÔTIE CHÂTEAU DE MONTLYS

2003 (PREBOTTLE) ★★ Floral scents drift on the nose, light pepper appeal. Tender wine with supple appeal, coffee touches on finish. 2012–13. Last tasted March 2005; bottled April 2005.

2002 ★ Light black jam aroma. Firm texture, with oak (60 per cent new) there at the end. Fresh cherry, black fruit. A northern wine, not a sunny one. Esp 2007; 2011–12.

2001 (CASK) ★★★ Gentle, quite ripe fruit nose, some spice; soft, plump palate, runs on well, gains quiet flesh at end. Violets here. Authentic wine, oak not evident. 2011–13.

CÔTE-RÔTIE LA FLEUR DE MONTLYS

2004 (CASK) ★★ Cooked, brewed aroma, earthy and pungent. Grilled taste, fruit understated. Fair elegance. Oak a bit severe at this stage. Esp from 2009; 2017–20. Last tasted March 2005.

2003 ★★(★) Well-knit bouquet, calm black fruits, has an earthy side, has lost its oak. Brewed, spicy, good depth here. Little sweet on finish. Tannins mean it should be left until 2007. Less "inky" than before, is gaining poise. 2014–17. Last tasted March 2005.

Export 15 per cent (1) USA, (2) Great Britain, (3) Japan

DOMAINE MOUTON

Le Rozay 69420 Condrieu +33(0)474 878236

See also Condrieu.

Jean-Claude Mouton started on the family farm above Condrieu in 1989, and has been busy since then planting and developing the family's Côte-Rôtie vineyards. He works one hectare split between *Maison-Rouge* (1998) and *Bassenon* (1990, called on the map the *Coteaux de Semons*).

He is also planting and gradually bringing along a further 0.78 ha on *Corps de Loup*. These are all southerly vineyards not far from the start of the Condrieu zone, their loose granite soil giving scented, refined wines that are lighter in colour and tannin than those from the northern end of Côte-Rôtie.

Jean-Claude has sandy hair and an intense look about him—a little like Vincent van Gogh without the beard. He acknowledges that the Viognier has little part to play in his red wines, especially as the vineyards are so near Condrieu.

"I don't think the Viognier contributes to a wine that is soft anyway. We have been destalking all or most of the crop, but in some years may cut that because we want more tannin in the wine." After at least three weeks' vinification, with a manual *pigeage* and pumping-over, the wine is raised over 18 months in casks, half of them new, the other half two to three years old. Fining and filtration are done.

CÔTE-RÔTIE

2003 ★★(★) Big, quite funky bouquet, broad with brewed fruit. Wholesome, earthy wine with a floral lining. Traditional; gutsy towards finish, shows its tannins. Genuine. Handles this year's 40 per cent–new oak OK. Esp from 2008; 2017–19.

2002 ★ Gummy fruit, reduced bouquet. Some dark flavour, tannins/acidity present. Raspberry hints, lies low. Aftertaste severe. From 2006, and hope; 2013–14.

2001 (CASK) ★★ Raspberry, pepper, and earthy notes; good firm fruit attack, some oak presence, quite promising.

2000 ★ Soft, black fruit/violet aroma; clear fruit, which runs on nicely. Tender, friendly wine with agreeable tannins. Drink early.

DOMAINE ROBERT NIÉRO

20 rue Cuvillière 69420 Condrieu +33(0)474 598438

See also Condrieu.

A prominent name at Condrieu, Robert Niéro planted 0.6 ha on the stones and schist of *La Viallière* in 1987, at the northern end of the vineyard, where his neighbour is Gilbert Clusel.

Since 2000 he has complemented this with a progressive planting of 0.1 ha per annum on what the locals call *Bassenon* (*Coteaux de Semons* on the map), right at the southern end of Côte-Rôtie; its soil is very like that of Condrieu, which is a tiny distance away.

Until 1994 the crop was sold to Guigal; now it is all bottled. It includes 5 per cent Viognier, which is fermented with the Syrah. After destalking, it is vinified in concrete, with *pigeages* and *remontages*, over around three weeks, the high temperature being 34°C or so. Yeasts are used if necessary.

Wood ageing lasts around 15 months, in casks of which 10 to 15 per cent are new. Fining and filtration are done.

CÔTE-RÔTIE

2002 harvesting was done early, from mid-September. The wine was light and was sold off in bulk.

2001 ★★ Raspberry jam nose, some truffle, soil; elegantly firm palate, well-wrought black fruit; bit upright but can progress, decent end tannin. From 2006–07; 2013–14.

DOMAINE MICHEL AND STÉPHANE OGIER

3 chemin du Bac 69420 Ampuis +33(0)474 561075

This is a fast-moving domaine. Unsurprisingly, it takes after the high-octane buzz and energy of its owners, the Ogier family. As father Michel, 60 in May 2003, eases himself into a role that he drily calls that of "consultant," Stéphane the son is out there, guns blazing, as he launches new cuvées, plants a vineyard on the way to Vienne, does some commerce in northern Rhône wines, and hares around, showing the wines at overseas dinners.

Born in 1977, Stéphane is one of the youngest growers in the *appellation*—Gisèle Vernay is younger, as is Benjamin Duclaux, but they have a father and elder brother on the case. The approach here is now overtly modern, with plenty of new oak, and is being lapped up by critics. The *Cuvée Belle Hélène* risks becoming a cult wine in the process, notably for those who blindly follow Maximum Score wines.

"New oak brings an element of oxygen," explains Stéphane, adding that he doesn't like to rack the wine from one cask to another. I would, however, make a formal bet with Stéphane that he will be using less new oak, and will be seeking less obvious scale in his wines, in 10 years' time. One hundred dollars or Euros should do the job.

FIGURE 6 Stéphane Ogier with his sparkling parents, Hélène and Michel, the sweep of the *La Landonne* slope behind them. (Tim Johnston)

You can't blame a young person in a hurry, though. And there's the point that Stéphane wasn't even very convinced about becoming a *vigneron* when he started out. "I did five years of studies at Beaune, and that was the turning point," he confesses. "I met and have chums from lots of different regions, and my *stage* in South Africa opened up my horizons as well." He worked on two vintages in Stellenbosch.

A tall, strong young man with a firm jawline, he went to work with gusto, giving up his rugby career with Ampuis in the process. "The first objective was to enlarge the vineyard, and then build a new cellar." He started full-time in 1998, and the pace has been hectic. By 2005 the Côte-Rôtie vineyard will amount to three hectares, broadly half schist, half granite. Three hectares is quite small these days if you are in a hurry, so there has been a lot of extra activity in the peripheral *vin de pays* areas.

The core plot is the 1.2 ha on *Lancement* (1979), above the *Côte Blonde*. There are six *lieux-dits*, the foundation ones being *Lancement*, 0.32 ha on *Côte Rozier* (1950s), and 0.4 ha on *Champon* (early 1990s). More recently, they have expanded in the south at *But de Mont* (1988) in Tupin and on *Besset* (2001) and *Gerine*

(1999–2000), either side of *Montmain* in Verenay, at the northern end.

In the 1970s this domaine was unknown, since it made no wine. Michel, who has a wry sense of humour and a natural charm, worked with his father on their mixed vines and fruit activities until his father died in 1970. The grape harvest was all sold to Guigal and Chapoutier. On his mother's side, five generations were involved in winemaking, but it wasn't economical, so Michel continued with the apricots, pears, and apples until deciding in 1982 that he could make the wine pay.

The domaine started with just *Côte Rozier* and part of the *Lancement* vineyard, a 1940s plot of Syrah that was in Hélène's family. Michel moved fast, from bottling half the wine in the first year, to all of it by 1987. He also had worked the vineyard without weedkillers before, but its expansion meant hiring people and working on a more time-saving basis. He vinified largely traditionally—no destalking; cap immersed in the juice with grills to push it down; 18 months in oak, none of it new, the oldest casks 10 years old.

The wine was clean, authentic and refined. At times it just lacked a little *gras*, or richness.

Even in poor years like 1993, it and the *vin de pays La Rosine* were very correct.

Stéphane wanted to move past this, however. "Dad's wine showed a lot of finesse, but it didn't necessarily exploit the potential of the grape," he explains. "For instance, I do *pigeages* and *remontages* over a week, and once the alcoholic fermentation has finished, I go back to immersing the cap, so the juice is always in the crop. I won't do punching after the alcoholic stage, because it produces too many rough tannins," he adds.

Stéphane has also increased the duration of the vinification in steel from two to three or four weeks to gain more richness. He is destalking 80 per cent now and prefers to place the more tannic wines in the new oak. From 2003 they have had a new temperature-controlled cask ageing cellar, a much longer building so the barrels are never more than two high.

It's clear his head is buzzing with ideas. He is adapting the vinification of the crop from the southern areas at Tupin, where the wines are naturally gentler; here there is a week of cool storage, followed by the vat held at a maximum of 29°C "to keep the wines expressing their best fruit." *Saignée* (bleeding off early juice to get more colour) is also a regular activity now. "It was vital to do this in a high crop year like 2000, even after all vineyard cutbacks," says Stéphane.

He is doing some *micro-oxygénation* on the *vin de pays* Rosine "to get early, clear fruit." External yeasts can be used if the situation—a slow-to-start fermentation—warrants them. Experiments on filtration show that the process takes out some of the tannic content, so the wines have not been filtered since 1997.

In 1997 the Ogiers added a second Côte-Rôtie, the Cuvée Belle Hélène, from the *Côte Rozier*. The name is significant, because it pays hommage to a central cog in the wheel here. Hélène is Michel's wife, whom he met when they both sang in the Ampuis choir "just a few years ago"! She radiates great energy and a bustling, "anything is possible" outlook. She is an intuitive person, of the earth, on the ball and

very open. She moves around at some pace, her tightly knotted blue apron a trademark, and galvanises those around her.

It's house policy to vinify the fruit from all the plots separately so the style of each *terroir* can be better known. The classic wine, Réserve du Domaine, contains about half *Blonde*, half *Brune* grapes. Like the Belle Hélène, it is pure Syrah. The Belle Hélène is chosen from cask tasting before bottling, and always runs to between six and eight casks. First made in 1997, there are up to 2,100 bottles in any year.

The classic continues to receive 18 months in cask, but 30 per cent are new, the rest one to four years old. Belle Hélène is aged for 30 months in new oak.

In 2001 Stéphane introduced two new Côte-Rôties, one of them a *négoce* wine. Because Lancement "terroir de Blonde" is from vines at the top of their largest *lieu-dit* at *Lancement*, it expresses the very rocky, thin topsoil there. "Its yields are naturally low, the grapes usually small and concentrated," says Stéphane. This receives 24 to 30 months in oak, 25 per cent new and 1,200 to 2,000 bottles are produced.

Stéphane has also gone into *négoce*, whereby he is buying crop from two sources at Verenay and vinifying it in the same way as the other wines—80 per cent destalked, a four-week process and then a 24-to-30-month ageing in half new, half one-year-old casks. There are 3,000 bottles of this pure Syrah wine called "Les Embruns." It is mostly from *Berthelon*, at the top of *Grandes Places*, plus *La Viallière* and *Montlys*.

Since the early 1990s, the Ogiers have made a benchmark pure Syrah *vin de pays des Collines Rhodaniennes* called "La Rosine." The vines are up at Semons, on the southern end of the *appellation* near Condrieu, and this vineyard has been expanded at some pace. There are now 5.0 ha, ranging from 1988 to the later 1990s in age, growing on pretty pure granite.

La Rosine receives 14 months in casks, 10 per cent new, the rest on their second wine after ageing the Côte-Rôties. It is always well fruited with enough tannic structure to raise it above the usual *vin de pays* level—excellent for summer barbecues, where its clear fruit comes into its own.

From 2003 the Ogiers have also made a white *vin de pays* from a little over a hectare of Viognier with a touch of Roussanne as well. This too is called "La Rosine."

Stéphane is also charged up about his project at Seyssuel, north of Côte-Rôtie and across the river. Here he is following in the steps of Messieurs Cuilleron, Gaillard and Villard, Chapoutier, Paret, and the Louis Chèze group. On a site called *Le Vieux Château* just under the château, 1.3 ha of Syrah were planted from 2002; this also makes a *vin de pays des Collines Rhodaniennes*. "The soil is more in the *Brune* style," he says, "so the wines will be longer-lived than the *Rosines*." The wine is raised for 14 to over 18 months in cask, one-third of them new.

CÔTE-RÔTIE

2003 ★★(★) Ripe, raisiny aroma, warm core to bouquet, a southern leaning. Fruit shows vigour, is punchy. Oak enters later. Serious structure, from 2008, but its richness guides it along well. 2016–17.

2002 ★★ Smoky, raspberry/bacon aroma. Some stuffing on palate—cherry maraschino fruit, pepper present. Licorice, quite structured end. Oaked tannins present, is quite international. Helped by 20 per cent Belle Hélène. 2013–15.

2001 (CASK) ★★★ Gently cooked blackberry fruit aroma, some reduction; tight *cassis* fruit start, closely knit. Solid end; oak handled well. Go straight to middle age, e.g., 2008; 2015–17.

2000 ★★★ Live, upright aromas, brambly/ olives, animal edge; has become more prune/ plum, less purely juicy. Good cohesion, jam textures. Esp 2005–06; 2013–15.

1999 (CASK) ★★★ Black fruits, spice, wide aromas; tight black fruit, grows well, leads to wide, sleek tannins. Very clean, decent body, quite modern. From 2006; 2012–15.

1998 ★★★ Smoky, powerful, brown earth bouquet; lot of crunchy fruit, good pungent flavour, muscular wine, evident tannins. From 2004; 2012–13.

1997 ★★★ Chocolate, red fruits, licorice aromas; fair weight, raspberries, nice fruit at end. Touch end tannin. 2007–09.

1996 ★★★ 2009–10

1995 ★★★ 2008–09

CÔTE-RÔTIE CUVÉE BELLE HÉLÈNE

2003 ★★★★ Well-founded bouquet, smoky, peppery, and persistent. Black fruit–chocolate mix, with violets, is sinewed. Pushes along to a mineral, dry, oak-influenced finish. Upright, a Bordelais of bearing. Will blossom, from 2009. 2019–22.

2002 Added to the classic cuvée.

2001 (CASK) ★★★★★ Profound, tight-knit, smoky blackberry nose; crunchy black fruit, pepper/licorice end. Substantial but harmonious. Tannins run around at end. From 2007–08; 2022–25.

2000 ★★★ Quite overt, toasted nose, oak on top of fruit/spice at moment. Chewy palate. Oak rules from halfway. Hope there's enough matter to allow assimilation. From 2006–07; 2018–19.

1999 ★★★★★ Lots of varied aromas— olive/anchovy/blackberry. Air brings more mineral. Lot of deep black fruit; oily, pine essence, suave texture. Great packing. Heated end, atypical. From 2007–08; 2019–22.

1998 ★★★★ Red fruits/pepper, compact nose; quite heated wine, touch of dryness. Sound, dense matter; oak flourishes at end, some burnt fruit there. Needs time—from 2005–06; 2013–14.

1997 ★★ Soft, nuanced blackberry aroma, oak discreet; supple wine, *cassis* fruits with some chew on finish. Stylish. 2009–11.

CÔTE-RÔTIE LANCEMENT "TERROIR DE BLONDE"

2003 ★★★ Notably ripe, soaked fruit aroma—jam and raisin together. Brewed, squeezy fruit, fleshy wine. Possesses the elegance and harmony of the place, then is pushed along by its oak. Just about enough matter to handle the oak. Tarry aftertaste is livened by floral touches. From 2007–08; 2019–20.

2002 Not made.

2001 (CASK) ★★★★★ Tightly packed nose, stylish, "singing" black fruits, *vrai*; black fruits/olives with well-founded richness, very deep. Good Syrah black fruit end. 2015–17.

CÔTE-RÔTIE LES EMBRUNS

2003 ★★★ Bright, full *robe*. Serious, grounded bouquet, mineral content, too. Stylish black fruits, ripe tannins in support. Good length, licorice finale. Esp from 2008; 2019–20.

2002 ★★ Quite dark, bright *robe*. Smoky bacon, firm bouquet. Well-knit palate, carries an upright appeal, cherry fruit has some depth. Likeable, live fruit. Acidity towards finish. 2010–11.

2001 (CASK) ★★★ Quite meaty nose; cleanly stewed black fruits; prominent, peppery tannins. Brewed fruit style shows *terroir* well. Very different from the classic, thus. Licorice end. 2013–15.

Export 50 per cent (1) USA, (2) Great Britain, (3) Switzerland

DOMAINE STÉPHANE OTHEGUY

Chemin Chez Maurice 38138 Les Côtes d'Arey
+33(0)474 589443

See also Condrieu, St-Joseph.

Having worked with Vincent Gasse for seven years, Stéphane Otheguy was ideally placed to take on the organic baton when M. Gasse took his retirement in 2004. "I am attracted by the different dimensions of wine," he says. "You can work outside, be the master of your product, there is conviviality, and then of course the organic side. As a way of preserving the environment while working in the agri-viticultural field, it is what I want to do."

His route into wine has been varied. He used to work with children, travelling around villages with old wooden games and statues, being the animator of community events that attracted young and old. But wine nibbled away at him,

and he went to study it at Mâcon before joining M. Gasse in 1997.

He is renting the Gasse stable of sites—*Côte Rozier, Leyat,* and a young plot on *Rozier,* along with *Bonnivière* and *Ritolas,* which are nearer the plateau. The oldest are *Leyat* and *Bonnivière*—both around 1945 and 1955—while the last two plots vary between 1985 and 1999.

His wines will follow their origins of place and vine. He is continuing the Vieilles Vignes of Vincent Gasse, drawn from the *Leyat* and *Bonnivière* sites, where the Syrah is all preclone *massale* quality. Then there is a wine from the sites of *Ritolas* and the bottom end of *Leyat*: these are clone vines dating from the 1980s. Lastly, there is a wine from *Côte Rozier,* also a Syrah clone plantation of the 1980s, but the soil nuance justifies it being prepared apart, according to M. Otheguy.

"*Côte Rozier*'s clones are the same as those on *Ritolas* and *Bas de Leyat,*" he says, "but the soil is rockier at *Côte Rozier,* and the wine's tannins finer and more elegant than the others'; their soil is heavier, and the wine a little rustic."

After destemming, and a vinification of two to three weeks, with cap punchings and one pumping-over a day, the wine is aged in used casks for up to two years.

DOMAINE CÉDRIC PARPETTE, FORMERLY RENÉ FERNANDEZ

8 rue Montlys Verenay 69420 Ampuis +33(0)474 561005

Dark, wiry, fast talking, and very southern in looks and name, René Fernandez finally achieved his aim of being a full-time *vigneron* in 1997. Born in Lyon, he would come south as a boy to pick fruit and by 15 was working on fruit, vegetable, and vine growing at Verenay.

"In 1971 the plain area was bought up to build the autoroute and the Rhône canal, so that meant I had to go and work in the public sector. It was 1986 when I was able to buy 2.5 hectares of abandoned vineyard, and for the next three years I cleared and planted 2.7 ha in my spare time. Just when I thought I might be able to start the wine properly, the bad vintage of 1993 came along, followed by the pests of 1994." In all this time, he was on his own.

He retired in 2003, to be succeeded by his son-in-law Cédric Parpette, who joined him on the 3.5-hectare vineyard in September 2002. Cédric has no family winemaking background but has done formal wine studies.

René started by renting vines on *Le Bourg* and *La Viallière* and would sell the crop to Guigal. Now the domaine comprises 2.7 ha on the south-facing *Montmain* (1988–90), topped up by 0.6 ha on *Le Plomb* (1996). The soil is largely schist, the slope extreme— around 35° to 40°. Six per cent of the holding is Viognier.

There are around 6,000 bottles of *Le Montmain*, the rest of the crop sold to Guigal. During the tasting, René moves around his cramped cellar, an old stable, with swift, neat movements. With his black hair slicked back, he looks like an Argentinian tango dancer. "Yes, I do like dancing very much," he says. "The slope keeps me fit, too!" *Allez* Gardel!

Since 2001 the crop has been destalked to make the wine more refined. Cédric ferments in concrete over 18 to 21 days, with *remontage* and *pigeage*. Ageing is in 600-litre *demi-muids* for a year, then a second year or so in 228-litre casks of one to eight years old. He fines lightly but does not filter.

CÔTE-RÔTIE LE MONTMAIN

2002 (CASK) ★★ Decent fruit on nose; peppery, chewy touches; maybe to 2011.

2001 (CASK) ★ Ripe enough, floral nose; black fruits, cool texture, some spice. Touch dry on end. 2010–11.

2000 ★★ Light spice, jam bouquet; tender, elegant wine, suave. Prune, red jam; lightly tannic aftertaste. More variety from 2004–05.

DOMAINE STÉPHANE PICHAT

6 chemin de la Viallière Verenay 69420 Ampuis
+33(0)474 483723

For the moment, Stéphane Pichat is the new kid on the block at Côte-Rôtie. Born in 1978, he works two hectares on his own in the northern hamlet of Verenay. His sites are varied—the high-up *Champon*, *Le Plomb* just below it, the well-known *Les Grandes Places*, and *Le Bourg*, which sits a little away from the *Côte Brune*. The oldest vines, dating from the late 1960s, are on *Champon*. Two to three percent of the vineyard is Viognier.

This is a family that reflects precisely the comings and goings of three generations in this part of the Rhône. Stéphane's grandparents made their living from fruit, vegetables, and a few vines at Verenay. His father worked for the Electricity of France, while he has returned to the soil.

"I hesitated between the electricity and the wine, I have to say," he comments, "but one week of electricity was enough for me!" He did work practice locally with Jean-Michel Gérin and Gilbert Clusel, plus a visit to the Sonoma Valley, and made his first wine in 2000.

After using whole crop in 2000, Stéphane destalked in 2001 and 2002. He ferments in steel, yeasts if necessary, and likes to do *remontages* and *pigeages*. He works a lot with new oak, which shows up in his wines. Cask ageing lasts 18 to 22 months, with 80 per cent new wood. He fines but does not filter. With the prominence of the oak, these are wines to drink strictly when they are mature.

With under 2,000 bottles, sales are only to private customers.

CÔTE-RÔTIE LE CHAMPON

2003 (CASK) ★★★ Well-founded potential on nose, dark aroma. Meaty, black fruit, tight-knit—a schist child. Solid, good *gras* and definition. Quite rigorous, masculine, can come along. From 2007–08; 2019–21.

2002 (★) Oak on bouquet, has a damp side, not fresh. Simmered mulberry fruit, but lacks flesh. Some length; end acidity apparent. Esp 2006; 2010–11.

2001 (CASK) ★ Ripe, stewed berry aromas, smoky; decent matter, berry flavours, chewy. Ends drily, rather hot. Hope oak softens. 2011–13.

2000 ★ Oily, bit spiced nose, supple; nice black garden fruit with oak drying it towards end. Fair flesh, heated end. 2009–11.

CHRISTOPHE PICHON

Le Grand Val 42410 Chavanay +33(0)474 870678

See also Condrieu, St-Joseph.
The talented Christophe Pichon makes his classic Côte-Rôtie from just 0.55 ha on *Rozier*, a plot that was planted between 1967 and 1969, on schist soil that contains minor amounts of loose granite. It holds 10 per cent Viognier.

The wine was first made in 2001 and averages around 3,000 bottles each year. "I rent the vineyard from an uncle who used to sell the crop to Guigal—it's useful to have an uncle in Ampuis," he admits.

In 2005 a second wine came on stream, called La Comtesse. This is from a rented 0.48 ha plot on the *Côte Brune* (1930s, 1991).

The grapes are 80 per cent destalked, and after a cool maceration lasting three to six days at around 12°C, the fermentation takes place in steel vats, with *remontages* and *pigeages*, and runs for 20 to 30 days, up to a temperature of 31°C. The young wine is then raised in 20 per cent new, 80 per cent one-year casks over 14 months. Fining and a light filtration are done.

On his outlook, Christophe comments: "I don't use outside yeasts, I don't inject oxygen, and these other modern tricks. I also don't want much new oak because it brings a loss of typicity. If you have the *terroir,* you shouldn't have to resort to these things."

CÔTE-RÔTIE

2003 (CASK) ★★★ Dark aromas, some rose hip, *typicité*—more to come. Jam style, but round and quite savoury palate. Open, some elegance, charm from the Viognier. Tannins ripe. Reduced at present. From 2006; 2014–16.

2002 ★ Tender floral/black fruit/leather aroma. Clear-cut light fruit on palate, not that sustained. Light tannins. Some length. Drink 2005–08, and be precise with the date.

2001 ★★★★ Expressive red fruit aroma, some Viognier warmth; refined structure, will be tasty. Very pure—bravo for first wine! Good balance, tannins work in well at end. 2010–13.

DOMAINE DE PIERRE BLANCHE

RN 86 Verlieu 42410 Chavanay +33(0)474 870407

See also Condrieu, St-Joseph.
Michel Mourier sells about 7,000 bottles of Côte-Rôtie a year. This comes from two sites, the *Côte Blonde* and *Côte Rozier*, representing a mix of the granite and schist soils. It is aged for two years in casks ranging from new to five years old.

GILLES REMILLER

12 route du Laca Verenay 69420 Ampuis
+33(0)474 560133

Within the rather chiselled face of the good-looking Gilles Remiller lies a wistful shadow. He has worked hard all his life, but things appear no easier. He has taken brave decisions, but the rewards are unclear. He carries a slightly solemn air, as if there are not too many guaranteed moments of satisfaction ahead.

The Remillers have been at Verenay, in the north of the *appellation*, since the nineteenth century. The family land was divided between successive generations, and it was Gilles' grandfather's generation, Jean and Louis, who took on the vineyards. Louis started to bottle in the 1960s and handed down his vineyard to his son Jean-Paul, who died in his early fifties in 2003.

Meanwhile Gilles' grandfather Jean worked a local vineyard, notably 0.75 ha on *La Viallière*, the local hot spot. Without a large vineyard to keep body and soul together, Gilles went off to live and work in the esteemed Indosuez Bank in esteemed Lyon, where he stayed for 15 years.

As wine prices rose, so did the temptation to return to Côte-Rôtie. Accordingly, in 1990 he started to work double time, reclaiming and scrubbing out old vineyards while continuing at the bank.

One of the early moves was to rent the land around the splendid Château de Montlys in the *commune* of St-Cyr, overlooking the Rhône. This area needed clearing and planting, and he worked with his cousin Christophe Semaska on this.

Since then he has revived plots on *Cognet* (0.3 ha, 1999) and *Montmain* (0.1 ha, 2001), as well as working 0.8 ha on the plateau at *Champon* and his grandfather Jean's plot on *La Viallière*. There is also 0.4 ha of Syrah Côtes du Rhône on the plateau.

These were years of great toil. Once he left the bank in 1993, Gilles realised his income wasn't enough from selling off his wine in bulk, which he had started in 1991 with his first vintage. Back to employment he went, therefore, and from 1996 to 2002 worked with Guigal. He looked after the slope vineyards that make up their Doriane wine at Condrieu—*Colombier* and *Châtillon*—for four years, and for the last two years was the man responsible for their Côte-Rôtie vineyard upkeep, a weighty role.

Now he is bang on his own. "I would like to have a worker to help me, because there's never enough time," he admits in his soft-spoken tones. "I get in people to help tie the young vegetation, and obviously do the harvest, but it's hard working on your own in the winters. I'm 45 now, and from a physical point of view, the best years to be in a bank are when you're in your 50s. The big drawback there of course is all the *Bonjour, Monsieur le Directeur* stuff and politics."

He destalks by preference, although well-ripened old vine fruit is left alone; advice is given by Stéphane Ogier, and vinification takes place in steel vats, applying yeasts to get the fermentation going. There is pumping over and punching down, and in a year like 2002, tannins are added.

Cask raising lasts 15 to 18 months, the wood new to seven years old. The best wine is chosen for bottling, which often means it is from the old vines of *La Viallière*. About 2,000 bottles are currently produced, the rest sold early on in bulk to local buyers.

CÔTE-RÔTIE

2002 (CASK) ★ Red fruits/pepper aroma; light, quite agreeable red fruit, tender overall. Young drinking.

2001 (CASK) ★★ Smoky, dense, stewed fruits nose; full-style palate, plenty of weight and tannin; violet, toasted end. Esp 2005–06; 2011–13.

Export (1) Great Britain, (2) USA

DOMAINE DE ROSIERS

3 rue des Moutonnes 69420 Ampuis +33(0)474 561138

A very unassuming, solid worker, Louis Drevon works a substantial seven hectares. The domaine was created in 1947 by his father, André, a small, southern-looking man. Until 1970 it mixed fruit and vine; by 1976 André had started to bottle a little, with the rest of the crop from his three hectares sold to Chapoutier.

André died in 2002. His son Louis is now in his early 50s and has the modesty of the true countryman. His holidays are spent in other French wine regions, and with no children to help, he employs three full-time workers.

The approach is very down the line; there is no supercuvée, just the one wine that is assembled early in the process, right after the malolactic fermentation. All the production is bottled. The wine is unpretentious and lies in the honest, middle ranks of Côte-Rôtie. Its flavours often run with stewed fruits rather than anything more subtle. "I seek a fruit imprint, but also a wine that can keep for 10 to 15 years," comments Louis.

There are 27 different plots; the largest single site is three hectares on *Rozier*, dating from the late 1940s. The other main site is the 0.8 ha on *Besset*, with fine decomposed *arzelle* forming a loose topsoil high above Verenay. *Rozier* is more centrally sited and consists largely of mica-schist; its crop ripens earlier. Louis says that his vineyard's average age is 35 to 40 years.

The vineyard work involves treatments when things go wrong; Louis had to spray against mildew in 2002, for instance. Three per cent of the crop is Viognier, which is vinified with the Syrah, therefore at a relatively more advanced stage of ripeness.

The crop has been destemmed since 1989 to cut out any green flavours. Since 1992 the cellar has been temperature controlled. Vinification lasts three to four weeks in concrete vats, with just some pumping-over (*remontages*). The vats work on the submerged-cap principle, so no punching down is needed.

Wood ageing lasts 12 to 18 months; the first six months are in 25-to-35-hl ex–Alsatian beer barrels, followed by a stay in casks, a quarter of them new, the rest two to three years old. Fining and filtration are done.

CÔTE-RÔTIE

2004 (CASK) ★★★ Oily, black fruits, sustained bouquet. Elegant, fine and rich palate, suave texture, pretty. Cooked black fruits show through, length is good. Oaked finale. A fine year and more savoury than 2003. Maybe a 14-to-16-year wine. Last tasted March 2005.

2003 (PREBOTTLE) ★★(★) Full, compact bouquet with no excess—well weighted, some heat and oak. Very northern, schist style, direct attack, with mineral present. Richness amplifies through the palate, extends well. Tar aftertaste. Drinks OK now with its richness. More from 2008, though; 2016–20. Last tasted March 2005.

2002 ★ Nutty, cherry aroma, soaked fruit without great depth. Direct, rather burnt, tarry palate, is a bit square. Clear-cut. Drink esp 2006–09.

2001 (CASK) ★★ Sweet raspberry, earthy, sound bouquet; stewed dark flavour, burnt tones, chewy. Leathery style. From 2007; can become interesting; 2012–14.

2000 ★★★ Rounded bouquet, blackberry/raspberry mix; nicely full, then tightens. More

chunky than expected. Southern aspect here, nicely ripe. Violet hint at end, texture is stewed, length good. 2010–13.

Export 30 per cent (1) Belgium, (2) Japan, (3) Great Britain

RENÉ ROSTAING

Petite rue du Port 69420 Ampuis +33(0)474 561200

See also Condrieu.

René Rostaing has to be termed the Mystery Man of Côte-Rôtie, a complex individual who rarely reveals his true self. Much is his restraint, and his inclination to walk alone. He has never been a member of the Growers Union, and when most of the village turned out to present their wines in the second, highly successful Découvertes en Vallée du Rhône in March 2003, M. Rostaing was to be found in London, showing his wines there.

Some of this restraint comes through in his wines, which are always tightly assembled and require time before they pan out. They bear a studied elegance rather than flamboyance and, in the best vintages, are notable for their stylish, lithe-fruited poise.

M. Rostaing married into wine, and his wife's vineyard inheritance plays a central part in this domaine's fortunes. These are some of the finest spots in the *appellation,* plum in the best sites. His wife, Christiane, is the daughter of Albert Dervieux and the niece of Marius Gentaz-Dervieux, two top veterans of the village's vineyards.

M. Rostaing worked in real estate—residential lettings—for many years. His first wine work was in 1971, when he started on a few vineyards of his own. "By 1975 it started to be more economical; we were helped by sales abroad, including to the USA, where Albert Dervieux had been selling since the early 1970s," he recalls.

He started to devote more time to wine in the early 1990s and finally went full-time to it by 2000. Now in his late 50s, he looks after 7.5 hectares spread across 14 *lieux-dits,* made up of

FIGURE 7 René Rostaing on his Condrieu vineyard at Sainte-Agathe, a south-facing sun trap above the Rhône. (Tim Johnston)

20 separate plots. As an example, his hectare on the *Côte Blonde* comes in two plots, both dating from the 1960s.

The Albert Dervieux vineyard amounted to 3.2 ha, the Gentaz-Dervieux to 1.2 ha. The latter's vineyard, which includes a choice plot on the *Côte Brune,* is being replanted bit by bit, and the main old Sérine vine plantation is now just left to *La Viallière.* "The whole Sérine debate is a pointless one, anyway," is his pithy comment on that matter!

The largest vineyards are his 1.6 ha on *La Landonne* (1970s), followed by around 1.5 ha on *Fongeant* (1970s) and by the 1.2 ha on *La Viallière* that was well-known thanks to Albert Dervieux. This vineyard is part 100 years old, part 20 years. Other holdings are on *Le Plomb, Boucharey,* and *La Roche.* His most recent development has been half a hectare at *Tupin,* in the south, from 2004.

The vineyard leans more towards the mica-schist, stone-covered aspects of the northern sites. Seventy-five per cent is on slopes, 25 per cent flat. M. Rostaing prefers to continue with terraced walls and points out that he probably has over one kilometre to maintain. "My three full-time workers have to spend a month per year on doing these up. Wall upkeep contributes about 5 per cent to the cost of a bottle," he states.

He is not a fan of late harvesting, as has become more fashionable in recent years: "The Syrah lacks acidity, and any start of overripeness makes the wines very heavy and lacking in vigour," he points out, with fair reason.

From 1996 he has made just three wines, a classic (20,000 bottles), the produce of 11 different lieux-dits: a Blonde (5,500 bottles); and a Landonne (7,000 bottles). The classic and Landonne are pure Syrah, average vine age 30 and 35 years, respectively, while the Blonde's vines, on the Garde site, date from the 1950s and contain 3 to 5 per cent Viognier. M. Rostaing gave up his single La Viallière wine because its crop size was irregular.

All three wines receive the same vinification and ageing, so, as M. Rostaing points out, "their differences come down to the *terroir.*"

He has destemmed part of the crop since 1994. The classic is 75 per cent destemmed, the single-vineyard wines between 35 and 50 per cent. The current style has been set since 1995; M. Rostaing has a battery of horizontal steel fermenting vats that allow automatic *pigeages,* or cap punching, with the vats themselves turning. A 10-to-12-day alcoholic fermentation is followed by a two-week maceration, when he lets the temperature rise to around 35°C. Only natural yeasts are used.

Ageing is done half in 228-litre casks, half in 550-litre *demi-muids.* Ten per cent of the oak is new, the rest between two and seven years old. In a big vintage like 1999, ageing lasts two years, in a quieter vintage like 2000, it lasts 18 months. Over the two years, there may be five rackings, the wine switching to and from the different casks. There is fining but no filtration.

The Landonne shows more openly early on, the Blonde being well packed but reserved. There is more of a gamey, leathery texture to the Landonne. In time, the Blonde often becomes more flamboyant. In the top years, like 1995 and 1999, both wines start to show their powers after six or seven years and can live for around 20 years.

Beyond Côte-Rôtie, M. Rostaing works two well-placed vineyards at Condrieu, and he ventured down to the Languedoc in 1996, when he bought a domaine between Nîmes and Som- mières, the village where Lawrence Durrell used to live. Domaine de Puech-Chaud has 13 hectares, mainly Syrah with some Mourvèdre, and 2.5 hectares mixed between 35 per cent Grenache Blanc, 40 per cent Rolle, and 25 per cent Muscat; the Muscat is going to have Rous- sanne grafted on to it. The soil is poor, sedimen- tary limestone. The red is aged a year in cask, and there are now a red and white Coteaux de Languedoc.

"For me, this area was the Far West, there's space down there that we simply don't have here," he explains. "You can have 20 hectares, just one owner, the vines all together, and it gives you a great chance to progress. It's an extraordinary challenge." As he talks, rare ani- mation appears on M. Rostaing's strong fea- tures, his usual piercing looks softening for a moment.

There's no doubt that rigour is a notion with which M. Rostaing is entirely at ease. Many years ago, this showed itself on a bitterly cold, above all damp January morning, when we were tasting in an outer room of his house. Our breath issued forth like that of dragons, and still the analysis of the wines continued at a very steady pace. True to form, M. Rostaing, clad merely in a dark-blue shoulder-buttoned French sweater, made no reference to the prevailing conditions, and was clearly enjoying the severity of it all, as his visitor shuddered and scribbled chaotically.

Likewise with his wines: "I prefer 2001 to 1999," he states. "1999 is a hot year; it's not typ- ical, whereas 2001 is more reserved." The fruit in his wines is always streamlined, sleek rather than plush. There is a Bordeaux side to them, evident in their construction and in their maker's outlook. And M. Rostaing's favourite Italian wine speaks again of his liking for rigour and reserve; it is Barolo, which takes time to develop and to be captured.

In 1997 only one wine was made, because the very hot, dry year robbed the other wines of their nuances, making them all too fat. The domaine had a wobble in that period, since the 1996s were also uneven. In the 2000s, the wines seem on better form once more, and the sensible decision in 2002 was to produce just one wine, called *Terroirs*, given the indifferent nature of the crop.

CÔTE-RÔTIE

2001 (CASK) ★★★ Quite full, broad red berry nose, tar; dark flavours, locked up right now. Fresh wine, full enough. Upright, leave alone till 2006–07. Fair length. 2015–18.

2000 ★★★ Open aromas, raspberry/cassis, bit of jam; straight elegance, red fruits present, nice licorice/vanilla length. 2010–12.

1999 ★★★★ Cooked plum, oily/leathery nose, plenty to come; quite round red fruits, generous but not plush. From 2006 will have more width. Length OK. 2014–17.

1998 (CASK) ★★★ Big, full, dense nose; good intense palate, well-balanced, spiced and tannic. Good length, clear dimension. 2010–12.

1997 ★ The only wine made this year: rounded, black jam–style bouquet. Fat, rich wine, heat at end. Tannins present, some final oak. Esp 2000. Length fair. 2004–07.

1996 ★★ 2008–11
1995 (CASK) ★★★★ 2011–14
1994 ★★★★ 2006–08

CÔTE-RÔTIE CÔTE BLONDE

2001 (CASK) ★★★★★ Floral/red fruit, lightly spiced nose; close-knit fruit, dumb, tannic edges. Complexity to come. Fair length, fruit returns with violets. 2017–21.

2000 ★★★★★ Wild strawberry/cinnamon/ pepper, charming nose; tight matter, lots of dense, partly spiced red fruit. Fruit more solid near end, quite complex. Oil/licorice end, long. From 2007; 2015–17.

1998 (CASK) ★★★★★ Very typical bou- quet, aromatic, floating, plenty in it. Quiet, ele- gant warmth; has plum, cedar, cinnamon. Lasts well, tannins well woven in. Esp 2004–05; 2013–17.

1995 ★★★★★★ 2012–16
1994 ★★★★★ 2008–11

CÔTE-RÔTIE LA LANDONNE

2001 (CASK) ★★★★ Black soil/violets bouquet; dumb black fruit, decent weight, straight wine; peppery, tarry end. Dark flavours overall. 2016–18.

2000 ★★★ Black fruits/earth, peppery nose; good grain on palate, black fruit widens second half, some tannin near end. Broad finish. From 2006; 2014–16.

1999 No *Landonne* due to hail.

1998 ★★★ Young colour at six years; pine/spice bouquet, violets. Mineral, dry-toned, assertive flavour, has a brittle black fruit side. Drinks younger than its age. Clear, elegant wine—reflects the Burgundian finesse of its cask days. Fruit is plum/cherry style. Can soften more. 2010–14.

1995 ★★★★★ 2016–20

Export 87 per cent (1) Great Britain, (2) Switzerland, (3) Germany

SAINT-COSME

Château de Saint-Cosme 84190 Gigondas +33(0)490 658080

See also Condrieu.

The energetic Louis Barruol from Gigondas has shown his skill at selecting good Condrieu and has repeated the formula at Côte-Rôtie. He sells 8,000 bottles and is very careful over his crop suppliers. "I work with three suppliers, their vineyards notably on *La Viallère* and *Les Grandes Places*. It's not a challenge to find the grapes, more to find the people who work well," he comments. The ratio now runs at 80 per cent northern sector, 20 per cent southern. The wine is raised in new oak for 15 months. "My wines often close up between two and six years old," states Louis.

CÔTE-RÔTIE

2003 ★★★ Meaty, touch gamey bouquet, also some floral tone. Well-filled palate, direct, nuanced fruit. Oak tightens the end. Rich, chocolate style core. 2013–15.

2001 ★★★ Black fruits, earthy underlay, plenty to come on nose. Tight-knit palate, tarry

finale, solid wine. Good black fruits definition. From 2007; 2015–17.

2000 ★★★ Raspberry, some floral edges on quite authentic, mild bouquet; good juice on palate, interesting, creeps up and broadens. Stylish. 2010–13.

DOMAINE JEAN-MICHEL STÉPHAN

69420 Tupin et Semons +33(0)474 566266

Jean-Michel Stéphan is the Independent Spirit of Côte-Rôtie, setting out his stall as the maker of unadulterated, at times innovative wines. He works in a cramped cellar with no adornments or signs around, and most usually it's children's toys that are spread around the outside.

Short, with curly brown hair and glasses, he could be the boffin of the class, and admits to a love for biology. He has continued a progression whereby his grandfather grew vegetables, his father apples, pears, and peaches, and he the vine, all at Tupin.

His cellar is on the site of the cold-storage rooms for the fruit and vegetables; it was being a chum of the Duclaux and Gallet sons that moved him towards growing vines and making wine. He studied at Belleville in the Beaujolais and took his first steps in 1991, spurred on by his passion for biology and plants.

"I make wines on the fruit, without sulphur," he states. "I want fruit and maximum freshness. The late Jules Chauvet in the Beaujolais would saturate his vats with carbonic gas until the cap rose, and vinification would take place around 10°C. That's what I do with one of my three wines, the one from Tupin that is called *Coteaux de Tupin*, while my plain Côte-Rôtie is made partly along those lines."

The plain Côte-Rôtie comes from four sites—the northern schist at Verenay, mixed in with crop from the gneiss of *Les Bercheries*, a degraded clay-chalk soil, plus *Tupin* and the *Coteaux de Semons*. He spreads around 10 per cent Viognier in layers through the steel vat so its aromas fan out, and cools the crop at 5°C for half a day so the skins remain firm before destemming. After five days at 14°C, the juice is then allowed to rise to around 31°C and vinification lasts another two weeks.

Jean-Michel calls this his semicarbonic method, and when questioned about the risk of reduction (the stink the Syrah can give when not oxygenated enough), he replies that two pumping-overs in the first week help to restrain this effect. "Anyway, reduction comes with the process; remember, the wine is not blocked in any way by sulphur, and the reduction aromas lessen in the bottle after 16 months' cask raising, where I use wood between two and six years old. You should also decant the wine, and it will remain good for three days in an open bottle."

On separate tastings, including blind ones, Jean-Michel's 2000 (see below) is an example of the wine's ability to step out of the ordinary, but it's a hard call to know when it will be showing well. Take low pressure—a damp, drizzly day, for instance: then you may have some of the earthiness and stinky side coming through. The Viognier presence is another issue—it can blanket the Syrah and leave the texture rather overstewed. These are the prices that praiseworthy natural handling demand—and the consumer should be aware of them.

For cross-reference, these are techniques used at Morgon by Marcel Lapierre and at Fleurie by Yvon Metras. They are the sort of progressive thinkers much needed in the often stagnant Beaujolais region; their wines can be superb but also have a hit-and-miss side to them.

Born in 1971, Jean-Michel now works 4.5 ha of Côte-Rôtie, with still a bit under 1 ha of fruit trees. He takes delight in his organic apricots and dreams that one day he might sell an apricot cordial to the bar of the Hotel George V in Paris.

His largest holding is the 1.5 ha on the Coteau de Bassenon (Coteaux de Semons on the map); Bassenon is in fact a derivative of the term "Bas de Semons." This is a 40° slope, with a lot of terraces cut into the soft granite or gneiss. The high part dates from 1987; the low part, of 0.87 ha, from 1896 and 1902. "These vineyards were kept going because the old-timers grew vegetables like peas beween the rows," comments Jean-Michel.

His other sites are Tupin (1965), Coteaux de Tupin (1980), Les Bercheries, and a tiny 0.3 ha up at Verenay (1992). "My cousin is useful to have up there!" he jokes. "The soil is silico-schist with a lot of sand, because it's low down the slope and so also holds little glacier stone debris. Rain filters through quickly there, and I find the vines ripen fast."

As someone who tries to be organic at every turn, Jean-Michel is planting massale-selection Sérine whenever possible. At present, his vineyard is around 60 per cent clone, 30 per cent Sérine, and 10 per cent Viognier; the last is also being regenerated, and at Verenay he has planted 500 young Viognier cuttings grafted from an old massale plant.

In vineyard upkeep, Jean-Michel picks the soil around the wood of the older vines and cuts the weeds on the surface. If he can look harassed by the burdens of his job, it's not a surprise given the expectations he places on himself. "In eight years I expect a large difference in quality to come through," he states; "there will really be a sense of terroir in the wines."

Deep down, he is desperate for this style of wine to be recognised: "My great wish is that carbonic gas use becomes accepted as giving a maximum of fruit, a perfection of the elements in a wine. My methods turn more on fermentation than ageing—oak ageing is just to add some polish to a wine," he almost pleads.

His search is for purity, which means he is dead set on swerving right away from the false modernism that he states was created by Robert Parker, the American wine writer. His confrères in this struggle he identifies as people like Dard and Ribo at Crozes-Hermitage, Hervé Souhaut of St-Joseph, the Domaine Mazel in the southern Ardèche, plus Thiérry Allemand at Cornas.

Two other Côte-Rôties come from this singular source; an accomplished Vieilles Vignes that has already built up a following in the United States, and a Coteaux de Tupin, first made in 2000. The Vieilles Vignes, first made in 1994, is from the rented 1902 plot by the Bassenon stream and contains about 5 to 6 per cent Viognier. This is crushed and destemmed, and fermented in steel—"with no yeasts, chaptalisation, enzymes, sulphur"—Jean-Michel reels off the foes! This spends around six days at 28°C, followed by a 15-to-20-day maceration, during which cap punching five times a day by foot ensures no drying out.

The malolactic occurs in the vat, and is succeeded by 16 months' cask ageing in three-year-old ex-Puilly-Fuissé casks. As with all his reds, there is no fining nor filtration.

The *Coteaux de Tupin* wine comes from his father's vineyard, planted in patches in 1941 and then between 1993 and 2000. This is pure Syrah and is in essence a carbonic maceration wine. Whole bunches are kept in a cold chamber for a day at 3°C, and the vat is then saturated in carbonic gas until the cap rises, whereupon the crop is held at 10°C for 20 days to allow intracellular fermentation. There are a couple of cap punchings on the last two days to ensure the sugars have finished their fermentation. Until 2003 this did its malo and ageing in new Allier oak casks over two years. From 2004 half is new oak, half two-year-old wood—a good move.

Jean-Michel produced his first domaine-bottled wine in 1994. Now there are around 8,000 bottles of the classic, 1,500 of the Vieilles Vignes, and 1,200 of the *Coteaux de Tupin*. When he has underage vines on the go, he makes a *vin de pays des Collines Rhodaniennes* via carbonic maceration. In 2001 this held good, core *cassis* fruit, a life of six years or so ahead.

A point of interest on these wines is their colour; they are not black wines, and it is a pleasure to observe dark red with purple patches in their *robes*. They are also long on the palate, with no props like new oak panning them out.

The Coteaux de Tupin is Jean-Michel's favourite: "I adore this style of easy-to-digest wine that slips down with pretty aromas, even if they aren't the usual ones," he states. This is a cleaner, more direct wine than the Vieilles Vignes, and is less broad on the palate.

CÔTE-RÔTIE

2002 (CASK) ★★ Brewed, peppery nose, more brewed than many southern-zone wines.

Well-defined, stylish fruit with rounded appeal. Persists well, good length. Drinks well now. 2010–11.

2001 (CASK) ★★ Light red fruit/pepper nose; tight-knit, good consistent texture of black fruit with some pepper edges. 2012–13.

2000   *Two tasting notes on the same wine:*

2000 ★★ Wild fruit, full, earthy aroma. Very ripe fruit, has a rustic, almost volatile side. Tastes a little flat—maybe high Viognier element stifling the Syrah. 2008–10. Tasted May 2003.

2000 ★★★ Black fruit jam/floral notes; elegant black fruit, good definition, quiet reserves of *gras*. Nicely assembled. Syrah blackberry/mulberry comes through, smooth tannins support. 2010–12. Tasted March 2003.

CÔTE-RÔTIE COTEAUX DE TUPIN

2002   Not produced.

2001 (CASK) ★★★ Alert, spiced wild red berry jam aroma; spicy, clear red fruit becomes more licorice/vanilla—oak kicks in. Expressive. 2011–12.

2000 ★★★★ Springy, simmering blackberry fruit aroma; smoky black fruit, very clear with leather/licorice fringes. From 2006; 2013–15.

CÔTE-RÔTIE VIEILLES VIGNES

2001 (CASK) ★★★★ Raspberry/licorice on a compact bouquet; refined, pure cut of fruit with some body around it. Satisfying length, cherries, some chew at end. 2016–18.

2000 ★★★★★ Dark; tightly packed aroma, floral/berries, some reduction. Brewed, earthy flavour. Spirited burst of berries on finish. Well-wrapped, harmonious, very good length, lovely. From 2007; 2013–15.

1999 ★★★★ Warm, ripe fruit/mint nose; lot of blackberry fruit, potent, well-charged elements; good length. More solid than floral. 2013–15.

1998 ★★ Earthy, strawberry/prune jam nose, plus reduction; cooked red fruits, tasty, approachable; some end spice. 2005–07.

Export 45 per cent (1) Belgium, (2) Japan, (3) Denmark

DOMAINE GEORGES VERNAY

1 route Nationale 69420 Condrieu +33(0)474 568181

See also Condrieu, St-Joseph.

Georges Vernay first made a Côte-Rôtie in 1970. The main wine, Maison Rouge, comes from the hill north of Condrieu and is from their 0.9-hectare vineyard (1924, 1972) of the same name. It is pure Syrah.

In 2000 a second cuvée was introduced, called "Blonde du Seigneur." This is also taken from vineyards off the southern, granite end of the *appellation*, as the title implies, namely 1 ha on *Coteaux de Semons* (1987) (aka *Bassenon*) and 0.65 ha on *Lancement* (1999). It contains 8 per cent Viognier.

The crop is all destemmed and spends three weeks in steel vats, during which time *remontages* and manual *pigeages* are done.

The Blonde du Seigneur is aged over 18 months in cask, 25 per cent of them new, the rest one to five years old; the Maison Rouge for 24 months in half new, half one-to-four-year-old oak. There is light fining and filtration.

If the Viognier is well ripened, it is included with the Syrah at the start of the fermentation; otherwise, it is introduced at the end of its vatting so its malo is done with the Syrah.

Both wines come in the refined house style, with a charming red-fruit elegance that in the Maison Rouge broadens into a fuller, more tannic constitution. "I am looking for finesse in our Côte-Rôties," states Christine Vernay, Georges' daughter; "that's why I destem, even in a very ripe year like 1999."

CÔTE-RÔTIE BLONDE DU SEIGNEUR

2002 (CASK) ★★ Light floral/mineral/oak aroma; medium-weight red fruits, light, fair style. Tightens at end. Eight to nine yrs.

2001 (CASK) ★★★ Crisp, pepper/black fruit nose, some floral; suave attack, then tannins come. Stewed black fruits/olive, fungal bits at end. Quite pretty. Esp 2005–06; 2011–12.

CÔTE-RÔTIE MAISON ROUGE

2003 (CASK) ★★★ Full, chocolate/raspberry bouquet, broad, oak hint. Pretty, scented berried attack; tannins grow, oak/licorice at end. Has some cut. Smoky aftertaste. From 2009; 2019–21.

2000 ★★★ Striking, pepper/floral/cassis bouquet; tarry, stewed-plum/strawberry fruits. Very clean; nice end richness, where red fruits flourish. Elegant, good definition. Esp 2005–06; 2012–13.

1999 ★★★ Chocolate traces, brewed black fruit, has lost its floral nature. Red fruits, on cusp before second stage. Tasty, has nice sinew. Tannins need till 2006; 2017–19.

1998 ★★ Mineral presence on bouquet; dry-toned year, cool texture. Bit medicinal, more flesh please. Air helps it to round. Leave till 2006; 2013–15. Last tasted Dec 2004.

DOMAINE VERNAY

Le Plany 69560 St-Cyr-sur-le-Rhône +33(0)474 531826

This domaine sits not far from Vienne's doorstep, to the extent that Daniel Vernay—no relation to the Vernays of Condrieu—feels he is on his own: a tall, almost beanpole man with silver hair, he says: "240 people lived here at St-Cyr 20 years ago; now there are 1,200, and not one *agriculteur* left, either."

It's a breezy spot 300 metres up, with a striking, sweeping view of the Rhône as it heads south. His cellars are outside the *appellation* zone, and his vineyards are all in the northern, schist area.

Daniel's grandfather grew vines and vegetables and reared animals, the grape crop being sold to Vidal-Fleury and Chapoutier. Born in 1947, he first made wine in 1975, and works with his younger brother, Roland, and his niece

Gisèle, a slim, pretty brown-haired woman born in 1980. Gisèle studied wine at Mâcon and admits that she was always heading for the family domaine: "I was always keen," she says, as she returns from a morning's vine tying, her features fresh from the sun and the breeze. "I'm the youngest winegrower here at Côte-Rôtie, and I'm also the first woman to sit on the committee running the Growers Union," she says without pretension.

There is momentum here, therefore, and Gisèle is not going to continue with the few fruit trees they still work—a mixture of cherries, apricots, pears, and apples. There will be 5.5 hectares by about 2007, and they have also started to plant some of the old Sérine variety from the Gilbert Clusel supply. The bottle quantity of 15,000 is likely to rise as well, with less wine sold off in bulk.

There are around five small cultivators at St-Cyr who sell crop to Guigal, and the only other registered bottler in this *commune* is Christophe Semaska, who works the vineyards around Château de Montlys. The *lieux-dits* are less known as a result: around 3 ha on *Bourrier* (planted 1950s, 1978, late 1990s), and half a hectare on *Montlys* (1987). These are well topped up by 0.7 ha on the more central *Rozier* (1950s), 0.2 ha on *Rochains* (1960s), and just under 0.5 ha on *Les Grandes Places* (1950s).

The all-Syrah wine is made without ritzy techniques by Daniel and Gisèle together; about half the crop is destalked, and fermented in concrete vats that allow planks to be laid across to permit pumping over. Vinification lasts about two weeks, only natural yeasts are used, and the top temperature is around 30°C. In 2002 a basic system of cooling and heating was installed.

The young wine is aged for 18 months in *demi-muids* of 550 litres, the wood ranging from one to 10 years old. The various *lieu-dit* wines are assembled just before bottling, when fining and a light filtration are done.

CÔTE-RÔTIE

2003 ★★ Brewed, prolonged coffee/cocoa/mocha aroma. Restrained weight, fruit on palate

is brewed, tannins have some bite, though are ripe. Sound, in the midbracket of Rôties. From 2007; 2014–15.

2002 ★ Fruit gum, reductive bouquet, some breadth. Fruit on palate quite clear, but wine is limited. Acidity evident. Some length. Has always suggested it was hard work to achieve even this. Esp 2006–09.

2001 ★★ Fair red *robe;* some cooked black fruit, earthy touches. Quite classic. True style, gentle wine, some spice. Decent cut. From 2006 so can round itself; has gained with ageing. 2012–14.

2000 ★★ Cooked, soft black fruit aroma, grows; pretty berry fruit with some kick, runs on correctly. Some end tannin, dry towards the finale. 2010–12.

1999 ★★★ Nice depth on bouquet; clear stewed fruit, damson/chocolate. Quite solid, earthy too. From 2005–06; 2011–13.

Export 20 per cent (1) Belgium, (2) Great Britain, (3) USA

J. VIDAL-FLEURY

19 route de la Roche 69420 Ampuis +33(0)474 561018

See also Condrieu, Cornas, Crozes-Hermitage, Hermitage, St-Joseph.

The Guigal conning tower is now turning its attention towards the oldest *maison du vin* in the northern Côtes du Rhône, the House of Vidal-Fleury, which dates from 1781. Bought by Marcel and his father, Étienne Guigal, in 1984, this house has continued on a steady, if not spectacular way since then.

From 2006 there will be new ageing premises, just below the last Ampuis *commune* vineyards at Le Combard. These comprise a two-story building for raising the wine, plus a spruced-up nineteenth-century family house for receiving visitors—all in a year's work for the Guigal family!

The original 1980s purchase was the first Big Step from Guigal and set tongues a-wagging. The patriarch had been acquired by the worker. Étienne had started out in a most modest way, employed by Joseph Vidal-Fleury and rising to become his cellar master and then his head *vigneron*. After 15 years chez Vidal-Fleury he left in 1946 to set up his own company, Ets Guigal.

Joseph Vidal-Fleury died in 1976, and the company started to wobble. M. Vidal-Fleury had run the business for an incredible 68 years, and so had experienced the changing work methods and attitudes of three generations. An hour spent with him was a wonderful education, for he possessed a Pandora's box of knowledge and anecdotes that was impossible to rival. Throughout, his confidence in the old methods had remained unshaken.

As he would frankly admit: "It is difficult for me to talk about new things. I am a believer in ancient processes, which I esteem to be the best, the most honest, and the most efficient. Wine just needs a lot of care, cleanliness, racking, and a minimum of chemical products. Like that, one makes very good wine." These words would be spoken from the antique leather chair sat in by Thomas Jefferson, adding to their lustre.

The Vidal-Fleury vineyard portfolio represented a leap forward for the Guigals: 10 hectares, seven of them already established on the prime *Côtes Brune* and *Blonde*, vineyards such as *La Chatillonne* and *Le Clos* on the *Blonde*, and *La Turque*, *La Pommière*, and *Pavillon-Rouge* on the *Brune*. These are all names within names on today's cleaned-up map, but they form the basis for some of Guigal's finest wines.

The one single-vineyard wine that has remained with Vidal-Fleury is La Chatillonne, from a terraced, full-south area of just under one hectare dating from the late-1960s and containing 12 per cent Viognier, bang on the *Côte Blonde*. It is luscious, extremely fine wine with all the charm and probing red fruit intensity associated with the best Blonde cuvées—very much a child of its *terroir*. Around 4,000 to 5,000 bottles are made.

Until the mid-1970s, Vidal-Fleury produced strong-bodied, slow-maturing, classically made Côte-Rôtie La Rolande as well as an excellent red Hermitage. Any red Vidal-Fleury dated before 1971 can make a first-class buy if still found at auction.

The boss since the new start in 1986 has been Jean-Pierre Rochias, a native of St-Étienne who worked first in the merchant trade at Châteauneuf-du-Pape, then at the House of Cordier in Bordeaux. He has tightened up the working practices and vinification methods and renewed all the oak ageing barrels. He is an experienced scout for the wines that form the main part of this business, including St-Joseph and Crozes, and also Côtes du Rhône from the southern Rhône. These are shipped in for wood ageing once they have finished their malolactic fermentations.

He likes finesse in his wines and cites the Syrah from the Gard *département* as an example. "In recent years, this has become very rounded by and large," he says in his sonorous tones. "It has greater acidity and a softer feel than the wines from the more rocky Vaucluse."

The Vidal-Fleury wines are released after longer-than-usual ageing, and Jean-Pierre makes an important observation on this: "If I were a young man again, I would study how to work with wood, how to master that. Everyone knows how to vinify now—that's not an issue. But wood ageing is all empirical—it's not technical like winemaking."

The two Côte-Rôties are aged quietly in 30 hl barrels for up to three years. The duration varies according to the vintage: the 2000 Chatillonne was bottled before the 1999, for instance. Only two rackings would normally be done. The Brune et Blonde (30,000 bottles) is made only from Guigal vineyards, with no outside sources. Its Syrah averages 40 years in age, and it contains 3 to 5 per cent Viognier. It is fined and filtered. "I think of the Médoc when I taste the Brune et Blonde," says Jean-Pierre Rochias, "and St-Émilion when I try the Chatillonne."

CÔTE-RÔTIE BRUNE ET BLONDE

2001 (BARREL) ★★★ Some pine/mineral/leather aromas, very vintage style; good chewy matter, plums, tar/pine end. Character to come, nice end tannins, minerality. From 2008; 2018–20.

2000 ★★★ Hearty, fat, *cassis* aroma, leather edges; openly rich, juicy stewed black fruit. Touch prune, tannin at end. Easy to like, rather stylish. From 2006; 2014–17.

1999 ★★★ Soft black fruit aroma, a bosky side to it; squeezy, cooked fruit, jam effect. Spice/licorice end. Nice clean, fine wine. From 2005–06; 2013–15.

CÔTE-RÔTIE LA CHATILLONNE

2000 ★★★★ Soft, violet, floral/pitch nose—classic. Ripe stewed plum fruit with grainy side; interesting mix of *gras* and mineral. Warm, generous from 2006; 2016–18.

1999 ★★★★ Oily, herbal/minty nose, good potential; stylish red fruit, nice local fullness. Good warm texture; thyme here, mint/licorice at end. Persistent. Tannins need till 2006–07; 2017–21.

Export 65 per cent (1) USA, (2) Canada, (3) Denmark

GÉRARD VILLANO

111, RN86 69420 Condrieu +33(0)474 598764

See also Condrieu, St-Joseph.

Gérard Villano likes his red wines to be natural and not interfered with by outside agents. He is happy to declaim, in a suitably loud voice given his robust frame, and often in a growers' meeting, "You can make concentrated wine without using new oak. Indeed, I find new oak vexes me considerably."

So his 18 months of ageing is done in casks of eight to 15 years old. It is taken from his 0.55 ha on the *Coteaux de Semons* and contains 10 per cent Viognier. Sixty-five per cent of the vines date from 1991, the rest from the early 1950s.

The bunches are fermented whole in fibreglass vats over an average of two weeks; he has been trying a four-to-five-day cool maceration so the Syrah can start off slowly, then gradually move up to 26°C. He does a manual *pigeage* with a wooden grill pushed down on to the cap,

and a *remontage* at the end of the fermentation. The wines are fined and lightly filtered before bottling.

CÔTE-RÔTIE

2002 ★ Light, floral aroma. Gentle, soft wine—clear fruit, some roundness. Length OK. Unpretentious and aromatic, no great core; early wine. 2009–11.

2001 (CASK) ★★ Truffle, burnt soil, violet bouquet; mint/raspberry with fair weight; nicely juiced, live licorice finish. Honest, genuine wine in a punchy way. Esp 2005–06; 2010–12.

2000 ★★ Oily, pine, *crème de cassis* aromas; well-founded blackberry taste, decent chewy, quite rich end. A sweat-and-toil wine, not one smarmed out by a press-button operator. Good oily end. 2010–12.

FRANÇOIS VILLARD

Montjoux 42410 Saint-Michel-sur Rhône +33(0)474 568360

See also Condrieu, St-Joseph.

"It's a *catastrophe*," declares François Villard. "Too many people want my Brocarde Côte-Rôtie, and I don't have enough to sell—I've only ever made 1,200 bottles a year since I started it in 1995."

His solution is to move into the *négoce* business of buying grapes and vinifying them himself. Since 2002 he has bought harvest, mostly Syrah, from 1.3 hectares of the *lieux-dits Fongeant, Grands-Taillis,* and *Côte Baudin,* adding in 2004 his first usable crop from *Le Plomb,* a vineyard he started to plant in 2000.

Looking to the future, François has also rented a 2.1 ha plot that needed clearing on *Le Plomb,* with Pierre Gaillard and Yves Cuilleron; they have 0.7 ha each, which will be on stream by 2006. His emphasis is therefore on the schist areas from the *Brune* up towards Verenay.

His merchant wine is named "Le Gallet Blanc" (8,000 bottles) after his vineyard chief, Frédéric, from whom he buys harvest. The Brocarde wine comes from a postage stamp plot of

0.22 ha; its Viognier content can run between 8 and 15 per cent Viognier.

The crop is usually just 30 per cent destemmed, although all the 2002 had to be done. Vinification lasts three weeks in steel, using only natural yeasts. Having performed twice-daily *pigeages* and *remontages* for some years, François cut back the *pigeages* from the 2004 level. He also cut down the final week's vat heating to below the 35°C previously exercised. These are good signs. "My tendency is to make less firm wines than before," confirms François. I could embrace him for that!

Ageing lasts 23 months in new oak. Until 1996 only half the casks were new. There is fining but no filtration.

CÔTE-RÔTIE LE GALLET BLANC

2004 (CASKS) ★★(★) Direct, broad, open aroma. Fruit is well structured, broadens mid-palate. Sound length, rich enough towards finish. Open early on. Only 3 per cent Viognier this year. Esp from 2008; 2015–17.

2003 (CASK) ★★★ Brooding, licorice/violet/smoky oak bouquet. Brewed damson style flavour; mineral side to finish. Big scale, for New World wine lovers. Looser, more varied by 2007; 2017–20.

2002 ★★ Minted, grilled black aromas, bit stern. Dark fruit, licorice palate, could have more middle, some width. Contains 15 per cent Viognier, 85 per cent destemmed, and some *saignée* for extra colour. From late 2005; 2011–13.

CÔTE-RÔTIE LA BROCARDE

2004 (CASKS) ★★(★) Scented, gamey and smoky aroma, fair persistence. Interesting mix of chocolate and brewed fruit, has a farmyard effect. Later picking gives a more raisin/prune aspect at the end. Can roll along, esp from 2009. 2019–21.

2002 Crop went into Gallet Blanc.

2001 ★★ Overtly oaked nose, fair black berried fruit with it. Decent weight of flavour, ends oaky, which adds to the tannins. Leave well alone till 2007 or so; 2015–17.

2000 ★★ Ripe, oily aromas, some damp/violet; quite warm red fruits, pretty full. Dries on second half; this is a worry; rather taut, hasn't evolved as expected. 2009–10.

THIÉRRY VILLARD

69420 Ampuis +33(0)474 561501

Dominique Villard is the daughter of Adolphe Royet, who was always a little outside the main limelight at Côte-Rôtie and who retired in 1997. Adolphe's son-in-law Thiérry Villard comes from Ampuis and worked as a welder until moving into wine. His family's business was vegetable selling, with a few vines as well.

A robust man in his early 40s with a bronzed face and a relaxed way, Thiérry worked his father's vines from 1989, helping him out in his spare time. From 1997 until 2002 he worked in the two jobs—welder and grower—to defray some of the costs of building up the domaine. Now he sells half his crop and 20 per cent of his wine to Guigal, the rest in bottle. The bottle proportion is growing.

There are almost three hectares, 75 per cent on *Maison Rouge* at Tupin (1975), from Adolphe Royet, the rest on the *Côte Blonde* (1991), a plot that had to be reclaimed and planted from scratch. There is 5 per cent Viognier.

The crop is destalked, and the wine receives a three-week vinification with the use of yeasts and modern techniques. Wood ageing in *demi-muids* of 600 litres lasts 14 months. Thiérry fines but doesn't filter.

The wine is called "Coteaux des Maisons Rouges." It may show more charm if left until around five to six years old. Thiérry has plans to develop his holdings into Seyssuel north of Vienne, and to make a Viognier *vin de pays* as well.

CÔTE-RÔTIE COTEAUX DES MAISONS ROUGES

2002 (CASK) Quiet, light early wine, light black fruit.

2001 Quite peppery, direct black fruit bouquet; dark flavour, rather stern, tarry; attack better than finish.

2000 Quite full, earthy nose, bit of game; medium weight, stewed fruit, dry finish. Bit plain.

VINS JEAN-LUC COLOMBO

La Croix des Marais 26600 La Roche-de-Glun +33(0)475 841710

See also Condrieu, Cornas, Crozes-Hermitage, Hermitage, St-Joseph, St-Péray.
Jean-Luc Colombo's merchant business buys young wine from the northern site of *Rozier* and raises it for 18 months in 20 per cent new oak, 80 per cent one-to-two-year-old casks. The wine is called "La Divine" and was produced in 2000 and 2001, but not in 2002.

It reflects the tight textures of the schist and contains some dark, peppery fruit. Usually it is a wine to drink from four or five years onwards, with a life of perhaps 12 years or so.

CÔTE-RÔTIE LA DIVINE

2000 ★ Smoked red fruits, tight jam aroma. Cooked dark fruits with some dry influences; end pepper. Not that fresh. Length only fair. From 2006; 2010–12.

LES VINS DE VIENNE

Bas Seyssuel 38200 Seyssuel +33(0)474 850452

See also Condrieu, Cornas, Crozes-Hermitage, Hermitage, St-Joseph, St-Péray.
The trio of Villard, Cuilleron, and Gaillard produce a *négoce* wine called Les Essartailles. This is 80 per cent crop from five sources, vinified at their premises in Seyssuel, plus 20 per cent bought-in wine from three suppliers.

Les Vins de Vienne works with northern and southern Rhône wines—a full range in the north, and Châteauneuf-du-Pape, Gigondas, Vacqueyras, Visan, Cairanne, and Côtes du Rhône in the south. On average they sell 200,000 bottles, the wines raised at Seyssuel.

The northern Rhône reds are a mix of crop (St-Joseph, Côte-Rôtie) and wine purchase (the rest). The casks are taken to the domaines before the malos have occurred. The Côte-Rôtie and the St-Joseph *rouges* are vinified in steel vats, with cap punching and pumping-over, the whole process lasting three to four weeks. Destemming is done only if necessary, with a split jury here: "Pierre Gaillard likes to destem because he likes finesse and aroma, and a silky side in his wine," says Yves Cuilleron. "François Villard and I prefer to leave the grapes alone— I like a robust side in my wines so they can keep."

The reds, which are produced in lots of around 5,000 to 10,000 bottles, are aged for 18 months, in new or very young oak. The house style is for overtly wooded wines.

The white wines are made from purchased grapes. Cask fermentation is followed by raising for a few months, with stirring of the lees. An ample style is sought.

The Côte-Rôtie Les Essartailles is pure Syrah and about half comes from the northern schist area, half from the loose granite further south. It is aged for the 18 months in 80 per cent new oak, the rest of the wood one to two years old. 12,000 bottles are produced.

CÔTE-RÔTIE LES ESSARTAILLES

2003 (CASK) ★★★★ Decent schist style bouquet; has cool flint in the violet/black fruit. Black fruit, peppery tang on palate, is rich, has a southern warm finish. Soaked berries, tannins evident. Modern wine, is sound, has potential. From 2007; 2017–19.

2001 ★ Hidden nose, firm tones; some black fruit; oak makes the wine firm for a Côte-Rôtie. Overtly dry, touch stern ending.

2000 ★★ Roasted fruit, lost its floral side, light pepper nose; now upright, tightening, quite warm red berry finish. Firm, schist style wine. Cool texture, can broaden. From 2006–07; 2011–12.

CÔTE-RÔTIE VINTAGES

Earlier exceptional vintages: 1953, 1952, 1949, 1947, 1945, 1929

1955 Excellent, charming wines.

1956 Mediocre.

1957 Very good.

1958 Mediocre.

1959 Excellent, exceptional balance and finesse.

1960 Poor.

1961 Excellent, wonderfully broad wines.

1962 Good. Gentle wines.

1963 Poor. A frost-hit year.

1964 Excellent.

1965 Poor.

1966 Very good. Wines that needed time.

1967 Very good, although less full-bodied than 1966.

1968 Mediocre, although a successful Guigal La Mouline.

1969 Excellent, truly memorable. A tiny crop, wines on a par with 1961, and maybe even greater finesse. Outstanding Guigal La Mouline.

1970 Very good. Gentle, well-balanced wines. Wonderful La Mouline.

1971 Excellent. Big, warm, and full wines.

1972 Mediocre. Poorly balanced, high-acidity wines, faded early.

1973 Good. A huge crop; well-balanced wines, mostly over by now.

1974 Mediocre. A second large crop. Light wines.

1975 Mediocre. Smallish crop, light wines. Best from Jasmin, Guigal.

1976 Very good. Full flavoured, they lived well, esp Guigal.

1977 Mediocre. Too much acidity; only easy wines for early drinking.

1978 Excellent, nay wonderful. Immense wines, packed with flavour. A hot September was vital. Note all the Guigal range, esp La Mouline and La Landonne, Gentaz-Dervieux and Jasmin.

1979 Fair. Soft wines from many, like Émile Champet and Jasmin. Excellent, long-lived Brune et Blonde, and La Landonne from Guigal, latter more exuberant than La Mouline.

1980 Fair. Easy wines short on tannin. No great depth. Best: Jasmin and La Landonne, La Mouline—both need drinking now.

1981 Mediocre. Rain during harvest sorted out the good and bad vinifiers. Good, short-term wines from Jasmin and Rostaing. The best were the concentrated wines of Gentaz-Dervieux and Guigal La Mouline.

1982 Good. A very dry, hot summer and intense heat during the harvest led to problems of overheated vats. Smaller-grower wines (no cooling equipment) prone to jammy flavours. A few very good cuvées: these accentuate finesse. Best: Jasmin (early bottling), Gentaz-Dervieux, Guigal (Brune et Blonde, La Mouline). La Landonne the most robust and backward of Guigal's Big Three. Drink up most wines.

1983 Very good. Powerful, chewy, tannic wines. As in 1982, harvesting in extreme heat, around 25 September, with further problems of overheated vats. Very good depth and notable concentration in the best cuvées. Very Rhône, no hint of Burgundy this year. Note: Gilbert Clusel, Gentaz-Dervieux, Joseph Jamet, Pierre Barge, Delas Seigneur de Maugiron, Guigal—La Mouline (very typical, lovely length, balance), La Landonne (great balance, intense, cooked fruit concentration, still in good, live form).

1984 Poor. A late flowering, lack of August and September sun, and high rainfall, so poor ripening. A small crop gave lean, light-coloured, often astringent wines. A few honourable exceptions: Burgaud, Jasmin, and Guigal's well-weighted La Mouline. Drink up.

1985 Excellent. A vintage of great all-round appeal, combining the merits of fleshy, succulent fruit with firm, ripe tannins and a delightful balance. The success was widely spread. The spring was quite dry, the summer very dry, and having been a month behind at the end of a very hard winter, the vines were only a week behind the schedule of a normal year when harvested. The wines blossomed with the great charm of a "singing" vintage. They are now starting to tire.

Note: Gentaz-Dervieux, Pierre Barge, Joseph Jamet for longevity, and Guigal's La Mouline and La Landonne (remarkable length on both).

1986 Good. A large crop, hit by rot and at times low ripeness. Acidity levels were above average. Careful sorting was needed, and then patient cellaring so the tannins and acids could meld together with the content. Note: Jasmin (elegant), Albert Dervieux (hearty Viallière, Fontgent) and the most solid wines from Burgaud, Gentaz-Dervieux, and Guigal's Big Three. La Landonne is perhaps the winner of the trio and can live past 2006. Drink up to avoid dry finishes.

1987 Mediocre. A difficult year—a variable summer, below-average temperatures, and more rain than desirable. Careful crop selection needed. The best were middle-weight, elegant wines with enough tannic support to keep them going for 10 years or so. Others were mean, and low on core. Note: Émile Champet, Joseph Jamet, Jean-Michel Gérin, Guigal La Landonne, Vidal-Fleury La Chatillonne.

1988 Very good. A smaller crop than even the rot-affected 1987, and wines that started with stern tannins through the drought conditions. Some fruit failure and hail at flowering. Harvesting started around 21 September. The wines were naturally full and bore a traditional strength, with game and animal notes developing as they aged. They finish with some dry minerality now, and are ideal for autumn–early winter dishes. They can live for 18 to 25 years.

★★★★★ Guigal La Landonne/La Turque, J. Jamet

★★★★ Burgaud, J-M Gérin Champin le Seigneur, Guigal Brune et Blonde/La Mouline, Rostaing Blonde

★★★ Gentaz-Dervieux, J-M Gérin Les Grandes Places, Jasmin, B. Levet, de Vallouit Les Roziers

★★ G. Barge, Delas Seigneur de Maugiron, Vidal-Fleury Chatillonne

1989 Good to very good. Another very hot and dry year, the drought hurting the vines until some welcome rain on 10 September. The *ban des vendanges* was called on 15 September, the earliest in 40 years. A larger crop than 1988 gave some very good wines, but they can be uneven. Some lack intensity and can be a little discordant. The best carry warm aromas now, and their searching tannins have blended in well, their breadth placing them ahead of 1988. Drink them towards 2008–12. Others have faded rather quickly.

★★★★★★ Guigal La Pommière/ La Mouline/La Landonne

★★★★★ Vidal-Fleury Chatillonne

★★★★ Burgaud, Chapoutier Mordorée, Gentaz-Dervieux, Guigal La Turque

★★★ Chapoutier, P. Gaillard, J-M Gérin Les Grandes Places, Guigal Brune et Blonde, Jasmin, Rostaing Blonde

1990 Good; very good in places. Some wines lacked balance and showed the effects of another year of drought, when a full, balanced ripening was not always easy to achieve. Maturity on the best slope sites was at times blocked, and the plateau vines from less noble spots did better. Flowering was a shade earlier than usual, but harvesting passed the 100-day rule in many cases due to the slow ripening. A section of the wines was medium weight, not especially tannic, and suitable for early drinking: flavours were a little stretched, fruit not clear-cut. The best are full, hearty, and a little obvious, with stewed fruits and forest aromas mingling now. They can live until 2010–14. Guigal picked later than nearly everyone—in 1990, with its sustained heat, he waited until 29 September, against 15 to 20 September for his neighbours.

★★★★★ Guigal La Mouline/La Turque/ La Landonne, Jasmin

★★★★ Clusel-Roch Les Grandes Places, Delas Seigneur de Maugiron, Gentaz-Dervieux

★★★ G. Barge, Burgaud, J-M Gérin
Les Grandes Places, Jamet

★★ E. & J. Champet, Chapoutier,
P. Gaillard, Jamet, Rostaing
Blonde/La Landonne

★ de Vallouit Les Roziers

1991 Very good. Underrated quality in an off year for Bordeaux—often the sign for Rhône fans to reach for the chequebook. Drought in July and August hurt the vines. Harvesting started at the end of September and was affected by very heavy rain on 29 September and 6–7 October. Often high levels of alcohol—several growers had to ask permission to be above 13°. The wines were awkward at first, appearing to lack intensity, and carrying uneasy levels of tannic acidity. They settled down well and have integrated into a complex assembly of clear fruit, sinewy, interesting tannins, and varied, second-stage aromas. They finish long and are classic in style. The best still have more to give and can live towards 2015–18.

★★★★★★ Guigal La Mouline

★★★★★ Guigal La Turque/La Landonne

★★★★ G. Barge, Clusel-Roch

★★★ Burgaud, Chapoutier Mordorée,
Paul Jaboulet Jumelles, Jamet,
Rostaing Blonde/La Landonne

★★ Chapoutier, Guigal Brune et
Blonde, Jaboulet Vercherre Brune
et Blonde, Jasmin, Rostaing,
de Vallouit Les Roziers

★ Gangloff

1992 Mediocre. Flowering ran over three weeks, which meant co-ordinated picking was difficult. June was indifferent, and rot started in early September. Two weeks of good weather followed, but on September 22 there were 50 mm (2 in.) of rain. Harvesting was done in fine weather after that. At least the crop was nearly ripe and held more degree than 1993. The wines lack middle body, and carry jammy textures, with no real bite. Some are plain dilute.

The best have cobbled-together juiced, red fruits that come across in an undemanding, squeezy way. Others project dried flavours as they age. Drink them up.

★★★★★ Guigal La Turque/La Landonne

★★★★ Guigal La Mouline

★★★ de Boisseyt Chol Côte Blonde,
Jamet

★★ Burgaud, L. Drevon, Jasmin,
de Vallouit Les Roziers

★ Delas Seigneur de Maugiron,
B. Levet, M. Ogier

1993 Poor for many; fair for the committed, well-equipped few. Flowering went well, but June lacked sun and was rainy at times. From mid-August it rained on and off for a month, leaving a mix of rotten and unripe grapes. Once the sun reappeared, some grapes became very overblown. Harvesting had to be done very fast, but in another month-long rain. "My worst ever year," B. Burgaud said. So dilute was some crop, just 9°, that the allowed degree was lowered. Light, pale, vegetal, and aggressive were many wines. The best, though, rose above the dull 1992s, and have more character. Their initial edginess has worn off and they carry medium-weight, grainy, mineral flavours. Bouquets have reached a peppery, dry-leafed stage. Drink them soon after opening, before their length starts to dwindle. The Guigal Big Three can live for 20-plus years.

★★★★★ Guigal La Turque

★★★★ Guigal La Mouline/La Landonne,
Rostaing Blonde

★★★ Rostaing La Landonne

★★ G. Barge, Clusel-Roch Les Grandes
Places, P. Gaillard, Gangloff,
B. Levet, M. Ogier

★ Burgaud, Clusel-Roch, Jasmin

1994 Good. Budding was very early in mid-March, but April was cold. The summer was variable, leading to more vineyard treatments than usual. Ripening was fair, but rain and grey weather on and off for two weeks from September 19 provoked rot and difficult harvest conditions. Modern cellar methods helped to ensure some wines avoided being too hard.

The wines emerged rather tricky—the aromas a little strict, at times edgy, the best spiced and dry toned. They are midweight, and took time to loosen their firm tannins and express some integration. Some lack flesh, and it was a year for the best sites and the oldest vines. These wines run along some of the lines of 1991, but on a lesser scale and without the same depth and balance. They can live towards 2007–15.

★★★★★ Chapoutier Mordorée, Rostaing Blonde

★★★★ G. Barge Côte Brune, Guy Bernard Vieilles Vignes, Chapoutier, Clusel-Roch classic/Les Grandes Places, Rostaing classic/La Viallière

★★★ L. Drevon, P. Gaillard, J-M Gérin Champin le Seigneur, Guigal La Mouline, Jasmin, de Vallouit Les Roziers

★★ G. Barge Du Plessy, Cuilleron, Gangloff, Jamet classic/Côte Brune

★ Guigal Brune et Blonde, M. Ogier

1995 Very good. A small crop, hit by a near-tornado in July and eight to 10 days of September rain. Harvesting had to be done quickly, since the rain returned. The vintage was marked by obvious, at first demanding tannins, which were not always as ripe as assumed. It is a robust year, with the best wines holding a well-layered power that is well founded inside the broadly full matter. Flavours are dark and dense, and the wines will live and develop well. Expect the best to run for 20-plus years—they are on the upright side.

★★★★★★ Guigal La Mouline/La Turque/La Landonne, Rostaing Blonde

★★★★★ Rostaing La Landonne

★★★★ G. Barge Côte Brune, G. Bernard Vieilles Vignes, Clusel-Roch, Paul Jaboulet Jumelles, Rostaing

★★★ G. Barge Du Plessy, Clusel-Roch Les Grandes Places, Dom Corps de Loup, L. Drevon, Guigal Brune et Blonde/Château d'Ampuis, Jamet, Jasmin, M. Ogier

★★ G. Bernard, Cuilleron Bassenon

1996 Quite good. A year that needed patience from drinkers because of the high acidities. The crop was too big, and if growers didn't cut back during the summer, they faced a lack of ripe content and low degrees. The weather was dry from July, which blocked the ripening on some vines. September was dry but not very sunny, with cold nights.

This is a mineral vintage, where the flavours are dry textured and not deep-seated. Some wines have made good progress, providing they had enough stuffing to smother the acidity. They are now at a stage of cloves/violet aromas, with red fruits and dry, peppered finishes. Textures are cool. Drink with autumn–winter food. The most robust can live for towards 25 years.

★★★★★ Guigal La Turque

★★★★ Burgaud, Guigal La Mouline/La Landonne

★★★ Clusel-Roch classic/Les Grandes Places, M. Ogier

★★ G. Barge DuPlessy/Côte Brune, P. Gaillard Rose Pourpre, Gangloff, Jamet, Jasmin, G. Vernay, F. Villard Brocarde

★ Chapoutier, P. Gaillard Brune et Blonde, Guigal Brune et Blonde

1997 Good, a plush year. The key was the very hot, dry weather of the second half of August, both days and nights. Acidity levels were low, the grapes very ripe. These are warm, easy, soft wines that deliver pleasure with few hidden corners. They are rich with often jam textures and open aromas, with plenty of floral scents in evidence. The wines have always been open, a little flattering even. "They never went through a closed spell," explains Michel Chapoutier. Some are overripe, but certainly there are no hidden corners. They are versatile with a variety of foods, given their sweet textures. Many should be drunk before about 2014.

★★★★★★ Guigal La Landonne, Jamet Côte Brune

★★★★★ Guigal Château d'Ampuis/La Mouline, Paul Jaboulet Jumelles

★★★★ Chapoutier Mordorée, Delas La Landonne, Guigal La Turque

★★★ Burgaud, Clusel-Roch classic/Les Grandes Places, Garon, J-M Gérin Les Grandes Places, Jamet, Jasmin, Dom du Monteillet Les Grandes Places, M. Ogier

★★ G. Barge Du Plessy/Côte Brune, Dom Bonserine Moutonnes, Delas Seigneur de Maugiron, Gallet, M. Ogier Belle Hélène

★ Bonserine Côte Brune/La Garde, Chapoutier, Guigal Brune et Blonde, F. Villard Brocarde

1998 Good, but an awkward year. Bad frost hit on Easter Monday, especially on the high slopes as well as the low plain areas. It was a severe, wintery frost, not a spring one. There was also hail, and yields were low. Ripening was not easy, and while growers waited, acidity levels fell. Early September rain helped to expand the grapes, but some growers were forced to chaptalise to raise the degree. A year that may be underestimated—if well worked, the tannins play a strong role and are softening up in a very becoming way. There is decent flesh in the best wines, but some do skip a beat in midpalate and can be a little edgy. A drier-toned year overall, whose evolution may occur in fits and starts. The top wines can live for 20-plus years.

★★★★★★ Guigal La Mouline

★★★★★ G. Barge Côte Brune, Guigal La Turque/La Landonne, Rostaing Blonde

★★★★ Clusel-Roch Les Grandes Places, Delas La Landonne, Guigal Brune et Blonde/Château d'Ampuis, Jamet, M. Ogier Belle Hélène

★★★ G. Barge Du Plessy, Burgaud, Chapoutier Bécasses/Mordorée, Clusel-Roch, Delas Seigneur de Maugiron, Garon, Jamet Côte Brune, Jasmin, M. Ogier, Rostaing classic/La Landonne

★★ Duclaux, J-M François, Paul Jaboulet Jumelles, J-M Stéphan Vieilles Vignes, G. Vernay Maison Rouge

★ Dom Bonserine La Garde/ Moutonnes, Dom Corps de Loup

1999 Wonderful, a Mighty Year, likened by the old-timers to 1947. Some hail in May and on June 2—just before flowering—served to do some of the *vendange en vert* work, cutting the crop back. In the northern sector, some growers lost at least 75 per cent—Clusel Roch on *Les Grandes Places,* for instance—and in the south, Semons was also hit. Regular but not large rainfalls through the hot summer were beneficial. The remaining grapes became very high in sugars, and ripening was so good on the central sites that the crop had reached 13.5° to 14° by early September—unheard of precocity. "In one week we gained 2°, twice what is normal, but we had to harvest fast to keep the acidity," D. Duclaux said.

The wines were straightforward to vinify, and are atypical; many display a Hermitage-style richness and an unusual oiliness. One could consider this to be a weather-climate vintage, not a *terroir* one. Jamet consider their wine will not show *terroir* aspects until much before 2010–12. So bountiful was nature that the wines of those growers who did little active work in the vineyards started out on a similar level to the hard workers, but ageing has begun to reveal more nuances between these uniformly full, warm wines with their swirling, ripe bouquets. Wonderful textures—the south came a-visiting this year.

★★★★★★   J-M Gérin La Landonne, Guigal La Mouline/La Turque/La Landonne, Jamet Côte Brune

★★★★★   G. Barge Côte Brune, Guy Bernard Vieilles Vignes, Burgaud, Chapoutier Mordorée, Clusel-Roch Les Grandes Places, Delas La Landonne, Duclaux, Garon, J-M Gérin Champin le Seigneur/Les Grandes Places, Guigal Château d'Ampuis, Jamet, Jasmin, M. Ogier Belle Hélène

★★★★   G. Barge Du Plessy, Guy Bernard, E. Champet, Delas Seigneur de Maugiron, Dumazet, Guigal Brune et Blonde, B. Levet, Rostaing, J-M Stéphan Vieilles Vignes, Vidal-Fleury Chatillonne

★★★   Clusel-Roch, Dom Corps de Loup, B. David, Paul Jaboulet Jumelles, Lafoy et Gasse, M. Ogier, GAEC Daniel Vernay, G. Vernay Maison Rouge, Vidal-Fleury Brune et Blonde, Vins de Vienne Essartailles

★★   Chapoutier Bécasses, J-M François

2000 Good, but not especially profound, wines. There was damage at Tupin from an enormous early June storm—soil slippage. There was a large budding, and by early July growers had to drop grapes. Even then, yields were high. On the *Brune*, drought slowed ripening. The summer was not consistently warm, and while growers therefore waited for the crop to ripen, rain appeared around 25 September. There was some rot.

Colour levels were indifferent, and growers in the southern areas bled early juice off (*saignée*) to boost them. Acidity levels can be above average, but the hope must be that some

wines come together as they age and gradually grow in depth. "They show a lot of aromatic finesse, and are more peppered than 1999," G. Barge reported. This is an open year of midweight wines but is not considered a top do by growers who see it some way behind their 1999s and 2001s, lacking their potential and complexity. There are wines that lack cut and nuance, with jam flavours early on. Tannins appear supple, but Philippe Guigal warns, "be careful about this vintage's amiable side—we find our wines are gaining in structure with the wood process." The leading, fullest wines should show well for up to 20 years, but should be monitored.

★★★★★   J-M Gérin Les Grandes Places, Guigal La Turque/La Landonne, Rostaing Blonde, J-M Stéphan Vieilles Vignes

★★★★   Clusel-Roch Les Grandes Places, Guigal La Mouline, Jamet Côte Brune, J-M Stéphan Coteaux de Tupin, Vidal-Fleury Chatillonne

★★★   G. Barge Du Plessy/Côte Brune, Dom Bernard Vieilles Vignes, P. & C. Bonnefond Côte Rozier, Dom Bonserine La Garde, Burgaud, E. Champet, Chapoutier Mordorée, Clusel-Roch, Cuilleron Terres Sombres, Dom Corps de Loup, Duclaux, Gangloff Sereine Noire, Gasse Lafoy Sophia, J-M Gérin Champin le Seigneur/ La Landonne, Guigal Brune et Blonde, Jamet, Jasmin, Y. Lafoy RG, B. Levet regular/Péroline, Dom du Monteillet Les Grandes Places, M. & S. Ogier classic/ Belle Hélène, Dom de Rosiers, Rostaing classic/La Landonne, Saint-Cosme, J-M Stéphan, G. Vernay Maison Rouge, Vidal-Fleury Brune et Blonde

★★   C. Billon Brocarde, Dom Bonserine Sarrasine/Moutonnes,

Chapoutier Bécasses, B. David, Delas Seigneur de Maugiron, Dumazet, J-M François, P. Gaillard Rose Pourpre, Gallet, Gangloff Barbarine, Garon, R. Fernandez, GAEC Daniel Vernay, Villano, F. Villard Brocarde, Vins de Vienne Essartailles

★ Dom Bernard, Colombo Divine, Cuilleron Bassenon, A. François, Paul Jaboulet Jumelles, Dom Mouton, S. Pichat

2001 Excellent, a vintage of constant development after an edgy start. Spring rain slowed down the growing cycle. It was even more necessary to drop grapes than in 2000—a copious year that for Jasmin resulted in a full 40 hl/ha. The most rainy moment of the summer was 14 July; otherwise it was dry. Some cold in July slowed ripening. Helpful rain fell in early September, and ripening took time as the month was not very hot. Unusually, harvesting was done 120 days after flowering—not the rule-of-thumb 100 days. The polyphenols therefore ripened more from the wind and the drawn-out process than from any hot sun. Rain by the third week of September and more on 29 September brought rot to any late harvesters.

At first, acidity levels were prominent, but these integrated since there was enough flesh to match the vivacity. Matter in the wines has become good and deep. There are typical cooked fruits and some game aspects, and an appealing, lively side comes through. The growers expect these wines to live long, and talk often of 15 years or even more. They fly the flag for direct, clear-cut flavours rather than the stewed ones so often found now to suit certain market tastes. The gain in structure points to at least 20 years for the top names.

★★★★★ G. Barge Côte Brune, Guigal La Mouline/La Turque/La Landonne, Jamet Brune, M. & S. Ogier Belle Hélène/Lancement "terroir de Blonde," Rostaing Blonde

★★★★ G. Barge Du Plessy, Dom Bernard Vieilles Vignes, Dom Bonserine La Garde, Burgaud, Chapoutier Mordorée, Clusel-Roch Les Grandes Places, Delas La Landonne, Guigal Château d'Ampuis, Jasmin, C. Pichon, Rostaing La Landonne, J-M Stéphan Vieilles Vignes

★★★ C. Billon Brocarde, Dom Bonserine Moutonnes, E. Champet, J. Champet, Chapoutier Bécasses, Clusel-Roch, Cuilleron Bassenon/Terres Sombres, Dom Corps de Loup Paradis, Delas Seigneur de Maugiron, Duclaux, P. Gaillard Rose Pourpre, Gangloff Sereine Noire/Barbarine, Gasse Lafoy Vieilles Vignes, J-M Gérin Les Grandes Places, Paul Jaboulet Jumelles, Jamet, Jasmin, Y. Lafoy, B. Levet Péroline, Dom du Monteillet Les Grandes Places, Château de Montlys, M. & S. Ogier classic/Embruns, Rostaing, Saint-Cosme, J-M Stéphan Coteaux de Tupin, G. Vernay Blonde du Seign-eur, Vidal-Fleury Brune et Blonde

★★ Dom Bernard, Dom Bonserine Sarrasine, L. C. Brotte, B. Chambeyron, Dom Corps de Loup Corps de Loup, B. David, P. Gaillard, Garon, Gasse Lafoy Sophia, J-M Gérin Champin le Seigneur/La Landonne, Meffre Laurus, Dom Mouton, R. Niéro, J-M Stéphan, Dom de Rosiers, GAEC Daniel Vernay, Villano, F. Villard Brocarde

★ Dom Boucharey, P. Faury, R. Fernandez, Gallet, F. Gérard, S. Pichat, Vins de Vienne Essartailles

(★) A François, B. Levet

2002 Fair. April frost hit the northern, St Cyr sector. After a very, very hot June, the summer deteriorated, with storms and wet weather in

July and August until mid-September. Rot was a constant problem. "In July, we stripped leaves from the two sides of plants to try to fend off the rot," J-M Gérin recalled. The unusual blight of grape worm broke out from mid-August and paved the way for much rot. Waiting for the crop to ripen, the growers welcomed a fine second fortnight in September, but the rot peril forced their hand. Those who picked around 15 September found their wines lacked core, and the sticky effect of chaptalisation was evident in them as a result. Every day after, with very hot weather between 18 and 23 September, was vital. A lot of growers used up the full allowance of 2° alcohol to be added by chaptalisation. "It was a fighter's year—we were battling all the way through," said G. Villano, who threw away 30 per cent of his crop.

Often the wines are taut and unrelaxed; many were notably short on the palate at first, though some have come on. Few wines possess great depth, but the best are respectable, likely to drink well around 2008 or so. Several wines are not integrated and their finishes unconvincing. This could well act as a Wake-Up Year, one when growers had to get out, think, and act: they could not afford to be lazy or formulaic. With the advances of the past 10 years, it will be interesting to see how the wine pans out compared to 1993, the most devilish recent year. "In 1993, we weren't experienced in such conditons, but in 2002 we were ready, so we harvested much faster," said P. Guigal, whose yield was 37 per cent down. Not a year for the big domaines who send their workers on holiday in August!

★★★★ Guigal La Mouline/La Turque/ La Landonne

★★★ G. Barge Côte Brune, P. & C. Bonnefond Rochains, de Boisseyt-Chol Côte Blonde, Chapoutier Mordorée, Cuilleron Bassenon, P. Gaillard, B. Levet Péroline

★★(★) Burgaud, Delas Seigneur de Maugiron, Guigal, Dom du Monteillet Fortis

★★ G. Barge Du Plessy, Dom Bernard, J. Champet, Chapoutier Bécasses, Clusel-Roch, Cuilleron Terres Sombres, Dom Corps de Loup Paradis, Duclaux, R. Fernandez, A. François, P. Gaillard, Gangloff, Garon, J-M Gérin Les Grandes Places, Jamet, Jasmin, Y. Lafoy RG, B. Levet, Dom du Monteillet La Pèlerine, M. & S. Ogier classic/Les Embruns, J-M Stéphan, G. Vernay Blonde du Seigneur, F. Villard Gallet Blanc

★ C. Billon regular/Brocarde, P. & C. Bonnefond, Dom Bonserine Sarrasine, de Boisseyt-Chol Côte Blonde, B. Chambeyron, Dom Corps de Loup Corps de Loup, P. Faury, Gangloff, Gasse Lafoy Sophia, J-M Gérin Champin le Seigneur/La Landonne, Y. Lafoy, B. Levet, Château de Montlys, Dom Mouton, C. Pichon, Dom de Rosiers, Villano

(★) Dom Corps de Loup Marions-Les!, Gallet, S. Pichat, GAEC Daniel Vernay

2003 Good, some very good wines. An extreme vintage given the rasping summer heat that brought the earliest-ever harvest date, the *ban des vendanges* proclaimed on 23 August; the grandparent generation was used to October in their working day. The year started with the severe frost of 7 April, that caused some growers to lose 40 per cent of their crop. In the north, the GAEC Vernay lost 30 per cent that morning. Thereafter the theme of dry weather and steady heat, that ratcheted up in early August, brought smaller and smaller cropping.

B. Levet lost 35 per cent. "It wasn't hail," he said, "just lack of juice in the grapes. Our highest was 14.5° from *La Landonne*." There was hail at St-Cyr-sur-le-Rhône at the end of July to add to the woes there. To show how fast the ripening accelerated, the end of July prediction had been for harvesting around 10 September. It was a tough year for the Viognier, and levels were down in the wines of the southern sector.

The wines are deeply concentrated, with brewed, stewed flavours. "It's no surprise—my grapes were the size of blueberries," G. Barge declared. There was a definite challenge with fermentations, the risk of the wine turning volatile was high, and malolactics broke early and fast. Some growers had difficulty finishing the fermentation of the sugars, and vigilance in the cellar was vital. "For me, it's a year to drink young," says Bernard Burgaud. "There are dry tannins around from the cooked grapes." Certainly, there are wines with an oxidative tendency that means a dryness on the finish, while the oak also adds to that dryness in some. This year there are few seasonings like pepper present; flavours run more on brewed and stewed soaked-fruit/smoky lines, with jam and fruit gum tastes, also tar, chocolate, mocha, and olive—unusual associations for Côte-Rôtie. What is missing is the fully sustained, calm richness all the way through the wines—very few are truly persistent, or truly balanced. Bouquets can be high toned—the alcohol effect pushing through. The most enjoyable have a degree of orderliness or restraint even alongside their well-packed flavours. These atypical wines may live longer than some expect—but for most, 18 years will be near the limit.

★★★★★★ Guigal La Turque/La Landonne

★★★★★ Guigal La Mouline

★★★★ Clusel-Roch Grandes Places, Delas Landonne, Jasmin, Dom du Monteillet Grandes Places, M. & S. Ogier Belle Hélène, Vins de Vienne Essartailles

★★★ P. & C. Bonnefond classic/ Rochains, Dom Bonserine La Garde, L. Clerc Pont de Tupin, Clusel-Roch, Duclaux, P. Gaillard Rose Pourpre, Garon, Y. Lafoy, B. Levet, Dom du Monteillet Fortis, M. & S. Ogier Les Embruns/ Lancement, S. Pichat, C. Pichon, Saint-Cosme, F. Villard Gallet Blanc

★★(★) Dom Bonserine Sarrasine, Chapoutier Mordorée, R. Desbordes, Jamet, Meffre Laurus, Château de Montlys Fleur de Montlys, Dom Mouton, M. & S. Ogier classic, Dom de Rosiers

★★ G. Barge Côte Brune, Dom Bernard, Burgaud, B. Chambeyron, Dom Corps de Loup Corps de Loup, Delas Seigneur de Maugiron, P. Faury, A. François, P. Gaillard, Château de Montlys

★ G. Barge Du Plessy, P. & C. Bonnefond Côte Rozier, Dom Corps de Loup Marions-Les!/Paradis, GAEC Daniel Vernay

(★) Cuilleron Terres Sombres

2004 Good, and some wines will be very good. Super September was the story of the year. The first two weeks of February saw some days of 20°C—the vines surged along. Come early March, north wind and frosts arrived, but luckily, too early to damage the vines; their growth stagnated, and the cool spring stalled the Syrah more than the Viognier. Water reserves were then OK—the *Reynard* stream held water in early March. Flowering was at the usual early June time, but the summer was not especially hot. It continued very dry, and the vines started to show signs of fatigue, bearing in mind the stress of 2003. In late July, nights were fresh, influenced by the north wind. The *veraison*, when the grapes change colour, was later than normal in August because of the dry conditions—"there was a blockage," said B. Burgaud. Between 10 and 19 August there were 98 mm (3.8 in.) of rain in four falls. "The rainfalls accelerated the *veraison* and the inflation of the grapes, which meant that we had to clear the leaf cover severely," commented B. Levet. "The richer soils like *Moutonnes* with its clay were better off, also the *Blonde*," Jean-Paul Jamet said. The rain spurred ripening, and mercifully, no more fell for five weeks or more. A south wind in early September was succeeded by a north wind that helped the grapes to contract again after the rain. By mid-September the phenolic ripening was making progress, and there was little rot to worry about. Many growers were harvesting by 23 September.

The wines hold very clear fruit flavours; this appears to be a tender but classic vintage, with the charm of a late-developing year in store. Acidity levels are interesting, and the wines should not need large amounts of new oak— their beauty lies in their simplicity. Aromas can be spiced, while on the palate the wines carry direct appeal, with red fruits in evidence on first inspection and some underlying richness. This is likely to be a vintage that can evolve gracefully, achieve varied flavours and aromas, and

run for 15 to 20 years. The earlier wines will start to show well around 2008, with many coming on stream from 2009. "These are wines of very frank flavours," commented Philippe Guigal.

★★★★ J-M. Gérin La Landonne

★★★(★) Tardieu-Laurent

★★★ Y. Lafoy RG, Dom de Rosiers

★★(★) F. Villard Brocarde/Gallet Blanc

★★ Dom Bonserine Sarrasine, B. Chambeyron, Dom Corps de Loup Corps de Loup, J-M. Gérin Champin le Seigneur, Y. Lafoy, Château de Montlys Fleur de Montlys

(★) Dom Corps de Loup Marions-Les!

2

Condrieu

VIOGNIER BURST INTO wine drinkers' lives in the 1990s, but for many new converts it was probably thought to be a New World wine, or one with a largely New World pedigree. Indeed, the northern Rhône would have been well down the list of likely suspects, since Condrieu is only a speck of a town, and its hills above the west bank of the Rhône have never grown a lot of Viognier, even in its pre–First World War heyday.

People have taken to Viognier because it leads the charge for wines that are musky, opulent, heady, luxurious. It is a Charles II, not a Cromwellian grape. Its broad apricot, pear, and floral aromas swirl around the glass, its texture is smooth and oily, and there is a prolonged, broad final flourish that makes it sumptuous in its own right, a sensual prelude to food.

The story of this variety's resurrection is extraordinary. In 1971 Condrieu's plantation of Viognier amounted to just 12 hectares, or only 30 acres. Its neighbour Château-Grillet, then France's smallest single *appellation*, covered a mere 1.7 ha, or 4.2 acres. It wasn't planted elsewhere in France or abroad, so with 13.7 ha it was on the verge of extinction.

But some naughty foreign enthusiasts had smuggled out the odd cutting to their homelands, so taken were they by this singular wine. Josh Jensen is not a man to argue with anyway, his Nordic origin well apparent from his tall, broad frame. This young Viking traveller had fallen prey to the Viognier's charms.

In 1970 he was a student at Oxford University. His home was California. He had discovered Condrieu and the Viognier while holidaying in France; that autumn he went to help for two days on the harvest at Château-Grillet. "I fell in love with the Viognier thanks to my payment of three bottles of Château-Grillet!" he remembers.

In 1983 Josh planted what he calls some of the first "serious" amounts of Viognier in California—two acres (under one hectare). He selected soil as close as possible to the northern Rhône—decomposed granite and limestone, 90 miles south of San Francisco, 25 miles in from the ocean, and 2,200 feet altitude.

Josh has stayed with his Viognier, and his quality control on it is high enough for him not to have issued a 1998, for instance. But the two veritable American pioneers, whose small plant-

Condrieu

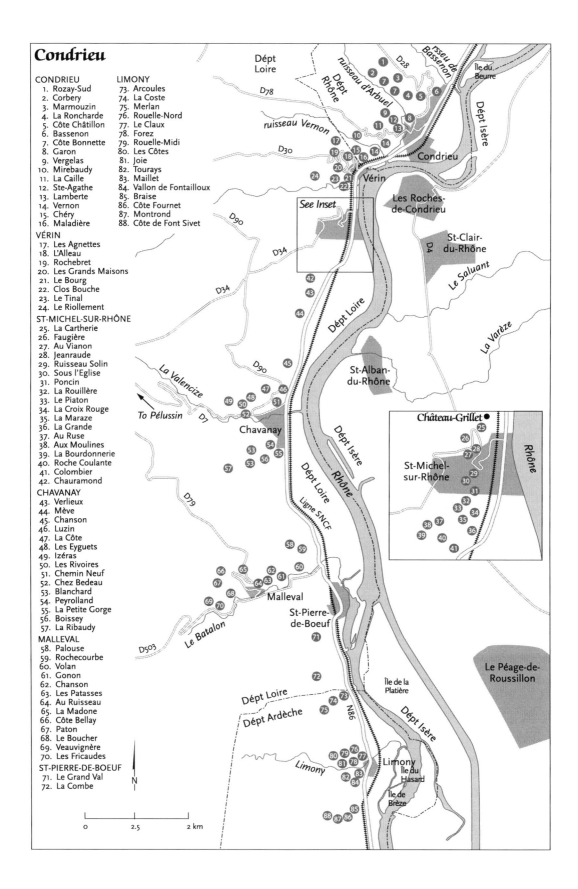

CONDRIEU
1. Rozay-Sud
2. Corbery
3. Marmouzin
4. La Roncharde
5. Côte Châtillon
6. Bassenon
7. Côte Bonnette
8. Garon
9. Vergelas
10. Mirebaudy
11. La Caille
12. Ste-Agathe
13. Lamberte
14. Vernon
15. Chéry
16. Maladière

VÉRIN
17. Les Agnettes
18. L'Alleau
19. Rochebret
20. Les Grands Maisons
21. Le Bourg
22. Clos Bouche
23. Le Tinal
24. Le Riollement

ST-MICHEL-SUR-RHÔNE
25. La Cartherie
26. Faugière
27. Au Vianon
28. Jeanraude
29. Ruisseau Solin
30. Sous l'Eglise
31. Poncin
32. La Rouillère
33. Le Piaton
34. La Croix Rouge
35. La Maraze
36. La Grande
37. Au Ruse
38. Aux Moulines
39. La Bourdonnerie
40. Roche Coulante
41. Colombier
42. Chauramond

CHAVANAY
43. Verlieux
44. Mève
45. Chanson
46. Luzin
47. La Côte
48. Les Eyguets
49. Izéras
50. Les Rivoires
51. Chemin Neuf
52. Chez Bedeau
53. Blanchard
54. Peyrolland
55. La Petite Gorge
56. Boissey
57. La Ribaudy

MALLEVAL
58. Palouse
59. Rochecourbe
60. Volan
61. Gonon
62. Chanson
63. Les Patasses
64. Au Ruisseau
65. La Madone
66. Côte Bellay
67. Paton
68. Le Boucher
69. Veauvignère
70. Les Fricaudes

ST-PIERRE-DE-BOEUF
71. Le Grand Val
72. La Combe

LIMONY
73. Arcoules
74. La Coste
75. Merlan
76. Rouelle-Nord
77. Le Claux
78. Forez
79. Rouelle-Midi
80. Les Côtes
81. Joie
82. Tourays
83. Maillet
84. Vallon de Fontailloux
85. Braise
86. Côte Fournet
87. Montrond
88. Côte de Font Sivet

ings occurred in 1981, both took out their Viognier in later years. Richard Minor of Ritchie Creek planted some vines on Spring Mountain in the Napa Valley, and a few weeks later, so did Bill Smith of La Jota, up on Howell Mountain nearby. Viognier never became a leading part of their more Cabernet portfolios.

Josh Jensen's Calera Viognier led the way in the United States, selling on the East Coast before others and gradually moving from being a hot, overcharged wine to a genuinely full one as the young vines grew up.

The United States has adopted the Viognier with open arms. In 2003, there were officially 2,089 acres (846 ha) in California—only about 40 times less than Chardonnay, but there you go! The Viognier Guild started in 1992 by a man from Georgia, Mat Garretson, has evolved into the annual Hospice du Rhône event held in Paso Robles and attended by growers from all over the world. Quality in the United States is improving all the time as the vines mature, but there are some danger signals—like the amount planted (one-fifth of California's total) on the fruit-bearing fertile lands of the Central Valley— jug wine capital of the state.

Now Viognier is grown commercially in countries like Australia, New Zealand, Italy, Chile, Greece, South Africa, the Valais in Switzerland, and the south of France—you name it. It's not just the obvious names now, either—Uruguay is growing Viognier, for instance, with the Toscanini brothers making a sound Viognier Reserva. And the august have joined in, too; in the south of France, the Domaine de Triennes is a joint venture between the principals of Burgundy's Domaine Dujac and Domaine de la Romanée Conti. Their Viognier is respectable, and will gain weight as the vines mature.

In California, Edna Valley and the Paso Robles area have become gathering points for progressive Rhône enthusiasts, the early pacesetter being John Alban, who produces two styles now, the more opulent Central Coast Viognier, and the more reserved Edna Valley Estate. Alban's fervour for Viognier is strong indeed: hearing of Yves Gangloff's loss of 75 per cent of his crop in 2003 through hail on the *Côte Bonnette* site, he suggested they make a wine together with Alban crop. Called Conversation, the wine was made with the help of e-mail. Gangloff communicated through his computer, sent Alban his Condrieu casks, and went to California for the final blending. In similar vein, Yves Cuilleron made a wine called Les Deux Cs with Morgan Clendenen—half his Condrieu, half her successful Cold Heaven.

Other notable names from California include Calera, Eberle, Garretson, Seth Kunin, McDowell, Frick Winery, Ojai (Ventura), Qupé (Santa Barbara), and even the large, but committed, Joseph Phelps operation. Way up north in the more temperate Washington State, Cayuse run by Frenchman Christopher Baron and McCrea Cellars have shown up well.

In Australia, Viognier is moving along at speed. In 2000, estimates were of around 50 hectares (123 acres) of Viognier planted, led by Yalumba, d'Arrenberg, Mitchelton (Central Victoria), Scarpantoni (McLaren Vale), Bannockburn (Geelong), Heathcote (Central Victoria), and Veritas (Barossa). By 2004 the area had grown to about 545 hectares (1,345 acres), about half of them planted in 2003 and 2004.

Yalumba, with a presence in the Barossa and Eden Valleys and Riverland, is far and away the biggest producer of the variety in Australia. Their Viognier vineyard has remained constant at 28 hectares since 2000, but purchases for their portfolio of Viognier wines that run from dry to sweet (noble rot) cover another 120 hectares.

Yalumba's pioneering of the variety stems from the curiosity of Peter Wall, their then production director who visited the Rhône in the early 1970s and became intrigued by the wines of Condrieu. Following his visit, a Viognier clone (free of leaf roll) was selected and imported from Montpellier. After quarantine, Yalumba started to mist propagate from this collection in 1979 and, by 1980, had enough material to plant 1.2 hectares in their "Vaughan" vineyard in Angaston (Eden Valley/Barossa) close to where the winery is situated.

Today the Vaughan vineyard stands at eight hectares, and is the oldest Viognier vineyard in Australia. It has served its purpose in other ways, since cuttings from it were taken and planted on various rootstocks in Yalumba's Heggies Vineyard, further up the Eden Valley at 550 metres' (1,815 feet) altitude.

Yalumba's accomplished winemaker Louisa Rose finds that the Eden Valley provides them with their best Viognier: "Our best grapes still come from the cool Eden Valley, on light grey sandy loam and gravel soils." The pH there is low (around 5.2 to 5.5), the soil tight with low amounts of readily available water.

"However, I think the jury is still out on what will be "the best region in Australia," she adds. "Cooler regions are tending to produce richer, more luscious wines with the typical apricot and spice flavours. Warmer regions are producing wines with more white flower and honeysuckle flavours—still with good luscious textures."

By 2004 other notable producers in Australia were D'Arenberg (the Last Ditch Viognier from McLaren Vale), Mitchelton (Central Victoria), Clonakilla (Canberra District), and Gary Farr. From just 2.6 hectares of Viognier in 2000, Mitchelton had increased to 12 hectares by 2004.

For the enthusiasts, selection of suitable soil is crucial for the Viognier. Whereas the vine on its home Rhône slopes enjoys a special 40 cm (16 in.) topsoil of decomposed granite, mica, and schist, in the Languedoc it is more likely to turn up in thicker soil, with a higher clay content. This is not favoured by the Condrieu purists, nor often by those seeking to make personal wines elsewhere. They—people like John Alban and Josh Jensen in the United States—generally agree on the need for thin soil, and higher elevations to avoid excess and sudden ripeness. Alban's Viognier grows in some of the rare Californian limestone outcrops, for instance.

Yields have risen in recent years due to the introduction of disease-resistant clones. Some USA growers talk of the one official 642 clone but seem sure that others are using different, more productive ones. In Australia a heat-treated clone has been found to have a lower virus index and may come more on stream. Certainly southwestern France and the Ardèche producers can double the usual harvest of around 30 hectolitres a hectare.

So Viognier is becoming a wine with a double landscape. There is the mass-produce section, aiming to satisfy an alternative to Chardonnay at low, supermarket prices, and the hand-crafted, unusually flavoured side. The first is taut, zesty even; the second is lush and spoiling.

New Zealand has joined the party, with Te Mata's Woodthorpe Viognier, while in the Valais, the source area of the Rhône in Switzerland, there has been Viognier action since 1989, when two producers, Benoît Dorsaz and Simon Favre, both started to grow the variety. The Dorsaz vineyard, unlike most of his compatriots, is on a base of gneiss, with a covering of limestone and loess deposits, standing at 500 metres (1,650 feet) near the town of Martigny. There are now around 20 Viognier growers in Switzerland, most of them working on the classic limestone of the southwest of the country.

Viognier outside France is often a big, heavy wine, with growers seeking maximum draping of the wine in lush flavours and high alcohol. Beyond the Rhône in France, notably in the Languedoc area, the wines are often much leaner and wiry. Cropping levels may well have a part to play; for the southern French, it's a grape with commercial possibilities. For many of the overseas producers, it's an emotional, intellectual ride to take up the Viognier's challenge and to see what can be done.

In France the first cuttings despatched outside Condrieu came from Georges Vernay: "Lord Gray at Hermitage—his L'Hermite vineyard is now with Gérard Chave—was probably the first to plant, around the mid-1960s. I also sent cuttings to Guy Steinmaier at Domaine Ste-Anne in the Gard, Paul Avril of Clos des Papes at Châteauneuf-du-Pape, the Mas de Daumas Gassac in the southwest and Domaine Ste-Apollinaire in the Vaucluse."

At Condrieu the vineyard moved on to 117 hectares in production by 2004. "By 2005, there are due to be 130 to 135 hectares in production," states former Growers Union President Philippe Faury. To have 20 per cent of the vineyard just past its fourth leaf represents a dangerous weighting for the quality level, so look out for a lot more sweet wines that can hide faults. M. Faury is noncommital on this, preferring to state that "a lot of the young vines are on abandoned slopes that used to be vineyards."

Such a rise is startling when compared to the dog days of the 1950s and 1960s, when the bright years before the First World War had faded into wistful memories. In 1940, when the *appellation* was formed, an area of 200 hectares had been designated for vine growing but had never been taken up.

To this day, the dim form of old, well-ordered terracing arising out of clumps of scrub and bramble serves as a ghostly reminder of that time. Famous slopes like the *Coteau de Chéry* were then fully covered by vines, with spare land just for the occasional tool shed. But by 1949 under 200 hectolitres of wine were being made. Although there were as many as 14 growers bottling their wine, the sums were tiny—1,500 bottles here and there—and the wider wine trade had little interest in such a small *appellation*.

By the 1960s the hillside of *Chéry* was a run-down, gloomy vineyard. A miserable eight hectares across the seven Condrieu *communes* were being worked in 1965; only 12 hectares were under vine in 1971. In 1969 the whole Condrieu vineyard yielded a miserly 19 hectolitres, 2,530 bottles, not remotely enough for even a single full-time *vigneron* to live off.

Prices were also poor for the wine called just *Viognier* in those days. Before the Second World War, the wine sold for eight to 10 francs; in 1968 it sold for just seven francs, meaning a grower like Pierre Multier at the Château du Rozay was desperate to sell his crop, without even vinifying it. When the Vernays opened their tasting room in the 1970s, the price of a kilo (2.2 lbs.) of cherries was five francs, the price of a bottle of Viognier seven francs.

During the 1970s a minor revival occurred, with a little land reclaimed for the vine. But the economics of winemaking here remained poor, especially given all the hard physical work involved.

So when Condrieu's name and price were languishing, little incentive existed for the young or middle-aged to leave their comfortable indoor occupations. Only a few old-timers or persistent, dyed-in-the-wool *vignerons* with long local connections continued to work the slopes, often doubling up with fruit and vegetable cultivation. Their fruit, notably cherries, plums, and apricots, was always ripe some time ahead of anything grown on the plain—just right for the early summer market in Paris.

By the late 1970s, things started to change. Commercially grown fruit under cover undercut the hillside produce, and the wine price crept up. Foreign interest grew. Even large vineyard owners like Vernay, Multier, and Delas set about reclaiming land for the vine.

During the 1980s there was extensive replanting, with 40-year-old ash trees and magnolias bulldozed away, stone retaining walls repaired, and the soil cleared of ivy and thick growth. By 1982 a minor rise to 14 hectares of productive vines indicated a trend that by 1986 had gathered speed to reach 20 hectares. The figure in 1990 was up to 40 hectares, by 1992 it had shot up to 60 hectares, and in 2004 the figure for vineyards old enough to produce Condrieu stood at 117 hectares, or 289 acres. Meanwhile, if one adds into the area planted all young vines not yet past their third leaf, it stood at 129 hectares in 2004 and 135 hectares in 2005—six hectares having been the recent annual expansion allowance.

There is a downside to this plantation fever: bad winemaking. Growers with just a hectare or so had often been selling their crop—they weren't winemakers. Now they had 60 to 80 hl of wine that they couldn't find a home for. As top grower Georges Vernay observed in June 1993, "too many people thought all you had to do was make the wine, bottle it, and customers would come beating at your door." He quotes the case of someone quite well known these days, forced to sell his wine to his neighbour Guigal.

Indeed, Condrieu's saviour in those tricky days of the early 1990s was Marcel Guigal. In most cases it was he who bought the wine, raised it, and moved it into the market. There was a time when at least half the wine moved through his hands.

The years 1992 and 1993 also marked a low point in winemaking practices at Condrieu. Too many growers were seduced by the "freshen up/lighten up" counsel of the *oenologues*. This crass approach meant that a musky, opulent varietal was being treated like a Sauvignon—all zest and zing and early hit. Low temperature fermentations ruled, and many of the wines lacked balance and true character: neither fish nor fowl. One of the few to stand outside was André Perret, whose wines flew the flag. But the drinker was still being charged between £20 and £24 (then US$31–US$37) retail for a bottle in spring 1995: often atrocious value.

In the mid-2000s the panorama is better, but I sense a quality pyramid with a wobbly base. Too many wines are being made in a sweet version; a late harvest or a partly blocked fermentation can be used to cover up young-vine fruit deficiencies, and can also act as a price rise tool, pro rata above the extra costs of production. Yields are also laxly being allowed to climb—permitted cropping has risen from 30 hl/ha in the 1970s to 37 hl/ha plus a top-up of 10 per cent now.

There is also the fact that it's hard to pin down a single Condrieu style, even in the dry wine. Variables include soil nuances—whether the granite is pure, clay, or limestone-topped for instance—exposure, altitude, and above all, *vigneron* cellar style. It's not as if the outlying *communes* of Malleval and Chavanay have a strong identity built up over decades. So a heavily oaked, clumsy wine from there could be extolled because of the lack of any local yardstick to set it against.

Viognier from other places and countries can also be compared now with Condrieu, and maturing vines and measured winemaking are closing the gap. So Condrieu must look sharp and not let the price-quality ratio become too stretched.

The village of Condrieu is indeed a suitable setting for such a soft, rich wine. The Rhône runs past the village in a gently curling arc, prompting its early name of Coin du Ruisseau (Corner of the Stream). Bounded by lush green undergrowth, the swirling waters here appear to be benign: there is no torrent, no crash of water on rock, just the oscillating patterns of its steady tow gliding across the surface.

Such apparent calm is reflected on the riverside. The quiet air is disturbed only occasionally—perhaps by chugging barges or a train hastening along the eastern bank, by the barking of a tethered dog, or even by a game of *pétanque*, with the "clink-clink" of the *boules* resonating in the unhurried stillness.

The village is crammed into a brief stretch of flatland between the river and the broad, gently rising slopes that build steadily up towards the Massif Central. It has more bustle, more character than Ampuis; it is more obviously a market centre than a wine community, partly because there are few signs indicating wine growers' cellars or domaines. There are nine growers with cellars inside the *commune* of Condrieu, but not many clues about them in the busy village: just one street name, the *rue du Cep*, gives a modest indication. A quick scan of the hillsides shows new patches of vineyards, their modern stake-poles intruding into what was previously lush and often overgrown vegetation.

The *appellation* remains a spread of many smallholders, despite the presence of a few large operators like Guigal. The 117-plus hectares in full Condrieu production are worked by around one hundred growers, many of whom sell crop rather than make and bottle their own wine. The latest number of bottlers is around 65.

HISTORY

The Viognier's origins are obscure. Some say that it was brought up from Marseille by the Phocaean Greeks around 600 BC. This is dubious, for it is more generally assumed that the Phocaeans—if they carried any vine with them—brought only one variety, the Syrah. Even this theory is under scrutiny, with DNA testing pointing to the Isère and Savoie as the origins of the Syrah—but where had it arrived from before then?

The other leading theory relies heavily on legend. According to this, it was the Emperor Probus who imported the Viognier from Dalmatia in AD 281, after the total destruction of the Condrieu vineyards by Domitian around AD 92. The latter, a man who combatted corruption, is said to have ordered the total clearance of the vines as retribution for a local uprising, fomented, it was claimed, by too much drinking of Condrieu's wine by the Gallic natives. Dalmatia is the most common choice among the most learned local *vignerons.*

There is no doubt, though, that wine was made at Condrieu during the Roman occupation. In the third century the poet Martial sang the praises of the "violet perfume of the wines of Vienne," and today's hillside terraces date back at least as long. Their heritage is hard to surpass, which makes it galling to see the cellar dominating the vineyard in some of the wines.

After the expulsion of the Romans from Gaul in the fifth century, it is thought that the vineyards went uncultivated until the ninth century. Even then only very little wine was probably made, all drunk locally. By the twelfth century, Condrieu belonged to the Church of Lyon, and was fortified by Renaud de Forez, its Archbishop. For the winegrowers there was payment of one obole, a unit of money, a year.

Thereafter religious conflict governed its activities—Viennois, Protestants sacking it—with the locals referring to Condrieu as "the Kingdom," and the bank opposite as "the Empire," alias France and Germany.

Slowly the wine's reputation spread more widely, and by the fourteenth century it was being shipped down to the Papal Palace in Avignon from the ports of Condrieu and St-Pierre-de-Boeuf. The fact that more than one port of embarkation was used would indicate that the wine was perhaps ordered several times. The first export recorded was to England by 1714.

P. Morton Shand relates that the Earl of Bristol then introduced it into his already well-stocked home cellar.

In the twentieth century the local support for Condrieu centred on the restaurant trade, then inextricably linked to the journey south to the Côte d'Azur. Vienne lay just south of Lyon and was a well-timed stage on any car journey in the days before the autoroute. The late Fernand Point, one of France's most famous chefs this century and precursor of the Bocuse-Troisgros school of cooking, considered Condrieu to be one of the country's three best wines, and his restaurant, the Pyramide, introduced it to many French and foreign gourmets. His mantle was subsequently taken up by the late Jacques Pic, at his famous three-star restaurant in nearby Valence.

The *appellation* was created in 1940, but it took until 1944 for the creation of a Growers Union, incorporating around 10 growers making about 200 hl. Georges Vernay's father, Francis, was Secretary and Treasurer. "The only growers who let the wine ferment through until it was dry in those days were Jurie des Camiers and Multier," recalls Georges; "they would leave it for a year or so. The rest of the growers didn't have the money for that, so would stop the wine with sulphur and sell it as *demi-sec* or outright sweet, especially for Christmas. My father would leave eight to 12 gm of sugar in his *demi-sec,* and Dézormeaux would make a sweet wine with 20 gm still in it." Georges adds that his father was always happy to see the wine go out the door, since it left space in his cellar for the next stage of his working year, the vegetables and fruit.

Of course the risk at this time was re-fermentation, and people had a variety of ways of ensuring this didn't happen. "There was the old aspirin trick," chuckles Georges. "The salicylic acid in it killed the fermentation dead, and it also didn't smell! You see, the sulphur risked decolouring the wine. There were only a few bad boys around doing this, though."

In those days there was no crop buying: everyone vinified their grapes. The restaurateurs would buy the wine early; Francis Vernay used to sell casks to André Pic to bottle at his restaurant, and Fernand Point would serve the wine young and gently sparkling because it didn't contain sulphur. So there was plenty of "variety" in the wines of Condrieu back then.

THE VIOGNIER

The Viognier is recognised as an awkward vine. With over 50 harvests behind him, now retired Georges Vernay explains: "I think first and foremost it's a case of soil. We have this curious topsoil, 40 cm (16 in.) deep, of *arzelle*—it's decomposed rock, mica, and schist, under which there can be some clay, as I have on the hillside of *Vernon*."

At Côte-Rôtie the Viognier doesn't do well in the northern, schist reaches of the *appellation*, but is still planted there to provide the Syrah with increased vinosity and warmth. Gérard Villano also found that some Viognier he had in clay-limestone at Condrieu did not prosper, either. Certainly clay soils are not ideal—loose granite is very much the dish.

The Viognier is a rambling vine, its foliage spreading easily, and therefore needing trimming in the summer. In the Rhône, only the Guyot method is allowed for its pruning, the shoots traditionally having been led along wooden stakes. Its training can also be along wires, but the challenge is that many of the terraces are short and the cost and labour involved in drilling holes make that option uneconomical. Where terraces are long or deliberately sculpted from recently cleared land, wire training is the natural choice—better aereation for the vines and less risk of rot.

Viognier at Condrieu suffers mostly from oïdium, with bouts of mildew and black rot possible. The other annual problem is the failure of the fruit to set after flowering: even when fully ripe, its grapes remain small.

Recently a more serious ailment has arisen, one mirroring the perishing of the Syrah. This is a parasite called esca that attacks the vine's

wood. "Either the vine dies quickly—in a matter of a week or two," says Christine, Georges Vernay's daughter, "or it suffers a slow death over a few years, sometimes giving fruit, then missing out." Her estimate is of a loss of as much as 5 per cent across Condrieu in 2004.

Similarly to the Syrah, the esca has most attacked vines planted between 1985 and 1990. It is also potentially significant that the product used to treat the esca mushroom, which is arsenic based, has been banned since the early 2000s.

The Viognier's growth pattern is another of its foibles. Back to Georges Vernay: "The Viognier is also difficult, full of caprice and never wholly predictable. Some years we can have a really successful flowering in June and expect a large crop. The weather may remain healthy right up to the time of the *vendanges*, and yet for some unknown reason the grapes will be shrivelled and undeveloped. You can't use fruit like that for your wine," he laments.

The vine's unpredictability is echoed by Louis Barruol, a new and welcome small-*négociant* face on the scene from Gigondas. "A year like 2000 is so big and almost wonderful, but in reality I prefer more balance, so that the violet, the velvety side with a touch of mineral, can come through. The trouble is, the Viognier doesn't give you the choice—the ripeness can explode, and rise by a whole degree in just four days. Even if you think you're ready to harvest, you can be caught out." The year 2003 saw another dramatic late ripening, necessitating a frantic dash home from holiday for some growers.

Talk around town has been that the National Institute for Appellations (INAO) is slowing down the growth of the vineyards from six to three extra hectares a year: if so, this is not before time. Too many young grapes lead directly to thin wines. "The Viognier needs at least 10 years if you are to secure depth in the wine," states Georges Vernay. "It's important to control the number of bunches, too; past 30 hl/ha, you can't be sure of quality."

The Viognier's best fruit is borne between the ages of 25 and 55, although growers continue with the vine beyond then. "If the vines are not damaged, they can still give a good crop at 90 or 100 years old," states Georges Vernay. "Half a hectare on our vineyard at *Vernon* dates from 1936, and it's still yielding around 30 hl/ha." André Perret is another optimist: "I reckon up until 80 years in my experience—with yields by then of around 20 hl/ha."

By contrast, Christophe Pichon at Chavanay had to take out some 70-year vines in 1991—a sad, but realistic decision: "The quality of the juice was wonderful, but by then we had got down to just 9 hl/ha, a yield that was uncommercial."

Yields have risen here since the 1970s in two spurts. The average for the period 1962–78 was approximately 17 hl/ha, just over half the total permitted. After the disastrously small crop of 1978—only 96 hl all told—the average rose firmly into the mid to high 20s hl/ha, then took off again near the late 1990s. Nowadays, in years free of great blight (unlike very dry 2003, frost- and hail-hit 2002), yields are now settled comfortably in the mid- to high 30s hl/ha (see table 4).

Two main factors are at work: the first is the jump in the permitted yield per hectare from 30 to 37 hectolitres, with on top a 10 per cent surplus allowed if asked for. Suddenly 41 hl/ha— allowed in a year like 2004—becomes the figure, which is not to everyone's taste. It's left to nature to regulate in this case, as she did in 2003 with the *commune* of Chavanay averaging 20 hl/ha, and the whole *appellation* 25 hl/ha.

The new growers, with no long-term horizon established, are even pushing hard for a base figure of 40 hl/ha, which would take the maximum up to 44 hl/ha. The words of veterans like Georges Vernay about risks to quality appearing above 30 hl/ha should be heeded. Any *appellation* that has allowed a rise in cropping density of over 50 per cent in the past 30 years can reasonably be accused of being greedy.

As to the plant itself, a study of 1812 by Cochard wrote of "a variety of vionnier [*sic*] known by the name red vionnier, because the grape, when ripe, bore a reddish colour." There

TABLE 4
Condrieu Yields in Recent Decades

1982	14 ha	390 hl	27.86 hl/ha
1989	40 ha	1,183 hl	29.57 hl/ha
1995	93 ha	2,175 hl	23.39 hl/ha
2000	105 ha	4,111 hl	39.15 hl/ha
2002	110 ha	3,575 hl	32.50 hl/ha
2004	117 ha	4,700 hl	49.17 hl/ha

was also a stated distinction between the Viognier of Côte-Rôtie and that of Condrieu.

Claudius Roux (1907) wrote: "It has a medium/fine leaf, five lobes and quite light green; bunches fair-sized, a little long, cylindro-conical, quite compact; round berries, medium-sized, ranging from light green (for the Viognier of Côte-Rôtie, a local subset) to golden yellow (for the Condrieu Viognier), transparent, juicy, very sugared and also used as an eating grape."

It was said to be synonymous with the Galopine of the Isère *département* across the Rhône. But the strains were not numerous, and the twentieth century saw a narrowing down in the sources for new stock.

That's why the other factor playing on yields has been the use of a disease-resistant strain of Viognier that has boosted average production. Georges Vernay first worked with his own cuttings from old stock in 1957, when the oldest vines in the *appellation* were those dating from 1915 chez Multier at the Château du Rozay. But the universe was limited, with just one plot from the 1930s providing healthy woodstock. So during the 1980s, a clone was taken up, called 642.

This has its drawbacks. "Clone 642 is very productive," states Philippe Faury, "and its wines are not greatly aromatic; its grapes are larger than our Viognier here, and it's mainly been planted in Languedoc." He adds that in the 1960s and 1970s, research on the Viognier centred on increasing its productivity, for the understandable reason that so little was planted anywhere.

Such a limited pool of stock has been a leading concern for one of the most conscientious domaines, that of Gilbert Clusel and Brigitte Roch, better known for their Côte-Rôtie. With just the one clone available, the Syndicat set out in the late 1990s to check out all the old vines. The point was that at Condrieu, only 20 years qualified as "old," for the simple reason that 30 to 50 years ago the vineyards were so tiny.

"We came up with 60 to 70 different plants, but a lot were diseased with their wood deformed," comments Brigitte Roch. "We took rootstock for 10 new plants from each old vine that screened healthy, and these, all numbered, were planted at ex-President of the Growers Philippe Faury's *Ribaudy* vineyard in Chavanay. They are intended to preserve and activate the Viognier heritage."

From 2004 a second clone was developed; 300 vines of clone 1042 were planted at St. Thomé, near Alban-la-Romaine in the Ardèche, after development by M. Pascal Blois at the Domaine de l'Espigouette.

In 2005 a third one, the 1058, was due on stream. Research is said to centre on improving quality rather than quantity in this second phase.

According to André Perret, there was a false Viognier in circulation for seven to eight years around the late 1980s: "Its foliage was wider and thicker and it grows very upright, almost rigid, rather than spreading like the genuine vine. The bunches are very tightly packed, and their taste was more rustic. Even the local nurserymen didn't know it, and sold it as Viognier."

This fake Viognier, now being sorted by grafting over the rootstock, brings to mind the *scandale* of the Viognier sold to California from Châteauneuf-du-Pape many years ago. Since its wine was sold as Viognier for a long time and it turned out to be Roussanne, there was much consternation for eminent growers and questors like Randall Grahm of Bonny Doon.

CONDRIEU VINEYARDS

The Condrieu *appellation* extends in a very straggling way over seven communities: Condrieu and, to the south, Vérin, St-Michel-sur-Rhône, St-Pierre-de-Boeuf, Chavanay, Malleval, and Limony. The distance between them brings a difference in the style of the wines. The central Condrieu village style is often overtly rich, with great, plush pear flavours and swirling aromas to match. The southern end of the *appellation*, which is 10 miles (16 km) and many gulleys later, brings out more minerality in the wines, with its younger, firmer granite cited as a contributing factor.

When the *appellation* was created in 1940, it was restricted to the *communes* of Condrieu, Vérin, and St-Michel-sur-Rhône. "It was decided by the geological map," recalls Georges Vernay. Such a pure decision is upheld by the fact the best sites, like *Vernon, Chéry, Colombier,* and *Clos Bouche,* all lie within this first area.

The total area qualified to produce Condrieu was raised to 320 hectares, then cut back to 220 hectares when the authorities realised that things were getting out of hand. With 130 to 135 hectares under vine in 2005, many of the top slope spots have now been taken.

There also exists an anomaly with growers in places like Chavanay allowed to use their land for Syrah and Viognier; in other words, the same vineyard can provide Saint-Joseph red or Condrieu. Pierre Gaillard at *Côte Bellay* and Stéphane Montez at *Chanson* both work this way.

The prime observation about the central Condrieu soil is that it is poor. The mid- to late-nineteenth century studies of V. Rendu (1857) and Ladrey (1873) show Condrieu as having lower levels of calcium, magnesium, iron oxide, and organic matter than Côte-Rôtie.

Like that of Côte-Rôtie, the shape of the Condrieu vineyards at the northern end, where the most traditional quality lies, is governed by a series of streams running off the Massif Central granite and down towards the Rhône. This creates a set of gulleys with some choice south-facing slopes above the streams.

The first of these is the *Côte Bonnette*. At the top end of the *appellation,* it and the *Côte Châtillon* have become the two best known sites here.

Bonnette is in two humps, mainly south-south-west facing, and contains largely decomposed granite or *gore*—sanded granite with quartz in it—with sticky red clay between a half and one metre down. There is more clay at the top of *Bonnette,* where the land is flatter; this area was used in the past not to grow vines but to graze cattle. Jean-Claude Mouton is one of the growers here.

Below *Côte Bonnette* runs the busy *Arbuel* stream, on its way through Condrieu and on to the Rhône. This part of *Bonnette* has become better known because high-profile growers like Gangloff and René Rostaing have plots on it, Gangloff having planted on the steepest area, which rises dramatically above his home beside the *Arbuel* in Condrieu.

Châtillon was discreetly known in the 1970s for its high quality from André Dézormeaux's vineyard, but Guigal's use of it to form half of his *Doriane* cuvée has increased its profile. It has stony, flinty, at times yellow-tinged soil with limestone and in the past it, too, was used for other purposes—vegetables and red grapes. Château du Rozay, Bonnefond, Mouton, and Gérard are other growers here. Across the road on the way up to Rozay lies *La Roncharde,* which also contains the small stones and a limestone content. Robert Niéro works plots on both *Châtillon* and *Roncharde,* while François Merlin has some late-1980s and Louis Clerc some early-1990s Viognier on the latter as well.

The wines from this portion of the *appellation,* which was not included in the 1940 decree area, accentuate rich, savoury elements that can coat the palate. The aromas they express are stone fruit rather than floral. François Gérard planted a hectare on *Côte Châtillon* in 1985, and finds that his wine's aromas shift from apricot and peach at the outset, on to a more floral side a little later on.

South of the *Arbuel* one moves into the true centre of the Condrieu vineyard. Georges Vernay is far too discreet to say this, but it's clear from his descriptions that he considers the area from the *Arbuel* to south of the *Vernon* stream to be his Fifth Avenue or Bond Street.

The first site, *Vergelas,* forms a modest start. This faces northeast and is nearly flat ground at the top of the hill, covered with red-grey clay. South of it, *Ste-Agathe* is more noted: a steep slope above the southern end of Condrieu itself that turns from southeast to south and is marked by powdery-grained granite with a few small stones. It is worked by Rostaing and Domaine Georges Vernay among others, and produces clear-fruited, quite direct wines.

At Condrieu, there are two top vineyards—*Vernon* and *Chéry.* They lie just a little south of the village centre. *Vernon* is formed of one main plot, a convex hill that is southeast facing, with severely tucked-in ledges that at most hold five plants across. Its topsoil is mostly *arzelle,* fine granite with mica mixed in, and to the eye it presents a small-grained, sandy layering. In a place there is some grey-blue, hard schist as well. The Domaine Georges Vernay is the sole owner on this front site, with 2.5 hectares planted; in time they expect to be cultivating four hectares or so there, the extra land requiring grubbing out and clearing.

Further into the valley, behind the Vernay vineyard on the same hill, are two plots worked by Yves Cuilleron and Vincent Porte, both of them about half a hectare. Cuilleron uses his grapes for his Vertige wine, and Porte in 2003 started to make a wine he calls Noblesse de Vernon.

The Genin-Valluit family, which owned *Vernon* in the past, also possessed land across the *Vernon* stream, and through their usage rather than the map contours, there became known another plot of the same name across the stream. This extends over into the full south-facing slope of *Chéry,* with the *Vernon* stream here so modest that it can fail to reach the Rhône in dry weather.

This south side of *Vernon,* where Clusel-Roch work a vineyard, is made up of different soil to the core northern part. There is more limestone, the surface whiter to the eye. This deeper, drought-resistant soil extends into *Chéry,* and is relatively nutritious when compared to a vineyard at Chavanay such as *Les Eyguets.*

The two famous *Vernon* slopes lie about 600 metres apart, and in 1934, when he was eight years old, Georges Vernay witnessed a rare show from an artist of the day. "His name was Henri le Funambule, a high-wire cyclist from St-Étienne. And yes, he did cross between the two slopes, there and back, on the high wire!"

Ever a wonderful raconteur, Georges recalls details with a photographic eye: "He crossed above the *Vernon* stream, and so that he could be seen, they had placed a French flag on the back of his bicycle. There were a lot of trees then, so they'd tied a smooth chain around a large almond tree on the north of *Vernon* and run it across to the oak tree we call *La Gaberte* on the south side of *Vernon*, where Yves Gangloff now works."

Chéry lies below *Vernon* at a slight angle to it, and its vineyard now covers seven hectares. The two-thirds of it nearest the N86 road looks due south, then it turns a little to the southeast. The slope runs in a gentle concave curve, ideal for full sun and regular ripening. At the summit it is very granitic, but the middle has a heavier soil, with clay and chalk mixed into the loose granite; lower down is more clay and marl mixed in with the grainy *gore*, on plots held by Villano and Gangloff. At the foot of *Chéry* runs a small stream, the *Alleau;* this holds water in the winter, but is dry by July and August.

Over the years *Chéry* has been made famous by the wines of André Perret more than anyone else; he has also been responsible for the winemaking of the Lyonnais Robert Jurie des Camiers's grapes from this *climat*. Robert Niéro, the Château du Rozay, Gaillard, Clusel-Roch, and Gangloff are other important names working on *Chéry*, Gangloff's vineyard straddling the *Vernon* plot.

Vernon's wine comes in a reserved, cautiously fruit-scented style—white fruits with some light spice. It is a wine of serious structure that opens and develops with age—the Georges Vernay is likely to be closed after four years, for instance. This contrasts with the broad, open aromas and rich texture of the *Chéry*, although the latter's musky richness can be encouraged

by a degree of later picking. Always full-bodied, the *Chéry* wines are also often marked by a nutty, chewy ending.

At the bottom end of *Chéry* lies *Maladière*, a series of craggy terraces above the supermarket Champion. Jean-Michel Gérin has a plot there.

The next big-name *climat* above the hamlet of *Vérin*, where the Rhône flows very close to the hill, is *Clos Bouche*. At its foot runs a busy stream, the *Vérin*, that flows through the village into the Rhône. *Clos Bouche* was known for years because of its Delas of Hermitage family connection. Delas own just under two hectares planted around 1960 here, on the dark-coloured, south-facing granite. Such a mature vineyard is now a prized asset, and this has always formed the basis of the Delas Clos Boucher Condrieu. As with wines off the very best sites, this benefits from delayed drinking, from three years on. In the best vintages, it carries a subtle but deep-seated richness.

South of Château-Grillet and beyond the *Vérin* stream is a pocket of less well known sites, but ones worked by promising growers like François Merlin and the ubiquitous François Villard. *Jeanraude* and *Poncin*, the latter another site in two parts, have blue-grey granite and mica that filters quickly; there is less piled-up topsoil, and these sites give rich, strongly floral wines with some minerality on the finish.

A little farther south, at St-Michel-sur-Rhône, are two vineyards that Georges Vernay would place in the top six; *Colombier* and *Roche Coulante* provide the real, thickly flavoured style of Condrieu. These are earthy wines, grounded in solid textures, with mineral touches on the end. Their soil is yellow, crumbled granite.

In the 1970s, *Colombier* produced tiny yields for André Dézormeaux, and while he often made an indifferent sweet wine, the raw materials were excellent. It is a place where a lot of cherry trees grew, casting many of the vines into shade, but now it is back to full vine cultivation; its ace card is a lovely south-facing position. *Colombier* makes up the other half of Guigal's Doriane.

Roche Coulante is also full south, and largely the classic *arzelle* or decomposed granite, with touches of clay. Talented Christophe Pichon considers its style to be complex: "*Roche Coulante* has spice touches, some apricot, and a sense of fat on the bouquet." There is also often honey on the bouquet, as well as a mineral side on the palate. Another grower here is Gilbert Chirat.

The next step south starts the area included in the *appellation* zone in its second phase from 1967 to 1969. This brings in the extended and high-profile *commune* of Chavanay. One of the first sites here, *Mève*, is worked by Christophe Pichon. Its soil is *arzelle* mixed in with patches of clay, and Pichon's plot is mainly easterly facing, making it cooler than some. "My plot at *Mève* gives straightforward wine, with an easy richness, and open, soft fruit and floral aromas," he says; "it also provides acidity."

The main split at Chavanay concerns the vineyards on the north side of the village and the south, which are separated by the Valencize River. The north side—its best-known plots *Chanson, Les Rivoires, La Côte, Izéras, Les Eyguets*—is made up of firmer granite than the south, where the main names are *Ribaudy, Peyrolland,* and *Blanchard*. "This gives the wines from *Ribaudy* and the southern side of the village more minerality," comments Philippe Faury.

The best-known site here is *Chanson*, again due to the work of André Perret, who has bottled a wine of that name for many years. *Chanson*'s rock is partly white to the eye, since it contains sand and limestone. This brings out a stone fruit, apricot-style flavour, with a minerality and freshness that set it apart from the core Condrieu vineyards. Other growers here are Merlin, Montez, and Verzier.

The other high-profile site here is *La Côte*, generated by the work of Yves Cuilleron. It covers a large area, comprising several hectares; it is a broad, southeast-facing, and in places windswept hill since it rises to 320 metres. There is poor, stony soil on a granite base, and like *Chanson, La Côte* also holds Syrah vines for red Saint-Joseph. Boissonnet and Betton are other growers here.

On the same extended hill above the Valencize River are some other *lieux-dits* that are becoming better known. *Les Eyguets* held Viognier in the dark days of the 1970s; it forms the heart of the hillside behind Chavanay and has an extremely sandy soil on top of very fine granite granules—poor, light terrain.

Just past and below it up the valley is *Les Rivoires*, where there is a stronger amount of clay and a deeper, more humid soil mixed in with the sand/rock elements; with its cooler soil, *Rivoires* tends to ripen behind *Eyguets*. Beyond *Rivoires, Izéras,* the most westerly site in this cluster, is home to 1939 Viognier of Yves Cuilleron. Philippe Verzier of Cave Chante-Perdrix also works a plot there, where some clay is mixed in with the granite.

South of Chavanay, *La Ribaudy* is tucked away from the Rhône corridor, a vineyard illuminated by the hard work of Philippe Faury over the past 25 years. The soil is stony, loose granite, and the wines are often restrained—more elegant than potent in the Faury style—with mineral edges. Gilles Barge is another grower here.

The role of the winemaker carries a direct impact on styles around Chavanay, especially because so many of the vineyards are young. What constitutes a true local wine is open to some debate, because there haven't been generations of trial and error. Take the comments of young Stéphane Montez, who works his wines hard in the cellar: "There are style differences just within the *commune* of Chavanay," he says. "*Boissey* in the south gives wines that are rich and fat, while *Chanson*'s wines from north of the village are finer and more aromatic."

The next two *communes*, St-Pierre-de-Boeuf and Malleval, sit cheek by jowl, Malleval lying upstream along the *Batalon* stream. The valley here seems to have been cut through by the incisive strike of a sharp knife; there are slabs of granite within the rocky outcrop, and the country is rugged, almost Spaghetti Western style.

Malleval's prime site is the south-facing *Volan*, where Rouvière, Paret, and Chapoutier have vineyards. Since 2004 Paret's three-plus hectares have been in association with Marcel Guigal, as well as his usual partner, actor Gérard Depardieu. Soil plays an extreme importance at *Volan* in the wine's style, since it is rich, with clay and sea fossil traces. The clay's water retention slows down the ripening. There is a lot of schist here, and this hard rock sets it apart from many nearby sites, which contain the typical loose, sanded granite.

This is a rare local vineyard with a documented past, connected to the newly restored Château de Volan and mentioned in manuscripts of the fifteenth century. The vineyard, said to have survived phylloxera, stands below the château on a mix of terraces and flat, sweeping land. Immediately evident are plenty of shiny, breakable schist stones lying on the topsoil. The wine from here is powerful, ripe, and often chewy—really meaty stuff.

Many of the Malleval vineyards are young, and this has a direct bearing on the wines, which I find can lack core. One of the older plots worked by Pierre Gaillard dates from the early 1970s on *Côte Bellay*. Gaillard describes the local granite as investing these wines with a cut and mineral texture.

The most southerly Condrieu vineyards lie in the Ardèche at the *commune* of Limony. They are typically represented by the work of a small grower like Pierre Dumazet, who does not imprint a lot of new oak on them, so allowing the *terroir* to come forward. These show exotically spiced and smoky touches that are not usually found in wines from the heart of Condrieu about eight miles (13 km) north.

Limony's Condrieu also expresses finesse and greater refinement than wines from Chavanay and especially Malleval. There is some talent coming through here—growers like Pierre Finon and Emmanuel Barou.

The best-known site here is the *Côte Fournet*, a south-southeast–facing, quite steep hillside that rises above the Limony stream. *Fournet*, where Dumazet and Louis Chèze both work, is gneiss, with crumbled sand; there is a topsoil of 10 to 70 cm (four to 28 inches) above the gran-

ite rock, and water drains fast from it. It is a good spot to achieve extreme ripeness, notes Pierre Dumazet, with dried stone walls adding to the heat of this inset little valley. For Dumazet, its wine style is mineral, with sound ageing prospects.

About 200 metres from the village of Limony, in the same valley as *Fournet* but with a more easterly exposure, is a site with a gradually growing renown, *Braise*. This contains slightly harder granite, with some loess and patches of clay present. It ripens a little ahead of *Fournet,* and its wine is more floral. Emmanuel Barou is a young grower here, along with the more established Louis Chèze.

The paradox at these southern levels of Condrieu's *appellation* is the growers' right to plant Syrah as well as Viognier on the same *lieu-dit.* On *Merlan,* for instance—a sound, south-facing hillside behind Arcoules—Anthony Vallet grows Viognier, and Chapoutier is busy planting it, while François Villard grows Syrah there for his St-Joseph red. A strange business, it seems.

Because Condrieu is not one compact vineyard like Hermitage, there are some nuances of climate in the *appellation.* Across the *appellation* the average annual temperature is said to be 11°C; this compares with the Marsaz weather station just behind the northern Crozes-Hermitage hills of 11.9°C per annum from 1972 to 2001. The 11°C is also pretty consistent across the whole Condrieu area.

While the southern region around Crozes is warmer, it is also wetter than Condrieu. The 1972–2001 rainfall average at Marsaz was 840.8 mm (33.6 in.), whereas a rainfall survey of 1987 showed a sharp divergence in the precipitation on Condrieu, as opposed to St-Pierre-de-Boeuf and Chavanay, other villages in the *appellation.*

Condrieu's average annual fall between 1957 and 1982 was 804 mm (32.16 in.); St-Pierre's between 1953 and 1982 was 717 mm (28.68 in.), Chavanay's between 1946 and 1965 was 713 mm (28.52 in.). This translated into 111 rainy days at Condrieu, and only 87 at St-Pierre-de-Boeuf, just 11 km, or under 7 miles, away (Lyon Station d'Avertissments Agricoles).

The wind is an important factor for Condrieu; according to Georges Vernay, it acts to chase away the cloud cover and bring sun, even if the temperatures are not usually in the high 30s°C, as they were in 2003. Indeed, the 2004 harvest was largely saved, then made by the prevailing north wind of September. Minor outbreaks of rot were headed off, then the grapes evolved steadily, with final alcohol levels in the wines often around the 14° mark.

CONDRIEU VINIFICATION

Dry Condrieu regained its roots in the late 1990s. The early 1990s saw a lot of experimentation, with fashion-conscious *oenologues* dictating the terms. Freshness was the word. So much Condrieu was sadly neutered in those days—bred for early vivacity, to the detriment of its core, ripe, musky qualities with a touch of comforting minerality and cut on the finish.

The crop was picked early, the wine frequently bottled in January at that time. Several growers blocked its malolactic fermentation, and the whole process was completed quickly. Now crop is picked later, with hints of noble rot even, and the majority of bottling comes after a year, in September. Lees contact is sought—with *bâtonnage,* or lees stirring, during the wine's upbringing—and more fullness is the goal.

Yves Cuilleron is someone who seeks extreme ripeness in his Viognier: "My first late harvest wine was in 1990; in 1992 there was a lot of rot, but when I pressed these grapes, expecting them to make a *vin de table,* I found their alcohol was much higher. So I've carried on with this. But you have to be alert in the vineyard if you're picking late—I do a lot of leaf dropping after rain to ventilate the grapes."

Most growers vinify in a mix of vat and 228-litre cask. The younger growers, with young vines, use more oak than the older ones. Frédéric Boissonet, the Bonnefond brothers, Thiérry Farjon, Gilles Flacher, Laurent Marthouret, and Stéphane Montez are all oak-only, and out of the generation ahead of them it is the regular modernists like Pierre Gaillard, Yves Cuilleron, Yves Gangloff, and François Villard who use plenty of oak. One grower, Alain Paret, uses a mix of 228-litre and 550-litre casks, and Yves Cuilleron's new dry wine, Vertige, actually receives a full 18 months of cask.

Fermentation along time-honoured lines is central to getting the Viognier grape to express itself. Low-temperature fermentation around 16°C does not suit it. The best results come from a more natural cellar temperature around 18° to 20°C, some of which can be done in cask. Too much young oak, and the wine lacks clarity. It's easy to overlook just how pure Viognier aroma and flavour are. While smells like honeysuckle, acacia, pear skin, and apricot are referred to, they are delivered with great definition, as are the pear fruit, honeys, and apricots on the palate.

A pre-fermentation skin contact, used very successfully by leading Condrieu men like André Perret and Marcel Guigal, also brings out the aromas more fully and truly, without any exotic jungle fruit smells. Allowing the malolactic to occur also helps the wine's natural fragrances and opulence to bloom. Perret, for example, leaves his Condrieu 12 months on its lees, during which time the malo takes place.

It's also noticeable that more mature growers have backed off the extreme use of oak in the past decade. Jean-Michel Gérin reintroduced 20 per cent vinification and ageing in vat in 2000; Philippe Faury's La Berne has been cut from 40 to 25 per cent new oak. Louis Barruol at St-Cosme has cut new oak from 100 to 70 per cent, the rest in vat "to obtain more fruit."

Generally growers like Gilles Barge and André Perret see the role of the stainless steel as providing the freshness, while the wood serves to bring the richness.

Marcel Guigal believes that there is a very delicate balance in the Viognier between keeping its fruit and still producing a wine that is typical of the region—hence the use of intracellular maceration and new oak. "The fruit leaves a Viognier wine quickly in my opinion," he comments, "which is why I seek to make full-bodied, firm-tasting Condrieus that still have a touch of lively fruit on the palate. By using half new oak on Doriane, for instance, I am adding to the wine's fullness—don't forget that it's common to harvest Viognier that measures over 14° alcohol naturally, and you're setting yourself against nature if you try to make a fresh, lively little wine from such ingredients."

The issue of oak and Viognier is very central to what will become of this wine in the future. My view is that Viognier does not need great amounts of new oak. Providing ripeness has been satisfactory, there is plenty of stuffing and potency in the wine for its flavour and texture to be thickly layered. Much of the Viognier's "work" is actually done in that early, impressive flourish on the palate. Oak gives it some extra length at first, but after three years or so, its effect retreats and narrows and then floats away, leaving a rather vacuous finale. The more new oak used, the more pronounced this effect.

Several growers privately talk about this, and one who is not frightened to come forward is Jacques Jaboulet of Paul Jaboulet Aîné. "As an *appellation*, Condrieu should have gone more for promoting its *terroir* than its grape variety, for expressing that in the wines. There are too many messed-up vinifications there, and glutinous late-harvest wines." No more to add to that, m'Lud.

So gentle oak application, using young, not necessarily new oak, would be fine in my mythical domaine. But I would also be determined to show the world the pureness and glorious musk of well-ripened Viognier, taken from soil to bottle with no barrel intervention. I would choose a site like *Chéry* for this *cuvée splendide*, knowing that its *terroir* brings an overt, charged earthiness. Such are dreams.

All this confirms the fact that Viognier does not need loads of cask input, since it is so well scented and flavoured on its own. Gradually a degree of reassertion of *terroir* will come through if the fall in oak use continues. With the vineyards maturing after their rapid growth, Condrieu should be producing more sustained wines over the next 15 years.

Generally the wines are fermented in the 16° to 20°C area. "If you go above 20°C," comments Phlippe Guigal, "you break the aromatic molecules, and the wine becomes heavier and more clumsy."

The duration of the vinification has increased, with growers now happy to let the malolactic fermentation take place. The malolactic is also important in governing the flavour of the wine, according to Gilles Barge: "There are grapefruit and citrus notes before the malo is done, and apricot and pear tones after it." So fermentation can run gently along for some months, although the main alcoholic process lasts three to four weeks. After it, a fining is often required because the Viognier generates a lot of vegetal protein and can need clearing of this.

Even once in the cellar, the Viognier can be given to caprice during fermentation. Gilles Barge points out that its sugars can ferment until the end of November, with the mustimeter dropping by only fractions. "Often the Viognier can surge on and then enter this very steady phase, when it pays to leave it alone. It's not good news for anyone trying to produce a zesty, fresh wine, as was the fashion in the early 1990s," he adds.

The wines are left on their lees now, with often a weekly stirring until the spring/early summer. *Bâtonnage*, or lees stirring, needs some care—too much, too often—and the grower risks making a wine that sits heavily on the palate. Most Condrieus are bottled in September, the earliest in April or May.

That is today, but how was Condrieu vinified a hundred years or more ago? Claudius Roux cites the studies of Cochard (1812) and Durand (1906) in his work of 1907. Obviously, some modern bells will ring with this, and to paraphrase him: Picking was done at perfect maturity, and even at the start of some rot; harvesting always two weeks after the neighbours, sometimes after All Saints (Nov. 1st). After pressing, the juice was placed in new casks of 275 litres. For the first week, a daily racking, with fining, followed by three to six further rackings. After each racking the cask was *muté*—alcohol placed in it—until there was one-third *eau-de-vie* and two-thirds dry white wine.

"This mixture was then stirred (*bâtonnage*), but always in good weather with a North Wind. Conditioned in this state, it was reported, the white wine could live for fifteen to twenty years. With age it became dry and maderised, taking the colour and taste of a Malaga. Any bottling could take place in March, when it was still very sugared. On a tasting level, it was compared with the Roussettes of Seyssel away to the east in Savoie."

Condrieu has always been made in dry and sweeter forms, according to prevailing tastes. One of the 1990s themes was the move towards late-harvested wines, their sweetness derived from the extreme maturity of the grapes often picked in late October or early November. Fifty years earlier there had also been a change in tastes, as witnessed by Georges Vernay. When he first joined his father in the family vineyard in 1944, the prevailing taste was just changing from a sweet and sparkling wine to a drier version.

These wines skipped past the *demi-sec* level and went straight on to sweetness in various forms—drying grapes *en passerillage*, late-harvested and even *vin de paille*. There are only a couple of growers still making a commercial Christmastime *demi-sec*, Yves Lafoy and Marc Rouvière. It's been abandoned by Gilles Barge and Georges Vernay, amongst others.

The two debutants in 1990 were Yves Cuilleron and André Perret; the former has stuck with his Ayguets late-harvested wine; the latter made one other sweet wine in 1997, and gave up. André Perret explains his view: "I wasn't convinced by the wine's ability to show well over time, like many late-harvested wines, because of its lack of acidity. These wines for me are very nice over the first two to three years for those who like their fruit to be sugared."

When there isn't marked new oak use, I find the sweet wines reinforce the floral side of the Viognier's aromas and bring out the spice on the palate. Often, too, there are brown sugar elements, and fruit pie connotations.

There's also disorder on the legislation front: "0.90 gm of volatile acidity is allowed by the *appellation* laws," says Yves Gangloff, "but there's always going to be more than that on a late-picked wine [his was 1.1 gm on 2001] because its raising takes so long. The law needs changing, since the 0.90 gm refers of course just to the dry Condrieu. The late-cropped wines need to have their own set of rules and constraints."

Already, of course, Alsace has forbidden the use of the words "Vendange Tardive" on these wines. So there's *moelleux*, *passerillage*, autumnal picking, and all allusions to ripe crop.

CONDRIEU

Condrieu is one of life's most ample, lush white wines, but the statement needs to be made that it can also age well. The much distributed view that it must be drunk within three to four years is untrue. In its youth, it is naturally more exuberant than in its middle age, the aroma card a strong component of its charm. But Condrieus of 20-plus years hold deep-seated flavours, a different style of aroma, and give plenty of pleasure.

Young Condrieu possesses a fine combination of powerful fullness and flowerlike delicacy. Its aromas are instantly striking. They evoke a highly singular series of scents and smells, a range of flowers and fruits. Acacia, irises, peonies can all be found; the Vernays even detect fermented yoghurt in their young wines. The fruit aromas centre on pear, white peach, apricot, greengage, and green apple. Often a prime sensation is that of slightly underripe pears or of eating the fruit near the pear skin.

On the palate good Condrieu should show overt stone-fruit flavours; peach and apricot are typical candidates, with pears present, too. In hot vintages like 2000, the sensation is that these fruits have been stewed. Other tastes to be found are melted butter and a custard, flan flavour. The inherent richness lasts for four or five years before tightening and settling towards a drier texture.

The finish on Condrieu should always be clear-cut. This is where minerality can come through, a dry-toned or pebbly prickle at the end, which helps the wine's definition: glowing and ample on the start, orderly and compact on the finish. Nuttiness is apparent on the finish of wines from the *Chéry* slope, spice is sometimes present, and at times saltiness can also come through. Another finale can be aniseed or fennel.

An important influence on the aromatic profile of the wine has been new or young oak. This levels the aromas down to more international "exotic fruits" scents—tropical fruits like pineapple, guava, and banana. The new oak can be absorbed after three or four years providing the raw material is sufficiently well ripened.

Another aspect of Condrieu, that can be found in wines from southern areas like Limony, is its minerality. This blends with a light spiciness and is apparent on the finishing stages of the palate. Whereas the opening is full and unctuous, the wine's ending is pointed and channelled in an unexpected way.

Exposure and altitude come into play on this, as well. Yves Cuilleron's wine from *La Petite Côte* is more mineral than that of Louis Chèze from the hotter *Braise* at Limony. The variation stems mostly from altitude, the higher, windier spots being fresher and gentler.

At times, there is also a tannic sensation in the wines. This comes through as a chewy finale, a suitable ending to wines that are often over 14° alcohol. Alain Paret talks about this and advises that his Lys de Volan wine should be left for two years to allow the tannins to settle. This is also something that is evident with the Coteau de Vernon of Domaine Georges Vernay and the Chéry from Robert Niéro. It also pops up in years of lower sun levels but correct ripeness, like 1996.

Another underappreciated aspect of the Viognier is its acidity. Bottles over 20 years old from more lively vintages like 1979 remain fresh and tight on the finish. Yves Gangloff agrees that he is often surprised by this: "There's always a challenge surrounding the balance of its alcohol, richness, the maturity of the grapes, and its acidity; this can lie between 3.0 and 3.5 pH, which I consider to be good. I often harvest a bit later, in successive pickings, and I'm often pleased by the acidity that goes with the sugar richness."

With the *appellation* spread over different *communes*, there is clear leeway for style differences. The traditional saying, according to Stéphane Montez, is that Chavanay's wines are the aromatic ones, Condrieu's the richer, more *gras* wines. Georges Vernay finds more fruit in the heartland wines right around Condrieu, with which I would concur. There are certainly more deep-seated flavours and a more prolonged, savoury side to the wines from there.

In local terms, most Condrieu is vastly different from its neighbour Château-Grillet. The latter is a wine that needs patient cellaring and is never as showy as Condrieu. An understated pear flavour is its closest point of comparison. One Condrieu, Vernay's Coteau de Vernon, is similar; it too is a wine that shows complexity and increased flavours after six years or more. Both wines can still show well beyond the age of 20, and both benefit from airing or decanting.

With such an essentially robust wine, it is often a good move to decant Condrieu. It is also wise to serve it lightly chilled, not straight out of a fridge where it has sat for many hours.

Viognier is subject to the dumb spell that hits so many white Rhônes a little after bottling. André Perret feels his wine can close up around July after bottling, just under two years old: he recommends they should be drunk from the start of their third winter. Gilbert Clusel echoes this, feeling his wine can lie low after 18 months, for as long as another 18 months.

Condrieu's evolution is an interesting one, and doesn't tally with that of many white wines. The wine's aromas change early on and lose the overt floral side; scents of rotted fruit come along, a more fungal, even cheesy note can be struck. A constant aroma that I find in all old Viognier is damp wool, evident still when the wine is over 20 years old. This tends to disappear after an hour or so.

After this early shift, the aroma profile holds stable. The wine changes early on, people give up on it, and then it doesn't evolve much more. Twenty-year-old Condrieu from the best places is not old wine. Analytically, it bears acidity, vigour, freshness, and clear flavours that come and go with air.

On the palate, dried fruits enter the equation with age. The wine becomes more sinewy and there are lime tart, honey, and cooked fruit connotations. Underlying the flavour is a body of southern ripeness that is not dry.

One of the few growers who openly supports ageing the Viognier is Jean-Michel Gérin: "Obviously the lively years like 2001 can help it to age. But the tradition of drinking the wine quickly came from the days of *moelleux,* the sweet version that risked re-fermentation if left too long. Nowadays the technology to make the wine is better than those late 1970s, early 1980s you talk about, and I reckon Condrieu should be considered as a wine that can do well over the course of some years."

Georges Vernay agrees: "If you vinify Viognier correctly, the wine doesn't get old," he says. "It keeps its floral aromas for three years, and then turns towards acacia and *tilleul* or lime."

The wines to which he refers, his 1979 and the 1983 Coteau de Vernon, have been quietly left over the years, and now are great fun to show to the band of doubters about the Viognier's keeping powers.

1979 Vernay, drunk in 2002: air moved the bouquet from damp wool, exotic fruit to a marked buttery, almost Chardonnay intensity with a tang of citrus. Salty aspects later. The palate started mineral, moved to buttery, then tightened and became more complex. Pears, a salty tang and lime notably, gave way to aniseed and some final heat after two hours. There were present young Viognier aspects, notably the pear flavour, but the the greatest change had occurred on the bouquet.

And a Coteau de Vernon from Vernay 1983, drunk in late 1995: very pale gold; dried raisin smells, a little cheesy. Tight, not lush. Fine-

boned wine, tucked up at first. Gains opulenece and floral side with air. A lovely breadth emerges, similar to old Marsanne in some respects. Dried, quite firm aftertaste. Can still run till around 2003–05.

In blends, even those involving the Syrah, Viognier is a bully. I remember the 20 per cent Viognier in a Côte-Rôtie of the late Robert Jasmin: the Syrah fruit and grip was flattened, with a pomade effect brought to the wine. Very careful amounts need to be lent to fellow white varieties like Grenache Blanc, Bourboulenc, and Clairette, also Roussanne. Grenache Blanc and Viognier, as sometimes encountered, are like a couple of Sumo wrestlers failing to reach a result. Acidity and neutrality are helpful for the Viognier. Roussanne can be a successful ally— an interesting example of this blend being Steve Edmunds's Los Robles Viejos white from California, where both varieties are cofermented in old oak.

There is now an extensive range of sweet Condrieus available. During the 1990s many growers widened their array of wines to run from dry to very sweet, the latter always involving new oak. For a grape that is so naturally potent and rich, this often comes out as overkill, with delicacy kicked out of the back door in favour of exhibitionism. Many of these wines are crazily heavy, laden with residual sugar. They aren't for pleasure or for gently convivial chats over a meal—it's all "bow down at the temple" time.

The sadness is that there are some genuinely made sweet wines, with a nobility of structure and a potential to age, but they are often lost in the great banal crowd. Pierre Gaillard and Yves Cuilleron achieve high quality, as does Christophe Pichon, for instance.

The craze for late-harvest wines, although they can't formally be called "Vendange Tardive," poses a dilemma. Here the gap between *terroir* and wine served in the glass is stretched to breaking. Tasting notes constantly refer to burnt brown sugar and oak, with some traditional touches of pear and apricot mixed in. Bergamot and orange marmalade also show up, and very few wines present the likelihood of a long life ahead.

These wines are anything but pure: they represent a forcing hand, a domination by the maker, and if written off as a bit of (very expensive) fun, then perhaps I should calm down. But nagging away is the thought that perception can quickly become reality, that the average drinker anxious for an immediate big hit for the big money considers this to be the real Condrieu, and once tiring of it, moves away to another, probably New World big hit. The grower mounts the risky catwalk of fashion. When budgets tighten, does the drinker remain faithful? And we move another step nearer laboratory wines—just throw in the usual man-made elements, and presto!

A more experienced and reasoned voice is that of Georges Vernay: "Overripeness suppresses aromas, and you pass a point of genuine Viognier expression. You'll never find any minerality in a wine made with extremely ripe crop, either."

The formula for these wines, which were propagated by the New Wave, younger growers during the 1990s, and which drew a lot of acclaim from some leading US writers, runs thus. The formula coefficient rises, by the way, in direct proportion to the size of the Bank Loan held with Crédit Agricole or similar.

$$D(A + B - C) + EF \times GH = £\$€ + I$$

where

A = young vines = less intense fruit

B = pick fruit late = more intense fruit

C = if fruit starting rot, sort and extract more from other berries

D = cool ferment in new oak barrels to prolong extraction

E = leave on lees and stir like crazy

F = complete malolactic

G = make maximum noise in the market

H = sell to fashionable places, max out on PR

I = rest feet on Bank Manager's desk, light up No 1 Havana

There's a final irony attached to these extreme-ripeness wines; they couldn't be made in decades gone by, for the simple reason that there were too many fruit trees and woods around the vineyards. "The birds—mainly blackbirds and thrushes—would eat all the grapes!" says Georges Vernay.

IDEAL FOODS TO ACCOMPANY CONDRIEU

Condrieu can pose problems for food because it is such a rich wine. But scratch away, ask the growers, have a few tryouts, and there is a great range of dishes that it can help to light up.

Pure, clean Condrieu—the more oak-free cuvées—is great as an aperitif. The oaked wines require food.

It's also one of those rare wines to be a great companion for fresh asparagus, as shown by a lush Guigal Doriane 1997, and with another awkward vegetable, celery. Christine Vernay supports asparagus as good with her Condrieu when it's young, as well as cardoons, the local winter vegetable. Christophe Pichon drinks his with artichoke hearts. It was an artichoke *purée* that the Restaurant Lucas Carton of Paris presented with a Vernay Condrieu: "The *purée* was done with lemon and ginger, the ginger to cut the lemon's acidity," recalls Christine Vernay.

Jean-Michel Gérin likes Condrieu with black truffles: "Simple truffle dishes, pasta with grated truffles, for instance, work well." A five-year-old Vernay Coteau de Vernon 1995 was a near-perfect match with a scrambled eggs/black truffle dish.

If dining locally, it's a treat with any pike *quenelles* dish such as the *quenelles de brochet* with lobster touches served at the superior Beau Rivage restaurant beside the Rhône.

With his Chéry, André Perret recommends langoustine tails and lobster. Langoustines—straight grilled—are liked by Christine Vernay, while Yves Gangloff also finds his Condrieu very good with warm lobster, but emphasizes that shellfish should definitely be avoided. By contrast, the restaurant Lucas Carton in Paris prepares a Coquille St Jacques (scallop) dish with its artichoke *purée* mixed with ginger. Philippe Faury also advocates scallops, just plain steamed.

Many fish are too delicate, but the most appreciated are monkfish and turbot, also salmon trout in sauce. Pierre Dumazet enjoys his full dry wines with a variety of sea fish, citing turbot and sea bass, while he finds the *moelleux* goes well with lobster. Sea bass and red mullet are mentioned by Christine Vernay as having the strength of flavour to accompany a Condrieu, and it also works well with smoked salmon, where richness meets its namesake.

Philippe Faury and Yves Gangloff like *poulet à la crème* (creamed chicken) with their wines, a view shared by Christine Vernay once her Condrieu is five to seven years old; a wild mushroom or *morille* sauce is also advocated for the chicken. In similar vein, Pierre Dumazet likes quail with his wine. A couple of growers talk about Condrieu with white meats, as well.

Several growers praise warm foie gras as a good complement for Condrieu of the dry kind; while I find the late harvest wines are oppressive, that is not the view of the older generation in the form of Pierre Dumazet, who suggests his *moelleux Myriade* with it. Louis Chèze sits neatly in between by recommending that his richer dry wine, the Cuvée de Brèze, be drunk with foie gras.

The Bernard brothers find Condrieu to be a good partner for the strong flavour of snails, as well as spiced food. François Gérard favours both *foie gras* and snails! Jacques Grange of Delas shares my view that Condrieu's warm richness is a good complement for spiced Chinese, Cambodian, Vietnamese, or Thai food, an observation that opens up enormous gastronomic frontiers.

Cheese and Condrieu can work. André Perret, Louis Chèze, and Pierre Dumazet like it with Roquefort, while many growers praise the local goat's cheese Rigottes de Condrieu. "Both firm and soft goat's cheese suit," says Jean-Michel Gérin, "but the wine must be fresh, and not too heavy in style," a view fully supported by Christine Vernay. That's also why André Perret prefers his more elegant Chanson for Rigottes, and Bernard Chambeyron his Condrieu with a cheese that isn't too strong—plumping for cow's milk *rigottes d'Ampuis*, conveniently made by his sister!

With dessert, Georges Vernay enjoys his Condrieu with apple pie.

THE PRODUCERS

DOMAINE DES AMPHORES

7 Richagnieux 42410 Chavanay +33(0)474 876532

See also St-Joseph.

Véronique and Philippe Grenier planted a tiny 0.15 hectare at *La Côte* in 2003 for their Condrieu. The domaine was registered as biodynamic in 2002, but had been working naturally for many years and is mainly a St-Joseph producer.

DIDIER ET GILBERT BADIOU

La Ribaudy 42410 Chavanay +33(0)474 870696

Didier Badiou is a neighbour of Philippe Faury at *La Ribaudy* near Chavanay, and also makes red and white St-Joseph.

DOMAINE GILLES BARGE

8 Blvrd des Allées 69420 Ampuis +33(0)474 561390

See also Côte-Rôtie, St-Joseph.

Gilles Barge turns out very sound Condrieu, which since 2001 he has called "La Solarie." It is made from just over one hectare, off three plots: 30-year vines on the *Côte Bonnette* just above the houses of Condrieu, and a mix of rented vines on *Blanchard* (1980s) and *La Ribaudy* (1990) at Chavanay a little to the south.

The Condrieu is always made in a mix of stainless steel and wood, with flexible proportions according to the year: half and half in 1996 and 2000; 65 per cent cask, 35 per cent steel in 1995. The steel provides the freshness, the wood, which is always four to five years old, the richness. A little lees stirring is done.

Gilles resolutely refuses to join in the low-temperature fermentation approach and has stayed at 20° to 25°C, a purely traditional approach.

The wine is bottled around the end of May, malolactic done. There are around 5,000 bottles.

The style is usually for refinement, without the full-on power found chez some of the younger growers. In the mid-1990s, the wine contained some later-picked crop but is now back towards a more measured, slightly drier form. The bouquets are always pretty and refined.

There used to be a *demi-sec*, just one or two casks' worth, but this was not really a commercial do and was dropped in 1998.

CONDRIEU LA SOLARIE

2004 ★★★
2002 ★★★
2001 ★★
2000 ★★
1998 ★★

EMMANUEL BAROU

Picardel 07340 Charnas +33(0)475 340213

See also St-Joseph.

The competent Barou family has worked *en bio* since 1975; Emmanuel made his first Condrieu in 1997, working the Limony vineyard of a retired local man. This is right at the southern end of the *appellation*, in a classic zone, one of the best within Condrieu.

He started with 0.3 ha on *Fontailloux* (1991), with a sandy-silty soil, and from 2004 he has worked 0.3 ha at *Braise*, on the decomposed granite.

The crop is decanted at 10°C and then vinified in cask, one-third new at around 18°C. It is raised on its lees, with a gentle weekly stirring until the malolactic has finished. Bottling is in June.

The wine reflects a stylish, unforced upbringing and leans towards the controlled version of Condrieu, with a tight finish. It will gain in richness as the vines grow up.

CONDRIEU

2004 ★★★
2001 ★★

MARIE ET PIERRE BÉNÈTIÈRE

42 Grande Rue 69420 Condrieu +33(0)474 861893

See also Côte-Rôtie.

Pierre Bénetière has moved up in the world. Imagine a flat Montmartre; take out the young, international crowd; replace them with retired provincial French people; drop in a row of plain, low houses; plonk down a jumble of casks, wooden stakes, and cellar tools; and presto!— until 2003 that was Condrieu's most offbeat vinification venue, the house and garage of Pierre Bénetière in Roussillon, a small town across the Rhône in the Isère *département*. His vineyard is probably only a little larger than Montmartre's, too.

In 2003 he shifted his cellars back to an old family house in Condrieu, a central location that had been the main wine store for several years. "I feel a little lost now that I have so much space," he jokes.

What did his old neighbours, used to quiet suburban living, make of it all? "Well, to bring in the grapes, I hire a truck for two weeks. Now in this tiny road a car usually passes every three hours, but when it's the truck and the grapes, lo and behold, a car comes along inside a minute!" Pierre Bénetière, clad in a check shirt and stout boots and often likely to take the counterview if he can, has a very wry sense of humour. He delights in reeling off the names of the past rugby greats from Wales, England, or France. Then he moves on to Roussillon's history, a note of chiding evident that the visitor is less than well informed.

"This is where Charles IX, Catherine de Medici's son, proclaimed the start of the Julian calendar in 1564, moving us to a 1st January new year, rather than Eastertime." He is also Protestant, so is outside the local crowd on that front, too.

"My friends all said it was an impossible task, to get land cleared and planted for vines, then to make the wine," he recalls in his nice, quietly gravelly tone. "That got me going, for a start. I studied oenology in Lyon, Paris, Dijon, Mâcon, and remember, my family were wine merchants at Condrieu. They sold local table and Algerian wines to the bars and cafés, so, like Obelix, I fell into wine pretty naturally."

In 1990, four years after starting to clear land, he planted 1.5 hectares at *Le Tinal*, complete with stone wall terracing, above Vérin and Château-Grillet. The soil is acid, with the classic shiny and slippery *arzelle* of very loose granite. He also planted 0.2 ha in 1994 at *Le Riollement*, deeper into the *Tinal* valley, where the soil is sandier and more schist covered. In the same years, Pierre also planted just over a hectare at Côte-Rôtie.

"The less I go to the vineyard, the better for me," is how Pierre describes his approach. There are no pesticides, nor insecticides, but treatment against fungal problems has to be done.

The one new piece of equipment after the cellar move has been a pneumatic press. The Condrieu is all oak vinified, the new oak content at 11 per cent, the temperature around 19°C. The wine spends a year on its lees. It tends to be full, with plenty of chewy, ripe matter. The bouquets can open when exposed to the air for a little while.

He also makes a little late-picked wine, which he calls Indian Summer in French. The grapes are picked until around 25 November and the production has risen from 80 litres in 1997 to 300 litres in 2000 (he skipped a 1998). The aim is to achieve a balance in a wine of this nature. It is a solidly filled wine, which can live and develop over time.

Behind the humour, one can sense that Pierre loves the wine he makes—he defends it in the cellar with little touches of detail—closing casks quickly or not pouring half a glass of young vat wine back into the casks. He admits that his wife, Marie, who works in an accountancy business, kept him for seven years, so maybe now he can settle and steadily build on his progress so far. The first adventures are over. As he approaches 40, the time is right for consolidation.

CONDRIEU

2002 ★★
2001 ★★★
2000 L'Été Indien ★★

Export 40 per cent (1) Netherlands, (2) Japan, (3) Great Britain

DOMAINE BERNARD

RN 86 69420 Tupin et Semons +33(0)474 595404

See also Côte-Rôtie.

Brothers Frédéric and Stéphane Bernard work a rented 0.7 hectare of Viognier, a vineyard on *Bassenon* that was replanted in 1987. It's right at the north end of the *appellation*, only 300 metres from their Côte-Rôtie vineyard on what is now officially called *Coteaux de Semons*. The *Bassenon* stream runs between the *appellations* at this point. The soil is a typical sandy *arzelle*, or very loose, grainy granite.

Their wine, Coteau de Bassenon, is around half steel, half oak vinified at 15° to 18°C, with twice-weekly lees stirring. It is raised in vat and cask until the malo has been done and is bottled in September. This is four months later than in the mid-1990s, and efforts have clearly been made to bring forth more depth in the wine than some of the taut offerings of a few years ago. They also destalked the Viognier for the first time in 2002: "We felt the stalks were adding a touch of greenness to the wine," comments Stéphane.

CONDRIEU COTEAU DE BASSENON

2002 ★
2001 ★

DOMAINE LAURENT BETTON

La Côte 42410 Chavanay +33(0)474 870823

See also St-Joseph.

Young Laurent Betton makes Condrieu from 1.7 ha high up at 320 metres on the exposed hillside of *La Côte* (1989–93), just above Chavanay, where his neighbours are growers like Yves Cuilleron. The southeast-facing hill has poor, sandy-stony soil on a granite base with quick drainage. The vines are trained on wires.

The wine is vinified two-thirds in oak (half new, half on year old), and one-third in steel at 18° to 20°C. It receives a year's ageing before release.

Laurent bottles one-quarter of his crop; the rest is sold to Guigal. The wine shows a mix of zest and light substance, the tone overall being of a fresh wine in a vintage like 2001.

CONDRIEU

2003	★★(★)
2002	(★)
2001	★

DOMAINE BOISSONNET

Rue de la Voute 07340 Serrières +33(0)475 340799

See also St-Joseph.

Building up their Condrieu vineyard are André and son Frédéric Boissonnet, who live outside the Condrieu zone in the more southerly village of Serrières, noted for its water jousting on the Rhône, which runs right past it.

Currently they work half a hectare, which is due to double by 2007. They also work plots planted in 1994 on the granite *La Côte* at Chavanay and at Limony.

The wine is vinified in cask, 15 per cent of it new, the rest one year old. A weekly *bâtonnage* is done, and bottling is in July. It possesses quite a rich, sometimes earthy bouquet, and a fair fullness on the palate. It is an example of the group of Condrieus whose vines need to mature more before their fullness can be deep-seated.

CONDRIEU

2003	★★
2002	★
2001	★

DOMAINE PATRICK AND CHRISTOPHE BONNEFOND

Le Mornas 69420 Ampuis +33(0)474 561230

See also Côte-Rôtie.

Father Charles Bonnefond had started to look ahead for his teenage sons Patrick and Christophe when he first cleared, then planted a hectare of Viognier on the *Côte Châtillon* in 1988. He was a *viticulteur* pure and simple, selling off any crop he grew.

The vineyard is a prime location above Condrieu, on the granite. The crop receives a 12-hour decantation and since 2000 has been fermented in new oak, with a bit of the lees from the decantation present to nourish and round off the juice. The temperature is held at 16° to 18°C. *Bâtonnage* is done on the lees until May, then the wine goes into vat, and is fined and bottled in July, the malo done.

"We don't want a superfat wine," explains Christophe, "which is why we harvest around 13 to 13.5°, not really late. We rely on the lees effect to achieve richness, and want the wine to be fresh rather than heavy and alcoholic."

This is supported by tastings; the wine has a zesty side in fresher vintages, a fairly modern approach in its vigour. It can be drunk quite early.

CONDRIEU CÔTE CHÂTILLON

2004	★★★
2003	★★
2002	★★
2001	★★

DOMAINE DE BONSERINE

2 chemin de la Viallière Verenay 69420 Ampuis +33(0)474 561427

See also Côte-Rôtie, St-Joseph.

This Côte-Rôtie house sells a little Condrieu via its *négociant* business, buying grapes from the good village of Limony and vinifying them. Fermentation and raising are done in oak, half of it new, and lasts 10 months. The aim is to work with very well ripened grapes that emphasize the Viognier's plush features.

The wine was formerly called "Père Capus," but is now called "Bonserine." It shows off ripe, cooked fruits.

CONDRIEU BONSERINE
    2004 ★★
    2001 ★

LAURENT CHARLES BROTTE

Le Clos rte d'Avignon 84230 Châteauneuf-du-Pape
+33(0)490 837007

See also Cornas, Côte-Rôtie, Crozes-Hermitage, Hermitage, St-Joseph.
Domaine du Versant Doré is the Condrieu sold by the Châteauneuf-du-Pape–based *négociant* house of Laurent Charles Brotte. Their merchant wines are carefully chosen, from top-end sources.

Christophe Pichon is the grower at Condrieu, and the wine carries his usual accomplished, quite reserved style. There are appealing spice and refined white fruit flavours present.

CONDRIEU DOM DU VERSANT DORÉ
    2002 ★
    2001 ★★★★

BERNARD CHAMBEYRON

Boucharey 69420 Ampuis +33(0)474 561505

See also Côte-Rôtie.
Bernard Chambeyron is better known as a member of a long-established Côte-Rôtie family. He made his first Condrieu in 1988, having planted 0.7 ha on the north side of *Vernon* in 1985.

The wine is vat fermented at a quite low 16°C for around two weeks and is then raised for six months, 75 per cent in oak (a tiny 8 per cent new, the rest five years old), 25 per cent in vat. There is a little lees stirring, and the wine is bottled with its malo completed. Around 3,000 bottles are made.

The wines are well made, with restraint. There is a correct pear/apricot local touch and a good mix of aromas. They are stylish and understated.

There is also a good vat-only Viognier *vin de pays des Collines Rhodaniennes* and an interesting *moelleux*, or sweet Viognier *vin de table*.

CONDRIEU
    2004 ★★
    2002 ★★★
    2001 ★★

DOMAINE DE CHAMPAL-ROCHER

Vignobles Rocher 2 rue de Belgique 69160 Tassin
+33(0)478 342121

See also Crozes-Hermitage, St-Joseph.
Eric Rocher, based in Lyon and holding diverse vineyard interests in both northern and southern Rhône, has 0.85 ha on *La Coste* at Limony, planted between 1999 and 2001.

The wine is part steel, part oak fermented and raised. The oak is two to three years old.

CAVE DE CHANTE-PERDRIX

Izéras 42410 Chavanay +33(0)474 870636

See also St-Joseph.
Philippe Verzier works 1.7 ha of Condrieu, with a tiny 0.2 ha on the prime *Chanson* site just north of Chavanay, the rest on the *Izéras* hill running west of the village near the Madone statue: there the decomposed granite has more clay mixed into it.

The Viognier was planted when Philippe started in 1988; "The vineyard contained quite a lot of hybrid vines for red wine and had been abandoned after the Second World War."

His Condrieu gets a little more oak than it used to—50 per cent is oak fermented (new to five-year-old barrels)—with the rest in stainless steel. Since 1998 he has extended the time on the lees by six months, with stirring as he goes. This ties in with his destalking of 60 to 80 per cent of the crop in any given year. Bottling is in September, the malo done.

He makes a sweet wine, a *moelleux* called "La Chevalière." Since 1995 he has also made a late-picked Condrieu called "Les Grains Dorés." The 1999 was less concentrated than usual and ended with 50 gm of residual sugar. The crop was 70 per cent rotted, the result of rain in the first two weeks of October, and was picked in the first week of November. It is vinified half in new oak, half in vat and bottled in the following September.

The dry wine is usually marked by pear flavours, and veers from a pebbly texture to a quietly fuller one in the best vintages. There are spiced elements present, too—an imprint from the Chavanay area. "I seek a pretty finesse of aroma, with a fullness of flavour," states Philippe. "My calling card is finesse rather than too much density."

The sweet Chevalière holds some exotic flavours without being too overdone, while Les Grains Dorés successfully combines fat textures with some acidity and can benefit from being left to come together over four years or so.

CONDRIEU SEC

2004 ★★
2003 ★★
2002 ★
2001 ★★
1998 ★★★

CONDRIEU LA CHEVALIÈRE MOELLEUX

2001 ★
1999 ★★

CONDRIEU LES GRAINS DORÉS

2002 ★★
1999 ★★★

M. CHAPOUTIER

8 ave Dr Paul Durand 26600 Tain l'Hermitage +33(0)475 082865

See also Cornas, Côte-Rôtie, Crozes-Hermitage, Hermitage, St-Joseph, St-Péray.

Chapoutier bought into Condrieu in 1994, with the purchase of an unplanted 1.5-hectare plot on the largest *lieu-dit* at Malleval, *Volan*. By 2004 one hectare of this had been planted, the rest of the site being still overgrown. The south-facing hill is pure granite, with some clay patches here and there.

The company also owns another three-hectare area on *Merlan* and the adjoining site of *La Coste* in the northern sector of Limony; this is being cleared and will be planted in the years to come.

Their own production now accounts for about 30 per cent of the wine and is added to by the purchase of grapes from nearby growers, most of them at Chavanay and Limony. From 2004 a further source of quality crop developed with the agreement to buy the *Chéry* vineyard harvest from Jean-Yves Multier that had made up his Château du Rozay. This includes vines that date between 1921 and 1950.

The regular Condrieu crop is pressed and lightly decanted, then 50 to 60 per cent of the juice is cask-fermented in oak one to three years old, the rest in steel vats. It remains on its lees until April, with regular *bâtonnage*, and is bottled in June.

The wine has shown early promise, with enough content to handle its oak. Its structure is above average, and it will be capable of decent evolution over five or six years. I expect this wine to grow in stature and fullness as the vines age.

CONDRIEU

2004 ★
2001 ★★★
2000 ★★

DOMAINE DU CHÊNE

Le Pêcher 42410 Chavanay +33(0)474 872734

See also St-Joseph.

When he set up in 1985, Marc Rouvière worked just 0.24 ha of Condrieu. He has now enlarged his holdings to 3.5 ha. His sites are right beside Chavanay, 2 ha at *Les Eyguets* (1970s, 1997), with a very sandy topsoil on the granite rock; 1 ha close to it on *Les Rivoires* (1990), where there is a stronger amount of clay and a deeper soil mixed in with the sand-rock elements; and 0.5 ha on *Volan* (1989) at Malleval, where the clay content in the schist brings a later ripening.

Marc likes to harvest late from *Rivoires* and *Volan*, and in 1999 he actually finished picking on 10 November, by which time the grapes were grey-blue and with little juice left. But their state of health was excellent and contributed to his late-harvest Condrieu called "L'Automnale de Condrieu." Since 1990 around 400 to 500 50-cl bottles of this have been made in vintages with noble rot; recently it was made in 2002, but not in 2000 and 2001. In future this wine will be called "Julien," after his son.

Marc makes three styles, one of them unusual. This is a wine to cater for the traditional Christmas demand; 1,000 bottles are made for locals, and the style is *demi-sec*, with a blocked fermentation. This is the same as Yves Lafoy's Condrieu, very much an endangered species these days (no comment). Marc recommends this with foie gras—boom boom!

The wines are vinified 70 per cent in vat, 30 per cent in cask, two-thirds of it new. Fermentation takes place at 19° to 20°C, "so my wines can last more. The Condrieu might be a little less expressive, but it will live longer," he comments. Bottling takes place at the end of summer, and Marc also recommends decanting his Condrieu.

These wines have moved into a solid league at Condrieu—reliable, with good core and a restrained fullness of weight. They carry a sound variety of flavours and are aromatic. Their oak content can be intrusive at times, when the aromas and early appeal should be unbridled: more gentle oaking would suit. Nevertheless, the *appellation* needs more such wines to broaden its quality spread.

CONDRIEU

2004	★★★
2003	★★★
2002	★
2001	★★★★
2000	★★★
1999	★★★
1998	★★★

LOUIS CHÈZE

Pangon 07340 Limony +33(0)475 340288

See also St-Joseph.

Louis Chèze got his Condrieu going in 1987 and 1988, when he planted three hectares of Viognier on a single Limony hillside that comprises the *lieux-dits Braise, Côte Fournet,* and *Montrond.* These are part terrace, part slope; the highest areas at above 200 metres are *Fournet* and *Montrond,* both sand-topped granite. The *Braise* is slightly heavier granite, with patches of clay.

Louis produces three wines; the Cuvée de Brèze and Pagus Luminis (Latin for "country of light") are both dry; the Grains de Camille is a sweet wine made in most vintages.

The wines receive nine to 10 months of ageing after the destemmed crop has been vinified in cask; Pagus Luminis is raised in 10 per cent new, 90 per cent one-to-two-year-old casks, the Brèze in 40 per cent new, 60 per cent one-to-two-year-old oak because the grapes are richer and riper. In healthy years, unlike 2002, there can be a skin maceration to extract refined fruit. Lees stirring continues until the summer.

The Brèze wine (4,500 bottles) is from crop off the sunniest, middle part of the *Braise* slope, while the Pagus Luminis (7,000 bottles), is taken from the higher levels, where the crop is a little fresher. Louis recommends drinking the Brèze with foie gras or cheese such as Roquefort, and the Pagus as an aperitif or with sea fish.

The late-harvested Grains de Camille comes in 50 cl bottles, and around 1,000 bottles were made in 1996, 1997, 1999, and 2000.

The Pagus Luminis shows pear and sometimes tropical fruits, with a generally assured elegance. The Brèze is more obvious, somewhat of a full symphony, with the grower's hand well in evidence. It needs time to settle its oak content.

GILBERT CHIRAT

Le Piaton 42410 St Michel-sur-Rhône +33(0)474 566892

"You move the domaine on from *vin de table* to *appellation* wine, but there's one item that people often underestimate—the commercial side. That takes at least ten years to develop." Gilbert Chirat took over his family domaine in 1984, which got him going before the many early 1990s start-ups, all coming to Condrieu the same way—via fruit and other activities like raising anaimals.

"We are the third generation here beside the village of St-Michel," he says, his short-cropped black hair and moustache giving him a classic French look. He speaks in a harmonious tone, his steady way that of a countryman. "We raised dairy cows, as well as peaches, apples, and cherries, but as long ago as the 1970s, wine started to be worthwhile."

He has kept his ambitions orderly, and works 1.8 ha of Condrieu, plus having 1.7 ha of Syrah and 0.3 ha each of Chardonnay and Viognier in *vin de pays des Collines Rhodaniennes*. His wife, Catherine, works in the public service sector in Vienne, and he comments on just how this village, near the plateau above the Rhône, has changed in the past few years.

"The population has doubled, and quite a lot of the new people go off to work in Lyon—people who came from the suburbs there to live here. We don't see them a lot—many of them don't attend village events." At times he, the man of the land, must feel a little solitary.

Gilbert learnt his trade on the ground, with only a brief stay at Agricultural College. He and his father started the vineyard in 1979 with cuttings from Georges Vernay; their plots are on *La Bourdonnerie, Roche Coulante,* and the evocatively named *Sous l'Eglise,* all in the *commune* of St-Michel. The soil is predominantly fine, decomposed granite, with a little more clay on *Bourdonnerie.* The main planting was done between 1984 and 1990.

Gilbert tries to leave the vineyard alone as much as possible; he doesn't use insecticides, and the main fears are oïdium and black rot. The wind up here keeps mildew in check.

He makes just the one wine, and is against too much oaking: "The Viognier doesn't need lots of new oak—it's very fruited and aromatic, so why bother?" He vinifies 60 to 70 per cent in steel, the rest in cask split between new and one year old. Since the 1990s, he has moved the fermentation temperature up to 17°–18°C, and now raises the wine for 11 months, with weekly *bâtonnage* until the end of May, before a September bottling.

The domaine sells around 4,000 bottles a year, with one-third of the crop sold to the *négoce* trade. Its aromas are usually more overt than its flavours, which can be tight and redolent of pear skins.

The *vin de pays* vineyards date from 1988–93 and grow at around 270 metres, close to his house and neat cellars. The Viognier St-Michel is an open, quite bouncy wine, and the Syrah St-Michel carries clear black fruit flavours. The latter is all destemmed and raised for a year, half in cask, half in vat. It is fined, not filtered.

Export 15 per cent (1) USA, (2) Great Britain, (3) Belgium

LOUIS CLERC

1638-1658 route de Gerbey 38121
Chonas l'Amballan
+33(0)474 563164

See also Côte-Rôtie.

Louis Clerc, a man in his 60s who started to bottle his own wine in 2003, works 1 ha of Condrieu. His plots are spread across *La Roncharde* and *Rozay-sud* at Condrieu, *Verlieux* at Chavanay, and also Malleval. They were planted between 1992 and 1993.

The wine is fermented and raised 30 per cent in oak, 70 per cent in steel vat, and bottled with the malo completed in March. It is full, with an honest local feel.

CONDRIEU

2003 ★

DOMAINE CLUSEL-ROCH

15 route du Lacat Verenay 69420 Ampuis
+33(0)474 561595

See also Côte-Rôtie.

This excellent domaine works half a hectare on the prime site of *Chéry*, with a link to the southern spur of *Vernon*. The soil is granite with mica bits in it. This makes it fast filtering and hot in the high summer.

Their Condrieu is made in 65 per cent cask (new to five years old), 35 per cent vat, with the temperature between 18° and 20°C, and is bottled with the malo done in early September. There is a weekly *bâtonnage* of the lees over three months.

The vines were planted in 1984–85, the first wine coming out in 1987. As one would expect, it is always elegant, and even a little subdued at the outset. It can live well, and starts to take on more variety and complexity after three years or so.

The year 2003 was most unusual, with so much of the crop dried out. As a result, four casks of dry wine were made, and one cask of "sweet."

CONDRIEU

2003 ★★★
2003 "sweet" ★★★
2002 ★★
2001 ★
2000 ★★
1998 ★★★★

VINS JEAN-LUC COLOMBO

La Croix des Marais 26600 La Roche-de-Glun
+33(0)475 841710

See also Cornas, Crozes-Hermitage, Hermitage, St-Joseph, St-Péray.

Jean-Luc Colombo has changed his Condrieu's name from an early "L'Aurore" to a current "Amour de Dieu." Around 3,000 bottles are produced, with the wine purchased from Chavanay.

After an all-oak vinification, it is raised for 15 months in one-to-two-year-old casks, with lees stirring.

It goes for the buttery, replete style of Condrieu, with plenty of fat and at times a blowsy presence to it.

CONDRIEU

2002 ★

DOMAINE DE CORPS DE LOUP

69420 Tupin et Semons +33(0)474 872345

See also Côte-Rôtie.

Martin Daubrée planted 0.6 hectare on the *Côte Bonnette* above Condrieu in 2003. He also has a further 0.3 hectare being cleared and planted close to Condrieu itself. The first serious bottling will be in 2008.

YVES CUILLERON

Verlieu RN86 42410 Chavanay +33(0)474 870237

See also Côte-Rôtie, St-Joseph.

This is one of the best domaines at Condrieu, and turns out big, flavour-packed wines in the modern style. Some are very overtly oaked,

FIGURE 8 A rare pause for Yves Cuilleron, who has energetically taken the family domaine on to the world stage. (Tim Johnston)

stuffed full of wood, but others achieve a correct balance between the raw materials of the land and the man-made implements of the cellar.

Although his grandfather Claude and uncle Antoine were growers and had made their own wine in the 1920s, Yves set out on other paths and studied industrial design and engineering. "I was 23, in the army in Alsace, and there were these guys from Bordeaux and Burgundy swapping bottles, so I gave them some Condrieu. They really liked it! It was the time when my family were talking about selling the domaine, so I decided to give it a go," is how he explains his conversion back to wine.

So in 1984 he took himself to the Mâcon wine school, then spent a year with the Courbis family, makers of St-Joseph and Cornas. "I was also aware of our past, which played a role, too," he continues. "My great-grandfather made wine, sold off in bulk, but we'd started to sell bottles as early as 1947. That was called 'Vin de Chavanay' Viognier and Syrah, because the St-Joseph *appellation* hadn't been created then. My uncle bottled all his wine, so the name was known when I started."

And off he went at speed. Yves is always running around, projects abound, and his dress sense remains stuck in a Charity Shop warp. His Parisian garments for an upscale tasting there ran to some old pin-striped trousers, a claret-coloured top, and a neck-high pullover. He's small, busy, and charming and doesn't care about such niceties.

Uncle Antoine retired in 1986, leaving Yves to take over. A major leap forward came in 1992 with the move of the cellars from Antoine's house to a much larger location just outside Chavanay beside the N86.

Quickly the vineyard cultivation rose from four hectares to 18 by 1995 and nearly 28 in *appellation* vineyards by early 2005—taking in Condrieu, St-Joseph, and Côte-Rôtie. His Condrieu holdings cover 7.7 hectares, a mixture of ownership and rental from mostly family members. There are 3.5 hectares on *La Côte* (1970s, 1989) at Chavanay; some of this needed replanting and clearing, having held vines since before the Second World War; his other main *lieux-dits* are around half a hectare each on *Vernon* (1980s, 1990s), plus *Ribaudy* (1991) and *Peyrolland* (1988) south of the village.

Yves is a worker bee, and his office, run by his sister Odette, is always in a certain state of fever. His cellars are impressive and the sheer cash investment is testament to his commitment. He has been in the vanguard of the northern Rhône's quality and marketing advance during the 1990s. He speaks with a fired-up enthusiasm, and his energies found a perfect outlet in the vineyard project of Seyssuel, the once Roman vineyard north of Côte-Rôtie on the other, east bank of the river. This is shared with Pierre Gaillard and François Villard, and has given birth to Les Vins de Vienne. He also became President of the Condrieu Growers Union in 2004, adding to his work load and responsibilities.

He describes his vineyards as being largely granite, with a lot of sand and little clay. The majority are in the southern sector of Chavanay and Limony, where the granite contains more iron and is stronger stone, more red in colour—"good for wall making," he confides.

Because his crop is always "overripe," Yves does no pre-fermentation maceration. Even for his dry wines, he likes a little noble rot. The juice is cask fermented, 25 per cent new, the rest one to three years old. This usually lasts three to four weeks but can tick along to March in some years. "I'm after a gradual fermentation on a fine lees to get the best results," he says. Bottling is in June.

La Petite Côte is his workhorse Condrieu (12,000 bottles), served up in a full-blown style, with oak residues and ripe pear, apricot, and honey tones. This is from his many plots at Chavanay and Limony.

Next up is Les Chaillets (4,000 bottles) from older vines on *La Côte* (1976) and *Izéras* (1939). This is much more refined than Petite Côte and possesses serious structure. Within the melted butter and pear aromas lies a cool grain, and the wine's development through the palate is classic—its flavours are deep, the length strong. The Viognier is shown in a true light in Les Chaillets, which is one of the prominent wines of Condrieu.

In 2001 Yves launched a Condrieu called "Vertige," with crop from his *Vernon* plot. This

dry wine receives 18 months' cask ageing, and Yves's reasoning runs as follows: "I'm convinced that a prolonged raising adds length and a more creamy texture to the wines. Since the southern wines of Condrieu are aromatic and fruited, I'm emphasizing those aspects." On the palate there is a fine combination of *gras* and finesse.

For his sweet Viognier called "Ayguets," Yves uses crop taken from the middle of young vineyards on *Les Eyguets* and *La Côte*, where the birds do not naturally gather. His vines here are also on wires, allowing greater ventilation. Called *liquoreux* by Yves, this is often harvested in four runs that can extend between mid-October and mid-November.

"I'm looking for potential alcohol of 20° to 22°," he explains. "That means 100 to 120 gm of residual sugar and 13° to 14° alcohol." He makes 4,000 to 6,000 50-cl bottles of this. It is full, with plenty of different flavours—pineapple, white fruits, honey—in evidence, as well as some spiced touches. Even in a year like 2003, the acidity level was interesting. The Ayguets label declares that it is a "sorting of noble rot and grapes that are *passerillés*," or dessicated.

Yves' *vins de pays des Collines Rhodaniennes* are well done; the Marsanne and the Viognier are fermented at a low 16°C and both express a full, buttery flavour, even in tricky years like 2002. The Viognier is very representative of the great grape, and its character puts some of the less exalted Condrieus to shame.

CONDRIEU LA PETITE CÔTE

2003 ★★(★)
2002 ★★
2001 ★★

CONDRIEU LES CHAILLETS

2003 ★★★ Melted butter, pear aroma, some minerality also. Cooked white fruits with the vintage heat at end; full flavours and width. Good Viognier display.

2002 (CASK) ★★★ Ample colour and bouquet; good *gras* and width.

2001 ★★★★ Peach skin/nut nose, peppery/spice. Gentle dried fruit skins/marmalade flavour. Elegant, good length, mineral/toasty finish.

2000 ★★★ Reserved nose, good potential. Grows nicely on palate. Persistent, quite complex. Tight, discreet lemony edges. 2011.

CONDRIEU VERTIGE
   2002 ★(★)
   2001 ★★★★

CONDRIEU AYGUETS
   2002 ★★★
   2001 ★★★

Export 40 per cent (1) USA, (2) Great Britain, (3) Japan

DOMAINE DE BOISSEYT-CHOL

RN86 42410 Chavanay +33(0)474 872345

See also Côte-Rôtie, St-Joseph.
Maker of St-Joseph and Côte-Rôtie, Didier Chol started to plant at Condrieu in 2000. His tiny patch of 0.12 ha is on two sites, *La Côte* and *Boissey*, with clearing on the latter continuing all the while—a vineyard that had not been replanted since phylloxera. The soil is the loose *arzelle* of the area.

The first wine was made in 2004, with the vineyard moving gradually towards half a hectare in the first instance.

MAISON DELAS

*ZA de l'Olivet 07300 Saint-Jean-de-Muzols
+33(0)475 086030*

See also Cornas, Côte-Rôtie, Crozes-Hermitage, Hermitage, St-Joseph, St-Péray.
The firm's connection with Condrieu goes back many years, with the late Michel Delas owning 3.2 hectares that are now run by his son-in-law Maurice Bruyère, who sells the crop to Delas.

There are three plots at Vérin and St-Michel-sur-Rhône; the main vineyard is the 1.93 ha of Viognier planted around 1960 at *Clos Bouche*,

which is on the dark-coloured, south-facing granite-schist hill of Vérin near Château-Grillet. The best wine from here goes into the Clos Boucher cuvée, of which there are around 6,500 bottles.

The other wine is called "La Galopine," of which there are 13,000 bottles. "Galopine" is the old local word for Viognier. This is made from the three sites together.

La Galopine was vinified in stainless steel from 2003 with fermentation at a pretty cool 16°C. It is and bottled after eight months, the malo done. It carries a quiet charm, with light pear and spice aspects, and is in the elegant rather than full-blown group of Condrieus.

The Clos Boucher was the Condrieu standard-bearer for Delas during the 1990s, and often delivered the goods. The oak content here has been raised, and now it is vinified and raised purely in casks, a mix of 10 to 20 per cent new oak, the rest one year old, for eight months on its fine lees. *Bâtonnage* is done by cask turning until the malo has finished. Bottling is in May–June, after light fining and filtration.

Clos Boucher possesses enough content to demand a little patience, mixing white fruits with some chewy, spiced textures. The spicy, grainy side to it gives it more subtlety than the full-blown Condrieus, and the finish can carry a tannic-style chewiness in a big year like 2003. The wine is not made when the vintage has been difficult—hence the Galopine 2002 benefited; full vintages like 2001 and 2003 can run on soundly for around 10 years.

Until 1997 there was a sweet wine called "Brumaire de Bruyère," made with late-picked grapes off the slow-ripening eastern end of *Clos Bouche*.

CONDRIEU LA GALOPINE
   2003 ★
   2002 ★★★
   2001 ★★★

CONDRIEU CLOS BOUCHER
   2003 ★★★★

2002 Not made.

2001 ★★★

DOMAINE LUCIEN DÉZORMEAUX

Au Colombier 42410 St Michel-sur-Rhône

This is a long-standing domaine that has always valued its privacy. Their vineyard is the sublimely exposed *Coteau du Colombier* beside the N86 at St-Michel-sur-Rhône.

There was some bottling here in the late 1940s, and I recall early encounters with the fairly eccentric André Dézormeaux at the start of the 1970s. André used to cultivate vines and fruit trees, but it was the peach trees that often gained the better of the argument for space on the *Coteau du Colombier*, which rises steeply behind the back door of his house. So intrusive were the trees, taking space and spreading shade, that in the abundant year of 1973 he produced a mere 891 litres of wine; as a comparison, Georges Vernay, whose vineyard was then four times bigger, came up with over 12 times as much.

Son Lucien took over in the latter half of the 1980s, the peach trees have been removed, and most of the crop is sold to Guigal, contributing to his Doriane cuvée.

One of the Dézormeaux family traditions that has persisted with the arrival of the new generation is the domaine's sweet Condrieu, called "Coteau du Colombier" *demi-sec*. This is sold strictly locally.

When carefully made by a man with well-established Condrieu roots like Lucien Dézormeaux, the *demi-sec* can really strut the Viognier in all its panoply of sumptuous appeal.

DOMAINE PIERRE DUMAZET

RN 86 07340 Limony +33(0)475 340301

See also Cornas, Côte-Rôtie, St-Joseph.
Stylish, active, and charming are the attributes of Pierre Dumazet as he works on in his late 60s. He continues a winemaking dynasty that has run since 1870, but one that has always

been based on a tiny, vertiginous vineyard that is still now only 0.78 of a hectare.

The original holding is on the *Coteau de Côte Fournet*, a steep-ledged crumbled granite-sand site at the very southernmost end of the *appellation*, 13 km (8 mi.) from Condrieu itself, where there is 0.48 ha. The oldest 20 per cent dates from 1930, half is from the 1950s, and the rest from 1970 and later.

Complementing this is 0.3 ha on *Rouelle-Midi* (1970s), a granite site that drains fast. M. Dumazet is the only established grower here, but its south-facing exposure has been noted by others and new planting is taking place.

Pierre's father, Marc, was an amazing stalwart and inspiration to the young, since in his 70s he would still look after the vineyard, make the wine, and sell it—all by himself. This was some feat given the immense steepness of their vineyard above the hamlet of Limony, a "blink and you missed it" spot on the N86. The Dumazets used to grow fruit as well as vines, and Pierre's grandfather would make spectacular journeys all the way to London in his 1930 truck to sell the fruit at the Covent Garden market.

The family still hold a big reunion at the time of the *vendanges*. Marc Dumazet would pick his grapes early in the morning before the sun rose high, and Pierre has maintained this system. He is also a late harvester by practice, with two pickings for all his whites to ensure maximum ripeness, the first at the end of September, the second up until mid-October.

In father Marc's time the vineyard was just over a quarter of a hectare. This was not large enough to support Pierre full-time, so he left to work in the metallurgy industry in Lyon, and when his father died in 1978, he was only lightly versed in weekend winemaking. Throughout the decades this domaine has been naturally worked, without chemicals, making "60 times more work as a consequence," in Pierre's words. Blessed with a mane of lush silvery hair and the throaty voice and chuckle of his father, he explains: "It's hopeless to not let the roots gain nourishment from the rock further down—you lose typicity if you don't work the soil and the roots rise higher and higher," he says.

He has expanded the wine range, part of it through vineyards, part of it through a wine négociant business, and became a full-time *vigneron* in 1990. So now there are also 0.2 ha of Côtes du Rhône Viognier and 0.3 ha of *vin de pays*. Pierre also has shared operations for leading northern Rhône reds. At Côte-Rôtie he vinifies the crop for a *viticulteur* who has 0.75 ha on the *Côte Brune*—a 20-year-old vineyard of 95 per cent Syrah and 5 per cent Viognier. At Cornas, the same method applies to a 0.8 ha holding of 38-year Syrah in the middle of the *appellation* and to a 1.2 ha vineyard called *La Roue* at St-Joseph, with 40-year Syrah.

The Condrieus Fournet and Rouelle Midi are vinified in 20 per cent new, 80 per cent two-to-three-year-old casks; the former is raised for 12 to 15 months, the latter one year. The lees are stirred once a week after the end of the primary fermentation for five to six months. "This brings more richness," explains Pierre.

Even at this small scale, investment has been made to control temperature, so the casks are kept around the 15°C level during fermentation. The wine stays on its fine lees until the malolactic, then may have a light fining and bottling in late August.

He is a very careful and thorough man, and his wines have become some of the most regularly successful at Condrieu. They are marked by an intense concentration of flavour and a good old-fashioned Viognier power—sometimes making them heady indeed. If I wanted a wine to flaunt the true aromatic opulence of Viognier, it would often be a Dumazet.

Pierre's three sons give him a hand at the weekends, and the youngest, near his mid-30s, is the one who may take over. Franck for now lives at Chambéry and sells foodstuffs, but has done agricultural, wine, and commercial studies.

The Cuvée Rouelle Midi is named after its 0.3 ha slope vineyard. This is vigorous, full, pushy wine. The Côte Fournet is more "Arts and Letters"—a buttery wine with floral notes on the bouquet. Its spice reflects the difference in style from the wines of Condrieu village itself. These Condrieus are pretty power-packed and can show a full flourish around the age of five or more.

Since 1995 Pierre has made a late harvest wine called "La Myriade" from crop on *Fournet*. This is called *moelleux* on the label and gives the family good exercise at well-spaced intervals, since its grapes are picked over about five weekends ending around Armistice Day, November 11.

The Cuvée de la Myriade varies a little from year to year; it can end up at over 16° alcohol, but with just 9 gm of residual sugar, as in 2000. It was not made in 2001, and the 2002 held 80 gm of residual sugar. It is vinified half in new oak, half in steel, and is kept for two years before release in 50 cl bottles.

M. Dumazet then goes one step further for his Myriade Cuvée de l'Extrème, which is made from the very last picking of November 11: there is 90 gm of residual sugar in this overt but accomplished dessert wine. It is for gentle sipping, quite different from the regular.

The range of lesser whites is also very good. The Viognier *vin de pays des Collines Rhodaniennes* La Seilleoise, also oak fermented and raised, is spiced, nicely fresh, and classy for its title. The Côtes du Rhône Cuvée du Zénith Viognier is refined, with a chewy, dried fruit texture and good length. It is oak vinified and raised over a period of a year and comes from land at the foot of the slopes in Limony.

CONDRIEU ROUELLE MIDI

2002 ★★

2001 ★★

2000 ★★

1999 ★★

CONDRIEU CÔTE FOURNET

2002 ★★

2001 ★★★

2000 ★★★

CONDRIEU CUVÉE DE LA MYRIADE

2000 ★★★

1999 ★★★

1999 *Myriade Cuvée de l'Extrème* ★★★★

Export 55 per cent (1) Great Britain, (2) United States, (3) Ireland

MAURICETTE AND CHRISTIAN FACCHIN

Les Grand'Maisons 42410 Vérin +33(0)474 595891

Looking back, Christian Facchin took a good decision when he went off to work in a TV/video shop in Vienne in the early 1980s. Apart from providing him with a living, the owner also had two charming daughters, and so provided him with his wife, Mauricette, as well! Her family had an abandoned vineyard at Condrieu, which since 1984 they have set about replanting and tidying up.

"The vineyard is a challenge," he reflects, "but is in a wonderful position, the vines running all the way around the old dried stone house." The house, which is on the hill opposite the Beau Rivage hotel, has been in Mauricette's family since the Revolution, and it was her great-grandfather who had been the last person to work the vineyard until 1930. There are now 1.2 hectares in production at *Les Grands Maisons*. There are also small plots on *Vernon* and *Rochebret*, the latter in the *commune* of Vérin, bringing a total of two to five hectares of Condrieu.

The wine is vinified half in oak new to two years old, and half in steel. It is bottled in April. A little more oak than usual was used in 2001 but was cut back in 2002. The Facchin Condrieu accentuates elegance, with a compact texture and some spice. It is promising wine. Around 6,000 bottles are produced, with the rest of the crop sold to Guigal.

The Facchins also work 1 ha of *vin de pays* vineyards for a Collines Rhodaniennes Viognier, vinified the same way as the Condrieu, and a Syrah, Le Gour d'Enfer, which receives 15 months in cask.

CONDRIEU LES GRAND' MAISONS

2003 ★★(★)

2002 ★★★ Floral, pretty aroma; elegant, refined flavour with mineral.

2001 ★★ Toasted, oak-marked nose, elegant, some spicy apricot. Dried fruit flavours, toasty end. Christian suggests to drink it in 2005.

Export 10 per cent (1) Great Britain, (2) Belgium, (3) USA

DOMAINE THIÉRRY FARJON

Morzelas 42520 Malleval +33(0)474 871684

See also St-Joseph.

Thiérry Farjon has increased his Condrieu vineyards at Malleval to one hectare; the sites are *Volan* (1989–92) with its sandy, partly granite soil, *Veauvignère* (1999) on more full granite, and the most recent, *Les Patasses* (2003). All are on the southern flank of the hill high above the *Batalon* stream.

The Viognier is oak-vinified at the low temperature of 14°C, the casks ranging from two to eight years old. Lees stirring lasts over three months, and bottling is done in May. Outside yeasts are used to provoke the fermentation at the low temperature. In some vintages he makes a later-harvested Graines Dorées wine.

His dry Condrieu carries the effects of young vines, and the 2001 and 2002 show the need for more middle-palate depth. Bouquets are pear fruit in style.

CONDRIEU

2004 ★

DOMAINE PHILIPPE FAURY

La Ribaudy, 42410 Chavanay +33(0)474 872600

See also Côte-Rôtie, St-Joseph.

Until March 2004 Philippe Faury was the President of the Condrieu Growers Union, and this quite cautious, bearded man with a friendly face and deep voice was an excellent diplomat for that job. He has the air of a lecturer or a man of letters, and lives in charming isolation in a hamlet above Chavanay, La Ribaudy: "25 people live here in winter, 30 in summer" is his form of census.

Ribaudy comes from the old phrase to *faire la ribaude*, as in ribald, party time. It was a place with a well, so its local importance was high. This is 300 metres up on the plateau, and the houses are marked by the firm brown of their granite stone; just beyond them there is the quiet warble of peaceful birdsong and rustling sounds from the wind in the leaves. The pastures indicate the legacy of cropping the land for different foods, and such polyculture is a welcome sight when one considers the balance of the local ecosystem.

M. Faury works three hectares of Condrieu. These are on *La Ribaudy* itself (1978–88) and *Peyrolland* (1983), both near his cellars and both marked by the loose, sometimes stony granite of the area.

He makes two dry wines—one with just the name "Condrieu," the other "La Berne" (2,000 bottles), which comes from his 25-year vines on *La Ribaudy*. The regular wine is vinified in 10 per cent new oak, 40 per cent casks two to five years old, and the rest in steel. Fermentation is kept at between 20° and 22°C, the casks receive lees stirring, and the raising lasts 11 months, with a September bottling, malo done. M. Faury has done a stirring, or *bâtonnage*, since 2000, and finds that it makes the wines richer. His taste is to drink his wines between two and five years old: "then you capture the mix of floral aromas and their young fruit."

Made since 1997, La Berne is vinified the same broad way, with more new oak—25 per cent, plus 25 per cent two to five years old, the rest in steel. The new oak proportion has been reduced from around 40 per cent in the late-1990s. Even so, in a big wine year like 2003, the oak clambers all over the bouquet, robbing it of its early flamboyance.

When he can, M. Faury also makes a Condrieu *moelleux*, a sweet wine; in recent years, it wasn't made in 1998 (frost) and 2002 (rot). In 2001 there were 1,000 75 cl bottles. The grapes for this are picked a little later, in early October, and are vat fermented at 16°C; with 30 gm of sugar left, the fermentation is blocked by sulphur, cooling, and filtration. It is released after a year in steel vats.

The late-picked wine, Cuvée Brumaire, is the result of four or five successive pickings from mid-October until early December; the juice is fermented in cask at a deliberately low temperature of 8° to 12°C, over two to three months. It is then aged for 15 to 17 months, half in new, half in two-to-five-year-old casks. This contains 80 gm of residual sugar per litre. The wine has been made consecutively from 1994, missing only 1998, 2000, and 2002. On average 1,000 half bottles are made. Mandarin and brown sugar flavours mark it out as a small sip wine that could even go well with chocolate.

The wines here are usually restrained and elegant, not the heavy, souped-up style that can often be found. They are ideal with food, better than when served as an aperitif. La Berne has more body and structure than the often rather tight classic, and repays a later drinking. Its aromas also expand nicely if allowed to evolve. A vintage like 2003 should live until about 2011.

CONDRIEU
- **2003** ★
- **2002** ★
- **2001** ★★
- **2000** ★★

CONDRIEU LA BERNE
- **2003** ★★
- **2002** ★★
- **2001** ★★★

CONDRIEU MOELLEUX
- **2001** ★★

CONDRIEU BRUMAIRE
- **2001** ★★★

Export 20 per cent (1) USA, (2) Great Britain, (3) Sweden

DOMAINE DE LA FAVIÈRE

Vintabrin 42410 Chavanay +33(0)474 872338

See also St-Joseph.
Pierre Boucher works just half a hectare of Condrieu on *Veauvignère*, a mixture of south-facing slope and terraces west of Malleval. There is some clay in the decomposed granite. This is a far-flung corner of the Condrieu empire, and the wines do not possess the core quality and depth to be found near Condrieu village itself.

The vines were planted between 1998 and 2003. The crop is fermented in steel at 15° to 18°C, and after fining, remains in vat away from its lees, until bottling in June, the malo done.

FERRATON PÈRE ET FILS

13 rue de la Sizeranne 26600 Tain l'Hermitage +33(0)475 085951

See also Côte-Rôtie, Crozes-Hermitage, Hermitage, St-Joseph.
The Ferratons from Hermitage offer a Condrieu, Les Mandouls, which is wine purchased when young and raised by them, 60 per cent in oak, 40 per cent in vat, for 10 months. It is bottled, its malo completed, in June. It carries a typical pear flavour, with sound acidity in a vintage like 2001 and agreeably elegant fruit in 2002.

CONDRIEU LES MANDOULS
2002 ★★
2001 ★★★

DOMAINE PIERRE FINON

Picardel 07340 Charnas +33(0)475 340875

Just a postage stamp of 0.3 ha of Viognier for this good white wine maker. His St-Joseph *blanc* is an accomplished wine, and his Condrieu is also refined, in the house style. The vineyard is at Limony, on *Côte-Fournet*, between Laurent Marthouret and Pierre Dumazet. Its granite slopes and terraces were abandoned after the First World War, but Pierre Finon and his father restored this tiny plot and made their first wine from it in 1998.

The Condrieu is 80 per cent new oak, 20 per cent vat fermented, and raised for up to eight months. It seems suited for early drinking. Its white fruits are offset by some discreet oaking. There is also a sound duo of whites in *vin de pays des Collines Rhodaniennes*, made from Viognier and Marsanne, that are vinified in stainless steel. These vines lie outside the *appellation* zones. The Marsanne is a fresh, refined wine; the Viognier carries some floral aromas and mixes roundness with a little citrus.

CONDRIEU
2001 ★★★
1999 ★★

DOMAINE GILLES FLACHER

Le Village 07340 Charnas +33(0)475 340997

See also St-Joseph.
Gilles Flacher cleared and planted a 0.8 ha site on the decomposed granite of *Rouelle* at Limony in 1992, the first wine coming through in 1995. The land was overgrown and is terraced, up between 200 and 250 metres.

The Condrieu is cask fermented and aged for seven months in 60 per cent new, 40 per cent one-year-old oak. The lees are stirred during the malolactic fermentation. The oak overlay can be heavy, a pity since Gilles shows promise with his whites, even though he is one of the less well known local growers; when his vineyards are a little older, his Condrieu will step up a gear, especially if the oak is cut back a little.

CONDRIEU
2002 ★
2001 ★★

PIERRE GAILLARD

Chez Favier 42520 Malleval +33(0)474 871310

See also Côte-Rôtie, St-Joseph.

Pierre Gaillard has moved his Condrieu on from one hectare in 1995 to 2.5 hectares now. He works four *lieux-dits*, the best known on *Chéry* (1988) in the heart of Condrieu, plus *Côte Bellay* (1973, 1995) and *Gonon* (1998), either side of Malleval near his cellars, and *Boissey* (1993) at Chavanay.

Pierre had planted at *Les Rivoires* at Chavanay, but in the early 1990s he did an enterprising swap with Michel Mourier of Domaine de Pierre Blanche there: his site on *Les Rivoires* for M. Mourier's on *Côte Bellay*. Then both parties had a vineyard close to their cellars.

The soils are all granite, notably at *Boissey*, where Pierre finds the wine heavier and notably aromatic. From the Malleval and Condrieu sites, there is more minerality, he says.

Although he loves to proliferate his cuvées—he makes three St-Joseph reds, for instance—Pierre makes just one dry Condrieu, which is sold under that simple name.

He aims to pick with a near-overripeness; the summer work of stripping leaves and excess vegetation comes into play here. He no longer does an initial *macération pelliculaire*, since his vines have aged beyond the point where that is worthwhile, so there is pressing, decantation, and vinification in oak.

Pierre was one of the first to vinify only in cask, but has withdrawn from the use of only new oak. "I have always felt that the wood can help a Condrieu to live a bit longer, towards four years," he says. The wine receives seven months in cask, 10 per cent new, the rest one to 10 years old, and a weekly *bâtonnage* (lees stirring)—"to develop richness and aroma"—before bottling in June, the malolactic done. The temperature is kept at 16° to 18°C.

The dry wine shows full aromas, and enough substance to need a little time to blossom. Its texture is usually warm and nicely oily, and it is very reliable from one year to the next.

His two sweet wines are a late-harvested Condrieu called "Fleurs d'Automne" and what qualifies as a *vin de table* called "Jeanne-Elise" because it is a Viognier *vin de paille*. Pierre is more skilled than most at making these wines,

which hold a proper structure to allow serious ageing and development beyond the flashy early symptoms.

The Fleurs in 2002 was made after four pickings, the last in early November. Most of the grapes must have noble rot or botrytis, but Pierre keeps back a few that are healthy or *passerillé* to help the freshness of aroma in the wine. Fermentation is in new oak at 15° to 18°C, and there is a six-month raising with weekly *bâtonnage*. In 2002 there were 210 gm of residual sugar in the wine, its degree 13.

Jeanne-Elise is prepared in the usual way of picking ripe but not rotted grapes and laying them on straw racks to dry until Christmas. They are then fermented in new oak and raised for six months. The complex and successful 2002 had retained 240 gm of sugar, its degree 9.5.

CONDRIEU

2003 ★★
2002 ★★
2001 ★★★

CONDRIEU FLEURS D'AUTOMNE

2002 ★★★

VIN DE TABLE JEANNE-ELISE

2002 ★★★★

DOMAINE MATHILDE AND YVES GANGLOFF

2 rue de la Garenne 69420 Condrieu +33(0)474 595704

See also Côte-Rôtie.

It's always hard to imagine Yves Gangloff getting through a day of heavy *vigneron* labour, especially one that involves uprooting trees and building stone walls. He's about as skinny as me, and his supremely tousled, floppy dark hair seems better fitted to his collection of electric guitars spread around his upstairs pad, where rolled-up lengths of fabric patiently wait their marching orders for the curtains that have still not arrived after 10 years in residence.

So there's room for flair here, and that's what is happening with his Condrieu as the vines and their master run on with age. As of 2005 there are two hectares of Condrieu, and let's hope the progress he is making continues. His recent wines have shown great fullness of flavour and are delivered with a chewy, ripe Viognier texture: that's prose for "They're delicious," by the way.

A native of Strasbourg, Yves' first vintage was 1987, with 1,100 bottles of Côte-Rôtie and 500 bottles of Condrieu. His father had been in the army for half his career, then had worked in textiles in Alsace, so there was no obvious vinous connection. Yves made his first move towards wine in 1980, signing on with Delas to work in their vineyards at Condrieu and Côte-Rôtie. There he stayed until 1987, planting some of his own vines as he went along. "All my first learning and habits came from the soil," he states.

The first planting in 1984–85 was on an important half hectare of *Chéry* that he managed to buy. Yves recognises that his timing was good. "I was lucky," he observes: "there I was in 1983, able to buy this old vines' site for 80,000 francs [£8,000 or US$12,500]." Curiously, this would only have risen by around 50 per cent by 1992, according to Georges Vernay, but by 2004 it would cost 15 times more in all probability.

Currently there are 0.53 ha of *Chéry* (1985) and 1.2 ha of *Côte Bonnette* (1989–91), with an increase of 0.1 ha each year until 2005 for *Bonnette*. The soil for both is very similar, but *Bonnette* is more purely granite, with a free-draining sandy topsoil. Because his *Chéry* vineyard is low down the slope, there is clay mixed in with the granite there.

Clearing and planting a vineyard on these steep gradients is not everyone's cup of tea, but for Yves the work was fulfilling: "I loved making the dried stone walls on *La Bonnette*; we had to clear woods from a plot left alone for 30 to 80 years without vines, and it took us three months to do just half a hectare—what a project!" Part of the site belonged to the Hospital of Condrieu, which had stopped making its own wine in the

FIGURE 9 Outside wine, Yves Gangloff's love is his Fender guitar. Friends tell him he should stick to making wine. (Tim Johnston)

1960s, while the rest had been home to apricot trees. Yields from here are low, around the 20 hl/ha mark.

Yves has always been a soft operator in the vineyards, without going to full bio levels: "I have one full-time worker with me, but would have to employ a lot of people for that."

The Condrieu is all cask vinified and raised, at a temperature that he lets run freely between 18° and 26°C. "I don't have the kit to cool the casks, but I'm also in favour of a higher level overall than most people. If the casks are this warm, there is likely to be more richness in the wine. I'm trying to work the *terroir* more than the Viognier."

The casks are up to 30 per cent new (a slight decrease), the rest two to four years old. No outside yeasts are used, the wine is raised for a year and receives a lees stirring once or twice a week until the malo has finished in April or May. A curiosity is Yves' use of 300-litre casks, aimed to raise the proportion of wine to oak and so soften the wood effect.

In achieving the undoubted richness that is now present in his Condrieu, Yves is deliberately avoiding some of the more recent associations of the Viognier, now that it is so widely planted. "I don't want the vulgar aromas that it can give—too much apricot and peach make me think of southern Viogniers. Stone fruits and some subtlety should be in the bouquet—lime tree and mineral notes as well."

Yves's wife, Mathilde, works in the cellar and on the business side; she too has an artistic look, with her henna hair and full figure. Her black motorbike sits outside the cellars. It's no surprise to learn that their daughter is a student of Chinese, their son a rock drummer who is also studying plastic arts. Yves and Mathilde's first notable impact on the community came in their very first vintage, when the labels showed reclining nudes, a man and a woman, the man holding the glass. This was the work of Yves's brother.

"I met Mathilde through him. In return for the use of the artist's studio at the Château d'Ampuis, my brother had to look after and keep up the building. Mathilde was from Vienne, and I met her there at the Château."

With his Côte-Rôtie also coming along well, it's time to ask Yves how he regards the past years: "For the first 15 years, I did nothing but work, and only in my 16th year did I realise where I lived! There's been a lot of improvisation as I've gone along, and there's still a big margin for progress. But by vinifying the plots separately, I was able to find out where the elegance or the power lay, so now I feel as if I'm just starting my real trade, and can be more accurate."

When cornered by tight questions, it's apparent that Yves thinks in a well-channelled way, one that is not always revealed under the sometimes floppy, "Baba Cool" exterior. His modesty is also charming: "I'm still surprised to see my name come up in tastings and the like."

In 1997 and 2001 Yves also made a late-picked wine, Les Vendanges de Noë (Noah). The two wines are different, since 1997 was so dry

late on that the grapes moved to a state of *passerillage,* or dried raisin, with just 15 to 20 per cent botrytis; whereas 2001 brought out a full botrytis, or rot. The 1997 held 90 gm of residual sugar, the 2001 a mighty 170 gm. Both were raised in new oak for 18 months. The wine comes in 50 cl bottles, and is sold in wooden cases of three, with an *N, O,* and *E* on each bottle. Exotic fruits and typical late harvest Viognier brown sugar elements are present.

Since 1996 Yves has vinified and bottled all his Viognier crop. Before then, part was sold to Guigal.

CONDRIEU CLASSIC

2003 ★★
2002 ★★
2001 ★★★★
1999 ★★★

CONDRIEU VENDANGES DE NOË

2001 ★★
1997 ★★

Export 30 per cent (1) USA, (2) Switzerland, (3) Great Britain

FRANÇOIS GÉRARD

Côte Châtillon 69420 Condrieu +33(0)474 878864

See also Côte-Rôtie.

François Gérard literally stepped into Condrieu in 1991, moving from Ampuis and starting up a wine made from his new doorstep vineyard, the *Côte Châtillon* (1985).

The crop is half steel, half oak-vinified. Four-to-five-year-old *demi-muids* of 600 litres are used, the temperature held around 17° to 19°C. The wine is left alone until bottling, the malo done, a year later. It is unassuming Condrieu, sometimes more interesting on the bouquet than the palate.

CONDRIEU

2002 ★★

JEAN-MICHEL GÉRIN

19 rue de Montmain Verenay 69420 Ampuis
+33(0)474 561656

See also Côte-Rôtie.

This action man works 1.8 hectares of Condrieu. Half a hectare is on *Maladière*, next to Vernon between Condrieu and *Vérin*, the rest on *L'Alleau* at Vérin. Both sites are granite and are split by a stream, with the *Maladière* having a full south exposure: this had been abandoned by his uncle after the 1956 frost and had to be completely cleared of scrub and trees before replanting in 1987.

His Condrieu is called "La Loye" (until 1997 "Coteau de La Loye"). Since the 2000 vintage Jean-Michel has moved back to using steel vats for 20 per cent of the wine, to gain freshness. The rest is vinified and raised in casks ranging from new to four years old over the course of a year. He has cut the incidence of new oak recently and has moved back to a fuller style, having bottled the wine in January in the early 1990s.

He likes a low, 15°C temperature for the fermentation, which can last three weeks or two months, according to the behaviour of the cask. The malos are done. "I want to make a Condrieu that is elegant and so can match food well," is how he explains his approach. The Loye is a wine that can start life quietly, and often shows spice in its make-up.

Every two to three years, Jean-Michel makes a sweet wine, called "Vendanges Suprêmes," with a November picking. The last vintages for this were 2000 and 1997.

CONDRIEU LA LOYE

2002 ★★
2001 ★
2000 ★★

E. GUIGAL

69420 Ampuis +33(0)474 561022

See also Côte-Rôtie, Crozes-Hermitage, Hermitage, St-Joseph.

Marcel Guigal's Condrieu has for more than two decades been a top example of the full-blown, oaked Viognier style. He added to his armoury in 1994, when he introduced his special cuvée La Doriane, the stimulus for which came from the sale of Patrice Porte's *Châtillon* vineyard in central Condrieu.

Guigal has been the dominant merchant at Condrieu for some time. Most of the pure growers have traditionally sold their crop or their wine to him, with smaller amounts going to Jaboulet, Chapoutier, and Delas. So he has been in a position to cherry-pick the best around. "Guigal buying around 800 hectolitres of Condrieu each year has been very important for the region," comments Georges Vernay.

From 2004 he stepped up a further notch by entering into a venture with Alain Paret and his usual supporter, actor Gérard Depardieu. The Guigal share is half, the other two one-quarter each, and the project concerns the reputed 3.5-hectare vineyard of *Volan* in the southern *commune* of Malleval.

Marcel admits that he "loves working with whites, which is very personal. Getting the cooling of them right is vital, as is the oak and the need to stir the lees. You can get right into whites in a way that sometimes you can't with reds." "Stylistically, we like *gras* and roundness," adds son Philippe.

The classic cuvée is made from crop bought from around 40 different sources. "We are not fans of a couple of *communes*," states Philipee; "Limony's wines we find a little green, and Malleval's altitude for us gives the wines an acid side." The rest of the area is scanned, and relationships endure. One of the new influences is St-Pierre-de-Boeuf, where the joint venture with Alain Paret and Gérard Depardieu has been formed. There the *Volan* site's fruit, which is vinified on its own, can go into the regular Condrieu, as in 2004, or will appear in the Doriane—all a matter of tasting and judgment.

After an eight-hour skin maceration, the wine is left at 5°C over a night, then vinified 33 per cent in new oak, 67 per cent in vat at 16°C.

The cask portion has its lees stirred once a week, and the wine is bottled in June.

Pear and musky elements circulate in this wine, and the expected openness of a Guigal Viognier on the bouquet. There are fewer oak traces than in the past, and after three to four years, the wine can show some fungal, pungent, almost cheese–dried fruit aromas.

Philippe likes to ferment between 16° and 18°C and slowly for three reasons: "First, there shouldn't be sugar left in the Viognier must—its natural character is to be drier than that. Second, you achieve a powerful but elegant bouquet like this, and third, you obtain lots of richness on the palate."

Previously the Guigals had tried fermenting at over 20°C, with no barrel cooling. "But you break the aromatic molecules, making the wine heavier and the aromas less refined. Plus the fermentation is too fast for finesse." And that finesse is something Philippe cherishes. In 1998 his new press was the latest Blucher, giving a very gentle, prolonged operation lasting over five hours rather than the previous robust two-hour circuit. This prompted the remark that "it was better spending a night here with my Condrieu, pressing it, than watching TV." Maybe Ampuis had better get some nightclubs!

So from 1997 the house started a two-and-a-half-to-three-month process, with as usual the malolactic fermentation completed in its own time. "If you block the malo on the Viognier, you get green apple smells, not white peach and apricot notes," he remarks.

Having started the Doriane on a half new oak, half vat vinification in 1994, the Guigals switched to all new oak for it in 1998, the temperature kept between 16° and 18°C. There is lees stirring and a total eight months' upbringing. Its crop comes from one hectare on *Le Colombier* (1973), the old Lucien Dézormeaux vineyard, a sheltered hill of fine-grained, decomposed granite just south of Château-Grillet. The other source is their one hectare vineyard on *Châtillon* (1983), above the village of Condrieu and opposite its church, with a more silico-lime-

stone topsoil. There are 8,000 bottles of Doriane in any vintage.

To Doriane *Châtillon* brings the aromatics, which the Guigals describe as lychee, white peach and apricot typically, and dried fruit length. *Colombier* adds the structure and density. In 1996, for instance, *Colombier* was brought in at 14.8°, very much the powerhouse of the wine, with the *Châtillon* at 13.5°. The *Colombier* style is altogether fatter, very rich and solid, with spiced, almost tannic tones. "*Châtillon* is a bit behind *Colombier* in its ripening," comments Philippe Guigal, "but its wine is more exuberant. *Colombier* is more reserved."

The two halves showed their differences when tried separately at just five months old:

2002 Châtillon fine, quite elegant bouquet; dried fruits, sinewy pear flavours, with apricot and honey. Fine, has a dried fruit skin, oak end.

2002 Colombier oily, hazelnut aroma; solid, austere, has a brown soil flavour/texture. Good depth, tight flavour, quite hidden wine, with mineral finale.

Philippe Guigal considers the Doriane to be an eight-to-10-year wine. I would say that it is always an imposing drink, its fullness obviously expressed. As such, it flourishes mightily early on, and it is not every vintage that contains the adequate acidity to permit a comfortable middle or old age.

Macération pelliculaire is still part of their routine: "We like it for the Viognier because it brings out its aromas," comments Philippe. The wines are fined and filtered before bottling, a sterile filtration being used because little sulphur is applied earlier.

In 1999 Philippe Guigal, encouraged by his father "to do his own thing," produced a sweet Condrieu called "Luminescence." "I said to him—you make the wine, find the name, and do the label yourself," recalls Marcel proudly. This was harvested on 14 September 1999 at 17.3° potential alcohol. Its malo was not done, with a 100-day fermentation that stopped on its own with 33 gm of residual sugar and 15° of alcohol.

Philippe cut down on the sulphur use in this, and instead of the usual higher-than-normal amount, made a filtration and then just a normal sulphur dosage. "Forty to 50 years ago, it was quite common for a Condrieu to have not finished fermenting before bottling," states Philippe; hence the sulphur use. The 1999 was bottled in July 2000.

Half new, half one-year-old oak casks are used for the wine. Luminescence is sold in half bottles, and is intended to be drunk as an aperitif or with foie gras. The second time it was produced was in 2003, when the grapes were picked on 21 August at 18.4° potential alcohol. The malo on this was also not completed, and the wine was bottled in July 2004, with 55 gm of residual sugar and 15° of alcohol.

CONDRIEU CLASSIC

2003 ★★★★ Big, broad, buttery bouquet; rich and extended palate, some oak and mineral grip at end. Great aromas in its youth.

2002 (EXAMPLE) ★ Fair aroma, some spice. Gentle, three-quarter-weight wine.

2001 ★★

2000 ★★

1999 ★★

1998 ★★

1997 ★

CONDRIEU LA DORIANE

2003 ★★★★ Tight-knit, solid bouquet. Chunky wine, needs till 2006 to unpick its lock. Banana-oak mix, then dried fruits/honey finale, some heat. 2013.

2001 ★★★ Cooler aromas than 2000, restrained pear; mineral, chewy dried skins, elegant and full, but burnt, rather abrupt oak finish. Let's see.

2000 ★★★★ Broad, deep nose, oak melding well; ripe, oily texture, unctuous and enough fat to beat the oak. Fabulous richness. Esp 2004–08.

1999 ★★ Oak, lemon drizzle on nose. Tasty, modern style on palate. Tight, with a toasted end.

1998 ★★★ Sustained, deep, flan-style flavour, some spiced, deft touches around it. Some floral/oak aspects on bouquet. Well worked.

1997 ★★★ Full-on bouquet, peaches, toasted, frilled almonds; very full and rich with a touch of final spice. Oak/honey mix on a long finish.

CONDRIEU LUMINESCENCE

1999 ★★★ Overt pear William on the bouquet, *bonbon* also; well-wrapped texture, the richness is direct. Mix of spice and oak towards finish. 37 gm residual sugar.

PAUL JABOULET AÎNÉ

Les Jalets RN7 26600 La Roche-de-Glun
+33(0)475 846893

See also Cornas, Côte-Rôtie, Crozes-Hermitage, Hermitage, St-Joseph, St-Péray.
The doyens of Tain l'Hermitage sold a Condrieu for the first time in 1995 after buying wine in the open market. From 1996 they had moved on to a buy-in of grapes, supplemented by the crop from their own vineyard in Limony on *Les Côtes,* a site well inset into the little valley off the Rhône corridor through which the Limony stream runs.

First planted in 1993, this had reached just over one hectare by 2004. The soil is decomposed granite, on the middle of a steep slope just south of the village that is the extension of the *Rouelle Midi* site. There are another two-plus hectares available for planting over time here.

The purchased grapes are brought in from nearby Malleval, so this is a "southern" Condrieu. Since 2002 the crop has been destemmed, as it has for the whole Jaboulet range as they seek increased finesse. Pressing follows, with cool storage at 10° to 12°C for a day to let the juice clear.

Vinification policy has darted around, which has not helped a consistent flow of wine style from one vintage to the next. In the late 1990s, the Viognier was vat vinified, then given a short, one-to-two-month stay in wood. The latest policy is a steel vat vinification, after which half the wine is placed in a mix of new and one-year-old oak for five months. The idea is to bottle quite early, with the malo completed, to keep the wine's fruit. The 2002 was understandably not exposed to oak because of its low degree, and Jacques Jaboulet's fear was that it would oxidise.

From 2001 the wine has been called "Les Cassines." It appears that with a reduced amount of lees stirring, the intent is for less obviously fat and sometimes heavy wine.

CONDRIEU LES CASSINES

2004 ★ Fresh, appley, spice, and iodine bouquet. Midweight palate, also fresh, a glimmer of matter, but impression is fleeting. More on show by early 2006; an airy wine now. Last tasted March 2005.

2003 ★★ Buttery, oily bouquet. Rounded palate, white fruits, pretty rich but rather flat, low acidity. Length sound, finishes with chewy texture. Early drinking because of the acidity level. Slight improvement since first tasted. Last tasted March 2005.

2003 ★ Baked apples, brown sugar aroma, broad, quite deep. Flan, *crème patisserie* flavour, vacates towards the end, a pity.

2002 ★ Pretty, quite full, also elegant bouquet—pear/wax, some Limony minerality. Restrained style, has a chewy, slightly fleeting middle. Touch of acidity on the finish. Better from 2005.

2001 ★ As usual a fat bouquet—melted butter/light pear, with a hint of mineral. Fair weight and dried fruits, quite broad. Peach skin/spice on end. Has gained some roundness on finish that was rather dry and taut.

2000 ★ May flowers, authentic bouquet; fat, ample taste, touch burnt halfway through. Fades after a promising start. Texture not very clear-cut.

JURIE DES CAMIERS

The Jurie des Camiers vineyard on *Chéry* goes back five generations and runs to around one and a half hectares. It has a prime southerly exposure, with a steep, 35° incline. The Jurie des Camiers are a family of industrialists from Lyon, and Robert, now in his 90s, used to have a silk factory that was forced to close in the face of Far Eastern imports.

Until 1982 the wine was made for them by the late Jean Pinchon; since then André Perret has vinified it in one-third vat, two-thirds new and recent oak. Around 1,500 bottles are sold by M. Jurie des Camiers under his own label.

It is a full, vigorous wine, as one would expect from *Chéry*; there are notable white fruit flavours, and a full butter-spice presence as well. It is a wine of classic structure that can still show great appeal after five or six years.

CONDRIEU COTEAU DE CHÉRY

1999 ★★★

JOCELYNE AND YVES LAFOY

8 rue du Vagnot 69420 Ampuis
+33(0)474 561926

See also Côte-Rôtie.

The active, wholehearted Yves Lafoy makes a wine in keeping with his respect for local ways, a *demi-sec* that is sold at Christmas time to locals.

He works 0.3 ha at St-Michel-sur-Rhône on *Au Ruse*, where the soil is crumbly *arzelle*, mica mixed in with the loose, sandy granite. The vineyard dates from the 1980s.

Yves describes its vinification as "bizarre." After pressing and decanting the juice, he cools it down to just 4°C, leaves it alone, and lets it warm up naturally in its vat; when there are around 30 gm of sugar left, he blocks it with sulphur, cooling, and filtration. Bottling is in December, for the Christmas holidays. It is sold to locals.

It shows a baked apple flavour, with a quite live finish and should be drunk within two to three years.

CONDRIEU DEMI-SEC
2002 ★

DOMAINE LAURENT MARTHOURET

Les Rôtisses 07340 Charnas +33(0)475 341591

See also St-Joseph.

The convivial Laurent Marthouret has one hectare of Condrieu, half on the *Côte Fournet*, half on *Braise*, that turns away east of *Fournet* on the southernmost outcrops of Limony. The terraced vineyards date from 1988.

He vinifies and bottles only the *Braise* crop; this is worked in oak, half new, half one year old, at around 19°C. It remains on its lees until bottling at the end of August. The rest of the crop is sold to the *négoce* trade.

The style is for potent wine, with plenty of weight and overt heat.

CONDRIEU
2002 ★
2001 ★★

GABRIEL MEFFRE

84190 Gigondas +33(0)490 123021

See also Cornas, Côte-Rôtie, Crozes-Hermitage, Hermitage, St-Joseph.

The Gigondas-based *négociant* produces a Condrieu in connection with Alain Paret, named "Laurus," from the *lieu-dit* of *Volan*. This is fermented and raised in the Meffre special size of 275-litre new oak casks. It is aged for eight months, with regular lees stirring.

The wine is broad and aims for overtly rich, fat flavours. At times these can be a little clumsy.

CONDRIEU LAURUS
2003 ★
2001 ★

DOMAINE FRANÇOIS MERLIN

Le Bardoux 42410
St-Michel-sur-Rhône
+33(0)474 566190

See also St-Joseph.

It is always gratifying to see a self-taught winegrower breaking through. François Merlin trained in agriculture, without a home background in wine, since his father was a chemical engineer. In 1983 he took a job working in René Rostaing's vineyard, where he continued, latterly half-time, until 1998, having started his own project in 1989. He also spent a useful six months chez Georges Vernay.

What he gathered together was a dispersed series of plots—no surprise given his lack of previous family connection with any vineyards. In all, he now works 1.8 hectares and is supported part-time by his wife, Nadine, a small, fresh-faced, and pretty blonde woman who, when not looking after their three children, is busy doing the office work, labelling, and vine tying in early summer.

François has half a hectare on *La Roncharde* (1987–89) at the northern end of the *appellation*, in the *commune* of Condrieu near the road up to Rozay. This was a plot that he cleared and planted all on his own, as he did with his 0.27 ha on *Jeanraude* (1987) a couple of miles (2.75 km) away next to Château-Grillet.

A short distance from *Jeanraude*, he works a further 0.3 ha on *Poncin*, where François Villard has a holding. This is important, for it combines vines from before the Second World War with some planted in 1996–97. Down in Chavanay, François also cleared and planted another 0.58 ha on *Chanson* in 1987.

The soil splits into two variations on the granite-gneiss theme. *Jeanraude* and *Poncin* have blue-grey granite that filters quickly; this gives rich, strongly floral wines. *Roncharde* and *Chanson*'s rock is more white to the eye, containing more sand and limestone. This brings out a stone fruit, apricot-style flavour, more robust than the floral wines.

Blessed with piercing blue eyes, François talks fluently about his life as a winemaker and is clearly a switched-on, bright operator. One senses plenty of determination here as he hits his 40s. "My first steps were to vinify and bottle a bit in 1990, while selling most of the crop," he says. "Now I'm selling just one ton of crop, and the rest is bottled for my Condrieu and St-Joseph." He built his new cellar himself, and all progress is entirely down to his own efforts.

He says his aim is "to make fresh, long, frank wines rather than unctuous ones. My time in the vineyard was a big help; it allowed me to observe the importance of *terroir*." Certainly his outlook is present in his wines, which bear a classic stamp of developing their flavour and persistence evenly through the palate. This is an STGT name to note for anyone seeking clear, pure local wine.

The classic Condrieu is made from the *Roncharde, Chanson,* and young-vine *Poncin* crop. It is vinified 50 per cent in casks one to three years old, 50 per cent in steel, at a temperature of 18° to 20°C; no outside yeasts are used. The oak wine receives a lees stirring until June, and the wine is bottled one year after the harvest. It is intended to be an open and fresh wine, and accentuates the simple pear fruit side of the Viognier. In a big year like 2003, more pepper comes through on the palate.

The top cuvée, Jeanraude, comes from old vines on *Jeanraude* and *Poncin,* both just south of Château-Grillet. It is 80 per cent made in casks one to three years old, 20 per cent in steel vat and is also bottled after a year. This is François's keeping wine. It is a definite cut above the classic, with pretty fullness and a pleasing length. It can also improve and blossom if left for three years or so.

A late-harvested wine, Douceur d'Automne, was made in 1997 and 1999, when conditions suited. This is taken from crop on the heavier soils, so it contains more acidity. It is all oak fermented and raised, and the 1999 held over 100 gm of residual sugar, with an alcohol degree of 13.5.

CONDRIEU CLASSIC

2004 ★★★
2003 ★★★
2002 ★★
2001 ★

CONDRIEU JEANRAUDE

2003 ★★★
2002 ★★★
2001 ★★

Export 20 per cent (1) Switzerland, (2) Great Britain, (3) Germany

DOMAINE DU MONTEILLET, STÉPHANE MONTEZ

Le Montelier 42410 Chavanay
+33(0)474 872457

See also Côte-Rôtie, St-Joseph.
Stéphane Montez has developed his father Antoine's Condrieu from being sold as crop to the Péage-du-Roussillon Co-opérative to being a domaine-bottled wine. His 2.5 hectares are made up of several different *lieux-dits*—the largest is *Chanson*, followed by *Boissey* and *Les Eyguets*, all at Chavanay, while he has a cluster further north at St-Michel comprised of *Chauramond, La Bourdonnerie,* and a recently scrubbed-out plot on *Sous l'Église*. Many of the vines date from 1982.

The classic wine is the Domaine du Monteillet; this is around three-quarters from *Chanson*, one-quarter from *Boissey*, the vines ranging from 1982 to 1998 in age. Stéphane destalks his crop and performs an early *macération pelliculaire* for nine to 12 hours for better fruit/aroma quality before pressing. The juice is stabilised at 12°C or so for a few days before cask fermentation. When the crop is good and healthy, Stéphane likes to keep the crop at 0.0°C (32°F) for as long as 10 days. "It helps to obtain richness and favours the development of secondary aromas that are more assured," is his reasoning on this technique.

The Monteillet is raised for 11 months, in one-third new, one-third one-year-, and one-third two-year-old oak. Lees stirring is weekly, except in the cool moments of the winter when it would rob the wine of oxygen. Bottling is in September.

The top wine, Les Grandes Chaillées, is from *Les Eyguets, Sous l'Église, La Bourdonnerie, Le Tinal*, the extension into the valley of *Clos Bouche* at Vérin, and *Chauramond* (2001). On average, these vines date from the mid-1990s. This is raised in the same way as the Monteillet and was first made in 1999.

There is a late harvest or selection of noble bunches wine called "Grain de Folie," made in 1996, 1999, and 2001. Picking is in late November, and the wine is raised for two summers in new oak, and the final wine contains around 70 gm of residual sugar. It should be drunk when well aged, perhaps around the eight-year-plus mark.

These are wines made in the modern way, reaching for overt declarations of ripe crop and a full, heady impact. Bouquets can reflect lychees and jungle fruits. The wines work well providing there is enough matter in the harvest to handle and absorb the oak. A year like 2003 has content, but should be left until 2006 before its broad appeal can break out and fly, away from the oak.

CONDRIEU DOM DU MONTEILLET

2003 ★★
2002 ★★
2001 ★★
2000 ★★★
1999 ★★

CONDRIEU LES GRANDES CHAILLÉES

2003 ★★★
2000 ★★★

CONDRIEU GRAIN DE FOLIE

1999 ★★

DOMAINE DIDIER MORION

Épitaillon 42410 Chavanay
+33(0)474 872633

See also St-Joseph.

On the hill south of Chavanay, Didier Morion rents a 0.7 ha vineyard of Viognier planted in 1988 on the schist soil of *Peyrolland*. This is supplemented by 0.3 ha of Viognier planted in 1999 and 2001 on *La Côte*, north of Chavanay.

The first wine was in 1994; this is fermented at 18 to 20°C, half in oak ranging from one to five years old, half in steel. It is raised over nine months, with *bâtonnage* for the cask portion, and is bottled with the malo completed.

Judging by the 2002 and 2001, the bouquets perform better than the palate here, and perhaps some later picking may suit in the years to come, especially as the vines grow up.

DOMAINE MOUTON

Le Rozay 69420 Condrieu
+33(0)474 878236

See also Côte-Rôtie.

The early 2000s saw the end of a long tradition of family innkeeping for the Mouton family. After 37 years at the helm, Thérèse, known to her customers as Jannette, and born in the Auberge du Rozay, which the family had owned since the 1700s, sold up and moved all of 50 metres across the road to the family farmhouse.

Her son, Jean-Claude, is gradually developing the wine business, while her husband continues with the farm, situated high above Condrieu on the plateau near the Château du Rozay. Wheat, maize, and cattle are the main activities, with Jean-Claude helping out his father until he retires, when he will move fully on to the wine.

The family work 2.2 hectares of Condrieu, as well as Côte-Rôtie and *vin de pays des Collines Rhodaniennes* of Syrah and Viognier.

The Condrieu is mixed between *Côte Bonnette* (1989), *Côte Châtillon* (1997), and *Mar-*

mouzin (1981–82), all nearby. Two wines are made, a Côte Bonnette and a Côte Châtillon. The Bonnette is vinified half in steel, half in cask two to three years old, with lees stirring and a June bottling. The Châtillon is cask fermented, the oak being one-third each new, one year, and two years old. It is also left on its lees, with *bâtonnage*, and is bottled in September.

Jannette is as sharp as a button, no doubt partly the result over many years of adding up the bills in her head; she has a fair, Celtic look and says she was often taken to be Irish. Her "drinking days" started young, for her father died when she was just six years old. "My mother didn't like wine, and so got me to taste the wine when I was eight years old. In those days—we're talking about the 1960s—the staple white was called just 'Viognier' and was sold in bulk, while our inn sold the '*vin rouge du pays.*' This was Syrah, with also a lot of Gamay sold, while there was another very popular sweet red wine called 'Mille' (one thousand), which was made from hybrid vines. The Gamay was fermented over two weeks, so was always dark.

"The first bottled wine from here I remember being sold was a 1960 Côte-Rôtie from our cousin Antoine Chambeyron. He bottled up a few and put a label on them. By the 1970s I sold a few more domaine wines, and by the 1980s listed probably half a dozen Côte-Rôties. Businessmen most often bought these. The wine that was hard to sell was the St-Joseph, especially the white. The locals were all used to Viognier, and found the Marsanne rough, and just about tolerated the Roussanne!"

All the family join in with the wine; mother does the office, Françoise, Jean-Claude's wife, does the pruning, tying, and some office work, and father helps in the cellar.

The wines are gradually moving upwards, and the intention is to bottle them all in time. The Châtillon can contain ripe fruit at its core, although its oak overlay brings in the usual exotic flavours that are not part of Condrieu. It would be more fleshy and relaxed if its oak quota were reduced.

The Bonnette has more grip and minerality than the Châtillon and is a more discreet wine —it was full and well done in 2003, a marked improvement on the 2001.

The Syrah *vin de pays* is made from 1.2 ha of 1981–82 vines, the Viognier from 0.25 ha of vines (1992) just outside the Condrieu zone. Both show promise.

CONDRIEU CÔTE CHÂTILLON

2003 ★★
2002 ★
2001 ★

CONDRIEU CÔTE BONNETTE

2003 ★★★

Export 30 per cent (1) USA, (2) La Réunion, (3) Great Britain

ROBERT NIÉRO

20 rue Cuvillière 69420 Condrieu
+33(0)474 598438

See also Côte-Rôtie.

Part of the limited second wave of people committing their futures to Condrieu, Robert Niéro set up on his own account in 1986. His wife, Claude, was a Pinchon, their family having under one hectare of Condrieu, which wasn't enough for her grandfather Émile and father, Jean, to work. Accordingly Jean had become a cheese seller, with a mobile shop on the square of Condrieu, until he was 50.

By the mid-1980s, Jean Pinchon was working 1.5 hectares, and since his death in 1990, the vineyard has been built up to three hectares of Condrieu, plus some Côte-Rôtie and *vin de pays*.

Robert, a tall, good-looking man, had worked in banking around Lyon, and his last three years at the bank between 1983 and 1986 meant mixing the finance and the wine, with a special part-time contract allowing him to do the two jobs. "I was very content at the bank, but now that I am in my early 50s, I'm glad I made the move" he comments. He is proba-bly quietly encouraged by his son Rémi, who as a trained mechanic, has chosen to work for a company that makes harvesting machines and has studied viticulture through a postal course.

"The years of the fastest growth here were 1985 to 1990," he recalls; "it was also a time when the cost of a hectare wasn't too steep—it would be £100,000, or US$165,000, now, for instance." Accordingly, he expanded the family vineyard to 3 hectares of Condrieu, spread across five *lieux-dits*. The *Chéry* holding is 0.8 hectare, the major part 1940, 0.3 ha of it from 1985. This is very decomposed *gore*, with no stones at all. It supplies his top wine, called "Cuvée de Chéry."

The largest site is the 1.7 hectares at *La Roncharde*; a rented 0.7 ha here dates from 1963, and the rest was planted between 1985 and 1998. Across the road is *Côte Châtillon*, a 0.27 holding (1987); both sites have a few more small stones than *Chéry*, the soil a little thicker.

Just south across the *Arbuel* stream, and still in the core Condrieu village area, lie their two other vineyards—0.27 ha on *La Caille*, planted in 2000–02, and 0.18 ha on *Vergelas* (1974). The latter is almost flatland at the top of the hill and contains some clay, of a grey to red colour, and no stones.

Robert was President of the Growers Union from 1996 until 2000. He has been involved in the project of setting up a conservatory for the Viognier, with cuttings taken from the healthiest older plants, which are now being grown at his successor Philippe Faury's vineyard above Chavanay.

The staple Condrieu has been called "Les Ravines" since 2000. It is made from the four plots outside *Chéry*. It is fermented in steel at between 16° and 18°C, and one-third is raised in one-to-five-year-old oak casks for nine months, with a July bottling.

The *Chéry* wine is also raised one-third in oak, two-thirds in vat. It gets two months more of cellar ageing, with about 10 per cent new oak and a September bottling.

Robert feels that Condrieu is best drunk when around three years old. Certainly, I have found his wines reticent at two years old, and that they show more if given extra time. They are never big hitters, though. The Ravines shows elegant white fruits and some floral aromas. The Chéry can carry a very solid structure with some near-tannic touches on the finish in a prime vintage like 2001. It accentuates the full, spiced side of Condrieu—typical of its hillside.

Robert's 0.37 ha of Syrah *vin de pays des Collines Rhodaniennes* Les Agathes grows next to *Vergelas*, just outside the Condrieu *appellation*. Sixty-five per cent dates from 1972, the rest from 1998. It is aged in three-year-old casks for nine months. It expresses black fruit and some pepper and is nice and direct.

CONDRIEU LES RAVINES

2003 ★★
2002 ★★
2001 ★★★
2000 ★

CONDRIEU CUVÉE DE CHÉRY

2003 ★★★
2002 ★★
2001 ★★★
2000 *Coteau de Chéry* ★★

Export 35 per cent (1) Great Britain, (2) Japan, (3) Belgium

DOMAINE STÉPHANE OTHEGUY (formerly DOMAINE GASSE-LAFOY)

Chemin Chez Maurice 38138
Les Côtes d'Arey
+33(0)474 589443

See also Cote-Rôtie, St-Joseph.
Stéphane Otheguy, the successor to Vincent Gasse of Côte-Rôtie, has continued with the rental of M. Gasse's Condrieu vineyard on the *Gonon* site at Malleval, a south-facing slope above the *Batalon* stream. There is just 0.2 ha

on the hard rock, acid soil. The vines date in part from 1997, in part from 1989.

The wine is used-cask fermented and raised, with *bâtonnage* every 10 to 15 days. It is bottled in July, the malo done. It carries marked mineral tones on bouquet and palate, with the clear-cut fruit typical of the Gasse wines.

CONDRIEU
2002 ★★

DOMAINE ALAIN PARET

Place de l'Eglise 42520
Saint-Pierre-de-Boeuf
+33(0)474 871209

See also St-Joseph.

Unexpected glamour exists at this domaine, its cellars on the main square of the very low-key village of St-Pierre-de-Boeuf, close to the Rhône. The imposing French actor Gérard Depardieu is a part owner of some of the 6.5 hectares of Condrieu worked by Alain Paret, a busy, friendly man now in his mid-50s.

It was the late 1970s when the two first made contact. "Depardieu had tasted one of my wines in a St-Étienne restaurant, who gave him my details," recalls Alain. "When he rang me, I hung up! I heard the voice and thought someone was pulling my leg. My wife dealt with his next call! We met, we're the same age, and we got on, and two or three years later we got together when Gérard inherited some land."

The Depardieu effect is strong: M. Paret's cellars on the small, dull square in St-Pierre-de-Boeuf are visited by an average of 4,000 people a month, the French coming from all parts and filling their car boots and their cubitainers and no doubt telling their dinner guests all about the wine's provenance. Alain has even had to take down his signs around the square to calm the throng.

The main site is on *Volan* (1980), a south-facing slope that runs above the *Batalon* stream as it heads for the Rhône. These nearly three hectares, since 2004 co-owned with Marcel and Philippe Guigal as well as Depardieu, contain a lot of schist with patches of clay. This hard rock sets it apart from their other sites, which are more the typical loose granite with a sandy, cystallised topsoil with many fissures allowing the roots to reach deep down. The *Volan* vineyard, said to have survived phylloxera, stands below the Château on a mix of terraces and flat, sweeping land. The muscular top wine, Lys de Volan, comes from here.

This is a rare local vineyard with a traceable past. Records show the purchase of a property at *Volan* that included a roughly 10-hectare vineyard in 1486 by Pierre Goran of Malleval. There is a Château de Volan, which has been restored by a family from Lyon. Dating from the 1790s, its cellars have vats hewn in to the rock; there are three cellars on top of each other, one for each year of an *élevage*. The Château's white wine was well reputed both inside and outside France.

Alain's other *lieux-dits* at Malleval are 2 ha on *Rochecourbe* and 1 ha on *Côte Bellay*, the latter near the village centre; at Chavanay, he works 0.8 ha on *Luzin*. All date from the early 1980s. Alain has backed off his extreme picking policy of the early 1990s. "I was waiting until the grape skins were very advanced, even a little cracked: I wanted more than 14° alcohol to achieve aroma and elegance, bearing in mind that the Viognier is different to other varietals and gives a tannin," he states. "The trouble was, my wines were a bit unbalanced by this, and since 1997 I have returned to the 14° limit."

The crop is fermented in a mix of steel and fibreglass vats at a maximum of 18°C until it reaches a specific gravity of 1040, about halfway through. It is then transferred to cask, with Alain increasing the proportion of 600-litre *demi-muids* over 228-litre casks. "This allows us to control the fermentation better," he explains, "and it ends up lasting a minimum of six weeks. Then we do a daily lees stirring, dropping it down to just once a week after four months. This also helps oxygenate the wine."

There are two dry wines, Les Ceps du Nébadon and Lys de Volan. Nébadon is raised in older oak—one-third new, one-third a year old, one-third two years old. Half new oak–raised until the late-1990s, *Volan* is now purely a new oak wine.

Bottling is done in June. The oak policy derives from the soil, according to Alain: "Nébadon is from the sandy granite, lighter soil sites than the Volan, so its more floral wine doesn't handle so much new oak."

Nébadon is a peaches and pears wine with a tender texture. By contrast, the Lys de Volan is a wine with shoulders, a wine with meaty aspects and heat derived from its schist. It shows overt, quite punchy pear fruit and can require waiting for three years or so before it displays its best qualities.

In certain vintages, Alain makes a special dried grape wine, a *passerillage sur souche*. Called "Sortilèges d'Automne," this comes from grapes picked after 15 October from the *Volan* vineyard. Alain doesn't delay picking for too long: "The old timers never waited too long, because they found that grey rot, not noble rot, develops if you do. I find that brings a mushroom taste."

Alain reckons that 750 kg of grapes brings just 130 litres of fermented juice. The final wine used to run at 16° alcohol, with a bit over 130 gm of residual sugar. But he has cut back the fermentation to 14.5°, to express the aromas more and subdue the overt alcohol effect.

The Sortilèges is raised for eight months in new oak, but Alain intends to increase this to two years: "I want to avoid an overly sugary taste, and make the wine finer and softer," he explains. The last wines were in 1999 and 2000, with just 200 to 300 50-cl bottles made. This mixes dried fruits, some spice and honey, and the sweet tones are offset by oak aspects on the finish.

CONDRIEU LES CEPS DU NÉBADON

2004 ★★

2003 ★★

2002 ★★

2001 ★

CONDRIEU LYS DE VOLAN

2003 ★★

2002 ★★

2001 ★★★

DOMAINE ANDRÉ PERRET

17 RN86 Verlieu 42410 Chavanay +33(0)474 872474

See also St-Joseph.

Put André Perret and the *Coteau de Chéry* together, and there are fireworks. With this old family vineyard, one of the best sites in the whole of Condrieu, André's touch can be supreme. His *Chéry* has been perhaps the most expressive, delicious Condrieu of the past 15 years and is one of the first names I would ever recommend to someone seeking the rich soul of this variety.

There is no show business here, just an orderly, neat cellar with a simple anteroom that often contains more children's toys than wine implements or artefacts. The cellar style is the man: a man of some caution with other people, not a chatterbox like some in the wine community, a man who lets the wine do the talking. His are practical talents, there is no loud philosophy worn on his sleeve, no large statements—just a job busily and well done. André's style is to stand quietly during a tasting, and any broad views have to be prised out of him.

Marriage and a new cellar in 1995, followed by having a growing family of two daughters around him, have settled André and strengthened his clarity of approach; I sense that he is now more self-confident about what works best in making his wine; there had been hints of following trends in the past, but it's always a main moment when a grower stops doing something before it's been talked about elsewhere.

André's grandfather Antoine came here around 1925, travelling the few miles south from Rive-de-Gier to marry into a wine family. A little wine was bottled in 1960–63, but the effort

FIGURE 10 André Perret's Chéry Condrieu extols the opulence of the Viognier. Here he dips into a young wine in the company of his wife, Dominique. (Tim Johnston)

was not deemed worthwhile, so the crop was sold to the Tain Co-opérative between 1963 and 1969. The domaine reverted to bottling its own wine under father Pierre in the early 1970s, when its only vineyard was on the *Coteau de Chéry*.

André was born in 1957 and first worked with his father in 1979, before running the domaine himself from 1985. His path into wine was circuitous, since he studied biology at Lyon University before moving on to a specialisation in viticulture at the Mâcon wine school.

His wife, Dominique, small and brown haired, was a *restauratrice* in Lyon. He married at 38, saying that he had decided on a *mariage tardive*.

His vineyard runs to 4.8 hectares, with a monumental three hectares on the prime, south-facing slope of *Chéry* (1948, 1988), where the topsoil of about 50 cm (20 in.) is loess and loose earth, the granite rock below it. There are also half hectares each on *Chanson* and *Chauramond* (1986), the latter a pure granite plot at 275 metres between Chavanay and Condrieu. The *Chanson* vineyard dates from 1960 and is just north of Chavanay village, its foundation rock schist. It grows around the house of a Lyonnais from whom André rents the land.

Recent expansion has come through his valiant clearing and planting of a 0.50 ha south-facing plot on *Verlieux*, which is on the back side of the *Bruyères* hill opposite his cellars at Chavanay. The granite here contains specks of quartz and has a sandy topsoil; it is very pure, which brings increased finesse in the wine.

He makes three wines, all dry. There is a classic (4,000 bottles), a Chanson (2,000 bottles), and a Chéry (8,000–10,000 bottles). The classic is part *Chauramond*, part the younger *Chéry* vines from 1989. André describes Chéry as more feminine than Chanson, founded on *gras* and power. Chanson he says is more mineral but can also age as well as Chéry, for about 10 years.

André is dark haired and quite broad and wears glasses. In the cellar he looks practical, perhaps a bit of a thinker. Outside, as he scampers away up the hillside, he's tough. The wee bit of extra flesh from good, regular home cooking does not hold him back. He lights up on the hillside—he's an outdoors man. And when it appears, the smile is broad.

His vinification has had some gradual adaptations over his 20 years at the helm. "Chéry and Chanson have very high potential ripeness if you leave them alone," comments André; "it's not always easy to calm them." He has therefore become careful about how much extremely ripe crop he picks; he played with this over most of the 1990s, dabbling on the fringes to broaden his Chéry cuvée, up to 30 per cent included each year.

He has gone back to seeking more freshness, as if that were what he wanted all along—a clarity of expression. "I'm down to 10 per cent when conditions permit," he says, "and all I want is a gain in richness, and the peach/apricot side of the aromas. Later picking is fine if you regard it as a pinch of salt in your dish—not too heavy-handed. Too much Condrieu wears expensive make-up these days."

If he destalks, it is on the young vine fruit, meaning that the classic wine is half destalked. It is 30 per cent fermented in three-to-four-year-old casks, 70 per cent in steel vats, and is bottled a bit over a year after the harvest. Like all three Condrieus, its lees are stirred until the malolactic has finished, but André has been reducing the incidence of this *bâtonnage* because he feels, quite correctly, that it results in a loss of finesse.

The classic Condrieu is a well-modelled wine, not a big one. "I use less cask in my regular Condrieu to gain in aroma and fruit, with a pureness of the violet and apricots in it," he explains. It is a wine whose straight fruit makes it good for aperitif time or for undemanding food like simply grilled chicken.

Since 1999 he has eased back the early fermentation temperature from 20° to 18°C, having installed a new cooling system. No outside yeasts are used. "This allows a gradual, not a violent, start, so there's a gain in finesse," he comments. Likewise, he also relished the challenge of his new pneumatic press in 1998: "It's softer on the crop, but you have to judge it just right. If the grape must is too clear you underplay the aromas."

Chanson is all cask vinified and raised, 10 to 15 per cent new, the rest up to four years old. From 2004 Andre increased its stay in the oak from 12 to 18 months. "It's a Burgundy style, really; what I'm doing is allow it two winters in the cellar; then there'll be a precipitation of lees and tartrates, so I won't have to filter." With just 2,000 bottles, he has the space to do this, something that is not so easy with the Chéry.

Chéry is vinified in one-third steel vat, two-thirds cask (20 per cent new to four years old), although the crop shortfall of 2003 (half was lost) allowed a full oak treatment. As with Chanson, the lees are stirred until around springtime. Bottling is in September. André actually says that the recent Chéry style is more citrus and grapefruit. He explains: "I'm now aiming for more refined wines without sacrificing too much richness. Maybe it's also something to do with my using less copper solution in the vineyards, as well." Since around 2000 he finds Chanson more mineral than before.

These two wines are frequently in the very top rank at Condrieu. Chanson is a live, clear-cut wine, its fruits well-defined, the finish marked by some tightening from its mineral content. Chéry is more an earth wine, displaying great fullness and grounded flavours, very much full of rich, stewed pear fruit. Chéry's aromas are more swirling, heavier, more *boudoir*—the quintessence of Condrieu.

André is not a man for a vast array of sweet wines: he has the mature vines and the locations to not need them. Once, in 1997, he made a dried grape wine, a *vin de passerillage*, which he called "Vendange d'Automne." This was fermented in cask, 30 per cent new, and bore 15° and 16 gm of residual sugar.

Along with Yves Cuilleron, he was one of the first growers to make a late-harvested wine in 1990; the grapes were picked 30 days late, and the wine was fermented and raised in oak for a year, bearing 15°. He renewed it in 1997, the very hot summer, but remained unconvinced and has not made it since.

He also quietly made a late-harvest wine in 1996 to celebrate the birth of his daughter Marie. Picking was in early November, there were 70 gm of residual sugar, and it was bottled at the end of 1998. It was a success, naturally:

★★★★★ Yellow, pronounced straw colour. Dried fruits, light honey, good grip; apricot/

quince/dried fruits on palate. A lot of beguiling glazed fruit flavours, clean ending.

André also makes red and white St-Joseph and a Syrah and Viognier Côtes du Rhône from vines planted on the granite of *Chauramond* in 1983—900 and 500 bottles respectively. There is also a series of single grape *vins de pays des Collines Rhodaniennes*—Syrah and Marsanne (both 1980s, from the sandy, free-draining plain near the cellars) and Merlot, first made in 2003. The reds are oak raised over a year or so, the Marsanne is half oak, half steel vinified.

There are times when André seems close to being overrun by so much work, and the vinification of his wines outside Condrieu can appear too modern and mechanical; even the Condrieus in 2002 have tasted unevenly at different times, so let's keep fingers crossed for the future.

CONDRIEU CLASSIC

2004 ★★
2003 ★★
2002 ★
2001 ★
2000 ★★
1999 ★★
1998 ★★★

CONDRIEU CLOS CHANSON

2004 ★★★ Honey, tangerine aroma, floral touches—has potential. Chewy, quite assertive attack, bold wine, dried fruits like the tangerine, citrus sources, also rounded flan flavour. Correct acidity, quite subtle wine.

2003 ★★★ Full fruit, stone fruit/brown sugar. Light top spice on nose. Golden fruits, quite elegant texture, then kicks on finish. Pear in a wine sauce taste. Chunky—over 15°. Not aperitif, when to drink is the question.

2002 ★★ Floral/stone fruit, roasted almonds nose. Palate bit taut, touch burnt on finish, caramel plus mineral. Acidity evident, more rounded from 2005. Liable to come and go.

2001 ★★★★★ Cowslip/butter aroma, cool mineral edge; tasty, elegant, stylish; white fruits/melted butter, good control, chewy aftertaste. Persists well. 2011.

2000 ★★★ Floral, delicate bouquet, clearcut. Mineral on palate, exotic fruits, some final heat. Tight-knit, interesting. 2010.

1999 ★★ But some re-fermentation problems.

1998 ★★★★★

CONDRIEU CHÉRY

2004 ★★★★ Elegant fat on bouquet, hint of oak, also mineral. Good broad start, buttery and rounded fruit and richness. Holds glycerine, with plenty of core. Restraint of the year adds elegance. Esp from late 2006; 2013–14.

2003 ★★★★ Quite suave, restrained, lime tart aroma. Tight palate—pineapple, toasted flavour. Good ensemble, sound elegance. Fruit skins and power here, younger Chéry vines helpful for freshness this year. Length sound. Needs food. 2010.

2002 ★★ Spice, white fruit/orange zest bouquet. Midweight, quite firm wine, not especially fleshy. Rather tart finish, some pear there. Lacks the usual width, small scale. From 2006, and hope.

2001 ★★★★ Warm, open, ripe nose, spiced apricot; quite fat texture, toasted end, flan dessert/apricot flavours. Touch of heat.

2000 ★★★★ Pear/dried fruits, floral and toasted topping on bouquet; stylish, more restrained than usual on palate, pretty flavour, finishes elegantly. Nutty, touch of end heat. Good length. 2006–07.

1999 ★★★★★ Full, elegant bouquet—pear/vanilla and good grip. Great combo of pear-flavoured fullness and final tightening, a tannic chew. Really compact wine, doing well after four years. 2008–09.

1998 ★★★★
1997 *Vendange d'Automne* ★★★

Export 50 per cent (1) Great Britain, (2) USA, (3) Japan

CHRISTOPHE PICHON

Le Grand Val Verlieu 42410 Chavanay +33(0)474 870678

See also Côte-Rôtie, St-Joseph.

It's always an exciting moment when you realise that a grower you have respected on previous visits is really moving up into the top league. Christophe Pichon is making exceptionally well styled wine now, full of local integrity and delicious, pure flavours. They are in the restrained, elegant school, with tight textures, their subtle quality making the drinker pause just a beat for quiet reflection.

This domaine is not far off being a benchmark for good Condrieu from the Chavanay sector. Now André Perret has a neighbour to keep him company at the top table! Christophe himself is a man with a quiet country grounding. He is dark-haired, brown-eyed, and pleasant looking, approaching 40, with a gentle, unhurried manner. His talk involves recollections and observations taken from the land around him, nothing that can be read up in a book: always the sign of a grower prepared to let the soil do the hard work, with just some steering from the grower's hand.

Until his retirement in early 2000, Christophe's father Philippe worked his own two hectares, most of them at *Roche Coulante*, the extension of the *Colombier* hillside just below St-Michel-sur-Rhône.

Now Christophe works the full four hectares, three on *Roche Coulante*, one on *Mève* a little south, plus some St-Joseph and Côte-Rôtie. *Roche Coulante* (1970–77) is a full south hill where Christophe's vines rise from 220 to 350 metres. This is decomposed granite, true *arzelle* with its sandy texture, and a tiny amount of clay and is one of the best-ripening places at Chavanay.

Mève (1987–91) is also decomposed granite, but with a little more clay, and is just about 800 metres away. It is mainly turned eastwards, with a little southerly exposure.

Christophe considers the *Roche Coulante* style to be more complex than *Mève*, even though its vines are older. "Roche Coulante has spice touches, some apricot, and a sense of fat on the bouquet. Mève is more straightforward, with an easy richness, and open, soft fruit and floral aromas. It also brings acidity."

This is a family that has always been close to the soil, but not always working vines. Christophe's great-grandfather worked vines, but his grandfather didn't. His father Philippe went back to growing vines in 1959 to make table wine, and it was only in 1976 that he moved on to the full *appellation* Condrieu. Until 1987 his other activities were fruit and vegetables, notably pears and apples and the local winter vegetable of cardoon that would be sold to supermarkets in the eastern regions of France.

Philippe's hand was then forced towards wine in 1975 by the creation of a new channel for the Rhône's water flow, which meant the compulsory purchase of his 10 hectares of fruit trees near the river. With some of the money from this, he was able to buy half a hectare at *Roche Coulante*.

"Everyone thought he was mad to do this in the mid-1970s," says Christophe. "Maybe Jean Pinchon was also doing a little planting then, but that was it. The INAO rule makers made no restrictions because it was so completely unfashionable, and really the worst obstacle then was the line of poplar trees beside the Rhône. These were blocking the circulation of the warm air off the river and led to frost on the hillsides. The Compagnie Nationale du Rhône now forbids any poplars from being grown on the plain beside the Rhone."

By 1980 Philippe was booming on with his vines, bottling from 1982 onwards, and was also the first grower to use a specially adapted caterpillar digger in the vineyards. After attending wine school at Mâcon, Christophe started up in 1987, when he was 22, and by 1991 had gone solo.

Friends, family—boosted by their five sons and one daughter—and one or two outsiders harvest the grapes, which are lightly pressed and cooled over six hours' decantation at around

FIGURE 11 Christophe Pichon's Condrieu is marked with pure flavours and elegant quality. (Tim Johnston)

12°C. No external yeasts are used, and fermentation takes place at between 16° and 21°C in 75 per cent vats of steel and fibreglass, 25 per cent in casks ranging from new to five years old. Since 2000 individual vat temperature control has been introduced, and Christophe can track the precise evolution of each plot's wine and better know its style for future reference.

Cellar ageing lasts a year, including *bâtonnage*, with the vat and cask wine assembled just before its September bottling, when fining and filtration are done. The ageing process has been extended by three months since the mid-1990s.

Christophe is very objective and honest about his wines. He hasn't made a *moelleux*, or sweet wine, since 1999. "It's less interesting to make, but there is a clientele attached to it," he admits. It's funny how some growers would have you believe it is the best, most complex wine in their locker. He first made this in 1990, and only if the year were poor, as in 1992, would it not be made. Apart from the *moelleux*, he has also made a full-on, late-picked wine, called "Patience" in 2000. This came from 20-year

Viognier that was picked six weeks after the regular harvest; 1,400 half bottles were made of a wine that received two years in new oak. Its quality approaches a *vin de paille*, with a life of over 30 years possible for the 2000.

This dedicated man is likely to continue to provide exceptional wines; his wife, Isabelle, helps in the office and does tasks like pruning and tying in the vineyard, while also bringing up the six children. Holidays are snatched days here and there, a weekend's ski-ing and a summer holiday somewhere like Alsace or Banyuls, never too far away from a vineyard.

There is also an agreement with Laurent Charles Brotte, the Châteauneuf-du-Pape *négociant*, to sell the Pichon wine, with mention of Christophe on the label. This, too, is well worth looking out for.

CONDRIEU
2004 ★★★★
2003 ★★★
2002 ★★★

2001 ★★★
2000 *Patience* ★★★★

Export 25 per cent (1) Japan, (2) USA, (3) Sweden

PHILIPPE PICHON

Philippe Pichon took his retirement in March 2000 and went south to live near friends at Montélimar. His wine was made from the *Roche Coulante* and *Mève* sites. The wine was bottled in August, 20 per cent raised in oak, with its malo done.

In some years like 1999 a *moelleux* was also made. His son Christophe has taken over his vineyards.

DOMAINE DE PIERRE BLANCHE

RN 86 Chanson 42410 Chavanay +33(0)477 572959

See also Côte-Rôtie, St-Joseph.
Michel and Xavier Mourier work 1.5 hectares of Viognier that they planted themselves in 1991. Part is on *Rivoires* at Chavanay, the other part at *La Madone* at Malleval, and in both cases the soil is granite.

The crop is vinified in casks that run from new to six years old, and is bottled in June. The wines have sound white fruit and are nicely understated.

CONDRIEU
    2002 ★
    2001 ★★★

DOMAINE PORTE VINCENT

8 rue Cuvillière 69420 Condrieu
Sceaportevincent@aol.com

Patrice Porte, now in his mid-40s, has seen the wheel of fortune turn through his career in wine. As a young man he set out on his own, with a fine vineyard on the *Côte Châtillon*. His father had been one of the old names at Condrieu, and the future seemed clear.

But selling his wine was a big problem, and he retreated to the employ of Guigal, selling off most of the *Châtillon* in the process. This plot now contributes to half of Guigal's successful and acclaimed La Doriane.

Patrice then turned to fruit cultivation—notably, cherries and apricots—but in 2002, with Condrieu wine prices high, he returned to the fold, working with his cousin Hervé Vincent and his brother Frédéric.

The three men cultivate 2.2 ha, spread across four sites—*Côte Châtillon*, *Bassenon*, and *Ste-Agathe* (all 1987–90), with 0.3 ha on *Vernon* (1980), which supplies the special Noblesse de Vernon wine. All are mainstream Condrieu *lieux-dits*.

Two wines are made. The classic is vinified and raised half in four-to-five-year-old oak, half in vat and is bottled in July or September according to the style of the year. There is some lees stirring.

The Noblesse de Vernon is oak handled—10 per cent new, the rest four to five years old. "We aren't partisans of new oak," says Patrice; "we simply don't like the taste." It, too, is bottled in July or September.

M. Vincent looks after the commercial side and also works 2 ha at Mormoiron in the Vaucluse, where he makes a Côtes du Ventoux.

Fingers crossed this time for Patrice: the Noblesse is certainly promising if the 2003 is a yardstick—a big wine with interesting spiced, dried fruit flavours.

CONDRIEU
    2003 ★

CONDRIEU NOBLESSE DE VERNON
    2003 ★★★

HERVÉ AND MARIE-THÉRÈSE RICHARD

RN86 Verlieu 42410 Chavanay +33(0)474 870775

See also St-Joseph.
Hervé and Marie-Thérèse Richard have built up their Condrieu holdings to three hectares since 1983, when they first planted vines. Two hectares are on *La Maraze* at St-Michel-sur-

Rhône. The soil is sandy granite. A little of their crop is still sold to Guigal.

The dry Condrieu is called "L'Amaraze," and is made only from crop off that *lieu-dit*. Since 1997 they have also made a *moelleux*, later-picked wine. The dry wine is fermented 30 per cent in oak one to five years old, with just a touch of new, the rest in steel or enamel-lined vats. The grapes are sometimes destemmed, and the wine is bottled in August.

L'Amaraze is slow-burn, fine wine that merits being left for over two years to allow the oak to integrate. The signs are quite promising here.

CONDRIEU L'AMARAZE

2003 ★★★
2002 ★★
2001 ★★

RENÉ ROSTAING

Petite rue du Port 69420 Ampuis +33(0)474 561200

See also Côte-Rôtie.

Since 1991 René Rostaing has produced a Condrieu, the stylish La Bonnette. This is taken from 0.6 hectare on the southwest-facing *Côte Bonnette*, on the left on the way to the Château du Rozay, and from 0.4 hectare on *Ste-Agathe*. The vineyards are split by the *Arbuel* stream.

The *Bonnette* vineyard was retrieved and replanted in 1987. The soil is very light, sandy granite, with bits of quartz in it—the whole known as *gore*—with a couch of red, sticky clay between half and one metre down.

Ste-Agathe was a south-facing vineyard planted around 1974 that M. Rostaing bought in the late 1990s—a rare chance to find such mature vines. The soil is decomposed granite, but there isn't the clay below. This makes its wine more classic, with white flowers and honey notes. The *Côte Bonnette* gives more powerful, formally structured, and mineral-tinged wines. When blended, the final wine expresses quiet richness, with a clean finish that shows off the fennel, licorice side of Condrieu and a marked degree of minerality.

M. Rostaing used to ferment in steel and raise the wine for its malolactic fermentation in new oak. But since 1998 he has changed his view: "Because the Viognier is very pure, I don't want to mask it or mess it about with wood, so I use only stainless steel, for maximum purity." The wine is bottled in July, the malolactic finished.

CONDRIEU LA BONNETTE

2002 ★★
2001 ★★★

CHÂTEAU DU ROZAY

Le Rozay 69420 Condrieu +33(0)474 878292

Jean-Yves Multier leads the way to the patch of terrace that he is laying just beyond his house. There is a small fountain of spring water behind it, and beyond runs the sweep of fields, pastures, and light hills on the way to Mont Pilat. His comment reveals much about him: "I may not be rich, but how can I want for more, when I can sit here with my friends, have the sound of running water behind me, a glass of wine in my hand, the late sun on our faces, and enjoy that view?"

He and his wife, Fabienne, a gentle, pretty woman from Lyon, live quietly with their three daughters in the old estate worker's house next to the Château du Rozay, an illustrious title for a property that is creaking at the seams. She likes pottery, gardening, and nature, and is well suited to the tranquil, rather withdrawn life here.

The drive up to the château is always inspiring: many a turn and bend along a road that passes at times lush vegetation, hanging strands of dark-green foliage, and some recently hewn vineyards. Then comes the openness of the plain, a deep breath of view and air, grazing animals, another world beyond the rumble of the Rhône Valley. Finally the château, its fading pink-coloured side bordered by a line of four splendid plane trees. Shutters are tightly drawn, draughts whistle through, the cream façade facing west is a closed book.

Here is a mild, reflective countryman who in 2004 had to take a hard decision: to build an expensive new cellar, or stop his winemaking and sell the harvest to a local *négociant*. His brother and sister inherited the château when their father died, and Jean-Yves the vineyard. With them requesting him to free up the cellar area in the château, his hand was forced. He gave up his winemaking and is now working under the Chapoutier direction.

"I couldn't afford the new cellar," he states; "it's as simple as that. Two frosts in 1998 and 2003 cut my crop enormously, and the outlook for wine isn't strong, either. I'm in my mid-40s, and have three young girls to bring up."

He made his first wine with his father in 1979, and throughout has also tried to maintain some form of decorum for the family home and its history. His genial father, Pierre, died in 1984, aged just 64, having suffered from tuberculosis in an epidemic that hit Lyon when he was a child. Pierre had been one of those *vignerons* who stand out by their zany enthusiasm for what they are doing in life. He would stride around the château and its cellar, dispensing information on Rozay or its wine or even Lyon and its traditions, clad in a jauntily angled cloth cap and wearing large green Wellington boots that seemed set to gobble up his small frame.

This left Jean-Yves, a mere 23-year-old, to take over. His older brother was not interested, nor was his sister, who lives in Lyon. Jean-Yves was then both the rider of heavy-duty German motorbikes, never under 1,000 cc, and a part-time one-man-show actor: anything but the usual. What he always held was a strong interest in the family home and its vineyards, perhaps even ahead of the daily nitty-gritty of winemaking.

"We've been here since 1890, a Lyonnais family who used Rozay as a secondary residence," he explains. "My great-grandparents manufactured braided uniforms and gilded vestments for the military and the Church— keeping good company, you might say. They also owned the *Clos de Chéry*, and I recently found an old, staged photograph of that vineyard dating from 1910. The women were harvesting in dresses with tight corsets and hats; there were two and a half hectares of Syrah and one and a half of Viognier, on a site called the *Descente du Mauvais Pas* ['descent of the bad step'], which are the ledges just below the château here.

"My father's real passion was agriculture, and he was never that keen on lugging around textile samples to his clients, especially as he had only one lung and a deformation of the spinal cord, which made it all very hard work for him. He had no grounding in wine, so taught himself, read a lot, and started having our crop vinified at the Co-opérative in Tain-l'Hermitage. At the time it was merely a complement to 40 hectares of corn and maize and a few sheep."

"The wine was bottled and sold through an intermediary under the title 'Château du Rozay' until about 1968," he recalls. "From 1969 to 1978 Georges Vernay vinified and bottled our wine, on average 1,500 litres from under one hectare, with the third that we kept sold to Yapp in Britain. Georges Vernay always helped my father tremendously."

The 2.8-hectare vineyard is held in five plots, headed by 1.5 hectares on *Chéry*; this plot contains 0.07 ha of Viognier planted in 1921. The average age there is around 65 years, the youngest vines dating from 1988. The other *lieux-dits* are *Corbery* (1980), next to the house, and *Côte Châtillon* (1986). The soil for all three sites is largely decomposed granite, but there are nuances between each one: *Chéry*'s is a lighter colour, with speckles of mica. *Châtillon* is more pale yellow to the eye, and *Corbery* is sandy brown, with black patches in the rock. Jean-Yves also grows 2.2 hectares of Syrah planted in 1981 on *Corbery*.

The Coteaux du Château du Rozay (8,000 bottles) was from *Corbery* and *Châtillon*; the Château du Rozay (3,000 bottles) was purely *Chéry*, essentially its old vines' element. The Coteaux was the soft, midweight wine; the Château was a more fully laden wine and, when on song, one of the impressive wines of Condrieu.

From 2004 Chapoutier have bought and vinified the crop from here. It forms part of their wine entitled simply "Condrieu," but from around 2006, they may start to make a wine from the oldest vines on *Chéry*; the vineyard is said to need some attention before then.

LES COTEAUX DU CHÂTEAU DU ROZAY
2002 ★

CHÂTEAU DU ROZAY
2002 ★★
2001 ★★★

SAINT-COSME

Château de St-Cosme 84190 Gigondas
+33(0)490 658080

See also Côte-Rôtie.

In 1997 Louis Barruol, a grower at Gigondas, energetic and open to ideas, started to produce a Condrieu. He went north to find *viticulteurs* with good sites and who didn't want to vinify themselves. The area sourced can range from Vérin to St-Pierre-de-Boeuf and Malleval.

Low yields are a must. The Vaucluse *département* is not included in the region allowed to vinify Condrieu, so the wine is made in the northern Rhône. After an all-oak start to his vinification in the late 1990s, Louis switched in 2000 to 30 per cent vat to achieve more fruit from the Viognier. Now he has settled on using all oak, one-third of it new. In February the casks are taken south to Gigondas, and bottling is done after completion of the malo and before the summer heat, around June. Three thousand bottles are produced.

The style is for a full wine that can show well for six or seven years.

CONDRIEU
2003 ★★
2000 ★★

CAVE DE SAINT-DÉSIRAT

07340 St-Désirat +33(0)475 342205

See also St-Joseph.

The Co-opérative has five stalwart members who supply Viognier from Condrieu, and the regular wine was first produced here in 1992. The sites are *Les Rochains* at Limony, mainly *La Combe* at St-Pierre-de-Boeuf, and *Champ de Four* at Malleval. This is vinified in steel vats, and is bottled before the summer heat.

The top Condrieu, the Domaine de Rochevine, is vinified half in steel, half in two-to-three-year-old oak and raised for eight months. This comes from a 1.5-hectare holding on *Les Côtes* at Limony.

The classic wine expresses fair pear and apricot fruit flavours, while the Rochevine is more angled towards exotic fruits; its intensity at times risks being overstretched, making the wine a little taut.

CONDRIEU
2000 ★

CONDRIEU DOMAINE DE ROCHEVINE
2001 ★

CAVE DE SARRAS

NO LONGER IN BUSINESS

See also St-Joseph.

This Co-opérative is supplied from the crop of just one member. The wine is called Domaine Jacques Vernay and comes from St-Pierre-de-Boeuf.

After decantation, enzymes, and yeasting, 90 per cent of the crop is fermented in steel, 10 per cent in oak, at around 17°C. The wine is stirred on its lees over the course of six months and is bottled with the malo done.

The 2001 was rather stretched, with some richness in it, but the overall effect was uneven. The 2002 was rustic, the 2003 the best of the three, a big constitution wine, with a chewy finale. Its fruit style is in the exotic arena— pineapple mixed with apricot.

CONDRIEU DOMAINE JACQUES VERNAY

2003 ★★

ÉRIC TEXIER

Bel Air 69380 Charnay +33(0)472 542618

See also Hermitage, Regional Wines, St-Joseph.

Éric Texier produces two Condrieus, which are unusually fermented and raised in acacia wood casks. The Janrode comes from the *Jeanraude* site at Saint-Michel-sur-Rhône, and the classic is mostly from *Vernon*, the loess part of it called locally *Le Pigeonnier*, not the schist, and *La Combe* at Saint-Pierre-de-Boeuf nearby. "The aim of the acacia is to bring forward more the white flower aromas of the wine, avoid the vanilla of oak, and the toast side," he comments.

The acacia casks are 30 per cent new, and the rest run up to four years old. Both wines are bottled in June after the harvest.

DOMAINE VALLET

La Croisette N86 07340 Serrières +33(0)475 340464

See also St-Joseph.

Father Louis and son Anthony Vallet have a smudge of Condrieu, precisely 0.4 ha, split between two sites in the south of the *appellation*. With gradual planting, this will rise to 0.75 ha by 2007. The greater portion is on the south-facing *Merlan* (1994), beside the hamlet of Arcoules, north of Limony; and precisely 0.164 ha was planted in 2004 on *Rouelle Midi*, a hill of good quality just west of Limony. Both have decomposed, slippery granite soil, with Merlan containing pockets of clay below the topsoil.

In future years, Anthony would like to make a late-harvested wine off *Merlan*, which lies in a typical small Ardèche valley and so has sound ripening potential.

First made in 1998, the wine is cask fermented, the oak 25 per cent new, the rest two to three years old. Weekly lees stirring is done until the malo has finished, and bottling is in May.

Anthony describes his wine as showing more white fruit than flowers on the bouquet—a typical trait of these southern-sector Condrieus. There are also fruits like banana present to inject a touch of the exotic.

CONDRIEU

2002 ★★

2001 (★)

DOMAINE GEORGES VERNAY

1 route Nationale 69420 Condrieu +33(0)474 568181

See also Côte-Rôtie, St-Joseph.

This is the home of the doyen of Condrieu, the vastly respected Georges Vernay, now retired and busy dusting down his old vegetable gardening skills. It has been a great relief to many that his transfer of the domaine in 1997 to his daughter Christine and her husband, Paul, has proved to be highly successful, for much of the welfare of Condrieu depends on the welfare of the Domaine Georges Vernay.

For some years the next move here remained unclear, and the domaine's wines suffered from some loss of direction in the early 1990s. The emergence of Christine has been a surprise, since she was an unlikely source a few years ago, when she was busy living and studying the history of art and literature in Paris. Her husband, the lively Paul Amsellem, was born and raised in Morocco until he was 10, and later ran a retail business selling baby clothing mainly in the Paris area—so no grounding in winemaking whatsoever for him. In 1996 they returned to the south, and Christine's first vintage was the 1997.

Since then these wines have performed really well. There is a finesse present now, the lighter touch of Georges' greatly refined daughter apparent. Christine and Paul make a good combination: she clearly dreams of the spires, the expressions of art, the Italianate; speaks Italian; and puts these shades into her wine. She has the dark eyes and southern air of her mother. Paul openly declares, "I am the Jew with a family of commerce; I can buy and sell things." Talkative, interesting, and a great party man with a rolling blues piano, he brings pep to the partnership.

It was Christine or nothing, really. Georges' sons, Luc and Daniel, had peeled away to do their own thing—Daniel to be a cowboy, raising and breaking horses in Colorado, Luc to run his own flying school. Which left the poised, cultured Christine, a woman whose knowledge of the arts and chic style fitted more naturally a Parisian *quartier* than a Condrieu vineyard ledge.

The vineyard runs to 7.5 hectares, placing them in the top three owners at Condrieu, with Guigal and Cuilleron. The top site is their fabled 1.7 ha on *Vernon*, which they bought in 2000 from a Lyonnais, having rented it for three generations. It is a fabulous spot, the convex arc of the hill enjoying a wonderful sunny exposure. The soil is the classic mica-filled granite, with some schist, of Condrieu. This is the source of their top cuvée, the Coteau de Vernon.

There are three wines. The classic is the Terrasses de l'Empire, a wine from mainly the *lieu-dit Ste-Agathe*, average age 40 years, plus *La Caille* next door—which together amount to a bit under five hectares. This makes Terrasses the nearest thing to a big-scale wine at Condrieu, with an average production of around 20,000 bottles. As such, it shows commendable character—solid and stand-alone in a big year like 2003, and nicely rounded in the more supple 2000 vintage. Nuts, dried fruits, and some chewiness combine to make this a wine that can live correctly for around 10 years.

It is fermented and raised at 16° to 17°C in 20 hl barrels that run up to 10 years old. The lees are stirred until the early New Year, and in April the wine is moved to steel vats until bottling at the end of May. Three new barrels were bought in 2003, slightly distorting the usual new oak proportion, which is never meant to be pronounced.

The Chaillées de l'Enfer was first made in 1992, from *Ste-Agathe* initially, then from 0.8 ha on *La Caille*, across the road from *Vernon*, and since bought by the Vernays in 1999. This is a *marque*, the source word *chaillet* meaning the flat terrace space between walls. The vines now total 0.8 hectare and date from 1957. The policy here is to work with extra-ripe crop. The wine is fermented and raised for one year in small casks, 25 per cent new, the rest up to five years old. It is bottled in January, 15 months after the harvest, and is sold in 50 and 75 cl fluted bottles.

The very first Chaillées de l'Enfer in 1992 told a story about Viognier longevity and showed that if the grower can succeed in capturing a balanced power from the Viognier, a long-lived wine awaits.

When drunk in September 1998, it was noted thus: "vanilla, tropical fruit bouquet, air moves it to pear drop sweets; very full palate, more definably Viognier here, the grape at its full, potent best. Still has new oak on finish. Aperitif wine, although with food would need strong-tasting fish. Does not seem six years old; the texture is fat and nicely luscious."

The Enfer is a more gourmand wine than the Vernon—it delivers the pleasure, the Vernon's complexity making the drinker stop and reflect. I find Enfer clams up and hides its early flamboyance between two and three years old, emerging with a tighter, sometimes drier texture in its second phase.

The mighty, rightly famed Coteau de Vernon has through thick and thin defended the domaine's name, even when the wines were going through a dull patch in the early 1990s, and outside *oenologue* advice was getting them to harvest early. It is vinified at a maximum of 18°C in casks, 25 per cent new, the rest up to five years old. Its ageing lasts longer than Chaillées, from 12 to 16 months. Around 4,500 bottles are made.

The Vernon is exceptional; the bouquet is usually directed towards dried fruits rather than floral nuances. The wine is very discreet when young, its flavour packed in tight-knit layers. There is a slow-burn emphasis on the palate, with some final tannic aspects as well. Stylistically, Vernon approaches Château-Grillet, especially in its aromas and its longevity. It is one of the only Condrieus to do so. It's above all a wine of subtlety, of gradually revealed nuances.

Christine Vernay believes the Vernon can live for 10 years, and especially enjoys drinking it when it is three to four years old: "Then it's possible to find some honey and licorice in the wine." With a British palate, I would attest that the Vernon can live comfortably 20 years, as with the 1983 drunk in 2003. It had held together well, its compact texture still in evidence. The usual aged Viognier declarations like slightly decomposing white fruit and damp wool were in evidence, but above all, the wine's discreet elegance was still there.

A couple of sweet wines were made here, in 1992 and 1994. The crop was vat fermented at 12°C until December, when the wine was taken gradually below zero, without icing up, to stop the process and leave 25 to 30 gm of sugar. The 1994 showed better balance than the 1992 and contained a little less sugar.

Winemaking policy in the last few years has established itself as aiming for elegance with correct fullness here. These wines will never be flashy and overheated. For instance, the 2000 crop was destemmed, the 2001, 2003, and 2004 left intact. "Leaving the bunches intact, we find, brings a more complete juice," observes Christine. "You also have to press harder if you have destalked, and we prefer to be more gentle." The policy is also to allow the malolactic fermentation to happen, although so low in acidity was 1997 that it was blocked in that year.

Christine is now the Madame of the domaine; Georges prefers to stay strictly in the background. He hasn't lost a jot of wisdom and can advise that potatoes should be planted on a waning moon to avoid excess vegetation, as well as recall with photographic clarity events from many decades ago. He is a strong-voiced, big, ruddy man now in his late 70s, ever the true

countryman, as his large hands and broad shoulders indicate.

He doesn't give a lot away when sitting talking in the confines of his shaded tasting room, but the moment he is up the hillside discussing his vines, out come the animation and sure instinct of someone whose winemaking spans several generations, with many hours of personal toil attached. The comments are usually delivered with a rumbling chuckle, the features always expressive. The debt to him from anyone who loves Condrieu or even Viognier wines is enormous; for me he is Le Grand Patron.

Apart from their St-Josephs and Côte-Rôties, the domaine also makes red Côtes du Rhône and *vin de pays des Collines Rhodaniennes* in Syrah and Viognier. The former is from plantings on the high, 320-metre level of *Ste-Agathe*, outside the Condrieu zone, which date from between 1958 and 1966. This is aged for 10 months in two-to-10-year-old oak.

The Viognier *vin de pays*, formerly Le Grand Terroir, now Le Pied de Samson, is from above 300-metres on *La Caille* and *Mirebaudy*. The vines date from the 1980s. This is steel vinified and gets a May bottling. It can be delightful, an early drinking wine, helped by its low, 30 hl/ha yields.

CONDRIEU TERRASSES DE L'EMPIRE

2003 ★★★
2002 ★(★)
2001 ★★★
2000 ★★

CONDRIEU CHAILLÉES DE L'ENFER

2003 (CASK) ★★★★ Scented, apple aroma, nice light touch. Quite firm palate, restrained texture with brooding power. Can become rich without looseness. Correct length, rich elegance, ways to go. From 2006; 2012–14.

2002 ★★ Pear aroma, fair potential; slightly tart start, but has some flesh, and on the finale. Apple/fruit skin taste. 2010–12.

2001 ★★★★ Nicely weighted, broad pear aroma, promising; mixed dried fruits, touch flat. Sound length, tightens well. Shows potential. Elegance/quiet power mixed, good nuances here. From 2004.

2000 ★★★

CONDRIEU COTEAU DE VERNON

2003 (CASK) ★★★★★ Pear with floral/almond/buttery side. Full attack, has broadened and become more profound in six months. More *gourmand* than usual at this stage, was more *en finesse*. Dried fruits/spice, is prolonged. Firms with air. From 2009; 2020–23. Last tasted Dec. 2004.

2002 ★★★ Compact, light acacia bouquet, some depth. Pebbly white fruit, more alive than usual. Elegant towards finish, salty tang there. Light mineral/honey mix on latter part. Lesser scale than normal, but has variety of flavours. 2013–16.

2001 ★★★★ Subtle nose, pretty pear, lovely discreet elegance; good pear/dried fruit sinew; structured wine, will live and gradually develop. Good apricot, heated touch. Esp 2006–07; can live till 2015–17.

2000 ★★★★ Caramelised fruits, mineral/custard, has gone past pear/floral. Good grip on palate, very profound. Some mineral/tannin near end. Great refinement, complex, stylish. 2011–13.

1999 ★★★ First yellow of age on *robe*; mineral/smoky, light pineapple aroma, variety to come; tasty, generous wine, exotic fruits present. Quite potent, ends firmly—oak/heat. Greengage aftertaste. 2011–13.

1998 ★★★★ Ripe bouquet—pear/apricot, mineral/butter, first damp wool signs. Tight buttery flavour, still hidden. Dry mineral/white pepper end, clear-cut. Appealing variety. 2012–14.

1997 ★★★
1996 ★★★★★
1995 ★★
1994 ★★★★

Export 20 per cent (1) Great Britain, (2) USA, (3) Switzerland

DOMAINE VERRIER

42520 Malleval +33(0)4777 572959

A domaine with young vines planted in the early 1990s, its nearly one hectare vineyard is just south of *Volan* at Malleval. The Condrieu is part vat, part oak vinified. The Condrieu of the Verriers will improve as the vines age.

The brothers work with Domaine de Pierre Blanche for vinification.

J. VIDAL-FLEURY

9 route de la Roche 69420 Ampuis +33(0)474 561018

See also Cornas, Côte-Rôtie, Crozes-Hermitage, Hermitage, St-Joseph.
Vidal-Fleury, part of the Guigal empire, produce 6,000 to 7,000 bottles of Condrieu a year. There are three regular suppliers from the *commune* of Condrieu and one from Chavanay.

The wine is bought once the malo has been done; if this delays, as in 2001, the wine is bottled with the malo blocked. It is a midweight wine, at times somewhat in the mainstream, and can repay being left alone to develop more openness: the 2003 improved well between six and 18 months old.

CONDRIEU

2003 ★★★
2001 ★

GÉRARD VILLANO

111, RN86 69420 Condrieu +33(0)764

See also Côte-Rôtie, St-Joseph.
One of the sad elements sometimes about eating out is to observe how little some old couples speak to each other when dining at a nearby table. There's no chance of that happening in the future with Gérard and Sylvie Villano. This is a duo with grown-up children who are still filling in each other's sounds and words and who chatter and chirrup merrily away to one another the whole day long. In Condrieu they

FIGURE 12 Sweet nothings and a zest for life—the inseparable Sylvie and Gérard Villano. (Tim Johnston)

are known as "Les Amoureux," and their lives have been a series of varied adventures, spent close together in each other's company.

Gérard could well pass for a strapping sailor, a bearded mariner of the waters with just a bit of extra girth. Whatever the weather, he never wears socks. His ponytail and glasses, his loud pronouncements, and his exotic past all qualify him as an *original*. Now that he's making wine, he is still inclined to ruffle some feathers with his trenchant views on what should or should not be allowed.

Gérard describes himself as a wanderer; he started life as a *patissier-chocolatier* but became fed up with the baking and making, and went on to be a computer expert in the days when each machine took up much of any room. "But I tired of city life," he comments, and proudly continues, "so then in 1978 I took five months of voluntary unemployment." He rolls the word "voluntary" around with great relish. City life was Marseille, his hometown, where he and Sylvie had gone just to have their children—"we felt they should be born in the same place as me."

That was the turning point in his life, for he became a sailor-chef, *matelot-cuisinier*, on the barges of the Rhône. For seven years, he worked on four different barges, each one with a crew of seven men. "Our typical cargo in those days was phosphate or coal, loaded on at Les Roches de Condrieu here and taken down to Lavéra, the port for Martigues on the Mediterranean. Each run like that would last about 24 hours.

"The most ferocious part of the Rhône is at Viviers, south of Montélimar, where the river is just one channel that runs between two cliffs. The stream there could bring the barge to a halt, and when we reversed, it was 'hang on for your lives' as we would set off at 20 kilometres an hour."

After seven years, Gérard had had enough of being cooped up with the same six men for days on end—he would work a week on, a week off—and he went off to Mâcon to do a wine and commerce course. His first harvest was 1986, starting with 0.9 ha mixed between *Ste-Agathe* and *Chéry*, and a tiny amount of Syrah on the *Coteaux de Semons* in Côte-Rôtie. He also revived his chocolate making, to keep some money coming in, and this continued until June 1997, a date Sylvie recalls with great precision.

Sylvie, small beside Gérard, with brown hair and marine eyes, and a regular winter jumper, explains the wine connection: "My family always made some wine for themselves here, and so it was a natural thing to do. At first we had to clear forest land at St-Michel. Now we handle the vineyards in as laissez-faire a way as we can, although the rain in 2002 caused so many weeds, that was testing."

Their hectare at Condrieu is split 0.2 *Chéry* (1950) and 0.8 *Poncin* (1990), the vineyard they had to clear. Their part of *Chéry* has some white soil, limestone and marl with the granite, while the *Poncin* is very decomposed granite involving a lot of thick sand with some clay, too. The grapes are all vinified together.

Elsewhere they continue to make some Côte-Rôtie, a red St-Joseph, and Côtes du Rhône Syrah and Viognier from vines in the Condrieu zone.

The Condrieu is simply made; after pressing—Gérard has an old wooden press that he calls "Monsieur 120 Years"—the juice is left to decant for 36 hours at cellar temperature and is fermented in cask at around 18°C. The wood is between eight and 15 years old, and houses the wine for around 10 months until an August bottling, the malo done. Work in the cellar is not at all flash—indeed the last cooling machine, a down-home affair, exploded!

Most of the white wine is bottled, the rest going to Guigal as crop or as wine to the merchant trade. The Condrieu is a fair wine, not always as well defined as it could be. White fruits are emphasized.

The Côtes du Rhône Sainte-Agathe is taken from a 0.3 ha plot on *Vergelas*; the red is a Syrah, the white a Viognier. The white is vinified like the Condrieu; the Syrah receives 18 months in used casks, with fining and filtration. The Viognier shows exotic fruit flavours, the red a firm live fruit.

CONDRIEU

2003 ★

2002 (★)

2001 ★

Export 5 per cent (1) Switzerland, (2) Belgium

DOMAINE FRANÇOIS VILLARD

Montjoux 42410 St-Michel-sur-Rhône +33(0)474 568360

See also Côte-Rôtie, St-Joseph.

If traditionalists were shaken up by Jean-Luc Colombo, they should get a load of François Villard! This man is in a hurry. Before 1985 he worked in the restaurant trade, then between 1985 and 1988 he was chef of the Vienne Hospital. By then his thoughts had turned to becoming a sommelier. "I did four hundred hours of classes, but I didn't take the exam. I thought it would be easier to become a *vigneron*!" On top of this, his father, a smallholder mainly growing cereals in the Isère, didn't even drink wine!

"I had been fired by an enthusiasm for wine since I was 20," recalls François, small, with a receding cropped haircut, southern looking, and very fast talking. "We grew a few hybrid vines, and I bought some books on winemaking and set off. I do admit that I was a kept man, by my wife, for 10 years!" As he speaks, his T-shirt catches the eye. Wasn't that the one I saw him wear to the gala dinner, under a dark jacket, in the Palais des Papes at Avignon? Maybe he buys six of them at a time!

François first planted in 1989, and his vineyards mix ownership with rental agreements. At Condrieu he works 3.9 ha from three different places, 0.9 ha on *Verlieux* at Chavanay, 1.3 ha on *Le Grand Val* at St-Pierre-de-Boeuf, and 1.6 ha on *Poncin/La Rouillère* at St-Michel-sur-Rhône. While he rents a few vineyards from 1982, the majority date from the late 1980s onwards.

The soil has slight variations between the three sites. *Poncin/La Rouillère* mixes granite and mica, and the wines show mineral touches; *Verlieux*'s granite and quartz provide floral tones. *Le Grand Val* mixes granite, quartz, and loess, which contribute to a wine that can live well.

François is not shy of extremes. Leaving his grapes to rot nobly, be they Marsanne for his St-Joseph or Viognier for his Condrieu, is one tac-

FIGURE 13 Fast talking, fast moving—ex-chef François Villard, a man of projects and dreams, at Condrieu and beyond. (Tim Johnston)

tic. For him, the botrytis brings complexity: "I want to go beyond the peach or apricot tones of normal Condrieu." He makes three wines, and two of them, the Deponcins and Le Grand Vallon, contain about 15 per cent noble rot grapes. The third, Les Terrasses du Palat, from the *Verlieux* site, runs at 3 to 5 per cent. Because it is a hot and early-ripening site, he has to pick before the sugar content goes off the scale there.

He laughs as he recalls his 1995 Deponcins: "It's a wine with enough minerality to support noble rot, and in 1995 we reached 35 per cent, which made it almost a late-harvest wine. That took five years to integrate." He recognises that his task has to be to balance noble rot with a reasonable degree, not one around the 15° mark, so there is a check on this rotting activity.

Big cellar work is also his dish. François would be lost without oak. "I have the minimum baggage, which means no other reference outside using oak," he states. He likes a cool decantation at around 8°C after pressing, and then swings into action on the wood. For Palat he uses 20 per cent new, 80 per cent one-to-three-year-old oak; for Grand Vallon it is 30 per cent new, the rest one to three years old; and on Deponcins it is 40 per cent new, the rest one to three years old.

After 30 days of cask fermentation at 15° to 18°C, he does a weekly lees stirring over eight months, assembles the different casks in August, and bottles up the wines in September.

These are wines made in the active manner. "I like concentration in my wines," he explains. "The first way is through low yields, the second through the vinification, so there is much stirring of the lees. Then the wines can handle the wood."

And it works. I have witnessed restaurateurs from Lyon visiting him to top up on supplies, the overt, sometimes confected taste going down a storm there. He also possesses a sharp eye and ear for the media, and is written up as one of Condrieu's Young Turks, even though he has now hit 40. He is very motivated and can hardly sit still, and confesses that his daughters are not interested in following his trail: "They don't think much of my job because they never see me!"

Of the dry wines, Le Grand Vallon is the most accomplished. Its fullness is well founded, and there is enough content to assimilate the oak; the result is a healthy cocktail of varied flavours, a stimulating mix. The Terrasses du Palat is more straightforward, with an open style and comfortable weight of wine. Deponcins needs patience—around three years—before it adds to its pear-apricot early surge; it is also a fleshy-textured wine.

There are two sweet wines here. The Quintessence is his formal noble rot wine, fermented and raised in new oak for most of a year. This is later-picked, often from *Le Grand Val*, although in a year like 2002 that means 20 September. It comes in 50 cl bottles, and François is fermenting it through more than in the late 1990s, so there are 40, not 110 gm of residual sugar. He has made this since 1994, except for the years 1995, 1998, and 2001. It can carry orange, bergamot flavours and also an interesting acidity in a year like 2002.

His second sweet wine, with no *appellation* status, is called Après Tout!!!. This is made from The Must of Partially Fermented Grapes, to give it its formal title. This is the result of severe late harvesting of leftover bunches, picked in December. The 1999, for instance, was Marsanne 57 per cent, Viognier 28 per cent, and

Syrah 15 per cent. It is fermented and raised in new oak for almost a year, and weighs in at 12° with 120 gm of residual sugar per litre. Apricot and golden syrup flavours combine here, but also a correctly clean finish is apparent, when the Viognier's typical pear fruit returns.

With his chums Pierre Gaillard and Yves Cuilleron he also exploits the Seyssuel vineyard on the Rhône's east bank up near Vienne. They have a burgeoning *négoce* business covering northern and southern Rhône wines, while he is also fired up about his several *vins de pays*. Ever the fast-tracker, he planted a bit under one hectare of Merlot on the sandy plain near the Rhône at Chavanay in 2000 and will be making a 70 per cent Merlot, 15 per cent Syrah and Cabernet wine in the future. This is in addition to his oak-raised Viognier *vin de pays*, a successful wine.

François's latest scheme is to open up the northern part of the Isère *département* at Bourgoin-Jallieu, about 25 miles northeast of Vienne. "The hills there are Jurassic clay-limestone, and I reckon they are ideal for Pinot Noir and Chardonnay," he says. These would be *vins de pays des Balmes Dauphinoises*, by the way.

CONDRIEU TERRASSES DU PALAT

2003 ★★★
2002 (CASK) ★★
2001 ★★★

CONDRIEU LE GRAND VALLON

2003 ★★(★)
2002 (CASK) ★★★
2001 ★★★★

CONDRIEU DEPONCINS

2003 ★★★
2002 (CASK) ★★
2001 ★★★

CONDRIEU QUINTESSENCE

2002 ★★
1997 ★
1999 *Après Tout!!!* ★★★

Export 40 per cent (1) Great Britain, (2) USA, (3) Japan

LES VINS DE VIENNE

Bas Seyssuel 38200 Seyssuel +33(0)474 850452

See also Cornas, Côte-Rôtie, Crozes-Hermitage, Hermitage, St-Joseph, St-Péray.
The Condrieu here is made from purchased grapes, which are vinified at the group's cellars near Vienne. The wines are cask fermented, raised on lees, and bottled after the malo has been completed. The source appears to be from young vines, but the wine is going in the right direction.

There are two dry wines, a plain Condrieu and a more expensive La Chambée, the former receiving 30 per cent new oak, the latter 60 per cent over nine months. The Chambée often shows rather standard oak-pineapple flavours, but the 2003 was more authentic, with more local apricot/flan style flavours and less obvious oak: hopefully, its rich elegance is a sign of the style for the future.

There is also a Cépées Caties, a sweet wine made from a mix of dried and noble rot harvest, termed *baies botrytisées et passerillées*. This is raised for nine months in new oak.

CONDRIEU LA CHAMBÉE

2003 ★★(★)
2000 ★★

CONDRIEU VINTAGES

Earlier exceptional vintages: 1949, 1947, 1929

1959 Very good.
1960 Poor.
1961 Very good.
1962 Mediocre.
1963 Mediocre.
1964 Excellent.
1965 Mediocre.
1966 Very good.
1967 Very good.
1968 Mediocre.
1969 Very good, tiny crop.
1970 Very good.

1971 Excellent.

1972 Good.

1973 Good.

1974 Very good.

1975 Very good.

1976 Good to very good. Notable Vernay Coteau de Vernon.

1977 Poor.

1978 Excellent, long-lived.

1979 Good. Have kept very well. Notable Château du Rozay.

1980 Fair. Notable Château du Rozay and Delas.

1981 Very good. Notable Vernay and Château du Rozay.

1982 Good, but lack of acidity. Exceptional Vernay Coteau de Vernon.

1983 Very good. Excellent Vernay Coteau de Vernon and Château du Rozay.

1984 Fair to good. Notable Guigal.

1985 Good, sometimes very good. Excellent early wines from Pinchon, Delas, and Dumazet; longer-keepers from Vernay and Château du Rozay.

1986 Fair. Best from Château du Rozay, Delas, and Pinchon.

1987 Fair. Best from Guigal, Château du Rozay, Dumazet, and A. Perret Coteau de Chéry.

1988 Excellent. Very full wines. Notable A. Perret Coteau de Chéry and Clos Chanson, Vernay Coteau de Vernon and Guigal.

1989 Very good. Long-lived wines, stylish, and firm flavoured. Best from Château du Rozay, Dézormeaux Coteau du Colombier, Guigal, Alain Paret Ceps du Nebadon, and Vernay Coteau de Vernon.

1990 Fair to good. A very dry year, a lot of crop. Not always well balanced wines—potent but lacked crispness, clear fruit. Good Vernay.

1991 Excellent. Well-timed rain led to good acidity levels. A small crop of very ripe grapes brought in before early October rain. Big alcohol, a rich year of very stylish keeping wines. Wonderful bouquets. Best: Guigal, A. Perret Chéry, Vernay Coteau de Vernon, also Niéro-Pinchon.

1992 Mediocre. A large crop, difficult ripening, rot. Six weeks of rain in June to mid-July.

G. Vernay: "the first year I have ever brought in Viognier that were all lower degree than the Syrah." Small-scale, light texture, subdued/confected Viognier year. Early-drinking wines.

An ignoble period at Condrieu—*oenologues* everywhere doshing out the same formulaic advice—which was really found out since the crop wasn't ripe. Vernay sold one-third to *négoce*.

Best: Guigal (EARLY) ★★★★ Vernay Coteau de Vernon.

1993 Fair. Vital to harvest before 22 September, when rains and the south wind came, bearing rot. Small crop, hit by spring hail and fruit failure. Bad year for young vines. Acidity levels better than 1994. Quite a few uneven wines, lean and lacking middle-palate depth. The best showed gentle aromas; some were live and attractive.

Best: stunning work from A. Perret ★★★★ Chéry, Chanson.

1994 Very good. Early ripening, a month ahead of 1993. Despite rain on and off during harvest, a ripe, healthy crop. Good year for the late harvesters who started to develop their new product. Often solid, quietly rich wines. Good aromas, wines expanded with age and air. Some low acidities, notably at Vernay, where malo blocked. More stylish, lower-key, and less heated than the 1995s.

★★★★★ Guigal, a great success with the first Doriane

★★★★ Delas Clos Boucher, Vernay Coteau de Vernon

★★★ Chante-Perdrix, Cuilleron Ayguets, A. Perret Chanson/ Chéry, C. Pichon

★★ Clusel-Roch, P. Gaillard, A. Perret, F. Villard Coteaux Poncins

1995 Very good. Poor flowering and strong May winds hit crop levels. The summer was very dry, with extreme heat in July–August, then two weeks' rain in early September. Yields were only around 23 hl/ha. Fermentations were slow to complete, but acidity levels sound. The best wines were firmly flavoured and showed excellent length. Aromas were opulent, in some cases bordering on the clumsy. At least 10 years' life for many.

⋆⋆⋆⋆⋆ A. Perret Chéry, Chanson

⋆⋆⋆⋆ Barge, Chante-Perdrix, Chapoutier, Clusel-Roch, P. Gaillard, Guigal Doriane, Rostaing

⋆⋆⋆ Guigal

⋆⋆ Vernay Coteau de Vernon

1996 Very good. On the surface, tricky, but a gradual ripening with no burning sun, was the key. The hottest period was in June. There was no real July heat, and August was cool, with a cleansing north wind. Some rain fell in July, but by October annual rainfall stood at four inches below average. The Viognier withstood the dry, cool weather better than the Syrah. The crop was larger than usual. The wines held plenty of aroma and were firm and full. The weather brought out more character and variety, and a fine-boned make-up in the wines, which can live. Some have the light tannin finish of these drier, less sunny years.

⋆⋆⋆⋆⋆ A. Perret Chéry/Chanson, Vernay Coteau de Vernon

⋆⋆⋆⋆ Cuilleron Petite Côte

⋆⋆⋆ Vernay Chaillées Enfer

⋆⋆ Guigal, Rostaing, F. Villard Coteaux Poncins

⋆ F. Villard Terrasses du Palat

1997 Good. The year of great sun and high summer heat, therefore low acidity. Hot nights as well as days contributed to extreme ripeness. The wines were opulent, heady, and richly textured and made a big first impression. They are more one-dimensional than the 1996s, but their oiliness, length, and sweetness make them a vintage to luxuriate in. A. Perret's wines were notably restrained.

⋆⋆⋆⋆ A. Perret Chéry

⋆⋆⋆ G. Barge, Guigal Doriane, A. Perret Chanson/Vendange d'Automne,

Vernay Coteau de Vernon

⋆⋆ Gangloff Vendanges Noë, Paul Jaboulet, Château du Rozay

⋆ Delas Clos Boucher, Guigal, F. Villard Terrasses du Palat/ Quintessence

1998 Very good. Thirty-five per cent of the crop was frosted in places. Marc Rouvière managed just 4 to 5 hl/ha, René Rostaing 8 to 10 hl/ha, while André Perret escaped it. Growers with vineyards in the valleys facing west suffered. Frost apart, it was a very healthy year, with no pests or setbacks from 8 July till the mid-September harvest. Aromas were varied and persistent. The wines were big and heady, and strong white fruit flavours dominated. Their texture was often firm and chewy. They evolved quite quickly.

⋆⋆⋆⋆⋆ A. Perret Chanson, Rostaing Bonnette

⋆⋆⋆⋆ Clusel-Roch, A. Perret Chéry, Vernay Coteau de Vernon

⋆⋆⋆ Dom du Chêne, Chante-Perdrix, Guigal Doriane, Paul Jaboulet, A. Perret

⋆⋆ G. Barge, Guigal

⋆ Saint-Cosme

1999 Good. The crop was bigger than 2000–01. There is uneven quality in the wines; ripening advanced slowly before two weeks of good weather at harvesttime. Some vineyards gained 2° in just a week, and then a lot of rain fell. Fermentations often stopped around 1020 specific gravity; the wines can be insipid due to the heavy crop, while some are high in alcohol and carry burnt tones. The best are full framed, quite rich, and potent—showy and imposing early on. Some have mineral tones as well.

⋆⋆⋆⋆⋆ A. Perret Chéry

⋆⋆⋆⋆ Dumazet Myriade Extrème

⋆⋆⋆ Dom du Chêne, Dumazet Myriade, Gangloff, Guigal Luminescence, Jurie des Camiers

Coteau de Chéry, Vernay Coteau de Vernon

⋆⋆ Dumazet Rouelle Midi, Finon, Guigal classic/Doriane, Dom du Monteillet classic/Grain de Folie, A. Perret, Château du Rozay

⋆ Cuilleron Petite Côte

2000 Very good. A sunny, fine year. A dry August blocked ripening in some places. Crop cutting back was needed. A large-scale year with very ripe crop, and low levels of acidity for several of the wines. Showing more finesse than 1999, the wines are tasty, buttery, and rounded. A perfect year for growers with lower-quality plots and young vines—the richness could hide faults. Some wines are high in alcohol.

⋆⋆⋆⋆ Guigal Doriane, A. Perret Chéry, Vernay Coteau de Vernon

⋆⋆⋆ Dom du Chêne, Cuilleron Chaillets, Dumazet Fournet/Myriade, Dom du Monteillet classic/ Grandes Chaillées, A. Perret Chanson, Vernay Chaillées Enfer

⋆⋆ G. Barge, P. Bénetière Été Indien, P. & C. Bonnefond Côte Châtillon, Chapoutier, Chèze Pagus Luminis, Clusel-Roch, Dumazet Rouelle Midi, P. Faury, J-M Gérin Loye, Guigal, Niéro Coteau de Chéry, A. Perret, Vernay Terrasses Empire

⋆ Paul Jaboulet, Niéro Les Ravines, Cave Saint-Désirat, Vins de Vienne Chambée

2001 Very good. 30 per cent less crop than 2000. Spring was early, flowering good. The early summer was moderate, with no extreme heat nor much rain, but good weather from mid-August. Despite two weekends of rain in September, the crop was healthy. This is a No Hiding Place vintage—there is more acidity than usual, with patience and judgment called upon. It is also a year that found out growers lacking experience, good sites, and mature vines. It was difficult to get the Viognier to ferment, normally a good sign. The wines have character and combine depth with some vivacity. They are very well scented. Some can end rather hot. Not a year where balance was easy to achieve if you picked late and very ripe.

⋆⋆⋆⋆ L. C. Brotte Versant Doré, Cuilleron Chaillets/Vertige, Gangloff, Dom du Chêne, A. Perret Chanson/ Chéry, Vernay Chaillées Enfer/ Coteau de Vernon, F. Villard Grand Vallon

⋆⋆⋆ P. Bénetière, Chapoutier, Chèze Pagus Luminis, Cuilleron Ayguets, Delas Galopine/Clos Boucher, Dumazet Fournet, P. Faury Berne/ Brumaire, Ferraton Mandouls, P. Gaillard, Guigal Doriane, Niéro Ravines/Chéry, Paret Lys de Volan, C. Pichon, Rostaing Bonnette, Château du Rozay, Vernay Terrasses Empire, F. Villard Terrasses du Palat/Deponcins

⋆⋆ G. Barge, Barou, P. & C. Bonnefond, B. Chambeyron, Chante-Perdrix, Chèze Cuve de Brèze, Cuilleron Petite Côte, Delas Galopine, Dumazet Rouelle Midi, C. Facchin, P. Faury classic/Moelleux, Flacher, Gangloff Vendanges Noë, Guigal, J-M Gérin, L. Marthouret, Merlin Jeanraude, Dom du Monteillet, H. & M-T Richard L'Amaraze

⋆ Dom Bernard Bassenon, L. Betton, Boissonnet, Dom Bonserine, Chante-Perdrix Chevalière, G. Chirat, Clusel-Roch, Gangloff, J-M Gérin Loye, Paul Jaboulet, Meffre Laurus, Merlin, Mouton Côte Châtillon, Paret Nébadon, A. Perret, Cave Saint-Désirat Rochevine, Vallet, Vidal-Fleury, Villano

2002 Quite good. An early setback in the southern area around Malleval was April frost. The summer was not very hot, with regular rain before September. Rot was present before the heavier September rains, which lost growers around Condrieu itself up to 25 per cent. The next menace was hail in early September on Chavanay and St-Pierre-de-Boeuf, where locals lost one-third of their crop. Ripening was held up by the rain, so growers waited until 20 to 26 September, hoping for the rot to dry. Some pickings in the first week of October were a successful late addition. Some growers achieved 14°.

Often the wines are three-quarter weight and nicely styled, and work on restrained flavours. Acidity levels are OK. Many show decent mid-palate fullness, and several can live for 10 years or so. It is a decent year for the late-picked crop wines, especially those of P. Gaillard. Overall, the vintage should not be lumped in with the "poor" tag that many associate with the Rhône this year.

★★★★ P. Gaillard Jeanne-Elise

★★★ G. Barge, B. Chambeyron, Cuilleron Chaillets/Ayguets, Delas Galopine, C. Facchin, P. Gaillard Fleurs d'Automne, Guigal Doriane, Merlin Jeanraude, C. Pichon, Vernay Coteau de Vernon, F. Villard Grand Vallon

★★ P. Bénetière, P. & C. Bonnefond, Chante-Perdrix Grains Dorés, Clusel-Roch, Cuilleron Petite Côte, Dumazet Rouelle Midi/Fournet, P. Faury Berne, Ferraton Mandouls, P. Gaillard, Gangloff, J-M Gérin Loye, Merlin, Dom du Monteillet, Niéro Ravines/Chéry, Paret Nébadon/Lys de Volan, A. Perret Chanson/Chéry, H. & M-T Richard L'Amaraze, Rostaing Bonnette, Les Coteaux du Château du Rozay, Vallet, Vernay Chaillées Enfer, F. Villard Terrasses du Palat/ Deponcins/Quintessence

★(★) Cuilleron Vertige, Vernay Terrasses Empire

★ Dom Bernard Bassenon, L. C. Brotte Versant Doré, Chante-

Perdrix, Dom du Chêne, P. Faury, Flacher, F. Gérard, Guigal, Y. Lafoy, L. Marthouret, Mouton Côte Châtillon, A. Perret, Château du Rozay

(★) L. Betton, G. Chirat, Villano

2003 Good to very good, but not a straightforward year. Frost hit on April 7. P. Gaillard made just 8 hl/ha—"Viognier is my most precocious variety, and it got hammered." Yves Gangloff lost three-quarters of his crop—his whole hectare on *Côte Bonnette* frosted. There was then no rain to speak of until a few brief showers towards the end of July. The second week of August was The Oven, with 42°C recorded, the highest on record. The *ban des vendanges* had been pencilled in for early September, but the Syndicat met on 13 August to advance it to the next day.

The Viognier looked like Syrah—brown—and tasted like the raisins on a cake. Clusel-Roch lost 50 per cent from the grapes being dried out, and so made a dry wine and a *vin de passerillage*. Because of frost and drought, A. Perret lost 50 per cent, as did Vernay. The Vernays harvested 20–30 August, with the last days of the month a little cooler and marked by some rain. Harvesting ran from daybreak to 1300 hours, otherwise it was too hot for pickers and grapes.

Quality is uneven, and it is a year where the best *climats* excelled—*Vernon, Chéry, Clos Bouche, Colombier.*

These are ripe, perfumed, low-acidity wines, though the last aspect does not obviously show through. Some finish rather heatedly. Colours are darker than usual, with gold glints present. Flavours can lack clarity and be clumsy. The wines may appear a little short as the early fruit surge calms down.

The wines should be served a little cooler than usual, around 8°C, not 10°C—if they become too warm, they quickly lose their poise and grip. Only a few can expect a degree of success in their second phase, from 2008 onwards, so don't tuck the wines away in a forgotten corner.

★★★★★ Vernay Coteau de Vernon

★★★★ G. Chirat, Delas Clos Boucher, Guigal classic/Doriane, A. Perret Chéry, Vernay Chaillées Enfer

★★★ Dom du Chêne, Chèze Cuvée de Brèze, Clusel-Roch classic/"sweet," Cuilleron Chaillets/Petite Côte, Merlin classic/Jeanraude, Dom du Monteillet Grandes Chaillées, Mouton Côte Bonnette, Niéro Chéry, A. Perret Chanson, C. Pichon, Porte Vincent Noblesse de Vernon, H. & M-T Richard, Vernay Terrasses Empire, Vidal-Fleury, F. Villard Terrasses du Palat/Deponcins

★★(★) L. Betton, C. Facchin Grand'-Maisons, F. Villard Grand Vallon, Vins de Vienne La Chambée

★★ Boissonnet, P. & C. Bonnefond Côte Châtillon, Chante-Perdrix, Chèze Pagus Luminis, P. Faury Berne, P. Gaillard, Gangloff, Paul Jaboulet Cassines, Dom du Monteillet, Mouton Côte Châtillon, Niéro Ravines, Paret Nébadon/Lys de Volan, A. Perret, Saint-Cosme, Cave Sarras Dom Jacques Vernay

★ B. Chambeyron, L. Clerc, Delas Galopine, P. Faury, Meffre Laurus, Porte Vincent, Villano

2004 Excellent, bringing out the richness and elegance of the Viognier, the best of the past 25 years. After some late December 2003 rain, it was very dry. The first half of June was warm, and flowering occurred then with a clear passage. There followed a cool period from the second half of June to a week into July, and the dry theme began to stress some of the vines.

Two or three storms in August brought 150 mm (5.9 in.) of rain, which the vineyard soaked up easily. The weather then turned dry and was dominated by a north wind and warm to hot conditions.

With atmospheric pressure high and stable, growers could afford to take their time with the harvest—passing through the vineyards on several occasions to finesse each plot.

Most growers started to pick between 16–23 September, with a risk of excess potential alcohol levels if waiting longer. André Perret terms it a classic year, balanced between the acidity and the alcohol, with a lot of fruit. Jean-Michel Gérin brought in a healthy crop of tight-packed, small spicy berries and chewy skins from *Lauve*.

Crop levels were abundant, with the full 41 hl/ha yield granted. Alcohol levels were often 14° or a little higher, with occasionally a little rot present.

Life was tricky for the late-harvested wines, however, with rains arriving around 10 October. This made sorting a complicated business. "We had acid, volatile rot rather than noble rot, so couldn't make our late-picked wine," said François Merlin.

For Philippe Faury, it is a vintage with balance and helpful acidity, which is quite rich in alcohol. "There are some apricot jam flavours and some exotic notes," he stated. Yves Cuilleron thinks along the lines of 2001, pointing to the mix of richness of sugars with underlying acidity. "One of the best of the last 10 years—fruit and elegance—I like it a lot," said C. Pichon.

There is a sound fullness in the wines, but a sense of balance—more than the 2003s. Flavours from those tasted are clear and the best sites have produced elegant and classic structures.

★★★★ A. Perret Chéry, C. Pichon

★★★ G. Barge, Barou, P. & C. Bonnefond, Dom du Chêne, Chèze Pagus Luminis, Merlin, Paret Lys de Volan, A. Perret Chanson

★★ Dom Bonserine, B. Chambeyron, Chante-Perdrix, Paret Nébadon, A. Perret

★ Chapoutier, Farjon, Paul Jaboulet Cassines

3

Château-Grillet

Château-Grillet 42410 Vérin +33(0)474 595156

The now celebrated, at the time ground-breaking, comedy show *Monty Python's Flying Circus* showed a dishevelled old tramp running up hill and down dale, gasping as he went, to announce momentous news—the start of the show. Except that he keeled over before completing the sentence. Will the herald from Château-Grillet complete the mission, which has been running for decades, or will he, too, keel over?

For there have been some signs of revival here since the late 1990s, and what has been an easy target for writers and journalists, myself included, may just be getting its act together. If an improvement in the wines can be consistently maintained, it is good news for anyone who supports the existence of small family enterprises.

The enterprise in question, of course, possesses a famous history and an exceptional setting. For years, it was France's smallest single *appellation*. There is a well-proportioned castle, with an annex of tiered granite ledges around it, a striking pale brown in winter, a fecund green in summer—as inviting a vineyard amphitheatre as could be imagined.

And there's the wine, severely misunderstood by those who expect it to compare directly with the affluence and opulence of the Condrieu wines that surround it. There is only one Condrieu to compare to Château-Grillet, and that is the outstanding Coteau de Vernon made by the Domaine Georges Vernay—a wine threaded with a steely texture when young, and one that takes several years to broaden its reserved pear-toned flavours; a wine of great longevity, too.

Intrinsically, there is much to admire and stir the visitor here. The place is certainly one. Its very completeness—the bowed and ledged curve of vines, every ledge filled with Viognier, the southward-facing inflexion of its hill drawing in the sun—is unmatched in the northern Rhône. The setting in an early summer month like May is entrancing. Deep-hued red roses and yellow roses climb up the walls, and there can be ranks of bright poppies splashed through the vineyard. Under the verandah, the fig and cherry trees promise future bounty.

The château's façade and walls were repointed and smartened up in 1999, and its pale grey shutters, the colour no doubt chosen after much family debate, offset them neatly. In keeping with this orderliness presides Isabelle Baratin, a very elegant, auburn-haired Lyonnaise. She is the youngest daughter of André Canet, who married into the owning family, the Neyret-Gachets, and ran the estate for over 30 years.

It appears that the *patronne* Madame Baratin has been making conscious efforts to improve the property on a number of levels—equipment in the cellar has been upgraded, the château's stonework tidied up, the cellar surrounds refurbished. She has also brought in Denis Dubourdieu to advise on the vinification. Dubourdieu is famed in Bordeaux for his advice on making fresh white wines, but appears open to what methods may best suit Château-Grillet with its completely different grape variety, soil, and climate.

HISTORY

Château-Grillet is an unusual, curious white wine. It is made only from the Viognier grape, and the whole *appellation* with its one owner and its single-vineyard status runs to just 3.8 hectares. It's also curious nowadays to observe its immediate surroundings outside the front drive—here is this famous wine tucked away slap-bang in the middle of an industrial corridor of the Rhône Valley, somewhere between Paris and the Côte d'Azur.

Only 100 metres away from the château stands the site of an ancient Roman community, traces of which were discovered at the turn of the century. One can only imagine that the Romans enjoyed a better view than that which now extends before the château, for across the river at St-Clair-du-Rhône there have been factories, including a large Rhône-Poulenc, since around 1920. An ICI chemical plant built in 1971 did not help, and streams of steam and smoke curl slowly south, aided by the light north wind. Below the château, trains rumble past at regular intervals, topping up the hum from the factory. From the shaded terrace of the old house, its splendid wistaria sprouting a care-free drape of pale mauve in early summer, all this makes an incongruous, curious scene.

The château and its vineyard have been in the Neyret-Gachet family since 1825, and in old documents concerning French, and not just Rhône, wines, Château-Grillet is often present. Its rarity and high price attracted attention.

An early price reference was the tariff of the Hermitage House of Macker for the 1817 vintage; while the reds of Hermitage and Côte-Rôtie were on sale for 350 and 300 francs a cask, Château-Grillet was offered at 240 francs, with Saint-Péray—then very reputed—at 180 francs. In 1821 it was priced at 180 francs against Côte-Rôtie at 200 and St-Péray at 150 francs a cask. These were the only mentions of it between 1805 and 1837, so it was obviously not offered every year.

Château-Grillet's domaine bottling tradition stretches back to 1830, when it was started by the Neyret-Gachet family—an order for bottles from the English court being recorded at that time. Before this date the wine had always left the property only in cask.

A later price reference comes from the Paul Jaboulet Aîné Wine Tariff of May 1891. This placed the 220-litre cask of Châteaugrillé (*sic*) at 500 francs for the 1889, 700 francs for the 1888, and 800 francs for the 1887. Only the Jaboulet Hermitage *blanc* was more expensive—50 to 100 francs a cask, and this pricing put Grillet on a par with Meursault of 1ère *qualité*, for instance.

Curiously, the same list offered a Chateaugrillé *mousseux* at 300, 350, and 400 francs a cask for the 1889, 1888, and 1887. There are no records at the château of this sparkling wine.

Writers of different nationalities and different times have also praised Château-Grillet with zeal. The French gastronome Curnonsky, writing in *Lyon et le Lyonnais gastronomique* in the 1920s, was moved to rank Château-Grillet as one of France's three best white wines. Curnonsky wrote:

"But of all the white wines made from the Viognier around Condrieu, the palm must go to a very great, exceptional, marvellous and suave white wine: the most rare Château-Grillet, a golden and flamboyant wine cultivated in a vineyard of less than two hectares, a wine above commercialization, just about untraceable and jealously guarded by its one owner. . . . This wine is quite simply the third (and rarest) of the five best white wines of France (and therefore the world). The wine of Château-Grillet is lively, violent, changeable like a pretty woman, with a flavour of the flowers of vines and almonds, with a stunning bouquet of wild flowers and violets, and reaching up to 15° alcohol. In short, *un très grand seigneur*!"

Beat that! Well, Maurice Healy, an Irish barrister and wine connoisseur, had a try in 1940 (*Stay Me with Flagons*, Michael Joseph, London 1940). He wrote:

"I once drank a Château-Grillet that was over seventy years old, and delicious. . . . I think the vintage was 1861 . . . it had preserved its vinosity, and the clean, pebbly taste was quite remarkable. It appeared to me to be of a majesty greater than that attained by Chablis, or any Burgundy except Montrachet."

So there has indeed been a glorious past for the wine. The château itself stands next to the village of St-Michel-sur-Rhône, a little to the south of Condrieu. Backed against a sheltered hillside, it carries a mixture of architectural styles. The château records date back to the reign of Louis XIII (1610–43) and indicate that it was then a small lodge or dower house. In subsequent years successive owners built on as the fancy took them, their main criterion seemingly being size rather than charm.

Up until the French Revolution, in 1789, the château stood on uninterruptedly royalist territory, looking across the Rhône towards the Dauphiné, the home of Republicanism. As such, the rent had to be paid to the Church, which was clearly liberal with its granting of planning permission. While the façade dates from the Renaissance, the cellar below, with its blocked-in window, is considered to date from the Middle Ages. In places the outer walls suddenly become as much as a metre thick, and judging by such defences, it is clear that

possession of the property was hotly contested when the Neyret-Gachet family, today's owners, moved in.

Thereafter the wine became well known in select circles, particularly outside France. In the 1830s Château-Grillet was sent on several occasions to both Moscow and Odessa, the price of four francs a bottle being charged to the Russians, while the home French price was only three francs a bottle. And in 1829 the Court of St. James's ordered two cases of 72 bottles each for King George IV; James Christie, the Lord Steward, wrote the following letter to the Wine House of Faure in St-Péray to secure the order:

"Gentlemen, I beg you will have the kindness to forward immediately the undermentioned wine for the use of His Majesty the King of England with directions to your agent at Bordeaux to ship it by the very first vessel for this Port, the Bill of Lading to be enclosed to me; the Invoice I request you will send to me and for the amount you may draw a Bill at thirty days Sight on the Lord Steward of His Majesty's Household, St. James's Palace. In selecting this wine I trust you will be careful that it is of the very first vintage and such as may be fit for immediate use." (R. Bailly, *Histoire de la Vigne et des Grands Vins des Côtes du Rhône*, Avignon Imp. F. Orta, 1978).

When first visiting Château-Grillet in 1973, I was conscious of the awe that surrounded the estate—this was indeed a visit to an inner sanctum, so be on your best behaviour. This was justifiable, because there had been some 1960s Grillets of great authority and class—the 1969 Cuvée Renaissance and the 1966 spring to mind. The Neyret-Gachet family, notably in the form of André Canet, also kept a very low profile, so little was known about the inner workings here.

Part of the problem of the château's perception stemmed from the incredibly high price charged for the wine. That imposed the burden of excellence year in and year out, which was never the case: 1969, 1972, and 1976 were good, but not the years in between. There was also a drive to plant and expand by M. Canet, who added the short rows of vines below the château in 1970. The vineyard needed sorting and tidying, but it was hard for quality to keep up. At the time, M. Canet admitted that Grillet was not a commercial enterprise in its own right. Indeed, how could it be—in the postwar years, there had been vintages like 1957 and 1958 with a crop of just two hectolitres each year; even the lauded 1961 came in at just seven hectolitres, or 1,000 bottles all told.

Château-Grillet limped along in the 1980s, often off the radar of the discerning wine market; a case of the 1988 in Britain was on regular sale at around £440, or over US$70 a bottle at that date, and to add salt to the injury, the bottles then contained 70, not 75 centilitres!

Quality remained uneven. Just when one thought that it might rise, out would come a nondescript wine; too often the wines were just depressingly dull and humdrum, and clearly the death of M. Canet in 1994 created a strong sense of uncertainty about the whole place. As it was a much envied property, rumours circulated off and on during the later 1990s about whether it might be bought by any number of voracious large wine businesses.

Now things seem to have settled, and perhaps everyone—the wine's importers and drinkers, the Neyret-Gachet family and wine writers, too—can look forward rather than back: fingers crossed for that.

CHÂTEAU-GRILLET VINEYARD

As at Condrieu, the Viognier is the only grape variety permitted, but in the 1930s the vineyard was less formally planted. Georges Vernay recalls the Neyret-Gachet family making a Gamay red wine for home drinking because the simple local reds were too rough.

Now the vineyard is completely full, except for the wonderfully exposed promontory that houses *caviste* and *chef de culture* Guy Couturier's prized vegetable patch—abundant with potatoes, aubergines, cardoons, and tomatoes that soak up the sun.

The Viognier is in irregular rows that crouch up above and all around the château in the form of an amphitheatre. There are three flanks; the most southerly is concave shaped and is split from the two others by a small stream running diagonally across the vineyard. The other flanks are concave and convex, and are wonderfully exposed, facing full south. They all benefit from great sunshine and warmth and are perfectly protected from the Bise north wind by their encircling hillside, which mounts steeply to a height of 240 metres. Across the road is a fourth patch of vines, cut off from the rest when the road was built many years ago and called *Rond Point*.

The family use unofficial place names for these sites; higher above the château is *La Cabanne*, while the top of the vineyard is *La Cartherie*, for instance. Under the house is *Sous le Jardin*.

All vineyard care remains manual: the depth of many of the ledges is only about one metre, and the vines run across them at intervals of 90 centimetres (three feet). The retaining walls are dry stone and need upkeep to stop erosion and soil slippage. Mauve irises grow on them in places. When defending the high price of the wine, the family is quick to point out that in Burgundy there are no terrace walls to keep and repair and that the fixed costs are therefore much higher. For instance, the heavy rains of October 1993 caused three walls to collapse into the vines.

The vines are all pruned in the Guyot way, with the shoot carrying seven flowers led across the two large, two small upright wooden stakes for every two vines. The soil is surprisingly light and powdery and makes movement on the hillside a slippery operation. In bright sunshine, tiny particles can be seen glinting here and there; these are little pieces of decomposed mica, also found in the Condrieu vineyards. So poor is it that there is less likelihood of rot here.

The man who steered Grillet along and brought order to it from the 1960s on was André Canet. M. Canet married into the Neyret-Gachet family—his wife was born in the château—and came to live at Château-Grillet in 1961 until his death in 1994. He was clearly a man of action, and a lot of planting took place in 1962; the vineyard had been left alone for a long time, and there were plenty of empty spaces in the rows—dead vines not replaced. He was a distinguished old gentleman, a full-time engineer by trade, who in the early 1960s devoted his evenings and weekends to Château-Grillet.

M. Canet never liked to be questioned about such unseemly subjects as expansion and pushing for a higher production. But they were clearly his first mission, ahead of a handcrafted quality for the wine, and for years the estate struggled to regain the balance between the extra quantity and a correspondingly high quality.

The vineyard was enlarged from 1.7 hectares in 1971 (when it was indeed France's smallest *appellation*, behind Romanee-Conti's 1.8 hectares), to 2.3 hectares in 1977, to 3.01 hectares in 1982, to 3.8 hectares by 1991, where it remains today. It is renewed a little at a time now; around 300 to 400 vines a year can be replaced, mainly plants that can be up to 80 years old and have run their race.

Its gradual increase came from the restoration of a series of little terraces adjoining the property, as well as by the purchase in the mid-1970s of the well-sited Régis Campo Viognier vines that stood below the château on the left of the approach road on *Rond Point*. M. Campo was a producer of Condrieu and one of his regular clients was the late Fernand Point at his restaurant La Pyramide in Vienne, a noted promoter of the wines of Condrieu.

The wine taken from this tiny vineyard is even more revealing. Several factors caused the dramatic yield increases shown in table 5. A combination of intensive plantation, pruning that left many buds per plant, early picking to avoid the least chance of late damage from rain, extensive use of clonal disease-resistant cuttings of the Viognier, and liberal use of fertilizer brought this vineyard metaphorically to its knees in the years 1983 and 1984. "Never mind the quality, what's the quantity?" must have

TABLE 5
Château-Grillet Yields since 1956
(litres per annum)

1956–60	1,160
1961–65	1,820
1966–70	4,455
1971–75	5,663
1976–80	7,840[a]
1981–85	10,000
1986–90	9,602
1991–95	10,280
1996–00	12,380
2001–04	7,550[b]

[a]Includes the tiny 1978 crop of 2,900 litres, at the time the smallest since the 2,600-litre harvest of 1969
[b]Includes the tiny 2003 crop of 2,400 litres

been the cry to produce those consecutive harvests of 13,700 litres and 14,400 litres.

On an *appellation* whose yield per hectare was then set at 32 hectolitres (from 1984 it was formally raised to 37 hectolitres), the averages of about 45 hl in 1983 and 47 hl in 1984 were scandalous—a seeming mockery of the French *appellation* laws, designed, one might have thought, to protect the interests of the consumer rather than feather the nest of the producer.

When asked about this, M. Canet would only say that too much fertilizer was used, *c'est tout*. Well, nature has a way of saying "enough," and in 1985, when early wet weather hampered the flowering, the vines, probably largely spent, produced only 5,300 litres in total, an average of under 18 hl/ha.

Yields of 110 hl (2001), 78 hl (2002), and 90 hl (2004) give some indication that a grip may have been taken on production, involving some green harvesting. The year 2002 brought large loss across the board at Condrieu, but the only way Château-Grillet will regain its lost heights is if matters are tightened up in the vineyard. I would like to see tighter crop control and slightly later harvesting to be sure that this can start to consistently happen.

Harvesting does not take long in this tiny vineyard. Four days around 20 September or occasionally early October are sufficient to clear the rugged terraces of their fruit.

With 10 grandchildren and a host of cousins, Grillet's harvest is now a family affair, and a team of 30 to 35 is assembled to work with the four permanent staff. The harvesters demonstrate laudable agility in bringing down the grapes from the sometimes highly restricted ledges. There is only one narrow and awkward approach stairway from the vines to the cellars, and this presents the final challenge to the flagging *porteurs*.

CHÂTEAU-GRILLET VINIFICATION

Upon receipt at the cellars, the harvest is crushed in a pneumatic press that was updated in 2002; there had been an old cast-iron vertical version until the mid-1970s. The juice is then left for up to 48 hours to settle in 20 hl enamel-lined vats before fermentation; this then takes place in 70 to 80 per cent enamel and 20 to 30 per cent 228-litre casks that range from new to four years old.

Fermentation temperature is controlled at 22° to 24°C, with the vats cooled in the old-fashioned way by circulating water over them. According to the maturity of the vintage, the fermentation lasts for 15 to 20 days. The young wine remains in vats to complete its malolactic fermentation and is then transferred around springtime to vats and casks for storage and development. The cellar has one-metre-thick walls, so the temperature is largely constant for the roughly 35 barrels.

Raising lasts 20 months, and the wine is assembled bit by bit as each container is racked. Over the course of the 20 months, a total of 20 to 30 per cent of the wine is exposed to oak, mostly old casks; in any year there may be a few new ones to replace worn-out wood.

Isabelle Baratin has kept the old winemaking outlook, that of "leave alone." One senses that she wants to keep a monument to her late father, but that has been a struggle. Around 1996–98, she was the sole vinifier, having

learnt at her father's knee. That meant no racking during the premalolactic and postmalolactic phases, so the wine stays on a fine lees in cask to allow a natural evolution. "We're not looking for primary aromas or flavours at all," is her comment.

Since 2000, there has been a change of structure in the way the château runs its vinification. For many years the late Max Leglise, an *oenologue* from Beaune, was the adviser, someone who contributed to the penchant for picking the grapes before they had been very well ripened. Now Denis Dubourdieu, the owner of Château Doisy Daëne in Barsac and a flying consultant winemaker, is the adviser. He first visited the property in 2000, and has certainly helped to tighten the vinification and cellar work.

Bottling takes place a little under two years after the harvest and is done by hand in lots of 2,000 bottles at a time. The whole process, therefore, will run over the course of three months. The wine is fined and lightly filtered beforehand. With the wine comes a slip of paper describing Château-Grillet as a "keeping wine" —needing a minimum of one year in the buyer's cellar, as well as decanting before drinking so that all its qualities can be appreciated.

CHÂTEAU-GRILLET

This is indeed a keeping wine, one of subtlety and restraint, so comparisons with mainstream Condrieu are simply not worth the effort. The most appreciated Château-Grillets that I have drunk have regularly been over 12 years old— spanning vintages from 1966 to 1991. But there have been many miss-out years, too.

During much of the 1980s and 1990s, the Grillet qualities had become more elusive. Looking back through tasting notes, I find that the most impressive bottles of Grillet drunk in the past few years have been the 1966 (drunk in 1986), the 1969 (drunk in 1989), the 1971 (drunk in 1985), the 1974 (drunk in 1987), the 1976 (drunk in 1985), the 1978 (drunk in 2003), the 1982 (drunk in 1987), the 1991 (drunk in

2003), and the 1995 (drunk in 2003). The 1988 and 1989 were both good when drunk young, similar to the 1998, which was unusually open right from the start.

The problem in the 1980s was that many wines were marked by a blurred quality of fruit, a sometimes sticky texture and a lack of clear definition in the Viognier aromas. Not that Grillet has ever been a flamboyant wine—its ace card is discreet elegance, a classy finesse unusual in wines of this region. During the 1990s the problem more commonly appeared to be lack of ripeness, making some of the wines dilute and attenuated.

Stylistically, and when on good form, these wines are worlds apart from the rock 'n' roll wines of Condrieu, especially the new-wave, late-picked, new-oaked ones. Whatever the vintage, all are reserved and subtle, their success depending on the level of richness in the mid-palate rather than blazing a trail on the attack. They possess a lot of bone and very little opulence, and the Viognier here is picked and vinified for elegance and an old-fashioned, gradual expansion when being drunk. All benefit from patient cellaring and from decantation.

At its best, Château-Grillet presents itself with a very pale straw colour, one that is more marked than in most modern-day white wines. In a strong, well-made vintage, the bouquet carries varied aromas, some of which are described as apricot, truffle, and honey. With age—eight years or more—the aromas turn more floral. On the palate a mixture of apricot and hot-climate fruits (orange, tangerine) can be called up, but the interesting observation is that they are different from the fruit connotations—pears, for example—generally attached to Viogniers made at Condrieu up the road.

The part ageing in used casks may have some impact on this, as well as the attachment to fine lees for perhaps as long as a year. As a dry wine these days, Château-Grillet carries with it a rich underlying fullness and undoubted depth of flavour. But all its notes are subtle, underscored and therefore all the more intriguing when the wine truly is on song.

M. André Canet presented himself as an imposing, austere personality, indeed the distinguished Gallic gentleman with his strong features, darkly tanned face, and confident, almost stern bearing. He would defend his vineyard stoutly, as would only be expected. "When I arrived, my first challenges were to reclaim the vineyard and keep its good name going. Some of the terraces had been long abandoned, and we were only making around 40 to 45 hectolitres per year. Between 1965 and 1970 we got on with this *défrichage*, clearing the terraces of plants like acacia, whose roots go incredibly deep. This was the area right at the top of the hillside above the château."

"My main work perhaps has been to try to maintain the perfumes of the wine. My personal taste is to drink it when it's about 10 years old, and I think it goes very well with meat—beef, veal, or a leg of lamb. Even though it's dry today, it still has richness underneath it. I consider it probable that when Curnonsky was writing, he was describing a semisweet or sweet Château-Grillet, which was the old style. That's also why he called it a poor traveller, as its sweetness made it less stable."

With age the wine intensifies its colour towards gold, and both the bouquet and the palate gain in richness and the underlying oiliness of the Viognier. On the aromas, there can be a very typical old Viognier damp-wool connotation, that disappears after an hour or so. On the palate, the finish can carry salty, iodine elements.

Château-Grillet has always used distinguished dark yellow and brown Rhine bottles that until 1987 were of 70-centilitre content. In days gone by, the Vigonier growers of Condrieu also used flute-shaped bottles, which were specially blown for them at a glass factory in St-Étienne. These have reappeared with the resumption of late-harvest wines at Condrieu.

Isabelle Baratin finds 15 years an ideal age to drink the wine, for good harmony and typicity:

"Chicken or chicken breasts in a cream sauce or with truffles are very fine companions, and I like sweetbreads and roast veal as well. Fish should be fine-flavoured—turbot, crayfish, or freshwater *sandre* (pikeperch) for instance—turbot in a champagne sauce, even. It also matches Coquilles St. Jacques, and there's a dish of them with grated almonds on a cream sauce that goes well. Foie gras is also good."

She continues: "Decant the wine, especially the vintages under five or six years old, and serve the wine in broad glasses at 12° or 13°, not too cold. And don't drink it as an aperitif!"

Tracking down bottles of Château-Grillet calls for sound sleuthing. Grillet works with one importer per country and keeps them all on tenterhooks over their annual allowance. Most of the overseas wine goes to Europe, plus the United States and Canada—that means Yapp in Britain receives around 40 cases (four times more than in the late 1980s), while the New York allocation is generally around 20 cases.

The Château also makes two *eaux-de-vie*, distilled from the fermentation leftovers. The Eau-de-Vie de Marc de Château-Grillet comes in a 70 cl bottle and is a 45° alcohol drink by law. It has an agreeable bouquet of floral tones and is nicely smooth on the palate.

The second *eau-de-vie* spends several years ageing in old barrels. This Eau-de-Vie de Vin Fine de Château-Grillet is also well scented, the bouquet showing earth and dry straw elements. It is fairly potent on the palate. This is sold in minuscule amounts.

CHÂTEAU-GRILLET VINTAGES

1965 Fair. A vintage that lived a surprising time—into the 1980s. (25 hl)

1966 Very good. Richly scented wine of great style and finish. (24 hl)

1967 Good. Wine with more body than finesse. (42 hl)

1968 Good. Better than many neighbours, nicely fruited. (67 hl)

1969 Excellent. Remarkable fruitiness, great length and elegance: Château-Grillet at its best. 1,730 bottles (46 per cent of the tiny crop) were made into a special Cuvée Renaissance. (26 hl)

1970 Good. More fruit than depth. 6,360 bottles (67 per cent of the crop) of the Cuvée Renaissance. (66 hl)

1971 Very good. A wine that blossomed with age. 3,670 bottles of the Cuvée Renaissance (55 per cent of the crop). (47 hl)

1972 Excellent. Similar to 1969, highly concentrated wine. (28 hl)

1973 Fair. An extremely large crop for its time. At this stage of the 1970s the wine would be in cask for its malo and would be bottled between 18 months and two years after the harvest, so there was longer contact with wood—18 months—than in the 1980s. (84 hl)

1974 Good. Good fruit and matter in the wine. (87 hl)

1975 Mediocre. (40 hl)

1976 Very good. A good set of aromas, and fine evolution over 20 years. (87 hl)

1977 Good, especially for an off year. (63 hl)

1978 Excellent, very rich wine from a tiny crop. Note from Dec. 2003: light wool aroma, typical old Viognier, with apricot; dried fruits, still pretty with live acidity, some heat. Still going well. (29 hl)

1979 Fair. Some richness, but always a lack of freshness. (97 hl)

1980 Poor. Hard and dull-tasting wine. Very large crop. (116 hl)

1981 Good. Sound Viognier depth on bouquet and palate. (75 hl)

1982 Mediocre. Light wine—victim of early harvesting? (91 hl)

1983 Mediocre. Rain in early September stampeded the owner into early harvesting; the sun came out afterwards to reward those of greater patience. Blatant overproduction resulted. Innocuous, boring wine. (137 hl)

1984 Fair. Harvesting took place in good weather after some rot had broken out. Lack of depth, very much in the vein of the Grillets of the 1980s. (144 hl)

1985 Good. Later harvesting—thank goodness. Greater substance than the two previous years, but once again there is a lack of thoroughness. It won't age like the wines from the 1960s and 1970s; one can find no reason why this should not happen in a favourable year like 1985. (53 hl)

1986 Fair. A difficult year to vinify, with quite a high acidity. Firm-textured wine, with some finesse, but balance a little unsteady. (91 hl)

1987 Mediocre. Bouquet was a bit damp and mushroomy. Lacks thoroughness on the palate, a pale offering. (97 hl)

1988 Very good. Greater extraction of ripe flavour, the raw materials have been allowed to develop. Depth and length sound. (57 hl)

1989 Excellent. Perhaps a return to previous standards here. Bouquet is pungent, musky. A full palate, with good length and breadth of flavour. (78 hl)

1990 ★★★ Bouquet has honeycomb touch, also floral content. Palate's round appeal, light apricot flavour shows some of the richness I recall from the past. Persists well, with tangy, decisive finish, and can broaden. Despite large crop, wine has sound enough depth. 2016–19. (158 hl)

1991 ★★★ Elegant, melted butter/flan bouquet with typical old Viognier damp wool, also very ripe figs. Good richness, with its usual restraint. Cooked fruits for tarts, light brown sugar at end. Some local heat, and ends drily, saltily. Going well at 12 years old; 2014–17. (111 hl)

1992 ★★★ Gentle aromas, appealing; fair weight, opens and gains with air. Honeysuckle, refined flavour. Delicate, a touch of sweetness. Not very long. (136 hl)

1993 ★★★★ Rain just before the harvest, but the Viognier had largely ripened by then. Well regarded by the owners. Damp wool, spice/cooked bouquet with coconut—is nicely broad. Pretty attack—springs out, full and vigorous. Fair length, burnt touch on end. Lime/quince aftertaste. Typical, good sinew, elegance. Clean, mineral finish. Pear flavour after 90 minutes. (88 hl)

1994 Rain after harvest. Not tasted. (108 hl)

1995 ★★★ Midweight, smooth aroma—bonbons, dried fruits, varnish. At eight years, very much middle-aged; also light caramel, butterscotch, pear—bouquet can develop. Damp wool, custard start, some burnt fruits, too. Quite heated at end, though air softens it. Elegant, restrained—shows the vintage with some mineral edging on finish. 2010–13. (71 hl)

1996 Poor. On several tastings in different places, the wine has been discordant on the palate. The scent is largely floral, gentle, and quietly sweet. But there is a sharp attack with a bitter, rather burnt edge and even after being left for an hour, nothing had changed. The penultimate bottle was bought "on offer" at the Swedish Monopoly in Stockholm and still cost £21 (US$32) in January 2001. (124 hl)

1997 (★) Pale yellow; simple soft butter/floral bouquet, hint of aniseed. Not especially deep, though gains some earthiness. Acid attack—bang! Green aspects, underripe fruit. Some ripe fruit like peach with food, but still has sharp side. Not tight-knit; the bitter side is putting-off. (131 hl)

1998 ★★★★ Subyellow; refined, slightly tannic pear skin bouquet—elegant, dry-toned. Warms and expands gently after 90 mins. Coconut flavour on attack, tight-knit and refined on palate. Its elegance brings back memories of the better years of yore. Just enough flesh and a firm, clean, light honey finish. Pear/quince, spiced plum on palate. Very young at five years. 2012–15. (93 hl)

1999 ★★ Usual pale, flinty colour; gentle honey/floral, also rotted, damp wool/damp hay bouquet. White stone fruits come through. Slightly singed on attack, though has a subtle warm thread. Bit more width after 50 mins., pineapple/dried apricot, too. Fungal tones, and more flesh on second day. Acidity on finish—is crop being picked quite early still? Definitely benefits from decanting. 2008–10. (147 hl)

2000 ★★★ Subdued pear, dessert tart aroma, some potential. Pebbly white stone fruit, restrained, understated richness. Smoky, quite decisive finale. Gradual expansion with air; the customary elegance here. Plenty to come; still tight-knit at four years. More expressive from 2008; 2019–23. (124 hl)

2001 ★★★ Gently ripe, light apricot, dried fruit bouquet, with a mineral touch. Nice warmth of texture; quite ripe matter, so some flesh. Refined, light pear length, some *gras* all way through. Structure OK. 2013–17. (110 hl)

2002 A lot of sorting was required and performed in the vineyard; harvesting ran over two weeks.

★★ (CASK) Fresh, nut/pear aroma, quite full, light oak. Oily texture on start, three-quarter weight, stylish and then kicks on, fills out. Heated, touch oak on finish. Skips a little in middle. (78 hl)

2003 The cycle started with frost on 8 April, the first serious amount since 1939–40. A very hot year, and the vineyard felt the heat. A little picking took place on 15 August, most on 19 August. The earliest date in recent times had been 7 September in 1976. The extreme vagaries knocked yields for six. (24 hl)

2004 Cold in early April, with north wind then. Mid-August was rainy, but since the berries were behind time, they did not suffer. With September fine throughout, the grape ripening accelerated and harvesting started on 22 September. The portents are for a pretty good vintage. (90 hl)

Export 30 per cent (1) Switzerland, (2) Canada, (3) USA

4

Hermitage

WHAT AN INSPIRATION. If ever in your life you want to take your friend, your lover, your child, or your favourite person to see a vineyard that converts them to the pleasure of wine, then please go to Tain-l'Hermitage. Imbibe the utter majesty of this hillside, from which a mighty spread of vines reaches for the sky, its beautiful exposure soaking up nature's efforts and whims. The sparkling, darting glance of the setting sun across its top, or a full moon illuminating its high outcrop, turns thoughts beyond its rich red wine; even a resister would be seduced. To think I actually walked up the hill, through the vines and the gulleys, and proposed to my wife here. As with the best feasts in life, I think it's taken 30 years to realise just what a special, stirring place this is for a vineyard.

Here, then, right beside the Rhône, is a truly spectacular home for a vineyard. The green mantle of summer vines is punctuated by the pale brown of stone walls that hold the terraces tight. A zigzag occurs as the vines rise across the hill's contours towards the broad summit and the famous little chapel of St. Christopher.

In winter the dour granite colours and the long lines of oddly contorted vine plants lend an air of lunar austerity.

It is a hill with its own daily community, a little different each day. Smoke curls up in places as cuttings are burnt, and people work and walk across it, all quietly cut off from one another—from a distance, human specks tracing little paths.

The Hermitage hill stands as the last declaration of the Massif Central range of the middle of France. Here is the anomaly of a granite outcrop on the "wrong" bank of the Rhône, its eastern side. This phenomenon occured many thousands of years ago. Then the Rhône flowed past the other, back side of the hillside; Hermitage was therefore a natural part of the granitic Massif Central mountain range that lies west of Tournon. At some indeterminate date the river changed its course and burrowed out today's beautiful valley. Its old route is now covered by the A7 autoroute, the axis to the Mediterranean.

This explains why the west side of the hill, its sites those closest to the northern exit of Tain, hold the most granite: *Varogne* and *Bessards* notably, the last-named turned south-southwest.

Hermitage

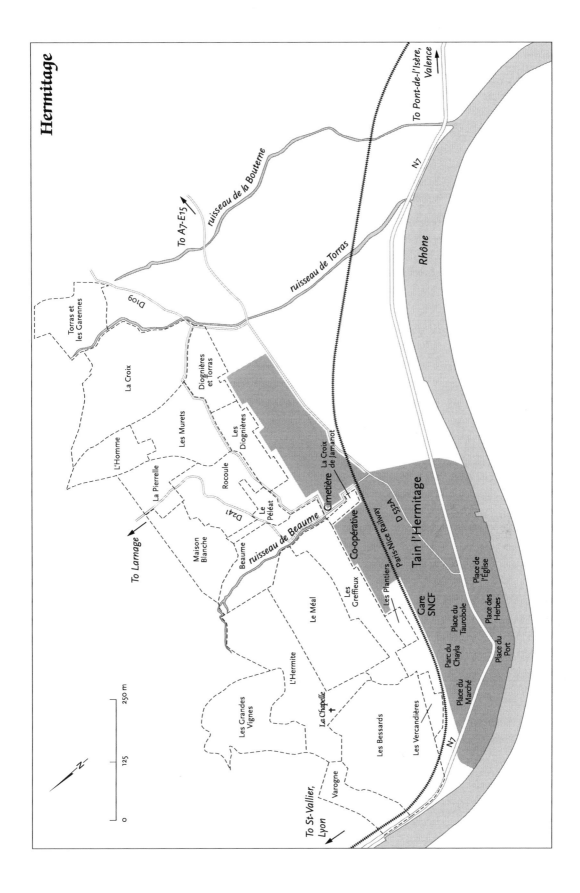

To A7-E15

ruisseau de la Bouterne

Torras et les Garennes

D109

La Croix

Diognières et Torras

ruisseau de Torras

Les Murets

Les Diognières

L'Homme

La Pierrelle

Rocoule

La Croix de Jamanot

Cimetière

Le Péléat

D241

Co-opérative

ruisseau de Beaume

Maison Blanche

Les Plantiers

D532A

Tain l'Hermitage

To Larnage

Beaume

Les Greffieux

Paris-Nice Railway

Le Méal

Gare SNCF

Place de l'Église

Place du Chayla

Parc du Chayla

Place du Taurobole

Place des Herbes

L'Hermite

Les Grandes Vignes

La Chapelle

Les Bessards

Place du Port

Place du Marché

N7

Les Vercandières

Varogne

To St-Vallier, Lyon

Rhône

N7

To Pont-de-l'Isère, Valence

N
250 m
125
0

Across to the east, on *lieux-dits* like *Beaume* and *La Croix*, the soil is more influenced by the Alps, with ancient glacier deposits in the form of *poudingue*—brown rolled stones mixed into a clay soil. The mighty hill is therefore marked by two distinct influences—the granite of the Massif Central on its western end, the glacial deposits of the Alps on its eastern end.

In the lee of the hill, wedged between it and the strong-flowing Rhône, is Tain-l'Hermitage, the unofficial capital of the Rhône wine industry. A small, busy town through the centre of which runs the old southern highway, the N7, Tain shares with Tournon on the opposite bank the privilege of housing some of the valley's larger *négociant* companies, and certainly those with most prestige. Houses like Chapoutier, Jaboulet, and Delas have traditions dating back to the early nineteenth century, and Jaboulet's move of their office and bottling operations in the early 1980s down the road to La Roche-de-Glun was the first major severance by any company of their full, close ties with Tain.

The town is still a noisy place, a convenient exit off the nearby autoroute for traffic heading north or south, and it can hardly be called charming. But one or two new restaurants and wine bars have sprung up, and the Saturday market in the Place de la Taurobole is a lively weekly event, attended by many small local suppliers from the wild Ardèche countryside across the river. Its contact with Tournon is close, too—there are pedestrian and vehicle bridges, the first of these a suspension bridge built in 1825.

HISTORY

Tain is acknowledged as having been a wine-producing community in Roman times, when it was an outpost of Lyon and went by the name of Tegna. In their works, the *Natural History* and the *Epigrams*, both Pliny and Martial mentioned the wine of Tegna, which would suggest that it enjoyed some fame.

Tain still displays a relic from its Roman days—an ancient chalk stone altar called a *tau-*

robolium that was used for the sacrifice and offering of bulls to the god Mithras. These sacrifices would last three days and were performed at the top of the Hermitage hill. The *taurobole* dates from AD 184 and, brushed up and renovated in 2004, remains the town's most jealously guarded possession, as the following story illustrates.

In 1724 a British traveller arrived in Tain expressly to buy the altar, claiming that its sale to England would help promote the *entente* that was noticeably lacking between the two countries. The town officials refused his request out of hand, however, and to make absolutely sure, took advantage of a dark night to carry off the taurobolium and hide it in the cellars of the Town Hall. The next day the British visitor was informed by grief-stricken, angered officials that the taurobolium had been scandalously stolen. The poor man took pains to console them and, as some sort of amends, bought a small barrel of their wine: to have kept the taurobolium and to have exported some of their wine in the process proved an eminently satisfactory outcome for the locals!

In the past, regional historians have contended that Hermitage may actually be one of France's oldest vineyards. They point to the possibilities of the Syrah vine being brought up the Rhône by the Phocaean Greeks, the invaders of Marseille around 600 BC. The word "Syrah," as in Shiraz in Persia, is the key to this. Recent DNA on the Syrah's Isère *département* origins leave the picture more obscure, however. The Isère is the region broadly northeast of Tain.

Hermitage swirls with several legends concerning the origins of vine growing and the name "Hermitage," whose old style was "Ermitage." These legends tend to vie with one another in romanticism, and were perpetuated to aid the sales of the wine in centuries gone by. One is the work of the Irish writer James Joyce, who claimed that it was St. Patrick who planted the first vines on the slopes of Hermitage, taking a quick break there on his way to convert Ireland. This is beautiful storytelling, but there is absolutely no evidence to uphold Joyce's theory.

In fact, one of the few written references to this tale does indeed come from another Irishman, Maurice Healy, in his *Stay Me with Flagons* (Michael Joseph, London 1940). In 1940 Healy wrote, with broad Irish charm: "Hermitage has an Irish link; there is a Clos Saint-Patrice there, which is supposed to be the site of a resting place of St Patrick on his way to Ireland . . . it is producing a red wine that would almost convert Hitler to Christianity."

The Irish tale must take second place to the much better known, oft-quoted legend that concerns the holy knight Gaspard de Stérimberg. This gentleman's name now appears on the labels of the House of Jaboulet's white Hermitage. Returning wounded in 1224 from a crusade against the Albigensian heretics, Stérimberg was making his way home when he came upon the Hermitage hillside; he climbed it, found it quite enchanting, and decided to stay—but of course had no roof over his head. As befits a knight, he dutifully applied to the then Queen of France, Blanche of Castille, for permission to build a retreat. This was granted, and he is said to have lived there for 30 years until his death. Various nineteenth century writers refer to his abode as a small house, a cell, or a chapel, and it is a chapel that still stands in solitary splendour near the top of the Hermitage hill.

A final local legend, attributed to Brother Benedict—of whom nothing else is known— dates from the time of the Roman persecution of the Christians, when a hunted priest is said to have taken refuge on the Hermitage hill: his basic source of nourishment, bread and cheese, was brought by the wild animals all around him. Nothing could be found to drink, however, and the holy man was on the point of death when the timely intervention of the good Lord saved him. As is well known, all *vignerons* eventually find their way into Paradise, and so there suddenly appeared a band of angelic growers ready with fruit-bearing vines that made wine overnight. The priest drank and was saved.

Between Roman times and the seventeenth century, Hermitage surprisingly disappears from the history books, but in 1642 it acquired a royal connection that eventually spanned three centuries. In that year King Louis XIII was touring the Rhône Valley, which at Tain reaches one of its narrowest points. The king's travelling companions advised him to descend from his carriage and be carried over the most dangerous part of the river, a large protruding rock. Of course, Louis' itineraries always allowed for impromptu glasses of wine, so when a subject offered him some of the local wine, he was quite happy to accept it and appreciate it at his leisure. The rock where he was forced to descend is known as the King's Table, for it was there that Louis decided that in future he would serve the wine at the Court of France—a decision that did much to advance the fame of Hermitage.

The seventeenth century marked the emergence of notable families at Hermitage. The Mure family came to Tain from the Vivarais in the Ardèche in 1653, when they bought a hostelry called Le Logis de la Croix Blanche. This started their commercial involvement with wine, and by 1695 they had established connections with England; by 1750 they were Hermitage's largest shippers abroad.

According to Charles Bellet (*Frais de la Culture de la Vigne au Coteau de l'Hermitage 1765*, 1915), "Mure de Tain" was the only owner to sell his wines advantageously to Bordeaux every year, wine known as Vin de Mure both in Bordeaux and Britain. "Others can't break into the market, so they are left with a local sale or no sale at all," he added. Apparently, Burgundy would also buy a lot and agree to fix a price with the English buyers.

The Mure de Larnage contact with England may well have been one with the ubiquitous John Harvey, first Earl of Bristol. He imported Hermitage in 1714, 1716, and 1738, and played a big role in making England the main foreign destination for Hermitage by the late 1700s. (C. Montez, *Le Monde du Négoce du Vin*, University of Lyon 1993). Perhaps Harvey had taken a bottle or two home to drink with his friends, since the owner of Tain's auberge was under orders to knowingly give bottles to English visitors to spread the word.

By 1759 Nicolas Bidet recorded that it was hard to keep up with demand from Bordeaux, stating that "the aim is to raise the degree of the Bordeaux and to preserve their wines' finesse" (M-L Marcelou, *Vins, Vignes et Vignerons de l'Hermitage 1806–1936*, University Lumière–Lyon 2, 2003).

The export wine was shipped via Bordeaux, which certainly helped the wine's notoriety. Indeed, the grip of Bordeaux on the Rhône was considered tight by the middle of the eighteenth century.

The route taken to Bordeaux is not entirely clear. Some regard the Rhône and the Canal of Languedoc as the likely way, a journey of 40 to 60 days and accounting for 8 to 12 per cent of the cost of the wine (Montez, *Le Monde du Négoce*). This would have meant that blending in any vintage could not have taken place much before Christmas. The wine was also subject to a series of different regional taxes as it moved along—no surprise, therefore, that its foreign buyers were aristocracy or rich gentry.

Another, overland route may have been north, then west, using some of the great rivers of France. This would have taken the wine up on the Rhône to Lyon, thence on the Saône to the Canal du Centre, thence to the Loire and down the Atlantic from its estuary. Water transport was cheaper than land.

By 1765 the main owners of vineyards at Hermitage were a series of aristocratic or noble families, several of them—like the Mures—from the Ardèche. The Count of Tournon, de Chirol, and the Marquis de la Tourette all came from Tournon across the river; other names were Deloche, d'Urre, Barbier Gallier, and the widow Bergier. (Marcelou, *Vins, Vignes et Vignerons*).

The Revolution of 1789 ended the involvement of the Tournon families, and the Mures, as seigneurs of Larnage, also had their domaines confiscated. They went into exile in Baden but returned in 1801 to recuperate their properties,

before moving to Paris later in the nineteenth century.

By the early 1800s, the nature of the hill's ownership was changing with the advent of bourgeois, "new money" owners alongside the old aristocratic survivors like de Gallier (the "de" added after the Revolution!), Durre ("d'Urre" elided—travelling in the opposite direction!), and Deloche (no change). In 1787 Jean-Pierre Monier had married Marguerite Jourdan, and their union had repercussions for the next decades. The Monier name still survives to this day on the Monier de la Sizeranne title of Chapoutier's red wine.

Charles Jourdan *père* created a merchant or *négoce* company in 1793 and by 1799 was calling himself a *cultivateur*—a new description, closer to the land, that had not been tagged on to any notables before. Jourdan and Monier were by 1801 said to be "owners of vines," selling their wine to the Netherlands and Hamburg, and an 1805 work by Gueymar-Dupalais recorded that "at Tain, there is considerable commerce, with a lot of export. The English take the majority of the wine in times of peace" (Marcelou, *Vins, Vignes et Vignerons*).

The English business was extremely important and was halted by the Continental blockade from 1806 onwards. By 1812 owners were desperate for outlets to sell their wine, and had set up the sale of about 200 casks a year to Switzerland and Belgium. "But the price was very low and hardly covered costs" (Marcelou, *Vins, Vignes et Vignerons*).

The alliance between vineyards and politics became close in these times. Between 1815 and 1848, all the Mayors of Tain were vineyard owners—including Jourdan, Bergier, Macker, and Bret (Marcelou, *Vins, Vignes et Vignerons*)

The Jourdans owned many different properties in Tain, and the running of the Mairie, or Town Hall, was orchestrated by them. Their group of allies included many of the notable wine families—Mure de Larnage, Monier de la Sizeranne, Macker, and Delacour. These people never called themselves *négociants*—"trade" was too vulgar a word—but proprietors, and the group was linked to Parliament (Montez, *Le Monde du Négoce*).

Bordeaux's influence over Hermitage continued well into the nineteenth century, with a growing range of export markets and a steady demand to beef up their own wines. For shipments to the many Dutch and Baltic customers, the Mediterranean port of Sète was out of the way, so casks would be shipped via the Canal du Midi to Bordeaux.

The Bordelais held a tight grip on people they no doubt regarded as their country cousins. Rules were firmly enforced. No wine was permitted to be shipped to Britain before Christmas, presumably so it didn't interfere with the export of Bordeaux's own wines. And if the Rhône wine was still in Bordeaux, unsold, by 1 May, it was ordered to be turned into *eau de vie*.

According to Jean-Antoine Chaptal in 1819, the "claret" sent to Britain from Bordeaux at that time was a mix of spirit wine, Bordeaux wine, Bénicarlos, and Hermitage. But the net may have been cast wider than that, for Cavoleau in 1827 cited Côte-Rôtie as being sent to Tain, and from there to Bordeaux to enter into the English mix.

André Jullien in 1822 also referred to the wine of Cornas as being used in Bordeaux to give body to the wines, and his work raises the issue of how many wines qualified under the broad title "Hermitage." He classed the wines from Crozes, Mercurol, and Gervans—all *appellation* Crozes-Hermitage today—as of the "second class of wines of Hermitage" (Marcelou, *Vins, Vignes et Vignerons*).

There is no doubt that trade with the warmer areas of France was habitual, with the Bordelais fretting about lack of body in their wines. Thiebaut de Berneaud wrote in 1826: "The Bordelais correct the light bitterness of their red wines and on the first lees mix with wines of l'Ermitage, also with Cahors and the best of the Gard and Hérault *départements* [around Nîmes and Montpellier]" (Marcelou, *Vins, Vignes et Vignerons*).

A fascinating glimpse of the links between Bordeaux and Hermitage can be pieced together at this time. There are few Hermitage records as compared to those existing in Bordeaux, so the cellar notes of Marc-Balthazar Macker (1796–1859) reveal many of the gaps in this puzzle. His father, Balthazar, lived until 1825 and started a cellar logbook that ran between 1801 and 1858.

Macker was an early vinifier, buying crop from 1825 under the impetus of the son and offering bottled wines on his 1835 tariff (Montez, *Le Monde du Négoce*). His house is now the Sorrel residence beside the N7 road, and Jean-Michel Sorrel's wine is vinified in its very old cellar. The house is redolent of those splendid times: the large residence beside the main road south to the Côte d'Azur, creeper strands and green shutters tangled together, crunchy gravel in the courtyard behind the gates, and an imposing line of lime trees bordering it. The Macker business ultimately evolved into Michel Ferraton's, with some of it also merging into Jaboulet and Chapoutier.

From the Hermitage end, it is clear that Bordeaux bought for a couple of prime motives—medicine and insurance. Occasionally, vanity may have swayed the decision, as the Bordelais sought to make star-studded wines with the help of a very good Hermitage year, what I would term a Glory Year. There is also a strict correlation that when Hermitage suffered a bad vintage, Bordeaux, too, was recorded as having a bad vintage: the patient lacked medicine!

Such was the case in some early-nineteenth-century vintages:

1816 Rhône bad, *Bordeaux terrible.*

1820 Bordeaux bought none, *Bordeaux very mediocre.*

1821 Rhône mediocre, *Bordeaux abundant, sad quality.*

1823 Rhône without quality, *Bordeaux light, perfumed wines.*

Some of the Northern Rhône vintages in the early decades of the nineteenth century appear thus in the Macker book. (Italics indicate my comments, with prime reference C. Cocks and E. Féret, the second edition of that august book, published by V. Masson et Fils 1868.)

1803 Nothing bought because of the War [with England]. *British market closed—so its importance clear.*

1811 Lowton [*sic*] came and bought all at 300 FF a cask. Côte-Rôtie sold also at 240 FF. *This was a great vintage in Bordeaux, the famous Year of the Comet. Glory Year.*

1815 Bordeaux bought all 550 FF; one of best ever, small crop, excellent. *Bordeaux low yield, but wines later deemed remarkable, like 1798, 1811 —excellent, good colour.*

1817 Bordeaux not buy—mediocre wine. *Bordeaux nearly as bad as the terrible 1816.*

1818 Bordeaux bought all 3 Oct at 650 FF. Average Year. *Bordeaux hard, disagreeable wines. Failed Medicine Year!*

1819 Bordeaux bought at 500 FF. Excellent, like 1811, 1815. *Bordeaux abundant, very good; rain at harvest. The year Julien Calvé (Calvet) left the Ardèche for Bordeaux to sell his wines; he later became the owner of Château Croizet-Bages.*

1822 Bordeaux mediocre and bought all at 700 FF. Excellent, abundant, grands vins. *Bordeaux good, though the reds a little hard. High prices. Medicine Year.*

1824 Bordeaux didn't want to buy. Mediocre wines. *Bordeaux terrible.*

1825 Eight days after harvest there remained not one single cask to sell, Bordeaux bought all at exceptional price of 850 FF. Harvest 25 Sept. *Bordeaux famous, slow developers. Insurance/ Glory Year.*

1828 Unfavourable wines for Burgundy + Bordeaux. Wines were *sucrés. First mention of chaptalisation and Burgundy. Bordeaux favourable, light, perfumed wines but deficient in body and colour. The price of under 100 FF for this Hermitage and the 1826 was the lowest of the period 1802–54.*

1829 Bordeaux not buy a cask. Green wines, lack colour. *Bordeaux very bad, cropping in the rain. A year when very cool, rainy weather at Hermitage prompted Macker to go round locally and buy a lot of old wines to pre-empt the bad Rhône vintage.*

1830 Bordeaux bought later. Good colour, very good. Revolution of July. *Bordeaux unfavourable —robust, coloured wines but hard, green.*

1831 Bordeaux not buy much. 225 FF at first, then 800 FF later—good success at Bordeaux. *Bordeaux August hail, excellent, very expensive First Growths, slow developers. Insurance Year.*

1833 Bordeaux bought later on. Wines bit closed, good quality. *Bordeaux robust, coloured but bit hard.*

1834 Best year of the century. Perfect wines. *Bordeaux very famous, better than 1831. Very small crop—frost, hail, rot taste but First Growths developed perfectly and lost this taste. High prices.*

1836 Bordeaux did not want to buy at first, but bought later at 200–380 FF. *Bordeaux despite body and good appearance, wines hard and green.*

1837 Bordeaux bought all at 200–300 FF. *Bordeaux very abundant, good quality, moderate prices—purchases done early.*

The cellar book came to light through Jean-Louis Grippat, the now retired *vigneron* of Hermitage and St-Joseph. His grandfather Léon Grippa found the book and himself kept harvest notes while he was *régisseur* of a property at Hermitage. "The wines had to be thick in those days," comments Jean-Louis, "because they were drunk old and weren't chaptalised much before 1830—and if they weren't transportable, they couldn't be sold. There were two very different tastes then—Bordeaux was looking for robust, full wines, Burgundy for light wines."

Hermitage's role as the medicine wine for Bordeaux lasted over 100 years, probably starting on a small scale in the second half of the eighteenth century and continuing until the advent of phylloxera, which hit Hermitage in 1877.

So close did the ties become that the Calvet dynasty was by 1840 running a branch office in Bordeaux. The old Calvet residence still stands just off the main Place du Taurobole, the home of JMB Sorrel. Its cellars are used by Chapoutier, and before the first railway line was laid in the second half of the nineteenth century, there was a direct track connecting them to the vineyard.

Other sources corroborate Hermitage's role of strengthening the finer wines of Bordeaux.

H. Warner Allen, in his *History of Wine* (David & Charles, London 1961), quotes from *The Letter Books of Nathaniel Johnston*, written between 1799 and 1809 to his partner Guestier in Bordeaux:

"I was averse to using Roussillon on our best wines, unless it be a gallon or two, and that if you could get a sufficient quantity of good Hermitage to put a couple of Cans of it, it would be better. The Lafitte of 1795, which was made up with Hermitage, was the best liked wine of any of that year."

At that time, according to Nicholas Faith in his book *The Winemasters* (Harper & Row, New York 1978), Johnston was taking leases on a number of vineyards close to the Rhône to secure his supply of Hermitage.

Another venerable historian, Edmund Penning-Rowsell, in his *Wines of Bordeaux* (International Wine & Food Society, London 1969), mentioned a Château Ausone 1880 he had drunk, "without much hope," in 1967:

"It was surprisingly good. The colour, though pale, was much truer than the previous bottle [of Ausone 1880], the nose was fruity, and the body had a fullness that did actually suggest a St-Emilion. It had been château-bottled, and perhaps was *hermitagé*."

A bottle of Château Latour 1873 that I drank in December 1998 also revealed potential Hermitage influences. The bottle had lain in a Scottish castle until 1990 and had not been moved since its importation in the nineteenth century. It had been recorked in July 1990; at the time of its first bottling, the custom was to soak the corks in *eau de vie* beforehand, but after a few decades, recorking is a common practice. The 1873 Latour was tasted alongside four other 1870s First Growths—1874 Lafite and 1878 Latour, Lafite, and Margaux.

Its colour was astoundingly dense, and the palate well sustained. My notes continued: "amazing that it is 125 years old. A bit of soft chocolate at the end. Full, manly wine (any Hermitage?), not a fruit wine—may not have the delicacy of fruit of the 1878 Margaux and Lafite, especially the Margaux. The tannins are evident

on the finish. Very typical of what I expect Latour to be."

Hermitage may have been used to doctor this wine, since 1873 in Bordeaux was a lousy vintage—a classic one to choose for a top-up from the Rhône. There was only 25 per cent of the usual harvest, with frost in April destroying most of the crop.

Bordeaux of course rarely acknowledged the role played by Hermitage, and a rare example appeared in the 1860s, when, according to the late M. Paul Gauthier of *négociant* Léon Revol at Tain-l'Hermitage, labels like Margaux would proclaim with some pride that they were "Château Margaux—Hermitagé." Lafitte and Haut-Brion were other châteaux cited as mixers of Hermitage (Jean Machon, 1835–36). Machon also cited that the ideal Hermitage for Bordeaux was not the one considered locally as the best mix. The usual classic was to combine one-third each the wine from the *Bessards*, *Greffieux*, and *Méal climats*, but for Bordeaux the mixture was half *Bessards*, half the other two. This is said to have given more colour and fullness.

By the mid-nineteenth century, a certain amount of finesse had also entered the blending equation, and blind faith in one source was not enough for some. Jean-Jacques Lausseure wrote in 1858 that the Burgundy *premier cru* wines were found not really suited to this mixing. "The Ermitages of 1855 denature them completely, take away their bouquet and freshness, and always end up dominating and absorbing the taste of the fruit—which is so precious in Burgundy" (Marcelou, *Vins, Vignes et Vignerons*).

Meanwhile, Hermitage held its own faithful followers, although records seem to indicate that much of it was drunk outside the immediate region. The grandson of a former French President records that the Court of Russia had been long drawn to the wine. When his grandfather M. Émile Loubet visited Tsar Nicholas in 1903, he was served red and white Hermitage at the imperial banquet. M. Loubet took this as a friendly sign of recognition that he came from Hermitage's Drome *département*, but the Tsar said, no, the wines of Hermitage had in fact been regular Romanov favourites since the time that Nicholas Boileau wrote his satire *Le Repas ridicule* in 1663. True to form, the cynic Boileau had commented not on the wine's worth but on its apparent falsification:

> Un laquais effronté m'apporte un rouge bord
> D'un auvergnat fumeux, qui, mêlé de lignage,
> Se vendait, chez Crenet, pour vin de
>   l'Hermitage.

> *A cheeky flunkey brings me my red wine brimful*
> *With a heady Auvergnat, which, mixed with*
>   *dregs,*
> *Was sold at Crenet's as wine from the Hermitage.*

Literary references are another indicator of the wine's following in these ancient times. The Frenchman Jean-Francois Marmontel records that he stopped in Tain in 1755 to buy half a dozen bottles of the white wine; they cost him only 50 sous each, but he was quite entranced by their "nectar bouquet" (*Mémoires d'un père*). The English novelist Henry Fielding (1707–54) obviously had a soft spot for the wine, for it crept into several of his works, *Tom Jones* included; and the Scottish author Walter Scott held no doubts about Hermitage's ability to charm. In *Charles the Bold* (1831) he wrote: "I shall have a snack with you, and I shall satisfy you with a flask of old Ermitage." The last two confirm the wine's profile in Great Britain.

Another prime source from within France was the famous French novelist Alexandre Dumas, author of *The Three Musketeers*. Travelling around the Midi region of France with his friend Jadin in 1834, he arrived one night at Tain-l'Hermitage. "The next morning," he wrote, "I was up first and went for a walk. On returning to the hotel, I took Jadin to the window and invited him to salute the hill that dominated the town. Jadin hailed it wholeheartedly, but when I told him that it was the hill of Hermitage, he immediately repeated his action quite of his own accord; . . . we both considered Hermitage to be one of the best wines of France."

The Hermitage that Scott and Dumas knew may well have been that of the House of Bergier,

prominent at the time in making and selling the wine, always with flair. M. Bergier came from a well-established vineyard family, and had been an artist and lawyer when young. His eight hectares were regarded as a "quite enormous" holding in 1863 (Marcelou, *Vins, Vignes et Vignerons*).

Bergier made a flamboyant impression on the people of Tain when he designed and had built a six-windowed pavilion, exactly on the lines of one of the smartest villas of Pompeii, that was located slap-bang in the centre of his Hermitage vineyards. From here M. Bergier could watch the river and town below, plus of course his vineyard workers.

The eighteenth and nineteenth centuries were also times of many more *clos*—iron gated enclosures—across the hillside, each one declaring a notable's holding. Only a few such gates survive today.

Jean-Louis Chave sees this epoch as having two driving influences: "In France the wine regions were closed in the sense that a wine was made linked to specific local history and background. In the Rhône, people were often poor, so wine was not invested in to allow it to improve—unlike Bordeaux. To make Grand Vin, you need money—from sources like the Holy Orders, royalty, nobles, or top bourgeoisie. Here we had our moment of flowering with the noble families, whose physical legacy were things like their walled or gated Clos and Pavillons on the hillside. This was a time of free expression, and was overtaken once the local textile, leather, and silk industries grew—when wine resorted to being commercial, and not special in the same way."

M. Bergier's vineyard was centred on the *climat* of *Le Méal*, and he further distinguished himself by putting up an enormous signboard painted red and white and marked "HERMITAGE, CUVÉE BERGIER." This was the forerunner of the large Hollywood-style wall announcements that today carry the names of Paul Jaboulet Aîné and Hermitage Chapoutier —free publicity in the heart of the vineyards.

Bergier was a keen promoter of his wines, and in 1862 presented both white and red Hermitage at an exhibition in "the Palace of the Cromwell road" in London. As an indication of Hermitage's spread of ownership and its renown, 26 domaines presented 91 red and white wines. The only surviving name today is that of Delas, Étienne.

Curiously, the oldest wine on show was a white 1822, which along with other whites from 1834 and 1848, was said to have become liqueur—evidently a prized taste at the time, for the younger 1850 and 1859 were commented upon as having a nutty, slightly bitter taste, "special to the Bergier wines."

This *goût de noisette* is what we nowadays regard as typical of, and essential to, good white Hermitage, the bitterness being exactly what can be found in Marsanne wines. One of the most notable reds shown, of which the oldest was the 1830, was the 1834, which had been harvested in very hot weather. A remarkably healthy crop apparently gave a wine that was still fermenting in the summer of 1835, much to the desperation of the Bergier cellar archivist. Macker's cellar book confirms the 1834 as the then best year of that century.

Prephylloxera was a flourishing time for Tain's merchant trade; there appear to have been fifteen *négociants* in 1872, with an infrastructure that brought in 42 barrel makers. Between 1840 and 1890 two of the important families, Calvet and Chapoutier, bought wine in cask, as was the general custom of the day. Towards 1900 they had moved to buying crop and vinifying it (Montez, *Le Monde du Négoce*).

Phylloxera is said to have started in the summer of 1874, with the vineyards of *Rocoules* and *L'Ermite* set to be taken out by 1876 (Marcelou, *Vins, Vignes et Vignerons*). The Macker cellar book records the advent of phylloxera in the region in the late 1870s, but wine production on the domaine continued until 1883. Chez Macker, it did not then resume until 1892. Phylloxera was the cause of the reduction in the number of *négociants* at Hermitage from 15 in 1872 to just nine in 1886, and started the process of shaping the Hermitage vineyard in today's mould.

The Chapoutier story started with the arrival in the Rhône Valley of an Ardechois forebear some time before the French Revolution. He then worked his way up to being a *caviste* at Vogelgesang before buying the company out, with a partner named Delépine, in 1808. The Vogelgesang family themselves associated with Calvet until 1878, when Calvet cut its links with the Rhône to concentrate its efforts on Bordeaux.

The Jaboulet roots here started with Antoine, who was born in Cornas in 1807. His first business was formed in 1834, and by 1846 he was working as a cellar master in Tain and was also a barrel maker. Two sons of his five children—Paul and Henri—created a *négociant* business in 1873, before going their separate ways and starting their own firms in 1882.

Their purchases of plots on the hillside commenced soon afterwards. In 1889 Paul Jaboulet bought 2.83 hectares split between *Bessards*, *Le Méal*, and *Rocoules* for 30,000 francs. Not to be outdone, Henri Jaboulet bought 2.36 hectares spread across six plots in the same year—the sites less auspicious, and nearer the eastern end of the hill—*Grands et Petits Rocoules*, *Maison Blanche*, and *Colombier*, for a justifiably lower 10,000 francs (Marcelou, *Vins, Vignes et Vignerons*). *Colombier* is what today is called *La Croix*.

Today's Maison Delas was created in 1882 by Philippe Delas and Charles Audibert, and by 1897 names that exist today also included Paul Jaboulet Aîné, Chapoutier, and their sometimes used subbrands of André Passat and Delépine.

By the eve of the First World War, the imprint of today's ownership was stronger still. Jean-Louis Chave towards 1912 bought a plot on *Bessards* for 600 francs, and both Jaboulet and Chapoutier bought into the vineyards of Crozes-Hermitage. At the same time, the old family names of Bergier and Mure de Larnage, the latter also the owner of the Tain chocolate factory, had retired from the vineyard.

Nevertheless, Hermitage held its renown until near the end of the 1800s, with a following in Britain, if silver decanter labels of the period are any yardstick. At that time, the white wine held a very strong name, and Jean-Louis Chave points out that in his great-grandfather's day—the early 1900s—the family wine would be sold to *négociants*, who were obliged to buy the red in order to secure the white.

However, the early part of the twentieth century signalled a sharp downturn in fortunes; young men failed to return from the Great War, and the vineyards suffered from the same lack of interest and manpower that affected Condrieu, for instance. Louis-Francis de Vallouit recalls that in 1914 the yield was around 8 hl/ha, presumably with a lot of vines poorly cared for.

By 1930 the number of *négociants* had fallen to four, and it was in these straitened times that the Co-opérative was formed in 1933. Signing up were 114 growers, with half of them working less than one hectare and only two-thirds owning the land they worked. The signatories' vineyards were at Crozes as well as Hermitage.

Four remained the number of *négociants* that existed in the early 1970s—Chapoutier, Delas, Paul Jaboulet Aîné, and Léon Revol; their role was still important, since after the Second World War, Hermitage was still a place where few bottled the wine themselves. By then, Hermitage was reduced to just a connoisseur's following—in France and beyond. Demand never greatly exceeded supply, and prices lagged a long way behind the Bordeaux *crus classés* and all the main Côtes de Nuits and Côtes de Beaune red wines.

Two of the smaller owners at this time were *originals*—idiosyncractic characters. Lord Terence Gray was a man of Irish descent, involved in the arts and spending much of his year on the Côte d'Azur, although he had houses in England and Ireland as well. His wine was bottled under his name, his main holding being on *L'Hermite*. From 1978 Gérard Chave had access to a large part of his crop, before buying his vineyard in 1984.

Madamemoiselle Chierpe's father, Marius, had been an owner since before the Second World War, with 1.5 hectares from plots on *Méal*, *Beaume*, and *Greffieux*. His wine was called "Cuvée des Moines," and held a respected following. When he died, his daughter took over and, while employing a *vigneron*, made the wine herself. It was her wine that was sold to the United States via Frank Schoonmaker, one of the first Hermitages to be shipped there.

"Her custom was to age the wine in cask, and then leave it in bottle using a conical cork stopper for two years," recalls Gérard Chave. "She would then put the wine in its final bottle with no SO_2 and no filtration—it was completely clear. Today's *oenologues* would tell you it was impossible to do that." And he produces a packet of today's conical cork stoppers that announces they are "for wine to be drunk soon"!

The Chierpe vineyard was dispersed after she died without children well into her 70s, with the simplicity that the plots went to the neighbours who had tended them during a protracted legal case. The *Méal* went to Paul Jaboulet Aîné, the *Greffieux* to Henri Sorrel.

In the 1970s, press coverage and reporting on the wine increased, as did international awareness of the Rhône and the value it offered, and Hermitage started to be bought by a wider audience. Single-vineyard growers suddenly found themselves visited by foreign buyers, and the media spotlight swung heavily on to the easy name, the one that could offer any sort of quantity with good quality attached—Paul Jaboulet Aîné. Utterances from this house served as a definitive vintage summary on the whole Rhône Valley for stay-at-home wine journalists, and all the while prices pushed steadily ahead.

By the mid-1980s, futures in Hermitage red wines had become a commonplace offering from mainly British and American wine merchants. Nowadays, Hermitage is the province of collectors for the most expensive wines, and drinkers for the less expensive.

HERMITAGE VINEYARDS

The Full Up sign applies to the Hermitage vineyards. The figure of 131 hectares reflects the hectare and a half rooted out and planted during the 1990s by Chapoutier and Paul Jaboulet, around La Chapelle. In the early 1970s, there were 123 hectares, so these advances have been eked out over time. The first increase for many years occurred in 1984, when Gérard Chave cleared 2.5 hectares around *L'Hermite*.

Oversupply of Hermitage is anyway impossible because production is severely limited, both by law and by the sheer physical layout of the famous hillside. Whereas the *vignerons* of St-Joseph and Côte-Rôtie altered their *appellation* size and allocation by local rulings, both Hermitage and Cornas are restricted by national legislation. This serves as an excellent quality control and acts to avoid the sort of plateau expansion or riverside flatland cultivation that has made some wines from Côte-Rôtie or St-Joseph unworthy of their price.

The hill is its own natural boundary, the Rhône at its feet, its main façade set on a bountiful south-facing exposure. It is convex in shape, and rises abruptly away from the centre of Tain to reach a natural point of focus at the chapel of St. Christopher, which in the night becomes an incandescent glow perched on a brooding dark shape. The great landmark of the Chapelle was put up in 1864 on the site of the one built in 1100 and destroyed in subsequent religious wars. It is 280 metres up on the site called *L'Hermite* and faces southeast.

The main flank, which rises to 344 metres at its summit, is home to the boldest, most tannic wines, notably on the site called *Les Bessards*. Its neighbours, *Le Méal* and *L'Hermite*, are Hermitage's other two top sites—vital elements in the composition of any proper red Hermitage. But these two are subject to other influences, not mainly the stern, very old granite of the Massif Central but the much younger residues of the Alpine glaciers and hills from a couple of million years ago.

The whole Hermitage vineyard steers gradually away from the river Rhône for about three kilometres (just under two miles) on a mainly west-east axis. This means that many of its other sites or *climats* are also south facing. After the rugged outcrops of the westerly sites, the hill lowers and gradually flattens in steps as it runs to the east. Within the main area, there are little amphitheatres—*climats* like *L'Hermite* and *Beaume* have their own small slopes that are more turned east-west. What they may lose in exposure, however, they gain in retained summer heat inside those amphitheatres.

Downriver from the central area runs a spur, half the height, and the home of the most easterly vineyards, those *climats* known as *Les Diognières*, *Les Murets*, *L'Homme*, *La Croix de Torras*, and *Torras et les Garennes*. There is also a stretch of completely flat vineyard running along the bottom of the hill, its exposure in marked contrast to the prime, higher spots.

The constant benefit of Hermitage's south-facing exposure is highlighted by the growers. "Like the Pinot Noir in Burgundy, we're at the northern extreme of the Syrah's ripening here at Hermitage," says Jean-Louis Chave, "so we have to do everything we can to achieve full maturity every year—it's not something we can take for granted. So the hill's south-facing situation is a present from nature for us."

This means that most of the *appellation* is naturally protected from the dominant north wind; only the plateau towards the east around *Maison Blanche* and *L'Homme* and the jutting out *Varogne* at the west end are exposed to such wind. This natural shelter is a feature shared by some of the St-Jean-de-Muzols vineyards like *Ste-Épine* across the river in St-Joseph.

Altitude also plays a role here. Above the chapel, the old property of M. Montgolfier was planted with Marsanne for the simple reason that it was hard to get the Syrah to ripen. There is a loss of perhaps 1° alcohol for every 100 metres of extra elevation above the lowest level of 126 metres—just a little above the Rhône at this stage of its route south to the Mediterranean. This shows through in the wine from a high site like *Gros des Vignes*, for instance.

The density of plantation also varies according to height: the highest and steepest sites like the top of *Bessards* and *L'Hermite* are planted at a classic one metre by one metre, meaning 10,000 plants per hectare. The lower slopes, where a caterpillar tractor can pass, are planted more like 1.3 metres by one metre, giving about 7,000 vines per hectare. If these sites yield the same amount of grapes, the plants higher up have been more rigorously pruned and worked, their juice inclined to be more concentrated.

The prime heartland of Hermitage, the spinal column of its wine, is *Les Bessards*, right on the turn in the river and facing south. Looking from the square in Tain, this is the area to the left of the chapel. It is the largest *climat* and comprises what the locals call *Grands* and *Petits Bessards:* for Chapoutier and Chave, *Grands Bessards* refers to the west side towards *Varogne*, *Bessards* to the central sweep of the hill, and *Petits Bessards* to the lowest part of the *climat*.

The word to associate with the whole of *Bessards* is "granite." There are a few alluvial stones on the lower reaches, and there are some limestone veins and clay patches running through this part of the hill, but the great force here comes from its granite in different stages of decomposition. Jean-Louis Chave, resident of the granite-strewn Ardèche, states quietly that for him, *Bessards* is the Ardèche.

The west end, around *Grands Bessards,* is truly hard granite, while higher up there is more decomposed, alluvial topsoil. The mid to low areas of *Bessards* are *gore*, with some clay influences. The middle areas are said by Chave to bring maturity and a silken texture to a final bottle of red Hermitage.

Technically, the soil's acidity here marks an important influence in the wines. "The pH on *Bessards* is almost neutral," states Jean-Louis Chave; "it hovers around the 6.8 to 7 mark. That invests the wine with breed and grain. The granite at St-Joseph across the river, for instance, is more acid with a pH reading nearer 5—that's why the wines are more simply fruited from there. Our revived vineyard at Lemps north of Tournon has a pH of over 7, and we're obviously very hopeful about it." He adds that the soil's acidity can suddenly change, and that the *Méal* pH is 8.5—a greater and beneficial alkaline influence there. For him, this provides one of

the most simple arguments in favour of blending the wine from different *climats*.

The low end of *Bessards* can be worked by small tractor or horse, but higher up the only aid is the pulley, which can allow a man to drive an awkward mechanised hoe or earth turner between the rows of vines. The pulley system dates from the 1960s, and can't even be used in some places, because the dry stone wall ledges are so close together. To weed between each vine in its row, only a pickaxe will do.

The walls are deliberately close together on *Bessards* because soil is in such short supply; in places, there is just a sprinkling on top of the rock, so keeping the walls close serves to limit some of the slippage that can happen after rain.

Bessards is a mainly Syrah site. It is where Chapoutier's Pavillon wine comes from, it is the main vineyard for Delas, and this *climat* also contributes to about one-quarter of Jaboulet's La Chapelle, as well as being the foundation wine for Gérard Chave's Hermitage, which is made from seven different *climats* across the vineyard. This is where the vine and the *terroir* combine in full sympathy and expression—it's where the granite performs its most unfettered role.

The fire of that stone shows through in black, square-framed wines. For Gérard Chave, *Bessards* "is our essential *climat*—you cannot make a Grand Hermitage without it. You can make a flattering Hermitage without it if you want. *Bessards* is the frame around which we work. The granite is what assures good ageing for Hermitage—it is the main factor; no granite— no long life."

For Albéric Mazoyer of Chapoutier, "the *Bessards* granite gives a rigorous, mineral impact in its wines—there is a tension in the wine from the granite. So you can find elements like smoky bacon, blackberry fruits, and gunflint in it. Surprisingly, the acidity in the wines of both *Bessards* and *Méal* is similar."

Philippe Jaboulet states that the finesse in their *Bessards* Syrah comes from the rotted granite, and contrasts with the power of their *Méal* Syrah. Their 2.6-hectare plot on *Bessards* dates from the 1950s and lies between Chapoutier and Delas.

For Jacques Grange of Delas, "complexity is the principal characteristic of our Bessards cuvée. Its richness sits well on a thoroughbred structure, and the bouquet releases a succession of aromas. It's full and absolutely not aggressive or overdone in any way."

Quite often I find an association with violets on the bouquet of a young Bessards—something far removed from the cooked fruit, jam aromas and raspberry flavours of Méal. Bessards has a much more evident smouldering intensity and grip, as well—the cool darkness of a big wine. In classic vintages like 1998, 1999, and 2001—when the tannins are noticeable—the fruit aroma is black berries mixed with a meaty side. In more awkward years like 2000, the aroma is a more advanced game style, with less clear fruit definition.

But as Bernard Faurie comments, even defining the wine of a Hermitage site as just one type is dangerous: "Twenty metres can be a long way at Hermitage, because the soils change so quickly —which is why I think the wine is so complete." Certainly, this gives great possibilities to a master assembler like Gérard Chave who can work with different shades of Syrah from his seven different *climats*. Tasting his high, very granite Bessards Syrah 2002, it is smoky, stout wine with a grainy length; the more water-retentive, clay plot in the middle of *Bessards*, by contrast, shows more fungal, earthy characteristics, and yet is from the very same year.

One of the few Marsanne plots on *Bessards* is worked by Delas; this is a one-hectare vineyard planted in the 1950s down at the bottom of *Bessards*, known to Delas as *la plaine des Bessards*. Its soil is more like *Greffieux*'s, with some granite stones and more vegetal, deeper soil than elsewhere. "It's no surprise that Marsanne was planted here," comments Jacques Grange of Delas; "it's a spot that doesn't suffer too much from drought, and there's less pure rock."

Around *Bessards* are some satellite sites, all granite influenced, but none of them as grand for reasons of exposure. To the west on another flank of the hill is *Varogne*, covered in stony, hard grey granite, the *lieu-dit* closest to the Rhône and also the frontier with Crozes-Hermitage. This faces due west, more so than *Bessards*, which it touches at its top end above some woods.

Varogne may be a next-door neighbour, but its wines are more simply peppered, less complete, and less tannic than those from *Bessards*. Exposure has a lot to do with this: it's a site that gets the north wind, and the sun arrives quite late in the morning, so the wines are never very high in alcohol. Dard et Ribo and Bied have holdings here, the latter's a disorderly jumble.

South of *Bessards*, next to the railway line, is a tiny walled enclosure called *Les Vercandières*. Jean-Louis Chave has some very old Marsanne and some Syrah growing near the top walled end on granite, while the railway end with more clay is worked by the Co-opérative.

Above *Bessards*, and to the right of the chapel is *Les Grandes Vignes*—called *Gros des Vignes* in everyday usage—which lies in the *commune* of Crozes-Hermitage. A high, terraced site that ripens 10 days behind the prime spots, its soil reflects the theme of brittle granite found at Tournon. Its wine is overtly black fruited and crunchy textured and has a firm length— structured and tannic. But the heartbeat of a Bessards is absent, meaning the wine is often upright and would benefit from blending with wine from a riper site. The Desmeure family have actually knocked down the terrace walls here to make labour (and erosion) easier, and Paul Jaboulet and Delas also work plots here.

The ideal counterpoint to *Bessards*, and the second great *climat* at Hermitage, is *Le Méal*. *Bessards* gives wine that is brooding and at times severe; *Méal* offers open, warm-textured Syrah and is the provider of gloriously sumptuous, rich wine that can hold animal and meat undertones stemming from the natural heat of its location. *Bessards'* relative austerity compared to *Méal* is partly explained by its slightly cooler setting; the effect of more granite and some extra height also invests its wines with an evident firmness.

Father Gérard Chave calls *Méal* more a wine of the south than *Bessards,* which is fresher and less oxidative. Son Jean-Louis agrees with Dad when observing that for him, it is difficult to imagine a Hermitage without the presence of *Bessards,* which is its backbone, the tight tannins derived from that granite.

Méal lies east of *Bessards,* their frontier determined by *La Ravine de Greffieux.* It is below *L'Hermite,* from which it is separated by a tiny valley. From the town the prominent row of cypress trees marks the top of the eastern end of *Méal;* another landmark on the east end is a white *maison carrée,* which may have been useful for romantic encounters in the past. It is just along from the Paul Jaboulet Aîné sign at the top. This painted wall was the subject of a locally famous practical joke some years ago, when the town awoke one morning to find the word HOLLYWOOD had been overpainted on it. The offending item was swiftly removed and the wall correctly repainted.

Méal is marked by glacier stones and loose soil, which provides the eastern influence on *L'Hermite.* Like *Bessards,* this site starts flat on its lower reaches, then takes off steeply as it rises; in places it is not terraced, meaning that its slope is about the steepest in the *appellation.* One of the ace cards for *Méal* is its wonderful curved shape, a real south-facing sun trap. It rises to about 240 metres.

The eastern end of *Méal* under the Paul Jaboulet sign is an all-Syrah vineyard belonging to Jaboulet; it is their showcase and runs across to the valley preceding the westerly flank of the *Méal* hill. The vineyard comes in four strips, the most easterly comprising about 1.4 hectares, with next to it going west a plot of 1.3 ha bought in the 1960s from Jaboulet Vercherre, the Burgundian *négociants.* Then there is a 0.6 ha strip bought by them in the 1980s from Madame Chierpe, who made one of the most fabled and idiosyncratic Hermitages, the Cuvée des Moines, a *Méal-Greffieux* mix, in the 1950s and 1960s. Finally, at the western end, there is a two-plus hectare plot bought from the de Boissieux family at the end of the 1960s. Jaboulet's total holding across *Méal* is 6.8 ha, making it their largest *climat.*

Méal and *Bessards* contrast through their rock influences, but they are also linked by what happened to the Rhône's climate at the end of the Tertiary Phase some 2 million years ago. That was the time when debris from the Alpine glaciers was brought down the Rhône valley via routes like the Isère River, and it was also the time when the Rhône ran at its highest point.

In today's formation, the high level at which the river deposited its load of silt, sand, and pebbles is thought to be around the cypress trees near the Paul Jaboulet Aîné sign, at about 240 metres. Similar deposits trace across to *Bessards;* above it, there is more granite with its thin, acidic soils, and below it, more alluvium with its limestone debris and soil with an alkali influence. Thus the wine fruit above the Rhône's ancient high point is darker and smokier, and the fruit below, from the alluvium, more stony area, is redder, like strawberry: the perfect delineation for *Bessards* and *Méal.*

Méal's light-coloured and small glacier stones heat it up well, and its siting in the middle of the hillside means it gets very hot. Its soil is deeper than that of *Bessards,* so its retaining walls can be more spread out. They are bound with concrete and made from the site's alluvial stones instead of being piled on top of natural granite outcrops.

The lower end of *Méal* runs down in a sweeping slope and contains a little more clay with plenty of stones present all over it. This soil is richer than higher up and is good for whites as well as reds. "*Méal* is the first site we crop at Hermitage, be it red or white grapes," states Albéric Mazoyer of Chapoutier; "its wines are very silken, full of ripe fruits."

Méal, with the help of *Péléat,* is regarded as the provider of flesh in the J-L Chave Hermitage. In the past, Marc Sorrel's father, Henri, produced a *Méal* on its own—the 1978 and 1979 were fabulous—and now Marc blends it with a little of his *Greffieux* crop to make Le Gréal.

Bernard Faurie also produces a tiny amount of *Méal* on its own, including a sumptuous 2001. For Jaboulet, *Méal* is the core contributor to La Chapelle—up to half in a difficult year, and always at least one-quarter of it.

Near the top of the hill, its back part positioned as if looking over the shoulders of *Bessards* and *Méal*, is the third great *climat* at Hermitage, *L'Hermite*. It is the eastern fold of the *Bessards* flank, so its western end is on the granite of that *climat*. It then runs above and across the top of *Méal* in the form of a little plateau, and is also home to the chapel of St. Christopher. From a distance its shape at the top is concave.

The rock starts to change here. Below and east of *L'Hermite* is the ravine that cuts off the main portion of Hermitage granite from the rest of the *appellation*; up around La Chapelle on *L'Hermite*, there are five folds in the hill, and these high spots contain this *climat*'s greatest amount of granite. On the western side, at the *Bessards-L'Hermite* boundary, there is full granite because the Rhône River 2 million years ago never reached that height on the hill. It is this part of *L'Hermite* that furnishes the Syrah for the Chapoutier L'Ermite wine and also supplies Delas with some of their best Syrah from a half-hectare plot.

Soils are mixed across *L'Hermite*. "It's a real meeting point," says Jean-Louis Chave, "with all four influences here. There is loess, crumbling granite, full granite, and Alpine residues." There are therefore sudden changes within the same row of vines. The purest loess sites in the eastern section of *L'Hermite* are mostly planted with Marsanne and Roussanne, and this is where Jean-Louis Chave grows most of the domaine's Roussanne.

"The granite isn't good for the Marsanne and Roussanne," affirms Jean-Louis Chave; "it gives too much alcohol. The loess releases floral aromas, while the clay-chalk gives more honey," he says. Chapoutier are well present on the loess, too, and call their Marsanne plot of over three hectares *Chante-Alouette*, although it is not formally entered under that name on *L'Hermite*'s eastern section on the map.

The largest influences on *L'Hermite* are the loess and alluvial stones of its central and eastern portion; these cover around the top half metre (20 inches) on top of the granite couch, which can descend for several metres. The pale alluvial stones, or *galets*, help to mature the grapes, and were brought here by glaciers, not rivers. To the eye, there is loose brown topsoil that has been blown from the east; piled together, it becomes compact and also contains some sandy, very light clay elements. I would place *L'Hermite* as one of the three best white wine sites at Hermitage—those that give the most luscious, ripe Marsanne fruit from mature vines—along with *Rocoules* and *Murets*.

"You have to judge picking the Marsanne just right," says Jean-Louis Chave, "if you want its wine to be oily. But if you leave picking too long, the wine becomes flat." The Chave plot on *L'Hermite* is 80 per cent Roussanne, a vine favoured in the time of Terence Gray, and it brings a natural vivacity to their crop here. "For us, *L'Hermite* is a site for white wine of balance and finesse," observes Jean-Louis. Chapoutier favour pretty late harvesting for their Marsanne, which expresses ample, nutty flavours if allowed to age in bottle—there is usually more impact on the palate than the bouquet, a feature of Marsanne.

The Syrah vines on *L'Hermite* are mostly planted on the granite areas and on the Alpine glacier residues or moraines of the *climat*, which is usually one of the last to ripen at Hermitage. Jean-Louis Chave, for instance, mistrusts the loess for Syrah: "It can be OK in about one year in 10—for instance in 2003, when it was so hot and dry—but I would never want my Syrah to grow in pure loess. It's a soil that has trouble living. Loess needs an accompaniment—either the glacier moraines with their stones and an alkaline influence or some granite—to give it life."

"*L'Hermite*'s red wines always carry freshness and spice," says Jean-Louis Chave. "In some vintages, there can be a lot of maturity, but still a sound acidity. Its tannins are usually quite tight and vivacious." I would add that on its own,

L'Hermite *rouge* shows stylish red fruits, is refined and warm, with a notably clear purity when tasted solo chez Chave. The wines are midweight and quite complex. In a ripe, low-acidity year like 1997, *L'Hermite* played an important role for Chave, since it added a little extra tannin—*climats* like *Péléat* and *Beaume* were soft and sweet that year.

Jean-Louis Chave has a subset on *L'Hermite* that he calls *La Mortine*, opposite *Bessards* and west facing. His family bought this vineyard, which is cradled in the bosom of the hill, from the late Terence Gray. He describes its Syrah wine as sometimes being full of jam flavours: "That's because it's indented in the form of an amphitheatre, so it gets very cold in winter and very hot in summer," he explains. It's a very mixed spot, with granite, loess, glacier *moraines,* and even *poudingue* (bundles of stones clamped with clay). Other growers on *L'Hermite* are the Co-opérative, and Guigal since his acquisition of the de Vallouit vineyards.

Further down the hill, below *Méal*, from which it is separated by high stone walls, and next to *Bessards* at the latter's bottom end is *Les Greffieux*, a site I regard as worthy without holding quite the same inspiration as the Big Three already mentioned. Here Chapoutier works 2.7 hectares, Paul Jaboulet have half a hectare, Guigal has a plot bought from de Vallouit, and there are some smaller *viticulteurs* present—Bernard Faurie, Pascal Fayolle, and Marc Sorrel and his brothers, who own a discrete Clos a little north called *Le Vignon*.

Greffieux runs in a flowing sweep alongside the town, right next to the Co-opérative, and its highest 40 metres rise up with sudden steepness towards *Méal*. At the top, there is a near-ravine.

Greffieux's soil contains some granite, but here there is more clay and also fine elements than higher up the hill. The granite seam runs along its western side, so much so that Bernard Faurie unofficially calls his *Greffieux* "*Bessards*" because the soil on that precise spot is so similarly full of granite. The clay outcrops occur more in its eastern side, with some siliceous

influences, too. At the bottom, the soil deepens, meaning that some Marsanne is present.

Greffieux is also stony, the alluvion stones on it being glacier residues with the Alpine influence present, the rock itself about half a metre (20 inches) down. In the hard-rock areas, *Greffieux* is fast draining; elsewhere, the clay influences mean that the vines do better in a very dry year like 2003, and for Jean-Louis Chave their fruit quality even exceeded *L'Hermite*'s in that vintage. "It's like *Péléat*," he comments, "what I call a maturity *climat*."

There is limestone in *Greffieux*, and the wine is refined by nature, and higher in acidity than many. Bernard Faurie speaks of its very perfumed wines. I reckon it doesn't give wines with the same high/low nuances of *Méal* or *L'Hermite*; the latter, as expressed in bottle by Chapoutier's L'Ermite has an elegance that floats. Some call *Greffieux* "the Côte-Rôtie" of Hermitage. The tannins never demand a long wait, and the wine opens and delivers earlier than that from its neighbouring *climats;* the one demand is to wait to let its acidity settle. When compared to less august sites to the east, *Greffieux* produces Syrah wine that is firmer and more soundly structured than any from *Les Rocoules* or *Diognières*, for instance.

Greffieux is mostly planted with Syrah; it is not considered a strong site for the white vines, although Marc Sorrel grows a tiny 0.2 ha of Marsanne that he planted in 1985. He reports that his *Greffieux* Marsanne usually comes in with a degree less of sugar than his *Rocoules* Marsanne—13° versus 14°. The Domaine des Martinelles also grow some Marsanne right at the bottom of the vineyard.

A defender of *Greffieux* from the past was the nineteenth-century wine writer A. Jullien, who rated it as one of his top three outstanding vineyards here. In the 1866 edition of *Topographie de tous les Vignobles Connus*, he listed his three outstanding vineyards: *Les Bessards*, at the western limit of the hill, producing a deep-coloured, sturdy wine; *Le Méal* next to it, with very small stones, chalky soil, and a fine, perfumed wine; and *Les Greffieux*, below *Le Méal*, producer of generous, supple wine. It was Jullien's claim that the ideal bottle of Hermitage was formed through a combination of these three growths.

Right below *Greffieux*, and opposite the train station on a flat stretch of sandy, stony land is a tiny *lieu-dit* called *Les Plantiers*. Marc Sorrel grows some Marsanne with his Syrah here, the vineyard dating from 1970. This Marsanne is cropped and fermented with the Syrah, and Marc finds that it adds marrow and suppleness to his end wine, the Gréal.

Greffieux, *L'Hermite*, and *Méal* are split from the rest of the vineyard, away to the east, by a natural boundary, the *Ravine de Beaume*. At the east end of *Méal*, across the valley, is what is called locally *La Forêt de Chapoutier*, a shady spot with woods on it.

The *Beaumes* stream here is more gently worked into the hillside than *Greffieux*'s and is more often drier. The path of this stream creates its own valley, helping to favour the south-facing side of the escarpment.

The central sites in this part of the *appellation* are *Beaumes*, with a high spur that touches *Maison Blanche*, and *Roucoules*. The top of *Beaume* (called *Beaumes* in everyday usage, but not on the map) is a little lower than *Méal*, as the hill starts to taper away to the east. From here to the eastern end of the *appellation* the land flattens and so becomes more workable by machine. There is a curious little troglodyte house on *Beaume*, melded into its rock outer face. The word *beaume* means "grotto" in old French. The bottom of *Beaume*—very flat land—is opposite the Tain cemetery. Along the *climat* the slope turns gently towards the east.

The soil at *Beaume* is clay-sandstone, with a marked presence of what the locals call *poudingue*, that is alluvial deposits from the Alps to the east. Its top area has more red clay than elsewhere; the lower, more southerly facing flank, more sand mixed in with the stones. *Beaume* wines hold an easy, direct fruit with evidence of tannic support. I find a sense of black jam fruit, a roasted style; it's a hotter wine than that of its neighbour *Péléat* lower down the hill, with a little more power in it. Chave, the

Domaines du Colombier and des Martinelles, and Chapoutier work vineyards here, the first two with only Syrah, the last two with Marsanne as well. Paul Jaboulet also work a small 0.3 ha spot of Roussanne on *Beaume*, as does Ferraton.

Snuck in between *Beaume* and *Rocoules* is a small, much esteemed site in an L-shape called *Péléat*. It is mostly low down the hill and, like *Beaume*, is largely marked by *poudingue*, with a mix of clay, silex, and a few *galet* stones—a fine soil that isn't heavy—just like its wine.

Gérard Chave and family own 95 per cent of this roughly one hectare that his father bought in 1930—its mostly Marsanne white vines have never been replanted. Yann Chave cultivates a small plot, as does a Co-opérateur.

Following the local custom, the growers speak among themselves of subplots within a site or *climat*; so the Chaves talk about the *Daru* plot on *Péléat*, or the *Mûrier* on *Rocoules*—the names referring to an old owner and a mulberry tree respectively. *Mûrier* is no more than 0.3 hectare, for instance.

Péléat gives a refined, elegant, and silky red wine, with a smoked bouquet. Its red fruit has a classic lithe, granite style without great flesh—it's akin to an upmarket version of the Gervans red fruits from one of the best granite sites at Crozes-Hermitage. There is often great flair on the finish, and a genuine tight-knit texture. "It has a lot of affinity with our style of wine," comments Jean-Louis Chave, "meaning that it's not too tannic or overtly rich. If left on its own, we find it needs help from a *Bessards* or *L'Hermite*, but in turn it can bring elegance to them."

There is also old Marsanne grown high up on *Péléat* that dates from the early 1900s, planted by Jean-Louis' great-grandfather. Its wine is reserved when tasted young, and contrasts with the open serenity and charm of the Marsanne from *Rocoules* just above it on the hillside.

In 2002 Jean-Louis Chave replanted part of *Péléat* with a *massale* selection Syrah. Notably, he set out to increase the density of plantation from his father Gérard's day—what he terms "the tractor generation." "I was determined to do this and to narrow the width between rows from 1 by 1.8 metres to 1.4 by just 0.8 metre. It took me four years to track down the tractor for this width, which I eventually found in Switzerland."

This easterly end of the vineyard becomes a fine area for the white wine, with a trio of good sites—*Rocoules*, *Murets*, and *Maison Blanche*. The first two provide richer wine than the last, which is higher up the hill.

Maison Blanche is on a brief plateau, and *Les Rocoules* descends below it on the same hill seam. *Rocoules*, which is split in two by the *route de Larnage*, is a mix of clay-chalk, with a lot of glacier stones. High up there is some red clay and also *galet* stones on the boundary with *Maison Blanche*, although *Rocoules'* soil is generally a darker brown. "The clay in the subsoil is useful," states Laurent Habrard, who works a plot in the middle of *Rocoules;* "it means it doesn't dry out too much, even in a vintage like 2003." *Rocoules'* planting is dominated by the Marsanne, in a similar way to the Syrah on *Bessards*. Paul Jaboulet also cultivate 0.3 ha of Roussanne here alongside their 0.8 ha of Marsanne vines, and have a large painted Paul Jaboulet Aîné sign at the top of the eastern end of *Rocoules*.

Marc Sorrel's white wines show off *Rocoules* to excellent effect, helped by his Marsanne dating from the early 1950s. These wines are blessed with strong fruit extracts and good, complex structures. His Marsanne usually ripens very well to around 14°, and so provides natural richness in his white wines. "We rely on *Rocoules'* clay-chalk for richness in our whites," confirms Gérard Chave, "while our *L'Hermite* site with its acid, loess soil supplies them with freshness."

Philippe Desmeure of Domaine des Remizières is also present on *Rocoules*, with his Syrah bringing warm, broad wine that is not especially marked by tannin (unless it appears later in oak cask form).

Above *Rocoules* and also touching *Beaume* in its western zone, *Maison Blanche* lies in the *commune* of Larnage and is given to white vines, a

logical step given how the two sites fit together. Paul Jaboulet cultivate 0.7 ha of Marsanne and 0.4 hectare of Roussanne here. *Maison Blanche* contains a lot of loess, a pale brown presence notably at the flat top end of the site, with clay-limestone strips for Desmeure's Marsanne vines and for Jaboulet's Marsanne-Roussanne mix. Another grower on *Maison Blanche* is Florent Viale, with some old Marsanne.

There is a strip of red clay covered in *galet* stones on the eastern side of *Maison Blanche* beside the road to Larnage; across most of the slope the soil continues as loess—poor and very dusty, and if this soil is not worked by the grower, it quickly loses life. There are more stones again on the southern end nearest the Rhône.

As at *L'Hermite*, the loess is considered best for white vines, and *Maison Blanche* brings freshness and vivacity to them. Marsanne from here shows a medium-plus weight and some refinement in a good year like 2001, but doesn't have the character to merit sole bottling.

Moving east, and touching *Rocoules*, is the third of these prime white vine sites, *Les Murets*. The soil here is very pale brown, fine, and powdery, topped with pale, sometimes grey stones that are of Alpine fluvioglacier origin. The official description is sandy-stony, fast-draining soil on top of *würm*, or deposits from the Ice Age glacial period. *Murets* is above *Diognières* and rises in a gentle slope until a set of terraces at the top, and can be higher yielding than other parts of the hill.

Murets wines, especially the mainly Marsanne-filled whites, can be absolutely delicious, the epitome of warm elegance. For many years, their distinction was well shown by Jean-Louis Grippat, a vineyard now in the hands of Guigal. *Murets* is also the source for Chapoutier's de l'Orée, which is made from 1920s and older Marsanne vines. Pascal Fayolle and Philippe Belle have Syrah growing here, the latter considering the tannins from this site to be always silky.

Above *Rocoules* and the western end of *Murets* is squeezed a small site, *La Pierrelle*. This upper-slope *climat* stands in the *commune* of Larnage, has a south-southwest exposure, and is marked by red clay and *galet* stones that accumulate and become larger lower down it. The site is a mix of slope and plateau, and Pascal Fayolle observed that lower down, the stones add to the heat and precocity. "Even so, our Syrah performed OK there in 2003, despite the extreme heat, because the lower soil is deep enough not to dry too fast." Some Marsanne from *La Pierrelle* has appeared in the Tardieu-Laurent white, bought from a local cultivator.

The bottom strip of vineyard underneath *Péléat*, *Rocoules*, and *Murets* is a "workhorse" site called *Les Diognières*. It is called a *sabot*, or hoof, locally because it descends gradually. Its sandy, siliceous, rather poor soil is covered with stones, a lot of them near the town until a final band of about 15 metres that contains heavy soil and only a few stones. To the eye, *Diognières'* soil is a light colour, reflecting its mix of clay-chalk with sandy elements, and it is stonier than *Murets*. It is largely flat, so its vines are most often trained along wires.

"Wire training may be convenient for some, but it makes the Syrah age more quickly than the stand-alone Gobelet stake system," says Gérard Chave about the wire system that is used by growers like Paul Jaboulet on their 1.1 hectare of *Diognières*. "The Gobelet training is more compact for the vine, and should branches die, there is more vine base to restart with," he adds.

A track runs across *Diognières*, and above it the land slopes upwards, gaining some extra exposure. Dotted along the track are small stone tool houses and sheds. This is a site where the Fayolle family from Gervans has long owned plots. "My grandfather Jules bought it in 1965, when it was overgrown," says Laurent Fayolle, who since the splitting in two of the family domaine in 2002, has worked just 0.3 ha of Syrah, on the abrupt slope high up on *Diognières*.

He admits that this land is tired: "The soil needs vegetal matter to restore it, due to the high-volume treatments and cropping of the 1970s." He also works 0.2 ha of white vines—

90 per cent Marsanne and 10 per cent Roussanne—on the neutral lime-silt ground at the flat bottom end of *Diognières*. The Viale family of Domaine du Colombier, the Domaine des Martinelles, Ferraton, and Michelas Saint Jemms also have plots on *Diognières*.

The *Diognières* reds are fruited, relatively acid wines that are perfect for adding freshness to some of the darker vattings. Their colour is dark red rather than purple, and if the crop is left to push for near extreme maturity, they can be broad and jamlike in texture. This is also a site that serves up whites with a degree of freshness in them. The Marsanne of Domaine des Martinelles grows in the lower, more overtly clay-chalk areas here.

The eastern extension of *Diognières*, near the outer housing of Tain, is a site that is rarely spoken of, *Diognières et Torras*. Paul Jaboulet's plot here covers 1.3 hectares. It, too, is clay-chalk with sandy elements.

Also in the *commune* of Larnage are *L'Homme*, above *Les Murets*, which covers about two hectares, and *La Croix*, neither of them a site mentioned or written of in previous centuries. There is a very different feel to this east end of Hermitage, away from the rugged grandeur and cool breezes around *Bessards*. It provides a curious sense of domestication that doesn't seem to fit with one's perception of how the wine should be.

L'Homme is a flat plateau and, like *La Croix*, across the original easterly approach road leading up to Larnage, reflects Alpine influences—clay-chalk, with very loose sandy soil and a few stones on its flat stretches. The clay content increases going down the hill, with plenty of small *galet* stones stuck together in the form of *poudingue*.

Both sites are worked by members of the Tain Co-opérative, with Dard et Ribo holding a tiny spot on *La Croix*, where Paul Jaboulet have several hectares, some of them among their first Hermitage purchases just after phylloxera.

La Croix is flat at the top, where its soil is richest and has some clay. It holds some limestone patches higher up near the village of

Larnage, and then descends in small stone-covered terraces until flattening near its bottom end; there is some more clay, with stones and silt at this end. In the best traditions of Larnage, it is windy up on the top plateau, and behind *La Croix* the land changes abruptly, the grip of the vineyards ends, and it's over to apricots.

Paul Jaboulet are important owners on *La Croix*, and their vineyard reflects the diversity of the soil between top and bottom. On the plateau with more clay they grow Marsanne from the 1950s, the vines single staked. On the terraced slope, they grow Syrah, and mixed in with the Syrah down at the bottom, there are two plots of white vines, including some Roussanne from the late 1970s.

The third stream in the vineyard is the *ruisseau de Torras*, in this easterly sector. This musters a little flow after rainfall, but it serves more for drainage these days. It splits *La Croix* from the most easterly *lieu-dit*, *Torras et Les Garennes*, a small round hillock out on its own. This is all but a Crozes-Hermitage site if one is objective.

Torras et Les Garennes' soil is a series of compacted old glacier moraines, with alluvial stones present. It drains very well, so drought conditions can be a problem. The hard rock lies around a metre (40 inches) or more under the surface here. This site used to be called *Les Signaux*, and Jaboulet have a holding here.

La Croix, *L'Homme*, and *Torras et Les Garennes* are all easier to work than the fully terraced, steep sites around *Méal* and *Bessards*. Their vines are largely wire trained, and small pulleys can be used to turn the soil if required. Across the *appellation*, much cultivation remains manual, and the men working for a domaine like Gérard Chave's will carry up 20 tons of horse compost in the winter for spreading across their vineyards. Likewise, the weeding between the vines, the tying of the young growth in the summer, and clearing of leaf cover to air the grapes are all done by hand.

In the 1980s the vines started to be sprayed by helicopter, freeing up considerable labour. This treats against mildew, oïdium, and spiders,

but its range is naturally restricted to plots away from housing—*Méal* rather than *Greffieux*, for instance. It is also restricted to a copper solution rather than acting as a distribution of insecticides: not fully organic but at least reasoned applications are done.

Otherwise the pattern is still much the same as it ever was—work runs from dawn to dusk, and under the early morning sunshine little bands of *vignoble* workers weave their way slowly up the hillside, where they spend the rest of the day. These specialized vineyard workers often belong to the large *négociant* companies like Chapoutier and Jaboulet, and traditionally pass down their expertise and their anecdotes from father to son.

One of the unusual developments of the very technical 1980s was the reintroduction of ploughing by horse in the lower reaches of the hill. Brothers Georges and Pierre Cotte have a farm a few kilometres away in the Drôme; Georges is wiry, small, and tucked up, not at all a talker, Pierre is robust and chatty: "The horse season is March to September," he explains. "The two horses sleep here in a little stable in the vines, which used to belong to Jean-Louis Grippat, until he sold it to M. Guigal."

"I started to labour when I was nine and a half years old," he continues; "I always loved horses and so kept them on, because the farm was mixed—cows, goats, corn, apricots, and asparagus until that was hit by blight. You won't find farms with horses nowadays around here; it's a pity."

The horses work a busy seven to eight hours a day, and cover *Murets*, *Beaume*, parts of *Méal* and *Greffieux*, *Rocoules* and *Maison Blanche*. They move at speed, the reins—a piece of rope —drawn round to their quarters and then around Pierre's and Georges' backs. The horses strain to go once they are set up at the start of a row of vines. Grunting noises and throaty commands break out—"*yap*"—"*doucement*"— "*hah*"—as they till beside the vines, the jingle of the plough offering a note of treble counterpoint. Behind them the blue-clad man staggers along at pace, striving to keep them in a straight line. "My nighttime cramps are the price of this work," says Pierre solemnly.

One hectare is completed in 18 hours; two trips are made for a full row of vines, so that each side of the vine has had the soil lifted and turned. Aereation and access for the rain are achieved by this when it is done in March, for instance. Growers who use the horses are Sorrel, Jean-Louis Chave, Guigal, and Bernard Faurie. Chapoutier have two horses of their own for the same work.

Hermitage red is obviously mostly made from the Syrah grape, although a maximum of 15 per cent white Marsanne and Roussanne are permitted to enter the fermenting vats at the same time. This is a decree designed to make the *vigneron*'s life easier—so that he can harvest a whole vineyard instead of having to return later to one or two white-grape vines.

There is a concrete benefit, though. As the Marsanne has quite a high glycerine content, its presence can give the red wine a little extra richness and profundity. "The Marsanne could well have been deliberately planted in the old days," says Jean-Louis Chave, "because people knew it would calm down the granite effect on the Syrah."

Apparently, few growers ever use much more than 5 per cent Marsanne in their red Hermitage, although they can be tempted to add more in years of Syrah losses from setbacks such as *coulure,* or malformation of the fruit. Marc Sorrel sticks to about 5 per cent, which represents the amount of Marsanne he has mixed in with Syrah on old plots, but recognises the extra oiliness brought to his red Gréal— what he calls its *moelleux.*

Red Hermitage is also easier to sell than the white, adding to the temptation to include white grapes. That makes it well possible that the sweetness of nineteenth-century red Hermitage that was so beloved by the Bordelais because it fleshed out their wines came from the Marsanne as well as the Syrah.

Temperatures on the top of the hill on a sunny summer's day are surprisingly high, with so many terraced walls all around absorbing and radiating the sun's heat. It is similar down at the foot of the vineyards, for there a low stone wall provides shelter as it runs along the curve of the hillside and is broken only every 45 metres or so by iron gates that indicate the entrance to a new *clos.*

A meteorological study conducted at the end of the last century revealed an average temperature in the vineyards of 13.9°C, a figure more normally associated with Mediterranean France: what it would reveal after some of the scorching summers since the early 1980s is anybody's guess. Nearby at the 160-metre Marsaz weather station, the annual average for the 30 years up to 2001 is just 11.9°C, for instance. Under such conditions the Syrah has every chance to produce well and in a more consistent way than it does at Côte-Rôtie: I expect a difference of a degree or two when travelling between the two *appellations* on the same day. Nevertheless, there is still a 10-day interval between ripening on the top and the bottom of the hillside.

The crucial times that make or break a vintage here are classic. As Bernard Faurie puts it, "August is when you make Grand Vin at Hermitage. You can catch up a bit in September, but you don't get to the heart of the matter. September heat also tends to burn the acidities." Of course, August 2003 was a month that dawned with the crop in superb shape, and although it was a sunny time, the vines simply couldn't handle the onslaught of temperatures that were 42°C in the shade.

By law, yields have the clause that allows an extra 15 per cent over the 40 hl/ha platform. This probably seemed a fairly distant end result when written in to the ruling, but the advance of superabundant clonal Syrah has made this more of a yearly reality. Jacques Grange of Delas is concerned about this: "We should be more rigorous with the 40 hl/ha. Above 30 hl/ha I find dilution starts. The sure yield if you want strong quality is 25 to 30 hl/ha."

Between one-quarter and one-third of all the wine is white, a surprisingly high amount since there are many enthusiasts who know the red well but who have never tried or even seen the white wine. As a quality white with the most interesting ageing possibilities, it still has trouble obtaining a following, although I sense that people understand it better than they did in the 1980s and early 1990s, when the fashion was for fresh white wines.

White Hermitage is and also should be made principally from the Marsanne—Chapoutier back it 100 per cent, as do proprietors like Guigal with the Jean-Louis Grippat vineyard and Philippe Desmeure, while Gérard Chave's whites are 80 to 85 per cent Marsanne. The exception to the rule is the House of Jaboulet, whose Chevalier de Stérimberg, a finer style of white Hermitage, is made up of 65 per cent Marsanne and 35 per cent Roussanne, admittedly down from the 45 per cent of the late 1980s. Ferraton also relies on around 40 per cent Roussanne for his limited edition Ermitage *blanc* Reverdy.

On the international stage, the Marsanne has become more accepted since the early 1990s, with its performance on estates like Victoria's Tahbilk in Australia or Qupé in California helping its image. At Hermitage, the formula of old vines and the naturally low yields they give—around 25 hl/ha—and growing the Marsanne in the loess or clay-chalk areas is a very successful one. From the past, I would highlight wines like Chave's 1985, the Grippat 1983, a host of Chapoutier Chante-Alouettes from the 1950s onwards, and even the utterly delicious pre-Roussanne wines of Paul Jaboulet such as the 1961 or 1967 Chevalier de Stérimberg.

Some Hermitage whites show a bitter side on the palate, which at times is their calling card. Jean-Louis Chave explains this as the result of low acidity mingling with freshness on the palate, and directly due to the Marsanne. He is a big backer of the Marsanne, and sees Michel Chapoutier's support for this variety as crucial at Hermitage: "I say Bravo to Michel—he could pull up his Marsanne vines and earn a lot more from the reds, but he stays with it."

Michel himself states that the Marsanne has a unique quality because bitterness features among its flavours. "Its structure is the bitter-

ness, and that's what makes it ideal for the marriage between food and wine," he enthuses. "Bitter is one of the most subtle gastronomic flavours, and often comes to people after their youth. Marsanne is the only grape variety whose wine can live a long time without much acidity present."

For his part, Bernard Faurie finds that the granite brings a gunflint or salty side to the Marsanne—an aspect apparent in his 2002 Hermitage *blanc*.

The Roussanne is said to have been popular until the end of the nineteenth or start of the twentieth century, indicating that it may have been replanted after phylloxera. But growers were put off by its low yields, with problems from oïdium and blight in its woodstock.

Michel Chapoutier comments that the Roussanne was never that widely planted. "It was prone to oxidation," he says. "White Hermitage was a keeping wine at that time, so the Roussanne was neither appreciated nor much planted."

This may explain why a *vigneron* like René-Jean Dard, of Dard et Ribo, goes to Savoie for his Roussanne—in clone form. As leave-alone and time-honoured a domaine as this would naturally incline towards working with hand-grafted *sélection massale* from healthy old vines, but M. Dard states that no selection has been done on the Roussanne of Tain.

Albéric Mazoyer of Chapoutier, a noted thinker and student of vineyard care, comments that he would choose kaolin or calcium if he had to plant Roussanne. "I'd go for the lower slopes of *Méal* or *Murets*," he says.

When carefully cropped, and taken off a good site, the Roussanne can perform with distinction. In the days following the rains of September 2002, there was still time for some consolidation in the ripening, and Chave's L'Hermite Roussanne from his late 1970s vines was very classy in cask before blending. Its tasting note read, "very elegant bouquet, exotic fruits from a two-year old not new cask, but real style, clear definition and great length."

HERMITAGE *ROUGE* VINIFICATION

As with all traditional *appellations*, winemaking at Hermitage has gradually evolved to take in more modern equipment since the late 1980s. Systematic temperature control has become more widespread, as has destemming. There is also more incidence of new oak than in the past, but in no way is this a dominating feature; indeed, with generally riper content than Côte-Rôtie, there is less new oak use pro rata here than in the northern neighbour.

The small domaines are generally those that stick with whole-bunch fermentation—Belle, Colombier, Faurie, Ferraton for his own domaine grapes, and J-C Fayolle. Even Marc Sorrel now destalks in uneasy years. As a rule, riper crop is being harvested than used to be the case in the 1970s and 1980s, making the wines more rounded. The destemming adds to this textural softness. Gérard Chave considers 1985 to be the important year for this: "Before then, not many wines were destemmed; after that year, textures gained in silkiness."

Some growers stick with wood fermenting vats—Chapoutier with the old open ones, the same as Faurie, Marc Sorrel, and Dard et Ribo. J-L Chave and Laurent Fayolle of Fayolle Fils et Fille have wood vats as well, younger and smaller ones. Open fermenting vats are inclined to bring Louis Jaboulet, the doyen of the *appellation*, out in a rash: he puffs and dismisses them as being something "from the Middle Ages"!

Otherwise, concrete vats are used by domaines like Belle and Ferraton, while Jaboulet ferments in a mix of concrete and steel. Steel is favoured by J-L Chave, Delas, and Martinelles. Concrete vats draw very different views from two of the main houses here. Gérard Chave forsook them in the early 1990s, with concern that they could lose temperature very quickly. Jacques Jaboulet, however, contends: "I prefer concrete as it provides better thermo regulation thanks to its thicker walls, and that can be pinpointed nowadays. I prefer steel for storing the wine, though," he adds.

There is certainly plenty of attention to the role of yeasts at Hermitage, and forward-looking operations like Chapoutier, Delas, and J-L Chave all exclude the use of external or cultured yeasts. For Chave, leaving the natural yeasts to do their own thing can mean a steady six-month fermentation for his whites.

Cuvaison lasts two to four weeks in general; those vinifying around the two-week mark include the Cave de Tain, J-C Fayolle, and Marc Sorrel. Those allowing three to four weeks for a steady fermentation and slow maceration are domaines like Belle, the Cave de Tain for the special Gambert de Loche, Yann Chave, J-L Chave, Delas, and Guigal. Jaboulet can run for three to five weeks, Chapoutier for four to six weeks.

Growers like a mix of cap punching and pumping-over (*pigeages* and *remontages*) during fermentation. J-L Chave practises the classic floating-cap vinification, so punches the cap down, while Delas, Chapoutier, and Guigal also run regular cap punchings. Those favouring pumping-overs include the Fayolles and Jaboulet.

Temperature control during vinification is kept at sensible levels, with overextraction not usually discernible in the wines of Hermitage. Jaboulet warm their young juice for eight hours at 35°C at the start of the process, then sustain the vats at 28° to 30°C, and it is rare for any grower to surpass around 32°C.

The duration of wood ageing has reduced overall since the 1970s, when it was often at least two years, in old casks or barrels, too. Many growers work around 15 to 18 months in cask—the likes of the Cave de Tain, Chapoutier for their special *parcellaire* wines, J-L Chave, Ferraton, Jaboulet, Remizières, and merchants like Gabriel Meffre and Ogier. Since the late 1980s J-L Chave have used only 228-litre casks instead of a spread of 550-litre and small barrels as well.

The longest cask agers are Guigal, who leaves his wines for 30 to 36 months, and his other firm, Vidal-Fleury (36 months in large old 20 hl barrels). Delas vary between 12 and 26 months according to the state of the vintage.

Most growers favour the 228-litre Burgundian cask, although a few prefer the *demi-muid* of 550 to 600 litres (Y. Chave, Colombier, B. Faurie, Martinelles, Ogier). The new-oak proportion is not excessive by and large: overt new-oak practitioners are the Cave de Tain (25 per cent for the classic, 100 per cent for the Gambert de Loche), Chapoutier (33–50 per cent new), Belle (60 per cent new), Yann Chave, Delas for the Bessards (50 per cent, but for the Marquise de la Tourette only 15 per cent at most), Martinelles (70 per cent new), Guigal for his special Ex-voto (all new), Remizières (80 per cent new), and Tardieu-Laurent (all new).

Often the new-oak proportion runs up to 20 per cent, and a typical cask rotation for J-L Chave and Jaboulet extends over five years or so. Consequently the wine is usually able to express grape tannins in the correct form, and so develop with greater and steadier softness than it would with more new oak present.

The attitude towards wood at Hermitage has generally been conservative, as if the growers realise that their raw materials do not need an outside boost or more "shoulders." Indeed, until 1991 Chapoutier was still using chestnut casks and had only started to use any oak in the mid-1980s. Chestnut is the traditional wood of the region, with supplies drawn from the Ardèche. Once installed as *patron*, Michel Chapoutier rid the house of chestnut, proclaiming, "Chestnut casks are lovely for barbecues."

Across the *appellation*, there is some fining but little filtration before bottling. Bernard Faurie, ever the reflector on such matters, tries not to filter but finds that such big vintages as 1995, 2001, and 2003 need filtration. "I generally filter a bit," he states. "If you don't filter, you have to do one more racking from one cask to another. Then the risk becomes a loss of fruit, but also a gain of length on the palate. For me, the danger of nonfiltered wines is that they are coarse and lack clear flavours if they haven't been well structured from the start."

HERMITAGE *ROUGE*

"To make a Grand Hermitage, it is indispensable that the wine has profoundness, harmony, and tannic structure," says Jean-Louis Chave, then proceeds to dig out examples of these attributes from his family's host of plots across the hillside. He also emphasises that red Hermitage is not a big wine: "We're at the northern limit of the Syrah's ripeness here. The hill facing largely south and low yields help, but it's a struggle to get everything in the vineyard ripe. That makes the wine not just a question of power but also of flesh and finesse."

A hierarchy exists here, although it is not formally recorded by a *cru* system. The inner circle belongs to those growers with vineyards on the prime westerly sites that contain granite, described by Gérard Chave as the one soil factor that ensures any Hermitage a long life. Chapoutier, Delas, Chave, and Paul Jaboulet Aîné are all firmly in this bracket. Marc Sorrel, Bernard Faurie, and the Fayolles at Domaine des Martinelles also have some exposure to prime *climats*—the likes of *Bessards*, *Méal*, and *Greffieux*. Then there are other Hermitages—more supple and less formally structured ones like those from Belle, Domaine du Colombier, the Fayolles, and Remizières.

Some Hermitage contains a site-specific name, a growing trend and one set to continue. The obvious exponents of this are Chapoutier, with their high-priced reds and whites; Delas have their special Bessards; Marc Sorrel has Gréal, a mix of *Greffieux* and *Méal;* and both Ferraton and Bernard Faurie term some of their wine "Méal," the latter by word rather than label. J-L Chave and Paul Jaboulet remain blenders across several sites, though.

Gérard Chave is steadfastly opposed to the use of site-specific names. Every year, he blends the wines from his seven red or four white holdings spread over the hillside. His intention is to make one definable style of wine, and he regards his greatest challenge as the successful integration of all the different cuvées from his plots: he positively licks his lips at the prospect of a little alchemy each year. So a thorough tasting in his musty cellars in Mauves reveals widely differing characteristics from the different *climats*—none of them on their own capable of representing the word or the place "Hermitage."

With better facilities has come greater consistency in the bottling of wines. The 1970s and 1980s were marked by growers performing bottling at different times, so the drinker was engaged in a game of potluck at times—not knowing whether the wine was an "early" or "later," and therefore more oaked, drink.

A famous case in point was Chave's red 1978, which has shown differently throughout its life. The earlier bottling holds more of a fruit underlay and shows itself more vigorously and freshly than the sometimes subdued later bottling, which is firmer, less flamboyant, and for most people, less impressive.

Red Hermitage is a wine of resounding character, inescapably noble when drunk once some maturity has evolved. It is capable of long life and of holding a sustained and warm texture during that time, something that sets it apart from the best of Bordeaux or Burgundy, for instance. The richness of the south hangs around even in old age, bringing the whisper of succulence right down to the aftertaste. The celebrated vintages like 1961, 1978, 1990 and 1999 are all likely to live for at least 50 years.

When young, *Hermitage rouge* is robust, rich in dark fruits—sometimes berries, sometimes more stewed fruit flavours. Tannin runs around the edges and often down the middle, but its texture has softened appreciably since the 1980s; indeed, I would highlight the greater mastery of tannic ripeness as one of the main steps forward in vinification here in my lifetime. Even top-rated Hermitage like Chave or La Chapelle can be drunk within four of five years given the improved balance in the wine; black fruits and warmth come through at that stage, but the complexity of later years is notably absent.

Because it is near the limit of a ripening zone, Hermitage *rouge* is not inclined to show its alcohol; levels of around 13° are common and are well integrated in the ripeness of the wine.

The colour of red Hermitage is a dazzler—brilliant purple, with traces of jet black. Age brings gentle red tones, usually prolonged into the third decade. The bouquet starts closed in the more complex vintages, ones like 2001, 1998, 1995, 1989, and 1983. The prime fruit aromas are often those of underripe black currants or raspberries, but with increased maceration times of up to six weeks nowadays, there are more stewed fruits and prune connotations than used to exist. Other "regulars" on the bouquet are spice, tar, pepper, and sometimes violets; leather and undergrowth aromas come along with age, and with extreme age, there are wafts of wax and tea. One should expect warmth and breadth in the bouquet in all except the rainiest of vintages—2002 and 1993, for instance.

Two of the most interesting recent vintages at Hermitage have been the 1999 and the 2001. Both are likely to be classic years, but their routes to their success were different. One could call 1999 a Sun Year, 2001 a Wind Year. The former's ripening was propelled by consistent bouts of sun and heat in August, but the vines had been nourished by rain before then. Acidity levels were correct but not high, and quantity was high, too. The crop was healthy and the vintage is full-bodied and indeed sunny. There is no doubting its richness and its deserved place as an excellent vintage.

2001 was a peskier do. Ripening of sugars and tannins got out of step, with the latter trailing. As a sign of the greater wisdom present at Hermitage these days as compared with the 1970s and 1980s, the growers waited for the polyphenols, or tannic acids, to catch up. Against a backdrop of dry weather, cool winds also played a part in gradually bringing ripening along. The effect was to provide the wines with clear-cut textures and in many ways more interesting tannins than the more sun-ripened ones of 1999. This will be a vintage that will also age well, maybe with more stopping and starting than the more straightforward 1999.

The broad 1999 palates show warm black fruits, and touches of spice and olive at times; the 2001s have a "darker" side, the black fruit holding a nervous energy, the licorice and tar effects of the tannins evident. The 1999s finish with a southern flourish, a satisfying lip-smacking oiliness. The 2001s are more mineral and grainy, and their potential will take longer to show through. They finish more tightly.

A cousin year to the 2001 was the 2004, an Indian summer year if ever there was one. After around six inches of rain in the first half of August, rot was on the agenda. But a stable barometer came to the rescue, with late August and September dry and sunny, accompanied by a prevalent north wind as well. This is a vintage where the growers could select when to pick without rushing, as the grapes developed steadily in the last five weeks of the cycle. As a result, the wines hold clearly defined fruit and a fresh, helpful acidity that will allow them to age well. They have less stuffing than the 2001s, however.

With age, red Hermitage acquires an uncommon equilibrium and a finesse that would have often been bet against early in its life. The full-bodied constituents demand time and patience to integrate and develop their rich, enveloping harmony. Great Hermitage 20 to 30 years old, from the best vintages and the best makers, stands alongside any of the best wines of Bordeaux, or of anywhere on earth for that matter. There are legends like La Chapelle 1961 and the J-L Chave 1952, both still ticking along, but other more recent wines can aspire to lasting greatness—La Chapelle 1978, J-L Chave's 1990, and his Cathelin of that year, for instance. Keep an eye on Delas' Bessards and Chapoutier's L'Ermite, both in a vintage like 1999, as well.

Any light vintage—meaning years like 2002, 1994, 1993, 1992, and 1987—is good to drink between four and 10 years old, although the wine can live for longer. Middle-weight years like 2004, 2000, 1997, 1996, and 1991 are accessible from five years old or so but have a longer ageing cycle in prospect—up to 15 or more years. Wines like the 2000 and 1997 are especially indicative of the change in texture of Hermitage compared with a few decades ago: they were easy to drink in their youth, something that would not have been possible with midweight vintages of the past like 1979, 1982, and 1986.

A couple of more tannic vintages that just miss the top grade are 1998 and 1995, the former more rich and gamey than the more mineral-toned latter. Both are capable of life for 20-plus years. The one-off 2003, with its soaking of jammy fruit and spread of high alcohol, is another vintage likely to live for over 20 years without undue difficulty.

HERMITAGE *BLANC* VINIFICATION

The rich, oily grape of Marsanne dominates white Hermitage, and growers are these days happy to accentuate its full qualities. It can be picked very ripe and is most commonly fermented in cask or a proportion of cask and vat. About the only grower who now regularly blocks its malolactic fermentation is Bernard Faurie, and there is more acceptance than in the 1970s and 1980s that even if the wine is low in acidity, its glycerol and power will see it through to a ripe and satisfying old age.

Just a few growers perform a cool decantation, leaving the juice at 10° to 12°C for up to two days; Chapoutier, Jaboulet, and Laurent Fayolle like to do this. Thereafter, the main variation is the amount of new oak used for fermentation and whether steel vats are used alongside the casks.

Those who use 75 per cent or more new oak include Belle, Guigal for his special Ex-voto, Remizières for their Émilie, Martinelles, and Gabriel Meffre. Often, there is a mix of new and young oak, as well as a combination of vat and oak. Chapoutier, for instance, combine 65 per cent vat with 35 per cent oak, or adjust it to 50-50 per cent for their main whites; their L'Ermite *blanc* is a high 80 per cent new oak fermented and raised. J-L Chave, with around 15 per cent Roussanne, favours 10 per cent steel with his oak, of which 20 to 30 per cent is new.

Reflecting on his use of 15 per cent Roussanne, Gérard Chave says, "Roussanne on its own lacks richness and can have an oxidative character without help from another variety. I like the mix with the Marsanne—you get extra complexity if you *cuisine* the two together."

With 30,000 bottles, the Cave de Tain is a front-line producer; for their white, they use one-third each new, one-year-old, and two-year-old oak and raise it for a year. Paul Jaboulet mix up 30 per cent new oak with young oak, after destemming the crop, although the new-oak proportion is rising. Their percentage of Roussanne at 35 is the highest in the *appellation* behind Ferraton's 40 per cent for the Reverdy Ermitage.

Jaboulet have moved their Chevalier de Stérimberg preparation considerably over the past couple of decades. In 1988 and 1989, new and one-year-old oak from the Jura and the Vosges Mountains was used, and the very full, glorious 1990 received a purely new oak exposure. This was in the line of many an experiment they have conducted since the 1960s. It's difficult to say whether their actions represented a bold, innovative policy or whether they were always chasing the market in order to sell the wine more easily.

Whatever the motive, Jaboulet first blocked the malolactic fermentation in 1963 and 1964; they were the first in modern times to plant large amounts of Roussanne in 1970; they turned to fermenting in stainless steel in the late 1970s; and they first used new oak in 1987. And yet, when a magnum of 1960s Chevalier de Stérimberg comes my way, as has happened, the wine is resoundingly full and fat, a delicious representative of the south—made before all these measures.

The traditionalists are growers like Marc Sorrel and Habrard: not for them the pleasures of new Allier or Tronçais casks. Their casks are five to 10 and three to four years old, respectively.

The 1990s saw a false move by several of the growers—the stirring of the lees, a Burgundian operation to extract greater richness from their Chardonnays. *Bâtonnage* became the chic thing to do during the white's raising, but the result at houses like Jaboulet left the wines flabby and similar across different *appellations*.

Now domaines have started to cut back on this practice, realising that the matter in the wine is rich in its own right, and more fragrancy and elegance can be obtained without this. Domaine Belle have abandoned it and now leave their white for 14 months on its fine lees, the Cave de Tain has cut back its *bâtonnage* to once a week, and Jaboulet thankfully have ceased doing it.

Those who stir the lees include Chapoutier, Guigal, Habrard, Remizières, Gabriel Meffre, and Tardieu-Laurent. Stylistically, most of these are houses whose style is for overtly rich, big wines with plenty of oak content. Habrard is the exception.

Most white Hermitage is bottled within the year. J-L Chave, Tardieu-Laurent, Colombo, and Guigal are the last to bottle, the first three after up to two years' raising, the last after sometimes three. Marc Sorrel's excellent *Rocoules* receives 18 months of *élevage*, but the norm is eight to 12 months.

HERMITAGE *BLANC*

"'Glycerol' is the most important word for white Hermitage," states Jean-Louis Chave; "acidity—we don't even look at that. Alcohol without glycerol would be too fiery and hot." The four Chave white-vine sites are therefore precise in the choice of soil for their vines—so they can ripen well and help to emphasize the oily aspects of this naturally rich, very long-lived, and often misunderstood wine.

When young, white Hermitage is often reticent on the bouquet; Gérard Chave talks of acacia or hazelnuts, and there are some dried white fruit and sometimes spiced connotations. But it is not an exuberant wine in the overt vein of Condrieu, for instance. It is a long-term player, and serving it at tastings to people who do not know it is a risky business—unless the wine is seven years or more old.

Albéric Mazoyer of Chapoutier is aware that their all-Marsanne white Hermitages frequently have a subdued or dumb bouquet in their first five years. "Early on they are not especially aromatic, so the wine must contain good *gras* and ample richness. That we achieve through late picking and restricted yields. Then you let the bouquet gradually come along in the bottle."

Many Marsanne-Roussanne wines pass through this "dumb" phase between about three and six years old; this sounds strange but is also observable with certain traditionally made white wines at Châteauneuf-du-Pape. One finds the colour correct—showing rich yellows—but both the bouquet and the palate fail to reveal the full extent of the aromas and the flavours, almost as if they were being held back by a magic hand. Returning to the same wine when it is seven or eight years old, one is often bowled over by its all-round appeal and complexity of taste, both elements acquired with age.

"All Marsanne wines undergo a crisis of adolescence," states the great Marsanne supporter, Michel Chapoutier. "In their youth, peach and apricot flavours are present, then the bitter side comes through between five and 10 years old, then the wine returns to a set of rich flavours."

The palate of a young Hermitage *blanc* works on a large scale. The texture should be oily and beguiling. It is not a fruit-first wine; flavours may include apricot and orange peel, but the latter often turns up in midpalate as the variety's traditional bitter side shows through when it is under 10 years old. Almonds and nuts are often apparent, along with butter and dried fruits.

On the way to old age, there unfolds an array of flavours like crème brûlée, lightly toasted nuts, and soft spices. Honey and pepper also show up as the wine ages. But the top treat is the texture—such sleek velvet, a caressing hand passed over you. It's why these traditional white wines do not need the usual chilling, and benefit from decanting to be coaxed out. A top white Hermitage drunk in its teens can be described from many different approaches—philosophi-cal, sensual, intellectual. Utterly delicious, such wines do indeed stop any conversation.

Remarkably, white Hermitage is also inclined towards big finishes; the best wines like J-L Chave, M. Sorrel's Rocoules, and some of Chapoutier's special *parcellaire* wines like L'Ermite and Le Méal can reveal chewy, almost red wine structures on the finish. Pepper accompanies some of this quasi-tannic display.

White Hermitage is credited in many books with almost the same remarkable keeping qualities as the red wine; this definitely holds true in outstanding vintages, made by traditional vinifiers like Chapoutier and Chave or by Paul Jaboulet Aîné before the mid-1960s.

For example, a 1929 white made by Gérard Chave's grandfather was astoundingly rich and still very long on the palate when drunk in the summer of 1986. Its vigour held after opening, with a warm variety of honeyed, dried fruit, and floral aromas emerging on the bouquet, and a classic white Hermitage nuttiness on the palate.

Similarly a 1961 white from Chapoutier tasted in April 1990 still held a good lustre to the eye, showed a lovely depth of nutty aroma on the nose, and on the palate possessed excellent finesse around a powerful, rich structure. The wine was still a bit closed!

The realistic length of life for a traditionally made white Hermitage is 30 years or more, and the wine's evolution over that time delivers a stream of pleasant surprises. A good move is to buy the wine in magnum to celebrate a child's birthday, and then wait for the 25th birthday—consumption of that present conducted *ensemble*, of course.

IDEAL FOODS WITH HERMITAGE *ROUGE*

Hermitage *rouge* is a wine for full flavours. When it is under 10 years old, beef is an ideal partner; JMB Sorrel recommends red meat that has been grilled or roasted. Michel Chapoutier likes a simple rib of beef with a sprinkle of pepper for the young wine.

The other obvious set of companion foods is game; birds like pheasant and partridge show well and profit from the wine's opulence, especially when it is up to 12 years old. Then its fruit is still vigorous enough to enhance any juiciness in the bird's flesh.

Bernard Faurie distinguishes between big, full vintages and more supple, lesser years. For the former, he likes red meats, pheasant, and jugged hare; for the latter, he suggests rib of beef, veal, and turkey. Michel Chapoutier thinks along similar lines, proposing partridge and pigeon for the less grandiose, more fruit-filled years. For the big 2003, his idea is a *boeuf marchand de vin*.

Jean-Louis Chave is another to distinguish by vintage style; for him, a fruit-finesse vintage like 1985 goes well with lamb, while the bigger vintages are more suited to venison.

Past 12 years old, one moves more towards fuller, denser dishes. A *daube* or beef casserole, meat stew or jugged hare are ideal. So, too, is classic rich game like venison and wild boar.

One of Gérard Chave's main dishes is his young goat, or *cabri*; this has sweetness in its flavour, and it is a wonderful companion for a Chave Hermitage *rouge* that is around 20 years old.

Jean-Louis, Gérard's son, admits that the family preference is to drink the wine nicely aged, around 15 years old. "Woodcock (*bécasse*) is our top of all dishes," he says.

Some growers prefer cheese that is not strong—so goat, creamy cheeses. Marc Sorrel likes Bleu de Bresse with his old-vine Gréal, and Tomme and Picodon also.

Specifically mentioning the 2003, with all its sweet richness, Bernard Faurie thinks black chocolate would go well—but not a cake. Chocolate courtesy of Valrhona, surely.

IDEAL FOODS WITH HERMITAGE *BLANC*

Hermitage *blanc* is a versatile wine because of its richness and its oiliness. It is less fragrant, less of a boudoir wine than the Viognier of Condrieu, for instance, and is always best drunk seated with good food.

2000 was such a fat year that the wine is delicious with Chinese food. The oiliness of the 1998s also beckons Chinese food, and a racy, luxurious combination would be to drink the Chapoutier Méal *blanc*, with its low acidity, with oriental cooking.

Michel Chapoutier loves the possibilities of mixing the Marsanne with spiced food: "Most spices come from the tannin family," he declares, "and I rate Marsanne as a great companion for spiced or fusion food—Indian or Asian, for instance." He suggests lobster, with its sweetness running well with the end bitterness of the Marsanne—"a wonderful marriage."

Vintages that are especially rich and contain very ripe grapes, such as 1999, are good not only with Asian cooking but also with rich French classics such as frogs' legs and snails in garlic.

Classic old French cuisine also accompanies white Hermitage well—using butter and cream to texture the food; wild mushroom dishes, pike or crayfish *quenelles*, *ris de veau*, or sweetbreads are all advised by Jean-Louis Chave. "It's a wine of gastronomy," he says, "ideal for traditional French cuisine with its base of butter or cream."

Because of its happy balance of power and elegance, most white Hermitage is the ideal accompaniment for chicken, veal, wild mushroom dishes, fish with heavy sauces, and very particularly, poached Scotch salmon. Here, Michel Chapoutier highlights chicken and fish in white sauces containing cream or butter. Jean-Louis Chave suggests a classic chicken from Bresse with a truffle, foie gras sauce.

And when around eight years old, Hermitage *blanc* is excellent to drink with game pâtés and *terrines*. At 10 years and older, it goes well with truffle dishes and with sweetbreads, Chave finds. Jacques Grange of Delas agrees: "I love it, at eight to 10 years, with truffles in all forms, when its mineral notes work really well."

Jean-Luc Colombo and I also share a liking for white Hermitage with black truffles—certainly its richness marches well with the pungent flavours. Colombo also likes his shell-fish, selecting scallops, crab, and lobster as good partners for the white.

Marc Sorrel suggests fish like turbot or sole in a butter or cream sauce for his rich Rocoules *blanc*. "The fish must not be too simple because otherwise the white overwhelms it," he observes. For his lower-key classic white, he proposes veal and pork.

Bernard Faurie is happy to drink his white as an aperitif up till about three years old, but also likes white fish like trout and sole.

Young Laurent Fayolle is keen on *pintadeau* —young guinea fowl in a grape sauce—and when the wine is older, foie gras.

Other dishes proposed by a range of growers include *lotte à la crème* (monkfish in a cream sauce) and lobster *beurre blanc* (lobster in a melted butter sauce).

I have found blue cheese—an English example is Shropshire blue—to draw the sting of the oak out of young, overtly oaked Hermitage; a cooler, more mineral flavour is the result. Another cheese supporter is Bernard Faurie, with his suggestions of Picodon and Tomme.

VIN DE PAILLE

Until the turn of the century another white wine was regularly made at Hermitage by ancient, painstaking methods—the Vin de Paille, which today is found in the Jura region of France, east of Burgundy, although the Hermitage growers have always possessed the right to make it. In modern times, Gérard Chave, Chapoutier, Michel Ferraton, Jean-Louis Grippat, and the Cave Co-opérative de Tain have all turned out some of this legendary wine.

Chave led the way in recent times, starting with an experiment in 1974. "We had always made a Vin de Paille," recalls Gérard, "but it was never sold commercially. In 1974 I showed it to a journalist who wrote it up, which created a demand for it, so I went and got labels and a bottle for it, which I found in Italy."

He is at pains to emphasize that it is an integral part of the history of Hermitage, and not at all part of the fashion to make wines with residual sugar or sweet textures. "It's always had its own *appellation* laws, so it isn't a curiosity," he declares. "It's a wine without norms and really against many of the rules of oenology."

For example, chez Chave it stays in cask for many years—laissez-faire rules. The 1996 was bottled in July 2002: "It was fermenting all that time; the cask chosen had been used for the white wine of the vintage, and so had some yeasts left in it," recalls Gérard. The 1997 remained in the oak until bottling in the winter of 2004, for instance. And its level of volatile acidity is also higher than that of the regular dry wine—around 0.9 to 1.0 gm per litre as opposed to 0.4 to 0.5 gm per litre. "You also don't need to sterile filter it before bottling," says Jean-Louis, with a deadpan face.

The Chave family has always made its Vin de Paille the same way and always with the same "infinite longevity." Gérard once drank an 1860 with Marc Chapoutier, grandfather of Michel, "and it was still formidable—a completely brown colour and extraordinary aromas."

Gérard recalls how events took place in 1974. "I had been thinking of trying this experiment for several years, and eventually selected the 1974 crop. I didn't leave the grapes on the vines particularly late, choosing to pick them at the end of normal harvesting. I then separated them one by one and laid them out individually on straw on the floor of the attic above the *cuverie*, or vatting room; I used the straw that ties up the vines against their support stakes in the vineyards.

"The grapes stayed in the attic for a month and a half, and I was careful not to let them dry out since this would have robbed them of their remaining concentrated juice. I remember that my parents always used to give us dried raisins on Christmas Day, having let the grapes completely dry out. Anyway, I then pressed the grapes and started off the fermentation. Normally I estimate that to make a bottle of my white Hermitage I need to use 1.3 kilograms of grapes; with the Vin de Paille I needed four kilograms for each bottle.

"The straw wine fermented in cask on and off for two years. I did no racking during this drawn-out fermentation, mainly because the must was entirely clean—the grapes had been especially healthy at the time of pressing so that there seemed no need to disturb the wine. Once the malo had taken place, I bottled the wine, and here it is."

Chave takes his grapes from old vines on *L'Hermite* and, because of that old, somewhat random plantation, has a little Roussanne mixed in. *L'Hermite* is also the source for Chapoutier's Marsanne, which grows on what the firm calls its *Chante-Alouette* subset, on the eastern end of the *climat*, where the soil is poor loess.

Chapoutier are careful not to let their crop ripen so far that rot sets in; "we're looking for a *passerillage* effect, not botrytis," states Michel Chapoutier. "That means dried grapes, but healthy ones." They also dry the grapes for the statutory minimum of 45 days, and ferment in new oak, leaving the wine for two to three years. The end wine averages 150 gm per litre of residual sugar, with an extreme of 170 gm in the very ripe, low-acidity year of 1997. 2,000 to 3,000 half bottles are made, against Chave's 900 to 1,000.

The Cave de Tain first produced a Vin de Paille in 1985, one they call "Gambert de Loche." This averages 900 50-cl bottles a year—two casks' worth—although the 1995 crop was so fine that nearly 2,000 half bottles were made in that year. It is produced in 80 per cent of the vintages, providing the crop is up to scratch: that ruled out 1992, 1993, and 2002, for instance.

The grapes come from a very old plot on *Méal*, where around half the Marsanne is thought to date from the 1880s and 1890s—in other words a postphylloxera plantation. They are picked and left open to the air for up to two months while they dry, and around 2 kg are needed to make 50 cl.

In the first years, the Cave harvested late but now picks the grapes at the same time as those serving for the dry wine, in order to preserve their health. The grapes are kept at the Gambert de Loche domaine in slatted wooden fruit boxes. "We tried straw and we tried hanging them up, but the wooden boxes are the best way to dry them," states the experienced vineyard manager, Daniel Brissot. Pressing is in late November.

The juice is fermented and raised in one-to-two-year-old casks for up to two years. The final wine can carry 80 gm of residual sugar in a cooler vintage like 1996, or 120 or 130 gm in a boiling vintage like 2003, making the latter wine come out around 18°. Often there are flavours of quince in this interesting wine, which is capable of outliving most of us.

One observation made by the now retired Jean-Louis Grippat, who vinified five vintages of Vin de Paille between 1985 and 1997, was an unusual one: "I found that the malolactic fermentation was done inside the grapes, on an intracellular basis, while they were drying out—something I hadn't considered." His wine's residual sugar level was around the 90-gm-per-litre mark.

When drunk in 1982, the Chave 1974 presented a lustrous dark gold *robe*, with a soaring bouquet of concentrated richness, the aromas most reminiscent of flowers and honey. Then the surprise—the incredible richness continued on to the palate and through to the aftertaste, but left a crystal-clear, bitingly clean finish. The flavours—similar to honey and fresh fruit jams, such was the concentration—ended with a winning dryness. There was no sense of the alcohol degree of 14.5°.

The nuttiness of the Marsanne is often found in the Vin de Paille, with greengage, dried fruits, honey, and some spiciness. Apricot and the flan side of the Marsanne are also often present. It is a wine of marvellous variety of both aroma and flavour.

The Vin de Paille is usually drunk as an aperitif, of such deep-seated complexity of flavour and lasting grace that it is a sipping wine. Indeed, the Co-opérative's informal title for it is "our Wine of Meditation"—so choose a good view. I would also drink it with spiced food.

After a meal the Vin de Paille can replace a cognac, according to some, and chocolate and bitter orange desserts are also recommended.

Probably the oldest bottles of Hermitage still in existence are of Vin de Paille. The Chapoutier family of Tain have an 1848 Vin de Paille, decanted in 1910, 1948, and 1977, in their personal cellar, while M. Max Chapoutier, the former head of the family firm, once recalled that until only quite recently, they had two even older bottles. Producing from the sideboard of the company's reception room a thickly blown old bottle with a faint, blurred label saying "Hermitage 1760," he related the following story.

"This bottle of Hermitage Vin de Paille was drunk by my father, Marc, in 1964. There were two other bottles of this wine, but in the late 1970s they were given back to the Cambourg family, who had originally made the wine, and they have since been drunk. The bottles had certainly moved around, as we had earlier given them to the Sizeranne family after buying a leading Hermitage vineyard from them some years ago. When my father drank this particular bottle, the wine, whose degree was around 17°, was in an impeccable state, showing plenty of full-bodied flavour, even though there was a little ullage."

THE PRODUCERS

DOMAINE BELLE

Les Marsuriaux 26600 Larnage +33(0)475 082458

See also Crozes-Hermitage, St-Joseph. The Belles have 1.5 hectares at Hermitage. The one hectare of Syrah is made up of 0.67 ha on *Murets*, 0.35 ha on *Diognières*. The half hectare of white is on *Diognières*, 75 per cent Marsanne and 25 per cent Roussanne. The vineyard is partly a family heirloom, mostly from the 1971 purchase

of the vineyard of the local grandee proprietor de Boissieux.

For the red, whole-bunch fermentation starts after a cool maceration and lasts a total of about four weeks in concrete, with temperature allowed to run to about 33°C, in pursuit of colour. It is aged for 22 months in 60 percent new, 40 percent one-year-old oak. It is a charming wine with a silken power inside it—capable of a very pretty flourish once aged for seven years or more. The finesse of *Murets* Syrah dating from the 1960s comes through clearly here.

The white is cask fermented in 75 per cent new, 25 per cent one-year-old oak, at 20°C. Albert feels the white varieties are specially suited to oak: "In many ways, I think they can take new oak in their stride more than the Syrah; I also feel the whites can age with more stability and continuity than the reds."

The white is raised in the oak for 14 months, and bottled after 18 months. Lees stirring has been stopped—the wine is now allowed to lie quietly. The white is a firmly styled wine that does not do itself justice if drunk young. It becomes more complete after around six years.

HERMITAGE ROUGE

2002 ★★ Coffee, brewed fruit bouquet, quite dense and meaty. Sinewed black fruit with a cool side, has some flesh, attacks well. Bit burnt at the end, some oak there. Fair length. From 2007; 2014–15.

2001 (CASK) ★★★★ Toasted, olive, suave fruit aroma; *Murets* finesse on attack, good ripe juice, length good, some end oak. From 2008; 2016–18.

2000 ★★★★ Toasted black fruit/oak nose, will be copious. Stylish, tasty black fruit, is full, authentic, juicy wine. Tannins/length good. Will open well. From 2007–08; 2015–18.

HERMITAGE BLANC

2002 (CASK) ★★ Buttery, compact nose; tight-knit, quite obvious richness, solid in its way. Good content, esp from 2008; 2014–15.

2001 ★★★ Light oak/honey aroma; pineapple, firm, has elegant matter within. Some nut, oak on top. Length OK. From 2007; 2015–17.

LOUIS BERNARD

Route de Sérignan 84100 Orange +33(0)490 118686

See also Cornas, Côte-Rôtie, Crozes-Hermitage, St-Joseph, St-Péray.
The Louis Bernard *négociant* business provides a red Hermitage. The crop receives a three-to-four-week vinification, with pumping-overs and *délestages*. The young wine is aged for eight months in cask.

HERMITAGE ROUGE

2002 (★) Full red *robe*; simmered ripe fruit aroma. Some flesh present, stewed berries. Some tannin. Fruit not very fresh, may tire early, seems a bit oxidative. Balance? 2009–10.

2000 ★ *Robe* is dull early on. Pebbly, dry-toned bouquet, lacks warm fruit. Dry texture straight off; some width in middle, tightens again on finish. Rather anxious, dry tendency. From 2005–06; 2010–12.

DOMAINE BERNARD ET GILLES BIED

Les Malfondières 26600 Mercurol +33(0)475 074447

See also Crozes-Hermitage.
The Bied family have 1.5 hectares of Syrah on *Varogne*, the intensely granite outcrop at the extreme west end of the Hermitage hill. There is a little limestone as well on the slippery soil. The oldest vines date from the 1940s.

Whole bunches are vinified in concrete for 12 days, with *remontages*. The wine is raised in used casks for 15 to 18 months. It is passable at times, risking dryness often. Less time in cask or the use of younger wood might help.

LAURENT CHARLES BROTTE

Le Clos rte d'Avignon 84230 Châteauneuf-du-Pape +33(0)490 837007

See also Condrieu, Cornas, Côte-Rôtie, Crozes-Hermitage, St-Joseph.

The Châteauneuf-du-Pape merchant selects carefully made wines from the northern Rhône, and is a reliable source. The crop is destemmed and fermented and macerated for three weeks in steel, the temperature held to 28° to 30°C. The young wine is aged for a year in large barrels of 50 hl.

HERMITAGE ROUGE

2000 ★ Clean, stewed fruit gums aroma, some earthiness also; decent midweight fruit, though has a stewed, reductive side. Fair length, shows refinement more than power and brio. Midrange Hermitage. 2009–12.

HERMITAGE BLANC

2002 ★ Discreet, harmonious, bonbon bouquet. Soft texture, some apricot/white fruit, degree of matter. Tidy; toasted end, flan/crème caramel aftertaste. Esp 2006. Not that long.

M. CHAPOUTIER

18 ave Dr Paul Durand 26600 Tain-l'Hermitage +33(0)475 089261

See also Condrieu, Cornas, Côte-Rôtie, Crozes-Hermitage, St-Joseph, St-Péray.
The 1990s were very important for Chapoutier. Let the wine do the talking, is the best way to handle rumours and domestic "events." Was the firm in a partnership with interests from the Loire or Australia? What exactly were the ownership structures for a plethora of new vineyards—in southwest France, the fringe of the Rhône, Australia?

What about the biodynamic noise being made—just how well looked-after were the vineyards? And what about the sudden departure in the late 1990s of Marc Chapoutier, Michel's brother, to the West Indies and thence back to France, where he now sells dietary products?

Beyond all the background music, Chapoutier moved on to a higher level of quality than had been the norm during the 1970s and 1980s. For an old family firm, this is a marked achievement, with Michel taking the lead of his doughty grandfather Marc, a man who had resolutely continued to be involved in the business until his death in 2000. Marc lived in the imposing *maison bourgeoise* called "La Ciboise" looking out on Tain's Place de la Taurobole and was a survivor of many rigours during the Second World War, including the arrest of his wife by Klaus Barbie and his torturers in Lyon. He ran the firm from 1937 until 1977, and his son Max was head from 1977 until 1990, when he retired due to ill health.

Now Chapoutier are making excellent, very authentic Rhône whites—streets ahead of any rivals of a similar size, indeed benchmark quality a lot of the time. Michel's backing of the Marsanne grape has never wavered and has allowed a true local expression to be sustained across the lesser *appellations* as well as the Great Hermitages.

The reds have grown up, too. In the early to mid-1990s there was often too much extraction, with too many wines tasting similar. Now they are usually more stylish and more nuanced, with a greater chance of expressing their place, or *terroir*. For many, it's as if they are more relaxed, more grown-up. The top range mixes finesse and power extremely well, although there, ironically, the danger of extraction, no doubt to please high-flying customers, rears up on occasion.

The challenge that remains is that of turning out genuine, good-quality, local-feel wines in volume, and not just excellent garage-style wines in lots of 3,000 bottles at a time. There are signs of this in some years with the Crozes Meysonniers, and may that trend widen.

Explaining the moves at the end of the 1980s, Michel says, "In 1989–90 I wanted to make more intense wines and to avoid the dilution that had beset us before then. In the following years, I wanted to go for finesse. Now I find too much obsession with extraction—it's so easy to achieve, too. If all the impression you get of a wine comes along in the first two seconds, you know it's not marriage but a passing passion."

Michel is a short man with punchy views that are expressed in classic French idioms. It doesn't take much to get him started, and he is happy to air his opinions. A Rhône merchant of the new-generation boutique operation "should be denounced" because he has clearly never set foot in the vineyards. France divides into two civilisations for wine: on the one hand, the group of Alsace, Burgundy, and the Rhône—"*paysans* who live off the soil"; and on the other, Bordeaux and Champagne—"wine is an amusement; they do not have personal contact with the *terroir*. The former group is more convivial, too," he states with conviction.

On to his biodynamic outlook, where he has benefited from his contacts with Nicolas Joly of Savennières and Lalou Bize of Domaine Leroy in Burgundy. "The soil must be apt to bring the complexity into the wine; the more bacteria and wild yeasts in the vineyard, the less you need to grow different vine varieties. You mustn't destroy bacteria in the vineyard—they are its mother. So you must apply your compost early in the winter cycle so it can be well assimilated, to avoid too much buildup of nitrogen and potassium, which are the precursors of illness like mildew and oïdium. The biodynamic approach allows you to multiply bacteria by the million and they can transfer the mineral into the vegetal."

"I'm very in favour of polyculture," he continues. "The land and its subsystem need these different activities. The Rhône has to a degree maintained its tree and fruit culture, unlike Bordeaux, which is purely *vinicole* now. A lot of plant illnesses come from having just the one activity. My Ardèche roots I feel; the Ardechois are interesting people. This isn't a travelling area—people don't move around like they do across plains. The mountains stop that—they're rough territory—so the people are obliged to respect their soil, and not to make mistakes and be too sweeping in their actions."

Michel practises this himself; he has some ducks, chickens, guinea fowl, sheep, and walnut trees. Sixty to 70 eggs come into the office and cellars a day! He raises his own lamb on his hill farm above St-Vallier and also marks down the vintage on all his sardines, honey, and mustards—yes, indeed.

Another one of Michel's high-profile and very sensible moves was to put Braille on the Chapoutier labels in 1995. Michel recalls that one mistake was observed after about four years by a blind visitor: "He told me one white wine label said 'red wine' instead of 'white wine'!"

One of the discreet but potent influences chez Chapoutier has come from Albéric Mazoyer, one of many children of an *agriculteur* from the Ardèche, the same west-bank region as the Chapoutiers. His father died suddenly when he was a young man, and he spent 10 years doing all sorts of work at Grenoble to be able to live, as well as having a mixed farm of fruit, cows, and vines in the Ardèche near Alba.

"I was always stimulated by understanding the level of connection between plants, soil, animals, and man—everything to do with biodynamic principles," he explains. Gradually he moved into wine full-time, and after working with Jean-Luc Colombo from 1989 to 1994, he joined Chapoutier in January 1995. A tall, willowy man, he is one of life's Seekers, and his thinking allied with that of Michel Chapoutier drives the philosophy of the Chapoutier house. His official role is technical director.

All the French Chapoutier vineyards have therefore been worked biodynamically since 1995; this goes beyond straight organic approaches into a more declared philosophy of active soil applications and a year's calendar linked to lunar phases. Nourishment of the soil is central to this thinking, with the distribution of minerals to help it. Rudolph Steiner, the Austrian thinker, was at the heart of this outlook. Some of his schools and homes for the disabled can be found in many countries of the world.

Another powerful influence is Frenchman Claude Bourguignon, whose credo is that the agricultural world must now cultivate the soil without eroding it and must better understand the linkage between soil, plants, microbes, animals, and mankind. Reflecting on Bourguignon's work and his writing, and the wide discussion it releases, Michel states, "To cultivate is the first act of gastronomy," a very Chapoutierian observation.

On resting or idle plots at St-Joseph, Cornas, Condrieu, and St-Péray, Chapoutier have planted wheat as a prelude to putting in the vines. This is a simple method of soil nourishment. The firm's practices are not to everyone's taste, however, and I have walked on their *Côte Brune* holding at Côte-Rôtie and observed a number of dead vines and non-fruit-bearing vines on what looks like an overgrown plot. Perhaps the local workforce there needs some stirring up.

Chapoutier also have two horses for vineyard work—especially in vineyards planted on a one-metre-square basis. They can be used on the intermediate slopes, with a small tractor for the wider plantations. On the top slopes the work is manual.

Chapoutier's Hermitage possessions are glittering and reflect just how long the family has been present in Tain—the longest of all today's wine houses. The story goes that the first Chapoutier came down to the Rhône from a village up in the Ardèche sometime before the French Revolution, and worked his way up from the position of simple *caviste* at a firm called Vogelgesang until he was in a position, with a partner named Delépine, to buy out Vogelgesang in 1808: shades of the Guigal story with Vidal-Fleury from the 1980s.

Twenty-six hectares of Hermitage are owned, and a further 5.5 hectares worked under internal family rentals. The 19.5 hectares of Syrah vineyards are imposing: on *Bessards—Grands* and *Petits—*Chapoutier have nine hectares; on *Méal* there are three hectares; on *L'Hermite*, just behind the chapel, they have 3.3 hectares; and on *Greffieux* 2.7 hectares. The Syrah on the full slopes of *Méal* and *Bessards* ranges from the 1950s back to the start of the twentieth century; the youngest plot is a hectare on *Bessards* planted in 1979–80. The *Greffieux* Syrah dates from the late 1940s, with just half a hectare dating from 1979–80. Two of the smallest Syrah plots are a tiny patch of 0.1 hectare on *Murets*, acquired in 2004, and a small amount on *Beaume*.

The white-wine portfolio of 12 hectares is geared around old Marsanne—not a trace of

Roussanne in sight. On *Chante-Alouette*, which is, strictly speaking, the east part of *L'Hermite*, there are 3.6 ha of Marsanne dating from the 1960s and earlier. Its loess and limestone influences are considered ideal for the Marsanne.

Elsewhere on *L'Hermite* there is 0.7 ha of up to 100-year-old Marsanne, vines that give cuttings for new plantations. There are also two hectares on *Méal* (1940s and older) and a plot on *Beaume* (1950s, 1960s), and on *Murets*, there are 4.8 ha (1918–1920s, 1960s). The high slopes here are the source for the Cuvée de l'Orée, the lower part of the *climat* gives Marsanne for the Chante-Alouette wine.

Central to the house policy is late picking. Grapes are expected to express their maximum potential. In the cellars there are seven 100-hectolitre open wood vats for the Hermitage and Crozes reds; the crop is destalked, and since 1997 there has been an automatic *pigeage,* or punching the cap, system, which runs on rails above the large wooden tuns that are 2.50 metres high. "No person's foot could get very far down," observes Albéric Mazoyer wrily. This system gets to within 40 cm (16 in.) of the bottom of the wood vats and alleviates the need for pumping-overs.

No cultured yeasts are applied, and a long, four-to-six-week maceration is favoured, the temperature kept at 30° to 32°C. There is just one *remontage* (pumping-over) at the outset. The wines vinified in their concrete vats— St-Joseph, the Crozes Meysonniers, and the Châteauneuf-du-Pape Bernardine—receive one or two *délestages*, or partial emptying and refilling of the vats.

The red Hermitage Monier de la Sizeranne is the workhorse wine, the one that achieves distribution in some numbers around the world, given its annual production of 29,000 bottles since the 2001 vintage (down from 35,000 once its *Greffieux* content was bottled apart). It is made from the house's own crop, mainly off *Bessards*, with some *Greffieux* and a little *Méal*. Its cask ageing runs for 18 to 20 months, the oak one-third each new, one year, and two years old.

For many years M. de la Sizeranne was the flag bearer for Chapoutier. It has never held the limelight like La Chapelle for Paul Jaboulet, and now it's four or five times less expensive than the Specific Plot wines, which in ascending order of price are Les Greffieux and Le Pavillon (2001 vintage retail price in Tain €126/£83/US$150), Le Méal (€143/£94/US$170), and L'Ermite (€147/£97/US$175). All are termed "Ermitage" on the label.

The original Big Three reds from the specific plots are Le Pavillon, Le Méal, and L'Ermite. They were introduced in 1989 and 1996 for the last two, with Les Greffieux coming onstream from 2001. Before 1989 Pavillon had been a blend of wines of 15 to 20 years old. The first trio was probably aimed as Hermitage's riposte to Guigal's Côte-Rôtie Trio of Turque, Mouline, and Landonne. On average, there are 7,000 bottles of Le Pavillon, 5,000 bottles each of Le Méal and L'Ermite, and 3,000 bottles of Greffieux.

The single-plot red wines also receive a long, four-to-six-week maceration after destemming —four weeks in 2003, six weeks in 2001, for instance. They are aged for 14 to 18 months in 40 to 50 per cent new-oak casks, the rest one to two years old. The 2000s were kept for longer than usual—the wines bottled in September 2002, after four months of extra cask raising; by contrast, the soft 1997s were bottled in February 1999. None of the Chapoutier reds has been filtered or fined since the 1989 vintage.

The Pavillon is drawn from Syrah planted just after the First World War above and below the Chapoutier sign on the lower east end of *Bessards*, in the middle of the slope just as it starts to rise steeply. There is a narrow band of limestone one and a half metres down here, which is said to add finesse. There is a little pavilion here, but it is in a ramshackle state and is to be restored to some glory.

The Syrah used in the Méal dates from the 1940s and older, up to around 80 years. "We can never be quite sure how old the vines really are," comments Michel; "you have to remember that nothing was planted between 1936 and 1944 here, so there is a gap in the vineyard's chronology." The Syrah for L'Ermite dates from the early twentieth century, while for Greffieux the vines date from the 1940s.

The first ploy with these special and very expensive wines is a very low harvest yield of around 15 hl/ha. Taking the excellent 1999 vintage as a vehicle for comparison, the Méal has the most open bouquet of black fruits; it shows raspberry and chocolate flavours, the fruits are often red, while the oak on the end is noticeable. Its fruit is often more red than the Pavillon's black fruitiness. This tallies precisely with the nature of the fruit that is commonplace from the *climats* of Méal and *Bessards*.

The Pavillon carries a pungent bouquet, reminiscent of soil, with leathery tones. The palate is densely packed, more closed than Méal, with vigorous black berries, plus good length and end richness. It is a typical child of the *Bessards* granite.

The L'Ermite red is always more closed and austere than Le Méal and needs longer to open up. It reflects the very poor, sandy nature of *L'Hermite*'s soil and its higher environment as well. L'Ermite's bouquet is lighter and grainier and is the most delicate of the three.

On the palate, L'Ermite is discreet and, while reserved, has *so* much to offer—plenty of quince tones, with good sinew. There is a penetrating potential. In 1999 it was the best of the three: the Pavillon was like the ebullient Playboy making a noise, and the Méal followed its usual pattern of being the most precocious of the three in its ripening, as well.

Tasting the special *parcellaire* wines together also reveals how well the work on the tannins is going. All the wines have very correct tannins, their length entirely appropriate to them, their integration a successful achievement. Only properly ripe grapes whose picking has been accurately timed can produce this quality. It's not a question of playing catch-up in the cellar afterwards to introduce tannin, be it from oak or pill—something that too many young growers succumb to these days.

The Pavillon tannins are tighter and more enclosed than those in the Méal, where the tex-

ture turns to a softer jam. Meanwhile Greffieux accentuates elegance and rather more flirtatious tannins. The L'Ermite tannins are suave and refined, nestling well into the core texture.

Since 1999 there has been a Hermitage *rouge* from younger vines called "Mure de Larnage." This comes from vines of under 25 years old, on sites like *Greffieux, Beaume,* and the bottom or *bas des Bessards*. Up to 4,000 bottles are produced.

Chapoutier is the House of Marsanne when it comes to their whites. They have wonderful old vines in great spots, so this often underestimated grape can show its qualities. The house plays to the grape's strengths, too, with a late picking and a vinification that brings to the fore its oily, ripe white-fruit qualities.

At the start of the 1990s it was fashionable for New Wave wine writers to snipe at grapes like this, as they became bemused by faddish, low-temperature white wine vinifications. Now these rich, nuts, cheese, and fruit combinations are allowed their place again at the top table, and Chapoutier have to be thanked for their good work on the Marsanne at Hermitage and St-Joseph.

The equivalent of the Sizeranne red, the Chante-Alouette white has been Chapoutier's standard bearer for white Hermitage for well over 60 years. There was a simple liquor shop near the Vieux Port in Marseille with a cache of forgotten, top-shelf wines in the early 1970s. Among its lurking treasures were Chante-Alouettes of 1947, 1952, and 1953—all affordable on a student wage and all still marvellous decades later. This has been a rock-solid wine, one that evokes the old glories of long-lived Hermitage in full measure.

The wine is mostly from the vineyards on the *Chante-Alouette climat*—on the map a part of *L'Hermite*—with a part from the low slopes of *Les Murets.* There are pockets of clay here, with loess blown in by the wind higher up the hill. The youngest vines date from the 1960s.

Chante-Alouette is vinified two-thirds in vat, one-third in oak, the casks since 2000 purely the 550-litre *demi-muid* size—33 per cent new, the rest two to three years old. The temperature is held at 18° to 20°C. Ageing continues half in vat and cask and lasts for around 10 months. The malolactic is always completed, and around 20,000 bottles are produced.

In the early 1990s—1992 and 1993 for example, admittedly not great years—Chante-Alouette was a little sanitised and lacked its current stuffing. It may have been affected by the start-up in 1991 of the special Cuvée de l'Orée, whose old-vine crop used to be part of it. It has also taken the hit of its L'Ermite special wine crop being absent since 1999. But it trucks along nevertheless. In its youth it now carries more elegance than formerly, but it's always been very reserved when young, and tasters may often underrate its ability to blossom and live on. Like all good Hermitage, it demands patience and will rarely give a proper inkling of its quality until eight-plus years old.

There are three special whites beyond Chante-Alouette. Le Méal (5,500 bottles) is the most spiced and can be extremely rich right to the finish. The de l'Orée (7,000-plus bottles) is the most full-on and opulent, with always a flattering attack that brings immediate, sensuous pleasure. L'Ermite (1,800 bottles) is powerful with also a mineral side to it; it is the most complex of the three, indeed the best wine. These sell for dizzy prices. For the 2001s, the Méal *blanc* retailed in Tain for €139/£92/US$165, the de l'Orée for €100/£66/US$119, and L'Ermite *blanc* for €186/£123/US$221!

For all three, the crop is deliberately left until it has achieved a virtual overripeness, or *surmaturité*. "This helps to overcome too overt a declaration of the grape's bitterness," says Albéric Mazoyer, "but it's a fine judgment to avoid too flat or heavy a taste."

After a cool decanting at 12°C, the *Méal* and *de l'Orée* are vinified half in oak, half in small stainless steel vats at a temperature of 18° to 20°C. The casks are 550-litre *demi-muids*, half of them new, the remainder up to three years old. L'Ermite (1,600–2,400 bottles) receives more new oak—80 per cent—with 20 per cent one year old.

Since 2000 only this 550-litre cask size has been used, replacing some of the 228-litre casks. "The wine oxidises less in these larger containers," explains Albéric Mazoyer; "they also make our work on the lees easier, the wines lose their gas less, and there is a softer wood effect on them."

The young wine of all three cuvées stays on its lees through the winter, the oak portion receiving lees stirring, and can ferment quietly at 18° to 20°C until Christmas. The vat side of Méal and de l'Orée receives a few small pumping-overs but is left a long time on its fine lees. All three are quietly raised for 10 to 12 months before bottling before or just after the next harvest.

The de l'Orée was first made in 1991 in its current vintage and site-specific form; in the 1980s, it was called "Cuvée de l'Orée" and represented a blend of five or six vintages, average age around 12 years. It is made from Marsanne planted around 1918 and cropped off *Les Murets*. It is a voluptuous wine, full and warm, with some dry tones on the finish and an oak influence discreetly present when young. With its flan and fruit pie aspects, it is more overtly full than Le Méal *blanc*. This can accompany classic fish like turbot, simply presented.

Le Méal *blanc* comes from vines at the very top of the Méal slope and was launched in 1997; the vineyard dates from the 1950s, so there are a few Roussanne plants mixed in with the Marsanne. This is a determinedly full wine, often with at least 14° alcohol and a couple of grams of residual sugar. It shows more spice and pepper touches than de l'Orée and is less open when young. It works well with fish in sauce, the sauce nicely creamy and rich.

L'Ermite *blanc* was first made in 1999 from 1920s and 1930s Marsanne, on *Chante-Alouette*, aka *L'Hermite*. The elegance of this wine is exemplary in a vintage like 1999, and its length and grip appeal, too. Showing signs of extreme ripeness, it is a wine to tuck away and let patience and time weave their magic, with fireworks possible at 10 to 15 years old. With some interesting acidity at times, L'Ermite *blanc* goes well with fish in a spiced sauce or any foie gras dish.

In 1999 a younger-vines white wine, the Mure de Larnage, was introduced, a pure Marsanne made from plants up to twenty-five years old. Its sources are *Greffieux*, the *bas des Bessards* and *Beaume*. Up to 2,700 bottles are made.

Chapoutier is one of the three main producers of Hermitage's long-lived white, the Vin de Paille. This is made from a main crop picking, where the grapes are left to dry out and become *passerillés*, with no botrytis in them, therefore. "We have to avoid botrytis at all costs," states Michel Chapoutier; "otherwise there is a mouldy taste in the wine." The bunches are usually taken from *L'Hermite*, including what Chapoutier call its *Chante-Alouette* section, with the best specimens chosen.

A minimum of 45 days of drying follows before pressing and a slow fermentation in new oak. The wine stays in cask for at least two, and up to three, years. In its final form, the Vin de Paille averages 150 gm per litre of residual sugar, its alcohol 14° to 14.5°. A really sunny year like 1997, with long hot nights, produced a wine with 170 gm of residual sugar.

The Vin de Paille is made every year, except when conditions are too bad such as in 1992 and 1993. 2,000 to 3,000 bottles of 37.5 cl are made each year, and are really collectors' items, since they retail in Tain at over US$100 each.

This expresses the surprising elegance of which the Marsanne is capable, especially when prepared in this way. The palate is more varied and expressive than the bouquet, with honey and dried fruits, and also light spice present as the wine ages; a long, clean, and tapering finish rounds it off well. It is capable of 25 years of life and considerably more in the greatest years.

Chapoutier have always produced their own *eau de vie* and grape marc brandy—very correct after-dinner drinks. In 1994 they actually bought the still on wheels from the man who used to rent it to them, and there is more control on the distillation as a result. Each *appella-*

tion's marc has been separately stilled since 1996, then aged for a minimum of 10 years.

The other northern Rhône vineyards, with the obvious exception of single owner Château-Grillet, are also well represented by Chapoutier. Their Crozes red Meysonniers has made progress recently, as have the two white Crozes-Hermitages, while there are impressive reds and whites in the shape of the special wines from Crozes-Hermitage and St-Joseph, namely Les Varonniers and the Les Granits red and white from the latter *appellation*.

With bold enterprise, the Chapoutier empire has grown way beyond the Rhône since the late 1980s. For years Michel's great-grandfather Marius would chunter about stooping to sell *vin ordinaire* after the 1930s purchase of the Domaine de la Bernadine at Châteauneuf-du-Pape; now Michel has a series of interests all over the world.

In the southern Rhône, the 62-hectare Domaine des Estubiers in the Coteaux du Tricastin, set in stony, fluvioglacial land, produces a red called La Ciboise, made from 75 per cent Grenache, 25 per cent Syrah; a special red cuvée called Château des Estubiers; and a Ciboise *blanc*.

Elsewhere in France, there are 14 hectares planted at Banyuls, near the sea and the inland valleys; this produces both a Banyuls from different sites, as well as a site-specific wine called "Terra Vinya." In the Côtes du Roussillon Villages, the Domaine de Bila-Haut runs over 70 hectares, with 10 planted in vineyards.

Michel is prone to excitement, and this emotion is in ample supply when he discusses the recent development in his home area of the Ardèche. Having planted 18 hectares of Viognier, with a *vin de pays des Coteaux de l'Ardèche* launched in 2001, the firm has also grown a variety of Swiss Valais origin, the Petite Arvine. "This is only grown outside Switzerland in the Piedmont," says Michel, "and we find the wine is full of minerality, with an iodine side to it as well."

The domaine is on volcanic residues with an underpinning of limestone and marl, at 350 metres. There is clay with basalt stones, and Michel calls it "a *terroir* for white wine." There is a dry Viognier and also a Vin de Paille–style wine called "Coufis de Paille" made from Viognier, bottled two to three years after harvesting and drying of the crop; 3,000 bottles of 50 cl each are produced.

Michel is also very fired up by his Australian joint ventures. One is at Mount Benson on the limestone Coast, where 35 hectares have been planted out of a possible 50. Syrah, Marsanne, Viognier, and Cabernet Sauvignon feature here on red sandy soil. The intention has been to avoid outright clay plots and so achieve wine of greater elegance and minerality than usually found off the clay. The Syrah was launched in 1998, and the domaine is set to become biodynamic.

Michel is also in partnership with Ron Laughton, owner of the Jasper Hill winery. Its wine is made half from Australian Shiraz planted in 1998, half from Rhône Syrah, planted in 2004. "We'll be able to compare how the two different sources of the same variety get on," says Michel. Forty hectares of land were bought in 1997, and now over 10 are planted in the Heathcote region of Central Victoria, including some Viognier. Called Cambrian Pty, the enterprise does not irrigate and relies on the deep red-clay soil to aliment itself.

Chapoutier have a third Australian business set up in 2000, jointly with their USA distributor Paterno and Mount Langi Ghiran. This is a project in the rolling-slope Pyrenees region of Western Victoria, where the soil is strong in clay with some pebble stones as well.

HERMITAGE MURE DE LARNAGE ROUGE

2000 ★ Quite peppery, wild fruit nose, some fat. Straight hedgerow red fruit attack; chewy towards finish, but dries there. 2008–11.

HERMITAGE MONIER DE LA SIZERANNE ROUGE

2003 (CASK) ★★★ Some pretty black fruit aromas, peppery edging. Prune, black fruits attack, with reserve. Savoury texture, oaked aftertaste; oak needs to integrate. Some end heat. From 2008; 2020–22.

2002 (CASK) ★★ Some stone fruit/spice, reserved aroma; tasty, bit sweet, blackberry fruit. Not very long, oak at finish. 12 years.

2001 ★★★★ Warm, ripe fruit/leather, has lost its burnt/reduction side; good sap, soaked black fruit, leather/licorice end. Honest; sound length, open early. 2017–20.

2000 ★★★ Chunky, oily, solid, spiced nose; firm, clear flavour, midweight, tannins OK. Fair, not esp striking. 2014–17.

1999 ★★★ Quite dark red; bits of pine, red fruit, raspberry aroma, quite direct. Three-quarter-weight wine, not showing a lot on the attack, decent grip of red fruits and licorice on the end. Stylish, can come along, has charm. 2015–19.

1998 ★★★ Fungal side to the bouquet, bit reduced; airing brings black fruit, pine, mint, quite potent though still reduced. Typical Hermitage aromas. Savoury wine, big flavours, warm fruit, spiced attachments. Decent fullness, good end matter, raspberries. From 2004; 2011–16.

1996 ★★ 2010–12
1995 ★★★ 2010–13
1994 ★★★ 2012–15
1993 ★(★) 2007–10
1991 ★★★ 2007–11
1990 ★★★★★ 2015–18

ERMITAGE LES GREFFIEUX ROUGE

2003 (CASK) ★★★ Hidden bouquet, some red berry. Dry-tinged black fruit, has the chocolate style aftertaste of the year. Oak finale. Good palate, can develop. From 2008; 2020–23.

2002 ★★ Black fruit aroma, quietly done, touch smoky. Quite well-knit palate, dark fruits; the oak makes it upright, leaves aftertaste dry. Touch extracted. Should grow into the oak that has gained ground in last year. Esp from 2006–07; 2014–16. Last tasted Dec. 2004.

2001 (CASK) ★★★★ Raspberry liqueur, white truffle nose; tasty red berries, fruit sparkles. Suave, with content. Elegant; nice length, lots of pleasure. From 2005–06; 2016–20.

ERMITAGE LE MÉAL ROUGE

2003 (CASK) ★★(★) Very dark; big, packed bouquet—ripe fruits, prunes. Dark flavours, a powerful, enforcer wine. Notably ripe fruit with pepper extras. Broad finish. Extraction wine. Dry leaning now. From 2008; 2022–24.

2002 ★★(★) Closed bouquet, some potential but a bit dusty, subdued red fruits—was taut. Midweight attack, with some tannic structure around it. Red fruits, some spice. Reserved but elegant, quite pretty wine. Length OK, just lacks real follow-on. Has softened quite fast. From 2006; 2013–15. Last tasted Dec. 2004.

2001 (CASK) ★★★★ Roasted, leather/smoke aroma; corpulent berry taste, red then black fruit. Great tannins, coffee end. Earthy, true wine. From 2007–08; 2021–24.

2000 ★★★★ Full, purple *robe*. Beeswax, prune, roasted aroma. Violets on attack, very full wine. Oak-aided tannins. Well-controlled density, licorice end. From 2008 to shake off the oak. Length OK. 2021–24.

1999 ★★★★ Smoked, bacon, and pine aspects, mix of black and red fruits; suave texture, good chewy wine, middle is full of black jam. Can offer more. Upright, has a lot of end tannin. 2017–22.

1998 ★★★ Burnt tones on nose, pine, resin, mulberry; pretty red fruits, quite ample on palate; red fruit gets through the oak, just. Quite square, pushes its southern origin. 2014–18.

1997 ★★★★★ Broad, smoked pine wood, bacon, and hung-meat bouquet; immediately delicous core fruit, very tasty, sweet extract. Red fruit, quince style, squeezed plum fruit, with a nice grainy surround. Discreet, finer than Pavillon. From 2007; 2016–22.

1996 ★★★ Touch of wood, dry fruit, kirsch, touch of iron; some red fruit, good spine through it, cherry flavour. Fine bone. Touch dry at end. Leave till 2003–05; can live. 2014–18.

ERMITAGE L'ERMITE ROUGE

2003 (CASK) ★★★★★ Very dark; rich bouquet, oily and full, black fruits. Notably rich, persistent palate. No rough edges at all, chocolate

style flavours, well sustained, has real follow-through and is very pretty. Touch of end tannin. From 2007; 2022–24.

2002 (CASK) ★★★ Light red fruit/rose flower nose; floral also on palate, stylish, fresh attack. Floats, not dark wine. From 2008?

2001 (CASK) ★★★★★ Overt berry nose, vanilla, oily; elegant, intriguing wine, suave tannins, some mineral, rich texture. Complex. Esp from 2007–08; 2021–25.

2000 ★★★★★ Decent red *robe*; elegant, subtle bouquet—roses, some fruit, has potential. Full, warm palate, then grows and deepens. Red fruits, with oak hints, is complex. Refined within the not overdone power. Nice end chewiness. 2023–27.

1999 ★★★★★★ Most reserved bouquet of the '99s—hint of black fruit, slight raspberry, light spice; quite warm, generous opening. Raspberry fruit, delicate, and makes you seek. Some oak smoke and end dryness. A Philosopher of a Wine, subtle, with complexity and potential. Most Bordeaux-styled of this year's wines. 2021–26.

1998 ★★★★★★ Reticent, then air brings ripe grapes, essence, oiliness, some smoke; discreet cooked stone fruit flavour, very harmonious tannins. Juice/leather mix. Again, the most complex of the Big Three, the one that makes the drinker seek. The finish is also like a fat Bordeaux. 2020–25.

1997 ★★★★★★ Warm, even, fine bouquet, generous. Succulent texture, ripe fruit jam, quince, touch of spice. Good length. Very lasting fruit, great pleasure. Touch of grainy tannin at end. Needs time to broaden. 2016–21.

1996 ★★★★ Floral, violet, leather aspects—bouquet has quiet substance. More charming than Pavillon, less direct. Good sap in the dark fruits, nice density and some pepper. Can be complex, has good length and grainy finish. 2016–20.

ERMITAGE LE PAVILLON ROUGE

2003 (CASK) ★★★ Very dark; smoky, full bouquet, peppered black fruits, with a ripe curl. Big black fruit flavour that persists, stewed in texture. End heat, bit dry there from oak. From 2007; 2019–22.

2002 ★★ Coffee/mint aromas, peppery top, quite extracted. Tight-knit, black berries flavour. Upright feel, oak is evident, masculine style. Some fruit to end, but lacks soul. Is more domestic than wild dog this year. From 2007, better when oak is less prominent; 2015–17.

2001 (CASK) ★★★★★ Black fruit/earth/truffle aroma; bright, upright black flavour, pepper/leather content. Tight tannins, have depth. From 2008–09; 2023–27.

2000 ★★★★ Tight, reserved nose, hints of black fruit/pepper. Quite chunky, square, unformed wine, with oaked, rigorous tannic finale. Will always be chunky rather than charming. Autumn drinking ideal. Esp from 2009; 2017–21.

1999 ★★★★★ Leathery, minty, smoky bacon, black fruit—interesting bouquet, can become complex. Lot of blackberry jam, is open, then wham! Oak takes over. Dense wine, good length and balance. 2019–24.

1998 ★★★★ Some red fruits on nose, touch fungal and reduced, also a slight floral, violet side; good early richness, nice and oily. Generous wine. Red fruits on an oily finale. Good width of flavour. Faster evolving than the 1999. 2017–21.

1997 ★★★★★★ Deep bouquet, packs a lot, still reserved; is potent and black fruited. Lot of clean black fruit on palate; tannins take over from halfway, are dark and well-modelled. More deep-seated than Méal, more masculine than L'Ermite. Wild black fruit. 2020–25.

1996 ★★★★★ Very black-purple; heated and spirity ahead of dark, damp aromas, inky; lissom but powerful dark fruit, cherries. Very big, manly, meat and black fruit combo that runs truly through it. Tannic finish. 2020–25.

1995 ★★★★★ Full *robe*; very smoky, full, broad bouquet—black fruit/chocolate. Upright texture, prune, pepper/licorice. Mineral aftertaste. Has a true *Bessards* feel. From 2007–08; 2020–24.

1994 ★★★★ 2011–17

1991 ★★★★★★ 2009–15
1990 ★★★★★ 2016–24

HERMITAGE MURE DE LARNAGE BLANC

2000 ★★ Fresh, quite buttery, bit formulaic nose; butter/nuts—quite straight, fresh end, oaked. Low-scale. 2010–12.

HERMITAGE CHANTE-ALOUETTE BLANC

2003 ★(★) Full, brewed and compact bouquet. Apricot, dried fruits flavour, the fruit ripe. Full enough, a bit got up. Acetate, bonbon towards finish, clumsy at this stage. Lacks length. Can only meld and improve from here. Try 2007. 2018–20.

2002 ★★★ Pungent bouquet—iodine, butterscotch, white fruits. Pretty peach-white fruit attack, with white pepper also. Length discreet, sound enough. Nice style, has acidity to live. Has blossomed and become more local. From 2007; 2017–19. Last tasted Dec. 2004.

2001 ★★★★ Broad, almost banana nose, light oak, floral; tasty, crème brûlée flavour, mineral present. Toasted end. Elegant, hides its power, length good. From 2007–08; 2018–21.

2000 ★★★ Ripe crop, mature fruit, custard aromas; tightly bound richness here, plus some mineral around the drier finish. Discreetly chunky wine, packs more than it shows. From 2008; 2016–20.

1999 ★★★ Elegant, direct nose, varnish hints; sweets/butterscotch flavour, elegant, just starting to move. Weight OK. From 2006; 2017–20.

1998 ★★★★ Touch of oiliness, faint citrus, raisin, nut on nose, attractive. Restrained weight, light apricot skin flavour, oak adds end toast, and is rich. Nice latent flavour, can develop over 6–8 years. 2013–18.

1997 ★★★ 2013–16
1996 ★★★★ 2014–17
1995 ★★★ 2015–19
1993 ★★★
1992 ★★
1991 ★★★ 2007–12

ERMITAGE LE MÉAL BLANC

2003 (CASK) ★★★★★ Buttery, pineapple, dried white fruits aromas. Golden flavour, really ripe fruit. Glycerol, large mass in the wine, alcohol peeks out. Masculine, fully charged, has its young banana, toast flavours, then raisin, dried fruits aftertaste. From 2008–09; 2024–28.

2002 ★ Bouquet bit forced, taut—sticky bonbon, some hazelnut. Down the line, lacks character. Leave and hope gains variety. End rather vacant. Bit aggressive. Lacked core when last tasted, too. From 2007; 2014–17. Last tasted Dec. 2004.

2001 ★★★★★ Buttery bouquet, full of potential and future variety. Chewy, full palate, has integrated after shaky start. Spice apparent, has an earthy, tannic feel to it. Enough acidity to live well. From 2009; 2020–25.

2000 ★★★★ Marked yellow; great width and life, lots of depth, some exotic fruits on bouquet. Fresh, apricot/ripe fruit attack, has nice flesh with a tighter, almost peppered finish, also pears there. Some red wine characteristics, solid, great. Big. From 2010; 2019–24.

1999 ★★★★ Honeysuckle/citrus mix, full nose; toasted elements, quite deep. Tight, closed, wait till 2008. Good length, promising. 2018–22.

1998 ★★★ Soaked citrus fruits, fair weight nose. Lush golden sugar, lime tart, a hammock wine, bit heavy; apricot end. Chinese food ideal. 2016–19.

1997 ★★★ Lightly cooked fruit, smoky, hint of lemon, oily; quite closed palate, flavour emerges at end, some pineapple. Taut, also peppery. Fair length. Can develop well. 2015–20.

ERMITAGE DE L'ORÉE BLANC

2003 (CASK) ★★★★ Butterscotch, replete bouquet, more to come. Stone fruit start, nutty flavour later. Sound, discreet length. Good Marsanne, has character and *typicité*. Marmalade, nuts on finish. Quite forward. From 2007; 2019–23.

2002 ★★★★ Bouquet buttery, quite full, with early-stage banana. Palate also buttery,

pretty full. Dumb now, much more open around 2008. Hazelnut aftertaste, tightens at end, length good. Acidity to last well, has body, just needs to integrate. Good Marsanne display. 2019–23.

2001 ★★★★★ Yellow; creamy, peach/apple pie bouquet. Very elegant, suave palate, great roundness. Notable for its soft oiliness; some end grip from the oak. 2017–20.

2000 ★★★★ Ripe, fat bouquet, opulent, broad, and open; heat, cooked fruit, white fruit jam, caramel, and crème brûlée. Dried fruit skins, some end spice. Finishes more drily than attacks. 2019–24.

1999 ★★★★★ Custard tart style, buttered, with floral hints. Full and elegant, some floral aspects, grilled almonds. Sound length. Live, alert, long finish. 2016–21.

1998 ★★ Quite golden; marked over-ripeness, butterscotch on nose; fat, rich wine, opulent, with burnt sugar, bit over the top. Sizzled butter, some dried fruits on end. 2016–20.

1997 ★★★★★ Almost straw colour; rounded, buttery bouquet, with some reserve, has potential; lovely texture here, already soft but has good structure. Persistent and is both full and fine. Rounder than Méal, very discreet, lovely. Still restrained, with oak edging. 2017–23. Last tasted March 2005, jereboam.

1996 ★★★★★ Marked yellow; lot of oiliness, white fruit, fat bouquet. Plenty of depth on palate, the richness has an appealing soft edge. Warm and refined, has southern tendencies. 2015–20.

1995 ★★★★★ Butter, light spice on bouquet. Palate is a winner—fabulously warm and rounded, the richness is thorough. The term "spherical" designed for this. Good balance and some acidity present, too. On top, vigorous form now. 2015–19. Last tasted March 2005, jereboam.

ERMITAGE L'ERMITE BLANC

2003 (CASK) ★★★★ Buttered, light spice, ripe fruit aromas. Full, nutty flavour with elegance. Gains a chewy fruit side, then oak takes over, adds a burnt effect. Stylish wine, hazelnut is appealing. Leave alone in its youth. From 2008–09; 2020–24.

2002 ★★★★★ Broad, pretty bouquet—marmalade/honey—can progress, is an ace card here. Stylish, elegant fruit, refined length. Attractive, persists well. Treads lightly but certainly. Understated richness, lime jam on end. Has settled in last year. Classic, harmonious wine. 2024–28. Last tasted Dec. 2004.

2001 ★★★★ Pretty yellow; tender floral/peach aroma. Elegant palate, stylish and then tightens, with some burnt oak on finish. From 2007 to smooth the finish; 2018–22.

2000 ★★★★★ Great depth on nose, almost Viognier, superripe crop, though fresh also; great richness, lot of interesting flavour—dried white fruit skins, butter, apricot. Very full, very good length, tightens well at end with a mineral touch. 2018–23.

1999 ★★★★★★ Full yellow; buttered nose, quite simple at this stage; good, creamy wine—peach flavours and spice, good fat within. Slight aniseed on end. Fab elegance, good length, and a clean finish. 2016–23.

HERMITAGE VIN DE PAILLE BLANC

1999 ★★★★ Apricot/gold *robe*. Very round, full aroma—some notably elegant fruit/floral aspects. Palate also elegant and varied: crème caramel, honey, vanilla, apricot, quince on finish, with some oak there. Pretty wine. 2024–30.

Export 60 per cent (1) Great Britain, (2) Japan, (3) USA

DOMAINE JEAN-LOUIS CHAVE

37 avenue Saint-Joseph 07300 Mauves
+33(0)475 082463

See also St-Joseph.

Where would Hermitage, nay the Rhône, be without the Chave domaine and dynasty? Much of Hermitage is taken up by grand *négociant* affairs—Chapoutier, Paul Jaboulet Aîné, and Delas—and a Co-opérative, which between them account for 89 hectares of the 130-odd in production, a large 68 per cent of the total. Her-

mitage therefore needs an emblem of proximity between *vigneron*, the place, and the drinker. There are domaines of just a hectare or so, but they are too small to represent the *appellation* with fidelity.

Consequently the Chave domaine, with its spread of plots and its adherence to blending to express the very place of Hermitage, is a vital part of the structure and expression of the *appellation*. There is much more to it than that, of course, since here flourish some of the best facets of the human race—skill, intuition, and wisdom that are woven closely into the nature around them.

The domaine Jean-Louis Chave, started in 1481, represents the attainment of quality that can be achieved without technological force and zealous ideology. It means that the Rhône has a family domaine that is worthy of inspection alongside any of the best wine producers in the world, and of course it lightens the Hermitage panorama with a glowing merit.

The 1990s were important moments for the domaine, the time when the new generation eased into the picture. Gérard Chave, born in 1935, started to work with his son, Jean-Louis, born in 1968 and named after his grandfather. Preparing the way for the *dauphin* was a matter handled with great deftness by Gérard, whose ability to be firm on detail but expansive on broad thinking meant that Jean-Louis was steered towards the running of the domaine with a sure hand.

If there has been a shift in approach, it is minor and reflects a largely seamless transition. Perhaps the red wines have become a little more *gourmand* than before, their tannins riper and softer, the harvest taken in at a state of plush softness. In a vintage like 2000, this was especially noticeable, but that year conditions presented specific problems. The challenge was indeed to secure tannins, with cropping levels naturally high and late August rain inflating the grapes. A form of self-motivation showed through, with Jean-Louis issuing the special wine called "Cathelin"—not an obvious vintage for it—exactly to show a cuvée with greater stuffing and tannin than the classic Chave Hermitage of that year.

The theme of soft grace continued in 2001, with the red Hermitage undeniably refined and a gloriously smooth feel to it. "2001 is my style of wine," explains Jean-Louis. "I like balance in a wine, and that's what we had to work to achieve in 2001. When you vinify, you have to follow the rules of oenology, and the only time you have liberty is when you assemble—the moment when you can ask yourself, 'What do I have to do to achieve equilibrium in the wine?'"

Jean-Louis has also taken up the family's long connection with the vineyards of the Ardèche, their homeland. While the Chapoutier family also came to the banks of the Rhône from the Ardèche, the outlook between citizens of the Ardèche and Drôme around here differs for logical reasons of terrain. The west-bank stretch is a series of valleys, rugged inlets, and craggy hills. The east-bank area broadens into fields of corn and fruit, with a sprinkling of vineyards, and a consequent degree of light industry that is not found in the Ardèche. There is more intensity on the Ardèche, more detachment in the Drôme.

Jean-Louis is therefore keen to capture the essence of the typical red wine of the northern Ardèche—the simple fruitiness of St-Joseph. He wants his wine to reflect the spirit of freedom and integrity that could be found 100 years ago across many of the little, often isolated villages of his home territory.

Hence his grand project to revive the old family vineyard up on a steep hillside at Lemps, just north of Tournon. He scampers happily across this excavated site, amidst the broken acacia, the tangled brambles, the tree stumps, and sees the return of an old, worthy heritage, its true local name *Bachasson*, the new maps calling it *Côte du Pouly*.

This project is a painstaking, well-nigh fastidious process, with two hectares being cleared out to achieve a plantation of 1.5 hectares. But the vines will grow where the vineyard used to be, before phylloxera and setbacks—that is what

is so essential to him. It is the retrieval of roots—literally and metaphorically.

In similar vein, in 2003–04 Jean-Louis planted 0.8 hectare of Syrah on the extension of Hermitage's *Gros des Vignes* in the *commune* of Crozes-Hermitage, not far from Paul Jaboulet's new vineyard. This is a south-facing site around the corner from the top of the Hermitage hill, beyond the east end of *L'Hermite*. This was his first move into Crozes-Hermitage, but the soil— fine, pale sand/loess—is well known to him.

The domaine has also edged towards activities beyond the sheer exploitation of its own Hermitage and St-Joseph vineyards, and Jean-Louis has developed a small, thriving *négociant* business for St-Joseph and Côtes du Rhône *rouge*. The tracking down of the St-Joseph brings him close, agreeable contact with artisans who still make wine in the simple, unaffected way, those who can be found having a social chat and a drink with friends in the cellar at the end of a working day.

Domaine Jean-Louis Chave has never been one for the high life or high lights. It is the outside world that makes the running here. Gérard Chave is well known all around Hermitage and has a confirmed band of followers outside France, particularly in Britain and the United States. However, he is a private man. He lives in a modest house where the family has always been based in the west-bank village of Mauves. There is a rusty, bent, smudged, and most crucially, small "J-L Chave *vigneron*" sign on the wall outside it, and there is no open-door policy to passers-by, or even high-profile magazine groups seeking glossy interview material.

Gérard holds old-fashioned principles on quality and commercial behaviour. He contends that any special cuvée must be accountable—to both producer and drinker. "All such wines should be numbered," he states forcibly. "Otherwise, how on earth does the drinker know what he is getting?" It's an indication that this is the sort of issue that gets him going. The debate on fundamental practices like organic production is already done and dusted, just seen as the way to work without making a fanfare about it.

Gérard delights in being left alone to think out his outstanding wines to the last detail, and then to be sociable over them with a close circle of regular friends. He projects a wide-eyed look when making a strong point, his voice modulating up and down, gestures aplenty. His list of likes is anything but material: "fishing, gastronomy, my friends, and dialogue." He takes keen delight in friendship, in the union of trust and respect, and is a happy man when entertaining and swapping stories. He started working here early, in 1955, when he was just 20, and by the 1970s was running the domaine, although his father, Louis, lived until 1981. One senses that he feels now he can relax a little with the baton handed safely over to Jean-Louis. It must have been something of a lonely fight in his early days at the domaine; Hermitage was not easy to sell in the 1960s and 1970s, and was seen as something of a country cousin by the "noble" regions of France like Bordeaux, Burgundy, and Champagne.

His son Jean-Louis does not reflect the radicalism of his birth year, the time of the student barricades in the cities of France. This countryman is a deep thinker, given to turning and turning possibilities and contexts in his mind. He admits that he is lucky to have arrived at a domaine with such a good reputation as his, but adds, "Continuity, not change, is the key to a good handover at a domaine."

When one is tasting with father and son nowadays, it's evident that the debate and the quest about what makes good wine flourishes easily and naturally. There is no ceremony as Gérard walks off into a dark recess and pulls out an ancient bottle to illustrate a point under discussion.

If anything taxes Jean-Louis more than anything else, it's likely to be on the issue of how his vineyard should faithfully represent the humble link between man and earth, its wine the happy outcome of that. It's not coy or clever marketing strategies and buffing up his international renown that fill his thoughts. His internationalism, anyway, was secured once and for all, through his marriage in 2003 to Erin Cannon

from St Louis, Missouri, a woman who had worked with Kermit Lynch, himself a Rhône fan since the 1970s and for many years importer of the Chave wines into California.

Jean-Louis is cautious, a man of very deep rather than abundant friendships. He likes to quest and try to get to the bottom of matters, and will never take the "easy option." This leaning towards perfectionism makes him open to learn, and to exchange beyond the commercial whenever he can. "We make Hermitage, not Chave," is how I have heard him almost apologetically open a talk to foreign wine writers.

As one of life's Questors, Jean-Louis can also be prone to overagonising on matters, and the joint efforts of his wife, Erin, and his father no doubt serve to jolt him back to everyday reality. "Just when I'm getting caught up on a problem or issue, my father will turn to me and say, 'Don't forget—wine is made to be drunk,'" he admits.

At Hermitage, the Chaves work 9.3 hectares of Syrah vineyards and 4.6 hectares of Marsanne (80 per cent) and Roussanne (20 per cent); these are spread across seven *climats* for the Syrah and four for the white vines. The average age of the Syrah is over 40 years, and for the whites it is 50 years.

The largest Syrah plot is *Bessards*, followed in size by *L'Hermite*, then *Péléat*; the other red-grape sites are *Méal, Beaume, Diognières,* and *Vercandières*. For his Syrah, *Bessards* is what turns Gérard on, and many is the time I have seen him wheel away from a cask as he samples the young wine from this mighty source. A very throaty "*ça va être bon . . . hah, hah*" precedes some muttered oaths of pleasure, but his straight declaration when pressed is: "*Bessards* is our essential *climat*; you can't make a *Grand Hermitage* without it. You can make a flattering Hermitage without it, mind you. *Bessards* is the frame around which we work."

In keeping with the family's outlook on life, there's a degree of unease about *Méal*'s obvious warmth and come-hither: "powerful and *en finesse*," says Gérard of his 2001, with Jean-Louis adding the rider "but it isn't really our style of wine."

The white plots are led in size by *Rocoules*, *Péléat*, and *L'Hermite* with its loess holding a lot of the Roussanne, then *Maison Blanche*. The overall white-vine plantation mix comes to about 50 per cent *Rocoules*, 25 per cent *Péléat*, 20 per cent *L'Hermite,* and 5 per cent *Maison Blanche*, with the *Rocoules* the other *climat* to contain Roussanne.

The *Péléat* is home to over 100-year-old Marsanne, a plot bought by Gérard's father in 1930 and never replanted. This provides an excellent rich but not heavy middle for the white once it has been assembled.

L'Hermite's Marsanne gives rich wine, with sometimes a buttery feel to it, and a nice clear grip on the finish. The *L'Hermite* Roussanne is restrained when tasted young and solo; its acidity and tight texture derive from its loess origins. *Rocoules'* Marsanne is a wine of finesse and nuanced flavours, with fair grip—more so than the often riper, fatter, more ebullient *Péléat* Marsanne. *Maison Blanche* is always the provider of vivacity in the wine. In its final form the Hermitage *blanc* is a combination of 80 to 85 per cent Marsanne, 15 to 20 per cent Roussanne.

Below *Bessards*, close to the northern edge of the town, is a walled enclosure called *Les Vercandières*. Jean-Louis Chave has some very old Marsanne and some Syrah growing near the top walled end on eroded granite, or *gore*. The soil is not rich, and its Syrah, even though it dates from the 1920s or 1930s, rarely goes into the bottled domaine wine—it forms part of the annual sell-off of part of the production to the *négoce* trade. However, in a vintage like 2004, when the lower areas flourished more than the higher slopes, the Syrah from here is considered as a possible entrant in the final domaine wine. The 1920s Marsanne from *Vercandières* can be added into the red at harvesttime.

Looking back, Jean-Louis calls 1988 a decisive year for the domaine; "that was when my father went for closer control of the maturity of the grapes in the vineyard, and I've taken it

from there," he says. Note that this was an outdoors policy of signal importance, not an indoors one that involved new cellar toys. Now, beyond the 10 full-time personnel on the domaine, a band of five young vineyard workers are called upon when soil or vine work demands it.

The challenge during the 1980s was for Gérard to raise his family business on to a broader, more extensive commercial footing without sacrificing all-important quality. During that decade, he acquired the late Terence Gray's plot on *L'Hermite*, built a new bottle storage extension, and installed an updated *cuverie*. Some of the wines of that decade have slipped earlier than expected—both the 1982 and 1983, for instance, could be considered quite fragile now, but Gérard toiled to maintain a meticulous approach throughout.

The cellar has been progressively modified since the early 1990s. In 1990–91 the first stainless steel vats were introduced, replacing the old concrete ones, where sharp loss of heat had been a danger. Three open wood vats stayed because they allow cap punching during fermentation: "Syrah from a site like *Péléat* is especially suited for cap punching," says Gérard; "it helps to bring out the wine's natural silkiness of texture."

Crop had been cooled down to around 15°C in hot vintages by water pumping, but in 1998 the vinification cellar received a formal, electronic cooling system, which the Chaves admit had to be well thought out. It functions at around 13°C—deliberately cool, so little sulphur is needed—and has brought ease of mind.

Harvesting lasts for two weeks and starts with the white crop. It is conducted with extreme precision, necessitiating many journeys to and fro in the van across the Rhône, the small collection boxes designed not to crush the grapes before entry into the winery. The grapes from each plot are handled separately and with great care. Since the changes to the cellar, the Syrah can now also be harvested alongside the white crop if it is ripe enough.

The Syrah is nearly all destalked, and has been since the 1980s. The old custom was not to destem in the 1960s, but before that the Hermitage crop had often been destemmed by hand. "My great-grandfather did hand destemming," says Jean-Louis; "in the nineteenth century, the *Grands Hermitages* were known for their class and nobility, and growers went to lengths to rid them of any astringence."

Some of the crop is still foot crushed in their four 50 hl open wood vats, a smaller size introduced in 2002. The rest is vinified in stainless steel vats. Great attention is paid to the temperature of the grapes upon entry to the cellar; "the one thing we don't want is for the fermentation to get cracking too fast," says Jean-Louis.

There is usually no formal pumping-over of the vats, but this can be done to irrigate the cap and, as in 2003, to give oxygen to the yeasts. During fermentation, the Chaves practise a regular cap punching, or *pigeage*. "Our method is the classic floating cap," says Jean-Louis, "both in the wood and the steel, where the punching is done by a pneumatic process, and of course our temperature control is better in the steel." The vats may go to a top temperature of 34°C.

The press wine is not systematically included, especially after a long vinification period—the *cuvaison* lasts for three or four weeks. It's a sign of the ingrained quality approach that each year the Chaves sell some of their Hermitage in bulk to merchants—wine that isn't suitable for their bottled red. In 2000, a year tricky for the tannins, it was 30 per cent.

Cask ageing in these legendary cellars lasts 18 months, with the percentage of new oak depending on the style of the vintage. In the full, classically styled year of 2001, a high of 20 per cent new 228-litre casks was reached. Generally the new-oak content runs at 10 to 20 per cent, the remaining casks one to five years old. There is a bit more oak present in the wines of the 2000 years than the 1990s, but in the background ring Gérard's trenchant words about much modern winemaking: "The uniformity imposed by new oak and overextraction are what I deplore the most these days."

Jean-Louis admits that he has edged back from new oak, saying, "It can educate and refine a wine, but if you have a wine with good, noble tannin of its own, you need less new oak." The 2003 Hermitage received 10 per cent new oak, for instance. Jean-Louis also points out that the new oak can save a racking from cask to cask, since the young wood performs its own micro-oxygen effect. This means there is less reduction in the Syrah—the stinky, rubbery smell that can be present if it is not exposed to air during preparation.

The wine from each of the seven Syrah sites is kept apart for the 18 months, "in order to achieve a further deep expression of the soil," as Jean-Louis puts it. The different sources are blended in July, then left in vat until bottling in September. The red wine can occasionally be fined with egg whites, but there is no filtration. The special, occasional Cathelin is chosen by tasting from cask to cask at the end of the 18-month raising period, and on average 2,500 bottles of it are produced.

"Elegance" and "warmth" are two words that occur often when writing notes on the Chave Hermitage *rouge*. The skill of the blender guarantees a *rondeur*—a savoury depth that makes their qualities understated when judging them against many of today's vinous monsters. The bouquets show warm cooked fruits, a gentle black berry in style, and are aided by the added dimension of leather and spice and sometimes the flutter of rose-hip.

The palate shows off the elegance to the full—the texture comes to the fore, and the flavour is invariably tightly packed. This is tribute to the harmony to be found when bringing together the wines of the different soils in one bottle. The wines are fleshy, and their quiet warmth precedes a tightening from the tannins present—tannins that tidy up the wine and keep it in defined shape. Later in life, there is more mint, more tea, even more restrained harmony within the wine. Like all the best wines, there is some mental work for the drinker to do to appreciate its true depth and range of qualities; their subtlety but sureness of presence are exemplary.

Jean-Louis Chave is at pains to emphasize that their Cathelin—named after their friend the painter, the late Bernard Cathelin—is not a special cuvée wine: try telling that to the international collecting market, where they are offered at over £500, or US$900! "It contains the same wines as the main cuvée," he explains, "but the percentage is different, and the seven sites are blended differently. It doesn't contain more new oak, and we make the selection late on, after the 18 months' cask raising. I'm not aiming at just more concentration; I'm also after more finesse and a bit more of all its elements." There are 2,000 to 2,500 bottles each time it is issued, and some Jereboams and Methusalems as well—some thought!

Cathelin actually came about because Bernard Cathelin wanted to paint a label for the Chaves. "So we made the wine for the label," chuckles Gérard—"that way round."

Cathelin was made in 1990, 1991, 1995, 1998, 2000, and 2003. "2000 was a challenging vintage," comments Jean-Louis. "The problem was to find the tannins: there was alcohol without the construction around it; it's fatter than 1997, all the same, what I would call silky. With our Cathelin, we wanted to show that it was possible to make a wine with a decent tannic couch in it. We didn't make it in 1999, as the wines were naturally balanced anyway and would have been too similar—the classic and the Cathelin. That's why we made it in 1998 and 2000—to show some contrast."

If there is a relative secret at this domaine, it is their Hermitage *blanc*. Not only is this long-lived, fabulously rich, and truly southern, it is also blessed with great finesse and complexity. I have seen expectant, seasoned wine writers attend Chave tastings, waiting for the real action to start when the youngest red is tasted. When the dialogue and tasting of four whites continues past the 30-minute mark, one is sure they are revising their attitude to this often overlooked wine.

Gérard himself is very attached to Hermitage *blanc*; it is a wine for which he has a definite soft spot because he holds it in such high esteem. "I want richness in white Hermitage," he says, "not acidity; I want depth. Remember, white

Hermitages can age very well even with a low acidity." Jean-Louis adds, "The white is a texture wine more than an aroma wine, and it must be given time to achieve this. 'Glycerol' is the key word for white Hermitage, not acidity." He openly relishes the cerebral and physical challenge of finding balance in a wine that is rich but low in acidity.

The white Hermitage is 80 to 90 per cent fermented and raised in casks, up to one-third new, the whole process conducted at natural cellar temperature. The rest of the juice is fermented in stainless steel vats at under 20°C to achieve freshness, notably if the vintage demands it, and also if Gérard feels that the must is not quite rich enough for the oak. Natural yeasts are involved, which can mean that the fermentation ticks along for over six months. "We're in no hurry," says Jean-Louis; "we actually want a long, slow fermentation, and that can last for a year sometimes."

Jean-Louis returned to the domaine from his learning travels in 1992, after which some lees stirring, or *bâtonnage*, was tried in 1994. It is not systematic, since Jean-Louis is fully aware of its dangers: "Hermitage *blanc* is so rich that you risk making it heavier rather than more refined—you oxidise it," he says.

The oak and steel portions are blended in the spring, 18 months after the harvest, but there isn't a fixed rule about keeping them apart before then; the 2003 from *L'Hermite*, *Rocoules*, and *Maison Blanche* were all kept longer than usual in oak because they were so powerful. Regular tasting and checking governs the next move. Jean-Louis emphasizes that the objective behind raising the white wines is to make the primary matter more elegant, not to secure extraction. The *élevage* in total usually lasts about two years. It risked excess only for a moment in 1996 and 1997, when the new oak proportion was a little oppressive early on.

Like the red, an amount is sold each year to the merchant trade—this can be 4,000 litres or up to 25 per cent of the white wine. "It's wine that doesn't correspond to our year's blend," says Gérard.

The white is a wine of abundant variety of flavour, a stream of sensations present when drinking it after some years' ageing in bottle. Dried fruits, honey, spice, apricot are all present, and there is often a flowing, grapey bouquet that evolves towards nuttiness. The Chaves have never succumbed to what they term "harvest fever," so a lateish picking contributes to the firm straw colour that his whites usually display. In 1989 he recalls that he started to harvest the Marsanne and Roussanne when those around him were already at the stage of distilling their grape marc. They started around 12 September; he finished on 10 October.

When to drink the white is a challenge for all lovers of this wine, for its richness makes it quite capable of showing well for decades. Jean-Louis offers the following: "Either young, when it is two to three years old, or from seven years onwards. It will always go through a closed phase after about three years."

"A rich year is capable of infinite life," he adds. "My best memories of the white come with the 1929, which from time to time I open with my father to see how it's doing." This is a wonderful wine, its relative freshness and silken texture a reminder of what could be achieved before the advent of technology. As Gérard likes to state: "The truth—that is what lies within old bottles." In judging such a wine, Gérard points out that in those days, the grapes would be harvested in the morning and would be brought by horse to the cellar at 10 o'clock at night, with pressing not before the following day.

The Chaves have also made a little of Hermitage's late-picked special wine, the Vin de Paille. This was publicly revived by Gérard in 1986 after some long intervals—previously it had been made in 1974 and 1952 and occasionally in between for home drinking. "You need ripe grapes, and the motivation to make it," says Gérard, with a shrug. Since 1986 it has been produced in 1989, 1990, 1991, 1996, 1997, and 2000.

There are normally two casks—450 litres, although in 2000 just the one cask was made. The Vin de Paille is always largely Marsanne,

Gérard Chave has brushed with Viognier, and it is not to his taste.

In 1989 "for amusement—strictly not commercial"—he made his first vintage of 150 litres of Viognier *demi-sec* off the Hermitage hill, from some plants on *L'Hermite* planted in 1936 by Terence Gray and a few on *Rocoules* planted in 1975 by Gérard himself.

This 18° wine showed floral aromas within a surround of dense weight and alcohol on the bouquet; on the palate there were dried fruits and extreme length—the wine was very big, in an aperitif style, with the Viognier showing the extraordinary opulent roundness which is its hallmark.

The wine had had very little sulphur mixture applied to it to obtain the residual sweetness. In 1990 a slightly drier, even more successful Viognier was made and bottled earlier, in July 1991. The experiments are now over, and Gérard took out the Viognier vines after 15 years.

"I found the wine's structure wasn't that great," he says, "and I just wasn't that motivated." He has passed on his dim view of the Viognier to his son Jean-Louis, by the way. "Stirring the lees of the Viognier at Condrieu is an aberration," claims the latter; "it makes the wine far too heavy." *Allez!*

with some Roussanne present, and most of the grapes are taken from *L'Hermite*. "The Marsanne is easier to work with because it is less prone to rot," comments Gérard, "whereas for the Roussanne you need a real top year, and particularly a fine late growing season. That's why we chose years like 1986, 1989, 1996—you can only make this when you have the materials."

After pressing in early December, the Vin de Paille is left alone, and in a year like 1996 when acidity levels were higher than usual, the wine fermented quietly for over two years. It can be left for literally years in cask, with fortnightly topping up of the casks. The 1996 was bottled in July 2002, the 1997 in the winter of 2004. Around 1,000 half bottles of 37.5 cl are made.

The Vin de Paille is something of a sacrifice, as Gérard states: "If you declare one hectare of Vin de Paille, you are obliged to deduct three hectares of normal *appellation* wine; it's an old rule written into the Hermitage text."

The Chaves also work five hectares of Syrah at St-Joseph, mostly above Tournon. This wine has amplified since its early vintages of the 1980s, when it could lack a little flesh. The vines now average around 15 years. In 2003 there was also planting of Syrah on an old Terence Gray Crozes-Hermitage vineyard at Larnage.

Gérard broke his knee in two places in April 2002, something that restricted his close day-to-day involvement in the domaine's affairs. His wife, Monique, petite and determined, has also loosened her grip on the office, and some relaxation for the pair is now well merited.

Gérard Chave Thoughts

Fining: "For the whites I fine with bentonite; if I use egg whites on them, I'll take out their tannins. I use egg whites on my reds since they have more and heavier tannins. In a year like 2001, with late ripening helped by the wind, we didn't fine the red, as we feared it would make the wine too dry."

Yeasts: "I very rarely add yeasts. I had to in 1982, when it was so hot both by day (35°C) and by night that I had to cool the wine. The yeasts then became tired, so they needed pepping up."

When to rack and taste: "With the Vent du Nord you have higher atmospheric pressure here, so the lees are more suppressed—further down. That's why I'll rack and do my tasting by preference when there's a Vent du Nord. When there's a Vent du Midi, from the south, I smell the lees more. And I like to bottle the wine by preference when there's high pressure, a Vent du Nord and an old moon descending. In tricky years like 2001, that was very important."

Cooking: "It's close to what I do. I've attended courses in Lyon with the *grands chefs* to improve my cooking—Monique approves! I managed to make a wine, a cuvée of red, that suited a lamb dish of the late Alain Chapel's."

HERMITAGE ROUGE

2003 *Beaume*—gummy fruit, ripe, chunky palate, blood! Quite long, grape skin ending. *L'Hermite*—knit fruit nose, cooked/brewed black fruit, rich prune flavour. *Bessards*—shoulders, chunky, penetrating fullness, chocolate, a wave of black lozenges with alcohol, more like the wine you make *pour s'amuser*. Gasping aftertaste. Good portents for indeed a manly wine, high rating.

2002 (CASKS) ★★★ Black fruit, light pepper, floating bouquet. Pretty fruit on palate, good core, early flourish then tightens. Drier-toned year. Quite meaty finish, plum/black fruit present, too. Length OK, some end tannin. Esp from 2008; 2020–24.

2001 ★★★★★ Oily, warm cooked fruit/olives, quite plush bouquet. Real elegance, lovely freshness combined with maturity—great style. *Beau Vin.* Silken texture, tannins are defined, oily, pretty. Good length, mineral aftertaste with some dried fruits. 2024–29.

2000 ★★★★ Touch game/animal bouquet, also sappy fruit, some advance. Stylish, loganberry style fruit, starting to vary, air will help it. Compact finish, tannins there, also raisin/floral aspect. Not a constant evolution wine, goes up and down, flourishes, then curls up at different moments. General progress, though. 2013–22. Last tasted Sept. 2004.

1999 ★★★★★ Dark red. Smoky, tight bouquet, rubber, nut, and tar. Delicious palate, flies out of the starting gate. Tightens and dries at end as oak bites in. Persistent, lasts well. Pebbly black fruit subdued overall now, but good purity. Serious structure. From 2007–08; 2022–28.

1998 ★★★★ Some matt on *robe* after five years. Game, red meat, nicely firm cooked fruit, peppery edges on bouquet. Blackberry debut, then becomes drier, peppered—shows the vintage. Red fruit—quince, raspberry aftertaste, some chewiness. Turning to a second phase. From 2006–07; 2017–21.

1997 ★★★★ Steady red colour. Rounded, ripe fruit jam bouquet, also rose hip/mushrooms—is still tight, though. Nicely warm, pleasure wine, with good richness, pretty red fruit like strawberry, some spice. Well-directed, tasty. Sound length, has quiet warmth. 2016–20.

1996 ★★★ Dry-toned bouquet, hint of black fruit with animal, leaves, tea—more upright vintage tones. Mature black fruit flavour; again has a minty, tea aspect. Bit stretched on finish, prominent minerality, rather taut. Some warmth on aftertaste, can still move around and on. 2013–17.

1995 ★★★★★ Red colour subdued, turning to matt after eight years. Promising, sunny year bouquet, warm/fat. Warm, fleshy wine, delicious. Like sucking a spiced fruit plum jam lozenge. Smooth texture, tightens a little on finish, good length. Declares its style openly, excellent fruit. 2014–19.

1994 ★★★ 2008–11
1993 ★★ 2008–09
1992 ★★★ 2012–14
1991 ★★★★ 2012–16

1990 ★★★★★★ Dark red, thin brick line at top; sappy, moist plum/fungal bouquet, tight overall at 12 years. Very dense palate, great richness—this is TEXTURE! Top Burgundian finesse here. Some heat on aftertaste to reveal its origins. Minted/spice elements on palate, raspberry fruit, Pinot Noir connotations (talked of by grandpa Chave). 2019–25.

1989 ★★★★ 2013–17
1988 ★★★★★ 2012–18

ERMITAGE ROUGE CATHELIN

2000 ★★★★★ Dark, lingering nose, smoky black fruit deep within, cool tone. Savoury, beguiling black fruit, clean and stylish. Nicely tight, great potential charm, cool texture, fruit very persistent. Esp from 2008. 2020–23. (2,000 bottles)

1998 ★★★★★ Purple/mauve *robe*. Brewed black fruit, more international than regular wine, touch of oak. Tight, dense palate. Black fruit, some heat. Less raspberry than before. Peppered, dry tone finish. Decent length, but dry. 2021–25. (2,500 bottles)

1995 ★★★★★ Dense, compact *robe*, more black than the regular wine's red. Warm, integrated bouquet, hint of evolution. Tasty, very vintage style—lot of black fruit, mint—almost fennel, aniseed. Dense, and full also on end, with a tickle of dryness there. Can be stylish around 2010—needs time to show its finesse. 2019–24.

1991 ★★★★ Intense *robe*, still solid in 2003. Very dense, sumptuous broad black jam aroma, some advance towards dampness. Moist, plush palate—oily black fruits, dry touch within. Scented tea leaf, smoky black fruit end, with mineral. Has an intense core, rich, with some restraint. 2015–18.

1990 ★★★★★★ Only small advance on *robe* at 12 years; dense, warm, sappy bouquet, live fruit here. More power than usual when five years old. Very pretty attack, bounces out—very tasty impact. Sustained and wide through the palate—very elegant fruit and fat. Suave, but tight on finish. More "inky" than the regular 1990, which is mild and plummy—the Cathelin has more fire and potency. Perhaps like a Hermitage of the nineteenth century. 2021–25.

HERMITAGE BLANC

2003 (CASKS) ★★★★ Big, complex wine, powerful content, e.g., from *Rocoules* at 15°–16°. Set to receive more oak this year, notably the *L'Hermite/Maison Blanche/Péléat* portions. Plenty of richness on show. Likely to run for at least 20 years.

2002 ★★★★ Melted butter aroma, light spice topping. Fair style, a dried apricot/almond mix is well sustained, elegant. Persists well, opens with air, orange marmalade end. Will show its worth and broaden over time. *En finesse.* 2021–26.

2001 ★★★★★ Elegant, fine bouquet—flan, white fruit, spice/apricot. Good balance here—spice/toasted aspect on palate, restrained middle richness. Has a red wine structure, with a tight, near-tannic end. Lot of life ahead, not a tearaway. More from 2009; 2023–27.

2000 ★★★★ Greengage/mint/aniseed and wax aromas, not so usual. Mix of orange/almond in middle, some burnt fringes—that bitter side of the Marsanne. Stone fruit style now, expect wax-honey, more variety later. From 2010; 2022–25.

1999 ★★★★ Meaty, broad, quite brewed bouquet—citrus/greengage, has moved from early floral. Honey/vanilla on palate, plenty of fat, bonbon, butterscotch. Slow burn; if drunk young, decant it. 2019–23.

1998 ★★★★ Apricot/white fruit, oily bouquet, less upright/tight than previously. Firm, good matter, poised to unfurl. Good frame, refined richness, has hidden power. Full, good length. 2014–19.

1997 ★★★★ Sappy, generous melted butter/pineapple, some dry cheese bouquet. Buttery start, then a touch of the bitter; orange peel/greengage fruit. Still has mineral and sinew within, good. Dried fruits end. Has absorbed its oak. Fermented for a very long time. Can tick over for many years. 2017–23. Last tasted March 2004.

1996 ★★★★ Gentle white fruit/apricot/quince aroma with mint, light butter. Restrained, even at seven years. Nice acidity, more live than most years, good length and warm, clear finish, with some heat. Very stylish, elegant. More open, more fat from 2008 on; 2014–17.

1995 ★★★★★ Nicely oily peach/spiced honey bouquet, very sappy, ripe. Wee touch of spice and verve in the white fruit, rounded with some almond on finish. Very good grip. Floral/honey at end, where it is almost tannic, plenty of chewiness. 2020–23.

1994 ★★★★ 2010–15
1993 ★★★★ 2009–13
1992 ★★★★ 2010–16
1991 ★★★★ 2007–13

1990 ★★★★★★ Some yellow on *robe*; very round, full bouquet—butter, honey—rich, even robust. Lovely, delicious fullness on palate, with good end grip. Fine mix of flesh and fresh. Long life ahead, is very persistent. 2017–22.

HERMITAGE VIN DE PAILLE

1997 (CASK) ★★★★ Syrup, honey, warm bouquet—still ticking over. Soft, floral palate, has a delicacy and style that bely its deep-seated richness. Last tasted April 1999.

1996 ★★★★★ Really broad, plunging bouquet—crème caramel, apricot, chunky orange marmalade. Palate—suave, generous, tightly packed with nice acidity that just ticks over quietly within. Great length, fresh finish. Apricot, burnt sugar flavours, pretty. 2027–32. Last tasted March 2003.

1986 ★★★ Gold, near-apricot colour, some fade; burnt aromas, butterscotch, alcohol, softens a bit with air. Tight grip on attack, acidity still evident. Fair sap on middle. Finishes dry, but hot, with fruit peel leave-behind. Last tasted Nov. 1997.

Export 60 per cent (1) USA, (2) Great Britain, (3) Belgium

DOMAINE YANN CHAVE

26600 Mercurol +33(0)475 074211

See also Crozes-Hermitage.

The great enthusiast Yann Chave works 1.5 hectares of Hermitage, all Syrah. This is 90 per cent on *Beaume* (1978), 10 per cent on *Péléat* (1988). The 25-year vines were planted at an unusual 1.50 by 1 metre spacing, a density that means he has to cut back yields.

The Syrah is vinified for three weeks and raised in new and one-year-old 600-litre barrels. It is bottled around February, 17 months after the harvest. The style is full, the ripe grapes bringing a quiet potency to the wine: there is good tannic definition as well. On average there are 7,000 bottles.

HERMITAGE ROUGE

2003 (CASK) ★★★★ Dark; brimming, sappy bouquet of mellow fruit. Savoury attack, good genuine richness, sustains well. Length good. Has curves, appeal. Red berry fruit has pretty texture. Balance good, will age consistently and well. From 2007; 2022–25.

2002 ★★ Light black *robe*; smoked, laurel/black fruit aroma. Leathery black fruit flavour, becomes chewy through palate. Low-key, best in young middle age—2005–07. 2012–13.

2001 ★★★ Solid, bright *robe*; grilled, fresh loganberry-style fruit aroma; tight, well-packed wine. Dark red fruits, sound length. Wait till 2008. Clean-cut, stylish, modern. Low-key, classic waiting vintage, not an overtly fleshy year. 2017–20.

2000 ★(★) Cooked plum fruit, bosky/spiced, then stewed aromas; big, square wine, red fruit is dry toned. Rather taut, uneven. Leave till 2006 to settle. Length OK. Fundamental wine, has fair matter, but needs patience and maybe luck. Drink with the pressure high. 2011–15.

1999 ★★★ Spice and varied dark fruits aroma. Very beguiling fruit, a light touch. Black fruit, calm wine, suave end. Some heat. Savoury wine, will roll along evenly. Esp 2004–08; 2010–12.

1998 ★★★ Smoky, tarry bouquet, with clear-cut berry within, cedar too. Nice mix of stern and fat on palate, well-ripened tannins support. Good, stylish fruit, the front taste is silky. Esp 2005–07; 2009–12.

DOMAINE DU COLOMBIER

2 route de Chantemerle 26600 Tain-l'Hermitage +33(0)475 074143

See also Crozes-Hermitage.
The Viales work 1.61 hectares of Syrah on three plots at Hermitage—*Beaume, Diognières*, and *Torras et les Garennes*. The vines were mostly planted by Florent Viale's grandfather Paul in the 1950s. There is also a recently bought 0.20 ha of Marsanne dating from 1942 on the west end of *Maison Blanche*, near *Beaume*.

From 1968 the family sold the red wine to Guigal, but in 1991 started to bottle and sell it themselves. Whole-bunch fermentation of the Syrah lasts around 18 days; the wine is raised in 600-litre barrels and bottled in early April—18-plus months after harvest.

The style is very clean and *en finesse*. Tannins are orderly and the wine is typically likely to age well over 10 to 16 years. It is usually good value. After a promising start in cask, the 2001 fell away, revealing a lack of content in the mid-palate when tasted in the spring of 2003—a trait also observable in the 2000.

The white is cask fermented and raised.

HERMITAGE ROUGE

2002 ★ Stewed bouquet, sappy sweet aspect. Undemanding, rounded jam taste—wild red berries. Ends more grainily, fungal, bit dry. No great finale. From 2006; 2013–15.

2001 ★ Black fruit, stretched nose. Sleek, modern flavour, bit dry at end. Suave, international style, not sure about middle matter.

2000 ★ Brewed, touch sweaty berries, dry/green also. Prickly fruit, three-quarter weight, bit stretched—not at ease. Burnt edges at end, fades rather. Uneven; balance? From 2006. Was harmonious in cask, hasn't moved along at all on this showing. 2012–13.

1999 ★★★★★ Lovely wild fruit aroma, mulberries with dry, resin edges; plenty of oily flavour, and a soaking of well-founded fruit. Piney aspect, acidity is good, will age. Esp 2005–06 for first hit; 2014–16.

1998 ★★★★ Black pastilles aroma, tight and holding back. Classic Hermitage, full with sinew, good tannic frame. Some end mineral, persistent flavour. Esp 2005–07; 2012–15.

RENÉ-JEAN DARD ET FRANÇOIS RIBO

Blanche-Laine 26600 Mercurol +33(0)475 074000

See also Crozes-Hermitage, St-Joseph.
These two purists have their main activities at Crozes-Hermitage; at Hermitage they work a speck of just 0.4 hectare on the stony, hard grey granite of *Varogne*, with its westerly exposure, the *lieu-dit* closest to the Rhône. This is a vineyard at least several decades old.

In 2004 they added an even tinier 0.09 ha, a plot at the end of François' garden on *La Croix*, away to the east towards Larnage. This was a site with old trees on it, its soil red clay covered in smooth *galet* stones.

The Syrah crop is given an extended, three-to-four-week vinification in an open wood vat and is raised in used casks for a year.

This is a very honest wine, its fruit quietly threaded within it; the outright granite origins are shown through its dry texture towards the finish. Like the best reds from the granite villages of Crozes-Hermitage, it is a gently fruited wine, not a powerhouse.

HERMITAGE ROUGE

2003 (CASK) ★★★★ Pretty, classic dark red/purple *robe*. Lovely warm fruit aroma—juicy, deep, stylish. Silken wine, refined ripe cherry fruit, touch of final oak when young. Smoky finish. Great elegance. Very good. From 2006; 2014–18.

2002 (CASK) ★★ Decent volume, tight bouquet; firm fruit, will become peppery. Clear texture, red fruit flavour, sound length. 9–10 years.

2001 ★★ Oily, sappy red fruit/floral nose, also earthy; fleshy, warm cooked plums, tightens under granite influence at end, dries. Gentle, savoury wine, lightly done. 2011–13.

2000 ★★★ Pretty, floral scent; harmonious, light-touch wine. Good length of fruit, raspberries aftertaste, nicely upright. Violet, truffle finish. 2013–16.

MAISON DELAS

ZA de l'Olivet 07300 St-Jean-de-Muzols
+33(0)475 086030

See also Condrieu, Cornas, Côte-Rôtie, Crozes-Hermitage, St-Joseph, St-Péray.
No more False Dawns. That's the heartfelt hope surrounding Delas Frères, one of the old grandee enterprises of the northern Rhône that spluttered its way through the 1970s, 1980s, and much of the 1990s.

New people kept being introduced, things were "on the move," promotional tastings were held—and still the wines lacked that essential *je ne sais pas quoi*.

Then in 1997 the company, which is owned by Deutz, themselves part of the Roederer Champagne empire, made a good signing, taking on someone in his early 30s with all to play for. Jacques Grange had done time at Colombo and Chapoutier, and his horizons were ready to expand.

He's a busy, motivated man and is now hauling Delas towards higher levels of quality, ending many of the uncertainties of the past 25 years. He's boyish looking, has a brief cut of dark hair and pale blue eyes and would make an inspiring teacher, even of the most complex or arcane subjects. A very lucid thinker and speaker, his is a well-organised mind.

"We've done 90 per cent of the work now," he says—"the easiest, most accessible part of the challenge. The last 10 per cent brings complete mastery of the situation, but must also allow more spirit for the wine itself, away from the confines of an organisation. That can mean that if you have two or three cuvées that suddenly need bottling, you just do them."

He has always been at pains to emphasize that a company like Delas should be judged on its high-volume wines, not on a select band of quasi-garage small-quantity productions. But it's clear that he would also love to have the small-domaine flexibility and commitment woven into the daily habits here.

"I seek precision more than details," he says of his approach. "The wines should be pure—that's what matters most. Details can help you get there, but you'd become a maniac if that was what took up all your attention."

This explains why the production of special cuvées made from specific plots is not just set on automatic pilot, whatever the vintage. There were no *vins parcellaires* in 2002, for instance, meaning the omission of wines like the Condrieu Clos Boucher as well as the Hermitage Bessards. In 2000, a tricky ripening year for the

Syrah, there were plot-specific white wines, but no reds from specific sites. The full range was produced in 2001, by contrast.

Jacques' early task was to tackle how the wine was made. The cellar was completely rationalised so that the grape reception could link directly to a series of open concrete vats (designed that way to allow daily cap punching, or *pigeage*), the crop taken there by a moving carpet, not by screw pumping. "My first tasks were very fundamental, ones like using the right equipment and doing the vinification in the right place," states Jacques.

He was also hot to amend the barrel ageing. "Our old 40 hl barrels did nothing to enhance the wine, and also brought out a floral bacteria that made a lot of the wines similar on the bouquet. Then there was the dryness often found in Delas wines once they were in bottle, although I knew the raw materials had been fresh." One cannot argue with this analysis, especially when learning that half a centimetre of tartar was found stuck to the insides of the barrels when they were removed.

Now the ageing cellar is full of 600 casks of 228 litres, of which a low 8 to 10 per cent are new in any one year. The water drains around the cellar, once prone to flooding, have also been sorted out. Time, money, and yes, attention to detail were required, but most of all this was a triumph of will. Masters at Deutz Champagne had to back these moves.

"I want to stay around our current 1.7 million bottles a year. That will allow us to be semi-industrial on one level, but also to keep some artisan touches in our work," says Jacques. "Here we are with yields around just 30 hl/ha—we don't need 8,000-bottles-an-hour machines. And I refuse to go to small growers, buy their cast-off cuvées, and then charge a lot for them."

The first Delas vintage with the fermentation and ageing elements sorted was 1999. Each vat is temperature controlled from a central station above. An observation surfaces here: "In your vat room you should be on top of the vats, not below them at tap level. This allows you to study the cap and take action on it according to what you

FIGURE 14   Jacques Grange, the man who got Delas to turn the corner. (Tim Johnston)

see without having to make a special effort," is Jacques' reasoning. So there are two foot *pigeages* a day done from above, and only when they are devatting do the team go down to ground level.

Part destemming started here in 1991, and now the Syrah is totally destemmed; it receives a pre-fermentation cool maceration over three to four days at 15°C. This serves to gradually, rather than abruptly, free the anthiosans and tannins from the grapes, which otherwise would be too abruptly freed and so be out of step if the temperature moved to 22° to 24°C in just a day. There's also the slight start of intracellular fermentation, which makes the wines more rounded, with fresher fruit as well.

Jacques is also adamant that indigenous yeasts must be used, which is encouraging in an operation of this scale. "We were using outside, cultured yeasts before. I want silk in our Syrah, not a herbaceous side, and would prefer to go quietly on the tannins. All our red crop is destalked, and should their tannins be abrupt, I would take the case on its merits and fine the wine with egg whites." Otherwise there is no fining.

Delas now take the trouble to distribute their harvest boxes, which were changed to 40 kg grey plastic with slats in them so the juice cannot hang around, warm up, and start to ferment. Their contractors receive these ahead of time.

The whites have also received a big shake-up. "Balance, freshness, and finesse are what I want in my whites," states Jacques. From 2003 they have been vinified in steel. The crop is collected in the slatted boxes so the entire crop can be pressed. "It's a lot of work, but we're not crushing or destemming now, which means that you don't go too far at the end of the press run," explains Jacques. "You also eliminate the first rather messy 30 or 40 litres. When we drain the grapes now, we lose 2 to 3 instead of 10 per cent of juice, and another 7 to 8 per cent at the press, which is the way round we prefer."

The key to realising the sea change occurring here is Jacques' statement "I don't necessarily want impressive wines; I want them to express *terroir* and what the climate permitted us in that year."

In pursuit of this, Jacques is working on the 14 hectares of Delas vineyards. There are 10 at Hermitage and two each at St-Joseph and Crozes-Hermitage. In 2002 he revived the skill of home cutting propagation, known as *sélection massale*, so he and his four-man vineyard team carefully marked out vines that were healthy and suited to giving cuttings for the next generation of vines. "The men have got out of the habit of doing this. Personally, I don't have much confidence in nurserymen. You can't be sure what's inside the clone you get from them—it could even be Chardonnay inside the wood. I prefer our men to do it themselves."

The team has also been prepared to spot signs of illness in the vines—mildew, oïdium, grape worm—so they can be on to those early and so spray less. Allied to this early warning system, from 2004 Delas have hired a helicopter for their own use in treating the vineyards. This means specific dates can be booked in and organic solutions can be applied. "The net result is three or four, not eight treatments," says Jacques; "we're only spraying if necessary, when the blight presents real danger to the vine."

Jacques is taking a more active line with their grape suppliers, too. These sources represent around 50 hectares across the northern Rhône. "From mid-August on, I spend three days a week visiting five or six growers a day. I'm looking at yield levels, and the growers can only harvest with our say-so. The right ripeness is crucial."

Delas owns vineyards at Hermitage in prime sites. This family silver was accumulated over the years since the firm's foundation in 1835 by a Monsieur Audibert and a Monsieur Delas, the former dropping out between the two world wars. Until 1977 it had remained independent as Delas Frères, but in the 1970s it had to be rescued from possible bankruptcy by the Champagne House of Deutz. Through some years of turmoil, when vineyards like Cornas were sold, they at least stuck with their prized locations at Hermitage.

Of the 10 hectares at Hermitage, 6.5 are owned, the rest rented from the Marquis de la Tourette, a resident of the Ardèche at the Château de la Tourette. There are a choice 7 hectares on *Bessards*, 2.5 hectares on *Les Grandes Vignes* or *Gros des Vignes*, and 0.5 hectare on *L'Hermite*.

Nine of the hectares are Syrah (mostly *Bessards*, with *L'Hermite* and *Les Grandes Vignes*) and one hectare is Marsanne with a splash of Roussanne mixed up within the plots. The Syrah side of the vineyard enjoys a nice maturity, with most of it dating from between 1963 and 1968; the most recent planting was 0.98 hectare at the top of *Bessards* in 1991.

The white vines are an interesting age—so the white Hermitage Marquise de la Tourette should indeed be good. The *pied de coteau* Marsanne at the bottom of *Bessards* dates from the 1950s, and the oldest plot of all in the vineyard is a half hectare of Marsanne dating from 1912 on *Le Gros des Vignes*.

The red Marquise de la Tourette is made wholly from Delas crop, and in a year like 1999 approaches the fabled wine of Hermitage's past, with loads of flavour and varied nuances—fruit, leather, tobacco, and spices all mingled together. The Tourette *rouge* has come on extremely well since the later 1990s and could represent very strong value for money in the coming years. About 35,000 bottles are made.

In a potent year like 1999 it is raised in cask for as long as 26 months, in a soft year like 2000 14 months, and in a year of struggle like 2002 just 12 months. Generally it receives 18 to 20 months, a touch longer than in the early 1990s. Its oak is 15 per cent new at most, the other casks one or two years old. In days gone by, there was never such vintage variation in the duration of the cask ageing—the "system" didn't permit it. Like most of the Delas reds, it is not filtered.

The *parcellaire*, or small-vineyard, wine at Hermitage is *Les Bessards*, from midslope on its granite heartlands, where there are touches of clay. There are about three hectares of vines in this middle spot, the oldest patch dating from 1946, and the very best fruit is selected for its 5,000 to 6,000 bottles.

Les Bessards was first made in 1990 and, since then, has only missed out in 1992, 1993, 2000, and 2002 for quality reasons. It is vinified in open concrete, the top temperature 30° to 32°C, with daily *pigeages* and *remontages*. This, too, receives 18 to 20 months in cask, half the oak new, the rest one to two years old. Since its first issue, the stay in oak has increased, but the new-oak proportion has been cut: in 1990–91 it was almost 100 per cent new-oak raised. This is never fined nor filtered.

Bessards is a wine of full, ripe, and sometimes southern tendencies. The texture is tight-knit, and beyond the evident chunkiness runs a range of black fruits and chewy tannins. But the heady potency of the south is absent, and the wine smooths itself out with great aplomb once it has passed eight years. Smoky and challenging when young, it is a worthy representative of the granite hill, a wine of evident grandeur.

The white Marquise de la Tourette ends up as about 95 per cent Marsanne, 5 per cent Roussanne. This is vinified in oak, half the casks

new, half one year old, at up to 20°C. Methods have changed for this, with fermentation in 550-litre *demi-muids* until 1976, and 450-litre casks and a purely new oak vinification applied in the early 1990s until the new oak proportion was cut to its current level in 1997. The Marquise de la Tourette *blanc* stays on its fine lees, which are stirred, until June and is fined and bottled in July, with the malo completed.

From 2003 the casks were turned to replicate the lees stirring otherwise done with a *bâtonnage* stick. This takes place over a couple of weeks late on in the ageing process; it means that gas is not lost from within the cask, and therefore a lower sulphur treatment is needed.

The Hermitage *blanc* Marquise de la Tourette has become much more consistent since the late 1990s, and emphasizes the full elegance that can be achieved here. It often shows the Marsanne's typical almond side, along with buttery and fruit aspects like lime and apricot. It can live past 15 years in most vintages, the best like 1999 running for 20-plus.

Beyond the northern Rhône, Delas also now produce a reliable red Côtes du Rhône, and in the southern Rhône, where they buy wine, not grapes, the coverage includes all the leading *appellations*, including Muscat de Beaumes, Tricastin, and Ventoux.

HERMITAGE MARQUISE DE LA TOURETTE ROUGE

2003 (CASK) ★★★★ Very dark; sizeable, tight-knit bouquet, ripe fruit with meaty side. Big scale palate—chocolate, crushed black berries. Ripe wine—tannins present but integrated. Solid, very compact texture. More character, diversity from 2008; 2020–24.

2002 ★★ Brewed fruit—older, middle-age style, light licorice, Subdued from bottling. Quiet black fruit on palate, widens near finish, fair juice. Length OK, some oak at end. Contains *Bessards'* best fruit. Can truck on, esp from 2007–08; 2016–19.

2001 ★★★★ Nose has volume—spiced, cooked black fruits; good potential, tight-knit black fruits/olives, tannins collect at end, laurel aftertaste. Traditional, typical. From 2009; 2017–20.

2000 ★★★ Quite prominent bouquet, black fruits, some tar, pepper. Tasty fruit, friendly warmth, nice tannins, not demanding. Black olives end. Agreeable, pretty full wine. 2012–16.

1999 ★★★★★ Pretty *robe;* spiced bouquet, some warmth, has complex tones—leather, dark fruit, polish. Tasty attack—great fat, has a lot of stone fruit, plums/prunes, also tobacco, cinnamon—great variety. Really authentic. I could imagine people drinking this, the perfumed wine of literature, out of a goblet 200 or 300 years ago. Dryish end. 2017–23.

1998 ★★★★ Quite open, smoky red fruits aroma, plus a ripe side—promising bouquet. Good upright, firm start, nice depth, and a real crunchy black flavour runs through it. Fruit and leathery, wood tones. Feet-on-the-ground wine, thorough. Genuine tannins, lot of promise. Esp from 2006; 2011–16.

1997 ★ 2011–15
1996 ★ 2005–09
1995 ★★★ 2009–12

HERMITAGE LES BESSARDS ROUGE

2003 (CASK) ★★★★★ Harmonious bouquet —smoky, tight fruit, lots of potential. Black fruit peeps out of a big mass of wine, this is a solid, knit, no chinks do. Licorice finale. Balanced, appealing, long life ahead. From 2008–09; 2025–28.

2001 ★★★★★ Very typical, burnt black fruit, woody tones, *garrigue;* chunky palate, great width, really solid. Deep core, tight olive/cassis. Oak on aftertaste. From 2010. Strong, clean wine. 2023–28.

1999 ★★★★★★ Very full *robe;* very deep, ripe oily bouquet, leathery possibilities, moving to second stage. Very wholesome texture, broad/full with round exterior. Palate hasn't moved. Replete with black fruit, oily and suave, spherical. Great balance, *Grand Vin.* Will always drink well, but more variety from 2009; 2026–31.

1998 ★★★★★ Young, closed nose—heated black fruit, pepper, herbs; solid black flavour, chunky, then gets sappy, then chewy tannins. Quite heated, typical, has good juice. From 2008; 2018–22.

1997 ★★ Very dark; ripe crop, plum/prune and alcohol on nose; black flavours, pure, good guts. Length sound, well-integrated tannins. 2014–20.

1994 ★ 2009–14
1991 ★★★★★ 2009–12

HERMITAGE MARQUISE DE LA TOURETTE BLANC

2003 ★★★★ Well-nuanced bouquet, flies along, is broad too. Good mix of butter-hazelnut on palate, white stone fruit also present. Length sound, nutty finish. Plenty to come, full without excess. Stylish. From 2008; 2019–22.

2002 ★★ Stewed white stone fruit bouquet, honeysuckle also, is open. Softer than earlier when held more spice/oak. Hazelnut-apricot character, some buttery richness. Some acetate tone in it, ends rather apruptly. Not integrated now, was more classy and elegant; in a dip. From 2006–07; 2016–20 Last tasted Dec. 2004.

2001 ★★★ Gently fat, buttery, oaked aroma, elegant. Overt, persistent richness, oak edging. Mineral, toasted end then buttery aftertaste. Clean. Esp from 2007–09; 2016–19.

2000 ★★★★ Yellow tones; nicely rich bouquet—stylish, very authentic, some apricot. Really lovely, delicious wine. Bang! Mixes white fruit/light cheese, nutty towards finish. Rich enough to live well. 2010–14.

1999 ★★★★ Ripe crop, broad bouquet in the making; rich, ripe flavour—butter/lime. Good fat on aftertaste, also decisive, lasts well. Still closed. From 2006–08; 2020–24.

1998 ★★ Very discreet bouquet, hint of honey, butterscotch, some ripe crop. Light nut on palate, quite firm texture. Reserved. Should unfold well, staying on the elegance more than the power. 2011–16.

Export 50 per cent (1) Great Britain, (2) USA, (3) Belgium

BERNARD FAURIE

27 ave Hélène de Tournon 07300 Tournon
+33(0)475 085509

See also St-Joseph.

Don't worry, Bernard! You make lovely wines, full of the authentic Hermitage qualities. Yours is a benchmark small domaine in a wonderful *appellation*. Hang loose!

Such words need to be addressed to the often fretful Bernard Faurie, a man completely without pretension and one who has toiled heroically since changing jobs in 1980. Until then he worked in a factory near Tournon, while his father looked after the family cherry and apricot trees and sold the wine from their 0.56 hectare of Hermitage to local merchants.

Bernard first had to learn to vinify the wine for his father and for his relation Jean Bouzige in nearby Mauves. Between them, the three elder members of the family each held 0.56 hectare. "It simply wasn't big enough for me to work when I came out of school," he recalls. The Faurie family used to be the large local *pépiniériste* before the Second World War, when they would supply around 200,000 vine plants a year up and down the Rhône Valley.

"My family has owned vines on Hermitage since 1935, and my aunt, Mme. Bouzige, says that nowadays it's the *grosse* Syrah—the Syrah 3309—which is the enemy vine," he says. "This is the one with fatter pips that gives enormous crops, and it's been particularly in evidence at Crozes-Hermitage since the mid to late 1970s." In his own vineyards, he is now trying to plant *massale*, or selected vinestock grafted off current healthy old plants.

Bernard is in his mid-50s. He has graduated to silvery hair, keeping his usual moustache, but his figure remains trim. He takes his winemaking very seriously, and as one of Life's Questors, sometimes borders on the hyperactive. He darts around his cramped, cluttered cellar, talking at speed with a marked southern twang, but his zeal hides a shy, hidden personality.

The cellar has had a recent makeover, to allow him to store and sell older vintages. For years it was a paradise of bits of equipment, a grandfather clock beside crates, wooden cupboards, glass *bonbonnes*, cases of wine, casks, electric heaters that may be needed, you never know. There are no signs of advertising material or promotional literature. Outside the cellar, a shiny yellow tractor is wedged into his front yard.

A snatch of dialogue is revealing: "What did you do for your 50th birthday?" "My wife gave me a surprise." "What was that?" (questioner thinking of spectaculars, Michelin starred dinners) "She got my good friends along." The man is modest and reserved: just like his wines.

Bernard exploits 1.7 hectares at Hermitage, of which he has two-thirds and his cousin Pierre Faurie one-third. He vinifies his cousin's grapes, and that wine is sold in bulk to merchants like Tardieu-Laurent.

Bernard is the fourth generation to work on *Les Greffieux*, a vineyard that makes up over half his area. Its oldest vines date from 1914, and it has been replanted here and there since then. "I find a good part of its soil very like *Bessards*," he says, "since there is a lot of granite, some very hard, and some of it more broken down into particles."

The rest of this site contains *Greffieux*'s orthodox soil of alluvial Rhône stones, a topsoil layer of 40 cm (16 in.) and underneath it the hard rock. The Syrah here was planted by his great-grandfather in the 1920s and 1930s. Both spots are very free draining.

Lastly, there is a patch of 0.2 ha on *Le Méal*, a vineyard planted by his father in the 1960s. Elsewhere, Bernard has also built up nearly two hectares of St-Joseph vineyards. In line with this expansion, he has two full-time workers to help him.

Bernard's approach to the vineyards is natural. His pruning is conducted according to the moon: "The first quarter of a new moon encourages too much leaf growth," he states in his quiet tone. He has never used weedkillers, and restricts treatments: in 2003 some people sprayed several times as usual against mildew and oïdium, but Bernard just twice. He is also a

FIGURE 15 Yes! Bernard Faurie relaxes for the camera. (Author's collection)

subscriber to the horse of M. Cotte; the plough serves to build up the earth around the vines in January and to free it in the spring, a practice known as *buttage*.

He likes to leave alone as much as he can in the cellar, too. The crop is fermented in whole bunches, and he is adamant about not resorting to outside yeasts to stimulate fermentation. "I tried outside yeasts one year, and the wine wasn't the same," he states.

Vinification lasts 18 to 21 days in wood vats, the temperature allowed to run to a maximum of 32°C. There is cap punching, some of it done by foot, and pumping-over.

Cask ageing lasts 18 to 24 months, three-quarters in 600-litre *demi-muids*, the rest in 228-litre *pièces*; 10 to 30 per cent are new (a slightly raised percentage since the early 2000s), the rest up to five years old. In pursuit of more fruit, he has cut the number of rackings during the cask ageing from three or four to just two.

Bernard works almost obsessively to avoid any dirt or risk of infection in his cellar at all times; he is one of the only growers I know who washes his *pipette* after each wine during a tasting. The net result for the visitor is that the going underfoot can get a little muddy, but this habit, of which he is not really conscious, shows just why this domaine produces such wonder-

fully pure wines. The grower's commitment to them is total and respectful.

The wines have not been fined since 1991, while Bernard watches the weather to see if he can avoid filtering: "Well, say there has been a high-pressure front for as much as two weeks. Then your wine can be clear, which means very little filtration in light years like 1993 and 1994. But once you're dealing with a big vintage like 1995, 2001, or 2003, you have to filter because the wines are so structured."

Since 1994 he has made three different reds, wherein the nuance of his three soils comes through. The classic is taken from the more granite, *Bessards*-style soil of *Greffieux* and can contain a little *Méal*. Then there are 600 to 1,000 bottles of a Greffieux, except that this word does not appear on the label, in true Monsieur Faurie fashion. This comes from the bottom of *Greffieux*, where the style is more on the fruit, without firm tannic support.

Lastly, the top wine is Le Méal; this started life, and continues today with just a code known to Bernard on the label, and the regular Hermitage title. Call for Inspector Clouseau *encore!* This is a beautiful wine; the 2001 hit the mark in a big way, with masses of sumptuous richness, and awakened memories of the old Henri Sorrel delights from his plot on *Méal* in the late 1970s.

"I find it is structured and fine at the same time," says Bernard, his word "structured" referring to the tannic presence. "It shows red fruits, is persistent on the palate, and can live well." He always harvests its crop last as a conscious way of achieving very ripe grapes. There is never very much of this prized wine—1,000 bottles in 2001, none in 2002, and 600 bottles in 2003.

The white wine is pure Marsanne, planted around 1960 on the *Bessards*-influenced part of *Les Greffieux* where the soil is very granitic and poor—it's not the most ideal location for the Marsanne. This is microwine, but not knowingly, "garagely" done. It's just because there has never been much. Bernard ferments the 600 litres in oak, 10 per cent of it new unless he has bought a new cask, when the ratio shoots up!

Bernard's well-installed worry meter works overtime on this task. He has cut back his white-wine cask ageing (no new oak at this stage) from at least a year to six to eight months, and bottles it sometime between April and June, before the next harvest. He also blocks the malolactic fermentation as a matter of course.

His whites get off to a slow start and are best left until middle age, around seven-plus years. Bernard has always worried even more than usual about mastering white-wine vinification, and it's true that these wines are not straightforward. They're elegant and understated, less fleshy than many, and somewhat in the shadow of the very good reds.

The succession of this domaine is in the hands of Bernard's two daughters: the elder, just past her mid-20s is Christine, a student of achitecture. She has edged towards wine by making her architecture project the design of a new cellar. The younger, Catherine, is a sports teacher and helps in the vineyard in the summer. We keep our fingers crossed.

HERMITAGE ROUGE

2002 (CASK) ★★ Quite tight, red berry fruits nose; expressive, clear red fruit, with sinew in texture. Delicate overall. Fair, chewy length. Making quiet progress. From 2007; 2012–14.

2001 ★★★★ Quite solid nose, stylish red fruits/toffee, dry hints; well-bound flavours, elegant red fruit, tannins woven. Good balance, authentic, classic structure; esp from 2006–07; 2017–20.

2000 ★★★ Gentle black fruits/violet nose, earthy too. Tight black fruit, pepper. Sound tannins, pure, mineral touches. Persistent, traditional. From 2007; 2014–17.

1999 ★★★ Some black fruit, tar on bouquet; vibrant early fruit, tannins appear at end, berry-tar finish. 2013–16.

1998 ★★★ Big, broad, sappy blackberry nose. Cautious attack, but is full, chewy. Good core matter, and end tannins. 2014–18.

1997 ★★ 2009–13

1996 ★★ 2014–18
1995 ★★ 2008–13

HERMITAGE LES GREFFIEUX ROUGE

2002 ★★ Some roundness on bouquet—compact fruit. Pleasant fruit on attack, then tightens. Pretty enough. Agreeable, early-style wine. Some meatiness on finish, shows a bit more claw there. In transition, tannins softening quite fast. From 2006–07; 2015–18.

2001 ★★★★ Raspberry, rose-hip, pretty nose; clearly textured, persistent red fruits, stylish, elegant, tightens well at end. From 2006; 2013–16.

HERMITAGE LE MÉAL ROUGE

2003 (CASK) ★★★★ Compact, well-filled bouquet—pretty violets, licorice, bosky, is balanced. Well-filled palate, black fruit with some cut. Works quietly, without excess. Stylish side will develop. 2009; 2021–25.

2001 ★★★★★ Raspberry/mineral bouquet—solid but not excessive. Good quality—lots of style, savoury and rich core, really delicious. Graceful, caressing wine with full red fruit. Very genuine length. Esp from 2008–09. *Grand Vin.* 2019–22.

1999 ★★★★ Polish, table wax aroma; dense start, then firm flavours. Assertive tannins, needs time. Lot of extract. From 2007; 2018–2022.

1998 ★★★★★ Lovely wild black fruit/tar nose. Full attack, masses of silky black fruit, orderly, long tar/oak finish. Great balance. 2016–21.

1997 ★★★★ Violet/woods aromas, warm, oily sap; ripe, oily texture continues on palate. Well-graded fruit—fine, tasty. Feminine Hermitage. Mushroom aftertaste. 2010–14.

1996 ★★★ Aromatic, sappy cooked fruit aroma, pungent. Nice red fruits, then tightens, dark berries prevail. Stylish extract. Will expand. 2010–15.

1995 ★★★ Violets, warm, deep aroma; good fruit attack, then becomes profound. Firm, full; good tannic chew on finish. 2010–15.

HERMITAGE BLANC

2003 ★★★★ Pretty, broad bouquet—honey, dried fruits. Warm, suave texture, orderly richness. Stylish wine, persists well. Length is very good. Has heat and fat and is harmonious. 2018–22.

2002 ★★ Discreet, hawthorn, custard cream aroma. Three-quarter-weight wine, weaves along, has some richness. Salty touches within, stylish, live finish. Good purity, faithful to the vintage; has lost its early oak. 2012–14.

1999 ★ Pretty, restrained, gentle bouquet; lightly spiced white fruits, understated like Bernard; nice length from the oak. Seems fresher than the 1998. Unusual taste of greengage, spice. I back it to show a lot more when eight years old or so.

1998 ★ Vanilla from new oak, quince, light spice on bouquet; white fruit is upright, almost taut. Almond flavours on rather burnt finish. Understated; leave till 2003 for it to emerge. 2011–15.

Export 70 per cent (1) USA, (2) Great Britain, (3) Japan

DOMAINE JEAN-CLAUDE ET NICOLAS FAYOLLE

35 route des Blancs 26600 Gervans +33(0)475 033483

See also Crozes-Hermitage.

After the 2002 split in the old Fayolle family domaine, Jean-Claude and son Nicolas have kept 0.8 ha of Syrah (1965–70) and 0.2 ha of Marsanne (1982), both on *Diognières*. The Marsanne grows on clay-granite, the Syrah on a more stony part of the *lieu-dit*. The plot had been in an abandoned state when bought by Jules Fayolle in 1965—showing how difficult it was to sell Hermitage in those years.

The red is whole bunch–fermented for two weeks, with a top temperature of 32°C. Yeasts are added, and there are two pumping-overs a day. Cask ageing lasts 12 to 12 months in a mix of barrel and casks that are up to 10 years old. The wine is fined but not filtered.

Since 2002 the white has been raised for six to eight months in 10-year-old casks once its malo has been completed. The Fayolles recommend drinking the white before it is four years old or once it is 10 years old, finding that the wine falls into a quiet spell in the interim.

Both wines are a trifle plain. Their *lieu-dit* is not front rank, but one feels the winemaking is perhaps too safely ensconced in traditional methods.

HERMITAGE LES DIONNIÈRES ROUGE

2003 (CASK) ★★★ Soaked raspberry *coulis* aroma, wild berries also; simmered jam flavour, is a meaty wine. Decent content within. Hints of Syrah reduction present at this stage. From 2006–07; 2019–22.

Known as Domaine Fayolle pre-2002

2001 ★ Clear fruit nose—violet/game black fruit. Simple, straight fruit flavour, some prickle. Tender texture, some tannic gain near end. Simple, but quite agreeable. Maybe more variety in 2005–06. 2011–12.

HERMITAGE LES DIONNIÈRES BLANC

2002 ★ Dried skins, minted nose, some potential. Decent body, quite interesting. Light nut, also heat on end. Still quite tight. 2010–11.

2001 ★ Ripe, lush, sweet-style nose; sappy, almost overripe taste, fair richness, bit old-fashioned, could have more cut.

FAYOLLE FILS ET FILLE

9 rue du Ruisseau 26600 Gervans +33(0)475 033374

See also Crozes-Hermitage.

Born in 1946, Jean-Paul Fayolle can now take more of a back seat and let his son Laurent and daughter Céline get on with the domaine that was created in September 2002. Out of the family's old 1.5 ha on *Diognières*, they have kept half a hectare, the other part staying with his brother Jean-Claude. It is a plot that Jules Fayolle bought in 1965 in an overgrown state, and was planted at that time.

On the abrupt slope higher up on *Diognières* is 0.3 ha of Syrah, This is clay-chalk, with some stones, and Laurent finds that the soil is a little tired: "It needs vegetal matter to restore it, due to the high volume treatments and cropping of the 1970s," he admits. The 0.2 ha of 90 per cent Marsanne, 10 per cent Roussanne is at the flatter bottom end of *Diognières*, where the soil is neutral, a siliceous, silt mix present.

In the past, the twin brothers Jean-Paul and Jean-Claude vinified their red and white entirely traditionally. Laurent is changing that for his branch of the family. The red can be destemmed, and is fermented in a modern oak vat for two to three weeks. The process can now start with a four-day cool maceration, and there are twice-daily pumping-overs, and cap punching. The wine is aged for 12 to 16 months in one-to-three-year-old casks and lightly fined and filtered.

After pressing, the white juice is decanted for two days at 10°C and then fermented in young oak for two weeks, with temperature control available in the cellar. It remains on its fine lees, with stirring, until after the malo and is raised for around 10 months, with a July bottling.

Clean and tidy, these are middle-rank Hermitages that are definitely best drunk in middle age when they have acquired some extra variety of flavour.

HERMITAGE DIONNIÈRES ROUGE

2002 ★ ★ ★ Quite dark black fruit, tar/violet nose. Clean texture, gentle middle flavour. Some oak/fungal notes at end. Low-key but pretty, some style here. From 2006; 2014–16.

HERMITAGE DIONNIÈRES BLANC

2002 ★ ★ Obvious oak, toasted top bouquet. Oaked palate, some richness, oiliness within. Fair apricot, exotic length, dried fruits aftertaste. Not especially full. From 2006; 2013–14.

FERRATON PÈRE ET FILS

13 rue de la Sizeranne 26600 Tain-l'Hermitage
+33(0)475 085951

See also Condrieu, Côte-Rôtie, Crozes-Hermitage, St-Joseph.

This is a family and domaine blighted by tragic fortunes. The son of the estate, Samuel Ferraton, had a motorbike accident in 2002 that left him in a wheelchair, just as his wife was about to have their baby. At the time his father, Michel, a long-standing *figura* at Hermitage, was in the middle of lengthy hospital treatment himself.

One smidgen of good fortune was that the Ferratons had signed a joint-venture agreement with Chapoutier in 1998: half of the business to work with their single-vineyard wines, half to sell *négoce* wines. At least there was some underpinning in terms of helping hands.

Born in 1972, Samuel joined his father in 1994, making him the third generation in the family affair. He had studied wine at Beaune and in the Jura. In his grandfather Jean's day, the original vineyard dating from 1946 was on *Diognières*, a postage stamp of 0.3 hectare split between Syrah and Marsanne. Father Michel bought up other *parcelles* over the years, and now there are two hectares on *Diognières* (mainly 1970s). These provide the crop for the Dionnières Ermitage red.

All the vineyards have been officialy worked biodynamically since 2000. The other holdings are two plots of Syrah—0.64 ha on *Méal* (1960s), and 0.2 ha on *Petit Méal* to its east, at the low, richer soil level of the site. These make up the domaine's Méal Ermitage.

On *Beaume*, there is a small 0.22 hectare mixed 70 per cent Marsanne, 30 per cent Roussanne dating from the 1960s, which constitutes the Reverdy white Ermitage, along with Marsanne and a little Roussanne from *Diognières* and *Méal*. The end wine of Reverdy approaches 40 per cent Roussanne, about the most in the *appellation*.

Always something of an outsider to the orthodox winegrowing community, Michel bought his quayside cellars in 1971 from M. de Boissieux, who owned vineyards at Crozes and Hermitage and who sold some wine in bottle until 1970. Born in 1941, Michel is a member of the old school, a man whose phrases can emanate from the nineteenth-century school of politeness. An *entracte* of a cigarette and a quick toot of white form part of a tasting for him.

With Michel, several visits are needed to piece together the trail of partial data and approximations that he supplies. But one has sympathy for him. Why shouldn't he be impressionistic? He's not a businessman. And there's always a sidelong comment, an afterthought that sets out an accurate home truth. If he were a race-horse, his trainer would let him run from the front.

Vinification here is traditional. Most of the Syrah bunches enter the open wood and concrete vats whole, with the Méal receiving a three-week fermentation, the Dionnières two weeks. There are twice-daily pumping-overs and some cap punching.

The family continue to use their 100-year-old press and place the young wine in cask for its malolactic fermentation. As the more robust wine, the Méal is raised one-third in new, two-thirds in one-to-three year-old casks for 14 to 18 months. The slightly lighter Dionnières is placed in one-quarter new, three-quarters one-to-four-year-old casks for the same period of time. There are a few 600-litre *demi-muids* in addition to the 228-litre casks. The wines are neither fined nor filtered before bottling.

Dionnières *rouge* shows good local feel and a traditional character in a vintage like 2001. Le Méal carries a wild side of unbridled hedgerow flavours and leathery side tones: the Chapoutier Le Méal is more measured, by contrast—more sleek.

The domaine white, Le Reverdy, is 50 to 60 per cent Marsanne, 40 to 50 per cent Roussanne. After a day's cool decantation, the juice is cask fermented, with half the oak new. Ageing in cask lasts 10 months, with lees stirring until bottling in July, the malo completed.

There are also a red and a white Hermitage—both called "Les Miaux"—that combine some of their own crop with the purchase of wine. The red Miaux is half and half, from a mix of *Diognières*, *Méal*, and *Beaume*. The different plots have their grapes vinified separately—

Michel considers this to bring out the typicity of the wine more strongly than would an earlier *assemblage*. Its crop is destemmed and fermented in concrete vats for three weeks with pumpings-over and a top temperature of 32° to 33°C. It is then aged in one-to-four-year-old casks for 16 to 18 months.

The white Les Miaux is pure Marsanne, cropped at very ripe levels from Méal and Murets. It is 60 per cent oak fermented in one-to-three-year-old casks, 40 per cent handled in steel vats. Storage on its fine lees lasts for 10 to 12 months, and it is bottled with the malo completed.

Elsewhere, the *négociant* business works with the other northern Rhône *appellations* except for Cornas and St-Péray. From the southern Rhône, there comes a Côtes du Rhône, Samorëns, in red and white—the red largely Grenache, the white 60 per cent Grenache Blanc and 40 per cent Clairette from Laudun in the Gard. There is also a Châteauneuf-du-Pape, Le Parvis, which is largely Grenache.

HERMITAGE LES MIAUX ROUGE

2002 (CASK) ★★ Mid colour; lightly toasted, strawberry fruit aroma, more fungal with air. Easy red fruit palate, not real depth. Discreet tannin, ends tar/licorice. Gains oiliness, oomph after 90 mins. The lesser sites on show. Esp 2007; 2012–14.

2001 ★★★ Pretty, open/sappy red fruits nose, direct. Cosy attack, broad, lacks some scale. Decent chewy, pepper end. 2013–15.

ERMITAGE LES DIONNIÈRES ROUGE

2003 (CASK) ★★ Bosky, peppery fullness on bouquet, on the stern side. Oily, black fruit attack, wine is a bit stretched, cellar work on top. Oaked aftertaste, bit bitter. Leave so can integrate, relax. From 2008; 2016–18.

2002 (CASK) ★★★ Stinky, black aroma; is very reduced, stewed black fruits, core is OK, pretty warm. Hard to judge like this.

2001 ★★★★ Deep bosky, wild/leathery nose; broad, upright, has local feel. Oily texture, core black fruit, pepper end. Good length, character. From 2008; 2019–21.

ERMITAGE LE MÉAL ROUGE

2003 (CASK) ★★★ Inky, chocolate, replete bouquet, upright, a touch extracted. Lots of black fruit, then oak on palate. Big content, can take the oak. Granite-style firmness here, with good core. Hope it will gain more angles, variety as it ages. From 2008–09; 2017–20.

2001 ★★★★★ Thorough, oily/fungal, game aroma; well-integrated fruit, rich wine. Nicely wild, fresh prune style flavour, smoky. From 2008; 2019–22.

2000 ★★★ Ripe fruit, burnt aromas, earthy, brewed side. Good hit of stewed fruits on attack, wild berries. Tar traces, a macerated flavour. Length OK, oak present. Tannins refined. Grilled with air, then recovers. Quite rich finale if you wait. Esp from 2006; 2013–17.

HERMITAGE LES MIAUX BLANC

1998 ★★ Very ripe, warm nose; quite fat, bit gluey, slight oxidised notes, stone fruit/nut end. Can tick along quietly. 2014–17.

ERMITAGE LE REVERDY BLANC

2003 (CASK) ★★★ High-tone aroma, but bouquet overall refined, harmonious. White fruits ease along palate well. Almost tannic chewiness on finish, interesting. Good and full, with structure. Clear fruit here, and oak not overdone. From 2007–08; 2022–25.

2002 ★★ Light gold *robe*, not looking fresh. High tone, custard aroma. Down the line, plain flavour, persists OK. Quite solid, best in second phase. Lacks flair, more on show 2007. Has never grabbed the attention, not enough here. 2012–14. Last tasted Nov. 2004.

2001 ★★★ Exotic fruit, cooked apple tart/dried fruits/butterscotch aroma—sustained, some style. Possesses good oiliness, juice—has ripe, refined white fruit. Some acidity, too, but oak well on top. Orange marmalade also. Marsanne's flan/custard flavour

subdued and oak needs till 2007 to meld. 2018–21.

2000 ★★★ Mild straw *robe*. Elegant, streamlined aroma—some oak, melted butter/spice. Gentle combo of juice and oak on palate. Refined, some width. Banana/vanilla aftertaste. Not assertive like a white from *L'Hermite*. Good with Shropshire blue cheese to draw the oak out, makes it more mineral. 2016–19.

1999 ★★★ Sleek bouquet, oak notes; decent core, oak surrounds. Quite stylish, can settle. Fair finesse. From 2007; 2014–17.

Export 60 per cent (1) USA, (2) Europe

ALAIN GRAILLOT

Les Chênes Verts 26600 Pont de l'Isère
+33(0)475 846752

See also Crozes-Hermitage, St-Joseph. Changes to his rental agreement at Hermitage mean that Alain Graillot produced no Hermitage under his own name from 2000 to 2003. "I have been waiting for the vineyard, planted in 1993, to become a little older," he says, having sold the wine in the interim to a northern Rhône *négociant*.

Previously he rented a tiny 0.12 ha site on *Les Greffieux* as well as working his own 0.12 ha plot there. The red 1989 was his first wine.

The wine was revived in 2003, and in 2004 there was enough for three casks—around 1,200 bottles. It is raised for 15 months in one-year-old oak.

HERMITAGE ROUGE

2004 (CASK) ★★ (★) Pretty solid bouquet, fair persistence, has potential; stylish palate, grows nicely towards finish. Soft richness, good around 2008–09. 2014–16.

1999 ★★★★ Good, clear intense purple; red fruits on bouquet, tightly knit. Departs with a lot of red fruits, really good, delicious. Fresh, very good fruit cut, is very pure. Stylish Hermitage, elegant. 2014–16.

JEAN-LOUIS GRIPPAT

The sale of the Grippat domaine and vineyards to Guigal in 2001 meant the transfer of 1.5 hectares of Hermitage—1.2 hectares of Marsanne planted in 1942 and 0.3 hectare of Syrah, both on the southeasterly *Murets climat*.

On average there were just five casks of red Hermitage a year. From 1995 the Syrah was 80 per cent destalked. Cask ageing ran over 18 months. These wines, like the whites, were elegant and, after closing up around three years old, would often show well from six years onwards.

The whites were fermented in a mix of vat and new oak, the oak to bring extra length. Storage was in vat, with three to five months in oak before bottling, the malo done, 15 months after the harvest.

Grippat was also a Vin de Paille maker—in 1985, 1988, 1995, 1996, and 1997—what he termed "900 half bottles for us, *en famille*," with the words "Vin de Table" on the label.

Both the 1985 and the 1988 held aromas similar to an essence extract of oils, rather like a light, not very pungent Gewurtztraminer from Alsace. The flavours were honeyed and rich, the finish clean. It was not a commercial reality, but was very succesful.

HERMITAGE ROUGE

1998 ★★★ Pretty purple/cherry; open nose, very correct ripe fruit aroma; very dark fruits, nice scale, lot of persistent elegance. Smooth tannins, good length. Very good. 2013–17.

1997 ★★★★ Black *robe*; red/black fruit nose, some licorice, good vigour; silky style of Hermitage, very orderly, elegant. Very good red fruits. Full, ripe, closed at present. Balance and acidity fine. 2012–16.

HERMITAGE BLANC

1997 ★★★ Restrained, floral, and oily aspects on bouquet; soft, tender attack, expands nicely, a real explosion of nuts, apricot, mango/ lychee almost. Lovely finish, also is quite fresh. 2007–12.

HERMITAGE VIN DE PAILLE BLANC

1997 Straw colour; grilled fruits, crème caramel bouquet. Palate—very good grip, lovely depth, delicious dried fruits. Light touch, the finish is quite dry. Very good.

E. GUIGAL

Château d'Ampuis 69420 Ampuis +33(0)474 561022

See also Condrieu, Côte-Rôtie, Crozes-Hermitage, St-Joseph.

Marcel Guigal has crept somewhat stealthily on to the Hermitage hill through his purchase of the vineyards of Jean-Louis Grippat and the two hectares that belonged to de Vallouit. Down in the town, the tongues are wagging, no doubt, as this potential predator from the north hoves into view.

March 2001 saw the purchase of Grippat's 1.5 hectares—a very choice 1.2-hectare plot of white Marsanne dating from 1942, the rest Syrah averaging 30 years old, both on *Les Murets*. The de Vallouit holding acquired in June 2001 was mainly on *Greffieux* (average 30 years), with some *Bessards* (average 90 years) and *L'Hermite*. It was mostly Syrah, with just a little Marsanne averaging 40 to 50 years. Between the two vineyards, Philippe Guigal reckons there is perhaps 3 per cent of Roussanne dotted about in the old plots.

Guigal has long presented very acceptable, long-lived Hermitage red and white. The wines used to be vinified at Hermitage, but since 2001 this has been done chez Guigal at Ampuis.

The classic red consists of a lot of *Beaume*, with *Méal* and a little *Bessards* in the mix. It receives a three-to-four-week fermentation and maceration, with twice daily cap punching (*pigeages*). It is aged for 30 to 36 months in cask, 20 per cent of them new. It is neither fined nor filtered. The new oak content was first introduced in 1994.

Now Marcel can also make a wine from his own property. This is called "Ermitage Ex-voto," a name from the Latin representing "in consequence of a wish"—a very Guigal composition. First made in 2001 and intended to be issued only in the best vintages, the red is composed of 30 per cent each of *Bessards* and *Greffieux* and 20 per cent each *L'Hermite* and *Murets*.

This is vinified in Ampuis in the same way as the classic, and receives 30 to 36 months in new casks. Ten thousand bottles are made, and in the lesser years its grapes will certainly help the classic Hermitage wine. Judging by the quality of the 2001, this will become a force in the Hermitage firmament in years to come. In 2002's tricky vintage, there was just one red wine, a mix of property and purchased wine, under half raised in new oak. Ex-voto *rouge* was again made in 2003.

The classic white Hermitage (95 per cent Marsanne, 5 per cent Roussanne) is drawn from the *Rocoules*, *L'Hermite*, and *Maison Blanche* sites. Thirty-three to 50 per cent of the crop is vinified in two-year casks, the rest in stainless steel. Unlike for their Viognier, the Guigals do not practise *macération pelliculaire* (intracell fermentation for direct fruit/aroma extraction), since they feel it doesn't suit the Marsanne and Roussanne. The temperature is held at 16° to 18°C. It receives a two-plus–year cask ageing, with lees stirring. "We taste as we go," comments Philippe; "that's why the 2001 received three years in cask, for instance." The tendency has been to increase the cask ageing: until 1995 it was just one year.

The top white Ermitage Ex-voto is made from 90 per cent *Murets* and 10 per cent *L'Hermite* crop. This is vinified in new oak and also receives two-plus years of quiet ageing. Like all the Guigal whites, it is fined and filtered. The 2003 was a very solid wine, with the depth that one expects from many Guigal wines.

HERMITAGE ROUGE

2002 (CASK) ★★★ Good, smoky, compact black fruit, dark aroma. Black fruits here, sound-enough depth, holds together well, rolls along. Cool, tangy flavour. From 2007–08; 2015–18.

2001 (CASK) ★★★ Fresh, direct, red fruit from granite/figs aroma; open, cooked ripe red fruits. Juicy with fungal end. Can please. 2013–15.

2000 ★★★ Warm, open, quite deep nose, reflects the year. Supple start, good compact stewed fruit, stylish. Oak is in support, end tannins are rounded. Clean, polished Hermitage. From 2005–06; 2014–17. (Composed of 60 per cent crop purchase, 35 per cent Grippat crop, and 5 per cent de Vallouit crop.)

1997 ★★★★ 2011–17
1995 ★★★ 2014–18

ERMITAGE EX-VOTO ROUGE

2003 (CASK) ★★★★ Very dark; ripe, succulent bouquet, very broad, floral surround. Sucrosity and black fruits attack, scale wine. Some end heat, quite potent. Mature fruit, is very full. From 2009; 2024–27.

2001 (CASK) ★★★★ Chunky, black fruit nose, olives/*garrigue*, rich; plenty of content, carries local berried richness. Wide, silky then tannic. Tasty, juicy. *Bessards'* quiet presence noted. 2022–25.

HERMITAGE BLANC

2000 ★★★ Stylish, fair weight aroma, limes; buttery start, quite rich, middle holds up, decent length. Toasted end. Sound. 2015–17.

1999 ★★★ Oily, full, butterscotch/oak aroma; toasted fruits, spicy, rather low-key, was more obviously rich. Clean, subdued finish. Two phases here: 2005–08 and 2011–13. Very good with Chinese food. 2014–19. (Grippat vines/purchased wine.)

1998 ★★★★ Greengages, beeswax, acacia on good, interesting bouquet; very refined flavour, great length, reserved still. Better around 2005–06 with oak absorbed. Nice kick at end, 14° wine. 2011–16. (Made by Grippat, bottled by Guigal.)

1997 ★★★ 2011–16

2001 ★★★ Full *robe*; ample, quite lush bouquet—pineapple, exotic, orange peel aromas, heady enough. Rich and profound, with a near-tannic side. Meaty wine, has shoulders. Sound length, heat on finish. 2007–08, expect oak still then. 2019–22.

DOMAINE HABRARD

Le Village 26600 Gervans +33(0)475 033091

See also Crozes-Hermitage.

Just half a hectare on *Rocoules* is enough for the Habrard family to make a very successful white Hermitage—pure Marsanne and full of typical flesh. Some of the vines are 100 years old, the rest 40 to 50 years, so it's no surprise that the wine is good.

"The vineyard is so old that there are some odd Roussanne vines sprinkled in," admits Laurent Habrard; his neighbours are Marc Sorrel and Jean-Louis Chave. Picking is quite late, usually towards the end of September. Until 1998 the family sold the wine to the Guigal family, but now they make 1,000 to 1,200 bottles themselves.

It is oak fermented, in casks of three to four years old, and raised for six to eight months, with lees stirring. After a short time in vat, it is bottled, malo done, in December, a little over one year after the harvest. "We used to raise the wine for two years, but we're working on what is best for it," admits Laurent modestly.

HERMITAGE BLANC

2002 (CASKS) ★★★ Oily, pear/varnish nose; stylish *gras*, elegant, apricot/nuts. Sound potential. 2014–17.

2001 ★★★★ Quite fresh, elegant floral/butter nose; plump, tasty attack, exotic fruits. Light spice, fennel end. Stylish, great length. 2019–21.

2000 ★★★ White stone fruit, butter/lime nose, some spice; measured warmth, sensuous, nicely full. Apricot/flan mix. Fruit has spiced edge. Rich, persistent. From 2006; 2014–17.

PAUL JABOULET AÎNÉ

Les Jalets RN7 26600 La Roche-de-Glun
+33(0)475 846893

See also Condrieu, Cornas, Côte-Rôtie, Crozes-Hermitage, St-Joseph, St-Péray.

In the 1970s, this family firm was the international yardstick for good Rhône, led by the well-known Hermitage La Chapelle. The reputation carried on into the 1980s, but the 1990s and recent years revealed a slipping of the mantle. Just as it was time to ask the question *Quo vadis, Maison Jaboulet?* the company was sold in late 2005 to the Swiss financier Jean-Jacques Frey. As quality levels in the Rhône have risen, and more and more expression of *terroir* can be found at the best sources, Paul Jaboulet Aîné had not run with the noble pack, and that was a pity.

On the one hand, there are world wine legends like the Hermitage La Chapelle 1961, 1978, and 1990, especially the first. The 1961 mixes with the all-time greats, according to Stephen Browett of international wine merchants Farr Vintners in London: "It's up there with 1945 Mouton, 1947 Cheval Blanc, 1961 Pétrus," he says. "If somebody rings up and asks for the greatest bottle of Rhône ever made, it would be La Chapelle 1961 that is recommended. That has made it the province of collectors now, though, not drinkers, and it is very scarce."

The 1961 sells for £2,000 (US$3,600) a bottle, while the 1978 is at £300 (US$540) and the 1990 a more modest £165 (US$300). But it's revealing that Browett continues with "People don't ring us and ask for young La Chapelle any more—the 1999 is there on the list at £27 ($US49) and not in demand."

The market can speak and be a poor arbiter of taste at the same time. However, there is no denying the inadequacy of the 2000 La Chapelle, which should never have been allowed on to the market. Simply too much wine was passed out as La Chapelle that year, a damning indictment on the company's culture. Looking back through tasting notes, I see that

La Chapelle can still be a very good wine—the 1995 and 1999 were in that category—but the trend has not been encouraging for some years now.

This is a sad do. Personally, Paul Jaboulet Aîné has been the cutting-edge Rhône *maison* in my lifetime, the trailblazer around the world. While Chapoutier were struggling along with uneven quality in the 1970s, Jaboulet were bounding ahead, their rich, true, warm 1960s La Chapelles bringing the very hearth of the Rhône into people's lives. Their wines were spread around the world and served at the greatest events, and were present in wine shops in places as far apart as Caracas, Hong Kong, and San Francisco.

Recently the cutting edge went missing. The vinification policy changed frequently and lacked conviction. It never set the agenda. Saddest of all, there was no longer the feeling that this was a vineyard owner with merchant interests—it was the other way around, with a lot of the wines workmanlike and lacking both flair and personal touch.

Under the new regime, the winemaking will be in the hands of Laurent Jaboulet, Jacques's son, who will be overseen by Jean-Jacques Frey's daughter Caroline, an oenologue in her late twenties who directs vinification at Château La Lagune.

I certainly wouldn't volunteer to run an old (founded 1834) family business; matters were complicated by their very nature here. The doyen of the old family firm and of Hermitage was the redoubtable Louis Jaboulet. Born in 1912, pale blue eyes flashing, he still interviews well: a bit of a joust takes place; answers are snapped back, suspicion about the validity of the whole exercise is not hard to detect. But his presence held this rather disparate family grouping together, even though he "retired" in 1977.

He is less in evidence these days, and the company is run by Louis' son Jacques, who deals with vinification and the buying-in of wines, and the two sons of Louis' late brother Jean—Philippe, who looks after the vineyard and crop purchases, and Michel, who works mostly on the commercial side within France and who joined the company late on, in 1984, after a career in engineering. Philippe is also the President of the Growers Union.

The great tragedy of the 1990s here was the sudden death in July 1997 of Gérard Jaboulet, the charming and much loved envoy of the firm, whose travels took him all over the world and who contributed mightily to the firm's earlier reputation.

Jacques' son Laurent studied at Beaune and is a qualified *oenologue* from the Dijon school. His first vintage was 1998. Slim, with dark hair and glasses, he is a keen young man. In his hands rest much of the future, for it's not the commercial side that needs attention, but the wine production side.

The firm's biggest recent step was to open a new bottle storage centre at Châteauneuf-sur-Isère, five miles from Tain, in June 2001. All the company's *Grands Vins* are stored in cellars that cover a full five or six hectares and have been hewn into the mountain. Vinification still takes place in Tain for the domaine wines, and at La Roche-de-Glun for the *négoce* wines, in a building extension completed in 2004.

Jaboulet's vineyard holdings are centred on the Hermitage hill, and its neighbour the Crozes-Hermitage *appellation*. At Hermitage they work 22 ha of Syrah, all but 0.6 of them their own vineyards. The most celebrated single *climat* is Le Méal, with 6.8 ha, most of it contiguous vineyards acquired in progressive stages from the 1960s to the 1980s.

There are also 7 ha on *La Croix* (often mistakenly referred to in books as *Les Murets*) on the eastern sector of the hill towards Larnage, and 2.6 ha on *Les Bessards*, 2.1 ha on *Rocoules*, 1.3 ha on *Diognières et Torras* (at the eastern extremity), 1.14 ha on *Les Diognières*, 0.6 ha at the top of the hill on *Les Grandes Vignes*, and 0.53 ha on *Les Greffieux*. What a spread! Never more than half a hectare is replanted in any one year. According

GÉRARD JABOULET—
AN APPRECIATION

If there was one wine that served as the international ambassador for the Rhône in the last 30 years, it was Paul Jaboulet Aîné's Hermitage La Chapelle. If there was one man who served as the international ambassador for the Rhône in the past 30 years, it was Gérard Jaboulet, who has died at the tragically early age of 55 years.

Gérard was known to wine lovers around the globe. He wore true Seven League Boots as he patrolled the continents extolling and showing the virtues of good Syrah from its home base of Hermitage. His generosity was almost legendary, his time for the enthusiast unlimited. In Hong Kong in 1997 a leading doctor approached me, triumphant that he had a detailed inscription from Gérard in my Rhône book, promising a future get-together that alas will not take place. Elsewhere in Asia—Bangkok, for example, not noted for its wine drinking—owners of restaurants would volunteer warm memories of Gérard's visit, made memorable by his openness and smiling outlook.

Gérard was the supreme ambassador: he was proud of the Jaboulet wines but never overstated the case. His annual tasting in London combined him not unnaturally with another of the legendary families of French wine, Hugel, also given to enthusiasm more than fanfare. His visits to the United States, where his liaison with Frederick Wildman stretched back many happy years, were regular and lively affairs: the French description *dynamique* fitted him well.

I know how respected he was by his fellow *vignerons*—not just in the Rhône but beyond. He was the 1997 President of the Grandes Familles du Vin, including the Mondavis, Torres, Prats, and Hugels. I remember, too, how he loved the tranquility of the river bank in Ireland for the moments when the globe-trotting paused.

Hermitage La Chapelle is the wine that has excited and delighted people around the world. Our thanks go to Gérard most of all for showing it, explaining it, enthusing about it, and giving people's lives the glint of high pleasure that we all need.

July 1997

to the family, the average age of their Syrah here is 35 to 45 years.

The mighty wine of La Chapelle is chosen by tasting of all the wines, with the best selected for it. The core contributors to La Chapelle, in their most frequent order of importance, are *Méal, Bessards,* and *Greffieux,* with *Rocoules* and very often *La Croix* from a subset there called *Murettes.* In exceptional, clement years, wine from *Diognières* will also be included, and in the very ripe vintage of 1997 all the wine tasted good enough to form La Chapelle.

The *Méal* contribution to La Chapelle is always at least one-quarter and, in a difficult vintage when ripening has been tricky, can rise to half, according to Philippe Jaboulet. It is interesting that comparative tastings of La Chapelle with the Chave Hermitage usually show the La Chapelle to be the more brooding, backward wine of the two, and yet much of it is from *Méal,* with its lush, full fruit. The contribution of *Bessards* is clearly important.

The wine is a registered brand, named after the little chapel of St. Christopher at the top of the hill on *L'Hermite.* It was Henri Jaboulet, Michel's grandfather, who bought the chapel from the French state in 1929, but there is some mystery as to whether the wine had existed as La Chapelle before that. The oldest current bottle the family now possesses is a 1919, with a black and white label. "But our account ledgers show La Chapelle existing in the late 1800s," comments Philippe.

There are 4.77 ha of white vines—65 per cent Marsanne, 35 per cent Roussanne. The main portion is the 2.2 ha on *La Croix* (1.5 ha Marsanne, including some early 1900 vines, and 0.7 ha Roussanne), as well as a choice 1.1 ha on *Rocoules* (0.8 ha Marsanne, 0.3 ha Roussanne), another 1.1 ha on *Maison Blanche* (0.7 ha Marsanne, 0.3 ha Roussanne), and 0.3 ha of Roussanne on *Beaume*.

The *La Croix* site reflects the typical soil changes of a plateau that descends towards the river. On the richer, more clay soil of the plateau, the Marsanne is grown, and right at the stony bottom, where the soil is more silted, there are two plots of Roussanne.

The Hermitage holdings are harvested each plot at a time—usually starting with the eastern end at *La Croix* and the lower site of *Diognières* near the town; "the soils there are deeper and so the grapes a little more fragile," states Philippe. *Bessards* and *Méal* are the last two to be picked—taking one and three days, respectively, to be harvested. Jaboulet are often the last to harvest at Hermitage.

All the red crop across the Jaboulet range is destemmed and crushed. Jacques Jaboulet first destemmed in 1967, and observes that this can allow two to three weeks of extra *cuvaison*. Each plot's fruit is vinified separately as well and raised on its own. Cultured yeasts are used for the white grapes, and for the reds when necessary; but care is taken to use a variety that restrains fast rises in temperature during fermentation.

Fermentation and maceration last three to five weeks, a rule that applies for all the Jaboulet reds. A mix of concrete and steel vats is used—the last wood vats were used in the 1970s. "I prefer concrete because it provides better thermoregulation with its thicker walls and its new temperature control systems as well," says Jacques Jaboulet. Fermentation runs up to 28° to 30°C after the vats have been heated to 35°C for eight hours to obtain colour.

Pumpings-over are done during fermentation, but not cap punching. "We decide on the frequency and duration of the *remontages* by

tasting," comments Philippe; "the first ones are done by a jet of wind that breaks up the 'cake.' We prefer pumping to punching because it avoids any risk of a bitter taste."

Cask ageing lasts up to 18 months, with two or three rackings as the Jaboulets watch out for signs of reductive smells in the Syrah. The new oak content varies according to whom you speak to, a regular feature chez Jaboulet. Some family members talk about 80 per cent new oak, others 20 per cent, and still others none at all, with the age range of casks for La Chapelle stated by Philippe to be one to five years old, with very little new oak. Laurent, the young winemaker son of Jacques, volunteers two-to-five-year-old oak and no new casks.

What is certain is that the 1985 La Chapelle received 17 months' oak, whereas the late 1990 La Chapelles were raised for 13 months. The 2000 received 15 months and was bottled in April 2002.

"La Chapelle spends less time in oak nowadays," says Jacques Jaboulet. "Our vinification process means the wines have lower acidity levels than before, so we have cut the Chapelle back to a stay of 11 to 16 months since around 2000." Jaboulet has also bought around 15 per cent of its casks made from Hungarian oak, supplied from François Frères. With a tighter grain, it is considered to give both the reds and the whites more finesse.

During the raising, there is a series of crucial family tastings from October until March to decide what wines will make up La Chapelle. The final wine is bottled two to three months after this, before the high summer heat, and kept in bottle until September. There is no fining and a light filtration.

The ex-cellars price of La Chapelle has risen strongly since the mid-1990s; who can blame the Jaboulets when it had reached the status of an international trading commodity as well as delicious wine? An example was the 1992 Chapelle, sold ex-cellars for 150 francs (£15/US$27) and on sale in Russian restaurants for 4,000 francs (£400/US$720). The 1995 ex-cellars was 140 francs (£14/US$25), a very stable price level, then the 1997 moved up to 230 francs (£23/US$41), with the 1998 220 francs (£22/US$40). The 2001's price continued the increase, selling to private clients for €58.60 (£39/US$70).

Quantities vary, more so because La Chapelle is decided by tasting and not by specific vineyard. In the later part of the 1990s, a high was 102,000 bottles (1997), with 80,000 in 1998 and 60,000 bottles in 1995. But things went badly wrong in 2000, when 107,000 bottles were produced—far too many. Jaboulet's reputation suffered as a result of this damage to its Crown Jewel.

The 2000 La Chapelle was a mystery, a lot less distinguished than usual; it started life very promisingly, but the process of selection must have gone wrong, since after bottling it came out as a very low-key wine lacking the usual colour, stuffing, and pedigree.

This prompted Jaboulet to produce three Hermitages for the first time in 2001. Michel Jaboulet explained: "We only made 55,000 bottles of La Chapelle in 2001, down from the usual 80,000. There is also a Petite Chapelle— of 40,000 bottles. This is the wine that didn't make it into the full Chapelle. And of course, there is "Le Taurobole," our new name for the Pied de la Côte, with around 13,000 bottles." The Petite Chapelle received the same ageing as the La Chapelle, and is not necessarily going to be repeated.

2001 aside, the second wine is Le Taurobole. This used to be called plain "Hermitage," and was first made as Pied de la Côte in 1990. It is taken from a mix of bought crop and wine and Jaboulet's own grapes and receives 12 to 15 months in casks, none new. In 2000, for instance, the 170 hl of La Chapelle that Jaboulet declassified went into Pied de la Côte. In 1997 all the domaine wine was considered good enough for La Chapelle, so some wine was bought in to keep Pied de la Côte present for that vintage.

I still feel a frisson of anticipation and excitement when a bottle of La Chapelle Hermitage is opened. It has long been such a classic wine that it's a treat one patiently waits for, and handles with a degree of reverence. It's not an indulgent, spur-of-the-moment drink. I like to think of vintages like the 1999 to warm my heart, also the 1995, 1991, and 1990; further back, special favourites have been the 1988 and 1978.

Its colour is usually a sound dark red with black cherry signs present. The young bouquet when on form combines different sensations— fruit, smoke, leather, even game. It is a beguiling mix. The palate declares black fruit and chewy tannins, and in the best vintages is tightly packed, showing its southern inclinations and demanding patience from its guardian. There is often a minty, licorice feel on the finish, which can be long and satisfying.

When thinking of why Bordeaux chased Hermitage to doctor and beef up its wines in the nineteenth century, the best examples of La Chapelle would be my explanation. The ripeness and warmth present, with the potential longevity and gutsy middle palate, would have served to transform some of the reedy Cabernets in rain-affected, poor-ripening years. So it is to be hoped that Jaboulet tends this precious part of France's wine heritage with due care in the coming decades.

All the white crop has been destalked since 1996: "We don't want the sap in these grapes pressed, so as to avoid any bitterness; we do a tiny press of only 2 kg pressure," states Jacques Jaboulet. The white Hermitage, Chevalier de Stérimberg, comes from around two-thirds Marsanne and one-third Roussanne; Jaboulet have been a supporter of Roussanne since the 1970s, when it was designed to introduce freshness into the wine. The creed of that decade was that Rhône whites needed to be fresher and less oxidative, and Jaboulet also blocked the malolactic and picked the crop early in those days to enhance the wine's acidity.

Philippe Jaboulet, a chatty man of pale, sandy hair and moustache, explains: "There are two factors behind the Roussanne—it brings a lot of finesse, especially at the start of the palate, and secondly, its natural acidity is better than the Marsanne's—if you pick them both at the same time. That means you can achieve a better-balanced wine and have better aromas." The Marsanne always ripens ahead of the Roussanne, and is about 0.5° alcohol stronger at the same moment. According to the vineyard layout, some Roussanne can be vinified with the Marsanne, in cases when the vines are mixed up together.

Since 1998 the principle has been for Stérimberg to be vinified in new or young oak, although over the years policy has been variable about this wine. Stainless steel, low temperature fermentation at 14°C, and a blocked malolactic were the tools for it into the mid-1990s, and from 1996 until 1998 fermentation was in stainless steel, with raising in oak. When the degree exceeds 12.5°, the Jaboulets ferment half of it in steel, and only near the end of fermentation place it in oak—as they did in 2001 with their 14° Stérimberg.

The pressed juice is left for 24 hours at 10° to 12°C to let any matter fall clear, and is then transferred to the oak. These days the casks are one-third each new, one year, and two years old, and the temperature is carefully controlled. The 2002 was kept to 16°C, but other years the high can be 18° to 19°C. So potent and low in acidity was 2003, however, that the new-oak proportion was cut back to one-quarter.

The young wine remains on its main lees until June, and thankfully, Jaboulet have now abandoned the lees stirring that coarsened so many of their late 1990s whites. "Lees stirring, or *bâtonnage*, was an experimental phase," says Philippe Jaboulet. "When we used it, the wines turned out to lack acidity and to be high in alcohol. Now we find the *grosse lie* can bring richness without the heaviness." He adds that typically, in a 228-litre cask, there may be five to seven litres of *gross lie* present.

Nowadays Stérimberg is bottled in June or July, at the same time as all the other house whites. Exceptionally, some of the Stérimberg 2001 was bottled in September, with the malolactics taking a very long time to occur.

Chevalier de Stérimberg has been a wine of changing styles over the years, as if Jaboulet cannot settle on its true identity. The 1960s were a glorious period, and the early 1970s too, but thereafter the wine became less regularly robust, rich, and glorious as those earlier wines. By the mid-1990s, the clear policy was to regain richness in the wine. This meant very late picking of extremely ripe crop, but it also brought the aforementioned, dreaded Burgundian practice of *bâtonnage*. The 2002 Stérimberg, however, showed a pretty classic style and the ability to develop steadily—good portents—while the 2003 was quite stylish. It must be stated that Jaboulet argue that the *terroir*, the local feel of the wine, returns after a couple of years.

Jaboulet do not make a Vin de Paille, but used to in the nineteenth century; indeed, the oldest bottle they possess is an 1847 Vin de Paille that is in a hand-blown bottle containing about 65 cl.

Outside Hermitage, Jaboulet have added to their traditional Crozes-Hermitage vineyards around the Domaine de Thalabert; part of the Domaine Roure, on the notable granite highlands of northern Crozes, was acquired in 1995, with some of the Ferraton plain–area vineyards in 1996. They also planted a hectare near Larnage on a hill site in 2003–04. If they can make the most of these excellent sites, so much the better.

Vineyards at Cornas (*St-Pierre*), Condrieu, St-Joseph, and St-Péray have also been bought since the early 1990s, so the firm should be capable of competing with the high-quality suppliers of the northern Rhône. It's a question of will and a strong, centralised policy in the future: the Rhône needs a thriving Paul Jaboulet Aîné.

HERMITAGE LA CHAPELLE ROUGE

2003 (CASK) ★★★ Dark *robe*; some soaked fruit aroma, is bound together, has floral traces, smoky. "Elegant," simmered red fruit berry flavour, as if primary tannins tamed in the cellar. Degree of tannin at the end, which is ripe and pretty soft. Length OK. From 2007–08; 2018–22.

2002 ★★(★) Decent bouquet, top aroma a bit dusty, some warmth within, stewed plums.

Fresh, minted fruit. Soft wine, no real high points. Some width and tannins. Has oak traces, then raspberry aftertaste. Fair balance, some structure, can drink quite early. From 2006–07; 2015–19.

2001 ★★★★ Quite dark purple/black cherry colour; stewed black fruit, minty and hung game aromas, leathery; fair packing of flavour, not very big scale. Blackberry/*cassis*, nice tannins alongside. Some southern character here, from 2007–08. 2023–25.

2000 ★(★) Some advance at top of *robe*, rather see-through. Fungal, bit overripe bouquet—stone fruit, overt cooked fruit. Cooked red berries attack, then lean interior, red fruits return. Berried, bosky texture. Short; dries and vacates. Lacks width. May have a tiny bit more around 2007. 2011–14. Fourth tasting, Jan. 2004.

1999 ★★★★ Dark plum core to *robe*, red at top. Brewed, smoky toasted nose—coffee/mocha, warm cooked stone fruit, deep/varied. Assertive, dry-toned texture with warm centre. Southern tones—raspberry fruit with good underlay. Some richness, oil at end. Upright at this stage, likeable punch. More prune flavour with air. Reminds me of 1960s/1970s Chapelles. Bit dumb now, was more exuberant. From 2007–08; 2022–26. Last tasted Sept. 2004.

1998 ★★★ Only fair *robe*, not as dark as 1999. Oily, warm, floral bouquet—soft fruit aromas. Gently stewed plum fruit, gains dimension though the palate; smoky, fruit skin presence. Its gentle red fruit not especially southern. Can sing, more boom from 2007. Has lost some earlier edginess. 2015–19. Last tasted May 2003.

1997 ★★★★★ Intense matt plum colour; warm, fat, rounded bouquet, some damp leaf, touch reserved, has brooding promise. Immediate appeal—the flavour runs around the mouth, great fleshy texture, brewed black fruit. A Pomerol-style Hermitage, *gourmand*. Soft fatness, good. A vintage where the year holds sway over the place. 2017–21. Last tasted April 2004.

1996 ★★★★(★) Sleek black colour, quite dark; upright, dry style bouquet—leaves, woods, mint, alcohol; tight, reserved palate, almost resiny, touch tough right now. Ends richly. Nice end fruit. Extreme contrast between the 1996 and 1997 tannins. Leave till 2006 or so. I back this to do well. 2018–23. Last tasted May 2001.

1995 ★★★ Solid *robe*, still well sustained. Warm, cooked jam aroma, dusty backdrop, decent—has potential to vary. Air brings rosehip, violet side. Good, firm Syrah expression on palate, with dry, minted texture of a dry vintage. Some body beyond the cooked black fruit. Funnels along rather, length is OK, not more. Leave till 2008–09 and maybe more width, but lacks richness. A subset of the 1983. 2018–22. Last tasted Sept. 2004.

1994 ★★★ 2011–14

1993 ★★ The Year of no La Chapelle. Jaboulet made only 300 hl from all its Hermitage Syrah, which came out with that plain name.

1992 ★★ 2009–12

1991 ★★★★★ 2013–17

1990 ★★★★★★ Stop-and-pause wine, no idle chatter. Full, still dark *robe* after 13 years. Herbal, meaty, even a little reduced still after one hour open. Tight, compact palate, tar and stone fruit. Much on the sinew, needs to unwind, still solid and unmoving. From 2008–09? 2021–25.

1989 ★★★★ 2016–20

1988 ★★★★★ 2009–13

HERMITAGE LE TAUROBOLE/
PIED DE LA CÔTE ROUGE

2001 *Le Taurobole* ★★ Fair sustained red colour; cool bouquet—light black fruit, some mineral, fair width. Berried, brewed fruit with width and openness. Red jam, some spice on end. Tannins well woven. The more simple *lieux-dits* feel to it. From 2008; 2015–19. Last tasted Jan. 2004.

2000 *Pied de la Côte* ★★ Correct red colour; quite open bouquet, mint, cooked fruit, tender aroma. Fine, suave, quite silky wine. Fruit could be more striking. Overall is bit sweet, facile, has raspberry tones. 2011–15. Last tasted May 2002.

1999 ★★★ Some burnt, leathery dark fruit aromas. Elegant palate, quite simple in its pleasure. Clean and direct, has some core. Nice, smoked fruit ending. Burnt edges on aftertaste. More varied from 2005. 2011–14. Last tasted May 2003.

1998 ★★ Reserved bouquet, some berries; dense attack, sets off well then dries. Black fruits. Fair length. From 2004; 2013–16.

HERMITAGE CHEVALIER DE STÉRIMBERG BLANC

2003 ★★★ Stylish, forward bouquet, white fruit/hazelnut, floral too. Facile, buttery taste, light spice, honey. Toast, dried skin fruit at finish. Likeable, polished, has good length. Just a little plain, no strong distinction. 2018–21.

2002 ★★★★ Full yellow *robe*; full, rich, buttery, white fruits bouquet. Pretty, rich attack—persists well, genuine *gras* here. Very correct; Marsanne influence good. Good length, salty aftertaste from the Roussanne. Meaty, near tannic ending, take-your-time wine, is evolving well. 2020–25. Last tasted Dec. 2004.

2001 ★★ Fat, ripe bouquet, overtly buttery, fair depth. Quite stylish—flourishes then retreats, oak comes along and brings drier tones. Bit withdrawn on end. Was more unctuous and heavy. May show more by 2007–08. Last tasted Jan. 2004.

2000 ★★ Big, oily bouquet—honey/toast/vanilla pods. Quite refined melted butter attack; caramel, some finesse, rather burnt finish. Rid it of oak by maybe 2005, and can be round and pleasant. Fat wine, length OK. I have found it heavy, clumsy in past. 2013–15. Last tasted May 2003.

1999 ★ Quite pungent, citrus/squeezed white fruit bouquet, open. Rather uneven palate —a degree of flesh but lacks some middle. Burnt aftertaste that I've found before. Not very thorough. 2009–10. Last tasted May 2003.

1998 ★ Understated depth of white fruit, some freshness on bouquet; tasty, warm rich-

ness, with an oaked finish. Must shake off the cellar overlay, so leave till 2003 or so. 2009–14.

1997	★★	2008–13
1996	★★	2013–17
1995	★★	2010–15

Export 60 per cent (1) USA, (2) Great Britain, (3) Canada

PATRICK LESEC

Moulin de Bargeton BP6201 30702 Uzès
+33(0)466 376720

See also Cornas, Crozes-Hermitage, St-Joseph.

In a venture with Philippe Desmeure of Domaine des Remizières, new-oak supporter Patrick Lesec has encouraged two overtly modern cuvées from this source, a red and a white Cuvée Émilie.

The red is usually composed of 75 per cent *Gros des Vignes* and 25 per cent *Rocoules* Syrah that is said to average 20-plus years old. It receives 16 months in 80 per cent new, 20 per cent one-year-old casks, and is raised with the help of *micro-bullage*—air injections—and modern technique.

The white is pure Marsanne from *Maison Blanche* and is fermented and raised for a year in 90 per cent new oak casks, the rest one year old. Its lees stirring can continue until past the malolactic fermentation.

The wines have sufficient juice to handle the oak, providing the vintage has ripened well. See Domaine des Remizières.

DOMAINE DES MARTINELLES

2 route de Vignes 26600 Gervans +33(0)475 077060

See also Crozes-Hermitage.

With 500 bottles of red Hermitage in 2002, Pascal Fayolle became the first "new" domaine to appear at Hermitage for many years. Before then, the domaine's wine and crop from their vineyards at Hermitage and Crozes-Hermitage would be sold to the regional merchant trade.

Pascal's great-uncle and grandfather worked vineyards here decades ago—indeed, his grandfather Louis bought his first plots in the 1950s. With just under six hectares of Hermitage, and access to quality sites like *Greffieux, Beaume,* and *Murets,* this is a domaine that should be capable of making its mark in years to come. There are 3.95 hectares of Syrah and two of Marsanne.

The vineyard's delineation respects the soil differences in the manner that the old-timers would employ: the Marsanne is usually in the deeper soils, often down at the bottom of the slope as on *Diognières, La Pierrelle,* and *Greffieux.* At the top of the eastern end of *Beaume,* there is some red clay that is also the venue for their Marsanne.

On *Beaume* there are two plots, one of 1.75 ha, the other 0.3 ha. The Marsanne (1970s) is on the eastern end, where the sand and stones are bordered by the red clay, while the Syrah (1970s) grows on the south-facing area of sand-stones. On the east end of *Greffieux,* near *Péléat,* there is 1 ha of mainly Syrah (half 1930s), with some Marsanne at the bottom of the slope near the road. On *Murets* (1960s) there is 0.3 ha of Syrah that the family bought in the 1980s.

The other sites include 1.5 ha on *La Pierrelle,* on the way towards Larnage; here the Marsanne grows higher up on red clay, and the Syrah lower down on the packed alluvial stone area. There is 0.75 ha of 1960s Syrah on *Diognières,* along with some Marsanne further down, and 0.4 ha of Marsanne on what the family terms *Haute Pierrelle,* a site that strays into *Maison Blanche* on its east end.

The red Hermitage is destemmed and fermented in horizontal steel vats for a minimum of three weeks. It receives 12 to 18 months' raising in 600-litre *demi-muids,* 70 per cent of them new. From 500 bottles of just one red wine in 2002, the domaine passed to 3,000 in 2004, with two qualities, a classic (2,200 bottles) and an older-vine, more site-specific Louis et Aimé (800 bottles). These are not fined, but are lightly filtered.

The prime source for Louis et Aimé is a vineyard they call *Rouméas,* after the old owner of their *Beaume* plot on the flatland on the right of the road up to Larnage. "We rented it from Madame Rouméas, then bought it from her in the 1960s—its oldest Syrah dates from the 1940s," says Pascal. "Grandpa used to go there on his horse to work the plot, and eat lunch in the small tool shed in the vineyards. While he was doing that one day, his horse escaped and ran off all the way up to *La Pierrelle,* my grandfather running after him—he couldn't catch up!"

The white Hermitage is 99 per cent Marsanne, and fermented in 80 per cent new, 20 per cent one-year-old *demi-muids.* It is bottled after the malolactic has taken place, meaning a stay in the cellar of eight months to one year. Its treatment shows a lot of good sense from Pascal, his established local roots coming to the fore: "I'm not seeking overripeness," he says, "so I press the whole bunches because I want fresh wines. The Marsanne is picked according to the ripeness of each plot, and we will return to the same plot days later if we have to."

In 2003 the smaller crop meant all new-oak fermentation, but there was flexibility in the approach after that. "I assembled 20 per cent of the vat Hermitage that would normally be sold in bulk with the oaked wine, since I felt the oak was too strong and took away the white flowers side of the Hermitage *blanc,*" he recounts. He also blocked the malo for that vintage.

HERMITAGE DOMAINE DES MARTINELLES ROUGE

2003 (CASK) ★★★ (★) Violets, full and well-knit bouquet. Black fruit shows at first on palate, quite tight then broadens and blossoms. Fruit is rich. Some grilled tones on the finish. From 2008–09; 2021–23.

HERMITAGE LOUIS ET AIMÉ ROUGE

2003 (CASK) ★★★★ Pretty, floral-inspired bouquet, a winner. Round, flowing wine, has class. Lot of tannins and sound richness here, can become charming. Violets reappear. Grilled finish from its oak. From 2008–09; 2022–24.

HERMITAGE BLANC

2003 ★★★★ Full *robe*; ample, dried fruits bouquet. Good, rich, and fat Marsanne, traditional style, well made with good juice. Runs on nicely. Pretty, nutted wine with classic *gras*. 2018–20.

GABRIEL MEFFRE

84190 Gigondas +33(0)490 123021

See also Condrieu, Côte-Rôtie, Cornas, Crozes-Hermitage, St-Joseph.
This Gigondas *négociant's* red Hermitage is taken from *Diognières* and *Greffieux*. The crop is destalked and macerated for 12 to 18 days, with temperature kept to a conservative 25° to 28°C. Ageing lasts 18 months in the usual Meffre 275-litre casks, which are new.

The white is drawn from *Beaume, Rocoules,* and *La Pierrelle*. It is 80 per cent Marsanne, 20 per cent Roussanne, and is fermented in new 275-litre casks for 15 to 20 days, the temperature controlled at around 18°C. The young wine is raised on its fine lees for eight months, with the lees stirred during that time.

HERMITAGE LAURUS ROUGE

2002 ★★ Minted, aromatic nose, smoky red berries. Likeable fruit—red berries, cool texture. Some end tannin, bit dry aftertaste. Fruit gum flavour, the vintage imprint. Middle of the road, OK. Has come together in last year. Esp from 2006; 2011–12. Last tasted Nov. 2004.

HERMITAGE LAURUS BLANC

2002 ★ Quite full *robe*; pungent, open bouquet. Its oaked start makes the wine upright, rather hard. Oak all through, dominates *terroir*. The bitter side of Marsanne increased by the oak. Can live and develop, but must shake off the wood—not a pleasure wine! From 2007; 2016–18.

2001 ★ Overt exotic banana, oaked bouquet; some fat on palate but still very oaked. Has sun in it, some sweetness. Burnt trimmings, final heat, no confirmed depth. From 2007; 2013–14.

DOMAINE MICHELAS SAINT JEMMS

Bellevue Les Chassis 26600 Mercurol +33(0)475 078670

See also Cornas, Crozes-Hermitage, St-Joseph. The Michelas family from Crozes-Hermitage work just half a hectare of Syrah on *Les Diognières*. After a three-week vinification, the young wine is aged for a year in a mix of new and one-year-old casks. There are 600 bottles a year.

HERMITAGE ROUGE

2002 ★ Some black fruit, smoky/leather side to dumb bouquet. Dark red fruit, some oak staining, gives a varnish effect. Quite a lot of end tannin, pepper/licorice too. Can meld together. 2010–12.

CAVES OGIER

10 ave Louis Pasteur 84230 Châteauneuf-du-Pape +33(0)490 393232

See also Cornas, Crozes-Hermitage, St-Joseph. There has been a satisfactory rise in standards at this southern Rhône *négociant*. In 1994 it was bought by Jeanjean, which heralded the start of the revival.

There is a simple red for supermarkets called Cuvée Oratorio. This is bought as young wine, just after the malo, and is raised for 16 months in 550-litre *demi-muids*, 40 per cent of them new, the rest up to six years old. It is fined but not filtered.

The top wine is Les Allégories d'Antoine Ogier. This is a Big Packaging wine—beware! The heavy, very high-punt bottle is made in a small Swiss factory.

Its crop is destemmed, and a long maceration is punctuated by cap punching. The wine is aged for about 14 months in 550-litre *demi-muids* and is bottled before the Oratorio to emphasize finesse.

HERMITAGE ROUGE CUVÉE ORATORIO

2000 ★ Square, solid, midweight nose; fair crunchy fruit, licorice, quite dry finish. Sinewy, fair length. Esp from 2006; 2011–14.

HERMITAGE ROUGE
LES ALLÉGORIES D'ANTOINE OGIER

2000 ★★ Tea/herbal, brewed black fruit nose; quite generous start, supple, fleshy middle. Quite clean ripe, raspberry-style fruit. Soft end licorice, some heat. Early drinking. 2010–13.

DOMAINE DES REMIZIÈRES

Route de Romans 26600 Mercurol +33(0)475 074428

See also Crozes-Hermitage, St-Joseph.
In 1981 the Desmeures bought 1.5 hectares of early 1960s Syrah on the firm granite of *Les Grandes Vignes*, above and to the right of the chapel of St. Christopher. They also work a bit over 0.5 ha of Syrah on *Les Rocoules* and 0.52 hectare of 96 per cent Marsanne, 4 per cent Roussanne (1970s) in two plots on *Maison Blanche*. The soil differs between the plots on *Maison Blanche*—one is loess, the other claystone, according to Philippe Desmeure.

Since 1996 there has been just one red cuvée, the Émilie, named after Philippe's daughter. This is usually bottled around February, 18 months after the harvest. It is raised for 15 months in 80 per cent new, 20 per cent one-year-old oak. The new oak has been encouraged by the merchant Patrick Lesec, who sells some of the wine under his own label. Young oak—casks of two to five years old—was first used here in 1985.

The red Hermitage here has always held an interesting, upright composition that requires ageing to soften. It has been a steady success for two decades, with bottles from the 1980s and early 1990s especially good value for auction bargain hunters. Nowadays the main fear surrounding it is the risk of overextraction, but providing the crop is harvested in a healthy state, this can be played down.

The white Cuvée Émilie is vinified and raised for a year in a mix of 60 per cent new and 40 per cent one-year-old oak. It is 95 per cent Marsanne, 5 per cent Roussanne. In the past it would spend 18 months in cask. Like the red, it is discreetly rich and can age well. It is best left for four or five years to allow the oak to integrate.

In 2003 the oakfest moved up a gear, with the issue of 3,700 bottles of a red called "Essentiel"; this was given what the family terms " 200 per cent" new oak—in other words, a switch during its 15 months' raising to a second new cask.

HERMITAGE CUVÉE ÉMILIE ROUGE

2003 (CASK) ★★ Very dark; chocolate, prune, full black fruit aroma. Big wine with oak presence on finish. Tightly packed. Rather dessicated, more flesh please. Is it oxidative? Oak needs three years. From 2007; 2016–19.

2002 (CASKS) ★ Ripe fruit aroma. Overt oak, searing on the palate, though ripe crop taste present, too. Medium weight. 2012–14.

2001 (CASK) ★★★ Tight, black berry nose, some fungal aromas. Black fruits, tar on attack. In the house style, has a tight structure. Good juice on the end, has pep, is alive. Quite upright, will age. 2016–20.

2000 ★★★ Pretty, sappy blackberry jam aroma. Fairly open blackberry flavour, has elegant tannic edging. Mineral/pepper residue. Live wine, fresh. Some tannins. From 2006; 2014–17.

1999 ★★★★★ Pretty *robe*; very smoky, lingering wild black fruit aroma. Berries and plums on attack, raspberries at end. Combines fullness and good acidity. Long and persistent. Tar and licorice, the *Grandes Vignes* plays a strong role. By Nov. 2002, had lost the oak traces on the finish. 2018–22.

1998 ★★★★ Bouquet quite stern but underscored with warm, ripe fruit. Plenty of substance, mixes very good style and refinement with a cosy punch. Good final burst of southern warmth. From 2005–06; 2012–16.

HERMITAGE CUVÉE ÉMILIE BLANC

2001 ★ Taut bouquet, apricot, fair depth. Oak-marked flavour, some core matter inside. Oak helps its length, quite an easy wine. Not very expressive, maybe more from 2007. Rather dry finish. 2012–15.

2000 ★★★ Nice fat, oily, and broad aroma; fat, rich style of wine. Apricots and honey, rich texture, stylish wine that handles the wood well. Oak still present after four years. Has some grip. 2012–14.

1999 ★★ Some floral aromas; suave, above all refined palate, elegant. Nice quiet matter here. 2008–10.

1998 ★★ Oak fills the bouquet after two years, some matter there as well; bit less rich than the 1999, slightly upright. Tight texture. Wait six years. 2008–12.

JMB SORREL

24 rue de l'Hermitage 26600 Tain-l'Hermitage
+33(0)475 078484

The Sorrel family, notaries at Tain since 1893, perpetuated some of Hermitage's nineteenth-century customs by planting a vineyard between 1910 and 1915. The mix of bourgeois capital and vineyard ownership was a strong one in Hermitage's developing years, and today this tradition lasts in active fashion through two of the late Henri Sorrel's sons, Marc and Jean-Michel.

JMB Sorrel stands for the three brothers, Jacques, Jean-Michel, and Bruno. Jacques lives in Paris, Bruno in Milan, and Jean-Michel in Tain, in an elegant mid-nineteenth century house built by the Calvet family. He is the third generation of notary, and his son may well follow him in that profession.

The vineyard is 1 ha: Syrah on a mix of *Greffieux* (0.65 ha) and *Méal* (0.2 ha) and 0.15 ha of Marsanne on the lowest part of *Greffieux* near the town. The vines are all vintage First World War, between 1910 and 1915. The red and white are both called "Le Vignon," after the walled Clos right beside the railway station; on the official map this is now called Plantiers.

Jean-Michel has been overseeing the vineyard since 1976; the first Le Vignon red was made in 1985; there are just 600 bottles of white and 3,500 of red. Jean-Luc Colombo is their adviser.

The Syrah has been 95 per cent destalked since 1991; it is vinified in fibreglass vats, with a floating cap, which allows a long, 25-day process. There are two to three *pigeages* a day and a pumping-over, with a top temperature of 32°C. A horizontal press is used, with the press wine added to increase the tannins. Ageing in four-to-five-year-old casks lasts two years, and there is a light fining but no filtration before bottling.

The white is vinified traditionally—used casks, a natural cellar temperature, wine left on its fine lees, and bottling in July, the malo done. The only recent innovation has been the lees stirring done since 2000.

"It's more a convivial than a commercial objective here," says Jean-Michel, a man of silver-grey hair and dark eyes, a counterpoint to the blonde hair and blue eyes of his wife, Michèle. "Each brother can have his 150-bottle allowance a year and keep the old connection with Hermitage." Jean-Michel has never wanted to use weedkillers, and set up ploughing by horse in his vineyard, a practice adopted by several of the growers on the feasible lower sites.

HERMITAGE LE VIGNON ROUGE

2002 (CASK) ★ Quite direct red fruit nose; red fruit, some *gras*, pepper/tannic end. From 2006–07. Midweight, direct. 2010–12.

2001 ★ Dark, leathery, rustic-style nose; cherries, pepper, some frame. Chewy, black flavour, some warmth. From 2007; 2013–15.

2000 ★★ Even nose, earth/leather, violet/truffle; elegantly full, rounded. Ripe fruit kept in check, earthy/heated end, midweight tannins there. 2012–14.

HERMITAGE LE VIGNON BLANC

2001 ★★ Rounded white fruit, nutty hint aroma; slight spiced white fruit, quite full. Clean, nice weight. Hazelnut, quince end.

Export 50 per cent (1) USA

MARC SORREL

128 bis avenue Jean Jaurès 26600 Tain l'Hermitage
+33(0)475 071007

See also Crozes-Hermitage.

La Femme du Boulanger is a Pagnol film masterpiece, made in 1938. The baker keeps getting up at four in the morning, holding conversations out loud, and baking his bread. The first suspicion the village has that all is not well comes when the local palates find his bread not as good as usual. It then turns out that his wife has left him.

Marc Sorrel's wine had that uneven phase from the late 1980s into the mid-1990s. This very private man only quietly implies the pain of his divorce, but it's true that his wines came back to form in the late 1990s. His confidence and commitment to push his harvest and to finesse the winemaking seem deeper than before, as if he has come to terms with himself now—that there has been some self-discovery. He can now be his own man, perhaps for the first time in his life.

We can all be thankful, for he possesses some fantastic locations on the Hermitage hill. His late father, Henri, made the occasionally fabled red wine, notably the 1978 and 1979, and Marc is getting into his own stride with sumptuous wine like his 2000 and 2001 white Rocoules and his most elegant recent Gréal reds. He is now in his early 50s and is striking out. His children, in their 20s, have no connection with winemaking—his daughter a speech therapist, his son working in sports management.

Descended from a line of public notaries at Tain, Marc Sorrel is a rare small-domaine grower with prime vineyard locations at Hermitage.

He makes two white and two red Hermitages from his 2.55 ha vineyard. The regular red is called just "Hermitage," like the white, while the special red is Le Gréal (5,000 bottles), the white Rocoules (2,000 bottles).

There are 1.8 ha of Syrah: the 0.8 ha on *Le Méal* (1928, including 5 per cent Marsanne) was planted by Marc's great-grandfather Félix, a notary as well. The remaining hectare is made up of plots on *Greffieux* (1984)—which gives the derivative name of his main wine Gréal—*Bessards* (1987), and the *lieu-dit* known as *Les Plantiers* (1970, with some Marsanne), right on the flatland between *Greffieux* and the railway line.

The Marsanne on *Méal* and *Plantiers* is cropped and fermented with the Syrah and makes up about 5 per cent of the *Gréal* red wine: "It adds marrow and suppleness to the wine," Marc says, reflecting an old Hermitage tradition of some white grapes often being present in the red wine.

There are just 0.75 ha of white vines—92 per cent Marsanne, 8 per cent Roussanne. The younger vine plot of 0.2 ha is all Marsanne on *Greffieux*, a vineyard that Marc bought in 1984 "when prices were still sensible" and replanted in 1985. Its first wine was produced in 1993. The 0.55 ha on *Rocoules* is about 85 per cent Marsanne, 15 per cent Roussanne, its vines dating from the early 1950s.

From 1990 Marc made efforts to work his vineyards in a reasoned way, with fewer treatments. He has since found that yields on less old sites like *Plantiers* have fallen. "I've also cut back on fertilizers to restrict leaf growth and excess bunches," comments Marc; "a side benefit from this has been less rot, because the fertilizers help to encourage very tight bunches."

The vineyard is also being tilled where possible: horsepower has returned. The accessible, gentle slopes of *Greffieux* are fine for this, but the *Méal* hill is too steep and too tightly planted, so there is no turning space for horse and man together. This work avoids having to apply herbicides, and turns and airs the soil.

Completing this revised policy is Marc's conscious decision to harvest later from the 2000 vintage onwards.

Naturally reserved, Marc will gradually open up if he sees enough of someone; some of his comments mark him out as different from many growers. He follows stock markets and is an inveterate player of newspaper competitions, buying 50 or 100 copies to make multiple entries. The payoff has been travel, a Limoges china collection, home cinema equipment, and other goodies.

FIGURE 16 Descended from a line of public notaries at Tain, Marc Sorrel is a rare small-domaine grower with prime vineyard locations at Hermitage. (Tim Johnston)

Marc joined his father, Henri, for many years Tain's Notary Public, in 1982. When the latter died in January 1984, he, the third son, left his business post to run the vineyard that had been left in equal portions to his brothers. Henri admitted that he always preferred being a *vigneron*, but that time was against him.

Until the early 1970s the Sorrel harvest from their 3.4-hectare total family holding was sold as grapes to local *négociants*, but during that decade Henri progressed to making an excellent red and white. The red Le Méals of 1978 and 1979 were wonderful wines of great breeding and appeal and were aged for 18 months in ex-Romanée-Conti casks.

Since 1998 the Syrah from all younger vines has been fully destalked, and it's in rot-affected years like 2002 that the whole crop is handled this way. The destalking issue had been vexing Marc for some time: "I considered the tannins on my 1995, 1996, and 1997 as too rustic, so now I'm destemming. In 1998 it was half, 1999 was so ripe that the stems were included, and in 2000 and 2002 I destemmed the whole lot," he

says. The proportion of destemming is always a lateral indicator of harvest quality, by the way.

Fermentation is in open wood and steel vats and lasts 15 days for the regular wine and three weeks for the Gréal. Outside yeasts are used, and since 2004 Marc has worked with an automatic cap-punching machine that is set to work morning and evening. He also pumps over the juice at the start of fermentation to activate the yeasts.

The classic red is aged for 16 to 20 months in five-to-six-year-old casks; the Gréal receives 18 to 22 months in oak of four to five years old. The final Gréal wine is always made up of 90 per cent Syrah off *Le Méal*, with the rest taken from the best fruit off *Greffieux*—a percentage that will rise a little as the *Greffieux* Syrah matures. There is no new oak, nor is there fining and filtration.

With the recent emphasis on waiting for great ripeness in the vineyard, the Gréal has become a wine in the more accessible, fleshed style. There are similarities with the sensuous warmth often apparent in the wines of Jean-

Louis Chave, without their tannic breeding. I would welcome a little more bite in the wines—a dose of George Saintsbury's manliness wouldn't go astray.

The whites are fermented and raised traditionally in oak. The temperature is held around 16°C, and the intention is to let nature take its course until the sugars are finished. The classic white (1,800 bottles, 100 per cent Marsanne) is raised for 14 months, its casks aged from five to ten years, while the Rocoules spends 16 to 18 months in five-year-old casks and is bottled gradually between May and July.

In some ways, Marc's flagship wine is his Rocoules *blanc*, a triumph for mature, oily Marsanne with just a hint of elegance imparted by its up to 15 per cent Roussanne. The fabled Hermitage richness that drew the Bordelais to eastern France in the nineteenth century is present in years like 2000 and 2001. It is a veritable sit-down wine, worthy of proper meal planning and good company. It is well capable of living and flourishing more than 20 years.

HERMITAGE ROUGE

2002 (CASK) ★★ Broad, friendly, suave bouquet. Wrapped-up black berry fruit, with quiet flesh. Correct enough, some length. Mid-plus weight. Esp from 2008; 2012–14.

2001 ★★ Decent black stone fruit/spice aroma. Down the line black fruit flavour, some tannic edging. No great width. Some end raspberry, grip. Esp from 2007; 2013–15.

2000 (CASK) ★ Quite prominent red fruits, spice bouquet. Some flesh, decent weight on palate, a bit down the line. Some end chew. Could be more expressive. 2010–14.

1999 (CASK) ★ Cool, even black fruit bouquet, some width. Decent live fullness here—red and black fruits, some leathery aspects. Tannins present, just skips a beat in the middle. Young vines influence here. 2011–15.

HERMITAGE LE GRÉAL ROUGE

2001 ★★★ Damp, bit vegetal nose, some peony topping. Earthy, midweight wine. Ele-

gant, lot of ripe crop here, soft feel. Oily finish. I'd like a bit more scale, robustness. 2015–19.

2000 (CASK) ★★★ Very dark; black cherries, nice depth of aroma; plump cherry/*cassis* on palate, then sleek tannins. Pepper touches. Feminine style of Hermitage, shows the elegance possible here. Nice length of black fruit. Esp 2006–07; 2014–19.

1999 ★★★★ Tightly packed, black fruit and olives aroma, harmonious. Really good, assured content on palate. Cool black fruit, bits of tar and berried fruit. Very elegant. Good end tannins. Funky wine. 2014–20.

HERMITAGE BLANC

2002 (CASK) ★★ Boiled sweet/pear drop bouquet. Forward wine—honey/stone fruit mix, decent richness. 2010–12.

2001 ★ Quite elegant, streamlined almond/ honeycomb nose. Restrained flavour, bit light, some length. Touch short, may do a little more with time. 2009–11.

2000 (CASK) ★★ Touch yellow; pretty bouquet, white fruits, floral, medium weight. Warm palate, then stops, is rather closed. Elegant style. Touch of oak. Quite sound. 2013–17.

1999 (VAT) ★★★★ Generous, still reserved nose, touch of citrus, cheese. Very sound, unflashy. Palate is weighty, lot of fat at the end, good width of flavour. Bit reserved, will become delicious with this richness breaking out. 2014–19.

HERMITAGE LES ROCOULES BLANC

2002 (CASK) ★★★ Creamy, nicely traditional bouquet. Sound attack, rich and oily, peach/ apricot flavour. Good length. 2013–16.

2001 ★★★★★ Floral/white fruit aroma, spice lurking. Tasty straightaway, yes! Good structure. Very elegant dried fruits, some nut. Length very good. Tightens discreetly on its warm finish. 2019–22.

2000 (CASK) ★★★★★ Gold hints; buttery and floral mix, tight bouquet. Very thorough, tightly packed wine. Lot of power but is subtle. Stylish, genuine wine, great *terroir* feel. A year of low acidity, but lots of rich matter to permit long life. 2020–25.

1999 (VAT, PREBOTTLE) ★★★★ Good live bouquet, lime cordial drink, hint of exotic fruits. Big opening on palate, toast, dried fruits, apricot. Very beefy, warm, but reserved finish. Structure good, final heat, very Marsanne oily texture. 2023–28.

Export 75 per cent (1) Great Britain, (2) USA, (3) Japan

CAVE DE TAIN-L'HERMITAGE

22 route de Larnage 26600 Tain-l'Hermitage
+33(0)475 082087

See also Cornas, Crozes-Hermitage, St-Joseph, St-Péray.

This establishment has undergone a suited revolution, the suit worn by the whirlwind tigress Julie Campos, a Yorkshire Terrier from Britain. Julie arrived in Tain after working in Chablis in 2000, and immediately set out on a determined drive for quality and consistent, even rigorous business practices. Out went the old guard like Michel Courtial, a man born in the cellars, whose father had also worked as Director of the Cave.

Vineyard practices were tackled. A green harvest letter was sent to all 295 full *appellation* and 121 *vin de pays* members, asking them to trim the crop. The policy included Julie spending half a day every three weeks to meet the *adhérents* and explain to them what was going on. Her office is spotless, very orderly, with all the corporate accoutrements—the briefcase, laptop, and neat piles of paper. With her short fair hair, snappy disposition, and firm look, Julie and her office are odds on to make even the most robust and grizzled of *viticulteurs* quaver!

People are surprised when they find out how much of the Hermitage hill is owned or directly rented by the Cave Co-opérative itself—20.7 hectares. Of these, just over 19 hectares form the purchase set up in 1956 by the late M. Louis Gambert, the Cave's President between 1933, when he founded it, and 1956. He died in 1967 without heirs and gave the Cave the right to buy his large holding—about one-sixth of the total *appellation*, a rare bounty.

His plots importantly give the Cave access to some of the best sites up at the western end of the hill, notably *Bessards* (0.7 ha), *Le Méal* (1.8 ha), and *L'Hermite* (2.8 ha). The largest holding, of 10 hectares, is on *La Croix* at the eastern end of the hill, surrounding the old Louis Gambert domaine. Its soil is *poudingue*, alluvion stones lying on red clay–chalk. The Gambert de Loche domaine has been renovated and brought back to life by the Cave for receptions—smart iron gates, a gravel drive, and the full monty.

Fourteen vinegrowers also send their crop to the Co-opérative; their vineyards amount to 9.75 hectares. The Cave's other plots lie on *Les Grandes Vignes, Greffieux, Beaume, Murets, Pierrelle,* and *Torras et Garennes.* Out of the 30-plus hectares under the Cave's control, a little over 24 are Syrah, the rest mainly Marsanne. The leading white site is *Maison Blanche* (3.25 ha).

Like all the members, the Hermitage growers are now expected to nip excess buds, prune in a recommended way, apply treatments on a central advice system, "so quality control starts early in the year, not just at harvest time," in the words of Julie Campos.

The Gambert legacy also serves a useful extra purpose, not to be sneezed at. If the price of a prime hectare of the Hermitage vineyard stands at around £275,000 (US$480,000), the Cave possesses pretty sound collateral if it ever needs to raise capital from the banks.

Under this one roof, therefore, is made over a quarter of all Hermitage—around 1,450 hectolitres—of which the Cave now bottles the majority, any extra going to the merchant trade. A lot of commercial activity centres on the Caveau shop; its over 80,000 visitors a year, one-third of them foreign, contribute to 11 per cent of turnover.

Three red Hermitages are offered, although the basic one is being reduced in favour of the next quality, known for years as "Nobles Rives," but renamed the simple classic wine of Hermitage. There can be a perfectly legitimate 5 per cent white Marsanne crop in them, following the practices of yore when the vineyards were a jumble of irregular plantings. The red wine is also easier to sell than the white.

The Syrah crop has been destalked since 1992, and its maceration lengthened from 10 to 15 days to up to 18 days. Concrete vats are used for the Hermitage fermentations, with punching of the cap and some *remontage,* or pumping-over.

The straight cuvée is destined for the French market; it is vinified for 12 to 15 days and is raised in oak for 15 to 18 months. Like the major reds, it is not fined, but lightly filtered.

The classic, or previously titled "Nobles Rives," is also vinified for 12 to 15 days. Its ageing lasts 15 to 18 months in casks, one-quarter of them new, the rest one year old. In rich years like 1999 and 2001 the stay lasts 18 months; in a softer year like 2000, it was 16 months. In the past, about one-third was raised in steel rather than oak, and the duration was a little shorter. Like all the reds, it is not fined, but is filtered.

Half the Hermitage is now placed in wood before its malo, the other half once the malo has finished. "The idea is to help bring volume and encourage the integration of the oak," states Alain Bourgeois, the *oenologue* from the Jura region.

The top red is the Gambert de Loche, of which there are 6,000 to 10,000 bottles. First made in 1992, it receives a maceration of 18 days, a total vinification period of over 25 days. Its crop is taken from vines dating from 1960–65, mostly on *L'Hermite, Méal, Bessards, Greffieux,* and some low-yielding plants on *La Croix*—east meets west.

After a selection tasting, the best wine is placed in Allier and some Tronçais new oak for 15 to 18 months. It is racked after its malo, then left alone for a year, before a spring bottling with a very light filtration.

The classic wine, aka Nobles Rives, started to improve and become more consistent from the early 1990s—vintages like the 1990, 1991, 1995 all did well, wines capable of a good evolution over 15 to 20 years and providers of great value. Their style was more "southern" and funky than

the current batch produced since the change of management.

The classic is now aimed at an audience that will drink it earlier, posing the contradiction that it will really show its local side only when mature—say from around six or seven years old. The Gambert de Loche, with its older vine content, is shaping up well to the challenge of an all-new-oak regime—again, provided the buyer is patient. There is a likeable richness about this wine, which if drunk before five years old, risks being too international.

The Cave has been making marked progress on its white wines, and at Hermitage around 30,000 bottles are made each year. The return to the traditional habits of cask vinification started early here, in the 1980s. The hand could be heavy with this, and a 1994 drunk in 2003 still bore oak on the finish.

The practice now is to vinify the white juice at up to 20°C, then age the wine for a year in one-third each new, one-year-, and two-year-old casks, with lees stirring. "We've cut back on the stirring," comments Alain Bourgeois; "it's just once a week—we tried daily stirring in 1998–99 and found it made the wine too flat."

The Marsanne crop for this comes from very old vines whose age is difficult to determine; they yield 25 to 30 hl/ha, and their grapes are picked ripe enough to achieve a degree of 13.5 or so. Generally the malolactic fermentation is done, although it was blocked in the low-acidity vintage of 2003. The 2002 and 2003 were both good, correctly full wines, which show promise for the future; they uphold the merits of good Marsanne.

The Cave is one of the few producers to issue Hermitage's special white wine, the Vin de Paille, which is also called "Gambert de Loche." This was first made in 1985, and averages 900 50-cl bottles a year—two casks' worth—although the 1995 crop was so fine that nearly 2,000 half bottles were made in that year. It is produced in 80 per cent of the vintages, providing the crop is up to scratch, which it wasn't in 1992, 1993, and 2002.

The Vin de Paille grapes come from a very old plot on *Le Méal*, where around half the Marsanne is thought to date from the 1880s and 1890s—in other words, a postphylloxera plantation. They are picked and left open to the air for 50 to 60 days—the law states a minimum of 45 days—while they dry; around 2 kg are needed to make 50 cl of this.

In the first years, the Cave harvested late but now picks the grapes at the same time as those serving for the dry wine, in order to preserve their health. The grapes are kept at the Gambert de Loche domaine in slatted wooden fruit boxes. "We tried straw and we tried hanging them up, but the wooden boxes are the best way to dry them," states the experienced vineyard manager, Daniel Brissot. Pressing is in late November.

The juice is fermented and raised in one-to-two-year-old casks for up to two years. The Co-opérative informally call this their "wine of meditation." It can carry 80 gm of residual sugar in a cooler vintage like 1996, or 120 to 130 gm in a boiling vintage like 2003, making the latter wine come out around 18°. Often there are flavours of quince in this interesting wine, which is capable of outliving most of us.

In the lesser wines, the Syrah and Marsanne *vins de pays des Collines Rhodaniennes* now form 15 per cent of the Cave's production. The Syrah is made in the Cave de St Donat, which was bought in 1986, where the village is famed for its Bach Festival every year. Yields have been trimmed towards 65 hl/ha from the usual 80 hl/ha. Some of these growers also own Crozes vineyards, that very often lie just across a track or road.

The Syrah is concrete vat raised for a year or more; it mixes assertive red fruits and spice and is a tidy wine. There is also a Pure Syrah for export, which is 10 per cent oak raised in American wood for four to six months. First made in 2001, this expresses black fruits and aromas, with a touch of end heat from the oak.

The Marsanne comes mostly from the east-bank Drôme area, with villages towards Romans-sur-Isère contributing. It is vinified in steel and bottled early, in January, its malo blocked for freshness. It makes good, simple drinking, with some weight on it even in a year like 2002.

HERMITAGE ROUGE (FRENCH MARKET)

2000 ★★ Gently cooked fruit, prune/berries/oak, worked over a bit; well-cut red fruit, oak end. Fades a bit. From 2007; 2013–15.

HERMITAGE ROUGE/LES NOBLES RIVES ROUGE

2002 ★★ Quite full *robe*; smoky, broad, compact bouquet. Interesting cooked red berry fruit on palate, some depth. Rather dry from its vinification and the oak. Decent structure, lively at two years. Esp from 2006; 2013–15.

2001 ★★★ Compact red fuits, smoky/minted outcrops on bouquet. Quite well-cut red fruit, plus decent stylish weight behind. Brewed middle texture. Fair width, tannins flourish on end, where is fresh. Oak/tar finish. From 2007; 2017–20.

2000 ★★ Warm, sappy fruit aroma, clean, bit of smoke; black stewed fruit, quite warm, clean-cut, tar end. Air narrows, dries it. 2010–13.

HERMITAGE GAMBERT DE LOCHE ROUGE

2003 (CASK) ★★★★ Black fruit, smoke, and bacon aroma—mixes minerality and ripeness. Full, savoury attack, real richness. Correct length, tannins hold it together. Black currant liqueur aftertaste. Drinks well and fully young. 2018–21.

2001 ★★★★ Smoke/leather with core black fruit aroma, good potential. Well-textured attack, wild fruits. Sleek black fruit through it, sophisticated style. More local feel around 2008. Sound volume, tannin here. 2020–23.

2000 ★★★ Stewed, ample bouquet, berry jam, overt. Compact start on palate, texture quite damp. Restrained warmth, rather too brewed. Has absorbed oak quite quickly. Tannins create interest at end, smoky finish. 2014–16.

1999 ★★★★ Dark fruits, light pepper/mint, full bouquet. Firm attack, compact, a closed big wine. Marked tannin, but rich towards finish. Plenty of chewy matter. Big, classic old-style

Hermitage, hearty. Affinity with St. Julien here. 2017–21.

HERMITAGE BLANC

2002 ★★★★ Apricot, honey, light spice bouquet, can develop. Restrained but stylish flesh. Some core richness with a tangy border. Agreeable texture. Good balance, length. Persists well, has pretty warmth. Good. From 2007; 2017–21.

2001 ★★★ Grainy, fruit skins, light spice aroma, *brioche* bread. Fair weight, but dumb. Some largesse at end—dried fruits/mineral. Tight-knit nuttiness on second half. Should evolve slowly, a wine of sinew more than flesh. 2017–20.

2000 ★★★ Creamy/buttery, white fruits, some spice on broad nose; fairly rich, oak couch last part. Apricot/peach towards warm finish. Can flourish elegantly. From 2007; 2015–17.

ERMITAGE VIN DE PAILLE GAMBERT DE LOCHE

1996 ★★★ Gold/yellow colour. Spiced fruit skin/raisin aroma, also damp wool, pineapple juice. Broad but controlled palate, has grip. Quince, touch salted finish. Burnt brown sugar flavour, plus light oak. Good acidity, finishes almost dry.

1991 ★★★ Very gold with orange hints; almond, citrus tones on nose; lots of flavours— quince paste, honey wax, roasted nuts, dried apricots. Still young, good length.

Export 30 per cent (1) Great Britain, (2) USA, (3) Belgium

TARDIEU-LAURENT

Rte de Cucuron 84160 Lourmarin +33(0)490 688025

See also Condrieu, Cornas, Côte-Rôtie, Crozes-Hermitage, St-Joseph, St-Péray.
Tardieu-Laurent raise one red Hermitage supplied by three producers. The wine is taken from *Beaume, Diognières,* and *Greffieux,* with a little *Méal* present.

The amount varies—17 casks in 1997, 12 in 2001, 7 in 2002, 20 in 2004. The wine is picked up from the producers at the end of the alcoholic fermentation and stored in the new-oak casks at Lourmarin for 15 months, then spends 9 months in one-to-two year oak. It is neither fined nor filtered.

The white Hermitage comes from just one proprietor and is half from *Beaume* and half from *La Pierrelle,* the high site towards Larnage. It is 95 per cent Marsanne, 5 per cent Roussanne, the vines dating from the late 1950s. It is vinified in Tardieu-Laurent casks and transported to Lourmarin in the early part of the new year. There is some lees stirring over the first three to four months. Like the red, it is cask raised for two years. Around 3,000 bottles are produced.

HERMITAGE ROUGE

2001 ★★★★★ Pure bouquet of bacon, smoky oak; very ripe fruit, too. Crushed fruit attack, compact black berry flavour, has a floral, smoked oak end flourish. Good length. Is nicely rich, good acidity to keep it going in principle. 2015–18.

HERMITAGE BLANC

2001 ★★★ Reserved aroma, some weight. Peach and pebbly fruit flavour, refined. Fair length. Hints of white pepper/pear/licorice. I'd like more guts. Oak on top still, there's an almost tannic finish. Esp from 2007; 2013–15.

ÉRIC TEXIER

Bel Air 69380 Charnay +33(0)472 542618

See also Condrieu, Regional Wines, St-Joseph. A red (3,000 bottles) and white (up to 900 bottles) Hermitage are offered by *négociant* Éric Texier. The red can be derived from his purchase of wine after it has received most of its two years' cask raising, or from a mix of outside wine and purchased crop. It is fined but not filtered.

The white can contain 5 to 10 per cent Roussanne. Both wines were first produced in 1999.

L. DE VALLOUIT

The House of de Vallouit, bought by Marcel Guigal of Ampuis in June 2001, owned 1.8

hectares on *Greffieux*, with some on *L'Hermite* and a tiny plot on *Bessards*. These had been purchased in the early 1980s and were 85 per cent Syrah, the rest Marsanne with just a touch of Roussanne.

Before then the house would trade wine as a merchant, and previous generations of de Vallouits would buy barrels of Hermitage from Louis and Jean-Louis Chave, father and grandfather of Gérard Chave.

The reds were not destalked and received a traditional vinification, with a three-year stay in wood. The top wine, Les Greffières, was made from old vines on *Greffieux* and averaged 4,000 bottles a year. This would usually have a dry side to it from the long cask ageing, but possessed underlying Hermitage *typicité* in its variety of peppered, often tannic flavours. The fruit style was often a throwback to the sweet, slightly faded ripeness of the 1960s. In the best years, the wines could live for over 20 years, but would not appeal to a modern audience reared on spotlessly clean, technically sound reds. The white Hermitage was vat fermented, aged six to eight months in old casks, and bottled before the next crop.

J. VIDAL-FLEURY

19 route de la Roche 69420 Ampuis +33(0)474 561018

See also Condrieu, Cornas, Côte-Rôtie, Crozes-Hermitage, St-Joseph.
Owned by Guigal since 1984, Vidal-Fleury have always produced good red Hermitage. "It's actually hard to get hold of," admits Jean-Pierre Rochias, the experienced Managing Director. "We get together the equivalent of around 3,000 to 4,000 bottles from two sources and raise the wine in 20 hl barrels for three years."

The wine is neither fined nor filtered.

HERMITAGE ROUGE

2003 (BARREL) ★★ Oily, bosky aromas, ripe fruit, overall attractive. Cooked, quite supple red fruits, suave wine. Length OK. Bit commercial; lacks freshness. From 2006–07; 2016–18.

2000 (BARREL) ★★ Tarry, black fruit/violet nose; stewed fruit, animal side, quite compact, reserved. Oily, bosky side to it. From 2008; 2015–17.

1999 (BARREL) ★★★ Full, rich, oily "dark" aromas; warm attack—wholesome berry fruit, has *gras*; mixed flavours, vanilla. Correct, clean end, authentic wine. From 2007; 2019–22.

1998 (BARREL) ★★ Prune, spiced leather aromas; chunky, dark cooked-up fruit, skins too; mineral, bosky notes this year. Good autumn wine, peppery end. From 2007; 2015–17.

VINS JEAN-LUC COLOMBO

La Croix des Marais 26600 La Roche-de-Glun
+33(0)475 841710

See also Condrieu, Cornas, Côte-Rôtie, Crozes-Hermitage, St-Joseph, St-Péray.
Jean-Luc Colombo from Cornas produces a red and white Hermitage for his négociant business—8,000 of Le Rouet Rouge and 4,000 bottles of Le Rouet Blanc. The red comes from *Le Méal* and *Greffieux* and is bought as wine before an 18-to-20-month ageing in 70 per cent new, 30 per cent one-year-old casks; there is more emphasis on young oak than there used to be.

The white Rouet is bought once its malo has finished; this is mainly from *Rocoules*, and is mostly Marsanne, with some Roussanne. After fermentation in a mix of vat and wood, it is raised at the grower's domaine for two years in 70 per cent new, 30 per cent one-year-old casks.

Neither red nor white was produced in the relatively tricky vintage of 2000.

HERMITAGE ROUGE LE ROUET

1999 ★★ Restrained berry/earthy aroma; red berry flavour, fair weight and length. No real brio, but has charm. Softer tannins from 2005. 2013–15.

HERMITAGE BLANC LE ROUET

1999 ★★★ Typical straw/warm south nose, with some oak/exotic—nicely tight. Misses a beat at start, fair weight, clean wine, oily length lasts well. Cleanly traditional, some final heat. Has developed with age. 2013–17.

LES VINS DE VIENNE

Bas Seyssuel 38200 Seyssuel +33(0)474 850452

See also Condrieu, Cornas, Côte-Rôtie, Crozes-Hermitage, St-Joseph, St-Péray.
The combo of Cuilleron, Gaillard, and Villard produce a red and a white Hermitage. The red, Les Chirats de Saint Christophe, is wine bought from two sources. It is aged for 18 months in 60 per cent new oak.

The white, La Bachole, is pure Marsanne. It is fermented and raised on its lees for nine months, with lees stirring. The 2001 was one-dimensional and short.

HERMITAGE LES CHIRATS DE SAINT CHRISTOPHE ROUGE

2003 (CASK) ★★★★ Sustained, full, peppery nose, good balance. Well-charged, upright Hermitage, the manly wine. Sound content, fruit is red berries, and has tannic structure. Very hidden now, from 2008. 2021–23.

2001 ★★★ Quietly full, smoky nose, peonies; bit narrow start, then broadens, has sound, chewy licorice length. Quite directed. 2013–15.

2000 ★★ Meaty/smoky, ripe nose, has moved past violets stage, though still stylish; harmonious attack, light cooked red fruits, less oak marking than at first. Correct tannins. Some end richness. Esp from 2005–06; 2011–14.

HERMITAGE LA BACHOLE BLANC

2000 ★ Modern, toasted nose, no identity. Rather gluey bonbon style on palate. Some fat, then oak at end, a bit of juice present. Lacks character. 2011–13.

HERMITAGE VINTAGES

Celebrated years from the old days are 1953, 1952— an outstanding J-L Chave—1949, 1947, 1945, 1943, 1933, and the astounding 1929.

Red wines tasted from these vintages include an impressive Chapoutier M. de la Sizeranne 1953; the Chapoutier and Chave 1952s; the rich, slow-to-evolve Chave 1947; and the Chave 1929— a wine that will never quite fade away.

Of the whites, the legendary Chave *blanc* 1929 has been the most remarkable white Rhône I have ever tasted. Tasted in 1984 and 1986, it was still opening up and revealing increased nuttiness of flavour after exposure to the air, and possessed incredible length. A 1952 Chave *blanc* was still elegant and chewy when tasted in 1984, and the Chante-Alouette from that year was also a beautiful wine.

It is well worth looking out for white Hermitage in the salerooms; there is obviously an element of risk, but these are wines that can show gloriously, with subtlety and allure, even in great age.

1955 Very good. Charming reds, long-lived whites.

1956 Mediocre. Many light wines.

1957 Very good. Full-bodied, overtly tannic wines.

1958 Mediocre. Pale, light wines.

1959 Very good. Some excellent wines—great harmony, long-lived.

1960 Mediocre. Mainly dilute wines.

1961 Excellent, on a par with 1929, 1978, and 1990 as the best of the century. Both the reds and the whites were mightily rich but also blessed with wonderful harmony and roundness. A memorable La Chapelle from Jaboulet, which is now showing age (just a touch of spicy dryness on the finish as it shortens up) but also a stunning complexity of flavour. The whites also possess extreme depth and warmth and are sometimes even younger than the reds. A memorable white Hermitage from Chapoutier: a wine of greater strength than most of its contemporaries, it will live easily for 45 years.

1962 Very good. Quite full, intricate reds with good balance. The whites are now tired.

1963 Poor. Wishy-washy wines.

1964 Very good. Firm, tannic, and gutsy wines. The best, like a still-potent La Chapelle, can live until at least 2005. The white wines were very full.

1965 Disappointing. Weak wines, just a few decent cuvées.

1966 Very good. Rich, well-balanced, chewy wines. A tremendous La Chapelle, full of local character. Very full whites, which should be drunk up.

1967 Very good. Well-coloured, fleshy wines, which softened very well, but are now tired. Note Chapoutier's M. de la Sizeranne. The whites developed striking dried fruit aromas and typical complex nutty flavours; the best can still be enjoyed. Note Jaboulet's Chevalier de Stérimberg and the Chave *blanc*.

1968 A disaster. Rain, storms, and very light wines, many of which were never bottled.

1969 Very good. Rich reds, which achieved great style, complexity, and length with age. Very successful Chave and La Chapelle—drink these up now. The rich whites need drinking.

1970 Very good. Rain was a problem. The reds were full, with mineral traces. They advanced faster than the 1969s, and are now fragile. The fine-boned whites became complex but are now tired. Note J-L Grippat.

1971 Very good. The reds started life with quite rich, well-founded flavours with some freshness present as well. They were never very beefy, and worked well on elegance more than power. They have tired by and large by now and need drinking up.

The whites aged very well and hung on to some of their early depth. Their impressive warm elegance set them apart from the big, voluptuous vintages. Jaboulet's Chevalier de Stérimberg can still show well.

1972 Excellent—for the best winemakers. The crop was small, afflicted by hail. Initially bursting with colour and flavour, the reds have evolved more quickly than expected. The refined Chave and the once exuberant La Chapelle should both be drunk. The whites were fruity and quite rich. They should be drunk.

1973 Good, although like 1972, parts of the vineyard were affected by hail. The reds were quite sturdy, with evident, sometimes acer-bic tannins. They should have been drunk. The whites were very well scented and well balanced.

1974 Fair. Quietly agreeable wines from the best domaines. They were lighter and simpler than usual, with rain a factor. Like the light, fruity white wines, they should have been drunk.

1975 Mediocre. A small crop with light, sometimes narrow reds. Ripeness was lacking, some rot at harvest time. The whites were better—with fair body and acidity to keep them going. Drink them up.

1976 Good to very good—but a vintage that fell victim of the growers' early hue and cry that it was quite exceptional after the hot summer. The reds progressed more rapidly than first anticipated, and have thinned out. They should have been drunk. The well-fruited whites did very well thanks to above-average levels of acidity.

1977 Poor. The reds lacked colour and extract after a wet summer. They were 10-year wines. The whites held together better—with rich aromas and dried fruit flavours. Drink them up.

1978 Excellent, approaching 1961 in dimension. A small harvest and very healthy grapes after a fine, dry summer. Wines that are therefore notable for their power, richness, and balance. The reds have held a dark purple hue well, while the bouquets are crammed with berry, pine, and essential oil aromas. Very firmly structured on the palate, the best are 40-plus-year wines. The La Chapelle is sensational, a full-blooded offering from Jaboulet, while Chave's red seems split into a more vibrant cuvée and a rather hard, subdued cuvée. Chapoutier was successful with M. de la Sizeranne, Sorrel's red Le Méal had an extraordinary bouquet and remarkable construction, and the Guigal was a solid, tight-knit wine, still ticking along in 1999. Wines from smaller domaines should be drunk before 2008 for safe results.

The whites were very good—full and succulent, with a rich frame around them. They should be drunk by 2009–13. Jaboulet's white Chevalier de Stérimberg did not live up to its name this year.

1979 Very good. A year of some intrigue since the wine improved after 15 years, then quietened down again, as if that flourish was its finest hour. The reds were not in the same powerful league as the biggest years, but developed very good fruit flavours during the 1980s and showed an appealing oiliness of texture; they are showing their age, with spices and coffee flavours coming through now. The whites developed tremendous apricot-inspired aromas and are long, full, and delicious. They can live for a few years more. Note the excellent red and white of the late Henri Sorrel, the reds of Chave and Guigal, and the white of Grippat.

1980 Fair. The harvest was interrupted by rain. The middle-weight reds became soft and elegant but now risk having passed their best. The Chave red was an unsung hero of the vintage. It is tender and very appealing, but needs drinking. The whites were excellent—very aromatic, very long. Note Jaboulet's white Chevalier de Stérimberg and Chapoutier's white Cuvée des Boys.

1981 Mediocre. An uneven vintage, from a very rainy year, better for the whites than the reds. The reds lacked extract—partly the result of heavy rain at harvest. They were often short on the finish and should not be kept for anything other than anniversaries. The whites showed good early aromas and lively fruit; they are now tired.

1982 Very good—the first scorching summer of the 1980s, and a large crop. The wines were rich, rounded, and well coloured. Prune and plum flavours abounded with age. Smaller growers had problems with cooling their fermentation vats, so some wines were rather jammy on the palate. The reds have passed the soft stage and are now becoming drier and fragile. They should be drunk by 2007–11.

The whites were sustained by high alcohol and dense flavours, but were a little short on acidity. Their texture was very unctuous. They can still show well until 2010. Note the reds of Chave, Bernard Faurie, Guigal, and La Chapelle; also the whites of Guigal and Chave (both very powerful) and the white of Grippat (elegant).

1983 Very good. A strong, dark vintage of concentrated, firm wines that evolved slowly. They didn't quite match their early promise, never having as much richness at their centre as was anticipated.

Early summer rain and some *coulure* (fruit failure) on the Syrah were succeeded by prolonged heat and drought. The reds were tight-knit, holding compact berry fruit edged by stout tannins. This is a classic "upright" year, whose textures have always remained on the dry side.

The Chave has reached a grainy, damson fruit stage and should be drunk by 2009–13. La Chapelle has always been a stubborn wine, replete with tannin. Some bottles have loosened, others remain tight and lacking fruit. They should live to 2011–15.

Also: de Vallouit Greffières (2008–11), Delas Marquise de la Tourette (2007–10). The Desmeure Domaine des Remizières and Fayolle Diognières are both still ticking over, with now funky overtones. The Sorrel Gréal is more fragile.

The whites were excellent. They held more acidity than the 1982s, were well balanced and very long on the palate. They can still show well towards 2008–11. Very good Chevalier de Stérimberg, Guigal, and Chapoutier whites.

1984 Mediocre. Lack of summer heat and August–September rains affected the vintage. The reds lacked colour, and aromas were sometimes narrow, even astringent. Growers who picked late and selected their harvest carefully—Chave, Bernard Faurie, and Delas for their Marquise de la Tourette, for example—succeeded in making wines whose soft fruitiness was very attractive. These should generally have been drunk by now.

The whites were lighter than the 1983s and 1982s, but their fruit and vitality were appealing. Some cuvées were dull, but the best—Chave, Grippat, Chapoutier's Chante-Alouette—were stylish, elegant wines. They should be drunk up.

1985 Very good. *Coulure* hit the crop, and the white harvest was almost half the size of 1984. The summer was hot, but interspersed with welcome bouts of rain; the reds were darkly coloured, but while the 1983s held severe tannins, the 1985s were marked by rounded, well-ripened tannins—no need for Chave to destalk his 1985 as opposed to the 1983. Bouquets were generous and warm. The fruit was exuberant, the wines full of southern ripeness, with good length at the finish.

Note: very good M. Sorrel Gréal, B. Faurie (drink them up).

Also a Chapoutier M. de la Sizeranne chock-full of fruit, and an immaculately balanced red Chave that has the longest life in prospect—up to 25 years or so. Good but not startling La Chapelle, which should be drunk by around 2009–11.

The whites are superb—excellent balance, good depth, and luscious flavours. Note Chapoutier's Chante-Alouette and Chave for the longest-lived cuvées. Jaboulet Chevalier de Stérimberg, M. Sorrel, and Grippat whites should be drunk.

1986 Fair. A vintage of varied quality, where the competence of the growers was tested. The best cuvées improved with age, shrugging off their early acidity and blatant tannins. Rain and warm temperatures at harvesttime upset the work of a hot, sunny summer and brought rot. Strict sorting was needed. The top wines were quite solid but lacked assured harmony, even with age. Their direction was one of pebbly, mineral textures rather than the *rondeur* of the 1985s.

Note: very well-made Chave, also Guigal (excellent length, firm tannins). The La Chapelle developed soundly in bottle, taking on deep-seated game and dark fruit flavours. It has the tightness of the year but broadens with air (2008–10).

The whites were good, the best—like Grippat—holding a combination of acidity and *gras*. Some bottles can still show a stylish maturity. The Jaboulet Chevalier de Stérimberg white missed out.

1987 Mediocre, but some charming wines emerged. A difficult vintage, with the summer short on heat, and rain present. The reds were a bit better than popularly assumed; colours were middling, and some cuvées had rather hot, uneven bouquets. But there were wines with pleasant fruit on the nose and some medium-weight flavours. They drank well in their first 10 to 12 years.

Note: Chave red, M. Sorrel, B. Faurie Méal.

As usual in a lesser vintage, the whites were superior and developed well. Bouquets were full-blown and flavours lush. They should be drunk soon.

Note: whites from Chave (full), Guigal and Desmeure (both elegant), Vidal-Fleury, Cave de Tain (full, good acidity), Chapoutier Chante-Alouette (ripe, slow-burn wine).

1988 Very good. A vintage of full-blooded, solid red wines, a very typical example of Hermitage's "manly" side. The harvest was very healthy after a long, dry, hot summer. The skins were thick, the berries small, and tannins evident. The reds were very dark and some held extreme tannins. Their content was pretty rich, and with age has become more mineral—in the habit of a dry vintage. Several will live for 25 years or more.

Note: Grippat, Chave, Chapoutier M. de la Sizeranne (2007–09), La Chapelle (2012–18), Delas Marquise de la Tourette (drink up), and Desmeure Remizières (drink).

The white harvest was affected by *coulure*; the wines showed great finesse and were full and chewy. Fruity and well balanced, they are still drinking well and should show nicely towards 2010–13.

Note: Chapoutier Chante-Alouette (finer than usual), Jaboulet Chevalier de Stérimberg (new-oak treated), Grippat (fine, medium-weight, drink), Chave (elegant, great fruit).

REDS

★★★★★ J-L Chave, P. Jaboulet La Chapelle

WHITES

★★★★ J-L Chave

★★★ P. Jaboulet Chevalier de Stérimberg

1989 Excellent. Another hot, dry year, where the firm tannins were accompanied by content that was a little richer than 1988's. The reds were fleshy and boldly textured, with spiced berry fruit and good, firm length. Colours were dark. They are warm and appealing in their middle age and can live for at least 25 years.

Note: M. Sorrel Gréal (back to form); B. Faurie Greffieux (2012–15); a La Chapelle that developed and broadened in the bottle, shaking off its early new-oak overlay; Chapoutier M. de la Sizeranne (middle weight, solid); Chapoutier Pavillon (intense, captivating); and a complex, rich and long Chave.

The whites were strongly scented, full of good fruit, and finished with sustained length. They can be drunk successfully towards 2010–14.

REDS

> ★★★★★ P. Jaboulet La Chapelle
> ★★★★ J-L Chave

WHITES

> ★★★★ J-L Chave
> ★★ P. Jaboulet Chevalier de Stérimberg

1990 Excellent, even superb. A vintage that approached the majesty and delicious depth of 1961. Its tannins were ripe and softer than the other great post–Second World War vintage, 1978—altogether a more fleshy, wholesome vintage right from the start. Yet another drought summer hit the growers, but this year the rainfall, although slight, came at just the right moments, notably in August. The harvest was a regular size and very ripe. B. Faurie reported vats of 14°, having started 22 September.

REDS

The red wines showed this ripe, grape-skin side on the bouquets. The wines were brimful with rich dark fruit flavours, and the best extremely well balanced. These are exciting wines, which in the hands of growers like Jaboulet (La Chapelle), Chave, and Chapoutier will become classics of great long life and enormous pleasure. The Delas Marquise de la Tourette was also very ripe and generous (2008–12). Chapoutier's M. de la Sizeranne was big, brewed wine, with long life (2012–17). Even the Cave de Tain produced a big, genuine wine (2011–15). "Nature was very generous," declared J-L Chave.

> ★★★★★★ J-L Chave classic/Cathelin, P. Jaboulet La Chapelle
> ★★★★★ Chapoutier Pavillon/M. de la Sizeranne
> ★★★★ Delas Marquise de la Tourette
> ★★★ Guigal
> ★★ Cave de Tain

WHITES

The whites were powerful, initially subdued wines, whose richness will drive them along for towards 30 years. The Chave and the Jaboulet Chevalier de Stérimberg were both full but well-integrated wines; some growers' cuvées risked being too corpulent and lacking in acidity.

> ★★★★★★ J-L Chave
> ★★★★ P. Jaboulet Chevalier de Stérimberg

1991 Very good. An underrated year, lying in the shadow of indifferent results in Bordeaux. There was April rain. Twenty-five per cent less crop than usual. Rain fell at the end of September. Some reds lacked acidity. Brooding nose, spiced, dark soup. Chocolate, *cassis*, plenty of guts and sève. Reds had interesting acidity and tannins that were ripe but not smooth. Challenging futures, all capable of living well. Early wines were upright but tannins loosened quite willingly. Wines to live 15 to 22 yrs; quality was well spread.

REDS

> ★★★★★★ Chapoutier Pavillon
> ★★★★★ Delas Bessards, Ferraton Miaux, P. Jaboulet La Chapelle

★★★★ Belle, J-L Chave, Dom du Colombier, Cave de Tain classic/Nobles Rives, B. Faurie

★★★ Chapoutier M. de la Sizeranne, de Vallouit classic/Greffières

★★ M. Bernard Réserve des Pontifes, Guigal

★ Graillot

WHITES

This was a very successful year for the whites, with that little extra acidity to pep them up. The crop was ripe, but not too burnt. There was a mix of aromatic finesse and complexity; firm, with good structures at first, they developed in fine style, and were always long on the finish. A year when their balance was in the mainstream, the wines not led by local potency. The leading lights can live to 2011 and perhaps beyond.

★★★★★ Chapoutier de l'Orée

★★★★ J-L Chave

★★★ Chapoutier Chante-Alouette, J-L Grippat, Guigal, P. Jaboulet Chevalier de Stérimberg

1992 Mediocre. There was more winter rain than recently. A small and quite precocious flowering. The summer was rainy and not very hot. Ripening was slowed by strong rain on 29 August, and the harvest struggled along in the last 10 days of September, with sustained rain from 27 September onwards. The high slopes were hit more than the low areas. Sorrel lost 30 per cent because of poor budding.

REDS

These were easy, early wines, led by light jam fruit flavours that lacked depth and conviction. Tannins were supple. Plum, cooked fruits were the style, not the black intensity of better years. Some were disjointed between their sweetness (chaptalisation) and the upright nature of the raw fruit. They should be drunk now.

★★★ J-L Chave

★★ P. Jaboulet La Chapelle, M. Sorrel Gréal, de Vallouit Greffières

★ Belle, Delas Marquise de la Tourette, B. Faurie

WHITES

Paul Jaboulet lost half their white crop, with rot in September a factor. Growers said ripening was delayed but wasn't easy to obtain. For those who sorted well and waited, results were good. The best were rich and warm, though some could be a little heavy. The Guigal *blanc* was well packed and likely to live for 15 to 20 years. The Chave blanc also showed rich, chewy matter, with lots of glycerol to keep it ticking along well.

★★★★★ Guigal

★★★★ J-L Chave

★★★ J-L Grippat

★★ Chapoutier Chante-Alouette, P. Jaboulet Chevalier de Stérimberg

★ Belle, M. Sorrel Rocoules

1993 Poor—a disastrous year. Rain started from the end of August; 1500 mm (60 in.) fell in six weeks, local vineyards were flooded, the Rhône burst its banks. Hail hit on 27 August. So much sorting was needed of rotted grapes that Chave hired 20 people to do that alone in the vineyards. Ferraton's cellars near the river were flooded.

REDS

Controversy surrounded the Chapoutier M. de la Sizeranne, the rating of which varied a lot between different wine writers. There was no La Chapelle. The wines inevitably lacked core, colour, tout. The best have early plum flavours but yield to the air after an hour. The best survivors should generally be drunk before 2005–07.

★★ J-L Chave, Dom du Colombier, P. Jaboulet

★ J-L Grippat

The year was sound enough for the whites because of their earlier ripening. They can represent good value also because the vintage as a whole is so written off. Acidity levels were above average, so they may live.

★★★ Chapoutier Chante-Alouette, B. Faurie

★ J-L Chave, M. Sorrel Rocoules

1994 Good, but an uneasy year where balance was hard to achieve. The year was quite cool. The crop was abundant, the Syrah marked by thick skins, and good apparent ripeness.

REDS

Early on the wines showed some good matter with a solid surround, but some, like those from Chave, lacked acidity and real core beyond the fruit. Tannins were in evidence and sometimes the wines were square framed. In a similar year the crop would be handled better today, with the growers more informed on the ripening of the tannins. Some wines were prone to decline rather abruptly and become grainy. A year to keep an eye on—drink most before around 2012.

★★★★ Belle, Chapoutier Pavillon/ M. de la Sizeranne

★★★ J-L Chave, B. Faurie Méal, P. Jaboulet La Chapelle

★★ Dom du Colombier, B. Faurie, Ferraton Miaux

★ Cave de Tain Nobles Rives

WHITES

The whites held solid dried fruit flavours, the Marsanne having ripened almost too well. "I think I harvested too late—the wine is too fat for its own good," said B. Faurie. The theme of low acidity was found at Delas, while Sorrel's white was almost rosé coloured. Paul Jaboulet picked early, so their whites were fresher—and disappointing.

★★★★ J-L Chave

★★★ M. Sorrel Rocoules

★★ Belle, Colombo Rouet Blanc, Guigal, de Vallouit

★ Cave de Tain, P. Jaboulet Chevalier de Stérimberg

1995 Very good. "It could have been exceptional," J-L Chave said. The yield was small, down about 25 per cent. Early September rain encouraged some evolution, but had it come two to three weeks earlier, it would have made the ripening spot-on. Chave harvested at end of September and reported the wines were nice to vinify, net and limpid.

REDS

The reds contained good levels of acidity, and tannins were firm, even austere, at the start. Time has mellowed these and the wines are starting to soften, their red fruit laced with a pebbly, white pepper content. They can live until 2017–24, but their dry feel means they demand careful food selection—winter game, for instance.

★★★★★ Chapoutier Pavillon, J-L Chave classic/Cathelin

★★★ P. Jaboulet La Chapelle

★★★ Belle, Cave de Tain Gambert de Loche, Chapoutier M. de la Sizeranne, Delas Marquise de la Tourette, B. Faurie Méal, Guigal

★★ Cave de Tain Nobles Rives, B. Faurie

WHITES

There was a very good crop of Marsanne, healthy and rich, so the Vin de Paille was popular. The wines were firmly structured, with plenty of ageing potential, and took time to loosen—over eight years in some cases. Chewy textures and spice tones are present in this full-bodied year that will live for well over 20 years in the best cases.

★★★★★ J-L Chave, Chapoutier de l'Orée

★★★ Belle, Chapoutier Chante Alouette, B. Faurie

★★ P. Jaboulet Chevalier de Stérimberg

1996 Good, although problematic. The summer was hot and dry, but August was fresh and rainy. Ripening was slow and hard to achieve. The north wind saved matters, along with a stable September. Quite high yields were another challenge. Acidities were said to be the highest in 50 years. "Any site that was not well exposed really suffered," G. Chave observed—"it was a year for the top locations, those that achieved maturity."

REDS

The wines were upright, grainy, and peppery. They finished firmly and did not hold a beckoning warmth. They are cool-weather drinkers, set alongside autumn/winter foods. Their bouquets are moving on to the damp, mineral tones of such a vintage. Their acidity will keep them ticking over, but the lack of core matter may make them sharp as they get older. Good, stable storage will count for much. Their longevity will hover between 17 and 25 years, except for the biggest wines like Chapoutier's Le Pavillon.

★★★★★ Chapoutier Pavillon

★★★★(★) P. Jaboulet La Chapelle

★★★★ Chapoutier L'Ermite

★★★ J-L Chave, Chapoutier Méal, B. Faurie Méal

★★ Chapoutier M. de la Sizeranne, B. Faurie, Vidal-Fleury

★ Delas Marquise de la Tourette

WHITES

The whites were centred on elegance more than outright power. They lacked some of the usual stuffing, but a quiet thread of *gras* ran through them. They may not be very big, but can live nicely, helped by a live, clear-cut feel.

★★★★ Chapoutier Chante-Alouette

★★ P. Jaboulet Chevalier de Stérimberg

★ Cave de Tain

1997 Very good, but not a purist's year, because the wines were all about flattery, not so much about structure and classic balance. August was very hot, with the added feature that from mid-August to the start of September, the nights were unusually warm. By the end of August, the ripening process had stalled— "there was a gain in sugar but not concentration," G. Chave observed. All the great wines of the vintage were those from the high vineyards, the fresher ones—so the role of *Bessards* and *L'Hermite* was very important. It was important to harvest late, around the fourth week of September.

REDS

Surprisingly, growers reported the quantity of tannin as similar to 1998 but in a much riper, softer form. Flavours are not clear-cut, and stewed jam textures are normal, with plush, mature berry fruits. The tannins do not show on the surface. These were wines that could be drunk without much delay, and were in great form by 2005, the best still not turned to an obvious second stage. Consequently, they may live and tick along softly for longer than expected—well towards 25 years.

★★★★★★ Chapoutier Pavillon/L'Ermite

★★★★★ Chapoutier Méal, P. Jaboulet La Chapelle

★★★★ J-L Chave, B. Faurie Méal, J-L Grippat, Guigal

★★★ Tardieu-Laurent

★★ Cave de Tain Nobles Rives, Delas Bessards, B. Faurie

★ Delas Marquise de la Tourette, Dom Remizières Émilie

WHITES

For the whites, it was of course a rich year. The Marsanne worked along a power line, with a fat, buttery style and some opulent white fruits. The wines' lack of acidity hovers as a potential problem, but this is set off by the integral richness. A classic year to accompany sauced fish and rich dishes like foie gras. They should run for at least 20 years.

★★★★★ Chapoutier de l'Orée

★★★ Chapoutier Chante-Alouette/ Méal, J-L Grippat, Guigal

★★ Delas Marquise de la Tourette, B. Faurie, P. Jaboulet Chevalier de Stérimberg

1998 Good to very good. A more wayward and therefore more interesting vintage than 1997. A small flowering occurred during cool weather. There was no lack of water for the vines, with well-timed bouts of rain in July, early August, and the final ripening stages. The summer was generally hot. Some hail affected crop levels, which were lower than usual. Chave's Méal yielded just 18 hl/ha against 38 hl/ha for the 1999. In mid-September, a storm dropped 65 mm (2.6 in.) of rain in a day. After September 26 the weather never came back to form, with rain storms and thunder moving in from the south. The wind influence through the year was from the north, a factor that helped the crop to gain concentration but also to lose acidity. The tannic ripening lagged the sugars, and it was important to wait to harvest.

REDS

The firm grape skins played a strong role in making this a more tannic, mineral-edged year. At first, the tannins seemed dominant, but they loosened within four years. Bouquets reflected crunchy black fruit aromas more than the usual red fruit, peppery ones; they are moving quite swiftly towards game, and *sous-bois*, undergrowth tones. There is a lot of lush content in the best wines. They may not live so long as first anticipated, but are classic meaty Hermitages with a wild side to them. Expect longevity towards 20-plus years, and great entertainment on the way.

★★★★★★ Chapoutier L'Ermite

★★★★★ J-L Chave Cathelin, B. Faurie Méal

★★★★ Chapoutier Pavillon, J-L Chave, Dom du Colombier, Delas Marquise de la Tourette, Dom Remizières Émilie

★★★ Chapoutier Méal/M. de la Sizeranne, B. Chave, B. Faurie, J-L Grippat, P. Jaboulet La Chapelle

★★ P. Jaboulet Pied de la Côte, Vidal-Fleury

WHITES

The whites were founded around rich and ripe Marsanne, with alcohol levels high enough to drive the wine along as it ages. Early on, they were tight and reserved, with the potential to develop an elegant complexity. They held correct acidity and this is likely to be a year that can show well over 20-plus years.

★★★★ Chapoutier Chante-Alouette, J-L Grippat

★★★ Chapoutier Méal, J-L Chave, Guigal

★★ Chapoutier de l'Orée

★★ Cave de Tain Nobles Rives, Delas Marquise de la Tourette, Ferraton Miaux

★ B. Faurie, P. Jaboulet Chevalier de Stérimberg

1999 Excellent. The surprise of a large crop and very high quality. The vintage made itself late on, at the correct moments; there was some rain during the summer, but August was hot and September fine. Growers found the crop healthy, the wines easy to vinify. There is greater acidity than the 1998, but ripeness is assured as well.

REDS

Colours were often bright purple. These are rich, potent wines, but not as fully fleshed as the 1990s. Their balance is very good. They work on all levels and are wines of great allure. The main *climats* were exceptional—a lot of solid power in the *Bessards*, and great persistence of the full fruit in the *Méal*.

★★★★★★   Chapoutier L'Ermite, Delas Bessards

★★★★★   Chapoutier Pavillon, J-L Chave, Dom du Colombier, Delas Marquise de la Tourette, Dom Remizières Émilie

★★★★   Cave de Tain Gambert de Loche, Chapoutier Méal, B. Faurie Méal, Graillot, Guigal, P. Jaboulet La Chapelle, M. Sorrel Gréal

★★★   Chapoutier M. de la Sizeranne, B. Chave, B. Faurie, P. Jaboulet Pied de la Côte, Vidal-Fleury

★★   Colombo Rouet

★   M. Sorrel

WHITES

The whites were borne along by extremely ripe Marsanne; Marc Sorrel cropped his *Rocoules* Marsanne at 14.8° against 14° more normally. They started closed and have remained slow to budge. They are going to live a long time, with succulent, broad flavours and plenty of chewy length.

★★★★★★   Chapoutier L'Ermite

★★★★★   Chapoutier de l'Orée, Guigal

★★★★   Chapoutier Méal, Delas Marquise de la Tourette, M. Sorrel classic/Rocoules

★★★   Chapoutier Chante-Alouette, Colombo Rouet, Ferraton Reverdy

★   B. Faurie, P. Jaboulet Chevalier de Stérimberg

2000 Good, but uneven. Early announcements rated it very good, but there were underlying problems—notably, a blockage in the ripening, then dilution. There was a rainy start to the growing season, and great heat in August. Excess crop was the bugbear, exacerbated by the end-of-August rain that pumped up the grapes. Like 1999, September was fine. It was essential to wait and cut the crop back severely—then more matter was present in the wines.

REDS

"It's too rounded a year, and lacks acidity," B. Faurie observed. "It was difficult to find the tannins," added J-L Chave; "there was alcohol without the construction around it, and the wines were even fatter than 1997 *chez nous*." The best are charming and show some tannic support. Colours are not very dark, and the wines are expected to evolve faster than 1998 and 1999. There is some elegance, with restrained fullness. The fruit is fair, but can be stewed and indistinct. The balance is fragile on some wines that can lack flesh and show burnt edges, especially from the lesser sites. Many will not drink pleasantly past 15 or so years, but the Chapoutier reds are more tannic and reserved than most.

★★★★★   J-L Chave Cathelin

★★★★   Belle, Chapoutier L'Ermite/Méal/Pavillon, J-L Chave

★★★   Cave de Tain Gambert de Loche, Chapoutier M. de la Sizeranne, Dard et Ribo, Delas Marquise de la Tourette, B. Faurie, Ferraton Méal, Guigal, Dom Remizières Émilie, M. Sorrel Gréal

★★   Cave de Tain classic/Nobles Rives, P. Jaboulet Pied de la Côte, Ogier Allégories Antoine Ogier, JMB Sorrel Vignon, Vidal-Fleury, Vins de Vienne Chirats St. Christophe

★(★)   B. Chave, P. Jaboulet La Chapelle

★   L. Bernard, Chapoutier Mure de Larnage, Dom du Colombier, Ogier Oratorio, M. Sorrel

WHITES

The whites are very full, with a lot of richness. For them, it was quite a classic vintage, and they have managed to absorb their alocohol levels well. "A year of texture for the whites," J-L Chave.

They are generous and buttery, and will show well by around 2006–07.

- ★★★★★ Chapoutier L'Ermite, M. Sorrel Rocoules
- ★★★★ Chapoutier Méal/Orée, Delas Marquise de la Tourette
- ★★★ Cave de Tain Nobles Rives, Chapoutier Chante Alouette, Ferraton Reverdy, Guigal, Habrard, Dom Remizières
- ★★ Chapoutier Mure de Larnage, P. Jaboulet Chevalier de Stérimberg, M. Sorrel
- ★ Vins de Vienne La Bachole

2001 Very good, sometimes excellent. Termed by G. Chave as a "more classic, understated year than 1999, with greater freshness," the vintage came together in its later season. August was very hot, and a divergence between the alcoholic and polyphenolic ripening occurred. It was crucial to be patient to avoid hard tannins. Ripening took longer than 2000, a factor that helped the vintage's complexity. Rain fell in early September, but the wise waited. Chave harvested a week later than usual, and Chapoutier ended 7–8 October, taking advantage of the lovely end season that was warm from mid-August to the end of September, when rain fell. Some growers had to cool the harvest on entry, so hot was it at picking time.

REDS

The juice in the grapes was well concentrated; the wines have good flesh and acidity and will keep well. They have a traditional character, with cooked elements and a leathery side well evident. Balance is good, and while they showed well early, they may close up around 2006–08.

- ★★★★★ Chapoutier L'Ermite/Pavillon/ Méal, J-L Chave, Delas Bessards, B. Faurie Méal, Ferraton Méal, Tardieu-Laurent
- ★★★★ Belle, Cave de Tain Gambert de Loche, Chapoutier M. de la Sizer-

anne/Greffieux, Delas Marquise de la Tourette, B. Faurie classic/ Greffieux, Ferraton Dionnières, Guigal Ex-voto, P. Jaboulet La Chapelle
- ★★★ Cave de Tain classic/Nobles Rives, B. Chave, Ferraton Miaux, Dom Remizières Émilie, M. Sorrel Gréal, Vins de Vienne Chirats St. Christophe
- ★★ Dard et Ribo, P. Jaboulet Taurobole
- ★ Dom du Colombier, Dom Fayolle Dionnières, JMB Sorrel Vignon

WHITES

A particularly good year for the whites—they were fresh and in no way heavy. "It's rare to have grapes at 14° with freshness—it's like 1991 this year," said G. Chave. Expect them to live and develop well over more than 20 years. They will be very stylish.

- ★★★★★ Chapoutier L'Ermite/Méal, M. Sorrel Rocoules
- ★★★★ Chapoutier Chante-Alouette/ de l'Orée, Habrard
- ★★★ Belle, Cave de Tain, Delas Marquise de la Tourette, Ferraton Reverdy, Guigal Ex-voto, Tardieu-Laurent
- ★★ P. Jaboulet Chevalier de Stérimberg, JMB Sorrel Vignon
- ★ Dom Fayolle Dionnières, Dom Remizières Émilie, M. Sorrel

2002 Fair for the reds. Good for the whites. Flowering was a stop-start affair, so some crop was lost, and the summer was poor, the July weather variable, with hail 20 and 21 July. Rot hit the grapes, especially if the grower allowed high yield levels. Consistent sorting was needed during the ripening cycle; "the indifferent weather meant the grapes were tired and degraded more than rotted," J-L Chave said. "From my point of view," observed L. Fayolle, "crop was quite healthy—it was a question of taking out secondary shoots to allow maximum ventilation more than leaf dropping." From the end of August to 12 September, hot and humid weather provoked outbreaks of acid rot, and even patient growers brought in crop at only 11 to 11.5°. What was left was fruit with small berries, though quite intense ones. J-L Chave lost half the crop, B. Faurie 60 per cent.

REDS

"These are small-scale wines." B. Faurie asserted. "They have quite clear fruit, but the usual rich centres and tannic length are absent." Chaptalisation was required, and flavours are indistinct a lot of the time. Dard et Ribo found the year accentuated the firm texture and pepperiness of their raw granite wine from *Varogne*.

The reds are often disjointed, their constituents out of synchronisation. They are uneasy and lack flesh—bringing in ripe crop was clearly a problem. A light hand with the oak was needed, and generally that does not intrude this year. The main problem is the lack of core, which means they will not persist well—so early drinking will be best. The best examples may live for around 15 years, and can show some tender flavours, the fruits more red berries than black berries this year.

   ★★★★ Chapoutier Pavillon

    ★★★ Chapoutier L'Ermite, J-L Chave, B. Faurie Greffieux, Fayolle Fils et Fille Dionnières, Ferraton Dionnières, Guigal

 ★★(★) Chapoutier Méal, P. Jaboulet La Chapelle

     ★★ Belle, Chapoutier M. de la Sizeranne/Greffieux, Y. Chave, Dard et Ribo, Delas Marquise de la Tourette, B. Faurie classic/ Greffieux, Ferraton Miaux, Meffre Laurus, Cave de Tain

      ★ Dom du Colombier, Dom Michelas St. Jemms, Dom Remizières Émilie, JMB Sorrel Vignon

   (★) L. Bernard

WHITES

Good. Poor flowering hit yields, but as so often in the Rhône, an indifferent year emerged favouring the white wines rather than the reds. Yields around 20 to 25 hl/ha meant the remaining crop intensified, and the robust nature of the Marsanne came through, with M. Sorrel reporting his grapes from his mature Marsanne at 13° natural. The Cave de Tain found better ripeness on their white crop than on the Syrah, and likewise a healthy 13° or more. Aiding the wines' longevity is a respectable acidity, and they show sound length on the palate. Fruit flavours can be spiced. While these wines are not heavily weighted, they have plenty of elegance and matter and bring echoes of 1991, another underrated vintage. Expect the best to live towards 2020 or beyond.

★★★★★ Chapoutier L'Ermite

  ★★★★ Chapoutier de l'Orée, J-L Chave, P. Jaboulet Chevalier de Stérimberg, Cave de Tain

    ★★★ Chapoutier Chante-Alouette, Habrard, M. Sorrel Rocoules

     ★★ Belle, Delas Marquise de la Tourette, Fayolle Fils et Fille Dionnières, Ferraton Reverdy, M. Sorrel

      ★ L-C Brotte, Chapoutier Méal, J-C & N. Fayolle Dionnières, Meffre Laurus

2003 Good to very good. The great heat was more of a challenge than a bounty, bringing the potential for wines that were unbalanced and too potent. Rainfall totalling 200 mm (8 in.) of rain in early December 2003, which brought some soil damage to young plantations, were a blessing in retrospect, bringing help for the 2004 water table. The hot and dry summer saw only some rain in early July. Even so, by early August growers said the crop looked superb. The week of 10–17 August was when the heat became wildly extreme—42°C (108°F) in the shade. This grilled the vine leaves and caused large loss of crop. It also meant the sugars were way ahead of the tannins in their ripening—Y. Chave had bunches of 15.3° Syrah, but the polyphenols representing skins and stalks in them lagged behind. When to pick was even more delicate than usual, since even the veteran *vignerons* were working in uncharted territory. "We were the first to pick at Hermitage, so we avoided the 17° vats that some had," recalled P. Guigal. "We finished picking on 29 August—we found the phenolic maturity OK by then, so why wait?" said J. Grange of Delas. Bringing green back to the leaves, 140 mm (5.6 inches) of rain on 30 August also freed the sometimes blocked polyphenols, but the high alcohol degree remained an issue.

REDS

Well, what would you expect? These are Big Wines. Look at Les Bessards. From tasting casks of this pre-assembly, the flavours are dark chocolate rather than clear fruit, the aftertaste can be gasping, with the degree roaming towards 16°. The hill soaked up the heat.

Vinification had to be a carefully judged affair. Any grower who was not vigilant would encounter a high risk of volatile acidity and stop-start fermentations. "I wanted to treat it perfectly normally, especially as the year wasn't at all normal—so we've played it low-key in the cellar, and done nothing unusual," said J-L Chave. Attaboy!

The colours are all very dark, like the fruit flavours—berries, prunes, the textures warm and rich. The aromas are broad and lasting—often there are meaty, ripe black fruit connotations, with smoke, pepper, and bacon sidelines. Where fruit aromas reflect red berries, the wines are from softer, more eastern *climats* like *Greffieux* or *Diognières*.

The best reds are naturally very full and have a persistent, savoury character, with ripe tannins that integrate well. Oak use can be a problem in some cases—crop may have been rich on analysis but was also tired. The oak may have served to squeeze it further, and combined with the lack of fresh vigour, means some finishes are dry.

Where next? That is the big question. Will the wines live and develop harmoniously? Some will suddenly evolve and loosen, and it would be sensible to try bottles in 2007, and the largest wines in 2008. Longevity past 2020 is sure for the leading wines but not by a long way.

★★★★★ Chapoutier L'Ermite, Delas Bessards

★★★★ Y. Chave, Dard et Ribo, Delas Marquise de la Tourette, B. Faurie Méal, Guigal Ex-voto, Dom des Martinelles Louis et Aimé, Cave de Tain Gambert de Loche, Vins de Vienne Chirats St. Christophe

★★★(★) Dom des Martinelles

★★★ Chapoutier M. de la Sizeranne/Greffieux/Pavillon, Y. Chave, J-C & N. Fayolle Dionnières, Ferraton Méal, P. Jaboulet La Chapelle

★★(★) Chapoutier Méal

★★ Ferraton Dionnières, Dom Remizières Émilie, Vidal-Fleury

WHITES

A big-scale vintage for the whites, with the Marsanne's glorious richness working overtime. The Roussanne wilted under the heat, its bunches often compacted and unusable. Bouquets can be spiced, with typical hazelnut and dried fruit content—they are prominent in their youth, but will close around 2007. Palates are charged with white fruit, *crème patisserie* flavours, and are solid—so much so, that there can be chewy textures rather like those of a red wine. Expect these potent wines to show well around 2010 and to run towards 2021–25.

★★★★★ Chapoutier Méal

★★★★ Chapoutier de l'Orée/L'Ermite, Delas Marquise de la Tourette, B. Faurie, Dom des Martinelles

★★★ Ferraton Reverdy, P. Jaboulet Chevalier de Stérimberg

★(★) Chapoutier Chante-Alouette

2004 Good, with the whites superior to the reds. Flowering was abundant, except in the very dry soils that had particularly suffered in the 2003 heat. July saw good weather, and with August bringing 150 to 200 mm (6–8 in.) of rain in total, growers got busy deleafing to permit ventilation. The north wind and fresh nights helped to stave off some rot problems. The aftereffects of 2003 were apparent in some places: "The lower areas down the slope did better than the higher sites, which were tired after 2003's dry conditions," said J-L Chave. This meant that cropping levels could be quite variable—some plots with only 10 hl/ha, others 40 hl/ha—a reduction that was noticeable from the flowering onwards. "There were very few setbacks for us—we were healthy before the August rain," reported P. Fayolle of Dom des Martinelles.

The reds are generally well-coloured, with open fruit, but not the body of the best vintages. Their tannins gained weight and presence inside the first year. Expect the reds to grow in stature with time; they should drink well around 2010–11 and beyond.

The whites have done very well; the crop was healthy and ripe and they possess good degrees and levels of richness. With decent acidity present as well, this is set to be a vintage that ages and evolves well, over 20 years or more. There are some comparisons with 1991 at this early stage. Note the Chapoutier trio of special whites, J-L Chave and Fayolle Fils & Fille.

PLATE 1. Early morning light on the Rhône at Le Port, Ampuis. (Tim Johnston)

PLATE 2. Clusel-Roch Syrah vines on the up-and-coming site of *Les Grandes Places*, Côte-Rôtie. (Tim Johnston)

PLATE 3. The *Côte Brune* at Côte-Rôtie—10 hectares of rugged rock and the heart of the fullest wines. (Tim Johnston)

PLATE 4. The 14-hectare *Côte Blonde* rises above the walled vineyard of *La Taquière*, Côte-Rôtie. (E. Guigal)

PLATE 5. Gilles Barge—the family home and cellars are opposite the steep climb of Côte-Rôtie's *Côte Brune*. (Author's collection)

PLATE 6. Marcel Guigal's gleaming triumph—the restored Château d'Ampuis. (E. Guigal)

PLATE 7. Gilbert Clusel and his wife, Brigitte Roch, on the schist vineyard of *Verenay* beside their cellars. (Tim Johnston)

PLATE 8. Marcel, Bernadette, and son Philippe Guigal in front of the La Mouline barrel in their Côte-Rôtie cellars—Marcel with tie and casquette, as usual. (Tim Johnston)

PLATE 9. The *Sainte-Agathe* vineyard high above Condrieu, the Rhône curling south past its hills and factories. (Tim Johnston)

PLATE 10. Allez, Georges! Georges Vernay, for so long the bastion of Condrieu, checking out his refined Côte-Rôtie with daughter Christine and son-in-law Paul. (Tim Johnston)

PLATE 11. Château-Grillet's Viognier vineyard rises above and beside the old house, its benign southeasterly siting helping ripening. (Tim Johnston)

PLATE 12. Isabelle Baratin's charming elegance is underpinned by her determination to defend the reputation of the famous Château-Grillet. (Tim Johnston)

PLATE 13. Why Hermitage contains granite—the Rhône now runs past the west side of the Hermitage hill (right of picture). Millions of years ago, it ran east of it (left of picture) and the hill was joined to the Massif Central granite. (Tim Johnston)

PLATE 14. A classic Hermitage view—the sweep down from *Le Méal*, Paul Jaboulet Aîné's prized vineyard, to *Les Greffieux*. (Tim Johnston)

PLATE 15. The mainly granite west end of the Hermitage hill—*Les Bessards*—with the soil rich enough at the bottom to nurture cardoons and leeks. On the right is *L'Hermite*. (Tim Johnston)

PLATE 16. Hard labour—Pierre Cotte and his sturdy mare put in full days during the growing season at Hermitage, here on *Les Greffieux*. (Author's collection)

PLATE 17. Michel
Chapoutier, the
driving force of
Hermitage, in his
biodynamic vine-
yard on *Les Bessards*.
(Tim Johnston)

PLATE 18. In horse racing, a good stallion stamps his stock. In wine, a good vigneron does the same. Gérard and Jean-Louis Chave. (Tim Johnston)

PLATE 19. Philippe Jaboulet on the plain of *Les Chassis* with his Crozes-Hermitage Marsanne crop. (Author's collection)

PLATE 20. The Rhône at Serves-sur-Rhône, the most northerly village of Crozes-Hermitage. (Tim Johnston)

PLATE 21. South-facing vineyards at Mercurol, southern Crozes-Hermitage. (Tim Johnston)

PLATE 22. The rushing Ozon stream at Arras, one of the many Ardèche water sources that create vine-growing valley slopes at St-Joseph. (Tim Johnston)

PLATE 23. "It's up to you, baby Antonin." Four generations of the Coursodon family in their garden beside the square of Mauves, St-Joseph. (Author's collection)

PLATE 24. "I plant and prune, but it's nature that does a lot more than me"— Philippe Desbos, Domaine de Gouye, St-Joseph. (Author's collection)

PLATE 25. The best climat at Cornas—the *Reynards* vineyard, with its subset *Tézier* under the cedars. (Tim Johnston)

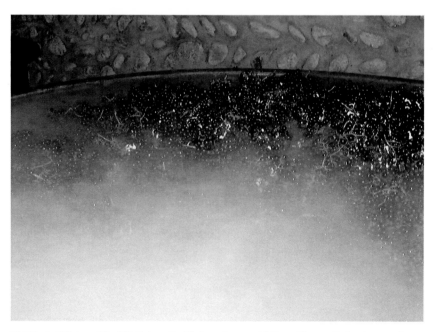

PLATE 26. "We have lift-off!" Carbon dioxide hovering over Thiérry Allemand's Syrah vat at Cornas. (Fabien Louis)

PLATE 27. Stubborn, dedicated, and talented—Thiérry Allemand on his *Tézier* vineyard at Cornas. (Tim Johnston)

PLATE 28. Supreme standards, a supreme sense of touch—the Clape family, Olivier, Auguste, and Pierre-Marie, in their timeless cellar at Cornas. (Tim Johnston)

PLATE 29. St-Péray is host to a lively local Wine Fair in early September, which includes a musical carnival through the streets and, yes, wine. (Tim Johnston)

PLATE 30. Clairette de Die's location in the pre-Alps is reflected in its colourful annual Wine Fair posters. (Author's collection)

5

Crozes-Hermitage

SHERLOCK HOLMES might have said, "Hmm, there's more to this than meets the eye," had he lent his analytical mind to Crozes-Hermitage. It's an *appellation* with no particular variety in it for most people—a relatively safe provider of middle-range, fruity Syrah reds. Nothing to get too emotional about: lots of vineyard space, so lots of wine, and regarded by some as a supplying a form of answer to New World fruit-bomb wines. Shove it on a restaurant chain's wine list—it'll nicely fill the French red category above the Côtes du Rhône.

If only life were that simple. This is an *appellation* where rockmen and -women should come and sniff around. It's something of a geologist's paradise. It's home to snow and snakes. There are soil divides that are very clear-cut. There are climate influences that vary sharply only five miles apart. It sits on the east bank of the Rhône, so in places its connection to Alpine glacier activity thanks to the conduit of the Isère River is direct and traceable. It's also compact. The 11 *communes* are close to one another, so the determined detective can pin down the impact of varied soil groupings on the wines they yield.

Shock news: *terroir* is alive and well at Crozes-Hermitage!

But that's fine theory, some would say—does it lead anywhere? Do the growers express notions of *terroir* in their wines? The answer to these questions is "no—not yet." What has happened in the evolution of this area since it received the extension of its *appellation* in 1952 is a simple commercial split between wines that are young and fruity and those that are more oaked and longer-lived. They're in pretty much the same marketing basket together, hitting two slightly different price points. Winemaking is pretty uniform, too, full of the standard *oenologue/* wine school practices.

Farms that used to grow fruit and vines now make a good living from wine alone, so why expect growers to question or explore beyond this status quo? As more of a romantic than a *commerçant*, my answers would be several:

· Wine bore the village or its main family's name in past centuries; the connection with its place was total. Why can't that be regained for the best plots?

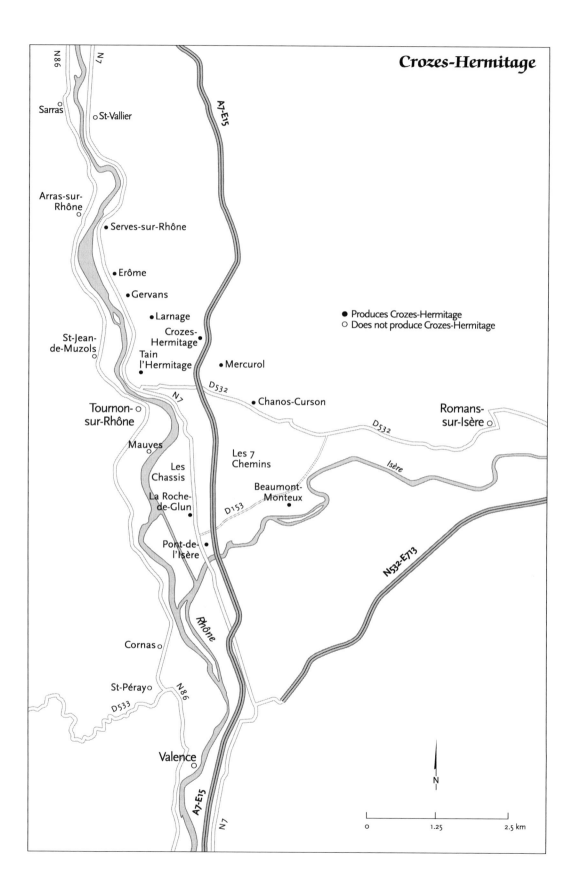

Crozes-Hermitage

- N86
- N7
- A7-E15
- Sarras
- St-Vallier
- Arras-sur-Rhône
- Serves-sur-Rhône
- Erôme
- Gervans
- Larnage
- Crozes-Hermitage
- St-Jean-de-Muzols
- Tain l'Hermitage
- Mercurol

● Produces Crozes-Hermitage
○ Does not produce Crozes-Hermitage

- D532
- N7
- Chanos-Curson
- D532
- Romans-sur-Isère
- Tournon-sur-Rhône
- Mauves
- Les 7 Chemins
- Les Chassis
- Isère
- La Roche-de-Glun
- D153
- Beaumont-Monteux
- Pont-de-l'Isère
- N532-E713
- Rhône
- Cornas
- St-Péray
- N86
- D533
- Valence
- A7-E15
- N7

N

0   1.25   2.5 km

- Consumer knowledge is making a fast journey through the bland and uniform in life and seeking out the more challenging as everybody knows more about everything.

- Would not a Questor grower gain more satisfaction from producing wine that expresses the purity of his best soil, with a greater level of challenge, than blending or selecting casks of the best-tasting wine for the special cuvée?

- A hierarchy of terroir may well emerge, but that would also stimulate increased pricing for the best places.

- Should not this *appellation's* quality be expressed through terms of soil and environment than through turbo-charged winemaking and flashy wine commentator endorsements? Real Life or the Soft Life?

So the argument is for greater expression of place in the wines from here in the next 10 years. Even a subtitle under the Crozes-Hermitage billing that reads *"vin de Larnage"* or *"vin de Gervans"* or *"vin de Pont-de-l'Isère"* would be stimulating. Why should consumers not be interested in the nuances that our planet can bring to its fruit? Do we lead too busy, self-important lives to shrug such matters aside as the preserve of sad Trainspotters?

An early lead in this direction came with the Domaine des Entrefaux's back label on their 2002 white Coteau des Pends, named after one of the most historically renowned sites for white wine in the *appellation*. Lo and behold—there was the name MERCUROL on the back, not the front of the bottle!

It's true that for many years Crozes-Hermitage bumbled along in the lee of Hermitage, a rather dowdy relation in name, producing red and white wines of a lesser stature and only moderate interest. There were very few growers making any sort of splash—bottles of Crozes from the 1950s are rare and, if they turn up, are likely to be from a merchant, not a domaine. Jules Fayolle was one of the early private bottlers

in 1959, which helped him to also export some of his wine.

The main footnote from the 1960s was the arrival from Algeria of the *pieds noirs*—escapees from the bloody conflict of the time as French rule ended. They were fruit farmers and set themselves up on the Chassis plain's open spaces. Their work gradually moved on to vine-growing, with the Cave des Clairmonts one of the first groups to bottle their own wine.

There was a marked instinct to remain hidden away at Crozes when I first visited it in the early 1970s. Only the Thalabert wine from Jaboulet stood out, with just four growers—Bégot, Fayolle, Roure, and Rousset—present in the northern granite zones, and two—Bied and Desmeure—on the flatter lands of Mercurol. People had no idea about sophisticated marketing, overseas sales, label requirements, or spreading the word beyond the vicinity.

That decade was also tricky for other reasons, as explained by *vigneron* Michel Ferraton: "The vineyards had been extended, you see, and there were a lot of young vines, plus yields were high. Those were dark days, because we risked getting a bad name."

One underlying motive for the opening up of the plain area of *Les Chassis* was its ability to give wines of higher alcohol than the Gervans area peopled in the 1970s by the Fayolles and Raymond Roure; the wines were more ebullient and less refined, as well, but could be sold at competitive rates because of lower labour costs.

The surge in planting was underway by the 1980s, a decade that heralded more enjoyable wines, younger growers, more independence of spirit. It was if this rather rustic backwater had received a makeover. Many wines were better made and less hit-and-miss. The emphasis was on fruit extraction and fresh appeal, with vigour still present. It was also plucky for Charles Tardy and Albert Belle to quit the Co-opérative, never an easy transaction, and prove that life could exist beyond it and the merchant network.

But the 1990s advances were not all beneficial. As a middle-ranking name in the Rhône hierarchy, Crozes is always likely to be prey to fashion whims as growers jostle to sell the wine in a crowded marketplace. At the start of the decade, it became more and more common to find severe vinifications, with modern techniques used with unstinting abandon by growers aiming to achieve strong colour and more "depth." This engendered a raft of formulaic wines, so diversity of *terroir* slipped away. Technique dominated touch.

New-oak use spread, without necessarily the right grape extract to go with it. And white wines were also subjected to this new regime of intense treatment in the cellar. The Burgundian practice of *bâtonnage,* or lees stirring, became widespread. This is done to obtain extra *gras,* or richness of extract. The malolactic fermentation was generally allowed to take place, too. The result was a raft of homogenous whites, with the same fat, white fruit flavours and at times sticky textures. Not much vintage variation was detectable, either.

Let's just remember that Burgundy is a northern vineyard region. Mean temperatures and sunshine hours are well below the Rhône. So why import a technique designed for cooler ripening conditions? It sounds like the old instinctive Rhône reaction of centuries gone by, when the area was the very poor relation of Burgundy and was commercially subservient to it— wines sent north to fill them out and so on.

A return to simplicity has to be urged for the first years of the new millennium. Let's have wine that grows in the glass and is capable of expressing its place of origin and its subtlety. May growers not pander to fashion—fashion in winemaking imported from ill-suited places and fashion from writers and commentators who uniformly extol the merits of the Big Wines they encounter at mass tastings.

Wine—food—company, folks!

Certainly, the Crozes region is buzzing with its increasing commitment to winemaking. In Tain this shows through with new wine bars that serve young, local start-up growers' Crozes wines and bistrots in some of the outlying *communes,* while there is even a wine tasting held on the Tournon-to-Lamastre steam train.

From the second edition of *The Wines of the Rhône,* 1983

To arrive at the Fayolles' farm, where they also grow apricots and cherries, it is necessary first to traverse the main Paris-Nice railway line, whose crossing near the centre of Gervans is always firmly placed in the down position. Shades of the France of old Jean Renoir films are recalled when a solemnly dressed and straightfaced *madame* emerges from a little house, waddles over with the utmost aplomb and slowly proceeds to wind up the level-crossing gate, no doubt swearing under her breath at the unwanted disturbance.

The late 1990s brought a welcome change of economics for the Crozes growers. "The year 1996 was our recent tough time," states Jean-Louis Pradelle, President of the Growers Union. "Then it was taking 16 months to sell one year's wine." By 2003 that lead time had reduced to eight months, but the future has again reverted to uncertainty. There's too much *appellation* wine sloshing around in France, with demand falling at home and abroad. A very small crop in 2003—37 per cent down from 2000 and 2001—alleviated stock levels, but there is a fundamental issue of who will buy all the wine when abundant vintages, those like 1999, 2000, and 2001, return and occur back to back. The year 2004 was abundant, incidentally.

"It was euphoria until 2003 here," states Jean-Louis Buffière, "and things have got tricky—more due to the general economic situation than the price of the wine, which I sell for €7.30 (£4.80 or US$8.50)."

Another factor stated by growers is the change of policy by the Tain Co-opérative since 2000 to sharply increase its proportion sold in bottle. The bulk element fell from 80 per cent to 30 to 40 per cent, and this squeezed the bulk wine price with around 5,000 hectolitres taken off the market. In its place, the new regime of sales obviously includes deals with supermarkets, where special prices are given—undercutting that side of the market for the smaller domaines.

Vineyard prices have pushed up in the meantime. A hectare bought by Yann Chave in 1996 cost 150,000 francs (£15,000/US$26,000), "and I was accused of inflating prices!" Now a rough estimate is that a hectare on a good site like *Les Chênes Verts* on the plain would cost 400,000 to 500,000 francs (£40,000–£50,000/ US$69,000–US$87,000) and a hectare on the hill terraces of Gervans perhaps 10 per cent less.

The vineyard grew to 1,325 hectares by 2003. "There are 15 hectares allowed for planting in 2003–04, against 30 the year before," says Jean-Louis Pradelle, "and a lot of demand for them. We favour plots that are already there for the expansion."

Locally, wine's progress from the late 1990s has caused employment changes. By 2003 the agricultural labour force, notably for apricots, was about even with the wine labour force, after years of being much more numerous. The Habrard family at Gervans estimate one person working half-time can look after his 10 hectares of apricots. Pruning the trees is the only slow job. But the rewards aren't great compared to wine. "Ten to 15 years ago, we earned a lot more from apricots than we did from wine," states Laurent Habrard. "In abundant fruit years, we probably lose money—there are no *appellation* rules for apricots here, so there is often overproduction—or terrible frost like in 2003," he adds mordantly.

Evidence of the continued desire, particularly among the young, to take a risk and have a go comes from a small but significant statistic that emerges from interviews with the Tain Coopérative over the years. In 1982 there were 550 subscribers cultivating *appellation* and *vin de pays* vineyards, in 1991 420, and in 2003 390— a very marked indication of a desire for autonomy, or to have the freedom to sell grapes in the open market. The movement started by the likes of Charles Tardy and Bernard Ange back in the 1970s and taken on by Belle and Viale in the late 1980s has been maintained by recent departing growers like Franck Farguier at the Domaine des Hauts Chassis and David Raydon at Domaine Les Bruyères.

White wine represents around 8 per cent of all Crozes, although growers are actually allowed to mix white grapes with the Syrah before vinification. "More growers are doing this because the red is easier to sell," comments Jean-Louis Pradelle. "They're allowed up to 15 per cent white content, but that's taking it too far, I think. If you add 10 per cent, you can lend extra richness to the wine."

Much of the production—and the perception of the wine's quality—lies in the hands of the Cave Co-opérative de Tain; it makes about 60 per cent of the wine. The collective Cave des Clairmonts accounts for 10 per cent, and the domaines make up the remaining 30 per cent. The last group includes the merchants who also own vineyards, like Chapoutier and Paul Jaboulet Aîné; Jaboulet produce 10 times more wine than Chapoutier and also Delas, by purchasers.

About 30 per cent of the wine is thought to be sold in bulk of some sort—from people filling a five-litre *cubitainer* to merchants from Burgundy dealing in vatloads. The non-Rhône proportion of buyers has fallen since 2000, guided by the Co-opérative's policy of favouring local purchasers.

THE VILLAGES

The *appellation contrôlée* area runs across 11 *communes* around Tain-l'Hermitage and derives its name from one of them, a tiny community whose agreeable red wine was in the past referred to simply as "Crozes." Tain serves as the unofficial centre of the *appellation* and is ringed by Crozes-Hermitage, Serves, Erôme, Gervans, and Larnage to the north; by Mercurol and Chanos-Curson to the east; and by Beaumont-Monteux, Pont-de-l'Isère and La Roche-de-Glun to the south. The villages all lie within easy distance of the main Paris-to-Nice highways, the old N7 that hugs the Rhône, and the *autoroute du Soleil*, the A7, that slices through the vineyards behind the mighty Hermitage hill.

Whereas all these were once villages in a gentle time warp, signs of a dormitory existence now show through on the plain area of the *appellation*. Beaumont-Monteux, for instance, has a well-attended school. The families work in Valence, Tain, or Romans, spread in different directions. The old village, too, is surrounded by a lot of new peripheral housing, bringing a modern, transient air to it, unlike the northern outposts of Gervans and Erôme, for instance.

Gervans rises out of the narrow plain, its main hills rising to the east. It is a jumble of stone houses, with some signs of renewal—new pointing, shiny shutters. Recent dropping of VAT on refurbishments has boosted such makeovers. Almond, cherry, and apricot trees—a burst of colour in spring—stand on its fringes. The centre is timeless; a dull, plain main square is just a tiny space, a primitive clearing for the Mairie, the streets are narrow, and children and grandparents stroll around on a Sunday afternoon.

The notice board in the Gervans square adds to the Vieille France touch. Apart from the usual electoral roll and village council coverage (a lot of *vigneron* family names present on that), two important country matters are addressed: the shooting season dates and the "places of destruction" of foxes, rats, weasals, mink, large rats, rabbits, pigeons, magpies, starlings—nature's villains assembled together!

In the face of supermarket competition, Gervans took action, and the *commune* built and opened a grocery store in 2002. It's also a bar and meeting place for the old-timers. But, wham—a touch down the hill, and modern housing is plonked down beside the vineyards on its outer edge.

Erôme's Place de la Mairie is even smaller than Gervans'; the railway cuts old Erôme in two, a series of bridges levered over it for access towards the hills. The church is simple, and big for a village this size. Around it are all the old street names of any small French community—Grande Rue, Rue du Ruisseau, Rue de l'Eglise.

Either side of the N7 sits "modern" Erôme in two halves of very plain structures.

There is heavy background music between Gervans and Erôme, which were just one *commune* until 1947, with Gervans a mere *quartier* of Erôme. Erôme had been the senior community with the administration and, importantly, the fiscal responsibility and tax charging. All this changed in 1968 when the Rhône hydroelectric dam opposite the villages was created. This was destined for Erôme, but its villagers didn't want the noise, pollution, and disruption, so to much rubbing of hands and "That'll do nicely," it was built between the villages, under the umbrella of Gervans. So Gervans escaped being charged taxes by Erôme, and received the revenues from the dam. Long faces in Erôme!

The most northerly village is Serves-sur-Rhône. Like Erôme, this looks ordinary on first inspection. The main village peels away off the N7, and suddenly revealed is a timeless row of neat houses either side of the road, their first floor terraces and metalwork intact. The Table du Roy's ornate portico is redolent of roaring times in past decades.

Still smudged on some old houses is lettering reading BOULANGERIE-ÉPICERIE, and on the social club, "MAISON pour tous." Nowadays it's bread on wheels here, with the van klaxoning its way along the main street, stopping every 100 yards. It's a chance for the locals to come out and catch up on a bit of chat. There are no obvious signs of prosperity, unlike at Mercurol, for instance.

The old village of Serves is hewn out of a steep granite escarpment, and a ruined castle sits above it. Part of the château has been smartly redone. Inhabitants of these northern villages are rather like the wines—there is more caution, more staring, the children hang out with just an extra hint of uncertainty drifting on the air.

Immediately north of Tain lies Crozes-Hermitage. On the way here the land is craggy, almost brutal, a feeling reinforced by the old-fashioned railway, the one chiselled passage through the rock, its open tunnels tired and stained. The road builders not surprisingly chose to build the N7 along the brief plain beside the Rhône. Here and there are spots of steep, at times terraced vineyards and, on the softer slopes, fruit trees. Whenever the Rhône curls away west, there is more space, and fruit is grown between road and river, on land that from 2009 cannot also be used for Crozes' vines.

The village of Crozes boasts new housing of various sizes, and has been "modernised": there's a road system, a trim public garden area, an enlarged Mairie. It's not as sleepy as it was; it looks like a Tain satellite now, even though official 1999 census figures show its population to be markedly older than either Gervans or Larnage.

The village has a curious shape, almost leaning on the wrong foot, at a tilt. The main square is away from the bistrot and the baker, across a narrow stream. There are quite steep rises in the land around it, so perspective is hard to secure. The area attracts serious walkers, kitted with ample rucksacks.

Down to the N7 the vines run along terraces. Along the top road from Crozes to Larnage, the vines run in straight, wire-trained rows. The soil is powdery loess, but the granite incidence starts to fall. Just one brief valley away is *L'Hermite*, the site near the top of the Hermitage hill, which tapers to the southeast from here.

Larnage is a white stone village—appropriate given the white clay on its slopes—and is trim and flower packed in summer. Tain's influences are marked here, not surprising given that the village sits just above it. Smart big houses stand here, and a lot of recent houses and villas are spread out all around the village. Its population is about double that of Crozes.

The square has been completely redone, with shiny Syrah-coloured lampposts; even the round No Parking bumps sport the same corporate colour. There are obvious signs of prosperity, like newly painted shutters and doors, but still the trusty clink of *boules* carry on the air of a sunny Sunday afternoon. There's a restaurant, Le Cep de Vignes, and a very plain church. The village feels out of a different time from Serves and Erôme.

Between Larnage and Mercurol, fruit production intensifies. The theme of new houses, lots of them, continues at Mercurol. There has been a vast transformation here in the past 20 years. An electronic sign advertises the village's Internet site. At night the smart façade of its church and the ruined tower above it are lit up. The heart of the village is now marked by the restored Hotel de la Tour on its orderly square, a baker, and the *tabac* along from it. Among the fallen on the First World War Monument is a Fonfrède, a name connected with today's Domaine des Chenêts.

The ridge between Mercurol and Chanos-Curson, its neighbour to the east, contains some of the best vineyards of this corner of the *appellation*. More will be heard of *Les Pends* as a great white wine site in years to come, restoring it to its early-twentieth-century fame. Some of its vineyards are terraced and enjoy a great south-facing exposure. Sprinkled in among them are one or two large houses and wooded clumps. Lower down, the vines run along gentle slopes to the main Romans-Tain road. The broad expanse of the vine- and fruit-bearing plain runs away south towards the Isère River.

Even here, side-by-side villages like Mercurol and Chanos-Curson do not overlap much; "people keep their attention on their particular *commune*," observes Jean-Louis Pradelle, and a Chanos-Curson resident.

Chanos-Curson has a new housing estate on its edge, an enforced wake-up to one of the sleepiest Crozes villages. An imposing stone-walled church looms over its little square, and old shuttered residences stand opposite it. Movement is slow, even at the start and end of the day. Grande Rue is a misnomer, and one of the few signs of change comes courtesy of the sheen of the new Post building.

Moving from Chanos-Curson to Beaumont-Monteux means crossing the heart of the plain. The alluvial stones show up towards the middle and beyond towards the south, and the feeling of intensive farming grows. It is confirmed by the Cave des Clairmonts' big and modern building with its different Parking signs for Bus and Car.

Beaumont-Monteux is scarred by the landmark of its old abandoned grain silo. Just to the south is a big, ugly electricity plant, and a lot of new housing has sprung up on the village periphery. A tiny fountain has been plonked down near the church—where is your soul, Beaumont-Monteux? A bar, hairdresser, and paper shop provide for a mix of needs; and beside the Isère is a quite veteran Electricité de France building. Beaumont runs to two schools, one public, the other private.

Downstream from Beaumont is Pont-de-l'Isère, and a major return to reality: the N7 cuts right through its middle. The autoroute is very close by, and a railway station as well. It feels like a town, much less intimate, the outcome of the mean streets of life. It is the ultimately plain place, with tool and packaging light industries, and the traveller no doubt gasps on seeing the oasis of Michel Chabran's polished Michelin-starred restaurant. It takes one back to the old gastronomic traditions of Roanne and Valence nearby—the industrial towns home to the three-star legends of their day, the Troisgros Brothers and Jacques Pic.

The Marché aux Fruits sign here speaks of the area's past and its still-important fruit-growing activities. But there is distance here between the place and the visitor, whereas a village like Gervans seems more pliant and approachable.

The most southwesterly village, just down the road from Pont-de-l'Isère, is La Roche-de-Glun. Part of it lies across the Rhône, even though the village is in the Drôme *département*. There is a host of small businesses here—two bakers, a pizzeria, a pharmacy, Bar-Hotel with PMU Turf facility, a second hotel. The church has been restored and the Mairie grotesquely enlarged, while nearby is a quietly remarkable small white-stone statue of Madonna and Child. It is called VOEU (vow), and its date is 15 August 1944, a poignant reminder of old conflicts and the faith needed to get through them.

HISTORY

The wine from these small villages is historically obscure. Very little is recorded about it until the eighteenth century, when, it appears, wine from the village of Larnage was sold on a fairly regular basis to England; this was called, not *vin de Larnage*, but *vin de Mure*, after Larnage's leading family, and it was always sent across to Bordeaux before being shipped north. This was not the first local wine to go abroad, however, for the white wine of nearby Mercurol was sent to England around 1309, according to village archives. To whom it went is not known.

The other great local claim, used with notable reverence in the 1960s and 1970s, when the wine's identity was obscure, came from the 1846 tasting panel of the Lyon Wine Congress: about the wines of Crozes-Hermitage and Hermitage their view was "If they are not brothers, then they are certainly first cousins." Just occasionally this is true—the fattest, most unctuous white of Marc Sorrel from very old vines being the best example. *Terroir* and exposure differences make the comparison untenable for the reds.

Some indication of those sites that were most reputed is given by the Paul Jaboulet Aîné Tariff of May 1891, offering the vintages 1889–91. There was Crozes red 1889 from their own vineyard at 500 francs per 220-litre cask; the other sites on the list were Gervans and Chassis, both listed as "Grands Ordinaires" and selling for 250 francs a barrel for the 1889. Below them, Mercurol, an Ordinaire wine, was 180 francs a barrel. All the wines were also offered in bottle. At the same time, a Cornas or St-Joseph cask was 400 francs, and a Châteauneuf-du-Pape 350 francs. The whites on the same list were all older and more expensive. The vintages offered were 1887–89, with Mercurol's 1887 220-litre cask priced at 250 francs, while the "Crozes" was on sale for 500 francs, the same as the Condrieu.

Paul Jaboulet Aîné were actively buying vineyards in small plots by the late nineteenth century. One record shows the purchase in 1892 of 0.15 hectare on the hill vineyard of *Corniret*, close to Crozes-Hermitage, for 200 francs. In 1913 Delépine and Chapoutier were also cited as "among the principal *viticulteurs* at Crozes" (M-L Marcelou, *Vins, Vignes et Vignerons de l'Hermitage 1806–1936*, University Lumière-Lyon 2, 2003).

The first official *appellation* decree came along in March 1937, when "wines from the reverse side of the Hermitage hill looking down towards the village of Crozes-Hermitage" were allowed to carry the title "Crozes-Hermitage." In practice, this meant—wait for it—Crozes-Hermitage on its own!

In July 1952 the area was expanded to cover the current 11 *communes*. This encouraged more widespread planting, with accessible lower slopes and the fruit plain around *Les Chassis* chosen as the most workable sites.

CROZES-HERMITAGE VINEYARDS

Slope versus plain. Breeze versus baking heat. High ground versus lowland. Snow versus sun. These are the themes that run across this *appellation*. The northern area—notably the villages of Serves, Erôme, and Gervans—stands towards the cool north-wind funnel, its soil is more laced with granite, and the configuration is one of high-up ledges, rocky Wild West–style outcrops and slopes. Here there are rolled stones and old glacial deposits, with some red clay. Cacti grow in the sunny, exposed areas. Above Serves stands a dark-red road sign of signal foreboding: Road closed at times of Snow.

The plain area is the flatland whose boundary is the River Rhône to the west and the River Isère to the south, a triangle whose apex faces east towards Romans-sur-Isère. Vinegrowing is more recent here and to a degree less "legitimate." Apricots crop well here (apart from 2003), as do cherries. But other countries can produce them for less, so they get replaced by more cash-yielding vines. The contrast when

trawling across this plain south of Tain is striking. There are the fruit groves still there, their black water pipes sticking out of the clay. The dry wind rustles around them. Rolled bales of hay strike oval poses in open-sided fields. It sure gets hot: two crows finish off a road-kill snake; the high summer air hangs heavy and parched.

And then, just a few miles away, one returns to the winding lanes, the pastoral edging to the slope vineyards, indeed the high hills at times rising above 300 metres: the granite outcrops, the dusty loess covering, the dried stone walls in the gulleys, the fresher texture to the air, the more temperate feel to the climate. Streams run off the hills and feed the Rhône, past Crozes-Hermitage, Gervans, and Erôme. This is also home to the wine of Crozes-Hermitage—but one of longer and more established pedigree, it must be said.

If the grower is on the plain, it's a lot more difficult to create well-structured noble wines from his *terroir*. That's why the plain producers excel in the nearest the northern Rhône comes to a New World–style open fruitiness—all-singing wines with some oaked extras for the older-vine cuvées. But if I want a wine that can age and bring forth unexpected and complex notes, then I would always seek out the slope men and be patient with their drier-toned wares.

There's also a marked difference between some of the plain and hillside people. On the plain there are some domaines run by practical farmers, not winegrowers seeking nuance. These properties are set in what also feels like farming country—massed ranks of commercial fruit trees, some vines, and long views away to snow-peaked hills. It's a long way from the narrow granite corridor of the northern sector.

The difference in tannin between these two sources is articulated by Yann Chave of Domaine Bernard Chave: "the *Chassis* plain's tannins are supple and *gourmand*—there's more black currant and jam texture. From Gervans they are straighter and harder-hitting, drier overall. Mind you, I wouldn't take a Gervans *coteau* from you if you offered it free—the wines are too hard for me!" That's why the southern Pont-de-l'Isère wines, with their flattering early roundness, are lapped up by the *négoce* trade.

Now a counter from François Ribo of Dard et Ribo: "The classic area of the *appellation* is the north, around Larnage and Crozes—the later-ripening sites. There's a different Syrah expression here, more refined and complex than the *Chassis* Syrah. The best expression of a variety does come when it's at the limit of its zone of ripening"—just like Pinot Noir in Burgundy, he could have added.

The sprawling plain of *Les Chassis* has Mercurol at its northern end, La Roche-de-Glun, hard by the Rhône, at its southern end, and Chanos-Curson on the eastern side of this triangle. Drought can be a problem here. The advance of wine prices led to replanting with vineyards, but there are still serious fruit plantations. It's a very different state of mind to grow fruit, and it's true that the land is not considered among the best by some of those involved in winemaking at Crozes. Their reasoning is perfectly logical.

The switched-on winemaker at Delas is Jacques Grange, an experienced local with track form at Chapoutier and Colombo before this post. He thinks there are specific challenges facing growers at Crozes. "The Crozes wines generally suffer because the grapes get so ripe and so there are acidity problems: that's the effect of the plain, which for me brings a heaviness into the wines. The soil in Larnage is a bit cooler, so later ripening there is more balanced.

"What this means is that people should pick earlier on the plain, and it's absolutely vital that they work the soil, and get the vine roots to work lower down. The sap needs to circulate and help get acidity into the grapes."

"Of course on the plain, life appears easy," he continues. "People get on their tractors and spray pesticides and herbicides, and that's it. In 2002 there were growers who by early summer had done two treatments when we hadn't had any rain—so at that stage there existed no threat from that." One of the main blights in this region is oïdium, more so than mildew or black rot, and this needs treating with sulphur. The plain is also marked by wire training of many of the vineyards, mainly to allow harvesting machines ease of passage.

Laurent Habrard is in a position to compare the time taken on the plain and the slopes. His family has over three hectares on *Les Chassis* and many plots across Gervans and Erôme. "We doubled our vineyard on *Les Chassis* with a new plantation in 1999; the old plot was staked, the new one trained on plastic runners. It took 100 hours to tie the stake vines in summer and just eight hours to attach the young vines."

Laurent's grandfather used to grow maize on the site, despite it taking him a long time to get there by horse. But clearly, it is tempting for the hillsiders to own some simple plain vineyards, and Laurent Fayolle from Gervans has just himself bought a hectare on a promising site called *Les Saviaux* at La Roche-de-Glun.

Local pressures for housing to serve Valence, and even Lyon, mean that these villages are not likely to stay as rural as they have been. On the plain, places like Beaumont-Monteux show the hard edge of modern, often soulless development. Three of the villages with hillside vineyards—Gervans, Crozes-Hermitage, and Larnage—have therefore mounted a defensive, quality operation of defining selected sites on the hills and clearing and planting them with up to 30 hectares. This shop-window exercise—what the French term "Opération Vitrine"—mirrors the work at places like Mauves and Serrières in the St-Joseph *appellation*.

At Gervans, the idea is to make one single 8.6-hectare vineyard on a hillside that mixes loose granite soil—little pebbles, almost gravel—with clay. "The site is called *Les Paillassonnes*, just south of the village and visible from river cruisers and from the road, which is an implicit part of the plan," comments Laurent Habrard. "There will be six vineyard owners, including Co-opérateurs, Pochon, and Fayolle; the land was used for shooting and for children's hideaway huts and was bought from 15 different owners. The gravel will bring finesse to the wines."

At Crozes, the Vitrine site is called *Méjeans-Pévin*, a confidential 2.4-hectare spot with some granulated soil. It is on the high ridge at over 300 metres to the north of the village of Gervans.

The site at Larnage, the third Vitrine, is called *Château-Verdurette*, 7.85 hectares on the east bank of the *Bousande* stream. The slope here can rise to 60 per cent.

These operations are state aided—all administration costs are handled, along with half the annexed costs, like drainage and access roads. After clearing what are in places heavily forested areas, the avoidance of erosion is a prime concern that adds to the overall cost.

At Mercurol a Conservatory of the Syrah has also been set up. This draws on cuttings from all the *appellations* between Cornas and Côte-Rôtie, and it took three years to spot which vines were healthy enough for the exercise. "It started with 1,000 plants," comments Jean-Louis Pradelle, "then was cut to 600 or so that were deemed good enough. These were planted on free-draining soil on the Mercurol terraces, and are worked by me and my brother Jacques. We are studying and comparing what works best."

Visually, the first observation on the northern area of the Crozes *appellation* is that the vineyards—the named sites—are not easy to spot. Often they are tucked away in confidential settings, a cluster of vines here or there. The hard economics of the relatively modest price of the wine means that this is no spotless, unbroken set of vineyards à la Côte-Rôtie or Hermitage.

The three most northerly villages—Serves, Erôme, and Gervans—are the main granite locations, with pockets of dusty loess here and there that are seized on for white wine cultivation. Further south, Crozes-Hermitage has some granite, but the influence of clay grows towards it and Larnage. Gervans' granite is gneiss and is sanded, while Larnage's granite has decomposed and altered more, bringing in stony soil rich in the local speciality of kaolin, a compact white clay that, once the preserve of fine porcelain, is now used for heat-resistant pizza ovens.

The most northerly vineyards are at Serves. There is very slippery, fine sandy granite above the village; terraced patches of vines mix in with dense woods and fruit trees, a lot of them cherry. On the pretty plateau at the top, cheese is made and foresters' houses peek out of the woods.

The polyculture in the north of the Crozes *appellation* is reassuring. Fruit trees stand right next to vines; scrubland, wild flowers, and woods surround some of the vineyards. There is a balance to nature's tapestry. The vines are almost all staked, and grass is left to grow around them to restrain erosion.

SERVES VINEYARDS

North of the village of Serves and close to the Rhône are the hill terraces at *La Rochette*, where white vines are grown by Nicolas Fayolle. The soil here is clay with some siliceous soil, and granite about a metre down. It is also fully exposed to the force of the north wind. Where there is denser red clay, the Fayolles grow their Syrah, remarking that the clay from these northern villages was often used for tile making in the past.

Laurent Fayolle sees Serves as a good place for white wine: "It has very heterogeneous soil—lime content until midslope, then sandstone-clay seams with fine particles," he explains.

Most of the Serves vineyards are worked by outsiders; Laurent Combier has vines near the château on *Les Garennes*, where there is a predominance of loess with a little more sand than at Gervans. Champal Rocher's vineyard is also on loess, a mix of clay and silted sand, against the backdrop of the northern granite.

An important local influence at Serves is its cool microclimate. This is because the village is set on the westerly extreme of its rocky outcrop, jutting out into the Rhône corridor. The rock face then tucks back in towards Erôme, a *commune* that is accordingly more sheltered. After the old château of Serves, there is a spur with more luxurious vegetation, lots of woods, and a colder climate.

"Serves is rather north and west facing too," adds Laurent Fayolle, "while between Serves and Erôme the slopes are more southwesterly. That's why the local rule of thumb is that if you keep the stalks on grapes from Serves they absolutely must be ripe, otherwise you risk austerity in the wine."

"There's always a 10-to-15-day delay in the north," affirms Laurent Combier, "so I pick my Pont-de-l'Isère crop and get that moving well before the rest—helpful for space in the cellar," he adds.

GERVANS VINEYARDS

Of the three granite villages, Gervans holds the most renowned sites. Its hill vineyards are on steep, well-exposed slopes and terraces overlooking the Rhône, and indeed the village possesses a situation nearly identical to that of Hermitage, with its southward-facing hillsides and generally granite topsoil.

The most noted red wine site at Gervans is *Picaudières* just northeast of the village at between 210 and 260 metres, where there's plenty of granite-*gore* with bits of light brown clay-limestone mixed in and stones and rock debris scattered around. Behind it runs the important stream of *Val de Gervans/Pévin*, which scoops up a lot of small tributaries on its way down to the village and the Rhône.

The *Picaudières* vineyard is very steep, with old terraces hewn out of the rotted granite. Ripening is generally excellent here, with degrees of 13 to 14 registered in 2003–04. *Picaudières* will become an important flagship name for Crozes in the future. Its quality has long been recognised by the locals, and its oldest Syrah vines date from the 1930s.

"The soil changes a lot round here on these hills," states Robert Rousset. "I know three of the *communes*—Erôme, Gervans, and Crozes—and the soil can change across a single plot with seemingly no reason. What I do know is that the best site is *Picaudières* because it faces full south, is sheltered from the north wind, and always ripens well."

Picaudières gives firmly structured wines with good core matter, and real oily appeal when the Syrah vines are old. The soil is colder than in the plain, leading to slower growth and naturally less alcohol. The mentality up here is also more reserved—more private and hidden than the growers down below whose every move can be seen! Having the Paul Jaboulet family buy the old Raymond Roure domaine was certainly a shake-up for the locals.

In general, the granite hillside wines are restrained, dry, and more peppery than the plain wines, their leaner tannins needing extra time to fuse into the core of the stone fruit. Colours are lighter than those from the plain. Red fruits and spice are also their marks. These are also sites that can give excellent, stylish white wines.

Next to and just south on the same hill flank as *Picaudières* is *Sassenas*; Rousset and Chomel are both cultivators on the former, which was the stamping ground of the 1970s legend Raymond Roure. Chomel also works some 1930s Syrah on *Sassenas* near his house, along with Paul Jaboulet, who look after part of the old Roure vineyard there. Its soil contains some loess with an alluvial stone presence.

Below *Sassenas* is a long-established white wine site called *Les Blancs*; Nicolas Fayolle, Chomel, Paul Jaboulet, and Habrard grow mostly Marsanne here that dates from the 1940s and 1950s; the soil is brown clay and quite deep. *Les Blancs* is a name to retain for the future.

Other sites at Gervans are *Merjurol*, also a *gore* spot broadly east of the village at over 300 metres and what the Habrard family calls *Barbari*, a loess slope suitable for white vines. The Fayolles of Domaine des Martinelles also have a respected plot of 1960s Syrah on *Tenay*, a sanded granite vineyard facing south-southwest that is part terrace, part plateau.

Maxime Chomel is in no doubt about the importance of hillside vineyards here: "It really matters," he declares. "I find 10-year-old vines from the full slopes give better quality than 50-to-60-year vines on the plain."

Other sites mentioned at Gervans are *Cafiot* (loess/granite areas), worked by Combier, and

La Tuilière, which has a mix of red clay and decomposed granite and is on slight-slope terraces. There is loess high up, where Rousset grows his tiny plot of Marsanne. Habrard, Rousset, and Combier have plots on the latter site.

Down beside the river is *Les Îles*, which is marked by small alluvion *galet* stones. As it is on the plain beside the Rhône, this is due to be declassified by 2009, with its Syrah due to deliver a *vin de pays*. Its soil is sandy-clay, rich and humid. Domaine La Batellerie works 50-plus–year-old Syrah vines here, as does Nicolas Fayolle.

The Gervans hillside style is for red fruits on the palate, a refinement of taste that contrasts with the Gervans wine made from the flatter land like *Les Îles* beside the Rhône, the village, and the N7 route. The latter wine displays more black fruit flavours with a violet finish, according to Laurent Habrard. I find the presence of the black fruits, with also some spice and tar from a spot like *Les Îles*.

ERÔME VINEYARDS

Gervans and Erôme were one *commune* until 1947, so the vineyards mainly straddle both villages. Rousset has a plot of Syrah dating from the 1950s, as well as Marsanne on *Les Vedias* immediately behind and above the old village of Erôme and beside *Les Picaudières*. A terraced site 130 to 180 metres up, its soil is granite with loess present in places, the loess chosen for his Marsanne, that goes back as far as 1923. This means it is one of the oldest Marsanne plots in the *appellation*, in company with some of the Larnage Marsanne around the château there.

Tout, another site at Erôme, also reflects the changing soils within a single site. Rousset grows his Syrah in the clay areas, and his old Marsanne in white clay–loess that has some stones present. Domaine La Batellerie also grows some Marsanne here.

Other Erôme *lieux-dits* are *Beaubrunet La Roux*, a granite site with some loess and, close to the village and the N7, *Les Mottes*, with deeper soil.

CROZES-HERMITAGE VINEYARDS

The Crozes-Hermitage hill vineyards are landscaped by the north-south water flow of the *ruisseau de Crozes*, which curls south of the village and flows into the Rhône. In so doing it creates a valley with some fine sunny hillsides suitable for vinegrowing.

The first easily visible site is *Les Pontaix*, on the left of the road up to the village from the N7. Chomel and Laurent Fayolle work vineyards here. The soil is stony clay with a little limestone, the highest point around 220 metres. "Syrah wines from *Pontaix* carry a tannic structure and can take oak," states Laurent Fayolle; "they show ripe red fruits and spice and are pretty rich." In places on *Les Pontaix* there are what the growers term *terres mortes*—pale granite, siliceous, sticky soil that is good for white grapes.

North of *Pontaix* and a little nearer the Rhône is *Les Cornirets*. "This has a different geological seam," explains Laurent Fayolle, who works an old Raymond Roure plot of 1940s Syrah; "it's very fine granite, with brown clay, and makes very fine wine. It's shielded from the north wind by the woods behind it."

Beyond *Cornirets* and close to the railway is *Les Voussères*, whose name has been given some exposure over the years by the Fayolle family. Its soil is sandy granite and fine clay and gives a very fruited, delicately tannic and structured red wine. Paul Jaboulet have a plot of 1960s Syrah here.

High up in the *commune* of Crozes, east of *Picaudières* and separated from it by a ravine is the plateau called *Quartier de Méjans*. The terraces here start at 270 metres and rise to 330 metres. The slippery granite is light, acid soil with gritty sandstone about. Rousset and Chomel work holdings here.

Further south are the vineyards that used to be worked by the Bourret family on *Les Côtes* above the village on the way to Larnage. This is a clay-chalk, later-ripening site at 250 metres, with its oldest Syrah dating from 1929. Dard et Ribo now work some of this.

A small site that perhaps contains some of the purest granite at a depth of about half a metre (just over half a yard) in the northern sector is *Chavanessieux*, close to *La Varogne*, the extension of the Hermitage hill above the N7 on the way out of Tain towards Crozes. This is worked by Chapoutier; it's noticeable that the aromas of this wine frequently show leather and earthy aspects, due in part to the firm granite couch, and also to the incidence of the cooling north wind on this exposed spot.

LARNAGE VINEYARDS

The *commune* of Larnage has a local speciality, the white clay or kaolin that is spread around the old château. As the soil is often deep here, the vines are not unduly affected by dry conditions. In full sun, the white soil can be dazzling to the eye, and the quarry still functions here. The Fayol factory in Tain produces the well-known Panyol ovens for bread and pizzas, proclaiming "Terre Blanche de Larnage" since 1840 as its emblem.

There are areas of gravel from old decomposed granite on top, as at *Les Terres Blanches*. Larnage is also known for its high wind incidence, notably above 200 metres, with the north wind, or Bise, dominating—helpful in 2002 with so much rot around.

Many of the plots at Larnage are small, spread out between lines of trees and recent housing. There is still small-scale fruit production here as well, and for long-established families like Olivier Dumaine's this means flitting between 30 different sites to work his six hectares. There were many more vineyards before the Second World War, but in the years following, apricots paid a lot better than wine. Estimates are that there are now about 60 hectares planted at Larnage.

Like all the Crozes villages, Larnage is poorly charted, and names abound that are known to growers rather than official maps. Around the château, to the east of the *Bousande* stream, are clustered sites that reflect the kaolin theme to

greater or lesser extent. One, called *Les Carrières* by Dard et Ribo, holds some 1920s Marsanne.

Ripening is delayed here, because of the cool soil that retains moisture—a bonus for roots and leaves in the drought of 2003—and also because the vines are in a small, well-aired valley. They may ripen two weeks behind the plain growers' plants.

"We find that the Marsanne off the kaolin gives wine of more rigour and decisive cut than much of the Crozes area—it's a different do," comments François Ribo. Sticking to the white wine theme, Larnage is also home to Marc Sorrel's half hectare of 1940s Marsanne and Roussanne on what he terms *Les Terres Blanches*; "that was an epoch when a lot of Roussanne was planted," says Marc. The Sorrel Crozes *blanc* is one of the fullest, finest wines in the *appellation* and reflects what good soil this is for white wine. The Domaine des Martinelles also make the most of some 1940s Marsanne here, that is topped up by a 1970s plantation, their two sites called *Tenay* (loess, sand) and *La Mine* (kaolin).

The red wine from this area is restrained in style but has good flesh, and some power, if picked nice and ripe or if taken from old vines. The Louis Belle cuvée from Domaine Belle, taken from a mix of kaolin and granite, is an example of this style. Tannins are less smooth, cooler, and more peppery than the obviously black fruited ones of the plain-area wines. The colour of Larnage Syrahs, especially on the classic cuvées, often stops at red, not a darker hue. The fruit also comes in a fine red berry style, with the lift sometimes of a white peppery side to it.

La Bouvate et Les Rennes holds some Syrah worked by Sorrel, whose neighbours are Desmeure, Belle, Dumaine, and Guigal. This site reflects the kaolin and small-stone topsoil theme. Dard et Ribo talk of another local site at 250 metres called *Le Pé de Loup*, where there is white gravel with a touch of kaolin, and also the *Quartier des Chaux*, which is a mix of loess with quite large alluvial stones and red clay: "It's a spot of transition where the Alpine influences come to bear quite strongly," remarks François Ribo.

There are areas of red soil at Larnage as well, where there is more granite. This brings very dark, concentrated wines, with a lot of richness at their centre, according to Philippe Belle. The Domaine des Martinelles of Aimé and Pascale Fayolle have a south-facing plot of 1960s Syrah on *Les Bâties* in this sector, where the soil is red clay and granite mixed, with a covering of stones. This soil is more meagre than the kaolin, which is where their Marsanne is planted.

MERCUROL VINEYARDS

East of Tain, and connecting to the broad *Les Chassis* plain, lies Mercurol, the largest *commune* of the *canton*. It runs away to the Rhône south of Tain and also extends down to *Les Chassis*. The connection to the granite and loess of the north is largely severed here, although it is the source for some of the best white Crozes. Mercurol's Coteau des Pends white wine was written about after the First World War, a fact relayed to Bernard Chave by his father, who was born in 1909.

The *Coteau des Pends* is the ridge running just southeast from Mercurol towards Chanos-Curson; the vines rise in a gentle sweep up it and enjoy a great south-facing exposure. The theme is white clay-chalk with pockets of red clay, the clay factor helping the whites. The topsoil is very fine on the slopes, with smooth, cream-coloured stones dotted about, the legacy of rock shifts away to the east. High up, the stones become larger and multiply. "We have always used any limestone areas at Mercurol for our whites," says François Tardy of Domaine des Entrefaux. Their Pends white is improving all the time.

The whites from *Les Pends* are floral, whereas there is more minerality in the Gervans whites, a characteristic shared by some of the Larnage whites as well, according to Philippe Belle.

Jean-Louis Pradelle, Domaine de la Tour, Florent Viale of Domaine du Colombier, Philippe Desmeure of Domaine des Remizières, and the Domaine des Entrefaux work white vine plots on *Les Pends*. "The problem of *Les Pends* is that there is too much Syrah growing on it," comments Florent Viale, whose small plot of Marsanne dates from 1902.

Mercurol's red wines are considered more tender than those from Larnage, which is why the Domaine des Remizières age their Larnage Syrah in more new oak than their Mercurol Syrah. Dard et Ribo also choose their *La Grace* site on the plain, where there is a sand-clay mix of soil, and smooth alluvial stones, for their fruity red wine called "C'est le Printemps."

On the plain, Mercurol is a mix of sandy-stony ground with pockets of clay underneath, so moisture is retained to some extent. Its northwest section of *Les Chassis* is noticeably stonier than Chanos-Curson's across to the east. The reds are not naturally very dark coloured—if they are, be aware that the grower has extracted pretty hard. They are easy, direct wines with fine tannins, somewhat like those from Beaumont-Monteux.

"As a rule the plain ripens a week ahead of the slope vineyards in hot years," says Jean-Louis Pradelle. The slope areas at Mercurol and Chanos are less windy, standing in the lee of the north wind. The higher areas are usually harvested by hand, the plain by machine.

CHANOS-CURSON VINEYARDS

Chanos-Curson has heavier soil than the Pont-de-l'Isère areas of *Les Chassis*. Like Mercurol, it is clay-chalk, but notably clay rich, water retentive, and so good for whites, while the reds can be marked by firm tannins with medium-weight red fruit. The Pochon wines confirm this, with the style of his reds helped by his holdings at Beaumont-Monteux. Growers can be dismissive of Chanos, not considering its red wine pedigree very strong.

For the whites, areas with a higher clay content and richer soil like Chanos-Curson and parts of Mercurol tend to give wines that are more powerful and live longer than those from areas further south like Pont-de-l'Isère and *Les Chênes Verts*. The last two hold more fine sand, which means their whites deliver flattering early flavours and aromas but don't necessarily have the structure to evolve interestingly.

LES CHASSIS VINEYARDS

The connecting theme across the southern areas of Crozes-Hermitage is the *Chassis* plain, also the home to hare and partridge. *Les Chassis* itself is close to the N7, with domaines like Collonge, Pavillon, and Gilles Robin nearby.

Now extra momentum is coming to this area from people like Yann Chave, who in the early 2000s planted 2.5 ha at a *lieu-dit* called *Conflans*, which touches the *Thalabert* vineyard of Paul Jaboulet. Its red soil is extremely stony and drains fast, and its clay content of around 15 per cent has an impact when compared with the *Saviaux* site away west nearer the Rhône at La Roche-de-Glun, according to Chave. "That's 5 per cent more clay than *Saviaux*, which actually brings a difference in the wines—it means they have a higher degree and are more potent and heady," he says.

Overall, the *Chassis* can reach up to 20 per cent clay, with sand and *limoneux* elements as well. Much of the higher clay content is around Chanos-Curson and near Mercurol, along the Tain-Romans road in the north. The stones here on the plain of *Les Chassis* increase the further south one goes.

The *Thalabert* domaine of Paul Jaboulet Aîné is an old farm a tiny way north of the meeting point of *Les Sept Chemins*; the vineyards here stand among dry stones and some brown clay-limestone. To the eye the soil can be red, with distinct layers to it, as Jean-Michel Buffière found when building a new cellar 100 yards from *Les Sept Chemins*. "Under the Alpine stones, there's about half a metre (20 inches) of earth, and then 20 to 30 metres of gravelly stones," he states.

"Until phylloxera, this area grew hybrid vines," states Laurent Combier, "and a lot of the land was uncultivated *garrigue*—outcrop. It was the 1960s that saw the fruit growing take off

with the setting up of an irrigation system by 1965, prompted by the arrival of the fruit farmers from Algeria. Now of course, it's often mixed fruit and vine, as it is for me."

Most of the *Chassis* is underpinned by the gravel couch, with around half a metre of alluvial stones of Alpine origin on the surface. Their density increases in the southern areas near the Isère River. The stones vary a lot in size but serve to heat up the soil and aid maturity.

Some of the oldest vines on *Les Chassis* are centred at *Thalabert* and just south at *Les Chênes Verts*. The 40 hectares of Syrah at *Thalabert* average 50 years old, with Jaboulet supposed to have been the first vinegrowers on the *Chassis*. The *Chênes Verts* plots date from the 1950s and 1960s, vineyards that Combier and Graillot bought from M. Guerrier, formerly associated with M. Borja of the Clairmonts group, and M. Dubarry. The *Chênes Verts* zone is very stony, with a notable pale brown, sandy presence in the earth; it is fast draining.

The wines of the southern *Chassis* and *Chênes Verts* are perhaps one degree higher in alcohol than those of the northern *Chassis*. These are wines with exuberant black fruits and often a smoked, tarry, or lard set of aromas. Cornu and Graillot's wines reflect this.

The west side of *Les Chassis*—around the domaines of Collonge and Michelas Saint Jemms —is found by some growers to give the reds a tar and geranium aspect to the wine that is not very refined. Hence these wines can be drunk early—the grapes ripen well there, but there isn't great structure from what is more farming than vine land.

BEAUMONT-MONTEUX VINEYARDS

The most southeasterly part of the *appellation* is at Beaumont-Monteux, the village right beside the Isère. The red from here is fine, with a clear-cut fruit—due, it is said, to its gravel-sandy soil. Domaine des Entrefaux age their Beaumont-Monteux Syrah not in small casks but in 60 hl barrels—"the small young wood is too strong for it," says François Tardy. "By contrast, I expect more tannic, chewy wines from the clay areas around Chanos and Mercurol," he adds.

Luc Tardy, the promising owner of Domaine du Murinais at Beaumont, finds minerality in his reds and claims that "it's not my vinification system—it's the *terroir* of Beaumont-Monteux." He adds that the only other place he knows whose wine gives such minerality is Alain Graillot's domaine around *Les Chênes Verts*, with its straight cuvée. "And yet, ripening there is usually six days ahead of us, as its soil is a lot hotter."

The alluvial stone presence continues at Beaumont; David Raydon observes that his *Bruyères lieu-dit* soil is sandy-clay with *galet* stones covering about 60 per cent of the surface, the same proportion as on *Les Croix* nearby, where the soil is a little deeper. *Les Croix* and *Le Port* are both very close to the Isère, with a marked small pebble stone content from the river's old links to the Alps.

A *lieu-dit* at Beaumont likely to gain more coverage in the future is *Les Pichères*, a site whose main vineyard was planted in the 1980s and previously worked with all the worst excesses of chemical applications and a sedentary approach. It has been bought by Maxime Graillot, whose first task has been to revive its tired soil. Ferraton also work a newly planted plot on *Les Pichères*.

The plain around Beaumont drains very quickly, so growers have to be watchful about which sites they choose for their white vines like the Marsanne, a thirsty variety. "Marsanne does well in clay because it likes moisture," comments Luc Tardy. "My father planted it here—in limestone—to overcome the problem of rot, since the wind provides good aeration here." As a result, they find their whites show ripe grape aromas and are less floral or perfumed than many white Crozes. Beaumont-Monteux and Pont-de-l'Isère are generally the two areas where there is least clay, rendering their reds aromatic, fruited, and not especially potent.

PONT-DE-L'ISÈRE VINEYARDS

Tucked into the southwest corner of the *appellation*, at the junction of the Rhône with the Isère,

Pont-de-l'Isère's soil is a mix of sand and clay with plenty of stones. As Laurent Combier says, "It's more meridional than the rest of the *appellation*, and our warm soil brings plenty of ripeness." The red wines are fruity, forward, and open. They carry often intense black fruit—such as black currant. Colours are dark, and in Combier's words, "you can feel the heat from the galet stones in the wines."

Les Pautus is just north of Pont-de-l'Isère close to the Rhône, a site from which Yann Chave takes his top wine, the Tête de Cuvée. Its stony soil is composed of 15 per cent clay with sedimentary earth and gravel underlay, and Chave's Syrah, averaging towards 50 years, is surprisingly old for its location. Gilles Robin works a plot here, too.

Another site spoken of within the Pont-de-l'Isère *commune* is *Les Grandes Blâches*, to the northeast of the village. It is also full of alluvion stones and is quite fast draining. In this area fruit trees are mixed in—apricot, peach, and cherry—and some cereal. The *appellation* runs down to the Isère here between Pont-de-l'Isère and Beaumont-Monteux, but there are just one or two small spots of vines alongside the river.

LA ROCHE-DE-GLUN VINEYARDS

The nuance of the soil towards the Rhône at La Roche-de-Glun, which apart from Delas' strikingly good Clos St Georges, does not figure much in specific, good-name wines, is that it is covered in alluvial stones much smaller than those on the best-known vineyard at Pont-de-l'Isère, Combier's *Clos des Grives*. There is more clay than at Pont-de-l'Isère, its nearest *commune*.

Here the youngbloods have gathered—Laurent Fayolle, Yann Chave, Emmanuel Darnaud, and late-starter Franck Faugier—the first three all concentrating on new vineyard development. The Fayolles planted a hectare of Syrah on *Les Hauts Saviaux*, due west of *Les Sept Chemins* towards the Rhône in 2003 and, like Yann Chave, are keen on this new source. "It's *galet* stone covered," says Laurent, "with a brown clay subsoil and less gravel than the

Chassis vineyard. There were fruit trees and some spring cereals here; the land hadn't been worked very hard and so is in good shape, full of natural nutrients."

"From here at Mercurol to La Roche-de-Glun is America," observes Bernard Chave, father of Yann. "The soil is different, the grass is different; there are so many stones, too." *Saviaux* is a plateau with even more sand than the other plateau area of *Les Chassis* around *Les Chênes Verts* and *Sept Chemins*, where Alain Graillot has his domaine.

"So far I'm finding that this makes its wines relatively more tender and less firm, with savoury tannins," remarks Yann Chave. "They don't have the vigour on the attack of the *Chênes Verts* area." I would state that the La Roche-de-Glun fruit style is more reserved, with perhaps more red fruits, than the gushing Pont-de-l'Isère style, with a touch more finesse as well.

The other sector at La Roche-de-Glun is the *Combe Close* plateau south of *Saviaux*, not far from the Paul Jaboulet Aîné installations beside the N7 road. There the stones are bigger, and one finds a thicker, redder clay.

CROZES-HERMITAGE
ROUGE VINIFICATION

Much of the Chassis plain is machine harvested these days, as opposed to the hillside granite sites of the northern sector. Some growers on the plain like Domaine des 7 Chemins make an exception for older-plot vines whose crop is destined for the special cuvée.

Those remaining with whole-bunch vinification are Graillot, Bied, Habrard (80 per cent whole bunch), and Belle for the special Cuvée Louis Belle and Ferraton for the top domaine wine Grand Courtil. Otherwise total destemming is the order of the day across the *appellation*.

Most growers ferment in concrete vats and like to perform pumping-overs and some cap punching. The trendiest, modern operations like the Cave de Tain and Cave des Clairmonts with their large-scale system use fancy steel

vats—the Cave's are 700 hl and combine storage with *cuvaison* functions, while Clairmonts can set all interventions at the press of a button. Gilles Robin on a small scale follows this path.

Open wood vats remain the province of just a few—Colombier, Dard et Ribo, Ferraton, Habrard, Sorrel, and Chapoutier for 30 per cent of their Meysonniers production. This is much reduced from the 1980s.

Fermentation and maceration times vary between two and four weeks. Chapoutier's special Varonniers is left for five to six weeks, while Jaboulet have actually cut back the duration for their Thalabert; in 1990 and 1991 its *cuvaison* lasted 40 to 44 days at a top temperature of 27°C. Now it is a 25-to-35-day process.

More growers are cooling the crop before fermentation; Delas, Laurent Fayolle, Graillot, 7 Chemins, and two newcomers, Domaine La Batellerie and Bruyères, like to work this way to permit a steady start to the fermentation and to aid early fruit extraction.

Intervention in the form of techniques like adding external yeasts and enzymes, tannin addition, and acidification exist, with the evidence of the last two often apparent when tasting vintages like 2002 and 2003. These techniques are not widespread, but there are domaines that are clearly open to all modern methods; the Cave de Tain, for instance, will micro-oxygenate vats to create a softer wine earlier, and Gilles Robin and the Cave des Clairmonts use *micro-bullage* to soften the tannins and reduce the possibility of Syrah reduction.

Oak use is widespread, with many classic cuvées now receiving some exposure to usually aged casks. Most producers work 9 to 12 months raising in oak or vat. Some of the wines from the plain that extol straight fruit are purely vat raised—Clairmonts in concrete, Michelas Saint Jemms and Robin's Papillon in steel. Luc Murinais on the plain at Beaumont-Monteux is another vat-only user for his straight Amandiers wine.

Casks of 228 litres, 400 litres (known locally as *pipes*), and 550 to 600 litres (*demi-muids*) are all used, with a few large barrels as well. Of the best-known names, Chapoutier uses vats only for his straight fruit Petite Ruche but gives one-third of the red Meysonniers exposure to three-to-five-year-old casks. Jaboulet's Thalabert is cask aged for 11 to 16 months in two-to-three-year-old oak, a reduction from the 18 months of the late 1980s, when up to 28 per cent of the oak was new. Alain Graillot's classic wine is 95 per cent cask reared, the casks up to six years old, with just 5 to 10 per cent of them new.

New oak is of course a subject for debate. It is creeping in, especially on the slight cliché of the "older/better/more noble" cuvée. The extremes come with the 60 per cent new-oak Cuvée Christophe from Domaine des Remizières, where Philippe Desmeure is working with Patrick Lesec for a wine largely aimed at the US market. Michelas Saint Jemms started their new special cuvée in 2003 at half new oak, a policy that Chapoutier use on their Varonniers.

Users of around one-third new oak casks are suppliers like Gabriel Meffre, where the effect is potent; Belle with the Louis Belle; young Emmanuel Darnaud (successfully, especially for a young grower); Combier with his Clos des Grives; Ferraton for his Grand Courtil; and Étienne Pochon for his Château Curson, a wine that is delicately and successfully handled.

Domaine du Pavillon-Mercurol work with 25 per cent new casks, Murinais with 20 per cent for the Vieilles Vignes, Robin for his Albéric Bouvet, and even countryman Robert Rousset runs at 20 per cent. Generally the wines stay in oak for around a year, although the Vins de Vienne leave their selected wines for 16 to 18 months in 20 per cent new, 80 per cent one-to-two-year-old oak.

The debate centres on whether the content of the wine is adequate for the oak imposition. Certainly, wines made from old or mature vines on restricted yields should provide adequate matter. The most successful alliances with size-able proportions of new oak are the Louis Belle, Clos des Grives, Varonniers, Château Curson, and the Pavillon-Mercurol. It's also noticeable that some domaines like Belle have actually cut the new oak exposure of the classic Pierrelles

down to 15 per cent, so there is reasoned thought occurring on this subject. The danger occurs when the same old formula is applied—age of cask, size of cask, stay in cask—when the vintage is not that good.

The special cuvées at Crozes are drawn from a variety of themes. Old vines is an obvious start point—the Louis Belle is from 20- to 100-year-old Syrah, for instance. Yann Chave, Olivier Dumaine, 7 Chemins, Bruyères, and Michelas Saint Jemms all select their special wines on this criterion.

The notion of *lieu-dit*, or site, names is still in its infancy at Crozes, so there are not many domaines that work along this precise definition. Not surprisingly, it is from the hills of Gervans that two come—the mighty Picaudières of Robert Rousset, which includes 1930s Syrah, and Chomel's Sassenas from the next-door hill. Chapoutier weigh in with their Varonniers from the granite at Crozes, while Combier's Clos des Grives at Pont-de-l'Isère is a rare southern plain example of precise location driving the wine.

The other route to a top *cuvée* is by cellar tasting; Étienne Pochon selects his Château Curson just at the end of the vinification, while Alain Graillot makes his judgment for his Guiraude after the wine has all spent a year in cask. Bernard Ange also works this way.

As a footnote, red Crozes-Hermitage is usually made entirely from the Syrah grape, although the inclusion of up to 15 per cent of white grapes is permitted at the moment of fermentation. The Cave Co-opérative at Tain and one or two other growers would sometimes take advantage of this ruling in past decades, but nowadays find it less necessary to do so because the white wine is selling well in its own right.

CROZES-HERMITAGE *ROUGE*

Given the range of *terroirs* at Crozes, it's sad that not enough vineyard definition comes through in the wines on sale. A few examples of the range that has existed by default over the years may illuminate this point.

The northern villages of Serves, Erôme, Gervans, and Crozes-Hermitage are broadly linked by the presence of granite, often in its sanded, decomposed form. Larnage I would also place in this camp, even though there is only a little granite there. The reds from this group tend to be more complex, their flavours more layered and less obvious than the wines off the alluvial stones and flat ground around Pont-de-l'Isère and Beaumont-Monteux, for instance. The latter run with exuberant fruit, but that fruit is more one-dimensional.

The Gervans granite effect used to be revealed via Raymond Roure's rustic winemaking, so wasn't always obvious. Today I would look to a young grower like Laurent Habrard for expression of place in the reds and whites from Gervans, to Robert Rousset for a sense of Gervans and Erôme together. The reds from here are never inky or very black—the colour is mainly red, the aromas reflect red fruits, too, often garden crops like raspberries. Beyond the red fruits of the palate lies a mineral, drier-toned finish. The tannins are generally noticeable at first, with an upright, slightly lean aspect. These are the least facile wines of the *appellation*, the ones that repay patient cellaring and a well-thought-out menu. Often lamb and game appeal.

Larnage reds expand if aired when young—providing they haven't been overextracted. Their frame is also somewhat drier and straighter than the reds from many of the *communes* on flatter land. Larnage Syrah bouquets tend to be fleshier and fuller than Gervans, and the tannins can be quite prominent.

The reds from the southern plain, by contrast, bring an overt fruit bounty, with varying degrees of tannins according to location. Over at Chanos-Curson, the wines are simply fruited, black currant being a regular association, and are good to drink young. Local grower Étienne Pochon distinguishes between the fruit style by vintage, though "in years of riper fruit like 2001, I find black fruits," he says, "while in years of less ripe fruit like 2002, there are more red fruits."

For pure fruit enjoyment, the area around Pont-de-l'Isère is notable. Even a Combier 1993,

In the 1970s, red Crozes fell into two categories: either it was a mass-production wine, utterly bland and almost soupy, with little Syrah *typicité*—a delight for a Burgundian *négociant* who could whack out large amounts to supermarkets. Or it was a rustically produced, hot country wine—a beefy, coarse peasant linked by name to the immaculate Hermitage. The one exception to this rule over the years, providing a thoroughbred class, was Paul Jaboulet's Domaine de Thalabert.

from a very dodgy vintage, displayed still live raspberry fruit on the palate when drunk at eight years old. In better vintages, these wines can have bouquets of black stewed fruit, plus touches like black olives—warm-toned aromas. The palate fruit is exuberant and is enjoyable soon after bottling.

This style demonstrates one of the ace cards held by Crozes-Hermitage. "For me Crozes is the nearest we come at Delas to a grape variety wine," is how Jacques Grange puts it when talking about their large-production red, Les Launes. This is reflected in most growers' classic cuvées, which are chosen for their direct fruitiness.

When aged, the *Chassis* style as shown by Thalabert gains earthy tones, a mix of game and fungal typical of the Syrah after 10 years; as shown by the 1983 Thalabert drunk in 2001, these earthy touches stay and mix in with brambly fruit sequences. The drier the vintage, as in 1983 and 1998, the more these tones of leather and outdoor decomposure appear. Thalabert has traditionally been an extremely long-lived wine for a red Crozes—the 1979, 1980, and 1983 were all wonderful when drunk in 2004.

The other style of Crozes, often derived from cellar work rather than from terrain, is the older-vine, cask-aged red wine. These are wines that show well from four or five years onwards, just as the early fruit-oak combination settles, and the fruit retains some verve. The special wines of southern growers like Pochon, Belle, Graillot, and Combier spring to mind as examples of this genre. Their tannic structure is sufficient to ensure decent evolution in good vintages like 2001, 1999, and 1998.

But there must be a word of caution. One aspect here, admittedly less severe than at St-Joseph, is that of young growers coming on stream and turning out technobabble wines. The previous generation was involved with what to plant, following decrees, mastering white wine vinification, tidying up their cellar work. This current generation is feeding off a high-price regime and lending their ears to advisers and image dabblers, the theory merchants, who dispense advice without responsibility. Suddenly a father-to-son domaine switches from the serenade to punk rock: a world of injected oxygen, lees stirring, high-temperature fermentation, max extract, and wines that fall apart after just 20 minutes' air.

Witness these notes on a red 1999 Crozes bought in a Tain restaurant in May 2001: "very dark, inky wine; nice black fruit freshness on nose; palate is more suspicious—a black jam flavour, not sure how true. Twenty minutes later this has dried and lost its richness. Thirty-five minutes, and the bouquet is hard, metallic—like the palate by now. How many books do I have to sell to pay for this rubbish?"

IDEAL FOODS FOR CROZES-HERMITAGE *ROUGE*

The first move is to separate young red Crozes from mature red Crozes, and the oaked, older-vine wines from the fresher ones.

Crozes hinges on live fruit when young, so it's a popular choice for several growers, including Cornu and Collonge, with charcuterie and a summer salad. Sylviane Borja of Cave des Clairmonts agrees, adding that it can be served lightly chilled and that a young, fresh vintage is ideal—2001 would be an example. "I think of the season, so I drink young Crozes in the spring—with thirst or with *saucisson*," says François Ribo.

Personally, I like young Crozes with grilled red meats and barbecues; its tannins are more streamlined than those of its neighbour St-Joseph and so pair off with the charry flavours better. Fruity, sunny vintages like 1997 or 1999 in the classic cuvées are good for outdoor picnics in the English summer. Laurent Fayolle is also a barbecue supporter, liking grilled *entre-côte* steak as well. Sylvie Robin suggests the wine be drunk when young with grilled beef, ribs of beef, chicken—even *à la crème*—and beef carpaccio.

Beef served straight is popular; a few *vignerons* select rib of beef with the wine served slightly cool. Bernard Ange likes roast beef with pepper and garlic, like François Ribo, who comments: "The simple flavours match the *gras*, suave, quite generous style of our reds." Catherine Berthoin of Domaine Les Chenêts suggests a winter combination, of "roast beef with my red-wine based sauce." Philippe Bourret puts forward beef *bourguignon* or a *daube*.

Lamb is another popular selection. Lamb in garlic with a special cuvée like the Clos des Grives when quite young is mentioned by Laurent Combier; "the oak and youth are soaked up by the sweetness of the dish," he observes. "Otherwise the wine would be a little tough. Alternatively, you wait for the wine to loosen, maybe decompose a bit, and choose a more game-based dish." Bernard Ange and the Cave des Clairmonts both suggest lamb with the classic version of their wines.

As red Crozes ages, the dishes suggested become more complex, the flavours more prominent. Étienne Pochon suggests his classic wine with age or his oaked Château Curson with lamb, red meat, and venison, as well as with a mushroom sauce; "I also find that truffled flavours go well with Crozes as the wine ages," he says. Jean-Louis Pradelle proposes a simmered, slow-cooked *daube* like lamb in olive tapenade or a game *civet*; "pheasant and sauced meats are ideal," he comments, a view supported by Cave des Clairmonts for their special Pionniers wine.

Wild boar and game are suggested by Sylvie Robin and Laurent Fayolle; the latter also likes pheasant with his wine when it is older. Another young grower, Yann Chave, finds his Tête de Cuvée splendid with partridge when about four or five years old. From the granite end of the *appellation* come traditional thoughts from Maxime Chomel and Robert Rousset—both select their special cuvées for pheasant, game, and red meats.

Guinea fowl is also put forward by some growers—including roasted in olives and garlic (Collonge). Duck lightly sugared with turnips, and duck with olives are other suggestions.

Étienne Pochon steps outside most ideas when putting forward Chinese and Indian food that is of course spiced. "I would choose a sunny year with ripe fruit, and drink that young with a dish like Peking Duck," he states.

Bernard Ange is also keen on two full-bodied dishes—couscous and paella—when his old vines wine has aged past six years.

Supporters of cheese crop up; Robert Rousset proposes local Picodon and blue cheese, while Sylvie Robin likes the wine when older with rigottes or Picodon. Philippe Bourret advises two blue cheeses—Bleu d'Auvergne and Roquefort.

I would add that young red Crozes from a year with a touch of acidity like 1996 or 2001 is also a sound companion for salmon.

CROZES-HERMITAGE *BLANC* VINIFICATION

Most growers work their white grapes with a fixed eye on their acidity levels. The Marsanne off the mainstream plain does not make naturally stylish wine, and that is why Luc Tardy chose the limestone section of his vineyard on *Colombier* at Beaumont-Monteux for his Marsanne. He has also planted Roussanne there.

As with the reds, there are therefore two intrinsic types of white Crozes—the hillside and the plain. The hillside wines carry more acidity and nuance, while the plain wines are intended for earlier drinking. For the plain growers, vinification is a stage when many think they can rec-

ompense for nature's deficit in the vineyards, and more oak is present in these white Crozes than used to be the case.

At the same time, confidence in the worth of the grape varieties has returned after clear doubts in the 1980s and early 1990s. In those years, growers were keen to block the malolactic fermentation to gain freshness; their aim was to fight accusations that their wines were "heavy." Less malo blocking occurs today.

Generally, white Crozes is bottled within the year, and these days the majority of the wines have finished their malos by bottling time. Domaines that block the malo in search of vivacity include the Cave des Clairmonts, Graillot, Murinais, and Pavillon-Mercurol—all on the southern plain.

The big suppliers like the Cave de Tain and Chapoutier ferment and raise the wine in mechanised steel vats, the former after crop cooling down to 5° to 6°C. Like the Cave de Tain, Chapoutier block the malolactic on their Petite Ruche and bottle it after about nine months.

For their Meysonniers, Chapoutier include a 20 per cent one-to-three-year-old oak cask fermentation, but the instinct for old established names like the two Fayolles and Ferraton is to stick with mainly vat treatment and bottling within the year. Under the Chapoutier linkup, Ferraton also block the malo for their white Matinière.

There is a vat-oak mix for fermentation for a hard core of sound names—Belle (50-50), Colombier (75-25), Combier (30-70), Dard et Ribo (33-67), and Sorrel (90/10). Belle and Combier favour mostly new or one-year-old oak, while Dard et Ribo, Sorrel, and Martinelles rely on older casks, the last named the *demi-muid* size of 550 to 600 litres.

Étienne Pochon, Yann Chave, the Cave des Clairmonts, Laurent Habrard, Robert Rousset, and François Tardy of Domaine des Entrefaux all use steel vats for their regular whites, the first named with a *macération pelliculaire* (intragrape fermentation at the start). Pochon is one of the first to bottle, by mid-April, and takes a precise line on the malolactic—he lets the Roussanne do it, "as it is more fresh by nature," and blocks it on his Marsanne. Chave, Habrard, Rousset, and Tardy all let the malo occur.

Those who favour heavy new- or young-oak exposure include Paul Jaboulet and Remizières. The Jaboulet Roure *blanc* is all new-oak treated, for instance. Domaine La Batellerie and Bernard Ange also rely purely on oak.

Other growers dip into oak for their special cuvées. Entrefaux's Les Pends is raised in new to three-year-old casks, the oak imprint a strong one when the wine is young. Combier's white Clos des Grives, a wine of abnormally high, 85 per cent Roussanne, is made half in new, half in one-year-old oak casks. Pochon's Château Curson white receives four months in new oak. Cave des Clairmonts' special Pionniers is purely oak raised on its lees until June.

CROZES-HERMITAGE *BLANC*

There are one or two areas that provide pedigree white Crozes, but a lot of this wine is pretty dull. The problem often seems to be a lack of integration in the textures and shortage of acidity. This can render the wines insipid and a little flabby. Many of them therefore need drinking within two or three years, often in their region of production.

It's a question of *terroir*, as so often. The north-south divide plays its part in the whites of Crozes. From the northern sector around Gervans come some dashing wines, their sinew and clear, lightly nutty white fruit flavours in contrast to the more clumping roundness of the whites of the plain. The combination of granite, hillsides, and often mature Marsanne is a good one, as expressed in the wines of domaines like Rousset, Habrard, and Laurent Fayolle.

Robert Rousset observes that the presence of loess on his sites around Erôme imbues the wines with more nerve—more cut—than the whites from places like Beaumont-Monteux on the plain. They are more hidden and less showy at the outset, but carry much the greater breeding. This cut or clarity is also apparent on the finish of wines from Crozes-Hermitage itself—they have a fresher, clearer finale than those from Chanos-Curson and the flatland. Up on the ledges and terraces, there is little mention of the Roussanne, either, as if no outside medicine is required.

Somehow the Marsanne at Crozes does not produce wines of a remotely comparable stature and class to those produced off the granite and clay on the Hermitage hill. The typical Marsanne aromas are often notes like white flowers and acacia, which become more extreme once the crop has been late-picked, even turning to honey and deeper tones. The Roussanne expresses dried fruit aromas more but is also often handled in new oak so there is an extra vanilla, taut element from that source.

There's no doubt that the gradual ripening cycle at Gervans, and the fresher climate there than on the plain, helps to give those wines off the loess and loose granite very good structure. It's also where Marsanne from the 1920s and 1930s grows, a sign that the grower was confident about the quality of the site, in this case the Rousset family on *Les Vedias*.

The whites from Gervans carry good bone, their stucture allowing a productive evolution. Drinking these around four to six years old can be very rewarding. Like the reds, they are drier and less obvious than the commercial whites from the plain vineyards.

The kaolin at Larnage is another area for good whites, such as those of Marc Sorrel, where mature vines are also a prime factor. Olivier Dumaine's Larnage Marsanne is up to 50 years old, and the result is some classic nutty and attractive depth in his Croix du Verre cuvée.

The Larnage whites are often full, and growers consider it worth letting their malos finish because they have plenty of vivacity in them when young. "They can digest the malo, take the oak, and then come together," says Philippe Belle, although neighbour Olivier Dumaine has not been satisfied with too much oak on his whites. The oak brings a grilled or smoked side, and Philippe Belle prefers to drink his whites after three or four years, so they can settle.

The *Pends* hill between Mercurol and Chanos-Curson is the third great location for white Crozes-Hermitage. It is sited due south, and rises in a gentle sweep, giving its vines excellent exposure.

These top white Crozes all possess greater steel than the often ordinary, flat-ground whites; their flavours are more clear-cut, expressing dried fruits and some nuttiness. Aromas are fruited, with the Pends sometimes more floral. They are capable of young and middle-aged pleasure, broadening and gaining in richness if allowed to age for four years or more.

Winemaking is more proficient than it was in the 1970s and 1980s, and that has made white Crozes more respectable across the board. Crop is picked at a riper stage than in those days, when the buzzwords were freshness and liveliness. Accordingly, there used to be a low-temperature vinification school, the growers using the then new stainless steel vats and working at around 15°C. Much of the time the malolactic fermentations were blocked and the wine issued in the spring. The hand of man usurped nature by some distance in those days.

The need for freshness is still apparent through the policy of an important Marsanne specialist, Chapoutier. A big supporter of the Marsanne, Michel Chapoutier usually goes all out for ripeness and traditional fullness. With his simple white Crozes, Petite Ruche, he foregoes that and has the malo blocked.

Another approach in the hunt for freshness and maybe a little more nobility comes through growers' attitudes to the Roussanne. Laurent Combier's special Clos des Grives *blanc* is 85 per cent Roussanne and is oak fermented and raised, with lees stirring, for a year. It possesses a rich core in a good vintage like 2001, but the oak needs about three years to integrate.

As to white Crozes' longevity, surprises can appear, with occasional fabulous performers that live for abundant time. Given how the wine has recently become variable, and often low in acidity, the Paul Jaboulet Aîné Mule Blanche 1978 put on a great show when drunk in March 2003. The tasting note ran: "Dried fruits, very tight bouquet, opens and fleshes with air. Marked salty tang on palate, also tight. Length very good. Dry-toned wine. Not a big, fat wine, more an elegant one. In good shape." The saltiness is a feature that I find at times in old Roussanne.

From an earlier age, a 1959 Paul Jaboulet Aîné *blanc* drunk in 1974 initially showed a hint of oxidation on the bouquet, but the palate developed richly with about half an hour's airing and left a strong hazelnut flavour on the finish—an excellent wine.

IDEAL FOODS WITH CROZES-HERMITAGE *BLANC*

The first stop with white Crozes is the aperitif, when the wine is young and classic, not oaked. Salads—simple or with nuts, cheese, or smoked duck—are also popular. In similar vein, a *terrine de volaille* (chicken paté) is appreciated, while Pradelle and Rousset plump for charcuterie, the former insisting that the wine not be served too cold—a minimum of 11° to 12°C suggested.

Several growers suggest plain chicken dishes as a good accompaniment, while white meats with sauce are liked by Cornu. Graillot puts forward white meats, too, as well as ravioles and asparagus. Ribo also suggests asparagus with *mousseline* or hollandaise sauce.

"Because the Marsanne lacks acidity, our oaked wine Pionniers is good with *poulet aux écrevisses* (chicken with crayfish)," says Sylviane Borja of Cave des Clairmonts—"even done in a white Crozes sauce as well. I like the white with creamed sauces, and *vol au vent*," she adds.

Cornu and Ribo are both independent thinkers and opt for Chinese food, both adding the rider—if it is not too spicy.

Clearly fish is a popular selection. Simple grilled fish with a younger wine from a nicely full vintage is suggested, but also fish in traditional buttered sauces. "Because the wines hold a white buttery style, they go well with fried Coquille St. Jacques (scallops)," says François Ribo. Laurent Fayolle and Maxime Chomel both enjoy trout or pike in sauce, but the latter says "not seafood—it kills its aromas." On the sea fish theme, Sylvie Robin proposes grilled *rouget* (red mullet) and steamed scallops.

Rich fish like salmon is also put forward, including a tagliatelle of smoked salmon, the pasta cooked al dente; fish *terrine* is another suggestion.

Local freshwater fish like *sandre* (pikeperch) is agreeable; Robert Rousset likes his *sandre* cooked in the oven, topped off with a white Crozes wine sauce. Sylviane Borja also goes for oven cooking for trout or *daurade* (sea bream). Langoustines are liked by Cathérine Berthoin.

"I am happy to try the wine with lamb or even venison that is only lightly cooked," affirms François Ribo; François Tardy puts forward the great delight of scrambled eggs with black truffles, while Stéphane Cornu suggests desserts to round off a meal.

Cheese is liked by some of the growers— for instance, St. Marcellin and other creamed cheeses. Sylvie Robin also likes Beaufort and Roquefort with her white Crozes.

THE PRODUCERS

DOMAINE BERNARD ANGE

Pont de l'Herbasse 26260 Clérieux +33(0)475 716242

Bernard Ange went solo in 1998, after nearly 20 years of association with Charles Tardy. He worked as a *caviste* in a Coteaux du Lyonnais Coopérative until 1979, and in the early 1980s the brothers-in-law were trend setters in producing more vigorous, fruited reds and whites than had been the norm until then.

Divorce intervened, however, and he now works 7.5 hectares of Crozes, six and a half Syrah (1983, 1994), and one hectare split two-thirds Roussanne and one-third Marsanne, dating from 1988. The vineyard's plots are grouped together on poor soil of gravel and Alpine residue at Beaumont-Monteux, at the easterly limit of the *appellation*.

"I wanted a more low-key existence," he comments. Still with his shock of black hair, he appears to have something of the child of the seventies in him. He has just turned 50, and his vineyard yields and cellar work remain largely of that era: yields are at the top end, the whites have their malolactic blocked, outside yeasts are used to stimulate fermentation, and there is no new oak.

But there have been changes. "We were in that period of the boom in weedkillers; now I'm much more careful about that and use a lot less, and also work the soil more," says Bernard. He has also taken part in the Larnage showcase vineyard operation, the Vitrine, through clearing and planting a plot on the slope of *Mortiers et les Chaux*, where the soil is clay marked with a stony overlay. His half hectare is next to Alain Graillot's plot.

His new home used to be called the "Hotel de la Plage" (the Beach Hotel), which of course is a comedy given how far it is from the sea. But Clérieux nearby had a shoe factory into the 1960s, and the workers would come to Pont de l'Herbasse for their recreation. There was a small waterfall on the River Herbasse and a patch of sand and gravel that amounted to the beach. The hundreds of workers would bring their families, eat *friture* (small fried fish), drink rosé, and play *boules* at the three hotels in the village. It was a pure *Vieille France* scene that can be conjured up through the line of the buildings to this day.

Two-thirds of the crop is machine harvested and therefore destalked. The one-third whole-bunches element is picked first, so its presence can add content to the vats. Vinification lasts two weeks in concrete vats, at a maximum temperature of 30°C, with *remontages*, light punching-down, and vat decantation as well.

Bernard's cellar is unusual—it is around 600 years old, hewn out of mollase rock, and is six metres high, a giant cavity. Cask ageing starts in January and runs for a year for the classic wine, 18 months for the Rêve d'Ange. Bernard uses a mix of barrel sizes—228, 400, and 600 or 650 litres. The Rêve d'Ange, the older-vine wine, is chosen by tasting, with about 5,000 bottles a year.

The classic red is fruited but sometimes modest, while the Rève d'Ange is clean and modern, with black fruits and an oak imprint in its youth. The white is fermented in 400-litre used oak barrels at around 18°C, the malolactic is blocked, and the wine is bottled in late April.

CROZES-HERMITAGE ROUGE

   2003 ★★ 2012–14
   2002 —
   2001 ★

CROZES-HERMITAGE RÈVE D'ANGE ROUGE

   2003 (cask) ★★★ Violets, black jam aroma, elegant, gradual. Black cherry flavour with oak/licorice surround. Clean, modern wine. Rasp of new oak now, leave till 2007. 2014–16.

   2001 ★★ 2008
   2000 ★★ 2006
   1999 ★★ 2007–08

CROZES-HERMITAGE BLANC

   2002 ★
   2001 ★★

Export 5 per cent (1) Switzerland

ARNOUX ET FILS

Cave de Vieux Clocher 84190 Vacqueyras
+33(0)490 658418

This southern Rhône domaine doubles up with some commerce; their Crozes red is indeed commercial, a simple wine that shows red fruits and a ripe, soft style.

CROZES-HERMITAGE PETITES COLLINES ROUGE

   2003 ★ 2009–10

DOMAINE LA BATELLERIE

RN 7 26600 Gervans +33(0)475 033452

   See also St-Joseph.

This domaine represents the adventure of the lives of Jean-Pierre and Hélène Mucyn, a young couple from Bar-sur-Aube in Champagne country. Jean-Pierre's grandparents came to France from Poland in the 1930s, and his father, despite being an *agriculteur* at heart, worked in the industrial laundry business to earn a living.

Jean-Pierre followed suit, working in the same line of business in Le Touquet and then in Paris, where he spent eight years with the large Initial company. "The breakthrough came when we were transferred to Beaune, where Hélène and I both took a viti-oenology course," he explains. His job had involved an awful lot of travel, and Hélène, a very fair, young-looking woman, reveals the anguish of it when she shakes her head quietly and says, "I was pining my life away, enclosed in our Paris flat with our three lively daughters."

Observing Hélène's evident energy of movement and snappy responses, it is clear she is mightily recharged by their change of life. She seems driven and fired. The small daughters burst out of the car after school and charge around outside with the family boxer, Rambo. Jean-Pierre, lush dark-brown hair and glasses, stands in great, heavy work boots, hands striped with paint, work trousers too short. He appears to be the calmer of the two, quite a serious man. Beside him is their log pile, assembled with crosswordlike precision in March; the world of suits and soft shoes is a long way from here. "I'm not superstitious, but I felt a calling to do this," he says.

Their path parallels that taken by the mid-1980s pioneers here, Alain and Elisabeth Graillot. The Mucyns liked the area for holidays and buying wine, and put the word out to Safer, the central land authority, that they were seeking a vineyard. Safer came up with over two hectares of abandoned land at Ozon, north of Arras in St-Joseph, and later a hectare of Crozes at Erôme, followed in 2004 by a hectare on *Les Chassis*, an old apricot grove near Pont-de-l'Isère that they have newly planted, with more land available for the vine in due course. The vineyard portfolio has been growing, and now stands at nearly 3 ha

ALBERT BÉGOT

Hats off to Albert Bégot. The man who in the early 1970s seemed an outsider, whose wine could be glorious or way off target, was decades ahead of the game. With his friend Maurice Combier, he was the first organic, truly laissez-faire grower at Crozes or in the region for that matter.

His wines invariably bore a surging purple *robe* and were quite different from the usually more astringent offerings often available in those days. On other occasions they could be spoilt by spending too long in old oak. Ah well.

Albert died in 1985, and his widow, Marcelle, took over the domaine's five hectares at Serves and Gervans until handing over to son Franck. Franck is more interested in other activities like architecture, and from 2004 the domaine's vineyards—organically worked since 1970—were let to Laurent Combier.

at Crozes, 0.7 ha at St-Joseph, and 1 ha of *vin de pays* Syrah/Gamay at Sarras across the river.

They started to work the Erôme site in 2001, a full south slope whose decomposed granite soil is mixed with loess and sand. There is 0.8 ha of mature Syrah (1970s) on *Les Mottes* and 0.2 ha of Marsanne (1970s) on *Tout* where the soil is sandy-clay with lime in it. The vines in both plots are trained up stakes, meaning a lot of hard manual work.

At Crozes, there is another 1970s Syrah plot on *Les Cornirets*, with a mix of decomposed granite and alluvial stones. In 2002 half a hectare of organic vineyard at Gervans was added, the site near the Rhône belonging to Franck Bégot, son of one of the first local growers to pursue organic practices, the late Albert Bégot. At present, the wine from this flatland Les Îles (its Syrah averages 50 years old) provides a sound base of black fruit and some spice and tar, allowing the gentler, more peppered slope wine from Erôme to fly expressively on the outer edges of the bottled wine.

"We are trying to be rational about the vineyard," states Jean-Pierre. "We work the soil when we can, cut grass, and so on." Hélène works in the vineyard, enjoying the space and the freedom. She learnt what to do with the Roussets, no doubt her sparky, talkative presence waking up the vineyards and cultivators of Erôme. Jean-Pierre deals with the cellar, and states that he is very keen on achieving fresh fruit in his wines—he's not a fan of the heaviness of old wines. "I want to express the elegance of the variety, and be attracted by the wine when I drink it *à table*," he says. The *oenologue* adviser here is Anne Colombo.

The crop is hand harvested, and the red Crozes is destalked, then vinified in steel and open concrete vats to allow cap punching. After four days of crop cooling, there is a four-week fermentation and maceration process, the temperature up to 33°C. Ageing is in used casks for 11 to 12 months. "If I had new casks, I would seek the grilled side they give to the wine—but I'm not really a new-oak fan," declares Jean-Pierre. There is just a light filtration.

The pure Marsanne white is cask fermented at around 16°C and left in three-year-old oak for a year, with lees stirring. Because the Marsanne contains a lot of protein, it is lightly fined.

The red *vin de pays des Collines Rhodaniennes* is 60 per cent Syrah, 40 per cent Gamay; in a year like 2001 it is a charming, friendly fruited wine.

The Domaine La Batellerie is beside the N7 road north of Tain and was an inn for 250 years, much attended by Rhône boatmen with the river just 100 yards away. The stables—now the cellar—housed the horses that pulled the barges. Once the disorder of the unfinished house and cellars is out of the way, these wines will move along nicely. Already the white shows an encouraging fullness, and the 2003 Crozes *rouge* promised well, too.

CROZES-HERMITAGE ROUGE

2004 (CASK) ★★
2003 ★★★ 2009–11

2002 ★★ 2008–09
2001 ★

CROZES-HERMITAGE BLANC
2004 ★★
2003 ★★★
2002 ★
2001 ★★

*Export 55 per cent (1) USA, (2) Luxembourg,
(3) Switzerland*

DOMAINE BELLE

Les Marsuriaux 26600 Larnage +33(0)475 082458

See also Hermitage, St-Joseph.
The bell chimes for some at 50. The call to arms. That must have been how Albert Belle felt in 1990 as he made the move to split from the Tain Co-opérative, which his father had joined in 1933. It's not straightforward unwinding the association with your local community venture in France, but Albert had been waiting for the day. Here was a fruit grower dying to be a vinifier.

As he takes you round his smart cellar, it's clear that Albert, a quiet, modest, still trim man is proud of his work and of his breakaway from the Co-opérative after the 1989 vintage. In his very down-to-earth way, he explains: "I always made wine, which we drank at home, and was keen to do my own thing, but thought it wise to wait while my sons grew up. The domaine just dealt in fruit crops before; now I can make the wine on a proper scale. It may not at first enrich the bank balance because of all the investement, but it's worth it in the end."

The sons are in harness now, the elder Philippe mostly on the vineyards and wine, with Jean-Claude running the still-thriving apricot business, except in disastrous summers like 2002. He has cut out cherries and instead now has a burgeoning and respected vineyard nursery business that sells cuttings mainly to growers in the Drôme and the Ardèche. Albert can now trot down to Toulon with his wife, Monique, and take her on an early summer cruise, but warns "I'm not yet fully retired!"

Philippe is the fourth generation in wine at Larnage. A man with short dark hair and glasses, he shows a firmly practical outlook. He was always passionate about wine and vineyards, and went off to Beaune for his studies, his enthusiasm encouraging his father to go it alone. "I want to take our quality up a notch or two and work with lower yields," he says. "In 2002 we rejected maybe 35 per cent of the crop through the year, not just in a rush at the end." He cites a group of youngish growers like François Tardy, Laurent Combier, and his brother-in-law Étienne Berthoin as sharing this view.

The domaine moved quickly into prominence once its own wine came out from the 1990 vintage onwards. The quality is extremely dependable and the wines develop nicely with patient cellaring. Like Domaine du Colombier, this is the sort of thoroughly good address, well-run by sensible people, that every *appellation* needs.

The Belles have 20.5 hectares of vineyards— all Crozes, except for a precious 1.5 hectares at Hermitage. There are 17 hectares of Syrah and 2 hectares of white grapes, split 75 per cent Marsanne and 25 per cent Roussanne. The vineyard age is a mix of 20 to 25 and 40 to 45 years. The apricot business, the fruit sold fresh across France, means they are doubly occupied between mid-July and mid-August.

The choicest vineyards are on the slopes of Larnage, 3.5 ha spread across 10 plots at up to 250 metres, where only hand and foot cultivation is possible. The Larnage *coteau*'s special white clay gives wines with more robust tannin than that of the finer wines from the granite. Another site at Crozes-Hermitage helps to make up the prized Cuvée Louis Belle. The Crozes vineyard for this wine is granite mixed with white clay and limestone.

Les Pierrelles is a 10.5 ha vineyard, bought in two stages in 1987 and 1991, the vines dating from the mid-1970s. This is mostly on the plain to the south at Pont-de-l'Isère, where the soil is made up of alluvial stones on clay; a little lies inside Mercurol. The vines date from the early 1970s and can be worked mechanically, including their harvesting. This *quartier* is noted for the overt fruitiness of its wines.

Crop is actively cut back each year, especially on the young vines, and organic composts are put down. Harvesting is as late as possible, which means around 10 October in a more tricky year like 1996. In 2002 the Belles harvested only by hand given the fragile state of the crop, and Philippe declares that they are gradually reducing the amount that is machine harvested: "It's for reasons of quality and to respect the vineyard," he explains.

Vinification of the reds has evolved only a little since 1990; over half the crop is now destalked on the Pierrelles, but the bunches are left whole for the special Louis Belle. After a cool maceration, external yeasts are used to move fermentation along on the Pierrelles, but only when necessary on the Louis Belle. The maceration lasts over three to four weeks in concrete and includes *remontages* and *pigeages*.

Both wines are aged for a year in cask: the Pierrelles receives 15 per cent new oak, a slight reduction from the mid-1990s, the rest three to five years old. The Louis Belle is aged in 30 per cent new oak, the rest one to three years old. Oxygen is introduced during the raising by dint of a clicker machine. Bottling is between 18 and 24 months after the harvest, with the final stockage in vat. A light fining is done, but no filtration.

The Louis Belle comes in part from vines planted by Philippe's grandfather; the fruit is gathered from 20- to 100-year-old Syrah off terraces and steep slopes, and 30,000 bottles are made. It can be a very full, long-lived wine with a good tannic declaration. The more tannic vintages like 1994, 1999, and 2001 need five or six years to soften, while the open years like 1997 and 2000 sing along well after four years.

From 1994 part of the white has been vinified in oak, the rest in steel. The oak proportion

has risen to 60 percent, split half new, half one year old. It is bottled in early September, the malo done, after 10 months of raising. Some vintages need leaving for four years or so to absorb the oak, and should run for around eight years.

CROZES-HERMITAGE LES PIERRELLES ROUGE

2003 Not made.
2002 ★★ 2008
2001 ★★★ 2010–11
2000 ★★★ 2011–12

CROZES-HERMITAGE LOUIS BELLE ROUGE

2003 ★★(★) Full, brewed bouquet. Raspberry, coffee mix on palate, solid wine. Fair juice here, is "dark" tasting. Tannins, oak need till 2008. Could close up; drink in second phase is best. 2013–15.
2002 Not made.
2001 ★★★ Nice depth, compact, clear fruit nose; plenty black stone, cherry fruit, overt tannins, oak adds to them. From 2007; 2014–16.
2000 ★★★ Still-tight black aroma, *garrigue* hint; nice, cool dry black fruit. Clean tannic ending. 2005; 2012–14.

CROZES-HERMITAGE BLANC

2003 ★★ 2012–13
2002 ★★ 2009–10
2001 ★★ 2009–10

Export 75 per cent (1) Norway, (2) USA/Great Britain/Japan

LOUIS BERNARD

Route de Sérignan 84100 Orange +33(0)490 118686

See also Cornas, Côte-Rôtie, Hermitage, St-Joseph, St-Péray.

The Louis Bernard red Crozes-Hermitage is fermented for up to four weeks, with pumping-overs and *délestages*. It possesses low-key fruit, and can need two to three years to settle.

CROZES-HERMITAGE ROUGE
   2003 ★ From 2006; 2010–12

DOMAINE ROLAND BETTON

26600 La Roche-de-Glun +33(0)490 658591

For 15 years Roland Betton would sell his crop to the Chéron family of Pascal Frères at Vacqueyras in the southern Rhône. From 2003 the arrangement changed to the harvest being vinified at La Roche-de-Glun and the wine being sold in bottle under his name.

There are three hectares of Syrah dating from the 1990s back to the early 1980s, and 0.5 hectare of Marsanne of a similar age. These are all southern-sector sites, with the emphasis on ripe black fruits in the red wines.

After hand harvesting, the red crop is cooled and receives a three-week vinification, with cap punchings. The classic wine is vat raised, and bottled in July. The special red, Vieilli en Fûts de Chêne is oak raised for eight months in 30 per cent new, 70 per cent one-to-two-year-old casks; both are fined and filtered.

The white is pure Marsanne, and after vat fermentation and raising for six months, it is bottled with the malo blocked.

CROZES-HERMITAGE ROUGE
   2003 ★★ 2011–12

CROZES-HERMITAGE VIEILLI
EN FÛTS DE CHÊNE ROUGE
   2003 ★★(★) 2011–13

DOMAINE BERNARD ET GILLES BIED

Les Malfondières 26600 Mercurol +33(0)475 074447

See also Hermitage, St-Joseph.
The only time I have tasted in the company of a live, on-the-hoof lamb, is at this understated domaine near Philippe Desmeure at Mercurol. Gilles Bied lives quietly in his own world, a true countryman not seemingly aware of large pro-

motional events like the successful, international Découvertes week in the Rhône.

The two-week-old lamb needed hand raising, so resided in the house. It trotted down the outside stairs from the kitchen and carried on straight into the cellar, by the way. It was last seen clambering over the boxed-up wine on a nearby pallet.

Grandfather Bied worked mainly fruit; Gilles' father, Bernard, moved on to wine, selling it in bulk to Chapoutier. A tall, slim, dark-featured man in his early 30s, Gilles attended wine studies at Orange and encouraged the domaine to start bottling from 1990.

They work 10 hectares of Crozes—nine of Syrah and one of Marsanne (1993)—as well as vineyards at Hermitage and St-Joseph. The Crozes vineyards are at Mercurol on a mix of gravel and stones, with some clay, while at Erôme their hillside holding is largely granite.

Whole bunches are fermented very traditionally in concrete, for about 10 days, at up to 30°C. Pumping-overs are done. Ageing lasts a year in casks from six to 15 years old, and the wine is filtered but not fined. It is also kept back for 18 months before sale.

The white is also fermented in concrete, at natural cellar temperature that can run above 20°C. It is bottled after 18 months in vat. When on song, it shows some floral/elderflower aromas and fair richness with nutty hints on the finish.

The domaine bottles around 15,000 bottles, and sells the rest, indeed the main part, to Guigal and Chapoutier. The red Crozes is the most interesting wine, a throwback to wild, funky days of the 1970s and 1980s. Very traditional, it shows cooked fruits and spices and at times a rustic side as well.

CROZES-HERMITAGE ROUGE
   1999 ★★ 2009–10
   1998 ★★★ 2009–10

CROZES-HERMITAGE BLANC
   2000 ★

MAISON BOUACHON

Ave Pierre de Luxembourg 84230 Châteauneuf-du-Pape
+33(0)490 835835

The Crozes red from this southern Rhône house, which is part of the Caves Saint-Pierre organisation, comes from the plain area in the south of the *appellation*. Called "La Maurelle," it is vinified with a semi–*macération carbonique* process to achieve as much fresh fruit as possible. It is raised in large barrels.

La Maurelle reflects its vinification, with an open, easy style, its soft fruit demanding early drinking.

CROZES-HERMITAGE LA MAURELLE ROUGE

2003 ★(★) 2012–13
2002 ★ 2008

PHILIPPE BOURRET

Place de la Mairie 26600 Crozes-Hermitage
+33(0)475 072069

A simple, bare house beside the Mairie in Crozes is home to bachelor Philippe Bourret, a man with wavy black hair who looks younger than his 45-plus years. He is the third generation to live in this house but has never nourished himself from wine alone.

"I'm the fourth generation to make wine, but when my father died in 1987, I was already working at the textile dyeing factory in Tournon owned by Liberty of London," he states. "I was doing well there, so I sold all except 0.08 ha of my father's three hectares. I left school in Tournon at 16, and the domaine wasn't big enough for me and my father." Now he is one of the 80 or so shareholders who bought out the design and dyeing business.

The vineyards were on *Les Côtes* above the village on the way to Larnage. This is a clay-chalk, later-ripening site standing at 250 metres. Its oldest Syrah dates from 1929, and Philippe reckons the average age is over 50 years. "I have 800 plants, trained on stakes," he says with a hint of pride.

The domaine first bottled in 1974, and Philippe's debut vintage was 1988, when he was working on his own. He does a whole-bunch fermentation in an open wood vat, with cap punching, for about two weeks. No yeasts are added. Ageing lasts 16 to 18 months in three-to-five-year-old casks, and he fines but does not filter his 400 bottles. These are sold to friends and tourists, all by word of mouth.

The wine is old-fashioned in style, and can benefit from airing.

LAURENT CHARLES BROTTE

rte d'Avignon 84230 Châteauneuf-du-Pape
+33(0)490 837007

See also Condrieu, Cornas, Côte-Rôtie, Hermitage, St-Joseph.

This Châteauneuf-du-Pape merchant's red Crozes is called "La Rollande." The crop is fermented in steel for two weeks at a maximum of 30°C and, after four months in concrete, receives eight months in old oak barrels of around 45 hl.

The 2001 held a mild red fruits flavour, but was a little short.

DOMAINE LES BRUYÈRES

Les Bruyères 26600 Beaumont-Monteux
+33(0)475 847414

The fourth generation on his family's farm, David Reynaud is moving it decisively towards being a fully fledged wine estate. He left the Tain Co-opérative after the 2002 crop, ending the family arrangement to supply it with grapes that had lasted since the early 1970s.

Tall, dark, and quite rugged, David explained that it was his grandfather Georges who planted six hectares of Syrah on *Les Bruyères* in the 1950s. "Before that we had been corn threshers serving farms for around 20 km (12 mi.) around, and livestock farmers. Part of our farm was also dedicated to apricots, peaches and with another farmer nearby we were two of the first cultivators of the kiwi fruit—in France it started here in the Rhône Valley," he states.

David's father was working in the Crédit Agricole Bank when his grandfather retired in 1988, and it was his mother, Marceline, who took up the reins. "She knew I had been inspired by my grandpa, even though I was only 13 then, so she planted five more hectares of Syrah and Marsanne between 1988 and 1999. She took out the wooden stakes and installed wire training to allow mechanisation as well," he remarks. For his own plantings, David has used cuttings from his grandfather's 1950s Syrah, a source of evident satisfaction for him.

The domaine is grouped in the southern area of Beaumont-Monteux and runs to 12.6 ha of Syrah, 0.6 ha of Marsanne, and 0.3 ha of Roussanne, as well as 1.5 ha of Syrah and Viognier *vin de pays des Collines Rhodaniennes* just outside the *appellation* at Châteauneuf-sur-Isère. The *Bruyères* soil is sandy-clay with *galet* stones covering about 60 per cent of the surface. An important site is *Les Croix*, which combines low-yielding 1950s Syrah and, more recently, 2.2 ha of Syrah and 0.3 ha of Roussanne, both planted by David between 2000 and 2003. Here there is deeper soil but the same *galet* presence as *Bruyères*.

The third site is *Le Port*, at the extreme south of the *appellation* just 100 metres from the Isère River; this is also clay-sand with a lower incidence of stones. All three sites are underpinned by white gravel that starts about 60 cm (two ft.) down, and which can be six to seven metres (20–23 ft.) deep, with the odd trace of sand at some levels.

David studied at the Orange Wine School and mixed six months at the Domaine du Rieu-Frais, maker of good Viognier in the southern Drôme, with a year's military service. He started on the domaine in 2000 and has all life's challenges ahead of him. His reasoning appears practical and properly thought-out, and he conducts himself well.

Reversing the normal family formula, David's father does the management and accounts, while his mother works on the domaine with one full-time person. A new cellar was com-pleted in April 2003 and David is working the vineyard organically.

The crop is hand harvested, and in 2003 two-thirds was destemmed. David says he is trying not to work with external yeasts, and prefers cap punching to pumping-over so the wine is disturbed less. *Délestages*, which involve partly emptying and refilling a vat, are off the menu for the same reason. After three to four days of premaceration cooling at 18°C, vinification in concrete lasts three to four weeks, and maintaining the "gentle is best" theme, a vertical press is used nice and slowly—just one press per vat a day.

The top wine, Les Croix, comes from old vines and is raised for 12 to 14 months in one-third each new, one-year-, and two-year-old casks; the regular red is raised in vat for eight to 10 months. Fining and filtration are done. Some of the production is sold to Rhône *négociants*.

The 2003 Les Croix reflected its southern zone with an easy squeeze of fruit present, a sweet-toned harmony that made it suitable for enjoyable drinking quite early. It had softened noticeably in its second six months, as if there had been micro-oxygenation.

The white receives a *macération pelliculaire*, an early fruit extraction, and is fermented two-thirds in steel at 16° to 17°C, one-third in oak. The oak portion receives once-a-week lees stirring, and after its malo has finished, the white is bottled in May. The respectable Viognier *vin du pays* was one-third oak raised from 2004.

CROZES-HERMITAGE ROUGE
2003 ★★

CROZES-HERMITAGE LES CROIX ROUGE
2003 ★★★ From 2006; 2011–13

CROZES-HERMITAGE BLANC
2003 ★

DOMAINE DE CHAMPAL-ROCHER

Quartier Champal 07370 Sarras +33(0)478 342121

See also St-Joseph.

The Lyon-based Eric Rocher has a 2.8-hectare Syrah vineyard planted between 1993 and 1995 at Serves-sur-Rhône. He is a larger owner at St-Joseph, across the river at Sarras.

The vineyard is on loess, a mix of fine clay and silted sand, against the backdrop of the northern granite reaches of the Crozes area. The wine, called "Chaubayou," is raised for 18 months in stainless steel vats. Its red fruits are reserved and carry a typical northern Crozes grain, with touches of white pepper, and a degree of coolness in the texture.

CROZES-HERMITAGE CHAUBAYOU ROUGE
2003 ★★(★) From 2007; 2012–14
2000 ★★ 2009–10

M. CHAPOUTIER

18 ave Docteur Paul Durand 26600 Tain l'Hermitage
+33(0)475 082865

See also Condrieu, Cornas, Côte-Rôtie, Hermitage, St-Joseph, St-Péray.
For over 30 years, Chapoutier have supplied likeable, openly fruited red Crozes. With only 10 hectares of vineyards, much of their wine is bought in from outside sources. Their one single-vineyard wine, Les Varonniers, has been made since 1994, but only in quantities of 5,000 bottles a year.

The main red, Les Meysonniers (100,000 bottles), has made progress in recent years, and is fuller and more consistent than before. It is made from 30 per cent Chapoutier crop, 70 per cent purchased wine, so the contract system is vital here to ensure reliable, high-quality supplies.

The company cultivates just over 10 hectares at Crozes, eight of them their own and two rented. The bulk of the holding—seven hectares —are on the Mercurol area of the *Les Chassis* plain; two hectares date from 1996, the rest from the 1950s and 1960s. All are Syrah.

The remaining three hectares reflect a growing interest in the northern, granite sector of Crozes. Just beside the west end of the Her-mitage hill, there has long been a plot of 1940s Syrah on the *Chavanessieux lieu-dit*, close to the *La Varogne* site of Hermitage. Now walls have been built higher up the hill, with more than one hectare planted here since the early 2000s. This is a windy, rugged plot, its crop contributing to the special Les Varonniers red.

Les Meysonniers is vinified 30 per cent in wood vats, 70 per cent in concrete. It is actively worked during *cuvaison*; there are pumping-overs, *délestages,* and some cap punching. It is raised for 14 to 16 months, one-third in three-to-five-year-old casks, two-thirds in concrete vats. It is lightly filtered.

There is agreeable and overt fruit in the Meysonniers nowadays; this is where evident progress has come through, a shrug-off of some of the old possible stalkiness that could appear in the wine. It can live for seven to 10 years but is ideal to enjoy when its fruit is flourishing.

The pure *négociant* red La Petite Ruche (130,000 bottles) comes mostly from purchased wine, its Syrah up to 25 years old. It is raised for eight months in steel and concrete vats. This usually comes from Mercurol and the more easterly end of the *appellation* around Chanos-Curson, with a touch of crop from the northern granite in it. Its style is easy, plenty of fruit and plump flavours making it what Michel Chapoutier memorably terms "more disco than baroque"—while he is equally quick to assert, quite correctly, that his Hermitage wines are definitely more baroque than disco.

The special red, termed "Crozes-Ermitage" on the label, is Les Varonniers. Its vineyard is west facing and terraced; the top soil is mainly sandy, with traces of silt and clay—all overlaying a couch of hard granite and then clay at around 60 cm (2 ft.) down. Yields are low here, 20 to 25 hl/ha, and the crop is always concentrated from the marked influence of the north wind. A small percentage of grapes from the oldest *Chassis* vines is included in this wine.

Its crop is destemmed and given an extended, five-to-six-week fermentation and maceration, like all the special Chapoutier reds. The temperature is held at 30° to 32°C, and it does its malo in cask. The Varonniers is raised for 18 to 20 months, half in new oak, half in casks one to two years old. It is bottled unfiltered.

Varonniers has become a leading red Crozes, even though it is very highly priced. It is much more complex than the typical plain-zone Crozes-Hermitages, with swirls of smoke and leather alongside the black, berried fruit. There are often animal and forest tones present, too. In the best vintages like 2001 and 1999, it is worth waiting for about seven years to allow its integration and complexity to come forward.

There are two whites, also Meysonniers and Petite Ruche. The Meysonniers *blanc* is largely composed of purchased Marsanne crop, with just a small Chapoutier domaine presence. The outside grapes are grown biodynamically on the plain of *Les Chassis*. The wine is vinified 80 per cent in steel vats, 20 per cent in one-to-three-year-old casks, and is bottled after 10 to 12 months, its malo usually completed.

The vinification of the white Meysonniers has switched around since the early 1990s; before then there was a two-year preparation, after which new oak was tried in part, and the picture now seems to have stabilised. Generally the developments have invested the wine with more grace, though at first there is often an exotic fruit feel that gives way to a couch of quiet local depth later on as the almond side of the Marsanne comes through.

The white Petite Ruche, 90 per cent Marsanne, 10 per cent Roussanne, is produced from wine purchased mostly from Mercurol, plus Larnage and Beaumont-Monteux. Chapoutier term this wine their "alluvial stone wine." It is raised in vat for nine to 10 months, and its malo is often blocked for freshness. It can be very successful, as in 2001, when it held genuine charm.

CROZES-HERMITAGE PETITE RUCHE ROUGE

2002 ★ 2006
2001 ★★ 2007–09
2000 ★★ 2005–06
1999 ★★ 2006–07

CROZES-HERMITAGE LES MEYSONNIERS ROUGE

2003 ★★★ From 2006; 2014–16
2002 ★★ 2008–09
2001 ★★ 2009–11
2000 ★★ 2007–08
1999 ★★ 2006–08
1998 ★ 2005–06

CROZES-ERMITAGE LES VARONNIERS ROUGE

2003 (CASK) ★★ Black fruit, smoked bouquet, cool feature here. Straight black fruit, some pepper, oaked finale. Clear, berried, upright fruit. Granite lends minerality. Bit dry beyond the tannins, best in second phase. From 2007–08; 2015–18.

2002 ★★ Wrapped-up bouquet, cool side—mocha, coffee bean, smoky. Dark fruit, quite severe extraction, oak override at end. Prune, black fruits, violets, bit wannabe. Some end heat. Mineral tinge through it. Was more compact. From 2007; 2012–14.

2001 ★★★★ Overt, funky, animal bouquet; dense fungal/black fruit, truffle taste. Live, loganberry finish. Structured, good wine. Esp 2007–08. 2016–17.

2000 ★★★ Warm, tight black fruit nose, harmonious. Clear fruit attack—berries, quite soft. Sound tannic finale. Esp 2004–05. 2011–12.

1999 ★★★★ Tight, brooding nose, forest smells/raspberry. Packed flavour—black fruits now, tar. Quite massive. Esp from 2007 for tannins; has absorbed the oak well. Fresh, smoky end. 2013–16.

1998 ★★★ Open, animal/red fruits–spice nose. Mineral. Red fruits palate, good tannins. Decent end *gras*. Tasty, has improved. 2011–13.

1997 ★★ 2007–10
1996 ★★★★ 2010–14
1995 ★★★ 2005–06

CROZES-HERMITAGE PETITE RUCHE BLANC

2002 ★
2001 ★★★

CROZES-HERMITAGE LES MEYSONNIERS BLANC

2003 ★ ★
2002 ★
2001 ★ ★ ★
2000 ★ ★
1999 ★ ★
1998 ★

DOMAINE JEAN-LOUIS CHAVE

37 avenue Saint-Joseph 07300 Mauves
+33(0)475 082463

Jean-Louis Chave has planted Syrah on the hillside behind Hermitage, in the *commune* of Larnage, on land used by the late Terence Gray to
make his own Crozes-Hermitage. First production will be around 2007.

DOMAINE YANN CHAVE

26600 Mercurol +33(0)475 074211

See also Hermitage.
This has been a rather overlooked domaine for
many years. Its location plum beside the noisy
autoroute A7 is a put-off—no charming, tranquil views here. But it has been completely revitalised by one of the best young men to appear
in the northern Rhône in the past dozen years,
Yann Chave.

He wandered into wine, too. Maybe that
should be done more often: study economics,
work in a bank in Paris, and suddenly realise
that life is not good. So he hightailed it south—
to work in a bank! "But I tried working with my
father, enjoyed it, and so did wine studies at
Nyons and Suze-la-Rousse. My first vintage was
1996, when I was 26." As he stands in his crin-
kled, rough, torn blue jacket and his clumpy
boots, with specks of Syrah stuck on his glasses,
it's fair to say the boy has come a long way since
Paris!

But he did not take on a big-name estate. The
family worked in agriculture, but had often been
on the move. "In the 1840s we had to leave the
Ardèche, where it wasn't safe to be the only
Protestant family in the village, and that took us

FIGURE 17 Banking in Paris—*pas pour moi, merci.* Yann
Chave returned to Crozes-Hermitage to revitalise the family
wine domaine. (Tim Johnston)

to Algeria. Then, in 1962 we escaped to France
from Algeria, where my great-grandfather had
started a vineyard. Back here my grandfather
grew cereal around Valence, but my father,
Bernard, preferred vines and ended up buying
this small farm here in 1969, with apricots,
cherries, and peaches as well." The grape crop
was sent to the Tain Co-opérative.

Now Bernard does the fruit, Yann the wine,
and it works well. Bernard is very wise and
knows his locations well—what the soil in different places can give—so he acts as a good tiller
on the family boat. Highly motivated, Yann
eases his tall, thin frame around the cellar and
studies his vineyard with a near-obsession for
signs that can educate him. He is a lucid thinker
and speaker, too, and can go a long way. He is
open-minded and soaks up all information that
can send him on the right path.

The domaine is expanding and changing as
new opportunities are spotted and taken. There
are 15.5 hectares of Crozes and 1.5 ha of Hermitage. The core Crozes is formed by 6.5
hectares at Mercurol, with 14-to-55-year-old
vines, and five hectares of 50-year-old vines at
Pont-de-l'Isère. Between 2001 and 2003 the
family planted four hectares on the exciting

green field site of *Les Saviaux*, a plateau south of the domaine at La Roche-de-Glun, where the soil is well nourished from growing corn and cereal and, before that, fruit. There is a little less clay than at *Les Chassis*, and the wines are more tender as a result.

There have also been 2.3 ha planted at *Conflans*, next to Jaboulet's *Thalabert*, on very stony red soil that drains quickly. This gives quite punchy wines.

The top red, the Tête de Cuvée, comes from a site called *Les Pautus* at Pont-de-l'Isère, across the N7 from Combier's fine *Clos des Grives* vineyard. Its Syrah averages 48 years in age, and the soil is composed of 15 per cent clay with sedimentary earth and gravel underlay.

Yann's 1.4 ha of white vines—70 per cent Marsanne, 30 per cent Roussanne—are at Mercurol on the west side of *Les Chassis*, one plot from 1963, the other 1978. The Mercurol soil is clay-chalk with some sandy-stony parts, so water retention is better than at the poorer, sandier soil of Pont-de-l'Isère. The classic white is pure Marsanne, while the special Rouvre is half Marsanne, half Roussanne from the 1963 plot.

From 1998 the vineyard was no longer sprayed with prepared solutions; the soil was worked to encourage root growth. Yann started to do manual grafting of new vines with the help of the Gonon brothers from St-Joseph—up to 700 plants in a season. Leaf control meant that the old foliage didn't rot into the soil, recycling any of the year's pests.

Treatments against grape worm were cut from four to six, to one or two, with sexual confusion practices introduced on the males with the female hormone. Yann did not want copper solutions to destroy a lot of microbodies in the soil, so gave up using those to treat against mildew. He explains why: "You can try a synthetic copper instead of lumping on the 15 kg per hectare that Elf Aquitaine used to recommend. Or, what I like, apply 2 kg of zinc, which is less heavy and stays less time in the soil. Then the vine wood looks better for it."

So he proceeds apace outside, and the notion of the summer holiday disappears over the horizon. "I harvest very late, which demands very healthy grapes. Going over two years without a holiday was not pleasing to my wife, but this demands day-to-day surveillance." Look at 1999: in early August there were too many bunches, so he cut them back twice in 12 days. Already in late June he had been nipping off extra shoots and excess leaf growth, which is called *éfeuillage*. "I bought a complicated machine to do this, which breaks down—but it allows the work to be done, and done properly, so the bunches aren't damaged and not too many leaves are taken off. It's work that must be done in about 20 days by early July, and manually we were taking a month to do it." Now Yann cites a gain in aroma and firmer berries better able to withstand wasp attacks.

To achieve this amount of detail, he has three people working on eight-month contracts and expands to a team of 15 for harvesting. His mother does the admin, and his father lends a hand, with around 70,000 bottles being made each year now—his whole production bottled since 1998.

Working in a cellar completely renovated and enlarged in 2002, Yann is pleased that the extra space and design allow him to treat each precise *lieu-dit* in its own right. He destalks the whole crop and punches down the *chapeau* three times a day to start the 18-day fermentation. For this he descends to chest level wearing fisherman's chest waders on a belt, and is gutted that he takes 45 minutes, longer than the half hour his bigger, stronger Tunisian helper takes for the job. His active, tiring intervention rather than using a switch is typical of his driven approach.

Yeasts are natural, and he aims for fermentation temperatures of 30° to 32°C for the reds (plus a small boost at the end for more extraction). Vinification lasts 14 to 18 days usually, though in 2000 the Tête de Cuvée required 27 days to achieve a crucial measured extraction, without too many bitter items on board from too much *remontage* and *pigeage*. "It didn't pay to be a robot in 2000," he says.

Ageing lasts just a year. The regular Tradition Crozes changed from being 30 per cent cask aged until 2000 to being steel tank raised: "The oak robbed it of fruit," comments Yann. Its grapes come from the western end of *Les Chassis* at Mercurol, and around 50,000 bottles are produced.

The Tête de Cuvée (12,000 bottles) is aged for a year in one-year-old 600-litre barrels. This size is larger than usual—Yann feels the Syrah is easily overrun by too much oak. Because there is no filtration, the wines are racked every three months.

In 2000 Yann did some micro-oxygenation to free up the Tradition red and loosen its tannins. He also was keen to avoid any Syrah stink from reduction, where the wine shows a lack of airing during its raising. This technique came in reaction to the 1999, which had been so big that it was closed—but then surely that is what each vintage should deliver—its own style?

The white wine changed course markedly in 2001; before that there was just the one wine, made from 70 per cent Marsanne, 30 per cent Roussanne. This was produced as a big wine, with late harvesting, lees stirring, and racking. But Yann found the Roussanne didn't take the air from the racking and developed a rotting pear aspect.

Now the classic is pure Marsanne, fermented in steel at between 16° and 20°C and bottled with the malo done at the end of June. The half Marsanne, half Roussanne Rouvre is vinified and raised in new, 600-litre casks for a year, with some but not daily lees stirring "so the wine doesn't become too buttery." The Rouvre was not made in 2002 because of the difficult harvest. The style is still finding itself here; the whites are generally tender and well formed and can be drunk over five to six years.

Since 2001 Yann has also used a synthetic silicon stopper on bottles of the white, which causes less oxygen flow and so could slow down the wine's evolution.

CROZES-HERMITAGE TRADITION ROUGE

2003 ★★ From 2005–06; 2011–13
2002 ★★ 2007–08
2001 ★★ 2009–11
2000 ★★ 2006–08
1999 ★★ 2007–09
1998 ★ 2005–07

CROZES-HERMITAGE TÊTE DE CUVÉE ROUGE

2003 ★★★(★) Crushed black berry, tar, ripe fruit aroma; tasty, live sleek fruit—*cassis* style, pushes all along the palate. Some final oak. Clean wine, plenty to come. Coffee aftertaste. Stylish from 2007–08; 2016–18.

2001 ★★★ Stylish brewed fruit/herbs aroma. Lissom texture, then tightens/darkens. Nose, palate fresh. Tannins still prominent. Good, sinewed fruit. Plenty of variety to come, evolving well. 2012–14.

2000 ★★ Dark cherry; nicely tight bouquet, mixes black currant, some pepper; quite full, has some nice tannic support—they needed till 2004–05 to settle. Clear-cut flavour, can express itself well in time. 2008–10.

1999 ★★★★ Dark fruit, leather, ripe fruit in a sustained bouquet; lovely black fruits flavour, juicy matter, good length, suave tannins. A rich, singing wine, great harmony and purity. High alcohol (14°), but you wouldn't know it. 2010–12.

1998 ★★ 2005–08

CROZES-HERMITAGE BLANC

2004 ★(★)
2003 ★★
2002 None made.
2001 ★★
2000 ★★
1999 ★★

CROZES-HERMITAGE ROUVRE BLANC

2003 ★★ Quite broad, honey/spice nose. Solid, compact, oak/spice end. Sit-down wine, dried fruits/raisins taste. From 2006.

2001 ★★★ Light toast, exotic aroma stage, orange marmalade. Decent richness, dried fruits; smoky finale, where oak grips it. Brown sugar, peach aftertaste. Stylish. Set to close up. 2010–11.

Export 70 per cent (1) Great Britain, (2) USA, (3) Belgium

DOMAINE LES CHENÊTS

Les Chenêts 26600 Mercurol +33(0)475 074828

This is a domaine that bottled its first wine in 1991 and continues with the local involvement of apricots. Catherine Berthoin's sister is married to Philippe Belle, and both families operate similar wine-fruit operations.

Catherine's father, Raymond Fonfrède, planted Syrah and Marsanne in 1962 and would sell his wine to Chapoutier. The domaine is now run by her husband, Étienne, a strong man with short-cropped hair in the French crew-cut style. There are 10 hectares of apricots, which are sold in the Paris market of Rungis, and 11.5 hectares of vineyards—2.8 of Marsanne (oldest 1964, average age 15–20 years) and 8.7 of Syrah (oldest 1960, average 20 years).

The Marsanne grows on the fine clay of the Mercurol slopes and near the village cemetery; the Syrah is mostly on the northern end of *Les Chassis* towards Mercurol, with plenty of clay and white *galet* stones. "The *Chassis* is windier, but ripens ahead of Mercurol," says Étienne. He widened his reach in 2000 and 2001 when planting 2.2 hectares of Syrah in the southern *commune* of Pont-de-l'Isère on a site called *Beausejour*, marked by the alluvial *galet* stones of that area.

Catherine, quite small and fair, looks after the paperwork, and there is one full-time employee. "We haven't studied viticulture or oenology," she says; "we studied with my father." Vineyard treatments are under review, since they are keen to cut them back. With all the vines wire trained, they were machine harvested since the 1980s until hand harvesting was carried out in 2004: "There was rot on the Syrah, so we could sort the crop carefully that way," comments Étienne.

The Syrah crop is vinified in concrete for around 20 days, with twice-daily cap punching. External yeasts are added. Cask ageing lasts 10 months in 15 per cent new oak, the rest up to six years old. Fining and filtration are done.

The classic white is enamel vat fermented, and bottled, its malo done, around June. The superior Mont Rousset is a plot-selection wine, fermented and raised in oak for 10 months—one-third each new, one-year-, and two-year-old oak. Honey aromas, nutty flavours, and oak are mixed here, with the oak needing three years to settle in a full vintage like 2001.

CROZES-HERMITAGE ROUGE
2001 ★

CROZES-HERMITAGE MONT ROUSSET BLANC
2002 ★
2001 ★★

Export 60 per cent (1) Belgium, (2) Great Britain, (3) USA

MAXIME CHOMEL

Chemin des Roches 26600 Gervans +33(0)475 033270

High above Gervans, panoramic Rhône views on his doorstep, Maxime Chomel can guard his privacy while he works quietly away. His domaine and its cellar building are at 210 metres, where the countryside mixes fruit tree terraces with pockets of woods and scrub and patches of vines.

He cultivates 11 hectares of Crozes and five hectares of apricots and continues a long line of family involvement in the land. "Chomels have been here since the 1600s," he says, a balding man in his early 40s. "I became an electrician at 15, but came back here after the army and started in 1984. When I was young, I'd helped my father on jobs like taking the horse through the vineyards, so I knew what was involved."

His father was a Co-opérateur at Tain, with only 1.8 ha, and the decision to build their own cellar in 1987 set Maxime up as a private grower. Seven hectares of his vineyards are at Gervans, with old Raymond Roure plots to help him, notably on the rotted granite or *gore* of the adjacent *Picaudières* and *Sassenas*; the oldest vines there date from the 1930s, partly planted by his maternal grandfather, the youngest from 1978. His 1.3 ha of Marsanne is on the nearby *lieu-dit* of *Les Blancs*, vines dating from the 1950s and earlier, growing on soil that is light and neutral.

In the *commune* of Crozes, M. Chomel has just over 3 ha of Syrah, in the *Quartier des Méjans*; his main sites are on the *gore* of *Merjurol* (1990s) and on *Pontaix*. He is solely a northern-sector Crozes-Hermitage grower, and his remaining small plots are 0.5 ha at Serves—low slopes with granite deposits—and 0.3 ha at Erôme, on flat land.

M. Chomel stresses the importance of hillside vineyards here: "It really matters," he affirms. "I find 10-year vines from the full slopes give better quality than 50-to-60-year vines on the plain."

In the early 1990s he decided to halt systematic chemical spraying in the vineyards, and now does just one anti-weed application in the spring. Since 1996 he has destemmed the crop, and vinification lasts 20 to 25 days in concrete vats, with the first vats yeasted to get the process going. There is pumping-over and a top temperature of around 33°C.

The wine spends its first winter in vat, then the regular quality red is aged for a year in a mix of 228- and 400-litre casks. The special Sassenas is left for two years; all the wood is between six and 15 years old. The regular is fined and filtered, the Sassenas is bottled unfiltered. Twenty per cent of all the wine is sold in bulk to a northern Rhône *négociant*.

After a day's decantation of the juice, the white Crozes is vat-fermented for two weeks at 18° to 20°C. It is bottled, malo done, after a year's raising in vat.

M. Chomel's regular red has local character and a chewy, more tannic structure than many an equivalent produced on the flatlands of Crozes further south. The ingredients for the Sassenas are good—70 per cent early-1950s Syrah, 30 per cent 1970s—but the finished wine can suffer from an excess of cask and thus lack freshness at times; its fruit is dark, its tannins quite evident. Traditional and faithful to its origins it may be, but less than two years in oak would perhaps benefit it.

CROZES-HERMITAGE ROUGE

2003 ★(★) From 2006; 2010–12
2001 ★★ 2009–11

CROZES-HERMITAGE SASSENAS ROUGE

2000 ★★ 2007–09
1999 ★ 2010–11

Export 30 per cent (1) Great Britain, (2) Belgium, (3) Netherlands

CAVE DES CLAIRMONTS

Quartier Vignes Vieilles 26600 Beaumont-Monteux
+33(0)475 846191

The hardworking Jean-Michel and Sylviane Borja must look back on three decades of endeavour and feel pleased. The Cave des Clairmonts was set up in 1973 and is the second-largest producer of Crozes behind the Tain Co-opérative.

It is a collection of families in a mini-co-operative with over 102 hectares of Crozes between them. Jean-Michel's father, Joseph, was a Pied Noir who had to improvise when he came over to France from Algeria in the early 1960s. He had worked in shipping agricultural produce, and found a Naval Commander ready to sell his overgrown 150 hectares of the Domaine des Clairmonts to him and a partner.

Sixteen hectares were planted on the alluvial terraces of Beaumont-Monteux in 1963–64, and the domaine developed through the linkup with two other families in 1973, one of them, the Defrances, still present. Now there are 10 people involved.

This is a southern, rolling-plains enterprise. There are 40 hectares at Beaumont-Monteux, 32.5 at Pont-de-l'Isère, 16 at La Roche-de-Glun, 13 at Chanos-Curson, and just under six at

Mercurol. At Crozes 95 hectares are Syrah and 7.65 are Marsanne, and there are another 5.5 hectares of vines for *vins de pays de la Drôme*—Syrah, Chardonnay, and Viognier.

Concerted efforts have been made to work the vineyards naturally. The grapes from the Borja domaine are grown biodynamically and its wine is sold to Chapoutier, while all the other domaines are now also biodynamic. M. Chanas is one of four ex-Co-opérateurs in the Cave. "Four of us bought the original Guerrier domaine in the late 1970s, and from 1998 I've used no weedkillers," he says; "that means I have to work the vineyard once or twice more, but it's a good policy." Beyond his 10 hectares, he also grows peaches, apricots, and nectarines.

The classic red is destemmed after machine harvesting, and its crop then fermented in two different ways. Seventy per cent is fermented in the latest steel vats for eight to 10 days, in search of direct fruit; here there are automatically triggered cap punchings and *délestages* (part vat emptying and refilling), as well as airing of the Syrah to avoid its closing in on itself and reducing in the stainless steel. The temperature is held around 25°C until a specific gravity of 1030 is reached, then it is allowed to rise to 33°C at the end of the fermentation. The remaining 30 per cent receives over two weeks in vat, with pumping-overs, cap punching, and *délestages*. The aim here is to achieve more tannic content and structure.

The two wines are brought together after their malolactic has finished, and are stored in concrete, with bottling according to demand—from June after the harvest until 21 months on.

The special red, Cuvée des Pionniers (up to 25,000 bottles), is concrete vat fermented and receives a three-to-four-week vinification, with pumping-over and *délestages*. The crop for it most often comes from La Roche-de-Glun and Pont-de-l'Isère, where there are vineyards planted in 1963–64 on the stone-covered, fast-draining terraces. Techniques are modern, with cap punching by nitrogen and *micro-bullage*, or air injection, in the casks.

The Pionniers receives a year in 20 per cent–new casks, the rest up to four years old, and is stored in bottle for another year or so. Like the classic, it is fined and filtered.

Since 1997 two whites have been made, both pure Marsanne. The classic is steel fermented at 16° to 18°C, raised in vat, and bottled in June, while the Cuvée des Pionniers is cask fermented, and raised in oak with lees stirring till June. The oak is 20 per cent new, then up to four years old. The malos are usually blocked.

Sixty-five per cent of the production is sold in bulk, 5 per cent in cubitainer at the cellars, and the rest, about 200,000 units, is bottled.

These are direct, fruited wines with no special pretension to complexity later in life. Their early fruit burst is more compelling than their second palate. The *Pionniers* red may lack a little soul but works quite well with its oak. Grape variety more than *terroir* comes through, mostly, at this domaine.

CROZES-HERMITAGE ROUGE

2003 ★★ From 2006; 2012–13
2002 (★)
2001 ★★

CROZES-HERMITAGE CUVÉE DES PIONNIERS ROUGE

2002 ★
2001 ★★
2000 ★★
1999 ★★

CROZES-HERMITAGE JARDIN ZEN CUVÉE ROUGE

2001 ★★

CROZES-HERMITAGE BLANC

2002 (★)
2001 ★

CROZES-HERMITAGE CUVÉE DES PIONNIERS BLANC

2002 ★
2001 ★ 2010

Export 60 per cent (1) Great Britain, (2) Netherlands, (3) Denmark

DOMAINE COLLONGE

See also St-Joseph.

This is one of the no-nonsense, larger-family domaines on the Chassis plain. The Collonges work 37 hectares of Crozes, mainly in the *commune* of Mercurol. Their domaine retains its rather battered yellow wind sock as a landmark and is one of those where practical farming prevails over detailed, questing wine philosophy.

The 33 ha of Syrah are on the sandy gravel of southern Mercurol and part of Beaumont-Monteux, with stones of varying sizes on the surface. The light brown topsoil is about 60 cm (2 ft.) deep, with the gravel underneath. The site is called *La Négociale*. The oldest vines date from the early 1970s and are all wire trained. There are 4 ha of Marsanne, as well as 2 ha of Syrah *vin de pays de la Drôme*.

Mireille Collonge is in her 50s and works with her brother Gérard and brother-in-law Léo Gigierro. Her son Florent, just past 30, works on the vineyard, and her daughter Christine, near her mid-20s, covers the office. They are both self-taught.

Wine has been made on the property since just after the Revolution, and Mireille is the fourth generation. "It used to be a mixed domaine, but we've kept only four hectares of apricots," she says. "Bottling started in 1974, but we were never Co-opérateurs—the crop was always sold to local *négociants*." Now only about 5 per cent of the wine is sold in bulk, and a house speciality is sales in large bottles, up to the six litres of a Mathusalem.

The red is machine harvested and receives a 12-day fermentation in concrete and some steel, with twice-daily pumping-overs. It is raised for nine to 12 months and is bottled, fined, and filtered from June onwards. It shows a rounded, easy red fruit style, with a touch of end tar—wine to get on with, a reflection of the southern area. The 2003 had more stuffing than usual.

The all-Marsanne white is fermented in enamel and concrete vats at 16° to 18°C and bottled with the malo usualy blocked in January. It is appley and not that inspiring.

CROZES-HERMITAGE ROUGE

2003 ★★ 2011–14
2002 ★ 2008–09
2001 ★ 2006–07

DOMAINE DU COLOMBIER

2 route de Chantemerle 26600 Tain l'Hermitage
+33(0)475 074407

See also Hermitage.

Every *appellation* needs its "engine room" domaines—those that keep turning out well-made wines without fuss and pretension. Colombier is one such estate.

Very tall, chatty, and charming, Florent Viale runs the wine side. His grandfather was a mixed farmer, with chickens, cows, and horses, plus vines and fruit. The family continues to cultivate fruit trees and since 1991 has bottled and sold its wine. Previously the Hermitage was sold to Guigal, the red Crozes to Ogier and to Burgundy, and the white Crozes to Paul Jaboulet Aîné—good addresses all. Now just about 10 per cent, from the young vines and the press wine, goes away in bulk.

The cellars are part of a pretty domaine at the foot of the east side of the Hermitage hill and have been there for three generations. Father Gaby, born in 1939, is a contemporary of Albert Belle, and both men set off on their own domaine wine track at about the same time. The Viales have always worked half in fruit, notably apricots plus some cherry and peach. Cherries are the least popular fruit from the angle of their harvest clashing with vineyard work in mid-May.

The vineyard holdings have grown in the past few years. There are over 13 hectares of Syrah for their Crozes, 1.9 hectares of Marsanne for the white, and a precious 1.81 hectares for the Hermitage.

The Crozes Syrah grows on gentle, tractor-friendly terraces around Mercurol and Tain. Colombier itself is right in the *commune* of Tain, with a filtering, sandy-sediment soil topped with broken stones. At Mercurol the soil is more red clay, with a couch of gravel about a metre down. Their Crozes runs over a dozen or so plots.

The Marsanne grows in four plots; many of the vines date between 70 and 100 years, their centre being *Croix du Torras*, right next to the most easterly slope of Hermitage, *Les Signeaux*, or *Torras et les Garennes* as it is now known. The other three plots are at Mercurol, led by a notable 0.3 ha of 1902 Marsanne on *Les Pends*. "We bought this in 1997," recalls Florent; "it's a fantastic old vineyard, but it took me four winters with my pickaxe to get it in better shape. The old owner would deliver the crop to the Cave de Tain." The other sites at Mercurol are *Mont Rousset* and *Creux Charbonnier*.

The outlook is practical. Spraying is done against grape worm blight, but likewise, excess leaves are cleared and the soil is banked and worked. "I adapt as necessary," says Florent: "I just want healthy vines."

Florent was a latecomer to the domaine, having worked off a serious amount of wanderlust. His travels took him to Central America and Africa, and he worked as a ski instructor in the Vercors mountains nearby, before a year's training in the Libourne near Bordeaux in 1988. He has a relaxed attitude and with his broad outlook is happy to chat beyond the subject of wine.

The Syrah is vinified whole in a variety of vats—concrete, steel, and wood; a 30-hectolitre open wood vat is from his grandfather's time, and Florent does a foot *pigeage* on this: "It's useful to help me judge the vintage quality because in the good years it's hard to break down the top crust; I wear my bathing trunks for that."

The Crozes is fermented for two weeks, around the 30°C mark, with the end temperature rising to 34°C before gradually descending to 22°C and devatting. Florent is careful about excess heat for the loss of fruit it can bring.

Ageing is 50 to 60 per cent in cask, with the *demi-muid* 600-litre barrel favoured, the rest in steel or enamel vats. The Gaby cuvée is selected from the best cask wine, one month before bottling around November, 14 months after the harvest.

The classic red shows soft fruit, with a sprinkling of tannin, a wine that is fine to drink when three to six years old, although it should last longer. The Gaby *rouge* (18,000 bottles) has more scale—increased black fruit and a tarry content. It gains leathery tones with age and drinks well towards 12 years old or so.

The white receives only a light decantation after pressing, and is then 80 per cent vat, 20 per cent oak fermented, and raised for 10 months. Since 1997 there has also been a Cuvée Gaby white (1,500 bottles), all done in new wood for a year when conditions lend themselves (there was no Gaby in 2000). Florent's comments on this are a relief to hear: "We started to make this wine with lees stirring, but the wine came out too massive and wooded, with low acidity and a loss of finesse. Now we let the malo occur."

CROZES-HERMITAGE ROUGE

2003 ★★ 2011–12
2001 ★★ 2008
1999 ★★ 2010–12
1998 ★★★ 2008–10

CROZES-HERMITAGE CUVÉE GABY ROUGE

2003 ★★ Grilled, imposing bouquet—soaked black cherries. Full, brewed dark fruits on palate, rolls along well, oak intervenes. Length OK. More together by 2007. 2012–13.

2000 ★ Bosky, wooded elements on nose, pine wood, dry; spritely early fruit, red berries. Slightly lean, fair length, though dries. Needs some time—not sure about balance here. 2006–09.

1999 ★★★★ Dark fruit/mint, pepper on a wholesome, full aroma; tightly packed black fruit propped up by sound tannins. Quite challenging as a young wine, drink from 2004. Sound, not flashy fruit, can gain complexity. 2010–13.

1998 ★★★ Varied, black fruits, tar and mint aroma, dry tones; earthy flavour, black fruit, tar and berry finale. After three years, tannins more prominent, is more punchy. Oily finish, tannins need to work out. 2009–11.

CROZES-HERMITAGE BLANC

2004 ★★
2001 ★★
2000 ★

CROZES-HERMITAGE CUVÉE GABY BLANC

1999 ★★★ Full yellow; dried apricots aroma, full; very rich, lots of exotic fruit here, plenty of fat. Luxury wine, cask effect on end. Towards mini-Hermitage. 2007–09.

Export 60 per cent (1) Great Britain, (2) USA/Canada/ Japan

DOMAINE COMBIER

RN7 26600 Pont-de-l'Isère +33(0)475 846156

See also St-Joseph.

Laurent Combier strides around the hangar behind his cellars, a busy, action man issuing comments and instructions to those around him. The tempo is not surprising. He runs a wine domaine and grows both table grapes and fruit—peaches and apricots. He also has a share in a Spanish vineyard and does some *négociant* wine selling as well. He's a compact, solidly made chap, flecks of silver in his dark hair as he approaches 40, who has continued the organic methods started by his father, Maurice, in 1970.

They left the Tain Co-opérative in 1989 in order to vinify the 1990 vintage themselves, and have not looked back. They expanded the vineyard quickly, doubling it from five to 10 hectares by 1992. There are now 19 hectares of Crozes—17.3 of them Syrah and 1.7 hectares white, split 70 per cent Marsanne, 30 per cent Roussanne—a single hectare of St-Joseph, five of table grapes, and 20 of mainly peaches, with some apricots.

In 2004 he took over the five hectares of old Albert Bégot vineyards at Gervans and Serves in the northern sector, a rental agreement confirming this source as a counterpoint to the 13 hectares of Syrah at Pont-de-l'Isère. These vineyards date from the early 1970s, and a part runs as far back as the 1920s.

"There's always a 10-to-15-day delay in the north," he says, "so I pick my Pont-de-l'Isère crop and get that moving well before the rest—helpful for space in the cellar," he adds. His sites at Gervans are *Cafiot* and *La Tuilière*, which share a loess soil with granite zones, and *Les Îles* down by the Rhône, which holds some small *galet* stones. His site at Serves is *Les Garennes*, where there is a predominance of loess with a little more sand than at Gervans.

Replanting has become a mix of selected *massale* cuttings and clones. "We let the soil rest three to four years, although I know seven years would be ideal," says Laurent. He also grows cereal in the interim: "It takes out viruses and lets the soil rest." Being organic, the vineyard work is often very labour-intensive. It takes six people three weeks to trim back surplus young shoots early in the cycle, for instance.

The domaine carries the emblem of the fruit-packed wines of the southern Crozes plain around Pont-de-l'Isère. The jewel is the hedge-lined *Clos des Grives*. This encapsulates Laurent's belief in running a balanced ecosystem across his domaine. The hedge is a dark-green pyracantha, which of course provides shelter for the vines, but also for the wildlife—hares and birds. His fruit trees are also helpful: "You do get a higher concentration of parasites when you work organically," says Laurent, "but the mix of fruit and vine is important. Blackbirds don't eat grapes, and the crows prefer cherries, so they're not a threat."

The *Clos des Grives* vines run east-west along neat wire-trained lines. The soil is deep red, with a lot of alluvial stones; the red clay-chalk is typical of *Les Chassis*, which extends away from here on to the vineyards of Graillot and Jaboulet. Four and a half hectares are Syrah averaging 50 years old, some of them planted by Laurent's

FIGURE 18 A longtime organic grower, Laurent Combier makes wine that carries the fruit-charged style of the flat, stony south of Crozes-Hermitage. (Author's collection)

The Syrah is vinified in steel with twice-daily pumping-over, cap punching at the start of the maceration, and an 80 per cent *délestage* (vat emptying and refilling). Laurent lets the temperature run to 32° to 34°C, then eases back to around 26°C for extra maceration. The malos are done in cask; the Combier receives 12 months in two-to-four-year-old casks, the *Grives* 14 months in 30 to 40 per cent–new oak, the rest one to two years old.

In keeping with the organic work in the vineyard, only light sulphur applications are done. "Here in the south of Crozes the pH levels can be quite high, more than at Gervans for instance, so we filter lightly to deal with any bacteria," comments Laurent.

The Combier white is vinified at around 16°C in 70 per cent oak (half new, half one year old) and 30 per cent vat and bottled in the spring. The Clos des Grives white, 85 per cent Roussanne, 15 per cent Marsanne, is fully oak fermented (half new, half one year old), with *bâtonnage* (lees stirring) until the spring. It is bottled after a year. Both wines usually complete their malos.

Laurent makes a third wine called "L" on the label, one aimed at the simple *bistrot* market. From 2004 this was made with home-grown grapes, mainly from the old Albert Bégot organic vineyards at Serves and Gervans that date from the 1940s and 1960s. The white version of L is pure Marsanne, made from grapes grown at Gervans; it is 70 per cent–vat, 30 per cent–young oak fermented.

Laurent employs four people full-time, while his wife, Ghislaine, runs the office and retail sales. Every year he trades around 30,000 bottles of organic red Côtes du Rhône from near Vaison-la-Romaine (a wine of 70 percent Syrah, 30 percent Grenache) and Syrah *vin de pays* under the title "Laurent Combier"; he has worked in the past with Jacques Frelin, a Béziers-based merchant, for his Crozes, but now bottles it all himself.

His overseas project came along in 2002, when he bought a 13-hectare domaine at Torroja del Priorat, the high, rocky northeastern Span-

grandfather Camille. These provide the special red Clos des Grives (23,000 bottles). The other 5 hectares of Syrah here average 25 years old, and make up the juicy regular wine Domaine Combier *rouge*.

In 1997 Laurent made his first Clos des Grives white (up to 3,000 bottles), then from 80 per cent Roussanne (1977) growing on *Les Blâches*, part of *Les Chassis*, and 20 per cent Marsanne (1982) from the *Clos des Grives*. His regular Domaine Combier white is from younger vines, the mix reversed—80 per cent Marsanne, 20 per cent Roussanne.

Laurent packed in a lot of preparation for the day the family went it alone. He studied viticulture and agriculture at Orange and also had stays in a variety of French domaines— Provence, Burgundy, and Châteauneuf-du-Pape. "We like to work with ripe grapes and let them have a long, 25-to-30-day maceration," he says, so he destalks after the hand harvesting. Natural yeasts are used, except in tricky years like 2002.

ish vineyard that has become very fashionable and known for its old Grenache. His partners are Jean-Michel Gérin from Côte-Rôtie and Peter Fischer from Château Revelette, also a high vineyard in the Coteaux d'Aix-en-Provence.

"We planted eight hectares in 2002–04 and also rented two properties of 12 hectares whose vines average 25 years old," says Laurent, a good strong gaze indicating his commitment to the project. "It was 60 per cent Grenache, 40 per cent Carignan, but we have added 10 per cent Syrah for our Rhône touch. The soil is schist, like that of Côte-Rôtie." The Grenache can be over 100 years old, with yields as low as 10 to 20 hl/ha. Their first, very respectable wine was made in 2002 and received a 16-month cask raising.

Laurent's work with Domaines Ott in Provence and also in Burgundy influenced him in his outlook to his wines: "I like my wines to be suave and fine," he states. "*Grand Vin* is not about power at all costs; it's about the finesse it can show. We want the same in our Priorat."

The classic red is a very good example of a fruity, quietly structured Crozes and travels with a definable vintage character. It's bottled at the end of May and is a wine good to drink over its first five or six years, but is notably fulfilling when young.

The Clos des Grives red is full of smoky black fruit, as if the breezes of the south are present. Its oak content can mean it needs some years to settle, but generally there is a sound, rich content. I expect it to show well for somewhere around 12 years or more—very much the full, sunny wine of southern Crozes.

A one-off in 2003 was Laurent's 1,500 bottles of Torride, a red Crozes from the most south-facing vineyards, where the grapes were often rather burnt. As a result, more than twice the amount were needed for each litre. After 13 months in new oak, it showed broad chocolate aromas and a mix of fruit and flowers—mulberries and violets—on the palate. With a heated finish, it is indeed a true vintage representative.

The classic white shows some of the Marsanne almond nuttiness, and fair elegance. Its

oak can provide the finish with extra punch. The Grives *blanc* demands around three years for the oak to assimilate, which it can in a good vintage like 2001. It is a wine that could make progress in the years to come, but its oaking will have to be carefully monitored in order to be in step with each year's maturity.

CROZES-HERMITAGE
DOMAINE COMBIER ROUGE
2003 ★★★ From 2006; 2013–15
2002 (CASK) ★ 2008
2001 ★★★ 2010–11
2000 ★★ 2007–08

CROZES-HERMITAGE CUVÉE L ROUGE
2003 (CASK) ★★★ From 2006; 2014–16
2001 ★★ 2007–08

CROZES-HERMITAGE TORRIDE ROUGE
2003 ★★★ 2011–13

CROZES-HERMITAGE CLOS DES GRIVES ROUGE
2003 (CASK) ★★★(★) Soaked, ripe fruit, Pez sweets, some heat on nose. Oaked black fruit, persists well, some refinement. Widens at finish. Abundant wine, less oak after two hours. From 2007–08; 2016–18.
2001 ★★★★ Healthy red fruit/raspberry smoked, tar aroma, potential. Smooth black fruit; elegant, fat texture. Tarry end. From 2006; 2011–13.
2000 ★★★ Open aroma, full of violets and berries; stone fruit, plums with good persistence. Lasts well, rounded wine. 2008–10.
1999 ★★ Nose quite dense—cooked black fruit/oak. Slight dry jam texture; oak grows with air. Needs time to sort, loosen. 2009–11.

CROZES-HERMITAGE
DOMAINE COMBIER BLANC
2003 ★
2002 ★★
2001 ★★

CROZES-HERMITAGE CLOS DES GRIVES BLANC

2001 ★★★ Very pretty, oak/spice nose; broad, has rich core. Modern style, clean. Vanilla/oak end, needs three years to settle. 2010–11.

Export 40 per cent (1) USA, (2) Great Britain, (3) Belgium/Switzerland

RENÉ-JEAN DARD ET FRANÇOIS RIBO

Blanche-Laine 26600 Mercurol +33(0)475 074000

See also Hermitage, St-Joseph.

These two are the troubadours, the Bohemians of Crozes. They eased into a small street-corner Tain courtyard in 1984, parked up their black Citroën 15, the detective Maigret's car, and set to work. There wasn't much cash, but there was plenty of inclination, a seasoning of artistry— and wines that were individual, one-off, and thoroughly genuine.

They neatly span the Rhône: François, born 1961, from Tain, and René-Jean, born 1960, from Tournon. They both have three children. They met at the Wine Lycée in Beaune. François is perhaps the air side of the partnership, a man with soft sandy, curly hair and glasses, with the look of the comedian Gene Wilder about him.

René-Jean, brown haired and bearded, with glasses and a short, stocky frame, is the grounded, doughty, and at times abrupt side of the equation. René-Jean's family owned a hectare of St-Joseph, and that was about it. Now they work a total of 7.5 hectares, mainly Crozes, with some St-Joseph and a smidgen of red Hermitage.

A visit to them is an honour because they do not feel inclined to swap tittle-tattle and tasting notes with journalists. Their cellar has moved to a gulley near Mercurol, a simple hangar beside a river. The bell sign reads DRR . . . . . . IING!, an expected artistic touch. It's the farm of the nearby nineteenth-century Château de Blanchelaine, now a locale making high-priced Manoukian sweaters. The contrast of the boule-vard destination of one product, with the likely simplicity of consumption of the other is wry. Certainly the domaine's standout black label, raw white lettering overprinted, is not going to be put up for chic awards.

It's clear that all they want to make is wine that is friendly and faithful to its origins. "We have projects to do *terroir* wines," says François, "but often they're so good, we drink them our-selves. What we like is natural wine because it's alive, wine that doesn't necessarily have to be kept—just drunk and drunk again." Their cellar, a clean jumble of casks and bottles, reflects this natural approach.

In 2002 they lost half their crop because of the conditions; the final sort was done in the vineyards by friends at the weekends in small teams of eight to 10. Overall the process took up to three weeks: "If the weather is good, we're in no hurry; we want to achieve the best ripeness we can," comments François.

They work five hectares of Crozes, which includes one hectare of Roussanne and Mar-sanne, notably at Larnage; one 0.6-hectare plot planted by them in 1986 contains soil that is a mix of glacial alluvial deposits, rolled stones, and red clay. The other 0.3 hectare of Marsanne dates from the 1920s and grows on *Les Carrières* in Larnage's speciality soil of kaolin, or white clay. Ripening is delayed here, because of the cool soil that retains moisture—a bonus for roots and leaves in the drought of 2003—and also because they are in a small, well-aired val-ley. These vines may ripen two weeks behind the plain growers' plants.

Their Syrah is spread across a number of sites. The main proportion is at Larnage, some at Crozes-Hermitage and Mercurol. Attempting to secure precise raw data here is to not really enter into the spirit of the domaine; a large part—two hectares—grows on red clay on *Les Bâties* at Crozes-Hermitage, a vineyard they bought off Philippe Bourret's father when Philippe decided to continue with his dye fac-tory work in Tournon. The Syrah here ranges from the 1940s to the late-1980s. Also at Crozes, there is half a hectare on the sandy granite of *Les Pins* (1994).

The Syrah at Larnage is half a hectare at 250 metres on *Le Pé de Loup*, where there is white gravel with touches of kaolin—here the youngest vines are 1988, the oldest from the 1930s. A 0.3 ha plot is in the *Quartier des Chaux* also at Larnage, southeast of the village towards the autoroute, which is a mix of loess with quite large alluvial stones and red clay: "It's a spot of transition where the Alpine influences come to bear quite strongly," remarks François.

The duo make an early, fruity Easter red wine called "C'est le Printemps," which comes from half a hectare on *La Grace* on the plain at Mercurol, where there is a sand-clay mix of soil, and smooth alluvial stones. "There's a tar/geranium side to the Syrah from Mercurol," states François, "so that's why we make this early wine—it's simply not as refined as the Larnage Syrah wines." The Printemps wine is half oak, half steel–fermented and bottled in March.

The outlook here is laissez-faire, patient; "we try to vinify by *terroir* and even by variety, without the fixed target of what final wine that crop will become," states François. He's a modest chap, a Paris Left Bank operator standing in a Rhône vineyard. His humour is cutting, a little mordant. He's very anti–techno wines—"these wines may be extracted, but after one glass they are nothing, and you have no desire to drink another glass"—and fits wine into the broader picture, where it is to be drunk with food and friends, over time. The style of grower he respects—established people like Thiérry Allemand, René Balthazar, and Hervé Souhaut and starters like Jean Delobre and Jean-Pierre Monier—endorses this.

His home reflects the man: it's on *La Croix* on the end of the Hermitage hill, the old domaine *vinicole* of the Salavert *négociant* business. It must please him that the view runs straight along to their little Pavillon on *La Croix*, with his own Hermitage vines beside it. Meanwhile in the garden near the house, his horse and his mule bite each other and contest the turf, a long-distance slugging match in progress.

For the main red Crozes, the Syrah is fermented with its stems in open wood vats and twice-daily *pigeages* (cap punching). The overtly declared policy is to use very little sulphur during fermentation. The wine is aged over 10 to 12 months, in a mix of used 228- and 600-litre casks. Policy is clear on these: "We don't want the wood to intrude—it serves just to let the wine breathe," explains François.

The red style here is for ripely fruited wines, but which are not flashily open. Their subtlety contrasts with the exuberant fruit of the plain at *Les Chassis*, for instance. There is often a touch of peppery restraint and a quiet outer boundary to them. The duo sell a lot to *bistrots* and wine bars in Paris, even though they don't make sales visits to them, and are aware that the wine should be an effortless companion for food. The red is often good to drink before its fifth birthday.

Marked emphasis and care are placed on their white wines, both from Crozes and St-Joseph; these are full and correctly southern, their texture intended to be rich and ripe. The duo like the Roussanne grape, and it forms two-thirds of their white Crozes. On its own, this reveals a peppery, spiced tone in the white fruits.

The Crozes white is raised one-third in steel, the rest in 228-litre casks that average 10 years in age; it is bottled, malo done, after 10 to 12 months. Since 2001 there have been 800 to 1,000 bottles of another white, called "K." This comes from the 1920s Marsanne that grows in the kaolin at Larnage, and receives a cask fermentation and raising for a little under a year. When the crop is ripe enough, as it was after a good wait until early October in 1996, there is a special white Crozes Cuvée Toto.

"It's all very well doing extra cuvées, but we take great care not to spoil the regular cuvées," is the realistic comment of François; "blending can create great, fruitful synergies if you get it right. Look at Gérard and Jean-Louis Chave."

CROZES-HERMITAGE
C'EST LE PRINTEMPS ROUGE

2003 ★
2002 ★

CROZES-HERMITAGE ROUGE

2002 (CASK) ★

2001 ★★

2000 (CASKS) ★★

CROZES-HERMITAGE BLANC

2003 (CASK) ★★★ Light, smoky fruit nose. Good clear fruit, chewy and spiced. Richness present, has good core. Interesting.

2002 (CASKS) ★★ Nutty, light honey nose; clear-cut *gras*, fair amount, some nuttiness. Sound for the year.

2001 ★★ Ripe, grapy nose, fig/dried fruits; full, fleshy plump flavour, almost oxidative. Expressive, ripe Marsanne.

2000 ★★

1999 ★★

CROZES-HERMITAGE CUVÉE K BLANC

2002 ★★ Stylish, warm cooked fruits/light honey aroma; surprising palate at first, seems oxidative but air helps it. Praline, dried grapes/apricot mix. Was more savoury earlier in life. 2008–10.

2001 ★★★ Salty/citrus refined nose, ripe; dried white fruits, gentle texture, bit bitter, fair length. Richer from 2005; light oak at end. 2010–12.

Export 40 per cent (1) Japan, (2) Switzerland, (3) USA

EMMANUEL DARNAUD

21 rue du Stade 26600 La Roche-de-Glun
+33(0)475 848164

One of the newest recruits to the growers' ranks at Crozes, Emmanuel Darnaud has plenty of energy and a switched-on mind. He is happy to say that he didn't undertake any wine studies and instead spent time visiting growers and asking plenty of questions. His diploma was in agricultural management, but when that finished, he admits that "I got the passion for wine" and went off to work with Bernard Faurie for four years.

FIGURE 19 A promising career ahead—Emmanuel Darnaud has started to make his mark at Crozes-Hermitage. (Tim Johnston)

He's a photogenic chap, quite tall, tousled, very fair hair done in the modern semiruffled style, dark blue eyes set in a clear face. His "friend" is Mlle. Christine Faurie, daughter of aforementioned Hermitage *vigneron* Bernard, and the future lies invitingly ahead for this very motivated man in his late 20s. If his 2003s are a guide, he is someone to keep a close eye on.

"I have Italian blood," he says, with no irony. "My grandparents grew apricots and a few vines here at La Roche-de-Glun, my father fruit and vines, but neither vinified the grapes—those my father sent to the Tain Co-opérative."

He started out with 1.5 hectares of Syrah—the smallest private domaine—split equally between *Les Haut Charissier* at Pont-de-l'Isère (1960s), a vineyard of some very old family friends 300 yards from Combier's *Clos des Grives*, and La Roche-de-Glun (1978). By early 2005, he had achieved one of his early goals—that of reaching five hectares of vineyards to bring the domaine towards a more economic footing.

Additions came through 1.25 ha of Syrah dating from 1998 at *Les Saviaux* at La Roche-de-Glun, 1.35 ha of rented 1982 Syrah at Mercurol on *La Négociale*, and over 0.5 ha of young Syrah (2000) at Pont-de-l'Isère. There is also some young Marsanne at Pont-de-l'Isère planted in 2000.

The Roche-de-Glun soil is marked by alluvial stones much smaller than those on the *Clos des Grives*. There is less clay than at Pont-de-l'Isère, its nearest *commune*, which makes it lighter, more filtering ground.

His two mentors were an uncle who is an *oenologue* and Bernard Faurie. "Bernard's work gave me the eyes of a *viticulteur*," he comments, while his uncle, Jean-Etienne Guibert, worked at the Cave de Tain for 30 years until sacked in recent big changes. His father is still a Co-opérateur, with 10 hectares spread between La Roche-de-Glun, Pont-de-l'Isère, and Mercurol, so Emmanuel can borrow a tractor or spraying machine from him.

As an indication of the generation gap, Emmanuel does not use weedkillers, unlike his father, Christian. "I try to turn the topsoil once it has rained, and use only contact products that do not enter the soil—they were much in use in 2003 with the baking weather." His approach is more logical than purely organic.

His first vintage was 2001; the whole crop was destalked, though this is not fixed for the future. With great personal and physical commitment, he does up to three foot-crushings a day in his concrete vats, some cap punchings, and only three pumpings-over—like Bernard Faurie. "I prefer to achieve colour and extraction by foot," he explains.

After about 20 days, the young wine is transferred straight to cask—Emmanuel works with 35 per cent new, the rest up to five years old, the sizes a mix of 228 and 300 litres. The larger size is to play down the oak influence, as Emmanuel admits, "I'd be happy with 600-litre casks, but I'm not big enough to move them." In 2002 he reduced the new and one-year-old oak proportion to 25 per cent each.

Committed to detail, he racks a cask, cleans it, and then reintroduces the wine into it; this is so he can track its precise influence. He uses French and Hungarian oak for the time being. The stay in wood lasts about 14 months, and there is fining and a light filtration.

His production runs at up to 20,000 bottles for two wines—7,000 bottles of his rounded, direct Mise en Bouche (no new oak), and 13,000 of his Les Trois Chênes, half of it taken from his new-oak casks. The Trois Chênes contains well-cut black fruit, with lightly grilled oak aspects when young. In good vintages like 2001 and 2003, it settles after four years and can show well at a mature stage, around six to eight years old. From such a young grower, it is a wine of considerable promise.

In 2002 Emmanuel made his first white wine, "probably" pure Marsanne because it's from a vineyard over 70 years old. The owner of this 0.12 ha south-facing site—just above the Crozes village houses near Les Balcons de l'Hermitage view—used to make the wine in his garage (without fanfare). Now he's getting on and prefers to go and walk in the vineyard; he also has another 0.35 ha of land for planting.

After a day's decantation, this is cask fermented, with a mix of ages for the casks. "I include an older cask—say, six years—so I can preserve some freshness and the oak isn't too intense," he reasons. His other casks are one or two years old. It is bottled, the malo done, before the summer, with a princely 800 bottles produced.

CROZES-HERMITAGE MISE EN BOUCHE ROUGE

2003 ★★★ From 2006; 2011–13
2001 ★★ 2010–12

CROZES-HERMITAGE LES TROIS CHÊNES ROUGE

2003 (CASK) ★★★★ Cool side to black fruit aroma, well-founded bouquet. Stylish palate—rounded fruit, well-packed, fat throughout. Jam/olive mix, southern effect. Very stylish wine. Oak impact lightly toasts it, not intrusive. From 2007; 2014–16.

2002 (CASK) ★ Medium-weight nose, stone fruit; fair depth, length. Has enough fruit to work with different oak influences (Allier, Hungary). Probably OK around 2006, needs time to integrate. 2011–12.

2001 ★★★ Yeasty, black fruit, some reduction, grilled notes from oak. Decent juice, restrained style with underplayed oak that needs a little time. Good black berry fruit, clear-cut. 2011–13.

CROZES-HERMITAGE BLANC

2002 (CASK) ★ Fair, light aroma; some middle *gras*, nicely warm.

Export 35 per cent (1) USA, (2) Great Britain, (3) Switzerland

MAISON DELAS

ZA de l'Olivet 07300 St-Jean-de-Muzols
+33(0)475 086030

See also Condrieu, Cornas, Côte-Rôtie, Hermitage, St-Joseph, St-Péray.

In 1996 Delas stepped into vineyard ownership, acquiring two hectares split between Gervans and Erôme, the northern villages of the *appellation*. At Gervans, the site is called Les Terrets, a hectare that is half Syrah, half Marsanne (both 1950s). Like their Erôme site that they call *Peichon* after the old owner, the soil is quite cold granite, with bits of loess (windblown silt and sand) present; these give a light hue to the vineyards. The Syrah vines from these two sites average between 35 and 40 years old.

In 2004 another 1.3 hectares came on stream, with an agreement to buy the crop from a site near *La Négociale*, on the west side of *Les Chassis*. This 1984 Syrah grows on alluvial stone soil and gives fruited rather than tannic wines.

The company also buys crop from a noble and little-known vineyard near the Rhône in La Roche-de-Glun. One of the most evocative vineyards in the Crozes area, this is the walled, slightly mysterious *Clos St. Georges*, that lines the small road away north from La Roche-de-Glun and the Rhône. It is a fabulous six-hectare site, surprising because it is set in country jumbled up with modest houses and scrappy land. The oldest plots are a little less than one hectare of 1950s Syrah, and another hectare of 1970s Marsanne, still stake trained on a subset called *Le Coteau*.

At *Le Clos* there is about a foot of clay-limestone topsoil with then a couch of quite large alluvial stones that are said to descend for a full 30 metres. One of the owners is the uncle of Emmanuel Darnaud, who set out to make his own Crozes in the early 2000s.

The *Clos* provides the house's *cuvée parcellaire* Crozes, which until 1998 was called "Clos St Georges," now just "Le Clos." This wine was not produced in 2000 and 2002, so the standard Launes cuvée could be given extra weight in those tricky years.

As with all the Delas reds, the Syrah is destemmed, and there is twice-daily cap punching by foot from above the concrete vats and some pumping-over. A pre-fermentation cold maceration at 15°C helps tannic extraction—four to five days to allow simultaneous tannic and anthiosan extraction. "The result is richer, more *gourmand* wines, fresher and more robust, too," according to Jacques Grange. Vatting time lasts two to three weeks, and no outside yeasts are used.

Delas produce three red Crozes—Les Launes (200,000 bottles), Cuvée Tour d'Albon (25,000 bottles), and Le Clos (7,000 bottles). The staple wine of Les Launes is largely made from purchased crop with a little bought-in wine. Forty per cent of it is raised in two-to-three-year-old oak, the rest in vat, for six to eight months, and bottling comes a year after the harvest. "The Syrah gets just enough oxygen from this to allow us to get round the reductive side of it, or to at least let it happen more gradually," explains Jacques Grange. "Any longer, and we risk drying out the fruit." This is a direct, drink-early wine.

First produced in 1988, the Tour d'Albon is made from 25 per cent Delas and 75 per cent outside crop, the latter coming from one supplier at Gervans, a neighbour of Raymond Roure in that prime area who also has vines above Crozes-Hermitage. This is an overtly granite-inspired cuvée. After four months in vat, the Albon is aged for 10 to 12 months in 228-litre casks that are one to three years old; until recently it was aged in large, old 70 hl barrels that have been shown the door. The Albon crop went into Les Launes in 2000 and 2002 to give a boost to the main workhorse wine.

Le Clos receives a year's ageing in 20 per cent new, 80 per cent one-year-old casks. Its richness, a far cry from the filigree pepperiness of the northern granite, is built around warm fruits, and it is a wine that gives wholesome pleasure. Its richness in 2003 was laced with a thread of mineral—a most satisfying whole.

The white Les Launes (23,000 bottles) is made purely from purchased crop. The wine's focus has changed since the early 2000s, with more crop taken from the granite areas of the north—notably the villages of Gervans, Erôme, and Crozes, with some Mercurol present, and from 2004, 0.6 hectare of Marsanne from *Le Clos*, a *massale* selection vineyard planted there in 2000.

From 2001 Les Launes *blanc* has been 90 per cent Marsanne, 10 per cent Roussanne. It was first vinified in steel in 2003, with just 8 per cent in oak, and fermentation takes place at between 18° and 20°C. It is bottled after eight months, its malolactic completed. It has shown well recently, with good vintage respect—the 2002 an easy, soft drink with appealing roundness, the 2003 showing quiet richness and some typical Marsanne almond flavour.

CROZES-HERMITAGE LES LAUNES ROUGE

2003 (CASK) ★★(★) From 2007; 2013–14
2002 ★
2001 ★★ 2008–09
2000 ★ 2007–08
1999 ★ 2006–08

CROZES-HERMITAGE TOUR D'ALBON ROUGE

2003 ★★ Chocolate, raspberry bouquet, plenty of sappy, brewed fruit. Lot of matter, tightly packed black jam, pepper and tannin uplift. Some reduction. Violets aftertaste, heat. Some concern that lacks freshness. From 2006; 2012–15.

2001 ★★★ Biggish, dense stewed red fruits nose; compact, cooked fruit, thorough/warm, good *gras*. Ripe end fruit. From 2007; 2013–14.

1999 ★★★★ Spicy, bacon/dry pepper nose; live, pebbly fruit—prune, kirsch, end tar/

some dry tannins. Structured. From 2007–08; 2013–16.

1998 ★★ Generous, ripe red fruit bouquet, touch of jam. Attack works well—fleshy feel. Just a bit short, pity. 2006–07.

1997 ★

CROZES-HERMITAGE LE CLOS ROUGE

2003 (CASK) ★★★★(★) Oiled, very knit nose, ripe fruit notably, potential. Big, broad black fruit, some mineral thread through it. Rich to the end, good tannic surge. Lot of quality, texture will delight. Slow-wait wine, lasts well. From 2008; 2017–19.

1999 ★★★★ Compact, ripe red/black fruits, tar, some animal aroma; full, with still some dry, upright touches. Blackberry/pepper end. The *gras* mixes with leathery/meaty side. From 2007–08; 2017–18.

1998 ★★★ Sappy, overt, almost Pinot nose; tasty red fruit attack, then throttles back. Cool black end flavour, liquorice. Great with autumn food. Esp 2003–07. 2010–12.

1997 *Clos St. Georges* ★★ 2005–08
1996 *Clos St. Georges* ★ 2005–07

CROZES-HERMITAGE LES LAUNES BLANC

2003 ★★
2002 ★★(★)
2001 ★★

OLIVIER DUMAINE

Chautin 26600 Larnage +33(0)4745 072150

See also St-Joseph.

The Dumaine family have resided at Larnage since 1650, but in the past three generations their living has moved out of wine and back to it again, following the economic trends of the moment. "My grandfather made a *bistrot* wine for Tain and Tournon," explains Olivier Dumaine. "But there were great moments of crisis around 1927–28—in the 1930s he had five years of stock. That's why my father Raymond went off to work for the Post Office. I came back to wine in 1987."

He started with fruit—mainly apricots—and wine; now there is more wine. He's a humourous man, whose dark hair contains elegant creases of grey; within the chatty, extravert style lies a lively mind capable of making serious, perceptive points. He wants to make honest wine without lots of garage cuvées, and one feels that his Beaune studies served him well—up to a point. His approach to a superior cuvée reveals his measured thinking: "I don't want it to be so far ahead of the classic that I lighten and denude the true, simple Crozes." As a result, there was none made in 2002, to defend the quality of the classic wine.

Until 2004 there was no destemming, another sign of a man of independent thought. But the crop that year wasn't ideally ripe throughout, so half was destemmed. "I wanted to refine my wines, and think it worked in 2004—there had at times been a bitterness apparent in some of the the wines that I wanted to avoid," he states. The wines are pleasingly noninterventionist and their fruit is nice and pure.

He works 4.5 ha of Syrah and 2 ha of white—90 per cent Marsanne, 10 per cent Roussanne—and 0.5 ha of some recent *vin de pays* Syrah. The Crozes Syrah averages 35 years in age, some of the vines much older, while the Marsanne ranges between 35 and 50 years. These are all inside Larnage, on the typical white soils, some of them with a little more red clay to the eye. All vineyard work is manual.

He makes two whites and two reds—a classic and La Croix du Verre from older vines. There are 1,500 bottles of the latter in white, which is 90 per cent Marsanne, 10 per cent Roussanne, with the vines dating back to the 1940s and beyond, and 4,000 bottles of the red Croix du Verre. Olivier uses no external yeasts and ferments for three weeks in concrete, with two *remontages* a day. Against the current mode, he restricts the amount of oak on the classic red—"I like the red fruits and pepper side of the Syrah," he says—so no more than 20 per cent of this wine is aged for eight months in three-year-old casks. La Croix is all wood aged, over 10

months in three-year-old oak. Both wines are fined and lightly filtered.

The whites are fermented in steel, with loose temperature control up to 20°C. Olivier has reappraised his approach to them: "My first years were very academic, and I wasn't getting what I wanted," he says; "I tried oak for the white but wasn't convinced." He leaves the whites for a year on their fine lees, without much stirring and intervention, and bottles both of them in September.

The classic red is indeed a red fruit, peppered wine, with just a hint of tannin: in the good years it drinks well after two or three years. The Croix du Verre follows the same red fruit style, with more dimension, notably from the tannins that bring an extra chewy texture.

Showing that Larnage is a good location for whites, the Dumaine duo perform well. The chewy elegance of the Croix du Verre reflects the mature Marsanne from a good site, in similar vein to the accomplished whites of neighbour Marc Sorrel.

CROZES-HERMITAGE ROUGE

2004 ★★

2002 (VAT) ★ 2009–10

2001 ★ 2008

CROZES-HERMITAGE
LA CROIX DU VERRE ROUGE

2003 ★★★ Deep *robe*; ripe black fruit bouquet with a jam, sweet, southern tone; is full. Rose-flavoured black fruits, savoury without being too plush. Elegantly compact, with detectable tannins towards finish. Decent definition. Unpretentious winemaking, more variety by 2008. STGT wine. 2012–14.

2002 Not made.

2001 ★★ Tight aroma; well-cut direct fruit, pepper in it, tannins within, chewy end. 2011–12.

CROZES-HERMITAGE BLANC

2002 (VAT) ★

2001 ★★

CROZES-HERMITAGE LA CROIX DU VERRE BLANC

2003 ★★★ Full, refined, broad bouquet—pear, white fruit influence. Full and stylish palate, well modelled, with elegant richness. Mixes local feel with clean winemaking. Marked STGT here. Chicken in sauce a delight with this.

2002 Not made.

2001 ★★★ Persistent, dried fruit/honey aroma; stylish, chewy, elegant wine. More open by 2005.

Export 50 per cent (1) Great Britain, (2) USA, (3) Canada

DOMAINE DES ENTREFAUX

Quartier de la Beaume 26600 Chanos-Curson
+33(0)475 073338

Behind the village of Chanos-Curson the road winds gently upwards, and there is a brief burst of countryside *à l'anglaise*—cornfields, hedges, trees. Then atop a ridge stands the Domaine des Entrefaux, which played an important role in waking up quality at Crozes in the 1980s.

The cellars' dry-stone exterior is set off in summer by a dazzling blue wistaria that dominates the whole courtyard. In early summer there are also white and violet lilacs in full bloom, and an abundant rose-coloured tamarisk giving the domaine an aspect of colourful fecundity.

It was formed in 1979 by brothers-in-law Charles Tardy and Bernard Ange, after the former left the clutches of the Tain Co-opérative and showed that private enterprise could work out well. From 1998 it has been run by Charles and his stout, chatty, and motivated son François, Bernard Ange having left to go solo in that year.

Their 26 hectares comprise 22 Syrah of between five and 40 years' age and 4 hectares of white (90 per cent Marsanne, 10 per cent Roussanne), on average 15 years old. The vineyard's developing maturity has played a marked role in bringing greater depth to their wines. The soil is half gravel and sand at Beaumont-Monteux and Pont-de-l'Isère, and half clay at Mer-

curol, where the limestone zones are used for the white vines.

Vinification and vineyard methods changed after 1998; one senses that François was keen to put into practice the more natural ideas of his generation, so they no longer machine harvest, something they practised between 1985 and 1997. The soil is worked more, sprayed less. Nor does François use outside yeasts in the cellar, while he works with the lees more than he used to, and no longer fines the whites.

Hand harvesting allows precise destalking—80 to 100 per cent for the Beaumont-Monteux grapes and 50 to 80 per cent for the Mercurol harvest. "We destalk the Beaumont Syrah because we're aiming for overt fruit," explains François, "while at Mercurol the vines are older, so we keep their stalks."

Vinification lasts up to three weeks in concrete, with pumping-over, punching-down, and some vat decantation. The Syrah is raised on the lees and stirred until May. The classic receives nine to 12 months in vat and barrel, the Machonnières 16 to 18 months in oak—10 per cent new, the rest two to three years old. There is no fining or filtration of Les Machonnières. In 2002 a *lieu-dit* wine, a red Coteau des Pends, was added to the lineup. It is made from young Syrah on that hill and is raised in new-oak casks for a year. This emphasizes clear-cut fruit with some core present in it as well.

The classic red usually carries black fruit and is tinged with peppery traces. It emphasizes the simple fruitiness of plain-area Crozes and is good to drink after a couple of years in the bottle.

This can appear under different names in different countries, notably the United States and Britain. The names under which they sell the classic are "Domaine des Entrefaux" and "Domaine de la Beaume," a name used for a chain of hotels in Britain.

The Machonnières, first made in 1998, is from two plots at Mercurol that are largely clay with a bit of chalk, the Syrah dating from the 1960s and 1970s, just above the white *Les Pends* vines.

The Machonnières red offers good variety of aroma and flavour; its scale is more obviously southern than that of the classic. The bouquet brings in olives and oily scents, while the palate contains tannins that give the wine life and structure. The cooked black fruits are present, with width and robust appeal from the start. It is a wine that can be cellared for 10 years or more and will deliver different textures during its life.

The classic white is 98 per cent Marsanne, 2 per cent Roussanne. A cool maceration precedes fermentation in steel at 15° to 17°C, which jogs quietly along for nine to 12 months, with bottling, malo done, at the end of August. It contains 10 per cent of the oaked *Les Pends* wine. Policy on the malolactic changed in 1998; it was first blocked from 1986 to gain freshness, but the aim now is for fuller wines. This aperitif wine sometimes shows ripe fruit traces that round out the palate.

The special-vineyard Coteau des Pends white (max 5,500 bottles) is in a style not much found at Crozes. It is two-thirds Marsanne, one-third Roussanne. It also represents a deeply rooted local heritage. "We have 100-year-old bottles of it in the cellar, and a label dated 1875," states François. The new label is taken from the time of my great-great-grandfather."

The Coteau des Pends *blanc* is vinified in casks that range from new to three years old. The oak presence is a delicate judgment, and I prefer the use of some older casks as well, as happened in 2002. Lees stirring lasts until March, bottling is at the end of August. These are chunky, oaked whites that need later drinking to encourage flavours other than international pineapple and exotic fruits. The 2002 was made in a welcome, subtle style, the year restraining the extracted content.

The Tardys have recently resurrected a quiet local tradition of black truffle collecting from the *Coteau des Pends*; François Tardy planted some oaks in the early 1990s and has found some truffles since, in the footsteps of his father and grandfather before him. Keep an eye on this

domaine—I back it to do well, but—please, François—take it easy in the cellar.

CROZES-HERMITAGE ROUGE
2003 ★★ From 2006; 2013–14
2002 ★(★) 2008–10
2001 ★★ 2010–11
2000 ★★ 2009–10
1999 ★★ 2008–10
1998 ★ 2006

CROZES-HERMITAGE
LES MACHONNIÈRES ROUGE
2003 ★(★) Very dark; grilled, international, and obvious bouquet—floats away rather than grips. Severe oak hit on palate, has some richness but is stretched, so clear danger that will dry later on. No real moment of harmony here. Southern, olive-flavoured finale. Hasn't yielded much in last nine months. From 2008; 2012–13. Last tasted March 2005.

2002 Not made

2001 ★★★★ Suave, stylish aromas; starts well—olives, southern *gras*, varied, full black flavours. Good end tannins, a serious wine. From 2006; 2016–17.

2000 ★★★ Expressive black jam fruit aroma. Cool black currant; middle is fat then touch of end acidity. Solid, honest. Tannins settling. 2010–12.

1999 ★★★★ Fungal tones on bouquet; tight attack, chewy, profound black fruit. Deep, lasting, tight-knit. Very good, very long. 2012–15.

1998 ★★★ Sappy, damp black aromas, earth; juicy, oily texture, warm black flavour. Mineral damp leaf/tobacco end, some tannin. Good. 2006–07.

CROZES-HERMITAGE
COTEAU DES PENDS ROUGE
2002 ★ Stand-to-attention bouquet, ripe black cherry fruit, oak. Quite sleek black fruit, tannic hue from the oak. Constructed wine, dry, kirsch elements at end. From 2006, but risk of dryness, core not esp ripe. 2010–12.

2002 ★★

2001 ★★

CROZES-HERMITAGE COTEAU DES PENDS BLANC

2003 ★★★ Elegant bouquet—dried fruits rather than 2002's floral tones. Stylish, restrained peach flavor, with a soft richness; long on glycerol. Attractive, honeyed finish that persists. Has taken its oak well now. 2013. Last tasted March 2005.

2002 ★★★ Honeysuckle, some white fruit, stylish and wide bouquet. Pear-style fruit, pretty, elegant, has nerve, goes beyond the plump. Minted, fair length. Good for the year, subtle.

2001 ★★★ Pineapple, jungly fruit aroma; firm attack, exotic fruits, chewy. Wide, chewy. Fair refinement, oaked finish. 2010.

2000 ★ Intense, ripe bouquet; butter/oak, nice middle juice. Oak very marked. Good matter, too oaky.

1999 ★

Export 35 per cent (1) Great Britain, (2) USA, (3) Belgium

DOMAINE JEAN-CLAUDE ET NICOLAS FAYOLLE

35 route des Blancs 26600 Gervans
+33(0)475 033483

See also Hermitage.

The splitting of the long-established Fayolle domaine in the northern area of Crozes came as a shock and provoked some confusion among the wine-buying and scribbling community. After all, Jean-Claude and Jean-Paul are twins, and very interchangeable at that.

The separation came from the 2002 vintage onwards, and each side of the family has its own cellar now as well. Jean-Claude and his son Nicolas cultivate two separate one-hectare sites of white grapes—pure Marsanne (1940s) on the brown clay of *Les Blancs* at Gervans and 80 per cent Marsanne, 20 per cent Roussanne (1993) on hill terraces at *La Rochette* in the *commune* of

Serves. The soil differs here—clay with some siliceous soil, and granite about a metre down.

They also have a hectare of Syrah (1991–92) on *La Rochette;* this grows on the denser red clay area of the *lieu-dit*. In the *commune* of Crozes, they work 1.15 ha of Syrah (1982) on a site that the family calls *La Grande Seguine*: its terraces are clay-granite with a covering of small alluvial stones on top. Finally at Gervans, there is a 0.3 ha patch of Syrah on *Les Îles* and 0.2 ha on *Les Voussères*—both sites sandy-clay and low lying, the former near the Rhône, the latter just next to the railway.

Nicolas sometimes gives the impression of a wandering mind; maybe there is something of the dreamer in him. He wears glasses, and has short-cropped dark hair, very much the facial image of his father. Born in 1970, he studied wine at the Mâcon and Beaune Schools, and is still finding his feet.

The Syrah is fermented in whole bunches for 10 to 15 days in a mix of concrete and steel. Outside yeasts are used, and there are twice-daily pumping-overs. There are two reds, the Grande Seguine, which is aged in used 600-litre casks and large barrels for 15 months, and La Rochette, raised for a year in used casks and barrels. Grande Seguine is fined and filtered, La Rochette only fined. Grande Seguine is the more robust wine, with its 1982 Syrah, while the Rochette is more expressive of soft red fruit, as befits its 10-years-younger Syrah.

The white Les Blancs is vat fermented at over 20°C, then raised for 10 months, also in vat. It is bottled with the malo usually done, except for low-acidity vintages like the 2003, when the old Marsanne side of its character came through well.

CROZES-HERMITAGE LA ROCHETTE ROUGE

2001 ★

CROZES-HERMITAGE LA GRANDE SEGUINE ROUGE

2003 ★★★ Prune, violet aroma, mineral glint. Refined black fruit, cool finale. Restrained, stylish future ahead. Tannins have the right bite. From 2007; 2015–17.

2000 ★ Fair even fruit nose; quiet stewed fruit, jam. Simple, touch sweet, red fruits, Gervans style. Some end grip. 2008–09.

CROZES-HERMITAGE LES BLANCS BLANC

2003 ★★★ Honeyed, quite ample bouquet, stylish. Buttery/flan attack—rich, agreeable texture. Classic Marsanne, some final hazelnut, touch of dryness there. Length OK.

2001 ★ Light, easy white fruit nose; nutty start, correct. Quite fresh, direct.

Export 6 per cent (1) USA

CAVE FAYOLLE FILS ET FILLE

9 rue du Ruisseau 26600 Gervans +33(0)475 033374

See also Hermitage.

Jean-Paul Fayolle's son Laurent is a switched-on young man who, with his older sister Céline, is likely to move this new domaine in the right direction. It has risen from the old combined Fayolle estate that was split at the time of the 2002 harvest.

Laurent, a dark-haired, slim young man has inherited his father's sonorous voice and explains some of the new approach: "We're looking for evolution in the vineyard. We are restricting treatments on the hill vineyards, and are growing grass in every other row, sowing in spring and autumn." He is a qualified *oenologue* from the Montpellier School and in 1999 spent half the year working in the southern Rhône and half the year in Victoria, Australia. He joined in 2000 and brings a widened perspective. Céline covers the commercial side of the domaine and has herself studied and worked in wine in the southern Rhône and the Ardèche.

Altogether they work 7.5 ha of Crozes and 0.5 ha of Hermitage. The main Crozes site is 3 ha of Syrah (averaging 32 years old) on *Les Pontaix*, a hill flank on the left side of the road up to the village of Crozes from the N7. The soil is stony clay with a little limestone, the highest point around 220 metres. The slope areas are wire trained, the high terraces staked. "These wines carry a tannic structure and can take oak," states Laurent; "they show ripe red fruits and spice and are pretty rich."

Just north of *Pontaix*, there is an old Raymond Roure plot, 0.83 ha of Syrah (1940s) on the *Clos des Cornirets*, that they bought in 1996. "This has a different geological seam," explains Laurent; "it's very fine granite, with brown clay, and makes very fine wine. It's a bit nearer the Rhône, and is shielded from the north wind by the woods behind it. I have to set my alarm clock early in summer if I'm working there—it gets very hot."

The other mature Syrah vineyard is their 0.7 ha on *Les Voussères*, at the bottom of the slopes between Gervans and Crozes. This is white granite soil with fine clay, the vines ranging between the 1970s and the 1950s. "Its wine is very fruited, with a fine structure," says Laurent; "you can drink it young, so we deliberately don't extract its crop much because of that natural style."

The family is enthused about a new project away from their natural base at La Roche-de-Glun. The hectare of Syrah on *Les Hauts Saviaux* was planted in 2003, and like Yann Chave, the Fayolles are keen on this new source. "It's *galet* stone covered," says Laurent, "with a brown clay subsoil, and less gravel than the *Chassis* vineyard. There were fruit trees and some spring cereals here; the land hadn't been very worked very hard and is in good shape, full of natural nutrients."

There is 1 ha of 90 per cent Marsanne, 10 per cent Roussanne (1950s) on *Les Pontaix*, present on what they call *les terres mortes*—white granite, siliceous, sticky soil that is good for white grapes.

There are three reds—Les Pontaix, Les Voussères, and Clos Les Cornirets, all named after their sites. Since 2000 the crop has been destemmed and precooling can run for four days at 12°C; after outside yeasts have been added, fermentation lasts for two to three weeks in concrete and steel. There are twice-daily pumping-overs and *délestages* (partial vat emptying and refilling) in the steel vats, with cap punching on the concrete vats.

Les Pontaix (15,000 bottles) is raised for 12 to 14 months, 60 per cent in 600-litre, 40 per cent in 225-litre casks of one to six years. Les Voussères (5,000 bottles) receives 10 months in large old barrels, while the Clos Les Cornirets (5,000 bottles) receives 12 to 14 months also, 60 per cent in 225-litre casks, 40 per cent in 600-litre *demi-muids*, both one to four years old. The wines are lightly fined and flitered.

The white *Les Pontaix* is 90 per cent vat fermented at 18°C, 10 per cent cask fermented and raised. It is bottled in June the following year. Laurent is not seeking to achieve fresh fruit with his white: "I've been working more on the lees and temperature control," he says, "and I feel this has helped the white to become more honeyed and more intense, without the bitterness that might have existed in the past."

Laurent did well with his 2002 Cornirets *rouge*, since it was an undeniably tricky vintage. The local feel of the wine comes through, with a true finesse present. "A lot of the top-of-the-range Crozes are big, high extraction wines," he observes, "while ours works on finesse and length." I'd expect this domaine to move towards the front rank in the next few years—the raw materials are in place.

In the notes, any wine from 2001 or earlier was made by the whole Fayolle family, before the splitting of the vineyard.

CROZES-HERMITAGE LES PONTAIX ROUGE

2004 ★★ 2013–14
2002 ★★ 2009–10
2001 ★★ 2010–11

CROZES-HERMITAGE LES VOUSSÈRES ROUGE

2002 (CASK) ★ 2009–10
2001 ★★ 2007–08

CROZES-HERMITAGE
CLOS LES CORNIRETS ROUGE

2004 ★★(★) Tarry aroma. Ripened fruit, with a restrained style—shows the finesse of the

year. Can sing when older. Esp from 2008; 2014–16.

2003 (CASK) ★★(★) Ripe fruit, violets bouquet. Cooked, plum fruits, warm and broad, some potency. Decent tannins present. 2013–15.

2002 ★★★ Compact, low-key fruit/licorice aroma. Three-quarter-weight black fruits, all clear and well formed. Very good fruit, with finesse here. Pretty length, too. 2009–11.

2001 ★★ Overt reduced, tar/raspberry aroma; quite clean, blackberry core, persists. Fruit gum style, fruit well inset. Warm, structured; tar end. 2011–13.

CROZES-HERMITAGE LES PONTAIX BLANC

2003 ★★★ Honey, white fruits bouquet. Good weight and density on palate, is refined as it rolls along. Nutty, quietly rich finale, dried fruits present. 2012.

2002 ★★ Light, soft butter, white fruit bouquet. Small amount of *gras*, quite sweet; fruit, then spice. Sound finish. Enjoyable early wine.

2001 ★★ Slight bonbon, nuts/honey aroma. Pretty full palate, firm-bodied, solid end. Licorice/violet mix present. 2009–10.

Export 20 per cent (1) Great Britain, (2) Netherlands, (3) USA

FERRATON PÈRE ET FILS

13 rue de la Sizeranne 26600 Tain l'Hermitage
+33(0)475 085951

See also Condrieu, Côte-Rôtie, Hermitage, St-Joseph.

The Ferratons make a domaine red Crozes, Le Grand Courtil, from their biodynamic vineyards, and a merchant red and white Crozes, both called "La Matinière."

The domaine vineyard is 2.5 ha of Syrah (1983, 1991) on *Les Chassis*, in its more clay-influenced Mercurol area. Another 1.8 ha of Syrah was planted in 2003 on *Les Pichères* at Beaumont-Monteux, where the soil is sandy gravel with *galet* stones on top.

Michel always maintained that his is a house of red wine, made in the traditional way, while

Samuel naturally inclined to slightly more modern methods that have brought more rigour to the winemaking. Many a firm statement from father, therefore: "My Crozes style is traditional, and I won't jump to attention and empty my vats when the *oenologues* say it should be done. A lot of Crozes has become uniform because of them." Warming to his task: "A white coat has never entered the house and won't while I'm around."

The domaine vineyard red, Le Grand Courtil, is mainly whole-bunch fermented for around 10 days in open wood and concrete vats, with twice-daily pumping-overs and cap punching. It is then aged for 14 to 16 months in 225-litre casks—one-third new, one-third two to three years old, one-third three to four years old—and bottled without fining or filtration. It can suffer from too much extraction, as occurred in 2001.

The *négociant* red and white are called "La Matinière." The red comes from Mercurol, Beaumont-Monteux, and Pont-de-l'Isère—the alluvial zone of *Les Chassis*—so is a purely southern zone wine, with no granite influences. It comes mainly from wine purchases, with just a little crop added to it. It is aged half in two-to-five-year-old casks, half in concrete vats for 12 to 14 months.

The white Matinière is purchased wine from Mercurol. It is steel vat raised for eight to 10 months and is bottled in June with its malo blocked for freshness.

CROZES-HERMITAGE LA MATINIÈRE ROUGE

2003 ★ 2008–09
2001 ★★★ 2012–13
2000 ★★ 2006–08

CROZES-ERMITAGE LE GRAND COURTIL ROUGE

2003 (CASK) ★★★ Ample, smoky bouquet, more to come. Quite extreme maturity, touch oxidative. Fully charged, earthy wine, meaty style, tannins aplenty. Lots here. From 2007; 2013–15.

2002 Lacks balance on this sample

2001 (★) Piny, resin-tinged, smoky black fruit aroma, big and extracted; tarry, hedgerow fruit wine. Acidity needs time to settle, elements uneven. Was more harmonious; extraction renders it dry at this stage; alcohol prominent, too. 2010–12. Last tasted May 2005.

CROZES-HERMITAGE LA MATINIÈRE BLANC

2001 ★★

DOMAINE ALAIN GRAILLOT

Les Chênes Verts 26600 Pont-de-l'Isère
+33(0)475 846752

See also St-Joseph, Hermitage.

Action man Alain Graillot did Crozes-Hermitage a strong favour when he took the plunge to leave successful international corporate life in 1985. Before then he had never made a drop of wine in his life.

A native of Vienne, with his parents later living in Burgundy, Alain had been bitten by the Syrah bug through buying wine from Guigal, Jean-Louis Grippat, and Paul Jaboulet Aîné. His arrival sparked the boom on the *Chassis* plain and the opening up of the fruity, lively side of red Crozes to thousands of drinkers, many of them outside France.

This is par for the course if you know Alain. He's what the French call *dynamique*, a charming, chatty man who relishes life inside and outside the wine trade. Hang gliding in the Vercors mountains; cycling weekends in Burgundy (no pit stops below Grand Cru level); travel to Laos, Iran, Cambodia; bullfights in Seville; cheering on Les Bleus at Twickenham—he pops up with great energy and creates a sense both of fun and of "everything is possible." His staunch ally is his slight, slim wife, Elisabeth, she too charming and possessing the sort of French style and femininity that weakens most hearts.

His vineyard is composed of 17.3 hectares of Syrah, all grouped around his cellars at *Les Chênes Verts* on the *Chassis* plain. Most were planted in 1973, the rest from 1978, so the 2005 average works out at around 30 years. The

FIGURE 20 First steps towards a wine dynasty—Alain and son Maxime Graillot on their *Chênes Verts* vineyard in the south of Crozes-Hermitage. (Author's collection)

white-vine area runs to 2.6 ha, made up of 80 per cent Marsanne, 20 per cent Roussanne (1980). The middle part of the *Les Chassis* here is very stony, the alluvial deposits of the Alps lying on a sandy, brown-coloured, and free-draining couch, what Alain terms "sandy-siliceous." "There was an excess of nitrogen in the soil from it having been a pig farm here before we arrived," says Alain. "That brought rot; now, it's more balanced because we've left the soil alone."

Alain saw the opportunity inherent in having some open space in the otherwise cramped northern Rhône, and was able to build house and cellars on the old farm site. He admits that when he started, his precise winemaking knowledge was about the same as that of most people who draw up their car outside a *vigneron*'s cellar, fill it up with bottles, and then disappear back to a town apartment.

His old work had been on the export side of a Paris-based company selling agricultural treatment products to areas like Latin America. At the age of 40 he decided to make the break, and in a memorable quote, when asked why he wanted to make wine, replied, "I wanted to make a Syrah wine, which I couldn't do with a full-time job."

His first wine, the 1985, was made with him taking six weeks off from his Paris job to use the harvest from his then rented vineyard. He also made a red St-Joseph from crop grown on the granite slopes of Andance across the river, and then duly returned to the boulevards. Both wines were very creditable.

Both Alain and Elisabeth are very convivial, but remain just outside the old local, more single-speed ways. Now, as he touches 60, Alain is fired up over what he calls his last big project—namely a one-hectare abandoned plot on a hill site at Larnage, *Mortiers et les Chaux*, that he cleared and planted in 2003 as part of the Crozes-Hermitage Vitrine vineyard operation. An early badge of honour for this site, one that seems apt for the Graillot style, is that its wall has been selected by the local graffiti artists, their handiwork visible from the autoroute A7 below.

This is an extension of the Hermitage hill, on the back side of it, the soil similar to *Beaume* and *Péléat*—alluvial stones and markedly more clay than on *Les Chassis*. The cuttings for this have all been hand selected from healthy old vines, some of them from Raymond Trollat, the veteran of St-Joseph. "It's a mini-*Méal* for me—it's got the rolled stones and a bit of white clay and compacted soil and is southeast facing," he observes.

The other clear spur to Alain and Elisabeth, who is always busy around the cellar, has been the arrival of oldest son Maxime, born in 1977, a big lad who after zero interest in the *métier*, has also caught the wine bug. He has bought vineyards at Beaumont-Monteux and built a cellar next door to the family home.

Meanwhile, Alain's renown has grown to a stage where he is asked to advise on a Venetian vineyard project (think about that carefully, please) involving the planting of Istriana and Malvasia. Some of the 4.5 hectares have indeed needed replanting, he reports, since their soil has been too saline.

Alain is satisfied with the progress of his vineyard since the mid-1990s. "There was too much potassium and nitrogen in the soil before, but now it's better balanced—mostly because I've done nothing with it," he states. "It's spectacular to see the difference in the musts when I'm fermenting. They can be rich but also bear natural acidities that in good years like 1999 and 2001 are much better than in other good years like 1989 and 1990."

To achieve this, there are four runs through the vines each year, notably in April–May when Alain harrows to admit moisture to the soil. "We have too much sudden rain, so we have to stop its evaporation, which becomes the classic problem faced by the growers who use weedkillers— for them the water doesn't penetrate and is burned off quickly by the sun," he says. Other contributory factors to his vineyard's health are burning cuttings on the spot and allowing grass to grow in August. "The vine's energy is now channelled towards ripening its grapes rather than its woodstock," he adds.

With much of the *Chassis* now given to machine harvesting, the Graillot operation has remained faithful to hand harvesting. The red crop is whole-bunch fermented in concrete vats after a cool maceration, relying only on natural yeasts and no added sulphur. Vinification runs for three weeks, with twice-daily pumping-overs and a top temperature of 32°C.

The classic red is aged for a year, at least 95 per cent in casks up to six years old. The special Guiraude is selected by *le patron* from cask at the end of that year and can run to 10,000 bottles. In any vintage the proportion of new oak is low, 5 to 10 per cent. Guiraude is produced in most vintages, exceptions being 1993, 1997, 2000, and 2002. The wines are filtered but not fined.

The classic red is always well coloured, black cherry style. The bouquets advance black fruits and southern olives in the big years, an undertone of tar sometimes present. Aromas are always open and striking when young, their immediacy bringing direct appeal. The palate fruit kicks along well, berried fruits with some licorice and tar towards the finish. These are wines for outdoors, picnics, or barbecues and are great liveners of any party. Drunk on the first fruit flush up to three years, they are highly entertaining.

The Guiraude is more serious, its flavours more deep-seated and persistent. Pepper and smoke come into the equation, and the wine takes longer to show up. Its tannins are also deeper. This is a wine for sitting down and more refined clothing and conversation. Whereas the classic can run for eight to 10 years, the Guiraude can evolve with pleasing variety for over a dozen years. Both wines can at times reflect a little pushing in the cellar—just the sense that extraction is on the cusp of being obvious.

The white is intended to be drunk young, and always has its malolactic fermentation blocked for freshness. Its crop is 80 per cent fermented in cask (new to 10 years old), 20 per cent in steel, and the young wine is lees stirred until January, when it is fined and then bottled in April. The malo is blocked by filtration. It is a regular wine, at times a little uninspiring due to its provenance. Bonbon sweets are often present in its bouquet, with white stone fruit on the palate. It should be drunk young.

In 1999 Alain made his first Vin de Paille, with white grapes from Crozes, not Hermitage. The grapes were eventually pressed on 15

December and fermented in new oak. Their richness is such that there is little trace of the oak—not surprising given that 8 kg of grapes were needed for each litre of wine! Three hundred half bottles were made.

Alain's wife, Elisabeth, was the major contributor here, separating the grapes in the cellar every day between 15 September and 15 December. "I wanted to call the wine "Elisabeth," but that wasn't her style," comments Alain, adding, "I always found a lot of these wines had their sugar detached, so I tried to be very patient with this."

The patience has paid off: a tasting note on his 1999 Vin de Paille: ★★★★★ Pretty bright gold; bouquet has hints of orange, very light butterscotch, tight and balanced. Clean and sweet, has a very controlled texture. Some dried apricots on the finish, has great balance and lovely integration of sugars and flavours.

CROZES-HERMITAGE ROUGE

2003 ★★★ Full *robe*; strawberry *purée* aroma, persists. Weighted wine, has a compact, tasty flavour. Some spice in the fruit, touch end tannin. From 2006; 2012–14.

2002 ★★ Straight fruit bouquet, sense of sweetness. Live, red cherry fruit, appealing palate, like a *cru* Beaujolais. Frank wine, take it on the up, no great length—delivers fruit. 2008.

2001 ★★★ Well-weighted bouquet, stewed berries, some oil. Tasty, direct black flavour, southern touches—black olives, spice, also licorice. Nice tannins. Esp now to 2006. 2009–12.

2000 ★★ Quite ripe, tarry, raspberry, and blackberry nose; ripe crop texture, black currant/tar. Dark and tight, some end tannins, modern style wine. Fair length. 2007–10.

1999 ★★★ 2008–10
1998 ★★ 2007–09
1997 ★ 2003–04

CROZES-HERMITAGE LA GUIRAUDE ROUGE

2003 ★★★★ Broad bouquet—lot of content, weighty but pretty aromas. Black fruits flavour, more variety and potential than just jam. Ripe,

chewy matter on finish. Has cut, can develop. 2017–20.

2002 Not made

2001 ★★★★ Ripe raspberry fruit, coffee touches, balanced nose. Classic structure, full, warm with richness, tannins present towards finish. Ripe black fruit with pepper. Marked oiliness. 2011–14.

2000 Not made

1999 ★★★★ Quiet, understated bouquet, smoky and floral; very wholesome attack, a lot of berried flavour and a long finish. Nice cool texture, good. 2012–15.

1998 ★★★ Tight packing of small berry fruit, smoke on nose; can develop, broaden. Tight cut of good flavour. Mixes red and black fruit, licorice on end, which is cool and chewy. Good length. 2009–12.

1997 Not made
1996 ★★ 2006–08

CROZES-HERMITAGE BLANC

2002 ★
2001 ★
2000 ★

Export 50 per cent (1) Great Britain, (2) USA, (3) Japan

MAXIME GRAILLOT

Les Chênes Verts 26600 Pont-de-l'Isère
+33(0)475 551349

Maxime is a bear of a young man, friendly and enthusiastic, a convert to wine fair and square now he has reached his late 20s. Born in 1977, he wasn't especially interested in wine in his teens and only gradually warmed to its possibilities.

Having studied at the Dijon Wine School, he set out on his own in 2004, working 5 out of 6 tired hectares in two plots of Syrah, both a mix of 1980 and 1990 plantings on a site called *Les Pichères* at Beaumont-Monteux. It is a sandy, alluvial stone terrain.

The vineyard Maxime took over reflected the notorious 1970s, make no mistake. The rows of vines were covered in black plastic—that has gone. Weedkillers were applied—they have stopped. Missing vines were not replaced—they have been. "I am working the soil now, but have to be careful because the vine roots are so near the surface," says Maxime. Plantation density was just 2,800 per hectare, with gaping 3.5-metre (nearly 12 feet) spaces between the rows to allow machinery through.

The crop is destemmed and receives a pre-fermentation cooling at 17°C for three to five days. The vinification lasts three weeks, with twice-daily cap punching at the outset. Ageing takes place in a mix of differently aged ex-Burgundian casks from domaines like Dujac, Arlot, and Romanée-Conti—from 2005, 10 per cent in new oak, the rest in one-to-four-year-old casks. It lasts about one year. In 2004, 8,000 bottles were produced; in 2005, 15,000 bottles.

"My main objective is to make a wine that is precise and clean and not try to get more out of the vineyard than I could expect," he comments with due reason. The 2004's fruit widens well after its first flush, and showed sound length. An early-style wine, it was a very tidy first effort.

Maxime is the only bottler of wine from this *quartier*, and in time may add a small *négociant* business, in the vein of Jean-Louis Chave or Stéphane Ogier at Côte-Rôtie. He will also move beyond bottling one-third of his harvest towards a full bottling run.

E. GUIGAL

Château d'Ampuis 69420 Ampuis +33(0)474 561022

See also Condrieu, Côte-Rôtie, Hermitage, St-Joseph.

The Guigals moved into selling Crozes in 1999. The main prompt was the acquisition of 2.5 ha of vineyards bound up in the de Vallouit purchase. These are in the *communes* of Larnage and Crozes-Hermitage. The family now rents or owns 11 hectares of Crozes-Hermitage.

The red is made from their own crop and wine bought from Gervans, with a little from Mercurol and *Les Chassis*. It is mainly large used barrel or cask raised for over two years. On recent showing, its fruit is open and the wine suitable for drinking in the rounded house style within five to eight years.

The white comes from bought-in wine. It is largely Marsanne (2003: 93 per cent, with 7 per cent Roussanne) and is vinified and raised in oak. Bottling is in April after the harvest, the malo done. Following the house imprint, it is best drunk with food rather than as an aperitif.

CROZES-HERMITAGE ROUGE

2002 ★★ Soft red fruits bouquet. Clear-cut black fruit, rolls along, touch tight on finish. Its freshness would please northern Europeans. 2010–12.

2001 ★★ Pretty, fruit gum aroma, some freshness with it; brewed wine, pebbly texture, just moving into second phase at three years. Wild strawberry flavour, some end oiliness. 2006–07.

1999 ★★ Quite deep, chocolate bouquet, brambly fruit also. Solid, black fruit on palate, chewy finish, long enough. 2010.

CROZES-HERMITAGE BLANC

2003 ★★ Floral, pretty bouquet, good content. Rich, nicely oily palate, almond nuts in middle, sound length. More open 2005–06, a food, not aperitif, wine. 2011–13.

2001 ★ Golden, bonbon nose; apricot, apple tart, boiled sweets flavour. Quite ripe, spiced end. Touch of oak.

DOMAINE HABRARD

7 route des Blancs 26600 Gervans +33(0)475 033091

See also Hermitage.

This is a domaine in the northern area at Gervans with a developing reputation. Father Marcel is moving towards his mid-50s, and his two sons, Laurent, nearly 30, and Emmanuel, mid-20s, are on stream behind him. The whites are especially notable—both the Crozes-Hermitage and the Hermitage are excellent examples of orderly, stuctured Marsanne and faithfully reflect their origins.

Fruit and vines have been the order of the day for four generations here. A notable card is that the vineyard is mature, averaging over 40 years in age. Apricots, peaches, and grapes have always been the crops. "My grandfather used to sell some grapes to the Co-opérative and keep the best to vinify and sell in bulk. He actually bought the vineyard from General de Gaulle's son-in-law M. de Boissieux," states Laurent Habrard, a friendly, chatty man with pale brown hair, gentle brown eyes, glasses, and a slight look of the teacher about him.

"Over 40 years ago, the Co-opérative told him—it's all or nothing with your crop—and he chose to leave them. From then on he vinified and sold the wine to the merchant trade and to customers who brought along their cubitainers. My father actually produced about 3,000 bottles a year, but his outlook wasn't for hard commerce. He preferred to receive people and have a chat over a glass and a *saucisse*, or to be in the vines, which he regarded as a holiday!"

Marcel, a solid, red-faced man with a flat hat firmly in place, nods silently, as he joins in the tail end of the conversation.

Around 15,000 bottles, or one-third of the crop, are domaine produced. Laurent started in 1998, and the bottled proportion is set to grow. Emmanuel, trained in agriculture, is responsible for the over 10 hectares of apricots.

The family works 11.7 ha of Syrah (average 40 to 50 years old) and 2.5 ha of white—90 per cent Marsanne, with the 10 per cent Roussanne (40 to 50 years) randomly scattered within the Marsanne in the old-fashioned way. Most of the white is on *Les Blancs* at Gervans, with some on *Barbari*, a loess slope. The most recent planting was in 2005 on the Vitrine vineyard site at Gervans of *Les Paillassonnes*—0.5 ha of Marsanne and 0.2 ha of Syrah. There are also 0.5 ha of almost pure Marsanne Hermitage and 0.6 ha planted in 2003 on the noted *Ste-Épine* hill at St-Joseph.

One-third of the Crozes Syrah is on *Les Chassis*, with two-thirds spread between Erôme and Gervans in a mix of hill and flat ground. "We have 50 plots!" says Laurent, which means a mix of flatland, half slope, and slope, most of them staked, which means manual working." The Syrah grows on a mix of rocky and largely clay soil; the Marsanne does very well in the very fine, dusty loess soil up near the old Raymond Roure domaine. "There's not a stone to be seen," says Laurent.

Laurent has an unexpected helper when making the wine. "My grandfather actually taught my mother, Marie-Thérèse, the art of vinification," he explains. "My father likes to be outside, not in the cellar, so Maman comes along to help me, and my brother Emmanuel has also worked part-time on the wine side as well as running the fruit since 2001."

The domaine-bottled wine is fermented in open wood vats, the wine sold to the *négoce* trade in a mix of steel and concrete. About 20 per cent of the crop is destemmed, and no outside yeasts or enzymes are used. The process lasts about three weeks, with a couple of *pigeages* a day. The aim is to be laissez-faire.

The domaine red is aged for a year, mainly in barrels up to 50 hl, and in 400-litre casks, all five years and older. The bulk wine stays just six months. The reds carry a refinement that places them a long way from the more tub-thumping black and bouncy flavours of the purely *Chassis* and southern Crozes areas. Peppery flavours and a sprinkling of refined tannins are evident. They are made to last and can run beyond 10 years in the best vintages.

The Marsanne and Roussanne are harvested late by preference. The crop is vinified and raised in steel, and bottled with its malo done in September, a year on. These are good wines: their white fruit has a nutty side, in best Marsanne fashion, and their aromas are delicate. Age expands them and makes them more substantial.

Laurent is keen to keep the price of his wines realistic: "I don't want surgeons or notaries to be the only people drinking our wine—I'd like it to be accessible to a large part of the population, so as we move to more domaine bottling, I'm trying to keep prices reasonable."

CROZES-HERMITAGE ROUGE

2003 ★★ Well-knit bouquet; raspberry fruit has a Larnage feel to it. Black jam fruit flavour, some sweetness. Tidy wine, length is good. Herbal, southern-climes end. 2010-11.

2002 ★★ Smoky, black fruit aromas; red fruits flavours, elegant, some spice. 2010–11.

2001 ★★★ Some earthy, fruit gum aroma; peppery, grainy flavour with some tannin—granite side of Crozes. Funky, tar aspects like a St-Joseph. Tannins evident on finish. Has character. 2009–11.

2000 ★★ Crabapple, supple, stewed nose; soft, strawberry style jam flavour, suave, easy, can sing. Fine, typical of Gervans. 2008–10.

CROZES-HERMITAGE BLANC

2003 ★★★ Floral, with latent fat on bouquet. Nicely rich, chewy palate, almonds there, sound width, pretty fullness. Some end alcohol. 2010–11.

2002 ★★ Fleshed white fruits, *crème patisserie* bouquet, rounded. White fruit/flan combo, nicely knit with good midpalate. Nice fresh end, pretty.

2000 ★★

1999 ★★

1998 ★★

Export 10 per cent (1) Canada, (2) USA, (3) Great Britain

DOMAINE DES HAUTS CHASSIS

Les Hauts Chassis 26600 La Roche-de-Glun
+33(0)475 845026

Franck Faugier started his own enterprise, the Domaine des Hauts Chassis, in 2003. It is a project that he had planned for a long time, since three previous generations had either grown grapes or made wine on the family domaine at Les Chassis.

"I waited until my father retired in 1998," he explains. "I had always wanted to work with my own domaine-bottled wine, while my father continued with the Co-opérative. I did wine studies at Bordeaux, but then worked in different fields such as sales for the Mars confec-

tionary company. I didn't want to join the domaine without being able to make the wine and sell it as well." Reaching 40 in 2005, he has exercised patience in his quest.

He has picked up the tradition of his grandfather, who used to sell his wine locally. In the 1950s and 1960s, wine and then harvest were sold to Paul Jaboulet Aîné, until his father joined the Tain Co-opérative in 1969.

There are 12 hectares, all Syrah and all on the stony *Les Chassis* in the *commune* of La Roche-de-Glun. The prize section is over four hectares of Syrah dating from around the 1930s, while another four hectares trace back to the 1950s and 1960s. The remainder are young vines.

Three reds are made—the classic, Ésquisse, is a young-vines, vat-only cuvée that is bottled in March. The next is Les Galets, made from the vines dating from 20 to 50 years. This receives a year in one-to-three-year-old casks. The top wine, Les Chassis, is selected from the best of the old vine plots each year and is aged for a year in new *demi-muids* of 550 litres.

"My vinification is based on plot selection," states Franck. "Twelve hectares—12 fermentation vats. I perform a pre-fermentation cool maceration and like to do plenty of cap punching and pumping-overs, two a day of the latter, with a postfermentation raising of the temperature to 32° to 34°C." Up to 15 per cent of the stalks can be retained.

CROZES-HERMITAGE LES GALETS ROUGE

2003 ★(★) From 2006; 2011–12

CROZES-HERMITAGE LES CHASSIS ROUGE

2003 ★(★) Full *robe*; mixed attack—black stone fruit, then oak, and a cool, oaked finish. Upright at 15 months. Leave till 2006, hope oak calms. Wee bit taut. 2012–14.

PAUL JABOULET AÎNÉ

26600 Pont-de-l'Isère +33(0)475 846893

See also Condrieu, Cornas, Côte-Rôtie, Hermitage, St-Joseph, St-Péray.

A big step forward for Paul Jaboulet Aîné came with their 1995 purchase of the core of the Raymond Roure vineyard and the rights to the name for the wines from 1996. Another part of the vineyard was transferred to M. Roure's nephew, Robert Rousset, who lives in the next village of Erôme.

M. Roure had been one of the great *originals*, a one-off with a legendary temper and fearsome aspect for a young foreigner climbing up his slope to see him in the early 1970s. This was raw, sharp-edge farming, with the clutter to endorse it, and lots of abundant apricot trees would populate the hot vineyard outside the backdoor of the cellar. When these required attention, which was mainly picking the fruit rather than anything more refined, the wine would go on hold. So the site was fabulous, and occasionally the wines, like the odd bottle of 1978 Les Picaudières, were mighty.

Jaboulet have embarked on a lot of tidying up across the more than seven hectares they bought. The apricot trees have been bade farewell, and replanting has occurred. Old vines remain, though. The oldest of the 3.1 hectares of Marsanne on *Les Blancs* exceed 100 years; "I know this because I found shoots buried 20 cm (8 in.) down in the soil, like they used to just after phylloxera," comments Jacques Jaboulet. These grow around Roure's house, on light, sandy ground with loess present that Jacques describes as "asparagus soil."

This is quite different from the richer ground of their other white vineyard, whose fruit goes into the Mule Blanche Crozes. 10,000 bottles of white Domaine Roure are made, and its style should be notably different from the Mule Blanche. Late 1990s winemaking was so powerful that the delicacy of this wine was not strikingly evident, but a greater sense of elegance has emerged more recently.

The 4.58 ha of acquired Syrah are in the *communes* of Crozes and Gervans. The Crozes-Hermitage plot is 2.4 ha on the sanded granite of *Les Voussères*, a 1960s vineyard of Syrah. The sites at Gervans are *Sassenas*, *Hauterives*, and *Les Blancs*. Over 2 ha of Syrah plus Marsanne and

Roussanne were planted in the late 1990s on *Les Blancs* and on *Sassenas*, while the *Hauterives* Syrah dates from the late 1970s. These sites are notably windier than Jaboulet's *Thalabert* vineyard on *Les Chassis*, and this freshness means that the Domaine Roure reds will always be more refined and less versed towards the plump jam textures of Thalabert. "This white soil for me signifies that you should drink the wine old," states Jacques Jaboulet.

In 1996 Jaboulet bought 2.83 ha on the *Chassis* plain from Michel Ferraton. This Syrah vineyard is adjacent to their *Thalabert* vineyard; 1.5 ha was planted in 1976, the rest a few years later. Its crop now contributes to the Thalabert wine.

Since the 1970s, the main emblem for Crozes-Hermitage around the world has been Jaboulet's red wine, Thalabert, which since 1980 has been called "Domaine de Thalabert." This is made only from their own Syrah crop, and around 200,000 to 230,000 bottles are produced in a normal year.

This is a jewel in Jaboulet's vineyard portfolio. *Thalabert* is an area of precisely 39.44 ha, its Syrah's average age around 50 years. In active production there are around 36 ha, the rest being part of the continuing replanting programme. The two largest chunks are over 20 ha on the *Conflans Nord lieu-dit*, with over 10 on *Les Chassis* itself. Because it is at the 7 Chemins meeting place, the former is in the *commune* of Mercurol, the latter in La Roche-de-Glun. In the early 2000s, the family also bought a neighbouring walled *clos*, the *Clos de Conflans*, which has the potential for a 5 ha vineyard.

The *Thalabert* vineyard is about one kilometre from the Jaboulet offices, in the middle to western side of *Les Chassis*. "The Jaboulets were the first family to plant vines on *Les Chassis*," states Michel Jaboulet; "it was a fruit farm, and we bought today's domaine in two gos." Before the Crozes-Hermitage *appellation* came into being in 1956, its wine was called "Côtes du Rhône Thalabert."

The vineyard at *Thalabert* is treated against pests from the air, and the mechanical theme also means that the Syrah is destalked, largely due to the machine harvesting across the *Chassis* plain. The crop is vinified in a mix of concrete and steel, and after the alcoholic fermentation at up to 28° to 30°C, there are a further two weeks or so of maceration. External yeasts can be used.

From 1990 greater extraction was sought, with must contact for 44 days that year and 40 days in 1991—a very long maceration, with the temperature controlled at around 27°C. This means that there are usually more stewed flavours in the 1990s and more lithe, "dark" flavours in the 1980s.

To some extent, Thalabert's vinification changes reflect the fact that there is frequently no fixed policy here. Take cask ageing, for instance: this lasted 18 months for the 1990 and 16 for the 1991. It has been 11 to 16 months since 2000.

New-oak policy for Thalabert was stepped up in the late 1980s, then relaxed again. The 1988 received 28 per cent new oak, the rest second-year casks, while the 1990 saw 35 per cent new oak. Since 1999 the oak is around five years old, against three-to-six-year-old casks in the mid-1990s and part new oak before that. Ten per cent of the oak can be Hungarian.

The Domaine de Thalabert is always endowed with great fruit extraction and a healthy purple Syrah colour. Throughout the 1980s it was consistently good, be it in lesser years like 1987, beautifully fruited years like 1985, or full-blown years like 1983 and 1988.

Thalabert set off well in the 1990s, with an enormously rich, succulent 1990 and a very successful 1991. Thereafter there were some wobbly years, the best being 1995 and 1998. What seemed less guaranteed was the core richness of the wine, with the extended macerations stretching the flavour away from relaxed warmth. This has continued and even deepened into the 2000s, with some of these wines dangerously dilute when tasted outside France. "Where is Thalabert going?" is a question that mirrors the questions surrounding the House of Jaboulet as a whole.

The best Thalabert generally develops a funky, animal side to it with some age; its fruits are often black and fat, a lush texture prevailing in overt, sunny years like 1997 and 1990. Stewed jams spring to mind, and in its current style it is a wine suitable for drinking earlier than in the past—at around four to six years old, although it can still live longer.

The Domaine Roure red runs to about 18,000 bottles. Like Thalabert, it receives a four-to-five-week *cuvaison* and is raised for 11 to 16 months in two-to-three-year-old casks. The aim seems to be to make an overtly ample wine.

The Roure red is more tender than Thalabert, the colour lighter and redder, the taste a little more lively and refined. The red fruits flavour can be topped off by a touch of minerality. The hauteur and restraint of the granite hill contrasts with the oily chunkiness of the Thalabert's alluvial plain. Signs of greater complexity and potential came through in the Roure *rouge* of 2001 and 2003.

In recent times, two other red Crozes have been produced as one-offs. The special cuvée Famille 2000 Jaboulet Crozes-Hermitage and the Vieilles Vignes 1996 were both taken from the domaine's oldest 1930s and 1940s Syrah, late harvested in October for extreme ripeness, and given an extended vinification.

CROZES-HERMITAGE CUVÉE FAMILLE 2000 JABOULET ROUGE

★★★★ Very dark; ripe bouquet moving towards overripe fruit smells, black fruits, like a pungent Merlot! Dense, berried fruit, warm, rolled-up flavour, the flesh of a mini-Hermitage. Lasts well. Esp 2005–06. 2010–12

CROZES-HERMITAGE VIEILLES VIGNES 1996

★★ Harmonious, plum jam bouquet; red fruits with jam texture, more so than the Thalabert 1996. Rather punchy ending; not easy to judge its evolution and best moment—still rather acid/raw on second half. From 2005–07? 2013–15.

Jaboulet also sell a third Crozes brand, Les Jalets. This is made from young vines on the *Thalabert* and *Roure* domaines, plus the harvest from their stony 5.75-hectare vineyard beside their La Roche-de-Glun offices, and from a mixture of purchased crop and young wine. The stones on this vineyard are Quaternary, a lot larger than the Alpine stones of the *Chassis*.

The Jalets *rouge* Crozes receives no oak. It's aimed to express a pure Syrah feel. It can be dull, as in 1997, 2000, and 2002, or a little more successful, as in 2001, when its perky red fruit was appealing. There is also a simply named red Crozes-Hermitage produced from outside sources.

For the Mule Blanche white Crozes, there are 6.8 hectares in equal measure of Marsanne (1950s) and Roussanne (1970). These are just north of the 7 Chemins crossroads and grow on very stony, alluvial ground mixed with some clay-chalk. The vineyard is named after one of the *Chassis quartiers* in the *commune* of Mercurol.

The final wine of Mule Blanche is 80 per cent from the Jaboulet vineyards, with the other 20 per cent from crop purchase. During the 1990s the Mule Blanche style changed. The grapes are picked late in overripeness to invest more fat into the wine, so it's often a full yellow colour.

The malo has also been revived. From 1964 the Jaboulets blocked the Mule Blanche malolactic fermentation to achieve freshness—remember that the common cry against white Rhônes in those days was that they were all flabby and oxidised. But in 1995 they started to do the malo again—"I want *gras* from these wines," explained vinifier Jacques Jaboulet.

For the vinification, Jaboulet have destemmed their white crop since 1998, with machine harvesting playing a role. Pressing is at around 8° to 10°C, which they say avoids oxidation and gives greater colour. The Mule Blanche is then slowly fermented at just 12° to 14°C in one-third each new, one-year, and two-year-old oak, while the 100 percent–Marsanne Roure *blanc* ferments and is raised partly in 80 per cent new,

20 per cent one-year-old oak, partly in vat. "We want finesse," states Jacques Jaboulet.

Mule Blanche's oak exposure has risen steadily since the mid-1990s—when the wine spent just four months in new or one-year-old casks. Bottling for both the Mule Blanche and the Roure *blanc* comes after 11 months. There are around 50,000 bottles of Mule Blanche and 13,000 of the Roure *blanc*.

The Mule Blanche carries ripe white fruit on the palate, and sometimes the texture is fat. The usual modern-style exotic fruits can parade on the bouquet at first, but these can give way to more nutty aspects and enhanced local feel after three or four years. While top vintages of past decades could live for 20 years or more, nowadays most Mule Blanche should be drunk within eight to 10 years.

The Roure *blanc* accentuates an oily fullness; dried fruits and some honey tones are present. The ripeness of the fruit is apparent, and the wine is best drunk with food because of this.

CROZES-HERMITAGE LES JALETS ROUGE

2003 (CASKS) ★ 2010–12
2002 (★)
2001 ★★

CROZES-HERMITAGE DOMAINE DE THALABERT ROUGE

2003 (CASKS) ★★ Full *robe*; late-picked fruit, black, sappy southern bouquet. Big-scale wine, overt black fruit, tar. Oak abounds, also alcohol—a snorter of a wine. Balance not sure; sweet, low acidity. From 2007; 2013–15.

2002 ★★(★) Subdued *robe*; fruit gum, southern Crozes aroma. Interesting red, raspberry fruit, some sinew, natural. Easy, tasty, length OK. Nice now, to 2008–09.

2001 Different bottles, different notes:

(★) *Robe* is dull; light floral side, gummy fruit, dilute bouquet. Subdued wine, ripe fruit use but is advancing and dries towards end. Stewed fruit/oak mix doesn't work well. Best drunk now or soon. 2008–09. Last tasted June 2004.

★★★ Smoky, black fruit/soil aromas; tasty and juicy. *Gourmand* wine, nicely broad—blackberry/raspberry. Some game aspects, good tannins. Now or from 2005–06; 2015–18. Last tasted Dec. 2003.

2000 ★★ Aromatic plum/prune nose, quite ripe; smoky, black jam palate, oily finish. Fruit gums, some width. Not a lot of mystery, has the one dimension. Quite persistent. Esp 2005–06. 2012–14.

1999 ★★(★) Very dark; full, grapey ripe bouquet, interesting potential; good weight, a soaked texture on the palate, decent tannins in support. Quite strong extract wine, risk that it is stretched. 2011–14.

1998 ★★★ Dark; overtly ripe harvest aroma, a leathery aspect also. Opulent, fleshy, ripe fruit flavour, cooked texture on it. More overt warmth than the 1999. Very soaked, luscious wine. 2010–12.

> **1997** ★★ 2007–09
> **1996** ★★★ 2011–12
> **1995** ★★★ 2012–14
> **1994** ★★★ 2006–07
> **1993** Dilute
> **1992** *Flatteur* wine
> **1991** ★★★★★ 2007–11

1990 ★★★★★ Usual oily texture here; cooked fruits bouquet, more leathery with air, starting to advance now. Pretty fullness on palate, good roundness. Black fruits evolving towards prune. Less flamboyant as it matures. 2011–14.

> **1989** ★★ Drink now.
> **1988** ★★★ Drink soon.

CROZES-HERMITAGE DOMAINE ROURE ROUGE

2003 (CASK) ★★★★ Minted, bosky bouquet, pebbly, northern granite side. Pretty fruit, clear and appealing definition. Length sound. Good mineral-tinged finish. Stylish potential. From 2007; 2017–20.

2001 ★★★ Tender raspberry, live aroma; refined red and plum fruits with a jam touch in midpalate. Flow of friendly tannins, mineral ending. Don't drink young, wait till 2006. 2016–18.

2000 ★★ Quite fine aroma, floral and some fruit, dusty bits; gentle red berry attack, has quite refined juice, more acidity than Thalabert. Chewy, licorice, ripe grape finish, touch stretched. Dry, rather powdery tannins need till 2005–06 to meld in. 2008–10.

1999 ★★★ Red quite tight, upright bouquet—the cooler Gervans effect; warm attack, supple with lots of soaked fruit matter, black currant everywhere. Some licorice on finish. Lot of fruit here, simple at present, can broaden. Sweet end. 2010–12.

1998 ★ Smoky bouquet, red meat, high aroma. Quite plump on palate—plums/prunes. Stretched, dries at end, thins out. Pebbly finish. 2006–07.

> **1997** ★★ 2007–09
> **1996** ★★★ 2009–11

CROZES-HERMITAGE MULE BLANCHE BLANC

2003 ★★ Quite warm bouquet—varnish, exotic, pineapple aromas. Oak/dried fruits palate —rich, its glycerol persists most of way, then tapers. Early, low-acidity wine, sound enough.

2002 ★ Light honey, buttered/oak bouquet, low-key. Flan flavour, quiet *gras*, oily texture. Oak tightens it quite fast. Some length; a food wine, soft and simple.

2001 ★★ Toasty, nutty bouquet. Quite juicy, fleshy palate, not too overdone. Elegant wine, reserved towards finish. Some richness and style, has done better with age. Sound length. 2008–09.

2000 ★★★ Quite yellow; delicate sides to the bouquet, fruit tart, custard. Palate mixes apricots, warm texture with dried fruits; warm. Drink soon, before 2007; sauced fish best.

> **1999** ★★
> **1998** ★
> **1997** ★

CROZES-HERMITAGE DOMAINE ROURE BLANC

2003 ★★ Quite broad bouquet—mixes honey, apricot, oak, some freshness. Interesting combo of flavours—spiced apricots, pear *eau de vie*. Ripe fruit use evident, also potency.

Some richness through it, ends with heat, slight gasp.

2002 ★★ Warm, soft bouquet, understated, some potential. Nice soft style, rounded with fair width. Correct Marsanne almond, bitter tinge at end. Decent midweight; gentle food wine. 2009–10.

2001 ★★ Nicely full, broad bouquet of spice/mineral; lot of fat on palate, citrus start, then white fruit. Honeyed end, fair length.

2000 ★★ Yellow; white fruit, lime/floral/buttery nose. Savoury, fat flavour, runs nicely; stone fruit, mineral end, has improved. 2010.

1999 ★
1998 Disorderly
1997 ★
1996 ★★

PATRICK LESEC

Moulin de Bargeton BP 6201 30702 Uzès +33(0)466 376720

See also Cornas, Hermitage, St-Joseph.
Patrick Lesec, ex-Californian restaurateur, has had a large impact on Philippe Desmeure's Domaine des Remizières. His wines are the red and white Cuvée Christophe that have been mainly sold to the North American market. The red receives 60 per cent new, 40 per cent one-year-old oak and is raised for 12 to 14 months.

The white is 90 per cent Marsanne, 10 per cent Roussanne; thankfully its new-oak proportion has been reduced to 30 per cent, the rest being one-year-old casks.

The Sélection Patrick Lesec wine is therefore the same as the Cuvée Christophe sold under the Remizières name. If oak is your style, this is the address for you.

DOMAINE JEAN MARSANNE

25 ave Ozier 07300 Mauves +33(0)475 088626

See also St-Joseph.
Jean and Jean-Claude Marsanne work a 0.8-hectare west-facing Syrah vineyard (1978–83) at Crozes-Hermitage, where the bottom slopes become flat plain. The soil is a mix of alluvial deposit, with some granite and clay.

The crop is destalked, only natural yeasts are used, and a traditional vinification lasts three weeks. The wine is raised for a year in used-oak casks and then in vat for six months.

It follows the house style of a light fruit, fine-toned texture.

CROZES-HERMITAGE ROUGE
1999 ★
1998 ★

DOMAINE DES MARTINELLES

2 route de Vignes 26600 Gervans +33(0)475 077060

See also Hermitage.
Moving away from the Cave de Tain and arrangements with local *négociants*, Pascal and Aimé Fayolle set off to produce their own domaine wine in 2003. They work 14 hectares in the northern sector of Crozes, and so are much larger than most domaines in the northern sector. Their holdings are in the *communes* of Larnage, Gervans, Erôme, and Crozes-Hermitage, with just a slope vineyard at Mercurol outside the main northern run.

"My grandfather Louis used to vinify here at the property," states Pascal, a man of sandy-coloured hair and blue eyes. "But he sold the wine to local merchants, like Léon Revol and Chapoutier. When Chapoutier said they didn't want the 1968 crop, he sent it off to the Cave de Tain, and we stayed with them until 2002."

Pascal was born in 1971, his father, Aimé, in 1946, so the time was right for the new approach, before Aimé's retirement. The family also work a healthy 5.95 hectares of Hermitage, whose wine would be sold to Guigal, so Martinelles can become an important extra name in that *appellation* as well. The outlook here is one of steady, unassuming application.

Les Martinelles is the site on the right side of the road running up to the village of Crozes-Hermitage from the N7; *Les Cornirets* and *Les Pontaix*, with vineyards worked by cousin

Fayolles, lie across this road, making it an enclave for the extended family. There are 3.5 hectares there, the soil clay-limestone beside the road with some granite a little higher up. Its Syrah was planted in 1975 and 1999–2000.

In all, there are just under 11 hectares of Syrah. For the special red Crozes Les Coteaux, the Syrah is taken from two sites, *Tenay*—part terrace, part plateau at Gervans on sanded granite—and *Les Bâties*, a granite–red clay and stony site at Larnage. The Syrah on both dates from the 1960s.

The red Crozes is vinified over two to three weeks; the classic wine (6,000 bottles) receives six to 12 months in used 600-litre *demi-muids*, the Coteaux wine (3,000 bottles) 12 to 14 months. A light filtration is done.

The regular Domaine des Martinelles *rouge* carries black fruit flavours with good ripeness present, even in 2002. It has more character than many of the classic-level wines of Crozes. The Coteaux does its name justice, the cool cut of its flavour issuing from its granite, with tannins to stabilise it. At times, it comes across as traditional and rather too earthy, as if clearer fruit expression would benefit it.

There are a little over three hectares of Marsanne, mainly from the Larnage white clay or kaolin. It is fermented in three-to-four-year-old *demi-muids* and is left on its fine lees until the malolactic has been completed. Bottling can be after eight months, with 2,400 bottles produced. This is full wine, with the imprint of good-quality Marsanne present, and its handling is not overdone.

The Fayolles are busy men, in the vein of the northern zone's mixed fruit and vine heritage. Their 17 hectares of apricots have a preharvesting in June before picking through July, and their five hectares of pears (*poire William*) are cropped in the second and third weeks of August. Then it's only a matter of time before the grapes need harvesting.

CROZES-HERMITAGE DOMAINE
DES MARTINELLES ROUGE

2003 ★★ 2010–12

2002 ★★(★) 2011–13

CROZES-HERMITAGE LES COTEAUX ROUGE

2003 ★★ Ripe fruit, raisin aroma. Mature fruit, a brewed style of wine, earthy. Almost a rustic nature. Tannins are present, just wonder if may tire earlier than expected. Has become funkier in last six months. 2010–12. Last tasted March 2005.

CROZES-HERMITAGE DOMAINE
DES MARTINELLES BLANC

2004 (CASK) ★★ Green apple, floral hints on bouquet—will settle and become nuttier. Palate rich, calm wine with good length. Rolls along well, good Marsanne expression. Promising.

2003 ★★★ Yellow traces on *robe*; subdued, ripe fruit bouquet. Full style, Marsanne allowed to run wild (well, is 2003). Plenty of flavour and texture, with nice end grip. Traditional, complete wine. 2013–15.

GABRIEL MEFFRE

84190 Gigondas +33(0)490 123021

See also Condrieu, Côte-Rôtie, Cornas, Hermitage, St-Joseph.

The red is sourced from the granite of Gervans. The crop is destemmed and receives a three-week vatting, the top temperature 28° to 30°C; there are three pumping-overs a day.

The wine is aged for 18 months in the special Meffre 275-litre casks, one-third new, the rest one to two years old. It is fined but not filtered. Until three to four years old, the oak can be a very potent presence in the wine. Thereafter, a softer tone of fruit emerges, the wine capable of living for 10 years or so.

CROZES-HERMITAGE LAURUS ROUGE

2003 ★★ From 2007; 2011–12

2001 ★★★ 2009–10

DOMAINE MICHELAS SAINT JEMMS

Bellevue Les Chassis 26600 Mercurol +33(0)475 078670

See also Cornas, Hermitage, St-Joseph.

Given the wide open spaces at Crozes-Hermitage, there are some domaines that give the impression of being businesslike and involved in volume operations. This domaine has grown a lot since Robert Michelas left the Tain Coopérative in the late 1970s. His family have been winegrowers at Saint-Jemms since 1851, and when he owned just 12 hectares of Crozes in the early 1980s, father Michelas used to express his hopes about his daughter Sylvie. She was then due to take her *sommelière* exams, which he felt would help her to promote the family wine.

Well, things have moved faster than that. "Since 1988, we expanded a lot in the cellar and in the vineyards," states Sylvie today. She is one of life's doers, no messing around. Hence there are 36 hectares of Syrah at Crozes, 1.7 of Marsanne and 0.3 of Roussanne.

The sites are largely in three zones: the Mercurol end of *Les Chassis*; the southern part of *Chassis* at Pont-de-l'Isère on *Les Blâches*—stony, alluvial land with a free-draining gravel substratum; and the white clay near the Château de Larnage.

There are also vineyards at St-Joseph, Cornas, Hermitage, and a *vin de pays*, along with apricots, peaches, and cherries in production. But there are also three brothers and sisters to help her—Florence and Corinne in the cellar and the youngest, Sebastien, who joined in 2001 and works mostly in the vineyards.

The Crozes Syrah crop is machine harvested, which serves to destem. The classic wine, Signature, is purely vat fermented and raised. External yeasts are used, and there is some pumping-over. The next red, La Chasselière, is made from Mercurol Syrah dating from 1958 and from older vines at Pont-de-l'Isère. This receives six to eight months or more in large barrels. In 2003 a special oaked wine was launched— receiving a year's ageing in half new, half one-year-old casks. The wines are fined and filtered.

The two *vins de pays* Les Grivelles—a Syrah and a Marsanne—come from the sandy soil of Clérieux, between Tain and Romans-sur-Isère.

The Crozes are accessible, commercial wines, usually good for early drinking. The fruit is in the easy, forward black/light tar style of the southern plain.

CROZES-HERMITAGE SIGNATURE ROUGE
2002 ★

CROZES-HERMITAGE LA CHASSELIÈRE ROUGE
2003 ★★ From 2006; 2011–13
2002 ★
2001 ★

CROZES-HERMITAGE SIGNATURE BLANC
2002 ★

Export 12 per cent (1) Belgium, (2) Great Britain

DOMAINE DU MURINAIS

Quartier Champ Bernard 26600 Beaumont-Monteux
+33(0)475 073476

It's hard to forget a young couple who have started to make their own wine in the house the family has occupied since 1683. An enterprise like this needs guts and determination: there's the wine, its perfection, and the accompanying headaches of getting the house into shape to be a good home for both children and wine.

This is the challenge facing Luc and Catherine Tardy. Their domaine stands on the plain outside Beaumont-Monteux, the main house dates from 1774, and its pretty courtyard is lined along one side by a typical seventeenth-century Dauphinois monastic top corridor.

The family's ace card in centuries gone by was the stream that ran through the land. The plain around Beaumont-Monteux is arid, so this house became the most important one near the village. Now the stables are used for wine storage, with plenty of space on site. The casks are in a cellar dating from 1801, and some of the bottle stock area was used for silkworms until around the 1960s. So the venue is wonderful for winemaking and is quite unlike the generally functional wine cellars of the Crozes *appellation*.

There are 13 hectares of vines south of the domaine, in four main plots, all of them within

FIGURE 21 Zeal and motivation to burn—Luc and Catherine Tardy in their Beaumont-Monteux vineyard on the southern plain of Crozes. (Tim Johnston)

Beaumont-Monteux. There are four soil types as well—clay on *Les Amandiers* and limestone on *Colombier*, then close to the Isère further south, the very gravelly *Les Croix* area and *Le Port*. Of the last named, Luc says, "It's very gravelly, but also rich in trace elements since cereal was grown on it; that's why any vine or fruit crops from there are very healthy."

One-third of the vineyard is under 15 years old, one-third 15 to 25 years, and the final third older vines. There are two reds: Amandiers, from 15-to-25-year-old vines and aimed to be fresh fruit wine; and the Vieilles Vignes, made from two hectares of 65-year-old vines at *Les Croix*, one hectare at *Le Port*, and 1.5 hectares on *Les Amandiers*—the last two aged 35 to 65 years.

Luc is a slim, wiry man with dark hair and wire glasses; one wonders how he takes the work. He is possessed of a clear mind and describes himself as more the intellectual and nervous end of the family. The youngest of five, he was the only child interested. "My father always took me into the vineyards, which I enjoyed, and those early memories served me well."

He works largely on his own, with his father lending a hand in the cellar. Born in 1971, he attended the Montpellier School and is a qualified *oenologue*. He moves around at speed, and likes frankness in wine and in life. "Too many wines are dirty because their makers have tried too many tricks. They end up lacking clarity—wine should resemble the grapes that go into it," he declares with a sharp-eyed look. His work is promising: Luc takes the process of making his wines personally—they represent him—rather like a father hoping his child won't let the family down.

Luc sent his crop to the Tain Co-opérative until 1997. In 1998 the new vinification cellar was built. The vats are concrete, and the crop is worked as whole as it can be after machine harvesting, which is done in the morning from 6 to 11 for freshness. Maceration is long—five days at 15° to 18°C, which leaves the yeasts quiet—followed by at least two weeks' fermentation at 30° to 32°C. "I do it this way," he explains, "so the cooling brings out colour and red fruits from the grapes. Then the warmer fermentation brings out a more stone fruit, prune aroma. I halt the maceration when I taste a marc effect coming through."

Until 2001 he made two reds; the Amandiers, is raised for 12 months in vat. This is meant to be a get-on-and-drink wine with some local feel, not too sleek. The Vieilles Vignes stays a year in oak that is one, two, and three years old.

He launched a third red in 2001, Caprice de Valentin, named after his young son. "I narrowed 150 casks down to seven by constant tasting and checking, and gave them five months extra in cask, again using mostly two-year casks."

In 2002 he had the good sense to drastically cut back the amount of wine he bottled: 17,000 bottles against around 60,000 in 2001. The 2002 Amandiers is indeed light, the prototype Vieilles Vignes a touch fuller. It's a year for raising the wine in the more tender *demi-muid* size of 550 litres, than for the smaller, 228 cl cask.

The Amandiers *rouge* holds fair tannins to accompany the fruit, giving it a little more structure than many basic cuvées; it can run for around eight years and has shown itself to be respectful of the vintage style. In general, the Vieilles Vignes carries blackberry fruit laced with some minerality and some pepper touches. It is gentler than the Pont-de-l'Isère special cuvées from vineyards a little to the west. It sets off fruited and can then withdraw and come back with extra complexity after five years.

Luc's white, named "Marine" after his daughter, is pure Marsanne, taken from a half-hectare plot planted in 1981 on the limestone of *Colombier*. Luc planted 0.7 hectare of Roussanne in 2000 there as well, and in future may add around 15 per cent to his Marsanne and bottle up the rest as its own separate cuvée. This is more arid soil than that usually found for most white Crozes.

It is vinified and raised over six to eight months in one-third a mix of new and one-year-old oak, two-thirds in vat. Luc picks late, just before the grapes turn towards rot. He then stirs the lees to gain richness. The malolactic fermentation is blocked to add freshness. My view is that these wines display finesse despite their active, modern handling thanks to the soil here. "I like whites that do well as an aperitif, more than being made for food," is how Luc sees it.

CROZES-HERMITAGE LES AMANDIERS ROUGE
2003 ★★ From 2006; 2011–12
2002 (★)
2001 ★★ 2010–11
2000 ★★ 2007–09
1999 ★ 2006–08

CROZES-HERMITAGE VIEILLES VIGNES ROUGE
2002 (CASK) ★ Light fruit aroma; light cherry jam, some end sweetness. Simple, drink with undemanding flavours. 2008–09.

2001 ★★★ Smoky-topped, cooked fruit nose; compact blackberry, nice cut. Easy density; mineral end. Best: second phase, from 2006; 2015–16.

2000 (CASK) ★★★ Evenly fruited nose; good clean matter, some cool, peppered tannins, violets, decent intensity. 2009–11.

1999 ★★ Dark fruit/oak, quite funky aroma; violet, has character, taut tannins. More zest than core *Les Chassis* wines. Bit stretched. 2006–09.

CROZES-HERMITAGE CAPRICE DE VALENTIN ROUGE
2003 ★★ Olives-kirsch mixed bouquet—full, grilled, and southern. Although oak prominent, has the richness to handle it so far. Black jam, olive tapenade flavour. A constructed wine, out of line with the norm here. Esp from 2008; 2014–15.

2001 ★★★ Ripe *robe*; grilled nuts nose, was black fruit; compact, firm *cassis*, fair mid-*gras*. Oily, smooth; dry end. From 2008; 2017–18.

CROZES-HERMITAGE MARINE BLANC
2002 —
2001 ★★
2000 ★
1999 ★★

Export 70 per cent (1) Norway, (2) Great Britain, (3) USA

CAVES OGIER

10 ave Pasteur 84230 Châteauneuf-du-Pape
+33(0)490 393232

See also Hermitage, St-Joseph.
The southern Rhône house of Ogier presents a Crozes red under its own name that is modern in style, a big extraction affair with an overt oak presence. It is aged for a year in 600-litre *demimuid* casks and comes in a heavy bottle.

CROZES-HERMITAGE LES ALLÉGORIES D'ANTOINE OGIER ROUGE

2001 ★ From 2006; 2010–11

Under the Caves des Papes title, there is a Crozes called "Oratorio." The 2001 was uneven, with some oily black flavour, but also a rather singed, withering effect on the palate.

DOMAINE DU PAVILLON-MERCUROL

Les Chassis 26600 Mercurol +33(0)475 079912

Set in his own independent groove, Stéphane Cornu, a slim man with a gambolling walk and a strong, piercing blue-eyed gaze, turns out some of the most fully fruited wines of the *appellation*. There's a latent artist in him, the person who doesn't give much of a fig about his public face and who lives life under his own terms. Now in his late 30s, he has married a woman whose natural, easy charm combines well with his busy, wired persona.

There's been a lot of work in progress chez Cornu for over a decade. This includes the property—the rather ramshackle farm building and the cellar—and also Stéphane's stubble, which at times breaks into full beard status. It's no surprise to learn that he works all alone—Stéphane has always appeared to juggle many a task all at the same time. The old cellar, for instance, used to be distinguished by an old, heavily wine-stained wooden table, no doubt cherished by its owner, and piled high with bric-a-brac, while wrenches, funnels, measuring sticks, and glasses lay around the periphery.

The cellar's structure, access, and interior have been worked on for two years, and the high-light is an open-hearthed fireplace, an antique. "Hey, Myrhiam," he calls to his wife, in his part gruff, part humorous way, "come over to the confessional." Over comes Myrhiam, her own startling pale blue eyes a match for Stéphane's. She is earth, the ground, and exudes human warmth. She looks after abandoned dogs and cats, to socialise them before finding them new homes. One of their hobbies is to take their horses and trap off to the Pavillon itself on its little raised ridge, and have a picnic, a bucolic picture well in keeping with their natures.

Stéphane learnt the trade on the job, outdoors, and works vineyards bought and planted by his grandfather in 1971, after he moved to Mercurol from the Ardèche. Pears and vines were both grown here, with his father, Alphonse, selling his own wine to Paul Jaboulet Aîné. The first bottling came in 1989.

Stéphane covers 12 hectares of Syrah and a hectare of Marsanne (1976, 1994). There are eight hectares around the domaine, whose name comes from the hunting Pavillon that stands next to the *Meysonniers* vineyard on the south end of *Les Chassis*. The soil there is draining, with a lot of smooth glacial stones. These Syrah mostly date from 1969 and 1971. In 2000 he planted a former peach grove with 2.5 hectares of Syrah at Mercurol, on clay soil with just a few stones. There are also about two hectares of 1995 Syrah on the more red-clay soil towards *Les Chênes Verts* near Alain Graillot. This last wine is sold to the *négoce* trade.

The domaine now works with *agro-biologique* status: "I worked the soil already," says Stéphane, "but the full organic licence came through in 2000."

After machine harvesting, the Syrah ends up 70 per cent destalked and is fermented in concrete over three weeks, using only natural yeasts, during which time the temperature can rise to 35°C. There is the odd *délestage* for extra concentration, but no pumping-over or cap punching.

There is just the one red wine, the Domaine du Pavillon, whose 35,000 bottles represent around 40 per cent of the production. The rest is sold in bulk. The Pavillon's stay in oak has increased since 2000; the malolactic now occurs in oak, not concrete, and the stay has extended from between eight and 12 months to 15 months, using 25 per cent each new and one-year-old oak, the difference up to four years old. There is now also just one bottling, and still a light fining and filtration.

"I like my wines to have the best possible length on the palate," states Stéphane, his head tilted to the right as he explains. "They may be penalised at first on their aromas, but after four to five years, they come into their own. That's why I don't cool the crop pre-fermentation, for instance." His wines are full, fruited, well-grounded, and very consistent.

When he makes a white—there was none in 2001 and 2002—Stéphane considers it capable of living at least 10 years, helped by ripening that takes it to a natural 13+°. In a vintage like 1999, this is abundantly true to its place, a big wine with depth and a nutty side to it. The white's 1976 Marsanne is on a slope at the *Chassis* end of Mercurol; the other, 1994 half grows on the flat *Conflans* area of southern Mercurol. Ten per cent is new-cask fermented; the remainder is fermented in enamel vats left at natural cellar temperature. It is bottled, with the malo blocked, after 15 months.

CROZES-HERMITAGE DOM DU PAVILLON ROUGE

2003 —

2001 ★★★ Funky, *cassis* leaf aroma, dense; lightly stewed black fruit, ripe, juicy, chewy. Accessible, quiet richness. Tannins sound. Flattens a bit with air. 2010–13.

2000 ★★★ Cooked fruit/raspberry/pepper nose; tight-knit black fruits, *gras* all through; full, good weight, floral side. Prune ending. 2011–12.

1998 ★★★ 2010–12

CROZES-HERMITAGE BLANC

1999 ★★★ 2012–14

Export 99 per cent (1) USA, (2) Switzerland, (3) Great Britain

DOMAINE PERRIN

The Perrin family of Château de Beaucastel at Châteauneuf-du-Pape produced one or two wines around 1998 as part of their merchant business. These combined wine and grapes bought by them. Quality was fair. This line has been discontinued.

ÉTIENNE POCHON

Château Curson 26600 Chanos Curson
+33(0)475 073460

Étienne Pochon matches his wines: he conveys finesse in his appearance and bearing, his voice is soft and harmonious and—presto!—his wines are like him, especially the Château Curson cuvée, which is some way ahead of his regular-quality red. In this top wine a little of his measured, sometimes intense outlook emerges. His life has moved on a step, too, with his marrying a Parisienne at a later-than-usual age and with two children born since 2000.

His domaine lies due east of Tain, off the road to Romans-sur-Isère. The Château dates from the late sixteenth century and has been in the family for 200 years, although not lived in recently. The views are sweeping here, with gentle slopes suited to machine working, rows of wire-trained vines, and maize, corn, and vegetables growing as well.

Étienne and his father, Edouard, expanded home production from zero to 50,000 bottles between 1988 and 1990. They had been Co-opérateurs with Tain from 1965 to 1987, selling their harvest. Like all subscribers, they were on five-year contracts that are difficult and expensive to break if the *viticulteur* wants to leave. They started to vinify from seven hectares in 1988 and now work 14.5 hectares of Crozes, split 10.5 hectares Syrah, three Marsanne, and one Roussanne.

The white grows all around Château Curson itself, on gravelly, largely sandy soil with some clay that is deep enough to retain water, unlike many parts of the main plain of *Les Chassis*. There are 12.5 hectares in the *commune* of

Chanos-Curson and two hectares at Beaumont-Monteux to the south, where the soil is very meagre and does not retain moisture.

Since 1995 they have bottled all their red and, since 1998, all their white wine. Their proportion of 30 per cent white is about three times the average for Crozes. While the reds outpoint the whites, there are just times when I wish a little more personal imprint from M. Pochon's hand would come through in them. The cellar techniques here seem to reflect the textbook rather than the full-blooded commitment of a Questor, but then, that's not the man he is. Perhaps he's a crack poker player in his spare time.

He explains his use of organic fertilizers and how he is moving towards a more natural combatting of pests. "I'm glad we have vines on the slopes and the plain," he says. "I get a decent maturity and some good acidity off the *coteau*, but on the plain the potassium levels have been diminished over the years through the use of chemical treatments, which gives less chance of a sound acidity."

Between 1988 and 1990 he tried some machine harvesting but gave it up in 1991 to secure a better sorting of the crop. "The costs are probably three times higher, but we can get that back from the bottle price. The southeast of France has suffered from acid rot, on top of the usual rot, and any grapes like that can only be discarded by hand." Likewise, he is aware of just how much the vineyard is inclined to produce if left alone—80 to 90 hl/ha, way above the 45 hl/ha base, 50 hl/ha buffer amount allowed. So there is plenty of cutting back and dropping of bunches during the ripening season.

The oldest Syrah vines, which date from 1964–66, stand all around the château and his cellars; their fruit is vinified apart to form a basis for the Château Curson cuvée, a wine from specific plots. The crop for both reds, the classic and the Curson, is destalked, and vinification is modern. Cultured yeasts are used to provoke fermentation in stainless steel, and there are twice-daily pumping-overs, as well as a *délestage* (part emptying and refilling of the vat) when the specific gravity hits around 1030.

"We've done this since 1999," comments M. Pochon; "it substitutes for a cap punching and can calm a vat's progress."

Since 2000 his basic red and white have changed names from "Domaine Pochon" to "Étienne Pochon." The Étienne Pochon red is mostly bottled in July, after six months' raising in casks of three to six years old. Like the Curson, it is both fined and filtered. This provides live fruit in its first couple of years before widening and becoming more earthy. It's a good example of the simple Crozes red that is good to drink inside five years or so. This regained its form in the late 1990s, although the very light 2002 should have been helped out by the Château Curson crop.

The top red cuvée, Château Curson (28,000 bottles), is very good, and a wine of star price quality in a vintage like 2001. It is chosen by tasting just after vinification and is raised over 11 months in oak that is one-third new, two-thirds one to two years old. Its elegant, spiced black fruit is woven into some oakiness when young, and it repays patient cellaring, blossoming well after four or five years.

The Marsanne in M. Pochon's whites receives a *macération pelliculaire*, with a gentler pneumatic press used since 1999. After destemming, the crop is vinified in steel at between 18° and 20°C and bottled in mid-April. In years like 2000 the malolactic fermentation was not done because the crop was very ripe and low in acidity. By contrast, he is more likely to let the Roussanne do its malo because of its higher intrinsic freshness, as happened in 2002. "I generally block the malo on the Marsanne," he reasons, "to keep a floral side to the wine."

The Étienne Pochon whites are 80 per cent Marsanne, 20 per cent Roussanne. M. Pochon recommends drinking them within five years; when they have more floral aspects like the 2000's, they are best on their own, as an aperitif. I would agree that their elegance and harmony dictate early consumption.

The Château Curson white (8,500 bottles) moves up a gear via one-third Roussanne that is vinified and raised in new wood for four months, with lees stirring. Just one-quarter of the Marsanne is vat raised, and the malo is not done.

Château Curson *blanc* veers towards the more mainstream, a sleek wine that lacks a little soul and is of course constructed around the god Oak—which makes it hard to know when to drink it if you want an integrated, harmonious wine with your food. I look back at early 1990s tasting notes of this wine and find that it was capable of freshness then.

CROZES-HERMITAGE E POCHON ROUGE

2002 (★)
2001 ★★
2000 ★ 2004–06
1999 *Dom Pochon* ★★★ 2006–08
1998 *Dom Pochon* ★★ 2004–06

CROZES-HERMITAGE CHÂTEAU CURSON ROUGE

2003 ★★(★) Bright, dark *robe*; oak and lissom black fruit mix on bouquet, direct and straight at this young stage. Usual elegant fruit on palate, with a light pepper presence. Fruits are red, show up again on final part. Oak, tar aftertaste. In thrall to the oak on the finish, so a little worry about it keeping its warmth. Much more expressive from 2007. 2013–15.

2002 (CASK) ★★ Calm, cherry fruit aroma; some pointed red fruit, fair length. Will be sinewy, dry toned. 2010–11.

2001 ★★★★ Elegantly full, oily/bosky mix; complete, good structure. Measured density, upright black fruit, good frame. From 2007; 2015–16.

2000 ★★★★ Slow-burn bouquet, leather/ jam mix; cooked, juicy black fruit, light new oak. Rich, oily end, elegant and spiced. Good *typicité*. From 2005–06; 2011–12.

1999 ★★★★ Southern, smoky black fruit bouquet—violets/herbs. Warm texture, packs good flavour. Has dimension, lasts well. Black fruits integrate well with oak. Going towards mini-Hermitage. 2011–13.

1998 ★★★ Earthy/fungal, black fruit bouquet—decant. Rounded, rich, then tightens near finish. Some end oak. Esp 2003–05; 2007–2010.

CROZES-HERMITAGE E POCHON BLANC

2002 ★
2001 ★
2000 ★★
1999 *Dom Pochon* ★★
1998 *Dom Pochon* ★

CROZES-HERMITAGE CHÂTEAU CURSON BLANC

2002 ★
2001 ★★
2000 ★
1999 ★★

Export 55 per cent (1) Great Britain, (2) Switzerland, (3) Belgium

DOMAINE MICHEL POINARD

Les Chassis 26600 La Roche-de-Glun +33(0)490 658591

The Chéron family, with interests in Vacqueyras, Gigondas, and Burgundy, moved into Crozes-Hermitage with meaning in 2002. They bought a 9.5-hectare domaine on *Les Chassis* from Michel Poinard, a Co-opérateur, then in 2003 acquired the Domaine Veau d'Or at Mercurol, and also developed the Domaine Roland Betton—like Poinard, in the southern sector at La Roche-de-Glun.

"We were finding it hard to get hold of grapes at Crozes-Hermitage—it's quite a closed area," comments Yves Chéron. "Crozes also has a price-quality rapport that makes it probably easier to sell than a Vacqueyras, for instance."

There are nine hectares of Syrah averaging 10 to 20 years in age, and half a hectare of Marsanne dating from the early 1990s. The core site is on the up-and-coming *Les Saviaux*, where the higher terraces are marked by clay.

The first wines were in 2004, made in a new cellar. There are two reds—the classic is vat-only treated, and bottled after eight months. The oaked wine receives eight months in new casks. Both are fined and filtered. The pure Marsanne white is vat fermented and raised, with an early March bottling, the malo blocked.

CROZES-HERMITAGE ROUGE
2004 ★★

DOMAINE PRADELLE

Le Village 26600 Chanos-Curson +33(0)475 073100

See also St-Joseph.

Jean-Louis Pradelle is a busy man. He has been President of the Growers Union since 1992, he runs his own domaine, and he is involved with his brother Jacques in an expanding nursery business selling young vine cuttings. A slim, wiry man, he's a fast talker, too, used to bustling on and getting things done as he hits 50 years old.

He and his elder brother Jacques are the third generation at Chanos-Curson. "Our father grew fruit and grapes and raised cattle but, in the 1970s, went towards making wine, meaning he left the Co-opérative. We both attended Beaune, and I started in 1977, making our first vintage with the 1978."

The vineyard has edged forward from 20 to 25 hectares since the early 1990s. There are 20.5 hectares of Syrah, average age 20 years, and 4.5 hectares of white—95 per cent Marsanne (average 20-plus years) and 5 per cent Roussanne (1998). The Syrah is spread among Mercurol for the largest amount, Chanos-Curson, and Beaumont-Monteux, growing in poor red soil, covered in stones. These plots produce quick, easy wines with fine tannins. The remaining 2.5 hectares are on the *Les Pends* slope of Mercurol, with more clay-chalk influence. All the white comes from here, too. The brothers also work one hectare of Syrah at Arras in the St-Joseph *appellation*.

The slope vines, which are trained up wooden stakes, are mostly those on *Les Pends*. These are harvested by hand, those on the plain by machine. "We had hail in 1992, so I bought a harvesting machine," recalls Jean-Louis. He makes two red wines, a classic and Les Hirondelles, and destalks all the crop. He vinifies simply—no yeasts are added, nor does he punch the cap or practise *délestages* (vat refilling). "I tried them over three years, but wasn't convinced," he says—"I don't want to make my wine uniform or technological."

Vinification lasts between 10 and 17 days—the contrast between 2002 and the much superior 2001. His classic red is aged for six to eight months in used casks, Les Hirondelles for 13 to 15 months, also in old casks. Unusually, Jean-Louis works with no 228-litre casks, only larger sizes up to 60 hl.

"Les Hirondelles comes from the older slope vines averaging 25 years and is more closed and tough when young," he explains. He makes about 20,000 bottles of it, fining and filtering both reds. Just under 10 per cent of his wine is still sold in bulk to local merchants.

The classic wine contains easy fruit, often red or raspberry in flavour, and fair appeal. The domaine makes correct, not heavily weighted wines; there is earthy fruitiness in them and tannins that lend unobtrusive support. The Hirondelles is a grounded wine, with stone fruit and some leathery connotations. It is worth drinking after three years' ageing and can run for around eight years. The white is vat fermented at 16° to 20°C for up to three weeks. It is a modest performer.

The Pradelle nursery business is now selling 350,000 plants a year, 80 per cent of them Syrah. "Demand for the Syrah has accelerated since 1998," comments Jean-Louis.

CROZES-HERMITAGE ROUGE
2003 ★★ 2010–12
2002 (CASK) ★
2001 ★ 2005–06

CROZES-HERMITAGE LES HIRONDELLES ROUGE
2001 (★) 2009–10
2000 ★★ 2007–08
1999 ★★ 2008–09

2003 (★)

2002 —

Export 35 per cent (1) Great Britain, (2) Japan, (3) Switzerland

DOMAINE DES REMIZIÈRES

Route de Romans 26600 Mercurol +33(0)475 074428

See also Hermitage, St-Joseph.

For 40 years this has been a low-profile, hard-working domaine that recently has edged into the broader international limelight. The house style is reserved; the Desmeures are true countrymen who like the world to come to them. It is something of a shock to see Philippe Desmeure, who runs the estate, clad in a blue jean suit in a smart hotel off the Champs-Élysées in Paris dispensing his wine to trade and press alike. Maybe he is being spurred on by his slim, blonde daughter, Émilie, who joined up full-time in November 2002.

Philippe is a nice-looking chap with brown southern eyes and a solid, firm frame. His wines are also often tightly woven, and upright; they are not at all showy, and possess a genuine, sometimes dry fruit core. They have been very good value for many years, always rewarding patient cellaring. Two developments in the past 10 years need highlighting, though: a notable increase in the use of new oak, which can be overpowering and which has been accompanied by more overt, hands-on winemaking; and a multiplication in the number of cuvées, which is also disconcerting.

The family work 24 hectares inside Crozes, six of them white grapes (90 per cent Marsanne, 10 per cent Roussanne). The core is at Mercurol, at *Les Pends*, where rounded *galet* stones rest on the clay-limestone soil, a slope site suited to white grapes. There is also a hectare of 1970s Syrah bought by Emilie on the *Gaubert lieu-dit*. At Larnage—*Terres Blanches*—and Crozes itself there are also slope vineyards, with other plots in the *communes* of Tain, on granite, and La Roche-de-Glun, the last being their fastest-ripening vineyard. In all there are maybe 25 plots.

At Hermitage they work two hectares of Syrah and half a hectare of mainly Marsanne. There is also a 2.5-hectare vineyard at Clérieux just to the east; this provides Syrah and Viognier *vin de pays de la Drôme*.

In the 1970s the domaine was led quietly forward by Alphonse Desmeure, whose crinkly smiling eyes have been passed on to his granddaughter Émilie. He cultivated fruit and vines across the sweeping land around the domaine, which lies north of *Les Chassis* backed by the low ridge that runs east from Tain to Romans-sur-Isère.

Alphonse would vinify and sell half his then four-hectare crop to the *négoce* trade, the other half going to the Tain Co-opérative, which he left in 1973. By 1978 all the wine was being domaine bottled. Unusually for the time, the Domaine des Remizières name was most founded on its white wines. In 1990 Alphonse ceded the reins to son Philippe, who at 34 had already spent 15 years working with his father. Since then six hectares have been added at Crozes, and the domaine is flourishing.

In 1987–88 they started to machine harvest their crop off the plain areas. Since 1993 they use their own machine, which crops the grapes for the basic red and for part of the Cuvée Particulière. "We can wait for maximum maturity, and then go quickly; we can also stop harvesting when it's very hot, which we can't with a manual harvest," explains Philippe. They do still hand harvest the Crozes slope vineyards and of course their Hermitage sites. Tasting their Crozes from the mid-1990s compared to the mid- to late 1980s, it is clear that later harvesting became a matter of new policy here.

Since 1996 the crop has been destalked and the vinification has been extended to 30 days in concrete vats, with two to three *remontages* a day. Half the cask stock is replaced every two years, with an increased emphasis on new oak. There are still some old, large barrels, but mostly it's young oak spread across the very tidy cellars.

The basic red Crozes, made from young-vine fruit on the plain, is raised in older, large barrels and bottled in November, just over a year after the harvest. It is a simple wine for early drinking.

The middle Crozes red, the Cuvée Particulière, is a selection of older, 35-year slope and plain vines. It is raised in a mix of large barrels and 600-litre and new, 228-litre casks for a year. Its fruit has an earthy side to it, and its tannins need a little time to meld: a wine to drink after three years.

The top Cuvée Christophe comes from 60-plus-year-old slope vines, 60 per cent from Larnage, the rest from Mercurol. The Larnage influence is interesting on this wine—the finer tannins, the cooler textures typical of Syrah from that village. This is raised for 12 to 14 months in 70 per cent new oak, 30 per cent one-year-old wood. The new oak use has been encouraged by the merchant Patrick Lesec, who targets the US market for many of his sales. The new-oak proportion has risen in recent times, hitting 80 per cent in the reduced-size vintage of 2003.

Cuvée Christophe shows black fruit and grilled, oaked effects when young. The fruit texture can be dry, with the tannins marking the finish. As a result, it is not a wine to drink early, and is best approached from four years on. Its style is overtly modern, and in a year of big heat like 2003 there is a marked tarry aspect to it.

In 2003 the domaine produced a one-off oak-fest wine, called "Essentiel". Taken from old Syrah at Lavnage, this was raised for 15 months in new oak, with 3,700 bottles made. Cuvées like this indicate an increasing eye is being kept on the dictates and tastes of the market, rather than on making a wine of simplicity that projects the *terroir* here.

The Cuvée Particulière white (100 per cent Marsanne from Mercurol that dates from the early 1970s) is vat vinified, then raised for 11 months in a mix of 600-litre casks and large barrels, with lees stirring. The special Cuvée Christophe comes from Mercurol—*Les Pends*—and the *Les Bâties* site at Larnage. It is 90 per cent Marsanne, 10 per cent Roussanne, the Larnage vineyards dating from the 1950s, the Mer-

curol from the 1960s. It is raised, with its lees stirred, for 11 months in 30 per cent new, 70 per cent one-year-old oak: the new oak proportion has thankfully been cut back. Both wines perform their malos.

These are fairly full white wines, which in a fat year like 2003 can handle the oak. The rub comes when the oak formula is applied and the grape matter lacks richness. The Cuvée Christophe is a wine to leave alone for three to four years as a matter of course.

Philippe insists that his white Crozes be given time: "They can live for 10 to 12 years; they're not early flatterers like the Crozes whites off the plain. They convey the steady ripening of the *Pends* slope at Mercurol, and benefit from patience."

The Viognier at the Clérieux vineyard for their white *vin de pays* was planted in 1995. The Desmeures have lowered yields from the 75 hl/ha allowed to around 40+ hl/ha. Two cutbacks are made—the first to help the growth of the remaining crop, the second to refine that. The soil contains a lot of stones and gravel, with patches of sticky gravelly clay. It's on a small south-facing slope.

This Viognier *vin de pays* is promising. The 2000 (sold Non-Vintage) held true Viognier aspects on the nose—pear/floral—and showed a genuine richness and pear flavour on the palate.

CROZES-HERMITAGE ROUGE

2002 ★ 2008–09
2000 ★

CROZES-HERMITAGE CUVÉE PARTICULIÈRE ROUGE

2003 ★★ From 2007; 2011–13
1999 ★ 2008–09

CROZES-HERMITAGE CUVÉE CHRISTOPHE ROUGE

2004 (CASK) ★★(★) Cooked fruit, floral tone on bouquet. Good integration on palate, flavor weaves along well. Has a pebbly feel, shows promise. Esp from 2008–09; 2016–18.

2003 ★★(★) Full, brewed nose, runs along coffee-pepper lines. Also big scale on palate, with oak assertion on finish. Rich, but oak in charge. Mocha finale. Esp from 2008, but will it hold its richness? 2013–15.

2001 ★★★ Pebbly, slightly airy nose, upright black fruit, modern style, needs time. Interesting fruit on palate, with dry, mineral edging. Granite, cool style, grilled and oaked. Structured tannins need time. Greater variety and expression later. From 2006; 2011–13.

1999 ★★ Black, firm, tar bouquet, some stink; full, tight wine. Has structure and quiet scale. Quite prominent, ripe tannins. 2009–11.

1998 ★★ Warm, promising, smoky black fruit bouquet; very dense, a lot of concentration for a Crozes. Middle is reserved, dry. Bit upright, less rich than 1999. 2008–2012.

CROZES-HERMITAGE L'ESSENTIEL ROUGE
2003 ★★★ From 2009; 2013–15

CROZES-HERMITAGE CUVÉE PARTICULIÈRE BLANC
2003 ★★
1999 ★

CRÔZES-HERMITAGE CUVÉE CHRISTOPHE BLANC
2003 ★★★ Orange, exotic aromas on pretty broad bouquet. Restrained start, then gains some richness. Spice-oak aftertaste—oak comes on strong. Broad and rich, can work itself into cohesion by 2007. 2011–13.
2001 ★
2000 ★★
1999 ★

Export 30 per cent (1) Great Britain, (2) Belgium, (3) USA

GILLES ROBIN

Les Chassis Sud 26600 Mercurol +33(0)475 084328

See also St-Joseph.
Born in 1972, Gilles Robin forms part of the younger generation making their own way at Crozes-Hermitage. Like Luc Tardy at Domaine du Murinais and David Reynaud at Les Bruyères, his family used to send crop to the Cave de Tain.

Gilles went solo in 1996 and gradually built a new, blue-shuttered cellar that connects with his new house south of Tain. He is a fourth-generation wine man; his great-grandfather worked at Paul Jaboulet Aîné and grew a few vines.

In the 1960s his father worked around five hectares at Mercurol, combined with fruit production; nine hectares were planted by his grandfather and father, two of them on *Les Chênes Verts* in 1946. Gilles has now increased the total to 12 hectares. All is Syrah, except for just half a hectare planted in 1995 and split 75 per cent Marsanne, 25 per cent Roussanne. These white vines are at *Conflans*, near the *Sept Chemins*, where the soil contains some chalk topped with small stones and is free-draining.

The main Syrah vineyards are on the full southern part of *Les Chassis*, mixing *La Terrace de Chassis* and a plot near *Les Meysonniers* behind his cellar, where there is a gentle slope. The soil is typical of *Les Chassis*, with alluvial stones lying on a half-metre-thick layer of clay-limestone that gives way further down to gravel and sand. Its wines show off overt, direct fruit.

There are 3.5 ha at La Roche-de-Glun where the soil is deeper, with a higher clay presence than at *Les Chassis*. Of this, 1.2 ha dates from 1946, 0.7 ha from 1970 to 1975, and 1.6 ha from 1996 to 1998, planted by Gilles. "These wines have more tannic backbone than my core *Chassis* ones," remarks Gilles.

He is quite a tall man with a solid upper body and light brown hair. His habit is to talk quickly, and he does seem to want things to move along at speed. His instinct since studying at the Montpellier Wine School has been to extract his reds, pushing the fruit, a practice that is detectable in other pupils from this wine school. This can render the wines uncomfortably dry if exposed to air for a couple of hours—a classic modernist phenomenon.

Gilles also spent three years in Savoie, an unusual destination, working with local growers, and so became well acquainted with varieties like the underestimated Mondeuse, and Roussette and Gamay. Now he has a secret weapon, his wife, Sylvie, who has joined him full-time on the domaine, with tasks ranging from vine tying, to running the office, to labelling. An ex-teacher, her wide-eyed look belies a quiet steel, and she admits that the last thing she used to think of herself as when they first met was a country girl. "I was very sporty, and only drank water; now look at me—doing a wine tasting course!" she laughs.

Meanwhile, Gilles is trying to work the vineyard in his grandfather's way—simply. So there are no herbicides; he plants barley in alternate rows and has worked the soil since 1995. The vines are triple-wire trained, but in 2000 he stopped using the harvest machine bought by his father in partnership with other growers. "The machine meant that 80 to 90 per cent of its crop was automatically destemmed, and I prefer to have the choice, although my summer wine from young vines, the Papillon, is fully destemmed here," he says.

Given the size of his frame, Gilles had the doors on his steel vats specially widened to allow him to get in and out of them. His cask-ageing cellar is an impressive sight, an addition to the domaine since 2000.

First made in 2000, the Papillon (25,000 bottles) is fermented for 18 to 22 days in steel. Gilles wants to extract the juice quickly for this, so is happy to use enzymes to encourage extraction. "I work particularly on the postmaceration stage, after the first week," Gilles explains. He doesn't cap punch or pump over, and gives the wine a simple six-month tank storage with light *micro-bullage* to inject some air to avoid any return of the Syrah's rather gassy, stewed tendency for reduction. Papillon is fined, filtered, and bottled in May. Its speedy process reflects its origin from Syrah vines that date from the early 1990s onwards, and Gilles describes it as his "thirst quenching, *bistrot* wine."

The top wine, Albéric Bouvet (35,000 bottles), named after his grandfather, is vinified for 28 to 30 days after a variable amount of destemming—100 per cent in 2002, 20 per cent in 2003, for instance. Enzymes are also used to break down the cells to obtain more juice, and

Gilles punches down the cap and pumps over. He ends with a process called *étampage*, whereby the cap is immersed with wooden punchers at the end of the fermentation and stays eight to 10 days in the bottom of its 80 hl vat. "You have to taste the wine to know when to take it out," says Gilles, "so you avoid the tannins becoming too dry." Although very clearly interventionist, he says his grandfather used this method as well. In the course of purchasing Gilles' wines in Paris and Stockholm in the past, it has been observable that they are inclined to dry out by the time of the second or third glass.

The Albéric Bouvet is aged for a year in 228-litre casks, 20 per cent new, the rest up to four years old. It does its malo in cask, there are three rackings, and the wine is fined but not filtered. It is an assertive wine, with extraction the first impact when drinking it. This means the texture is taut, and one has to hope that time softens and broadens it. It is not the style of wine with which I feel at ease.

Since 1998 he has made a white wine, Les Marelles; this comes from deeper, more clay soil in the *commune* of Mercurol, so Gilles considers this a wine that expresses straight fruit rather than its place. Gilles admits that he is still seeking the best way to vinify this. In 2001 it was all oak vinified and raised, in 2002 all vat treated, and in 2003 half and half, the oak a mix of new and one year old! The 2004 formula broadly followed 2003, with the half vat proportion complemented by one-to-two-year-old oak.

It is raised on its lees until March and is bottled after a year in November, the malo completed.

CROZES-HERMITAGE PAPILLON ROUGE
2004 ★★(★)
2002 ★★
2001 ★★

CROZES-HERMITAGE ALBÉRIC BOUVET ROUGE
2003 ★★★ Mixed bag of aromas—coffee, warm plum fruit. Rounded, fleshy start, runs towards a chocolate finale, with dried fruits,

pepper, prune elements. Tannins softer by 2007. Modern, has correct integration, length. 2014–16.

2002 ★ Smoked, dense bouquet, stewed black fruit, a little forced. Rather heated attack, as if stretched. Quite big wine, has width but not grip. Taut from its early acidity. Try from 2007; 2011–12.

2001 ★★★ Meaty, open bouquet, red fruits present. Wide blackberry flavour, fruit runs well. Spice-herb–black olives mix at back of palate. Has scale, plus the freshness of the year. 2010–12.

2000 ★ Modern, rather spirity nose; taut black fruit, lissom and straight. Some heat, dry-toned, bit forced.

1998 ★★ Dark; dark, tarry bouquet, has ripeness, hint of young vines; bit disjointed, not a safety-first wine, brambly, peppered fruit, needs air to broaden. 2006–07.

CROZES-HERMITAGE LES MARELLES BLANC

2004 ★★

2002 ★

Export 60 per cent (1) Great Britain, (2) Switzerland, (3) USA

DOMAINE ROUSSET

Route de Gervans 26600 Erôme +33(0)475 033038

See also St-Joseph.

Maybe Robert Rousset was a Master Mariner in his previous life. He makes a firm physical impression: a tall, strong-framed man in his mid-50s, with thick grey hair, a deep voice, and a rolling walk. His face tells an outdoor story, and he looks good for it.

His roots are good, too. His uncle is octogenarian Raymond Roure, he of the wild Syrah rides in the 1970s, and once possessor of some of the most prized sites in all Crozes-Hermitage. Ten generations have lived in his house in the low-key northern village of Erôme and many of the vineyards are mature. I recall his father, André, making a sparkling white wine in the early 1970s, as a local top-up to his red and

FIGURE 22 Doughty Robert Rousset makes one of the best Crozes-Hermitages, Les Picaudières, from the granite hills of the north of the appellation. (Tim Johnston)

white Crozes. The flagship site is an old Roure vineyard, the 1.1 ha on *Picaudières* at neighbouring Gervans, which they bought in 1996, with Paul Jaboulet taking its other part.

There are 9.5 ha of Crozes, plus a 0.5 ha of St-Joseph. The family worked in fruit and vines in decades gone by, but it was Robert's father who moved the emphasis towards wine in the 1960s. Just 2 ha of apricots remain today. Vineyard practices are natural, without fanfare and special labelling. A 17-year-old mare tills the soil on the 1.5 ha of flatter terraces, up to five times in a normal year.

The *Picaudières* vineyard is very steep, with old terraces hewn out of the rotted granite. The oldest vines date from the 1930s, with a new batch planted to rejuvenate it in 1997. This supplies the fruit for the special Picaudières cuvée, of which there are up to 4,500 bottles.

Erôme and Gervans were one *commune* until 1947, so the vineyards mainly straddle both villages. A common theme is their antiquity, a prized feature for a Crozes-Hermitage domaine. At Erôme, there are 1.5 ha of Syrah (1950s,

1988) and Marsanne on *Les Vedias*. This terraced site is 130 to 180 metres up and is granite with loess present in places. The loess areas are home to the Marsanne, which is a mix of 1923, 1933, and the 1950s. "The Marsanne does very well in the loess," affirms Robert.

Tout, also at Erôme, is a mainly Marsanne site—1.1 ha, with just 0.2 ha of Syrah. The Marsanne is the same mix of ages as those on *Les Vedias*; the Syrah dates from the 1960s. The Syrah grows in clay, the Marsanne in white clay–loess that has some stones present. Another Erôme *lieu-dit* is *Beaubrunet La Roux*, where there is a hectare of Syrah (1970s, 1998) on granite with some loess.

Nearby at Gervans, the Roussets also have a tiny 0.3 ha plot on *La Tuilière*—0.2 ha of Syrah (1950s) on granite covered with some stones and 0.1 ha of Marsanne (1950s) on loess, near the summit.

In the *commune* of Crozes, on the high site of *Méjans*, the Roussets have 1.5 ha of Syrah (1978). The terraces here start at 270 metres and rise to 330 metres. The slippery granite is light, acid soil with gritty sandstone about.

"The soil changes a lot round here on these hills," observes Robert in his deep tones. "I know three of the *communes*—Erôme, Gervans, and Crozes—and the soil can change across a single plot with seemingly no reason. What I do know is that the best site is *Picaudières* because it faces full south, is sheltered from the north wind and always ripens well."

Robert adds that his Picaudières *rouge* often has an animal, robust side rather like a Hermitage, especially in big vintages like 2003 and 2001. "In the 1940s my grandparents sold it to the best restaurants of Valence; they would load up their *demi-muid* of 600 litres on to the mule and ride their horses down there to deliver it." He started to bottle some of the wine as early as 1967.

The Syrah crop has been destemmed since 1990, and is vinified with twice-daily pumping-overs, followed by cap punching—the punching a necessity in the tricky vintage of 2003 with so much sticky, sugary crop. With destemming, the process lasts longer, from 15 (in 2003) to 25 days now, and the top temperature is kept to a peak of 32°C.

The classic red and the Picaudières both receive 12 to 15 months' cask ageing in 20 per cent new, 80 per cent two-to-five-year-old oak. The wines are filtered but not fined. The classic shows signs of modernism—the black fruit/grilled aromas—but there are some respectable tannins present, too. The domaine is advised by the Jean-Luc Colombo stable, but their influence is quite measured, notably on the Picaudères.

This is a domaine to keep an eye on. Robert is a grounded, rural man, his instincts the natural ones of the countryman—a vineyard more than a cellar man. He studied agriculture, but not wine as a young man, before starting work in 1967, when he was 18. His son Stéphane joined the domaine in 1994, when he was 21, after wine school studies in the Beaujolais. The two mens' outlooks provides a good balance of approach, and quality is enhanced through their working some prime hillside sites as well.

All the wines are structured, with ageing beneficial. The classic red can run for eight to 10 years and has more substance than many straight Crozes reds. The Picaudières is a wine of genuine breed and character and evolves well, the ageing bringing along added complexity. It is one of the most distinguished red Crozes, and while its flavour lacks the variety of a Hermitage, it is certainly better than many of the more formulaic wines from the lesser, easterly areas of the nearby hill. The Picaudières' depth comes from its *terroir* and its old vineyard, thank goodness, and not from cellar extraction.

The classic white is steel fermented at 17° to 18°C and raised in vat for a year, its malo done. The Vieilli en Fut de Chêne was all new-oak handled when first made in 1999, with lees stirring and bottling after one year. Robert felt the new oak intruded too much, so when next made in 2002, he had decided on 60 per cent oak, 40 per cent vat for this.

The whites are stylish, reflecting the qualities of the northern well-ventilated, granite
zone. "The terrain here is very good for whites,"
says Robert, "they're more structured than most
white Crozes, and we've also got old vines."

CROZES-HERMITAGE ROUGE
2003 (CASK) ★★(★) From 2006–07; 2017–18
2002 (CASK) ★★ 2010–11
2001 ★★ From 2006; 2011–12

CROZES-HERMITAGE LES PICAUDIÈRES ROUGE
2003 (CASK) ★★★ Scented, upright black
fruit aroma, some alcohol, power. Direct black
berry fruit flavour, plenty of vigour, clean winemaking. Oak edging. Gains earthiness, local feel
through the palate. 2007 on, oak within by
2008. 2015–18.

2002 ★★ Earthy, lightly truffled aroma, with
black berry/raspberry. Black fruit attack, chewy
after it with oak impact. A wine for its second
phase, needs patience. Berried, truffly aftertaste,
has length. From 2006; 2012–14.

2001 ★★★★ Raspberry/black currant, bit
fungal nose; structured black berry fruit, stylish,
with potential. Light peppery tannins, cool textured finale. Length good. From 2006. Serious
wine. 2016–18.

2000 ★★★ Grilled, sappy black fruit, mineral edge nose. Grilled black berry fruit, with
grain/bone. Light tar end, fruit persists. Mineral, light violet end. Has character. 2010–12.

1999 ★★★★ Reserved, brooding black
fruit/peppery/meaty nose. Very full, tight-knit,
rich wine, animal touches. Slight mineral aftertaste. Tannins well involved, stylish depth. From
2006; 2017–19.

CROZES-HERMITAGE BLANC
2002 ★★★ Broad, oily, light butter nose.
Structured, wide flavour, with grip. Chewy/
some heat near end. Can age. 2008–09.

2001 ★★ Light honey/mineral nose; refined
white peach fruit, slight spice length, nutty end.
Good weight, pretty. 2008.

CROZES-HERMITAGE
VIEILLI EN FUT DE CHÊNE BLANC
2002 ★★ Light toast, fair depth on bouquet.
Some middle richness, oak surround, dried
fruits. From 2005 to let it integrate, needs to.

DOMAINE DES 7 CHEMINS

Les 7 Chemins 26600 Pont-de-l'Isère
+33(0)475 847555

Jean-Louis Buffière is a busy man, flitting
between vineyards on Crozes-Hermitage's broad
Chassis plain and an 80-hectare peach and
apricot domaine west of Arles at St. Gilles.
"Fruit is still more important than wine here,"
he says, an action man, quite short, with mouse-
fair hair. "Sixty people work down there when
we're picking what comes to about 1,500 tonnes
of fruit."

Sept Chemins is the central point on the *Chassis*, marked indeed by a seven-road crossing
point. The domaine is a stone's throw away
from it and was bought by Jean-Louis' maternal
grandfather in 1920. "Phylloxera had knocked
out a lot of the vines—yes, there were vines here
then—and my grandfather replanted around
five hectares in the 1930s," he states.

The vineyard runs to 12 hectares, in four
plots on *Les Chassis*. The soil is covered in old
alluvial Alpine stones, with about half a metre of
earth, then a very deep gravel couch that can
descend as much as 20 to 30 metres. In the La
Roche-de-Glun area, the soil is sandy with some
silt and no gravel. The vines date between the
early 1970s and 1999 and are trained on wire;
the majority are machine harvested. The Syrah
for the old, 30-plus–year vine Cuvée des 7
Chemins, is hand harvested.

Vinification lasts for 20 days in concrete vats,
with no outside yeasts, and cap punching followed by pumping-overs. Top temperature is
not extreme, 28° to 30°C; recent moves have
been to cool the crop and to achieve a longer fermentation, with the temperature held around
25°C for much of the time. From 2004 the wine
has been all oak raised for a year, the casks

20 per cent new, 80 per cent up to four years old.

From 1945 Jean-Louis' father, Louis, held a longstanding contract with Chapoutier to sell crop and wine; Jean-Louis took over in 1980 and started to sell some bottled wine to private customers from 1990. Now about one-third is bottled—around 35,000 bottles—and the rest goes to Gabriel Meffre (Domaine 7 Chemins) and to Guigal.

The bottled red reflects its place—the fruit is lively, sometimes peppery, and runs on to a chewy finale. It is a good wine to enjoy in its youth, but can also last into a second stage of evolution.

Jean-Louis is looking ahead and has just built a new cellar, encouraged by his son Jérome's interest. In his early 30s, Jérome is married to the granddaughter of the legend of the 1960s and 1970s, Raymond Roure from Gervans; a student of viticulture, he is in charge of the vineyards and helped to make his first wine in 2003. Jean-Louis' other son, Rémy, is also set to take part in the enterprise.

A little white is made from half a hectare that is 85 per cent Marsanne, 15 per cent Roussanne planted in 1975. This is vat fermented, then raised for a year in one-to-two-year-old casks. It shows orthodox, and a little clumsy, modern oak and exotic fruit tones and is best left for three years to avoid the oak.

CROZES-HERMITAGE CUVÉE DES 7 CHEMINS ROUGE
   2003 ★
   2002 ★★ 2008–09
   2001 ★★ 2009–11

CROZES-HERMITAGE BLANC
   2002 ★

Export 55 per cent (1) USA, (2) Belgium, (3) Switzerland

MARC SORREL

128 bis avenue Jean Jaurès 26600 Tain l'Hermitage
+33(0)475 071007

   See also Hermitage.

Marc Sorrel's aim and achievement with his red Crozes is a direct, fruited wine. He places emphasis on his decision in 1998 to change to destalking at least half the crop. The tannins are now smoother, and the wines work on a pleasing, direct level. They are ideal to drink over roughly their first five years.

The important point here is the youth of the Syrah vineyard and how its soil particularly favours white-vine varieties. The one hectare of Syrah was planted in 1990–91 on a respected site at Larnage, *La Bouvate et Les Rennes*. This is on the typical soil there that the locals term *Les Terres Blanches*. This is clay with a lot of kaolin, a clay derivative, in the soil. It is white to look at, dazzling to the eyes in full sun, with a very gravelly topsoil, and is what Marc Sorrel terms "good for brick making." This vineyard is near Desmeure and the old de Vallouit plot.

Marc's half hectare of white vines is here, too. Planted in 1945, it is half Marsanne, half Roussanne. "That was an epoch when a lot of Roussanne was planted," says Marc. "People liked its aromatic side, but the great problem was its failure to handle oïdium—the Marsanne was much less prone to it." The *terroir* is good here, the vines are mature, and yes, Marc's Crozes *blanc* is one of the fullest, finest wines in the *appellation*.

First made in 1993, the red is vinified for two weeks, with some *délestages* (part emptying and refilling of the vats) and automatic cap punching. It receives 13 months in used casks and then a few months in steel tanks before bottling between April and June, some 20 months after the harvest. There is no fining or filtration.

His white Crozes is much more the dish: this continues a tradition of great fullness and a wholesome, broad flavour. At times—1994, 1999—this approaches mini-Hermitage status, a genuine accolade for Crozes white, which can often be dull and flabby. The old vines, which Marc first rented in 1990, yield between 25 and 30 hl/ha, well below the usual. This is a case of the classic old vines–low yields mix.

The crop is mostly vat fermented, and the young wine is then raised in used casks for up to 14 months, during which time it does its malo. A brief stay in vat precedes an April bottling, two springs after its harvest. It is lightly fined.

CROZES-HERMITAGE ROUGE

2002 (CASK) ★

2001 ★

2000 ★

1999 ★

CROZES-HERMITAGE BLANC

2002 ★ Broad, earthy/buttered nose; gently cooked fruit, some life, fair weight. Malo not done.

2001 ★★★ Ripe, grapy aroma; fleshy, warm, full. Persistent *gras*, honey aftertaste, nicely buttered. Serious wine. 2010–12.

2000 ★★ Gentle, touch of honey aroma. Tight white fruit, smoky end, tight-knit wine. Stylish, can develop well. 2008–09.

1999 ★★★★ Wholesome, full nose, potential. Chewy, partly spiced white fruits, tiny cask at end. Very orderly, good grip, interesting.

CAVE DE TAIN-L'HERMITAGE

22 route de Larnage 26600 Tain l'Hermitage
+33(0)475 082087

See also Cornas, Hermitage, St-Joseph, St-Péray.

The Cave is the Big Fish at Crozes—a little under 2 million bottles a year are made, or 70 per cent of all the wine, so it plays a vital role in determining the public's perception of the *appellation*.

It handles the crop of 204 members across the Crozes-Hermitage area, including a legacy of 3.35 hectares at Mercurol and Larnage. The Larnage vines are old—a hectare of Syrah (pre-1943) and a half hectare of Marsanne (1970, 1988) on *La Bouvate et Les Rennes*, a site near the Château de Larnage. The Mercurol plot is Syrah, planted on *Les Chassis* in 1991. The members' vineyards are largely southern, although there are useful amounts in the granite hills of the north (see table 6).

TABLE 6
Cave de Tain-l'Hermitage Member Vineyards
(size in hectares)

Northern zone	
Crozes-Hermitage	36
Larnage	31
Gervans	28
Erôme	14
Serves-sur-Rhône	3.5
Tain	2
Southern zone	
Mercurol	230
Beaumont-Monteux	218
Chanos-Curson	103
Pont-de-l'Isère	90
La Roche-de-Glun	80

Vineyard manager Daniel Brissot estimated that the average vine age in 2005 was 15 to 20 years for their Syrah and 30 to 50 years for their Marsanne. "We will plant a couple of hectares of Roussanne in the future," he says, "but the Marsanne is old and of such good quality that it's very difficult to take them out. The Marsanne does very well on the loess of Larnage and Crozes, and even in the drought year of 2003 we cropped a good quantity."

The main red is the classic, formerly known as Nobles Rives, with about 1.8 million bottles a year. There have also been cuvées selected by supermarket buyers at a cheaper price—in a good vintage like 1999, these reach ★★ status.

At the top end, the main wine is Les Hauts du Fief, first made in 1994—a southern, *Chassis* wine, mostly from Mercurol. The Cave are also launching further top-end Crozes reds from precise sites and are keen to highlight the northern, granite zone for these.

The Syrah has been destalked since 1991–92 and is vinified over around 10 days. A type of *délestage* is done for the hotter vats—juice is taken out, cooled, then reintroduced. Since 2002 the air-conditioned vinification building has allowed the application of robotic cap punching for the 700 hl steel vats, whose top half is used for vinification and bottom half for storage of the wine.

The basic red is made mostly from young vine grapes. Its fruit can be a little raw, rather out of step with its plump style of bouquet. When well chosen by the supermarket buyer, it provides value for money and is suitable for drinking before about six years old. These supermarket selections are sometimes titled as being from the Cave de Tain, but also from Les Vignerons Réunis, Tain.

The classic, formerly Nobles Rives red, is raised two-thirds in steel or lined concrete vats, one-third in wood that is not new. Since 2002, very large, 120 hl and 150 hl barrels have been used for the wood ageing; these will function over the course of 10 to 15 years. There is just the one, large underground cellar built in 1999. The process lasts six to 10 months: the shorter time is when the tannins are supple, as they were in 1999.

The Cave is also happy with the effects of micro-oxygenation on the red wine, notably for the easy supermarket cuvées, but also, strangely, for the top Hauts du Fief, where *terroir* and local feel are emphasized in its marketing. Alain Bourgeois explains: "We do the micro-oxygenation before the malo on the small oak portion. We find it makes the tannins more rounded, stabilises the colour, and helps to develop the richness and volume of the wine."

The special cuvée red, Les Hauts du Fief, is made from the crop of 20 to 30 growers, who each year are asked to tend their vineyards in pursuit of low yields and methods as natural as possible. This includes picking a week later than other Cave members. The amount of wine is limited to around 20,000 to 25,000 bottles a year.

After its malo has been completed in wood, 60 per cent of the Hauts du Fief receives a year's ageing in 400-litre casks one to three years old, the rest in 228-litre casks of the same age range. It is lightly filtered.

There is just one classic white Crozes, made from pure Marsanne; again, this used to be called "Nobles Rives." Its crop is cooled to 5° to 6°C, filtered, then fermented in steel at 18° to 19°C, a little higher than previously. It stays in vat and is bottled as early as possible, with the malo usually blocked.

"We place priority on freshness in our white wine," states winemaker Alain Bourgeois, adding, "Our new equipment has allowed us to obtain more freshness naturally, even when the malo has occurred." Given the mature age of the Marsanne, blocking the malo runs against playing its natural richness to the full: the grapes can be picked not too late if they are worried about acidity, and receive some oak—all perfectly traditional and laissez-faire.

CROZES-HERMITAGE CLASSIC/NOBLES RIVES ROUGE

2003	★★	2011–12
2002	★	2006–07
2001	★	2008–09
1999	★	2007–09
1998		2004–07

CROZES-HERMITAGE SÉLECTION PREMIÈRE ROUGE

2003 ★★ 2009–10

CROZES-HERMITAGE HAUTS DU FIEF ROUGE

2003 ★★ Soaked, ripe fruit nose, prune jam, southern leanings. Black, oily flavour, some violets, *garrigue* later—olives, then tannins. Taut from the oak, makes it dry, cutting. From 2008; 2015–16.

2001 ★★ 2009–10

2000 ★★ 2009–11

CROZES-HERMITAGE CLASSIC/NOBLES RIVES BLANC

2003 ★(★)

2002 ★★

2001 ★★

DOMAINE DE LA TOUR

La Beaume 26600 Mercurol +33(0)475 074341

Starting out as an agricultural worker, Luc Arnavon built up his wine domaine from 1983, juggling fruit and vine cultivation. He worked entirely on his own, with three daughters between 13 and 20 in the background, and would wear a crumpled look on his dark, southern features at times when the sheer weight of tasks piled up around him.

It was therefore not entirely surprising to hear that in 2003 the domaine—called "Veau d'Or" locally—was bought by the Chéron family, who are known for their Gigondas and Vacqueyras holdings under the Pascal name and who also have vineyard interests in Burgundy. M. Arnavon will stay on and work the vines, and the apricot trees will be rented out. Perhaps the final straw for him was the five hours of frost in April 2003 that wiped out the crop from his five hectares of apricots.

The domaine will also move to bottling all its production. A new cellar has been built, a cooling system installed, and harvesting has returned to being done by hand. Some Marsanne has also been grafted with Syrah to increase the exposure to red wine, so the domaine is moving towards seven hectares of Syrah and 0.85 hectare of Marsanne.

The prime asset is one hectare of 1958 Syrah, whose average age across the whole vineyard is 18 years. Some Marsanne dates from 1973, the rest 1983 and 1996. The soil is the red clay of Mercurol, largely on flat ground with a slight slope on *Les Pends*, source of the top white. All the land can be worked by machine.

Vinification has moved past the traditional, with the crop destemmed since the first new-regime vintage of 2004. The crop is macerated at a cool temperature, and cap punching is done. The classic Veau d'Or red is raised only in vat now for eight to nine months, with greater emphasis on fresh fruit. A second-level wine called "Les Hauts de Mercurol" was introduced in 2004 that will be raised in 20 per cent new oak, 80 per cent vat for nine months. The Cuvée Marius remains, with its raising shorter, at nine months, in a mix of new, one-year, and two-year-old oak. All the wines are fined and filtered.

The classic white is still vat fermented and raised for six months, but its malo will be done. The Cuvée Les Pends is now fermented and briefly raised in new oak until a March bottling, the date as before.

The past style was towards the raw, bosky side of Crozes, something from days gone by. Now one can look forward to a greater sequence of quality from one vintage to the next.

CROZES-HERMITAGE CLASSIC ROUGE
1999 ★

CROZES-HERMITAGE MARIUS ROUGE
1999 ★

CROZES-HERMITAGE BLANC
2001 ★

Export 5 per cent (1) USA, (2) Great Britain, (3) Belgium

J. VIDAL-FLEURY

19 route de la Roche 69420 Ampuis +33(0)474 561018

See also Condrieu, Cornas, Côte-Rôtie, Hermitage, St-Joseph.

The Ampuis house of Vidal-Fleury, owned by Guigal, produces both white and red Crozes. The white (6,000–7,000 bottles) is pure Marsanne and comes from two suppliers in the *communes* of Tain and Gervans, at the granite end of the *appellation*. The malolactic is usually blocked, and the wine receives three months' cask ageing. It accentuates the gentle side of white Crozes, with some quiet nuttiness on the aroma. The 2003 did well to be pretty refined, with a subtle richness.

The red spends two years in 20 to 30 hl barrels. It is only lightly fruited and not a wine that impressed in 2001 or 2002. The 2003 is promising, with clear black fruit and sound definition.

CROZES-HERMITAGE ROUGE
2003 (CASK) ★★★ From 2006; 2015–16

CROZES-HERMITAGE BLANC
2003 ★★★
2001 ★★

VINS JEAN-LUC COLOMBO

La Croix des Marais 26600 La Roche-de-Glun
+33(0)475 841710

See also Condrieu, Cornas, Côte-Rôtie, Hermitage, St-Joseph, St-Péray.

Colombo's classic red Crozes, La Tuilière, is a mix of fruit from the granite and open plains. It is 25 per cent from Gervans, 75 per cent from Pont-de-l'Isère and Beaumont-Monteux. He buys the wine young and raises it, one-quarter in three-year-old casks, the rest in vat, for 10 months.

La Tuilière is a wine best enjoyed in its youth, with a straightforward, dark-red fruit style that is given interest by the peppery, pebbly end brought by the Gervans granite. The 2001 was variable on different tastings, though; one was ★★, another bottle much more vacant and rather short.

Since 2002 there has also been a wine intended for longer keeping from the hillsides of Gervans, Les Fées Brunes. This is raised for a year in two-to-three-year-old casks.

The white Crozes, Les Gravières, is 30 per cent from Gervans, 70 per cent from Pont-de-l'Isère and Beaumont-Monteux. This is also bought as young wine and is aged for six to nine months, 40 per cent in one-year-old oak and the rest in steel vats. There is a little Roussanne mixed in with the Marsanne, and the malo is completed. Les Gravières *blanc* accentuates the potential richness that can be achieved here with ripe crop, and is a warm, mature style of white.

CROZES-HERMITAGE LA TUILIÈRE ROUGE

2001 ★★? 2008?

CROZES-HERMITAGE LES GRAVIÈRES BLANC

2001 ★★ 2007

LES VINS DE VIENNE

Bas Seyssuel 38200 Seyssuel +33(0)474 850452

See also Condrieu, Côte-Rôtie, Hermitage, St-Joseph, St-Péray.

The merchant business of growers Yves Cuilleron, Pierre Gaillard, and François Villard produces one white and two red Crozes. The white, Les Chaponères, is pure Marsanne from the southern sector; it is cask fermented and receives a weekly lees stirring, with bottling 10 months after the harvest. Thirty per cent of the oak is new, the rest up to two years old.

The classic red receives 10 months' ageing in two-year-old oak. The top red, *Les Palignons*, is raised in 30 per cent new, 70 per cent one-to-two-year-old oak for 14 to 16 months. It is made with crop from the southern sector, notably the *communes* of Pont-de-l'Isère, La Roche-de-Glun, and Chanos-Curson.

CROZES-HERMITAGE ROUGE

2000 ★

CROZES-HERMITAGE
LES PALIGNONS ROUGE

2003 ★★ Dark *robe*; light prune presence on nose, southern herbs also. Agreeable fruit, sweet-tinged on palate. Runs on freshly. Length good, also its richness. Has softened and advanced quite rapidly. Last tasted March 2005.

2001 ★★ Fresh, black fruit bouquet, oak evident. Quite dense, juicy black fruit, clear-cut and likeable. Lively wine. 2009–11.

2000 ★ Tar, red stewed fruit nose; tasty stewed start, oak tightens the finish, dries it. Some core here. 2006.

CROZES-HERMITAGE
VINTAGES

The best years before the 1980s were 1979, 1978 (exceptional, especially the Thalabert), and 1976. Before that, 1973, 1971, 1969, 1967, 1966, 1964, 1961, and 1959 were all good or very good. The 1978 and 1979 Thalaberts were both still in fair shape in 2004.

1980 Good. A classic sleeper vintage written off too early. Bouquets became smoky and leafy-bosky, textures oily, with red fruits. Thalabert still showing very well in 2004.

1981 Fair. Difficult ripening. The reds lacked body.

1982 Fair. Many short-lived, stewed reds and low-acidity whites—hit by the high heat of both the summer and harvesttime. A turning-point vintage for switched-on growers who realized the urgency of the need for temperature control in the cellar.

1983 Very good. Firm tannins a feature. Very striking, leathery, smoky aromas emerged. Great autumn drinking. Reds still on the go. Excellent Thalabert, also good Tardy and Ange reds. Rich Paul Jaboulet Mule Blanche *blanc*.

1984 Mediocre. *Coulure* on the Syrah. Lack of colour, aroma, and genuine body. Better for the whites—some well-scented wines.

1985 Very good. The key was a very fine late summer. The reds were packed with warm fruit and ripe, agreeable tannins. Excellent Thalabert, Les Voussères from Fayolle, and Tardy and Ange *rouge*, and a very good debut red from Graillot. The Paul Jaboulet Aîné Mule Blanche *blanc* was powerful and rich. The reds now show age, with very seductive fruit and rounded flavours. "Wines that sang"—a classic sun vintage.

1986 Fair. A variable vintage: a very dry year then produced rain at harvesttime, which started early, around 17 September. The reds held dry tannins; the fruit was often lean and taut. The best cuvées settled after five years. The whites were better, showing fresh aromas and lively fruit, although some were short. For the reds, note Graillot La Guiraude and Cuvée Particuliere from Alphonse Desmeure. A low-key Thalabert this year. Most are now past their best.

1987 Mediocre. A rain-affected year. Some rot hit the harvest, which turned out better, fuller red wines than first expected. Middling-weight wines with open but not very deep aromas and some hot finishes. They have peaked. The whites were a little unbalanced, and light. A successful Thalabert from Paul Jaboulet.

1988 Very good. A dry summer that produced a solid, classic vintage with depth and marked tannins early on. The reds evolved into a chewy, cooked fruit, leathery stage. The best names are still drinkable in 2005. The whites were delicious, full of firm flavours, with excellent balance. The Thalabert was marked by new oak, a departure for Paul Jaboulet, but had settled after four years.

1989 Very good. Drought once more was a central part of the vintage's makeup. The summer was again very fine and too dry, leading to some robust tannins. The best reds contained concentrated fruit with well-built tannic support. They broadened well and gained complexity with age. The best can be drunk until around 2008. Note Graillot La Guiraude, Pochon Château Curson. The whites were attractively weighted and aromatic.

1990 Excellent. "The growers had it easy," stated Alain Graillot. The year was very dry, but rain fell at opportune moments, particularly in August. The heat of the year shows in the fully juiced, sometimes rich jam flavours. Bouquets are full and prolonged, now at a damp earth, prune stage. The fruit is very ripe, almost overmature and tannins were very ripe. Textures from the plain—Graillot, Thalabert—are thick and sweet. The outstanding Thalabert will run over 20 sumptuous, very rich years or so. The whites were good and full, with evident southern warmth, but they lacked acidity. They should have been drunk by now. Note Dom Remizières *blanc*.

REDS

★★★★★ P. Jaboulet Thalabert

★★★★ Graillot, E. Pochon Château Curson, Dom Remizières Particulière

★★★ Bérard Cuvée Prestige, Chapoutier Meysonniers, Combier Clos des Grives, Delas Tour d'Albon

★ Dom Remizières

1991 Good. The summer was respectable, but its heat was not sustained enough to ripen the grapes, and rain was an occasional problem. "We had extraordinary late and fast ripening between 15 and 31 August," said A. Graillot, pointing to the key to the vintage. The first harvest rains came in early September, with heavy rain on 7–8 September. This brought rot for the later harvesters, but levels of ripeness were mostly sound, without showing high sugar levels. The reds showed lively, elegant fruit from the start and were less replete than the booming 1990s. The tannins played a sound role, lending a quiet frame to the ripeness and helping the length. Bouquets, full of wild berries at first, ran into bosky, mixed dried fruits with time. A very likeable vintage that was always underestimated through false linkage with the problems of Bordeaux and Burgundy. Good names like Louis Belle and Graillot's Guiraude need drinking by now, but Thalabert can run towards 2010–12.

A top year for the whites: they were well constituted, with chewy fruit and good levels of acidity, too. The Marsanne was very expressive, with plenty of the nuttiness present when it is well ripened. Elegance ruled among the early-drinking cuvées.

REDS

> ★★★★★ P. Jaboulet Thalabert
> ★★★ Belle Louis Belle, Combier Clos des Grives, Graillot Guiraude, Dom Remizières
> ★★ Belle Pierrelles, Dom du Pavillon
> ★ Chapoutier Meysonniers, Graillot, Cave de Tain Nobles Rives, de Vallouit Château de Larnage

WHITES

> ★★ Graillot, P. Jaboulet Mule Blanche
> ★ Chapoutier Meysonniers, Dom Remizières

1992 Mediocre. Crop levels were hit by a poor flowering, July to mid-August was wet, and there was also early July hail. The grapes inflated and lacked sugar, and incidences of rot occurred. Sorting was essential at harvesttime. The fruit on the reds was tenuous and often fuzzy and overbrewed. Chaptalisation was used to gain degree and prop up the wines, but they were never long *en bouche*. Adding to the confusion was the new trend of high-temperature extractions this year, imported from the Médoc, topped up by increased new- or young-oak use. With the fashion of late harvesting gaining ground, this was a strange vintage with *terroir* out of the frame. The reds developed very fungal aromas over time, but should have been drunk by now.

The whites were delicate and flattering. Their fruit stopped short and they were for early drinking.

REDS

> ★★★ Ferraton Matinière
> ★ Delas Tour d'Albon

WHITES

> ★ Graillot, M. Sorrel, Dom du Pavillon

1993 Poor. The crop was abundant and needed green harvesting. The summer was fair, not more, but the problems came in a rush with hail on 27–28 August at Mercurol and around *Thalabert* on *Les Chassis*, with pouring rain from 7 September. The Rhône broke its banks.

The reds were pale and dilute, finishing thinly. Aromas were stretched, some burnt aspects present. Most wines were edgy, just one or two showing midweight dark fruit—modest lunch-wine status for them. They are past their best.

The whites were a touch better, often the case in off-vintages in the Rhône. They were also prone to lack depth, but aromas were superior to their slight flavours. Some turned gold and oxidised within three years. Sorrel did well from his higher, windier site at Larnage, helped by mature vines as well.

REDS

> ★★ Dom du Colombier Gaby
> ★ Combier, de Vallouit Château de Larnage

WHITES

★★ M. Sorrel

1994 Fair. Ripening was uneven; some growers found they could pick early, but the grapes were often fragile. Rain in the third week of September signalled the end of the cycle. The classic cuvées from the plain showed expansive early fruit, but they lacked real depth, and many slid into early anonymity. Balance was hard to find, with tannins inclined to be firm and the wines rendered more angular by the lack of richness and midpalate substance.

Some special cuvées bore enough content and compatible tannins to live for 12-plus years. Given the delicate grape matter, Paul Jaboulet cut their Thalabert cask stay from 18 to 12 months.

The whites were better—fairly full, with open bouquets. The traditionally made wines held good density and length: a vintage when the best northern sites like Larnage and Gervans far outranked the plain.

REDS

★★★★ Belle Pierrelles/Louis Belle, Chapoutier Meysonniers

★★★ P. Jaboulet Thalabert

★★ Dom du Colombier

★ de Vallouit

WHITES

★★★★ Ferraton, M. Sorrel

★★ Dom du Colombier

★ Delas, Dom du Pavillon

1995 Very good. The Syrah crop was limited by some indifferent flowering and by the onset of rain around 5 September. Ripeness was thorough if the grower was patient, and Graillot even went for *surmaturité*—overripeness—for extra richness. Tannins were firm thanks to the hot, dry tenor of the summer. The early fear was that the wines would be tough, especially if the grower had not waited long enough for the

polyphenolic ripeness. By 1999 classic wines from the plain like Pont-de-l'Isère and Chanos-Curson had blossomed and showed delightful roundness and warm fruit—real singing wines. Textures became sappy and oily. The top reds should live to 2010–12.

The whites were pretty full, with fair core. The ripeness meant that some of the plain wines lost their grip after seven years. Again, a better year for the northern sites; interesting complexity developed with age here. They can run towards 2005–07.

REDS

★★★★ Graillot Guiraude

★★★ Belle Louis Belle, Chapoutier Varonniers, Graillot, P. Jaboulet Thalabert

★★ Belle Pierrelles, Combier Grives, Dom Remizières Particulière

★ Dom des Entrefaux, R. Michelas Hautes Blaches, Dom du Pavillon, Pradelle

WHITES

★★★ Belle

★★ Dom Collonge, Dom du Pavillon

★ Dom Pochon, Cave de Tain

1996 Fair. The summer's weather broke down after a lovely June and a very quick flowering. July and August were very rainy and humid, so vegetation pushed on, but the grapes were not nourished. Ripening was a slow, uneven process. Rot hit in early September, but some alleviation came via the north wind. The problem of lagging phenolic ripening made it essential to be patient—sugars had reached their legal level by early September, by contrast. The crop was large and needed sorting, and some growers waited until early October. There was some chaptalisation to boost degree. Acidity levels were way higher than both 1995 and 1997, making this an edgy year. There wasn't enough secure fruit to allow the wines to tone down and round out comfortably, and textures are indistinct, often dry toned.

The classic reds showed some live fruit early on, though a dry side as well; lack of length was often a problem. The special cuvées were cast in similar vein, with a touch more middle content. This is not a year when cellaring brings forward great surprises, but the acidity levels mean that some wines can live for 10 to 13 years.

The whites were low-key, but their fruit showed well early on. It was important to harvest them well into September, so the early whites were inclined to be dilute. Those who waited made wines with more degree than the reds, giving them extra substance.

REDS

★★★★ Chapoutier Varonniers

★★★ P. Jaboulet Roure, Dom Pochon

★★ Jacques Frelin, Graillot Guiraude, P. Jaboulet Thalabert/Vieilles Vignes, Dom du Pavillon, Cave de Tain

★ Belle Pierrelles, Combier, Delas Clos St. Georges, Fayolle Grande Seguine/Voussères, G. Robin Albéric Bouvet

WHITES

★ Belle, Fayolle Les Pontaix, P. Jaboulet Roure

1997 Good. A pleasure year, in sharp contrast to the tetchy 1996. The vintage's style was made by the prolonged high heat of August and notably by the unusually warm nights that ran into mid-September. There was no rain either, so the vines did not switch off. Growers with higher vineyards in the northern sector fared best. Acidities are low, and the wines were warm and expressive from the start—easy to like. Some show very jammy flavours and work on a likeable single level of quite sweet berry fruit. "The style is fat, but I find less matter than the 2000s, which were a bit similar," Yann Chave

said. The reds will be best drunk until 2007–09. The whites struggle to show true depth and length *en bouche*. They were early drinkers, supple, broad and easy.

REDS

★★ Chapoutier Varonniers, Delas Clos St. Georges, P. Jaboulet Roure/Thalabert, Cave de Tain Hauts du Fief

★ Delas Tour d'Albon, Graillot, Cave de Tain

WHITES

★ Fayolle Les Blancs, P. Jaboulet Mule Blanche/Roure, Tardy et Ange

1998 Very good, a vintage of oily, robust character. August was too hot, and the grapes dried and gained thick skins. Ripening was early, acidity often low. Rain fell in the late stages of the harvest. The crop was small, affected by cool weather at flowering. Tannins were marked early on but have advanced quite fast. The fruit style is brewed, with dark, woody edging. Colours turned matt and subdued quite fast. There is now a sappy, leathery, nicely oiled texture in the best reds. Animal tones on the bouquets are typical of this year, along with an earthiness in the texture. It is a year that worked well for the special cuvées, since there was plenty of content for the winemaker to work around. A vintage to enjoy now; the fullest wines may live towards 2010–12.

The whites were less even, and some lacked genuine depth and balance. The best were stylish, well-knit wines with character and fair acidity. These have evolved and broadened well.

REDS

★★★★ Belle Louis Belle

★★★ Bied, Chapoutier Varonniers, Dom du Colombier classic/Gaby, Delas Le Clos, Entrefaux Machonnières,

Graillot Guiraude, P. Jaboulet Thal-abert, Dom du Pavillon-Mercurol, E. Pochon Château Curson

★★ Chapoutier Varonniers, B. Chave Tête de Cuvée, M. Chomel, Grail-lot, Habrard, Dom Pochon, Dom Remizières Christophe, G. Robin Albéric Bouvet, Cave de Tain Nobles Rives

★ Chapoutier Meysonniers, B. Chave Tradition, Dom Entrefaux, P. Jaboulet Roure, J. Marsanne, Vignerons de Tain

WHITES

WHITES

★★ Combier, Habrard

★ Chapoutier Meysonniers, B. Chave, Delas Les Launes, P. Jaboulet Mule Blanche/Roure, E. Pochon classic/Château Curson, G. Robin, Cave de Tain Nobles Rives

1999 Excellent. Lovely warm to hot weather, with the critical aid of well-timed bouts of rain. August heat was not excessive, and the ripening proceeded so evenly that some growers achieved a natural degree of 14.3 on their Syrah, which is very rare. The one drawback was the large crop, meaning that growers had to drop grapes to pre-serve acidity. The wines have all-round fullness, with a brewed, touch heated middle. Tannins are present but can ride on the back of the core extract. There are hints of jamminess in some wines, "usually present if the grower was idle in the vineyard," in the words of Delas' Jacques Grange. The vintage will live well, and the spe-cial cuvées can look ahead to a flourishing mid-dle-to-later age—out towards 2014. The north-ern sector did especially well, carrying better acidity than the plain; it thus avoided any of the soupiness shown by some of the latter wines.

The whites were very good, potent wines, with the Marsanne full of oily, fat flavour if cropped patiently from the best sites. Aromas were floral from the plain wines, and they showed well early on. Expect the best like Sorrel to live for 10 years or more.

REDS

★★★★ Chapoutier Varonniers, Delas Le Clos/Tour d'Albon, B. Chave Tête de Cuvée, Dom du Colombier Gaby, Dom Entrefaux Machon-nières, Graillot Guiraude, E. Pochon Château Curson, Rousset Picaudières

★★★ Graillot, P. Jaboulet Thalabert, Dom Pochon

★★ B. Ange Rêve d'Ange, Bied, Chapoutier Meysonniers/Petite Ruche, B. Chave Tradition, Cave Clairmonts Pionniers, Dom du Colombier, Combier Clos des Grives, Dom Entrefaux, Dom Murinais Veilles Vignes, Pradelle Hirondelles, Dom Remizières Christophe, Cave de Tain Hauts du Fief, Vignerons Réunis de Tain

★ M. Chomel Sassenas, Delas Launes, J. Marsanne, Dom Muri-nais Amandiers, Dom Remizières Particulière, M. Sorrel, Cave de Tain Nobles Rives, Veau d'Or classic/Marius

WHITES

★★★★ M. Sorrel

★★★ Dom du Colombier Gaby, Dom du Pavillon-Mercurol

★★ Chapoutier Meysonniers, B. Chave, Dard et Ribo, Habrard, P. Jaboulet Mule Blanche, Dom Murinais, E. Pochon classic/Château Curson

★ Dom Entrefaux Les Pends, Graillot, P. Jaboulet Roure, Dom Remizières Christophe/Particulière, Rousset

2000 Good, but not a straightforward year, and time has revealed inconsistencies. The main problem was that ripening moved at two speeds, the sugars running ahead of the tannins. July was cool, and the weather improved only around 10 August, when it became too hot. Mildew was an unusual blight this year. September was fine, until 65 mm (2.5 in.) of rain 19–22 September; this was mitigated by the north wind, so grey rot held off. It was essential to not pick too soon—something that caught out the typical trigger-happy machine harvester. Again, the crop was large—so it was vital to green harvest to avoid dilution.

REDS

Acidity levels were often low, colour levels were below average, and the low tannins meant a lack of structure for some. The style of the wines is rounded, undemanding; they showed easy fruit right away, and that made them a good buy when eating out. With age, it's clear the fruit on some of the classic-level wines is more edgy than first seemed likely, with a failure to sustain all through the palate. The wines have advanced to a more bosky, secondary stage, with the special cuvées best drunk by 2009–11 for the most part.

★★★★ P. Jaboulet Famille 2000, E. Pochon Château Curson

★★★ Belle Pierrelles/Louis Belle, Chapoutier Varonniers, Combier Clos des Grives, Dom Entrefaux Machonnières, Dom Murinais Vieilles Vignes, Dom du Pavillon-Mercurol, Rousset Picaudières

★★ B. Ange Rève d'Ange, Champal-Rocher, Chapoutier Meysonniers/Petite Ruche, B. Chave Tête de Cuvée/Tradition, M. Chomel Sassenas, Cave Clairmonts Pionniers, Combier Domaine, Dard et Ribo, Dom Entrefaux, Ferraton Matinière, Graillot, Guigal, Habrard, P. Jaboulet Roure/Thalabert, Dom

Murinais Amandiers, Pradelle Hirondelles, Dom Remizières Christophe, Cave de Tain Hauts du Fief

★ Dom du Colombier Gaby, Delas Launes, J-C & N. Fayolle Grande Seguine, E. Pochon, Dom Remizières, G. Robin Albéric Bouvet, M. Sorrel, Vignerons Réunis de Tain, Vins de Vienne classic/Palignons

(★) J-C & N. Fayolle Rochette

WHITES

The whites carry obvious, openly fruited bouquets and were immediately likeable. Their matter was rich enough to allow them some evolution, although the plain wines will advance ahead of the northern sector.

★★★ P. Jaboulet Mule Blanche

★★ Chapoutier Meysonniers, B. Chave, Dard et Ribo, Habrard, P. Jaboulet Roure, Dom Remizières Christophe, M. Sorrel

★ Bied, Dom du Colombier, Entrefaux Les Pends, Graillot, Dom Murinais, E. Pochon classic/Château Curson

2001 Excellent, ahead of 1999 with better acidity and, ultimately, balance than that vintage. The winter was wet, but not cold. Seventy millimetres (2.8 inches) of rain fell in early May, and the cycle fell behind. The summer was patchy, and a large storm on 14 July was followed by two months of dry weather, with August very hot. Sugars and polyphenols ripened more in step this year—gradually. The north wind played a strong role in helping the ripening. Philippe Belle remarked, "We had a lovely end season, all the way from mid-August to the end of our harvest in late October. There was a lot of concentration in the juice, with small berries; the combination of heat and wind worked well, especially as the soil was not too dry." Rain each week after 15 September was not a problem given the small size of the berries. "We even had to cool the harvest when we brought it in—we were picking in 25° to 30°C," recalled Yann Chave.

REDS

The ensemble of fruit and acidity renders these wines most enjoyable; the clear-cut nature of the fruit shows off the Syrah's young berry fruit vigour to great effect. "This is a very *sympathique* year," said Alain Graillot; "it's at the same time ripe, but it also retained some austerity, so there's a classic side as well." Bouquets are full, leaning towards dry-toned rather than fat aromas. The vintage is coming along with age and will evolve very well given its acidity and balance. There is also enough rich content to handle and absorb new-oak raising. The tannins on the special wines need four or five years. A life of at least 15 years beckons here.

★★★★ Chapoutier Varonniers, Combier Clos des Grives, Delas Le Clos, Dom Entrefaux Machonnières, E. Pochon Château Curson, Rousset Picaudières

★★★ Belle Pierrelles/Louis Belle, Y. Chave Tête de Cuvée, Combier, E. Darnaud Les Trois Chênes, Delas Tour d'Albon, Ferraton Matinière, Graillot Guiraude, Habrard, P. Jaboulet Roure, with some Thalabert ★★★, others (★), Meffre Laurus, Dom Murinais Vieilles Vignes, Dom du Pavillon-Mercurol, G. Robin Albéric Bouvet

★★ B. Ange Rêve d'Ange, Chapoutier Meysonniers/Petite Ruche, Y. Chave, M. Chomel, Cave Clairmonts Pionniers/Jardin Zen, Dom du Colombier, Colombo Tuilière, Combier L, Dard et Ribo, Delas Launes, E. Darnaud Mise en Bouche, O. Dumaine Croix du Verre, Dom Entrefaux, Fayolle Fils et Fille

Pontaix/Voussères/Cornirets, Graillot, Guigal, Dom Murinais Amandiers, E. Pochon, Dom Remizières Christophe, G. Robin Papillon, Rousset, Dom des 7 Chemins Cuvée 7 Chemins, Cave de Tain Hauts du Fief, Vins de Vienne Palignons

★ B. Ange, Dom La Batellerie, Dom Chenêts, Dom Collonge, O. Dumaine, J-C & N. Fayolle Rochette, P. Jaboulet Jalets, Dom Michelas Saint Jemms Chasselière, Ogier Allégories Antoine Ogier, G. Robin Albéric Bouvet, M. Sorrel, Cave de Tain Nobles Rives

(★) Ferraton Grand Courtil, Pradelle Hirondelles

WHITES

The whites are also excellent, full of rich matter and backed by a driving level of freshness. Their early sinew is integrating and making them excellent to drink in the period 2005–08. The best will live towards 2012–14.

★★★ Chapoutier Petite Ruche/Meysonniers, Y. Chave Rouvre, Combier Clos des Grives, Dard et Ribo K, O. Dumaine Croix du Verre, Entrefaux Les Pends, M. Sorrel

★★ B. Ange, Dom La Batellerie, Y. Chave, Dom Chenêts Mont Rousset, Colombo Gravières, Dom du Colombier, Combier, Dard et Ribo, Delas Launes, O. Dumaine, Dom Entrefaux, Fayolle Fils et Fille Pontaix, P. Jaboulet Roure, Dom Murinais, E. Pochon Château Curson, Pradelle Hirondelles, Rousset, Cave de Tain Nobles Rives, Vidal-Fleury

★ Cave Clairmonts Pionniers, Combier, J-C & N. Fayolle Les Blancs, Ferraton Matinière, Graillot, Guigal, P. Jaboulet Mule Blanche,

Dom Remizières Cuvée
Christophe, Pradelle,
E. Pochon, Dom Veau d'Or

2002 Mediocre—no surprise, given the series of hurdles presented by the weather through the year. The first big frost since 1975 sent temperatures down to −5°C in four hours in the early morning of 8 April—the day later reached 15°C. The main sufferer was fruit, but vines were hit as well. July was variable, with hail on 14 July and in early August. A windless summer with rain present set up conditions for rot, with hot and humid conditions from the end of August to 12 September unleashing a lot of rot on the Syrah.

"The plain was where the worst troubles were—some plots had acid rot; it was a year when the harvesting machine should have been banned; it was just not capable of sorting the rot like there was," reported J. Grange of Delas. "The grey rot meant you couldn't afford to wait to pick as you might usually like to have done," said Y. Chave. 65 millimetres (2.5 inches) of rain on 9 September added to the woes. Graillot lost 40 per cent of the crop; Dard et Ribo 50 per cent; Combier and S. Cornu both lost 30 per cent. "It wasn't the final rain that was dire—it was all the lead-up factors on top," recalled L. Combier.

The plain was savagely hit, more than the northern hillsides. "I carted crop away from my vineyard on Beaumont-Monteux and dumped it elsewhere to decoy the flies," L. Tardy stated. Dom des Entrefaux also lost 75 per cent of the Beaumont-Monteux portion of their crop. The slope vines carried less rot, but Rousset still struggled to achieve 12° for his prime ripening vineyard of *Picaudières*. A lot of the wines hovered around 10.5° to 11°, and needed at least 1° of chaptalisation.

REDS

Unquestionably a light vintage, its fruit light and often tenuous. Some Mercurol reds show lean red fruit flavours, in a firm cherry style. The better wines come from the northern sec-

tor. Many of the reds risk drying out, with their lack of true, well-founded core a problem. Where oak has been excessive or clumsily applied, the problem is aggravated. Northern-sector wines from Larnage and Gervans contained a degree of integration, but worked on a reduced scale, the main granite wines offering a 10-odd–year life, the softer Larnage wines a couple of years less. Quite rightly, there were fewer than usual special wines, and those southern domaines that produced the usual duo provided the market with ignoble "classic" offerings.

★★★ Fayolle Fils et Fille Cornirets

★★(★) P. Jaboulet Thalabert, Dom Martinelles

★★ Dom La Batellerie, Belle Pierrelles, Chapoutier Meysonniers/Varonniers, Y. Chave, Delas Launes, Dom Entrefaux, Fayolle Fils et Fille Les Pontaix, Graillot, Guigal, E. Pochon Château Curson, G. Robin Papillon, Rousset classic/Picaudières, Dom des 7 Chemins Cuvée 7 Chemins

★ Cave de Tain Sélection Première, Chapoutier Petite Ruche, Cave Clairmonts Pionniers, Combier, Dard et Ribo, E. Darnaud Trois Chênes, O. Dumaine, Dom Entrefaux Coteau des Pends, Fayolle Fils et Fille Voussères, Habrard, Dom Michelas Saint Jemms Signature/Chasselière, Dom Murinais Vieilles Vignes, Pradelle, Dom Remizières, G. Robin Albéric Bouvet, M. Sorrel

(★) Cave Clairmonts, P. Jaboulet Jalets, Dom Murinais Amandiers, E. Pochon

WHITES

The vintage was better for the whites, especially because the summer was not too hot, so there is a floral side present. Again, the southern area suffered most from rot, with some crop there halved and under 11°. The Marsanne did better than the Roussanne, and those who waited until near the end of September, like Dard et Ribo, achieved fair ripeness in their old Marsanne. The northern-sector whites held more stuffing and Laurent Fayolle brought in crop at up to 12°.

There are graceful floral elements on the best bouquets, and the textures are pliant, with a few of the usual hazelnut flavours present. Often these are wines for aperitif or for gentle foods. The best should be drunk by 2010–12.

   ★★★ Dom Entrefaux Coteau des Pends, Rousset

  ★★(★) Delas Launes

    ★★ Combier, Dard et Ribo regular/K, Dom Entrefaux, Fayolle Fils et Fille Pontaix, Habrard, P. Jaboulet Roure, Rousset Fût de Chêne

     ★ B. Ange, Dom La Batellerie, Bouachon Maurelle, Chapoutier Meysonniers/Petite Ruche, Dom Chenêts Mont Rousset, Cave Clairmonts Pionniers, E. Darnaud, O. Dumaine, Graillot, P. Jaboulet Mule Blanche, Dom Michelas Saint Jemms Signature, E. Pochon classic/Château Curson, G. Robin Marelles, Dom des 7 Chemins, M. Sorrel, Cave de Tain

   (★) Cave Clairmonts, Collonge, Dom Murinais

2003 Very good. A most unusual year, with wines displaying aromas and flavours that are not normally found in Crozes-Hermitage, thanks to the extreme heat and intense ripening process. The story of the summer is quite simple—hot and dry, with crop losses starting by July as the heat moved well into the 30s°C. "The extreme heat burnt the skins and shrivelled the grapes—we suffered from evaporation everywhere," said R. Rousset, who cropped just 18 hl from his 1.1 ha on the hill of *Picaudières*. Many domaines lost half their crop—hillside and southern sectors alike: Harbrard, Dom Batel-

lerie, 7 Chemins. Harvest dates lurched suddenly forward as growers moved to save what they could—Rousset on 18 August was not alone. There was a storm of 100 mm (4 in.) on 26 August that helped to unblock the phenolic acids that had trailed the sugars in ripening. One of the later harvesters was Y. Chave, who started 3 September after the rain: "We worked in 25°C, not 35°C, with the Syrah coming in at 14.3°—more like Languedoc—but that wasn't too obvious."

REDS

Vinifications needed plenty of surveillance, with such ripe grapes ready to ferment at top speed. Acidification was required for several, otherwise the wines would have died, and the risk of volatile acidity lurked in the background. The wines are generously filled, Birth of Venus in shape, and both northern and southern sectors have enjoyed a bounty of flavour this year. The wines have emerged with greater style than might have been foreseen at the outset, and their early vigour is appealing.

Bouquets show southern *garrigue* aromas, with plenty of savoury dark fruit present. Unusual aromas this year are ones like chocolate, toffee, even cocoa and mocha. So ripe and grilled were the grapes that some vat-only wines show the dried raisin effect that could be taken for oak. Some minerality cools the aromas of the granite-based wines of the northern sector. There is so much squeezy fruit sweetness on the palates that this is a vintage that will appeal to young people not used to drinking wine. The sweet, packed black fruit flavours hold jam and truffly, earthy aspects at times.

Tannins are evident, and prolong the palates. Some alcohol and oak effects stuck out after 15 months, more from the southern-sector wines. There is generally more definition and stylish content in the northern-sector wines; they show some localised restraint, with cooler, more mineral finishes. The *négociant* wines can approach the quality of some of the domaines this year—all are sweet and full and, at least when young, taste quite similar.

The main debate is how long the reds will live—whether they can hold together and develop variety and a degree of complexity over time. Most will drink fine from 2006–07; a few need to be set aside until 2008. The open, early wines should be drunk by 2011–12, the longest-lived can run to 2018–21.

REDS

★★★★(★) Delas Clos St. Georges

★★★★ E. Darnaud Trois Chênes, Graillot Guiraude, P. Jaboulet Roure

★★★(★) Y. Chave Tête de Cuvée

★★★ B. Ange Rève d'Ange, Dom La Batellerie, Belle Louis Belle, Dom Les Bruyères Les Croix, Chapoutier Meysonniers, E. Darnaud Mise en Bouche, O. Dumaine Croix du Verre, J-C & N. Fayolle Grande Seguine, Ferraton Grand Courtil, Graillot, G. Robin Albéric Bouvet, Rousset Picaudières, Vidal-Fleury

★★(★) R. Betton Fûts de Chêne, Champal-Rocher, Delas Launes, Fayolle Fils et Fille Cornirets, E. Pochon Château Curson, Dom Remizières Christophe, Rousset

★★ B. Ange, R. Betton, Dom Les Bruyères, Chapoutier Varonniers, Y. Chave, Cave Clairmonts, Collonge, Dom du Colombier classic/Gaby, Delas Launes/Tour d'Alban, Dom Entrefaux, Habrard, P. Jaboulet Thalabert, Dom Martinelles classic/Coteaux, Meffre Laurus, Dom Michelas Saint Jemms Chasselière, Dom Murinais Amandiers/Caprice Valentin, Pradelle, Dom Remizières Particulière/L'Essentiel, Cave de Tain classic/Hauts du Fief, Vins de Vienne Palignons

★(★) Bouachon Maurelle, M. Chomel, Dom Entrefaux Machonnières, Dom des Hauts Chassis Galets/Chassis

★ Arnoux et Fils, L. Bernard, Ferraton Matinière, P. Jaboulet Jalets, Dom des 7 Chemins

WHITES

All growers reported the Marsanne to have been in doughty form, resisting the drought well. This was a vintage when it could parade its unbridled richness, not surprising with some growers cropping their last batches at 15.5°. Cellar restraint brought forward the best wines, with some balance in them. The wines are ripe, oily, fully charged. The Marsanne nuttiness comes through, as does a full power. At 15 months, plenty of oak is apparent, and also alcohol at times.

Bouquets are ample and broad, sometimes potent. Any freshness detectable comes from the northern sector. At times, finishes can carry kirsch, heated elements and can also taper away, the wines' low acidity obvious. These are wines that will live for 10 years, although some will continue if they were not overworked in the cellar. All demand drinking with food rather than as an aperitif, and their marriage with Asian cuisine would be particularly interesting this year.

★★★ Dom La Batellerie, Dard et Ribo, O. Dumaine Croix de Verre, Dom Entrefaux Coteau des Pends, Fayolle Fils et Fille Pontaix, Habrard, J-C & N. Fayolle Vielles Vignes, Dom Martinelles, Dom Remizières Christophe, Vidal-Fleury

★★ Belle, Chapoutier Meysonniers, Y. Chave Rouvre, Delas Launes, Dom Entrefaux, Guigal, P. Jaboulet Mule Blanche/Roure, Dom Remizières Particulière

★(★) Cave de Tain

★ Dom Les Bruyères, Y. Chave, Combier

(★) Pradelle

2004 Fair, with a lack of uniformity in the wines and often dilution on the palate. The winter was very dry, with no frost to contend with. It was then very dry until 1 August. In all, just 100 mm (4 in.) of rain fell between 1 January and 1 August. This was bad news for any vineyards where the grower normally applied weedkillers or ignored the working of the soil—the vines were stressed. "Ripening was completely blocked before the mid-August rains came—the wet weather was vital," L. Fayolle asserted. Around 150 mm fell in two storms between 10 and 25 August, with some hail on the plain at *Les Chênes Verts*. Thereafter it was fine, but not at all hot for a week in early September that centred between 18° to 20°C, marked also by the Bise Noire, the version of the north wind when the clouds are black.

Some flat-ground growers like Dom Chenêts suffered rot in places and chose 2004 for their first year of manual harvesting. The trick was to relax and wait this year: "Most unusual—we could choose when to pick with no hurry. We harvested for one day on 21 September, then left it until 27 September, and were one of the last to finish a week after that. The later picking brought a gain not in degree but in overall maturity and phenolic ripeness," said A. Graillot. "We kept a very close eye on the weather forecasts because we were waiting through September for the phenolic ripening that had been slow," commented Émilie Desmeure. Yields reverted to more normal levels a touch under the maximum allowed.

REDS

The best reds contain clear fruit, with agreeable cut and definition, a marked contrast with 2003. These are "air" wines, with floating red fruits, a live character, and quiet *gras*. I expect them to gain in matter as they age. They fall between 2000 and 2001 in style—with more balance than the 2000s—and, while in a similar fresh vein, they are more approachable early on than the originally tauter 2001s. The best cuvées from older vines will live for around 15 years.

★★(★) Fayolle Fils et Fille Cornirets, Dom Remizières Christophe, G. Robin Papillon

★★ Dom La Batellerie, Fayolle Fils et Fille Pontaix, M. Poinard

★(★) Tardieu-Laurent Vielles Vignes

WHITES

The whites are very good, and may become impressive with time. The profile of the vintage suggests a good level of acidity, with a healthy crop that carries genuine content. "Our Marsanne was extraordinary," reported F. Viale of Dom du Colombier: "not one spoilt grape, even on the last harvesting that brought in bunches at 13.5°." Balance is good in these wines; with a mix of richness and freshness, they finish long on the palate. Plenty will be charming early on, and the best will enjoy a healthy evolution of more than 10 years.

★★ Dom La Batellerie, Dom du Colombier, O. Dumaine, Dom Martinelles, G. Robin Marelles

6

St-Joseph

I HAVE A SOFT SPOT for St-Joseph. Some of my earliest memories of young Syrah come from standing 30 years ago in the cramped, musty cellars of Trollat and Coursodon and breathing in the raw hedge fruit aromas, their tangles of blackberry mixed up with tar and pine oil. There is a clear-cut simplicity, a flight to freedom, in these wines that is absent in the more grounded, serious duo of nearby Cornas and Hermitage. The St-Josephs seem like the tearaways of the granite slopes, their neighbours the more formal suits.

On a more equitable level, St-Josephs also possess a poise and a frame that places the best of them ahead of their other neighbour Crozes-Hermitage. People can say "The two wines are just different," but in the glass they are choosing to ignore that vital word—"tannin." Much of St-Joseph's west bank of the Rhône is composed of the granite outcrops of the Massif Central. Among the few east-bank granite stragglers from that seam are the west end of the Hermitage hill—fabulous sites like *Les Bessards*—and the best Crozes-Hermitage villages like Gervans. Elsewhere much Crozes comes from an old fruit-bearing plain, *Les Chassis*.

Which leads us on to tannin. The tannic structure brought out by the granite is one of order and definition. It places a frame around the wines that keeps them tidy, subtle, and ready for an evolution that turns fulsome youth into complex middle age. The tannins give these wines a slightly pesky side, the fruit is grainy, a little taut at times, but always the aroma is vibrant and layered, never monotone.

So here is a country cousin wine which can rise to the occasion, but which above all expresses a very important Syrah style for anyone wanting to check out this grape's credentials. Syrah and granite is a good pairing, especially if the granite is laced with minor influences such as a little clay, and its pH level is neutral. It's grandiose at Hermitage, voluptuous at Côte-Rôtie off the *Côte Blonde*, grave at Cornas, and here—well, it's lively, unleashed, and often delicious.

But St-Joseph today has run ahead of its legal status. The name refers to a hillside near Tournon, and the original idea behind this was to reflect the Syrah wine made in a few core villages north and south of the central fulcrum of Tournon, the town opposite Tain l'Hermitage. The main villages—Mauves, St-Jean-de-Muzols,

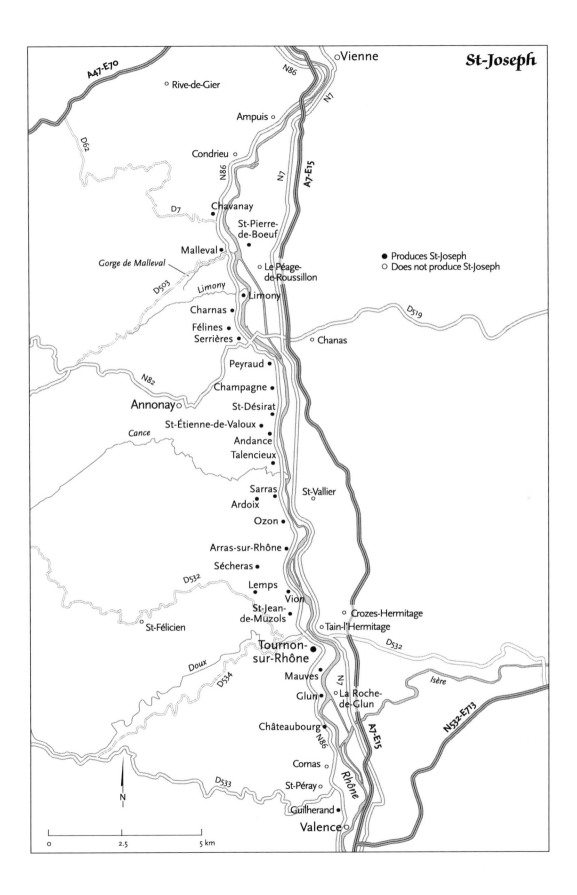

St-Joseph

- Vienne
- Rive-de-Gier
- Ampuis
- Condrieu
- Chavanay
- St-Pierre-de-Boeuf
- Malleval
- *Gorge de Malleval*
- Le Péage-de-Roussillon
- Limony
- Charnas
- Félines
- Serrières
- Chanas
- Peyraud
- Champagne
- Annonay
- St-Désirat
- St-Étienne-de-Valoux
- *Cance*
- Andance
- Talencieux
- Sarras
- St-Vallier
- Ardoix
- Ozon
- Arras-sur-Rhône
- Sécheras
- Lemps
- Vion
- St-Jean-de-Muzols
- St-Félicien
- Crozes-Hermitage
- Tain-l'Hermitage
- Tournon-sur-Rhône
- *Doux*
- Mauves
- Glun
- La Roche-de-Glun
- Châteaubourg
- *Isère*
- Cornas
- St-Péray
- Guilherand
- Valence

● Produces St-Joseph
○ Does not produce St-Joseph

Rhône

A47-E70, N86, N7, A7-E15, D62, D7, N86, D503, Limony, N82, D519, D532, D532, D534, D533, N86, N7, A7-E15, N532-E713

N

0   2.5   5 km

and Tournon itself—possess a sound viticultural past, their best hillside locations proven through the hands of many generations.

Created in 1956, the St-Joseph *appellation* was enlarged in June 1969 from six villages to 25. At a stroke, the vineyards became spread over nearly 40 miles, not six. Different locations, soils, and microclimates were brought into the equation. Vineyards rose from a total area of 97 hectares in 1971 to 640 hectares in 1992 and surged on to 904 by 1999. In 2005 the figure stood at around 990 hectares.

This is a vineyard that has grown more than 10 times in just over 30 years. In 2004 alone, around 15 hectares were planted at Sarras, to integrate into the Co-opérative's already large and often indifferent output. The immediate implication is this: large amounts of young vines now grow on sites that cannot all be good —and if their fruit is handled by novice *vignerons*, there is little certainty that good wine will be the outcome. In late 2004 one eminent grower commented darkly that in the next 10 years, St-Joseph will either firm up and really become a strong *appellation*, or it will disintegrate.

This severe case of plantation fever was allowed by people acting more from vested interests than long-term wisdom. Getting people to jump on the wine bandwagon while it was rolling sweetly along was simple, but the long-term effects have had to be dealt with.

We are talking economic and social change here. St-Joseph is essentially an Ardèche wine. The Ardèche is a proud *département* where the people have always lived rugged lives—at least before they could sell their farms to foreign tourists for vast prices. Livings were made not on a grand scale but by chiselling out the income from crops and fruit trees and animals, what the French call *polyculture*. There has always been a delicate balance between these sources: if prices moved higher for one, then it was invested in. There would be a few cutbacks elsewhere, a change of plantation, and life moved on. There was never one clear winner.

Wine changed that. Neighbours could see those who had stuck with wine for generations suddenly doing well, starting broadly during the 1980s, when the outside world first paid close attention to the Rhône. Prices moved up, not in a straight line, but the economic case became clear. Wine was the winner. Fruit, goats, vegetables—hard work all of them—made less sense, with polytunnels in Spain or Morocco adding to the sense of threat.

The stampede of indiscriminate planting finally provoked action from the Syndicat des Vignerons de St-Joseph. From early 1992 new legislation was designed to cut back the total area potentially available for vineyards from 7,000 hectares to under 3,500 hectares and, over a 30-year period, to reduce the incidence of vines planted in unsuitable sites—mainly on flat ground at the foot of the slopes and on high ground above 300 metres.

When the measures were announced, opportunists planted at speed to enjoy the supposed benefits of selling *appellation* wine from easy-to-work sites—high plateaus and flat plains, notably. The vineyard area under vine has now grown by 55 per cent since 1992! There were also anomalies, as pointed out at the time by then Growers Union President M. Amorique Cornut-Chauvinc. "I can think of one place—Charnas, near Limony—where there are 50 hectares of good vineland that should have been allowed originally in the *appellation*," he commented.

The measures meant that after 30 years—by 2021—poor sites would lose their right to produce St-Joseph and be downgraded to *vin de pays*. In the meantime, a series of special "shop window" zones of better exposure were planted in different *communes*, starting in 1990–91.

At Serrières, Paul Jaboulet Aîné form part of this Vitrine scheme, along with family domaines like Vallet, Boissonnet, and the Cave de St-Désirat. Two and a half hectares of hillside land were reclaimed for the vine. Likewise at Sarras, the Domaines Bonarieux and La Garenne, covering 3.3 hectares and four hectares respectively, were planted right above the village by the Co-opérative. Other *communes* with Vitrine projects included Vion and Arras, and the broad scheme ended in 1996.

Mauves was a little different, with its Vitrine operation held up by the bypass road construction. There, 30 hectares were set aside for this, an operation that was in full swing in 2004–05 on hillside locations opposite the village. Most of the growers are involved in this scheme. Such redevelopment of special areas will be a slow process judging by the average cost, however—probably over £30,000 (US$54,000) per hectare over a three-year period.

Jean-Louis Chave from Mauves pointed out some of the wobbly economics at work: "The cost in 1996 was US$45,000 to US$60,000 per hectare—vast given the price of wine then of US$2.50 or so per litre in bulk! The best domaines would be getting three times that price, but it's still a vastly uneven equation, and depends heavily on a buoyant price for the wine." The price of the wine has indeed risen since then, but so has that of the land!

Price increases encouraged a cavalier approach among some growers, as well. The average price per litre sold in bulk between 1980 and 1988 was 12-13 francs, between 1988 and 1998 18 francs and yet between January and September 1998—frost that year had cut the crop—it rose to 30 francs. For 2003 it ran around the equivalent of 32 francs, and for the 2004 campaign, the figure hovered around 28 to 31 francs, with a tendency to ease in view of the economic situation.

At the Cave de St-Désirat, Jean-Luc Chaléat calculates that in 1998 a cultivator with one hectare received revenue of around 70,000 francs (£7,000/US$10,500) before costs; by 2003 this had risen to 110,000 francs (£11,000/US$16,500). "This may encourage bad habits," is his ominous comment.

There are still some anomalies, though—pretty glaring ones. At Chavanay and Limony, growers can plant Roussanne and Marsanne to make white St-Joseph, but also Viognier to make Condrieu, which they know they can sell for a lot more. Sites like *La Côte* and *Les Rivoires* qualify for this strange dual allowance.

Some welcome tightening came out of the important INAO, the central French wine organ-

isation, from 2002. Alain Paret commented memorably that some growers were going to find their buttocks tightening with this! "Yields are being properly controlled—if there are too many bunches, the wine will be declassified," he states. "And people will be expected to replace dead plants—it's better to have many vines with a few bunches than a few vines with an overload of crop," he adds.

The average production of St-Joseph per annum over succeeding five-year periods since the creation of the *appellation* in 1956 is shown in table 7. From the growers' point of view, working methods have been tightening in some places. "I reckon it was around 1996–97 when I started to do canopy management, and drop grapes," says Laurent Marthouret, a grower in his 30s at Charnas. "This happened around me as well, helped maybe by having at last run down our stocks. 1993 had been a problem year that took a long time to sell. Things really got moving with the low-quantity, high-quality year of 1998."

But the slowdown in sales of 2003–04 put pressure on a lot of the recent start-ups, and anyone deep into the banks will find life difficult as stocks remain in the cellars. The stock figure rose every year from 1999 (end August, 37,499 hl) until 2003 (end August, 51,239 hl, an alarming 37 per cent rise). The year 2004 was abundant, and if 2005 followed suit and prices were to shift downwards—well, perhaps I should banish such outlandish thoughts here and now.

TABLE 7

Average Annual Production of St-Joseph (in hectolitres)

1956–60	1,404
1961–65	1,664
1966–69	1,873
1970–74	3,073
1975–79	4,980
1980–84	11,807
1985–89	17,838
1990–94	24,477
1995–99	29,568
2000–04	33,190

So for some years to come, St-Joseph will remain an *appellation* whose red and white wines need to be chosen from a nucleus of sound growers. The fast expansion of the past 15-plus years has meant there is a wide spectrum between the best and the worst wines here.

Statistically, around 30 per cent of the wine is sold through merchant or *négociant* channels; Co-opératives account for 40 per cent—notably those of St-Désirat, Tain l'Hermitage, Sarras, and a little from Péage de Roussillon; and domaines run to about 30 per cent.

Unfortunately, St-Joseph is also the northern Rhône *appellation* most guilty of turning out banal, short-lived techno wines. These are often made by growers using young vine fruit, recently starting their own production, and taking short-cuts. I have thrown away hundreds of francs or even Euros sitting in restaurants trying the unknown St-Joseph from round the corner. All too often there is a dazzling, black currant opening on the aroma and a puckering second black currant surge on the palate—which totally disappear after an hour's airing. The wines then become hard, mean, and aroma free. They are cellar wines, not nature's.

While St-Joseph's true merit can be often hidden, the good stuff is well worth investigation. The red is pure Syrah, while the white, making up about 9 per cent of the total, (2004 figure) is a mainly Marsanne—some Roussanne mix.

St-Joseph is an *appellation* of two distinct zones. Wine styles differ centred on a north-south divide that occurs around the village of Sarras. The southern sector, which comprises the start-up villages of 1956, gives wines of often ripe appeal, which carry berries, tar, and smoky aspects. Their tannins vary according to the amount of granite, and its acidity, that is present in the vineyards, but they are usually well founded within the wines.

The northern-sector wines are more peppery, their black fruit more taut. Tannins are often leaner, and the wines' texture is generally drier than that of the southern sector. This is a simplification, with many subtexts and nuances available, but acts as a general rule.

Chavanay is the northern "capital," and with its neighbour Malleval, it turns out Syrahs that are less showy when young than the southern-sector wines, their fruit more tightly knit; they need time to loosen and to gain extra variety of flavour beyond the straight dark berries and mint. "It's younger granite in the northern area," says Jean-Luc Chaléat of the St-Désirat Co-opérative. "It's less decomposed, and there's more pepper in the wines. Here we have the crumbled granite, and the wines are less angular from here down to the south of the *appellation*. The only exception is around Châteaubourg, where there are outcrops of limestone."

Even the tannic structures can be different from one place to another along this west bank. The tannins from the site called *St-Joseph*, beside Tournon, hold more density and finesse than those from Mauves across a little stream. In turn, Chavanay's tannins are drier and tauter than those from Mauves, lending the wine extra reserve.

Apart from the fact that ripening is earlier and easier at Tournon and Mauves, the age of the vineyards plays a role in distinguishing between there and Chavanay. Vineyards and growers are better established in the southern sector—wine has been a going concern, a sole activity, for several decades now. Not so at Chavanay, as can be witnessed by the roadside stalls still selling fruit and vegetables and other local produce along with the wine. There is only a tiny area planted with Syrah dating from the 1920s and 1930s in the northern area, while the south has more and older vineyards.

Other factors count. One wine may come from a full hillside vineyard, the other a plateau plantation; one slope may face southeast, the other straight east as it runs away from the Rhône. The vines may be 50 years old in one place, five years old in another. One grower may be laissez-faire in the cellar, the other an interventionist. But mostly, all roads lead back to the old and established cry of *terroir*, and climate. The buyer needs to know the domaine and follow those who can make grand wine in top years and good wine in difficult years.

As an important voice in local affairs, the Guigal viewpoint is worth a listen on the subject of *terroir*. Philippe explains that they source their St-Joseph red from Tournon and Sarras, with a little from St-Désirat: "We find the reds from the northern Chavanay area carry a green pepper aspect and can be rather bitter at times."

Another danger to St-Joseph's name comes from the increasing incidence of special cuvées. If some of the best growers with the best locations insist on making three or even four different red wines, the bottom of the pile suffers. That spells dilution for the basic St-Joseph wine, not the Cuvée Prestige or whatever. And which wine is more likely to be widely distributed and act as the unofficial flag bearer? Well, the wine sold in greater quantity—the regular, basic wine. The Cuvée Prestige is targeted at a minority of wine writers—probably ahead of consumers, even, which is a pretty pass to reach. Then, the reasoning goes, the domaine can become acclaimed and all its wines can be sold for higher prices.

There is room at most estates for an Old Vines cuvée, and that's it. The Old Vines will usually be from a specific site, often high on a craggy granite hillside, with naturally lower yields. If these wines are not too messed about by new wood and extreme extraction techniques in the cellar, they are noble. They and their regular *cuvée dauphins* are the reference points for St-Joseph: names like Gonon, Gripa, and Perret spring to mind.

HISTORY

Tournon stands wedged between rock and river on the Rhône's Ardèche side, its right bank, and carries a long feudal tradition that brings with it references to the role of winemaking. A 1292 charter granted by Odon of Tournon to its citizens stated that "it was absolutely necessary to let flow the production of wine before foreign wines arrived in the town": foreign meant anything not local in those days. Three miles up the road (local, therefore) at St-Jean-de-Muzols, its

eleventh-century church celebrates wine with the adornment of grapes on the top of its columns.

By the fifteenth century, Tournon had moved into royal circles as a wine-producing area under the reign of Louis XII (1498–1515). Then, according to Elie Brault, in his *Anne et Son Époque*, the monarchy would allow only its very own wines to be served at the Court of France. There were at the time three royal vineyards, those of Beaune and Chenove in Burgundy and the much-esteemed Clos de Tournon.

The wine of Tournon remained in royal circles for some years more, for it is recorded locally that King Henry II (1519–59) always kept a personal reserve of several barrels. The style of the wine he so liked can be judged from a quotation of 1560 by the first head of the College of Tournon, now one of France's oldest secondary schools, who praised the "delicate and dainty" wine of Tournon and Mauves, which was sold as far away as Rome and which the princes and king of France were prepared to acquire for themselves at no little cost.

The first written mention of St-Joseph as a vineyard came in 1668, when the inventory of the College of Tournon was sought by Louis XIV, who was looking to reform the universities. As a wealthy institution, the college played a central role in winemaking here. The King's Councillor was informed that "the Jesuit Fathers of Tournon [at the college] cultivated a vegetable garden, as well as a vineyard called St-Joseph," which was said to cover some "25 *fessoirées*," the equivalent of 10 hectares. This vineyard, at a place called Ryf de Leys, seems to be just south of what today is the *lieu-dit Peygros*, where Bernard Gripa works a vineyard. The college also owned vines on Hermitage's *Les Murets*.

Later on, when the college was enlarged in 1777, what is today's Lycée car park was the vineyard plot exchanged for that part of *Le Clos* vineyard that was to be built on. But only a dozen years later, the Revolution was to change things forever.

The Day of Reckoning for the college came in 1790, when, badly in need of revenue, Talleyrand decided that his sequestration of the clergy's goods would be followed by their sale. Eventually, in January 1793, the vineyard came up for sale. It was to go under the hammer as one lot, but the locals submitted the reasonable request that it be sold in plots. Their reasoning was in full support of the notion of *terroir*: "This vineyard is on the plain and on slopes with different degrees of quality and value, and may also be too large for just one *citoyen* to buy. If split, all the plots should contain both plain and slope"—very egalitarian.

This is how the Tournon vineyard's future shape came to pass. The lots were bought by notables, one of them a doctor, another the ex-Mayor of Tournon, and many of them related by blood or marriage. The plot of one Antoine Maurice belongs to Guigal now that he has bought it from J-L Grippat, while another plot can be traced directly to Roger and Syvlain Blachon today.

Meanwhile Mauves' repute was evident, and its wine cropped up in French literature of the nineteenth century. The celebrated French writer Victor Hugo (1802–85) had evidently encountered, and enjoyed, the wine, for he mentioned it in *Les Misérables*. Describing a social gathering, Hugo wrote that, in addition to the ordinary table wine, there was served a bottle of "this good wine of Mauves." Hugo hastened to add that no more than one bottle was brought out because it was "an expensive wine."

This is supported by the Purchase Book of Mauves' most famous merchant, called Ozier, which was found by Jean Gonon; it showed an 1849 invoice for a cask of 1847 St-Joseph selling for 100 francs and a cask of 1847 Cornas selling for just 50 francs.

Scanning through the Macker cellar book from 1805 to 1837, one finds Mauves to be the one village mentioned from today's St-Joseph; its price per barrel was more usually below that of Cornas in the most celebrated years. In 1825, for instance, Cornas reached a high of 200 francs, Mauves a high of 120 francs. In more regular vintages, they were not far apart—Cornas 100 francs versus 96 francs in 1812, 72 francs versus 50 to 60 francs in 1832, when the Gervans wine (today Crozes-Hermitage) was sold for 60 to 65 francs, and 55 to 60 francs for Cornas versus 50 to 55 francs for Mauves in 1836.

Mauves' wine clearly held its aficionados, without a sense of grandeur—much like today. Amusingly, in a book titled *Souvenirs de l'Ardèche* of 1846 (Ovide de Valgorge, Editions Camariguo, Nîmes), the following is scathingly written: "As for the wine of Mauves, it is far from possessing the advantages of Saint-Péray, St-Joseph and Cornas. It has less vinosity than them, and is flat, without taste and even rough. It is a wine of cabaret."

Following the habits of the Ardèche *département*, wine was not the only crop from these hillsides and craggy openings. Fruit and vegetables were also main contributors to a family's income, coming and going as prices moved. A well-known wine family like the Gonons at Mauves still work around a hectare of apricots, the Coursodons as many as 10 hectares, and there was an important fruit Co-opérative outside Mauves until the 1970s: specialities were apricots along with cherries and pears.

At St-Jean-de-Muzols, the wine culture ran deeper than at Mauves, and fruit was regarded in a wholly practical light. Cherries were the preferred crop, since they brought cash in early in the summer season. Apricots represented a longer wait and were less favoured.

Mauves was also celebrated for its onions, the flat, sweet, rose-coloured variety. Every year on August 29 there is the popular Onion Fair at Tournon. What killed off large-scale onion production in the late 1970s was the labour costs, with at least two weedings needed each year.

Looking back, therefore, it's at Tournon and at St-Jean-de-Muzols that the deepest viticultural roots exist—villages that were more wholly dependent on the vine than Mauves with its fruit and vegetable sources. Scratch the surface at St. Jean, for instance, and there are still people like Trollat, Fogier, Jean-Claude Farge, and André Margisier who have always known only vines and small, damp cellars. Amidst all the industrial zones and new houses with their swanky terraces, these are people mightily respected by the remaining country folk, whether the wine comes in bottles, containers, or straight from the *pipette*.

Interestingly, south of Mauves, it's Cornas that has the most *vinicole* culture of all these Ardechois villages. As Jean-Louis Chave put it once: "There's a lot of *sagesse* [wisdom] around at Cornas. It's a pity that some young growers arrive and don't take account of their context." Before the Second World War, the wine was sold around the region as Côtes du Rhône, with the occasional shipment further afield. The Courbis family would sell casks to Paris—five or six at a time would be sent on the train there for private consumers.

In 1956 the original *appellation* St-Joseph area was founded on a six-mile stretch of land taking in six villages—Glun, Mauves, Tournon, St-Jean-de-Muzols, Lemps, and Vion. When looking for quality, it is worth remembering these names—their vineyards and most of their *vignerons* were producing wine considered superior to ordinary Côtes du Rhône upwards of 30 years ago.

The 1969 legislation brought in the following villages, from south to north: Guilherand, Châteaubourg, Sécheras, Arras-sur-Rhône, Ozon, Ardoix, and Sarras, which is opposite St-Vallier. Then the northern area, all new since 1969, is made up of Talencieux, Andance, St-Étienne-de-Valoux, St-Désirat, Champagne, Peyraud, Serrières, Félines, Charnas, Limony, St-Pierre-de-Boeuf, Malleval, and Chavanay.

Along the link road, the N86, many of these villages have modernised themselves since the early 1990s: miniroundabouts, street lighting, one-way systems, nearby supermarkets—and the closure of locally owned shops. Chavanay is no exception. The visitor should seek out the older part of the village, since new housing has burgeoned all around it, but a hamlet like Malleval, with its tiny, cramped streets, has remained largely unchanged, while there is rocky charm at Arras as well, where the busy Ozon stream bisects it.

ST-JOSEPH VINEYARDS

The St-Joseph *appellation* runs for 64 kilometres (40 miles) from north to south, so its soils and local climate vary importantly. There is a marked difference in the texture of the red wines in the northern sector, centred on Chavanay, from those of the southern sector, centred on Tournon, and there are subset variations even within nearby villages.

History is a good start point here. The core area is Glun to Vion: the six southern-sector villages named in the 1956 *appellation* decree represent the classic form of St-Joseph—a series of little valleys that run down off the mainly granite Ardèche plateau, their streams feeding the Rhône. The south-facing slopes of these valleys constitute fine sites for growing vines. Even when wine prices were low, as in the 1960s and 1970s, some of these slopes remained as vineyards, and now possess a proven pedigree with their mature vines.

Out of this bunch, three *communes* distinguish themselves—from south to north: Mauves, Tournon, and St-Jean-de-Muzols. Glun, Vion, and Lemps, where access was often more awkward, fell mostly by the wayside, and only since the mid-1990s have young men returned to grub out abandoned patches and recommence their vine culture.

After the expansion of the *appellation* area in 1969, a new centre of gravity sprang up at St-Joseph. I would call this the village of Sarras, on which the north-south axis turns. Climate is perhaps the key observation here, although the granite in the northern sector is younger and less evolved than that of the south.

Just as Hermitage Syrah often ripens more easily than Côte-Rôtie Syrah, so with Mauves and Chavanay, 30 miles apart. The reason Delas for many years bought the crop for their St-Joseph from just Mauves, Tournon, and St-Jean-de-Muzols was that they found the northern sector rarely achieved the same level of ripeness that could be found on their doorstep.

Raymond Trollat has a white oak tree growing in his vineyard at St-Jean-de-Muzols. This drops its leaves, unlike its neighbours the green oaks. Pointing out what amounts to a demarcation line, he observes that north of Arras there aren't many green oaks or cicadas. "The green oaks are southern trees," he says; "their leaves never fall." Agreeing with this, another countryman in the form of Étienne Becheras, resident of Arras, adds that crickets are usually present in his village, but not in Sarras three miles further north.

Robert Michel, a longtime figure at Cornas, works a vineyard in the *commune* of Ardoix, west of Sarras. "The vineyard is at 350 metres," states Robert. "It's a lot 'colder' than Cornas, with longer winters, and is usually two to three weeks behind our Cornas vineyard—a big difference for just 30 kilometres (19 miles) apart." This comes through in the wine, which is tightly closed when young.

Fabrice Rousset of Domaine du Château Vieux is a promising young grower with a vineyard at Arras and another at Tournon. "Tournon ripens about eight days earlier," he comments— "they're both hillside sites, but Arras is windier. I find the Arras wine is soft and red fruited, the Tournon is more robust and tannic. In 2002 the more backward Arras vineyard survived the September rains better because the grape skins were tougher when the rain came. Tournon had more rot that year," he adds.

President of the Growers Union Joël Durand reckons there is a week's difference in ripening between Glun and Châteaubourg in the south and Chavanay in the north. "But if Chavanay gets rain and we don't, then that can be reversed," he observes when discussing the impact of summer storms down the length of the St-Joseph area.

Joël extends the north-south difference to the white wines of St-Joseph, and which dishes they are most suited for. For him, the southern-area whites around Mauves are ideal with a *feuilleté* of wild mushrooms, notably morilles, in a cream sauce; with the Chavanay whites, which hold more acidity, he recommends fish like a *filet de sandre*.

While granite is the prevailing theme along the length of the *appellation*, there are plenty of variations and local nuances. Right down in the south, from Guilherand to Châteaubourg, there is a seam of limestone. The Courbis family work chalky-silty vineyards near their cellars in Châteaubourg, but granite soil on their holdings at Glun.

Some growers consider Guilherand an anomaly: the nearest vineyards are Châteaubourg, over five miles north, and its limestone-influenced soil, sometimes grey in colour, is thought to be best for white wines. There are also sites with low sun levels here, and its crop is largely supplied to the Tain Co-opérative.

Châteaubourg benefits from good siting in the key areas. The prime hill *lieu-dit* is *Les Royes*, just north of the Cornas boundary. The soil here is limestone plus clay, with not much granite in evidence. This also explains why half the Courbis production was in white wine in the early 1980s—it is good ground for whites, and the oldest Courbis Marsanne dates back to the 1940s. The *Royes* vineyard is stunningly steep, even by northern Rhône standards, overlaid with jagged chalk stones. It is high up, between 200 and 270 metres. The Courbis point out that its shelter from the wind is a factor in the ripening process. Like many of the granite-ledged vineyards that branch off into the Ardèche hills, it is a sudden, hidden world away from the high-wind, high-velocity tempo of the main Rhône corridor. Since its launch, the Courbis special Les Royes white has shown itself to be a wine of serious pedigree.

The other cited vineyard at Châteaubourg is *Lautaret*, an east-southeast–facing slope just above the village, where the soil is largely granite, with a minor, diminished limestone presence. The eastern side of *Lautaret* is notable for giving wine with a firm, tannic feel.

As one of the original six *communes*, Glun holds a very low profile today. Most of its vineyards have been worked by growers from other villages—Courbis and Durand from Châteaubourg, Bernard and Robert from St-Péray, and Coursodon from Mauves. Since 1995 three more figures have popped up there—David Raydon, whose wife's family are from Glun; Laurent

Chomat, who is working some old family holdings; and François Luyton.

The Durand brothers' holding on *Gouyet* at Glun is in one of the sheltered valleys off the main Rhône corridor, an area opened up by them since 1990. It is south-southeast facing and is marked by the granite. The limestone residues have by now tapered away around Châteaubourg, to be replaced in places by gravelly outcrops and some loose sand-granite areas whose soils are not very deep. Many of the vineyards here are high—with Domaine de Fauterie's four-plus hectares, first cleared and planted in 1981, standing at between 300 and 380 metres.

Elsewhere at Glun, Stéphane Robert of the Domaine du Tunnel developed the *Terres Blanches* site, granite mixed with some clay, between 1997 and 2002; his highest vines here are 310 metres, the lowest 230 to 250 metres, so there is a natural freshness in the grapes.

Discussing how the style of the red wines changes between Châteaubourg and Glun, Laurent Courbis, the vinifier of Domaine Courbis, observes: "We find that more spiced wine with greater acidity comes off the limestone, as well as a more assertive, tannic side than the Syrah off the granite. The aromas from the limestone are also more *garrigue*, or herbal Mediterranean; while the colour tends to be more purple from the granite, more dark cherry from the limestone."

Moving north, the pulse quickens. Mauves. A village of a hundred memories, one of the trio that sits at the top table, inhabited by people of the land, not measly newcomers. The cast of characters is strong—the good doctor Florentin, his family faithful to the horse in his vineyards; the crinkly faced outdoorsman Gérard Courbis; the thoughtful, dedicated Gonon brothers; the Marsanne family, shy purveyors of their own vine cuttings these several decades; the Coursodons, the ex-Mayor's family with the wily, charming Gustave having lead the way in the 1970s; the Chaves, resplendent in their detail and considered approach; and the tenacious, reserved Bernard Gripa.

And yet many of these growers possess more acreage at Tournon than they do at Mauves, which was always a mixed fruit-and-vine community. The St-Joseph Vitrine vineyard project to create a shop window for Mauves has brought together these growers in a way not often seen before, and is due to thrust into the limelight some of Mauves' prime sites.

Contrary to first impressions, Mauves is not chock-full of vineyards. Its *commune* actually continues some way back into the Ardèche plateau where there are farms and dairy herds. In the 1970s, expansion here was not always precisely judged, so there are some sites that are both high up and a little northerly facing.

At present, the two leading *lieux-dits* are *Montagnon* and *Paradis*. *Montagnon* is opposite the north part of the village, *Paradis* the next site south, just 100 yards apart. *Montagnon* is a loess–crumbled granite site, with no rock near the surface, making it good for whites and less tannic reds. Chapoutier, the Gonons, and Jean-Claude Marsanne have holdings here, and Coursodon in some slightly more clay patches. Chapoutier's Syrah dates from the 1950s, and Marsanne's is even older.

Paradis, known thanks to the Coursodon Paradis St-Pierre wine, is firm granite, with Rhône alluvion stones spread across it. There are pockets of clay further down the hill, where the Coursodons choose to grow some of their Marsanne. It is mainly east facing—meaning it loses the sun in early evening. As such, its crop must be waited for pending ripening, although its acidity serves a useful purpose in a scorching year like 2003. At the top, the vineyard is bordered by dense woods.

At the southern tip of *Paradis*, the Coursodons grow some 1930s Syrah at up to 260 metres, and can enjoy the luxury of a couple of work or rest cabins at the bottom of the vineyard. Other growers here include Gérard Courbis and his son Ludovic, Jean-Claude Marsanne, Gripa, and Lantheaume, while Chapoutier have been planting on this site. The *Paradis* reds show more tannic content than those from *Montagnon*. For Jean Gonon, the typical *Mauves* red contains more acidity than that from Tournon and can live for longer.

The most southerly site at Mauves is a *lieu-dit* being opened up by the 30-odd–hectare plantation for the Vitrine vineyard operation. This is *Les Côtes Derrière*, officially known simply as *Les Côtes*. A three-kilometre (nearly two-mile) access road has been built for this, as well as a lot of new walls—the Chave walls notably are an impressive handmade sight.

Côtes Derrière is pretty firm granite; in tasting its wine alone, it is the sort that can bring energy to a blend—*cassis* fruit, with warm edging and a buzzy mineral aspect, and also quite tight tannins. Coursodon, Chave, and Gérard Courbis are growers here. Chave also has a plot on the next site, *Chalaix*. The stream of *Chalaix* runs below *Les Côtes*.

Above *Côtes Derrière*, to its northwest, lies a higher and windier site, *Guillamy*. This can ripen 10 days behind *Côtes Derrière*; its wine has a lively fruit whose cut is apparent even in a hot year like 2003.

In a similar approach to the hard granite–schist hillsides of the north of Côte-Rôtie, a recent trend at Mauves has been to take out the old terrace walls and so create a slope that can be worked with small caterpillar tractors. In this case, the density of plantation rises from around 7,000 to 9,000 plants per hectare, on the basis of 0.9 metre downwards and 1.15 metre across.

Heading north, the boundary between Mauves and the next *commune* of Tournon is marked by the *Oliviers* stream, also officially called *le ruisseau des Roches* by some growers and *le ruisseau des Aurets* by the Ordnance map! This flows just north of *Montagnon*. I have also heard this boundary named by its landmark of The Syrah Bar. The north flank of this valley presents a wonderful sun trap, and on it is a vineyard noted for its ripening quality, *Les Oliviers*.

This valley is quite narrow, with the *Oliviers* stream often running dry in summer. *Les Oliviers* is a much appreciated site likely to become better known in years to come. There is granite at the bottom, but much of the soil is a clay–*galet* stone mix, which gives very rich, only

mildly tannic wines. This makeup sets it up well for white wine, the style here being rich and rounded, sometimes a little low in acidity.

Since the late 1980s, growers have taken note; Blachon planted his Marsanne on some of the loess areas of *Les Oliviers*, while Ferraton did likewise with a straight Marsanne-Roussanne split. The Gonons grow Syrah and both Marsanne and Roussanne here, where the growers are a roll call of big names: Blachon, J-L Chave, Coursodon, Ferraton, Jean-Claude Marsanne.

Next to and above *Oliviers* is another prized *climat*, *Dardouille*, whose name in old usage means "touched by the rays of the sun." This runs up to around 250 metres, and is the extension of the *Oliviers* hill, pushing a little further into the valley. *Dardouille* is slanted southeast, *Oliviers* more full south.

Being a little higher, *Dardouille* is more granitic than *Oliviers*, although there is some dusty loess, as well as clay in its lower reaches. Jean-Louis Chave describes the clay as "good quality," since it gives the wines a core that is not so present off the full granite of a site like *St-Joseph*. Growers on *Dardouille* include Blachon, Gérard Courbis, Chave, and Bernard Faurie. The last named has his old Syrah from the 1950s here. The Coursodons grow their Marsanne in the heavier clay-*marne*, where it mixes with the granite. One unusual sight on *Dardouille* is that of a few beehives that sit among fruit trees tended by a local man.

The *Oliviers* Syrah is always rich and generous, but Jean-Louis Chave cautions about the risk of excess fatness, which can render it rather flat. *Dardouille* Syrah is a little more restrained but still works well on its own, without the obvious need for blending, thanks to the clay content in its granite; "otherwise the granite solo can make the wine tight, harder, and more acidic—less easy all round," comments Gérard Courbis.

Beyond these two reputed *climats* runs another stream to create its own next valley. This is the *ruisseau des Champs* in everyday usage, official name the stream of *Lay*. A slightly broader valley than the *Oliviers*, this is home to the *climat* of *St-Joseph*, much noticed for obvious reasons of name and because its front hillock is in full view of the N86 road south of Tournon.

Big guns have vineyards here, too. Chapoutier is near the road, with a sign to tell the world. Guigal works the old Jean-Louis Grippat plot. Coursodon has Syrah from the 1920s, as does Bernard Gripa, who uses its fruit to source his old-vine Berceau wine; both growers enjoy the best, full-south exposure. The *St-Joseph climat* turns from south through southeast to an easterly exposure. The soil is decomposed granite with some stones and clay—more clay, for instance, than is found in the more austere surroundings above Tournon on *Chapon* and *Le Clos*.

On the east-southeast slope, Chapoutier grow the 1950s Marsanne and Syrah dating from the 1930s and 1950s that go into the special Granits white and red wines. Roger Blachon's 1960s Syrah is here. The *St-Joseph* fruit style is generous, with black fruits and plenty of oily texture obtainable once the Syrah is 30 years or older. Aromas can reflect violets. For Pierre Coursodon, the tannin content becomes firm from here once the vines are old, and the wines accordingly need time.

Next to *St-Joseph* going north is the flat site of *Les Rivoires*, opposite the old fruit-selling complex for Mauves. This, too, continues the sandy granite theme. Jean-Claude Marsanne, Bernard Gripa, and the Roussets from Erôme across the river count among the growers here; the Syrah fruit is less supple than the *Oliviers-Dardouille* area, and has more sinew in it. The old Marsanne fruit from here is very rich, and in most vintages can handle the oak put its way.

The high vineyard in this enclave is *Peygros*, which touches both *St-Joseph* and *Rivoires*, and is quite easterly facing. Chapoutier planted some Syrah here in 1998, where the granite soil is generally poor as it rises to the top of the hill at around 300 metres. In the lower reaches, the soil is a little heavier. *Peygros* is the other source for the Gripa Berceau red wine, the Gonon brothers have a holding on what they term *Croix*

de Peygros, and Stéphane Robert of Domaine du Tunnel managed to acquire some 1920 Syrah here in 1994. Bernard Gripa points out the difference between his two sources, *St-Joseph* and *Peygros:* "The *St-Joseph* has more finesse, whereas the *Peygros* is more angular, with more obvious tannins." Both sites have a lot of granite high up, but the *St-Joseph* is more sanded and fine lower down.

Below *Peygros* is the *Javignas* site, a mix of granite and stones on a steep incline; the soil in places is quite rich, with clay, and also has some thick sand from the granite's erosion. Bernard Gripa has a holding here.

Hovering in this *Valleé des Champs*, west of *Peygros*, are Dard et Ribo; their plot contains only a little sandy granite and is mainly alluvial stones and red clay. Both Syrah and Roussanne are grown here. "It's like the Gonon family's *Coteau des Oliviers* to look at," comments François Ribo, "and is also good for whites because there's no worry about drought there." The red wines are often less coloured, apparently due to the red-clay influence.

All these hills conform to the geological logic of possessing the most granite and the poorest ground higher up, with stony areas in midslope, and then some clay and deeper ground in the middle to lower areas. But the Tournon plots also receive more sustained sunshine than the central Mauves sites, which accumulates to a marked edge in ripeness over the course of a year.

Above Tournon and its cramped streets rise high the most obvious signs of its granite inheritance. The awkward, slippery ledges here are a dull, rather sullen brown in winter, then burst into green fecundity in summer. The granite here is firmer and less degraded than that found on the *St-Joseph* site towards Mauves, strong enough to supply the stones for the ledge walls.

The sites here like the *Vigne de l'Hospice*— more properly termed the *lieu-dit* of *Chapon*— *Le Clos*, and *Les Petites Pierres* all produce wines that are more marked by dark flavours and almost wiry tannins than those from the Mauves–southern Tournon slopes. The rigidity of the contours here seems to eke its way into the wines.

Chapon is the high, visible vineyard whose main southeast-facing section of 0.6 hectare is in the form of an inverted trapeze. The word *chapon* means "young vines" in old French, and since the J-L Grippat acquisition, this site has been rented by Marcel Guigal from the Hospice of Tournon. Near the top of this steep incline is a raw block of granite with a few vines above it. The vineyard here reaches around 250 metres, while further west around the hill and away from the Rhône, the old de Vallouit vineyard rises to 300 metres, also on *Chapon*. The top area gets hot, since there is some protection from the north wind, whereas its neighbour *Le Clos* is more exposed.

Chapon's soil is rotted granite, what old growers like Jean-Louis Grippat call *gore;* "it contains porous sandy elements, some of them quite big," he states. He adds that for him, the *Chapon* wine is in texture similar to that of *Bessards* from Hermitage, obviously without the dimension. "It gives a rigorous wine, with marked tannins and blackberry fruit that has a freshness within it," he says of his old plot.

Marcel Guigal has accumulated a fair collection here by acquiring access to or outright ownership of the Grippat and de Vallouit vineyards: he exploits around 2.6 hectares on *Chapon*, the only grower to work this site.

It's no surprise that the well-financed Tain *négociants* Jaboulet and Chapoutier turn up here, on an expensive *climat* like *Le Clos*, which is separated from *Chapon* by some scrub. Jaboulet started to plant on *Le Clos* in 2001, with three hectares possible over time. Their vineyard is further into the valley than that of Chapoutier, who bought five hectares of land on *Le Clos* in 1997, two of which are now planted with Syrah. *Le Clos* is generally skewed east-southeast, and Marcel Guigal also has a holding here.

"Our vineyard on *Le Clos* had lain idle for 30 years, so its soil was well rested," comments Michel Chapoutier, adding that it used to be worked by the monks of the Abbey of Tournon.

Its loose granite is full of large particles; it is light, fast-draining terrain, although there are one or two bits of clay present. Here the wines are a bit less long-lived than those from *Chapon*; there is a meaty side to them, the fruits are black, and the tannins a touch more rustic and less densely enveloped than those in the *Chapon* Syrah.

The next valley north of Tournon is a major one, the broad *Doux* riverbed its spine. This leads to St-Jean-de-Muzols, the third of the trio of top villages, and no more than four miles from Mauves. The often straggly Doux River can become a dangerous, flooding torrent in unceasing rain, as was experienced in December 2003. St-Jean-de-Muzols is well protected from the north wind, tucked away just off the main Rhône corridor, encouraging sound ripening in its grapes.

The most celebrated *climat* at St-Jean-de-Muzols is *Ste-Épine*, a bonny granite hillside 200 metres up. Nearest the Rhône, there is an easterly fronting, and then the hill turns more southeast. It is a hill also covered in woods and abandoned terraces, its plots scattered across it. The heart of *Ste-Épine* is tucked into the Doux valley, "but," states Delas' Jacques Grange, "it is in fact on the same geological route as *Les Bessards* on the extreme granite tip of the Hermitage hill, having been cut off from it by the Rhône. It's a bit cooler and windier than *Bessards*."

Indeed, the *Ste-Épine* wines have a cool fruit texture, their sinewy, pebbly tannins needing time to blend. They are wines for thoughtful rather than carefree drinking. Jean Gonon talks about these wines' sometimes meaty aspects, and finds them less mellow than the wines from the less decomposed Tournon granite. His plot here ripens around five days behind his *Montagnon* holding at Mauves, for instance.

It took Eliette Desestret's grandfather 11 years to clear one hectare on *Ste-Épine* and make an access route to it, in the days of working with one's hands and with oxen, and this is a *climat* gaining notoriety due to various growers like Delas selling a site-specific wine. The domaines of Michelas Saint Jemms, Romaneaux-Destezet, and Habrard from Crozes-Hermitage also work plots here.

The Coursodons and Delas rent the ex-Mayor of St-Jean's terraced vineyard at the west end of *Ste-Épine* and a little below it, whose subset name is *L'Olivet*. This dates from the 1930s, and Jacques Grange of Delas has a curious observation on the Syrah fruit from this vineyard: "To the eye it's not the same as the Hermitage *petite* Syrah—the berries are smaller. I can only really put this down to the fact that the climate is a little cooler at St-Jean-de-Muzols." The Delas sales shop is the old *Olivet* farmhouse, and the hill rises above the road across from their cellars beside the Tournon-to-Lamastre steam train line. This decomposed granite site, with its easterly, then southeast-facing exposure, brings red fruits into the wine, according to Jérome Coursodon.

To the east of *Ste-Épine* and closer as the crow flies to the Hermitage hill is what I call Trollat's slope. The sites here are *Aubert* and *Pichonnier*, worked for decades by the Trollat family. The southeast-facing *Aubert* vineyard dates in parts back to the First World War for its Syrah and also holds Marsanne from the 1950s, as well as sundry outlying varieties planted in the random way of the past—the odd Clairette and *inconnu* here and there. The vines grow in a very fine grainy schist topsoil, the granite well broken down with a loess content below it. The *Aubert* site is at the top of Trollat's hill, while *Pichonnier* is behind the cellars. The Gonon brothers from Mauves have bought some of the *Aubert* plot, which is southeast facing. They also have vines on *Martinot*, a more east-facing site a touch further north, where there is fine granite and two bands of loess at the middle and low level of the hill.

Jean Gonon distinguishes between the St-Jean-de-Muzols and the Tournon granite in the following way: "The St-Jean granite is composed of very small particles, it's not as rich as the Tournon soil. The Tournon granite contains some mica and has larger grains, as well as some clay—it's less degraded." The Syrah from the sunniest, full south St-Jean sites is marked by brambly, often black fruits and is intrinsically pretty generous—there is little sense of the northern zone's toughness or taut texture from this core area of St-Joseph.

In similar fashion, the Syrah off the curved east, gently southeast hillside of *Roue* behind and east of *Pichonnier*, carries red fruits and an inherent softness; longtime locals Elizabeth Fogier and Jean-Claude Farge work vineyards here, as well as Philippe Michelas. It is a vineyard that loses the sun by 5 or 6 PM in August, and the lower degree and tenderness of its wine come as no surprise. Across the valley from *Roue*, and higher, at up to 321 metres, is the most northerly noted *lieu-dit* of St-Jean, *La Gouye*; protected from the north wind, it yields red wines that are also marked by a softness of fruit, and its Marsanne performs very well, too.

Close to Tournon running north are the last two original *appellation communes*, Vion and Lemps, whose soil is full granite. More could be heard of these spots in the coming years, especially Lemps, where Jean-Louis Chave is resurrecting the old family vineyard hundreds of years old on *Les Côtes de Pouly*, also known locally as *Bachasson*. The upper flank of the Lemps valley is all south facing and encourages a microsystem including exotic plants and scrub foliage.

Jean-Louis compares the neutrality of this valley's granite with that of *Bessards*, the site that brings the backbone to the best red Hermitage across the river. As with *Ste-Épine* at St-Jean-de-Muzols, this is another reminder of the link between the Massif Central and the west end of the Hermitage hill many thousands of years ago, when the Rhône used to flow behind that hill.

Dard et Ribo also crop a small amount of Syrah at Vion, where the lower slope location means the soil is full of sanded granite.

While the fruit nuances shift between local sites around Mauves, Tournon, and St-Jean-de-Muzols, there is also the question of comparison with Hermitage across the river. To some extent, a few of the St-Joseph sites share some of the same granite foundation, but they do not yield wines to rival the depth and fullness of their neighbour across the river. Exposure is certainly a factor: the top sites above Tournon do not enjoy the same wonderful exposure to the sun of the Hermitage hill, especially its high *Bessards* and *L'Hermite* areas. Outside high summer, the sun disappears behind the top of the Tournon hill, home of *Le Clos* and others, by midafternoon, for instance.

The other, more just comparison is that between the southern sector of St-Joseph and its northern equivalent. The southern style is for wines that are warmer and more embracing than than the upright, peppered wines of Chavanay and neighbours. They are more instantly open, the northern wines more reserved.

The northern wines' richness is on a less intense plane and doesn't have the blackstrap, tarry tones of some of the Mauves-Tournon axis wines. 1999 was one of the few vintages when I felt the northern Syrahs achieved a comfortable, natural depth, one that allowed makers to stand back and let the fruit do a complete, natural job. This area also survived 2002's early September rains better than the south, where the riper, softer grape skins absorbed more damp and rot.

Thanks to the climate shifts down the 40 miles of the *appellation*, the Mauves-Tournon–St-Jean tannins are often riper and more mellow. A further difference is that the vines in the north are also younger and often from more modern clones. A biodynamic grower from the northern sector at St-Désirat, Jean-Pierre Monier comments: "Our 3309 clones are too productive, so we're planting Richter on our *massale* selection cuttings taken from old local Syrah."

Philippe Guigal also observes that the methoxy-pyrazine levels from the soil are different between Chavanay and Tournon. This results in an overtly green-pepper aspect in the wines of Chavanay, which is much less evident at Tournon. Based at Côte-Rôtie, Gilles Barge also expects to find a difference in the wines from Chavanay. "Any pepper and spice are typical of them," he notes.

Moving north past the central axis of Ardoix, tucked away off the main Rhône corridor and Sarras, there has been a considerable amount of planting; indeed the slopes are often coloured by yellow bulldozers and earth diggers, the yellow indicating fever, perhaps.

At Serrières, Paul Jaboulet Aîné have redone the *Les Rouasses* site north of the village that they took over in 1993. The hill turns from east through to southeast and forms part of the St-Joseph Vitrine operation, to encourage planting in the best spots. The Vallet and Boissonet families are the noted local growers here, and they joined in with the Cave de St-Désirat to plant 2.5 hectares of Vitrine between 1996 and 1997.

"*Les Rouasses* had been abandoned for 90 years," states Anthony Vallet, "and we, too, planted here in 1993. On our site, it's *gore* mixed with clay and has fewer granite particles than our Condrieu vineyards. It gives big, tannically structured red wines." In a part of *Les Rouasses* with a greater limestone content, the Boissonnets chose to plant half a hectare of their Marsanne.

Another site at Serrières is *Le Grand Moure*, southwest of the village, where there is decomposed granite on the way to Annonay. Its wines are supple and easy.

Next, at Charnas, there are some good white wines coming through, the Roussanne doing well in some of the limestone outcrops that exist within the generally sandy granite environment. Most of the domaines are on the plateau, their growers young men. The vineyards mix plateau and hillside exposure, the quality patently more evident once the more granite hillsides are exploited. Flacher, Finon, and Laurent Marthouret show promise around here.

Limony has been a sound source of Condrieu for many years, with some prime, steep south-facing hillsides. The grower who has made more of a name for this *commune* since the 1980s has been Louis Chèze. The soil is classic, partly decomposed granite on the hill slopes, with pockets of stones. But the soil is less full of fine particles than the southern sector around St-Jean-de-Muzols, the granite rockier and a little younger.

Sites to note here include *Buis*, a very granite hill where Chèze, with some old-for-the-area 1950s Syrah, and Pierre Gaillard have plots, *Pangon* and *Montrond*. Jaboulet have also moved in and since 1999 have planted Syrah, Marsanne, and Roussanne on the *Rouelle Nord* site, and Chapoutier have joined in with Syrah on a site called *Les Vignasses* that they bought in 1995, the vines a mix of 1983 and 1995–96.

Moving north into the *département* of the Loire and getting closer to Mont Pilat, the terrain around Malleval becomes very rugged. Two *lieux-dits* stand out here—*Cuminaille* and *Coteau de Rochecourbe*. Pierre Gaillard makes good red wine from *Cuminaille*, a sanded granite hillside that he first planted in 1981. Thiérry Farjon also has a holding on *Cuminaille*. Michel Mourier and Alain Paret are two sound names working the firm granite *Coteau de Rochecourbe*. This steep hill at the southern entrance to Malleval rises from 125 to over 280 metres, and had been abandoned after the Second World War when many locals went to work in factories nearby.

Chavanay is the capital of the northern sector of St-Joseph, just four kilometres (2.5 miles) north of Malleval. This is the "young area" of St-Joseph, one in full expansion with plenty of planting and plenty of newcomers attempting to join in on the wine boom. The country mixes plateau and hillside, so there are good and indifferent sites here.

Up on the sparsely inhabited plateau above Chavanay, there are a few farms dotted around. Views stream away to the broad, dark shapes of the mountains west. Land has been reclaimed for vines on either side of the curling road up. But if the glass is the arbiter of quality, tasting shows that the vines up on the plateau simply do not give the full, berried, thicker concentration of the fruit that comes from the slope granite ledges.

The fruit from here is more fragile. There isn't so much blackberry and warmth in the red wines. So it's reassuring that a grower like Hervé Richard has the confidence to allow the finesse and more angular style of wine to come through in his whites and reds—he is in a minority in not playing a game of cellar catch-up to beef up his wines unnaturally. As these vines age, more fullness will come. But the plateau and hill sites are not comparable, and certainly some of the former should be giving *vin de pays* only. Hopefully, they are among those due to be phased out by around 2010.

There is an accompanying problem derived from the number of start-ups around here since the mid-1990s. Lack of experience shows through in the more angular, less obviously ripe vintages like 2001 and 2002. Here there are wines that veer towards hardness, wines that give the word "tannin" a bad name. Ripening of the polyphenols for the tannic extract has at times not yet been mastered, indicating that people pick too soon, and may also use excess young oak that acts to further dry the wines.

There are names that count here, obviously, as well as vineyard sites that conform to the essential tenets of good exposure, good soil, helpful climate. *Les Eyguets, Les Rivoires, Izéras, La Côte,* and *Les Vessettes* are all core names. The first four are all adjacent along the broad flank of the hill above the Valencize River that runs through Chavanay. *Rivoires* lies below *Eyguets*, and its *gore* soil is a little deeper than the *arzelle*, or granite granules, of *Eyguets*. *Rivoires* is worked by good growers like Didier Chol and André Perret. It gives Syrah of upright tannins but also elegance; Didier Chol remarks that there can be a petrol-style bouquet in some vintages.

La Côte has become prominent thanks to Yves Cuilleron. His Condrieu holdings here exceed three hectares, but they also show up what seems an anomaly—the same slope site can grow Syrah for St-Joseph or Viognier for Condrieu. The hill itself mixes stones with the decomposed granite and benefits from a full south-southeast exposure. It is also windy, and Yves notes that his highest spots, at around 300 metres, help out acidity levels in the rest of his domaine crop.

Les Vessettes contains some of the north's oldest Syrah, planted by Yves Cuilleron's grandfather in 1936 and 1947. The soil is generally the reddy, quite strong stone granite of the area around Chavanay, with some decomposed zones. Domaine Georges Vernay, with Syrah, and Pierre Gaillard with Roussanne are other cultivators on *Vessettes*.

Other sites around Chavanay are two of André Perret's and, a little nearer the Rhône, *Grisières*, a granite site that holds some venerable 1920s Syrah, and *Chanson*, clay-sand on top of a schist couch, which also holds Viognier. South of Chavanay, *Boissey*, granite with the hard rock close to the surface, is an old 1940s Syrah vineyard worked by Domaine Georges Vernay, while further west and high up is *La Ribaudy*, where Philippe Faury is the prime grower.

The most northerly St-Joseph vineyard is on *La Voturerie*, where François Merlin grows some Syrah. A mix of plateau and slope, it is sanded granite in composition.

While many of the vineyards of St-Joseph are young, dating from the 1980s onwards, encouragement comes with more growers prepared to work the soil carefully. Spraying has become less frequent, and soils are more respected than before. Alain Paret is an example, no doubt prompted by the arrival of his son at the domaine. Since 2001 he has stopped using insecticides and has grown grass on his lower slopes to restrict erosion. Half a dozen sorts are grown, adapted to granite slopes.

Those who go the whole way to organic or biodynamic production within St-Joseph are less numerous; names that spring to mind are Emmanuel Barou, Laurent Combier, Dard et Ribo, Ferme des Sept Lunes, the Domaine des Amphores, Chapoutier, and Jean-Pierre Monier, while the domaines like Gonon, Marsanne, and Jean-Louis Chave also conduct such practices without specially announcing them.

The rub comes when looking at cellar practices, where the good outdoor instincts of the younger generation often drift away towards easy production and activist methods. Overextraction is indeed alive and well, notably in the northern sector, with the new-oak syndrome prominent.

TABLE 8
St Joseph Ban des Vendanges

2004	8 September
2003	20 August
2002	10 September
2001	10 September
2000	7 September
1999	6 September
1998	7 September

The Syrah accounts for 92 to 93 per cent of the total plantation—the ratio of red to white wine at St-Joseph has hovered around this level over the past 25 years—and is generally used on its own to make the red wine. Since 1979 a maximum of 10 per cent of white grapes, the Marsanne and the Roussanne, can also be put to the making of the red, provided that they are all fermented together at the same time.

It is not quite clear why this change of ruling should have occurred; one suspects that it is a purely commercial decision, rather than one totally inspired by a desire to seek a softer quality of wine. The red St-Joseph is much better known and easier to sell than the white, so the inclusion of white grapes in it would mean that there was that much more to sell.

The formal harvest declarations, the *ban des vendanges*, for St-Joseph have been early recently (see table 8), when compared to the 1970s. Of course, 2003 was a record date by some way, but it was more normal over 30 years ago to harvest in the second half of September.

ST-JOSEPH *ROUGE* AND *BLANC* VINIFICATION

Most Syrah crop is destemmed, and the vinification of the classic red wines is usually a 10-day to two-week affair, with cap moistening by punching or pumping-overs. Stainless steel, temperature-controlled vats abound.

Grapes from the older vines or better hillside vineyards may macerate for three or four days longer. Their wine is more likely to be aged in cask, a fair proportion of it young or new. The duration of the cask ageing does not often run for more than 12 to 15 months.

Growers from the traditional villages like Mauves and St-Jean-de-Muzols have remained more faithful to old or used casks than those in the north; the latter group have newer installations since many among them have started up in recent years. There is also the influence of the shining lights of that area—growers like Yves Cuilleron, Pierre Gaillard, and Louis Chèze—who are modern vinification, new-oak exponents. The contrast between them and Raymond Trollat or Jean-Claude Marsanne could not be greater!

The *demi-muid* cask size of 550 to 600 litres is also preferred in the southern sector, against the 228 litres of the north. Everywhere, there is less fining and filtration than in the 1990s.

The whites are usually vat vinified, allowing a direct fruit expression. Cask treatment is growing, with the Roussanne often selected for oak. Some *bâtonnage*, or lees stirring, is done, but less relatively than at Crozes-Hermitage.

ST-JOSEPH *ROUGE*

St-Joseph *rouge* is a wine I most often choose for quiet enjoyment and regular drinking, one that will prove to be a good friend rather than a respected acquaintance. For example, I recall the now retired Jean-Louis Grippat referring to his very fruity 1985 classic cuvée as "a wedding wine."

St-Joseph *rouge* is a wine of two phases. When young, its charm lies in the black fruit, buzzy style—fruit with a touch of pedigree that gives its texture some licorice, pepper, or spice limits. It comes directly at the drinker, a no-nonsense fruitiness at its core.

When left to age, a more measured variety of flavours develops. Spice and pine come through, the oiliness of ripe years shows up, the fruits become more supple as the tannins subdue. There are more earthy connotations, as the Syrah takes on its middle-aged apparel.

It's well worth ageing suitable vintages to enjoy this extra dimension—the 1980 and 1983 reds from Coursodon were doing well when last tried in 2004: both slow-burn vintages that needed their tannins to drop back into line. After 20 years they had become classic examples of aged Syrah from more upright, hidden corner vintages.

Such evolution is observable, but extreme. Drinking a red St-Joseph from the mighty 1999 vintage in 2006–08 would land pretty much dead centre, but the wine could obviously show well after that. Taking a sunny year as an example, the 1990s are wonderful now, the 1997s as well, since their acidity levels were modest. The 1997s, with their overtly soft blackberry or black currant fruit, work well with spiced food. The most structured years like 1999—full of ripe fruit and tannic support—are the ones for autumn dishes, including pheasant and casseroles.

Examples of thoroughly aged St-Joseph *rouge* also include a 1967 Coursodon red drunk in 1986; this still carried rounded fruit on the palate, and good length, while a 1971 Coursodon red drunk in 1991 had a still ripe, southern-sweet bouquet, with some delicate fruit and a tender, drying finish. Likewise a 1971 from de Boisseyt–Chol drunk in 1995—this still carried some richness on the palate, with plenty of extract still there, even though the alcohol was starting to assert.

A well-looked-after wine from a top vintage should last for 12 to 15 years. At 10 years or more, the difference between a St-Joseph Syrah and a Cornas Syrah is that of the feather, the floating texture of softness in the St-Joseph against the grainier, more mineral side of the Cornas.

Personal preference is the key factor: for those who thrive on fruit and the richness of youth, these are wines to drink between two and seven years old. As Bernard Gripa from Mauves puts it: "The problem with the Syrah is that it loses its fruit quite quickly." This is strictly true, for the vigour naturally subsides, but the French and British palates generally differ here.

Other drinkers will enjoy the animal musk, *sous-bois* smells, and aged Syrah complexities that develop in the bottle—without much drying out—after more than seven years. The chosen style of the winemaker should also be considered, as well as the particular cuvée he has packaged up.

IDEAL FOODS WITH ST-JOSEPH *ROUGE*

Young St-Joseph made in the straight classic style—little or no oak, younger vines—is a fruit-filled wine, good for companions like charcuterie. "It's very versatile," says Stéphane Robert, a view shared by Joël Durand. "You can marry St-Joseph reds with a lot of foods, because they possess fruit and some depth as well," he comments. Gilles Flacher considers it good with all meats when young, and opts for sauced meats and game when the wine is older—five years or more.

Sylvain Bernard makes a specific young vinification wine, Solstice, in the rosé way; this is aimed at all summer dishes when the weather is hot, bringing in charcuterie and quiches. Raymond Trollat and Elizabeth Fogier are both veterans who consider it normal to slice off some charcuterie when drinking and tasting their wine, while Laurent Courbis states, "I am happy to drink the red through a whole meal if more tender meats like veal are served." For Jérome Coursodon, young St-Joseph *rouge* is great "on the rocks"—chilled—with a hamburger.

I consider St-Joseph excellent with lamb, notably *gigot*. Laurent Courbis and Jean Gonon both highlight lamb—the latter suggesting a rack of lamb and even lamb with lightly spread mustard covering, cooked in the oven.

Sylvain Bernard is an *amateur* of his classic wine with veal in autumn, and finds it goes well with grilled meats. I would suggest St-Joseph from the southern sector and a sunny, ripe year—low in tannin—for barbecues or summer picnics. Hervé Souhaut of Romaneaux-Destezet

advises white rather than red meats with his red St-Jo.

Guinea fowl and grilled quail are mentioned as good by Sylvie Chevrol of Domaine Michelas Saint Jemms and Jean Gonon, respectively.

I am very happy to pull out a bottle of red St-Joseph with pasta dishes—meat or mushrooms being very sound companions. I would choose the fruit-forward classic wines, or the years with ripe, not very noticeable tannins for these flavours, and I would drink the wine before it was four years old.

Stepping on to stronger meats, there are fans of beef: the Coursodon family like the wine with red meats, while Sylvain Bernard points to his more tannic Les Combaud for beef *bourguignon* or *daube*. "I like beef when the wine is full-bodied, like a 2001," says Joël Durand; Roger Blachon is another beef man, while Stéphane Robert advocates *entrecôte à la crème* and *filet mignon*.

Duck has its supporters—Durand and Gonon, for instance—with *magret* mentioned, and there is major consensus among the ranks of the older growers on game. Roger Blachon plumps for game, and highlights *marcassin*, or young wild boar; the Coursodons, the Courbis family, Étienne Becheras, and Philippe Desbos all agree. Blachon extends the age of the beast with the age of his wine, so for him a full-grown wild boar, or *sanglier*, should be accompanied by an eight-to-nine-year-old wine. Philippe Desbos adds in venison, while Hervé Souhaut opts for birds, nominating pheasant and partridge. Jean Gonon suggests a pigeon *pot au feu*.

On the less obvious front, Laurent Courbis would eat tuna or eel in a wine sauce with his red St-Joseph, and the Coursodons like chocolate cake with the young wine. "Chocolate cake is fine when the wine is two or three years old, but note the chocolate should be dark and bitter, not sugared," says Jérome Coursodon.

Cheese is not frequently suggested, although the Blachons would choose a Tomme goat cheese, the Coursodons a creamy goat cheese.

ST-JOSEPH *BLANC*

White St-Joseph has made strides since the 1980s; growers have sorted out those plots that suit the Marsanne and the Roussanne, and control their vinification better. The result is wines that may not often be exported but that present sound value for money, meriting a little ageing and decent food to accompany them.

It is not always the granite that provides the answer for these wines, however. The limestone areas around Châteaubourg have rewarded the Courbis with wines like their special *Les Royes*, which has gained in stature in recent times. At Mauves, *Montagnon*'s loess element prompts white vine plots, while the clay lower down on *Paradis* is the home of Coursodon's Marsanne. Some of the limestone spots around Charnas have also provided a good foundation for the burgeoning whites from that northerly village.

On the Mauves-Tournon boundary, the *Les Oliviers* and *Dardouille climats* both contain clay elements here and there; the Coursodons grow their Marsanne in the clay-marne areas, likewise Blachon and Ferraton. *Oliviers* will become better known for its whites in the future, as the vines mature.

Dard et Ribo also like the red clay areas of the *Vallée des Champs*, the next one along from *Oliviers*. They grow Roussanne, not Marsanne, there.

So granite is not necessarily the answer, but one noted wine made from such ground is Les Granits, by Chapoutier. Here the 50-year-old vines, the late picking, and oaked treatment accentuate its fullness; it is a big, fat wine that can at times veer towards excess. Gérard Chave is one grower who doubts the granite for the Marsanne: "There are only a few *terroirs* round here that suit it—the best plots have been well known within St-Joseph over the years, places like *Les Oliviers*. Mercurol at Crozes is a good site as well. Marsanne from the granite can be too alcoholic and *gras*."

Marsanne remains the foundation grape, but Roussanne has its definite supporters. Three domaines that produce Roussanne-only wines are Pascal Jamet at Arras, Pierre Gaillard at Malleval, and Dard et Ribo from their base in Crozes-Hermitage. Jamet's 2000 was very successful, but he is aware that every year there is the risk of oïdium attacks and poor flowering. Gaillard's wine can show honey and floral aromas, while the Dard et Ribo Roussanne is often deliberately picked late; it is more spiced than the usual Marsanne wines, with dried fruits and honey also to the fore. Vinified in a calm, low-sulphur way, it is very beguiling.

There is the usual north-south divide with the whites, as expressed by André Perret up at Chavanay. "We have good acidity here; the wines are less heavy and less thickly textured than the St-Jean-de-Muzols and Mauves wines, which are more potent. To get results here, you have to push the ripeness and even take risks—otherwise the wines can lack structure and fat."

When soundly vinified, white St-Joseph shows more exotic aromas and more marked fruit than white Hermitage—peaches and apricots, and sometimes greengage, can be present on the bouquet. The palate is well weighted, with more richness and breadth on the palate than a St-Péray, its nearest comparison. The fruity chewiness on the finish is particularly appealing. While St-Joseph can hold a light almond or nutty backdrop, St-Péray expresses more a tangy iodine near its finish.

Good white St-Joseph shows extremely well after two or three years, and as it ages towards eight or 10 years old, it acquires greater richness and fullness of flavour. Notes of damson, quince, and apricot skins can be found then. Any Roussanne content adds a tingle of spice, sometimes honey, too.

Compared to its white neighbours, St-Joseph stands on its own. These fruit sensations mark it apart from Hermitage, which has more nuttiness and obvious depth of richness in it. And there is no contest between aged white St-Joseph and aged white Crozes-Hermitage.

St-Joseph is more stylish, more structured and upright, and much classier, also holding a better acidity often than white Crozes. Crozes outside the villages of Mercurol, Larnage, and Gervans struggles to impress after an early flourish.

The nearest comparison is with St-Péray, but even there the growers don't all agree. Stéphan Chaboud finds the Marsanne at St-Joseph adapts better to wood than the Marsanne harvested from St-Péray: "St-Péray is a fresher, more mineral wine, better suited to aperitif drinking, for instance," he comments. Bernard Gripa makes both wines, but doesn't quite concur: "St-Péray runs along the lines of the white St-Joseph, but can live even a little longer," he says. "I give St-Péray 10 years plus," he says, "St-Joseph a little less."

Drinking bottles of Jean-Louis Grippat white St-Joseph that were 15 years or so old, I have found them possessed of lovely, almost floral delicacy. I would also be keener to leave alone in the cellar a white St-Joseph from the relaxed south of the *appellation* than the more worked northern area.

IDEAL FOODS WITH
ST-JOSEPH *BLANC*

An easy first port of call for white St-Joseph is the aperitif; that is the view of the Coursodons for a young wine, while Philippe Desbos of Domaine de Gouye likes it with nuts such as almonds on the side. Courbis and Blachon also propose the aperitif, but I would prefer the wine with food.

The range of foods is, like the red, varied. To start with, fish: several growers mention sauced fish. The fatter the wine, the better this last mix, extending to even a *gratin* of seafood with a cream sauce. Sylvie Chevrol of Michelas Saint Jemms suggests scallops. Straight grilled fish works very well, or when given a few herbs like fennel or *marjolaine* (marjoram). The young wine, up to four years old, does nicely for this. With his unusually rich 2003 pure Roussanne,

Pierre Gaillard counsels turbot or bass in sauce, or white meats like *blanquette* of veal or a chicken fricasée. In years of greater acidity like 2002 or 2001, he recommends fish in simpler, often grilled form. The Coursodon family like their white with fish—but not shellfish, they underline.

Martine Blachon opts for a seafood *gratin*, while Philippe Desbos considers a trout in almonds as a good partner. Joël Durand makes a distinction by geography: with the Chavanay whites that hold more acidity, his preferred dish is fish such as a *filet de sandre* (pikeperch); for the southern area whites, he suggests a *feuilleté* of *morilles* (mushrooms) with cream sauce. Étienne Becheras, a fisherman, selects eel—steamed or in a parsley sauce.

The white is also a good companion for charcuterie, a *saucisse* of Lyon or *caillette* being suggested by the Coursodons. Spanish Pata Negra ham and chorizo are other good complements, setting up the palate and the appetite for later dishes.

The Gonon whites from the southern sector live extremely well, and, rarely for a local domaine, they keep back bottles to check this out: "The oldest successful white we have tried was a 1964 drunk in 1984," recalls Jean, "while we also found the 1972 in good shape when drunk in 1995." They are definitely food rather than aperitif wines—white meats, *ris de veau* (sweetbreads) with mushroom and a cream sauce, and even spiced dishes go well.

White meats like veal and pork are also suitable, and a mainstream idea is chicken in sauce, when the wine has a little age. Laurent Marthouret thinks of smoked salmon, chicken, and salads, while Gilles Flacher goes for snails and frogs' legs, too.

"When the wine is around five to eight years old, I like asparagus with it," comments Pierre Coursodon.

Cheese is suggested by Martine Blachon and Sylvie Desbos—the former plumping for a blue cheese, the latter a Tomme made from goat cheese.

THE PRODUCERS

THIÉRRY ALLEMAND

22 impasse des Granges 07130 Cornas +33(0)475 810650

See also Cornas.

Having sent his crop to the Tain Co-opérative for several years, Thiérry Allemand's agreement expired after 2004. His vineyard is in the deep south of the *appellation*, on the clay-limestone of Guilherand. The soil makes the wine's tannins firm and noticeable beyond the black fruits. The wine will be home bottled in future.

DOMAINE DES AMPHORES

7 Richagnieux 42410 Chavanay +33(0)474 876532

See also Condrieu.

When asked what she did before working in this Chavanay domaine, Véronique Grenier has a simple answer: "I was at school." She takes care of the office and sales side, and is very switched-on. Husband Philippe, who is in his early 30s, works the vineyard and cellar. Philippe moved the family farm on to wine in 1994, their previous activities having included raising chickens and goats.

He now works 4 ha of Syrah on three sites around Chavanay and 0.35 ha of Roussanne and 0.05 ha of Marsanne planted by him in 1995 on *Monteillet* above Chavanay. The Syrah is on sandy granite covered in stones; the Roussanne on stony, sometimes bare and sandy ground with the granite close to the surface.

Like many young people who started in the 1990s, he is pressing on with enlarging his vineyards, and in 2003 planted a tiny 0.15 ha at *La Côte*, to make Condrieu. There are also 2 ha of *vin de pays des Collines Rhodaniennes* that bring a Viognier and a Syrah.

The domaine was registered as biodynamic in 2002, but had been working naturally for many years.

The Syrah is 70 per cent destemmed, and fermented over a total of 20 days, with active working of the cap, pumping-overs, and *délestages*. The classic wine is raised half in casks two to three years old and half in vat, and shows pretty and pure fruit on the palate—a wine to drink young.

The most expensive red, La Cuvée des Mésanges, is a specific-plot wine, the crop selected beforehand in the vineyard. It is cask raised for 18 months, in a mix of 25 per cent new oak, the rest three to five years old. It can struggle to hold its local warmth in the face of the oak overlay, which renders the finish dry. Neither red wine is fined, but both are lightly filtered.

The white St-Joseph, 95 per cent Roussanne, 5 per cent Marsanne, receives a *macération pelliculaire*, then is stabilised at 7° to 10°C for five days. It is fermented 80 per cent in vat, 20 per cent in new acacia wood. It is then left on its lees, with stirring, until bottling around late May.

ST-JOSEPH ROUGE
  2001 ★ ★

ST-JOSEPH LES MÉSANGES ROUGE
  2002 ★
  2000 ★

ST-JOSEPH BLANC
  2003 ★ ★
  2001 ★ ★

Export 8 per cent (1) Austria, (2) Switzerland

PAUL ARMELLIÉ, CAVE DE CHANTEL

42520 Malleval +33(0)474 871409

Modern-style wine; in less ripe years, the fruit can lack core.

ARNOUX ET FILS

*Cave de Vieux Clocher 84190 Vacqueyras
+33(0)490 658418*

See also Crozes-Hermitage.

This southern Rhône domaine doubles up with some commerce; their St-Joseph reflects the supple features of the southern zone, and is a wine to drink within five to six years.

ST-JOSEPH LES ECHAMPS ROUGE

2003 ★

DOMAINE GILLES BARGE

8 Blvrd des Allées 69420 Ampuis +33(0)474 561390

See also Condrieu, Côte-Rôtie.

A mainstay name at Côte-Rôtie, Gilles Barge also works 1.5 ha of Syrah near the hamlet of La Ribaudy above Chavanay, at the *Clos des Martinets*. This enclosed, walled vineyard had been abandoned in the early 1960s after being inherited by the brother and sister Martinet. The *clos* stands up at 280 metres, its 600 metres of walling affording the vines great shelter. Replanted in 1990, its soil is sandy-topped granite.

The crop is 30 to 40 per cent crushed, without destalking, and fermented for 12 to 14 days—about two weeks less than the Côte-Rôtie. Problems with the crop in 2002 and 2003 meant it was all destalked. First made in 1994, the wine is aged in large, 12 hl barrels, and bottled 10 to 12 months after the harvest.

Gilles Barge aims to show the lively aromas of Syrah in its youth: "I am looking at a four-to-five-year wine when making it." Martinets is a consistent, honest wine that has the breeding to reflect its place and its vintage. It carries a northern St-Joseph tightness in its black fruits. If drunk when two to three years old, it goes well with barbecued food, while leading vintages like 2001, 1999, and 1998 can live for 10 to 12 years.

Off a patch of 0.25 ha, he also makes around 1,000 bottles of pure Marsanne white, the vines planted in 1992.

ST-JOSEPH CLOS DES MARTINETS ROUGE

2001 ★★★
2000 ★★
1999 ★★
1998 ★★★

1997 ★
1996 ★★

DOMAINE EMMANUEL BAROU

Picardel 07340 Charnas +33(0)475 340213

See also Condrieu.

An organic enterprise since 1975, this domaine is emerging as a sound address for carefully made, natural wines. Emmanuel's grandfather arrived on the plateau at Charnas in 1920, and the farm's main activity then was peaches and cherries, with just a few vines. The organic side came through because his father, Alexis, never found enough flavour in his cherries once they had been sprayed.

Alexis made *vins de pays* and in 1990 tracked down some abandoned sites to plant his first St-Joseph vineyards. Bottling started in 1994, and after studies at Orange and Carpentras, Emmanuel joined up in 1997.

Their two hectares of Syrah—there is no white—were planted between 1990 and 1999, except for a tiny 0.2 hectare dating from 1975. They are mostly at Limony, with its crumbled granite soil, and a little at Charnas, where the granite is stone covered and harder.

The reds are all destemmed, and fermented without external yeasts in steel and fibreglass vats over 20 to 25 days after a three-day crop cooling. Emmanuel punches the cap during fermentation, and does a *délestage*, or partial vat empty and refill, halfway through the fermentation. Ageing lasts 12 to 15 months in two-to-four-year-old oak. He fines and filters lightly.

There are 6 ha of *vin de pays*—4.2 ha Syrah (1973, 1993), 1.2 of Viognier (1997), and 0.6 of Marsanne (1988). These *vin de pays des Collines Rhodaniennes* are led by the good, consistent Syrah Cuvée des Vernes and a gentle, correct Viognier. The Vernes Syrah is also raised 12 to 15 months in four-to-five-year-old oak, while there is also a nonwood Syrah. The whites are made one-third in oak, two-thirds in steel.

In his early 30s, and with the look of a moto rocker with his 1950s-style curly brown hair and

FIGURE 23 Over 30 years of organic farming: Emmanuel Barou assesses the clear fruit flavours of his St-Joseph with father Alexis. (Author's collection)

black shirt, Emmanuel put up a new cellar in 2002. It was an old stable and its 60 cm (23+ in.)–thick walls provide natural cooling, very much in tune with the outlook of the domaine. He is calm, almost reticent, and his wine is like him. There is clean elegance about the fruit in both the St-Joseph and the Syrah *vin de pays*. This is a name to watch.

ST-JOSEPH ROUGE

   2004 ★ ★ ★

   2003 ★ ★ ★

   2002 ★

   2001 ★ ★ ★

Export 10 per cent (1) USA, (2) Switzerland

DOMAINE LA BATELLERIE

RN7 26600 Gervans +33(0)475 033452

   See also Crozes-Hermitage.

The northern newcomers to vine growing, Jean-Pierre and Hélène Mucyn, work 0.7 ha on very steep, loose granite terraces at Arras—0.3 ha Syrah (1997–98) and 0.4 ha Roussanne (1997–98). The vineyard is fast draining, east and south facing. Just to the north at Ozon, they also planted 0.8 ha of Syrah in 2003.

The crop is destalked, precooled, and then given a four-week fermentation and maceration. Oak ageing lasts 11 months. The 2003 showed sound richness and subtle tannins, and is a promising wine to drink from 2007.

First produced in bottle in 2004, the white, 100 per cent Roussanne, is fermented in three-year-old casks and left on its lees for just about a year.

ST-JOSEPH ROUGE

   2003 (CASK) ★ ★ ★

DOMAINE ÉTIENNE BECHERAS

Le Prieuré 07370 Arras-sur-Rhône +33(0)475 070297

Étienne Becheras is not a man for undue ceremony and publicity. In winter he plonks a woolly sock on his head and hauls his large, ex-rugbyman frame off to his natural habitat, the vineyards. His broad forearms speak of plenty of hard work, and he reserves his warmest comments for operators of the old, natural school, people like Pascal Perrier, whose domaine is shrouded in a mix of Gitanes smoke and a countryman's habits.

He is the fourth generation to work the vines; his father, Paul, had been a director of the nearby Cave de Sarras since 1962, and Étienne took over from him there between 1984 and 1994. He was born in 1964, his family having worked fruit and vines at Arras in previous decades, but as he hit 30, he wanted to create his own wine *exploitation*.

Now he works 3 ha of St-Joseph, and 1.5 ha of *vin de pays* split 60 per cent Viognier (1996), 40 per cent Syrah (1989). The oldest plot is 0.5 ha of Syrah close to Arras in the *commune* of Vion on a lower-midslope site called *L'Iseran* (1970s), where the soil is decomposed granite, similar to St-Jean-de-Muzols. At Arras he planted 0.5 ha of Syrah in 1991 on the *Le Prieuré* slope behind his house—an abandoned vineyard that required clearing. This, too, has filtering, loose particle granite soil.

He also tends 1.5 ha on *Garde Poule*, a south-facing *gore* slope 250 metres above Arras, a vineyard planted between 1995 and 1997. The Marsanne and Roussanne (both 1997) for his white St-Joseph are split evenly here—under 0.5 ha of them. There are also plots low down on the rich ground beside the N86 road.

Arras is the gateway to the south of the France if one follows the old observations of nature. "It's true, we have crickets here, but Sarras doesn't," comments Étienne. It is a pretty pale-brown stone village that straddles an inlet valley of the Ardèche, with the vines mainly on the terraces above it, and the fruit—mostly apricots and cherries—on the fertile plain down by the Rhône.

Étienne doesn't care for marketing and got-up wines; his childhood bore witness to lots of eel fishing in the Rhône, notably before the building of the hydroelectric dam in the 1970s,

and his tutors were not always armed with a fly to catch the fish! "We used to clean up the eels by keeping them for two weeks in a mountain stream, so they got over being in the Rhône," he chuckles.

Bottling started in 1994, and the whole production is now sold that way. The Syrah is destemmed, then fermented with no outside yeasts in a mix of enamel and concrete vats for 15 to 23 days, the maximum temperature 32°C. M. Becheras relies on *délestages*—emptying and refilling a third or half of the vats—to homogenise and cool the liquid, and also does some pumping-over.

For now, there is just the one red, titled "Le Prieuré d'Arras" on the label; this is raised for 12 to 14 months in one-to-seven-year-old old casks, most of them 400 litres. It is fined, but not filtered. This is a good wine, a really solid, full offering that is honest and expressive in the local vein, with a touch of flair as well. It contains sound tannins and the black fruit has an earthy side to it. It drinks well from three or four years old and can live for around 10 years.

The white derives from around 70 per cent Marsanne, 30 per cent Roussanne, and is fermented in steel at around 15°C, then spends four to five months in one-year-old casks. *Bâtonnage* (lees stirring) is not approved of—"it quite simply gives the wine the taste of the lees, especially as I vinify in vat beforehand," he explains.

The Syrah and Viognier *vins de pays* are both vat-only fermented and raised, the former bottled in May, the latter three months after the malo has completed, usually in the spring. The 2003 Viognier was a hearty wine with plenty of flesh.

ST-JOSEPH ROUGE LE PRIEURÉ D'ARRAS ROUGE

   2004 ★★★
   2003 ★★★
   2002 ★(★)
   2001 ★★★

ST-JOSEPH BLANC

   2003 ★★

Export 15 per cent (1) Benelux, (2) Switzerland

DOMAINE BELLE

Les Marsuriaux 26600 Larnage +33(0)475 082458

See also Crozes-Hermitage, Hermitage.
Since 2001 the Belles have rented a 0.5 ha vineyard on the south side of Tournon at the *St-Joseph* site. It is steep and terraced, southeast facing, made up of firm granite with hard rock only 40 cm (16 in.) down. The vines date from the 1950s and later.

Whole bunches are fermented for three to four weeks, and the wine is aged for a year in 40 per cent new, 60 per cent one-year-old oak. It is fined, but not filtered. This is a serious domaine, and their St-Joseph lives up to that billing. It carries sound black fruits, enough richness to cope with the oak, and is a promising newcomer to the top ranks of St-Joseph. The 2002 can live for 10 years or so, the very thorough 2001 for around 15 years.

ST-JOSEPH ROUGE
2002 (CASK) ★★★
2001 ★★★★

LOUIS BERNARD

Route de Sérignan 84100 Orange
+33(0)490 118686

See also Cornas, Côte-Rôtie, Crozes-Hermitage, Hermitage, St-Péray.
The Louis Bernard group produces a red St-Joseph, but no white.

DOMAINE LAURENT BETTON

La Côte 42410 Chavanay +33(0)474 870823

See also Condrieu.
Laurent Betton is a young, first-timer to wine. He trained and worked as an electrical mechanic, then spent over 10 years with Jean-Michel Gérin at Côte-Rôtie, and started the domaine in 1993.

He makes red St-Joseph from his 1.8 ha of Syrah planted on *La Côte* above Chavanay between 1991 and 1998. The soil is classically poor, a mix of large sandy particles, loose granite, and stones.

The crop is destalked and fermented over a total of 17 days, with 11 months' ageing in 40 per cent casks of one to four years' age, 40 per cent large barrels, and 20 per cent vat. Fining and filtration are done. Laurent bottles his whole crop.

This is a domaine still finding its feet. The 2003 red was some way in advance of previous vintages, a soaked, southern wine in style, on the power.

ST-JOSEPH ROUGE
2003 ★★(★)

Export 20 per cent (1) Great Britain, (2) Belgium, (3) USA

DOMAINE BERNARD ET GILLES BIED

Les Malfondières 26600 Mercurol +33(0)475 074447

See also Crozes-Hermitage, Hermitage.
The Bieds from Crozes-Hermitage have a two-hectare Syrah vineyard at *Les Champs*, between Tournon and Mauves. Its soil is a mix of granite and clay.

A 10-day vinification of whole bunches is done, followed by a year in used casks. The wine can contain agreeable black fruit, with a touch of tannin, in the best years. Its style is traditional.

ST-JOSEPH ROUGE
1999 ★★

DOMAINE BLACHON

31 chemin des Goules 07300 Mauves +33(0)475 086112

The Blachon family have been making wine in Mauves for five generations and were even bottling some of it before the First World War. Roger resumed bottling in 1984, and son Sylvain continues with both wine and 10 hectares of apricots and a few cherry trees.

They work six hectares of St-Joseph. Their most noted sites are the hill of *St-Joseph* (1960s),

Les Oliviers (1988), and *Dardouille* (1960s). There are 5.4 hectares of Syrah, and 0.6 hectare of younger Marsanne on *Les Oliviers* and *Dardouille* (1988–91).

Roger first destalked after the rain-sodden harvest of 1993, and most crop is now treated this way. Vinification lasts 15 to 25 days in concrete vats, with cap punching and pumping-overs, the temperature running to a maximum of 30° to 32°C. The red is aged for a year in 225-litre casks that are one to six years old, and is fined but not filtered.

Two reds are bottled, a classic from the lower slope–plain areas, and a Coteaux, from the best hill sites. A little wine is sold to local merchants. The classic is a simply fruited, gentle wine, its soft texture typical of this area. The Coteaux contains more tannin and structure, and a nice, natural, unforced style. It should be drunk over seven or eight years.

The white is half oak handled for six to eight months, and bottled 15 months after the harvest, the malo done. It, too, shows sound local fullness, with a typical dried fruits flavour.

ST-JOSEPH ROUGE
  2003 ★★
  2002 ★
  2001 ★
  2000 ★★

ST-JOSEPH COTEAUX ROUGE
  2003 ★★(★)
  2001 ★★

ST-JOSEPH BLANC
  2003 ★★
  2001 ★★

Export 10 per cent (1) Belgium, (2) Switzerland

ANDRÉ ET FRÉDÉRIC BOISSONNET

Rue de la Voute 07340 Serrières +33(0)475 340799

  See also Condrieu.

Serrières is a bustling village right beside the Rhône and is the gateway towards the historic city of Annonay. It has a strong water jousting tradition, and generally has not been known for its wine.

The latest generation is the one that increased winemaking. In the two main families, both Anthony Vallet and Frédéric Boissonnet have wanted to move more towards wine than fruit after taking over from their fathers. "My grandfather Joseph made a little wine but sold most of his crop to the Cave of Péage-de-Roussillon," comments Frédéric Boissonnet, a sturdy, deep-voiced man. "My father, André, was more interested in cereals and fruit—notably maize and peaches. I always liked the festive side of wine—to eat and drink well—and wanted to give it a go on my own."

The connection with the Co-opérative ended in 1990, and by 1995 all the crop here was being bottled. There are six hectares of Syrah and 1.5 hectares of white, 85 per cent Marsanne, 15 per cent Roussanne. The oldest vine site is *Cime de la Côte*, a terraced hillside vineyard on loose, free-draining granite just west of the village. The other prime site is *Bus*, at St-Désirat, where the soil is a little deeper, although the theme remains that of granite.

The Boissonnets understandably pride themselves on their early-seventeenth-century vaulted cellars inside Serrières itself. After 80 per cent destemming, the reds are fermented for up to three weeks, with cap punching and pumping-over. Ageing runs for 12 months for the classic red and for up to 18 months for the special Cuvée de la Belive, 10 per cent of the oak being new. Cuvée de la Belive (4,000 bottles) is derived half from old vines on *Côte de la Cime*, and half from 10-year-old hillside vines, some of them on *Bus*.

In 2003 a third wine was launched, called "Extrême": made from only old-vine fruit, it is raised for 18 months in new oak; 1,800 bottles are produced. The style of the reds here is generally modern; the Belive 2002 was a full wine, good for its vintage. It carried some typical local pepperiness within its black fruits.

Half a hectare of the Marsanne grows in some limestone-influenced soil on *Les Rouasses* at Serrières, a part of the village's Vitrine operation—or showcase vineyard. The white is fermented and raised in cask, 90 per cent a mix of one- and two-year-old oak, with up to 10 per cent new. It is bottled around nine months after the harvest, the malo completed, with lees stirring during the raising. This is an interesting wine, with decent depth present.

ST-JOSEPH ROUGE
    2003 ★(★)

ST-JOSEPH CUVÉE DE LA BELIVE ROUGE
    2002 ★★★ 2011–13
    2001 ★

ST-JOSEPH BLANC
    2003 ★★★
    2002 ★★
    2000 ★

Export 15 per cent (1) Belgium, (2) Canada

DOMAINE DE BONSERINE

2 chemin de la Viallière Verenay 69420 Ampuis +33(0)474 561427

See also Condrieu, Côte-Rôtie.
This French-American domaine at Côte-Rôtie buys a mix of crop and wine to produce their red St-Joseph. The sources are mainly Charnas and Malleval, with a little from Chavanay.

Half the wine is raised for 10 to 14 months in casks, 40 per cent of them new; the other half is vat raised. It shows quite refined, soft fruit, with a tickle of tannin in a year like 2001; it is drinkable after three years.

ST-JOSEPH ROUGE
    2002 ★★
    2001 ★★

HERVÉ BORDE

07340 Charnas +33(0)475 340715

Hervé Borde learnt the trade chez his neighbour Daniel Roche at Charnas on the northern plateau. Like M. Roche, he favours a protracted ageing in cask. His Cuvée Morgane sees a little new oak. The wines are very traditional, and can finish rather drily.

DOMAINE BOUCHER

Vintabrin 42410 Chavanay +33(0)474 872338

This domaine has been bottling since 1975, and now 90 per cent of the crop is bottled. Michel works with his son Gérard. The family have been winemakers at Vintabrin since the late eighteenth century, mixing that activity with fruit growing and animal keeping.

They work three hectares of Syrah, planted between 1973 and 1993, and 0.75 hectare of 65 per cent Marsanne, 35 per cent Roussanne, planted in 1988. They also make a small amount of Condrieu.

The regular red St-Joseph is aged for 18 months in oak casks of two to five years. The top red, Cuvée Panoramique, is raised for 20 months in new oak. The white St-Joseph is vinified at a cool temperature and in a vintage like 2001 was fresh, zesty, with fair depth. There was a slight lack of flesh.

PATRICIA BOUCHER ET THOMAS PUTMAN

42520 Malleval +33(0)474 871525

Patricia, the daughter of Pierre Boucher of Domaine de la Favière, is near her mid-20s and met her boyfriend, Thomas Putman, at wine school in Beaune. He is from the north of France, and his parents are not involved in wine at all, working in the French electricity company EDF.

They are starting out, with all possibilities ahead of them. He is tall and slim, she a pretty chestnut-haired woman, and they started at La

Favière in 2004. Thomas has worked chez André Perret, and on his own account has planted at Chézenas near St-Pierre-de-Boeuf.

Their own *vin de pays des Collines Rhodaniennes* is called "Les Collonges"; this is 90 per cent Gamay (1952), 10 per cent Syrah, from a 0.4 ha sandy, fine soil site called *Collonges* at Pélussin. The 2002 showed promise and decent fruit, rating ★★.

LAURENT CHARLES BROTTE

Le Clos rte d'Avignon 84230 Châteauneuf-du-Pape
+33(0)490 837007

See also Condrieu, Cornas, Côte-Rôtie, Crozes-Hermitage, Hermitage.
The top red wine of this Châteauneuf-du-Pape *négociant* is Marandy, a vineyard with a schist presence. The crop is destalked, and vinified over three weeks, with pumping-over. A quarter of the wine receives a year's ageing in two-to-three-year-old casks, the rest staying in large, 50 hl barrels.

It is a wine with southern St-Joseph black fruit charm, some olives and a sappy texture present: sound wine There is a mainly Roussanne white with some rustic tones in it.

ST-JOSEPH MARANDY ROUGE
  2003 ★(★)
  2001 ★★★
  1999 ★★

DOMAINE DE CHAMPAL-ROCHER

Quartier Champal 07370 Sarras +33(0)478 342121

See also Condrieu, Crozes-Hermitage.
This is a domaine backed by the ability to invest, which, providing the money is thoughtfully spent, bodes well for the future. It stands high above Sarras at the end of the southern reaches of St-Joseph—a brown, dried-stone wall domaine in great isolation. There are cows in the distance, and wonderfully pure birdsong carries on the clear air around it.

The Rocher family come from the Giers valley near St-Étienne. Eric's grandfather Pierre

was a small-scale wine seller and would buy grapes from the Vaucluse that were transported on the railway to be fermented locally. After the Second World War, his father, Claudius, moved the business to Lyon, where it remains.

There are 21 hectares of St-Joseph, made up of 93 per cent Syrah, 4 per cent Marsanne, and 3 per cent Roussanne, planted between 1987 and 1989—their crop all goes into the red wine—as well as 4.5 hectares of Viognier *vin de pays* and about three hectares of Crozes-Hermitage. The family also owns the 20-hectare Domaine du Moulin Blanc at Tavel in the southern Rhône and works 0.85 ha of Condrieu.

The domaine was bought in 1987; it was flanked by pasture, and now the land to the west is vineyards giving *vin de pays*, to the east St-Joseph. The soil can be very sandy, with the usual granite traces, and the Rochers created a series of broad, gently sloping terraces to permit tractor working.

The wine is sold in a mix of bulk and bottle. The red, Terroir de Champal, is aged 18 months in already used casks and barrels.

The house style is for clear, clean-cut wines that carry a sleek fruitiness and a hint of tannin and provide good drinking from three years on. Half the wine is sold in bulk.

ST-JOSEPH TERROIR DE CHAMPAL ROUGE
  2001 ★★
  2000 ★
  1999 ★★

Export 10+ per cent (1) USA, (2) Canada, (3) Switzerland

CAVE DE CHANTE-PERDRIX

Izéras 42410 Chavanay +33(0)474 870636

See also Condrieu.
Since he started at the tender age of 19 in 1988, Philippe Verzier has established a good name and a sound following. His family have lived on the plateau at Izéras above Chavanay since 1828, and he is the fifth generation to work here: he has moved more towards wine and

home bottling, although there is still some fruit and cereal production. Philippe's father, Jean, would sell the crop to the Péage-de-Roussillon Co-opérative. Now 98 per cent is bottled.

The domaine is right beside a statue of the Madonna, from which there is a commanding view of the Rhône going south. A hum of traffic and the noise of local factories mask the more localised cricket and birdsong sounds of summer.

Eighty per cent of Philippe's seven hectares are high up, near the domaine. The St-Joseph's 4.6 hectares of Syrah were planted between 1967 and 1992; 0.6 hectare is on slope sites, the rest can be worked mechanically. The soil is fine, crumbling, and free draining, the loose granite mixed with mica traces.

The white vines are split 85 per cent Marsanne (1978), 15 per cent Roussanne (mid-1990s). Philippe also cultivates 1.7 ha of Condrieu and 0.9 ha of Syrah and Gamay nearby, which provide correct *vins de pays*. He tries to restrict his vineyard treatments: he applies a copper substitute before flowering and a sulphur treatment after flowering, and also works the soil between his vines.

Philippe is a neat, fit, self-contained man. His previous sports were volleyball and running, and he looks as if he works to keep himself in shape. His domaine sits a little apart from the mainstream, and one gets the impression that he is happy to live a private life. One of his great pleasures is the cinema, an unusual hobby for a *vigneron*. He's also one of the growers who thinks ahead to the toil of a Wine Fair, and so turns up with a swish swivel chair to help him through the day—another instance of being a little apart.

The red wines from up here on the plateau are more overtly spiced and dry textured than the Syrahs from Mauves and the core of the *appellation* near Tournon. Philippe makes two reds. The regular comes from 1985 Syrah, a wine whose oak exposure has been cut back. Until 1996 it was all cask raised, but he found this too oppressive, and now just half is aged for a year in casks that are changed every eight years.

His old vines' cuvée is called "La Madone," made from the 1967 Syrah. This is aged over 16 months, on a 70 per cent oak, 30 per cent vat split, 10 per cent of the oak new; the Madone's duration in cask has also been cut back. Both reds are fined and filtered. The regular red shows direct, but sometimes taut black fruits; the Madone displays smoky, peppery aromas, and it is worth waiting three years to allow its fruit to soften.

About half the white St-Joseph is cask raised for 11 months. This is elegant and good: it often shows nutty flavours and has enough structure in the best years to be full of mature flavour at around five years old.

ST-JOSEPH ROUGE

2002 (★)
2001 (★)
1999 ★★
1998 ★

ST-JOSEPH LA MADONE ROUGE

2003 ★
2002 ★
2001 ★★
1998 ★★

ST-JOSEPH BLANC

2002 ★
2001 ★★
1999 ★

Export 20 per cent (1) USA, (2) Great Britain, (3) Switzerland

M. CHAPOUTIER

18 ave Dr Paul Durand 26600 Tain l'Hermitage
+33(0)475 082865

See also Condrieu, Cornas, Côte-Rôtie, Crozes-Hermitage, Hermitage, St-Péray.
Chapoutier work 11 hectares of mainly central St-Joseph vineyards based around Tournon and Mauves; 7.5 hectares are Syrah, 3.5 hectares Marsanne.

One of the top sites is *Le Clos*, on the steep hillside above Tournon, which was purchased in 1997. There are five hectares of land here, of which two are now planted with Syrah. "The vineyard had lain idle for 30 years, so its soil was well rested," comments Michel Chapoutier, adding that it used to be worked by the monks of the Abbey of Tournon. This is southeast facing, and its loose granite is full of large particles; it is light, fast-draining terrain.

There is also an important three-hectare plot on the south slope of the *lieu-dit St-Joseph* nearer Mauves; this contains Marsanne from the 1950s and Syrah dating from the 1930s and 1950s that goes into the special Granits red wine. Nearby there is also a plot of Syrah on *Peygros* (1998).

At Mauves, there is a mix of Syrah and Marsanne on three hectares of *Montagnon*; the Marsanne dates from between the 1970s and 1990s, the Syrah from the 1950s. These grow on the flat part of this loess-granite site.

Beyond Tournon and Mauves, there is one hectare north at Limony, on poor granite soil; bought in 1995, this Syrah vineyard dates from 1995–96 until 2001.

The two workhorse wines have for years been the red and white Deschants. The red Deschants (25,000 bottles) is made from 60 per cent purchased wine, 40 per cent grapes that include some of the Chapoutier crop. The wine and grapes that are bought in come from the more southern area stretching between Arras and Mauves, taking in those *communes* as well as St-Jean-de-Muzols, Tournon, and Lemps.

Deschants receives a 15-to-18 day vinification with twice-daily cap punching, followed by 10 to 12 months' ageing, 40 per cent in oak, 60 per cent in vat. The oak is a mix of 550-litre old-wood *demi-muids* and some three-to-five-year-old casks.

Deschants *rouge* has been a regular friend to many Rhône enthusiasts over the decades. It is reliable without hitting the heights and so is often a value choice when eating out. It carries a certain reserve in its fruit, conveying some dryness of texture that tallies with its origins. It is good to drink from around four years old and

onwards in the best years. It holds together well usually for eight to 10 years.

The top red St-Joseph, Les Granits (up to 4,000 bottles), extols its granite origins, as the name implies. It is made from selected pickings of Chapoutier's best crop from 1930s and 1950s Syrah on the *lieu-dit St-Joseph*. Extreme maturity is sought for both this and the white Granits. The soil at the *St-Joseph* site near their big vineyard sign on the way to Mauves is very poor, stony granite with a sandstone texture to it. As Chapoutier like to explain, their biodynamic approach includes allowing ant and worm life to break up the stone, which permits increased root growth, with a good twist on the roots as they descend.

The house destalks all the Granits crop, which would seem to go against the benefits achieved on the stalks by extreme ripeness. Fermentation is in concrete vats, maceration lasting a month, with a few pumping-overs at the outset, and the cap punched down. The wine is then kept in one-third each of new, one-year-, and two-year-old casks for 14 to 18 months, the longer stay applying in a firm vintage like 1998.

Michel Chapoutier often finds a mineral texture on this wine. It is wild, tarry, fungal, big-scale wine—a vintage like 2001 can live for over 15 years, needing time to settle its power. Licorice and deep black fruits are often evident on this, one of the big structure, full-on red St-Josephs.

The white Les Granits is one of the most sensuous whites of the northern Rhône. It mixes a fleshy, oily texture with a local fullness that is not too sophisticated for its own good—its potency derived from its granite home. The first surge on the palate can often provide a glimpse of a Hermitage from a lesser year. Although it sells at a high price, it is the sort of wine that makes you feel you can have a darned good time when drinking it.

Picking is deliberately late, playing to the Marsanne's rich strengths, a feature enhanced by low yields of 20 to 25 hl/ha. The vineyard dates from the 1930s and 1940s, with very few recent plantings, and sits on the south end of the *St-Joseph* slope. The topsoil is loose, decomposed granite, but only just below is the hard granite itself—very poor soil, similar to *Bessards* on the Hermitage hill. Production is 5,000 to 6,000 bottles.

It is a good, ripe example of pure Marsanne from old vines. First produced in 1995, it is made half in 550-litre *demi-muids* (70 per cent new, the rest one to two years old), half in vat, with *bâtonnage* (lees stirring) and the malolactic done, like all the whites. Ageing time is 10 months.

The mainstream white, Deschants (18,000 bottles), is an improved wine. It comes from Marsanne vines dating from the 1960s and 1970s. It is mostly composed of purchased crop, with some Chapoutier grapes. The range of vineyard is, like the red Deschants, from Arras down to Mauves. One-quarter is vinified and raised in oak ranging from new to four years old, over the course of eight to 10 months, the rest is vat treated.

The Deschants white fruits are often clad within a pebbly texture, the drier tone of St-Joseph coming through when set alongside Crozes *blanc* from across the river. It carries a more local feel than it did in the 1990s.

ST-JOSEPH DESCHANTS ROUGE

2003 ★★
2002 ★★
2001 ★★
2000 ★★
1999 ★★
1998 ★★
1997 ★
1996 ★★

ST-JOSEPH LES GRANITS ROUGE

2003 (CASK) ★★★★ Tight-knit bouquet, plenty for the future, a cool side from the granite; balanced, measured black fruit, stylish and can vary. Good pedigree, has nuance. Grilled finale (oak). From 2008; 2019–22.

2002 ★★★ Minted, tar, black fruit/oak nose; chocolate style flavour, brewed fruits, assertive

content. Grilled side from the oak, but has rich core. Structured wine, more settled by 2006–07. 2016–18.

2001 ★★★★ Fungal, spiced red fruits, potential on nose; chewy, tight black fruit/licorice. Dry end. Lot of scale, from 2007. 2018–20.

2000 ★★★ Tarry, cooked black fruit bouquet. Juicy core, *joli*. Quite tannic, chewy with licorice on end. Big wine. From 2006; 2011–12.

1999 ★★★ Chocolate, powerful, ripe fruit aroma; pebbly black stone fruit, clear-cut. Fair length, licorice/dry oak end. 2012–14.

1998 ★★★★★ Very good black, oily/smoky pine aroma; funky palate—fruit sap with smoked/mineral touches. Oily tannins reappear on finish. Great combo of textures and flavours. Esp to 2010; 2016–17.

1997 ★★
1996 ★★★

ST-JOSEPH DESCHANTS BLANC

2003 ★★
2002 ★
2001 ★★
2000 ★★
1999 ★

ST-JOSEPH LES GRANITS BLANC

2003 ★★★ Oily, rich, buttery nose. Pretty rich wine, broad, a touch extracted, some oak evident. Length OK, chewy finale, overt Marsanne breadth and fullness. 2012–14.

2002 ★★ Yellow; exotic banana/oak nose; three-quarter weight, fine. Esp 2006; 2011–13.

2001 ★★★★ Broad butter/floral nose; full, juicy palate, with some restraint. Rich, oily wine, Marsanne *arriba!* Lasting, nutty end. From 2005–06; 2016–19.

2000 ★★★ Creamy, custard-style aroma. Thorough flavour, white fruit/light nut. Approaches white Hermitage in style, on a lesser scale. 2011–13.

1999 ★★★ White pepper/truffle/light spice bouquet; nice, clean density, has *gras*; white stone fruit, spice/heat end. 2015–18.

1998 ★★★★★ Open, tropical, sweets/white truffle aromas; tighter palate—flan, lime, honey/vanilla end with mineral. Complex. Lot of variety. Could get an oxidised side, but power will win. 2017.

1997 ★★

1996 ★

AURÉLIEN CHATAGNIER

Les Barges 42520 Saint-Pierre-de-Boeuf +33(0)474 317553

In his early 20s, this fair-haired, pale-eyed young man studied at Beaune and has worked with François Villard. He started his St-Joseph in 2002 and also has a tiny plot of Viognier at Limony to make Condrieu. The half hectare of St-Joseph Syrah is split 0.2 hectare at Charnas and 0.3 hectare at Malleval, on the plateau where loose sanded granite is the prime soil. The vines' average is 15 to 20 years.

After a cool, three-day maceration at 6° to 7°C, the vinification involves cap punching and pumping-overs and runs for three weeks. Only natural yeasts are used, and there is no filtration. Cask ageing lasts 12 months, in 25 per cent new, 75 per cent one-to-two-year-old oak.

Both the 2003 and 2004 show promise; the 2003 red was a fleshy, warm wine with clean lines, drinking well by 2005 but capable of eight years' life; the 2004 will drink well from 2008—it is a well-filled wine of earthy appeal.

Completing the picture are two half hectares of respectable *vin de pays des Collines Rhodani-ennes* made from Syrah and Gamay, grown at Charnas.

ST-JOSEPH ROUGE

2004 ★★(★)

2003 ★★★

DOMAINE DU CHÂTEAU VIEUX

26750 Triors +33(0)475 453165

Set in the Drôme *département* past the old shoe-making centre of Romans-sur-Isère, this old family domaine moved into making St-Joseph in 1994. Its local habitat is woodland, *vin de pays*, and asparagus: all around the tiny village of Triors, with its fine Château and Abbey, the soil is poor and sandy. The landscape here has also been marked by state-financed schemes of the last 30 years to encourage a lot of tree planting.

The Rousset family was one of the few here to stick with vineyards, and they still own 10 hectares of *vin de pays de la Drôme*. It was the son Fabrice who wanted to move up a grade, so he went for a mix of buying and renting superior vineyards, and very shrewdly chose mature plots of Syrah. His first was 0.8 ha at Arras, on a clay-limestone slope, his second 0.7 ha opposite the renowned hill of *Ste-Épine* inside the Tournon boundaries—where there is schist mixed with the clay-limestone. The Arras vineyard dates from the mid-1950s and 1968, Tournon from the 1920s and 1983.

The Syrah is handpicked and 70 per cent destalked. Fabrice, a small, slight man with light-brown hair has an unassuming approach, and says he vinifies "like my grandfather." There are no external yeasts, and no control of heat or cold. "We can go up to 37° or 38°C, and we open the doors if necessary, just like in the old days," he remarks. Vinification lasts 20 days, with cap punching by foot and twice-daily *remontages*, or pumping-overs.

Named "Vieille Vigne" on the label, the St-Joseph is aged for 18 months in cask, using three-year-old oak, and is filtered. It is gently and purely made, giving promise for the future. It carries style and authenticity. In both 1998 and 2003, two reds were made, but Fabrice is not sure he wants to repeat this—when made, the "special" is called Les Hauts and comes from the 1950s Syrah.

The *vin de pays* Syrah is largely destalked by dint of being machine harvested. This comes in two styles; the Vieille Vigne de la Drôme, from 50-year vines, receives 18 months in cask and the regular two years in large old barrels. Both are very good value for money.

The white *vin de pays* is made from Marsanne and Viognier, with some Roussanne coming through. It is steel fermented and bottled in the spring, with its malo blocked. It is respectable.

Export 10 per cent (1) Belgium, (2) USA

DOMAINE JEAN-LOUIS CHAVE

37 avenue St-Joseph 07300 Mauves +33(0)475 082463

See also Hermitage.

The Chaves have long worked a few vines at St-Joseph, as if keeping their eye in with their native Ardèche. Jean-Louis has taken this alliance with his roots a stage further since the mid-1990s, and the vineyard has grown from 1.5 to five hectares.

It is split about one-third each across four *communes*. The oldest vines are on slopes at Tournon, with some dating from before the First World War, some from the early 1980s, and most from 1992–93. The soil there is granite mixed with clay.

At their home villages of Mauves, on more acid granite slopes, there is a 2003 vineyard constructed on *Les Côtes* as part of the Vitrine operation, and another holding on *Sapelias*. Within Tournon, there are plots on *Dardouille* and *Les Oliviers*, and *Pichonnier* at St-Jean-de-Muzols.

On the ruggedly hewn granite terraces of the Chave family's origins at Lemps, a total of 1.5 ha was planted every other year from 1996 until 2002. Jean-Louis considers the Lemps site, called *Bachasson*, to contain a neutral soil make-

up comparable with the prime granite *lieu-dit* of *Bessards* on the west end of the Hermitage hill.

The crop is destemmed and receives a three-to-four-week vatting, with cap punchings. The young wine is raised for 15 to 20 months in two-to-three-year and older casks.

Father Gérard would call his St-Joseph red "an amusement," and this is the broad spirit in which the wine should be taken—a wine to drink in free quantities, with its fruit leading the way. Under Jean-Louis, the wine has become a little plumper than in the past. It always carries a frank fruitiness with a fresh bouquet. Typically it is a wine that should be drunk within around eight years, and because of its warm texture, it can work well with a variety of dishes. It reflects well its unpretentious Ardechois origins.

J-L CHAVE SÉLECTION

37 avenue St-Joseph 07300 Mauves +33(0)475 082463

This is the *négociant* business of Jean-Louis Chave, the top Hermitage producer; the St-Joseph is called "Offerus," the Côtes du Rhône "Mon Coeur." In countries like Norway, where his importer Christopher Moestue is an ex-harvester and old friend, there is a small amount of red Crozes-Hermitage. The family connections across the St-Joseph area run far and wide, and sources range from St-Jean-de-Muzols to St-Désirat and Sarras, with varying degrees of granite influence on the wine. Mauves and Tournon account for about half the wine.

There can be nine suppliers of the Offerus, with most of the wine vinified in each person's cellars. It is raised for 12 to 14 months in casks of three to six years old, and around 50,000 bottles are made. It follows its vintage quite faithfully—the 2000 delivered straight black fruits, the 2001 an added tannic element that would reward some cellar patience.

The Mon Coeur, made from Syrah and Grenache, is raised in a mix of 225- and 600-litre casks and in vat for 11 to 12 months. Jean-Louis likes a cooler area like Vinsobres for his Syrah, the cool approach also reflected in the inclusion of some Grenache from high-up Buisson in the Vaucluse. There are around 40,000 bottles of Mon Coeur Côtes du Rhône. It emphasizes live, direct peppery fruit, and has the makeup to show well for seven or eight years.

ST-JOSEPH OFFERUS ROUGE

2001 ★★★

2000 ★★

CÔTES DU RHÔNE MON COEUR

2001 ★★(★)

2000 ★★(★)

DOMAINE DU CHÊNE

Le Pêcher 42410 Chavanay +33(0)474 872734

See also Condrieu.

This is the sort of domaine that St-Joseph needs for its long-term future. Marc and Dominique Rouvière have worked to place it in a strong second wave of quality properties following the standards set over the years by the Gripa, Coursodon, and Chave families.

The Rouvières are first-generation winemakers from Lyon. In such circumstances much of the domaine's success is down to the raw determination of the *vignerons.* Marc Rouvière's parents were small-business people, and his interest in the countryside was kindled when they took him outside Lyon for his holidays. Accordingly, he went off to the Mâcon Wine School at 16. He would spend his days off school with growers in Pouilly-Fuissé, and after further commercial studies, Marc launched on the search for affordable land to realise his dream.

By 1984 he set up a small wine shop in Lyon: "I worked with a Co-opérative near Nîmes for my bulk wine, plus some Beaujolais and Mâcon

properties, and would also get bottles in from my mates," he recounts. "One day a client walked in and said 'What, you have no St-Joseph?' Luckily it was the Wine Fair at Chavanay the next Sunday, so I managed to buy some there for the client. But more importantly, I heard from Philippe Faury there that there was a property for sale because the grower had died in a cellar accident with his wine press. Things went from there."

Dark-haired and compactly built, Marc is obviously passionate about his winemaking and his vineyard work. He likes to receive people at his cellars, a form of test to check that they have been keen enough to find him up at 300 metres on the plateau above the valley, stuck away in the straggle of houses and hamlets up there. His open and friendly manner contributes to his practical work ethic. "I've still a lot do," he states suddenly. "Such as what?" "The vineyard walls will keep me going for another 20 years—the old owners never kept them up."

He tells his tale with gusto: "Dominique and I married on 19 October 1985 and off we went on our adventure. She had been a postwoman, and had also to accept that the house was so run-down it couldn't be lived in!" A slim, vivacious woman with bright eyes, Dominique works on the commercial and office side. He appears to be the grounded person, she more the spirit of the air, but both share a strong sense of purpose.

"We chose the name 'Chêne' for the domaine," he adds, "because 'Rouvière' means a plantation of oaks in ancient French, and because there were a lot of oaks here, one of which we left when we came here."

This high land has always mixed fruit, vegetable, cereal, and vinegrowing. As wine prices have risen, the Rouvières have sold off the apple trees and enlarged the vineyard from 4 to 14 ha. Their St-Joseph holdings are now 1.5 ha of Marsanne and 6 ha of Syrah, plus a healthy 3.5 ha of Condrieu vines. Three hectares of Syrah *vin de pays des Collines Rhodaniennes* complete the picture.

The St-Joseph sites are mostly at Chavanay—*Le Pêcher, Les Eyguets,* and *Les Rivoires,* with a

FIGURE 24 What an adventure! Marc and Dominique Rouvière have built up their Domaine du Chêne to be a leading name at St-Joseph and Condrieu. (Tim Johnston)

plot at St-Pierre-de-Boeuf on a steep slope called *Biez*—light, crumbled granite with more clay than the Chavanay sites, which are poor, with only light topsoils above the base rock. The wine from *Biez* is more marked by tannins than the Chavanay Syrahs.

Most of the property is planted with traditional *massale* Syrah, except for clones on the *Rivoires* site. The land is worked in all spots except for *Rivoires*. The Massif Central outcrops influence the soil, which is very sandy on the plateau around the domaine. Marc has planted alfalfa and mustard to correct the soil; as he sees it, "the alfalfa has a lot of roots, so brings with it a lot of organic matter and serves to loosen up the soil. This takes five to six years for full effect." He is a follower of Claude Bourguignon's philosophy of active nourishment and working of the vineyard.

The wind is potent up here, split equally between north and south. Their 21-metre roof went flying in the storms of late December 1999. "It's rare to have still days here—the north wind actually combines the Mistral with the wind from the centre of France—so we have to do a thorough *palissage* to stop shoots breaking," comments Marc.

A strong part of Marc's outlook is his delayed harvesting for both red and white crop. This often starts around the end of September, so the grapes are as mature and sugary as possible.

The reds, around 40 per cent destalked in normal years, are vinified in concrete over 15 to 20 days, with *remontages* done. Ageing is in casks aged two to four years and lasts 12 to 15 months for the classic red. There is no fining and only a light filtration. The classic holds a fresh, fruit-led style, with no great fat in it. Its peppery nature and sometimes lean tannins are typical of Chavanay.

The Anaïs, named after their daughter, is selected at the press, then raised in the previous year's white-wine casks for 18 to 24 months. It is usually made from 30-to-50-year-old Syrah. There was none made in 2002. This has gained in stature in recent years, and its oily, full texture is very enjoyable. The fruit has become more generous and is now deeply rooted in the wine, allowing more local feel to be present. A very good vintage like the 2001 can show well for over 10 years.

The white is fermented at 19° to 20°C, "so it can last a bit longer." It has always been pure Marsanne (1980s); in 2003 about 10 per cent extra Roussanne was planted. It is half new-oak, half vat fermented, and is bottled in September, the malo done. In a light year like 2002, it is bottled in July. The 2001 was much better—a serious wine with nutty/apricot elements and plenty of structure—with the 2003 similarly full. Its quality shows off the Rouvière penchant for white wines, since the Condrieu from here is nowadays very fine.

The Syrah *vin de pays* carries live, berried fruit in a dry and direct way, and is ideal for barbecues and grilled foods.

ST-JOSEPH ROUGE
  2002 ★★
  2001 ★

ST-JOSEPH ANAÏS ROUGE
  2003 ★★
  2001 ★★★★

ST-JOSEPH BLANC
  2004 ★★
  2003 ★★(★)
  2001 ★★★

Export 30 per cent (1) Great Britain, (2) Belgium, (3) USA/Japan

DOMAINE LOUIS CHÈZE

Pangon 07340 Limony +33(0)475 340288

See also Condrieu.

"Must keep busy" should be on Louis Chèze's coat of arms. This quiet-voiced, smiling man moves discreetly, speedily, indeed almost glides along, but is rarely still. He loves to plant vineyards, to keep developing new sites, is often late for meetings, and is clearly counterbalanced by his open, alert, and friendly wife, Béatrice—her good, deep laugh runs alongside his discreet smile; her broad sense of matters accompanies his pinpointed searchings, his view of going straight to the goal. His proposal to Béatrice in 1985 ran as follows: "so come along and help me—there's work to do!"

The latest project is Seyssuel, north of Côte-Rôtie, where he has gathered his brother-in-law and Laurent and Pascal Marthouret to join in with him—younger growers like Laurent Marthouret. The slope vineyards are south of the ruined Château, and the total plantation, a mix of clone and *massale* Syrah, has reached six hectares, with the first wine vinified chez Louis in 2003. "I'm a friend of Gaillard and his friends, so I thought I would join in, too. I'm the veteran of our group, which we call 'Les Vignobles de Seyssuel,'" he states.

His father, Marius, a founder of the St-Désirat Co-opérative, used to send his hectare's crop there for vinification. Cereal, fruits, asparagus, and cattle were more important up here on the plateau in those days. "When I started in 1978, my target was 10 hectares," confides Louis, "but I like to plant—I see a nice plot and I think that will fit in nicely!"

So now he's up to 22 hectares. At St-Joseph there are 11 hectares of Syrah, a mix running from those he planted in the late 1990s up to rented plots dating from the 1950s; these include a one-hectare, 50-year Syrah vineyard on *Buis* at Limony, where the hill is very pure granite. Yields hover around a low 25 hl/ha.

The three hectares of white are 40 per cent Roussanne (1993–98), 60 per cent Marsanne (1978). There are also six hectares of Viognier, Marsanne, and Syrah, each one producing its own *vin de pays*; these grow around his domaine and just outside the *appellation* area. And he has three hectares of Condrieu at Limony.

Louis' three reds start with the Cuvée Ro-Rée; this comes from several plots and vines aged 10 to 15 years. The Cuvée Prestige de Caroline is mostly from *Buis* and *Pangon*, both sites at Limony, its vines 25 to 30 years old. The Cuvée des Anges is from *Buis* and *Montrond*, their vines 40 to 50 years old. All the plots are mainly granite based.

The Syrah is destemmed, and Louis finds only *remontages* (pumping-overs) necessary, rather than cap punching as well. Since the late 1990s, he has used no external yeasts, and favours extended macerations in the steel vats—

20 days for Ro-Rée, 30 to 35 for Caroline, and 40 days for Anges—with a maximum temperature of 34°C. "I do a cool crop maceration first, which permits long vatting," he says; "I find the tannins are nobler if achieved in this way, rather than by cap punching."

Ro-Rée and Caroline are both aged for a year, the former in two-to-four-year-old casks, the latter in 25 per cent new, 75 per cent one-to-two-year-old oak. The Cuvée des Anges, first made in 1995, receives 18 months in new oak.

The white is also called "Ro-Rée"—60 per cent Marsanne, 40 per cent Roussanne. It is cask fermented, 15 per cent of the oak new, and raised over nine months, with *bâtonnage* (lees stirring). Its fruit is pleasant, and it's a wine that can be enjoyed in its youth.

Louis' Côtes du Rhône *blanc* is made from Viognier planted inside the St-Joseph *appellation* area, and is another oak-fermented wine.

In the mid-1980s, this marked itself out as a progressive domaine when its Cuvée Caroline was launched with a higher-than-usual proportion of new-oak exposure. Louis has worked closely with Jean-Luc Colombo, the avant-garde *oenologue*, since 1984. The wines still reflect this tendency towards overt oak influence, and when young, some of them dry noticeably on the palate after being open for an hour or so, with their aromas moving fast from black fruit to gaminess.

The Anges is emphatically a wine that should be drunk only from its middle age onwards; this is a cellar-constructed wine, going way past the straight fruit of typical St-Joseph. After six or seven years it shows an increased variety of aromas and flavours—notes like mocha, mineral, and prune come along, as the oaken grip subsides.

ST-JOSEPH RO-RÉE ROUGE

2002 (CASKS) ★
2001 ★★
2000 ★★

ST-JOSEPH CUVÉE PRESTIGE DE CAROLINE ROUGE

2001 ★

ST-JOSEPH CUVÉE DES ANGES ROUGE

2001 ★★
2000 ★★★

ST-JOSEPH RO-RÉE BLANC

2001 ★★

Export 33 per cent (1) USA, (2) Great Britain, (3) Belgium

DOMAINE CHIROL

Les Lacs Est 07340 Charnas +33(0)475 340673

This is a traditional, fourth-generation domaine at Charnas, where Bruno Chirol, in his mid-50s, works four hectares of St-Joseph. "I used to sell to the merchant trade until around the mid-1990s," he states, "and I don't believe in oak for either red or white wine."

He has plots at Limony and Charnas, the former for his *vin de pays des Collines Rhodaniennes Viognier*, made in the old-fashioned, sweet style. The 3.5 ha of Syrah was planted by his father Ferdinand in the early 1970s, as was the Marsanne for the 0.5 ha of white St-Joseph.

The crop is fermented in whole bunches, with M. Chirol foot punching the cap and pumping over the vats. The wine stays quietly in vat until bottling in November, around 14 months after the harvest. The white is bottled at the same time, its malo done.

DOMAINE LAURENT CHOMAT

Le Rioudard 07300 Glun +33(0)475 085925

Just 40, Laurent Chomat's sole activity until 2001 was fruit growing—apricots and some cherries. "I recuperated a half-hectare vineyard that had been planted by my grandfather in the 1970s," he states. This is on *Champs Longs*, in the southern area of Mauves, a granite site with grey oxide stones. It has been supplemented by another half hectare planted by M. Chomat on *Le Dessous du Chemin*, near the N86, where there is more clay.

The crop is destemmed, and vinification lasts up to three weeks, with cap punching and pumping-overs. Only natural yeasts are involved. The wine is raised for 18 months in four-year-old casks and is fined but not filtered. The 2003 bore a pretty local feel, its supple red fruits in the Mauves tradition, with some tidy tannic support. The 2004's fruit was clear-cut, and that is a wine to drink towards its eighth to 10th birthday.

ST-JOSEPH ROUGE
2003 ★★

DOMAINE COLLONGE

La Négociale 26600 Mercurol +33(0)475 074432

See also Crozes-Hermitage.
The Collonge family from Crozes-Hermitage have made St-Joseph since 1985. They work 5.5 ha of Syrah (1970s, 1988) on the sandy granite of *La Treille* at Ozon, between Arras and Sarras, north of Tournon. There is also half a hectare of Marsanne of the same age. It is a hill vineyard that ripens two weeks behind the Crozes.

The red is called "La Treille"; the crop is destemmed, and fermented for 12 days, with twice-daily pumping-overs. It is vat raised until June and bottled with fining and filtration. It is middle-of-the-road wine.

The all-Marsanne white La Treille is vat fermented at 16° to 18°C and bottled early, in January, the malo usually blocked for freshness.

ST-JOSEPH LA TREILLE ROUGE
2001 ★

DOMAINE COMBIER

RN7 26600 Pont-de-l'Isère +33(0)475 846156

See also Crozes-Hermitage.
Laurent Combier made his first St-Joseph in 1994 from a 0.6 ha vineyard he cleared and planted in 1990 on the *Blondel* site at St-Jean-de-Muzols. This is a slope along the Doux valley, beyond the Delas cellars. The vineyard is south-southeast facing at 220 metres, the vines

DOMAINE DU CORNILHAC

Philippe and Marielle Salette must be contenders for the best-looking northern Rhône couple. His blue eyes must come from roots on the plateau of the Ardèche, and his dark, trim good looks counterpoint Marielle's striking tall blondeness. The couple met in the musty surrounds of Raymond Trollat's tiny, dark cellar across the hill—a memorable *lieu de rencontre*.

Until 2002 Philippe made his own wine, having extended the family domaine from fruit towards vines after the death of his father, Fernand, in 1996. The only catch was that he was also a full-time vet, with a practice in Valence. He then decided that he did not have the time to keep going with both the vineyard care and the winemaking, and from 2002 sold his organic crop to Chapoutier, where Marielle, a trained *oenologue*, used to work.

"I didn't have the time to make the wine as well as look after the vineyard—all in my spare time away from the vet's surgery," he explains. "It was frustrating, but now I have my full energy on the vineyard, and planted half a hectare in 2004."

Philippe makes a lucid connection between his two worlds: "I like alternative medicine like homeopathy and osteopathy on animals, so that links with the vineyard's biodynamic structure. I call my Ardèche job *'agricole'* and my Drôme job *'animal'*!"

His red wines were dry toned, with good quality of fruit, sometimes a little lean. Their slightly peppered, upright texture stood in line with their rocky origins and a life of eight to nine years was possible for them.

trained along traditional stakes on the local loose, sanded granite. As with his Crozes and his fruits, Laurent works the vineyard on organic methods.

The crop is vinified in a small wooden vat for around three weeks, and raised for a year in one-to-two-year-old casks. The tannins in these reds invest them with more grip than Combier's Crozes counterparts. They show well after three years and have enough content to age and develop for up to 10 years.

ST-JOSEPH ROUGE
2002 ★★
2001 ★★

DOMAINE DE LA CÔTE SAINTE-ÉPINE

17 chemin Côte Ste-Épine 07300 St-Jean-de-Muzols
+33(0)475 088535

This domaine possesses one mighty ace card in its hand—a precious hectare and a half of neighbour and cousin Raymond Trollat's vineyard. Eliette Desestret's family have been winegrowers for four generations, leading back to her great-grandfather Baptiste Trollat. But her husband, Michel, did not work on the land—he was a manager with Black & Decker in the Isère until the factory closed in 1987 and he lost his job. Thus started his winemaking venture.

There are two *exploitations* now—father and son. Michel's son Mikael, a slim, willowy man now nearly 30, has studied at Beaune, and gave his parents the encouragement to press on with the wine when he started up in 1996.

Michel works four hectares, while Mikael has 2.1 hectares, including the 1.5 hectares from Trollat on his wonderfully exposed hillside. A further 0.35 hectare has been cleared around and above the cellars for planting.

Mikael is helped by the age of his vines—the *Aubert* vineyard of Trollat ranges from 20 to 90 years old, while the *Ste-Épine* site goes back almost 100 years. A small 0.2 ha of the *Aubert* holds Marsanne aged between 30 and 55 years. The soil is granite, 200 metres up, with an east and southeast exposure. It took Eliette's grandfather 11 years to clear one hectare on *Ste-Épine* and make an access route to it, in the days of working with one's hands and with oxen in support.

Mikael seems shy and very self-effacing alongside his imposing mother. Both domaines

now bottle all their wine, Michel having started this in 1985.

The red crop spends two days at a cool 15°C and is about 20 per cent destalked. The juice is pumped over and the cap punched in their steel and wood vats, with an end-of-fermentation temperature of up to 33°C. Ageing lasts 15 to 18 months, mostly in *demi-muids*, with some casks. All the oak is three to four years old. There is no filtration.

The red seems to be a wine waiting to take off; its fruit can be interesting—more on a sinewy than rich texture—but the ensemble can be a little awkward, the harmony unsure. I would expect some improvement to come.

The white is vinified in a mix of cask and *demi-muid*, and bottled in March once the malo has normally finished. Nutty and peach fruited, it has agreeable fullness.

Father and son have different labels, which both accurately state "M. Desestret" on them, as well as the words "Vieilles Vignes."

ST-JOSEPH ROUGE
2004 (CASK) ★★
2001 ★
2000 ★★

ST-JOSEPH BLANC
2001 ★★

DOMAINE COURBIS

Route de St-Romain 07130 Châteaubourg
+33(0)475 818160

See also Cornas.

This has become a big operation, a domaine with important holdings in both St-Joseph and Cornas, as well as 17 hectares of Bergeron apricots spread across plain and plateau. Its hillside vineyards are outside the original St-Joseph *appellation* zone, but the sites are quality ones, with a strong local nuance of limestone instead of the usual heavy granite orientation. These *terres blanches*, the local term for the limestone his ability to shoot a grand line leaves one guessing about its ratio of truth to humour. Now past his mid-70s, he has changed very little in the 30 years I have known him. He stoops, his hat is still askew, he remains faithful to his *papier maïs* French cigarettes. He walks softly around, but the wit is piercing. He clearly likes to get in the way of his sons, to have something to do, to stir things up a little. He and Gustave Coursodon have always been good friends, and go back many decades.

Twelve of their 18 hectares of Syrah are at Châteaubourg, on the prime hill site of *Les Royes*; the soil here is limestone plus clay, with not much granite in evidence. This is the end of the limestone seam that runs north from Guilherand and Crussol next to St-Péray. The *Royes* vineyard is stunningly steep, even by northern Rhône standards, overlaid with jagged chalk stones. It is high up, between 200 and 270 metres. The Courbis point out that its shelter from the wind is a factor in the ripening process. Like many of the granite-ledged vineyards that branch off into the Ardèche hills, it is a sudden, hidden world away from the high-wind, high-velocity tempo of the main Rhône corridor. The remaining six hectares of Syrah lie just north of Châteaubourg at Glun, where the granite reasserts itself strongly. This is also quite high, up to 230 metres.

Laurent Courbis is the vinifier, while Dominique runs the vineyard and administration. "We find that more spiced wine with greater acidity comes off the limestone, as well as a more assertive, tannic side than the Syrah off the granite," states Laurent. "The aromas from the limestone are also more *garrigue*, or herbal Mediterranean, and the colour tends to be more purple from the granite, more dark cherry from the limestone."

The red grapes are hand harvested, and destalked before 15 days of maceration for the classic wine and 22 days or so for Les Royes. The process includes the trio of cap punching, pumping-over, and partial emptying and refilling of the vats (*délestages*). The classic is aged for a year in three-to-four-year-old casks; Les Royes

areas, are found almost nowhere else in the *appellation*, and invest the wine with increased zest.

Maurice Courbis' family have been viticultural at Châteaubourg since 1587, so he says, for

FIGURE 25 Both skilled raconteurs, Maurice and son Laurent Courbis make a very good white St-Joseph that comes from one of the few limestone vineyards in the northern Rhône. (Author's collection)

is also aged for a year in casks that are one-third each new, one year, and two years old. Both reds are fined and lightly filtered.

The classic is usually well fruited, and suitable for drinking inside seven or eight years. The Royes is a much bigger wine, with stewed berry flavours, and plenty of rich content. It is best left for three or four years, and can drink well over 10 years or more. Its quality is very consistent.

The four hectares of white vines on the *lieux-dits Les Brets* and *Les Royes* are 95 per cent Marsanne, 5 per cent Roussanne, the oldest 1942–44, the average around 35 years. They are both clay-chalk sites with a noted limestone content, and stand within sight of the family cellars.

The white grapes, notably for the special Les Royes, are left on the vine as long as possible to secure maximum maturity. They are pressed and left to decant for 48 hours at 15°C. The classic white is then 30 per cent fermented in steel at 17° to 18°C, 70 per cent in a mix of new, one-year, and two-year-old oak. The cask fermentation was started in 1994. This classic wine is raised in a mix of vat and cask for a year before bottling, its malo done.

The special Les Royes white—pure Marsanne dating from 1975—is now a confident performer with a genuine pedigree. First made in 2001, it is all new Allier oak fermented and raised. It is lees stirred once a week until its malo is done in May/June, and is bottled 18 months after the harvest. After the site selection, only the best casks are used for this, with something over 3,000 bottles produced. The *Royes* is a leading St-Joseph *blanc*; there are tasty dried fruits mixed in with the oak, and the *ensemble* can perform very well after four years or so—rather than being drunk early.

Laurent professes to wanting a bit more acidity in his whites, just to help overcome any too obvious plumpness brought on by their terrain. He doesn't normally expect the whites to keep, but they do: a 1991 drunk in 1999 held a level yellow colour and showed every chance of living for 15 years. The bouquet mixed greengage, honey, and light Riesling-style petrol. There was ripe fruit on the palate, with a lurking almond touch that was likely to develop.

When the central part of the current cellar was built in 1980–81, half the Courbis production was white, a very high proportion for the Rhône. It is notable that these whites have grown in quality in recent years, due to older vines, better winemaking aided by a new steel vattery in 2002, and the change away from vat to cask fermentation and ageing.

ST-JOSEPH ROUGE
- 2003 ★★
- 2002 ★★★
- 2001 ★
- 2000 ★★

ST-JOSEPH LES ROYES ROUGE
- 2003 ★★★ Black fruit, leather, licorice on bouquet. Well-modelled palate, suave black fruit, some sucrosity, a fruit pastille effect, followed by oak. Definite southern, herbal connotations. Modern wine, can become more local by 2009. From 2008; 2015–17.
- 2002 ★★★
- 2001 ★★★
- 2000 ★★★
- 1999 ★★★
- 1998 ★★
- 1997 ★

ST-JOSEPH BLANC
- 2003 ★★
- 2002 ★★★
- 2001 ★★

ST-JOSEPH LES ROYES BLANC
- 2003 (CASK) ★★★★ Full, replete bouquet, white fruits. Custard/caramel flavour on attack, white fruit with a spice/mineral edge. Stylish length, very good grace in the wine. Has developed well. 2014–16.
- 2002 ★★★(★)
- 2001 ★★★

Export 35 per cent (1) Great Britain, (2) USA, (3) Canada

GÉRARD COURBIS

07300 Mauves +33(0)475 083184

Gérard Courbis is the second generation of his family in wine at Mauves, and also grows apricots and cherries. He works four hectares of St-Joseph; his largest site is on *Dardouille* in Tournon, where his Les Oliviers holding is also rented—from a canny Mauves family.

His Mauves vineyards are on *Le Paradis, Les Côtes Derrière*, and above it, *Guillamy*. There can be a 10-day difference in the ripening between the latter two, since *Guillamy* is higher and windier than *Côtes Derrière*, its firm granite making it free draining.

Gérard is a crinkly-faced man with curly grey hair, a countryman of the old school who makes just the one red wine. He is naturally content that his son Ludovic is starting out on the wine road—they share a joint venture of a hectare on *Dardouille* and on *Le Paradis*.

The Syrah is all destemmed and fermented plot by plot in concrete for 15 to 17 days, with no external yeasts. Cap punching is done by foot, and there are some pumping-overs. Cask ageing in seven-to-eight-year-old oak lasts about one year.

The wine comes with red fruits and a sinewy texture near the finish as the tannins kick in. It is ideal to drink around three or four years old, and a more tannic year like 1998 started its evolution to a funky side later—around 2004. This is honest St-Joseph, with no pretension—agreeable local wine.

A little under 5,000 bottles are produced each year, with the rest sold to the local *négoce* trade.

ST-JOSEPH ROUGE
- 2003 (CASKS) ★★
- 2000 ★
- 1999 ★★
- 1998 ★★

DOMAINE COURSODON

Place du Marché 07300 Mauves
+33(0)475 081829

The Coursodon family at Mauves is one of the original sources of very good red and white St-Joseph. New blood came along in 1999 in the form of Jérome, born in 1974, grandson of Gustave, a prime motivator and man-about-town for St-Joseph since the 1960s, who very sadly died in July 2005.

One has only to compare the family domaine today with its appearance in the 1970s to realise that this has been a Rhône success story. Gustave was very active over the years in showing his wines at regional Wine Fairs and in spreading the St-Joseph name, always working out of a restricted little cellar bang under his house. He also grew apricots, and there are still 10 hectares in production.

In the 1950s, before the *appellation* was set up, he would sell by the bottle to Paris and in cask to local cafés: the wine was called simply "Côtes du Rhône *rouge*" then. With a beret frequently perched on the top of his head, and a lot of sidelong glances accompanying his comments, he always looked like the cheeky Frenchman. By his early 80s, he claimed to have evolved his headwear—opting for a cap, turned severely to the right.

The Coursodons live on the main square in Mauves, and these days there is a spacious office and tasting room, and a large walk-about cellar. Jérome spent plenty of time in vineyards abroad before returning to St-Joseph, speaks English, and is tuned into the wide world of wine. I would hope and expect the domaine to continue to flourish if everyone keeps a correct sense of proportion in the future.

By vineyard, this is a heartlands domaine, in precisely the core places set out in the original 1956 decree. They have vineyards dotted about on the slopes and the plateau above the village of Mauves—55 per cent of the total—and also at Tournon (25 per cent), St-Jean-de-Muzols (15 per cent), and Glun (5 per cent).

From Gustave's three hectares in the 1970s, the domaine has grown to 15.6 hectares, all of them St-Joseph, spread over about 15 plots. There are 13.2 hectares of Syrah and 2.3 hectares of Marsanne, with a splash of 0.1 hectare of Roussanne planted in 1998. At Mauves, the prime *lieux-dits* are *Le Paradis* (some 1930s Syrah), a largely granite site, and *Montagnon*

The Coursodons' Mauves vineyard caused certain problems for Gustave's grandfather in his day, as Gustave explained. "Since my father Antonin was both Mayor of the village and owner of a fair-sized vineyard, the Germans had no hesitation in occupying our house early in November 1942. As we depended on our vines for our existence, like everyone else, we had to carry on as usual in order to earn our living.

The Germans certainly accounted for a lot of our wine, but overall I would say that the Occupation didn't directly hamper our daily working of the vines, except for the time when an aeroplane fell on them. Our house was burnt down in August 1944, when the Germans retreated, and there was quite a lot of machine gunning in those final days."

(1950 Syrah), which is loess-granite but in their plot more marked by clay. Their prime Tournon sites are *St-Joseph* (some 1920s Syrah and 1950 Marsanne) and *Dardouille*, the latter good for the Marsanne (1989, 1993) thanks to a heavier clay-*marne* content with the granite.

At St-Jean-de-Muzols, their holding is on *L'Olivet* (1920s) above the Delas offices. This was a vineyard that Gustave first worked in the 1960s, when the threat of housing lay heavily on the land there. The Glun soil is more small stone–gravelly than the other areas, with sand elements, and the half hectare of Syrah there dates from 1960.

Each generation here has played a key role in moving the domaine along. After Gustave's early brio, it was Pierre's turn to get down to the hard physical work of reclaiming parts of the vineyard abandoned since his own grandfather's time. He started in 1972, aged 22, a tall, good-looking dark-haired man, quieter than his father. One of his challenges was to rebuild terraces that had crumbled for over 20 years. This in turn necessitated constructing a road to gain access to the *parcelles*, quite apart from the arduous task of clearing and replanting. Some of the plots were very high up at the top of the slopes and plateau area above Mauves.

The next generational leap here came with the broadened view brought in through Jérome's attendance at the Wine School of Montpellier and his sojourns on estates in South Africa, where he worked with Lamotte and their Syrah, and in Alsace. Pierre had been entirely self-taught, taking over from his father in the immediate hands-on way expected in earlier days.

No doubt Gustave was immensely pleased when his great-grandson Antonin was born in 2003, and already Jérome has plenty of plans. A young man with a slightly narrow face, fair hair, and fair skin, he explains where he is looking: "I'd like to plant on the southern hillsides of Mauves, where there's a nice amphitheatre," he says. "I don't want lots of wine, but a good 50,000 to 60,000 bottles that are nice to drink."

Reflecting his generation's awareness, he believes that 70 to 80 per cent of the work is done in the vineyard. He chose *massale*-selected vines taken from healthy old Syrah for his planting between 2001 and 2003 (but in so doing, found out for himself that this old Serine suffers from *coulure*, or fruit failure). He is also active on canopy management and vegetation work for reasons of wind, air, and light exposure.

There are four reds, except that in 2002 just one wine was made due to the poor harvest. The classic (30,000 bottles) is assembled from all four different *communes* with their different soils. It is largely composed of young-vine fruit, all of it destalked. A cold pre-fermentation at 12°C over four days starts the process of extracting aroma. This is followed by a two-to-three-week maceration at a maximum of 28°C, which once the sugars have finished, is raised to 33°C for a final two or three days to get hold of the tannins.

Ageing takes place in a mix of sizes—228- and 600-litre casks, and large barrels. The classic is aged in mostly 15-to-20-year-old wood for around a year, with just 3 per cent new each year. This is what I would term an amiable wine, but its core has been reduced by the proliferation of different cuvées. Its fruit is simple and

down-the-line, and the nicest recent offering was the 2002, when all the other sources helped it out due to the tricky vintage.

Of course, time and economic necessities march life along, but it's worth recording the destiny of the Coursodon 1983 red, when there was of course just one wine made. Drunk in 2003, the notes read as follows:

1983 ★★★★ Red *robe* still, some turn on it. Pretty red fruit attack, tasty, jam style. Can broaden, still has ways to go—tannins have absorbed well by now, leave chewy finale. Good till 2009.

The second red, L'Olivaie (9,000 bottles), is taken from Syrah dating from the 1940s on *L'Olivet*. This is destalked and then vinified like the regular; its ageing in a mix of barrel and 228-litre and 600-litre casks, 15 per cent of them new, lasts 12 to 15 months. It can be big, quite chewy wine and in a vintage like 2001 closes up after an initial fruit burst, and is then best left until four or five years old.

The red Paradis St-Pierre (3,000 bottles) comes from three sources: the oldest vines from the 1920s and 1930s on *St-Joseph*, *L'Olivet*, and *Paradis*. Its crop is only half destalked, the wine also aged for 12 to 15 months in 600-litre *demi-muids*, 15 per cent of them new. This is my preferred wine, since it combines well-packed fruit with sound tannins and respects the vintage quite closely: hence the 2000 was more juiced and charming than the more demanding 2001. Both can develop over 12 years or more.

In 1997 a top wine, La Sensonne (4,000+ bottles), was introduced. The fruit is taken from a site that the family calls *Sensonne*, which is at the southern end of *Paradis*. This is an 80 per cent–new oak wine, selected from all their old-vine sources at the end of the fermentations. It is raised on its lees for 12 to 15 months with lots of intervention—stirring once a week in the cask. "The lees bring out the fat in the wine—that's what interests me," is how Pierre describes his approach to this wine. It has been produced in conjunction with Patrick Lesec, the ex-restaurateur, whose Selection Wines are all overtly oaked.

Jérome is aware of a tight rope he walks in his use of new oak: "I want to find casks that bring clear and fresh flavours, not the outright taste of wood," he volunteers, "but that's not easy." Certainly there are grounds for saying that unless the vintage has been enormously ripe and full, any St-Joseph of either red or white colour tends to bow down before the wood and be rather unpleasant to drink in its early years. Oak here needs a lightness of touch.

The Coursodons either fine or filter most years, although the 1999s were bottled without either. Jérome prefers not to fine, and *La Sensonne* is always left alone before bottling.

On the whites, Jérome feels progress has been made since they started to use a pneumatic press on a riper grape crop in 1999: "Before that we would crush the white crop before it went into the press," he says; "the effect has been to get away from the herbaceous and slightly bitter side that the Marsanne can show." Under Gustave white wine had never been much of a priority, with just a few casks for drinking at the domaine, and Jérome is taking this challenge seriously.

There are two whites, a classic and a Paradis St-Pierre. The former is vinified in stainless steel at 18°C after a 24-hour decanting, and bottled by May, its malo completed. The Paradis St-Pierre *blanc* (3,000 bottles), first made in 1987, is cask fermented, the oak new to five years old. It receives weekly lees stirring until May and is bottled by September, its malo also done. It comes off three sites—the *Paradis* and *St-Joseph* granite, with a little *Montagnon* (1950s).

With the Paradis *blanc*, Jérome's idea is to work the lees to achieve richness while profiting from the granite soil for the wine's freshness on the finish. Its content is nice and full, helped by the mature Marsanne; the length is usually good, and as a serious wine, it can run well for up to 12 years or even longer, as witnessed by a 1989 drunk in 2004. Its tasting note was "praline, almond bouquet, light cheese aroma; light almond palate, reflects a sunny year, touch apricot, toast end. Evolves nicely, shortens after 90 minutes."

In the 1990s the Coursodons made a few *vins de paille* for family and friends. These "straw wines" were made from late-harvested Marsanne in 1990, 1991, 1997, and 1999, just as is done at Hermitage, where the wine is legislated for in the *appellation* rules. Containing 140 gm/litre of residual sugar, the 1997 ★★★ was a wine of total pleasure: a golden *robe* preceded a bouquet that mixed caramel, butterscotch, and light honey. The palate was a drink of aromatic brown sugar, with lovely length and a soft finale.

Meanwhile, in 1996 they actually made a Syrah version, harvested on 31 October and pressed on 26 December: "We needed about 300 kg of grapes for about 32 litres," recalls Pierre. This was an experiment, and will probably stay that way! The bouquet of straw and quince was followed by an uneven strong red grape flavour, noticeably like a fortified wine. A touch of Syrah flourished at the end, the length was fair, but overall—well . . .

ST-JOSEPH ROUGE

2003 ★★
2002 ★★
2001 ★
1999 ★★
1998 ★

ST-JOSEPH L'OLIVAIE ROUGE

2004 (CASK) ★★★ Mocha, roasted aromas mingle with red berries—bouquet is deepseated. Likeable fruit at start, is elegant in midpalate, length good. 2007 on; 2014–16.

2003 ★★★(★) Black fruit, pepper/floral mixed bouquet. Good fruit, with real core, has a mineral side. Very long, stylish too. 2019–23.

2001 ★★★ From 2005–06; 2012–14
1999 ★★★

ST-JOSEPH PARADIS ST-PIERRE ROUGE

2004 (CASK) ★★★ Raspberry coulis aroma, good and harmonious. Fruit declares well on palate, possesses a good core. Supple, red jam flavour, is more open than usual. Sound length, but hasn't the usual brio. Refined overall. 2015–16.

2003 ★★★(★) Oily, simmered black fruit bouquet, very round, lots of supple warmth. Big palate, but well handled—a mass of black jam flavour, good tannins and grip, too. Decent length, tightens on finish. From 2007; 2017–19.

2001 ★★★
2000 ★★★
1998 ★★

ST-JOSEPH LA SENSONNE ROUGE

2004 (CASK) Grilled black fruits aroma, licorice present. Good, oily content, is pretty rich. Oak overlay and finale, can probably handle it. Esp from 2009; 2016–18. Too early to score.

2003 ★★★ Baked aspect on bouquet, olives, raisins, southern style. Quite oily, savoury attack —black fruit with violets, a warm disposition. Fair length, some restraint here, has a grapey finish. From 2006; 2013–15.

2001 ★★
2000 ★★
1999 ★★★

ST-JOSEPH BLANC

2004 ★★
2003 ★★
2002 ★
2001 ★★★

ST-JOSEPH PARADIS ST-PIERRE BLANC

2004 ★★★
2003 ★★★
2002 ★
2001 ★★★

Export 35 per cent (1) USA, (2) Canada, (3) Switzerland

DOMAINE YVES CUILLERON

Verlieu RN86 42410 Chavanay +33(0)474 870237

See also Condrieu, Côte-Rôtie.
Yves Cuilleron has become an important name at St-Joseph and Condrieu. His partnership with Pierre Gaillard and François Villard has gained widespread media coverage, along with the story of how they opened up a very old vineyard location lost in the mists of time at Seyssuel, north of Côte-Rôtie. Their funky New World–style wines also bring eager press coverage.

Yves Cuilleron works just over 11 hectares of Syrah and nearly four hectares of white St-Joseph, 2.4 hectares of it Marsanne, the rest Roussanne planted since the early 1990s. Some of the Syrah dates from his grandfather Claude's time, at *Les Vessettes* near Chavanay—around 0.4 hectare planted in 1936 and 1947. The soil is generally the reddy, stronger stone granite of this area around Chavanay, with a few zones that are more decomposed. His highest vines are just over 300 metres, which helps acidity levels, especially in dry years like 2003.

Yves tries to work the vineyards as naturally as possible, but there are limits. "I have to continue with weedkillers," he states. "I now have 17 workers—manual work to dig the weeds would mean another five or six people, and would bump up the cost by about 35 per cent." He has tried growing grass between the rows to counter erosion, but found his vines suffered too much from the competition.

"My uncle never used insecticides, and neither do I," he continues. "And I don't like putting down much compost, because it makes the plants grow too much. As for using only natural yeasts, I don't use any external ones for the reds, but for the whites it's more delicate. It can be difficult to finish their sugars—I don't want 7 to 8 gm of residual sugar. In that case we'd be obliged to sterile filter to stop them breaking out, and then you mask the *terroir* that way. We may use yeasts at the end of the vinification."

There are three reds; they are vinified in steel vats, with cap punching and pumping-over for up to four weeks. He destalks only if necessary—in lesser years, notably. All the reds are raised for 18 to 20 months, but in differently aged casks. Blending of the different plots is done just before bottling.

The classic, Les Pierres Seches, is aged in two-to-five-year-old wood and filtered. This is an early-drinking, fruit-forward wine that is sometimes a little taut.

L'Amarybelle, from *Eyguets* and *Le Pêcher*, is raised in one-to-two-year-old oak. Like the Serines, it is not filtered. It is often marked by black currant fruit, with smoky, tar, and oak sidelines; it can show well for around 10 years.

The old vines' wine is Les Serines, which combines fruit from grandfather's vineyards with that from the late 1960s nearby at *La Ruty*. This receives only new oak. The Serines is suitable for Yves' oak policy, since it contains sufficient core matter to absorb the external tannins and displays attractive fruit persistence. The Serines steps up a gear on the Amarybelle—its black currant fruit is oilier and more profound, and it has more secure tannins that permit a healthy development. It has power, tar, and heat within it.

I find that Yves' most flamboyant winemaking usually comes with his white wines, contrary to what one normally finds. There are three whites; house policy is to harvest these often in early October, to obtain high degree, so there is no prior maceration. "In 1992 there was a lot of rot, and when I pressed the more rotted grapes, out they came with a higher degree than the healthy ones," he explains, and he has continued with this delayed picking ever since. "I do a lot of leaf dropping to ventilate the bunches after rain, which is vital if I pick late," he adds.

The whites are cask fermented, 25 per cent of the oak new, the rest up to three years old. "We do a very careful decantation because after that the lees are left alone," says Yves. "I'm looking for a gradual fermentation rather than eyeing the temperature, so we run over three to four weeks, and sometimes into March, before the sugars are finished." Bottling is in June.

The classic white, Lyseras, is half Marsanne, half Roussanne, made from the youngest vines. This is the concocted member of the party—flashy cellar treatment, oak, and instant fullness from the ripe fruit, a wine not easy to drink on its own.

Le Lombard is pure Marsanne, the oldest planted in 1967. It is taken from the *Bois Lombard* site, officially called *Verlieux*. This is refined, with some floral tones on the bouquet, and a gradual broadening possible after a stylish, soft white fruits youth.

Saint-Pierre is a Roussanne wine from vines planted in the early 1990s on the *Digne* site at St-Pierre-de-Boeuf. It is vinified to show a lot of up-front flavour, and will become more structured once the vines grow older. In a vintage like 2002, it has enough acidity to live and to gradually settle itself.

ST-JOSEPH LES PIERRES SECHES ROUGE
2001 (CASK) (★)
2000 ★★

ST-JOSEPH L'AMARYBELLE ROUGE
2002 ★★
2001 (CASK) ★★
2000 ★★★

ST-JOSEPH LES SERINES ROUGE
2003 (CASK) ★★★(★) Inky, full bouquet, tightly packed. Clear, clean, nicely worked fruit, touch of end sweetness. Oak hints, the sweetness is beguiling. Has plenty of *gras* and good length. Will close up. From 2007; 2016–18.
2002 ★★★
2001 (CASK) ★★★
2000 ★★★

ST-JOSEPH LYSERAS BLANC
2002 (CASK) ★★
2001 ★
2000 ★★

ST-JOSEPH LE LOMBARD BLANC
2003 ★★
2002 (CASK) ★★★
2001 ★★

ST-JOSEPH SAINT-PIERRE BLANC
2003 ★★
2002 (CASK) ★★
2001 ★★

RENÉ-JEAN DARD ET FRANÇOIS RIBO

Blanche-Laine 26600 Mercurol +33(0)475 074000

See also Crozes-Hermitage, Hermitage.
These two *originals*, who seem well-suited to the ambience of an Arts Festival, work nearly two hectares of St-Joseph—1.4 ha of Syrah and 0.6 ha of Roussanne.

Part of the vineyard is in the *Valleé des Champs*, next to the hill of St-Joseph itself, just south of Tournon. The slope has only a little sandy granite and is mainly alluvial stones and red clay. Both Syrah and Roussanne are grown here. "It's like the Gonon family's *Coteau des Oliviers* to look at," comments François Ribo, "and is also good for whites because there's no worry about drought there."

They also crop a small amount of Syrah at Vion, where the lower slope location means the soil is full of sanded granite. Their third vineyard, of both Syrah and Roussanne, is on the nearby sandy granite soil of St-Jean-de-Muzols. This very rotted granite is called *gore*. The house policy is to seek as ripe a crop as possible, and this location is often harvested in early October. The colleagues harvest gradually, with friends and small teams of up to 10 people, over the course of two to three weeks. "If the weather is good, we're in no hurry," says François.

The Syrah vines range between 45 and 60 years old; their crop is whole-bunch fermented in open wood vats. Cask ageing lasts 10 to 12 months. This can show dry, peppery flavours, with a touch of black currant. It is reserved in style, not at all a populist "extract wine." Such words bring a shudder to these two genuine growers, for none of their house wines is remotely forced. With its more floating texture than the plush, jam flavours often found at Mauves, for instance, the Dard et Ribo St-Joseph can provide agreeable, reflective drinking for five or six years.

When conditions suit, as in 2000, 2001, and 2003, the St-Jean vineyard provides the white Cuvée Pitrou, a wine that depends on good weather in September and October. The waiting game comes at a price—a yield of only 20 hl/ha against their average elsewhere of 35 hl/ha. Pitrou is fermented and raised in used wood for 11 to 12 months. It is fat, nicely oily wine with dried fruits and exotic flavours. When the weather does not play ball, just the one white wine is made from here and from *Les Champs*.

The straight white, one of the rare Roussanne-only St-Josephs, is two-thirds fermented and raised in wood, one-third in stainless steel. After 10 to 12 months of ageing, it is bottled about 15 months after harvesting. This is very pretty, with a mix of honey and white fruits enhanced by some spice. Both whites repay decanting before drinking.

ST-JOSEPH ROUGE
2003 (CASK) ★★★
2002 ★
2001 ★★

ST-JOSEPH BLANC
2003 (CASK) ★★★
2002 (CASK) ★★★
2001 ★★
2000 ★★

ST-JOSEPH CUVÉE PITROU BLANC
2003 (CASK) ★★★
2000 ★★★

DOMAINE DE BOISSEYT-CHOL

RN86 42410 Chavanay +33(0)474 872345

See also Côte-Rôtie, Condrieu.
This family secured its vineyards at Chavanay in 1797, after the French Revolution, as is stated on their literature and labels. The domaine is run by Didier Chol, a musician with the shape of a band leader, a convivial fellow whose retired rugby player's frame fits him well. He lives his life within his local community, a fair way removed from treading the boards in search of global publicity.

As the baritone player and President of the Music Society of Chavanay, Didier's music trips are to places like Menton on the Riviera, with his teenage daughter and son playing clarinet and trumpet—the fifth generation of his family to play in the band. "The fact that there are people of 14 and 80 years old in the band allows a certain apprenticeship of life that is beneficial," he says, wisely.

A lot of Didier's wines are sold nearby; these trips are to Fairs at low-key places like Montbrison to promote sales, and there is a large private customer and restaurant following. The wines used to reflect this, with often robust flavours and a downhome character. Recently they have gained in elegance—perhaps a new press is a factor.

Until 1950 this had been run as a typical *polyculture* domaine, but in that year Didier's father, Jean, moved it over to purely wine, and the family have moved on from there. Didier's St-Joseph vineyards cover 5 ha, 85 per cent Syrah, all at Chavanay. They average 20 years on slopes at *Les Eyguets* and *Les Vessettes*, with 15-year-old vines on *Les Rivoires*. These are all core names. *Rivoires* lies below *Eyguets*, so it has soil a little deeper than the *arzelle* (granite granules) of *Eyguets*.

The whites grow on two sites, *Izéras* and *Le Calvaire*, both granite, with the Roussanne on the latter: "It's more easterly facing than *Izéras*," explains Didier, "which means it's fresher and gives wines with better grip." Among the whites comes a most unusual local speciality, a sparkling *méthode champenoise* made from Clairette. Didier's father learnt how to make this in Champagne, and the house have made it since 1947. Clairette was a widely planted grape around Chavanay in those days, some of it made into semisweet wine.

Didier is not an instinctive destalker, but grudgingly now destalks about half the crop for extra softness. Vinification lasts three weeks in steel, with *remontages* and *turbo-pigeages*. The domaine is notable for the duration of the cask ageing—two and up to three years in casks. Some of the classic wine stays for the three years and is sold a lot to the Rhône-Alps restaurant trade, which forms a large slice of the business. There is no fining or filtration.

There are three reds—a classic, made from several sites, notably *Izéras* and *Vessettes*; Les Garipolées, mainly from *Eyguets*, with a little from *Calvaire* and *Vessettes*; and the roughly 5,000 bottles of Les Rivoires, first made in 1998 from that *lieu-dit*. This sees 30 per cent new oak for its two years in cask. The lighter cuvées of St-Joseph, aged for two years, are made into the pure Syrah Côtes du Rhône.

The classic shows jam fruits in the sunny years, and a little more spice in the more tannic years; it is sound and honest local wine. The Garipolées is more upright in texture, with some leathery, tarry aspects. It needs time to soften and is a wine for autumn/winter drinking. The Rivoires carries full aromas, black fruits, and some southern herbal hints, and its good depth on the palate allows it to move along for 10 years or more.

The white is made from 60 per cent Roussanne (1988) and 40 per cent Marsanne (1968). The proportion varies according to ripening, so the 2002 was 60 per cent Roussanne, the 2001 40 per cent, for instance. It is two-thirds fermented in steel at around 14°C, with the rest in cask at around 18°C. Didier does not like the malo to be done—"it takes out the freshness and leaves the wines flat," he comments. All the wine is then raised for nine months in oak. It is fresh, dry wine, and not as interesting as the principal reds.

ST-JOSEPH ROUGE

 2002 (CASKS) ★
 2001 (CASK) ★
 2000 ★

ST-JOSEPH LES GARIPOLÉES ROUGE

 2002 ★★
 2001 ★★

ST-JOSEPH LES RIVOIRES ROUGE

 2003 ★★(★)
 2002 (CASK) ★★
 2001 (CASK) ★★★
 2000 ★★

ST-JOSEPH BLANC

2002 (★)

2001 ★

Export 8 per cent (1) Switzerland, (2) USA, (3) Japan

MAISON DELAS

ZA de l'Olivet 07300 St-Jean-de-Muzols
+33(0)475 086030

See also Condrieu, Cornas, Côte-Rôtie, Crozes-Hermitage, Hermitage, St-Péray.

The bedrock to Delas' St-Joseph is their rental of two hectares close by their cellars and offices, bang in the central St-Jean-de-Muzols territory. Since 1988 they have worked 0.65 hectare of Syrah that they planted then on the granite of the south-facing slope above their cellars, *L'Olivet*.

Just 200 metres away, they work a fine 1.4 ha on the *Côte Ste-Épine*, 1.1 ha of it Syrah, 0.3 ha Marsanne, the vineyard dating from the 1930s. The farm and the area around it here were bought in the 1970s by Noël Passat, then the Mayor of St-Jean-de-Muzols. He allowed the conservation of the slopes as vineyards, with the lower areas given over for small businesses. Delas now rent the vineyard from him.

There are three reds; the classic cuvée, Les Challeys, runs up to about 80,000 bottles. Jacques Grange explains what he is looking for from this wine: "I want a wine that is representative of the whole, long St-Joseph zone. So I buy crop from Limony, Chavanay, and Malleval on the schist and decomposed granite of the north as well as from the more southerly villages of Vion and Lemps, where the soil is sandy grained granite."

All the Syrah is destalked. There are two *pigeages* (cap punchings) a day and some pumping-overs, and the vinification lasts for over two weeks. The Challeys is aged for eight to 10 months, 60 per cent in vat, 40 per cent in two-to-three-year-old casks.

In 2002 there was just one red, a Challeys, a wise move given the indifferent nature of the crop. It meant that one very solid wine, good for

the vintage, emerged. The Challeys appears to be on the rise; there is greater depth in its black fruits than previously, and it carries a pretty authentic local stamp, with its pebbly tannins present. There is enough matter in the wine for it to develop into a successful middle age around five years old.

The next red up is the François de Tournon, a 20,000-to-25,000-bottle wine made from crop bought in the southern area of the *appellation*—the tight six-mile stretch between Mauves and Vion. Aged in casks of one to three years, it is bottled around 18 months after the harvest. First made in 1988, this has a very different texture to the St-Josephs of the northern area: there is more softness and a squeeze of warmth, a little more delicacy. It is wine that in vintages like 2000 can live for eight years. In vintages when the core Challeys wine needs a helping hand, like 2001 and 2002, François de Tournon is not produced.

The top wine is Ste-Épine, a specific-plot cuvée whose 3,500 bottles are the result of the elimination by tasting of all possible casks that could go into it. "*Ste-Épine* is in fact on the same geological route as *Les Bessards* on the granite extreme of the Hermitage hill," comments chief winemaker Jacques Grange, "and was cut off from it by the Rhône. Though it is south facing, like *Bessards*, it's a bit cooler and windier. I also notice that its grapes don't look the same as those from Hermitage—the berries are smaller, which I can only put down to the slightly cooler climate on this west bank of the Rhône." He adds that when making the Ste-Épine, he is looking for an affiliation with *Bessards*, so is happy that it has some obvious tannins when young.

Ste-Épine does its malo in cask, and altogether stays 16 to 18 months in oak—10 per cent new, the rest one to two years old. It is also brought out only in the best all-round vintages, appearing in 1998, 1999, 2001, and 2003. In between it helps out Les Challeys. It is not fined or filtered. This carries brooding, intense black fruits, with oily, smoky edges and plenty of healthy tannin. As a stylish, complete wine, it rewards patience and carefully thought-out dishes. It can live for a good 12 to 15 years.

The white Les Challeys (15,000 to 18,000 bottles) is made from crop bought from the mainly northern area *communes* of St-Pierre-de-Boeuf, Serrières, and Charnas. It is 80 per cent Marsanne, 20 per cent Roussanne. It is vinified at around 16°C and raised in steel, then bottled with the malo finished in May after the harvest. This has made welcome progress since some dodgy offerings in the late 1990s.

The special white Ste-Épine is made in tiny amounts—600 to 1,200 bottles. It is pure Marsanne, from the 1930s Passat vineyard. There are just two to four casks of this, with one-year-old oak used for fermentation and raising; its lees are stirred and it is bottled at the end of June. Peach fruits and subtlety combine here—a savoury but refined wine possessing good sinew.

ST-JOSEPH LES CHALLEYS ROUGE

2003 ★★
2002 ★★★
2001 ★
2000 ★
1999 ★★

ST-JOSEPH FRANÇOIS DE TOURNON ROUGE

2003 (CASK) ★★★ Mulberry/violet mix on bouquet, agreeably rounded. Good fruit quality here, like fruit pastilles, a pretty sweet presence throughout. Correct end tannins bring some control, definition. From 2007; 2017–19.

2001–02 Not made
2000 ★★★
1999 ★★★
1998 ★★★
1997 ★

ST-JOSEPH STE-ÉPINE ROUGE

2003 (CASK) ★★★★ Dark *robe*; olive/toffee, southern-style bouquet. Well-knit elements on palate—some herbal, nuanced black fruit. Tannins ripe and integrated. Length good, has structure and balance. From 2007–08; 2019–21.

2002 Not made
2001 ★★★★
1999 ★★★
1998 ★★★★
1997 ★

ST-JOSEPH LES CHALLEYS BLANC

2003 ★★
2002 ★★
2001 ★★★

ST-JOSEPH STE-ÉPINE BLANC

2003 ★★★ Melted butter, agreeable, stylish bouquet. Harmonious, nicely ripe Marsanne with good fat and vinosity. Typical Marsanne nuttiness runs through it. Evolved white fruit aftertaste. 2008–10.

2002 Not made
2001 ★★★★

OLIVIER DUMAINE

Chautin 26600 Larnage +33(0)4745 072150

See also Crozes-Hermitage.

Olivier Dumaine made his first St-Joseph in 1990; he works half a hectare of Syrah split between Vion, the first hamlet north of St-Jean-de-Muzols; Tournon; and St-Jean itself. The Vion vineyard is at 250 metres and averages 50 years, with some vines much older. The crop is destalked, and the young wine raised in two-year-old oak for nine months, then bottled with a light filtration. Around 2,000 bottles are made.

DOMAINE DUMAZET

RN 86 07340 Limony +33(0)475 340301

See also Condrieu, Cornas, Côte-Rôtie.

One of the long-standing quality names at Condrieu, Pierre Dumazet also produces a red St-Joseph from 1.2 hectares at *La Roue*, one of the main slopes at St-Jean-de-Muzols. This Syrah is nearly 40 years old.

There is no destalking, and after three weeks' vatting, the wine is aged in seven-to-eight-year-old casks for about a year. It is neither fined nor filtered.

The wine is called "La Muzolaise": it has a genuine feel, a link with its *terroir*. "Its relative austerity is its normal style," comments M. Dumazet. It is a wine that ages nicely and can gain finesse in so doing. There are peppered aspects to it, and its flavour also has the fruit gum side that can be found at St-Jean-de-Muzols from domaines like Fogier and Gouye. It is usually worth waiting for three years or so for the wine to come together.

ST-JOSEPH LA MUZOLAISE ROUGE

2001 ★★★

1999 ★★

DOMAINE DURAND

2 impasse de la Fontaine 07130 Châteaubourg
+33(0)475 404678

See also Cornas.

This domaine combines fruit and wine, and the villages of Cornas and nearby Châteaubourg. It was set up when father Noël Durand did the decent thing and married his local girlfriend—he from Châteaubourg, she from Cornas.

Like many an Ardèche family, the parents lived simply and ruggedly. Up on the plateau they kept cows and grew fruit, including cherries, with the Rhône basin giving wine and apricots.

The couple had two sons, Joël and Eric. Joël started to work with his father in 1988, prompted by the spur of rising wine prices. A new cellar, including a vaulted ageing room, was completed by 1996, and the property's activity is now 80 per cent wine, 20 per cent apricots—10 hectares of the Bergeron variety that gives fine fruit.

The domaine is tucked in the lee of the Château de Châteaubourg, the village being a turnback to old, sleepy days of trust. There are open boxes of tools, fruit lies on tables outside, garage doors are wide open. Around are classic street names—Grand'Rue, Impasse de la Fontaine—with the half-hourly toll of the church bell bringing a sombre, reflective tone.

For St-Joseph the brothers have two very steep vineyards, four hectares at Châteaubourg, with older vines dating from 1978–80, and three hectares at Glun just to the north in a valley off the main Rhône corridor, where the vines date from 1990, 1998, and 2000.

At Châteaubourg the prime site is *Lautaret*, an east-southeast-facing slope just above the village, where the soil is largely granite with a minor limestone presence. The eastern side of *Lautaret* is notable for giving wine with a firm, tannic feel. Both vineyards combine a mix of terraces and slope. *Lautaret* is a very sunny spot, and from 2003 the brothers have made a plot-specific wine from here, its mineral side traceable back to the limestone. The axis at Glun is more south-southeast facing, on a site called *Gouyet* in a sheltered granite-based valley just off the main Rhône corridor.

As a specialist in fruit growing and in trees, Joël's inclination has been towards viticulture since the start. Nearly 40, he has great respect for what is brought in from the fields—a countryman's outlook. A solid-looking man with curly greying hair, his face is strong, his look steady; he took on the duties of the President of the St-Joseph Growers Union in 2000, and this is clearly an important role in such a straggling *appellation*. "I was the union's administrator for three years, and now I'm happy to be involved right at the heart of what will be good for St-Joseph in the future," he states.

He has been working on the lack of magnesium in their vineyard, and his focus has fixed on their leaf management more than in the past. "We don't want excess leaves obviously, because they absorb too much and the grapes' exposure is poor; but you have to avoid too much direct sun. We've been fertilising with cattle dung mixed in with elements like cocoa powder and grape *marc*, which we put down in January or February: then we can get good balance between leaves and grapes."

Seven years younger, a slim, determined man, his frame rather like a jazzman's more than the rugby fullback player he once was,

FIGURE 26 Organic measures in the vineyard, modern winemaking in the cellar—Eric and Joël Durand are a bright force at St-Joseph and Cornas. (Author's collection)

Eric shares his brother's frank, open look. He started in 1996, when his father retired. He has done wine studies at Mâcon, and from him come the modern urges. Since 1994 they have destemmed in the crush, all the more sensible thanks to the youth of many of the vines. The duration of the macèration that follows in their concrete vats is governed by the quality of the harvest—the top Syrah fruit received 28 days in 2001 and 21 days in the rain-affected 2002.

Since 1998 the brothers have been trying to move away from adding external yeasts. Less yeasting also brings less reduction, or closing-up of the wine, due to the lees being less active. While this marks a sound, natural outlook, there is also a lot of intervention during the winemaking, prompted, one thinks, by their *oenologue*. Daily cap punching, twice-daily pumping-overs, partial vat emptying and refilling, and aeration are all on the agenda.

Eric is a doer, not a romantic: "I started to like wine when I did my chemistry studies at school. What caught my imagination was how it is made and how it evolves," he says. He's a fast talker, a man in a hurry with some early greying

hair and nice-looking features. He hops around the cellar at great speed.

The red Les Coteaux is raised for a year—75 per cent in one-to-four-year-old 228-litre casks, the rest in steel—then may be fined and lightly filtered. It represents a vigorously fruited style of St-Joseph—grilled aromas, black fruits, traces of oak—and so has a bouncy youth that then settles into a more measured stride around five years old.

In 2003 they started a Tête de Cuvée wine made from the best site—the core of *Lautaret*, called "Cuvée Lautaret." Its fruit lingers well, and it will reward patient keeping so an early austerity can soften.

The domaine also makes a *vin de pays de l'Ardèche* from their young vines at St-Joseph and at Cornas. Fruity and forward, it is bottled in April, and is made whenever they have young, noble vines available.

ST-JOSEPH LES COTEAUX ROUGE

2003 ★★★
2002 ★★
2001 ★★★
2000 ★★
1999 ★★

ST-JOSEPH CUVÉE LAUTARET ROUGE

2003 (CASK) ★★★

Export 45 per cent (1) Germany, (2) Quebec, (3) Belgium

DOMAINE THIÉRRY FARJON

Morzelas 42520 Malleval +33(0)474 871684

See also Condrieu.

Thiérry Farjon has retraced his grandparents' footsteps in planting his own vineyards and making wine on the plateau near Malleval. He worked for four years in restaurants, but his wife, Miryam, had her own career, so there was never the chance of running their own diner together. His parents had not found it economical to live off the land and so worked in a weaving factory in the Lyon area. They had kept the family land, though, even if it was in an overgrown state.

At 22 he went off to wine school in the Beaujolais for two years, and returned to work for Pierre Gaillard for nearly four years. He admits that between 1989 and 1998 Miryam kept him: "I made my first wine in 1992, and life was very difficult. But I can now stand on my own economically." He used to visit 15 Wine Fairs a year to sell his wine, and still appears at places like Vacqueyras on the national holiday of July 14. His drive is evident: all the carpentry in his cellars, built between 1995 and 1998, is his.

A down-the-line, reserved man, he has planted all his vineyards himself. His St-Joseph Syrah covers four hectares; one hectare dates from the mid-1970s, the rest from the 1990s, all in the *communes* of Malleval and Chavanay. He also has 0.6-hectare split 65 per cent Roussanne, 35 per cent Marsanne (1994, 1998). The soil is poor—very fine sand with a granite underlay. His *vin de pays* is made from Roussanne and Chardonnay, supplemented by any underage crop from young St-Joseph vines. This can be successful, even in a difficult year like 2002.

The red crop has been destalked since 1998. After a week's cool maceration, it is fermented over two-plus weeks; cap punching is done. The three reds are aged for 14 to 17 months, but in differently aged casks—the *cuvée normale* in oak of two to 15 years; what he terms Ma Sélection, wine usually taken from two sites, *Les Patasses* and *Cuminaille*, receives 25 per cent new oak (down from 50 per cent until 2003), and the top Grande Réserve is all new oak. Thiérry remarks that the Grande Réserve can come from *Les Patasses*, which contains some schist and is also a Condrieu site. He selects the top two wines just before bottling, and fines and filters all three.

The white is fermented in two-to-eight-year-old casks at a low 14°C. Lees stirring lasts three months and it is bottled in May. External yeasts are used because of the low temperature. I would back this vineyard to give good results, with white wines of structure, from around 2012 when the vines are older. Already there is an interesting combination of white fruit and nuttiness.

The reds are less impressive, and one has to think that three wines is too many. In 2001 lack of ripeness appeared an issue, as it did with several of the northern St-Josephs. Modern cellar techniques and extraction processes hover in the background: the wines need to smile more.

ST-JOSEPH ROUGE

2003 ★★
2003 (★)
2001 ★

ST-JOSEPH MA SÉLECTION ROUGE

2003 ★★

ST-JOSEPH BLANC

2004 (★)
2002 ★★
2001 ★

Export 30 per cent (1) Germany, (2) Japan, (3) USA

BERNARD FAURIE

27 avenue Hélène de Tournon 07300 Tournon
+33(0)475 085509

See also Hermitage.

The hardworking Bernard Faurie makes excellent, classical St-Joseph from his cramped cellar on the edge of Tournon. He is best known for his Hermitage, but the red St-Joseph is extremely authentic and finely made.

The two reds are made from 1.7 ha, with another 0.4 ha to come from new planting. His vineyard is on rather inaccessible granite slopes near Mauves—the *lieu-dit* called *Dardouille*. The soil is decomposed granite, with some clay in the lower reaches. Part of the vineyard dates from the 1950s and 1960s, the rest from 1986. The Marsanne element, planted in 1986, grows on the severe rock areas of *Dardouille*, where the granite is thicker, the stones larger than on his Hermitage sites.

Two reds are made, a classic and a Vieilles Vignes that was first made in 1990. Whole bunch fermentation lasts 15 to 17 days in open wood vats, with cap punching and pumping-over; the press wine is added six months later and both receive 18 months' (the 2000) to 24 months' (the more robust 1999) ageing in a mix of 12 and 30 hl barrels. There is no fining, only a light filtration. There are around 4,000 bottles of each wine.

Both reds are delivered *en finesse*, with an elegance of fruit and a cool lightness of touch. The fruit is nicely sprinkled, with some dry touches on the classic, while the Vieilles Vignes is more considered, the fruits darker, the tannins more evident. It can live for eight to 12 years. These reds happily reflect their place more than their *vigneron*.

There are just 800 bottles of the pure Marsanne white. This is fermented and raised in oak ranging from two to five years old until April after the harvest. In the past, new oak has been used, but Bernard has moved away from such outright stylisation in the wine. He likes to block the malo before bottling. This is an ele-gant wine, in the house mould. Bernard finds that the granite invests the Marsanne with a gunflint, salty aspect.

ST-JOSEPH ROUGE

2003 ★★★ Open, scented black jam aroma, cool touch to it. Berried fruit, a violet imprint, length sound. Tucked up at end, needs time, e.g., from 2007. Stylish wine, not forced. 2014–16.

2002 (★)
2001 ★★
1999 ★★★
1998 ★★★

ST-JOSEPH VIEILLES VIGNES RED

2002 ★
2001 ★★★

ST-JOSEPH BLANC

2003 ★★(★)
2002 ★★

DOMAINE PHILIPPE FAURY

La Ribaudy 42410 Chavanay +33(0)474 872600

See also Condrieu, Côte-Rôtie.

Philippe Faury forms part of the important second wave of quality at St-Joseph, growers who have now established their names and who therefore follow in the early tracks of Coursodon, Chave, and the now retired Jean-Louis Grippat. This is a domaine where quality should be consistent from year to year; I have a slight preference for the whites.

There are six hectares of Syrah, dated between 1963 and 1993, at *La Ribaudy*, with a little on *La Gorge*, where more clay is mixed in with the granite. The 1.5 hectares of white on *La Ribaudy* are 60 per cent Marsanne, 40 per cent Roussanne, and date from 1978 and 1988.

M. Faury took over from his parents in 1979, when the domaine was a fruit and wine enterprise. He was born at La Ribaudy and is the third or fourth generation there. In the early days, he had just 2.5 ha of Syrah at St-Joseph, plus 1.5 ha of *vin de pays*, the red being made from Syrah and Gamay, the white from Chardonnay and Marsanne.

Before coming home to work, his job was in the Isère *département* across the Rhône, selling cereals and fertilizers. His first task was to clear and plant old sites on *La Ribaudy*'s walled ledges that had been abandoned after the Second World War. Besides the cherries and peaches, his father had made wine, which he sold to Rhône Valley cafés and to the miners of St-Étienne in their homes.

He is now helped by his wife, Danielle, and by two full- and one part-time helper. He was also President of the Growers Union at Condrieu for some years until 2004.

The white St-Joseph is vinified 70 per cent in steel, the rest in oak two to five years old. It is fermented at around 22°C, and raised over 11 months before bottling. Its white fruits are discreet, the wine generally soft—in the house style.

There are two red wines; the regular is 60 to 80 per cent destemmed, and vinified in concrete for 18 to 20 days, with twice-daily foot *pigeage*, or cap punching: "I prefer black feet to a *turbo-pigeur* machine," he comments laconically. Oak ageing lasts 12 to 18 months, half in *demi-muids* of 600 litres, half in 228-litre casks, 10 per cent of them new.

The special La Gloriette (6,000 bottles) is made from 35-year Syrah off *La Ribaudy*. It is vinified like the regular red, with 18 months in casks, 15 to 20 per cent of them new, the rest one to 10 years old, with some *demi-muids* as well. M. Faury is not a fan of new oak and likes to keep the proportion at sensible levels. This is a gently assembled wine, its black fruit presented in a low-key, easy way. It can do fine for around eight years.

ST-JOSEPH ROUGE

2003 ★★★
2002 (CASK) ★
2001 ★

ST-JOSEPH LA GLORIETTE ROUGE

2003 ★★★★ Dark *robe*; southern, near-*garrigue*-style bouquet—violets/herbs. Essence of black fruits, warm but not sweet, well composed, correct structure. Tinge of end oak, balance pretty good, tannins, too. Complexity to come. STGT wine. From 2006–07; 2011–14.

2002 (CASK) ★★
2001 (CASK) ★★
2000 ★

ST-JOSEPH BLANC

2004 ★★
2003 ★★(★)
2002 (CASK, STEEL EXAMPLES) ★
2001 ★★

DOMAINE DE FAUTERIE

10 ave Charles de Gaulle 07130 Saint-Péray
+33(0)475 800425

See also Cornas, St-Péray.

Tall, with very pale green eyes, a wearer of quietly stated casual clothing, Sylvain Bernard must set the ladies' pulses racing. As for his origins, he says he is actually "a mix of olive oil and butter": his father was from Alès in the south, his mother from Besançon north of the Jura region, which is where his St-Péray colleague Stéphane Robert was brought up.

Now in his early 40s, Sylvain is well capable of passing for 10 years younger. He was born in Valence, where his father was big in textiles. He spent spells at Gérard Chave over a period of some years, and after two years at Beaune Wine School, promptly went off to the Antilles for 18 months of boating. Perhaps someone then had a word in his ear, for he came home and with his father's help started to buy land and plant on it.

The St-Joseph vineyard at Glun on a site called *Combaud*, high at between 300 and 380 metres, was first planted in 1982, then in 1984 and 1987. This lies between Mauves and Châteaubourg, very much in the southern sector of the *appellation*. The 4.86 hectares have started to reach an interesting age, with no young vines since the late 1980s. The vines grow on sanded granite soil that is not very deep and contains some scattered stones. Sylvain also has holdings at St-Péray and some very old plots at Cornas.

After 18 months with Jean-Luc Colombo, he made his first wine in 1985. At that time he lived in a farmhouse beyond the precipitous hill of Crussol that towers over St-Péray, but has since moved to the town itself. Sylvain approaches life with a relaxed attitude, a trait that shows up in his accessible, easy-fruited wines. He has been bottling all his crop since near the start.

There are three red St-Josephs, one of them more an *amusement* than anything else; this is called "Solstice," first made in 2001 by the rosé *saignée* method of bleeding the juice off the skins after only a few hours. This is vinified in steel and bottled in May—an early, simple "red fruit on top" wine.

The other wines, the classic and the principal Les Combaud, are vinified for eight to 12 days; the former receives 10 months' raising in four-to-six-year-old casks, the latter, selected from old plots to provide a more structured wine, stays for 12 months in two-to-four-year-old casks. It was first made in 1998, and the final selection is done just before bottling. Both are unfiltered.

The classic is well made, the emphasis on an easy style of fruit and roundness—it drinks well at two to four years old. The Combaud (4,000 to 5,000 bottles) is the more tannic wine, but can still be drunk well around five years old. The fruits are well-founded, the tannins peep out on the finish. There was no Combaud produced in 2002, and because the 2003 risked being very potent, some of the classic was included to cool its ardour.

Sylvain also makes a very sound white Côtes du Rhône (80 per cent Marsanne, 20 per cent Roussanne) in some years, from his St-Péray vines.

ST-JOSEPH ROUGE

   2003 ★

   2002 ★

   2001 ★

   2000 ★★

ST-JOSEPH LES COMBAUD ROUGE

   2003 ★★(★) Gutsy, meaty bouquet, has a black fruit surround. Charged wine with *cassis* fruit evident, a gum-chewing aspect. Slight reduction in it. Seems to hold plenty of tannin. From 2007; 2014–16.

   2001 ★★

   2000 ★★

Export 20 per cent (1) USA, (2) Great Britain

DOMAINE DE LA FAVIÈRE

Chez Favier 42520 Malleval +33(0)474 871525

See also Condrieu.

Pierre Boucher is the only nondrinker of wine or indeed of any alcohol that I can recall in the Rhône. Indeed, he has never touched the stuff. He's a slight man whose family have lived in this tiny plateau hamlet since before the French Revolution. His only neighbour is Pierre Gaillard, who bought his house off M. Boucher's parents.

There are three hectares of Syrah (1968, 1973, 1993) and half a hectare of Marsanne and Roussanne (1983). The soil is light, free-draining sandy granite. From 1983 M. Boucher, who also has a small Condrieu vineyard, has specialised in wine.

At 54 M. Boucher looks as if he has had a hard life, with his crumpled features, lined face, and slight frame. He admits in his soft voice that he is not passionate about wine, and it turns out that he was under obligation to get going on the wine when his father died when he was just 18. He worked for many years on his own, and in 2004 was no doubt relieved to have been joined by his daughter Patricia and her boyfriend, Thomas Putman, who both studied at the Beaune Wine School.

There are two reds, the regular only vat vinified and stored, the top one called "La Favière"; this is whole-bunch fermented in enamel vats for up to two weeks, with cap punching and pumping-over. Half the wine is raised in two-to-six-year-old oak for 12 to 15 months, the other half in vat, then oak. The reds are filtered, but not fined. The Favière is markedly better, a tarry, local wine, with some overt tannins.

The whites are vinified in steel at 16° to 18°C and raised away from their lees before bottling in June, the malo done. They, too, are traditional.

ST-JOSEPH LA FAVIÈRE ROUGE

2004 ★
2001 ★
2000 ★

ST-JOSEPH BLANC

2004 ★
2000 ★

LA FERME DES SEPT LUNES

Charbieux 07340 Bogy +33(0)475 348637

One of the most confidential domaines, high in the craggy outcrops of the Ardèche plain, houses a man whose generous blonde hair occasionally worn in a long, artistic style, earring, and considered movements bring to mind a mature rock performer.

Impressions are one thing, reality is another. Jean Delobre is pursuing a goal of organic wine, feeling his way, trying what works best with no book of rules from "school." He went organic in 1997, when still at the Cave Co-opérative of St-Désirat, from which he extracted himself in 2001.

He is soft-spoken and reflective. He works a family farm, Les Sept Lunes, that for 70 years has been mixed. M. Delobre stopped the cattle rearing but still has some cereal and apricot production. Around him spreads land that is home to autumn dish food like deer and wild boar—as well as foxes. The wine is vinified in an enormous, high stone-walled barn that used to serve as the cattle food store.

The St-Joseph vines are in the *commune* of Peyraud, just south of Serrières. Before joining the Co-opérative when it started in 1961, his father would sell his *vin de table* to the miners of St-Étienne away to the west. Now there are over five hectares of St-Joseph—all Syrah dating from 1976 and from the 1980s except for a recent 0.7 ha of half Marsanne, half Roussanne. There is also a hectare of Syrah *vin de pays*. The soil is sandy granite, the vines all wire trained.

The red is fermented in concrete vats in his new cellar, with destalking if necessary. Low amounts of sulphur are used as he continues the organic bias in the cellar. Early on, there are some pumping-overs of the cap, and he does a foot punching himself. Ageing is in a mix of cask and *demi-muid* (550 litres), from three to six years old. The classic red receives 12 months, the special *Pleine Lune* 15 to 18 months. There is no fining nor filtration.

Explaining his approach, M. Delobre states: "I work with very little sulphur because I want the greatest multitude of yeasts to perform in the vat as I start the fermentation. This also lets the wine develop more complexity of aroma. Later on, it also implies that the buyer should store the wine in a constant temperature cellar."

There is a very elegant and well-founded simplicity in these wines. The 2002s made progress and gained weight after their cask phase, and the fruit throughout is very clear-cut and wholesome. The 2001 was open on the bouquet early on, but more reserved on the palate, and merited keeping until 2005. As with many organic wines, it is a good idea to decant them before drinking.

The aim is to harvest the white crop after the Syrah so that it is invariably very well-ripened. Half each Marsanne and Roussanne, it is is vinified in two-to-three-year-old oak and raised on its lees, with a weekly stirring, and bottled once the malo has finished, which in extreme cases like 2001 and 2004 can mean September. The white grapes are picked deliberately late, their alcohol equivalent 13.5° or higher. The Roussanne has greater stature than the Marsanne once vinified—they are assembled at bottling time. Nutty flavours and some decent content show this wine to be promising.

The domaine is at 350 metres, which plays a definite role in the wines' style. "Up here we are later than those whose vineyards face full south, lower down, and it's windy," comments M. Delobre, adding that this helped in the awkward year of 2002.

This is a rare example of an unspoilt, working hamlet, not a haven for the retired or fussy. There are 15 families, and Bogy has its own school, linked to the next-door village. The neighbours drop in for a toot of wine at the end of the day, the farmer opposite joining in with someone who labours in similar fashion to him.

ST-JOSEPH ROUGE
2003 ★★★
2002 ★★
2001 ★★

ST-JOSEPH PLEINE LUNE ROUGE
2003 ★★★(★)
2002 ★★★

ST-JOSEPH BLANC
2002 (CASK) ★★

FERRATON PÈRE ET FILS

13 rue de la Sizeranne 26600 Tain l'Hermitage +33(0)475 085951

See also Condrieu, Côte-Rôtie, Crozes-Hermitage, Hermitage.
The Ferraton family work a tiny 0.2 ha on the prime site of *Les Oliviers* (1988, 1990), on the boundary between Tournon and Mauves. The vineyard is half Marsanne, half Roussanne and is cultivated using biodynamic methods.

After a cool decantation, the juice is fermented in casks, 50 per cent of them new, and left for 10 to 12 months, with some lees stirring until March. There are just 1,200 bottles of white Les Oliviers a year. This shows off the oily fatness of the Marsanne to good effect, with a zesty, rather iodine input from the Roussanne— a good combination. Its oak just needs four

years to settle, but the wine has very good ageing possibilities—over 10 years.

Their *négoce* red and white St-Josephs are called "La Source." The red comes from Chavanay and Mauves, and is fermented in open wood and concrete vats for 15 to 18 days, with twice-daily cap punching. Ageing lasts 15 months, half in two-to-three-year-old casks, half in concrete vats. There is no fining or filtration. It shows red fruits and a meaty side in a prime vintage, but can dry fast once opened.

La Source white is pure Marsanne, mainly from Tournon. It comes from a mixed purchase of grapes and wine. After a day or two of cool decantation, the juice is vinified at 18° to 20°C in steel, with just 5 to 10 per cent in oak. The two elements are assembled at bottling time in July. Its fruit is pretty, and it can live nicely for around eight years in a good vintage like 2001.

ST-JOSEPH LA SOURCE ROUGE
2002 ★
2001 ★

ST-JOSEPH LA SOURCE BLANC
2001 ★★

ST-JOSEPH LES OLIVIERS BLANC
2003 ★★★ Ripe, buttery, typical Marsanne bouquet. Good juice, with a wholesome flavour, very correct Marsanne display. Tinge of end bitterness. Nice poise and style, has character, balance. Bit taut from its oak. 2012–13.
2002 ★★★
2001 ★★★

DOMAINE PIERRE FINON

Picardel 07340 Charnas +33(0)475 340875

See also Condrieu.
Another good grower tucked away high on the plateau west of the Rhône is Pierre Finon. This is also an estate that has moved away from traditional local *polyculture* towards wine as its mainstream activity. Cereal growing, cattle, and dairy,

plus a few vines were the Finon family's staple goods. The cereal was sold to the Co-opérative at Annonay, while the fruits, such as cherries and apples, were sold in the markets of Serrières and Charnas nearby. Any grapes were either made into basic table wine, or the small St-Joseph proportion sold to the Co-opérative in St-Désirat.

Mont Pilat is only a few kilometres away, and there is a hideaway feel to the little village of Charnas. But wine has partly helped to revive its community. Four or five young *viticulteurs* live on the plateau with their families, and in 1997 the village school was revived. It now looks after 75 children. But that is the limit of the *risurgimento*: the small café is run by an 80-year-old woman who serves local builders or friends out of her kitchen, and after the school run is over, there is hardly movement from human or canine.

Pierre has a look often seen on the Ardèche plateau—soft brown hair and clear blue eyes. He is the fourth generation to grow grapes and got going on his own in 1986, renting and buying vines and vinifying their fruit. He studied agriculture, and his wine knowledge has been built up along the trail.

The domaine has been developed to 11 hectares, six of them in St-Joseph, a tiny 0.25 hectare at Condrieu, and the rest in *vin de pays des Collines Rhodaniennes*: the last named comes in Syrah, Viognier, and Marsanne with a fourth wine called "La Galère." This is 90 per cent Gamay, 10 per cent Syrah, but the Finons have found it easier to sell wine called "Galère" rather than Gamay!

The St-Joseph is spread across a lot of plots. The prime sites are on slopes at Charnas and Félines, where the soil varies between granite and sand, with schist and stones. All the vines are trained along wires. The Syrah accounts for 5.5 ha, the 0.5 ha of white St-Joseph having been all Marsanne until 10 per cent Roussanne was added in 2002.

Frost is a fear up here at 300 metres, as is hail, but the fact that the Finons' plots are dis-persed serves to lessen the hail risk. Wind plays a more prominent role up here than down by the Rhône and whips across the open pastures.

The crop for the three reds is destalked, and fermentation runs over 18 to 20 days, with manual *pigeage* and *remontage* twice a day. Yeasts are added if necessary. The young, 12-to-15-year-old Syrah vines' fruit is half cask reared (three-to-six-year-old wood) over a year, half vat raised. Like the other reds, it is fined and lightly filtered. From 2003 it has been called "Jouvencelles."

It is direct, fruity wine that is faithful to its vintages—the 2001 fresh, with live black fruit, the 2000 easier, with cooked jam, and lighter. The style starts to show some of the warmer, less peppery aspects of the mid- to southern St-Joseph vineyards, but some bottles can have the problem of drying out after exposure to air.

The older vines' fruit—from 1978 Syrah, the wine called "Les Rocailles"—is all raised in oak, 15 per cent of it new, for a year. This contains sound, clearly defined black fruits and sufficient tannin to evolve well.

The top wine, Le Caprice d'Heloïse, named after his daughter, is made from mid-1970s Syrah in exceptional years. It is chosen from different plots at Charnas and receives 18 to 20 months in one-to-two-year-old oak. They produce 2,000 bottles.

The 90 per cent Marsanne, 10 per cent Roussanne white is vinified at around 20° to 22°C, with oak alone used since 2001—the casks half new, half one to two years old. Since 2001 half the crop has been destalked, for reasons of increased finesse, and since 2004 a *macération pelliculaire* has been done at the start of the vinification; "I'm very satisfied with this—it has brought more richness into the wine," comments Pierre. Raised for up to eight months in cask, this is a successful wine, its nutty flavours mixing well with stone fruits like peach and apricot.

The Syrah *vin de pays* is attractive, easy wine for early drinking. A fresh, refined white *vin de pays* is made from Marsanne.

ST-JOSEPH ROUGE

   2003 ★★

   2002 (★)

   2001 ★★

   1999 ★★★

ST-JOSEPH LES ROCAILLES ROUGE

   2003 ★

   2001 ★★★

   2000 ★★

   1999 ★★

ST-JOSEPH BLANC

   2004 ★★★

   2002 ★★

   2001 ★★

   2000 ★★★

Export 25 per cent (1) Great Britain, (2) USA, (3) Germany

GILLES FLACHER

Le Village 07340 Charnas +33(0)475 340997

See also Condrieu.

The Flacher family have been *viticulteurs* since 1806, and it was Gilles' grandfather who would vinify the wine, then sell it in bulk and to private clients. Bottling here started in 1980, and the whole crop is now sold in bottle.

Gilles, a short, quite dark-haired man, moved the domaine along from 1991. He studied mechanical engineering, but then went off to Mâcon for a one-year wine course: "Our farm was in *polyculture*, but the fruit side didn't interest me." He is a reserved person, careful with his words, which come with a keen look—one senses he is a determined worker. His wife, Nathalie, does the accounts and all the lighter vineyard work, while his father, Louis, helps in the vineyard and in the bottling process. Harvesting is mostly a family affair.

There are 4.3 ha of Syrah (average 1983), above Charnas, on decomposed granite with mica traces. Half is terraced or staked, the other half is on slopes with wire training that allows mechanical work. There is 0.7 ha of white—60 per cent Marsanne, 40 per cent Roussanne, average 1988; the Roussanne grows on more limestone soil with some loose granite present.

Condrieu has been made since 1995, as well as *vin de pays des Collines Rhodaniennes* in Syrah and Viognier. The Viognier is a decent, peppery wine.

The modern cellar was built in 2001, allowing temperature control and more working space. The red has been destemmed since 1994 and vinified at a maximum of 28° to 30°C in steel over 20 to 25 days. External yeasts are used. For the one year of wood ageing on the regular wine, the casks are around two years old. The Cuvée Prestige receives a year in half new, half one-year-old wood. Fining and light filtration are done.

The classic red expresses sound fruit and can be drunk young, while the Prestige has to cope with its oak before its clear black fruit can sail along—often it's best to wait for three years or so. It can live for 10 years.

The white is cask fermented and raised in half new, half one-year-old oak. It is controlled at around 18°C, and left on fine lees for around seven months, with *bâtonnage*. "I started the oak around 1997 to bring extra richness and roundness—fruit rather than the floral side that comes with steel," says Gilles. It is a stylish, firmly flavoured wine with a good oak-fruit proportion, and shows that Charnas is a sound source for refined white St-Joseph.

ST-JOSEPH ROUGE

   2003 ★★(★)

   2001 ★★

ST-JOSEPH PRESTIGE ROUGE

   2001 ★★

   2000 ★★★

   1999 ★★

ST-JOSEPH BLANC

   2003 ★★

2002 (CASKS) ★★
2001 ★★★

Export 15 per cent (1) Switzerland, (2) Belgium,
(3) Great Britain

DOMAINE FLORENTIN

51 avenue du Midi 07300 Mauves +33(0)475 086097

This is the most unusual domaine in St-Joseph.
For years it has stabled a working horse to tend
its strikingly composed vineyard, which lies just
off the N86 south of Mauves. The vineyard is in
the shape of an amphitheatre and conjures
images of a relaxed, sunny epoch with its hunting pavilion shaded by a large cedar tree beyond
the first semicircular rows of Syrah vines.

Alas, such is officialdom, especially that of
the Swiss variety. For years known as Clos de
l'Arbalestrier, the domaine was obliged to
change its name with the 2001 vintage since it
clashed with the name of a Swiss wine merchant.

It is indeed a single Clos of four hectares that
was bought by Dr. Émile Florentin in 1956. The
estate dates back to 1528. The Florentin family is
one of doctors; Émile is now 93, and his son
Dominique works in homeopathy in Valence.
Dominique's main attention is on the vineyard,
his sister, the pig-tailed and energetic Françoise,
deals with administration and commerce, while
the cellar master–manager, René Despesse, has
been present since 1982.

The prime vineyard is wonderfully sheltered
and receives the sun from a dip between two
hills. There is a sprinkling of apricot and cherry
trees, but the vines have held their rainbow pattern since 1914, since they follow the run of a little stream—also a tactic to attract as much
south-facing sun as possible. Their average age
is 50 years, including the fifth hectare planted
across the road on the terraces of the *Coteau La
Carrière*, a vineyard that belonged to Mauves'
grandee *négociant* Ozier, who flourished in the
nineteenth and early twentieth centuries.

Of the total 5.5 hectares, one hectare is split
80 per cent Roussanne, 20 per cent Marsanne,

these vines averaging 25 years old. The soil is
alluvial with mica-schist topsoil and is very draining. The whole vineyard is worked naturally.

Vinification is traditional. The Syrah has
been destalked since 1985, on average about 80
per cent. Fermentation occurs in open wood
vats with two *pigeages* per day, and a *remontage*.
Ageing sets the domaine apart from it neighbours—this still runs over three winters, in
600-litre casks around 30 years old, plus some
barrels of 17 to 30 hl. There is no fining or filtration, and up to to five different bottlings occur
from February onwards.

Twenty per cent of the production is white.
This is fermented in used casks and is raised on
its fine lees over two winters. The proportion
can change according to the vintage conditions,
since the Roussanne can suffer from oïdium
and problems at flowering; 2000 was 60 per
cent Marsanne, 40 per cent Roussanne, while
2001 and 2002 were both 60 per cent Roussanne, 40 per cent Marsanne. The two varieties
are aged for a year apart, then assembled.

The reds are traditional, almost in a time
warp. They are undoubtedly marked by their
upbringing in wood for three winters. The wood
appears well looked-after, but the length of the
stay can reduce freshness and introduce dry elements if there is not enough initial *gras* or fatness. Smoky red fruit flavours can be found,
and a chewy, drying texture near the finish.
They should be able to run towards 10 years old,
but they will not be fresh enough for lovers of
modern wines.

The whites here are full and generally well
defined. They can also live well. Their fullness is
a reminder of the best St-Josephs of the 1970s
and 1980s—plenty of character, with a certain
rustic vigour in them. They are good—wines
that need food rather than being served as an
aperitif. They can live for a good eight to 10
years.

ST-JOSEPH ROUGE

2002 ★★
2001 (CASK) ★

2000 ★★
1999 ★★
1998 ★★

ST-JOSEPH LE CLOS BLANC

2003 ★★ Elegant Marsanne-inspired bouquet—nuts with a full, quite *gras* style. Rich matter, as if deliberately later picked. Broad wine, needs food, has a traditional fullness. Fair length, with an assertive, nutted finale. 2009–11.

2002 (CASKS) ★
2001 ★★★
2000 ★★
1999 ★★★

Export 20 per cent (1) Great Britain, (2) Belgium, (3) USA

ELIZABETH FOGIER

La Roue 07300 St-Jean-de-Muzols +33(0)475 082213

A veteran now, Elizabeth Fogier took over from her father in 1967. "In those days, you had to prove yourself as a woman," she says. "I actually learnt with my mother, and in those days we sold the wine in bulk. From 1983 we bottled it ourselves." She has been a mainstay of the St-Jean-de-Muzols wine culture, which has retained unpretentious roots in the making of simple, unfussy wines.

Elizabeth lives a farmer's existence, surrounded by her hens that pick at every nook and cranny. She has very pale auburn hair and glasses, and confesses to finding the current wine fashion not her style: "You're thrown out if you don't destalk and your wine doesn't taste of wood," she comments with complete accuracy.

Her tiny cellar is full of old *demi-muids*, where the wine spends a year. She vinifies traditionally, in concrete vats with whole bunches, and does not filter. The wine is gentle and simple, in the vein of the southern St-Josephs where the fruit is more soft than peppery.

For decades she has lived off two hectares on the *lieu-dit La Roue*, which rises behind her house. Some of its Syrah was planted in 1900.

She now restricts herself to just 0.4 hectare and has rented out the remaining 1.6.

She potters around outside the house, weeding nettles, her fragile health not stopping her from continuing with the activity she is so used to. Once in the cellar, she leans against her barrels and talks. A carefully dressed middle-aged couple arrive from Savoie, their shiny new Citroën parked outside. They hesitantly pick their way past the hens and stoop into the cellar. Elizabeth's life goes on in its timeless way.

ST-JOSEPH ROUGE

2002 (CASK) ★
2001 ★
2000 ★★

DOMAINE DE GACHON

rue Centrale 07370 Sarras +33(0)475 232410

Pascal Perrier's family farm at Sarras goes back to 1522, and he is one of the Vieille France characters of St-Joseph, along the lines of Raymond Trollat, a generation ahead of him. One senses his hair is permanently tousled, his voice stuck in a deep register with the encouragement of a few local cigarettes. There is a moustache to complete the "only in France" look.

He works five hectares of Syrah and was plunged into winemaking at just 13 years old, after his father, a Co-opérateur at Sarras, died in a tractor accident. "I started to vinify in 1966, and that's what I like to do best. It was a big challenge to learn how to vinify when I was so young, and I have stuck to a traditional approach since then," he states. In 1983 he started to bottle part of the wine and still sells half of it to local firms like Jaboulet and Delas.

Accordingly, the grapes are vinified whole, a process lasting three to four weeks in a mixture of different vats—steel, enamel, and fibreglass. The wine is raised for six months, 70 per cent in 600-litre and 30 per cent in 225-litre casks. He fines but doesn't filter before a June bottling.

His Syrah dates from 1976 on the high, flatter areas at 300 metres, and from 1990 on the slopes. The high ground is gneiss, a gradually decomposing granite, while the low ground is not surprisingly more fully crumbled granite. The vine roots can penetrate up to 2.5 metres in this soft rock. There is a week's difference in the ripening due to the altitude.

These are wines that convey blood and toil—there isn't a trace of urban chic in them, nor would I expect them to appeal to people like that. The fruit is wild and rather unpredictable, and the wines have plenty of hidden moments in their course through life. They appear to need patience, coming into their own from four or five years onwards. Winter food, a log fire, and no early commitments the following day—off you go.

FIGURE 27 Pierre Gaillard made his first wine in 1985; now he has a commanding name at St-Joseph and has widened his interests beyond the Rhône. (Author's collection)

ST-JOSEPH ROUGE

2001 ★
2000 ★
1999 ★★★
1998 ★★★

Export 60 per cent (1) USA, (2) Belgium, (3) Japan/Denmark

PIERRE GAILLARD

Chez Favier 42520 Malleval +33(0)474 871310

See also Condrieu, Côte-Rôtie.
Walking around Pierre Gaillard's immaculate air-conditioned underground ageing cellar, you wouldn't think that this was one of the men who laboured on the hot Côte-Rôtie hillside in the early 1980s working to build Marcel Guigal's *La Turque* vineyard.

He has made giant strides since those days of employment. The vineyard portfolio has grown in the northern Rhône, and also includes his ownership of a Banyuls Grenache vineyard in the southwest of France. The cellars are state of the art, and the whole business seems so well set that it could have been going for several decades.

Born in 1955, he has lived on the windy plateau above Malleval since 1986, having made his first wine, a St-Joseph, the year before. There

was nothing much in his pedigree that suggested wine. A Lyonnais, his parents worked in the SNCF (French railways) and with a leaning towards the outdoors, Pierre got work as a parks and gardens cultivator in the Paris region until his early 20s.

Driving him then was a desire to make agriculture or viticulture his life, so he went off to study at the wine schools of Beaune and Montpellier, during which time he became a friend of Gilbert Clusel from Côte-Rôtie. "That drew me there," he recalls, a big, open-faced chap with broad shoulders, and a calm manner behind the light brown eyes. "I was 24 when I joined Vidal-Fleury in 1979, and I stayed there for seven years, working for Marcel Guigal after he bought it."

He had struck out in 1981 with a few plantings done in his spare time on a sandy granite plot at Chavanay called *Clos de Cuminaille.* "I bought 2.3 ha first, then added to it in 1992," says Pierre of his prime St-Joseph vineyard of 3.85 ha. "It has a 30° slope, but I was able to take out four large terraces and make it workable by tractor." A tiny amount of Côte-Rôtie was made in 1986; to show how hard it is to break into a vineyard like this if the grower does not possess limitless funds and heavyweight contacts, Pierre started off there with just 0.25 hectare.

His St-Joseph vineyard has risen to 10 hectares, eight Syrah and two Roussanne. Apart from *Cuminaille*, he works 1.5 hectares on the granite of *Buis* at Limony, where Louis Chèze is a neighbour, and the rest is spread around *Côte Bellay* (1990) and on the plateau around his house, both at Malleval.

The Roussanne is in three plots—on Malleval's plateau at *Les Dries* (1994), on its slopes at *Chatres* (1999), and on *Les Vessettes* (1996) at Chavanay. Pierre's is one of the rare St-Josephs *blancs* to be made only from Roussanne.

With the smart cellar and ageing building put up in 2002, and his wife, Pascale, retiring from teaching at the Malleval school to deal with the commercial and client side, this is now a thorough family business. The eldest of their three children, Jeanne, has studied oenology, and there is a buzz about the domaine. Add in the 15 hectares of the Domaine Madeloc at Banyuls for its sweet wine, along with Pierre's partnership with Yves Cuilleron and François Villard in the Vins de Vienne project, and there's plenty to go on with for the next few years.

Despite all the facts and stats, Pierre remains a countryman at heart. It's clear that he likes to reason out very carefully any course of action, and his way is to absorb, then act. Of the Vins de Vienne trio, he is certainly the country boy, and he talks about the next step in the evolution of his domaine with an eye to this outlook: "Everybody knows how to extract their grapes now—it's the details in the vineyard that are going to make the difference from now on. I'm looking to achieve a notion of balance in every single site wine I make, which means not extracting too much and paying attention to the vintage."

That said, his vinification is modern and active and involves hundreds of oak casks. The Syrah crop is mainly destemmed and receives a week's pre-fermentation cooling at 6° to 8°C, with a daily pumping-over. "I'm seeking to stabilise the colour and achieve fresh fruit aromas that help me when selling it at a young age," he explains in practical terms. The bottom of another vat is used to reheat its neighbour, and Pierre reckons on a seven-to-eight-day alcoholic fermentation, prompted in part by external yeasts, with thrice-daily cap punching and pumping-overs.

The final temperature is a high 35° to 40°C. There follow *délestages*, or partial vat emptying and refilling, to oxygenate the liquid and reactivate the yeasts to finish any lingering sugars.

After this, Pierre continues with a three-week maceration at 30°C to smooth out the tannins. Finally, the wine is placed in oak, 25 per cent of it new, to run its malolactic fermentation. Modern techniques are used during the 18-month cask ageing, as he explains: "I used to rack every four months, but now I rack the wine from one cask to another after the malo, then I micro-oxygenate the cask (injecting small ampules of air) instead of racking it again." He started this in 2000, and says that it makes the wine dry out less and staves off the stinky reduction smell that the Syrah can be prone to.

There are three reds; the classic comes from plots in all three *communes* Chavanay, Malleval, and Limony. It is aged for 18 to 20 months in 20 per cent new oak casks, the rest two to five years old. Like the others, it is bottled unfiltered and shows off frisky black fruit with some heart to it.

Les Pierres is selected from the best sites of *Cuminaille*, *Buis*, and *Bellay* and is all aged in new oak for 18 to 20 months. Pierre contends that each site brings its own style—*Bellay* being the base of its elegance, *Buis* similar but a little more alcoholic, and *Cuminaille* providing the power side. Les Pierres has tannin/oak surrounds to the fruit and is agreeable to drink from three years on.

The Cuminaille also receives 18 to 20 months in cask, but its proportion is 30 to 40 per cent new, the rest up to five years old. It has always been a wine of rich character, and with its vineyard maturing, it is likely to broaden in the next few years. It is an energetic wine, its fruit deep, complex, and live, and when it hits the mark, as in 2001, it displays a very fine pedigree. I recall the 1990 as another triumph from this vineyard, but quieter years can intervene.

Pierre's handling of new oak has a defter-than-usual touch—perhaps aided by his time chez Guigal. Given the natural tendency of the vineyard to produce quite powerful wines, there is a pretty refined marriage between the vineyard and cellar elements here.

For the white, Pierre likes to pick his Roussanne with some advanced maturity in the grapes, somewhat like his friend François Villard; this can mean harvesting around mid-October. It is oak fermented, 10 per cent of the casks new, the rest one to three years old, at 16° to 18°C. To develop richness and aroma, he stirs the lees once a week for six months, then filters and bottles the wine with its malo done in June. It is quite rich in the modern style, capable of evolution over a few years.

Pierre also makes a pleasing Viognier Côtes-du-Rhône which is oak fermented and raised over six months. This comes from 1.5 hectares on the granite of Limony and Chavanay. There are Syrah and Viognier *vins de pays des Collines Rhodaniennes* from a hamlet called Ternay nearby, made in the house style—these are both oak raised.

ST-JOSEPH ROUGE
  2003 ★★
  2001 ★

ST-JOSEPH LES PIERRES ROUGE
  2003 ★★★
  2002 ★★
  2001 ★★★

ST-JOSEPH CLOS DE CUMINAILLE ROUGE
  2003 ★★★ Lightly oaked, stylish nose, elegant width, some tar. Interesting, well-defined fruit, earthy support, some complexity. Tannins need till 2007. Good style, with a red fruits finale. Four months' less cask this year to gain freshness. 2014–17.
  2002 ★★★
  2001 ★★★★
  2000 ★

ST-JOSEPH BLANC
  2003 ★★

  2002 (CASK) ★★
  2001 ★★

Export 50 per cent (1) Great Britain/USA, 2) Belgium

DOMAINE GASSE LAFOY

16 route de la Roche 69420 Ampuis +33(0)474 561789

See also Côte-Rôtie.

The learned Vincent Gasse from Côte-Rôtie worked an organic 0.3 ha Syrah vineyard (1983) on the granite beside the Malleval plateau until handing it on in 2004 to his successor, his ex-employee Stéphane Otheguy.

The wine received a two-week fermentation and two years' ageing in used casks, and was bottled unfined and unfiltered. It is marked by the cool, pure texture of this area, enhanced by the simplicity of the winemaking. It can live for eight to 10 years in the best vintages.

ST-JOSEPH ROUGE
  2001 (CASK) ★★

DOMAINE GONON, PIERRE ET JEAN

34 avenue Ozier 07300 Mauves +33(0)475 084527

Pierre Gonon was a mainstay at Mauves for many years, making sound, understated wine. He became ill in 1989 and handed over the domaine to his sons ahead of time, and they have moved it right into the top league. Jean, in his late 30s, has worked here since 1986, and Pierre, in his mid-30s, since 1988. They are a delightful pair, always brimming with smiles, and chatty to all comers, although Pierre's more solid presence betokens a leaning for the tranquility of the vineyard and his spare time hobby of *la chasse*.

In 2002 they finished building a new cellar, so that all their wine is now housed under one roof. It has a postmodern entrance and then, bang!—you're into the traditional old cellar, all in one short walk down a spiral staircase. Tradition, too, comes with the relief to find a domaine whose self-belief is such that only one

FIGURE 28 Top men—the skilled and modest brothers Gonon, Pierre and Jean, in their Mauves cellar, not a new cask in sight. (Author's collection)

white and one red are made, both called "Les Oliviers," and that uphold all the best virtues of the *appellation* system.

Father Pierre was farsighted in his commitment to white wine, and first planted some Marsanne in 1958; the first wine bottled by the domaine was indeed their 1964 *blanc*. "Few people had any commitment to the vineyard then," says his son Jean, "and the sale of the wine was tricky. My great-grandfather grew vines and sold his wine to one *bistrot* in Valence—30 casks a year, not bad going! My grandfather Émile worked in the office of the Mairie because by then there weren't enough vineyards left to make a go of it. It was down to my father to get things moving again."

Their two hectares of white varieties, 80 per cent Marsanne (core from 1958) and 20 per cent Roussanne (core, 1974), now average 30 years. They are above Tournon, 200 metres up on the *Coteau des Oliviers*. This has long been renowned as a top site, and before the St-Joseph *appellation*'s creation in 1956 its wine was sold as Vin des Oliviers. The vineyard contains old Rhône stones and red clay, with only a little sanded granite. "It gives whites that are fat, with

lowish acidity, and that can age well," comments Jean Gonon, a man with a malleable frame, short dark hair, and glasses that give him a measured, precise look.

The red is made from 5.5 ha of Syrah, 3.5 ha of them at Tournon, 1.2 ha bought from Raymond Trollat's sister at St-Jean-de-Muzols on the *Aubert* hill, and the rest at Mauves. The Syrah on *Oliviers* was planted in 1971 and 1974, after the Marsanne.

The family has more vines at St-Jean-de-Muzols than their home village of Mauves, and Jean comments that it is unusual for a domaine St-Joseph to come from all three of the main *communes*—"it's a good spread of soils and exposures," he observes. Apart from *Les Oliviers* and *Aubert*, these are led by *Montagnon, Martinot, Côtes des Rivoires* (the flat end of *Rivoires*), and *Croix de Peygros*.

The highest Tournon vineyard, at 308 metres, marks an interesting difference from the vines from around 100 metres lower: the highest slope is sunnier, but also fresher and windier, with a poorer, more purely granite soil. Its wine bears very striking red berried fruit, and a good structure; the lower wine, whose fruit ripens earlier, has a sappy, plump, straightforward character. "I always wish this wine had more minerality, but there you go—that's the *terroir* effect," sighs Jean.

The brothers deliberately like to harvest as late as possible, and the approach is traditional, starting with fermentation in open wood vats. They use only indigenous yeasts and see something of a generation gap on this important aspect: growers in their 40s are more inclined to yeast their vats, the younger ones less so. "For me, the main problem of outside yeasts is how they make so many wines banal and similar," is Jean's pithy view. "We yeasted only in 1984 and 1992, and you know how dodgy those vintages were."

There are two foot punchings a day throughout the two-to-three-week process, and a daily pumping-over at the start. The Gonons have increased the time their red spends on its lees, leaving it there even after the malolactic has taken place.

The red is aged for 13 to 15 months in 600-litre casks and, when there is enough harvest, a trusty 12 hl barrel, with two bottlings between November and June, up to 21 months after the harvest. The oak can be one to 40 years old, according to Jean. The red is not filtered, but can be fined.

The red Les Oliviers (8,000 bottles) is always a wine of pedigree, one that takes its time to open. Reserved early on it may be, but the fruit quality is invariably very clear and wholesome. The tannic presence is also very correct, allowing the wines to develop at a gentle, calm rate. These wines reflect the best virtues of careful and natural family winemaking.

After pressing and fermentation in ex-Burgundy casks that range from three to 15 years old, the white (8,000 bottles) stays on its lees, with once-a-week stirring until the first heat in May. It is left to repose until August, then bottled around the time of the next harvest. Usually 80 per cent Marsanne, 20 per cent Roussanne, it is very successful: the 1950s Marsanne provides a most satisfying persistence of flavour

and classy texture, a tasty oiliness on it. The roughly 1970s Roussanne is a little livelier, less fat but more complex, with hidden corners of dryness. The two combine extremely well.

Their whites live extremely well, and—rare for a local domaine—they keep back bottles to check this out: "The oldest successful white we have tried was a 1964 drunk in 1984," recalls Jean, "while we also found the 1972 in good shape when drunk in 1995." They are definitely food rather than aperitif wines—white meats, *ris de veau* (sweetbreads) with mushroom and a cream sauce, even spiced dishes.

The Gonons have been selecting cuttings from their own rootstock. They take the trouble to do this since it allows continuity in the vineyard and a better control of yields than bringing in outside clones. "The payoff is that the wines contain more richness," according to Jean Gonon.

"Simple is best" is clearly the motto of this domaine. Jean Gonon is both modest and level-headed and is also capable of very frank self-appraisal of his wines. "Holidays are partly a side issue because I like what I do," is a revealing statement. Their vineyard work is all manual, from the *massale* rootstock selection, to the tying and training of the vines, to each of their wooden stakes at first waist-, then head-level as the vegetation grows high in June, and anticipated shoots have to be nipped out. No wire-training lines are used.

The brothers also respect the moon's cycle for pruning, for instance. They prune on the old, waning moon since this favours the descent of the sap back towards the roots. They also start their pruning in mid-January, contrary to those who have nowadays started to prune in November, as can be seen when driving through the vineyards all over France. "The roots keep going between November and January, and should be given help at a well-timed moment," is how Jean Gonon puts it.

Respect for this domaine also comes from the fact that what Jean and Pierre Gonon know comes from life, from handed-down views, from ways that have been spoken about for their relay. It leads to a well-balanced outlook when dealing with the nature that surrounds them.

The final extra string to the brothers' bow is a fruity, lively Syrah *vin de table* called "Les Îles Feray," which receives the same handling as the red St-Joseph.

ST-JOSEPH ROUGE

2003 (CASK) ★★★★(★) Compact, harmonious bouquet, cool granite inflections. Good, vigorous wine—develops well, ripe end tannins, good structure and authority. Plenty to come. From 2007; 2017–20.

2002 ★★★ Minted, upright, peppery nose; cutting texture, steely black fruit. Tight now, can loosen its tannins. Peek of black berry fruit, pepper on finish. From 2006; 2012–14.

2001 ★★★★ Black fruit aroma, some spice, quite closed. Compact, black berried fruit, pretty. Licorice, chewy tannins on finish, gains quiet momentum. Good length. 2015–18.

2000 ★★★ Touch red fruit/meat, good width, jam touches on bouquet. Really good, supple Syrah, Mauves in a nutshell. Red jam, nice fruited finish. Charming, much softer, sweeter than a Chavanay red, for instance. Esp 2004–07. 2009–11.

1999 ★★★ Bright dark colour; bouquet now includes some animal with black fruits/pepper, black currant leaf. Ripe fruit start, baked prunes/olives, has loosened a little. Quite oily/leathery end. Tannins still prominent. From 2005–06; 2012–15.

1998 ★★★

ST-JOSEPH LES OLIVIERS BLANC

2003 ★★★★ Pretty honey, floral, touch of tight apricot aroma. Big flavour here, apricot, then orange peel end. Compact, scale wine, broadens and has great width. Good heart to it, with some elegance. Chewy finish. 2014–18.

2002 ★★★ Honey/spice mix with light flan aroma; buttered, soft white fruit flavour, good calm wine, more open from 2006. Some end grip, a degree of tannin. Time will enrich it. Quiet phase now. 2012–14.

2001 ★★★★★ Broad aroma, fennel, smoky, and plenty of potential. Delicious peach/apricot attack, wide and fleshy. Lovely richness, with buttery notes. Aniseed/licorice end. Warm, well-directed finish. Has opened up with great flair. 2011–14.

2000 ★★★ Lime tart, buttery aroma, less floral than earlier in life. Warm dried white fruits taste, clear flavour and good length. Some end minerality. 2010–12.

1999 ★★★

1995 ★★★

Export 25 per cent (1) USA, (2) Belgium/Norway, 3) Great Britain

DOMAINE DE GOUYE

Gouye 07300 St-Jean-de-Muzols +33(0)475 085824

Philippe and Sylvie Desbos form part of the confidential local wine culture that still exists at St-Jean-de-Muzols. It helps that their domaine is up a very narrow, steep, winding road above the village, tucked away with sweeping views extending out from its intimate courtyard.

Philippe's grandmother moved here in the 1930s from the plateau, and vines were already a part of the family's life then, as one plot of Syrah dating from the 1890s attests. Philippe and Sylvie bought out the other family members in 1992 and set to work on the vineyard. "We used to grow cherries and apricots, but the cherry harvest clashed with the tying of the vines, so we dropped them," says Philippe, a man of curly brown hair, pale blue eyes, and nineteenth-century moustache who is in his early 40s.

The four-hectare vineyard is all around and above the farmhouse; its *Gouye lieu-dit* is set back from the main Rhône valley, separated by a ravine from the better-known *Aubert* and *Pichonnier* sites of Raymond Trollat. Philippe is the only grower on *Gouye* and benefits from his father Jean's legacy of about three hectares of

Syrah planted between 1955 and 1975. Philippe planted half a hectare of Syrah in 1993, and there is half a hectare of Marsanne (1960, 1980, 1993) as well as a few *vin de table* vines on the plateau.

The topsoil is a typical decomposed granite, about 50 cm (20 in.) deep before the rockface. All work is manual, and father Jean even worked with a horse until the 1980s. The vines are staked, the old vines at a density of 10,000 per hectare, the more recent ones at 6,500.

Given the traditional approach to the vinification, it is a surprise to learn that Philippe not only studied at the Montpellier Wine School but also later worked with Jean-Luc Colombo. For the latter he was involved in the mobile bottling project rather than the new-oak purchase division!

Whole bunches are fermented, with no outside yeasts, in a mix of wood and concrete for two weeks, with manual punching of the cap or pumping-over twice a day; the maximum temperature of 33° to 35°C is allowed after the specific gravity has fallen to 1020. After pressing in the 1868 vertical press that is one of Philippe's pride and joys, the young wine is raised for nine to 12 months in casks of four to 12 years' age, although Philippe is gradually easing their average age down.

The red that he likes the best is bottled, with fining and filtration, the rest sold to local *négociants*. There are around 7,000 bottles. It displays typical red fruits—cherry with some pepper touches—although the deepest vintages like 2001 have more brambly black fruit aspects. The association with fruit gums is a regular feature, and the wines can run well for 10 years or so. They are true to their place, helped by the low level of cellar intervention.

The white has recently been fermented half in vat, half in cask due to the crop shortfall; normally a lower percentage sees the used oak. Its juice is kept at 18° to 20°C and left undisturbed on a fine lees for a year before bottling—around 1,000 bottles are made. The small amount is a pity, because this is lovely wine, a mix of dried white fruits and almonds on the palate and lightly spiced butter on the bouquet. In a classic local way, it builds to a chewy touch on the finish, with a salty tang also sometimes present.

Philippe also works a vegetable garden with great pride, except when his hens have got round the wire and feasted, and there are goats, too, which will end up eventually on the table. I don't meet many of his kind these days, people with a steady outlook. His pause to reflect before answering a question tells a tale, as he remarks with a piercing look, "I have always tried to the maximum in the vineyard without ever knowing what will happen; I plant and prune, but it's nature that does a lot more than me."

ST-JOSEPH ROUGE

2004 ★★(★)
2003 (CASKS) ★★★
2002 ★
2001 ★★

ST-JOSEPH BLANC

2003 ★★★
2002 ★★
2001 ★★★

DOMAINE ALAIN GRAILLOT

Les Chênes Verts 26600 Pont de l'Isère
+33(0)475 846752

See also Crozes-Hermitage, Hermitage. Alain Graillot's St-Joseph arrangements have changed and reduced the scale of his exposure to this *appellation*. He used to work 2.5 ha, but his rental at Andance has ended and he is now left with 0.7 ha at St-Désirat. This slope vineyard on decomposed granite dates from 1988 and touches the *Rochevine* hill above the Coopérative.

Alain has also planted 0.7 ha at St-Jean-de-Muzols, 14 terraces cleared out of an old forest on *Le Grand Pont*. The soil is also decomposed granite, and Philippe Desmeure, also based in Crozes, is his neighbour. This will come on stream in 2007.

Vinification starts with destalking—"to get round the firmness that the granite brings," says Alain. After a cold maceration, there is a three-week fermentation in concrete. Ageing lasts one year, in 10 per cent new casks, the rest up to six years old. There is a light filtration.

The wine holds peppery edges, its black fruit restrained by some worthy final tannins. It can live for around eight years.

ST-JOSEPH ROUGE

2004 (CASK) ★★
2002 (CASK) ★
2001 ★★
2000 ★★★

DOMAINE BERNARD ET FABRICE GRIPA

Le chemin de Halage 07300 Mauves
+33(0)475 081496

See also St-Péray.

This is an accomplished domaine, one that sets many a standard for authentic St-Joseph from the granite heartlands around Tournon. Bernard Gripa, a cousin of the now retired Jean-Louis Grippat, is an interesting man, very thoughtful, and an articulate provider of perspective on local winemaking and issues thereof. Dark haired and slightly cross-eyed, he is a good listener, and only gradually reveals his inner thoughts.

In 1997 he was given impetus by the arrival full-time of his switched-on son Fabrice, then 24. This young man bodes well for the domaine. Over four years, coming and going from home, he learnt the ropes at houses like the noted Leeuwin in Margaret River, Western Australia, and French domaines like Virginie in the Languedoc.

Fabrice has a clean, open view about the changing Rhône: although his family domaine is largely traditional in outlook, he regards the modernisers like Jean-Luc Colombo and François Villard as having served to alert growers in their

FIGURE 29 "Do things properly and pay attention to details," is still Bernard Gripa's work credo after almost 40 years on the family domaine. (Tim Johnston)

appellations to wake up and improve their standards. He thinks as his own man already: "The challenge is to pass beyond having big matter in the wine to having finesse in it. Concentration doesn't necessarily make a *Grand Vin*," are his wise words. He gives firm looks when he expresses himself, a hearty, base-toned laugh at the ready, his forehead crinkling as he does so: this is a man who means business.

Bernard doubled the size of his vineyard during the 1990s. Now there are seven hectares of Syrah and 3.5 hectares of white vines (80 per cent Marsanne, 20 per cent Roussanne) at St-Joseph and two hectares at St-Péray (80 per cent Marsanne, 20 per cent Roussanne). The expansion has been handled responsibly; many times I walk in the vineyards and see shoddy work fuelling the growth of the vineyards, shortcuts taken—vines subject to erosion and crumbling ledges. For Bernard, the redoing of the walls high on *Paradis* is the only way to work. "It took three men a whole winter," he says, "and we needed 700 tons of stones to redo half the walls." A plot of 1.2 hectares will start production from 2006 here.

"I started at 17 in 1963–64," comments Bernard, "and in those days a lot of the wine was sold to *bistrots*. My father had a very good client in Vienne, and the wine would be sent off to him in 600-litre barrels. The client would fill his own bottles and sell it as Vin de Mauves—that had as much drawing power as St-Joseph, as the St-Jo name wasn't known then. This was a species of bar that has largely disappeared around here since then—a real *bistrot à vin*; they didn't sell beer, pastis, or fruit juices," he adds with a wry smile.

"We were typical of many *vigneron* families in that way," he continues. "This arrangement stayed in place until the *bistrot* closed in 1974, so we then switched to selling to local *négociants* like Vérilhac and Chapoutier. Since 1974 I've been bottling the wine here and I now sell a lot to the French restaurant trade. That's why we like eating out so much, and have holidays that include visits to places that sell our wine."

Once up and running on the subject, Bernard loves to discuss wine in detail. For his reds, he likes some stems present "because it means the vats behave better." It's the young vine fruit in particular that is destemmed. "Even if the grape is ripe, but the stem isn't—we destalk," is the house position, "to avoid any green, herbaceous effects." So in 2001 half the crop was destalked, and in 1999, 80 per cent, for instance.

The crop is fermented 70 per cent in open wood, 30 per cent in stainless steel. This lasts three weeks, with a mix of *pigeages* and *remontages*. Cask ageing has been cut to barely a year, with 15 to 20 per cent new oak used. The November bottling for both reds comes with light fining and filtration.

The regular red is taken from the younger vines, many of them planted on *St-Joseph* and *Peygros* since the early 1990s, as well as from *Rivoires*. This represents a very reliable, securely grounded St-Joseph, with some late-harvest effect. Much of its work has been done beyond the cellar, which sets it apart from many of the more techno, modern St-Josephs from further north. Bernard is clearly out to make wines that can aspire to a genuine second stage in their development.

There are only 2,000 bottles of the top red, Berceau, which like the white is taken from the oldest 1920s vines on the *lieu-dit St-Joseph* plus a little from *Peygros*, whose oldest vines date from the 1950s. Bernard points out the difference between the two sources: "The *St-Joseph* has more finesse, whereas the *Peygros* is more angular, with more obvious tannins." Both sites have a lot of granite high up, but the *St-Joseph* is more sanded and fine lower down. *Peygros*, a high hill at the southern exit of Tournon, has heavier soil on its lower reaches.

Berceau *rouge* is a big wine, with dark fruits and earthy surrounds. Its spicy, chewy texture makes it a wine to set aside while the tannins subside, but it is a leading example of the structured, keeping red St-Josephs that can live for 15 years or more in the best vintages.

Since 1989 Bernard has fermented some of his select white Le Berceau in new oak—now it may run up to 20 per cent, the rest of the casks up to four years old. "When I started fermenting in wood, I found the older casks had an oxidising influence," he states. "We wanted to increase the oak on Le Berceau to gain richness and structure and to get away from the primary notes of many white wines. That meant ours could live longer, as well," he adds.

This pure Marsanne wine comes from the *lieu-dit St-Joseph* (mostly 1920s, some 1980s) plus some 50-plus–year Marsanne on *Peygros*. Bernard controls the temperature at around 18°C and likes to have the malolactic done—"despite the relative lack of acidity, I find the wines finish better with the malo done," he comments. After 10 months in cask, it is bottled in early September. Le Berceau *blanc* is driven along by its oak when young, although its apricot and white fruit richness manages to handle it quite well.

His regular St-Joseph *blanc* is 80 per cent Marsanne, 20 per cent Roussanne. It is fermented and raised 70 per cent in vat, 30 per cent in one-to-five-year-old oak for eight months, and is bottled before the heat of summer at the end of May. It is pretty and stylish, in the modern vein.

2003 ★★★★
2002 ★★
2001 ★★★
2000 ★★
1999 ★★★
1998 ★★

ST-JOSEPH LE BERCEAU ROUGE

2003 ★★★ Complete, black fruited, warm bouquet. Good depth on palate—cocoa, coffee, with black fruits. Locked up by some ripe end tannins. Good wine, genuine depth, intense and a touch sweet. 2013–14.

2002 (CASK) ★★ Quite wide nose; *cassis* fruit, end tar/tannin, pretty.

2001 ★★★★ Full black currant, light pepper, floral nose. Delicious! Lots of fruit, plus spice, tannins well set. Mineral/chewy. Esp from 2007. 2015–17.

2000 ★★★ Animal, reduced aromas; broad black flavour, gradual upping of tannin/width. Fair depth, mineral, true. From 2006; 2012–13.

1999 ★★★★ Cooked black fruits nose, potential; suave, fresh black fruit, peppery tannins, interesting; can close up. 2014–16.

1998 ★★★

ST-JOSEPH BLANC

2003 ★★(★)
2002 ★★
2001 ★★
2000 ★★

ST-JOSEPH LE BERCEAU BLANC

2003 ★★★ Nutty, full bouquet, some oak. Big, full wine on palate, flan, *crème patisserie* flavours, mineral touch on finish. Fat texture. 2012–14.

2002 ★
2001 ★★★
2000 ★★★

Export 15 per cent (1) Netherlands, (2) Belgium, (3) Switzerland

DOMAINE JEAN-LOUIS GRIPPAT

From the 1970s this was the reference domaine for much St-Joseph, with special emphasis on the white wines. It was sold to Marcel Guigal in 2001, as Jean-Louis Grippat took what seemed a surprising early retirement and headed for the hills on his racing bike. His last vintage was 2000.

"At 59, I was a tired man," he commented in a very matter-of-fact way. "I was tired of the administration and all that side of things, as was my wife, Ghislaine. My daughter Sylvie may not stay in the wine trade; we'll see"—as of 2004 she hadn't. Jean-Louis had also been working since he was 14.

So ended a notable chapter. Highly respected by his contemporaries, Jean-Louis had always let his wines do the talking. Their success spread the word about St-Joseph far beyond French shores, in the twilight years of the 1970s, before the Rhône was opened up. Their sophistication and elegance had always surprised those who considered St-Joseph as a rustic country cousin of the big shots like Hermitage and Cornas. And when he let you get to know him, Jean-Louis was the most articulate of growers, his wines bearing the traits of detail and close reflection.

His 1999 and 2000 were transferred to the Guigal cellars in April 2001 for their final ageing and bottling. For Guigal this was a major breakthrough, one that also allowed him to buy his first Hermitage vineyards.

Near the end of Jean-Louis' career, the Grippat reds were being cask raised for 18 months for the Vignes de l'Hospice and nine to 10 months for the regular St-Joseph. The Vignes was a wine of great elegance and southern aspects—flavours like olive tapenade would appear—with violets and blackberries present: a wine to drink around six to nine years old.

The pure Marsanne white St-Joseph was vat fermented, with a raising of 15 months, three of them spent in cask. The malo was completed. The very elegant whites, often marked by floral scents on the bouquet, could show well for up to 15 years in the biggest vintages.

Jean-Louis was also enterprising in making a *vin de paille* in 1985, 1988, 1995, 1996, and 1997: "900 half bottles for us."

E. GUIGAL

Château d'Ampuis 69420 Ampuis +33(0)474 561022

See also Condrieu, Côte-Rôtie, Crozes-Hermitage, Hermitage.

Marcel Guigal's purchase of the prominent Grippat estate, appropriately signed on the Day of St-Joseph, 19 March 2001, was a big breakthrough for the man from Ampuis. Grippat's best vineyard is on the near-vertiginous hill of *Chapon* that rises above Tournon, and benefits from fantastic exposure. This vineyard is the heartland of this straggling *appellation* and provides Guigal with a great flagship.

From here will come his top red of the three produced, the Vignes de l'Hospice. Its decomposed granite topsoil is classic northern Rhône, its physiognomy creating hard work after any heavy rain, when masses of newly funnelled rivulets appear. Each ledge has room for only two to eight vines, hemmed in by the stone walls. It's cramped working, with two stakes to train the vine, two branches on each one; these have to be tied three times with straw from halfway up the five-foot stake.

Altogether Guigal bought seven hectares of St-Joseph from Grippat—five and a half of Syrah, one and a half of white Marsanne.

The *Vignoble de l'Hospice*, right above the building itself, was until 1970 worked by three *vignerons*; its wine would be vinified under the control of the Benevolent Hospital of Tournon and given to the patients and staff. Jean-Louis Grippat started to work its 0.6 hectare *en fermage* from the early 1970s until passing it on to Guigal. Its vines were planted in the early 1900s, and its local subset name is *Le Chapon*.

Grippat also had 1.5 ha on *Le Clos des Hospitaliers*, near the cemetery of Tournon, and 1.5 ha of Marsanne and 2 ha of Syrah on the *lieu-dit St-Joseph*, close to the Tournon-Mauves boundary.

In 1998 another 0.8 ha was planted near the *Hospice* after a full operation to clear abandoned terraces. Grippat's remaining vines stood around his cellars on the way to Mauves.

Marcel Guigal's second advance into St-Joseph came via his acquisition of the three hectares of de Vallouit vineyards, also in 2001. The *Vignes de l'Hospice* puzzle was then neatly completed, for de Vallouit, too, was an owner here. Now the bottom right half hectare is rented from the Hospice of Tournon (1913), the middle 0.8 hectare is the recently planted ex–J-L Grippat vineyard (1998) and the left-side hectare is the 50-year-old de Vallouit holding that dates from the 1950s.

De Vallouit's vineyards were a mixture of ownership and renting, and also included one hectare above the Hospital at Tournon on a *lieu-dit* called *Les Petites Pierres*, next to Gripa's Le Berceau—right in the heart of the prime hillside there. So steep is the slope that there is a full 100-metre drop from top to bottom of this vineyard, which provided the crop for the de Vallouit Les Anges cuvée. The Syrah here was planted around 1955.

De Vallouit was also present on the *lieu-dit St-Joseph*, so that Guigal now works about three hectares of Syrah and 2.5 hectares of white vines there. Meanwhile, there was also a white-wine plot at Sarras in the de Vallouit portfolio—95 per cent Marsanne, 5 per cent Roussanne.

There are three Guigal red St-Josephs and two whites. The classic red is drawn from the vines on the low slopes and land near Grippat's old winery south of Tournon and augmented with crop bought in from Mauves and Tournon, and a little purchased wine from *communes* like Sarras and St-Désirat. The classic red crop is all destalked and, after a three-week vatting, is aged for two years in two-to-three-year-old casks. It is lightly filtered. The second wine is Le Lieu-Dit St-Joseph de St-Joseph, from the place of that name. "There are two olive trees in the vineyard, so warm is it," says Philippe Guigal. This receives two years' new cask ageing and is lightly filtered; around 1,700 bottles are made. The top red, the Vignes de l'Hospice (12,000 bottles), is raised in new oak for two years and is neither fined nor filtered.

The classic white is 95 per cent Marsanne, 5 per cent Roussanne. This contains around 15 per cent crop from the old de Vallouit and Grippat vineyards, 10 per cent bought-in crop, and the rest wine bought from six sources—mainly Tournon and nothing more northerly than Arras. Bottled in November, a little over a year after the harvest, it is raised half in vat and one-quarter each in new and one-year-old oak. The malo is completed on this and the top Lieu-Dit St-Joseph white.

The Lieu-Dit St-Joseph *blanc* is 95 per cent Marsanne dating from 1968 and 1973 and 5 per cent Roussanne. This is bottled a year after the harvest and is raised half in new, half in one-year-old oak. Exceptionally, because the crop was under half, the 2003 received only new oak raising for its 4,500 bottles.

ST-JOSEPH ROUGE

2000 ★★

ST-JOSEPH LIEU-DIT ST-JOSEPH ROUGE

2002 ★★ *Grillottes*, soaked cherry aroma, tar also. Taut black fruit presence, dry from the tannins and new oak. Cool texture, fair length. From 2007; 2014–16.

2001 ★★★★ Round, calm black fruit bouquet; succulent dark fruit, nice stylish width, good juice. Very charming, pure pleasure. 2011–12

2000 ★★★ Rounded black fruit, Tournon warmth, touch pepper; good, intense dark fruit, esp on attack; quite good length. Tannins ripe enough. 2011–12.

1999 ★ Dark, rather foxy nose, dense, leathery style has come early. Chocolate tones on palate, broad mass rather than clear fruit definition. Little cut on finish. Not like usual Grippat style (he vinified it). Dries out with air.

ST-JOSEPH VIGNES DE L'HOSPICE ROUGE

2003 (CASK) ★★★★ Dark *robe*; compact black jam bouquet, has a friendly, live side. Blackberry

fruit, lovely disposition, round with ripe tannic edging. Very broad, rounded, long, and warm. From 2008–09; 2018–20.

2002 ★★★ Oaked, balanced bouquet, tight packing. Floral/black fruit mix on palate—pretty middle, some *gras*. Runs on towards a tangy finish, fruit is tasty. Burgundian style. From 2006; 2016–18.

2001 (CASK) ★★★★★ Dense, tightly packed, mocha, funky nose; delightful core fruit, good structure, intensifies halfway. Fresh, pretty end. Length good. 2016–18.

2000 ★★ Grilled, upright black fruit aroma; refined behind initial austerity. Oak is stern; pepper/liquorice end. From 2007; 2011–13. Vinified Grippat, new oak–raised Guigal

1999 ★★★★ Full, big leathery/smoky bouquet; fulsome, tasty black fruits, good chewy texture, broad tannins. From 2007. 2016–19. Vinified/aged Grippat, bottled Guigal.

ST-JOSEPH BLANC

2004 ★★★
2003 ★★(★)
2002 (CASK) ★
2001 ★★
2000 ★
1999 ★★★★

ST-JOSEPH LIEU-DIT ST-JOSEPH BLANC

2003 ★★★ Lightly toasted, elegant apricot/pear bouquet. Refined richness, treads lightly with a mix of apricot and hazelnut. Rich, but has grip. Toast/honey aftertaste, touch burnt on end but can settle. From 2006; 2014–16.

2002 (CASK) ★★★ Some lime tart/mineral touches too; pretty, good structure, quite open, can flourish. Oaked length. 2010–11.

2001 ★★ Buttery, very ripe bouquet; warm, rounded, fair *gras*. Peach stone, nicely burnt vanilla, smoky dried fruit end. Fair length. 2009–11.

2000 ★ Light floral aromas; elegant palate, gentle white fruit. Stops a little short. Wee bit dull.

1999 *J-L Grippat blanc* ★★★★ Mix of floral and boiled sweets on bouquet; quiet fullness, good persistence here. Very good. Bottled by Guigal shortly after the purchase.

PAUL JABOULET AINÉ

Les Jalets RN7 26600 La Roche-de-Glun
+33(0)475 846893

See also Condrieu, Cornas, Côte-Rôtie, Crozes-Hermitage, Hermitage, St-Péray.

Jaboulet have spread their wings across St-Joseph since the early 1990s. Their first move was to buy a plot on a granite-based site called *Les Rouasses* at Serrières in 1993; this was the vineyard that supplied their occasional Cuvée Personelle, its 80-year owner having retired. It was stripped and replanted, the terrace walls redone, and the vines trained on stakes. The hill turns from east to southeast and forms part of the St-Joseph Vitrine operation to encourage planting in the best spots, which was conducted at Serrières in 1996–97. There are now 2.5 ha of Syrah, and its first wine was made in 1997.

In the same transaction, Jaboulet acquired the right to buy a terrain on *Rouelle Nord* at Limony—limited to an annual plantation allowance of 0.1 to 0.15 ha, rising to a total 3.5 ha. This had been overgrown, and between 1999 and 2002 a total of 0.5 ha of Syrah, 0.8 ha of Marsanne, and 0.3 ha of Roussanne were planted.

The third and very important vineyard is the one in the plum, firm granite heartlands of St-Joseph, at Tournon, where there are just over 3 ha of land available for planting. At present 0.8 ha has been planted since 2001 on *Le Clos des Hospitaliers* and *Les Petites Pierres*, both of them southeast-south facing. These sites held vines until phylloxera, and are now being revived, dried-stone walls and all.

The Syrah crop is destemmed and fermented for two to three weeks, with pumping-overs. Cask raising lasts for 12 months in two-to-three-year-old oak, some of it Hungarian.

The red wine is called "Le Grand Pompée": it is a quote from Victor Hugo, *La Légende des Siècles*. It shows the house leaning for stewed fruit flavours and a certain expansiveness of texture.

It is marked by black fruits and a degree of tannin when young. The first vintage to contain the fruit from the Serrières vineyard was the 2000, with some beneficial effects.

The white Le Grand Pompée has in recent years been markedly yellow-coloured, fat, and oily. Its malolactice fermentation has been completed since the mid-1990s. It is made from mostly Marsanne and is sourced 40 per cent from Jaboulet crop from Limony, the rest from purchased crop stemming from Malleval and Arras. It is raised for four to five months in one-third new oak, two-thirds vat—a welcome cut-back on the oak.

It is buttery—butterscotch and bonbon flavours present—and would be improved by more decisive flavours and perhaps less cellar extraction in pursuit of its fat. The 1995, for instance, contained some Roussanne and a much more clear-cut texture, but recent policy has not sought that style of wine. The 2003 promised more fullness and style than for some time, however, so perhaps this trend can be kept going.

ST-JOSEPH LE GRAND POMPÉE ROUGE

2003 (CASK) ★★★ Reserved, quite full bouquet—violets, ripe fruit, alcohol traces. Ripe fruit core with some tannin—fruit likeable, has definition. Some end heat. No great nuance, but enjoyable, also persists fine. From 2006–07; 2015–17.

2001 (CASK) ★
2000 ★★
1999 ★★★

ST-JOSEPH LE GRAND POMPÉE BLANC

2003 ★★★ Mixed, smoky bouquet—spice, lavender, mint, flowers. Evenly weighted, with style. Grows gradually through palate, ends nicely chewy. Rather a red wine structure. Charming young, interesting. Persists well, hazelnut aftertaste. 2008–10.

2002 ★
2001 ★
2000 ★

PASCAL JAMET

RN 86 07370 Arras-sur-Rhône +33(0)475 070961

After completing studies at Beaune in 1990, Pascal Jamet led a double life. From 1992 until 2001 he was an Inspector of nurseries and vineyards based in Lyon for Onivins. This work would take him on trips to Savoie or the southern Rhône to check up that people were playing the game with their vineyard plantation areas and were behaving and logging everything correctly.

In the meantime he was keen to make his own wine, and planted his first Roussanne in 1994 high above Arras, a tiny village beside the Rhône that lies opposite the northern extremity of Crozes-Hermitage. In 1997 he planted his first Syrah, a hectare on a site called *Les Vachers*, as well as Syrah, Merlot, and Viognier at the less likely spot of Portes-les-Valence on the outskirts of Valence. His wife Catherine's family has land there, and 2.8 hectares were planted on a mix of limestone and rolled stones in 1998. From 2003 Cabernet Sauvignon joined the lineup.

Pascal's parents would send their St-Joseph crop to the Co-opérative at Tain, a practice that he stopped in 1999 when he made his first bottles of the 2000. Since then he has planted around the ruin of the old feudal castle, and in so doing has restored this 0.6 ha plot to vine.

Slim, wiry, with tousled, curly dark hair, Pascal is now in his mid-30s. He works 2.5 hectares of St-Joseph, with another hectare set to be in production by 2007. Most of the soil is decomposed granite, with the sandier parts chosen for the Roussanne. Catherine, petite with tumbling fair hair and glasses, is an active helper in the vineyard.

Together they have deliberately planted a Syrah clone with small pips. Three-quarters of their vineyard is Syrah, one-quarter Roussanne. "We have no Marsanne, since we much prefer the Roussanne, but it's an abominable producer—every year it suffers from oïdium," laments Catherine.

There are two reds. After destemming, their crop is vinified for up to three weeks in steel, with *délestages*, and the young wine raised for a year in casks three to six years old. Both are fined, but not filtered, and the Jamets consider them better if given air. The Spéciale, called "Côte Sud" until 1999, contains 10 per cent Roussanne, fermented with the Syrah for extra richness. It is mainly from a site called *Les Traverses*.

The classic red shows grilled notes on the bouquet, its black fruit mixed in with licorice flavours. The Spéciale displays pretty fruit and some oiliness when first opened, but can dry quickly once in the glass.

The white Roussanne wine is 10 per cent oak fermented, receives lees stirring, and is bottled in April. This broadcasts tropical fruits, with some mineral tones present, too.

The *vin de pays* Grand Beliga is made from 60 per cent Syrah, 30 per cent Merlot, and 10 per cent Viognier. This is aged in oak and is more accomplished than the slightly dull Syrah-Merlot blend of the straight Beliga. There is also a botrytised Viognier *vin de pays*, its grapes picked from mid- to late October. This shows decent apricot flavours and a grapy aroma, while in 1999 Pascal amused himself by making a Roussanne from overripe grapes—picking when the sugar level was at 17°. This held pear and caramel flavours, with a firm finish.

These are wines that come with a nicely artistic label, and the Jamets are clearly working hard at making a name for themselves. But the wines often lose their grip and dry with air, tending to curl up after being open only an hour or so. This comes from the extraction process.

ST-JOSEPH ROUGE
  2002 ★★
  2001 ★

ST-JOSEPH CUVÉE SPÉCIALE ROUGE
  2001 ★
  1999 *Cote Sud* ★

ST-JOSEPH BLANC
  2001 ★
  2000 ★★

Export 10 per cent (1) USA, (2) Great Britain

GEORGES LAGNIER ET FILS

RN86 Verlieu 42410 Chavanay +33(0)474 872446

The Lagnier family sells their wine on the N86 roadside at Chavanay, and also grow fruit. There is a simple red and white St-Joseph, as well as a Condrieu.

DOMAINE MARSANNE

25 avenue Ozier 07300 Mauves +33(0)475 088626

See also Crozes-Hermitage.

This is one of the stalwart, thoroughly unpretentious domaines at St-Joseph, with wonderfully located vineyards on the slopes above Mauves. Jean is the last of three brothers whose existence was always discreet, mainly because they were so often in the vines rather than entertaining in the cellar. When there were three pairs of hands, all rootstock cutting and graftings were taken from their own vines, a naturally labour-intensive activity that most people could not be bothered about back in the dog days of the equipment-obsessed 1980s.

Jean and son Jean-Claude, a willowy man in his late 30s, work "between 4.5 and 5 ha": 0.8 ha on the plain beside the village of Crozes-Hermitage, the rest at St-Joseph. There is 0.5 ha of white Marsanne planted in 1990 on the sunny site of *Les Oliviers*, the rest is Syrah. The plots are equally split between Mauves and Tournon. "For the white vines, we chose a site where there was a mix of clay and sandy granite, with some stones. It resembled Larnage in the Crozes area, which is a good white address. The alkaline helps a lot," states Jean-Claude.

Their red plots range from the *Côte des Rivoires* (1998) on the cusp between Mauves and the Tournon hill—overt granite—to *Les Oliviers*, which is a much appreciated site likely to become better known in years to come. There is granite at the bottom, but much of the soil is a clay–*galet* stone mix, which gives very rich, less tannic wines. Other noted sites are *Le Paradis* and *Le Montagnon*, just 100 metres apart. *Paradis* is firm granite, bringing tannic wines,

while *Montagnon* is more loess, making it good for whites and less tannic reds. The vines are very old—some 100 years, others 60 or 70 years.

Jean is slim and modest and flashes a friendly smile; he started work at 15 and is now nearly 70. He is most at ease discussing outdoor matters and being self-deprecating: "No, we don't usually export: we don't own any young casks for that!" The yard outside the cellar reveals a cornucopia of different items, a wonderful disorder that may occasionally be called upon for active service. A banana tree completes a jumbled, offbeat picture.

Jean likes to work in the simplest way possible—he is a true, gentle countryman. Very self-effacing, his gaze is cast away as he explains: "I want the vine to receive as few treatments and *engrais* as possible. In the cellar I also want to be natural, for example with the yeasts." He is working organically, but would cringe from ever uttering such a modish term for his decades of honest application.

Jean-Claude, shock of black hair prominent, started full-time in 1991. He is the fourth-, maybe fifth-generation winemaker in the family. The domaine started to bottle in 1970, and sticks largely to selling to private clients and the restaurant trade.

The white is vinified at between 14° and 17°C and mostly raised in stainless steel. "We always pick the white grapes quite late," comments Jean-Claude, "which is why they are full-bodied. We also tried wood with it, but aren't sure about how well it works for the white." The wine stays on light lees, with a little stirring, until bottling by September. It is hearty, overtly full wine—another example of the merit of *Les Oliviers* for the Marsanne grape. Since they switched back to natural rather than selected yeasts and reduced the lees stirring, the quality has risen.

Since 1995 they have been increasing the destalking of their Syrah crop, reaching 100 per cent in 2000 and 2002. "The consumer these days wants softer wines," states Jean Marsanne, rather sadly, as if renouncing old practices is like bidding farewell to ancient friends. "If you keep the stalks on, you have to go out and find clients for that style," he adds.

Vinification lasts three weeks in 60 per cent steel, 40 per cent open wood vats. The process is traditional, and no outside yeasts are used. Wood ageing, which lasts 12 months, has been something of a challenge here. The Marsannes use a few more 600-litre *demi-muids* than 225-litre casks for this ageing, with the youngest wood five years old. Bottling occurs after 18 months, after a brief stay in vat. Around 15,000 bottles are produced, the other half of the wine sold to nearby *négoce*.

In the past the ageing sometimes made the wines lack freshness and appear a bit rustic, a dry second half on the palate hampering enjoyment. The domaine now is in some transition, as Jean is likely to let Jean-Claude, with his Beaune studies behind him, come to the fore. But the bond and respect between father and son is commendably strong, and a revolution here would never be suitable.

These are quite rustic wines, but there is a trend towards more softness in them. They can take one back to a previous era, when the fruit and flavour were marked by wild, sometimes bosky fruit. Tannins can be tarry and a little severe. But there can also be a degree of finesse that comes from a generally laissez-faire approach in the cellar. They live quite well, if vintages like 1991 and 1986 are references—both still showing in 2001. Fatter years like 2000 will need earlier drinking. Red fruits and some pepper are often found. Dry finishes can be a concern.

ST-JOSEPH ROUGE
2004 ★★(★)
2003 ★★
2002 ★
2001 (VAT) ★★
2000 ★
1999 ★★
1998 ★★

ST-JOSEPH BLANC
2003 ★★(★)
2002 ★★
2001 ★★
2000 ★★
1999 ★

Export 5 per cent (1) USA/Switzerland

DOMAINE LAURENT MARTHOURET

Les Rôtisses 07340 Charnas +33(0)475 341591

See also Condrieu.

Broad-shouldered, good-looking, with great big pale-brown eyes, Laurent Marthouret has the easy manner of a countryman who is not surprised to suddenly host a gathering of locals when a hailstorm hits his hamlet. Bottles are opened and the chat runs gently along—upstairs there are fellow growers, downstairs there are local chums who are helping to green harvest. The late afternoon takes its course.

Laurent's father had a smallholding and sent his crop to the St-Désirat Co-opérative. Indeed, he worked on the railways, since the land did not yield enough. Since starting in 1989, Laurent has moved the domaine to making only wine now, and bottles all his crop except for a small part sold to Chapoutier and a bit of bulk sold to Jean-Louis Chave.

His St-Joseph is made from 2.5 ha of Syrah (1973, 1990) on light, granite-sandy soil and 0.5 ha of Marsanne (1989) growing on similar ground. The *vins de pays* are Marsanne, Roussanne, and Viognier for the white, Syrah for the red, growing across 3 ha on the plateau.

The reds are all destemmed, and receive an 8°C cool maceration before fermentation at up to 30°C, the whole process lasting up to four weeks. The classic, Les Rôtisses, comes from vines towards the plateau and is aged for a year in cask, 10 per cent new, the rest up to five years old. The Cuvée de Pierre, from hillside crop, receives a year in 30 per cent new oak, the rest up to two years old.

The white is oak fermented, a little of it new. "I restrict the use of new oak because this soil gives minerality already," comments Laurent. Having destemmed, he leaves the wine on its lees for some time, with low use of sulphur, and bottles it at the end of August.

The whites are well founded, and reveal character and nice richness. The reds are more strained and can lack comfortable fruit. There are signs of dryness and grilled nuts that may come from the extraction process.

Laurent is one of the three growers involved with Louis Chèze in a new vineyard at Seyssuel, north of Vienne. This will make a Syrah *vin de pays*.

ST-JOSEPH LES RÔTISSES ROUGE
2002 (CASK) ★
2001 ★

ST-JOSEPH LA CUVÉE DE PIERRE ROUGE
2002 (CASK) ★
2001 ★
2000 ★

ST-JOSEPH BLANC
2001 ★
2000 ★★
1999 ★★

Export 15 per cent (1) Belgium

PASCAL MARTHOURET

Les Coins 07340 Charnas +33(0)475 341582

A beanpole of a man with fair hair, Pascal chose 2002 for his first vintage. He works 1.8 ha of Syrah and in 2004 started to make a half Marsanne, half Roussanne white.

PIERRE MEALY

07500 Guilherand-Granges

A dark, chunky man, Pierre Mealy has worked with Sylvain Bernard since 1998. He rents a 0.2-hectare plot on *Les Rivoires* (1987) in the

commune of *Tournon*. The red is a robust, honest wine, on the evidence of the 2003.

ST-JOSEPH ROUGE
2003 (CASK) ★★

GABRIEL MEFFRE

84190 Gigondas +33(0)490 123021

See also Condrieu, Cornas, Côte-Rôtie, Crozes-Hermitage, Hermitage.
The Gigondas house works with Alain Paret in the northern area for their red Laurus. The crop is destemmed and vinified for 22 to 28 days with three pumping-overs a day, the top temperature a guarded 30°C.

Cask ageing lasts 15 to 18 months in the Paret cellars in Meffre casks of 275 litres, one-third new, the rest one to two years old. This size imparts more oak than Paret usually expects, since his preferred cask size is the more gentle 600 litres. The wine contains lively fruit, but the oak means that it needs three years or so to settle.

ST-JOSEPH LAURUS ROUGE
2002 (CASK) ★

DOMAINE FRANÇOIS MERLIN

Le Bardoux 42410 St-Michel-sur-Rhône +33(0)474 566190

See also Condrieu.
Keen and talented François Merlin works 1.2 ha of St-Joseph in addition to his Condrieu. The vineyard is on *La Voturerie*, at the north end of the Chavanay area, which makes it the most northerly vineyard in St-Joseph.

A half hectare is plateau (1968); 0.7 hectare is slope (1997) just below it. The soil is a mix of granite and sand. François has planted about 25 per cent with *massale* Syrah: "It's a small producer, and fears frost, but I want to work with it for quality. I have insurance by using clone Syrah for the rest," he adds.

He picks before 10 o'clock in the morning, and starts with a cool maceration for a couple of days. For the first five days of fermentation, there is cap punching every two hours (by day, not night!). François also pumps over, and keeps the temperature to 30°C at most. Cask ageing lasts a year in one-to-four-year-old oak. There is no fining or filtration.

Peppery black fruit that is firmly in the Chavanay style comes through, with the wine likely to gain from being put aside for around three years. This is a promising domaine.

ST-JOSEPH ROUGE
  2002 (CASK) ★★
  2001 ★★★

DOMAINE ROBERT MICHEL

Grande Rue 07130 Cornas +33(0)475 403870

See also Cornas.
Robert Michel, a longtime notable at Cornas, first made some St-Joseph in 1996. His vineyard is in the *commune* of Ardoix, west of Sarras, near the very pretty Ay Valley. Planted in 1988, the Syrah grows on dark-coloured granite with mica and quartz mixed in—very dry terrain on two sites called *Les Blâches* and *Les Devès*.

"The vineyard is at 350 metres," states Robert. "It's a lot 'colder' than Cornas, with longer winters, and is usually two to three weeks behind our Cornas vineyard—a big difference for just 30 kilometres apart." This aspect comes through in the wine, which in a tannic year like 2001 is tight when young, with pebbly, upright fruit; it merits cellaring for two or three years before it opens properly. The 2002 was a much softer wine.

Robert's half-hectare Syrah vineyard was planted in 1988 and 1990. The crop is destemmed and receives a three-week vinification and a year's ageing in a mix of 550- and 225-litre casks that run up to five years old. The wine is called "Le Bois des Blâches."

ST-JOSEPH LE BOIS DES BLÂCHES ROUGE
  2002 (CASK) ★★
  2001 ★★

PHILIPPE MICHELAS

chemin du Marquis 07300 Tournon +33(0)475 080561

Philippe Michelas is a neighbour of Elizabeth Fogier on the hillside of *Roue* at St-Jean-de-Muzols. He ferments his Syrah for two weeks and raises the wine in three-to-four-year-old casks for a year. At times one feels it could be fresher.

ST-JOSEPH LES GOUTELLES ROUGE
  2002 ★

DOMAINE MICHELAS SAINT JEMMS

Bellevue Les Chassis 26600 Mercurol +33(0)475 078670

See also Cornas, Crozes-Hermitage, Hermitage.
The Michelas family from Crozes-Hermitage work five hectares of St-Joseph—3.5 of Syrah (1980s) and 1.5 of Marsanne (1980s). The vineyards are on the loose granite of *Ste-Épine* above St-Jean-de-Muzols.

The red Sainte-Epine is fermented for around two weeks, with pumping-overs. It is aged for six to eight months in large barrels and some casks. This shows off the sinew of *Ste-Épine* in its texture, the reserve of this site, and is sound wine.

The white Sainte-Epine is fermented in enamel vats at 19°C, briefly stored, then bottled in January, the malo done. It is open and pretty in a soft year like 2002.

ST-JOSEPH SAINTE-EPINE ROUGE
  2003 ★
  2001 ★★

ST-JOSEPH SAINTE-EPINE BLANC
  2002 ★★

DOMAINE MONIER

Brunieux 07340 Saint-Désirat +33(0)475 342064

If you want to drink organic—or strictly speaking, biodynamic—family-made wines, look no further than here. Like Jean Delobre at Ferme

FIGURE 30 Wine in all its simplicity—Jean-Pierre Monier and son Guillaume in their cellar on the plateau above St-Désirat. (Author's collection)

des Sept Lunes, Jean-Pierre Monier was a member of the Co-opérative at St-Désirat until 2001. He, too, works organically, with vineyards also high up, at between 300 and 340 metres. And he, too, shows considerable promise.

His has been another mixed domaine, with the cherries and apricots gradually abandoned since they do not pay. His great-grandfather raised goats, sheep, and cows and fed them homegrown hay and beetroots. His vineyards were laid out in alternate rows of vines and peaches, an unusual configuration.

Jean-Pierre, a slim, wiry man just touching 50, started in 1977. The hybrid vines had been taken out by then, replaced by Syrah in the loose, sandy granite. He now works four hectares, all Syrah except 0.27 hectare of Marsanne, which was planted in deeper, more siliceous soil.

His wines all derive from specific plots. There are two top sites for his Syrah, each just half a hectare. *Les Serves* (1977) holds quite degraded granite, with fine particles of earth ranging from just 1 to 5 mm (up to three-sixteenths of an inch), and is very fast draining. *Terres Blanches* (1978) has some clay at 30 to 40 cm down (12 in. or more), mixed in with the granite. Roussanne is due to be planted in the near future, and there is one plateau hectare of

vin de pays—80 per cent Syrah, 20 per cent Marsanne dating from 1985.

As an organic worker, Jean-Pierre runs his vineyard with thoughtful care. It is south-south-east facing on slopes and can be tractor worked. "We actively nourish the vineyard," he explains, "say with 4 gm of silica [silicon dioxide] twice a year, applied to the soil, the leaves, and the air according to the phases of the moon and 'fruit days' on my biodynamic calendar." To encourage root growth, a brew of cow dung is used, for instance.

He follows the writings of Maria Thun, who has spent 40 years studying and experimenting on this subject. A grated-horn solution is also applied three of four times a year to develop the humus in the soil; this is done from his tractor.

One can only be pleased to meet such a person. Here he is in a tucked-away area of a middle-ranking *appellation*, exercising the greatest consideration for a pure development of the soil and natural qualities of his vineyard. His quiet rationale and self-assurance about his work are commendable, and it's pleasing to hear that his son Samuel, in his early 20s, is studying at Beaune, prepared to take over the baton one day.

Jean-Pierre, an easy smiler with a friendly face, recounts how he used to be regarded by the villagers of St-Désirat down below on the plain. "We depend on St-Désirat," he says, "but when I was at school down there, they would call me or anyone from up here at Brunieux a *bouseux*—yokel, or cow patter! They were prosperous from their fruit crops, especially cherries, and parents didn't want their children to play with children from the poorer plateau. Mind you, our name for St-Désirat is 'Le Petit Nice.'"

Because the soil is worked from March onwards, it is left alone after mid-August, with grass growing between the rows. Any weeds are removed the following March. The middle of August sees green harvesting of up to half the crop, since the Moniers are adamant about low yields, aiming for 25 hl/ha. "Our 3309 rootstocks with the clones are too productive," states Jean-Pierre. "So we're planting Richter on our *massale* selection cuttings taken from old local Syrah."

Harvesting is largely a family affair: Jean-Pierre vinifies on his own, while his wife, Carnation, dark and Spanish, covers all the office work. Fermentation is in concrete, and for the moment the crop is destalked. There are no external yeasts, "because we don't yeast," says Jean-Pierre; "we have different aromas according to their *terroir*, but also due to the climate pattern of the year."

He starts with a six-day cool, 10° to 12°C maceration, then heats to 25° to 30°C for a three-week fermentation. Daily cap punching is done, and perhaps one partial decantation and refill of the vats—a *délestage*—to encourage fermentation of the later-progressing areas in the vat.

The wine spends 11 months in cask, 20 per cent new and 80 per cent two to three years old. There is no racking, so the wine stays on its fine lees until a light filtration before the October bottling. The white was first made in 2002: this, too, is fermented in 20 per cent new, 80 per cent older oak.

The classic red, or Tradition, made when the crop size is regular, comes from around five different plots. Of the top two reds, Terres Blanches is intended as a longer-lived wine. This, in particular, benefits from decanting: it

has a full, quite southern aroma in a good year like 2001 and some well-muscled fruit. A bottle tasted when already open for eight days was still very fine.

The Les Serves carries soft black fruit—a gentle wine that usually drinks well early on. Its fruit texture is very clear and agreeable in a tricky vintage like 2002, while the 2003 carried more scale and power.

ST-JOSEPH TRADITION ROUGE
  2002 ★

ST-JOSEPH LES SERVES ROUGE
  2003 ★★(★)
  2002 ★★
  2001 ★★

ST-JOSEPH LES TERRES BLANCHES ROUGE
  2003 ★★★
  2001 ★★★

ST-JOSEPH BLANC
  2002 ★

Export 5 per cent (1) Switzerland

DOMAINE DU MONTEILLET, STÉPHANE MONTEZ

Le Montelier 42410 Chavanay +33(0)474 872457

See also Condrieu, Côte-Rôtie.

The drive to this windswept domaine on top of its outer Pilat plateau—impressive broad views lancing down to the Rhône below, flocks of goats tinkling their bells—does not prepare the visitor for the fevered state of activity once inside it. Here works Stéphane Montez, whom some friends must call the Whirlwind, the original man in a hurry, projects tumbling forth from his person.

The family's granite stone farm, the farm machinery, the sheep, goats, the Rigottes cheese, the moorland feel—all give the clue that wine used not to be the only activity here. Ten generations of Montez have lived here,

FIGURE 31 Go Go! Stéphane Montez knows only one speed—fast. Here on the plateau next to his domaine above the Rhône. (Author's collection)

making some wine since 1712. Stéphane's father, Antoine, now approaching 60, started work at 17, with an emphasis on peaches and plums, the latter sold to the Jura to make tarts.

Antoine had around three hectares of vines in the St-Joseph area, and sold their crop to the largely fruit-processing Co-opérative of Péage-de-Roussillon. His wife, Monique, recalled that he also grew what the locals called "Cugnette," the Clairette de Chavanay, which was made into a semisweet wine "and sold like hot cakes" to private customers and cafés. This was stopped around 1975.

Stéphane likes to crack quick jokes and is constantly on the move, except when he has had an operation on his knee ligaments. Even then, he discharges himself from the recuperation centre after only one of the five weeks— "too much to do here," he says, shifting on his crutches.

Dark, with brown eyes, he is a sparky person, prepared to deliver a few bottles personally to the one-star restaurant in Tain, or investigate a Châteauneuf-du-Pape tasting in Avignon. The third child, he has hit 30 and is the one interested in making wine, while his brother

Christophe is the writer on it, having published theses on the region's past wine structures for the University of Lyon.

His Syrah runs over 5.5 ha, and averages around 20 years old, the oldest dating from the 1960s. The soil here is stony granite, the granite decomposed under the surface. The white St-Joseph is taken from 0.7 ha of Marsanne (1980, 1990) and 0.5 ha of Roussanne (1999). Since 2004 he has also bought the crop of another four extra hectares after his neighbour's suicide.

His route in coming home to work has been more varied than those of most of his neighbours, and his leaning towards modern vinification methods and overt oak use reflects this. "I studied for five years at Mâcon," he explains in his rapid way, "then moved on via Switzerland to Dorking in England and the Denbies Wine Estate, where I spent four months." Living in England opened his eyes to the New World, and how inexpensive were their wines, so Australia was the next step, with six months at Brown Brothers north of Melbourne.

On the travel went—the Barossa and Hunter valleys, five months at Joseph Phelps in the Napa, five months at Stellenbosch, and finally back to Chavanay for the 1997 vintage. "I live from day to day," he says, "so the travel was often linked from one suggestion or contact to the next."

His vineyard work involves grassing 70 per cent of the rows between the vines and rotivating them. Dung comes from their sheep and goats. Young vines are placed on terraces, especially for his Côte-Rôtie and Condrieu. "The best *terroir* represents a combination of soil, subsoil, sun, micro-climate, the grape variety, the reverberation of the sun off the stones, and the person," is how he sees matters.

There are four red St-Josephs, their Syrah destalked since 1990, encouraged by the success in destalking their hailed-on crop of 1986. Vinification lasts three weeks in steel, with cap punching; the juice spends five days at 23°C and is then heated to 30°C.

The simple or classic red, just called "Domaine du Monteillet," is taken from vines dating between 1986 and 2000 on *Montelier* and *Mève*; the traditional red, La Cabriole, is from four main sites—*Montelier, Blanchard, Champaillère,* and *Ribaudy,* the Syrah dating between 1988 and 2000. Both wines are raised for 15 months in four-year-old casks. The Cabriole can require three years to integrate and settle; the Monteillet is for early drinking, with black fruits prominent rather than any great depth.

The Fortior wine is mainly from *Blanchard,* where the granite-based slope is steep but the soil a little deeper than on *Montelier.* Its Syrah dates from the 1970s, and the wine is aged for two years in between 40 and 60 per cent new oak, the difference made up of casks that are one to three years old. Three-quarters of the new-oak casks are in the 580-litre *demi-muid* size. "I like this size—I rely on one barrel maker whom I trust implicitly," Stéphane says, "and it's a size that makes the wine less dry than the small casks." He has even arranged a two-tier system and lifting mechanism for the *demi-muids,* which of course are not easy to move.

Fortior is a wine with a direct style of fruit, and an evident modern character in the more potent years through the oaking. The 2002, a more restrained vintage, showed the fruit in a live, persistent form that was very agreeable.

The top red Cuvée du Papy is made mostly from early-1970s Syrah on *Chanson,* where the steep hill is terraced, and on *Verlieu.* It is aged for two years in up to 60 per cent new oak, with 40 per cent in one-to-three-year-old casks. There is no fining, and a light filtration if a little deposit is left behind. *Papy* bears rich black fruit at its heart, but always needs around five years to shake off its oak overlay if the drinker seeks a balanced flavour. Constructed in the modern way, it regains some of its roots if left to age.

There are two whites; the classic is 75 per cent Marsanne (1970s) off the *Boissey* site south of Chavanay, 25 per cent Roussanne (1998) from two sites, *Mève* and *Montelier*—the former north of Chavanay (also allowed to grow Condrieu Viognier), the latter beside the domaine and now sanded after the rock on it was ground down during the 1998 excavations. This is raised in casks aged one to two years for 10 months, with lees stirring. In a vintage like 2003, it is fat and wholesome with some power. The oak is lightly noticeable in the first couple of years.

La Cabriole *blanc* is 85 per cent Marsanne (1980), 15 per cent Roussanne (2000) from the *Mève* and *Blanchard* sites. It receives the same 10 months in cask as the classic.

Stéphane's *vin de pays* is called "Les Hauts de Monteillet"; part of this is made with 1959 Syrah growing in Côtes du Rhône vineyards near St-Michel-sur-Rhône, the rest with young *appellation* vine fruit. It is aged in six-year-old *demi-muids.* There can be a Viognier or Roussanne, as well, should there be any young vines.

ST-JOSEPH DOMAINE DU MONTEILLET ROUGE
2001 ★
2000 ★★

ST-JOSEPH LA CABRIOLE ROUGE
2001 ★ Jam-style black fruit aroma; even *cassis* fruit flavour, oaked towards end. Can open up. 2008–09.

ST-JOSEPH FORTIOR ROUGE
2002 ★★★
2000 ★

ST-JOSEPH CUVÉE DU PAPY ROUGE
2003 (CASKS) ★★★ Rich heart in bouquet. Good black jam fruit on palate, agreeable, has length. Some final sweetness, but overall possesses grip. From 2008; 2016–19.

2002 ★★★ Decent, complete, broad bouquet—truffly/smoky. Sound body on palate—is coming together. Clean, northern zone black fruit, some richness. Leave till 2007 to absorb the oak; 2015–16.

2001 (CASK) ★★ Broad, oak smoke nose; good matter inside the oak, from 2007. Firm at this stage. 2012–14.

2000 ★★ Smooth black aroma; *cassis* go-stop-go on palate. Needs to settle; "made to keep." 2011–12.

1999 ★ Mint/leaf, black jam bouquet—softens with air. Clear fruit, spice edges, then dries. Two hours air, and it crumbles, gets taut, loses flesh.

ST-JOSEPH DOMAINE DU MONTEILLET BLANC
2003 ★★★
2001 ★★

Export 50 per cent (1) Great Britain, (2) Russia, (3) Ireland/Switzerland

DOMAINE DIDIER MORION

Épitaillon 42410 Chavanay +33(0)474 872633

See also Condrieu.
Small and fair, with a Celtic look about him that is quite often found on the west-bank plateau around the Ardèche and Loire *départements*, Didier Morion always wanted to work outdoors. His family raised animals and grew cereal and fruit, and his grandfather made his own wine. Didier saw wine as the way forward and went off to Belleville in the Beaujolais to study it.

Having commenced with 2.5 hectares of Syrah, M. Morion now works six hectares of Syrah at St-Joseph, led by plots on the Chavanay sites of *Mève* and *La Ruty*; both contain decomposed granite that drains quickly after rain. With a little planting every year, the Syrah dates from 2004 back to 1968. There is also half a hectare of Marsanne (1986) on *La Ruty*.

The red crop is 80 per cent destalked, and two wines are made; the classic is raised 60 per cent in three-to-six-year-old casks for 10 to 12 months, and the special Les Echets, from the granite-stony site near the Malleval-to-Chavanay road, receives 15 months in casks ranging from new to three years old. The pure-Marsanne white is fermented and raised half in vat, half in one-to-four-year-old casks, and is bottled by June, its malo completed. Its lees are stirred during the raising period.

M. Morion also makes a Syrah *vin de pays des Collines Rhodaniennes* from two hectares on the plateau.

ST-JOSEPH ROUGE
2003 ★★

ST-JOSEPH LES ECHETS ROUGE
2003 ★

ST-JOSEPH BLANC
2004 ★★

DOMAINE DU MORTIER

Le Mortier 07340 St-Désirat +33(0)475 342305

This domaine moved on to making St-Joseph in 1982, under Guy Veyrier, who is now in his late 50s. Before that, the wine from their 1972 Syrah had been sold in bulk, along with their wine from hybrid vines.

The vineyards are all in the *commune* of St-Désirat, which is dominated by the local Co-opérative. There are 5.7 ha of Syrah (1972, 1985, 2000) and 0.8 ha of Marsanne with a splash of recent Roussanne.

The impetus here shifted in 1997 with the arrival of the independent-minded nephew, Didier Crouzet. Tall and well built, he has a dry sense of humour, which no doubt stood him in good stead in his previous work in the social services for children in Lyon.

"I changed when I was 30," he says, "and went back to school in Mâcon, which I found stimulating." That was in 1998, and he now regards the vineyards as both his work and his sporting leisure. "Put a 25 kg [55 lb.] spray machine on your back, and you'll know you've been sporting!" he laughs.

Didier has quietly reduced the amount of treatments, and now turns the soil around the base of the vines with a pickaxe and uses no insecticides. He has to continue with weed-killing, however—doing this manually is too much for him and his one full-time helper.

The soil is loose, often sandy granite with gneiss in parts, and the vineyards are 80 per cent terrace, demanding manual working. The more recent terracing contains wire training for the vines, while the older vines are attached to stakes. The highest plateau vines, around 300 metres, also ripen about two weeks behind his full south–facing slope areas.

Didier became involved in the vinification from 1996. He destems up to 80 per cent of the Syrah according to ripeness and works only with natural yeasts. He starts with a cool, 6°C maceration and has been trying to work some vats without sulphur. Vinification lasts up to five weeks, with a maximum temperature of only 28° to 30°C after the cool start. Ageing runs over a year, half in new to four-year-old casks, half in vat. There is no filtration on the red.

It's refreshing to find someone with an off-centre optic here, willing to back his own judgment rather than follow the fashion around him. These are well-made, individual wines of a good, consistent level and well-expressed fruiti-ness. They can live well for around 10 years.

The white is fermented in new oak between 12° and 15°C and stays on its lees until May, usu-ally once the malo has finished. It is bottled after one year. Its white fruits are agreeable, with a lit-tle depth.

There are 2.5 ha of *vin de pays des Collines Rhodaniennes*; this is largely Syrah (1988), with some Gamay (1998), growing on the plain. These wines are not oaked. The Syrah is pep-pered, and shows an assured black fruit texture; it can also age nicely over six or more years.

ST-JOSEPH ROUGE
   2002 (CASK) ★
   2001 ★★
   2000 ★★
   1999 ★★★

ST-JOSEPH BLANC
   2002 (VAT) ★
   2001 (VAT) ★

Export 30 per cent (1) Germany, (2) Great Britain, (3) Belgium

DOMAINE STÉPHANE OTHEGUY

Chemin Chez Maurice 38138 Les Côtes d'Arey
+33(0)474 589443

See also Condrieu, Cote-Rôtie.
Stéphane Otheguy, the successor to Vincent Gasse of Côte-Rôtie, has continued with M. Gasse's small 0.3 ha St-Joseph Syrah vineyard (1983) at Malleval. It is worked organically.

The crop is mostly destalked, and after pre-fermentation cooling, it ferments for two weeks or so, with manual punching down and some pumping-over. Naturally, no outside yeasts are used. Ageing is in casks at least two years old and lasts up to two years. There is neither fining nor filtration.

DOMAINE ALAIN PARET

place de l'Eglise 42520 Saint-Pierre-de-Boeuf
+33(0)474 871209

See also Condrieu.
Alain Paret came into wine aged 23, after his father died in 1972. The influences on him before then had been diverse, even though his family grew fruit trees, notably cherries, and sold coal. "We were from St-Pierre-de-Boeuf, and even though my education was to be an accountant, I had the virus of the soil in my

blood," he says. "My parents were determined that I should have the accountancy option, but it was left on one side after my father died."

He was also fascinated by big machinery and bulldozers. So, when buying an abandoned vineyard at Malleval, he was able to excavate it quickly and cheaply. "In those days land was still cheap—I recall it around 5,000 francs (US$850) per hectare!" he explains. "This was for sites that grew vines in the 1850s and over the years had been left as people perished in the wars, and then others, in the 1960s and 1970s, left to work in the chemical factories around here."

The first hectare was on the *Coteau de Rochecourbe*, at the southern entrance to Malleval, planted in 1974, not a prosperous time. "No one really wanted this plot—it was almost given away," Alain recalls. A nice-looking man, with an open face, light-brown eyes, and gently greying hair, he explains that the vineyard had lain abandoned after the Second World War as the men went to work in factories like Rhône-Poulenc nearby.

Since then it has been expanded to 15 hectares, with a little under a hectare of Marsanne in it. This is deliberately picked and vinified with the Syrah to boost richness and alcohol in the wine. The soil here is quite hard granite, the site is sheltered from the north wind, and the vines average 20 years old.

In the early 1980s Alain moved into Condrieu by sharing a seven-hectare vineyard with France's leading cinema actor, Gérard Depardieu. Since then he has moved on to Languedoc and joint ventures in the southern Rhône. One can sense the palpable relief that his son Anthony has joined him full-time. Even though he moves around the cellar at speed, he is 55, "my legs are tired," and he had been considering giving up. "Anthony was a successful mason but at 23 caught the wine virus, and now he's 26, has done all the exams, and is here!" says Alain.

In 2001 he stopped using insecticides, and has grown grass on his lower slopes to restrict erosion. Half a dozen sorts are grown, adapted to granite slopes. "I'm conscious, though, that in drought years like 2003 the grass competes

with the vines for moisture, and there's the possibility of a taste of nitrogen from the grass. But against that, you also allow rain to penetrate more easily, and the vine roots search lower down for any humidity," he comments in his fast-talking style.

The Syrah has been destalked since 1996, after urging from the USA market. "The market leads the maker, and I have to follow, so the wines are more rounded, but I wasn't fully in favour," comments Alain. The fermentation process lasts about three weeks, at up to 28°C, with automatic *remontages,* or pumping-overs of the vats. Since 1999 Alain has also exercised a partial emptying and refilling of the vats (*délestage*). "It allows you to free up the colouring matter and the tannins, and brings a gain in oxygen, to counteract any Syrah reduction smells," he observes. He is also a practitioner of the fashionable *micro-bullage,* which injects oxygen into the cask to save on having to rack it. "It also preserves the lees for longer, and you don't have to use sulphur dioxide," is how Alain views it.

M. Paret likes to keep experimenting and is using more 600-litre casks for his ageing—"the aromas last better, and the wines are more sprightly." The different reds each receive their own precise cask raising. The fruit-forward Syrah cuvée is Les Pieds Dendés. It is taken from *Les Tavardes,* where the soil at the top of the slope is sandy, and the wine from it soft. This receives eight months in a mix of vat and oak, the casks varying between 225 and 600 litres.

The red St-Joseph Les Larmes du Père is from the *Rochecourbe* hillside; about 80 per cent is stored for 12 to 14 months in one-third each new, one-year-, and two-year-old oak; the rest is vat raised. It shows leathery/oily aspects on the bouquet and has a sound local feel.

The red Cuvée 420 Nuits comes from *Rochecourbe* as well. It is aged in new *demi-muids* for 420 nights, a little longer than the *Larmes du Père,* following the custom of Alain's grandfather. The aim here is for a long-keeping wine, a policy enhanced by the use of the *demi-muids* rather than smaller casks. If the year is ripe enough to be naturally juicy, this modern-style wine works well. *420 Nuits* is capable of a seven-to-11-year life. Like all the reds, it is fined and lightly filtered.

Alain also sells around 100 hl of his St-Joseph to Gabriel Meffre at Gigondas for their Laurus wine. Meffre send their own 275-litre casks to him for its one-year ageing. The Cuvée Laurus is taken from selected plots, the grapes chosen on the vine.

The white St-Joseph Les Larmes du Père (2,500 bottles) is 80 per cent Marsanne, 20 per cent Roussanne. It, too, comes from the *Rochecourbe* hillside at Malleval. It is cask fermented in two-year-old oak at up to 18°C, then raised until a May/June bottling, with lees stirring. Alain finds this difficult to sell locally—"everyone wants Viognier."

His Côtes du Rhône Valvigneyre red is made from Syrah off the crumbly granite at nearby Limony. Two-thirds is aged for eight to 12 months in two-to-three-year-old casks. This works well at present, but plans are afoot to make the tannins softer and more modern. There are also a Syrah rosé and Marsanne white of Valvigneyre, taken from vines above the *appellation* zone.

Alain shares a Côtes-du-Rhône Villages with a friend at Laudun in the southern Rhône, Innocent VI. This is 90 per cent Syrah, 10 per cent Grenache. It receives eight to 12 months in two-year-old *demi-muids*.

This is not his only southern venture. There is also his domaine at Cournonsec in the Languedoc, 15 minutes from Montpellier, near Bouzigues. Here there are 53 ha of Syrah, Merlot, and Cabernet Sauvignon and 7 ha of Viognier, planted in 1989 on a plateau at 250 metres. The vineyard is covered in the rolled stones of the Cevennes mountains.

Le Cinquet is a pure Syrah, raised 60 per cent in vat, 40 per cent in cask. Pastourou is a dry white wine for men, and Pastourelle is a sweet white wine for women—stereotyping, or what?!—both from the Viognier. Part of these Viogniers are cask aged, and a lot is sold to Great Britain and Denmark.

There is also a *vin de pays d'Oc* Viognier Pastourou, its vineyard dating from 1995, the cuttings for it supplied from the old nursery in Limony. It is not yet inspiring.

ST-JOSEPH LES LARMES DU PÈRE ROUGE
    2002 (CASKS) ★★
    2001 ★★

ST-JOSEPH 420 NUITS ROUGE
    2002 (CASKS) ★
    2001 ★★

Export 70 per cent (1) Japan, (2) USA, (3) Great Britain

DOMAINE VINCENT PARIS

chemin des Peyrouses 07130 Cornas
+33(0)475 401304

See also Cornas.
Vincent Paris' vineyard is, like his uncle Robert Michel's, in Ardoix, a granite valley west of Sarras. He planted just under a hectare here on the *Quartier de Corme* in his debut year of 1997.

The crop is destalked, and fermented over two to three weeks. The wine is half vat raised, half cask aged for a year, the casks dating from two to 10 years old. There is no fining or filtration.

"I'm seeking a wine that is easy to drink," he comments accurately, since his wine contains springy, live fruit; "I'm located north of the main St-Joseph area, and high up, around 300 metres, so I'm not trying for big-scale wine."

ST-JOSEPH ROUGE
    2002 (VAT/CASK) ★
    2001 ★★
    2000 ★

CAVE LES VIGNERONS RHODANIENS, PÉAGE-DE-ROUSSILLON

35 rue du Port-Vieux 38550 Le Péage-de-Roussillon
+33(0)474 862069

This is a very low-key Co-opérative that has around 50 hectares of St-Joseph and Condrieu in production. There are both red and white St-Joseph.

DOMAINE ANDRÉ PERRET

RN86 Verlieu 42410 Chavanay +33(0)474 872474

See also Condrieu.

In 2000 André revived an old vineyard that his father had been obliged to abandon in 1950 because he lacked the time to work it. This 0.45 ha is set on a series of steep, small terraces at *Les Bruyères-sur-Verlieu,* the soil composed of a slippery granite topsoil, with quartz and sandy elements. This has been a stimulating project for him, the sense that his own imprint will be, on the hillside, an important one for him. For the moment, its crop enters the classic red, but will be bottled on its own in years to come.

He now works 4.5 ha of Syrah and 0.58 ha of white St-Joseph, split 50 per cent Marsanne (1982), 50 per cent Roussanne (1963), both at Chavanay. The main Syrah sites are *Grisières* (1920s, 1960s), *Les Rivoires* (light, decomposed *gore* that can suffer in drought), and *Chanson* (clay-sand on top of a schist couch). The last two were planted in 1982.

There are two reds, a classic and the old-vine Grisières. The Syrah crop is steel-vat vinified after a full destemming and a premaceration cooling at 14°C. Fermentation and maceration run for three weeks, the top temperature held at 28° to 30°C.

André has become an active cellar interventionist, and on some wines like his red Côtes du Rhône, which is sold locally, that can lead to disappointment—the wine drying and becoming vacant after only an hour or so. Recently there have been pumping-overs, cap punching, and *délestages* (partial emptying and refilling of the vat) "for better fruit extraction and because I worry about the Syrah reducing and making the aromas too animal."

The classic red is aged for a year in oak—10 to 15 per cent new casks, the rest four to six years old. It is bottled in two stages. The *Grisières* is aged for 18 months in anywhere between 20 and 50 per cent new oak, the rest one to three years old. Both wines are lightly fined and filtered.

Les Grisières is chosen by tasting. It has been made since 1988. "But the plots are similar each year," comments André, "from a mix of 40-to-70-year-old Syrah at Chavanay." Its alias is the Vieilles Vignes Cuvée. There are 4,000 bottles of this, which I would term a connoisseur's wine, not an overt crowd pleaser: it is tight and withdrawn when young, but usually carries the potential to develop and broaden away from its early berried fruit. None was made in 2002 because of the dicey vintage.

These St-Joseph reds usually have good grip and are structured to age well. Their texture is the typical dry style of black fruit from the northern St-Joseph reaches around Chavanay; in really ripe years like 1999, this fruit shrugs off some of its reserve and can be absolutely delicious.

The wines can be demanding when young, with evident tannins. I find that they greatly reward patience and have generally become more consistent in recent years. André admits that "since 1990 I have put in great effort on the reds." My worry for the future is overextraction, which may lead to taut and "me-too" grilled and roasted features.

The white wine's composition varies with the vintage; the 2000 was 60 per cent Marsanne, 40 per cent Roussanne, the 1999 50-50. The ratio changes according to the respective maturities of the two varieties. In 1999 and 2003 André assembled the Marsanne and Roussanne before their fermentation: "I had been finding that the Marsanne became reduced after a year or two, so included the Roussanne at that stage for freshness," he comments. André is a fan of the Roussanne, and its proportion is high because he finds it brings finesse, is more floral and less heavy than the Marsanne on its own.

The white is generally vinified one-third in oak, two-thirds in steel, but in small-quantity years like 2003, it is all oak treated. The new-oak proportion runs to 20 per cent, the balance one to four years old. Since 2000 the fermentation has been nearer 18°C than 20°C, with a new cooling system installed: this is considered to have brought a gain in finesse. Bottled after a year, the malolactic done, it is one of the leading St-Joseph whites, with good respect for the style of the vintage.

ST-JOSEPH ROUGE

2004 (CASK) ★★

2003 ★★

2002 ★

2001 ★★★

2000 ★

1999 ★★

1998 ★

ST-JOSEPH LES GRISIÈRES ROUGE

2003 ★★★ Warm, broad bouquet—violets, scented black jam, truffly. Has moved on from straight grilled aromas. Lot of warmth, richness, and roundness. Tannins thoroughly integrated; the shape is *gourmand*. Can drink well consistently, but leave till 2007 for more expression. 2014–16. Last tasted March 2005.

2001 ★★★ Solid dark *cassis* fruit, earth/animal nose; meaty, oaked wine, live with guts. Quite complex. Length to grow. 2013–15.

2000 ★★★ Quite dark; oily, ripe fruit nose. Rounded palate, has sap but also bite—good pedigree. Reserved when young. 2010–12.

1999 ★★★★ Rich aroma, deep. Great fruit, lovely straightaway, *cassis* flavours. Some tannin. Well-structured. 2010–13.

1998 ★★

1997 ★

1996 ★★

ST-JOSEPH BLANC

2003 ★★★

2001 ★★★

2000 ★★★

DOMAINE CHRISTOPHE PICHON

Le Grand Val Verlieu 42410 Chavanay +33(0)474 870678

See also Condrieu, Côte-Rotie.

Christophe Pichon works 1.7 ha at St-Joseph, a holding accumulated over the years and based around his father's single hectare planted between 1977 and 1979 near the family home at Verlieu.

One-tenth of a hectare was planted in 1990, the rest between 1999 and 2001. The Syrah vines all stand inside the Condrieu *appellation* zone on the *Verlieux lieu-dit*, as they are entitled to, and grow on the typical granite, with outcrops of clay. They are mainly on the midslopes, with the complement on the top slopes. The new plantations have brought with them the need for more access roads recently, involving extra hard work. The preferred subplot for the Pichons is what they call *La Palisse*, a prime midslope vineyard that was planted around 1997.

The crop is 80 to 100 per cent destalked, crushed, and fermented in steel vats after three to six days at 12°C. The vinification lasts 20 to 30 days, with *remontages* and *pigeages*. Ageing lasts a year in casks that are one to two years old. Fining and a light filtration are done. Around 7,000 bottles are made. The wine holds the rather upright style of black fruit that is typical of the Chavanay zone, and can be drunk from three years on in the best vintages.

ST-JOSEPH ROUGE

2004 ★★

2003 ★★

2002 ★

2001 ★★

DOMAINE DE PIERRE BLANCHE

RN 86 Chanson 42410 Chavanay +33(0)477 572959

See also Condrieu, Côte-Rôtie.

A conversion on the road to Rome, here. Michel Mourier's family had been *négociants* for four generations, but the extension of the St-Joseph vineyard zone in 1989 gave him the chance to break out and become a vineyard owner and producer.

"I'm pleased to have built up something," he says in his soft tone. He has the look of a tall, calm, bearded teacher, perhaps the master in charge of choristers, and at a distance appears better suited to the gravitas of growing vines than of hustling bottle sales for a merchant business.

With his son Xavier keen to make wine, the impulsion was there to move along as owners. The domaine now consists of 10 hectares of St-Joseph, eight in Syrah and two split 80 per cent Marsanne and 20 per cent Roussanne. The vines were all planted by father and son on previously overgrown sites, and are naturally young, the oldest Syrah dating from 1990, the whites from 1993. The soil is generally granite, with a touch of loess in places. The Mouriers also own a small vineyard at Condrieu.

The reds were half destemmed in 2002 for the first time, and are vinified in glass-lined concrete vats over three weeks with *pigeages* and *remontages*. Ageing lasts 12 months in casks that range from new to six years old. Fining and filtration are done.

His top red, Cep d'Or, comes from the very granite *Coteau de Rochecourbe* at Malleval, a steep, two-hectare vineyard that rises from 125 to 280 metres. This wine stays in cask for 20 months, the oak ranging from new to six years old. Cep d'Or performed very well in the slightly awkward year of 2000—full of oily, lasting fruit.

The white is fermented and raised in oak that also runs from new to six years old (new therefore is 15 per cent). Lees stirring occurs early on. Bottling is around June, once the malo has been done. It is fat and buttery, a sound wine.

ST-JOSEPH ROUGE
  2001 (CASK) ★

ST-JOSEPH CEP D'OR ROUGE
  2000 ★★★

ST-JOSEPH BLANC
  2001 ★★

Export 25 per cent (1) Belgium, (2) Switzerland, (3) Great Britain

DOMAINE PRADELLE

Le Village 26600 Chanos-Curson +33(0)475 073100

See also Crozes-Hermitage.

Brothers Jacques and Jean-Louis Pradelle from Crozes-Hermitage have made a red St-Joseph since 1990. This is from a half hectare at Arras, almost straight across the Rhône from them.

They planted this Syrah vineyard in 1986, on an easterly-facing slope that mixes granite and alluvial stones. The wine is aged for just over a year in barrel, and 2,500 bottles are made.

DAVID RAYDON

rue du Midi 07300 Glun +33(0)475 088871

Glun seems to slip through the net in despatches from the St-Joseph front; vineyards there are often worked by outsiders like Sylvain Bernard of St-Péray, and some of the land was also given over to apricots in the 1970s as wine was not deemed economical.

David Raydon arrived here in 1995 and set up on his own in 2000. He is from Vallon Pont d'Arc in the southern Ardèche, but his wife's parents are from Glun, where they worked both fruit and vines. "My wife's grandfather would ride his horse to Valence to sell his *vin de pays*, a whole day's work," he recounts, "and the cellar here has been in use since at least the 1950s."

A slim man with curly black hair, he works 1.5 ha of Syrah; "Glun was never reputed for its whites," he adds. There are two plots: 0.6 ha on *Le Pont* (1998) to the south of the village, an east-facing terraced site on stony, decomposed granite; and 0.9 ha on *Le Grayzard* (1996), a flatter site at the bottom of the slope.

Born in 1971, David did not mark out wine as his first destination; he was an industrial designer for three years, but found that it wasn't for him. "I preferred to work outside," he says; when one sees his none-too-robust frame, it's clear he didn't take the soft option.

A sense of quiet keenness is given out. Holidays as a boy with his uncle on his seven-hectare vineyard in the Ardèche influenced him, and when a student in England for a year, he spent his evenings gardening in old people's homes.

Vineyard treatments are organic, with just one weedkiller application. The harvest is manual, ripe crop sought. Whole bunches are foot crushed, and the vinification process lasts two to three weeks. David states that in 2004 he stopped using external yeasts, and also restricts his sulphur use in the cellar—so is clearly making efforts to work as naturally as possible.

There are pumping-overs at first, then cap punchings, the top temperature cut back to around 32°C since 2000. Cask raising lasts 16 to 18 months in two-to-eight-year-old casks, and there is no fining or filtration. The production is moving from 5,000 to 8,000 bottles over time—all the wine sold this way to private customers.

The 2001 was markedly better than the 2002 and showed the brambly, supple fruit of the southern St-Joseph sector—an agreeable wine with pleasant tannic content.

ST-JOSEPH ROUGE
2001 ★★

DOMAINE DES REMIZIÈRES

route de Romans 26600 Mercurol +33(0)475 074428

See also Crozes-Hermitage, Hermitage.
This extremely consistent domaine is best known for its Crozes and Hermitage, which have been reliable, if lately overtly oaked, wines for many years. Their St-Joseph was first made in 1997, the core vineyard being a rented two hectares on *Les Eygas* at Sécheras, where the granite is marked, the Syrah dating from the mid-1960s. This was augmented by a half hectare planted in 2000 on the decomposed granite of *Le Grand Pont* at St-Jean-de-Muzols. There is also enough Marsanne and Roussanne for a barrel of the white, split 70 per cent–30 per cent respectively.

The red is destalked, and fermented in concrete vats with some *remontages*. It is aged in 40 per cent new oak, 60 per cent one-year-old casks

for 12 to 16 months. There is a light fining but no filtration. It can show tangy black fruit, but is also rendered dry at times by the oak.

In 2003 a special, even more oaked cuvée, L'Essentiel, was made, raised for 15 months in 60 per cent new oak, 40 per cent one-year-old oak. It was a one-off to reflect the richness of the vintage, and presumably, its powers of dealing with oak.

ST-JOSEPH ROUGE
2004 (CASK) ★★

ST-JOSEPH L'ESSENTIEL ROUGE
2003 ★★(★)

HERVÉ ET MARIE-THÉRÈSE RICHARD

RN86 Verlieu 42410 Chavanay +33(0)474 870775

See also Condrieu.
This is a progressive domaine that has stayed low profile for many years due to its continuing involvement with fruits. The father, Martial, a small, chirpy man who retired in 1992, had largely worked on the plain beside the Rhône growing grapes to make table wines and cultivating apricots, plums, pears, and cherries.

His son Hervé planted vineyards in Condrieu and St-Joseph from 1983, and now works four hectares of the latter, including 0.6 hectare of white (80 per cent Marsanne, 20 per cent Roussanne). His sites are mainly around Chavanay—*La Côte, Le Pêcher, La Pension*, and *Les Nouelles*, the last a vineyard dating from 1968 and used for his Vieilles Vignes wine, called "Les Nuelles."

He set up full-time in 1989, and makes a white and two reds, the classic and Les Nuelles. The Syrah has been mostly destalked since 1993—"for finer, franker wines." No external yeasts are used, and vinification is in steel or fibreglass for 15 to 21 days, at around 28°C, with a maximum of 30° to 32°C. Ageing lasts 12 to 15 months for the classic and two years for the *Nuelles*. "We're not inclined towards new oak," states Hervé, slight with sandy fair hair. "So we stick to only 10 per cent on the *Nuelles*, the rest of the casks up to 10 years old." There is no filtration. The *Nuelles* shows clear, likeable fruit, an unhurried wine that can show nicely for around 10 years.

Destalking of the white grapes is becoming more commonplace. The crop starts its fermentation in vat until a specific gravity of 1020, when 20 to 30 per cent is placed in oak, one-tenth of it new. It is bottled in August, the malo done. Hazelnuts, apricot, and quiet richness are in evidence here.

Hervé is self-taught, topped up by an accelerated wine course in 1986. Marie-Thérèse, blessed with jet-black hair and dark features, also learnt on the ground. Together they like to do their own thing and not rely on too much outside advice from *oenologues*. "We want to express the *terroir*," he says, "and finesse is a good element in that."

ST-JOSEPH LES NUELLES ROUGE

    2002 ★★★
    2001 ★★
    2000 ★★

ST-JOSEPH BLANC

    2002 ★★
    2001 ★★
    2000 ★★

Export 20 per cent (1) Belgium, (2) Great Britain, (3) Japan/USA

GILLES ROBIN

Les Chassis Sud 26600 Mercurol +33(0)475 084328

See also Crozes-Hermitage.
Better known for his Crozes, Gilles works a rented 0.2 ha vineyard of Syrah (1966) between the *Berceau* and *Rivoires* sites at Tournon. The soil is dry, decomposed granite. There is enough crop for two casks; this receives whole-bunch fermentation, with cap punching, for two weeks.

Called "Cuvée André Péleat," this is aged in one-to-two-year-old casks for 18 months and is fined but not filtered before bottling. If the vintage offers good, ripe crop, as in 2001, this works well, and the wine should be left for about four years to come together. Otherwise it risks drying out soon in the glass, as the extraction tires it—the case in the weak 2002.

ST-JOSEPH CUVÉE ANDRÉ PÉLEAT ROUGE

    2002 ★
    2001 ★★★

DANIEL ROCHE

Le Village 07340 Charnas +33(0)475 340550

Daniel Roche, a man in his 60s, makes very traditional, gamey red St-Joseph. Aged in older casks, it is best for winter drinking. His Cuvée Spéciale is raised in very large barrels and is taken from his prime sites.

ST-JOSEPH CUVÉE SPÉCIALE ROUGE

    2000 ★

DOMAINE LA ROCHE PARADIS

Les Vessettes 42410 Chavanay +33(0)474 872626

Mireille and Claude Combe make traditional red and white St-Joseph, with sometimes rustic-style flavours.

DOMAINE ROMANEAUX-DESTEZET

Les Romaneaux 07410 Arlebosc +33(0)475 085720

Paris meets the Ardèche here: St-Cloud, the leafy west-of-Paris suburb with a racecourse, and Arlebosc, set in the craggy, river-pierced hills of the Ardèche. Step forward Hervé Souhaut, a soft-voiced man around the 40 mark with thick black hair and a calm manner, and his wife, Béatrice, *petite*, dark, and stylish, with a generous smile.

It was in Lyon that they met, while Hervé was studying biology and starting to get the taste of visiting local *vignerons*. Béatrice's family come from near Arlebosc and, besides vineyards up

FIGURE 32 Seeking the organic solution—Béatrice and Hervé Souhaut in their St-Jean-de-Muzols vineyard. (Tim Johnston)

the Doux valley there, had a farm and vineyard at the St-Jean-de-Muzols site of *Ste-Épine*.

Hervé is going straight at his challenge—he works organically, hardly uses any sulphur in his cellar preparations, and is trying to revive the old glories of the Arlebosc vineyards that today produce a *vin de pays de l'Ardèche*. "There have been vines above the River Doux there for hundreds of years, and some old plants are still around," he recounts. "In 1970 there were 100 hectares of vineyards; now it's less than 10. Arlebosc used to supply 70 per cent of the St-Désirat Co-opérative's needs in Gamay in those days, with a recognised name, too. Béatrice's family had a cellar and some vines to encourage me and I've planted Viognier and Roussanne."

Now he works 1.1 ha of St-Joseph, 0.7 ha of it bought from veteran Elizabeth Fogier—a Syrah vineyard dating from around 1900 on *Ste-Épine*. The 0.4 ha is on *Pitrou*, above Dard et Ribo's plot. Its Syrah was planted in 2001 on previously overgrown land, its soil a typical local crumbly granite. He is moving this vineyard towards official organic status—the *Ste-Épine* vineyard had received weedkillers for some time, although ironically the soil had been worked with a mule before then.

Hervé worked with Dard et Ribo for a year when he started out in 1990, and it's clear they

inspired his approach, along with other noninterventionist growers like Marcel Lapierre at Morgon in the Beaujolais. In his Arlebosc cellars, he even has the press that used to belong to the "softly, softly" approach's guru Jules Chauvet.

His core *vin de pays* is his 1.4 ha of Gamay that dates from the 1920s to the 1950s. There are 1.5 ha each of Roussanne and Viognier (both 1993) on the schist half slopes at Arlebosc, all of them in full organic production.

The St-Joseph crop is not destemmed, and ferments and is then raised without sulphur. Vinification can last two to four weeks; the cellars are at 400 metres, which helps the cooling during the young wine's maceration, with the temperature around a gentle 25° to 26°C. Hervé does some mechanical cap punching in the steel but not the wood vats.

The wine is aged for seven months in four-to-five-year-old casks, and bottled with neither fining nor filtration. "The only time I add some sulphur dioxide is a little, around 25 mg per litre, when bottling," says Hervé. As with many of these organic wines, airing or decantation is suitable before drinking to free them up. They are not yet in a regular groove from one year to the next; the best vintages have rounded black berry flavours and are gentle in texture, with some tannic support.

The top Gamay *vin de pays* La Souteronne is vinified in the same way, with a lesser one receiving *macération carbonique* for straight fruit extraction. The Souteronne is a good wine for aperitif drinking. Syrah grapes are also bought in for a sound third red *vin de pays*.

The white *vins de pays* is cask fermented and raised on a fine lees, but not stirred, until bottling a year after the harvest. Its Roussanne freshness leads on the bouquet, and a fair Viognier richness on the palate: a serious wine for food.

Politics entered Hervé's life in a big way in 2002. He is of course an outsider, and he found it strange that his St-Joseph from that vintage was deemed volatile and unacceptable for anything higher than *vin de pays* status. It certainly didn't taste volatile, and analysis finds it within the limits allowed. It's clear that this incident has caused him much pain—he was obviously sailing along until its advent.

ST-JOSEPH STE-ÉPINE ROUGE

2003 (CASK) ★

2001 ★★

Export 50 per cent (1) Japan, (2) Switzerland, (3) Belgium/Netherlands

DOMAINE ROUSSET

Route de Gervans 26600 Erôme +33(0)475 033038

See also Crozes-Hermitage.
Robert and son Stéphane Rousset, based at the granite end of Crozes-Hermitage, work a cousin's half-hectare vineyard on the Tournon-Mauves border. The Syrah dates from the 1950s and grows on the granite terraces of the good *Rivoires lieu-dit.*

Their first wine was in 1997. The crop is destemmed, and vinification lasts up to three weeks, with pumping-overs and cap punching. Ageing lasts a year, half in vat, half in two-to-five-year-old casks. The wine is filtered but not fined.

It can show expressive fruit with a sinewy texture in the good years, and reflects well the difference in composition and style between Crozes and St-Joseph.

ST-JOSEPH ROUGE

2003 ★★★

2002 (CASK) ★

2001 ★★

CAVE DE SAINT-DÉSIRAT

07340 Saint-Désirat +33(0)475 342205

See also Condrieu.
A father and son, Georges and Jean-Luc Chaléat, have had a profound impact on events at this Co-opérative situated in the middle of fruit-bearing flatland between Serrières and Sarras. It was one of the first in the northern Rhône to crack the quality whip and tighten up vineyard practices and cellar techniques.

Saint-Désirat is one of the rare local villages with its own distillery. This is best known for its pear, as well as apple, apricot, and cherry, *eaux-de-vie*. The secret weapon is its Ardéchois speciality, chestnut *eau-de-vie*. Until 1982 the Co-opérative was known as St-Désirat-Champagne, named after the two local *communes*. Champagne has a splendid twelfth-century Romanesque church, whose priest is often in Rome. But that wasn't good enough for the Champagne producers who kicked up a fuss and ordered the name to be dropped!

Ninety-five of the Cave's 150 members work 230 hectares of St-Joseph and three hectares of Condrieu, as well as lowland or plateau *vin de pays* in Gamay and Syrah for the reds and Marsanne for the white. The largest St-Joseph growers work eight to 10 hectares. The Domaine Rochevine is their jewel. This 18-hectare vineyard was created in 1990 and has its own *chef de culture* to look after it.

The local soil is crumbly granite, "so we are obliged to make erosion-restricting walls over hundreds of kilometres" in the words of Jean-Luc Chaléat, the director. "It costs around £90, or US$155, to redo a square metre," he adds. "We have two Portuguese who spend the whole winter doing nothing but this. Most of our planting in the last 15 years was on the trickier midddle slopes with such walls—the easier top- and bottom-slope sites had already been taken."

With the Cave founded by his father in 1960, Jean-Luc's presence since 1979 makes him the archivist for it and the village's wine heritage. An engaging man, he explains that "before 1969 we had only *vin de table* here. We've stopped planting Gamay, and most of the Syrah was put in between 1970 and 1990, so it's around 25 years old now."

"The big challenge for me in 1979," he continues, "was to get all three sides—vineyard, cellar, and commerce—moving along, which meant I had to be a bit authoritarian. The cultivators didn't necessarily see the importance of these broader issues. The danger of our region is now that if things go too well, people forget that life is not that straightforward."

The manual harvesting was a great saviour in 2002, when the Cave lost 30 per cent of the crop. Since 1998 there has been near-total destemming, and maceration and fermentation last around three weeks, mostly in steel. Thereafter there are differences in the ageing process by wine type, although all the reds are filtered but not fined.

The basic St-Joseph *rouge* is suitable for chilled drinking when young. This is raised in vat and bottled 16 to 20 months after the harvest. It has for long been reliable, a gently and well-done wine.

A small 15 per cent of the red Cuvée des Mariniers, a wine aimed at the restaurant trade, is wood aged, and bottled 15 months after the harvest. "The style here is for fruit and freshness," comments Jean-Luc—"a versatile wine to run through a meal from the charcuterie up to the cheese."

The Cave has moved towards more special-site wines; one of these is from the *Côte Diane*, a 15-hectare, east-facing plot of sanded granite that was planted in 1970 and 1975. Its wine is raised for 10 to 14 months in two-to-four-year-old casks—10 months for the 2002, 14 for the 2003, for instance. The Côte Diane *rouge* is more discreet and relaxed and benefits from a little time to ease the oak inside it. It shows spicy, peppery aromas, and should be drunk within around six years.

The Domaine Rochevine *rouge* comes from the terraces behind the Co-opérative. Its wine is raised for a year, half in vat, half in oak—15 per cent of the wood new, the rest two years old. Presented in a heavy bottle, this can be uneven, the softness and the oak not necessarily in sync, and excess extraction a potential problem, as in 2003. When harmonious, it shows red fruits on the palate.

The top red St-Joseph, Ex Septentrio, was first made in 1999. Its grapes are selected from different plots that date from the early 1980s. This, too is aged for a year, its casks 60 per cent new, 40 per cent two years old. It shows tight black fruits on the palate when young, and smoky aromas.

The three whites vary between 70 and 80 per cent Marsanne, with 20 to 30 per cent Roussanne. These are grown on spots that have a little loess in with the loose granite. "Loess here isn't good for the Syrah," states M. Chaléat, "but then nor is it very good for the whites—it should be just for fruit, but people didn't know that at the time," he laments. The loess works well on the *L'Hermite* site at Hermitage, however.

The white St-Josephs receive a *macération pelliculaire* if the crop is in good condition— eight to 12 hours of storage to help aromatic extraction. After pressing, the juice is steel-vat fermented, and the classic is bottled around eight months after the harvest, its malo done. This is a very agreeable wine that shows white fruits and can be drunk early on, including as an aperitif.

The special Côte Diane *blanc* is partly oak raised after its primary fermentation; it spends up to eight months in three-year-old casks, with *bâtonnage*. This is a good wine, with broader, more sustained flavours than the classic, and light oak touches apparent.

Bag-in-the-box sales have run since around 2000; these are popular with the young; the older folk prefer the petrol pump, and a yarn or two with it.

ST-JOSEPH ROUGE
2001 ★

ST-JOSEPH CUVÉE DES MARINIERS ROUGE
2001 (★)
2000 ★

ST-JOSEPH CUVÉE CÔTE DIANE ROUGE
2000 ★★

ST-JOSEPH DOM ROCHEVINE ROUGE
2003 —
2001 ★

ST-JOSEPH EX SEPTENTRIO ROUGE
  2002 ★★
  2000 ★

ST-JOSEPH BLANC
  2001 ★
  2000 ★★

ST-JOSEPH DOMAINE DE ROCHEVINE BLANC
  2004 ★★

ST-JOSEPH CUVÉE CÔTE DIANE BLANC
  2002 ★★
  1999 ★★

Export 12 per cent (1) Great Britain, (2) Canada, (3) Norway

The *vins de pays de l'Ardèche*—Syrah and Gamay in red, Marsanne and Viognier in white —come from plateau or plain vines.

ST-JOSEPH LES FAGOTTES ROUGE
  2003 (CASK) ★★

ST-JOSEPH DOMAINE DE BONARIEUX ROUGE
  2003 (CASK) ★

ST-JOSEPH CUVÉE CHAMPTENAUD ROUGE
  2003 (CASK) (★)

ST-JOSEPH DOM DE LA GARENNE ROUGE
  2000 ★

CAVE DE SARRAS

NO LONGER IN BUSINESS

See also Condrieu.

In the more southerly sector of St-Joseph, opposite St-Vallier, the Sarras Co-opérative was set up in 1960. It has 150 members who work about 300 hectares, making it an important cog in the St-Joseph wheel—perhaps a fifth of the total production, with plenty of new planting.

The Cave established two special named vineyards in 1992; these are called "Domaine Bonarieux" and "La Garenne" and cover 3.3 ha and 4 ha, respectively, right above the village. They stemmed from the Vitrine, or vineyard shopwindow reclamation programme.

There are six red St-Josephs. Many of these are overextracted and collapse after exposure to air. Oak use seems mechanical, too, sticking to a modern formula, when the matter may not merit such obvious handling.

The Domaine de La Garenne showed some quality in 2000, while Les Fagottes *rouge* 2003 was a potent wine, where the extreme oak imposition was luckily matched by a rich interior. As such, it is a wine that cannot be drunk enjoyably in its youth and needs five years to soften.

The Les Fagottes white, pure Marsanne, is vinified and raised for 10 months in steel.

CAVE DE TAIN-L'HERMITAGE

22 route de Larnage 26600 Tain l'Hermitage
+33(0)475 082087

See also Cornas, Crozes-Hermitage, Hermitage, St-Péray.

Fifty-two growers send their crop to the Tain Co-opérative, a fall from the 65 of the early 1990s, indicating the keenness of some to go solo. The total vineyard area amounts to about 140 hectares, 10 per cent of them planted with white vines.

The most northern *communes* are Ozon (2 ha), Arras (26 ha), Sécheras (10 ha), and Lemps (1 ha). There is plenty of granite across all these sites. In the heartland area around Tournon, the vineyards are led by St-Jean-de-Muzols (30 ha), Vion (19 ha), Tournon (18 ha), Glun (13 ha), and a small 0.7 ha at Mauves. The outlying area right at the south of the *appellation* is Guilherand, just below St-Péray. The 20 hectares here reflect the limestone influence of the Crussol hill.

Vineyard manager Daniel Brissot estimates that the average age of the vines is 10 to 12 years; the oldest plots are at St-Jean-de-Muzols, Tournon, and Glun. The white crop is mainly Marsanne, with some good performers on the limestone at Guilherand.

The Syrah is destemmed and receives a two-to-three-week vinification. This includes automatic cap punching in the Cave's 400 hl steel fermenting vats, and micro-oxygenation for the simple supermarket wines.

The classic red wine (formerly known as "Nobles Rives") is half oak raised for 10 to 12 months, mostly in 400-litre casks that are one to five years old, the difference made up of 225-litre casks. It is lightly filtered, and 400,000 to 500,000 bottles are made each year. It has fair black fruit and is a pretty straightforward wine, rewarding a little cellaring over three years or so.

The special Esprit de Granit, first made in 2001, is raised for 15 to 18 months in one-to-three-year-old casks, with also a light filtration. Its fruit is soft from the start, encouraged by its micro-oxygenation; in large-scale vintages, its more grilled features stem from its modern vinification. The 2002 is for drinking by 2008; the 2001, 2003, and 2004 can all live for around 10 years.

The white St-Joseph is made from Marsanne only. One-quarter is vinified in two-to-three-year-old casks, the remainder in steel vats at 16° to 18°C. It is raised for a year before bottling, and since 2000 its malolactic fermentation has been partly blocked. From being often indifferent in the 1990s, it shows a higher level of quality these days, a wine for fairly early drinking.

ST-JOSEPH ROUGE
2003 ★★(★)
2002 ★
2001 Nobles Rives ★

ST-JOSEPH ESPRIT DE GRANIT ROUGE
2003 (★)
2002 ★★
2001 ★★

ST-JOSEPH BLANC
2003 ★(★)
2002 ★★
2001 Nobles Rives ★★

TARDIEU-LAURENT

rte de Cucuron 84160 Lourmarin +33(0)490 688025

See also Condrieu, Cornas, Côte-Rôtie, Crozes-Hermitage, Hermitage, St-Péray.
According to the vintage, Tardieu-Laurent source their St-Joseph from two or three villages—Sarras and Châteaubourg (a neat combination from the north and south of Tournon) as well as Saint-Pierre-de-Boeuf in the northern sector. Their wine, Les Roches, is a Vieilles Vignes cuvée, the vines 25 to 60 years old.

In 2002, when Sarras and Saint-Pierre supplied the wine, it was aged in their Tronçais new oak for 15 months, then another seven months in wood of one to two previous wines. There is no fining or filtration.

Les Roches is good, keeping wine that repays four or five years' cellarage. The black fruit contains good sinew and is nicely juiced. It can show well for over 10 years.

ST-JOSEPH LES ROCHES ROUGE
2004 ★(★) 2011–12
2001 ★★★

ÉRIC TEXIER

Bel Air 69380 Charnay +33(0)472 542618

See also Condrieu, Hermitage, Regional Wines. The 2002 from this négociant was an early, respectable wine with some fruit presence. It is aged for just over a year in casks, one-third each new, one year, and two years old. There is also a pure Marsanne white St-Joseph, fermented in cask. Both the red and the white come from Serrières and Charnas.

ST-JOSEPH ROUGE
2002 ★ From 2006.

DOMAINE RAYMOND TROLLAT

Quartier Aubert 07300 St-Jean-de-Muzols +33(0)475 082717

One of the enduring legends of the rural Rhône, Raymond Trollat has remained a countryman down to his roots. With his woolly blue bobble hat, unchanged these many winters and substituted in summer with a white canvas campers' version, he has toiled on his sloping vineyard, exposed high above St-Jean-de-Muzols, since 1959. Born in 1931, he chose to get married in 2000, to Ginette, who says "he took only 20 years reflecting on whether to marry me." They married in a joint ceremony with another couple aged 67 and 65, and the day rolled on with meals in Crozes-Hermitage and Tain.

He has never known another life or really another place. It is his kingdom. People come to him, part pilgrimage for some. In his tiny, dark cellar he relaxes against one of his faded brown barrels, legs crossed, pruning knife shearing off cuts of *saucisson* to hand out to his visitors and friends. At moments of emphasis, the bobble hat is pushed higher up his forehead, his head tilts to the right, his southern tones broaden, and his eyes dart to convey his comment. "I call it Raymond's *bistrot*," says his friend Alain Graillot.

Walking with him in the vines, he gives glimpses of the now often lost mannerisms of a true countryman: the way he handles the vegetation, his instinct for assessing the state of his plants, his deep-grained knowledge of the land and what to expect from it, the way his cantering dog is spoken to. Having visited him over the course of 30 years, I can imagine just how much this vineyard contains of Raymond's musings, observations, hopes, and sweat—bucketloads of the last. "I like to walk around and work here," he says.

"I think of everything and nothing," is Raymond's simple explanation about what runs through his mind. He can see across east to the snow-capped Vercors range; the profile of the Chapelle at Hermitage stands out against the skyline. The birdsong calls out distinctly above the low rumble of traffic down below. The one element of shade is his white oak tree at the top of the vineyard, what he terms "the cooler."

There is a tinge of sadness here, since Raymond is slowly retiring, now that he is past 70. And he will continue to live in the house here.

FIGURE 33 One of the last of a breed, the impeccable and modest Raymond Trollat in his vineyard on *Aubert* above St-Jean-de-Muzols. (Author's collection)

And he will look out of the window and see someone else working his vineyard.

Until his father, Ernest, died in August 1996, he worked four hectares. His sister's share was rented out, then sold to the Gonon family in 2003. A further 1.5 hectares were let out to his neighbours the Desestret family, and he remains with his final hectare on the *Aubert* site. It's mainly Syrah, with some Marsanne, but while walk through the vines, Raymond points to a Chasselas "post-1918" and maybe the odd Pinot as well.

Proving the truism that good wine often comes from difficult places, the vineyard is largely schist, a very acid terrain, and can get very dry. At 230 metres it stands very exposed, mostly to the south wind that prevails during summer with its humid breezes. Across the Rhône lie the similarly high granite outcrops of Crozes-Hermitage, linked thousands of years ago to this Massif Central extension.

The family started winemaking in 1664 at Iserand, about eight miles north, the resident *vigneron* serving its Château. After stays at Lemps and Sécheras, Raymond's great-grandfather started here.

One doesn't like to think that the end of the line is coming here. Raymond's cutting back means he has stopped formal exportations, and there are now about 5,000 bottles a year—"just to drink with my friends!"

The whites have always been fermented in old barrels, their malolactic blocked, and bottled in August. Nothing has changed for 40 years. Aromas are often gently floral. Flavours can be honeyed and nutty, with stone fruit present. There is barely a human imprint on them.

The red is made from whole bunches, fermented in a mix of concrete and open wood vats, with a foot *pigeage* over 12 to 15 days. "The stalk is fundamental," says Raymond. "There aren't many of us now who still believe in it—Auguste Clape, René Balthazar"; his voice trails away.

The wine is aged in a mix of 550- and 225-litre old oak and chestnut barrels for 12 to 15 months before bottling. Some wine stays in vat for two years—since 2001 Raymond has tried resin-based containers as well. There is neither fining nor filtration.

He is critical of poor oak handling in the past around here. "There always used to be too much old wood; I remember being given a cask from another grower and it took me three weeks to soak it and revitalise it with water. It ended up as the log cabin for a neighbour's dog!"

ST-JOSEPH ROUGE
  2001 ★★
  1999 ★★★

ST-JOSEPH BLANC
  2001 ★★★
  2000 ★★

DOMAINE DU TUNNEL

20 rue de la République 07130 St-Péray
+33(0)475 800466

See also Cornas, St-Péray.
Stéphane Robert's first access to a St-Joseph vineyard came in 1994 with his purchase of 0.3 ha on the granite of *Peygros* in the southern area of Tournon—Syrah dating from 1920. He planted a further 0.2 ha here in 1996.

At Glun, where the granite is tinted with a little clay on the *Terres Blanches* site, he planted 1.2 ha between 1997 and 2002; the highest vines here are 310 metres, the lowest 230 to 250 metres, so there is a natural freshness in the grapes. His other holding is 0.2 ha on the clay of the plain next to Mauves (1950s vines).

His nearly two hectares are mostly young, therefore, which is why he destalks up to 90 per cent of the crop. Vinification lasts two weeks, with pumping-over and cap punching, and cask ageing runs for 14 months, in four-to-six-year-old casks. Fining and a light filtration can be done.

The red is a bonny wine, with some warm black fruit and correct late tannins; it is best drunk within six or seven years.

ST-JOSEPH ROUGE
  2003 ★★
  2002 ★★
  2001 ★★

DOMAINE VALLET, LOUIS ET ANTHONY

La Croisette N86 07340 Serrières +33(0)475 340464

See also Condrieu.
This domaine should be set to move along well with the arrival of son Anthony, a gentle, unassuming man, to work with his father, Louis. With just two hectares of vines in 1989, Louis left the Co-opérative de Péage-de-Roussillon and started to bottle part of his production the following year.

The St-Joseph area has grown since then to 6.8 ha of Syrah and 1.0 ha of 60 per cent Marsanne (1970s, 1994), 40 per cent Roussanne (1993, 1999). The plots are all at Serrières in four zones. Their oldest dates from the 1970s on *Les Vieilles Vignes*, where the Syrah grows on light, granite soil. *Les Rouasses* is another important site, restored to vines in 1993 as part of the St-Joseph vineyard Vitrine operation; its *gore*-clay mix also gives structured wines, and the white vines are planted in its most clay areas to encourage richness in the wine.

The domaine still works fruit and vine. On the plain they have 25 hectares of mainly maize, as well as cherry and apricot trees. Wine makes up about 70 per cent of their business.

Another site for their Syrah is *Charamelain* (1989), south of the village. This has clay, and the slope is gentle enough to permit machine work. *Le Grand Moure*, southwest of the village, has decomposed granite soil with stones and gives supple, easy wines.

Anthony, a very slim, dark-haired man born in 1975, is clearly a countryman; he likes to fish and to row, reflecting his Serrières river roots. But wine clearly inspires him, and his enthusiasm bodes well for the future. He studied at Mâcon and Davayé.

The red crop is destemmed and receives a nearly three-week vinification. The classic is aged for one year in three-to-four-year-old casks. It is a simply expressed fruit wine and appears in step with its vintage style.

The special Cuvée des Muletiers, named after the men who would transport the wine up the plateau for sale in St-Étienne, is taken from their 1970s *Vieilles Vignes* plot. This receives more cap punching and a raising of 18 months in casks, up to 30 per cent new or one year old, the rest three to four years old. The Vallets deliberately seek ripe flavours and crop for this wine.

The Muletiers holds soft fruits, no doubt connected to the policy of late picking its Syrah; the tannins are present but undemanding. The 2003 was given new oak because Anthony was confident the matter was rich enough to handle it, so this wine is on a bigger scale than previous years.

The white comes from two sources with different styles; *Les Rouasses* (80 per cent Marsanne, 20 per cent Roussanne, 1994) provides copious, rich wine from its clay-influenced soil, while the schist *Les Côtes*' Marsanne (1989) is fruity and more direct. It is half oak, half vat vinified. It shows white stone fruits and some live appeal when young, and is sound.

Anthony has also got together with the patrons of Serrières' most famous hotel-restaurant, Schaeffer. This top establishment has been owned by Bernard and Joelle Mathé for many years, and now they have done the decent thing and planted a hectare on *Les Rouasses* with the Vallets and a third friend. The first wine will issue forth in 2006.

ST-JOSEPH ROUGE

 2002 ★
 2001 ★★
 1998 ★★

ST-JOSEPH CUVÉE DES MULETIERS ROUGE

 2003 (CASK) ★★★
 2002 ★
 2001 ★★
 2000 ★★

ST-JOSEPH BLANC

 2003 ★★
 2002 ★★
 2001 ★

Export 10 per cent (1) Belgium, (2) Great Britain, (3) USA

DOMAINE DE VALLOUIT

This house and its vineyards were bought by Marcel Guigal in 2001. De Vallouit worked 2.5 ha, a mixture of ownership and renting, at Tournon and Sarras. The top red was Les Anges, aged in casks for two and half years. The white was 95 per cent Marsanne, 5 per cent Roussanne from a plot at Sarras. Both wines expressed traditional flavours, the fruit at times brewed up and somewhat lacking in freshness.

DOMAINE GEORGES VERNAY

1 route Nationale 69420 Condrieu +33(0)474 595222

 See also Condrieu, Côte-Rôtie.
Georges Vernay's family makes two red St-Josephs from a 1.45 ha vineyard at Chavanay, spread over three plots—0.75 ha on *Ribaudy* (1985), 0.4 ha on *Les Vessettes* (1980), and 0.3 ha on *Boissey* (1940–41). The soil is granite, with the hard rock close to the surface.

The crop is destalked, and the aim on the classic wine is for a fruity, direct drink. Both wines receive a three-week vinification in steel vats, which can include a *délestage*—"we find it breaks up and airs the cap, so helps the fruit," comments Christine Vernay. The classic is raised for 10 months in 225-litre casks, 10 per cent of them new, the rest up to 10 years old.

In 2001 they introduced a new cuvée, La Dame Brune; this is made from the old vines on *Boissey*. This receives 18 months in cask, 30 per cent new, the rest one to two years old. Both wines are lightly filtered.

The classic red displays lively, pebbly black fruit and proper tannins that need a little time to settle. The Dame Brune has floral tones on the bouquet, and its texture is agreeably oily, with some oak lurking in the background. Its elegance will be well expressed from four years old onwards.

ST-JOSEPH ROUGE

    2003 (CASK) ★★

    2001 ★★★

    2000 ★★

ST-JOSEPH LA DAME BRUNE ROUGE

    2002 ★★

    2001 ★★★

DOMAINE VERRIER

RN 86 42410 Chavanay +33(0)477 572959

Brothers Jean and Bernard Verrier are fruit and vine growers. They work closely with Michel Mourier of Domaine de Pierre Blanche, who helps with vinification and sales.

They make two reds, the top one La Pilatte. This receives two years' ageing in 50 hl barrels and is a specific-plot wine from early 1980s Syrah at Malleval.

J. VIDAL-FLEURY

19 route de la Roche 69420 Ampuis
+33(0)474 561018

See also Condrieu, Cornas, Côte-Rôtie, Crozes-Hermitage, Hermitage

Vidal-Fleury offer 60,000 bottles of red and 2,000 to 3,000 bottles of white St-Joseph. The red is sourced 80 per cent from the northern St-Joseph sector, 20 per cent from the south. "The north brings the Côte-Rôtie style that we like," comments Jean-Pierre Rochias; "the south adds roundness and charm."

It is raised by Vidal-Fleury after the young wine has done its malolactic fermentation with the growers and spends at least two years in 20-to-30-hl barrels. From 2006, following the opening of the new Vidal-Fleury premises near Ampuis, it will also be aged in casks. It is a fair but not very inspiring wine.

The white is pure Marsanne from the northern Chavanay region and spends three months in oak. It has ripe fruit and some pleasant honeyed content.

ST-JOSEPH ROUGE

    2001 (★)

ST-JOSEPH BLANC

    2001 ★★

GÉRARD VILLANO

111, RN86 69420 Condrieu +33(0)474 598764

See also Condrieu, Côte-Rôtie.

St-Joseph is where Gérard Villano really hangs loose. This large presence of a man, ex–chocolate maker, former Rhône River barge man, goes to town with his red wine here, loving its wildness and raw fruit.

As he tastes in his telepathic way with his wife and greatest chum, Sylvie, there are grunts and mutters of pleasure as they inspect another cask or bottle of their prized Syrah.

We come to the 2000, which brings the following observations.

Gérard: "My St-Joseph is always quite animal, especially as it ages."

Sylvie: "Yes, what about the 1995?"

Gérard: "Ah, [*low grunt, chuckle*] that wasn't a wine in the bottle, but a wild boar!"

Be ready, then, for "a wine that comes in all its splendour, not hidden by outside elements." The Villanos work 1.1 ha on the *Coteau de Blanchard* (1963, 1973) at Chavanay and have made a red St-Joseph since 1992.

There is no destalking, and a traditional fermentation over two weeks or so. No outside yeasts are used. Ageing occurs over 18 months in used casks eight to 15 years old. Fining and a light filtration are done. It is tarry and punchy when young, but softens nicely after three or four years. Gérard adores this with a rib of beef done on the barbecue. Don't argue!

ST-JOSEPH ROUGE

2002 (CASK) ★

2001 ★★

2000 ★★

DOMAINE FRANÇOIS VILLARD

Montjoux 42410 Saint-Michel-sur-Rhône
+33(0)474 568360

See also Condrieu, Côte-Rôtie.

The go-go François Villard (I'm sure some Anglo-Saxons call him Frankie) works 3.5 ha of Syrah and 0.65 ha of white vines (60 per cent Marsanne, 40 per cent Roussanne), all of which grow on granite-based land. Following his example at Côte-Rôtie, he also buys Roussanne crop from Sarras for his white wine, the Mairlant, which is intended to be half Marsanne, half Roussanne.

François' first Syrah vines grew on a *lieu-dit* called *Merlan* at Limony. He has 1.35 ha there (1990, 2000), with 0.9 ha at *Verlieu* (1944, 1999) and 0.55 ha on the *Cotayat* site (2001–03) at St-Pierre-de-Boeuf, and also a new vineyard at Félines—its soil is very decomposed granite, with a sandy texture.

The Syrah is up to half destalked, with François admitting that he would like to work with whole bunches; in 1999 he managed 80 per cent intact crop, for instance. "The trouble is, the granite at St-Joseph demands more destalking than the schist at Côte-Rôtie," he observes—"the flavour is noticeably firmer."

Vinification lasts three weeks, with cap punching and pumping-overs for eight to 10 days. No external yeasts have been added since 1995, and once the maceration is over, the vats are heated up to 35°C for a week to gain extract.

The red Reflet is aged for 23 months in new oak, then bottled without fining or filtration. Such a long stay in new oak marks this out as an overt stab at modernism, but with many of the vines immature, this becomes more explicable. The 2001 was successful, when the vintage contained sufficient natural extract to handle its oak. Patience is vital if these wines are to reveal their capabilities, and leaving them until they are at least five years old is a good idea.

In 1997 François went even further, leaving some of his Syrah 40 months in cask, a wine he called "Le Grand Reflet." This was tough going when tried, its overall impression one of dryness.

One of this domaine's specialities is its late cropping, which marks both its Condrieu and its St-Joseph. According to the year, there can be 15 to 30 per cent botrytis on the St-Joseph grapes to add an extra unctuous layer to the wine. The Mairlant white is vinified and raised for 11 months in cask, 30 per cent new, with a weekly lees stirring for eight of the months. Pineapple, marmalade, and tropical fruits swirl around this wine, as unbridled as its maker. Its 40 to 45 per cent Roussanne content (unusually 60 per cent Roussanne in 2004) adds another, sometimes salty dimension.

ST-JOSEPH REFLET ROUGE

2003 ★★★ Dark, purple *robe*; oily bouquet—black fruits/olives, southern. Modern-style black fruit, all nice and clean, then comes an oak influence that lends dryness. Plenty of black fruit core, is rich. Don't touch till 2007–08; 2015–17.

2002 ★

2001 (CASK) ★★★

2000 ★★★

ST-JOSEPH MAIRLANT BLANC

> **2003** ★★
>
> **2002** ★★
>
> **2001** ★★

VINS JEAN-LUC COLOMBO

La Croix des Marais 26600 La Roche-de-Glun
+33(0)475 841710

See also Condrieu, Cornas, Côte-Rôtie, Crozes-Hermitage, Hermitage, St-Péray.

The Colombo merchant business provides two red St-Josephs, Le Prieuré and Les Lauves. The former mixes wine from Chavanay in the north and Sarras and Tournon further south. It is vinified in steel for a month, then aged for 12 to 18 months in one-to-three-year-old casks.

Les Lauves comes from 1950s Syrah grown in the St-Jean-de-Muzols area, and is aged for a year in one-third new, two-thirds one-year-old casks. About 7,500 bottles are made.

Le Prieuré is intended for earlier drinking than Les Lauves. It shows black fruits with some spice and licorice and, in a good vintage like 2001, needs three years or so to settle. The Lauves is more a textural wine, with smoky, tasty dark fruit, which evolves into a more measured licorice-style overlay after three years.

ST-JOSEPH LE PRIEURÉ ROUGE

> **2001** ★★

ST-JOSEPH LES LAUVES ROUGE

> **2001** ★★★

LES VINS DE VIENNE

Bas Seyssuel 38200 Seyssuel +33(0)474 850452

See also Condrieu, Côte-Rôtie, Crozes-Hermitage, Hermitage, St-Péray.

Here there are two reds, a classic and L'Arzelle, the special wine selected on the basis of tasting. They are made from 80 per cent purchased grapes, 20 per cent bought-in wine, with the emphasis on the northern sector between St-Désirat and Chavanay. The classic receives 10 per cent new oak over 10 months, while the Arzelle is raised in cask, 40 per cent of them new, for 14-plus months.

The classic red shows straight fruit, while the Arzelle is more oak marked and needs a ripe fruit vintage to be able to come together.

The white L'Élouède is made from 80 per cent Marsanne, 20 per cent Roussanne. From 2001 it has come from purchased grapes, having been bought as wine before that. It is oak fermented, 30 per cent of the oak new, and bottled after 10 months. It is wholesome, rich, and buttery—not typical, but pleasing.

ST-JOSEPH ROUGE

> **2003** ★★
>
> **2000** ★

ST-JOSEPH L'ARZELLE ROUGE

> **2003** ★★
>
> **2001** ★
>
> **2000** ★★

ST-JOSEPH L'ÉLOUÈDE BLANC

> **2000** ★★★

ST-JOSEPH VINTAGES

> **1961** Excellent.
>
> **1962** Very good.
>
> **1963** Poor.
>
> **1964** Very good.
>
> **1965** Poor.
>
> **1966** Very good.
>
> **1967** Excellent.
>
> **1968** Poor.
>
> **1969** Very good.
>
> **1970** Good. Whites were very good.
>
> **1971** Excellent.
>
> **1972** Good, particularly for wines made in Mauves.
>
> **1973** Good, despite the very large crop.
>
> **1974** Mediocre. Better for the whites than the reds.

1975 Mediocre. Poor ripening, rain at harvest.

1976 Good. Decent reds, rich whites.

1977 Poor. Light wines after a cold, rainy summer.

1978 Excellent. Superb balance, lots of matter for reds and whites.

1979 Good, a vintage that progressed in the bottle and lived well.

1980 Good, and underestimated, a late ripening year. Reds gained complexity, nuance. The best can still taste well, e.g., Coursodon in 2004.

1981 Fair. Harvest rain—some vigorous reds, but uneven whites.

1982 Fair. Early-September harvest. Often overripe wines, jammy textures. Some correct cuvées. Not a long-lived year.

1983 Very good. Much larger crop than 1982. Marked tannins from the dry weather—big, firm reds. The best names will still be showing. Elegant whites.

1984 Mediocre. A cold bout of –10°C in February. Light colours, lack of ripeness. Fresh whites that aged better than the reds.

1985 Very good. A sunny vintage. Some overheated wines, but mainly they held warm fruit and open appeal. Excellent, rich whites.

1986 Fair. Hail was a problem. Some austere reds, with patience needed. The best were gamey and chewy. "Very tannic and hard to sell" (Jean Marsanne). The whites were more generally successful. Drink them up.

1987 Fair. After a rainy summer, the year was saved by a splendid, hot September. Early, easy-drinking wines. A coming-of-age vintage for several young growers around Chavanay, whose meticulous cellar work proved their merit for future reference—growers like Didier Chol and André Perret. Very good whites, e.g., ★★★ B. Gripa Le Berceau.

1988 Very good. Solid, dark, tannic wines with substance—more complete than the similar 1983s. The best are still going, from Tournon, Mauves, St-Jean-de-Muzols, Chavanay, and Châteaubourg. The whites were thorough and lived well, now tiring. Note ★★★ Coursodon red Paradis St-Pierre.

1989 Very good, although parts of the vineyard suffered more from the drought than in 1988. A very large crop. Less assertive tannins than the 1988s, but good fruit expression, on the wild, racy side. Another keeping year, but drink generally before 2006–08. The whites did very well, held up by a good cross between freshness and ripe depth. They can live towards 2007. Note:

> ★★★★ de Vallouit red Les Anges, J-L Grippat red Vignes de l'Hospice
>
> ★★★ J-L Grippat *blanc*

1990 Excellent. Not far off the now legendary 1978. A large, healthy crop. Intense fruit surrounded by lovely ripe tannins, plus higher-than-usual alcohol. Some growers sought near-overripe grapes to emphasize the oiliness and lush texture possible when growing Syrah—e.g., Louis Chèze 1990 Cuvée Caroline. The reds are delicious and have aged in a nice even way, with no rough edges.

REDS

> ★★★★ Rocking red Clos de Cuminaille from Gaillard
>
> ★★★ L. Chèze Caroline; succulent B. Gripa classic; wild/full Dom de Gachon; tarry, firm J-L Grippat classic; rich, heady Trollat.

REDS

The whites were rich and fat, sometimes just too opulent to be easy to drink.

> ★★★ J-L Grippat
>
> ★★ Dom Courbis—both very rich

1991 Very good. Different levels of ripeness within a single vineyard posed challenges; there was some rot around Tournon. These are more refined reds, with less overt richness than the 1990s; sound core extract was supported by just about ripe tannins. Some reds have dry, pebbly textures. Slightly higher acidity gave these wines the chance to live well. The northern area excelled—Chavanay, Malleval, Limony, St-Pierre-de-Boeuf. Drink these reds up.

REDS

★★★★ P. Faury, B. Gripa classic/Berceau,
J. Marsanne, A. Perret Grisières,
de Vallouit Les Anges

★★★ Coursodon L'Olivaie

★★ de Boisseyt-Chol, Gonon Oliviers,
Trollat

★ Cuilleron Cuvée Prestige

WHITES

Very good whites—they were well balanced
and complete, with high natural levels of alcohol. They show more finesse and complexity
than the really big 1990s. A good keeping year,
they should also be drunk.

★★★★ B. Gripa Le Berceau

★★★ Dom du Chêne, Gonon Oliviers

★★ Coursodon L'Olivaie, Dom Courbis, L. Chèze, J-L Grippat

1992 Fair. Rain and a cool June were a problem, with also rain around Tournon at harvesttime. There was some failure on the flowering,
then rot appeared. Growers struggled to achieve
genuine ripeness. The crop was reduced, but,
looking ahead, the water table was restored with
the rain.

The reds were mild, inoffensive wines that
carried a *confit* texture: easy, gentle jam paste
flavours, sometimes a touch floral, but rather
short and fragile on the finish. Many Syrahs
bore sweet textures and fuzzy, indistinct fruit.
Bouquets advanced quickly to more fungal
tones. One or two reds drunk in 2004 have still
just about held together, but they should be
drunk straight after opening.

REDS

★★ Delas François Tournon, B. Gripa

★ de Boisseyt-Chol, Dom Gouye

WHITES

Low acidity for the whites meant they needed
early drinking; at the outset they showed fewer
obvious flaws than the reds.

1993 Poor. Hail in the Tournon area on 23
August, then rain, rain, rain, falling in buckets
in September. Inevitably the wines lacked core.
It was a struggle to select acceptable grapes.
Austere at first, the reds were often thin on the
finish. They should have been drunk by now.

REDS

★★ J-L Chave, J-L Grippat

★ C. Pichon

WHITES

The whites were relatively better—but should
have been drunk by now.

★★★ B. Faurie

★ J-L Grippat

1994 Good, even though rain at harvesttime
set nerves on edge. Yves Cuilleron reported: "By
28 August I had the same maturity and concentration as 20 September 1993. So when the
rain came, the harvest was already ripe and
healthy—meaning it wasn't badly hit." Some of
the tannins in the northern reds were firm, also
a feature for those who delayed harvesting. The
tannins were softer around Tournon and
Mauves. There was a good, berry fruit expression on the best reds. The split is between wines
that were charming, with clear fruit extraction—
living up to eight years—and those that were
stubborn, more fungal, and closed initially.
These will live for 12-plus years.

★★★ Chapoutier Deschants, P. Gaillard
Cuminaille, A. Perret Grisières

★★ J-L Chave, Cuilleron, de Boisseyt-
Chol, C. Pichon, Cave St-Désirat

★ Cave Chante-Perdrix

WHITES

Some whites lacked acidity. There was a fair
amount of richness in the best. Drink them now.

★★★ P. Gaillard

1995 Good, but the tannins in some wines
were pretty severe. There was fruit failure at

flowering. Rain fell at harvesttime, bringing some rot and loss of degree, especially around the centre-north area. The reds were generally firm, and moved quite soon on to secondary, leather, and game aromas. The best are gradually opening, but their style makes them autumn wines for ripely flavoured dishes. Beware some dry tannins.

REDS

 ★★★★ J-L Chave

  ★★ G. Barge, J-L Chave, Coursodon, G. Flacher, Gonon Oliviers, B. Gripa, Vallet Muletiers

   ★ Graillot

WHITES

The whites were generally elegant and well perfumed. The best were well knit, with a steady evolution ahead of them. Many lacked the long-term potential of the reds. Drink now. The best, such as the Gonon, can run past 2012.

 ★★★ Gonon Oliviers, P. Jaboulet Grand Pompée

  ★★ Cave Chante-Perdrix, P. Gaillard, A. Perret

1996 Quite good, but quality was patchy. Lack of balance was a problem, as genuine ripeness was difficult to achieve. Yields needed active restraint. A dry summer with a hot June, and still no real rain in August and early September, meant tannic ripening was delayed. The north wind in August concentrated and thickened the grape skins. Chèze was still picking in mid-October. Some wines lacked alcohol, and are taut, lacking flesh on the middle palate. The best course is patience and the hope that the wines will round out. The best reds show restrained flavours, quite firm fruit, and fine tannins. Their secondary phase—earthy/fungal tones this year—is under way. They should be drinkable towards 2010–12.

REDS

 ★★★ Clos Arbalestrier, Chapoutier Granits, L. Chèze Anges

  ★★ G. Barge, Dom de Gachon, Chapoutier Deschants, A. Perret classic/Grisières, G. Vernay

   ★ J-L Chave Offerus, B. Gripa, A. Perret, Cave de Tain Nobles Rives

WHITES

The vintage was difficult for the whites, since the acidity levels were not often supported by enough extract. Wines with later-picked fruit held more flesh. The best can still be drunk with pleasure now they have softened.

  ★★ J-L Grippat

   ★ Chapoutier Granits, Gonon Oliviers

1997 Good, but marked by low acidity, so this is not a keeping vintage. Ripening was straightforward compared to previous years. Heat was the key factor, day and night. The extreme mid-August heat burnt the grapes' acidity. Ripening occurred at different speeds between the sugars and polyphenols, so the tannin ripeness became a worry. A lot of the reds are sweet and a little jammy. The best are oily and warmly fruited. Many are ideal lunch wines, also good in restaurants because they are open and easy to drink. L. Chèze recalls, "We had such good weather at harvesttime that I could pick just three days a week and let it run over a month." Top wines can run to around 2010, many drink sweetly now.

REDS

 ★★★ L. Chèze Anges

  ★★ Clos Arbalestrier, Chapoutier Granits, Coursodon Sensonne, Cuilleron Les Sérines, Ferraton Source, B. Gripa, J-L Grippat Vignes de l'Hospice, Tardieu-Laurent Les Roches

★ G. Barge, Cave de Tain, J-L Chave, Chapoutier Deschants, Dom du Chêne, Dom Courbis classic/Royes, Coursodon classic/Paradis St-Pierre, Delas François Tournon/Ste-Épine, B. Faurie, J-L Grippat, P. Jaboulet Grand Pompée, A. Perret Grisières, Trollat

WHITES

The best whites were fat and opulent, but dogged by a lack of freshness. After an early flourish, they have not held up very well, especially if constantly stirred on the lees and given a busy time in the cellar. They reflect the Marsanne in its traditional, full-on guise, so this is a year when the richness drives the wine rather than the acidity. They are wholesome, and good now, with floral aromas, and nuttiness in the flavour.

★★ de Boisseyt-Chol, Chapoutier Granits, Coursodon Paradis St-Pierre, Trollat

★ G. Barge, Chapoutier Deschants, Dom du Chêne, Dom Courbis, B. Faurie, J-L Grippat, P. Jaboulet Grand Pompée, Dom Mortier, Cave de Tain Nobles Rives, F. Villard Côtes Mairlant

1998 Very good. Mid-April frost hammered some villages, notably St-Jean-de-Muzols, where Trollat lost 85 per cent of his crop. The old vines on exposed slopes were often hit. Hail just before flowering hit at Glun and Châteaubourg in mid-May: Durand's yields were halved. Late harvesters were hit by a run of bad weather after September 26. It was a year to destalk. Even so, some of the wines show tough tannins. There remained a core of concentrated, bold wines, with firm depth, good length, and correct tannins. The top cuvées from older vines were often markedly more structured than the classic or regular wines. Age has brought forward an oily richness and these are great wines for spring/autumn foods. They should live to 2012–15.

REDS

★★★★★ Chapoutier Granits

★★★★ Delas Ste-Épine, J-L Grippat Vignes de l'Hospice

★★★ G. Barge, J-L Chave, Dom du Chêne Anaïs, Delas François Tournon, B. Faurie, Dom de Gachon, Gonon Oliviers, B. Gripa Berceau

★★ Cave Chante-Perdrix Madone, Clos Arbalestrier, Chapoutier Deschants, Dom Courbis Royes, G. Courbis, Coursodon Olivaie/Paradis St-Pierre, B. Gripa, J-L Grippat, J. Marsanne, A. Perret Grisières, Vallet

★ Cave Chante-Perdrix, Dom Courbis, Coursodon, Meffre Laurus, A. Paret 420 Nuits, A. Perret, Cave de Tain

WHITES

The Marsanne grape ripened well for the whites. The best are full, well-scented, and quite potent. Their richness is evident. A very small crop for Chapoutier's Granits. These will show well until 2010-plus.

★★★★★ Chapoutier Granits

★★★ Coursodon Paradis St-Pierre

★★ Blachon

★ Dom Courbis, J-L Grippat, P. Jaboulet Grand Pompée, A. Perret

1999 Excellent, in the best hands. But there was variation. Some tannins are a little dry and can make the wines finish sternly. The crop was abundant, with enough acidity to allow good ageing. The wines are complete and often potent. The northern sector around Chavanay achieved above-average ripeness, so their wines contain more fat and flesh than usual. The fruit is well expressed and has a great, clean cut to it. There are some really classic longevity wines here, a real treat lying in store over 12 to 16 years. The wines are big and unbridled and, for Joël Durand, possess a rather rustic, at times southern *garrigue* side to them. The classic cuvées were great value for money.

REDS

★★★★ B. Gripa Berceau, Guigal Vignes de l'Hospice, A. Perret Grisières

★★★ Chapoutier Granits, Dom Courbis Royes, Coursodon Olivaie/Sensonne, Delas François Tournon/Ste-Épine, B. Faurie, P. Finon, Dom de Gachon, Gonon Oliviers, B. Gripa, P. Jaboulet Grand Pompée, Dom Mortier, A. Perret, Trollat

★★ Clos Arbalestrier, G. Barge, Bied, L. C. Brotte Marandy, Cave Chante-Perdrix, Dom Champal-Rocher, Chapoutier Deschants, Dom du Cornilhac, G. Courbis, Coursodon, Delas Challeys, Dumazet Muzolaise, Durand Coteaux, P. Finon Rocailles, G. Flacher Prestige, A. Perret, Dom Remizières

★ P. Jamet Côte Sud, J. Marsanne, Dom Monteillet Papy

WHITES

There were some excellent whites, too. The best were full, chewy, mineral, and persistent. Their structure is sound and will permit ageing. Flavours were ample and, in the best hands, refined as well—e.g., J-L Grippat, whose wine was bottled and sold under the Guigal label. Drink to around 2012–15.

★★★★ Guigal-Grippat

★★★ Clos Arbalestrier, Chapoutier Granits, Gonon Oliviers

★★ G. Barge, Dom Courbis, L. Marthouret, A. Perret, Cave St-Désirat Côte Diane

★ Cave Chante-Perdrix, Chapoutier Deschants, J. Marsanne

2000 Quite good. Quality was uneven, due to a series of problems rather than one big

event, although the large crop was a prime challenge. Light hail at St-Jean-de-Muzols in early July "actually helped to order the vines," according to Philippe Desbos, but there was rain and some oïdium at harvesttime at St-Jean and Chavanay after a hot August and sometimes humid September. Heavy rain in early September at Chavanay inflated the grapes—adding to the yield challenge. "You had to green harvest this year," said Philippe Faury. There were outbreaks of mildew, too, in the southern sector.

REDS

Some wines carry sound fruit depth, others are edgy, their fabric fragile. The overall texture is *en rondeur*, and the best northern wines held good juice. "A tender, charming year," Jean Gonon dubbed it. They will be best drunk earlier than 1999 and 2001—by around 2010–12. A year that missed the benefits of a north wind and high pressure in the late season.

★★★ Chapoutier Granits, Dom du Château Vieux, J-L Chave, L. Chèze Anges, Dom Courbis Royes, Coursodon Paradis St-Pierre, Cuilleron Amarybelle/ Serines, Delas François Tournon, G. Flacher Prestige, Gonon Oliviers, Graillot, B. Gripa Berceau, Guigal Lieu-Dit St-Joseph, A. Perret Grisières, Dom Pierre Blanche Cep d'Or, G. Vernay, F. Villard Reflet

★★ Clos Arbalestrier, G. Barge, Blachon, Chapoutier Deschants, J-L Chave Offerus, L. Chèze Ro-Rée, Dom Courbis, Coursodon Sensonne, Cuilleron Pierres Seches, de Boisseyt-Chol Rivoires, Dom Côte Sainte-Épine, Durand Coteaux, Dom Fauterie classic/ Combaud, P. Finon Rocailles, E. Fogier, B. Gripa, Guigal classic/ Vignes de l'Hospice, P. Jaboulet Grand Pompée, Dom Monteillet Vignobles/Papy, Dom Mortier, H. & M-T Richard Nuelles, Cave

St-Désirat Côte Diane, Vallet
Muletiers, G. Vernay Villano,
Vins de Vienne Arzelle

★ Dom des Amphores Mésanges,
Dom Champal-Rocher, de Bois-
seyt-Chol, G. Courbis, Delas
Challeys, P. Faury Gloriette,
Dom Favière, Dom de Gachon,
P. Gaillard Cuminaille, J-C
Marsanne, L. Marthouret Pierre,
Dom Monteillet Fortior, V. Paris,
A. Perret, D. Roche Spéciale,
Cave St-Désirat Mariniers/
Ex Septentrio, Cave de Sarras
Garenne, Vins de Vienne

WHITES

The whites were fat and full, more so than the
1999s. "It's a nice year for rounded wines, not
very long-lived," Bernard Gripa. The wines can
be nicely frank and direct, playing a good, early
fruit card. Drink by around 2008–10.

★★★ Chapoutier Granits, Dard et Ribo
Pitrou, P. Finon, Gonon Oliviers,
B. Gripa Berceau, A. Perret, Vins
de Vienne Élouède

★★ Clos Arbalestrier, Chapoutier
Deschants, Cuilleron Lyseras,
Dard et Ribo, Ferraton Oliviers,
B. Gripa, P. Jamet, J-C Marsanne,
L. Marthouret, H. & M-T Richard,
Cave St-Désirat, Trollat

★ Boissonnet, Dom Favière,
Guigal classic/Lieu-Dit St-Joseph,
P. Jaboulet Grand Pompée

2001 Very good in the south for most growers, very good in the north for the best growers.
There was not much summer before mid-May,
with a lot of rain in early May. It was very hot—
even too hot in August near the end of the
ripening cycle. It was not easy to achieve a balanced ripening, notably on the young vines,
with tannic ripeness a struggle. Early September was cool, bringing a blockage of grape maturity for some. Early September rain in the southern area was not too damaging, because the
grapes were healthy. Two weeks of north wind
made the vintage, bringing slow, dry ripening
and concentration into the grapes. There was
rain between the harvest runs, with the second
bout in early October causing crop degradation.
"You had to harvest before the end of September," said both B. Gripa and A. Perret. Another
year when yields had to be restrained.

REDS

The wines are live, direct, vigorous. The southern sector contains more flesh than the north,
where inexperienced growers were found out,
with sharp tannins evident. "Fresh nights
helped this year—it's super, with drier and more
direct wines than 2000," said Jean Gonon. "I
find the fruit ripe and warm, with more finesse
than the '99s," added Joël Durand. There is
plenty of fruit in the wines, but the fruit texture
is well grained rather than plump and facile.
Tannins are sound, and the vintage will live
well, its structure a classic one. The regular
wines are showing well after four years; the special wines will perform well from 2006–07. The
best will live for 18 years or so.

★★★★★ Guigal Vignes de l'Hospice

★★★★ Belle, Chapoutier Granits, Dom
du Chêne Anaïs, Delas Ste-Épine,
P. Gaillard Cuminaille, Gonon
Oliviers, B. Gripa Berceau, Guigal
Lieu-Dit St-Joseph

★★★ G. Barge, E. Barou, E. Becheras,
L. C. Brotte Marandy, Dom du
Château Vieux, J-L Chave Offerus,
Colombo Lauves, Coursodon
L'Olivaie/Paradis St-Pierre,
Cuilleron Serines, Dom Courbis
Royes, de Boisseyt-Chol Rivoires,
Dumazet Muzolaise, Durand
Coteaux, B. Faurie Vieilles Vignes,
P. Finon Rocailles, P. Gaillard
Les Pierres, B. Gripa, F. Merlin,
Monier Terres Blanches, A. Perret
classic/Grisières, G. Robin André

Péleat, Tardieu-Laurent Les Roches, G. Vernay classic/Dame Brune, F. Villard Reflet

★★ Dom des Amphores, Blachon Coteaux, Bonserine, Champal-Rocher, Chapoutier Deschants, Cave Chante-Perdrix Madone, J-L Chave, L. Chèze Ro-Rée/Anges, Colombo Prieuré, Combier, Coursodon Sensonne, Cuilleron Amarybelle, Dard et Ribo, de Boisseyt-Chol Garipolées, B. Faurie, P. Faury Gloriette, Fauterie Combaud, Ferme Sept Lunes, P. Finon, G. Flacher regular/Prestige, Gasse Lafoy, Dom Gouye, Graillot, J-C Marsanne, R. Michel Bois des Blâches, Michelas Saint Jemms Ste-Epine, Monier Serves, Dom Monteillet Papy, Dom Mortier, A. Paret 420 Nuits/Larmes du Père, V. Paris, C. Pichon, D. Raydon, H. & M-T Richard Nuelles, Dom Romaneaux-Destezet Ste-Épine, Rousset, Cave de Tain Esprit de Granit, Trollat, Dom du Tunnel, Vallet classic/Muletiers, Villano

★ Blachon, Boissonnet Belive, Dom du Chêne, L. Chèze Caroline, Dom Collonge, Dom Courbis, Coursodon, Dom Côte Sainte-Épine, de Boisseyt-Chol, Delas Challeys, Farjon, P. Faury, Dom Fauterie, Dom Favière, Ferraton La Source, Dom Florentin, E. Fogier, P. Gaillard, Dom de Gachon, P. Jaboulet Grand Pompée, P. Jamet classic/spéciale, L. Marthouret Rôtisses/Pierre, Dom Monteillet classic/Cabriole, Dom Pierre Blanche, Dom Romaneaux-Destezet, Cave St-Désirat regular/Rochevine, Cave de Tain Nobles Rives, Vins de Vienne Arzelle

The whites have been excellent, helped by the mix of gradually ripened fruit and helpful acidity. If left to ripen properly, alcohol exceeded 14.5°. Freshness with sustained richness makes a rare combination; these will live extremely well, and merit serious interest for the future. Drink towards 2016–18.

★★★★★ Gonon Oliviers

★★★★ Chapoutier Granits, Delas Ste-Épine

★★★ Dom du Chêne, Dom Courbis Royes, Coursodon classic/Paradis St-Pierre, Delas Challeys, Ferraton Les Oliviers, G. Flacher, Dom Florentin, Dom Gouye, B. Gripa Berceau, A. Perret, Trollat

★★ Chapoutier Deschants, Cave Chante-Perdrix, L. Chèze Ro-Rée, Dom Côte Sainte-Épine, Dom Courbis, Cuilleron Lombard/St-Pierre, Dard et Ribo, P. Faury, Ferraton La Source, P. Finon, P. Gaillard, B. Gripa, Guigal classic/Lieu-Dit St-Joseph, J-C Marsanne, Dom Monteillet, V. Paris, Dom Pierre Blanche, H. & M-T Richard, Cave de Tain, Dom du Tunnel, Vidal-Fleury, F. Villard Mairlant

★ Dom des Amphores, Blachon, Cave St-Désirat, Cuilleron Lyseras, de Boisseyt-Chol, Farjon, P. Jaboulet Grand Pompée, P. Jamet, L. Marthouret, Dom Mortier, Vallet

2002 Fair to good for the reds, with the northern sector around Chavanay performing well—an underestimated vintage. Fair for the whites, with one or two good wines. The dire frost of 8 April hit high spots like Arras, where 80 per cent of the possible crop was lost. The annual cycle otherwise started well—north wind and healthy vines before May. There was rain at flowering, and the summer was patchy, lacking a sustained spell of fine weather. Localised hail fell—e.g., Sarras at the end of June. Early August, hail hit the crop at Mauves and Tournon during its *veraison*, as the grapes' colour changed. Rain then and more hail on 6–7 September brought on rot, especially on the precocious areas. The high vineyards struggled to achieve degree. It became hot around 10 September, which allowed some catching up, notably the cooler zones like the Chavanay plateau areas. "The tougher, less mature skins in the later-ripening areas helped those grapes to handle the rain," Yves Cuilleron commented, "but you had to wait." Growers like Faurie lost 55 per cent, Coursodon 50 per cent—so just one wine was produced by the latter.

REDS

Growers used *saignée* methods to increase colour (running off some first juice). The fruit often has a tenuous centre to it, the style light red/peppery, with some green aspects apparent among less skilled *vignerons* in the northern sector. Textures were firm if new oak was used. "For me, it's like 1996, but that was harder at the outset," said Yves Cuilleron. Certainly, acidities are higher than usual, and growers also had to chaptalise to gain degree. Where there was rot, the drinker suddenly hits vegetal notes or aromas. The best northern growers performed well, with their wines gaining weight and integration during 2004: they hold good tannic structures and can be potent, with enough matter for the oak. Several show peppery aspects, and some can be taut. "I find it best around Mauves and Châteaubourg," Laurent Combier. The southern-zone reds are soft, ideal for lunch and restaurant drinking, and should be drunk by around 2009–11. Many wines will drink well around 2006; the best will live until 2014.

★★★ Belle, Boissonnet Belive, Chapoutier Granits, Dom Courbis classic/Royes, Cuilleron Serines, Delas Challeys, Ferme Sept Lunes

Pleine Lune, P. Gaillard Cuminaille, Gonon Oliviers, Dom Gouye, Guigal Vignes de l'Hospice, Dom Monteillet Fortior/Papy, H. & M-T Richard Nuelles

★★ Chapoutier Deschants, Dom du Chêne, Combier, Coursodon, Cuilleron Amarybelle, de Boisseyt-Chol Rivoires/Garipolées, Durand Coteaux, P. Faury Gloriette, Ferme Sept Lunes, Dom Florentin, P. Gaillard Les Pierres, B. Gripa classic/Berceau, Guigal Lieu-Dit St-Joseph, P. Jamet F. Merlin, R. Michel Bois des Blâches, Monier, A. Paret Larmes du Père, Cave St-Désirat Ex Septentrio, Dom du Tunnel, G. Vernay Dame Brune

★(★) E. Becheras

★ Dom des Amphores Mésanges, E. Barou, Blachon, Dom Bonserine, Cave Chante-Perdrix Madone, Dom du Château Vieux, J-L Chave, L. Chèze Ro-Rée, Dard et Ribo, de Boisseyt-Chol, B. Faurie Vieilles Vignes, P. Faury, Dom Fauterie classic, Ferme Sept Lunes, Ferraton La Source, E. Fogier, Graillot, J-C Marsanne, L. Marthouret Rôtisses/Pierre, G. Meffre Laurus, P. Michelas Goutelles, Monier, Dom Mortier, A. Paret 420 Nuits, V. Paris, A. Perret, C. Pichon, G. Robin André Péleat, Rousset, Cave de Tain classic/Esprit de Granit, Vallet classic/Muletiers, Villano, F. Villard Reflet

(★) Cave Chante-Perdrix, Farjon, B. Faurie, P. Finon

WHITES

The Marsanne crop resisted the rain better than the Syrah; it was also a small crop—half size for meticulous growers like the Gonons. The flavours are soft, with the risk that they skip a beat in midpalate. Aromas are quite warm. There is some Marsanne richness to be found, and one may expect the leading names to offer better integration of flavours and longer finishes by 2006. The best wines contain good core fullness, although some finish a little uneasily. Many of these wines are set to combine with light foods and are not up to handling big flavours. The fullest wines can live towards 2012–14.

★★★(★) Dom Courbis Royes

★★★ Dom Courbis, Cuilleron Lombard, Dard et Ribo, Ferraton Oliviers, Gonon Oliviers, Guigal Lieu-Dit St-Joseph

★★ Boissonnet, Chapoutier Granits, Dom Courbis, Cuilleron Lyseras/ St-Pierre, Delas Challeys, Farjon, B. Faurie, Ferme Sept Lunes, P. Finon, G. Flacher, P. Gaillard, Dom Gouye, B. Gripa, J-C Marsanne, Dom Michelas Saint Jemms Ste-Epine, H. & M-T Richard, Cave St-Désirat Côte Diane, Cave de Tain, Vallet, F. Villard Mairlant

★ E. Barou, Cave Chante-Perdrix, Chapoutier Deschants, Coursodon classic/Paradis St-Pierre, P. Faury, Dom Florentin, B. Gripa Berceau, Guigal, P. Jaboulet Grand Pompée, Monier, Dom Mortier, E. Texier

(★) de Boisseyt-Chol

2003 Very good for the reds, good-plus for the whites. Phew, what a scorcher! January was cold and dry, with a lot of subzero days. February started warmer, but was cold from 10 to 20 February, with some rains. It was then very dry until the end of March, with a drying north wind in the first half of April. Frost on the slopes was an early setback—around high spots like Charnas and Malleval, some *vignerons* lost half their crop. The frost also hit old vines at St-Jean-

de-Muzols, and Cuilleron suffered losses at St-Michel-sur-Rhône. The weather was fine from April onwards, except for an unsettled spell from 15 to 24 May. Flowering was one week ahead of the usual at Châteaubourg, with the first flowers out by 14 May. The heat then persisted with a large upsurge in early August, prompting unheard-of harvest dates, but also very reduced yields. The Coursodons started on 16 August, one of the first at Mauves, and had ended by 27 August—"so we didn't acidify the wines," P. Coursodon reports. The Gonon yields were just 20 hl/ha for the Syrah and 23 hl/ha for the white—"no hail, just heat," J. Gonon said.

P. Jamet lost 50 per cent: "I started to pick my Syrah on 14 August and had to chill it in the fridge for a day at 4° to 6°C. By harvesting so early, I obtained extra acidity." Other growers lost 50 to 70 per cent of their crop.

REDS

The Syrah vinifications were tricky—there were blockages, with late release of sugars and such low levels of malic acidity that the malos were done before the end of the sugars—hence a strong risk of volatile acidity. The granite helped acidity levels, as opposed to Crozes-Hermitage's plain, for instance. The southern-zone wines can be big and beefy, sporting 14.5°, but tannins are well wrapped in the best cases.

The northern-zone wines have their usual black fruit but with a sweet, fruit lozenge aspect this year—compact and succulent. They are big and rich—fleshy enough to handle oak—and this is a notable year for this area. Many of these northern reds are likely to close up around 2006 and then bound along from 2007–08. "The wines are New World in style, and I expect them to make themselves quickly," asserts P. Gaillard.

The southern-zone wines show some herbal-olive aromas, and the best are vigorous, well-filled wines with good tannic definition. There is also a sweet richness in these wines, but a word of caution is that some have very low acidity and an uneven structure. "I find the St-

Joseph reds can be less extreme, less obviously southern than some of the Hermitages," comments J-L Chave. The northern-zone wines may end up living longer—towards 2018–20.

Floating around both zones are wines from less talented growers who, at the very least, need to sharpen their acidification techniques—poor work that can bring a rasping sensation on the end palate.

★★★★(★) Gonon Oliviers

  ★★★★ Chapoutier Granits, Delas Ste-Épine, P. Faury Gloriette, B. Gripa, Guigal Vignes de l'Hospice

★★★(★) Coursodon L'Olivaie/Paradis St-Pierre, Cuilleron Serines, Ferme Sept Lunes Pleine Lune

   ★★★ E. Barou, E. Becheras, A. Chatagnier, Dom du Château Vieux Les Hauts, Dom Courbis Royes, Coursodon Sensonne, Dard et Ribo, Delas François Tournon, Durand Coteaux/Lautaret, B. Faurie, P. Faury, Ferme Sept Lunes, P. Gaillard Les Pierres/Cuminaille, Dom Gouye, B. Gripa Berceau, P. Jaboulet Grand Pompée, Monier Terres Blanches, Dom Monteillet Papy, A. Perret Grisières, Rousset, Vallet Muletiers, F. Villard Reflet

★★(★) L. Betton, Blachon Coteaux, Chapoutier Deschants, Dom Courbis, de Boisseyt-Chol Les Rivoires, Dom Fauterie Combaud, G. Flacher, Monier Les Serves, Dom Remizières L'Essentiel, Cave de Tain

   ★★ Blachon, Dom du Château Vieux, Dom du Chêne Anaïs, L. Chomat, G. Courbis, Coursodon, Delas Challeys, Farjon classic/Ma Sélection, P. Finon, P. Gaillard, Dom Gouye, J-C Marsanne, P. Mealy, A. Perret, C. Pichon, Cave de Sarras Fagottes, Dom du Tunnel, G. Vernay, Vins de Vienne classic/Arzelle

 ★(★) Boissonnet, L. C. Brotte Marandy

   ★ Arnoux et Fils, Cave Chante-Perdrix Madone, Dom Fauterie, P. Finon Rocailles, Dom Michelas Saint Jemms, Ste-Épine, Dom Romaneaux-Destezet Ste-Épine, Cave de Sarras Dom Bonarieux

 (★) Cave de Sarras Champtenaud, Cave de Tain Esprit de Granit

WHITES

It is obviously a high-alcohol, low-acidity vintage for the whites, which therefore run on power rather than balance. It is a year for Marsanne, with the Roussanne suffering and drying out from the heat—Domaine La Batellerie lost 70 per cent at Arras, with P. Jamet's Roussanne a wipeout there. There are nutty, buttery flavours, the ripe fat of the Marsanne very typical. Some wines are agreeably chewy on the palate, with heat on the aftertaste, although some live, "fresh" finishes indicate traces of acidification. Many of the whites can show to 2007–10, with a maximum likely of 2012–15.

  ★★★★ Dom Courbis Royes, Gonon Oliviers

   ★★★ Boissonnet, Chapoutier Granits, Dom Courbis, Coursodon Paradis St-Pierre, Dard et Ribo regular/Pitrou, Delas Ste-Épine, Ferraton Oliviers, Dom Gouye, B. Gripa Berceau, Guigal Lieu-Dit St-Joseph, P. Jaboulet Grand Pompée, Dom Monteillet, A. Perret

★★(★) Dom du Chêne, B. Faurie, P. Faury, B. Gripa, Guigal, J-C Marsanne

   ★★ Dom des Amphores, E. Becheras, Blachon, Chapoutier Deschants, Dom Courbis, Coursodon, Cuilleron Lombard/St-Pierre, Delas Challeys, G. Flacher, Dom Florentin Le Clos, Vallet, F. Villard Mairlant

 ★(★) Cave de Tain

2004 Fair to quite good. The story of the year until August was the dry weather, which hit the hillside vines on free-draining sandy granite especially. The vines on deeper soil at the foot of the hills fared better. The dry weather showed in some vines suffering leaf loss. In early to mid-August the rain came in three visits, totalling around 150 mm (6 in.); some hail was reported in the southern Tournon area around *Dardouille*. "There was some hail and rot—it wasn't a regular ripening. We found some Syrah plots abundant, others lacking yield," reported J. Gonon. Hail on 17–18 August at Glun robbed S. Bernard, Dom de Fauterie, of half his crop there in 15 minutes. C. Pichon at Chavanay spoke of the need to drop a lot of bunches at the end of August as rot had started, and that was an important issue heading into September. The fine late season in September allowed some catching up in the ripening, and what had seemed a strong and widespread rot probability receded over the month. Crop levels are near the permitted 40 hl/ha.

The reds in November lacked colour, but by early 2005 had stabilised and carried quite prominent tannins in some cases around the central to northern zone. They can be quite heady. "For me, the 2004s are more marked by power, the 2001s by finesse, but there is some cross-reference between the two vintages," says J-L Chaléat of Cave de St-Désirat.

There is some decent matter in the reds, but they will need time to come together and gain weight. At present, they are for keeping in the midterm, not the long term.

★★★ E. Barou, E. Becheras, Coursodon L'Olivaie/Paradis St-Pierre/ Sensonne

★★(★) A. Chatagnier, Dom Gouye, J-C Marsanne

★★ Dom Côte Ste-Épine, D. Morion, A. Perret, C. Pichon, Dom Remizières

★(★) Tardieu-Laurent Les Roches

★ Coursodon, Dom Favière La Favière, D. Morion Les Echets

WHITES

Early-August hail hit the white crop of Gonon and neighbours around the Tournon-Mauves boundary, but the Marsanne ripeness was sound, B. Gripa reporting cropping of 13° grapes on 14 September.

The wines are fresh, with open, live bouquets and will become elegant as they settle. This could be an interesting year for wines of character and a jaunty early style, far removed from the heavy overlay of the 2003s. There is enough richness in the better examples to indicate some later complexity.

★★★ Coursodon Paradis St-Pierre, P. Finon

★★★ after P. Finon, Guigal

★★ Dom du Chêne, Coursodon, P. Faury, D. Morion

★ Dom Favière

(★) Farjon

7

Cornas

LONG BEFORE TECHNOLOGY came along and made red wines black at the touch of a button or two, the trusty, granite-filled slopes of Cornas were doing it nature's way. Back in 1763 the village priest, a Monsieur Molin, had been moved to record: "The mountain of this village is most entirely planted with vines which produce a very good black wine. This wine is much sought after by the merchants and is very heady."

Until the late 1980s, Cornas remained something of a Last Frontier in the northern Rhône's lineup of Big Red Wines. Côte-Rôtie and Hermitage were made in larger quantities and were much better known. Cornas was their rather wild country cousin, its aficionados more likely to favour the alternative than the mainstream. Since then, its press coverage has widened, its price has risen, and bottles of this undeniably dark wine are easier to find.

The wine's "blackness"—an unbridled fullness—is encouraged by the vineyard's setting. An aerial view such as that depicted in the very useful *Oz Clarke's Wine Atlas* (Little Brown/ Websters 2002) shows just how this vineyard is well tucked away from the main cooling draughts of the Rhône corridor. In the words of grower Joël Durand, "It's an enclave, outside the river's valley influence."

There are also warm southern air currents that arrive from the Toulaud Valley south of St-Péray; they hit Cornas but, just to the north, are blocked by Châteaubourg's rocky outcrop right beside the Rhône. This makes the Cornas ripening easier than that at even nearby Tournon, the heart of the St-Joseph *appellation*. Durand grows both Cornas and St-Joseph Syrah, and remarks that his Cornas stems are always paler than those of his St-Joseph, as if their ripening has been more constant and assured.

The figures support this. Cornas is usually the most precocious vineyard in these parts, its full-slope sites ripening at least a week ahead of Hermitage; such precocity can occasionally have its drawbacks, as the early April 2003 frost hit parts of the vineyard hard.

The other constituent bringing its relative austerity is its link to the Massif Central—the granite never far below the surface of its hills. This provides the minerality, the imprint of pebbly texture that is frequently present on the finish. Where the wine is at its richest, on prime

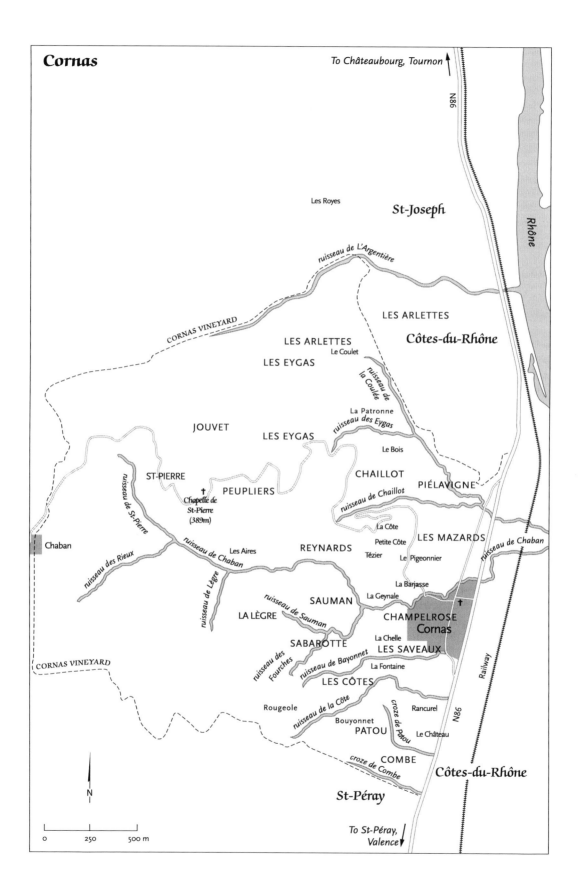

Cornas

To Châteaubourg, Tournon ↑

N86

Les Royes

St-Joseph

ruisseau de L'Argentière

CORNAS VINEYARD

LES ARLETTES

Côtes-du-Rhône

LES ARLETTES

LES EYGAS

Le Coulet

ruisseau de la Coulée

JOUVET

LES EYGAS

La Patronne

ruisseau des Eygas

Le Bois

ST-PIERRE

PEUPLIERS

CHAILLOT

PIÉLAVIGNE

ruisseau de St-Pierre

† Chapelle de St-Pierre (389m)

ruisseau de Chaillot

La Côte

Petite Côte

LES MAZARDS

Chaban

ruisseau des Rieux

ruisseau de Chaban

Les Aires

REYNARDS

Tézier

Le Pigeonnier

ruisseau de Chaban

ruisseau de Lègre

La Barjasse

ruisseau de Sauman

SAUMAN

La Geynale

LA LÈGRE

CHAMPELROSE

†

Cornas

SABAROTTE

La Chelle

LES SAVEAUX

ruisseau des Fourches

ruisseau de Bayonnet

La Fontaine

LES CÔTES

Rougeole

ruisseau de la Côte

croze de Patou

Rancurel

Bouyonnet

PATOU

Le Château

CORNAS VINEYARD

COMBE

croze de Combe

Côtes-du-Rhône

St-Péray

N86

Railway

To St-Péray, Valence ↓

N

0   250   500 m

sites like *Thézier*, the role of clay patches at one-plus metre down is a contributing factor.

Cornas lies to the south of the main area of the St-Joseph *appellation*, on the same west side of the Rhône, and with St-Péray marks the end of the northern Rhône. It is a small village that has undergone some superficial changes brought on by proximity to busy, industrial Valence just across the river. Since the late 1970s, new housing has sprung up—the view from the vineyards now includes groups of bold orange-coloured roofs, intruders into the previous soft pastels of light-brown Ardèche tiles.

But Vieille France is a stubborn creature. The arrival of the mobile *boucher-charcutier* in the Place de l'Eglise still stirs up a commotion. It provides the perfect backdrop for some impassive watching of the visiting stranger. Indeed, suspicion about a new face generates the question—undoubtedly tax related—"Are you from the Water Authority?"

Times move on, though, and the old *épicerie* has now closed—run for over 40 years by the Dumien winemaking family. There are still a baker and a smoky *bar-tabac*, joined now by a remodelled pharmacy and a hairdresser, and even two schools, one private, one public.

On the village streets, there are signs of the old community; the gossipers continue their social speculation, and an old man with a stick walks slowly along the rue Pied la Vigne and into the Place du Pressoir. A flash of colour whirls past him, a roller blader heading down into Grande Rue.

Towering over the village is its church. Its lank spire is visible for miles around, and the patch of ground around its front door is the village centre. Much of the window glass was donated by the de Barjac family. "The church took over 20 years to build and was finished in 1870—it was when my great-grandfather was Mayor and a Senator," states the now retired Guy de Barjac. Inside the church is a memorial plaque to those fallen in the two world wars. Many of the names are from old wine-growing families that still work the slopes above Cornas.

The cemetery down the road confirms this—a Balthazar married to a Verset and so on.

Meanwhile on the hillside, life is often unchanged as well. At the top of the *Reynards* hill, which looks down on the village, the call of a male deer can be heard from the bordering woods. After the soil has been turned, wild boar come rumbling through to satisfy their taste for its likely spoils. Just a quiet step away from the road, there is still a reassuring continuity across the open land.

That continuity is evident in the wine community in a way that exists nowhere else in the northern Rhône. The Cornas vineyard exercises a venerable draw on the children of growers. They leave the village because there isn't enough to live off here, but back they come to pick up the baton from the previous generation. Often they have become successful elsewhere.

François Michel, the Mayor and a grower, was one of the Cornas *appellation*'s founders in August 1938. His son was more involved in politics than wine, so the vineyard was rented out until 1988, when grandson Jean-Luc Michel returned home, forsaking a successful career. "I left the village in 1969 and my career was in the vehicle side of the army, outside France as well," he explains. Jean-Michel was born in the house above their cellars and decided to return in 1987, when he was 40. "After six months with the Courbis family, I went back to being a student and spent a year at Valentin near Valence studying wine and agriculture," he says; "people didn't salute me there!"

Jean-Luc has now handed on the domaine and its expanded 3.5 hectares to son Johann and daughter Chrystelle, who work full-time on it and are proud to do so. Jérome Despesse is another example of a young Cornasien who works the week in the Rhône Valley selling corks but returns to tend the family vineyard at the weekend.

Among the older generation, Bernard Blachon, Alain Verset, and Bernard Maurice all work elsewhere, but have kept their hectare or so in the vineyards and continue to make their own wine.

As for those whom the French call *les anciens*, well, they are a case apart at Cornas: not for them the notion of early retirement and sightseeing around the world at 55. Indeed, the habit of working on until the body can take no more is ingrained. The implicit hierarchy of the veterans is shown when Louis Sozet, 68, comments, doffing his hat, that "Noël Verset still goes up the hill to work his vineyard, and he's 84!"

Among the old wine families, there is also a network of intermarriages. Noël Verset's late wife, Aline, was René Balthazar's sister; the other sister is married to Marcel Juge.

Two of the families here, the Michels and the Lionnets, have been making wine for over 400 years. Many of the growers are fifth generation, indicative of the move down from the plateau to the plain and its polyculture in the later eighteenth century.

HISTORY

Cornas' precise wine tradition goes back a good thousand years. A Latin document of AD 885, from the canonry of Viviers, records wine being made by an unnamed religious order—the first definite mention of the wine of Cornas. Local rumour claims the wine had earlier been appreciated by the Emperor Charlemagne as he passed through the village in 840.

Further evidence of Cornas' "holy" origins comes in the register books of the St-Chaffre-de-Monastier Abbey, also in the diocese of Viviers. Here it is stated that "a nobleman named Léotard gave to the Abbey of St-Chaffre a field measuring four manses and a vineyard, on the condition that the brother responsible for the order would offer his colleagues a fine annual dinner that included lampreys and big fish." This agreement ran between the years 993 and 1014, but unfortunately it is difficult to be precise about Léotard's generosity, for the ancient measure of a manse has long since disappeared from use.

The lamprey tradition is said to have stemmed from the saving of some lost boatmen on the

FIGURE 34 Grande Rue, Cornas, with the local landmark of the church spire. (Tim Johnston)

Rhône over a thousand years ago, and today there is still a little chapel beside the Rhône on the rough site of the event.

The religious orders were probably cultivating only small vineyards at this time; the local church documents point out precise boundaries and geographical situations, and the description "a vine" occurs frequently in the old, often Latin, writings.

The nineteenth century was a time when this part of France was generally poor; there aren't many grand houses nearby. The de Barjac family were important seigneurs, and to this day retired *vigneron* Guy de Barjac lives in the family home in the village—a pale stone house with a brief courtyard, not noticeably grand at all.

The agricultural structure was that the residents of the plain villages like Cornas would generally own hill vineyards and grow crops on the easy-to-work, fertile land near the Rhône. The poorer residents of the plateau would be their workers, descending the hill to earn a living beyond their basic domestic polyculture. Thus it was an achievement—hard-earned spurs indeed—to be able to own a little vineyard on the hillside and to eventually live in the village. This is broadly how Cornas developed towards today's composition.

In the nineteenth century, Cornas may have been shipped to Bordeaux to make those wines more robust, if A. Jullien is to be believed in his work of 1822 (cited in M-L Marcelou, *Vins, Vignes et Vignerons de l'Hermitage, 1806–1936*, University Lumière–Lyon 2, 2003). The Tain *négociant* Macker's cellar also tracks Cornas prices by the cask between 1805 and 1836. These were very steady, with a range of 65 francs up to the one-off of 200 francs in the record-priced vintage of 1825. This made them two to two and half times cheaper than Côte-Rôtie, and usually four to five times cheaper than Hermitage.

By the twentieth century, the wine was drunk locally and, if travelling outside the region, was normally being sent for medicinal purposes. Before the *appellation* was created in 1938, there were two barrelmakers at Cornas. "They worked with 200-litre casks that would be sold to Burgundy," states Marcel Juge, "but gradually the merchants went further south to the Châteauneuf-du-Pape area when in search of a filler wine for their local Pinot."

With the growers' network naturally limited to a few *bistrots* and friendly cafés, Cornas remained a simple, local wine, even though entitled with full *appellation* status. Commercial help was needed, and came in the form of the wine *négociant* system. This gave the spur to its distribution.

By the 1950s the local *négociant* houses had started to spread the wine around the region, just as they were doing with the white wines of St-Péray. Vérilhac, Delas, and then Paul Jaboulet Aîné worked with Cornas, which explains why the rare bottles of Cornas dating from the 1950s that one used to find in cities like Marseille, Avignon, or Aix-en-Provence were from houses like Vérilhac—the *vignerons* had limited commercial contacts and so did hardly any of their own bottling.

The first person to bottle his domaine Cornas was a man who worked on the SNCF, the French railways, and who owned a choice part of the *Reynard* vineyard—a subsite called *La Geynale* that is now partly worked by Robert Michel and by Auguste Clape.

Georges Bessenay started to bottle some of his own wine in 1952–53, which was quite a departure for the time. "Well, the market was part *pichets* in Lyon, part *négociants* for a later bottling," comments Auguste Clape. "Either way, we didn't need to bottle—the *négociants* would bring their 600-litre *demi-muids* to the cellars and take the wine away in them. That's one of the reasons there are no splendid cellars at Cornas—everything is on a very modest scale. The only bottling that would take place was for weddings and family events. Otherwise the wine would go away in cask to private buyers 18 months after the harvest, and they would bottle it themselves with a *mise en bouteille par l'acheteur* (bottled by the buyer) label. The wine would sell out very early on," he recalls. "In 1957 it was all sold by November, and with a tiny

The Second World War brought problems for Cornas as the growers went off to fight. There was also a bad frost in 1939, which meant that a *vigneron* like the late Roger Catalon made only 375 bottles from his one-hectare plot. "My vineyard was, like many others, abandoned after I was made a prisoner of war near Trier. But I managed to escape in February 1941, and came straight back to my *boulot*," he would say. M. Catalon was a typical Cornas grower: he started his winemaking immediately after passing his education certificate at 13. He remembered the 1940s as being depressed years for Cornas. "The *cafetiers* of Valence and Vienne would take our wine as *vin de Cornas*, but they really only wanted a wine of no more than 11° to get their customers to drink more—we were selling a wine passed up and down the zinc counters in those days."

crop, prices soon doubled. I had started to bottle a little in 1955, and increased this from 1958 to 1960 onwards."

The crop of 1957 was 453 hectolitres—60,000 potential bottles all told, but the immediate postwar years had been even more precarious. In the run of vintages from 1946 to 1949, the total annual crop for Cornas had been 588 hl, 994 hl, 135 hl, and 360 hl. These were indeed tough days for any grower, so thoughts of bottling represented luxurious daydreaming.

Joseph Michel was another of the first home bottlers around 1956, on a small scale. "Usually the buyers were locals or Lyonnais, so it was a big surprise to find people from the Vendée in northwest France and Switzerland coming to buy the wine," states his son Robert.

Another to join in a little from 1958 was Marcel Juge, selling to private clients. "The *bistrot* trade continued healthily in those days as well," he recalls, "because the café owners of Vienne paid more than the *négociants*."

In the late 1960s, fortunes started to look up a little. The year 1968 had been a disastrous vintage nearly everywhere in France, and Burgundy was going through a rocky period, with expensive, irregular-quality wines. Marc Maurice, whose son Bernard continues with their small vineyard, recalls that as he picked what he could of the 1968 crop, there were three vintages of unsold wine in his cellar. For him, lower down the ladder at Cornas, revival did not start until around 1978.

It was in 1968, that even Noël Verset, now regarded as one of the old pillars here, had to take work in Valence. "I did two jobs for seven or eight years from 1968 on," he recalls; "I worked the morning in the vines, then I would be in Valence until 10:30 at night unpacking parcels from railway wagons." He fails to add that he was then already in his mid-50s.

Around 1969–70 some export orders trickled through as buyers began to look beyond the classic areas like Burgundy. But the vineyards lived under menace of land development, and matters came to a head in 1977. A water reservoir was built on the hill not far from *Patou* close

to the St-Péray frontier; this opened the way to build houses next to it, and some were put up.

Next came the proposal for further development. The village council held heated debates on the subject. Certainly there were growers in favour of licensing construction, but just as certainly men like Auguste Clape, Robert Michel, and Alain Voge stood firm. The project collapsed due to the lack of consensus, and the vineyards—and the reservoir, still in situ today—survived. And the price of a hectare of the vineyard today? Higher than the price of a hectare for development!

I recall the 1970s as tough years; Cornas was locked in a time warp. All the growers seemed ancient. Young people had no desire to sweat it out on the hillsides, and the only newcomers to the ranks were Robert Michel and Jean Lionnet, both born into local wine families. Robert's apprenticeship had started with his much-respected father, Joseph, when he was 18, but both he and Lionnet were over 30 by the time they got going under their own steam.

Jean Lionnet found those early years hard: "My first wine was in 1976, and until 1980 I depended on my wife Suzanne's work in Valence—she fed me for those four years," he remembers; "the year that helped me to get going was the good 1983 vintage."

By the early 1980s, under 20 of the 60 vine growers actually bottled their wine, although increased fame and prices during the 1980s raised that figure to around 30, as well as bringing in some of the first new blood to work the Cornas hillsides for many years. Precisely two men, Thiérry Allemand and Jacques Lemenicier, started out in 1982, and because neither had an inheritance to rely on, their progress was a mix of rental agreements and grubbing out of forgotten plots.

The late 1980s saw the emergence of Jean-Luc Colombo; however controversial his loud statements and his revved-up style, Colombo did shake up Cornas and prompted outside attention to be focused on the *appellation* as well as steering fellow growers to review their methods.

The 1990s brought big swings in the vineyard's fortunes. In June 1993 Auguste Clape reported that it was difficult to sell the wine: "There is a lack of support from the *négoce* trade for some of the small growers who are used to selling them their wine in bulk"—a comment that applies to Beaujolais in the 2000s.

At this stage, Cornas from a merchant or the Co-opérative retailed in France for 36 francs (£3.60/US$5.40) and the wine of a grower like Clape was in the 60-to-70-franc range (£6–7/US$9–10.5), all taxes included. Young growers with heavy capital commitments were renting out their vines to obtain cash flow and cultivating only the core part.

Robert Michel recalls that "we had to wait until the early 1990s for a real increase in demand, and that became more marked from 1996 on. The wine is well known now, with strong demand."

By 2001 that demand had led to the famous case of the Noël Verset hectare. Here swirled drama, greed, and vanity—all on display as people chased this illustrious site on the largely central *La Sabarotte*. In 1995, 0.45 hectare of the vineyard had been offered out at the hectare rate of 500,000 francs, or £50,000, making a total asking price for the precise site of £22,500 (US$36,000).

By 2001 the size available had grown to one hectare, and alliances made with Burgundians, Americans, Rhodaniens—all sorts—had been formed to get hold of it. Its price by then had quadrupled to FF2 million, or £200,000, or US$320,000—for just one hectare of Cornas!

Do the sums: likely number of bottles—perhaps 5,000 bottles a year. Assuming a basic goal of money back in five years, the price of a bottle had to be £8 or US$14—before five years of working costs and a margin were factored in, as well as depreciation. So what sort of price was this going to make the end wine before it had even left the cellars? Dizzy, or what?

The other big issue raised was of course the financing, and the exclusion of ordinary local growers from the event. No Cornas grower could possibly afford such a price, so outside money was forced to be present. Growers were linked with their overseas importers, and meanwhile, in the best French tradition, the acquisition by the Tardieu-Laurent grouping was blocked by the Agricultural Land Group SAFER, in the public interest. Such goings-on!

The outcome in 2002 was that the land—the vineyard on sale finally 1.2 hectares—was split between the Courbis family from Châteaubourg and the Clapes of Cornas. The hectare rate worked out at £229,000 (2004 exchange: US$389,000). By 2003 the theoretical price for a full-slope hectare of Cornas had risen again to around FF2.6 million (£260,000 or US$415,000).

At 104 hectares by 2005, the Cornas vineyard is still small when compared with the past. In 1927 when vineyards were being abandoned because of the shortage of men to tend them after the First World War, a local document described the annual village wine production as around 5,900 hectolitres. In 1999—an abundant year—the figure reached only 4,029 hectolitres.

What has changed in the past four decades is the density of production, and for once, the figures do not lie. The most abundant harvest in the 1970s—the 1973—yielded 2,029 hectolitres, with an average for the decade of 1,458 hectolitres. In the 1980s, the average figure rose dramatically to 2,179 hectolitres, the most bountiful year of 1989 providing 3,082 hectolitres. That is a rise of just under 50 per cent on the 1970s. But in the same period, the vineyard did not grow nearly as fast: 1971, 53.4 hectares; 1982, 66.8 hectares; 1989, 70 hectares—only just over 30 per cent.

The trend of more intensified production continued in the 1990s. In that decade, production levels averaged 3,055 hectolitres, when the vineyard surface area expanded from 74 hectares in 1991 to 93 hectares in 1999. So, while the vineyard was enlarged by nearly 26 per cent, average production rose by 40 per cent.

Former Growers Union President Pierre Lionnet has firm and reasonable views on the density of some of the new planting at Cornas.

"Since the late 1980s, I've been worried by the bad new custom of planting only about 4,000 plants a hectare, with wide spacing and wire training to allow easy working," he says.

"The true slopes' density is a minimum of 8,000 plants per hectare," he continues. "What these new moves mean is that each plant is expected to produce double, which isn't good for quality, obviously," he states with great conviction. "There's also no legal block on expanding up on to the plateau," he adds, an aspect that mirrors the rules at Côte-Rôtie. Within the delineated area of Cornas, up towards the plateau past *St-Pierre* are pasture and cows grazing, for instance.

The vineyard has also become a lot younger. Between 1990 and 2003, 33 hectares were planted, meaning one-third of the *appellation* is under 15 years old. The growers may often be old, but not all their vines! Most new vines have been clones, not a hand selection from current old vines, so production has been encouraged that way, too. If the grower receives state aid to help to finance planting, certified clones have to be used. Hmm.

The increased planting is spread around, according to Pierre-Marie Clape, President of the Growers Union. "Possibly there has been relatively most on sites like *Le Coulet*, *Chaillot*, and *St-Pierre*," he says—meaning the northern area. But there is also plenty of activity on the heights of sites like *Sauman* and on *Rougeole* beside St-Péray.

Yields are set at 40 hl/ha plus a potential extra of 15 per cent, although in reality the average extra usually comes to 10 per cent. Thus a total of 44 to 46 hl/ha can be considered. This level has been held in the mid- to low 40s despite pressure from some modernist growers in the late 1980s for amounts as high as 57.5 hl/ha; a dossier presented to the Paris central office of the Institut des Appellations d'Origine requested that much—to the dismay of older growers like Auguste Clape and Maurice Courbis.

Despite such concerns about planting and yields, the single most encouraging sign at Cor-

Like Guy de Barjac, who used old Syrah cuttings of his own to continue with the true local variety, Petite Syrah—the same as at Hermitage, but not the same as the Serine of Côte-Rôtie—Marcel Juge is wary of what he calls the recent clonal variety—"recent" meaning that it was introduced around the late 1960s and early 1970s.

"The Petite Syrah that we have here is still the old, small one. The new clonal variety produces larger grapes that are less affected by *coulure* [fruit failure] and have longer stems and branches. Their wines have less degree and colour—look what has happened on the plateau at Côte-Rôtie where it has been widely planted. As it's so naturally productive, the new version doesn't need to be pruned in the Guyot way to encourage it—it can be pruned *au Gobelet*," he observed in 1981.

nas in the 2000s is that the young are back in force, and a good thing, too. Stéphane Robert and Vincent Paris have both excavated some highly precipitous slopes on *Sauman*, a young man's activity; Paris has also planted on *Patou*, along with the Durand brothers. Then there's Matthieu Barret with a young vineyard on *Eygas*. All are taking advantage of the extra planting allowances accorded to young growers under the rules of the Growers Union.

There are also the young returnees—people like Jérome Despesse, and brother and sister Johann and Chrystelle Michel. They have taken up their families' vineyard heritage here and show clear motivation. The way ahead for Cornas lies clear and open.

CORNAS VINEYARDS

The vineyards of Cornas are spread to the west of the village, and it is notable that from north to south they barely extend more than three kilometres, or under two miles. There were 104 hectares planted in 2005.

There are three zones: a northern one reflects granite but also the limestone seam that runs up the eastern, Rhône River side from St-Péray. Its wines are often fresh, also due to the relative height of the vineyards, at 250-plus metres. Tannins are generally marked, notably from the lower ends of the slopes, where more clay is present. If there is any rusticity in a Cornas, it can derive from this more limestone-influenced zone.

The central zone is where the prime south-facing exposures exist, populated by the oldest vines; their ease of accessibility ensured their continued cultivation in the hardest times. Here is the core granite area, the gneiss of granite in evolution, with touches of clay. The wines here are the fullest and most sustained, with abundant tannins that are rich and usually well absorbed.

The southern zone contains some of the most precocious sites, and the granite here is often sandier and more decomposed than the central zone. These wines are aromatic and supple and, to a purist's eyes, would risk lacking the tannic sinew that should be present in a potentially long-lived Cornas.

Through the vineyard the Ardèche hilly influence wiggles unerringly. The Cornas *appellation* dips and rises across a series of small valleys, where streams burrowed out a trail thousands of years ago. These are a notable factor in assessing the layout of the vineyard, since they bring with them turns in the hills and changing exposures.

There are 11 such streams from north to south, the principal being *Chaban*, that runs through the heart of the village and picks up several of the subsidiaries on its way to the Rhône. From north to south, the others are *Coulée, Eygas,* and *Chaillot* all on the east side of the vineyard; *St-Pierre* and *Rieux,* the first tributaries of *Chaban* in the west, *Lègre, Sauman, Fourches, Bayonnet,* and *La Côte.* All have helped to define the shape and exposure of the vineyard sites, and where the best chances lie of achieving full ripeness.

As another general rule, the slopes hold more granite high up, and more clay low down. All are pretty well protected from the winds of the main Rhône corridor.

The village is situated at a point where the Rhône Valley is very broad and the vineyards are set well back against the valley's western flank. This means the heat level in the vineyards can be well ahead of other parts of the northern Rhône.

As a rule of thumb, Cornas expects to be a full 1.5° of alcohol ahead of Côte-Rôtie by 10 September, which makes the readings of 1999 even more startling. "That year we and Côte-Rôtie were at the same level of maturity in early September, which makes it clear why their vintage was so successful," recalls Auguste Clape. He also offers the saying that 20 to 30 mm (around 1 in.) of rain between 15 and 31 August makes the harvest ideal.

In 2003, of course, matters went to major extremes. The raw sun burnt up the grapes and provided Cornas with a Languedoc-style crop, full of potent, extremely ripe flavours. Young vines with short root systems suffered in 2003, but even though the laws allow for their irrigation up to three years old, that's not much in use. "Try lugging up and down a 20-litre watering can, which is what the word 'irrigation' means at Cornas," joked Robert Michel.

The Cornas *micro-climat* is often overlooked by vintage chartists, who, governed by events in Hermitage and Côte-Rôtie, lump together the different *appellations*. A year like 1977 is remembered at Cornas for the very reason that ripening was poor. On the other hand, 1993 was a vintage when Cornas' ripening profile came to the fore.

This was a year of tremendous amounts of September rain. Jaboulet made no 1993 Hermitage La Chapelle, for instance. Cornas was luckier. Readings by the Chamber of Agriculture on 6 September showed the sugar level at Hermitage to be equivalent to 11.2°, with Cornas at 12.8°. Cornas made the best wine in the northern Rhône that year. A Pierre Lionnet 1993 drunk in 2003 was still in good shape, for instance.

The *micro-climat* also means that growers can throttle back on their treatments. "I never actually treated against rot," recalls the now retired Guy de Barjac. "For me, the two main problems were *cicadelles* (locusts) and *ver de la grappe* (grape worm), and these can be attended to by lighter treatments."

At the top end of the *appellation*, the boundary with St-Joseph is marked by the *Argentière* stream, the nearest St-Joseph *lieu-dit* being the noted *Les Royes*, which is worked by the Courbis family.

The most northerly site reflects the merits of the French *appellation* system. For wine purposes, *Les Arlettes* is actually 90 per cent outside the *appellation*, since that part of it holds a lot of limestone from the seam that runs down into the village to *Pied la Vigne*—it's the northern spur of the Crussol chalk. This land can produce plain red Côtes du Rhône, but not Cornas.

The more degraded, weathered granite, or *gore*, part of *Les Arlettes*, contains some clay as well and is allowed to make Cornas, with Matthieu Barret and Jean Lionnet present on this site. Jean Lionnet finds its wines harder to drink young than those from the sunny, decomposed granite areas like *Combe* and *Patou* in the south of the *appellation*.

Its neighbour is *Le Coulet*, an east-facing site that runs behind the wooded limestone hill here at the top end of the *appellation*. Its granite is mixed with clay-chalk. Although its slope is quite steep, the land can be worked by mini-Caterpillar tractors. *Coulet* is mostly owned by the Barret family; the top half is worked by Matthieu Barret, the bottom half by Jean Lionnet under rental. Colombo works a small plot here, too.

Coulet's wines are usually fresher and a little more acid than those from the main area near the centre of the village. They emphasise black currant rather than hearty grilled flavours. A subsidiary site on the southern end of *Coulet* is *La Patronne*, which is also jointly worked by Jean Lionnet and Matthieu Barret. It is bordered by the *ruisseau des Eygas* at its southern end. Since the late 1980s, there has been a fair amount of planting on *Coulet*, with the presence of broadly spaced wire-trained vines set out on its terraces.

The largest site in the northern area is *Les Eygas*, which touches *Le Coulet* and rises higher up. This is well set back from the river corridor and is cut in two at the top by some trees, giving it good shelter. It is 80 per cent terraced and faces east-southeast. Its southern part is small, with Sozet and Chaboud present there. This is a rocky-sanded granite vineyard, running up to 300 metres or so. Any rain here filters away quickly, and there is a tiny stream, the *ruisseau de Bornes*, that runs from the northern reaches of *Eygas* into the *Argentière* stream, separating Cornas from St-Joseph. *Eygas* is late ripening, often 10 days behind the hillsides nearer St-Péray. The relative acidity of the soil and the altitude here ensure a fresh style of wine.

Growers on *Eygas* include Chaboud, Courbis, Colombo (who has his house high up in the vineyard), and Louis Sozet, who has rented out some of his 1920s vineyard to Stéphane Robert of Domaine du Tunnel and sold a little land to Matthieu Barret. The Courbis brothers' hectare-plus was a vineyard until the Second World War, after which it was abandoned because it is high—around 300 metres—a little way from the village, and a late ripener, with the attendant risks. This 1991 plantation ripens about two weeks behind their most precocious site of *Champelrose*.

One of the highest *lieux-dits* at Cornas is the tiny, isolated southeast-facing site of *Jouvet*, set between *Eygas* and *St-Pierre*. Its vines run up to 380 metres and grow on hard granite. It was an abandoned site with a ruined farm on it until some planting in 2002 by a Tain Co-opérateur.

The *Eygas* granite theme connects to that of its relative neighbour *St-Pierre*, about 800 metres away to the southwest and separated by a brief burst of meadowland. Well tucked away out of sight and high up at around 320 metres, this has become an exciting new vineyard since given prominence by Paul Jaboulet Aîné. Their 4.7 hectares are in a very steep bowl on the west side; Chapoutier have also acquired land here, and are planting a little each year across the road from Jaboulet.

Teysseire and Jacques Lemenicier are Jaboulet's neighbours here; the latter has the largest part of his vines on *St-Pierre*. These ripen around two weeks behind his plots on *Pigeonnier* and *Saveaux,* lower down and further south —all due to the altitude. Lemenicier finds his *St-Pierre* wine—from young vines, like most here—to be very aromatic, with plenty of raspberry. It is also evident that the relatively high acidity in the *St-Pierre* granite makes its grape juice very balanced, possessing good harmony.

There is a second side of *St-Pierre* to the east, separated by some apricot trees and a small farmhouse, and close to the chapel that stands at 380 metres. Here Jean-Luc Colombo works 1.5 ha.

In the more westerly sector of the *appellation* lies *Les Aires,* a rocky, gneiss-granite *lieu-dit* close to the stream of *Chaban* just after it has taken on the flow from the *ruisseau de Saint-Pierre.* It is on the east, valley side of the hill of *St-Pierre,* with a farm in the middle, and is worked by M. Combe-Dimanche, a well-known Co-opérateur, and by Vincent Paris.

Peupliers is an under-one-hectare subsite of *St-Pierre* just east of the Chapel of St-Pierre. It has granite at its southeast side and more clay as it turns east, with a tiny water source. It is worked by Vincent Paris and Colombo.

South of *Eygas* runs the stream of the same name, and after a ravine and some woods, there is a *climat* that is talked about with great respect by the growers, *Chaillot.* This is where the vineyards start to get closer to the village. Noël Verset and René Balthazar have always worked vineyards here, but there has been a lot of replanting since the mid-1970s on, encouraged by the possibility of using Caterpillar machines to work its lower areas.

The vineyard sets off facing east, then turns south and south-southwest; it runs in three folds, the outside two concave. The western and central folds are both granite, a lot of it decomposed with a *gore* topsoil, while the lower eastern one contains more limestone and clay. Of the last named, Auguste Clape admits that it would be "a lovely place to make white wine if we were allowed." The clay touches can run up to halfway up the hill.

Chaillot lies to the right of the road that wiggles up to St-Romain-de-Lerps and is on a more northwesterly flank of these Ardèche outhills. Across the vineyard here, the greatest incidence of granite is high up, with the lower areas showing more traces of limestone and red clay. It seems that the limestone shift that formed the jagged Crussol outcrop beside St-Péray did not reach the high spots of Cornas, leaving them more granitic and acid as a result.

Many of the top growers work plots on *Chaillot*—Allemand, Clape, Colombo, Courbis, Durand, Balthazar, Robert Michel, Noël Verset, and Voge, plus Elie Bancel and Pierre and Corinne Lionnet. "Tannin" is a key word when judging the wines from *Chaillot*: the higher granite sites provide what Auguste Clape terms "structured, complete wines with elegance." The Durand brothers concur, saying their *Chaillot* from high up is rich in tannins with a dry minerality, perhaps from the later ripening. The tannic presence becomes less marked the lower one goes down the hill.

The main zone of *Chaillot* ripens well and its wines can be quite low in acidity—from growers like Allemand and Verset they are big, gutsy wines, with rich but integrated tannins present. "My *Chaillot* is always more full-bodied and slow to come round than my *Sabarotte,* for instance," comments Noël Verset, referring to his old holding in the southern zone.

Another factor helping ripening at *Chaillot* is, in Jean-Luc Colombo's view, the role of the trees that line the whole northern and western boundaries of the vineyard. He compares their protection to that found on the Ott estate in Provence and at Château Rayas at Châteauneuf-du-Pape.

For Robert Michel, whose vineyard contains some clay and dates only from 1978, the wines from here are rich, but the tannins can be tough, so he often destems. Auguste Clape observes that the lower reaches of *Chaillot* provides wines that are heavier and less elegant than those from the core and higher up. René Balthazar is not a late harvester, so his view on *Chaillot* is a little different: "For me, it gives red-fruited wine, not especially tannic, and some violet; the tannins are soft enough to allow the wine to be drunk young."

A tiny site tucked into *Chaillot*, and rather hidden behind the central fold, is *Le Bois*, a granite-sanded spot. It is opposite the end of the plateau of *Les Arlettes* and is slightly northeast facing. Thiérry Allemand's old-vines crop from here is usually picked later than most, and Pierre Lionnet also has a small holding here.

The action near the village hots up running south and east of *Chaillot*. Along the eastern limit is the now reduced area of *Pied la Vigne*, where housing has intruded since the 1960s. This is clay-limestone, quite a flat area. Growers here include Pierre and Jean Lionnet, Clape (some vines dating from 1890), Voge, Durand, Courbis, and the Tain Co-opérative. For Pierre Lionnet, its wines come out with some rustic, punchy tannins; blending them with wines of greater finesse is desirable. Again, the limestone corridor from south of Crussol hugs this eastern limit of the *appellation*, which is the nearest part of Cornas to the Rhône.

On the west and south sides of *Chaillot* runs the stream of that name, with a large ravine separating it from some of the top *climats* within the celebrated *Reynards* site—*La Côte*, *Tézier*, and *Petite Côte*. Below *Reynards* is *Les Mazards*, which is under the wall that runs beside the road to St-Romain-de-Lerps and quite near the village. *Mazards*—old name *Mazasse*—mixes two rock and soil types: granite and clay-limestone, the granite a firm presence 60 to 70 cm (2 ft.) down. The theme is of granite high up and clay mixed with sand lower down.

The northern area of *Mazards* is very steep, but lower down the land is flat—with half a metre of sandy granite that has over time descended off the slope lying on top of red clay, which helps its rainfall retention. Machine work is possible here in the lower area, where Pierre

Lionnet cultivates an extremely old family plot. "My *Mazards* Syrah makes the fruit come out in my wine—for me it's a provider of fresh raspberry or black currant."

The landmark here on the line between the high and the low areas is a small, ruined sandy-coloured house called "Le Pigeonnier" that used to be the old hunting house of the de Barjac family and that now belongs to Thiérry Allemand. This is one of the subsets within the *Mazards climat*, where the vineyard is so well known—and thus so good—that local usage has come to identify precise spots within it. *Reynards* is the champion *climat* at Cornas for subsets within its area.

Le Pigeonnier mixes some sand and clay, with decomposed granite at its top point. Chaboud and Lemenicier grow vines here, the latter referring to the peppery style of their wine. Like its close neighbour *Petite Côte* on *Reynards*, its wine also bears some tannic austerity.

The lower-slope vines on *Mazards* are markedly more drought resistant than those higher up. Auguste Clape recalls the experience of both 1989 and 2003—two drought summers. "In 1989 a mere 2 to 3 mm (0.08–0.12 in.) of rain fell at Cornas between April and the harvest in September—less than 2003," he recalls. "That year the average weight of a bunch of Syrah taken off the high slopes was 250 grams; bunches picked at the bottom of the slopes weighed 410 grams." The other side of the coin here was the 2002 vintage, when the bottom area of *Mazards* was rotted!

Growers with plots on *Mazards* include Franck Balthazar, Matthieu Barret, Dumien-Serrette, the Durand brothers, Pierre and Corinne Lionnet, Vincent Paris, Stéphane Robert of Domaine du Tunnel, and Voge.

Wine from *Mazards* follows the soil, as one expects at Cornas. The high granite areas bring out cooked *cassis* or black currant fruit, with plenty of volume and richness. The lower sand-lime areas emphasize red fruits, with a lighter composition and less of a tannic structure than the wine from *Chaillot* or *Reynards*, for instance. There is also higher acidity than *Reynards*.

Rising some five kilometres (three-plus miles), high up in the woods and running through the heart of the village, the *Chaban* stream acts as an important vineyard defining line; south of it the names are worthy and provide top-grade Cornas. But there is a whisper of magic absent from them in my mind; one factor perhaps is that these *lieux-dits* are not always on main hillsides nor so full-south facing. Wines like the Courbis Champelrose and the Dumien-Serrette Patou are often wonderful, but there isn't quite the majesty about them of wines from the core areas like *Reynards* or *Chaillot*, which lie at the heart of any bottle of top-grade Cornas.

Asking the name of the stream uncovers a typically Cornasien exchange.

Author: "What's the name of the stream?"

Vigneron: "The Stream."

When it has a name, the locals mostly refer to *Chaban* as the stream of *Reynard*. It rises on the plateau of *Chaban*, passes in front of *Les Aires*, past *Reynards* and *La Geynale*, then splits *Barjasse* and *Champelrose* before running through the village. It has already been fed by the *Rieux*, *Sauman*, and *Fourches* burns, and just before the Rhône, something over 1 km (1,100 yds.) away, it scoops up all the northern burns as well—*Eygas*, *Chaillot*, and *Coulée*. After heavy rain, it becomes a busy torrent for a few hours.

In the village, a tiny patch of vines is observable beside the *Chaban* stream; these are on a site called *La Coulèyre* and stand right outside the front door of their owner, M. Combe-Dimanche, who sends his crop to the Tain Co-opérative.

Reynards runs behind the top of the hill visible from the village, and has an excellent south-southeasterly exposure. As with the other hill flanks at Cornas, the highest vines here go up to 260 metres or so, the *coteau* starting at around 125 metres. The soil here is granite with a bit of gneiss, very fundamental rock. There is some clay topsoil and the odd patch of limestone. The clay content helps to preserve the water reserves, which is a vital asset in drought years like 1989 and 2003. The presence of clay

and limestone also acts as a moderating influence on the granite's acidity and contributes to the quality from here, the best source of wines in the *appellation*.

Some of *Reynards* is home to real veteran vines: Robert Michel's core vineyard dates from 1910, precisely on *La Geynale*, also the name of his top wine, which is the extension of *Reynards* with strong granite in it. "*Reynards* gives wines that are elegant, contain a lot of pepper, and hold good tannins—so I don't destem its crop," he says.

For Auguste Clape, his *Reynards* wine is marked by violets on the bouquet and lots of tight tannins that need time to unbundle. There are often chewy, tarry aspects on the finish, too. Other growers on *Reynards* are Allemand and cultivators who sell to Jaboulet and the Tain Co-opérative.

Reynards is replete with subset names: *Tézier*, *Geynale*, *Barjasse* or *Cayret*, *La Côte*, *Petite Côte*, *Les Baumas*, and *Reynards*, whose title of course gives the whole corner its common name and whose slope is behind the front flank presented by *Tézier*. These are hallowed areas—the oldest vines, the sunniest slopes, the muscle providers in any good Cornas, but also the bearers of the richest grapes.

Placing *Reynards* in context with the much-esteemed *Chaillot climat*, Auguste Clape observes that *Reynards'* possession of some clay makes its wine more complete and more savoury. "Even though there are spots of clay on *Chaillot*, like where Robert Michel has his vineyard," he adds. Thiérry Allemand's plot on *Chaillot* also contains clay, and for him, this makes its tannins harder than those from *Reynards*, meaning its wine can therefore live well. "The texture of *Reynards* for me is more mineral because of the granite presence in my spots there," he adds.

The hill's flank starts with *La Côte*, the most east-southeast-facing site. These sandy-granite 2 to 3 hectares are tended by Bancel, Clape, Colombo, and a Tain Co-opérateur. Auguste Clape describes La Côte as a wine of red fruits, well ripened in style; there are olives and some warm, southern tones, with an elegant roundness on its finish, and some tannins peeking out.

Just south on the same flank is *Petite Côte*; this holds a lot of granite high up, but lower down there is clay close to the surface. The clay is thought to help introduce a spiced element into the red fruit, and also to encourage its tannic content. Growers here are Allemand, Clape, and Colombo.

Moving round to a more purely southeast exposure, at a level opposite the cemetery and in full view of the community, is the *Coteau de Tézier*. This hillock rises to precisely 241 metres at its top, which is marked by a little ruined stone hut used in the past for tools and horses.

Tézier is the epicentre of the *appellation*, the blue cedars above it, visible from the village, acting as its main landmark. With seven to eight hectares, it is the largest subset of *Reynards*. The soil here is again strongly granite based, with a covering of decomposed stone, and so susceptible to drought. Growers here are Allemand, the Durand brothers, Paul Jaboulet, and Voge. For the Durand brothers, their *Tézier* Syrah planted in 1990 provides a savoury, almost Pinot Noir aspect to their wine. Broadly, the style of *Tézier* resembles that of *La Côte*.

Underneath *Tézier* is a small *monopole* vineyard of Alain Voge, called *Les Baumas*, something over one hectare. Alain usually refers to this simply as *Reynard*. Also below *Tézier* is *La Barjasse*, named after the leading de Barjac family.

Barjasse lies very close to the village at around 130 metres, and its alias is *Le Cayret*. This is another site with vines dating from around 1900, and after Guy de Barjac's retirement, the vineyard was in part bought by Colombo and part worked under rental by Sylvain Bernard of Domaine de Fauterie. Alain Voge also has a small plot on its two to three hectares. It lies across the *Chaban* stream from Matthieu Barret's cellar.

Another grower on *Barjasse/Cayret* has been Marcel Juge, whose vineyard dates from the 1950s. This is engine-room wine—"robust and

good to blend as a central part of a wine made from various sites," he says. Cooked black fruits are in evidence here, with chewy finishes.

Turned more full south comes *La Geynale*. There are two soils here: high up it is mainly rotted granite or *gore*; lower down it is a mix of crumbled loess, stones, and clay. *Geynale* is about four hectares, best known thanks to Robert Michel's fine wine of that name, and is also worked by Barret and Alain Verset.

The *Reynards* name itself runs to five or six hectares and is the most south-facing flank of the hill, making it one of the most sheltered sites at Cornas—another spur to ripening. Growers here are Allemand, Clape, two Co-opérateurs, and a supplier of crop to Paul Jaboulet. Some of the Clape vineyard is typically old, dating from the 1920s.

Reynards' wine is robust, its tannins marked when young, but at its centre is a full, cooked fruit aspect that melds well with age.

The *Chaban* stream separates *Reynards* from two sites south of it—*Sauman*, which is set right into the flank of the hills, and *Champelrose*, which is nearer the village. The two sites are themselves split by another stream, *Sauman*, that flows into *Chaban*.

Champelrose's vines extend right beside the village, at the level of the pharmacy, until ending at the western extreme in a row of evergreens. It is on lower flatland, and its soil is heavier and deeper than many—a mix of sand and clay without any hard rock. It gives quite potent wines full of red fruits, with an earthy element to the flavour. The tannins are less present than those from the *Reynards* sites. Growers on *Champelrose* include the Durand brothers, Courbis (with some 1919 Syrah), Juge, and Noël Verset.

Sauman is a vineyard that rises steeply from around 130 metres up to over 300 metres. This brings into play the effect of altitude here, and a rule of thumb is given by Bernard Blachon: "Altitude is very important at Cornas; once your vineyard lies above a line twice the height of the church, your ripening will be delayed."

Sauman is still covered in plenty of woods and has recently been one for the young men like Vincent Paris. He planted here in 1992, first clearing what he calls its quite coarse ground of its pine trees in 1991. The *Sauman* slope is dauntingly steep, reaching 65° in places. There is a mix of exposures here, some vineyards southeast facing, and others, including those of a Co-opérateur from Tain, more northwesterly facing. Vincent Paris and, below him, the Durands are on the east-northeast section, where there is still a granite influence but the rock is less hard and the topsoil deeper.

Stéphane Robert is another young man toiling to plant here, on the southeasterly part of the slope. He has found traces of old terraces here from many decades past. On this turn in the hill, the granite is very hard, and it is poor ground with little soil. The aspect here is rugged to the eye—this is a "new frontier" site. Next to it, *Reynards* basks in a full south exposure, and Vincent Paris finds his *Sauman* vines ripen around five days behind his *Patou* and *Mazards* sites, for instance. In baked years, the freshness is an asset—otherwise, well, no.

West of *Sauman* and below the *Chaban* stream is another high vineyard, *Lègre*, marked by loose soil on top of its schist and hard granite. It is an expanding site, thanks to Paul Jaboulet Aîné and Franck Balthazar, who first planted there in 2002 and 2003, respectively. The Jaboulet project on *Lègre*, like Balthazar's, is a long-term one, with a small increment each year. Balthazar is on a subset of *Lègre* called *Rougeole* a short distance from its southern tip.

Rougeole abuts the most southwesterly spur of *Les Côtes* and extends into St-Péray, meaning the site can produce red and white wine. Here the vineyard rises past 300 metres, and some of the highest land was formerly home to cereals and cherry trees. The Tain Co-opérative has bought terrain high up here in a long-term venture to gradually plant and develop this granite site.

South of *Sauman* is *Sabarotte*, the first of two parallel hills, the other one *Les Côtes*, that overall are a mix of granite and sand. The stream of *Bayonnet* runs between them, passes by the bottom of *La Chelle*, and crosses the southern part of the village.

Les Côtes is divided in three parts—*Les Côtes* itself at the top and two subsets, *La Fontaine* in the middle and *La Chelle* at the bottom end. The *Sauman* stream, fed by the tiny *Les Fourches*, runs between the two hillsides of *Sauman* and *Les Côtes*.

Sabarotte is fringed on its western and top sides by severe woods, newly forested land that used to hold vineyards. The old growers recall a few parts being tilled after the Second World War, but these were gradually abandoned. *Sabarotte* runs to about 2.5 hectares and is named after the small house built on the hill in 1903. It is largely split between Clape and Courbis, notably after the sale of Noël Verset's plot. Elie Bancel is also planting a small holding here. The Courbis family work the higher section and Clape the lower, more sheltered part.

Sabarotte came to prominence in the late 1990s, when Noël Verset put his holding here on the market. For years it was partly owned by Verset and a notary's wife, who let it out to Delas. The 1.2 ha of Verset vines were jointly bought by the Clape and Courbis families in 2002, the latter also having bought the Delas plot earlier.

Some of these vines date from 1914. After the age of 50, their wastage rate would be about 50 plants a year from the 8,000 to 10,000 per hectare. The soil is mainly granite high up, around 200 metres, with a bit more clay in the lower reaches, where the Clapes work. The topsoil of sandy granite runs about one to 1.2 metres (up to four feet) deep before hitting the hard rock. "It's very slippery to work in dry weather," comments Pierre-Marie Clape, "and when it rains, the water filters through it quickly." The hill is organised into gentle terraces, each one holding 10 to 12 vines from top to bottom.

Sabarotte's wine is often a mix of black currant and red fruits, with some acidity, and tannins that are a little more overt than *Reynards*'. For Pierre Clape, the acidity makes the wine quite firm, while the Courbis cuvée is regularly rich and oily. Noël Verset nods his head vigorously when describing *Sabarotte*'s wine: "It's a very good site—wine of great finesse."

Turned a little northeast of *Sabarotte* and separated from it by a line of rock is *La Fontaine*. Its ground is schist, firm granite, with often very little topsoil. Its wine abounds in chunky, robust tannins, and is very full-bodied—altogether a more tannic wine than that from *Sabarotte*. Voge celebrates this site with his Vieilles Fontaines cuvée, his Syrah here dating from 1925.

Below *Fontaine* lies *La Chelle*, which is less sloping. Its wine is quite refined, without prominent tannin. Growers here are Juge, Stéphane Robert, and Sozet.

At the southwest end of *Les Côtes*, high up at 250 metres and facing southeast is one of its subsets, *Bouyonnet*, named after an old farm. Because access to it was not easy, it was abandoned in the old days. Now Fumat and Jean-Luc Michel have planted on its *gore* soil; at its top is a line of woodland.

Across the *Bayonnet* stream lies another *Les Côtes* subset—*Le Craux*, a thick rock vineyard belonging to the Courbis family. Apart from the big names like Clape and Courbis, growers on the main *Les Côtes* site that runs towards St-Péray include Courbis, Despesse, the Michelas family from Crozes-Hermitage, and Alain Verset. This follows the high-low pattern of holding decomposed granite at the top, then broken, stony granite on the midslope, and more clay at the bottom. Franck Balthazar, Johann Michel, and Co-opérateurs from the Tain Cave also work plots here.

Adjoining the easterly tip of *Les Côtes* and *La Fontaine* is *Les Saveaux*, which starts a run of small sites close to the N86 road and near the village. The vineyards are on gentle lower-slope areas here and often flatland, so wire training is the order of the day. They possess less nobility than the best full-slope locations at the core of the *appellation*. Stéphan Chaboud, for example, relies on his *Les Saveaux* grapes for his regular cuvée wine, the one that highlights accessible fruitiness.

Saveaux is very sandy, the *gore* granite well crumbled and the sand persisting to a depth of at least two metres (over 6.5 feet). It is very free draining. The name *Saveaux* comes from "Les Sept Veaux"—the Seven Veals—indicating the presence of a farm here in days gone by.

Saveaux's wines are what Joël Durand calls "seductive Cornas." The site is a precocious one, one of the first to ripen at Cornas, and the wine is fruited, elegant, and not especially potent. Other growers here are Ghislaine Fumat (who has some veteran vines), Allemand, Lemenicier, Johann Michel, and Jean-Louis Thiers.

The next flank of the hill above *Saveaux* rises and becomes *Patou*; the two sites touch at the southern point of *Saveaux* next to the N86. The only change to the original *appellation* rules came in the mid-1950s, when the southern sites like *Patou* and its next neighbour *Combe* were extended to include the final 50 yards or so that took them alongside the N86. This yardage may not be formidable, but at least there aren't houses built on this space.

Patou is split from *Les Côtes* by the *La Côte* stream. There is a north-northwest spur to *Patou*, where Jean-Luc Michel has a one-hectare plot, then comes a line of trees, followed by the main east-southeast terraced section. Here at the southern exit of the village, the soil is mostly classic granite, but there are spots of schist with mica in it where the Durand brothers work, as well as patches of white clay where the Clapes have some vines. The topsoil is loose and the rock crumbly, so the vine roots descend well here. *Patou* can get very hot because it is in a south-facing fold in the hill—its wine was very southern in style in 2003, for instance.

There are two named subsets within *Patou*, both near the N86—*Rancurel* and *Le Château*. *Rancurel* is opposite the service station, and is worked by the Durands and Vincent Paris, the latter using wire training on his mini-terraces. *Le Château* is a walled *clos* with no vines— an early nineteenth century bourgeois house stands here, with grass and trees around it.

Even though *Patou* runs down the eastern flank of the *appellation*, it is still a helpful kilometre or so (1,100 yards) from the Rhône. It escapes the air currents that run between the Tain-Tournon divide and that are deviated by the limestone hill of *Les Arlettes* sticking out about two kilometres north of the Cornas vineyards at Châteaubourg.

Like several sites at Cornas, some of the *Patou* vineyards were never cultivated after the loss of life in the First World War; it is on just such a site that the Durand brothers planted between 1999 and 2003, when they made a rental agreement with Guy de Barjac. Likewise, the young growers like Paris and Michel have also brought it back to life.

Gilbert Dumien-Serrette's main site, and the name on his bottle, is *Patou*, reflecting the 1920s vineyard he works here. Other growers on *Patou* are Voge and Bernard Maurice. The bottom area is flatland, and more wire training is likely in the years to come.

Patou is a *lieu-dit* that ripens well; its wine is more substantial than that of *Saveaux* and is rich and ripe, with a well-founded *gras*. It is less tannic than a core site like *Reynards*: again, the hierarchy implicit in the land comes through in the glass.

The most southerly *lieu-dit* at Cornas is *Combe*, a mix of terraces and flatland near the N86. It is south-southeast facing and marks the frontier with St-Péray. The soil here is, once more, sandy granite, the most granite higher up, with a couch of red clay between one and two metres down, notably near the road. Both *Patou* and *Combe* have a small drainage canal beside them, called locally a *croze*. The rotted *gore* soil here means the wines are less tannic than those from the northern, harder granite extremes of the *appellation*. Consequently the wine's texture is quite supple, approachable at a younger date. Aromas also reflect floral, violet connotations.

Names on *Combe* include Bernard Blachon, Durand, Juge, Lemenicier, Pierre Lionnet, Stéphane Robert, Thiers, and Voge.

In terms of vineyard work, the young of Cornas appear to carry a sense of responsibility towards their heritage. It is obviously a challenge to make such difficult terrain pay if going flat out for natural applications and remedies. It is often most economic and sensible to apply weedkillers on some gradients, since working the soil encourages slippage and erosion.

One concession to modernism that saves much labour is helicopter spraying, which was introduced in 1990. About 25 growers subscribe to this, which means that around 30 of the 100-plus hectares planted are treated against mildew and oïdium in this way. Around three treatments are applied between mid-May and mid-June as a rule. No insecticides are used.

Another advance from the 1990s has been the return by some growers to selecting their Syrah by cuttings taken from their own best old vines. This is labour-intensive, which is why it fell from use in most places over the past 30 years. The Clapes have been practising *sélection massale* again since 1998. This maintains diversity in the vineyard and also carries the merit of being a very precise, local solution.

There are three to four main clones across Cornas, and Auguste Clape feels there should be more. Such clonal overlap made its mark with a 0.3 ha plot of theirs on *La Côte*. This was planted in 1979, at the start of the clone revolution. "There are only two clone types in this vineyard, against 13 in our 1987 plantation next door between *La Côte* and *Geynale*," says Auguste Clape. "It means there is a lot more balance in the younger wine." Certainly this was clear-cut when tasting the two 1998s side by side before blending: notable balance and a suave fruit tone from the younger vineyard, and a bumpy, tough wine from the older site.

"If you really want to get it right," continues M. Clape, "you must do a microvinification of the fruit from each cutting, to really check it out. And that's extremely complicated." The other point made by son Pierre is that you automatically increase crop size if you plant the stock only from healthy vines. It's no surprise to hear that neighbours also practising *sélection massale* are Jean-Louis Chave and the Gonon brothers at Mauves.

There has also been a change in the rootstock used since the 1970s, when SO4 was popular for its high-yielding qualities. Its vine wood grows quickly, so its vines age and die more quickly. "People prefer the 3309 rootstock now—it has a better root structure," says Matthieu Barret—a view confirmed by another young grower, Johann Michel. Ninety per cent of Cornas' vines are now grafted on to the 3309 rootstock.

CORNAS VINIFICATION

What in those days was known as a hot, dry summer—1989—merited a declaration of harvest around 10 September. In the 1970s and 1980s, it would often take place around the middle of the month. The latest date that Auguste Clape can recall was 1950, when he started on 1 October. The earliest was 2003—22 August.

Recent vintages (see table 9) show the clear effects of the warming up of temperatures in the past 40 years. As holdings are small, most growers can bring in their crops to the cellars within three to eight days of intensive work by family, friends, and some temporary labour. Because there are long family roots here and plenty of smallholdings, early September is indeed a time of local celebration for the *vignerons* and their relations.

If one looks back over Cornas for more than 30 years, the mid-1990s onwards seem to be when the winemaking tidied itself up considerably. This was when fruit became purer and clearer, when cask handling was cleaner, when tannic ripeness improved. The Cornas of the 1970s was certainly more volatile than today—these days it's a surprise to come across a sweaty wine.

Another side effect of better winemaking has been the emergence of clearer, drier flavours, which can be construed as a minerality of texture. Wines are more approachable earlier in their lives—vintages like 1997 or 2000 were perfectly drinkable after three or four years in many cases. Cuvées from older vines would usually merit keeping back longer, but as noted

TABLE 9
Recent Cornas Harvest Dates

2005	21 September
2004	18 September
2003	22 August
2002	13 September
2001	10 September
2000	8 September
1999	10 September
1998	8 September
1997	4 September
1996	7 September
1995	9 September
1994	6 September
1993	9 September

earlier, at least one-third of the vineyard is now very young.

The traditional vat at Cornas is small, open concrete, with whole bunches worked on. The whole bunch growers who can justifiably be called more traditional are classic names like Balthazar, Clape, Dumien-Serrette, Fumat, Juge, Pierre and Corinne Lionnet, and the Versets, Alain and Noël. Thiérry Allemand also works with mainly whole crop, while Robert Michel splits by vineyard site—his *Reynards* is fermented whole, his *Chaillot* up to half destemmed. Alain Voge, likewise, is a part destemmer.

The modernists who destem and therefore later on are more likely to use young oak that may include new casks are names like Matthieu Barret, the Cave de Tain, Chaboud, Chapoutier, Colombo, Courbis, Delas, Durand, Paul Jaboulet Aîné, Jean Lionnet, and Thiers. Part destemmers are Fauterie, Lemenicier, Vincent Paris, Domaine du Tunnel, and the Michels at Vignobles d'Abondance.

Some growers like Colombo, Delas, and Jean Lionnet are premaceration coolers of their crop; Cornas is also a village where the use of cultured yeasts is quite restricted. Certainly the innate quality of the grapes most years plays a part in this, but there is also an awareness of trying to be laissez-faire among many growers, old and young.

More steel vatting is apparent these days, with younger growers like the Durands having thermo-regulated steel vats, and the Courbis family likewise. These modern-style vinifiers will also let the entire fermentation and maceration process run for up to 25 days. A veteran like Louis Sozet, by contrast, is a mere eight-to-10-day man. Colombo is an avowedly high-temperature extraction man—up to 35°C—whereas the more traditional growers run towards 30° to 31°C.

Pumping-overs are common, and for the traditional school, cap punching is normal. *Délestage*—part emptying and refilling of the vat—has been adopted by Barret, Colombo, Courbis, and Jean Lionnet in the past few years; no doubt avoidance of reduction—stinky, animal smells—in the Syrah is one aim, although Allemand would contend that using little or no sulphur solves that.

The tradition at Cornas is raising in used casks for 18 to 24 months. I reckon that by 2012 this will be less common, and that 18 months will be more the top end. The more modernist producers work around 12 to 16 months. While 228-litre casks are the norm, a couple of growers, Blachon and Dumien-Serrette, use the old Cornas *pipe* of 400 litres. The *demi-muid* of 550 or 600 litres has its supporters because it is gentler on the wine—the Durands, Pierre Lionnet, Robert Michel, Sozet, and Noël Verset all favour this size. The Clapes remain faithful to their 10-to-12–hectolitre barrels, while Vidal-Fleury, owned by Guigal, also like large barrels and keep their wine for up to three years in them.

New oak is not as widespread at Cornas as it is Hermitage, or indeed at Côte-Rôtie. Only a handful of growers use 90 to 100 per cent new oak—Colombo, Tardieu-Laurent, and Vins de Vienne. Generally there is a judicious sprinkling of 10 to 20 per cent new oak, as witnessed by the Cave de Tain, Delas, Durand, Rocherpertuis, and Voge. An interesting young man with potential, Jérome Despesse, is the rarity of a whole-bunch fermenter but user of 20 per cent new oak.

Two growers like to be outside the mainstream in their low sulphur use—Thiérry Allemand and Matthieu Barret, the latter also happy to make noise that he is the first organic grower at Cornas. Allemand also does a a few days *macération carbonique* on some of his crop to seek extra fruit and finesse, while he doesn't rack his wine during its 18 months' stay in cask.

There is some fining, but most Cornas is sold unfiltered.

CORNAS

Taste a full cross-section of Cornas these days, and it is clear that the wines are now much tidier than in the late 1980s or early 1990s. Fruit extraction is much purer, helped by closer vineyard care and more assiduous cask treatment and handling. Support roles are played by destalking and cap punching during fermentation, keeping the cap moist.

Such moves have actually opened the door to release extra *typicité*, the local imprint of minerality, a restrained, pebbly dryness most commonly found on the finish.

The classic style of wine from the centre of the vineyard—the area broadly opposite the village—is said by Auguste Clape to be one of grilled or cooked fruits, with prune and coffee touches, plus a good tannic structure. He adds that this is achieved when the grapes are well ripened. "When there has been a ripening without any blockages during the summer season, there can also be a lot of elegance in the wines from *Tézier* and *La Côte*," he adds.

Wine made from older vines—rarer than it was 30 years ago—is also notable for its oily, ripe texture on the early part of the palate. This is followed by the usual tightening of texture as the tannins kick in towards the final stages. With the climate ever warmer, I detect more overt fatness and glycerol in Cornas of the past few years. If growers seek a state of near-overmaturity in the crop—thankfully, not yet widespread—this can lapse towards dulled flavours.

Cornas is therefore a little nearer the mainstream than it used to be, but it is still apart from the other Big Wines of the northern Rhône, Hermitage and Côte-Rôtie. There is a grainier feel to it than that presented by the red fruits and warmth of Hermitage, while the more delicate fragrance of aroma on Côte-Rôtie is softer and more airy than the violets that can be detected on the Cornas bouquet.

I expect a leathery side to the cooked black fruits here, with prunes brought to mind and bosky elements. The dryness circling the wine is another differentiation from its neighbours and is one that is rarely thrown off, even with age. Years like 1990 and 1978 are the exceptions to this—so grandiose that local nuances are submerged under a display of glorious natural ripeness.

At times there is a wax polish effect on the bouquet, found in wines like some of Robert Michel and Thiérry Allemand. "I find this waxed wood aroma goes once it has been aired for a day or two," states Robert.

As the initial big cooked fruits effect settles, Cornas develops a more harmonious side. The austerity of the Syrah settles, and plum and dried fruit flavours emerge on the palate, while the bouquet gains in depth and complexity.

Years of slow ripening and an intrinsically dry texture are ones that can provide great pleasure if left well alone to mature. The glamour surrounds years like 1990 and 1999, for instance, but I look back to vintages like 1980 and 1981 as ones that were generally lumped in with Bordeaux and given a rough (non-Rhône) press. Both mellowed in good style, with their dry leaf–mineral tones prominent, supported by an understated local warmth.

Another vintage in this vein is 1995. The Clape Cornas was locked up at first, and again, parts of the press gave it the thumbs down. But as an expression of Cornas, it is wonderful—the correct early tannins just gradually loosening their grip. After 10 years, there was striking purity and clarity of flavour, a true example of Soil to Glass Transfer—my title for wines made in the noninterventionist manner.

Thirty years ago Cornas was a wine that demanded cellaring. With its fruit now often more direct and clear-cut, earlier drinking is feasible. Sylvain Bernard is not one of the old-timers, having started here in 1990, so maybe his view is unbridled by a sense of history: "I like to drink Cornas when it is five to seven years old," he says, "or capture its extraordinary fruit when it's just one year old." The Granit 30 wine of Robert Michel's nephew, Vincent Paris, is another cuvée aimed at providing direct fruit.

As its structure eases past its 10th birthday, Cornas reveals greater complexity. The secondary aromas of game, mushroom, and dampness become prominent from six years or so, and then soften back towards a gently cooked fruit, sometimes roasted tone that can come in towards 20. Here is old Syrah, with its pleasing southern warmth allowing a noble length on the palate. Whereas Hermitage can hold this Syrah sweetness at very advanced ages—40 or 50 years—Cornas, the more modest country wine, retreats towards dryness and overt minerality on the finish with great age.

Whether Cornas can live until great antiquity is doubtful, even though a bottle from the 1890s (the last number was missing off the label) was still going along when tasted by the magazine *Gastronomie & Tourisme* and reported in its March–April 1993 number. This was from Audibert & Delas of Tournon, and the tasting note read: "very dark ruby; still going—is rich and complex, has an agreeable 'chocolate' flavour of tannin."

IDEAL FOODS TO ACCOMPANY CORNAS

The typical suggestion for a Cornas is a game dish. But there are other options. One optic is to select foods according to the age of the wine. This brings in beef and lamb.

When the wine is young—in its first five years—Robert Michel, Thiérry Allemand, Auguste Clape, and Stéphane Robert suggest *gigot d'agneau* (leg of lamb), and *côte de boeuf* (rib of beef). Jérome Despesse favours grilled beef, and Jean Lionnet opts for barbecued lamb or beef for the young wine.

"I like spiced red meat to capture its youthful power and unctuousness," says Joël Durand, while another young man, Johann Michel, plumps for undercooked beef.

For the smaller vintages—1992, 1993, 1997, 2002—Auguste Clape proposes young Cornas as a good partner for veal. Matthieu Barret selects charcuterie, while Jacques Lemenicier suggests drinking young Cornas after a good bar of chocolate!

With older Cornas, the game options cluster together. Big flavours merit the complexity of the wine and are enhanced by its dark, cooked fruit flavours. The suggestions here are classic—dishes like wild boar and hare. A litany of growers put forward these—Bernard Blachon, Matthieu Barret, Marcel Juge, Johann Michel, Robert Michel, Noël Verset, Stéphan Chaboud, Jean Lionnet, Pierre Lionnet (when the wine is 15 years old), Stéphane Robert, and Elie Bancel. Auguste Clape adds the proviso that the vintage should be firm—meaning years like 1989, 1995, and 1998.

Venison appeals to Bernard Blachon and Johann Michel. For Sylvain Bernard and Jacques Lemenicier autumn dishes and sauced meats go well, while Stéphan Chaboud puts forward red meats in a mustard sauce. More simply, Louis Sozet likes plain roast meats.

Beef when prepared in a *bourguignon* sauce is ideal with an older Cornas for Elie Bancel, Jérome Despesse (five to eight years old), and Marcel Juge. Duck is the choice of Jean Lionnet and Matthieu Barret, both growers in the more limestone-influenced north of the *appellation*.

Game birds are proposed by a handful of *vignerons*; Johann Michel suggests pheasant, and Auguste Clape puts forward partridge, pheasant, and woodcock with a 10-year wine from an easy vintage like 1997. Jean Lionnet is another woodcock supporter.

Less obvious suggestions are *saucisson* from Noël Verset—no doubt thinking of having the odd glass in his cellar—quail in sauce from Pierre Lionnet, and a meat paté from Bernard Blachon.

Almost the last word goes to Thiérry Allemand: "Older Cornas suits lamb cutlets with flageolets, and take note—I consider cheese too dry for Cornas." In that last view, he is out of step with the body politic.

Alain Voge, for one, would disagree: "Strong cheese such as Roquefort, Bresse Bleu, or nicely matured goat cheese can go well," he states. The local Picodon is proposed by many old-timers—Elie Bancel, André Fumat, Louis Sozet, Noël Verset, Jean Lionnet, and Pierre Lionnet.

Cheeses that are mentioned run across a broad selection—Bleu d'Auvergne (Bancel); Roquefort (J. Lionnet, J. Despesse, Marcel Juge —"they soften out each other"); Munster (Johann Michel, M. Juge); Reblochon and Saint-Nectaire "when the wine is young" (J. Despesse); Tomme (J. Lionnet, J. et C. Michel—"when it's four to five years old"); St-Marcellin "when the cheese is mature" (P. Lionnet).

Two young growers follow part of the Allemand line on cheese: "I would restrict to goat," says Vincent Paris; Matthieu Barret would eat only mild cheeses, not strong ones like Picodon.

Sylvain Bernard is a lone voice in proposing a chocolate dessert with his Cornas.

THE PRODUCERS

THIÉRRY ALLEMAND

22 impasse des Granges 07130 Cornas +33(0)475 810650

See also St-Joseph.

Just one or two new names have come through at Cornas in the past 15 years. Maybe it's the prospect of lugging up the sweaty hillside and scrambling around on the slippery ledges that puts people off. So a certain intensity of will and stubbornness of outlook do not go astray when tackling these vineyards.

Cue Thiérry Allemand. No doubt a Terribly Angry Young Man in his early days, he still qualifies as Pretty Angry. He likes to do things his own way, searching for the correct solution but constantly impeded by life and officialdom. His wines are throughly good, so maybe he just needs to be revved up by a good bout of petty form filling if he is to perform at the top level.

He started out very much in the slow lane—no parachuting in from a family inheritance here. It was 1982 and—a teenager among the middle-aged and old—he created a 0.26 ha vineyard on *La Côte*, next to Auguste Clape. Precisely 0.16 ha of this held old plants dating from 1961. The rest was overgrown and needed scrubbing out.

Allemand's next step in 1984 was to fell and root out some very large fir trees on *Chaillot*. These were removed mechanically—another first for him—and a further 0.45 ha vineyard came into being. The trick was repeated in 1987 with more clearing of fir trees, this time on *Tézier*, and an extra 0.45 ha once again.

So straightaway Thiérry was involved with three big-name sites in the vineyard, but there were too many young vines. Balance was needed. The potential for quality was thus upped by his shrewd purchase of some old vines (dateline 1905–08) from Noël Verset in the 1980s and his brother Louis in the early 1990s, plus some from very small cultivators on *Reynards* that dated from 1934.

Now Allemand has reached 4.15 ha. These include vines on *Le Bois*, next to *Chaillot*, where the slightly northerly facing means slow ripening and cropping in early October. There are three wines, Chaillot (6,000 bottles) from vines under 40 years old, the older-vine Reynard (6,000 bottles), and his sulphur-free version of Reynard (2,000 bottles). The splitting by age of vines means that from the same site of *Tézier*, for instance, the young-vines (1987) fruit goes into *Chaillot*, and the 1960s- and older-vine crop goes into *Reynard*.

Nowadays, Thiérry Allemand is an established name and has an international following. I have even met self-styled American "Bordeaux collectors" in his cellar! But he has retained the slightly short fuse and pesky manner that often distinguishes the Questor from the Complacent. "Once I've got all these tiresome dossiers

out of the way—divorce and taxes—I say I'll be at peace," he has observed. The "I say" is the clue here.

He is an Ardechois—naturally, given his rugged temperament. He was born in 1963, and his father was an electrician from Vernoux, his mother from Cornas. His grandfather had done simple vineyard works for the St-Joseph grower Jean Maisonneuve at nearby Mauves, the nearest the family came to the soil since they didn't own any land. As a teenager Thiérry worked in the electricity generation business in the Drôme while waiting to do his military service. Life was not good, but salvation was at hand.

He went to see *le père* Joseph Michel, father of Robert, and was given "not only a job but the passion for wine. I joined him in May 1981, and he died in 1985, but set me on my way."

This very driven man then juggled three activities, to the extent of having one week's holiday in 10 years. By day he worked chez Robert Michel, by night he helped Noël Verset pack his wine, and at the weekends he worked in his own cellars. In 1993 he was still putting in two days a week at Michel, even though he was starting to break through.

Not surprisingly, Thiérry has never been a member of the Growers Union. "I have always worked on my own, and I don't have an agricultural diploma," is his rather tenuous explanation. He goes his own way by doing his own rootstock grafting—very time-intensive and bad for any holiday company seeking his business. Occasionally his parents help with tying the vines or taking out excess bunches. Until the late 1990s, they were the only extra pairs of hands.

Now he has a young assistant, a good strong lad who combines pickaxeing the vineyards for planting with devising graphs that track flowering dates, vat readings, and so on. In 2001 Thiérry also broke out of his small cellar beside the N86 road and moved to 400 metres up on the plateau at St-Romain-de-Lerps, from where there are stunning views across to the Vercors Mountains and Die. This allows him a privacy that he relishes. With this new cellar on the go, there is the gradual sense of some system entering life at this domaine.

Ever the individual, Thiérry was the first person at Cornas to use wire to train his vines. And yet he is ambivalent about it: "It's a done deal from the start, once you have trained the vineyard that way. It's more economical, but doesn't help quality. The Guyot stick training means more trips to attach the vegetation." So he uses wire for the younger vines.

He is working the equivalent of 10,000 plants a hectare, against the now quite common 5,000 to 6,000: thus he doesn't have to stress his vines to achieve his yields—they can work at half the rate. The almost crazy side of his nature comes through when he decides the walls of his *Reynards* vineyard need remounting, stone by stone.

The vineyard is tended on a mix of treatments and natural weeding—the older vines are weeded. He also makes use of the helicopter service to spray against mildew and oïdium when the vegetation is in its younger stages. His pruning is aimed to restrict yields to the 25 to 30 hl mark, to achieve which he also has to drop crop around late July.

A doughty man of lone spirit, Thiérry has a lightweight Zapata moustache, which can add to the sense of struggle he gives out. He would rather risk late harvesting than have to chaptalise underripe crop, as happened to some growers in 1996, for instance. He finished harvesting on 13 October that year, two weeks after many others. The vineyard must do the work, not him: "the notion of *terroir* is all-important."

Again, in the cellar he is on the outside through his very low sulphur dosage in his vats, something he has practised since 1992. In 1996 and 1997 he used no sulphur, but had to resort to 2 gm per hl in 1998, having lost a vat the year before: as always, the risk is taken if he thinks the reward warrants it. "I seek fruit above all, plus the respect for old methods," is how he sums it up. As a limited-issue proof of this policy, he has made 2,000 bottles of a sulphur-free

wine simply called "Cornas" since 1998. Its fruit is taken from *Reynards*.

By and large Thiérry works with whole crop. If the year is a little underripe, some destemming is done. Or, as in 1996, the *vin de presse*, the pressed wine, is kept apart from the main *vin de goutte* until late on, when it has developed. It's a sound policy, but adds extra work. He also uses some *macération carbonique* to extract fruit and to secure finesse, very unorthodox at Cornas. This lasts for two to three days at the start of the fermentation. There is indeed a pureness of fruit in his wines, with a very clean-cut feel to them. Limiting chaptalisation plays a big part in this.

Anxious not to give away too many State Secrets, Thiérry keeps his young wine in steel and wood until its malolactic is done around March (though the 2001 took a year). Then it stays in wood for 18 months, or two years if the ageing process has been slow, as in 2001. No further transfer or racking takes place: the wine is left alone. The Syrah is a grape that often requires aereation to eliminate the threat of reduction (the stinky aroma that is sometimes found all over a wine). So Allemand runs against the grain on this. His answer is simple: "I know all these people studying for Master of Wine (in English!) are taught that the Syrah reduces if not properly aired. But if you don't add sulphur, you can leave it alone." He politely omits the "So there!"

The Allemand wines distinguish themselves by the purity of the extract, a comment that crops up often in my notes. The other ace card is the understated richness that allows the wine to gradually assemble itself in a most harmonious way. There is no excess pushing from the *vigneron*. I find the Reynard is the more structured wine, as in 2000. Chaillot is more open and easy, less profound and nuanced, but its depth was notable in 1998. Reynard sums up the often demanding side of Cornas, and its minerality—this is no facile, lush wine. Often there are aromas of wax and polish, reminders of very aged Bordeaux.

Just one wine was made in 2002.

CORNAS

2002 ★★(★) Licorice, smoky black fruit, grilled touches. Good outcrop of crisp cherry fruit, clear definition, quite upright. Bit limited on finish. 2011–13. "A wine to drink, not keep," says T. A.

CORNAS REYNARD

2001 (CASK) ★★★★ Some oak on nose, nicely intense black fruit. Good structure, wine with grip. Fruit is tight knit, has clear texture. Tannins here, too. Unusual oak due to a one-off purchase of casks this year. Esp from 2009; 2016–10.

2000 ★★★★ Full purple; rather medicine, cleaning polish bouquet, like the *Chaillot* in a way, more compact. A lot of chewy matter on palate, well structured. Tannins show from the start. Direct wine, a good example of Cornas and its mineral side. Leave certainly until 2006 or so. 2017–21.

1999 ★★★★ Very dark, purples. Reserved bouquet with potential. Broods a little, also has a polish, wax effect. Good sinewy fruit on palate, a varied flavour of berries and stone fruit. Some violet on the aftertaste. Tannic. Quite long. More robust than the 2000. Leave until 2007 or so. 2018–23.

1998 ★★★ Dark colour, dulling a bit as it evolves. Taut, upright bouquet, woody hints, brambly fruit also. Overt chewiness and dry-edged texture. Quite austere. Has some flesh, but maybe not quite enough. Demanding wine —leave until 2007 and cross fingers it will unwind and broaden. 2016–20.

1997 (NO SULPHUR) ★★★ Not *en vente commerciale*

1997 (SULPHUR) ★ 2008–10
1996 ★★★ 2010–13
1995 ★★★★★ 2011–17
1994 ★★★★★★ 2015–18

CORNAS CHAILLOT

2001 (CASK) ★★★★ Quite soft bouquet— violets/truffle scents. Tasty, warm, stylish palate, harmonious. Pretty fruit all through. Great style, balance. 2013–16.

2000 ★★★ Good purple; bouquet mixes dustiness with marzipan, floor polish. Good cut of fruit on palate, is live and perky. Touch of violet on the dry-toned flavour. Nice enough length. May be a bit overworked, not especially profound. Leave till around 2005–06. 2012–14.

1998 ★★★★ 2015–18
1997 ★ 2005–07
1995 ★★★ 2006–11
1994 ★★★★★ 2012–15

Export 60 per cent 1) Great Britain, 2) USA, 3) Japan

FRANCK BALTHAZAR

1 impasse des Basses Rues 07130 Cornas
+33(0)475 800172

René Balthazar is content that his son Franck has returned to Cornas and the family vineyard, after working in an engineering company in Valence. He is much too self-effacing to say as much, but his crinkly, smiling face tells its own story.

Franck, a dark-haired, solid-looking man in his later 30s, started with the 2002 harvest, working the family's 1.5-hectare vineyard. "In my grandfather's day, there were three hectares," he says, "but half were rented. He grew cereal and vines—a bit like communion—the vines on spots like *La Côte* and *Chaillot*." Franck has set about enlarging his area and raised the vineyard to two hectares by 2005.

René chips in that his father bought the *Chaillot* vineyard in 1930, after coming down to Cornas from the plateau near St-Romain-de-Lerps.

"He was a corn thresher, and made his wine, too," he says, "which he sold in the spring to cafés, especially a big one at Annonay. I started a little bottling in the mid-1970s, but you can't say there was ever a tradition of long cask ageing here."

The vineyard's core hectare-plus on *Chaillot* dates from the First World War; there is 0.36 ha on *Mazards* (1959, 1961), and Franck started to

FIGURE 35 A typical son of Cornas—Franck Balthazar left his job in engineering to return to the family vineyard, with father, René. (Tim Johnston)

plant 0.1 ha a year over five years in 2003 on *Lègre*, at its southern extreme near *Les Côtes*, where the subset is called *Rougeole*. This was overgrown land, with loose topsoil above some very firm granite. He is sculpting out terraces for the vines to allow soil work and so avoid the use of weedkillers.

Whole bunches are fermented for two weeks in concrete, with twice-daily cap punching by foot and some pumping-over near the end. The 1954 press is still used, and ageing in 600-litre *demi-muids* ("they keep the wine's perfumes better than the 225-litre casks," says René) lasts for 16 to 24 months, since there are four bottlings per vintage. The casks are bought when they are 10 years old. The wine is lightly fined, but not filtered.

The wine is usually well scented—violets and dark fruits, with plenty of depth and an evident tannic presence on the palate. It can be drunk from four or five years on, and in the best vintages can live for up to 20 years. For authentic Cornas and an instinct of its pure nature, this is a good address.

The cellar's oldest artefact, an engraved beam, has the date 1736 on it, but its two tiny rooms are earlier than that. The house is right beside the church, and has become a completely different work environment for Franck. "I worked with a machine company in the textile

trade in Valence," he explains, "and this included six-week stays giving practical support near Shanghai in China. I did an eight-month wine course in Tournon, and now this is my life."

CORNAS

2003 (CASK) ★★★ Violet/stewed fruit/tobacco nose; open, springy fruit, expressive with nice tannins at end. Meaty, has cut. Good early, also from 2007–08; 2018–20.

2002 ★★ Medium-depth *robe*; smoky, Cornas dry, red fruits bouquet. Calm, easy scented fruit, good purity. Elegant, pretty lesser-scale wine. Correct mineral side. Fruit good now, or from 2007 for more variety, game presence. 2014–16.

2001 ★★★★ Raspberry/violet/earthy clear bouquet; robust ripe fruit, good cut. Ripe, well-set tannins. Pure wine, fresh end. Classic year. From 2006; 2018–21.

2000 ★★ From 2006; 2011–14

Export 60 per cent 1) Quebec, 2) Japan, 3) Belgium

ELIE BANCEL

43 Grande Rue/N86 07130 Cornas +33(0)475 402553

This is another family that has clung tenaciously to its small set of vineyards at Cornas.

Elie Bancel's father was a vineyard worker at the now defunct domaine of Robert Jaboulet, and Elie worked for many years on the French railways to supplement his living.

Now past retirement age, he works three sites, the original legacy being 0.25 ha on *Pied la Vigne* (the oldest 1920s, average 40 years). The others are 0.5 ha on *La Côte* (average 40 years) and 0.25 ha on *Chaillot* (average 45 years).

His sons have two tiny plots of 0.2 ha each— Alexis on *Les Côtes* and Dominique on *Chaillot*. Just 1 ha for the family and for Elie's son Dominique, therefore, but the same old pull of Cornas. Dominique has worked with local *vignerons* and looks set to continue the legacy at the domaine.

Elie, a man with an open, cheerful face, grey moustache and outdoor cheeks, does things a little differently in the vineyard—he grows fruit, vegetables, and flowers. Two rows of strawberries, echalotte onions for spring cropping, and bright red and yellow roses light up his holding on *La Côte*. "We eat the fruit and veg, they keep the soil tight, and they all look nice, so why not?" he explains quietly, adding that thyme also grows well in his vineyard.

The grapes are fermented whole in concrete vats for 12 to 15 days, with twice-daily cap punching, and *remontages* (pumping-overs) near the end. Ageing lasts 18 months in 225-litre casks one to six years old, and while there is a light fining, there is no filtration.

Up to 2,000 bottles are produced, with the rest of the wine sold in bulk in the spring to Chapoutier. The bottled wine is a down-home, chunky do, with red fruits and plenty of guts in the best years. It can be variable from one vintage to another.

CORNAS

2001 ★★ 2012–14

GUY DE BARJAC

One of the regulars at Cornas over many years, Guy de Barjac and his family can be traced as

> "One day in the 1980s there came to Cornas an extraordinary visitation that you more likely see outside Notre-Dame," recalls Guy de Barjac. "A bus of Japanese tourists—40 of them from the city of Nagoya—pulled up. Well, you can imagine this caused a commotion in Cornas—all those people, their cameras, the bus blocking the road. . . . They had come to see me, having read about me in a book, and they all came down into my cellar." He pauses at the thought. "They eventually ordered 60 cases of my wine."

vineyard owners way back to the fifteenth century. The site in question is Barjasse, where he owns 1.13 ha that have been in the family since 1475–80. This is a prime area of Cornas.

Now retired, Guy has turned his intellect to vastly different fields. He loves parchments and medieval manuscripts and reads Latin as a hobby. He is also known for deciphering twelfth-century documents in Gothic script.

The de Barjac home is what was called in the village "La Grande Maison." Its 1760 cellar is probably the oldest intact in the village.

Rentals have been made with younger growers such as Domaine de Fauterie, Colombo, and the Durand brothers for *Barjasse* and the other vineyard on *Chaillot*. It would be entirely in the village tradition were the time to come when M. de Barjac's family, his grandchildren for instance, take these up again.

The de Barjac wines were always very stylish. Neither fined nor filtered, they were elegant, with a genuine roundness of texture emerging earlier than from some of the neighbouring estates' wines. A long life would be 15 years.

MATTHIEU BARRET

45 rue du Ruisseau 07130 Cornas +33(0)475 800825

One of the youngbloods at Cornas, Matthieu Barret is setting out to make a splash by being the first organic and biodynamic grower at Cornas. His pedigree is local: his grandfather Jacques was Mayor in the 1960s and planted quite widely in the 1970s.

Matthieu's father, Guy, is an engineer with Shell near Marseille, so there has been a jump of a generation here. Matthieu left the Cave de Tain and made his first wine in 2001: "I was working organically, but they weren't interested in doing anything with that," he states, a short man with dark hair and beard, a definite activist.

His mother's side ran a hotel on the plateau above Tournon in the 1920s, as well as having vines at Cornas. Jacques, who died in 2000, built up the property to nine hectares and rented out half of it to Jean Lionnet while sending the rest of the crop to Tain. The cellars are for the moment still at his great-grandfather's house beside the *Chaban* stream, close to the *Geynale* part of the *Reynards lieu-dit*.

Matthieu speaks like a whirlwind, occasional cigarillo in hand, rapid bursts of speech lancing out—just 30, ready for the interview, unable to restrain himself, tugging at the leash of life: "I spent summers here with grandpa when I was small and went on to study biology at Aix-en-Provence, then on to Montpellier and Beaune for wine. I didn't like putting weedkillers down —so that was my first task. I want the grapes to express themselves, to have tannic balance, not maximum tannins. For me, Cornas can have finesse—the *gore* and its draining soil allow that."

Since 2005, when the Jean Lionnet rental agreement finished, Matthieu has worked what is for Cornas a large holding—9.9 hectares of Cornas and 1.7 hectares of Côtes du Rhône. Currently, three-plus hectares are in the northern sites of *Le Coulet* and *Les Arlettes*. The land is degraded granite—*gore*—with little soil, near the top of the hill at 250 metres, and mostly wire trained on terraces. Part dates from 1920, most from 1970, and the youngest from 1980–90.

He also works half a hectare on *Eygas* (2000–01), a very rocky granite site sold to him by Louis Sozet that had never held vines; 0.3 ha

on *Mazards* (1920s, 1970s); and 0.27 ha on *Reynards* (1930s, 1940s). He has been planting Roussanne and Viognier in the Cornas zone, and from 2005 has made a *vin de table* with them.

Destalking is between half and total—2003 was the latter given the dried state of the crop— and vinification lasts two to four weeks. As Matthieu does not like to work with a pump, he foregoes pumping-overs, so he punches the cap himself and also performs a weekly *délestage* to "oxygenate rather than to extract."

Oak ageing lasts 18 months in three-to-eight-year-old casks. He bottles two wines, the classic Brise Cailloux and the special Les Terrasses du Serre. The former has a go-go style of fruit, while the Terrasses holds deep-rooted fruit and tannin. Neither is fined or filtered.

The price policy here is top end, among the most expensive half dozen at Cornas. The wine is sold in only wooden boxes—for one, two, or at most six bottles. Because Matthieu works with very little sulphur dioxide during the vinification, the wine gains breadth and guts once open. The word that springs to mind here is "elegance"—the fruit is very harmonious, the textures compact. The wines exemplify the recent development of cleaner winemaking at Cornas, but still carry some of the somewhat meaty depth expected of them. Aromas often resemble violets.

CORNAS LES TERRASSES DU SERRE

2003 (CASKS) ★★★ Light pepper/violet, overt aromas; clear fruit, upright, glad no stalks present. Elegant, promising. 15-year wine.

2002 ★★★ Bosky, upright, pebbly black fruit aroma. Compact, gum fruit taste, good matter within, decent early fruit, dries a touch at end. Esp from 2007; 2016–18.

2001 ★★★ Elegant, light cooked red fruit, violet/grilled aroma. Compact matter, good core, some meat. Clean finish. From 2006; 2014–16.

Export 80 per cent 1) Great Britain, 2) Japan, 3) USA

LOUIS BERNARD

Rte de Sérignan 84100 Orange +33(0)490 118686

See also Côte-Rôtie, Crozes-Hermitage, Hermitage, St-Joseph, St-Péray.

This southern Rhône *négociant* produces his Cornas in co-operation with a local supplier who vinifies it under mutual scrutiny. The grapes come from the southern area of Cornas.

The crop is destemmed and receives a three-to-four-week vinification, with daily pumping-overs as well as *délestages* (part emptying and refilling of vats).

CORNAS

2002 Not fresh flavours nor aromas.

2000 ★★★ Thorough, typical bouquet—woods/wild berries. Big wine, tasty, open. Raspberry fruit. Vibrant, rounded, has tannins. 2014–16.

BERNARD BLACHON

8 rue de Clarenson 07130 Cornas +33(0)475 402211

Bernard Blachon, a dark-haired man in his later 40s, works in a factory in Guilherand nearby and, at the weekends, is out looking after his hectare on *Les Combes*. "My fellow workers envy me my Cornas vineyard—there is definitely a cachet attached to it," he says.

The family vineyard was split four ways, leaving him with not enough to exist on. He knows the vineyard was planted by his father, before precise documentation existed, so this is another old-vine domaine.

"It gives me great satisfaction to be in the vineyard," he says; "I have my three sons to help, just as I helped my father when I was a teenager." He first bottled part of the wine in the early 1970s, and sells at local markets.

"My vineyard is on rotted granite or *gore*," he states, "which puts the wine into the second, softer group at Cornas. The northern area around *Chaillot* has harder rock, and the wines up there are tougher."

He partly destems, and vinification in the cellar under his house lasts two weeks, with no outside yeasts added. Ageing runs for 18 to 24 months in 400-litre casks called locally *pipes*. There is a fining but no filtration.

CORNAS

2002 ★ Reserved, light black fruit scent, can come along. Nicely unforced black fruit gum flavour, then tightens, acidity shows through. Fruit a bit dull. From late 2006; 2012–13.

2001 ★★★ Suave loganberry fruit/floral aroma; stylish, soft black fruit, touch of violet, genuine. Slight tannins. 2010–12.

LAURENT CHARLES BROTTE

route d'Avignon 84230 Châteauneuf-du-Pape +33(0)490 837007

See also Condrieu, Côte-Rôtie, Crozes-Hermitage, Hermitage, St-Joseph.

The southern Rhône *négociant* Brotte has offered a Cornas off and on over the years. The latest comes from a younger grower, Matthieu Barret, who is working vineyards previously let by his father to Jean Lionnet. Its fruit is well worked, and elegance rather than power is the calling card.

CORNAS LES ARLETTES

2003 ★(★) Bright purple; peppery, spiced, full bouquet, some bosky undertones. Pretty early fruit, then marked tannins. Lacks comfortable middle flesh; not harmonious, rather dusty end. More stylish and better before bottling. 2013–16.

2002 A tale of a wine tasted in March and December 2004, the former savoury, refined and ★★★, the latter tasted twice and very dry, with plentiful acidity. If on form, the wine can show OK from 2006 and live till 2012.

2001 ★★★ Full *robe*; varied aromas—oily, pine/damp earth/violet. Full, oily and meaty flavour, good content. Tightly packed, quite ripe, mineral end. Esp from 2007; 2016–19.

DOMAINE CHABOUD

21 rue Ferdinand Mallet 07130 St-Péray
+33(0)475 403163

See also St-Péray.

Better known as the doyens of Saint-Péray, the Chabouds work one hectare of Cornas scattered across eight plots—talk about microvineyards. They have been making Cornas since 1993, their holdings being a mix of ownership and rental, some of them from the late Roger Catalon.

For his regular cuvée, Stéphan relies on fruit from lower slope areas, notably *Les Saveaux* towards the south of Cornas, where the soil is sandy, and *Le Pigeonnier*, a subset of *Mazards*. These vines are aged between 10 and 40 years.

He first made a Réserve in 1999; for this, he takes fruit from *Mazards* and *Eygas*, the former right in the heart of the main slopes, the latter in the northern area and added in since 2000. The vines range between 40 and 50 years here. The usual 3,000 bottles were reduced to just 1,000 in 2002 due to adverse ripening.

Most of the crop is destemmed, and vinification lasts three weeks in a mix of concrete and steel vats, the maximum temperature around 30°C. The regular and the Réserve both receive 12 to 14 months' ageing, the former in four-to-eight-year-old casks, the latter in one-to-three-year-old casks. They are fined, but not filtered. The regular has soft tannins and is an early wine, drinkable from three years on.

Stéphan Chaboud is aware of the greater drawing power of Cornas, "which has helped us sell some more of our St-Péray." His aim is for a wine that can be drunk within four to five years, so his regular cuvée carries light tannins and is open and direct. "I'm learning about Cornas," he admits; "I'm not qualified yet." His Réserve wine carries more stuffing, and judging by the 2001, is moving up a gear. It carries some chewy, mineral-style elements and can run for 10 to 14 years.

CORNAS

2002 (CASKS) ★ From 2006; 2010

2001 ★★ 2010–12

2000 ★

CORNAS RÉSERVE

2002 (CASKS) ★(★) From 2006; 2012–14

2001 ★★★ From 2008; 2013–15

M. CHAPOUTIER

18 avenue Dr Paul Durand 26600 Tain l'Hermitage
+33(0)475 082865

See also Condrieu, Côte-Rôtie, Crozes-Hermitage, Hermitage, St-Joseph, St-Péray.

Since 2000 Chapoutier have been planting on the three hectares of land they own behind the chapel of *St-Pierre*, in the north of the *appellation*. Their vineyard lies across the road from Jaboulet's and is also strongly influenced by the granite.

Approaching 0.7 ha is now planted, and this crop now adds to their other sources: mostly grape purchases, plus a little bought-in wine from vineyards such as *Eygas* nearby and *La Côte*.

The crop is all destemmed and is fermented in small concrete vats for about 10 days, with cap punching and pumping-over. A two-week maceration follows. Ageing lasts 13 to 15 months in one-to-four-year-old casks.

The style is for rich, warm textures here—wines that are full and appealing, with sufficient tannic support to ensure a steady development. They are easily approachable—either for a wholesome hit when very young or after five or six years when the oily, gamey side comes through.

CORNAS

2003 (CASK) ★★ Tight, a block of stewed fruit aroma. Dense wine, raspberry fruits, still very enclosed. Tannins ripe. Sound enough, length OK. Leave so can diversify. From 2007; 2018–21.

2002 ★★★ Live nose, violets, earthy; round fruit, sound three-quarter weight. More jam texture than usual. Esp from 2006; 2012–14.

2001 ★★★★ Big bouquet—oily/leathery/ wild berries/pepper; lively, prolonged fruit, mineral/dry end, very *terroir*. Tasty. From 2006; 2016–17.

2000 ★★ Bosky, varied nose, pine, smoky leather/spice. Very Ardèche granite style. Surprising midpalate flesh, red berry attack, is just a little stretched. Tannic chew at end. 2012–15.

1999 ★★ 2013–15

AUGUSTE ET PIERRE-MARIE CLAPE

146 RN 86 07130 Cornas +33(0)475 403364

See also St-Péray.

There should be a stone to Auguste Clape in the northern Rhône. A stone would suit more than a statue—it would be more fundamental and less pretentious. The legend on it should read something like "Wisdom, Integrity, and Humanity." For this is an exceptional person. Extending over 30 years I have observed the always understated work he has done for Cornas and its *appellation*. He is also an exceptional learning post, for he is one of the few growers I have ever met who succeeds in bridging the connection between man and nature.

There isn't an overt policy or out-loud statement of intent. It's more a feel, one that leaves a few clues if you are lucky enough to spend time with him. There is his strong belief in letting time do a lot of the work: an appreciation that Cornas—the very place—is as it is. He, the grower, is an attendant, now lucky enough to have his son Pierre-Marie to have taken over from him. It's almost an honour for him to be able to take fruit from the rugged soil and transfer it to other people's daily lives in a form that carries all sorts of historical, sensual, and emotional connotations.

This makes him a genuine, practising child of nature. There is an inner calm in some of those who work the soil that metropolitan dwellers seek to fulfil through courses, books,

and even therapy. Here it exists in an active, functioning state. Belief on the one hand, listening on the other. No closed walls. The true philosopher born of the exceptional opportunity that winemaking can confer.

Auguste's family were *vignerons* in the early 1900s, but life was tough. Owners of 100 hectares of vineyards in the southwest Aude *département*, they were caught up in the serious demonstrations of 1906–07 over the wines' failure to sell. These riots turned neighbours against one another—troops in the army versus growers. The property was sold as a result, and Auguste's grandfather became a Notary in Valence until invalided out of the First World War. Arm and leg paralysed, he took up a smallholding in the Ardèche, near Vernoux, which revived the family's contact with farmwork.

Meanwhile his father worked in Valence, across the river, in the Bank of France. Auguste was born there on 13 July 1925. In his early 20s he spent two years working in the Tarn et Garonne region, cultivating what he calls "the best table grapes of France," but not making any wine.

His wife, Henriette, was from Cornas, where her family owned five hectares of vineyards. Three and a half were inside the Cornas *appellation*, notably on *La Côte* and *Pied la Vigne*, the remainder just outside, serving for a 10° Côtes du Rhône de l'Ardèche. After their marriage, Auguste set to work on these vineyards, his first harvest the 1949. The oldest plot at that time dated from 1890, planted in the postphylloxera regeneration.

Auguste Clape is the arch example of a man whose wines are always faithful to their vintage, their style in tune with what the weather and growing conditions have delivered. A refusal to intervene too much brings the benefit of letting the vine sort out its cycles over time: years of drought, of abundant vegetation, of copious flowering, and so on are guided by observation, thought, and then deft touches. For 2000 Auguste Clape is formal in his view: "Those who failed to drop grapes were not pardoned.

They got away with it in 1999 thanks to the general high ripeness, even though those wines actually lacked refinement in their structure. We were cutting back the crop on our 60-year vines in 1999—it was that abundant."

So nothing is taken for granted, and it pays to be calm, to be open-minded and to not join in the rush to make a lot of wine and to sell it for a lot of money. Consistent quality is an attribute without price on its head.

Like his friend and neighbour Gérard Chave, Auguste Clape has always been a waiter when harvesting. He knows that genuine ripeness is essential. "When to pick the grapes is the hardest question I have to answer," he admits. But nor is he one to push ripeness to extremities, following the mode for such jammed-up wines. In 1989, for instance, he waited for eight days after the *ban des vendanges* before harvesting. In those days that was the action of a man strong in self-belief, apart from the crowd.

Always ready to learn, Auguste was in his 50s when he went back to school to study the theory of viticulture at the celebrated Beaune Wine School in Burgundy. There he survived the new-oak philosophy, for he is a traditionalist on this subject. He explains: "I was happy fermenting in open wood vats during most of the 1970s, but there was no *tonnelier* around here to repair them and maintain them, so I turned to concrete. As for ageing casks, here you need neutral wood with no tannin in it. The Syrah must breathe—it needs the wood to allow it to loosen and avoid reduction—and 18 months in older casks does the job nicely."

In 1989 Auguste was joined by his then 40-year-old son, Pierre-Marie. As with many small family holdings at Cornas, the problem of the succession of the Clape estate had vexed his supporters, and it was a great relief to many when Pierre left his job in Valence as a teacher of mechanical engineering. He is a solidly framed man with glasses and a greying black beard. His voice is gravelly, no doubt useful when addressing the Growers Union in his role as President.

Pierre's son Olivier has moved to full-time status after helping out in between ski-ing work

Located in the Ardèche *département*, Cornas' natural source of wood in the past used to be chestnut from the hills to the west. But an involuntary experiment of ageing his 1973 in oak and chestnut proved to M. Clape that chestnut was not right for his wine's stockage. He mistook the identity of one of his barrels and so had one lot of chestnut-aged wine on his hands. The difference between the "oak wine" and the "chestnut wine" was marked; both bore a similar bouquet, but on the palate the "chestnut wine" was dominated by the tannin emanating from the wood of the barrel.

By contrast, the youthful fruit and grapiness of the "oak wine" were much in evidence, and this barrel appeared to have the greater future. M. Clape found that wines matured in chestnut came round after about two years but were unlikely to attain the smoothness and suppleness of flavour of wines matured in oak. It is interesting to think that until the late 1980s the very traditional Ardechois family of Chapoutier at Hermitage depended almost entirely on chestnut for the raising of its wines.

stints in Val d'Isère, and although also a student of mechanical studies, he seems to find wine potentially interesting. He has studied business as well. With Pierre's wife, Geneviève, in the office, this is still a true family concern.

The Clapes work 5.38 ha of Cornas, owning 4.8 of those. They have a resounding 3-plus ha on *Reynards*—0.46 ha on *Tézier* (1983), 0.86 ha on *La Côte* (1954), 0.33 ha on *Petite Côte*, 0.68 ha on *Geynale*, and 1.2 ha on *Reynards* itself. The oldest vines date from 1900, the youngest from 1990.

The remaining plots are split between 0.25 ha on *Les Mazards* (1920s), with 0.64 ha on *Patou* (1989, 1999), 0.36 ha on *Pied La Vigne* (1890), 0.6 ha on *Sabarotte* (half the old Noël Verset site), and 0.06 ha on *Chaillot* (1975). The family also work another 0.9 ha of Syrah and Marsanne Côtes du Rhône, 0.51 ha of *vin de table*, and a tiny patch of St-Péray.

In 1995 they bought a plot of 1980 vines from Robert Michel, facing southwest and straddling *La Geynale* and *Reynards*. The price for this—FF500,000 or US$80,000—would now be around five times higher. The Clapes' comment on this vineyard is revealing: "We are still working this out; the bouquet is different from ours, more pointed, more acetate almost, although it isn't volatile. It may be the yeasts from that site, which explains why we have fermented the crop in with our 25-year-old-vine fruit from *Petite Côte* so their yeasts can work on it." This statement about "still working it out" was made eight years after the purchase!

This remains one of the traditional domaines. There is no destalking, although the ripening excesses of 2003 obliged them to destalk some of that harvest. The crop is fermented over about 12 days in concrete vats, with no added yeasts. There are two cap punchings a day and some pumping-over, and the maximum temperature rises to about 33°C.

The first press wine is added; thereafter the Cornas spends 20 months in the trim, curved *foudres* of their cramped cellar, which has not changed one iota in 30 years. The barrels hold 10 to 12 hl; "we paid for them as 12 hl or 1,200 litres, but found they only took 1,100 litres—the supplier used thick wood!" remarks Auguste wrily.

The UK wine for Yapp receives between 19 and 20 months, the rest up to two years. There are five to six rackings during this cask ageing. The younger-vine Cuvée Renaissance is raised for 18 to 20 months, the red Côtes du Rhône for 10 months. The Clapes fine with egg whites, but do not filter.

The domaine Cornas is assembled from five to six sources one month before bottling, and the process of tasting the different constituents in M. Clape's intimate, musty *cave*—with just the right amount of mushroom growth on the walls of the innermost cellar to keep him happy—is a fascinating exercise.

The precision of their blending is extreme. If either father or son finds a wine atypical—for example a *foudre* gives a wine too full of black-currant flavour, they won't blend it in, and instead it will go to a lesser cuvée. They are very respectful of what the wine should be like, with an innate clarity that comes from years of experience. Auguste's view is that in less ripe vintages like 1992, 1993, and 2002, Cornas shows black currant fruit. In ripe years, like 1999, the associations are black cherries, olives, truffle, and chocolate.

Reynards often gives violets on the bouquet right from the start, while *La Côte* is more reflective of well-ripened red fruits like raspberries "if the year has not been too hot," according to Pierre. "If the year has been hot and the crop very ripe, there is more black currant from *La Côte*."

CORNAS

2003 (CASKS) ★★★★(★) Shaping up to be a wine with a lovely heart from *Reynards*, and not excessive in style. The best sites moderated the outlyers. There are some chewy, full tannins. 2020–23.

2002 ★★★ Midweight bouquet—red fruits, some fungal aspect. Pretty fruit, rocks off well, good definition. Some end weight. Can live, has acidity, length OK. Now to 2007, then will retreat as usual; 2018–22. Last tasted Dec. 2004.

2001 ★★★★★ Full *robe*; handsome, peppery, black fruit aroma, well founded. Elegant fruit, very good structure, classic tannins grow through it. Oiled texture, then pepper and drier. Black fruit persists. Has length and width, very classic Cornas. 2024–28. Last tasted Sept. 2004.

2000 ★★★ Open, brewed fruit bouquet. Fruit gum flavour, three-quarter-weight wine, gains width. Chewy tannins at end, licorice presence. Just skips a touch before finish. From 2006. Less complete than August 2003. 2019–23. Last tasted Sept. 2004.

1999 ★★★★★★ Dark, purpley. Red fruits, smoke, lot of potential on the bouquet. Very good harmony on the palate, excellent balance. Fruits run straight through, persistently, and there is reserve in the wine. Can live very well because the tannins are well in support. 2023–28.

1998 ★★★★ Really big, chocolate-style bouquet, damp earth, black fruit jam, some freshness. The palate is also led by *confit*, cooked black fruits. Although a little withdrawn, there is a good centre here. A touch of sweetness, quite low acidity. Needs airing. 2013–17.

1997 ★★ Less colour than 1997–98. Red fruit jam aroma on bouquet, quite clearly defined. Softer texture than usual, black fruits are prominent early on with some agreeable depth behind them. Touch bitter on end. 2007–10.

1996 ★★★★ Lively red fruit, licorice bouquet. Upright vintage style on the palate, some mineral with the good red fruit persistence. This is interesting. Has similar acidity but less ripeness than the 1997. Live wine, has a good future. 2013–17.

1995 ★★★★★★ One of my favourite wines for its wonderful purity. Austere at first, written off by some critics, the wine has developed a lovely elegance with a clear fruit trail coursing quietly through it. Gentle cooked fruits; minerality persists on the nose. Light pepper and ingrained spice accompany the fruit. Typical *in extremis*. The fruit will advance on the minerality in its middle age. 2020–25.

1994 ★★ 2010–13
1993 ★★ 2005–09
1992 ★★★ 2010–12
1991 ★★★★ 2016–18

1990 ★★★★★★ After 11 years first touch of game on bouquet, a fantastic pure example of Syrah! Maturing red fruit, also some *garrigue* herb. The Clapes say it was more on truffles and the ripe fruit of Hermitage, so not strictly typical when younger. Such *gras* and fullness on the palate—lasting way past the finish. Still very good grip—it's young. Prunes, chocolate. Is reopening after a more closed, younger phase. A Clape: "The only year of my life when all the *cuves* reached 13° natural." *Grand Vin*. 2014–18.

1989 ★★★★★ 2012–14 may be underdoing it!

1988 ★★★ 2010–15
1987 ★★ 2006 if in magnum.
1986 ★★★ 2007–10
1985 ★★★★ 2008–11
1984 ★★★ 2006–10
1983 ★★★★ 2007–10
1981 ★★★★★
1979 ★★★★★ 2006–08
1978 ★★★★★★ 2010–15. Rich but subtle, top wine.

From 1998 there has been a second Cornas, the Cuvée Renaissance. This actually got off to a bad start in 1997, when much of it suffered from cork taint and had to be scrapped. It is made partly from vines dating from the mid-1980s and early 1990s, on *Geynale* and *Tézier*, and partly from older vines on the lower sites of *Mazards, Patou,* and *Pied la Vigne*.

It is raised in barrels similar to the main wine and bottled in the spring 18 months after harvesting. Again, it is the result of meticulous blending of different *foudres*.

Even though the Clapes say this is intended to be a more accessible and earlier wine than the classic, it still carries the house style of natural reserve when young; even the 1999 held a grainy, pebbly texture, accompanied by some streamlined fruit, nice and direct. The tannins on the end lend grip and serve to give it a healthy structure, allowing ageing over around 12 years.

CORNAS RENAISSANCE

2002 ★★(★) Peppered, grainy, red fruit bouquet. Refined fruit wine, sound cut. Fresh, pretty, wine for barbecues when young. Length OK, some tannins here, has some *gras* for the future. Esp from 2006–09; 2014–16.

2001 ★★★ 2015–17
2000 ★★ 2010–12

There is also a Syrah Côtes du Rhône, which is taken from a plot of less than one hectare at *Goulin* (1979) and 0.2 ha on *Grand Plantier* (1890, 1895), which borders St-Péray: some vine age for a mere Côtes du Rhône! Added to this can be the grapes from young Cornas vines that date from the early and mid-1990s or any Cornas that the Clapes deem unsuitable for the principal wine.

This is aged in cask along with the Cornas, and bottled around July after the harvest. It is medium weight, with touches of cooked fruit, and a light pepper and spice on the bouquet. In years like 2000 its fruit leads, so drink it within four to five years; in years like 1999 and 2001 it is more reserved and tight, mixing well-founded fruit with a light tannic persistence. The 2001 will be open from around 2004–05. The 1998, with its typically dry tannins, actually needed to be left for three to four years. According to the vintage, these wines can be drunk until up to eight to 10 years old.

Then there is a Syrah *vin de table*, the grapes grown on half a hectare of the plain outside the Cornas *appellation* zone near the railway, so on the river side. It can be mixed with any under-age Cornas fruit—up to four years old. The vines grow on clay sprinkled with rolled alluvial stones. This is indeed easy to drink—a vibrant bouquet preceding an amount of tasty rounded fruit.

The Clapes have a few vines south of Cornas, on the lowland between the N86 road and the river. These are mainly 25-year-old Marsanne, with a sprinkle of Viognier, and make their white Côtes du Rhône. The soil is gravelly and draining. Small concrete and stainless steel vats are used for the fermentation, at around 17° to 18°C. After the malolactic is finished, the wine is bottled around April.

This is *joli vin*—easy to drink over two to three years, with an agreeable light warmth in it. Its southern location comes through with a degree of around 12.5 to 13 and the finish can be suitably firm and clean. Only about 500 bottles were made in 2002—half the usual amount.

Export 75 per cent 1) USA, 2) Switzerland, 3) Great Britain

DOMAINE JEAN-LUC COLOMBO

La Croix des Marais 26600 La Roche-de-Glun
+33(0)475 841710

See also Crozes-Hermitage, Hermitage, St-Joseph, St-Péray.

The Mr. Motivator of Cornas, Jean-Luc Colombo has definitely enjoyed ruffling a wide range of feathers since his arrival with his *oenologue's* laboratory in 1983.

Always ready to have a go, Colombo at the outset sold materials like casks and wine presses to make ends meet. This topped up the income from his winemaking advice service to growers. A native of the fishing village of Carry-le-Rouet, west of Marseille, he had come back to southern France from Bordeaux. "I did stints in different châteaux for a bit over a year, with people like the Lurton family," he explains, a man of thick black hair and constant movement. His wife, Anne, from the southwest rugby town of Béziers, was (like Jean-Luc) a pharmacist, so it made sense in 1984 to start an advisory oenology service.

Their early clients were local—from Cornas and Saint-Péray. One of the first was Louis Chèze, now known for his Condrieu and St-Joseph. "All he made in those days was 30 hl of Gamay!" recalls Anne, a neat woman with short chestnut hair. "Our first thoughts were actually to open a pharmacy since Cornas didn't have one," she explains, "but the process was very slow, so we switched to wine; we liked the originality of the Syrah here and the hillside vineyards."

In 1987 Jean-Luc started his own winemaking, with just 2,000 bottles. By 1988–89 he had reduced the number of consultancy clients (and raised the price to those remaining!) and moved towards making his own wine across the board. He was certainly happy to cause a stir among the local *vignerons*, with his straight talking (a lot of it, as well) and his "get the job done" mentality. In the rainy year of 1992, he harvested late and very fast—"I got in 40 people—wham!—over our four hectares, and picking just spilled into a second day," he recalls.

Their Cornas vineyards run over 6.4 ha and have been increased steadily over the years. The main portion is in the northern sector. Their new house lies right beside the 2.5 ha on *Eygas*,

FIGURE 36 Innovation, drive, cultivation of the media—Jean-Luc Colombo, the man who shook up Cornas. (Tim Johnston)

high and winding up an inner flank of the hill, in a windy spot with sensational views. The specific subplot is called *Moutet*, where the soil is sandy decomposed granite; Colombo cleared and revived much of this plot from 1989, adding on to some old parcels dating from the 1920s, 1950s, and 1970s.

The Colombos also work 1.6 ha on *Chaillot* (1920s, late 1970s) and a recent 1.5 ha on the eastern section of *St-Pierre*—a south-facing spot with 1 ha dating from 1999–2000 and the 0.5 from 1989.

Two of Jean-Luc's best sites are plum in the middle of the *appellation*: 0.4 ha at the foot of *Cayret*, also known as *Barjasse*, where there is a little clay mixed in with the granite; and 0.2 ha of choice old vines from the 1930s on *La Côte*. Jean-Luc bought this from a Balthazar in 1990.

Outside Cornas there are three hectares of Syrah aged between 15 and 40 years, which makes their Côtes du Rhône Les Forots. These are also in the northern area of Cornas, at *Les Arlettes* and *Le Coulet*, where there is more limestone and clay mixed up. The limestone comes from the seam running between the Crussol hill and the next village north, Châteaubourg.

Because much of his soil around *Chaillot* and *Eygas* was fast-draining gore, Jean-Luc was quick to spot the chance to use a mini-Caterpillar to work the vineyards and so save time and money. He was not a herbicider, applying an early system of the reasoned fight (*lutte raisonnée*) against maladies.

Another early touch was his use of aluminium, not wood, stakes, to train the vines—the wood usually covered in creosote for preservation; likewise the production of his own straw to tie the vines, and the planting of apricots right at the top of the hill where the land "was no good for wine."

A man never at a loss for words, Jean-Luc recalled his first trips to the Rhône: "I started to go up the valley in 1977–78, buying the wine of growers like Jasmin and Chave. All the time I was thinking about the process and what was required for top quality. Apart from the vineyard care needing to be more detailed than before, the equipment had to correspond. If all the best restaurants serve up their napkins newly cleaned for you, then so should I as a wine grower. So top-quality wood, paper, boxes, and expensive corks were all necessary for the packaging."

The Colombo wines are very expensive, in part a result of this approach. The use of Bordeaux casks (now alongside Burgundian ones), the Bordeaux-shape bottle, and the paper wrapping around it are also techniques for being noticed, and justifying those higher prices. But the reality always lies safe and sound within the bottle, and that is where judgment is delivered.

So, stylistically his wines are a cross-breed. The notion of *terroir* is not faithfully adhered to, but neither is it given a beating. Clearly Colombo's main axe with Cornas of the past has been the dryness of the tannins, and much of his work has been geared to subduing that. Destalking, high-temperature extraction, and the use of young oak to replace the stalk tannins are all part of his campaign.

By 1992 Colombo was using 80 per cent–new Bordeaux 225-litre casks for his Ruchets, the remainder one-year-old oak, for an 18-month ageing. Still largely his method today, this was a vast departure from the norm of the time. Tasting such oaked Cornas *chez lui* then was to hit an impenetrable mass of resistance, the oak striking out early and late on the palate, with just a brief interim of local *gras* winking out for a moment. This shifted the grower's responsibility in dramatic fashion. Suddenly the requirement was mastery of oak, its source, its preparation, its degree of *chauffage,* and how long to raise the wine within it, given the vintage's ripeness. Wow!

The passing of time has softened some of the extremities and a degree of middle ground has been met. Certainly, Colombo could never be accused of raising his wines in tired oak barrels! With time, too, his wines have gradually melded, but their texture remains outside the traditional Cornas minerality. Given their treatment, they are correctly fleshier than the old-school wines, their texture more oily and supple. They also require less ageing than the wines of men like Clape, Balthazar, and Dumien-Serrette to become soft and rounded.

Since the late 1990s, Anne has largely run the vinification, and she says that they have changed it a little. "The crop is still all destalked, but we cool it now, to allow it up to three days to get its fermentation started; we start quite low, around 17° to 18°C, and this gradual start leads to a more gentle fermentation. Empirically, we find this aids richness and aromas."

She does also use outside yeasts when necessary: "I think the yeast implanted in any cellar often plays a greater role than the floating yeasts in the vineyards," she states. Fermentation runs for at least three weeks in stainless steel, with pumping-over and partial vat emptying and refilling (*délestage*) but no cap punching. Experiments have also been made with *micro-bullage* (oxygen input) during the maceration to promote fermentation and to ease the tannins.

Three domaine Cornas are produced. Terres Brûlées (6,000 bottles) mixes crop from *Eygas,* along with the bottom part of *Chaillot*. It is aged for 18 months in 75 per cent new, 15 per cent one-year-old casks. It reflects brewed, cooked fruits and needs a little time to settle.

The Louvée Cornas (1,000–2,000 bottles), first made in 1996, comes from *La Côte*; it, too, receives 18 months but in 90 per cent new, 10 per cent one-year-old oak. This is a fleshy, quite opulent style of wine, but can wither after exposure to air.

Until 1996, his core, Ruchets brand was 80 per cent from *Chaillot,* 20 per cent *La Côte*. Now it is purely from *Chaillot* (7,000 bottles). It is kept for 18 months in 90 per cent new, 10 per cent one-year-old oak. All three wines are egg-white fined, but not filtered. There are often stewed fruits on the *Ruchets* bouquet, and the palate can be tarry, with black fruits present.

Since 1995 the Colombo business has also provided another Cornas, 6,500 bottles of Les Méjeans; sources for this include the sites of *Eygas, Saveaux,* and *Le Coulet*. This is raised for 18 months in 75 per cent new, 25 per cent one-year-old oak. This shows light black fruits and a fair weight on the palate and is drinkable after four years or so.

The *négociant* business started in a small way in 1994, with a full range developed from 1998. Mostly wine rather than crop is bought, often from clients of their oenology advice service.

The Rhône range covers Hermitage red and white Le Rouet, Cornas Les Méjeans, St-Joseph Les Lauves, Crozes-Hermitage, red and white Côtes du Rhône Les Figuières (white 55 per cent Viognier, 45 per cent Roussanne). From the south come Châteauneuf-du-Pape Les Bartavelles and Tavel. From the Colombo domaine, the Syrah Côtes du Rhône Forots is aged for 10 to 12 months in two-to-three-year-old casks.

Jean-Luc is less often at Cornas these days; the most visible member of his team is the talented Croat Igor Paladin, and one senses Jean-Luc has difficulty keeping up with the details of his own empire. Some of the early brio seems missing, although a project to gain full *appellation* status for the Côte Bleue vineyards near his home village west of Marseille is under way, with the respected Mas de la Dame domaine from Les Baux.

The early heady oxygen of publicity that he closely cultivated two decades ago seems as if it may have shimmied away into the upper ether. A trail of disjointed remarks and curiously tilted observations hang in its place, while his dog gnaws at the logs lying beside the roaring fire in his sitting room.

CORNAS LES MÉJEANS

2001 ★★ Dumb, light black fruit nose. Compact, clean flavour, some fresh berry. Fair end weight. A bit plain. From 2006; 2014–16.

CORNAS TERRES BRÛLÉES

2001 ★★★ Lightly meaty nose, cooked red fruits. Soft attack, gains sinew from halfway. Fair mineral red fruit late on. Drinkable early. 2013–15.

> **2000** ★★ From 2006; 2013–15

CORNAS LA LOUVÉE

2001 ★★★★ Smoky, full black fruit aroma. Soaked fruit, good core, persists. Genuine, oily length, good balance. From 2007; 2017–19.

> **2000** ★★ 2011–13

CORNAS LES RUCHETS

2001 ★★★ Sappy, smoky stewed fruits nose. Mint/oily start. Finesse more than power. Quite wide blackberry/licorice end. From 2006; 2016–18.

> **2000** ★★ 2011–13
> **1999** ★★ 2010–12

Export 50 per cent 1) USA, 2) Switzerland, 3) Great Britain/Netherlands/Germany

DOMAINE COURBIS

Route de St-Romain 07130 Châteaubourg
+33(0)475 818160

See also St-Joseph.

The Courbis family is one of two wine families in the village immediately north of Cornas, Châteaubourg. They have been producers of Saint-Joseph for over 400 years but ventured into Cornas in 1982. Their first outright purchase was in 1986, and now they cultivate 5.4 ha spread over three main *lieux-dits*. This domaine is capable of growing in grandeur once several of its vineyards are older, and providing the sons want to push quality as far as it will go.

One of their purchased sites was the centre of an ongoing saga, namely that of the "Noël Verset hectare." Father Maurice Courbis, a teenager during the Second World War, and possessed of a mordant sense of humour, has very few flies on him. His timing was impeccable in 1986, when he bought the 0.67 ha vineyard of a notary's wife that had been worked by the Delas *négociant* house.

Digging out the records, he states that he paid 120,000 francs (£12,000 or US$20,500) for this 1947 plot on *Sabarotte* in the central-southern zone of the vineyard. Then along came the Verset hectare in the late 1990s. To and fro swirled the rumours; Cornas had become hot property and all sorts of buyers, many of them international, were said to be interested. Eventually the deal was signed in 2002, and the Courbis family emerged with another 0.58 ha of *Sabarotte*, the other part of the vineyard bought by the Clape family. This plot contained many vines dating from the First World War period.

This time the price was higher—11 times higher. Habitual yellow-papered cigarette end in hand, Maurice reverts back to the archives: "We paid 198,183 Euros and 72 cents for the 0.58 ha," he proclaims. This translates into £229,000 (US$389,000) for a sole hectare. These grapes contribute to their single *Sabarotte* wine, first made in 1988, first labelled that way in 1990.

Their other main sites are on the flat ground at the foot of the slope of *Champelrose*, a hectare from 1919 and 0.9 ha of 1998–99 vines. The erosion over time means the decomposed granite has a clay subsoil here.

On *Eygas* they have 1.1 ha, dating from 1991: *Eygas* was a vineyard until the Second World War but was then abandoned because it is high —around 300 metres—a little way from the village and a late ripener, with the attendant risks. For the Courbis, it is about two weeks behind their most precocious site of *Champelrose*, and its wine "is always the most vivacious that we make," comments Laurent.

The other sites are *Chaillot* and what they call *Cros* in the south of the *appellation*, 50 metres south and below *Champelrose*.

The approach is businesslike for their three Cornas wines. Despite calling the vinification "classic," the family destalk the crop and ferment in 50 hl steel vats. All plots have been vinified separately since 1990 so they can learn more about each one's characteristics.

Vinification lasts three to four weeks, with twice-daily pumping-overs and cap punching. There have also been two *délestages* (partial vat emptying and refilling) every vintage since 2000.

Champelrose (8,000 bottles, their classic wine) is raised for 12 to 14 months in two-to-three-year-old casks, although half the casks were new in 2003 as an experiment. The second wine, Les Eygats (7,000 bottles), is raised for 12 to 16 months in 25 per cent new, 75 per cent one-year-old casks. The top wine, Sabarotte (5,000 bottles), is aged for 16 months in 65 per

cent new, 35 per cent one-year-old oak. All are fined and lightly filtered.

The brothers Laurent and Dominique describe Cornas as containing more prune and jam flavours than their St-Joseph from just a few kilometres away. "The St-Jo, which has a shorter maceration than the max 30 days for the Cornas, shows more black currant and red fruits," explains Laurent. "We have to filter the St-Jo more tightly, too, since we find the Cornas more resistant to bacteria."

Laurent's aim is for elegance in their wines. I would describe the Champelrose as sometimes lacking in true Cornas soul and funkiness, more disposed to show off modern, "cleaned-up" winemaking. The Eygats is also sometimes this way, but it can hit the mark with its tannins on show and a local style, as in 1999. The Sabarotte is consistent, classy, often sumptuously textured, and definitely reflects the nuances of its place on the hillside.

CORNAS CHAMPELROSE

2003 (CASK) ★★ Aromatic, ripe fruit nose. Suave, quite fleshy, ripe wine. Rich, not especially tannic. From 2007; 2015–16.

2002 ★★★ Black fruit, smoky, live bouquet, quite full. Well-composed black fruit, tannins present, with acidity. Likeable early fruit, leave till 2007 to come together. Fair length. More here than before, going the right way. 2018–20.

2001 ★★ Violet, cooked fruit, reduced nose. Pleasant attack, subdued tannins, some pepper at end. Fair weight. From 2006; 2013–15.

2000 ★★★★ Quite firm, pebbly/peppered nose; lissom, elegant attack, good juice, very good core. Red fruit with meaty parts. Great as young wine but is serious. Some oak. Esp from 2007; 2015–17.

1999 ★★ 2011–13
1997 ★ 2007–09

CORNAS LES EYGATS

2003 (CASK) ★★★ Grilled, oaked aroma. Supple start, then tannins direct it. Clean Cornas, has warmth/fullness. From 2008; 2018–19.

2002 ★★(★) Bright, showy *robe*; cautious black fruit aroma, more expressive by 2007. Brewed, earthy black fruit palate, bit reduced. Decent width, runs on well enough. Hedgerow fruit aftertaste, some elegance. From 2006–07; 2016–19.

2001 ★ Live raspberry/earthy nose. Attack bit stretched. Clean, modern Cornas. Plums, quite chunky end. Lacks true core and dries from its oak. From 2007; 2015–17.

2000 ★★★ Some pepper on a compact bouquet, granite freshness, too. Good accessible red fruits, with fair depth. Violets on finish. Stylish, clear-cut wine. 2012–15.

1999 ★★★★ 2014–15

1997 ★★ 2010–12

CORNAS LA SABAROTTE

2003 (CASK) ★★★★ Oily, scented fruit aroma; notably ripe flavour. Violets, good warm matter, with finesse. Grilled end, good absorbed tannins. From 2008; 2020–22.

2002 ★★ Toffee style, raisin bouquet, some depth. Black fruit with some *gras*. Soaked fruit texture at end, is a bit stretched, macerated a long time. Oak dries it at end, isn't very calm. Was more savoury and fresher. From 2006; 2015–17.

2001 ★★★★ Ripe brewed fruit nose, silky violets; wide matter, oily/tannic pep second half. Blackberry/game mix. Grilled/oak end. From 2007; 2018–21.

2000 ★★

1999 ★★★ Oily, soaked fruit nose. Rich, cooked fruits, full with more to give. Clean, mineral end. Not quite as fleshy as 2001. 2013–15.

1998 ★★★ Very purple; bouquet mixes fruit with animal aspects. Has a masculine density. Probing black flavour, good depth, tannic support. Good length, some final heat. Gutsy, promising. 2013–15.

1997 ★★★ Dark, black at its core. Nice degree of finesse on bouquet—softly cooked fruit, hints of mint and brambly fruit. Good mix. Good, peppered surge of fruit on attack.

Tannins last well, are true. Three-quarter-weight year. Fruit pure, lasts well. 2010–12.

MAISON DELAS

ZA de l'Olivet 07300 St-Jean-de-Muzols
+33(0)475 086030

See also Condrieu, Côte-Rôtie, Crozes-Hermitage, Hermitage, St-Joseph, St-Péray.
Delas have always had close ties with Cornas. But, just at the wrong moment they relinquished them, and have been regretting it ever since.

In the 1960s, Delas worked several hectares here, and until 1979 they actually owned one hectare, but the wine was difficult to sell. So their holding on the *lieu-dit Reynards* was sold to Auguste Clape and Maurice Courbis, two of the local stalwarts.

From 1980 until 1993 they dabbled in the buying of crop. Then, along came another change of direction. The crop was deemed unsatisfactory because there was too much young-vine fruit in it, so only wine was bought from 1994 to 1996. All the while the final wine continued under the name of "Chante-Perdrix," with around 15,000 bottles a year.

Of course, Delas had not endeared themselves to the locals, and since 1997 have been easing gradually back towards crop purchase from three growers. By 2003 Chante-Perdrix had become 70 per cent crop vinified by Delas, 30 per cent bought-in wine. The production now varies between just 2,200 bottles in 1998 to a more regular 10,000 to 15,000.

"I place great emphasis on Cornas," states Jacques Grange, who had to try to tidy up the situation when joining Delas in 1997. "So that's why I work closely with our three suppliers from mid-August on, in the vineyards, tracking quality so we bring in the best possible grapes."

From 2004 the grapes have been taken from two hectares, on *La Côte* (1940s), *St-Pierre* (1998), and the wonderfully south-facing *Reynards* (1988), ironically next to their old vineyard. At 350 metres, *St-Pierre* ripens around a week after the other two sites.

The crop is destalked and receives a three-week vinification in concrete vats. There is a pre-fermentation cool maceration at 15°C over four to five days, and two *pigeages* are done per day during the alcoholic fermentation, with some pumping-over. The wine is raised during 15 months in casks, 10 per cent of them new, the rest of one to two years old. There is neither fining nor filtration.

Chante-Perdrix is a *négociant* wine with the important extra of local character; cooked black fruits and tannins mingle well in its youth, and I look back to vintages like 1990 and 1978, when the wine upheld the somewhat drooping Delas flag—both magnificent wines. Leathery and correctly restrained textures show this *appellation* still holds its place in the heart of the company. The wines live for 10 to 15-plus years.

CORNAS CHANTE-PERDRIX

2003 (CASK) ★★ Grilled aroma, ripe, raisin character, fruit subdued. Red berry flavour, a flourish, then oak and tightens. Lot of oak/tannin on finish. Less generous than was. From 2008; 2017–20.

2002 ★ Matt *robe*; biscuity, black fruit bouquet, rather airy. Bosky black fruit flavour, upright, not fleshy, pepper aftertaste. Reduction-tinged wine. Plain, bit short. Has withdrawn in last year. Await gamey stage, e.g., 2006–09. 2012–16.

2001 ★★★ Live, meaty/leathery nose, touch rustic. Tight black flavour at first, really good juice in it, tasty, quite oily. Firm, solid wine, truly made. Will be gamey. From 2006; 2013–16.

2000 ★★★ 2011–12
1999 ★★★★ 2014–18
1998 ★★ 2007–10

DOMAINE J. DESPESSE

Vieux Village 10 Basses Rues 07130 Cornas
+33(0)475 800354

Jérome Despesse is one of the bright young things showing a welcome return to their roots at Cornas. In his early 30s, he works for the cork makers Armorim, covering the Rhône Valley for them, and is clearly enthusiastic about his little 0.6 ha vineyard.

His father, Charles, is from the old school, with a rugged, outdoor look and offering up few words. Jérome, tall with brown hair and a chatty approach, is now the fourth generation working their vines.

Half the vineyard is Cornas, on *Les Côtes*, planted by Jérome's grandfather and replaced one vine at a time when the need arises; the other half is on the plain at *Les Perousses*, where Syrah planted in the early 1980s grows on clay-chalk, *galet* stone soil. The latter makes a very sound, early-drinking Côtes du Rhône red.

Charles looks after the vineyard and Jérome makes the wine, which has been bottled since 1991. Whole bunches are fermented in open concrete, with cap punching and pumping-over, to a maximum temperature of 30°C. No outside yeasts are used. Ageing runs for 11 to 18 months in 225-litre casks, 20 per cent of them new, the rest three to five years old. The wine is fined but not filtered. The 2001 was promising, with definite local character, and the 2002 very correct for its year.

CORNAS

2002 ★★★ Nice, wild berry, bit of jam aroma. Pretty, rounded wine, fairly knit. Grows through palate, sound finale. OK richness. From 2006; 2015–17.

2001 ★★★ Clear, scented nose, black fruit/olives, some mineral; pretty, oily wine, suave, stylish texture. Fruit persists, wholesome. Good character, *typique*. Some tannin, has gained body in last year. From 2006; 2017–19.

DOMAINE PIERRE DUMAZET

RN 86 07340 Limony +33(0)475 340301

See also Condrieu, Côte-Rôtie, St-Joseph.
Pierre Dumazet, best known for his Condrieu, makes Cornas from 0.8 ha on *Chaillot*, the plot

dating from the 1960s. The first wine was produced in 1989. He vinifies the crop of the vineyard owner, on a partnership basis, in a most traditional way.

Whole bunches are fermented; "we tried destemming, but it hurt the ageing potential of the wines," he explains. Vatting lasts about three weeks, and ageing runs for 15 to 16 months in casks that are around 10 years old. Conversely, the 2001 was softer than the more tannic 2000—both respectable wines with local feel.

CORNAS CUVÉE CHARLEMAGNE

2001 ★★ Brewed black fruit, some restraint, floral tones also on bouquet. Elegant black fruit, refined texture. Violet-fruit mix flows well. No obvious tannins. 2010.

2000 ★★★ Potent bouquet—blackberries, red meat, black earth. Deep solid wine in the drier, more upright style. Violets, tobacco on the finish. Good grip. Tannins need until 2006 or so to soften. Great around 2008. 2012–15.

DOMAINE DUMIEN-SERRETTE

18 rue du Ruisseau 07130 Cornas
+33(0)475 404191

Gilbert Serrette's domaine is the epitome of Cornas: small, unassuming, and meticulous. It's clear that toil has brought its rewards here. Gilbert, a native of the Jura in eastern France, came to the Rhône when he was four, his father working at the St-Péray merchant Paul Étienne.

Gilbert married Danielle Dumien in 1967, and recalls, "I knew nothing about wine then. I had worked in metallurgy. I learnt from my father-in-law, Henri, as we went along. He was very fair and free with me—he even let me try the Jean-Luc Colombo methods for two years in the mid-1980s, but we reverted to the old ways after that." He speaks of his traditional methods with pride.

Henri died in 1994, but had already seen the domaine progress to bottling in 1983, having sold bulk wine to Delas, Chapoutier, and Paul Jaboulet Aîné before that. Gilbert went full-time on the wine in 1999.

The family operate with great modesty. Their home lies across the small stream of *Chaban*, which runs through Cornas, while the tiny cellar stands in the lee of the church. Gilbert opens the high gate to the cellar yard, and there rises the spire, the inspiration and heart of Cornas, right behind the building.

Madame Serrette does the labelling, taking 100 bottles at a time up to the house to work on. She is well known since her mother ran the village *épicerie* for 40 years, just next to the church. Harvesting is done over three days by 25 friends and family members: all examples of a timeless, personal wine family.

M. Serrette cultivates 1.8 ha, split 1.6 ha between *Patou*, on the southern end of Cornas towards St-Péray, and just 0.2 on *Mazards*. *Patou* dates in part from the 1920s. In the late 1990s he extended by 0.3 ha, and these young vines have just come on stream.

Vinification is traditional: full bunches, stalks included, are foot crushed, and then there is up to three weeks' fermentation in neat concrete vats. He works with a submerged cap on his large vat, with *pigeage* (punching down) on the two smaller ones. Pressing is done in a vertical wooden press.

Wood ageing is in part 225-litre, part 400-litre *pipes*, an uncommon size used also by the Tain Co-opérative. It lasts 16 months. The oak is aged between two and 15 years.

The style is for very clean, pure wine. It can be drunk successfully quite young—around five or six years old—but can evolve also. It's apart from the more austere, uprightly tannic style of Clape. Gilbert Serrette, a short man with a hint of the Paul Newman eyes about him, is very open and very thorough, and also very modest. "I've had a breakout from being in wine . . . I love it," he says, his sparkling eyes belying his later-50s age.

His triumph is the quality of the fruit. This means the wines will always be interesting: they don't have to be locked away at the back of the cellar. As they age, they expand on the finish.

CORNAS PATOU

2003 (CASK) ★★ Bosky, varnish high-tone aroma. Potent wine, alcohol tinges the flavour, gives it a top kick. Mint/eucalyptus finale, almost New World. Atypical Cornas. From 2007—needs to settle. 2017–19.

2002 ★ High tone, pine/bosky aroma. Minty, wooded style, front-of-palate wine, full extract. Cool texture, dry, oaked finale. Some width. In a retreat phase now. From 2007; hope won't dry. 2014–16.

2001 ★★★★ Wide, oily, quite deep nose—violet/toffee/licorice. Black stone fruits, stylish, warm texture. Tannins tighten at end, juicy aftertaste with mineral. Good balance. From 2007; 2015–19.

2000 ★★★ Brewed black fruit/violet, some heat on nose; stewed black fruits, then more mineral. Some tannin, fair length. From 2006; 2012–15.

1999 ★★★★★ 2014–18
1998 ★★★ 2012–14
1997 ★★★ 2009–11

Export 65 per cent 1) USA, 2) Great Britain

DOMAINE DURAND

2 impasse de la Fontaine 07130 Châteaubourg
+33(0)475 404678

See also St-Joseph.

Brothers Éric and Joël Durand form part of the more modern-styled Cornas movement. The domaine, also known as GAEC du Lautaret, is in energetic hands that have taken it towards wine, away from its previously dominant fruit business.

The Cornas connection stems from their mother's side; their uncle used to send the crop from his four hectares at Cornas to the Tain Co-opérative. From the lowest part of the slopes, at *Mazards* and *Saveaux*, this wine is distinctive because it comes off more draining soil where

the vines, now over 40 years old, can suffer from drought and also ripen slowly. It is light and aromatic, and some is still sent to the Co-opérative to help cash flow.

The domaine's Cornas has risen to five hectares since 1999, with two hectares planted in the southern site of *Patou* between 1999 and 2003. This new vineyard, in part rented from Guy de Barjac, is on land abandoned during the First World War, and presents a different soil makeup from the clay-chalk areas of the extreme north of Cornas—largely granite, with sandy and schist zones mixed in. Their holding abuts Alain Voge and Gilbert Serrette.

The other three hectares are spread around: a hectare on *Chaillot* (1973, 1988), where there is a mix of granite and clay-chalk; a hectare on *Champelrose* (1970s, 1988); and one hectare across small plots around the main hillside—notably 0.35 ha on *Sauman* (1990) and 0.15 ha on the prime granite site of *Tézier*.

The crop is destemmed and lightly crushed. An 18-to-25-day maceration follows in thermo-regulated vats; there is pumping-over and some cap punching, but in a tricky year like 2003, when hail and drought were significant factors, only a soft pumping-over was done. The young wine does its malo in wood, with the classic Cornas receiving 12 months in casks, 10 to 15 per cent new, although the "sublime" 1999 stayed for 15 months.

The brothers have increased to 20 per cent the proportion of larger casks—600-litre *demi-muids*. Éric prefers this size for its gentler effect on the more fragile cuvées. In a closed year like 1998, the wine received air by clicker in the cask to open it up. The brothers try not to filter, in which case a light fining is done.

In 1999, a special Cuvée Prestige wine was made for the USA market, from *Tézier* and *Champelrose*; there is due to be a Tête de Cuvée, top wine, produced in the future here.

Overall the domaine style is for approachable wine, drinkable within five to six years. As Eric observes, "You can't make wine in the ancient style like Clape does if your vines are only 20 years old; but our wines like the 1994 can easily run for 10 years."

2003 ★★★★ Smoky, soaked dark fruit aroma, some sweetness. Savoury, oily fullness; blackberries run through. Big, wholesome; tannins ripe and support its structure. Rich without the dryness of some wines. *Chaillot* has played a main, temperance role. From 2006–07; 2016–19.

2002 ★ Quite big, soaked bouquet, prune/oak, bit heavy. Macerated fruit style, fruit persists OK. Oak brings peppery finish, dries it. Not at ease now, has moved around in last year, fruit was clearer. From 2006; 2011–13.

2001 ★★★ Grilled/berries, black fruit nose; suave black fruit, licorice. Decent finesse, correct length. Quite fine/accessible. From 2006; 2014–17.

2000 ★★★ 2014–16
1999 ★★ 2007–10
1998 ★★ 2008–12
1997 ★★ 2007–11

CORNAS PRESTIGE

2000 ★★ Aromatic, floral/earth, farmyard bouquet; savoury; style is modern, quite sleek, tannins streamlined.

1999 ★★ More overt oak, needs till 2005 to integrate: dark, dry, sinewy aroma. True style, solid Cornas. This is the chunkiest wine they make. Acceptable tannins but a touch dry. 2012–14.

DOMAINE DE FAUTERIE

10 ave Charles de Gaulle 07130 Saint-Péray
+33(0)475 800425

See also St-Joseph, St-Péray.
Sylvain Bernard, the youthful-looking 40-something man running this domaine, ventured into Cornas in 1990. His rental agreement with Guy de Barjac gave him access to a wonderful old vineyard, 1.4 ha at *Le Cayret*, locally called *La Barjasse* after this old village family, where some of the vines were planted around 1900.

Of this site 0.4 ha was acquired by Jean-Luc Colombo, so that Sylvain now works a total of 1.13 ha; there is another 0.5 ha available for planting by 2005. There are two soils here—high up it is mainly sandy granite, while lower down it is a mix of loess and stones. "There are a lot of 100-year-old vines, which I replace with *massale* selection plants when I have to," comments Sylvain, adding that the average age is now about 80 years.

Since 2000 he has destemmed about 30 per cent of the crop; 1999 was vinified from whole bunches, which made the wine more pointed and drier toned, a well-chosen vintage for this laissez-faire tactic. But the issue of wine that is accessible seems to weigh on Sylvain's mind.

He often does a *saignée*, or bleeding off of early juice, to enhance the colour on his Cornas. Fermentation lasts 10 to 15 days in stainless steel, the top temperature 32°C. Only natural yeasts are used, and Sylvain has also attempted to minimise sulphur use in the more awkward vintages like 2002 and 1993.

Ageing lasts 15 to 18 months, in 225-litre casks that are three to five years old, with three rackings. He fines but does not filter. His Cornas is more towards the stylish end of the spectrum, but retains a quiet fire at is centre. Its turns nicely gamey with age, its tannins usually well present to support its smooth evolution. In the best vintages like 2001, 1999, and 1995, it can live for 15 to 20 years.

CORNAS

2003 (CASK) ★★(★) Well-filled bouquet—sucrosity, black jam fruit, oak. Oily, soaked, slow-extraction wine, quite sweet, rich. Tannins are rounded. Funky, naughty style. From 2008; 2016–19.

2002 (CASK) ★ Gentle cooked fruit/meat nose; compact flavour, floats, some width/tannin. One-dimensional at present. Also have found an unbalanced edge on this wine, so be careful. Esp 2006–09.

2001 ★★★ Broad, quite meaty, cooked berry/marzipan nose; fruit/spice/leather combo is good. Full, elegant too. Pepper/heat end. 2012–15.

2000 ★★

1999 ★★★

GHISLAINE FUMAT

2 rue des Bouviers 07130 Cornas +33(0)475 404284

Typical smallholders at Cornas, André and Ghislaine Fumat work one hectare, split half on *Les Côtes* and half on *Les Saveaux*. "The vines were planted by my grandfather," comments André, a bright-faced man who looks younger than his mid-60s. He has worked the vineyard since he was 20, and most of the responsibility now lies with Ghislaine.

Whole-bunch fermentation in concrete lasts for eight to 15 days, with cap punching and pumping-over, and is followed by 18 to 24 months in used 225-litre casks.

The Fumats also grow fruit and vegetables, and their wine shows well in the best years, with plenty of local soul.

CORNAS

2002 ★ Soft, floral-tinted bouquet. Fleeting red fruit, light tannins follow. Drinkable young. 2009–10.

2001 ★★★ Smoky, full nose; quite intense black fruit, chewy towards finish, red fruits there. Traditional, true. From 2005–06; 2012–15.

PAUL JABOULET AÎNÉ

Les Jalets 26600 La Roche-de-Glun +33(0)475 846893

See also Condrieu, Côte-Rôtie, Crozes-Hermitage, Hermitage, St-Joseph, St-Péray.
Jaboulet stepped up their commitment to Cornas in a big way when they bought 3.8 hectares at the *St-Pierre* vineyard from an unusual owner, a man involved in outdoor publicity and billboards, in 1993. The vineyard was added to in 2004, when most of another hectare of 1990 Syrah was acquired from Jacques Lemenicier, their neighbour on the west side of *St-Pierre*.

The year 1994 saw their first wine, called Domaine de Saint-Pierre. This is Jaboulet's biggest and fullest red wine behind Hermitage La Chapelle, and is a mighty, robust Syrah for long ageing.

Planted in 1985–86, the original vineyard is close to the village of St-Romain-de-Lerps. Here the Ardèche starts to reassert its wildness, with sweeping drops into tree- and scrub-covered gorges and gulches. The road is narrow and winding, the sense of isolation a surprise so soon after the busy Rhône corridor. The vineyard is steep, its surface crumbling, the vines settled into a brief amphitheatre. It faces away from the Rhône and surrounding it lies pale-green grazing pasture.

The wind billows around these hills, a reason given for placing the region's old Leper Station at St-Romain-de-Lerps. The tiny, rounded chapel of St-Pierre used to comfort the lepers and was a point of annual pilgrimage for the farmers and growers of Cornas until 1945. They sought the blessing of their crops here.

Given its altitude, the *St-Pierre* vineyard is late ripening. This can mean that timing the harvesting is a matter of fine judgment. In 1999 most growers harvested around 17–18 September, and a few waiters a week later. Jaboulet were the last to harvest and managed to just escape the worst of the 150 mm rainfall (6 in.) that dropped on 25 September. In 1998 the difference in ripening between two of their Cornas sources, *Reynards* for the regular wine and *St-Pierre,* was a full three weeks.

The wine is made like their La Chapelle Hermitage: the crop is totally destemmed, and over 18 to 21 days there is a daily *remontage.* Cask ageing is a little different, with no new oak; Burgundian casks aged one to three years house the wine for 12 to 15 months. There is no fining, and sometimes a light filtration. In a full-quantity year, there are about 13,000 bottles of *St-Pierre,* but a crop like 1998 fell to a small 7,000, bottles due to the frost attack, and the 2003 to 3,000 bottles.

St-Pierre is a wine that helps one to keep faith with Maison Jaboulet. It is always beautifully full, an assertive drink when young, with the winemaker not afraid to declare its tannic content. Ripe crop is also a hallmark of the wine, giving it a sappy, oily inlay that at times can veer towards the excessive. It ages well; often at least 20 years of development lie ahead.

Following their moves at both St-Péray and St-Joseph, Jaboulet grubbed out and in 2002 planted a plot on the *Quartier La Lègre*, in the southwest of the *commune* of Cornas, but not visible from village level.

The area of 9 ha can be gradually brought along; it took them four years to reach 0.6 ha planted. After two years to clear the site, there is only a small allowance each year, now down to 0.03 ha, to prevent headlong planting across any *appellation*. This vineyard is more southerly than their prized *St-Pierre* site and a little less high—280 to 300 metres against 300 to 320 metres. It is in the shape of an amphitheatre, and faces part east, part south. The soil is also schist, with some solid granite present as well.

Their Grandes Terrasses, a name first used in 2000, is 10 per cent own crop, 30 per cent bought grapes, and 60 per cent bought wine. Their crop comes from a rented 0.56 ha vineyard of 1957 Syrah on *Reynards*.

The crop is destalked and destemmed, and vinified, with pumping-overs, in concrete. It is raised in used oak for 10 to 12 months.

The 1980s Cornas were often big and rumbustious wines, more local in their feel than many of the stable's other runners. The Grandes Terrasses has stuck to that tradition of showing more leathery, pepper, and mineral tones than the overtly richer St-Pierre.

CORNAS LES GRANDES TERRASSES

2001 ★★★ Leathery, prune, subdued grapeskin bouquet; damson, puckery black flavour, minty oil edges. Ripe fruit with some Cornas reserve. From 2007; 2016–17.

2000 ★★ Cooked fruit, leather/floral bouquet; easy feel on palate; moves towards overt fruit with pepper, mineral touches. Some fullness, a direct wine. From 2005–06; 2010–12.

CORNAS

1999 ★★★★ 2014–17
1998 ★

CORNAS DOMAINE ST-PIERRE

2003 (CASKS) ★★★★ Herbal, brewed, tarry bouquet, has potential. Southern wine, depth and sun in it. Elements harmonious, some earthiness at end, length sound. Full, not excessive. From 2007–08; 2020–23.

2001 ★★★★ Very ripe crop aroma, drying black skins/pepper; full, leathery, dry-flavoured, though some *gras* within. Mineral finish. From 2008; 2016–19.

2000 ★★★ Discreet aroma, some ripe grape, also game/earthy; violet notes on palate, tight structure. Red fruits, pepper/licorice end. Chewy finish. 2013–16.

1999 ★★★★★ Very broad nose, prune/violets/smoke. Full palate, overt berried fruit. Tannins restrain finish, add some dryness. More complex than 1998. 2016–21.

1998 ★★★★ Dark *robe*; very varied bouquet—leaf, woods, cough syrup, oiliness. Lot of prune/blackberry flavour. *Gras*, generous, very full throughout. Fruit is cooked nicely. 2014–18.

1997 ★★★★ Dark plum; ripe grape smell, porty. Ripe, rotting elements. Minty, earthy, good plush, tasty wine. Fat, ripe flavours, juicy texture. Not many hidden corners, not typical Cornas. 2012–16.

1996 ★★★★★ Sustained dark colour; oily black fruit nose, stewed black plums/mint. More peppered, controlled than 1997–98. Good feel, has integrity. Sound structure, persistent; acidity will keep it alive. End tannins agreeably demanding. 2017–21.

1995 ★★★★★★ 2012–18

DOMAINE MARCEL JUGE

Place de la Salle des Fêtes 07130 Cornas
+33(0)475 403668

Marcel Juge has moved into the veteran stage, now in his mid-70s, but is still dishing out forthright opinions and plenty of alleged village anecdotes. He lives in a modern villa-style house beside the Salle des Fêtes, a simple sign showing his name hanging askew on the mesh fence.

Thin and wiry, he possesses a precise mind, and has always been ready to champion causes. He was President of the Growers Union for several years and has fixed views on aspects of his trade: "I remember M. Colombo experimenting with different Syrah clones planted in different soils and vinified separately—catastrophe! You have to blend the clonal wines, not keep them apart," he exclaims.

He also detests the taste of oak and, very sagely, loves glycerol: "You should be able to smell richness in a wine—it's not a sugar or a sweetness, it's a proper ripeness."

His wife was born a Balthazar; her Clarenson family has been at Cornas since at least Louis XIV, and the road up to the vines beside *Champelrose* is the Chemin de Clarenson. "One of her family was the conductor of the Presidential Train," he avers with energy. He left school at 16, and looking back, comments, "I'm glad we've got over being exploited and have got the value back for our wine; the British in Paris saved Cornas, you know—people like Steven Spurrier, Tim Johnston, Mark Williamson. They served the wine in the wine bars and the Academy of Wine and that led on to its export. People compared Cornas to a Côte de Beaune and realised it was cheaper and often better."

"Who knows what's going to happen with my vineyard?" he trills out loud. "My daughter works with the French Railways, the SNCF, and my eldest grandchild is only just 20, so it's not clear." He has rented out part of his 3.5 hectares vineyards at St-Péray and Cornas to Stéphane Robert of the Domaine du Tunnel.

His main Cornas holding is two-plus hectares on the southern site of *Combe* (1960s), close to St-Péray. Its light sandy granite soil gives wines that are aromatic, with some stuffing. His other main sites are 0.3 ha on *Champelrose* (1970s) and 0.15 ha on *Cayret* (1950s), also known as *Barjasse*.

Marcel is mostly down to just one wine these days; in the past there were various, with his own system of coding—"Cuvée C" for his Coteaux or hill wine, taken mainly from *Combe*, and "Cuvée SC" or "Super Cuvée" for his top hill wine from the oldest vines. When he makes the latter, there are maybe 800 bottles.

He ferments whole bunches traditionally, with a floating cap, pumping-over, and foot punching during 12 to 15 days. The grapes from the different sites are assembled at the outset. "My casks are up to 50 years old," he heralds, when talking about the 18-to-24-month cask ageing process. He neither fines nor filters.

His wines have never been overtly tannic and are best known for their fruit and more restrained composition. This has helped his many sales to the restaurants of Lyon.

CORNAS CUVÉE C

2003 (CASKS) ★★★ Smoked black fruit/meat nose; firm, square attack, crunchy fruit, dark wine. From 2008; 2015–17.

2002 ★(★) Lightly stewed fruit aroma. Rounded raspberry, fair appeal. Tannins appear at end. Light but agreeable, red fruits reappear. Esp 2007; 2010–12.

2001 ★★★ Burnt/grilled, cooked fruit nose; earthy black fruits, deep/roasted. Chewy, brewed wine. End violets/tannin/heat. From 2006; 2016–18.

2000 ★★★ Expressive, floral scent; supple, charming red stone fruit, broad but compact. Pure enough, length good. Drinks well now. 2012–14.

CORNAS CUVÉE SC

2003 (CASK) ★★★ Broad, brewed black fruit nose; big attack, potent, violet/*cassis*, more heat than usual. Big but not out of control. From 2009; 2016–19.

2000 ★★★★ Raspberry/earth/meaty nose; pretty red fruits, tasty, clear width. Peppery tannins, length good. True local feel. 2017–20.

JACQUES LEMENICIER

Quartier des Grays 07130 Cornas +33(0)475 810057

See also St-Péray.

In among the gnarled veterans of the hillsides is Jacques Lemenicier, brief beard and pony tail, more like the rock music man than the country music follower. He came to Cornas at nine years old, his parents from Annonay and no vineyard connection in the family.

"I was 17, and thought I'd work with Alain Voge to earn my living—I didn't have any great aim beyond that," he recounts. It was 1982, and Jacques also helped out a local man related by marriage to his sister. "He had a car accident in 1983 that ruled him out of work, so I have stayed with those vines ever since," he continues in his soft tones.

Gradually he grew his vineyard area through rental and purchase; so tight was the cash that he ran a fast delivery company between 1994 and 2002. After divorce, he was also obliged to sell the youngest hectare of his *St-Pierre* holding (1990) to Paul Jaboulet Aîné in 2004, and is now working 2.8 hectares of Cornas, just over two hectares of St-Péray, and a little 0.3 hectare of *vin de table* vines. He also works two hectares of apricots.

His largest plot is on the granite of *St-Pierre*, where he started with the rental of one hectare in 1984—a site he cleared and planted himself in 1982, next to the Jaboulet vineyard. Since the 2004 sale, he has one hectare there and another five that can be planted in stages in the future. All the vines date from this time.

One of his choice older *lieux-dits* is his 0.7 ha on *Pigeonnier*, part of *Mazards*. The oldest 20 per cent dates from 1903, the rest is a mix of 1950s and recent renewal. On *Saveaux* (1950s), he has 0.5 ha and on *Combe* 0.35 ha (2002).

All the crop is destemmed except for the oldest vines' fruit off *Pigeonnier* and *Saveaux*. The core crop is fermented in thermo-regulated vats, with outside yeasts to provoke the process, for 21 to 25 days. It spends a year in casks that are two to eight years old. The top sites' wine is fermented in open concrete vats, with twice-daily cap punching, for 15 to 21 days.

Jacques makes just one bottled wine, which is broadly equivalent to 65 per cent *Pigeonnier*, 35 per cent *St-Pierre*. It is fined and filtered. Thirty to 50 per cent of his wine is sold off in bulk.

"I still need to buy and build a cellar, so I'm not there yet," says Jacques, who has just hit 40. He has recently divorced and was robbed three times in a year as well, so life has not been straightforward. He is another who seeks elegant wines rather than big-extraction, tannic ones.

CORNAS

2003 (CASK) ★★ Fruited, light toast/cherry nose; accessible, grainy fruit, some pepper/end tannin. 2012–15—not a big-style wine.

2002 ★★★ Sound, quite compact bouquet, harmonious black fruit, more varied by 2008. Upright, well-ripened fruit style. Some richness within and through it. Pebbly finale, esp from 2008; 2016–18.

1999 ★★★ 2013–17
1998 ★★ 2011–14

Export 25 per cent 1) USA, 2) Japan, 3) Quebec

PATRICK LESEC

Moulin de Bargeton BP6201 30702 Uzès

See also Crozes-Hermitage, Hermitage, St-Joseph.

The merchant Patrick Lesec started to provide the market with a Cornas from 1996. The Cuvée Sarah comes from *Chaillot* and is raised for 16 months, half in new, half in one-year-old oak.

The other Cornas, Le Vignon, is said by him to come from that *lieu-dit*, although no such name exists on the map. This is raised for 16 months in half new, one-quarter each one-year- and two-year-old oak.

PIERRE LIONNET

160 route Nationale 07130 Cornas +33(0)475 404210

This retiring man—"friends call me a 'publi-phobe'"—is not often seen out and about, although he was President of the Growers Union in the early 1990s. "I don't attend Wine Fairs, and sell by word of mouth," says Pierre Lionnet, a man with neat grey hair who is in his late 50s.

He represents one of the oldest winemaking lines at Cornas, tracing back to at least 1575. "We have always owned our sites on *Pied la Vigne, Mazards,* and *Chaillot,*" he says and is proud that this is purely a family affair still. His wife, Odile, ties the vines and harvests, and his pretty daughter Corinne, in her early 30s, has got the wine bug, and started with him in 1998.

He works about 2.25 ha; the 0.6 ha on *Mazards* is a very old vineyard mainly dating from 1910, with a topping of vines planted in 1968. The 0.8 ha on *Pied la Vigne* are high up there, part 1960s, part 1970s, growing on its clay-chalk soil. The 0.45 ha *Chaillot* vineyard planted by his father Michel in the 1970s is high up near the top of the hill, on terraces. The fourth site of 0.4 ha is on *Combe,* in the southern reaches, and dates from the 1940s.

These four sources represent a good spread across the *appellation,* and in the time-honoured way, he makes just one wine, called "Terre Brûlée"; there are 6,000 to 8,000 bottles of this usually, and the rest of his wine is sold in bulk to the *négoce* trade.

The vineyard has long been worked naturally, the soil turned once or twice between December and March by a little Caterpillar that can reach about 25 cm (10 in.) down.

Until 1986 Pierre worked in an agricultural supplies company and helped out his father in his spare time. He learnt his trade that way, since his early studies were on general agriculture, not wine. His vinification is traditional—a four-day gathering of family and friends to pick the crop, and whole-bunch fermentation for about 12 days in concrete, "with no added gizmos—no yeasts, no tannins, no enzymes"—he

emphasizes in the soft tones that bely his firm beliefs.

There is twice-daily cap punching, punctuated by a pumping-over in the middle of the day; the temperature is kept to a maximum of 30°C. In a healthy year the press wine can be included. Ageing runs over two winters, for 15 to 18 months in mostly 600-litre and some 225-litre casks that are between four and 50 years old. There is neither fining nor filtration.

His wine is marked by cool, sinewy red fruits, with the violet tones on the aroma that often show up at Cornas. Tannins are live and present, and this represents solid, traditional Cornas without being in any way aggressive. As such, they are not for young drinking, and perform well from six years onwards.

CORNAS

2003 (CASK) ★★ Dense bouquet, dried leaves to come; brewed fruit, different texture to normal, southern, rocky outcrop time. From 2009? 15 years, maybe.

2002 (CASKS) ★★ Floral/meaty mix on nose; quite firm red fruit, cool texture, some tannin. Fair length. Esp 2006–07. 2012–14.

2001 ★★★ Stewed, raspberry/meat-edged aroma; raspberry fruit, live and chewy, with sinew. Correct, genuine, has mineral/fungal touches. Some end acidity. From 2007; 2017–19.

1999 ★★★ Stewed black fruits/violet on deep nose; stylish, tasty raspberry fruit, good fresh, mineral end, bit of heat. Tannins sound. True wine. 2017–20.

BERNARD MAURICE

6 chemin de Clarenson 07130 Cornas +33(0)475 404313

Bernard Maurice is the fourth generation of his family to work their tiny 0.68 ha vineyard; his father Marc has one of the little painted tin Cornas *vigneron* signs outside his house in the southern part of the village, with their vines also set in the southern sector.

Half the holding is on *Patou* (65 per cent 1940s, the rest gradual replanting) and half on

Combe (65 per cent 1914, the rest later replanting). Bernard works in an office in Valence and admits, "I'm also watching the weather when I'm there, looking out of the window a lot, rather like school!"

Marc lived off the land and rented enough vines to work 2.5 hectares. He is in his mid-70s, and started to do some bottling in the 1960s, moving on from selling to friends and *bistrots* in Valence.

Whole bunches are fermented in concrete for two weeks, with a traditional crushing. Ageing lasts 18 months in five-to-10-year-old casks, and while there can be a fining, there is no filtration before bottling.

CORNAS

2002 ★ Some violet, quite pretty aroma. Red fruit flavour, with a meaty side. Can soften the finish. Respectable. 2011–12.

GABRIEL MEFFRE

84190 Gigondas +33(0)490 837007

See also Condrieu, Côte-Rôtie, Crozes-Hermitage, Hermitage, St-Joseph.
The crop for the Meffre Laurus is destemmed and undergoes a three-week fermentation and maceration, the top temperature kept to 28°C. The wine is aged for 14 to 16 months in new 275-litre casks. It is fined, but not filtered. It is cleanly made in the modern style, and is easy to drink when around three to four years old.

CORNAS LAURUS

2001 ★★ Midweight bouquet, cooked fruits, tar/rubber, start of fungal phase. Gummy red fruits, fair flesh, compact overall. Modern style, though some local definition. Tidy, is OK now. 2010.

DOMAINE MICHEL CHRYSTELLE, JEAN-LUC, JOHANN/VIGNOBLES DE L'ABONDANCE

52 Grande Rue 07130 Cornas +33(0)475 405643

See also St-Péray.

Jean-Luc Michel would think of Cornas when he was posted abroad with the French Army; he worked in the transport division, having left the family vineyard at Cornas as a young man in 1969 "because there wasn't enough for me to live on."

Eighteen years later he returned as a 40-year-old to work on the 1.19-hectare vineyard, which had been let out in the meantime. A six-month apprenticeship with the Courbis domaine in the next village of Châteaubourg was followed by a year at school near Valence studying agriculture and viticulture.

He set about enlarging the vineyard, and now his children Johann and Chrystelle work just under three hectares of Cornas and 0.4 ha of Syrah and Chardonnay *vin de table*. The original vineyard on *Les Saveaux* (1973, 1988) was topped up with 1 ha on *Patou* (1990), also in the southern sector. Johann joined in 1997, Chrystelle in 2001, and between 1997 and 2003 the family planted 0.3 ha on *Bouyonnet*—gore soil on this subset at the southwest end of *Les Côtes*—0.2 ha alongside it on *Les Côtes* itself, and 0.23 ha on *Chaillot*.

From 2005 the domaine has been operated under the three family members' names, instead of the formerly unwieldy *Les Vignobles de l'Abondance*.

Johann is a friendly man just into his 30s and has a nice sense of humour; he is solidly made, an impression increased by his strong forearms and short-cropped black hair: it's no surprise that he played local rugby for 17 years. He has ideas and enthusiasm for his career: he'd like to keep some wine back and be able to sell mature vintages; he also wants to build a cellar to allow more work on raising his wine. His training was commercial, and he has learnt his wine skills on the ground.

His tall, slim elder sister, Chrystelle, did agricultural studies, and between them their outlook is sensibly calm and unfussed. The wines turn out with a consistent style, nothing too overdone about them. They can be punchy when young—1999 and 2001, for instance.

Their only wire-trained vineyard is *Saveaux*, also their most precocious. This can be worked mechanically, but elsewhere the young generation tries to restrict the use of insecticides and apply plain copper treatments. In his short career, Johann has experienced two wildly different harvest dates—2001 ran from the end of September until 10 October, while 2003 was started on 20 August!

The policy is for partial destalking and a 15-to-21-day vinification, with only pumping-over and a top temperature of 30°C. Cask ageing runs for 12 to 18 months in one-to-10-year-old oak. Part of the wine is sold in bulk to the *négoce* trade. The bottled wine is filtered, but not fined, since it is left strictly alone once it is in cask.

This is an understated domaine, with a potentially promising future ahead of it.

CORNAS

2003 (CASKS) ★★★ Black jam aroma, not typical Cornas. Red berry attack, some late tannin to provide pepper and a prop. Full, no excess. Good length, some style. From 2007–08; 2019–21.

2002 ★ Reduced bouquet on different bottles, some fruit roundness underneath. Red berry fruits on palate, but very stinky again. Length fair, gentle wine. Needs decanting. Can break out, e.g., 2007. 2011–13.

2001 ★★★ Earthy-style red fruit Syrah/toffee aroma; solid, with cooked fruit finale, thorough tannins. Mineral, bit dry end. From 2006. Has traditional punch. 2015–18.

2000 ★★ 2013–14

1999 ★★★ From 2006; 2016–18

DOMAINE ROBERT MICHEL

Grande Rue 07130 Cornas +33(0)475 403870

See also St-Joseph.

Robert Michel officially took over from his father, Joseph, in 1975, and at the time—aged 29—he was one of the only young vignerons at Cornas. It can't have helped him to soldier on without any great momentum around him; his

FIGURE 37 Robert Michel's Cornas has always been honest and full, very much in the mainstream of traditional quality here. (Tim Johnston)

only contemporary was Jean Lionnet, a year older than him. This situation has changed now that his nephew Vincent Paris, Matthieu Barret, and Stéphane Robert are all leading the charge for younger growers.

He started in the vineyards in 1964, so is a senior commentator on events and changes at Cornas. He is also a retiring man, living a quiet life tucked away in his confidential house set just off the Grande Rue. On a baking hot, still July day, when there is not much he can do for the vines, he stands in the brief courtyard modelling an aeroplane that will eventually fly through radio control.

He married when in his 40s a woman from outside the region named Vivianne Perraud, but they recently divorced, and their joint *négociant* business of Michel and Perraud, dealing with Cornas and St-Joseph from outside sources, has been wound up. So it's back to what he knows best—the intimate features of his own vineyard. Robert has never lost his countryman's way, stating that "work in the vineyards is a pleasure for me—it's a chance to observe and think." His comments at times seem locked in a state of bygone innocence, touchingly so.

His holdings run to four hectares of Cornas, plus half a hectare of St-Joseph and a half hectare of Merlot for a *vin de pays*. The Cornas comes from just two sites: *Reynards*—granite with a bit of gneiss, very fundamental rock—where the core vineyard dates from 1910, with plantings from the 1960s and 1980s; and *Chaillot*, granite mixed with some clay, dating from 1978.

Robert destems according to the site: "*Reynards*, especially *La Geynale*, gives wines that are elegant, contain a lot of spice, and hold good tannins—so I don't destem," he says. "*Chaillot* I usually destem 30 to 50 per cent—the wines are rich but their tannins are tough, not so elegant, and if not destemmed, can be a little hard."

His vineyard care has softened over the years: a lot fewer herbicides, notably. "I stay with wooden stake training, even though wires are allowed, because the slopes are so steep," he comments. Harvesting takes a week, with some family and regulars in the 15-person team.

There are two wines, the Cuvée des Coteaux, made mostly from *Chaillot*, and La Geynale, from his oldest vines on what is the extension of *Reynards*. In the United States, Robert's *négociant* business has sold Les Genêts, which is another label for La Geynale. Half of the wine for La Geynale comes from a rented plot, with the rental agreement expiring in 2008, so the future of this wine is not assured after that. Robert has dropped his Pied de Coteaux, renting out this vineyard near the N86 to Vincent Paris.

His two-room cellar under the Grande Rue continues unchanged. The first room dates from the thirteenth or fourteenth century and was one of the first baptised vaults. Its walls contain old Roman stone tools and stones from the Rhône. "Cornas is one of the few remaining places where vinifications are still done in the village," says Robert, a man whose sandy hair has now largely receded. "I wear glasses, and I still have fit legs!" he jokes.

Fermentation, with no added yeasts, is in open concrete vats, the top temperature now a lower 30°C; the whole process lasts 20 to 25 days. From 1997 he moved on to also using larger *demi-muids* of 600 litres, for the richness and elegance they bring. Some 225-litre casks up to six years old are still on the go, with new ones bought from Tardieu-Laurent's cooperage. But there is no specific desire for a new-oak influence, its maximum presence in any year around 10 percent. The wood ageing starts after the malolactic has been completed, around December, and lasts a year.

There is no room to bottle, so Robert uses a travelling bottler who sets up shop beside the N86 in the month of March. He neither fines nor filters.

The Cuvée des Coteaux shows live berry fruits and is clearly intended as a more racy offering than the noble La Geynale. The Geynale is really likeable, authentic wine. It is not as well known as some of the big names, but I find that Robert's recent vintages have shown great local feel, the fruit nicely brewed, the tannins in order. Old vines with respectable cropping levels are always a winning formula, and as the Cornas vineyard has grown younger, this wine stands out all the more.

Robert's Merlot is grown on the plain of Cornas, near the Rhône, where the *galet* stones are similar to those found across the river at Pont de l'Isère and Beaumont-Monteux. "I chose Merlot because it is an early ripener and I wanted a wine in contrast to my Cornas," he explains simply.

Joseph and his son Robert Michel find their way of life both varied and stimulating. As Joseph said in 1980: "I wouldn't change my profession for anything. It is a good feeling to see your own wine, finished and bottled up, and then to see to whom it is going and whether it is likely to be appreciated. I used to sell almost completely to the trade, but more and more of my clients urged me to bottle it myself and sell it direct to them. An average order is around 30 bottles. What I really enjoy is having the people come to me: then I meet all sorts and nationalities. We even had a visit from a man who had read your book in Cairo, so life is full of surprises!"

CORNAS CUVÉE DES COTEAUX

2002 (CASK) ★ Light white pepper/red berry nose; thrusting red fruits; aftertaste is OK. Fair width, weight. Ideal for restaurants. 10 years or so life.

2001 ★★★ Near-polish aroma, tight, ripe black fruit; marzipan, black berry fruit, live feel. Raspberry, tar end. Promising fruit. STGT wine. From 2006–07; 2014–17.

CORNAS LA GEYNALE

2002 (CASK) ★★ Violets/roses, some earth on charming nose; scented flavour, red stone fruit, sinew. Chewy end, good cut, upright style. From 2005–06; 2012–14.

2001 ★★★★★ Great, typical bouquet—earthy, violet, typical; pretty ripe attack, oily, nicely modelled. Granite purity, light heat, some end tar. Classic, very good. From 2007; 2020–25.

2000 ★★★ Violet, stewed fruits, slight reduction on bouquet; pebbly black fruit—stewed plums in a very Syrah style. Mineral/dry surrounds, is clear on the finish. Fleshes out with air, broadens well. Esp from 2006–07; 2014–16.

Export 50 per cent 1) Great Britain, 2) USA, 3) Japan/Switzerland

DOMAINE MICHELAS SAINT JEMMS

Bellevue Les Chassis 26600 Mercurol
+33(0)475 078670

See also Crozes-Hermitage, Hermitage, St-Joseph.

This down-the-line Crozes domaine work two hectares of Cornas, on what the family terms *Les Murettes* (1950s), on *Les Côtes*, and on *La Combe* (1978), the most southerly *lieu-dit*.

The wine is fermented and macerated for three weeks, with pumping-over, and then raised for a year in half new, half one-year-old casks, although the lighter-than-usual 2002 was sensibly raised in 25 hl barrels. Called "Les Murettes," it is fined and filtered. It is the domaine's most consistent and often best wine.

CORNAS LES MURETTES

2003 (CASK) ★★(★) Smoky, brooding nose, leafy/truffled. Black fruit has vigour, persists. Very soaked wine. Tight-knit, pebbly at end, pepper too. Esp from 2007–08; 2019–21.

2002 ★★ Violet, black jam, pretty full nose, some Cornas minerality there. Modern, black fruit style, licorice/light pepper. Fair length. Bit constructed but OK, has some appeal, flesh. From 2006–07; 2015–18.

2001 ★★ Reserved bouquet, light meat/smoked fruit. Quite dense cooked fruit, rather spotless wine. Drier finale, some tar aftertaste. From 2006; 2013–15.

CAVES OGIER

10 avenue Louis Pasteur 84230 Châteauneuf-du-Pape
+33(0)490 393232

See also Crozes-Hermitage, Hermitage, St-Joseph.

This southern Rhône *négociant* offers a Cornas from time to time, and it can be very satisfactory.

CORNAS LES REILLOTS

2000 ★★★ Rubbery, stewed fruits, raspberry; compact, brewed fruits, black berries. Some heat, good cut. OK length. 2013–16.

DOMAINE VINCENT PARIS

Chemin des Peyrouses 07130 Cornas +33(0)475 401304

See also St-Joseph.

It pays to have connections in a vineyard like Cornas, with the cost of start-up from scratch formidably high. Vincent Paris got going in 1997, when he was 23, and was helped in his enterprise by being the son of Robert Michel's sister Marie-Jeanne.

A determined man, tall and slim with a soft voice, light-brown hair, and piercing, pale-blue eyes, he studied for two years at wine school in Mâcon-Davayé. "I have always been keen on wine," he remarks, "and maybe I'm a bit of a maniac when it comes to care in the vineyards and cleanliness in the cellar; that's probably why I work on my own!"

He is moving fast; he works vineyards at Cornas and St-Joseph, has a Merlot *vin de pays*, and has built most of his new cellar on the river side of Cornas single-handed. He is also keen to use information technology in spreading the word about the domaine. It's no surprise to hear that he is winding down his two hectares of apricots.

At Cornas he has three hectares; two sites lead the way—half a hectare of 60-year-old vines and 1.4 hectares (1997) on *Patou*, and a postage stamp 0.2 ha of 90-plus-year-old vines on *Mazards*. The remainder is on *Sauman* (1992) and a brand new plantation (2003 onwards) on *St-Pierre*. For the first three *lieux-dits*, the soil is largely granite; at *St-Pierre*, the high slopes are stony, the lower slopes sandy. Vincent finds that *Patou* and *Mazards* ripen around five days ahead of *Sauman*. "*Sauman* had to be cleared of pines in 1991 and is quite coarse ground," he adds.

About one hectare of *Patou* is flat enough to allow tractor working, and on that slight slope Vincent grows grass. Elsewhere he has to apply weedkiller in spring, but for the later weeds he uses the manual pickaxe to clear around the vines. Otherwise there are no insecticides or chemical applications.

Vincent started out vinifying chez his uncle Robert, and 2001 marked his first wine from his own cellar. He destalks all crop except for the oldest vine fruit from *Patou* and *Mazards*. In a mix of concrete and polyester vats, he pumps over the juice and stirs the cap, the effect being like a light crush. "I don't add yeasts, and I keep sulphur use low, up to 4 gm for instance," he says. "The *brassage* [stirring] adds carbonic gas to make the vat turn, and I do it over the course of three weeks," he explains.

Vincent's intention "is to make wines that hold a lot of perfumes, and finesse, though with some tannin also." This ties in with the young school thinking of people like Matthieu Barret and is why he switched to a cool maceration start to his vinification from 2001 on.

In 2000 he launched two wines: His young-vines wine, Granit 30, is raised for a year—one-third in vat, two-thirds in used casks. The carbonic gas brings out a lot of fruit, and this is a straight get-up-and-drink wine, tannin not forming a part of its plan. "I deliberately play the fruit card on this because the vines are quite young," he explains.

His Vieilles Vignes wine, the Granit 60, is all cask raised for a year, the oak also two to eight years old. There is no fining or filtration when bottling occurs 18 months after the harvest.

The Granit 60 especially will benefit from being left to age; young, it is somewhat mainstream—with age, more variety and layering of flavour will arrive.

The Merlot was planted beside *St-Pierre* in 1999. Its wine is firm and straightforward.

CORNAS GRANIT 30

2002 (CASK) ★ Nose—grilled notes, some fruit under; fair fruit, midweight, some sap. 2010–12.

2001 ★★ Firm, grilled, ripe/full nose, black fruit; compact, clean modern-style fruit. Suave/direct, up front. Fair length. 2010–12.

2000 ★★ Open, even olive/fruit nose; nice red fruits, modern. Open, quite straight/clear; peppery edge, oily; length OK. 2008–10.

CORNAS GRANIT 60

2002 (CASK) ★★ Red fruits/pepper, quite cool aroma; squeeze of black fruit, bit raw near a toasted end. Good effort, some length. Can move along. From 2007.

2001 ★★★ Grilled, dark fruit nose; clear fruit, bit burnt; clean, could have more soul, but quiet warmth evolving. Bit stern. Fair scale, modern style, leave till 2007. 2013–16.

2000 ★★ Overt berry/violet nose; evolution bringing more interest, middle red fruit, some gaminess taking over from almost metallic early side. Fair length. 2009–11.

Export 50 per cent 1) Great Britain, 2) USA, 3) Belgium

DOMAINE DE ROCHEPERTUIS

48 rue Pied la Vigne 07130 Cornas +33(0)475 403601

See also St-Péray.

Jean-René Lionnet hung up his wine spurs after the 2005 vintage. It surprised me that he did not receive bigger headlines in the media, simply because he turned out wines of a good, very consistent standard every year, both red and white. They were clean and not in the funky, local style, but his Domaine de Rochepertuis wine notably developed variety and depth with age.

His domaine is at the northern edge of the village. Next to it is one of the rare grassed spots in Cornas, a chicken run, and a couple of goats; a sheep as well to lighten the atmosphere. It's normally just fruit, vine, or houses at Cornas.

M. Lionnet appears to have his feet well on the ground. This is not a showy domaine—hence its low-key profile. He is an energetic man with a deep, gravelly voice, brilliant clear blue eyes and a mat of white-grey hair that makes him resemble Derek Jacobi playing the Roman Emperor Claudius. His big hands catch the eye, their size an indication of the work necessary in these craggy vineyards.

Now approaching 60, Jean owns 4.5 hectares and for many years has rented another 4.5 hectares of Cornas from the Barret family, whose son Matthieu started to make his own wine from the 2001 vintage. The rental agreement ended after the 2005 harvest, and the Barret family are once more working these 4.5 hectares.

He is the third wine generation of his branch of the Lionnets. The other, older branch, represented by Pierre Lionnet, has been making wine here for over 400 years.

During the late 1980s Jean took radical steps to change his vinification and outlook. He became a moderniser. This carried extra impact because of the size of his nine-hectare *exploitation*—which makes him one of the big hitters of the *appellation*: he was cultivating six hectares in the mid-1980s.

Half his vines are 40 to 90 years old and half 16 to 30 years—so his raw materials are top grade from an age point of view. The epicentre is in the most northerly part of the *appellation*, around *Les Arlettes*. There the 35-to-40-year-old Syrah grows on soil notably marked by the about 25 per cent limestone-chalk content mixed in with the granite, the limestone increasing the further north one goes. That is why Jean's 1.7 ha of *Les Arlettes* that lacks granite is set outside Cornas in simple Côtes du Rhône land.

His other main location is about three hectares at *Chaillot*, 55-year-old Syrah growing on granite mixed with a clay topsoil. This ripens ahead of *Les Arlettes* and is a superior *lieu-dit*. M. Lionnet finds that wines from the most granite parts of the northern part of the *appellation* are less easy to drink when young than those from the southern part of the vineyard, just below the heart of the village.

Since 1987 Jean has made a top wine, the Domaine de Rochepertuis, chosen from his full-slope vines. His regular Cornas comes more from the lower slopes than from any set of young vines; the latter's wine, making up about 20 per cent of the production, tends to be sold in bulk to local *négociants*.

Indicative of the limited demand for Cornas that ran well into the 1970s, Jean started to bottle a tiny amount of his wine only in 1976, and it wasn't until the 1985 harvest that he extended the process.

His turning point came in 1987, when he built a new cellar, concentrating heavily on stainless steel and completely changing his vinification. He was closely advised at the time by Jean-Luc Colombo, and his great achievement was to secure a full form of Cornas that gained in local robustness the longer it was aged in bottle—without some of the unstable, sometimes volatile elements of the purely traditional wine.

Since about 1990, vinification has started with a cool, 10°C temperature for a week. "As in Burgundy," he comments, "I want to obtain the most possible fruit so the wine can be drunk in its first two years, and then age well after it has gone through a quiet period." Outside yeasts are used to provoke fermentation.

The destemmed crop then spends around 25 days in stainless steel at up to 28°C; Jean does a *remontage*, or pumping-over of the cap, three times a day until finally once every three days. Since 2002 he has also done two *délestages* (partial vat emptying and refilling) during the maceration process: "They bring extra colour and maybe help the tannins to be finer," he explains, adding that he racks only twice instead of four times a year druing ageing as a result. The *jus de presse* and the core *jus de goutte* are kept separate; the wine is racked and then kept at 20°C to obtain the malolactic, which in 2003 was done in cask—the small crop allowing the space for this.

All the bottled Cornas is oak aged for 12 to 14 months—the regular wine in five-to-six-year-old 225-litre casks, the Rochepertuis in 20 per cent new, 80 per cent one-to-five-year-old casks. Fining and a light filtration are done before one bottling run in April.

"In those early days I had to take a deep breath and get rid of my family's nearly 100-year-old casks," he comments. "All my casks are Bordelais, with Allier wood, and a medium heating used. There was a large amount of learning to be done in those days of the late 1980s, I can tell you!"

Eight thousand to 10,000 bottles of regular Cornas are made, and 10,000 to 12,000 of Domaine de Rochepertuis. Chapoutier and Jaboulet buy the bulk wine.

Jean's red Côtes du Rhône is from 1.7 ha of 1970s Syrah that grows on a rented plot in a ravine on *Les Arlettes*, near the plateau above the main hillsides. The ★★ 2001 was a typical example, its lively black fruit ideal for barbecued food and drinking within its first five years.

CORNAS

2003 (CASK) ★★ Red jam fruit/violet aroma; wine with stuffing—cooked fruits, some richness, and a firm end. From 2008; 2016–18.

2002 (CASK) ★★ Floral/black fruit/varnish nose; light, clear cooked black fruits, some width/*gras*. Some end tannin, agreeable. I'd like more flesh. From 2006; 2012–14.

CORNAS DOMAINE DE ROCHEPERTUIS

2003 (CASKS) ★★★ Dark berried, oily/varnish aroma; peppered, cooked black fruit, which persists. Hefty, has tannins, is dark wine. From 2009; 2018–22.

2002 (CASK) ★★★ Grilled, gunflint, smoky nose, cool texture, clear-cut fruit, tight berries/violets. Fair width, end heat. From 2007; 2016–19.

2001 ★★★ Violets/grilled nuts nose; berried fruit/licorice/mint. Compact, elegant, chewy, quite rich. Sleek tannins. From 2005–06; 2013–15.

2000 ★★★★★ Woods/fruit/fungal mix on nose; intense, but restrained. Live berried fruit, mineral aspects. Firm end. Good character. From 2006; 2016–18.

1999 ★★★★ Sustained, brewed nose—black fruit/tar/woods; tight-knit palate, crunchy fruit, potential. Grip, balance good. Stimulating oil/black flavour. Esp from 2005–06; 2016–19.

1998 ★★★★ 2012–15

Export 50 per cent 1) Great Britain, 2) USA, 3) Belgium

LOUIS SOZET

25 rue du Ruisseau 07130 Cornas +33(0)475 405113

Touching 70, Louis Sozet is indicative of the game, "never retire until you have to" attitude at Cornas. "I had two hectares but I'm dispersing them now," he says. "I'm down to 0.8 ha, on *Eygats*, my aunt's old plot, and *Champelrose*, both of them having some 1919 vines and a few later ones as well."

A stooped man with a windswept, outdoor face, he sells a fair part of his 2,000 bottles at the Cornas Wine Fair in early December every year. He mans his stall on his own for two days, lugs around 36 bottles at a time on a trolley, and proclaims that he'll "keep going, making a bit of wine, as long as God permits."

His great-grandfather lived in Cornas, but was a typical smallholder with a few cows; vineyards were out of his reach. He started work at 14 and was on his own by the age of 21, in 1960. "Before I first bottled some of the wine in the early 1980s, we sold it to nearby *bistrots* and *négociants*; I had a hectare of apricots then, but I've rented them out, too." The beneficiary of his vineyard rentals is Stéphane Robert of Domaine du Tunnel.

Since the late 1990s he has destemmed, and ferments the crushed grapes in concrete for eight to 10 days, with one or two pumping-overs. The wine is raised for 21 months in a mix of used 550-litre and 225-litre casks and is filtered without a prior fining. It is a good example of honest, local-feel Cornas.

CORNAS

2002 ★★ Pretty, blackberry, smoky bouquet. Scented black stone fruit flavour, some warmth. Bosky towards finish, some acidity. Likeable, some guts, honest wine. 2010–12.

2001 ★★ Reserved red fruit/floral, slightly smoked nose; punchy, vigorous red fruit, fresh texture, tannins evident. 2011–13.

CAVE DE TAIN-L'HERMITAGE

22 route de Larnage 26600 Tain l'Hermitage
+33(0)475 082087

See also Crozes-Hermitage, Hermitage, St-Joseph, St-Péray.
The Tain Cave is a hidden force at Cornas, with its 15 Co-opérateurs working around 19 hectares —not far off 20 per cent of the *appellation*. The top sites are 2.7 ha on *Les Mazards*, 2.5 ha each on *Reynards* and *St-Pierre*, 1.8 ha on *Chaillot*, and 1.6 ha on *Saveaux*. The vines are in many good, central areas and average somewhere over 30 years in age.

The Co-opérative also has the right to plant a further 10 hectares in the future. The aim is to establish a showcase vineyard little by little over the coming years.

The crop is destalked and receives a three-to-six-week maceration; 80 per cent of the wine is raised in 228-litre casks (10–15 per cent new, the rest one to two years old) for 18 months. There is no fining, but a light filtration.

"Our big task at Cornas is to master the tannins," comments winemaker Alain Bourgeois; "we're after a wine that fully expresses the wild side of the Syrah, something of a juxtaposition."

The wine has become more modern in recent years, via the grilled notes on the bouquet. On the palate, its fruit can be whole-hearted with correct support tannins, and it stands in the "sound wine" category. A life of 15 years or so is possible in vintages like 2001 and 1999.

CORNAS PREMIÈRE SÉLECTION/LES NOBLES RIVES

2003 ★★ Full, soaked ripe fruit, peppery aroma. Raspberry attack, fair warmth. Fat and rather southern style, lacks the usual Cornas cut. Oak renders it a bit hard now. Herbal ending, some warmth. From 2007; 2015–18.

2002 (CASK) ★★ Midweight prune/oak/leather nose; cooked fruits, assertive tannins, upright texture. Not very deep, can be OK by 2007. 2013–14.

2001 ★★★ Grilled/black fruit/mineral aroma; black fruit/pepper mix, sound flesh at core with good tannins. Nicely rich. From 2006; 2016–18.

2000 ★ 2009–12

1999 ★★★★ From 2006; 2015–17

TARDIEU-LAURENT

Route de Cucuron 84160 Lourmarin +33(0)490 688025

See also Condrieu, Côte-Rôtie, Crozes-Hermitage, Hermitage, St-Joseph, St-Péray.
Michel Tardieu and Dominique Laurent know exactly whom to visit in Cornas, and their wine reflects the central situation of the vineyards chosen. Two of their past suppliers have been Noël Verset and Robert Michel, impeccable sources who furnished the *négociants* with their wine just after it finished its primary, alcoholic fermentation.

They recognise that Cornas has especially helped to make their name since they started with the 1994 vintage and just 10,000 bottles of all wines. What they have done is to refine the wonderful raw material from these slopes. The older-vine fruit is often from the old Petite Syrah, not a Syrah clone: it can be finer and less coloured than the modern produce. The clean new wood for the ageing works into the tannins and can serve to harmonise them that much earlier.

They work with just two suppliers for their Vieilles Vignes wine, and two or three for their Coteaux. Amounts are limited: around 3,000 bottles of the Coteau and 2,400 of the Vielles Vignes.

The wine is raised over 15 months in new-oak casks, the wood chosen by Dominique Laurent. "The new wood is a very good anti-oxidant that allows us to work without sulphur dioxide—that's why we use it, not to make a new-wood taste," says Michel Tardieu. Any elite Tronçais casks are now from their own sources. Stored in their fifteenth-century cellars at Lourmarin on the edge of Provence, the wine is racked as little as possible. Nonintervention is the policy.

In the richest years like 2001, the Coteaux remains in the new oak for another seven months. Otherwise it is transferred to oak a year or two old for its remaining ageing. It is made from *Chaillot* vines that date from the 1950s.

The Vieilles Vignes comes from near-100-year-old vines on *Chaillot* and 80-year-old vines on *Geynale*. Its stay in new oak has been cut from 24 to 15 months since 2003, with the remaining nine months now spent in one-to-two year-old casks. I can hear my sigh of relief as I write these words. The 2004 Vieilles Vignes held excellent and bouncy core fruit, with the oak less apparent than in 2001 or 2000, the latter a vintage that struggled under the weight of its oaking. Michel Tardieu's summary of the two wines is that the Coteaux is "more a wine of fruits and spice—fruits such as blackcurrant or raspberry. The Vieilles Vignes is a wine of greater minerality, one that can reflect the soul of the northern Rhône."

Given the problems of the 2002 vintage, the Coteaux was produced, but not the Vieilles Vignes. Exceptionally, it was raised in the Domaine Laurent Tronçais oak. The second wine in 2002 was Les Grandes Bastides, part of their new range where half the casks are new Allier oak. The vines for this are 20 to 40 years old.

CORNAS COTEAUX

2004 (CASK) ★★★(★) From mid-2008; 2019–21

2001 (CASK) ★★★ Good width, refined bouquet—cooked fruit, damp earth. Discreet, but has sound content, loganberry style. Good, fresh end. Esp from 2006; 2012–14.

1998 ★★★ 2008–10

1997 ★★ 2006–09

CORNAS VIEILLES VIGNES

2004 (CASK) ★★★★★ From 2009; 2020–23

2001 (CASK) ★★★★ Open, raspberry nose, smoked; red berry flavour, wide, tasty. Very live, has sinew; chewy, tarry end. Potential. From 2007; 2015–17.

2000 ★★ Brewed, fungal, peppery black fruit aroma; upright, with oily middle. Pine/ cedar. Sleek fruit, firm oak-aided tannins. Bit forced. From 2006; 2013–15.

1998 ★★★★★ 2016–23

1997 ★★ 2007–11

Export 70 per cent 1) USA, 2) Great Britain, 3) Luxembourg

JEAN-LOUIS ET FRANÇOISE THIERS

Le Biguet 07130 Toulaud +33(0)475 404244

See also St-Péray.

Jean-Louis Thiers' domaine is south of St-Péray, and he started to make Cornas from its southern sector in 1984, spurred on by a rental agreement with Marc Maurice, whose son Bernard works in an office in Valence.

He has a little under one hectare split between *Combe* (1950s at least) and *Saveaux* (1920s, 1950s). These areas can give a direct black fruitiness, without the overt, brooding tannins that the northern, rocky land of Cornas can bring.

The crop has usually been destemmed since the mid-1990s, although 2000 and 2001 were ripe enough to allow some stalks into the vat. Fermentation is in open steel and lasts three weeks, with a mix of pumping-overs and cap punchings. Ageing is 60 per cent in oak, using one-to-four-year-old casks, and 40 per cent in steel. There is fining, but no filtration.

they come from the warm southern zones, not the most structured central granite areas. They can be drunk from around five years on, and are capable of 15 years or so of sound life.

2003 (CASKS) ★★(★) Full *robe*; well-set fruit on bouquet, also violet, herbs, oak. Big, constructed wine, a Californian. Some end minerality, rare for the year. Meaty, full, earthy. Oaked finale. From 2008; 2020–22.

2002 (CASKS) ★ Jam fruit/earth aroma; direct, live red fruit, gets chewy, fair amount here. Best early for its fruit. From 2006; 2010–12.

2001 ★★★ Compact fruit/licorice/mineral nose; clear black fruit, can broaden by 2006, some guts, but typical Cornas restraint. Dark fruit/tobacco end. From 2007; 2017–19.

2000 ★★★ Suave, spiced black fruit, more gutsy with air. Tasty, intense black spiced fruit, oily. Cool, elegant feel, typical minerality. Smooth oak, smoky bacon end. 2014–16.

DOMAINE DU TUNNEL

20 rue de la République 07130 St-Péray
+33(0)475 800466

See also St-Joseph, St-Péray.

The sensible and promising Stéphane Robert is another of the younger brigade at Cornas, where he started his involvement by renting vines in 1994, when he was just 24 years old.

He now cultivates almost 3.5 ha of Cornas; his core site is his rented 1.5 ha on *Combe* in the south (sanded granite, more granite higher up), the oldest vines from the 1900s, the youngest from the 1980s. His most feverish activity has been on *Sauman* (very hard, pure granite), where he planted 0.9 ha between 2002 and 2003; "there were traces of old terraces here from maybe the 1950s," he comments.

The other sites are 0.5 ha on *Mazards* (2000–01), 0.4 ha on *Eygas* (1920s), and 0.25 ha on *Champelrose*, a mix of 1900s and 1970s vines, and a smidgen on *Cayret*, or *Barjasse*, in the heart of the *appellation*.

Stéphane destems around 60 per cent of the crop and ferments for 15 to 18 days in steel vats in his St-Péray cellars. He alternates pumping-over with manual cap punching. The wine is raised for 14 months in four-to-six-year-old casks and can be fined and filtered according to the vintage. In his best years (2003, 2001, 2000, 1999, 1998, 1996), Stéphane also produces 500 to 2,000 bottles of a Vin Noir that he now calls "Cuvée Prestige," made mainly from the old vines on *Combe* with the same ageing as the classic wine.

"For me the most important factor in the cellar is the temperature of the vinification—ahead of any cap punching or pumping-over," says Stéphane. "To extract well, I reckon you need a peak of 35°C for maybe four to five hours, then you must keep the vat at 30°C for a week to fix the colour and have the correct concentration." He is not a lover of new oak, and his wine, while clean and modern in its young texture, is capable of expressing *terroir* if drunk from five years old on.

CORNAS

2002 (CASKS) ★(★) Violet alongside stewed fruits aroma, some charm. Full, fruit flows along. Broad, ripe tannin finale, raspberry aftertaste. Lasts OK. Touch overdone, not sure. From 2007; 2016–19.

2002 ★★ Compact, suave berried aroma. Evident probing blackberry fruit, light tar, minted end. Some richness, though tannins quite tough right now. Length OK. More variety from 2007. 2014–18.

2001 ★★★ Very berried, meaty aroma; ripe fruit, a meaty, full wine, has sap, richness. Live, peppered. Promising. From 2007; 2018–20.

CORNAS CUVÉE PRESTIGE

2003 (CASKS) ★★ Dark *robe*; chunky, meaty, ripe grape–skin bouquet. Good, homogeneous black fruit attack, the ripeness of the year; raisin juice. Imposed oak tannins on finish, hope won't dry. From 2007–08; 2019–21.

2000 ★★★ Very dark; stewed, soaked jam nose. Supple start, berried jam with kick. Juicy, overt, some end tannin. Early style. 2010–12.

1999 (named "Vieilles Vignes") ★ Reduced nose, black fruit/tar; dense, berried/tar palate, red fruits, but stretched, taut. 2008–09.

L. DE VALLOUIT

See also Crozes-Hermitage, Hermitage, St-Joseph.

De Vallouit bought just under one hectare at Cornas in 1988, a vineyard dating from 1955. The crop was never destalked (except for 1993). Winemaking was traditional, with cask and barrel ageing for two and a half years at least. There was a light filtration.

Called "Les Médiévales," the wines were generally softly textured, more than most Cornas. There was fair authenticity. With age, more gamey, down-home aspects became apparent. In the house tradition, the wines sometimes lacked freshness.

ALAIN VERSET

140 Route Nationale 07130 Cornas +33(0)475 404123

Alain is the son of the late Louis Verset and therefore part of a well-known wine family. He works in a factory that makes public-sector refuse bins at Guilherand, south of St-Péray, while his father and grandfather Emmanuel were full-time on the domaine. "It's both a pleasure and work for me in the vineyard," he says of his weekends—"perhaps a custom or religion; I always saw my father and grandfather working the vines, so it's normal to follow them."

He has a little over one hectare on *Reynards, Mazards,* and *Les Côtes*; "some vines are from 1923, but it's hard to know just how old they are," he says. He has also planted 0.3 hectare of young vines on *Les Côtes* and *La Côte.*

This remains a domaine barely big enough to support a full-time presence; Alain is approaching 50 and has five children. He sells in bulk to *négociants,* with only 900 bottles produced at the domaine per annum.

Vinification is traditional—whole bunches fermented for 10 to 15 days in concrete vats under the family home, and some pumping-overs. No outside yeasts are used, and ageing lasts 18 to 24 months in four-to-five-year-old casks. Alain fines but doesn't filter the wine.

His own first vintage was 2000, and he prefers to drink the wine when it's three to four years old.

CORNAS

2000 ★ Ripe stewed fruits aroma; hearty attack, violets, red fruits. Decent length, local feel, pliant tannins. Some end heat/rusticity.

NOËL VERSET

Impasse de la Couleyre 07130 Cornas +33(0)475 403666

Noël Verset has been a quiet pillar of Cornas for decades. Born in 1919, he is always rumoured to be on the brink of retirement. Now that he is in his mid-80s, there is a gradual air of finality since his grandson François did not take to winemaking after studying at Beaune, and now lives in Savoie, where he has followed religious studies. One son-in-law who is a professor of horticulture is the gleam of hope on the horizon here, where, despite a car accident in 1996, Noël has soldiered on, held in high esteem by locals and fancy overseas experts alike.

The epitome of working rural France, Noël dresses all in blue. Small, crinkly-faced, and bald, he comes across as canny (the Scots' word for artful), and his wine reflects this, too. His first grape harvest was in 1931, when he was 12, after he left school with his certificate. He then worked with his father, Emmanuel, until 1943, the year after his marriage, when he embarked on renting a vineyard for himself.

His first ownership came in 1948, when he bought the Domaine de la Sabarotte from M. Delaygue, the local Cornas *négociant.* Subsequently he took over from his father, Emmanuel. Noël's firsthand experience is immense, and he likes to continue to work: "My father lived to be 100, and we say in the family that wine replaces penicillin," he says in his high, chirpy-toned voice.

As befits such a long-standing presence, he has worked away for decades on old vineyards—*Chaillot* he has tended since 1956, for instance. After selling off his nearly 1.3 ha on *Sabarotte* to Messieurs Courbis and Clape, he remains with 0.5 ha on *Chaillot*, a 1912 vineyard bought in 1931 by his late wife Yvonne's parents, and 0.2 ha on *Champelrose*—"not much more than 50 years old!" There are few *vignerons* anywhere who will know plots of land so intimately in the decades to come.

All work is manual—the grapes are worked whole, with foot crushing at the reception. The 15-to-18-day vinification is punctuated by twice-daily *pigeages* and *remontages*, small concrete vats used for the fermentation. "In 2000 I had two American girls helping with the harvest, but I remember them most because they added a lot of style to the foot punching of the cap during the *pigeages*," he laughs. Likewise the press is manually operated in his compact cellar.

M. Verset uses 600-litre *demi-muids* for the 15 months' wood ageing: he has always preferred sizes larger than 228-litres, given his laissez-faire approach: "The wine ages more slowly, and just has more time." These barrels are four to five years old when bought—no traces of new oak. Two bottlings are done, without filtration, after 18 and 24 months.

Cornas' old-timers have many thoughts to share on the passage of time in their trade. M. Verset sold a tiny amount of wine in bottle in the 1940s, but most was sold to merchants and the local restaurant trade in April after each harvest.

In the 1930s, school ended for many at 12, so Noël joined his father in 1931. "In those days the vineyard owners lived in the village and employed workers who came down from the Ardèche hills. Nowadays what has been lost is the sense of community as well as a sense of fun in the winemaking."

M. Verset's wine is genuine: the extract is thorough, the texture often oily, with woodland berries as a regular note. After four years or so, the bouquet can gain gamey aromas, going past a mild pepperiness. The palate is full, with a touch of flesh rather than too much austerity. Sometimes there are quite rustic hints of volatile acidity. They are wines that should be drunk around the six-to-12-year mark.

And just to shock the marketing consultants and gurus, the pale gold label with twirls for years carried the words "Grand Vin des Côtes du Rhône." These "experts" would of course say the wine was unsaleable with such an association attached to it.

These days in a low-crop vintage like 2003 there were just 1,300 bottles, the rest of the wine sold to Tardieu-Laurent to age down in the Lubéron.

Less and less of M. Verset's wine will be seen as he takes a backseat. The gnarled metal plaque on his front entrance was taken down in 2004, and just a few drops will be made by him and his family for their own drinking in the future.

CORNAS

2002 (only *Chaillot/Champelrose*) ★★ Floral, blackberry, earthy nose; accessible—floats without *Sabarotte*, berry/herb mix, prolonged, quite direct fruit now. Fair width/length. Drinks OK now; 2011–13.

2001 ★★★ Oily, stewed grapes, varnish side, too; bold wine—core is black stewed flavour, muddy tannins, dried fruits end. Traditional, potent, bit burnt. From 2006–07; 2013–15.

2000 ★★★ Very dark; raw, floral-violet bouquet with smokiness, some reserve. Lovely flavour, easy to like. Quite advanced ripeness and openness, towards a volatile edge. Tasty early on. 2009–11.

1999 ★★★★ Broad, red fruits, meaty/farmyard nose; red fruits/pepper flavour, violet/mushroom end. Length good. Tasty, hearty. 2016–18.

1998 ★★★★ 2010–13
1997 ★ 2007–11
1996 ★★ 2006–10

Export 1) USA, 2) Great Britain, 3) Japan/Canada

J. VIDAL-FLEURY

19 route de la Roche 69420 Ampuis +33(0)474 561018

See also Condrieu, Côte-Rôtie, Crozes-Hermitage, Hermitage, St-Joseph.

The house of Vidal-Fleury, owned by Marcel Guigal of Ampuis, patiently raise their Cornas over two to three years in 70 percent large barrels, 30 per cent casks. The wine is bought from two regular sources, topping up on occasion from two others. The firm produce 5,000 to 6,000 bottles. It is usually a full, quite chunky wine, with plenty of wild cooked fruits present as well—"dark wine."

"The vineyards are all in the central strip of the hillside, at between 150 and 200 metres up," states the boss, Jean-Pierre Rochias.

CORNAS
1996 ★★ 2014–16

LES VINS DE VIENNE

Bas Seyssuel 38200 Seyssuel +33(0)474 850452

See also Condrieu, Côte-Rôtie, Crozes-Hermitage, Hermitage, St-Joseph, St-Péray.

The Cuilleron-Gaillard-Villard trio produce just one Cornas, called "Les Barcillants," which comes in their trademark heavy bottle. In 2003 they switched from buying wine to grapes for this, which receives an 18-month ageing in half new, half one-year-old oak. Around 6,000 bottles are produced.

CORNAS LES BARCILLANTS
2001 ★★ Midweight bouquet, harmonious. Fair matter, can handle the oak, integration OK, and finishes correctly. Esp 2006–07; 2013–15.

2000 ★★ Quite upright, some black fruit aroma; elegant, not esp deep wine. Cooked red fruits, light tannic fringe. Clean, earlier drinking. 2009–11.

ALAIN VOGE

4 Impasse de l'Equerre 07130 Cornas +33(0)475 403204

See also St-Péray.

In the early 1970s, I recall Alain Voge as the new kid on the block, a rare fresh-faced bird among the old-timers. Even then his personal style was restless and busy—a new cuvée here, another small plot there. He has always been a bustler, getting on with a new technique or fiddling with the vinification of one of his wines. No doubt the old'uns raised an eyebrow or two in those days at what they saw as his antics, and that was a full 10 years before the Jean-Luc Colombo cyclone hit town!

Alain has almost had two lives, since he underwent a liver transplant in 1998. That has not dimmed this most enthusiastic of *vignerons*. His bright face and darting eyes have stayed with him, as has his *casquette* cap, and he has remained game for his work, although obviously weakened now he is past his mid-60s. To that end, he signed an agreement in 2004 to convert his domaine into a registered company, and his friend Albéric Mazoyer of Chapoutier was installed as manager while keeping his important post chez Chapoutier.

Alain left school at 17 and spent two years in the army in Algeria: "I learnt to live there," he says somewhat ominously. His father, Louis, died in 1965, when he was 26, and by then the domaine was turning more towards wine. "Until the early 1960s, we had everything," he recalls; "apricots, pears, cherries, wheat, pigs, and three goats for cheese and the meat from the young kids."

His father was also the local distiller, with a mobile alambic that served the whole area. Alain continued with it until 1980, giving himself a lot of extra work as well as a series of 04.30 starts.

In those early days of the 1970s, his resolute late mother would help him on most tasks in the cellar and the vineyard. His wife and four workers are now involved, and he makes good, sensible wines. They are always close to the mark, with the proviso that he can suddenly change an element of the vinification.

He started automatic cap punching, or *pigeage*, on the wines in 2000, making the fruit sleeker than before. The wines regularly show

FIGURE 38 Still chatty, still busy, still young at heart—Alain Voge with Albéric Mazoyer from Chapoutier, now a joint-venture partner. (Tim Johnston)

good local feel with honest, often violet, plum and spice flavours. They also often have a dry-toned finish and are classic wines for autumn and winter. Their likely life is usually between 12 and 18 years. They are never overalcoholic or too heady, but the top ones are expensive.

Since the early 1990s, Alain has doubled to six hectares at St-Péray and moved up to seven hectares at Cornas. His 12 Cornas plots are classic names, their vines old as well: these include *Les Mazards* (1970s), *Chaillot* (1970s, 1980s), *Reynards* (1983), *Les Côtes* (1925), *Combe* (1925), and *Saveaux* (1960s). His prized site of *La Fontaine* is part of *Les Côtes*, dating from 1925. He also makes a *vin de table* from 1970s Syrah on the plain near the river.

His work in the vineyards is practical—he applies weedkillers and insecticides, along with treatments against mildew and oïdium. He has never been drawn into the laissez-faire school.

There are three different Cornas wines, based on the age of the vines. The classic cuvée comes from vines planted around 1985, while the Vieilles Vignes is from 25-to-80-year-old vines. Their crop is 70 to 80 per cent destemmed, and fermentation is in stainless steel, lasting for up to three weeks. The classic receives 10 to 12 months' cask ageing, the wood five to six years old. Vieilles Vignes receives 18 months. "Brand new oak is too much for Cornas," says Alain, "so I stick to a max of 10 per cent new for these two wines." Fining and a light filtration follow.

Vieilles Vignes' fruit is sleeker and more harmonious than that of Vieilles Fontaines, with a more corpulent side to it. It tightens on the finish in the best Cornas tradition, its tannins present without excess. I would normally expect it to evolve well over 15 years or more.

The top wine, Les Vieilles Fontaines, is selected at harvesttime, and is usually a mix of *Les Côtes* and *Chaillot*. Quantity varies between nil (2002), 2,000 bottles (2003), and 5,000 bottles (1999, 2000). Its crop is about half destemmed, and the wine stays at least two years in casks that are 15 per cent new, the rest three to four years old. In big vintages like 2003, 1998, and 1990, the ageing ran to 27 months.

Vieilles Fontaines is a rich, big wine, and one of the leading Cornas. Vigorous, chunky, and often powerful, it is best to start drinking it after five to seven years.

CORNAS

2002 (CASK) ★ Smoked raspberry aroma; black fruit starts, then skips. Could have more matter. Licorice end.

2001 ★★ Black berries/earthy, smoked aroma; vigorous black brewed fruit, decisive. Light tannins. Great for restaurants. 2013–15.

1998 ★★★ 2011–13

CORNAS VIEILLES VIGNES

2003 (CASK) ★★★ Overt black fruit/grilled nose; solid, ripe grapes taste, oily end. Has southern warmth/herbs. An unusual vintage. From 2009; 2021–24.

2002 (CASK) ★★ Toasted/black fruit nose. Quite rich, rolls on nicely. Good fruit, some end chew, acidity also. From 2008; 2014–16.

2001 ★★★★ Bursting, full *robe*. Dry-toned bouquet on surface, profound below—a comfortable ease about it. Black currant fruit palate, some high tone present, fairly oily. Dry, pebbly feel on finish. On the fruit, pretty now, though can go a lot further. Length good. 2019–23.

2000 ★★★ Crunchy black currant/raspberry, warm nose; open wine, harmonious black fruit, persists. Correct mineral finish. 2013–15.

1999 ★★★★ Big, warm nose, potential. Juicy, tasty attack, very *gras*. Very good core matter here. Rich and well balanced. 2016–19.

1998 ★★★ 2012–15
1997 ★★ 2010–13
1996 ★★★★ 2010–15
1995 ★★ 2006–08

CORNAS LES VIEILLES FONTAINES

2003 (CASK) ★★★★ Full, persistent raspberry nose; bounding fruit, lots of vigour. Grilled, rich, big wine. Prune/raspberry mix. Heated end. From 2009; 2021–23?

2001 ★★★★★ Solid nose, dark fruit/raspberry, oily; full, broad attack, lots of fruit and content. Big, plenty. Pepper, licorice end. From 2008. Vigour, length good. 2021–24.

2000 ★★★ Grilled, prune/meaty aroma; quite suave cooked fruits. Pebbly, tannic end, mineral touches. Chunky, has character. 2013–15.

1999 ★★★★ Broad, warm nose—violets, elegant black fruit. Sustained clear black flavour, earthy touches, sinew, warm licorice end. Punchy. From 2007; 2021–24.

1998 ★★★ Upright, chocolatey, reserved bouquet. Powerful tannic presence with oak apparent. 2015–19.

1997 ★★★ 2010–14
1996 ★★★ 2013–16

Export 20 per cent 1) USA, 2) Great Britain, 3) Japan

CORNAS VINTAGES

1955 Good.

1956 Good. Soft, well-balanced wines.

1957 Very good. Robust, tannic wines.

1958 Mediocre.

1959 Good. Well-balanced, ripe-tasting wines.

1960 Good.

1961 Excellent. Big, full wines. Small crop, hit by *coulure*.

1962 Excellent. Only a touch behind 1961.

1963 Poor. Terrible weather, similar to 1993. Rot.

1964 Very good. Notable de Barjac.

1965 Mediocre.

1966 Very good.

1967 Excellent. Big wines, full of tannin when young.

1968 Poor. Rot.

1969 Very good. Quite marked tannins. Long-lived A. Clape.

1970 Good. Large crop.

1971 Excellent, close to 1961. Very small crop, hit by *coulure*; failure of the flower to turn to fruit. Full-bodied wines of notable balance. Top-class A. Clape and Joseph Michel.

1972 Very good.

1973 Very good. Prices ex-cellars doubled to 12 francs a bottle. Elegant wines.

1974 Fair. Best from A. Clape and Joseph Michel.

1975 Fair. The style is similar to 1981.

1976 Very good, for the most part. Drink up.

1977 Poor. A cold year, with *coulure* and an underripe harvest. Many high-acidity, pale wines lacking in core.

1978 Excellent, indeed magnificent. Tightly packed berried fruit and now well-absorbed tannins, aromas on the game/fungal edge. Great harmony and a life towards 2015 for the best. Note A. Clape, Delas Chante-Perdrix, and Paul Jaboulet.

1979 Good. Low-key wines. The best were elegant and broadened with time. Drink up. A lovely A. Clape.

1980 Very good. An underrated, sleeper vintage, with dry, interesting textures. Classic autumn wine to drink with game. Near the end of the road now. Note A. Clape, de Barjac, and Juge.

1981 Good. An indifferent summer with difficult ripening. More spice than usual, a certain fire here. Upright wines. Time has improved their balance. Drink up. Note de Barjac, Juge, R. Michel, and A. Clape.

1982 Good. The wines were extremely difficult to vinify, given intense heat day and night in September. Low acidities, fast-evolving wines. An unusually sensuous Cornas vintage. Note de Barjac, Noël Verset, and A. Clape.

1983 Very good. Tannic, quite stern wines. Their aromas have become suitably fungal and darkly spiced. After a warm start, the flavours taper towards a dry finish: true Cornas style encouraged by the tannins of the year. Note A. Clape, Voge, Balthazar, de Barjac, and Paul Jaboulet.

1984 Fair. *Coulure*, late ripening, and harvest rain. Some meagre wines, but the best were discreetly rounded. Drink up. One of the best "off-vintage" wines ever made by A. Clape—still ticking over well in 2001. Note also de Barjac and Delas.

1985 Very good, on the whole. The proviso is due to low acidities, meaning the wines were at times too supple. Colours and aromas were strong, as was alcohol with higher-than-usual levels—13° to 13.5°. The best were very stylish,

and need drinking. Note A. Clape, Juge, Jean Lionnet, de Barjac, R. Michel Geynale, N. Verset, and Paul Jaboulet.

1986 Fair, with some bright points. The end-of-September rain arrived too late, and the crop was large. The main problem is lack of depth, with insufficient fruit to counter some severe tannins. Note de Barjac, M. Juge (a delightful, fine Super Cuvée), and Paul Jaboulet. The A. Clape showed fine red fruit in the taut vintage style after 15 years.

1987 Poor. The growers had to play poker with the weather. Cutoff was 2 October, the start of some days of heavy rain. Harvesting after that date meant much diluted wines; growers who picked earlier made wines with attractive, easy aromas and simple, rounded fruit. Age has brought out the *confit* aspect. Note Jean Lionnet and de Barjac, also A. Clape.

1988 Very good. Spring rain helped the vines to come through a dry year. Some mildew in midsummer. Very solid, dark wines, with good mineral typicity. Life until 2010 or so for the best. Note A. Clape, Jean Lionnet, Voge, Noël Verset, de Barjac, and René Balthazar.

1989 Very good, a real slow-burn vintage in the best Cornas tradition. More stuffing and greater acidity than 1988. The summer was affected by drought (just 2 mm of rain from April to harvest), and the very large crop was marked by small grapes with very thick skins. Fits nicely between the drier-toned 1988s and the richer, more opulent 1990s. Note A. Clape, Noël Verset, Chapoutier, Lionnet, de Barjac, and most front-rank growers. Most can still show well until 2010–12.

1990 Excellent, a year with greater depth and balance than 1988 and 1989. A very dry and hot summer, with a vital 20 mm (0.8 in.) of rain at the end of August. Growers had to take care to combat some oïdium. The harvest was wonderfully ripe. High alcohol, low acidity, and ripe tannins in the wines: so ripe that the suave, rich texture is not a usual Cornas one. While powerful, the wines are well balanced; their richness and depth are greater than most years of the 1980s and 1990s, and they will live and show splendidly for more than 20 years.

★★★★★★   A. Clape, Delas Chante-Perdrix

★★★★   P. Jaboulet, Allemand Reynard

★★★   J. Lionnet Dom de Rochepertuis

★★   Colombo Ruchets, Voge Les Vieilles Fontaines

1991 Very good. Typical earthy/black fruit bouquets, solid flavours with clear-cut, fresh fruit. "Best year in last 10" for Dumien-Serrette. Most can live until 2008–12. It was a mineral-lined vintage, its tannins needing a few years to integrate. The wines were showing very well in their mature state in 2005.

★★★★★   P. Jaboulet

★★★★   A. Clape, Dom Fauterie, Voge Vieilles Vignes

★★★   Colombo Ruchets, J. Lionnet Domaine de Rochepertuis

★★   de Vallouit Médiévales

1992 Fair. A difficult year, with a lot of rain from the end of May until mid-July (300 mm/12 in. in June). August hail hit the south of Cornas, the first bad hail since 1955. Bouts of rain followed into September. No Cornas from Marcel Juge. Compared by A. Clape to 1984—no rot, but a lack of ripeness and inflated berries. The best wines needed time to expand. They fell between roundness and austerity but lacked depth. Flavours are truer and more cutting than the 1993s. A vintage that has become more interesting as it has aged. Expect the A. Clape to run towards 2010–12.

★★★   A. Clape

★★   de Vallouit Médiévales

1993 Mediocre. But Cornas was actually better than its neighbours like Hermitage. August was fine enough, but storms every week from 10 September till late October sealed many people's fate. There was much rot, with conditions likened to 1963. *Millerandage* (partial crop fail-ure) hit some. The late rain made ripening difficult, and the wines often have a *confit*, jammy texture. Early consumption was the ticket for these easy-styled wines. You had to harvest early and then chaptalise. The best, like Allemand and P. Lionnet, should be drunk by about 2009.

★★★   Allemand Reynard, P. Lionnet

★★   Allemand Chaillot, Chapoutier

★   A. Clape

1994 Good. Not an easy year, with ripening difficult to achieve. Very typical Cornas wines, mixing the earthy robust flavours with an upright tannic surround—delightful. There is a lot of dark and chewy matter as well, but some wines can be rather abrupt. They are often on the mineral side, with a pebbly texture. "Like 1983 and 1989 in their tannins," A. Clape finds. There is a danger of lack of body, which will reveal dry textures with age. Expect the best to live until 2015 or so.

★★★★★★   Allemand Reynard

★★★★★   Allemand Chaillot

★★★   Dumien-Serrette

★★   A. Clape

★   de Vallouit Médiévales

1995 Very good, a misunderstood year due to its often rasping tannins early on. There was less crop than usual—poor flowering, *coulure*. July was very hot before the *veraison*, but not after it, highs around 28°C only. North wind and cloud were factors that, with the modest temperatures and dry summer, meant the grapes were small. Comparisons with 2001 here—the manner of the ripening. There was a bit of rain during the harvest around 20 September. Very ripe crop.

These are tight, packed wines that need time to emerge and expand. Many found them "dry" early on. The red fruit content was sound, but the tannins ruled. "Like 1988," pronounced A. Clape. By 2005 the best had opened well, settling into a broader groove than before. They are ideal for autumn-to-spring drinking, in the finest classic ways of Cornas. Expect longevity of 20-plus years for the best.

★★★★★★ A. Clape, P. Jaboulet St-Pierre

★★★★★ Allemand Reynard

★★★★ Dom Fauterie

★★★ Allemand Chaillot, Chapoutier, P. Jaboulet

★★ Voge Vieilles Vignes

1996 Good. The old vines produced well and served to overcome some of the narrowness of flavour from the younger-vine fruit. Ripening was difficult, with a blockage late on. The weather was often cool. Harvesting started in early October. The wines are dry toned, their early austerity in sharp contrast to the more overt, warmer 1997s. Growers needed old-vine fruit to bring in welcome roundness. These wines can live well through their acidity and may pay to drink later than expected. Something of a sleeper vintage that can balance itself better with time. Bouquets show true fungal, organic aspects as they evolve and tannins are absorbed. Most should show well towards 2010–12, the best several years longer.

★★★★★ P. Jaboulet St-Pierre

★★★★ A. Clape, Voge Vieilles Vignes

★★★ Allemand Reynard, Juge Cuvée C, Voge Vieilles Fontaines

★★ Colombo Ruchets, N. Verset, Vidal-Fleury

1997 Good. A year of notably low acidities. Hot days and nights were responsible during August. Any well-exposed sites saw the sugars rise in August, but there followed a blockage in the ripening—no exchange between grapes and the plant, so everything just stopped. It thus took three weeks to gain 1.2° alcohol, against a more normal 3°. Several of the wines should be drunk ahead of the more resistant 1996s and 1995s. Textures are unusually squeezy and sappy—Cornas with a smile. Most are heading for drinking by 2006–10, the odd wine can run towards 2014 or so.

★★★★ P. Jaboulet St-Pierre

★★★ Dom Courbis Sabarotte, Dumien-Serrette, J. Lionnet, Voge Vieilles Fontaines

★★ A. Clape classic/Renaissance, Dom Courbis Eygats, Durand, Tardieu-Laurent Coteaux/Vieilles Vignes, Voge Vieilles Vignes

★ Allemand Chaillot/Reynard, Dom Courbis Champelrose, Cave de Tain Nobles Rives, N. Verset

1998 Very good. Easter frost on the lower slopes, the most productive areas, took out about 20 per cent of the crop. Bouts of oïdium and *coulure* (fruit failure after flowering) added to the woes. Hail was the next severe problem, leading to some growers like Voge and Chaboud losing between 40 and 50 per cent of their harvest. But from mid-July the weather bounced back, and nearly two months of fine, hot conditions preceded harvesting, with the odd sprinkle of rain.

The wines hold lower acidity and degrees than 1999, and drier, firmer tannins from a very hot, baking-dry August. Some wines had a grilled side from the hail, but ageing has moulded them well. Bouquets are earthy and advancing in an open, flourishing way. There are cooked black fruits on the palate, and some oily, leathery tones coming through. The vintage has come along well, and while most wines are drinking well now, they should perform well until past 2015.

★★★★★ Tardieu-Laurent Vieilles Vignes

★★★★ Allemand Chaillot, A. Clape, P. Jaboulet St-Pierre, J. Lionnet Dom de Rochepertuis, N. Verset

★★★ Allemand Reynard, Dom Courbis Sabarotte, Dumien-Serrette, Tardieu-Laurent Coteaux, Voge classic/Vieilles Vignes/Vieilles Fontaines

★★ Chaboud, Delas Chante-Perdrix, Durand, J. Lemenicier, V. Paris

★ P. Jaboulet

1999 Excellent. Very healthy but large crop. Even the old vines had to be cut back via green harvesting. The north wind dried out the abundant grapes and played a key role. It was a warm year with only light amounts of rain, well-timed at the end of April, a couple of falls in July and 20 mm (0.8 in.) in mid-September. According to A. Clape, "There wasn't much stress for the vines, just like 1990." The vintage's success came about in September. With the warm extract came an exceptional acidity level—pH of 3.6 against 3.7 or 3.75 average—and there is a long life ahead.

Bouquets are varied and interesting; Alain Voge finds plenty of violets in the wines. Great *gras* is present in the wines—they are more generous and rotund than most young Cornas. A lot of depth, with a well-marked but ripe tannic presence. Tannins are denser than the 2001s'. More warmth than usual in the wines. "There's overripeness, almost too much, so it's not such typical Cornas, on the same lines as 1990," says Thiérry Allemand. Many of these wines will run well towards 2014–18, the best stayers like A. Clape, Allemand, and the Paul Jaboulet St-Pierre into the 2020s.

★★★★★★ A. Clape

★★★★★ Dumien-Serrette, P. Jaboulet St-Pierre

★★★★ Allemand Reynard, Dom Courbis Eygats, Delas Chante-Perdrix, Dom Fauterie, P. Jaboulet, J. Lionnet Dom de Rochepertuis, Cave de Tain Nobles Rives, N. Verset, A. Voge Vieilles Vignes/Vieilles Fontaines

★★★ Dom Courbis Sabarotte, J. Lemenicier, J. Lionnet, P. Lionnet, Vignobles d'Abondance

★★ Chapoutier, A. Clape Cuvée Renaissance, Colombo Ruchets,

Dom Courbis Champelrose, Durand classic/Prestige

★ Dom du Tunnel Vieilles Vignes

2000 Good to very good. Of the northern Rhône Big Three, Cornas is my favourite. The key was to cut back yields. There were contrasts early in the year—a cold April and very hot May meant a precocious flowering, at least a week early in late May. Sun was in short supply in June–July; there was rain around until mid-July, but it was not very cold. Ripening was tricky, with fragile skins on the inflated grapes. Extreme early-August heat made the skins hard and lowered the acidity levels.

It is often a flattering year, with less tannic structure than 1998 and 1999, more similar to 1997 without the cosy roundness. Some show a cool feel in their texture, and minerality comes through on the finishes. Quality was homogenous. Too many wines showed reduction. Tannins are discreetly present but not demanding, and since the fruit is attractive, these wines can be drunk well already after five years. I expect most to run towards 2014–18. Not a vintage with shoulders, but its charm shows just how much the winemaking at Cornas has made strides in the past few years.

★★★★★ J. Lionnet Dom de Rochepertuis

★★★★ Allemand Reynard, Dom Courbis Champelrose, Juge Cuvée SC, GAEC Michel Abondance

★★★ Allemand Chaillot, Louis Bernard, A. Clape, Dom Courbis Eygats, Delas Chante-Perdrix, Dumazet Charlemagne, Dumien-Serrette, Durand, P. Jaboulet St-Pierre, Juge Cuvée C, R. Michel Geynale, Ogier Reillots, J-L Thiers, Dom du Tunnel Prestige, N. Verset, Voge Vieilles Vignes/Vieilles Fontaines

★★ R. Balthazar, Chapoutier, A. Clape Renaissance, Colombo Terres Brûlées/Louvée/Ruchets, Dom Courbis Sabarotte, Durand

Prestige, Dom Fauterie, P. Jaboulet
Grandes Terrasses, V. Paris Granit
30/60, Tardieu-Laurent Vieilles
Vignes, Vignobles d'Abondance,
Vins de Vienne Barcillants

★ Chaboud, Cave de Tain Nobles
Rives, A. Verset

2001 Excellent. A very mild winter was followed by terrible weather early on, and there
had been no summer by mid-May, which was a
rainy and cold month. Ripening was behind
time, but growth caught up in the first, very
hot two weeks of August. Most harvesting
started on 15 September, in dry conditions that
served to increase the degree. It was an awkward year to get the ripening right—picking too
soon meant hard tannins. The north wind
helped gradual ripening, so much so that
Robert Michel considered the grapes riper than
the 1999s.

These are classically structured wines, the
depth in them measured and not too obvious
and sunny. The tannins are indeed ripe and well
integrated. The magic word "balance" is apparent. Textures lean towards the sinewy, chewy
black fruit style, with freshness present. Aromas
reflect violets and will become varied with age.
Richness is restrained, with plenty of leather
and mineral. "There is very good *typicité*," says
Gilbert Serrette—"it's exceptional in my book."
"As it's a very full year," says Michel Tardieu,
"we used extra new oak."

For Robert Michel "*terroir* speaks a lot in
2001—the vintage is a real guide to what Cornas really is." Expect these wines to age wonderfully well—25 years for the best. Much enjoyment lies ahead.

★★★★★ A. Clape, R. Michel Geynale,
Voge Vieilles Fontaines

★★★★ Allemand Reynard/Chaillot, R.
Balthazar, Chapoutier, Colombo
Louvée, Dom Courbis Sabarotte,
Dumien-Serrette, P. Jaboulet St-
Pierre, Tardieu Laurent Vieilles
Vignes, Voge Vieilles Vignes

★★★ M. Barret, B. Blachon, L. C.
Brotte Arlettes, Chaboud Réserve,
A. Clape Renaissance, Colombo
Terres Brûlées/Ruchets, Delas
Chante-Perdrix, J. Despesse,
Durand, Dom Fauterie, G. Fumat,
P. Jaboulet Grandes Terrasses,
Juge Cuvée C, J. Lionnet Dom
de Rochepertuis, P. Lionnet, R.
Michel Coteaux, V. Paris Granit 60,
Cave de Tain, Tardieu Laurent
Coteaux, J-L Thiers, Dom du Tun-
nel, N. Verset, Vignobles d'Abon-
dance, Vins de Vienne Barcillants

★★ E. Bancel, Chaboud, Colombo
Méjeans, Dom Courbis Champelrose, Dumazet Charlemagne, Meffre Laurus, Dom Michelas Saint
Jemms, L. Sozet, V. Paris Granit
30, Voge classic

★ Dom Courbis Eygats

2002 Uneven, the best good. Quantity was
down after a poor flowering, and very variable
levels of ripening on any single vine. The summer was quite rainy and not very hot. Rot
became the main menace as the vines struggled
for ripeness. "I hadn't seen rot like that for a
long time—the one-third on the top slopes was
healthy, the third on the midslopes had some
rot, and the bottom third had to be thrown
away—so I lost net 40 per cent of my crop,"
reports R. Michel. The high slopes were helped
by the wind, but all growers reported losses—
Allemand 40 per cent, S. Bernard 30 to 35 per
cent ("My harvest took three times longer than
usual with all the sorting"), Clape 25 per cent.
Degrees were low, sometimes barely over 10, so
chaptalisation was the order of the day.

When tasting the wines together, one feels
there has been a struggle to get their elements
to integrate. Acidities are live and the wines are
on a reduced scale—apt for less weighty dishes
than usual (roast lamb rather than beef stew, for
instance). It is not a year for plentiful new oak,
since there isn't the stuffing. The fruit connotation is red berries, with colours subdued. Their

bouquets will turn gamey and fungal around 2008. The acidity levels mean some wines will evolve and stay on for 12 years or so, but this is not a vintage to make old bones.

★★★ M. Barret Terrasses du Serre, L.C. Brotte Arlettes (but some no score), Chapoutier, A. & P. Clape, Dom Courbis Champelrose, J. Despesse, Dumien-Serrette, J. Lemenicier, J. Lionnet Dom de Rochepertuis

★★(★) A. & P. Clape Renaissance, Dom Courbis Eygats

★★ F. Balthazar, Dom Courbis Sabarotte, Delas, J. Lionnet, P. Lionnet, R. Michel Geynale, Dom Michelas Saint Jemms, V. Paris Granit 60, L. Sozet, Cave de Tain, Dom du Tunnel, N. Verset, Voge Vieilles Vignes

★(★) Chaboud Réserve, Juge Cuvée C

★ B. Blachon, Chaboud, Dom Fauterie, Dumien-Serrette, Durand, G. Fumat, B. Maurice, R. Michel Coteaux, V. Paris Granit 30, J-L Thiers, Vignobles d'Abondance, Voge classic

2003 Good, some very good wines: Cornas as broad, southern wine this year. The last serious rain of the year fell in March. On April 8 frost hit, notably the lower slopes and the flat ground, where some growers lost half their crop. May was dry, and flowering passed off fine in early June. Twenty millimetres (0.8 inch) of rain fell at the end of June and early July on Châteaubourg and Cornas. The second half of July's heat was high, but there were pockets of light rain—12 mm (0.5 in.) on July 12—then hail 27 July and 1 August, not everywhere but notably on *Geynale, Sabarotte, Les Côtes, Mazards, Chaillot, Patou*. Despite the hail, 45 minutes of rain on July 27 helped the vines generally. Allemand and Clape lost 50 per cent, R. Michel 55 per cent, Fumat 65 per cent. The heat made the young vines suffer—their wines lack core and can be hot. "The high heat stopped all ripening, with the phenolic ripening

lagging the sugars. That's why some growers had to pick with high sugar levels, but low phenolic ripeness as well," says Clape. Some growers started to pick on 20 August. Twenty millimetres (0.8 inch) of rain on 29 August helped to freshen the crop of those who hadn't already picked. Clape started 27 August on *Patou*.

Vinifications were not straightforward—these were uncharted waters because there was so much sugar and so little juice in the grapes. Voge destemmed his whole crop because the stems were too dry and the skins dehydrated—and even traditional growers had to hire equipment to destem. Clape destemmed one-third: "We started doing it, but didn't succeed in separating many of the dried-up bunches, so reverted to whole bunches for the rest of the crop." A lot of *vignerons* had to yeast a lot and use their small vats because their fermentations were blocked. Allemand had some grapes still fermenting a year later, and there was talk of vats of 16°-to-17.5° Syrah.

Needless to say, the 2003s are low-acidity wines, with unusual, brewed-up compositions. There is a *garrigue*-style influence on some, with herbal aspects and an absence of the traditional Cornas clear-cut minerality. These are homogenous, tightly packed wines, with a big mass of matter; after three years, they have gained some roundness, their fruit taking on a more succulent texture. The flavour centres on black jam, and their sucrosity is very apparent. The wines are not fresh, and some finish with heat. The debate is how long they will live. Rigorous and severe early on, the best show signs of extending past 12 to 14 years. "The best wines from the full slopes have enough matter to age properly," says Auguste Clape. The impression is also of more new-oak use than usual, with the casks bought and a small crop upping the ratio. A sense of place is hard to perceive this year, just that the wines come from somewhere hot. Patience is the best guide for this tricky and challenging year.

★★★★(★) A. & P. Clape

★★★★ Dom Courbis Sabarotte, Durand, P. Jaboulet St-Pierre, Voge Vieilles Fontaines

★★★   M. Barret, F. Balthazar, Dom
      Courbis Eygats, Durand, Juge
      Cuvée C/SC, J. Lionnet Dom de
      Rochepertuis, Vignobles d'Abon-
      dance, Voge Vieilles Vignes

★★(★) Dom Fauterie, Dom Michelas
      Saint Jemms, J-L Thiers

  ★★ Chapoutier, Dom Courbis Cham-
      pelrose, Delas Chante-Perdrix,
      Dumien-Serrette, J. Lemenicier,
      P. Jaboulet St-Pierre, J. Lionnet,
      P. Lionnet, Cave de Tain, Dom
      du Tunnel Prestige

 ★(★) L. C. Brotte Arlettes, Dom du
      Tunnel

2004 Good, perhaps some very good. The
winter was even drier than the previous year.
The spring was difficult, with a lack of heat and
a marked cool spell in April that stopped the
vines. May and June were hot and dry, with a
fast flowering 8–10 June. July was dry and quite
hot, and the vines started to toil, with leaves yel-
lowing, especially after the heat rigours of the
2003. There was no mildew, and only light
oïdium. A large storm on 12–13 August was welcome, and two other storms brought August
rainfall to around 160 mm (6.3 inches). Rot
broke out on flat ground like *Mazards*, but the
north wind dried the rot, and from then on

there were sun and wind until the end of the
harvest, which started around 20 September for
Clape. "Our first two to three days were very hot,
but then it was OK, and we finished by 29 September," recalled P-M Clape. The lower-lying
and young vines were very abundant this year
and needed some cutting back. The vintage made
itself late on, and its freshness was also enhanced
by the cool nights, even in August. About the
last harvesters were Paul Jaboulet, on their cool
St-Pierre site: "We finished on 5 October, and it
rained on 6 October," said Philippe Jaboulet.

The wines are classically formed, with well-
cut fruit, and some tannic minerality in support.
They have clean lines and are stylish and mus-
cled from the best sites and the oldest vines. It is
a vintage for the lover of classic Cornas, in which
the tannins need time to settle and the wines
hold good definition. Acidity levels are better than
usual—their pH of 3.7 is good for Cornas,
unlike the 3.8 to 4.15 experienced with the 2003s.
The wines are not enormously full, but will do
well over a period of 16 to over 20 years. Tastings before all the wines were bottled revealed
vintage front runners in the shape of Thiérry
Allemand, Domaine Clape, Domaine Courbis
(Les Eygats), Domaine Durand (Empreinte),
Jacques Lemenicier, Tardieu-Laurent (both
Coteaux and Vieilles Vignes), Jean-Louis &
Françoise Thiers, Domaine du Tunnel (Vin
Noir) and Voge (Vieille Fontaine).

8

St-Péray

CAN ST-PÉRAY be the Comeback Kid? It's not exactly a burning question around the international wine highways and salons, but it is one of importance to this old, forgotten, and sometimes down-at-heel *appellation* across the Rhône from busy Valence.

Ah, the wiles of prejudice. If St-Péray had never made sparkling, indeed pukka *méthode champenoise* wine, then it would not have been known in the past hundred years. If St-Péray didn't make that same sparkling wine now, then it would stand a much better chance of acquiring wider fame and fortune.

One only has to track down old cellar books to see that St-Péray was one of the big wines of the Rhône in the nineteenth century, before and after phylloxera. The cellar book of the Hermitage merchant and owner Macker shows a cask of St-Péray 1805 as fetching 90 francs a cask, against Cornas at 75 francs and Côte-Rôtie at 140 francs. This was the table wine, in the days before the sparkling version. In the great vintage of 1811, the Year of the Comet, St-Péray was selling for 140 francs a cask.

The Chaboud family's order book for 1889 shows a bottle of sparkling St-Péray selling for 2.25 to 2.75 francs, the dry white for three francs—both the 1885 vintage. At the same time, Condrieu cost two francs, Château-Grillet 2.50, Cornas two, and Crozes 2.25. Pommard and Corton were just three francs, with Côte-Rôtie 3.50, Hermitage white 3.50, and Hermitage red four.

So the late 1990s initiatives here to relaunch the still white wine, rather quaintly termed *vin tranquille* by the locals, represented a latter-day lifeline for this vineyard. It was led by a collection of leading owner-*négociants* like Paul Jaboulet Aîné, Jean-Luc Colombo, Chapoutier, and also the Cave Co-opérative of Tain l'Hermitage. Countries targeted were the Netherlands, Belgium, Britain, Germany, the United States, and of course France.

But there is a side of me that feels that this is all rather imperious behaviour by the so-called knowing international palates and experts. You see, St-Péray makes its own fun in its own, local way; its sparkling wine is offbeat internationally. But it has a confirmed local following. It also has a funky, raucous village fair over a full weekend every year, fuelled by just this "good times" wine, visitors from across Europe in attendance.

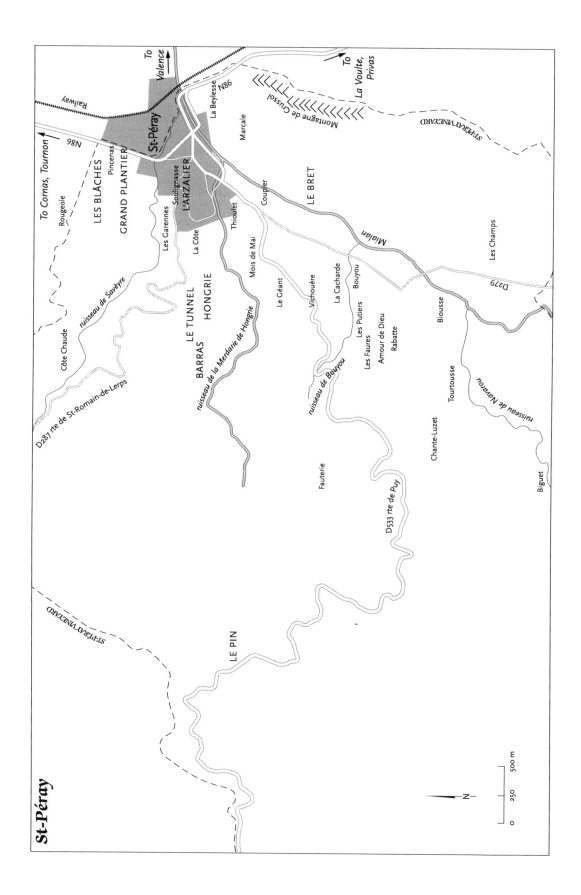

St-Péray

To Valence
Railway
To Cornas, Tournon
N86
Rougeole
LES BLÂCHES
GRAND PLANTIER
Pincenas
St-Péray
Soulignasse
L'ARZALIER
Les Garennes
La Côte
Thioullet
La Beylesse
N86
Marcale
Montagne de Crussol
To La Voulte, Privas
ST-PÉRAY VINEYARD
Coupier
LE BRET
Mialan
Les Champs
D279
Côte Chaude
ruisseau de Savèyre
D287 rte de St-Romain-de-Lerps
BARRAS
LE TUNNEL
HONGRIE
ruisseau de la Merdarie de Hongrie
Mois de Mai
Le Géant
Vichouère
La Cacharde
Bouyou
Les Putiers
Les Faures
Amour de Dieu
Rabatte
Biousse
ruisseau de Bouyou
Chante-Luzet
Tourtousse
ruisseau de Nauzon
Biguet
ST-PÉRAY VINEYARD
Fauterie
LE PIN
D533 rte de Puy

N

0   250   500 m

The locals know how to enjoy themselves and their sense of community.

So maybe it's more than a wine, but a way of life that is being besieged here in the name of wine correctness. Time to shift in one's seat, perhaps.

St-Péray is also a village edging ever closer to the industrial sprawl of Valence, just a quick trip across the river. Climbing up in the vineyards on the road west to St-Romain-de-Lerps, there are the new houses—right in the vines. Indeed, vines have become a sort of chic accoutrement to some homes: a little *allée* of vines can be used to mark the driveway, or a token row or two can be left to stand on their own. There is continuous pressure on the vineyard area, as witnessed by the disappearance of a *lieu-dit* like *Lardet*, while *Le Bret* hardly survives as a vineyard. Consequently, the Growers Union has formally protected two outlying sites, *Rougeole* and *Chante-Luzet,* for vineyards only, the former representing an important land purchase by the Tain Co-opérative.

There is therefore some question about just how much of a true wine location is St-Péray. Land here is continually encroached on for housing and development. Yet until the early 1990s roads behind the village were still lonely and represented the visitor's best chance of immersion in a world of escape, for St-Péray itself is not a pinup—it is a working place with little pretension to beauty. The main square is large and shaded by irregularly spaced plane trees, and the nicest old houses are topped by soft-coloured local Ardechois stone. But that's about it, and every year the suburban encroachment grows.

This is the incongruous setting for the Rhône's most incongruous wine, which shares its favours between still and sparkling white. Not a drop of red is made here. And yet the *appellation*'s soul, its hillside vineyards, possess exceptional *terroir*. These vineyards can produce cracking white wine, capable of acclaim, and more would be made were some of the tidying up done elsewhere in the Rhône over the past 20 years to be brought to bear.

Tidying up comprises rigorous vineyard management, a reduction in treatments, and more organic working methods. It also includes ensuring the plantation is renewed on a rolling basis, sticking to the prominent, around 30 per cent, role played by Roussanne here. St-Péray is home to some of the best Roussanne in the northern Rhône, not only mature vines but younger vines taken from fine old rootstock as well.

The cleanup also implies a mix of modern cellar methods, such as air conditioning, with the careful respect for what works well and isn't too interventionist. Already there are sad signs that some people see St-Péray as an easy way to create a low-production, high-priced, Super League wine—chock-full of new oak, heavily extracted, complete with a flashy label—little to do with the raw elements of its noble place.

Progress towards better-quality wines has been gradually achieved, but even so, the vineyard remains tiny. In 1971 it was 56 hectares. By 1982 it had fallen, when the outlook for here and Cornas appeared bleak, to 48 hectares. Since then it spent the 1990s hovering around the 63-hectare mark, and in 2005 stands at 64 hectares, with four hectares of young vines to come on stream.

Sixty per cent of the wine is made in still form, 40 per cent sparkling. The sparkling wine remains very localised, and only 3 per cent is exported, mostly to Britain and the Netherlands. The still wine is 17 per cent exported, mostly to the United States, Britain, and the Netherlands. To most Rhône enthusiasts around the world, St-Péray remains unknown territory.

Anyone wishing to visit St-Péray when its soul is laid bare should consider the first weekend in September every year, when the thoroughly noisy, rampant Fête des Vins de St-Péray is held. Processions, samba, music, wine handed out, dressing up—the Full Show!

HISTORY

Strange to observe, these minute vineyards carry both lengthy historical and popular traditions.

The still white wine attracted attention from two Roman writers: Pliny, in his *Natural History*, Book XIV, Chapters 1 and 2, and Plutarch, in Book V of his *Table Talk*.

Little is then heard of St-Péray until the nineteenth century, when it went through a gilded period of fashionable popularity, boosted by the advent of the sparkling wine in 1828. This was the brainwave of Louis Faure, son of the founder of St-Péray's first merchant in wines, and became the drink of cavalry officers. Before that, the young Napoléon Bonaparte had been stationed as a cadet at the garrison of Valence and in later years spoke of the still St-Péray as his first wine discovery.

Lamartine, Alphonse Daudet, and Guy de Maupassant are all said to have referred to the wine in their writings, and a vaudeville entertainer called Marc-Antoine Desaugiers (1772–1827) even wrote a song entitled "Le Voyageur de St-Péray," which went as follows:

A vous, je m'adresse, mesdames,
C'est pour vanter le Saint-Péray.
Il est surnommé Vin des Femmes,
C'est vous dire qu'il est parfait.
La violette qu'il exhale
En rend le goût délicieux
Et l'on peut dire qu'il égale
Le nectar que buvait les Dieux.

To you I address myself, ladies,
It is to praise St-Péray.
It is nicknamed the Wine of Women,
Which means that it is perfect.
The violets that it exhales
Give it a flavour of delight
And one can say it matches
The nectar that the gods would drink.

The key to the spreading of its name in those days was simple, according to Jean-François Chaboud, whose family has a collection of sales books tracing back to the nineteenth century. "The Champenois were buying the degree, the alcohol in our wine," he says. The 1816 vintage, all still wine then, had been bought by Champagne to boost their indifferent vintage. St-Péray even fetched the highest price of all Rhône wines that year. The wines would be loaded on to barges at Tournon, transshipped at Lyon from the Rhône to the Saône, and thence on to Chalon-sur-Saône, whence the journey continued by land.

While the still wine had probably been bottled in the late eighteenth century, the sparkling wine's debut in 1828 was aided by steamboat transport becoming the form of shipment for local goods. This proliferated the wine's distribution. Remember that it was sparkling, and opening a bottle signified celebration, the good times. Consequently the wine became fashionable around Europe, with records showing orders for the King of Würtemberg and for the French Consul Generals of both Russia and the United States, as well as a shipment sent to China in 1838 via Calcutta.

The most famous story about St-Péray's sparkling wine concerns the German composer Richard Wagner. In a letter from Bayreuth dated 2 December 1877, he wrote as follows to a leading *négociant* house: "Will you please send me as soon as possible those 100 bottles of St-Péray wine which you offered me." Wagner was then busy composing *Parsifal*, and it is popularly presumed by local *vignerons* that passages from this opera must have originated at the bottom of a glass of their wine.

Either side of the First World War, there were around 15 *négociants* in St-Péray, and it is said that five of them accounted for 75 per cent of all bottle sales (C. Montez, *Le Monde du Négoce du Vin*). This merchant group was thwarted by the domaine owners in a famous case of 1933. The merchants had been pushing to open up the *appellation* area, bringing in the plain and southern lands, and they also wanted the wine to be made from red grapes or low-grade vines. They were defeated, their pushy outlook a revealing one since their own demise was to occur in the next 30 years.

After the Second World War, St-Péray retained its standing through the presence of a mix of merchant houses and local growers. Although they had lost young men during the war and were gradually being whittled away, the *négociants* served to spread the word and to keep the distribution of the wine quite secure. But by the

1960s, life was tough selling just local Rhône wines. Philippe Jaboulet, whose family of course own marvellous vineyards at Hermitage, a much bigger name, takes up the story: "There were eight or nine *négociants* in St-Péray in the 1950s, but they started to disappear in the 1960s. Drinkers lost the habit of sipping a heavy, quite alcoholic sparkling wine at 4 PM with their cakes, or taking it as a dessert wine, so it slid from view."

And local really meant local. A *négociant* like Vérilhac, whom I recall being well respected in the early 1970s, would offer fine, aged Cornas beyond his St-Péray, but little or no Côte-Rôtie, for instance. The instinct would be to sell table wine from the Ardèche as the main cash cow. Such a parochial outlook was of course a reflection of drinkers' tastes as well. It was hard to sell wine from even 30 miles away.

So obscurity came a-calling. Even America's great Rhône enthusiast Robert Parker felt compelled to describe St-Péray as "the Rhône Valley's viticultural dinosaur" (R. M. Parker Jr., *The Wines of the Rhône Valley and Provence*, Simon & Schuster, 1987). Part of the problem attached to promoting the wine was the limited amount made. In the 1980s the annual average was just 2,315 hectolitres. In the 1990s, this fell to just 2,191 hectolitres. Years like 1998—ravaged by frost and hail—did not help, with a mere 1,493 hl produced. Poor continuity of supply has stemmed directly from this.

Jean-Louis Thiers believes that the *appellation* made some economic progress in the 1980s, but it was from 1990 that things picked up. For him, "it was a problem of communication—we growers needed to talk more about our wine," he says. Nevertheless, as someone who makes three-quarters of his wine in sparkling form, he is aware that its sales remain confined to the local Rhône-Alps region.

"We get our local clients back every year because they want to celebrate a birthday or anniversary," observes Guy Darona about his sparkling wine sales, "whereas the still wine clients you might only see once every three years."

Until the postwar years, St-Péray used to be a barrel-making centre for the northern Côtes du Rhône, with a prosperous community of four *tonneliers*. Sadly, 1973 saw the retirement of the last of them, M. Vinard, who at 65 decided that he had worked hard enough and long enough all by himself.

A grey-haired, slight man who belied his years, M. Vinard explained that he took over from his father. Methods had not changed in his time, and 90 per cent of a *tonnelier's* work today remains entirely manual. Over the years the wood used has undergone changes. Decades ago it was entirely oak, but in the 1950s and 1960s there was a trend to much more chestnut, taken from the Ardèche and the Isère. But now there is a fashion for oak again, with the difference that much of it is no longer imported from Austria and Russia; instead, nearly all of it now comes from the rest of France.

A *tonnelier's* time is divided between carrying out repairs and making new barrels. Much the hardest and most skilled work is the repairs, and it is the lack of experienced hands for this that *vignerons* most regret. To repair the area around the stopper or underneath the metal bands of a 585-litre oak barrel is a difficult operation. "Some of the barrels I used to be sent were as much as a 100 years old," said M. Vinard. "It is very precise and delicate work to graft on to the grain of such old wood."

M. Vinard found no one prepared to take over his work, and at a time when it was not fashionable to use new oak, his business closed down. Nowadays the demand for oak is there, but not for the careful restoration of old barrels that existed in the more thrifty and traditional days of M. Vinard.

Just how hard it can be to sell this white wine is illustrated by Stéphan Chaboud's decision in the early 1990s to reclassify two of his St-Péray hectares as Syrah Côtes du Rhône. "It meant me having another colour, another wine to sell, so I could reach a wider clientèle," is his simple explanation.

Sylvain Bernard tells a similar tale: having made two Domaine de Fauterie St-Pérays in 1999, he made just one in 2001; about half his production from his St-Péray vineyard—around 5,000 bottles—went into a white Côtes du Rhône that year. "You can sell St-Péray if you get people to try it," he says, "which means it has to be sold personally to individual customers."

Nowadays there are about a dozen small growers making and bottling their own wine. There are only four domaine makers of sparkling St-Péray, and two of them—Thiers and Darona, both men moving towards 50—have two daughters and three sons, respectively, but none of the children is as yet interested. Then there are merchants who may have a few vines—Jaboulet, Chapoutier, plus Delas, Colombo, Tardieu-Laurent, and Les Vins de Vienne. The St-Péray *négociant* side has reduced to nothing. Half the wine is made at the Cave Co-opérative of Tain l'Hermitage, which is the fifth source for the sparkling wine.

ST-PÉRAY VINEYARDS

There are three themes across St-Péray's roughly 64 hectares of vineyards—granite, limestone, and clay. The granite areas are nearest Cornas and at the high points of sites like *Hongrie*, with a further group in the west on *Fauterie*, *Chante-Luzet*, and the *Côte du Pin*; fine, sanded granite shows up southwest of the town on sites like *Les Faures*, *Rabatte*, and *Biguet*.

The limestone clusters around the sheer hill of Crussol with its ruined castle. Much of the clay is found in the southern areas that drift away west from the main Rhône valley, notably near the Mialan River on a site like *Biousse*, with some clay also beside the N86 road.

With marriages and inheritance playing a usual prominent role in the vineyards, there are several Cornas growers who have small plots at St-Péray, most of them adjacent to the southern Cornas vineyards. A small drainage canal (called

a *croze*), the *Croze de Combe*, splits the two *appellations*.

The main site in the north is *Grand Plantier*. This area, which includes *Grandes* and *Petites Blâches*, has some acid soil, and its feature is *gore*, or sanded, quartzy rotted granite, the hard rock about a metre or two down. The bottom part of the slope contains clay-limestone, the top terraces hold more decomposed granite around 150 to 180 metres, and there is also a little flint. On its west side is a stream called *Les Grandes Blâches*, and right up the hill here, housing takes over. In between there are cherry and apple trees dotted about, and bushes nearer the road: no obvious delineation for the vineyard.

Growers here include Clape, Lionnet, Voge, and Juge, whose 1910 Marsanne vines are let out to Stéphane Robert, Co-opérateurs, and down on the lower, clay area near the N86, Lemenicier. For Alain Voge, *Plantier* makes a wine to drink younger than that from central areas like *Hongrie*: "The granite wines at St-Péray don't live so well," he affirms.

The Co-opérative accounts for eight hectares split between *Grand Plantier* and, above it, the subset of *Pincenas*, which lies to the west of *Grandes Blâches*. *Pincenas* is also sandy granite, but the soil is a little deeper. Alain Voge's family has long owned a plot here. Otherwise, little ground remains for vines, the rest of the area now built on.

A young grower from Cornas, Johann Michel, has planted on *Petites Blâches*, reviving a vineyard abandoned in the 1960s. Above him, another young man, Stéphane Robert, works an old Marsanne site on *Grandes Blâches*, just where the high granite mingles with the lower clay areas. Growers are happy to work a little higher up the hill if it brings extra freshness to the wine. The view on the wine from the granite parts is that it is "dry and a little more acid than further south," according to Stéphan Chaboud —the effect of the granite. Much of *Grandes Blâches* is overgrown with scrublike green oaks.

A little apart from *Les Blâches* to its west, tracing within the valley, is a site for the future, *Rougeole*. This crosses into Cornas and is a granite spot where the Cave de Tain is clearing and planting land that it bought in the early 2000s.

Just one vineyard remains near the heart of this ever expanding village. Stéphane Robert's *L'Arzalier* vineyard is termed *Coteaux de Gaillard* by the locals; this is naturally a precocious site of 80-to-100-year-old Marsanne, with clay soil covered in some alluvial Rhône stones. Its wine is full-bodied.

The other nearby vineyard that still exists near the village lies across the *Merdarie* stream just before it becomes the full Mialan River. This is *Marcale*, where Jacques Lemenicier works 0.6 ha of Marsanne. Its soil is clay-chalk with silt present, a heavier, water-retentive site. He is the only, indeed the last, grower here.

The first of the valley streams running from the west, the *Savèyre*, defines a new flank to the vineyard, which brings in one of the top names, *Hongrie*, a well-sited south-southeast–facing vineyard bisected by the winding road up towards St-Romain-de-Lerps.

Up above and behind the village, *Hongrie*'s upper soil contains some rotted granite, its mid- and lower soil holding more white-yellow clay, quite fine, with a little limestone in it; the clay's moisture retention is very beneficial in a drought year like 2003. It is the clay-limestone areas that were chosen by the Chabouds when planting Roussanne here.

These vineyards rise above the stream of *Merdarie*, which later joins St-Péray's prime river, the *Mialan*, just beside the town centre. The name *Hongrie* derives from the tanners who used to work in this quarter of St-Péray. Growers here include Voge, Chapoutier, Chaboud, and the Tain Co-opérative.

Alain Voge finds *Hongrie*'s wine rich, with mineral touches and a grilled almonds flavour, its minerality confirmed by Stéphan Chaboud. *Hongrie* wine can also age well—eight to 10 years. "There's no doubt that it is helped by the rich soil with some carbonates in it," says Albéric Mazoyer of Chapoutier, "which makes it a good vineyard for the Marsanne."

Because of its importance, *Hongrie* runs to some subnames, sites connected to the main site. *Géant* is worked by Chaboud, Stéphane Robert, and Chapoutier. *La Côte* is on the left of the St-Romain-de-Lerps road as it winds upwards, on the east side of *Hongrie*, and is worked by Chaboud and Voge, the former with some Marsanne dating from 1903, the latter with some 1930s Marsanne. It is an irony that the wine from such old, established prime vineyards should prove so difficult to sell.

La Côte is granite higher up, but mostly clay-limestone with a narrow patch of pebble stones. Running from about 150 to 250 metres, it benefits from a full south exposure and finer-than-usual soil—some limestone, flint, and decomposed granite on top of a clay subsoil on its terraces, the granite more degraded than that at Cornas. It is Alain Voge's favourite of his three sites at St-Péray: "It gives wines that age well, with a lot of matter in them, plus some minerality," he states. "I consider them to be fresh and also notable for their length."

Both *La Côte* and *Hongrie* retain humidity well, unlike the outright granite areas of the *appellation*. In a vintage like 2003, their grapes were markedly fatter and bigger than those from the more granite sites. As a rule, the clay-limestone areas at St-Péray are the ones that invest the wines with minerality; a grower like Chaboud has his eight plots mostly on clay-limestone.

Running between *La Côte* and another subset of *Hongrie* called *Thioulet* is the *Thioulet* stream, which holds water all year and runs into the *Merdarie* stream. Stéphan Chaboud is the only grower on *Thioulet*, where he has a painted sign among a precious group of 1907 Marsanne.

On the west flank of the *Côte* slope, and closer to the *Merdarie* stream, is a site called *Soulignasse*. This contains clay-limestone and is worked by Chaboud.

Close to *Hongrie* is *Coupier*, a clay-based site with some sand and *galet* stones; these pebbles form part of the roughly 100 metres–wide band of *galet* stones that crosses from *La Côte* into *Coupier* over about half a kilometre (0.31 mile). Growers here include Colombo, Thiers, Chaboud, and the Co-opérative.

Tucked against the free-flowing Mialan just south of the village at the start of the road to Le Puy, and opposite the hill of *Hongrie,* is another top vineyard, *Chemin de Mois de Mai.* It is just 100 metres from the *Coupier* site. This gulley runs away from the road, and here there is clay-limestone, with sedimentary loess. In one part, worked by Stéphan Chaboud, there is a sudden outcrop of alluvial *galet* stones mixed in with the sanded clay-limestone. The Mialan valley acts as a funnel for wind—more of a factor than alongside the Cornas frontier.

The Marsanne does well here, where growers include Thiers, Lionnet, and Chaboud. Given the rich nature of its wine, Thiers uses *Mois de Mai,* where his oldest vines date from the 1950s, as a foundation for his *vin tranquille.*

Beside *Mois de Mai,* a little to the northwest, is a mature vineyard that was for years worked by Jean Lionnet. This 0.7-hectare plot on *Les Combes* dates from the mid-1950s and is mostly Marsanne, growing on granite outcrops. Colombo is set to work these vines when Lionnet retires.

A little to the west of *Hongrie* is a site revitalised by Stéphane Robert since the early 1990s, officially termed *Barras,* but *Le Tunnel* to the locals. Stéphane chose its rotted granite (*gore*) vineyard for a large part of his Roussanne; its granite is more sanded and decomposed than at *Grand Plantier* on the Cornas boundary, for instance. "You don't hit the hard rock until four or five metres down, unlike Cornas, where the blue rock is maybe only a metre below the surface," he points out.

In its early years, Stéphane finds his *Barras* Roussanne to be very aromatic and refined. *Barras* is east facing, another higher site at around 250 metres, with a consequent gain in freshness for the Roussanne. The Tain Co-opérative also receives crop from here.

At the apex of the limestone triangle formed by Crussol beside St-Péray is a vineyard next to the N86 road, just south of the village. *Beylesse* is a cool site, with an east-northeast exposure. It is terraced, its soil limestone with sedimentary loess and broken stones—very much

the Crussol chalk seam influence apparent. The Crussol hill, marked by its ruined castle, is where the young Napoléon climbed to prove himself in his youthful days. This area produces the *appellation's* lightest wine, which is blended with other sources—all the grapes go to the Tain Co-opérative.

Running generally to the west, the road to Le Puy rises and reveals more inset valleys, where changes have been made since the 1990s, when Chaboud planted on *Vichouère.* This is a big hill, and Chaboud's vines are on the lower part facing south; they also extend around to the west behind the hill. The soil is clay-limestone with some sand present. Next to Chaboud, facing full south, is the young Paul Jaboulet Aîné vineyard. This has risen out of the traces of a long-abandoned site and contains sanded granite mixed with patches of clay. Both growers recognise the value of the wind here, with some fresh evenings possible at around 200 metres. This is a classic northern Rhône polyculture spot, with apricots growing next to the Chaboud vineyard. *Vichouère's* wine, with its clay-limestone influence, shows floral aromas, and is fuller than that from *Hongrie,* where minerality weaves into the richness.

A little south from here, split by another tiny stream called the *Bouyou,* are three sites, *Les Putiers, Les Faures,* and across a small track from them, *Amour de Dieu.* This area has long mixed fruit and vine growing and is where Guy Darona has most of his vineyards. These are largely sheltered from the north wind through lying outside the main Rhône corridor and enjoying a south-facing exposure. Marsanne is planted here.

Les Putiers is in a cool zone, with some north-facing slopes on the folds of the valley; sand is mixed with outcrops of clay. Co-opérateurs are present here, as well as Darona. *Les Faures* is the *lieu-dit* around the Darona farm, its soil sanded, loose-stone granite. These rolling, south-facing slopes can be worked mechanically. Darona remarks that the granite is good for his still wine, bringing a clear-cut, gunflint style to the bouquet. *Amour de Dieu* is more plateau land, also south facing.

Darona's cousin Bernard Gripa also works vines on *Faures* and *Amour de Dieu*, and refers to his plot within the latter as *Rabatte*. This is also sandy, with well-decomposed granite. Roussanne dating from the 1960s grows here as well as the Marsanne. The subsoil is profound, however, and the Gripas find *Rabatte*'s wine richer than that from their rockier granite St-Joseph sites a little further north near Mauves and Tournon. *Rabatte* is the main constituent of their special Figuiers cuvée. It is from this site that they will select cuttings for their future Roussanne plants in the next 10 years.

Broadly following the road to Toulaud, southwest of St-Péray, lies a further set of different *lieux-dits*, those nearest the Mialan—namely *Biousse* and *Tourtousse*, both largely clay. Guy Darona finds the deep clay on *Biousse* not so good for the Marsanne's ripening, and so uses these higher-acidity grapes for his sparkling wine. Lemenicier has a small plot of Marsanne on *Tourtousse*.

A little west and higher up towards 230 metres, the granite theme returns at *Chante-Luzet*. Colombo planted Roussanne here in 2003, and Lemenicier also has young vines, a straight mix of Marsanne and Roussanne, on this site.

Near the *Navarou* stream on the hilly run southwest towards Toulaud are the most southerly vineyards, where Jean-Louis Thiers is the King. *Biguet* is a gently rolling Marsanne-only sandy-granite vineyard around his hamlet. Its wine is light in style, and Thiers uses it for his sparkling St-Péray. "It gets dry in summer here," says Jean-Louis, "because the soil is schist and sandy granite, which drains very fast."

The other southern outpost is nearer the Rhône and therefore perpetuates the Crussol limestone theme. Somewhat in the lee of Crussol, and therefore not an early morning sun receiver, *Les Champs* has limestone mixed into the clay, with some loess. The major owner here is the President of the Tain Co-opérative, plus Thiers.

The most westerly locations lie into the hills on the way to Le Puy and high up. Moving towards the Massif Central zones, the granite influence becomes pronounced. *Fauterie* was scrubbed out and planted at 320 metres and above between 1984 and 1987 by Sylvain Bernard. Its soil is more like his St-Joseph vineyards, with a preponderance of sanded granite. This *terroir* in the west is thought to bring roundness to the wine.

Further on, out on its own, is the *Côte du Pin*, which rises to nearly 520 metres. This is worked by Chapoutier with a joint-venture involving Anne-Sophie Pic, the accomplished *restauratrice* and daughter of the late Jacques Pic in Valence. It is largely granite-based soil, with patches of flint. With a hint of humour, the local term for this site is the *Auberge de Pin*.

One of the prime characteristics of St-Péray has always been the high level of Roussanne present here. Even back in the dark days of the 1970s, when standards and reputation were both often poor, growers stuck with the Roussanne, despite its flaws. It was regarded as the natural grape for the sparkling wine—its berries smaller but its degree higher earlier in the cycle than the Marsanne, according to Marcel Juge.

Its drawback is economic rather than quality linked. It suffers from oïdium, which can knock the crop badly, and also costs more to treat. But the Roussanne can also flower poorly, so crop levels are a lot more variable than those for the Marsanne, a tougher vine. The sanded granite of *Rabatte* is a suitable home for the Roussanne in these parts.

The usual proportion of Roussanne remains around 5 to 10 per cent. In the case of Sylvain Bernard, a full 30 per cent of his 2.8 hectares is grown with Roussanne, "but they're all mixed up with the Marsanne, so it's not practical for me to make a pure-Roussanne wine," he states.

Looking back, Jean-François Chaboud is disappointed with the Roussanne; he reintroduced it in the early 1970s to his vineyard, but says, "it wasn't economic—prone to disease and always the worry that it would oxidise when you were raising it in the cellar." "On the positive side," he adds, "its wine is richer and has more character than the Marsanne's."

Roussanne has become a big hit in the southern Rhône, led by the fantastic, mature vineyard at the Château de Beaucastel; but using it on its own at St-Péray is not the answer, according to Bernard Gripa. "I wanted to make a pure Roussanne," he says, "but I found that it gave a lot of bouquet that was firm and lively, but on the palate it skipped a beat in the middle. The Marsanne was able to fill that gap with its richness."

Marcel Juge, who since 1998 has rented out his *Plantier* holding of Roussanne mixed in with Marsanne, a vineyard planted in the 1950s, sees the Roussanne-Marsanne story as a conflict of generations. "The wines they were champagnising in the 1950s were already 12.5° to 13°, which meant that quite a few literally exploded in the cellars after the *tirage*," he says. "The younger generation of the 1960s and 1970s didn't want this to happen, so took to planting in the heavier soils, and using Marsanne not Roussanne, with larger spacing between the rows." "The old-timers were basically faithful to the Roussanne—they liked and wanted to make a heady Champagne-style wine. Indeed, they called the new lower degree sparkling St-Péray 'lemonade,'" he adds mischievously.

Stéphan Chaboud has stayed with a pure Roussanne, however, while Stéphane Robert from the Domaine du Tunnel makes one as well. Stéphan Chaboud also makes a half Marsanne, half Roussanne wine, Assemblage; "the Roussanne starts off the palate well, then the Marsanne's length comes into its own," he remarks.

Now, just to confuse the issue, the laws decree that St-Péray can be made from three grapes—the Marsanne and Roussanne, plus the Roussette. The trouble is, that while the *vignerons* refer locally to the Roussette, the identity of this vine has never officially been made clear. When discussing the problem of the Roussette, some growers are apt to declare that the word "Roussette" is merely a local term for the Roussanne vine. Others bravely suggest a difference, without being able to specify it.

One man who is able to shed light on the exact nature of the Roussanne vine is Jean-François Chaboud. In 1972 he received some Roussanne cuttings from the late Dr. Philippe Dufays, the viticultural expert who owned Domaine de Nalys at Châteauneuf-du-Pape and has since been able to observe this plant's characteristics as compared with Marsanne and the Roussanne grown at Hermitage; the latter, he avers, is distinct from the Roussanne that he is growing.

"My Roussanne is distinguished by a series of jagged insets on the leaves—much more than the Marsanne—and also has a lot more veins on it than the Marsanne leaves. The Roussanne grape is also more pointed than the Marsanne, and while a bunch of Marsanne will weigh a little over one kilo, the Roussanne gives only about half as much fruit per bunch." Certainly, the usual Roussanne leaf is rounded, as opposed to inset.

"This Roussanne," he continues, "even in a normal year gives less juice than most other local vines and, because the berries are small, has a high proportion of pips to juice. I find that it is extremely susceptible to attacks of oïdium and the grape juice easily risks becoming oxidized at the precise moment of harvesting. We therefore make sure that its grapes enter the press completely intact. We have raised our plantation of Roussanne from one to 2.5 hectares since the early 1990s, and it is mostly planted on the clay-limestone of our *Hongrie* vineyard. For me, this wine doesn't really live much more than a couple of years, which convinces me further that this Roussanne variety is not the same as the one planted on Hermitage hill."

For his part, the skilled and thoughtful Bernard Gripa considers that his Roussanne—20 per cent of his two hectares—is a vine that comes "from the exterior—perhaps it's Savoyard by origin. I planted it myself, but find that it doesn't compare necessarily with the few *ceps* that you find elsewhere at St-Péray," he comments.

Stéphane Robert observes that his Roussanne's berries are small and rose coloured and have big pips. His plants are susceptible to attacks of *coulure*, when the fruit fails to form after flowering. Its yield is often variable, but its degree superior to the Marsanne's.

In the St-Péray conservatory vineyard set up in the early 2000s, there are 25 different Roussanne plants alongside 80 Marsanne; these have all been hand selected from 80-year-old vines that have been tested healthy. The Roussanne comes from Châteauneuf-du-Pape and Savoie, the Marsanne from St-Péray, Hermitage, and St-Joseph. These provide cuttings for future planting. Roussanne clones exist, but so productive are they that, as is so often the case, they demand grape dropping during the summer cycle.

Meanwhile, a vehement defender of the Marsanne, and not a man seduced by the apparent glitziness of the Roussanne, is Alain Voge. An inveterate fiddler with his wines and their composition, he has come down firmly on the side of the Marsanne—provided it is exposed to oak. "If you know how to work with Marsanne, it gives you stunning wines," he affirms. "If you vinify it in oak, it gives fresh wines. You may get a little tannic matter from the wood, but you'll give the wine a longer life because Marsanne is a variety that is oxidative by nature. I've always found that my vat-only Marsannes never lasted so long as the oak ones. The oak needs to be mainly new, mixed with a few casks that are, say, two years old. Then you obtain more minerality and richness," he concludes.

Grapes intended for the sparkling wine are picked earlier than those for the still wine. "I pick when they are around 11°," observes Guy Darona, "and aim for 12° to 12.5° for the still wine. The sparkling process, the *tirage*, adds a degree or so, anyway."

For makers of the still wine, harvest dates circle around mid-September and beyond in normal years. Recently, early dates fell in 1999 and 2003. Stéphan Chaboud had considered his harvesting on 2 September 1999 to be early

until 2003 came along—18 August was his start date then!

ST-PÉRAY *NATURE* VINIFICATION

The prime theme since the early 1990s has been the increased use of oak, which has also led to many growers offering two styles of wine—"classic" and oaked. Obviously oaked wines are offered by the Gripas with their Figuiers, and by Voge with his Cuvée Boisée, a name also used by Lemenicier. The merchant businesses of Vins de Vienne and Tardieu-Laurent also use plenty of oak.

Even a conservative like Guy Darona started an oaked wine in 2000; his *Jardin des Faures* is 60 per cent oaked, while Sylvain Bernard first used 20 per cent oak in 2000.

The upshot is generally that the wines have returned to their full roots, by dint of being allowed to perform their malolactic fermentations and being left alone longer before bottling. Paradoxically, one of the early bottlers in the month of April is Pierre Clape, a noted conservative from Cornas, while Stéphan Chaboud also does a first bottling run around then.

What the oaked wines then demand is a long stay in bottle to come together and to evade the oak cloak. Often this period of delay will amount to a good five years. But the wines are of course launched on to the market with early consumption in mind.

One grower who has cut the oak exposure on his pure Roussanne is Stéphan Chaboud; "I find that St-Péray doesn't adapt so well to oak as St-Joseph," he says, "so I prefer to preserve the wine's more natural freshness." But he does oak the Roussanne on his Marsanne-Roussanne mix wine, as do nearly all the growers using this minority grape.

The fact that growers are prepared to wait for over a year before bottling is an interesting sign that they are not trying to deny St-Péray its local style. In the 1980s, there were attempts to freshen it up in the cellar, following the vogue of the time. The Co-opérative, users of oak since 1998, now bottle after 15 months, Colombo after 21; most bottle in the stretch between May and September, within the year.

Fermenting vats are generally steel, with some enamel, and just one or two concrete and fibreglass units. Fermentation temperatures vary between 16° and 20°C, although Lionnet is usually a cooler operator; he also picks quite late, a trait of Paul Jaboulet Aîné. A typical decantation after pressing lasts a day or two, the temperature held around 12°C.

Lees stirring is in flux. It became fashionable in the late 1990s but, in my view, encouraged confected textures. There was simply too much formulaic and sheeplike behaviour then, and the extra richness that might have been provided was swamped through too much stirring, making the wines clumsy. The Gripa family for one have reduced the incidence of lees stirring, and withdraw the wine off the lees a little sooner now. Paul Jaboulet Aîné likewise have cut the amount of stirring they do, thankfully.

ST-PÉRAY *NATURE*

The still wine of St-Péray should show floral tones like hawthorn blossom, acacia, or honeysuckle on the bouquet, any fruit being white, like plums. With age, at the second stage of advance, there can be beeswax or buttery aromas and sometimes a salty tang. The palate is often marked by a dryish, stone-fruit skin texture. Apricots and lime tart can come to mind, as well as the almond nuttiness found more commonly at Hermitage, and some honeyed tones on the finale. The mainly Marsanne wines often display a chewy texture late on the palate—almost a tannic side. Some growers also refer to finding quince jelly on the end palate.

The latter part of the taste brings out a minerality of texture. Any firmness on the end palate is what Stéphan Chaboud terms "the wine's typical gunflint character." The mineral touch is something not encountered in neighbouring Marsanne-led wines, and marks a liter-

ally firm difference between St-Péray and St-Joseph whites. This minerality comes from soil changes, and is also encouraged by the acidity of the Roussanne, in the view of Bernard Gripa.

He makes both St-Péray and white St-Joseph, and compares them thus: "St-Péray should be *pur et dur*—meaning that it has a clean fruit with a firm mineral side to it. Ideally, I like it to go past that and have an extra richness, but that's not easy to achieve. The hot years often bring low acidities, so those wines can't live and develop properly. If well vinified, St-Péray should live for 10 to 15 years. I expect St-Joseph to be more fulsome and often more open, also more elegant. It's not the higher Roussanne content at St-Péray that on its own makes the difference; it's also the richer soil, with pockets of limestone, that brings greater acidity."

This view is backed by Jacques Grange of Delas, who feels that in regular years St-Péray holds more acidity than St-Joseph, which allows its richness to hold on for longer.

I find the clay-chalk wines the most structured, and the longest *en bouche*, with more nuance than the granite wines. A Hongrie, for instance, is usually quite rich, with a tangy, mineral presence; by contrast, a wine from the more granite *Grand Plantier* near Cornas I would expect to be dry, with more nerve and sinew in it.

When fermented at average temperatures, around 17° to 20°C, the wine is gentler and more reserved than the lower-temperature wines. The latter bring out aromas of tropical fruits, grapefruit, pineapple slices, and so on after a year or two. There can be a soft touch of *noisette*, or hazelnut, on the palate.

For the oaked cuvées, the advice is to wait, unless buying them for the overt oak overlay. Three years is not enough; some of these intrinsically elegant Marsannes can need five or six years to meld.

A Roussanne wine on its own comes from Chaboud, whose domaine has been making one for some decades, and from Stéphane Robert, who introduced one in 2003. Colombo's Belle de Mai, first produced in 1999, is 90 per cent Roussanne. The Chaboud Roussanne is a fresher wine than their Marsanne, enhanced by the decision of son Stéphan to give up any oak use, and its flavours are less plump.

The attack on the pure Roussanne palate is always lively and elegant. Honey notes are present even when young, along with some of the apricot that might also be found in the Marsanne wines. When aged for eight to 10 years, the Roussanne's attack continues on its lively way, but the early flourish subsides rather suddenly and the wine can finish rather emptily. Flan and sugar notes are present on the palate, and furniture polish can even appear on the bouquet.

Regular Marsanne-dominated St-Péray can age well. A 1988 Marsanne from Chaboud drunk in 2003 was still full of beans. The aromas had become citrus, the attack was mineral, and the flavour reflected quince with a marked salty tang. The citrus side is a regular feature of the ageing process. The oldest St-Péray Stéphan Chaboud has drunk was a 1970, which showed signs of oxidation in 1995; "once the wine is six years old, you get another 10 years of good, mature-style wine, but then the risks rise," he says.

For their part, Fabrice Gripa and father, Bernard, consider that at 10 years the wine starts to show overt petrol and smoked aspects like a Riesling. For them, the wine goes to sleep at four years, passing through an oxidative phase, coming and going towards eight years of age. This makes it sound as if a lot of bottles must be bought to keep track!

Jean Lionnet, more the modernist, feels that his wine is best drunk as an aperitif when young: "It needs only a simple companion at that stage, when there are exotic fruits on the bouquet, but after about four years I would turn to white meats—when it's at what I call a honey wax stage."

St-Péray's nearest white-wine neighbour is St-Joseph. M. Lionnet believes there is more decisive fruit in the latter, whereas St-Péray acquires a fatter, more buttery aspect when it ages, almost placing it at that stage of life closer to white Crozes-Hermitage from across the river.

IDEAL FOODS WITH ST-PÉRAY *NATURE*

"St-Péray is more a wine for food than St-Joseph —there's an easier marriage, a wide choice of dish," comments Bernard Gripa. "I find shellfish awful with St-Joseph, for instance, but passable with St-Péray. I rate St-Péray best with grilled fish, and fish in sauce," he says. As he and his wife, Lucette, dine out often, that is advice worth noting!

Confirmed supporters of shellfish are Jean Lionnet, Guy Darona, and Jacques Lemenicier, "and especially when the vintage is small, the wine goes well with oysters," states Auguste Clape. *Coquille St. Jacques*—scallops—are rated a good dish by Alain Voge and, when done in the oven, by Stéphan Robert. Langoustine tails are mentioned by Alain Voge as a good companion, too.

A sea fish theme, such as turbot in a cream sauce, is also suggested by the Clapes. Bernard Gripa also favours raw or cooked salmon— "the wine's minerality cuts through it very well," he says.

Another angle is to drink it young, with freshwater fish. Jean Lionnet and Sylvain Bernard talk of grilled freshwater fish, especially when the vintage holds good acidity, as in 2001 and 2004. Jacques Lemenicier goes for straight grilled trout. The Jaboulets recommend a grilled fillet of *sandre* (pikeperch) with almonds.

Jean-Louis Thiers, Sylvain Bernard, and Stéphan Chaboud suggest drinking St-Péray as an aperitif when the wine is young; for Chaboud, his Marsanne is a better straight drink than his Roussanne. Stéphane Robert opts for quiche lorraine on a spring or summer's day with the young wine.

Charcuterie has its supporters, like the Clapes. "I like it with charcuterie because it's a rich wine," states Marcel Juge, while Stéphan Chaboud favours charcuterie with his wooded wine.

A more unusual but promising suggestion comes from Sylvain Bernard, who puts forward Chinese vegetables cooked in a wok as a suitable partner for a full vintage like 2003.

As the wine ages, accompaniments change. White meats become popular, with Guy Darona, Jean Lionnet, Sylvain Bernard, and Jean-Louis Thiers talking of chicken, usually in sauce, such as a creamed tarragon. Alain Voge favours veal, but not grilled or roasted—more Milanese—or sweetbreads.

Roast or stuffed rabbit is also liked by Thiers and Darona, while Bernard Gripa recalls: "Jacques Pic used to do rabbit in a St-Péray sauce, whereby the mineral side of the wine worked very well—that gunflint effect."

When it reaches five or six years old, Darona and Juge consider the wine to come into its own with fish in sauce, while Alain Voge speaks of *pageot* and Mediterranean fish like red mullet. Alain is also keen on serving his full, oaked Fleur de Crussol with foie gras. Another oaked wine, the Stéphane Robert Prestige, is considered good with freshwater *sandre à la crème*. As a footnote, the growers recommend that their oaked wines be served less cool than the regular wines.

On the cheese front, Comté is liked by both Sylvain Bernard and Alain Voge; the former also chooses Beaufort and fresh goat Tomme, the latter Gruyère. Jacques Lemenicier suggests goat cheese from the Ardèche for his Cuvée Boisée, while the Jaboulet family opt for Saint-Marcellin.

With dessert, Sylvain Bernard recommends a full year like 2003 as the complement for a rhubarb tart. When it is eight to 10 years old, Guy Darona finds his wine works well with chocolate gateau and apple tart, while at 15 years, Jean Lionnet counsels truffle dishes, and Sylvain Bernard suggests drinking the wine on its own.

For his pure Roussanne, Stéphan Chaboud opts for white meats, creamy cheese like Brie and Vacherin, or mild Camambert.

ST-PÉRAY *MÉTHODE CHAMPENOISE* VINIFICATION

The first difference between the still and sparkling wines is the need for higher levels of vivacity in the sparkling wine crop. Its grapes are therefore picked ahead of the crop intended for the still wine, especially as any semblance of rot would be fatal for it. In a year like 2003, this meant harvesting on 19 August for Jean-Louis Thiers, 10 days ahead of the still wine crop.

The sparkling St-Péray must by law be made exactly as Champagne, with even the yeasts used in the wine coming from that famous wine region: these are sent down from the Institut Oenologique de Champagne in dried form and are rehydrated by the growers.

It is mostly made from Marsanne. Jean-François Chaboud's experiments with using a marked amount of the Roussanne grape in the sparkling wine were not successful in the past. "I once tried making a sparkling wine composed half-and-half of Marsanne and Roussanne, but it simply didn't work; the wine was unbalanced, lacked acidity and simply wasn't lively as I would have hoped," he comments. Now he sticks to a maximum of 20 per cent Roussanne on his Cuvée Prestige.

The crop intended for the sparkling wine is not destemmed and is fermented at 16° to 17°C, usually in stainless steel. It starts life just as a regular still wine, although the degree is lower. Jean-Louis Thiers also blocks the malolactic at this stage to preserve essential freshness.

The next step is the addition of the *liqueur de tirage* in March or April—before the big heat of summer—when the wine gains its bubbles. Darona adds around 22 gm of sugar per litre, Thiers 21 gm, and Chaboud 20 gm, in a process that runs for about three days. By law, the *tirage* must be done in St-Péray, so Alain Voge is the last of the Cornas growers to bother with the sparkling wine: it means transferring his wine to St-Péray for that express task.

The blend of sugar and yeasts sets off a further fermentation, the carbon gas from which creates the sparkle in the wine, as well as boosting its alcohol level. The rules then dictate a nine-month stay in bottle after the *liqueur de tirage* addition, but Jean-Louis Thiers, for one, doubles that.

Guy Darona also works with a long lead time, releasing his wine around four years later. "You get a prettier set of bubbles," he states, "and the wine becomes more the finished article, stabilising its acidity by then." Stéphan Chaboud takes a similar view and releases his wines—both dry and *demi-sec*—after over three years.

The bottles are stored on their sides for these extended stays but, as for Champagne, have to be tidied up before bottling. The process of collecting the particles from the fermentation in the neck of the bottle is called *remuage*, or turning. Here the bottles are transferred nose-down, to wooden holders known as *pupitres*, or school desks. The *pupitre* is made up of two pieces of wood, each containing 60 holes, which stand leaning in on one another like an inverted cone. The bottles are placed neck-first into these holders, at first in an almost horizontal position.

The *pupitre* is a *champenois* implement said to have been thought up by the Veuve Clicquot when she was (obviously) messing around with her kitchen table—having it cut in half, for instance. It has become more standard at St-Péray than the old local *treteau de remuage*. This is a trestle table with four trays on top of each other, a large affair 1.5 metres high, with holes for 120 bottles on each level. Only very occasionally does one see a *treteau de remuage* in a St-Péray cellar nowadays.

When the bottles are put in their wooden *pupitres*, the wine in them is far from clear, for the secondary fermentation has brought with it a large amount of dead yeast cells and sediment. For a month the bottles in the *pupitres* are turned in pairs by a deft flick of the wrists: every day they draw nearer to the vertical, and the sediment inside them starts sliding slowly down towards the neck.

"Turning" is one of the most skilled, and least pleasant, tasks in the whole elaboration of a sparkling wine, and it continues in its original form at St-Péray because there is only a limited amount of wine being made. The experienced *caviste* in Champagne would turn as many as 50,000 bottles a day using both hands, but

there are now platforms that do the job mechanically inside a week in any of the big Houses.

By the time the bottles are in a near-vertical position, the sediment is well lodged in their necks. The next operation is disgorging, or *dégorgement*, and corking. The bottles are placed one by one, with their necks frozen, on a rotating disgorging machine, which whips off the tightly sealed cap. The upper liquid slowly starts to run out, and with it the sediment, and the bottle is immediately topped or "dosed" with a mixture of either cane sugar or concentrated must and St-Péray, half a centilitre per bottle.

It is then passed straight on to the corking machine, as the grower naturally does not want to lose all his good hard work and fine bubbles. This is the moment when a *demi-sec*, or sweeter wine, can be made through the simple addition of more concentrated must to the solution.

Guy Darona and Jean-Louis Thiers make both a *brut* and a *demi-sec*. Darona explains: "Since 2000 we have used a concentrated must which gives more fruit than the sugar cane of old. This is done at the moment of disgorging—there is 0.5 cl of *liqueur* for the *brut* and maybe 3 cl of liqueur for a bottle of the *demi-sec*. It gives almost a Pineau de Charentes effect." Jean-Louis Thiers admits that he is reducing his *demi-sec*, after it revived a little in the 1980s, while it makes up one-fifth of Darona's sparkling wine.

It is also frequent for the sparkling wine to contain wines from different vintages, just as in Champagne. Thiers never gives his 20,000 bottles a vintage to achieve a consistent style; his sparkling wine is still a large 75 per cent of his production. Guy Darona puts a vintage on the relatively limited amounts of sparkling wine that he sells to private customers at the cellar door.

Producers of sparkling St-Péray have whittled down in the past 30 years and now include the Tain Co-opérative, Chaboud, Darona, Thiers, and Voge. A young relative newcomer like Stéphane Robert of the Domaine du Tunnel is not drawn to the sparkling wine, which is perfectly understandable. The Co-opérative, for instance, sells most of its sparkling wine locally, and young growers inevitably do not have the local retail network set up for such sales by one or two bottles at a time.

ST-PÉRAY *MÉTHODE CHAMPENOISE*

St-Péray *méthode champenoise* is a country-style wine, very regional in its way. After a little time in bottle to settle down and lose an early raw, sometimes green aspect, the wine becomes rounded, and in the best examples can follow through with a sound, clean finish. Characterized by a firm, sometimes light straw colour that is darker than most modern white wines, the sparkling carries a fragrance of apples or faint flowers; at times, in the fullest wines, this becomes more like an earthiness within the aroma.

The palate should contain a green or white fruit flavour, backed by some tartness and liveliness. The finish should be rounded and not too sharp. There are times when I find the *mousse* not very well integrated, with a looseness after the early flavour that makes the finish too frothy and clumsy. In good examples, there is a nuttiness present that is typical of the Marsanne.

But beware—St-Péray sparkling is not a wine that should be specially cellared to obtain greater roundness and complexity like nonvintage champagne from good houses: it tends to tire and become flabby after six or seven years.

"Sparkling St-Péray must never be heavy," says Jean-Louis Thiers, "because it's an aperitif wine." He recommends drinking it in the two to three years following its *dégorgement*.

IDEAL FOODS WITH ST-PÉRAY *MÉTHODE CHAMPENOISE*

While it has been known to take the sting out of bad hangovers, St-Péray *méthode champenoise* is best served well chilled as an aperitif. Jean-Louis Thiers is someone who drinks it strictly in that form.

Locals talk about serving it with fish and shellfish due to the live acidity in the wine; also chicken in cream sauce, vegetarian dishes, and cold buffets.

Stéphan Chaboud's father, Jean-François, opts for raw or cured ham as a good companion for the sparkling, and also mentions quiche lorraine.

Twenty to 30 years ago more people drank sparkling St-Péray with dessert. Stéphan Chaboud finds that his *brut de brut* works well with apple or pear tarts more than red fruit ones. He also enjoys it with sorbets, ice cream, and *îles flottantes*. He notes that it should be served more chilled, around 8° to 10°C, than the still wine.

THE PRODUCERS

LOUIS BERNARD

Route de Sérignan 84100 Orange +33(0)490 118686

See also Cornas, Côte-Rôtie, Crozes-Hermitage, Hermitage, St-Joseph.
This southern Rhône *négociant* has moved into St-Péray with the issue of a wine made in conjunction with a local grower who vinifies it for them at a cool temperature. It contains some Roussanne. This St-Péray carries dried fruit flavours and oaked tones, not always in harmony.

DOMAINE CHABOUD

21 rue Ferdinand Malet 07130 Saint-Péray +33(0)475 403163

See also Cornas.
Off a busy street in the village of St-Péray is the key reference point for the *appellation*. Light and shade prevail in high summer: its pretty garden bursts with bright red roses, a splendid 300-year-old cedar tree casts flares of cool shade, and magnolias light up the small park. Their bounty reflects St-Péray's old status as the village of escape from Valence, a place for leisure and relaxation.

FIGURE 39 Stéphan Chaboud has continued his father's fight to keep St-Péray known and appreciated. (Tim Johnston)

This is home to the Chaboud family. Stéphan Chaboud is President of the Growers Union; his father, Jean-François, has also been an activist; and this domaine's work with white and more recently red wines has always been strong.

Their St-Péray comes from 8.5 hectares, six Marsanne and 2.5 Roussanne. These are spread across eight different plots, seven of them on the generally clay-limestone of the *Hongrie* quarter of the *appellation*, with one on *Vichouère*, where there is more granite.

Apart from the 1.5 hectares on *Vichouère* (1992)—next to the young Paul Jaboulet Aîné vineyard on the way to Le Puy—notable specific sites are *Le Thioulet*, which contains 0.4 ha of Marsanne dating from 1907, and *La Côte*, arguably the top site because of its mix of old vines and midslope exposure, where the Marsanne dates from 1903.

The soil across the hill of *Hongrie* is white clay-limestone, and Stéphan finds its wine more mineral than that taken from nearer the N86 Cornas road down on the plain, where there is more clay. There the wines are drier and a little more acid. On the good *Chemin de Mois de Mai* site, there is a further half hectare.

Stéphan is a busy man, since he has fruit interests—1.5 hectares of apricots and four prized cherry trees—as well as wine commitments elsewhere. There are also 1.5 hectares of Syrah at St-Péray, which makes two red Côtes du Rhônes (a straight and an oaked version), and one hectare at Cornas. In his mid-30s, he studied for two years in Champagne, and his outlook has not remained parochial. He realises that the broader distribution of St-Péray by the *négociant* firms can only be beneficial.

A stout lad, with tousled hair and generous features, he exports only a little; indeed 70 per cent of his sales are directly to private customers. He took the decision to reclassify a two-hectare plot of his Marsanne in the 1990s as land for the Syrah Côtes du Rhône—a move that allowed him to reach a wider audience.

The Chabouds' tidy cellar is nicely spread out through different rooms. These date from 1750 and were redone in 1798 and 1815, their last restoration. Hence they are naturally cool, 12° to 14°C. Today there is an incongruous mix of modern fuse boxes on the walls, with old, battle-scarred wooden *pupitres* for the sparkling wine, and mottled cellar doors.

Stéphan likes to work his Marsanne and Roussanne separately. "They ripen at different times," he says, "and doing it this way helps me to decide how to assemble them later on." He makes four still wines, which are usually sound and also live well. Cutting these back, however, might help him to make a really good wine rather than a series of correct, sensibly pleasing ones.

He has a pure Marsanne from slightly younger vines that is vat fermented and raised. There is an interesting pure Roussanne, also only vat vinified and raised, bottled with its malo completed. He follows his father in making this Roussanne wine, but has dropped any oak exposure to retain freshness in the wine.

Commenting on his use of oak in general, Stéphan draws a distinction between St-Péray and St-Joseph white: "I find St-Joseph adapts better to wood. St-Péray is more mineral and fresher than St-Joseph, so I am keen to go along with that," he says.

The Cuvée Assemblage is 50-50 Marsanne-Roussanne and is vat treated. Lastly, there is a Cuvée Boisée; here the minimum 20 per cent Roussanne content is fermented and aged in new oak for a year. With half its Marsanne content also new-cask fermented, the end wine represents about a 40 per cent new-oak exposure. The malos are usually completed for all these wines. During the raising, Stéphan stirs the lees daily for a month, then cuts back to once a week, and once a month before the two bottlings—March/April, then June/July.

Stéphan's penchant for a lot of different wines continues with his sparkling St-Péray, since there are five of these, which takes us into the realms of the obscure. In 2000, 2001, and 2003 he made a 50 per cent Roussanne, 50 per cent Marsanne Cuvée Prestige; there are also an 80 per cent Marsanne, 20 per cent Roussanne Cuvée Arnaud; a Brut Grande Réserve *brut de brut*; a pure Marsanne classic that comes in *brut* or *demi-sec* form; and a wooded wine called Cuvée Louis Alexandre, first made in 2002. The last named is pure Marsanne, and 40 per cent of it is raised in new oak for a year after its fermentation, before the addition of the *liqueur de tirage*.

The crop intended for the sparkling wine is not destemmed, and is fermented at 16°C, then bottled for its taking on of bubbles in March/April. After three years of storage, the wine's elaboration is completed with a disgorging and another two months in the cellar before release.

The Chaboud sparkling St-Péray is very stylised, with a robust, full flavour to it, but equally a long and attractive finish that sets it apart from many of the other wines. Stéphan bottles the sparkling wine around March/April, like the other growers.

Reflecting the low profile of the *appellation*, 70 per cent of the Chaboud sales are private; only a little is exported. The sparkling wine also comprises the major part of the production.

Of the two red Côtes du Rhônes, the classic is vat raised and the special receives six to eight months in cask. The former is a light, easy wine, the latter carries a degree of structure for slightly longer keeping.

The Chaboud wines often reflect honey aromas, and carry sound richness in vintages like the complete 2001. The straight Marsanne can live for up to nine years, and the Boisée should be left for at least five years in a good year. The pure Roussanne is a fresher wine, with a refined texture and some spiced aspects.

ST-PÉRAY ASSEMBLAGE

2001 ★★
1999 ★★

ST-PÉRAY MARSANNE

2003 ★★
2001 ★★

ST-PÉRAY ROUSSANNE

2002 ★
2001 ★★

Export 10 per cent (1) Netherlands, (2) Quebec, (3) Japan

LES CHAMPS LIBRES

La Tratoule-Les Champs 07300 Tournon
+33(0)475 071574

A small *négociant* business run by René-Jean Dard of Dard et Ribo, this served a very faithful Roussanne-inspired 2003, stylish and without the potential excess of the vintage.

ST-PÉRAY

2003 ★★★

M. CHAPOUTIER

18 ave Dr Paul Durand 26600 Tain l'Hermitage
+33(0)475 082865

See also Condrieu, Cornas, Côte-Rôtie, Crozes-Hermitage, Hermitage, St-Joseph.
Since 2001 Chapoutier have owned 1.5 hectares on *Hongrie* at St-Péray, another endorsement for the *appellation*. The vineyard is all Marsanne planted in the 1970s and has been worked organically since 2004.

Seventy-five per cent of their St-Péray comes from this biodynamic vineyard, the rest being bought in as wine. Up to 85 per cent of the crop is steel fermented at 18° to 20°C, the rest is oak vinified, with lees stirring and a raising for both sources of eight to 10 months. "We leave all the wine on its lees for the winter," explains chief manager Albéric Mazoyer, "and use small vats to emphasize the lees' role as an anti-oxidant agent."

In a year like 2001—full of content—the wine shows a flourish in its first two years, then slides into anonymity, but will revert to showing off more deep-seated and varied flavours around five years old. The fruit style is plum or apricot —white fruits—and in the good years like 1999 and 2001, the length is good, a life of around nine years possible. The 2003 accentuated the full, *crème patisserie* side of the Marsanne, a wine of plenty that should be left until 2006 to develop a greater variety of flavours.

In time, there will be two wines, one of them made purely from their own crop and produced in association with the restaurant of Anne-Sophie Pic at Valence.

ST-PÉRAY

2003 ★★★

AUGUSTE ET PIERRE-MARIE CLAPE

146 RN 86 07130 Cornas +33(0)475 403364

See also Cornas.
The Kings of Cornas, the Clape family have made St-Péray since 1967. The tiny 0.23 ha vineyard is on light slopes of mixed clay and granite on the high part of *Grand Plantier*, just beside the southern Cornas vineyards. It is 99 per cent Marsanne, a token sprinkling of 1 per cent Roussanne, of some age: two-thirds are 55 to 65 years old, one-third is 15 years old.

The wine is still, and while a year like 2002 provided 800 bottles, the norm is nearer 1,200. The crop is fermented at around 17°C in concrete, then raised in stainless steel before bottling with the malo completed in April.

The quality is very consistent, with peach and apricot fruits present, and any richness gently placed on show. Bouquets can reflect honey and flowers. Most vintages can be drunk inside six to eight years.

The Clapes also make a simple, very correct white Côtes du Rhône from 20-year-old vines which are all Marsanne with just a smattering of Viognier. These grow at the southern end of Cornas, between the road and the river, on draining, mainly gravel soil. It is vinified in lined concrete, transferred to stainless steel, and bottled with the malolactic done in late April. It should be drunk inside five years.

ST-PÉRAY

2003 ★★★

DOMAINE JEAN-LUC COLOMBO

La Croix des Marais 266600 La Roche-de-Glun
+33(0)475 841710

See also Condrieu, Cornas, Côte-Rôtie, Crozes-Hermitage, Hermitage, St-Joseph.
Jean-Luc Colombo is another who started with the 1999 vintage. At first, he chose to buy crop and went for 100 per cent Roussanne split

between two sites, *Chante-Luzet* and *Chemin de Mois de Mai*, where there is loess, on the road towards the hills of the Massif Central.

Between 2001 and 2003, Jean-Luc planted a half hectare of Roussanne on the granite of *Chante-Luzet*, on a hillside in the southern Toulaud area. The domaine vineyards now total almost two hectares, and Jean-Luc is also taking up some of the old Jean Lionnet vineyards as the latter retires.

Called "La Belle de Mai," this now 90 per cent Roussanne, 10 per cent Marsanne wine is fermented and raised on its lees in 80 per cent new, 20 per cent one-year-old casks for up to 21 months. The new oak incidence has risen since launch.

The 10,000 bottles are aimed at the top end of the market—half is sold abroad, the rest at the leading restaurants in France. This is a wine that needs patience to absorb its overt oak overlay, and it gradually reclaims a sense of *terroir* if left for four years or so.

The wine carries a *robe* more yellow than most and conveys buttery flavours that are tinged with mineral and spice. It is a wine for serious food, its oak requiring patience to assimilate into the main body. Like some St-Pérays, there can be licorice touches on the finish. In a good vintage, it can live for 10 years or so.

ST-PÉRAY BELLE DE MAI

2001 ★★★

GUY DARONA

Les Faures 07130 Saint-Péray +33(0)475 403411

The approaches of Valence show themselves imposingly on the way to Guy Darona's family farm; it used to be tucked away on a hillside in a beautiful rolling valley that leads southwest towards Toulaud. These days there is new housing en route, often fronted by thick, fast-growing dark hedges, grilled gates, and satellite dishes.

Now it's the farm that seems out of place; there are still some fruit trees around the house and cellars, and further away there are three

hectares of apricots beyond their vineyards. As the urban world rolls on towards them, it's sobering to think that the Daronas, related to Bernard Gripa of St-Joseph, have lived here for seven generations and yet seem the least likely locals now.

Monique Darona, Guy's mother, recalls the *champagnisé* wine being made here in her youth in the 1930s, and at its peak her late husband Pierre was selling 40,000 bottles a year. "In the 1930s, it was called just a sparkling wine, before the *appellation* was created, and most people drank it with dessert, as it was mostly sweet in those days."

Guy chips in, with his quite thick local tones: "Making it sweet helped to cover up its acidity, because ripening in those days was often not a great success—there was less mastery of the vineyards. Now we track the ripening better so the *brut* version can come out well." He is slim with short dark hair and moustache, heading for 50, very much a man at ease in his locale here. He started out at 18 in 1974, and has gradually shifted the domaine towards making more still or *vin tranquille* than sparkling wine.

Owning six hectares at St-Péray, he works another five under rental, making him an important source. Five hectares are on *Les Faures*, around the house, where there is sanded, loose-stone granite. The 90 per cent Marsanne, 10 per cent Roussanne vineyard (early 1980s) is trained along wires on rolling slopes that can be worked mechanically. The granite is good for the still wine and provides its gunflint style.

The next-largest site is three hectares on *Les Putiers* (average 20 years), all Marsanne growing on flatter, clay-sanded soil. There are also 1.5 hectares on *Biousse*, all Marsanne, where the soil is deep clay, and 1.5 hectares on *Rabatte* (85 per cent Marsanne, 15 per cent Roussanne), where the soil is loose sand–decomposed granite with limestone traces.

Guy observes that because his little valley is away from the main Rhône corridor, his vineyards are largely sheltered from the north wind; their often south-facing exposure also helps maturity. He works the vineyards as naturally as possible, including the sowing of clover seeds between the vines at the end of the year. "When I started, we tilled the ground, but were losing so much soil in erosion that we couldn't carry on doing that," he explains.

His still white is pressed and decanted for up to two days before fermentation in enamel-lined vats at 18° to 20°C; the classic wine is also raised in vat for six (2001) to 12 (2002) months before bottling, the malo done. The special Jardin des Faures, first made in 2002, is 60 per cent oak raised for six months with lees stirring and is bottled 10 to 12 months on.

The classic still wine carries good local character, following the vintage style faithfully. A vintage like 2002 was soft, the 2001 more structured, with a dumb phase appearing at three years. A floral, dried-fruit youth is then superseded by a more complex, nutty, honeyed second phase. The wine can live nicely for 10 to 12 years. The Jardin des Faures carries a more mainstream, exotic fruit/oak flavour.

Guy does his *tirage* for the sparkling wine in April, using around 22 gm of sugar per litre. He works with a long lead time, releasing his wine around four years later. "You get a prettier set of bubbles," he states, "and the wine becomes more the finished article, stabilising its acidity by then."

Half his wine is now sparkling, a gradual decline from 70 per cent in the early 1990s. Guy puts a vintage on the wine he sells to private customers, and apart from his own still wine, he also sells crop and wine to local merchants.

ST-PÉRAY

2002 ★★
2001 ★★★

MAISON DELAS

ZA de l'Olivet 07300 St-Jean-de-Muzols
+33(0)475 086030

See also Condrieu, Cornas, Côte-Rôtie, Crozes-Hermitage, Hermitage, St-Joseph.
Delas returned to making St-Péray in 1999, after an interval of six years. "It's difficult to sell," states Jacques Grange candidly, "so I don't mind putting it into the Côtes du Rhône in light years

like 2002." In a better vintage like 2003, the wine is a mix of purchased crop and young wine. The house produces 2,000 to 3,000 bottles.

When produced, it is half Marsanne, half Roussanne, and the source is a plot near the village itself, *Grandes Blâches*, so the influence is more granite than clay. The vines date from at least the 1930s, so the Côtes du Rhône gets a treat every now and then!

The must is bought just after pressing, and the wine is raised on its fine lees for five to six months in 60 per cent one-year-old casks, 40 per cent vat. Recent years have shown some chewy white-fruit flavours on the palate, with a correct dried fruit/mineral tightening on the finish.

ST-PÉRAY

2001 ★★
2000 ★★
1999 ★★

DOMAINE DE FAUTERIE

10 ave Charles de Gaulle 07130 St-Péray
+33(0)475 800425

See also Cornas, St-Joseph.
Sylvain Bernard's 2.75 ha of St-Péray are grouped on the *Fauterie* site. This is a very high vineyard that was scrubbed out and planted at 320 metres between 1984 and 1987. Its soil is more like his St-Joseph vineyards, with a preponderance of sanded granite.

The mix is a high 30 per cent Roussanne, 70 per cent Marsanne. After pressing and a 48-hour decantation, 80 per cent of the juice is fermented in steel at 18° to 19°C, the rest in three-year-old oak, which was introduced in 2000. The wine is raised on its fine lees for eight months, but left alone, with no lees stirring. In September the vat-oak elements are assembled and bottled.

The wine is bottled later than it used to be, and as the vineyard has grown up, the wine has been gaining in depth. "Rich, rounded whites are what I like to make," explains Sylvain, with part of his approach guided by a tendency to harvest late. In soft vintages like 2002 it is floral, while in fuller years like 2001 and 1999 there is more spiced fruit, with a clean, mineral finish and a life of 10 years ahead. The unusual 2003 weighed in at 14.5° and showed plenty of the spiced fruit with the added presence of dried banana aromas. It was rather extreme, almost a late-harvest style. Greater freshness would be welcome in the future here.

ST-PÉRAY

2003 ★

2002 ★★ or nil (varies). Some can be oxidative, gold-coloured.

2001 ★★★

LA GRANDE COLLINE

BP 12 07130 Cornas +33(0)475 586289

This is the enterprise of young Japanese Hirotake Ooka, who spent time with Thiérry Allemand after a stint in Bordeaux. The 2003 was an all-Marsanne wine, fermented and raised in cask. It was uneven when tasted in December 2004.

DOMAINE BERNARD ET FABRICE GRIPA

Le chemin de Halage 07300 Mauves +33(0)475 081496

See also St-Joseph.

The meticulous Gripa family have for years made one of the most stylish still St-Pérays, wines that have good structure and tight textures that need a little time to unfurl. Son Fabrice is adamant about this side of their wines: "You must leave St-Péray alone when young," he says. "It gains minerality and complexity with age, and our 1992 and 1996 are showing very well in 2004."

They work two hectares, 80 per cent Marsanne across seven plots and 20 per cent Roussanne across four plots—the result of several hundred years of ownership. The main site is *Rabatte*, a subset of the *Amour de Dieu lieu-dit* near their cousins the Daronas' cellars: a hill with degraded rock, a pH of 7.5, and soil a little heavier than at St-Joseph. "We find the acidity in our St-Péray higher than in our white St-

Joseph," observes Bernard, the father; "there's more limestone at St-Péray." The vines are wire trained, and while the topsoil is sanded granite, the soil below is deep.

"The white vines, especially the Marsanne, prefer sites of better water retention like *Rabatte*, so we plant them on that heavier soil," comments Bernard Gripa. "The soil there handled the 2003 drought better than our sites at St-Joseph," he adds. The oldest vines on *Rabatte* were planted by Bernard's father in the 1940s and 1950s.

The regular wine, 80 per cent Marsanne and 20 per cent Roussanne, has moved away from a purely vat fermentation. One-third is oak handled, 20 per cent of which is new, while the rest is vinified in steel before a May bottling, the malo done. There is a pleasing dry pebbly flavour in the regular wine: gently weighted, it is good both as an aperitif and with cold meat and salad dishes.

The special Les Figuiers, first made in 1997 from largely *Rabatte* crop, is made from 60 per cent Roussanne from the 1960s and 40 per cent Marsanne dating from the 1940s and 1950s, vinified apart. It has recently moved to an all-cask fermentation—using 20 per cent new oak each year in rotation. It is raised on its lees until September after the harvest, with a decreased incidence of *bâtonnage*; this is mostly undertaken between the primary fermentation and the end of the malolactic.

Fabrice says this lees stirring is "to help the wine to integrate with its wood," but Bernard may have had a say here, wanting to retain some of the wine's freshness. As he says, "the fine lees lose their benefit after a certain time." Figuiers has more chewiness and grip than the regular and is a more complex wine with good length in its best years like 2001 and 2003.

"We find the Roussanne has vivacity and finesse, but lacks a touch on the midpalate," states Bernard Gripa. "The Marsanne can supply that, which is why we mix the two rather than just make a pure Roussanne."

A bottle of the 1996, made with the then full Marsanne-Roussanne mix, showed in 2001 how these wines can progress from a discreet start. There was a mineral aspect, something of a salty tang, with the dried fruit aromas. The palate held *tarte tatin* (apple pie) and cooked white-fruit, plummy flavours. This was likely to live towards 2007. Likewise, the 1987 showed very well and was still discreet when tried in 1993. Note that both these were lesser red wine vintages, with a higher degree of acidity in the wines.

"We reckon there are often two stages of ageing with St-Péray," comments Bernard Gripa. "After four years, you get the first oxidative stage, and another one after eight years. The wine comes and goes and, at these ages, can be a little dumb. But there's no doubting their ability to live, provided they are from a mix of Marsanne and Roussanne."

There are 5,000 bottles of both wines. The classic usually carries a rounded bouquet, and the palate a typical sense of white fruit and almond fringing. The finish is clean, very much in the house style. It is a wine to drink within seven or eight years.

The *Figuiers* is one of the most serious wines of St-Péray; the mix of 40-odd-year-old Marsanne and Roussanne vines is a trump card and stands up well to its oaking. It is a wine I would always prefer to drink in its second, more varied phase, around the age of five or six. With age it acquires an extra salty, clear-cut dimension, and can live for at least 12 years in the best vintages. The 2003, for instance, is quietly rich with a tangy flourish on the end, a wine of genuine structure.

ST-PÉRAY

    2003 ★★★★
    2001 ★★
    2000 ★★

ST-PÉRAY LES FIGUIERS

    2003 ★★★★
    2002 ★★
    2001 ★★★
    2000 ★★

PAUL JABOULET AÎNÉ

Les Jalets RN 7 26600 La Roche-de-Glun
+33(0)475 846893

See also Condrieu, Cornas, Côte-Rôtie, Crozes-Hermitage, Hermitage, St-Joseph.

To move into St-Péray, Jaboulet entered into a novel accord with the local Town Hall. They had started work on the wine's revival through the pure *négociant* route, buying in crop. The next step was a 99-year agreement with the Town Hall, in partnership with the Growers Union. The idea was to construct a showcase vineyard, so technicians from the Chamber of Agriculture were called in to select the most healthy 50-to-60-year-old plants to give cuttings for the vineyard. Their inspections were both visual and technical, in the search for the best-quality stock.

An unusual attribute of this vineyard is the use of as many as 200 different Marsanne varieties. Philippe Jaboulet explained: "We are not using clones. The plan is to conserve the Marsanne species, so these cuttings have been taken from a wide range of different sources. We have tapped into old plots in the Ardèche and the Drôme, either side of the Rhône here, but also Savoie and Switzerland near the Alps and Châteauneuf-du-Pape. The plants were multiplied by a nurseryman, and the plants' development is being tracked statistically." If the quality is anything like the largely Marsanne wine from Cave Imesch at L'Infer in Switzerland, then so much the better.

The vineyard lies off the main St-Péray hillside on a site called locally *Pouzat*, but officially *Vichouère*, in the corridor running west off the Rhône valley. It has meant rebuilding terraces long since crumbled, and planting on a mix of slippery, sandy granite with patches of clay. The vineyard is east-southeast facing, with Stéphan Chaboud working the neighbouring, more westerly-facing plot. At 250 metres, there is some evening freshness here, helpful for acidity. Started in 2000, the vineyard had reached 1.27 ha on its third leaf. It is 80 per cent Marsanne and 20 per cent Roussanne.

Their first wine was produced in 1999, 90 hl of pure Marsanne. This was bought-in crop, while their own vineyard grew up. Now the formula for their 400 hl a year is a mix of their own crop, purchased wine, and purchased grapes.

Jaboulet have two suppliers, whose Marsanne vines date from between the 1920s and the 1940s. The Jaboulet vineyard provides the 10 per cent Roussanne present in the final wine, which is called "Les Sauvagères," a local patois name for Marsanne. Vinifier Jacques Jaboulet confesses to being a Roussanne supporter at St-Péray, and concurs with Stéphan Chaboud about its prime facet when he says, "I like it better here than the Marsanne because it brings more richness."

Following the current house style for their whites, the grapes are picked at extreme ripeness. Vinification is in stainless steel, with the young wine receiving three to six months in casks that are two to four years old. The lees are stirred, and the wine is bottled with its malolactic completed. The average production has now settled down around 50,000 bottles.

Stylistically, this wine is a one-off if compared to the regular makers of St-Péray, such as Gripa, Lionnet, and Clape. All their wines are less oaked, more restrained, and longer-lived. Efforts appear to have been made to cut the incidence of oak, a positive step, with the wine gaining in finesse. The 2002 showed signs of greater core freshness than usual, as well. There were spiced elements, and decent length on the wine, which can run towards 2007. The 2003 was solid all the way through, in the big-wine style, and can show well between 2007 and 2009.

ST-PÉRAY LES SAUVAGÈRES

    2003 ★★★
    2002 ★★
    2001 ★★
    2000 ★★
    1999 ★★

JACQUES LEMENICIER

Quartier des Grays 07130 Cornas +33(0)475 810057

    See also Cornas.

Better known for his Cornas, Jacques Lemenicier works just over two hectares of St-Péray across five sites. On the heavier clay soils, he has 0.6 hectare of Marsanne on *Marcale* and 0.3 hectare on *Tourtousse*, with a half Marsanne, half Roussanne 0.2 hectare on the lower, clay end of *Plantier*, beside the N86 border with Cornas.

The rest of his vineyards are all 50 per cent Marsanne, 50 per cent Roussanne; on the road to St-Romain-de-Lerps, he has 0.4 ha, and on *Chante-Luzet*'s granite he has 0.6 ha of vines planted in 2002–03.

Most years (but not the weak 2002), Jacques makes two still wines, one of them oaked. His Cuvée Traditionelle, made from 90 per cent Marsanne, 10 per cent Roussanne, is vat fermented at 16°C and bottled in June, the malo done. The Cuvée Boisée is half new, half one-year-old-cask cask fermented at around 20°C, and stays in oak, with lees stirring, until the end of July, with an August bottling, malo done.

The Traditionelle can be a big, full wine in a good vintage, with a chewy, near tannic side to it. The *Boisée* shows toasted, cooked fruit aromas, and some fruit along pineapple lines. It is suitable with food—served chilled with fish soup, or warmer with veal or poultry. Its Marsanne style is mature and carries the traditional, slightly oxidative tones of the variety.

ST-PÉRAY TRADITIONELLE

    2001 ★★★

ST-PÉRAY CUVÉE BOISÉE

    2002 ★★
    2001 ★★

DOMAINES MICHEL, JOHANN ET CHRYSTELLE

52 Grande Rue 07130 Cornas +33(0)475 405643

    See also Cornas.

Johann Michel and his sister Chrystelle from Cornas cleared and planted a site on *Les Petites Blâches* in 2004. There was a vineyard here in the 1960s, but it fell into abandonment. They have up to a hectare available, and the mix is 50-50 Marsanne-Roussanne.

DOMAINE DE ROCHEPERTUIS

48 rue Pied la Vigne 07130 Cornas +33(0)475 403601

See also Cornas.

Genial, frequently smiling Jean Lionnet has always made very consistent, sound-quality St-Péray. He works 2.5 hectares in *métayage*, meaning that the vineyard owner retains one-third (sent to Tain's Co-opérative) and Lionnet two-thirds of the crop he brings in.

Much of his vineyard is nice and mature, knocking on for 50 years. A plot of 0.7 hectare, mostly Marsanne, is low down on *Les Combes*, where there is granite, on the border with Cornas. The rest of his vineyard is on the clay-limestone *Quartier Le Mois de Mai*, one of the gulleys that run off the road to Le Puy; there is a plot of Roussanne planted in the mid-1990s here. Overall, he reckons his wine is made from 20 per cent Roussanne, 80 per cent Marsanne.

From the early 1990s M. Lionnet has partly destalked his crop and left the juice to decant for 36 to 48 hours. Fermentation is started in stainless steel, and he then vinifies 40 to 50 per cent of his wine in new oak, the rest in fibreglass vats. He has long liked low temperatures for fermentation, bringing a fresh immediacy to his wines. The vat wine ferments as low as 13° or 14°C, and the casks at natural cellar levels of about 16°C. The malolactic is done, with up to 10,000 bottles produced in May.

M. Lionnet's low-temperature style works especially well when the crop is rich and ripe, as in 1999 and 2003. He likes to pick late: "I need that ripeness to handle the oak," he says; "the more matter in the grapes, the more I use new casks. I don't want the oak to overrun the wine, but for me it brings roundness and fat into the wine." He also maintains that the wood lends St-Péray a greater life.

The wine of a grower like Lionnet is marked by its exposure to new oak, but these are wines that drink well over two to six years and that can provide good value for money over that time. They are generally full, with flashes of exotic fruits that settle over time as the elements integrate.

ST-PÉRAY

2003	★★
2002	★★
2001	★★★
2000	★★
1999	★★★

CAVE DE TAIN L'HERMITAGE

22 route de Larnage 26600 Tain l'Hermitage
+33(0)475 082087

See also Cornas, Crozes-Hermitage, Hermitage, St-Joseph.

Numerically, this is the dominant force at St-Péray, accounting for nearly half the wine. The Co-opérative's 10 grape growers cultivate just over 30 of the *appellation's* 64 hectares and account for 1,200 to 1,300 hl of wine. Twenty-five to 30 per cent of this is sparkling and is mostly sold locally. The Cave is doing its best to coax this *appellation* along and has also bought a 14-hectare plot on *Rougeole*, a *lieu-dit* that straddles Cornas and St-Péray and that is being cleared and gradually planted.

Just two of the 30 hectares are Roussanne. Because of its low mortality, the Marsanne is often several decades old. Holdings range across sites such as the esteemed *Hongrie, Putiers, Barras,* and *Beylesse* (the limestone site beside the N86 at the southern entrance to St-Péray).

There are eight hectares split between *Le Grand Plantier* and the adjacent *Pincenas*; the former—a lower-slope site—is marked by loose decomposed topsoil, with the granite one to two metres down. The latter is also sandy granite, but the soil is a little deeper. There are also

5.5 ha on the loess soil of *Petit Champ*, which is close to the Crussol limestone influence.

After pressing and a 12-hour decantation, 30 per cent of the still juice is fermented in new to two-year-old casks, 30 per cent of them American oak. "We use the American oak because we feel it brings roundness and so balances the freshness of a typical St-Péray," explains winemaker Alain Bourgeois. He also raises the new-oak content if the crop is very ripe, as it was in 2001.

Wood was first used in 1998, its wine blended with the stainless steel–fermented wine in September for bottling around December, 15 months after the harvest. The malolactic can be completed, but was blocked in the low-acidity year of 2003, for instance. The wine can serve as a refined aperitif in a year like 2002, or accompany fish dishes in a fuller vintage like 2003. The use of oak appears to have been successful recently, and the wines can show fine over six to eight years.

ST-PÉRAY

2002 ★★★

2001 *Nobles Rives* ★

TARDIEU-LAURENT

Route de Cucuron 84160 Lourmarin +33(0)490 688025

See also Condrieu, Cornas, Côte-Rôtie, Crozes-Hermitage, Hermitage, St-Joseph.
Tardieu-Laurent stepped into St-Péray for the first time in 2002, but then could not find a satisfactory source in 2003 and 2004. They resumed in 2005, working with 50 per cent Marsanne dating from the early 1900s and 50 per cent Roussanne from the mid-1970s, growing on the clay-limestone, granite-flecked site of *La Côte*. The wine is fermented and raised for 12 months, half in new oak, half in one-year oak.

ST-PÉRAY

2002 ★★

JEAN-LOUIS ET FRANÇOISE THIERS

Le Biguet 07130 Toulaud +33(0)475 404244

See also Cornas.

"I'm not a man who likes towns," says Jean-Louis Thiers, a slim, active, balding man in his later 40s. He lives alongside five other families in a tiny hamlet called Le Biguet south of St-Péray. Twenty years ago the drive here was still an adventure, but new housing has gradually encroached along the way, until the final stages, when the land rises to 175 metres and a couple of farms indicate the end of the line.

Barley and corn are grown here, along with apricots, and higher up there are chestnuts and goats grazing on hills topped with dense, rather brooding woodland. With the *Navarou* stream beside his house, the panorama here is simple, peaceful, and potentially lonely.

"It gets dry in summer here," says Jean-Louis, "because the soil is schist and sandy granite, which drains very fast." A small part of the St-Péray *appellation* is in the *commune* of Toulaud, and Jean-Louis works three hectares there and another two hectares within St-Péray.

Biguet is the Toulaud site, a sloping Marsanne-only vineyard around his hamlet that Jean-Louis planted in 1975 through to 1980. He also works 1.5 ha on *Le Mois de Mai* (1950s, 1980s) and 0.5 ha on *Les Champs* (1988), under the Crussol hill. Both are pure Marsanne and reflect the Crussol influence with limestone mixed into the clay.

Jean-Louis' father, André, ran much more of a mixed farm—he always made a little wine, but would class himself as more of an *agriculteur*, a well-known face at six in the morning at the Mauves fruit market, selling his cherries and apricots. Jean-Louis still works around two hectares of Bergeron apricots that are picked in mid-July. There was also dairy and beef during the 1970s, and the move to wine came when Jean-Louis attended wine school in Beaune for two years.

"We used to sell everything to the local merchant Cotte-Vergne, but in 1980 I felt that rising prices gave us the chance to do our own bottling ourselves," he recalls. Now everything is bottled except for the part of his crop that is sold to Les Vins de Vienne.

Jean-Louis has remained faithful to the sparkling St-Péray, which continues to form 75 per cent of his wine. The crop for this is harvested eight to 10 days ahead of the still-wine grapes—the 2003 date, the earliest on record, was 19 August. After a classic white wine preparation—pressing and stainless steel fermentation that ends with the malo being blocked for freshness—the *tirage* of 21 gm of sugar per litre is added over three days in April.

While the ruling is for at least a nine-month raising for this second fermentation, Jean-Louis allows double that. He never gives his 20,000 bottles a vintage, to allow a consistent style, so any finished wine contains a mix of ages if necessary. His *remuage* process lasts for four weeks in the *pupitre* racks and is followed by the disgorging.

"Sparkling St-Péray must never be heavy," says Jean-Louis, "because it's an aperitif wine." He recommends drinking it in the two to three years following its *dégorgement*. His wine shows apple and flan aromas with some white fruit, pear-peach flavours. Although it is full, there is some delicacy, reflecting the house style.

There are about 5,000 bottles of still wine; since 2000 he has cooled the must and fermented in a mix of enamel and steel at 18° to 20°C. It is bottled in May with the malo usually done. It can be rich with an elegant trimming in a vintage like 2001, with spice/ mineral aspects, and the appealing salty tang on the bouquet. The 2003, too, carried local feel, with a correct Marsanne bitter side on the finish. The Biguet St-Péray is good value for money and carries no traces of modern pretension.

Jean-Louis also makes a simple Syrah country wine from a half-hectare vineyard nearby.

ST-PÉRAY

2003 ★★★
2002 ★★
2001 ★★★
2000 ★★
1999 ★★★

SPARKLING ST-PÉRAY

NONVINTAGE (largely the 2000) ★★

Export 10 per cent (1) Belgium, (2) Great Britain, (3) Japan

DOMAINE DU TUNNEL

20 rue de la République 07130 St-Péray
+33(0)475 800466

See also Cornas, St-Joseph.

Stéphane Robert works 1.5 ha of St-Péray, the first new entrant to the village in many years, one who uses the old *négociant* Vérilhac cellars. He started as a complete outsider—his father an insurance executive; his birthplace Besançon, famous as a setting in Stendhal's tragic *Le Rouge et Le Noir*; and his early upbringing in that Jura region not far from Switzerland.

In 1982, when he was 12, Stéphane came to live in St-Péray, following his father's posting to cover the south of France sales region from there. "My first interest was agriculture," he states. "When I started to study it, I came into contact with the sons of *viticulteurs*—families who were making *vin de pays* in the south of the Ardèche, for instance, nothing fancy. There was also a Jura grower who was a friend of my father's."

So after wine studies at Orange and Mâcon, he commenced work with Jean-Louis Grippat of St-Joseph and Hermitage in 1993, while building up a vineyard that he could work on himself. A quarter hectare of Cornas was rented in 1994, and plots were bought at St-Péray and St-Joseph. Finally Stéphane left Grippat and set up the Domaine du Tunnel, named after a railway tunnel near his *Barras* site between St-Péray and Vernoux, in 1996.

He's a tall, dark-haired man with a calm air and generous smile. He also listens well, a good sign for the future. Traces of his hard work are evident high up on the steep Cornas slope of *Sauman*, where he has grubbed out very tricky granite terrain. He is trying to do the job properly, using stakes on the hills, and a near-traditional density of 8,000 plants per hectare on *Sauman*. His Roussanne is a *massale sélection* from old vinestock from Savoie.

FIGURE 40 Welcome new blood at St-Péray and a busy vineyard constructor at Cornas, Stéphane Robert is his family's first *vigneron*. (Author's collection)

Now he handles over six hectares between the three *appellations*, while his fair and slim wife, Sandrine, keeps busy running the office, dealing with shop clients, and joining in with the harvest. Common sense seems to be the order of the day here—outside yeasts were tried on the white grapes but have been abandoned—and there is no new-oak overlay. "I'm achieving naturally low yields of 25 to 30 hl/ha at Tournon, for example, simply because the vines are old," he comments, adding that he vinifies by *lieu-dit* and assembles only just before bottling.

His main St-Péray site is *Barras*, where he has planted everything—0.7 ha of Roussanne (1998, 1999, 2002) and 0.2 ha of Marsanne (1994). This is a rotted granite (*gore*) vineyard—the decomposition of the rock greater than at Cornas. Stéphane finds its Roussanne wine very aromatic and refined. *Barras* lies in a small valley tucked away off the Rhône corridor, and in best Robert tradition, the vineyard is quite high up at 250 metres, above *Hongrie*. This compares to his vines high up on *Sauman* as well.

Stéphane also rents 0.3 ha from Marcel Juge on *Grand Plantier*; this is the low, quite flat end of the loose-granite slope. There is a mix of Marsanne and Roussanne, the wine from here being rich due to the vines dating from at least the 1950s.

In 1993 Stéphane bought a small 0.2 ha terraced plot on *Les Grandes Blâches* at a point on the slope where the higher granite starts to meet the lower clay. This Marsanne vineyard dates from 1930 and used to provide the wine made by René Balthazar and sold to local *négociants*. The wine from here is rich.

His fourth plot is *L'Arzalier*, a vineyard that is to all intents and purposes in the village. Called the *Coteaux de Gaillard* by the locals, this is a precocious spot of 80-to-100-year-old Marsanne, with clay soil covered in some alluvial Rhône stones. The wine from here is full-bodied.

He makes three wines, a 100 per cent Marsanne regular; a Marsanne-Roussanne Prestige that varies between 60 to 80 per cent Marsanne, 40 to 20 per cent Roussanne; and a pure Roussanne that he launched in 2003. The Prestige is from *Grandes Blâches*, *L'Arzalier*, and a little *Grand Plantier*, the Roussanne coming from young vines on *Barras*.

After destemming and pressing, there is a 24-hour decantation at 12°C, and the fermentation starts off in stainless steel. At a specific gravity of 1040, about halfway, Stéphane draws off the Roussanne intended for the Prestige and continues its fermentation in new oak, with lees stirring, until its malo is finished early in the new year. The rest of the Prestige—its Marsanne—is raised in five-year-old casks.

The classic and the Prestige are bottled, malos done, in August. The Roussanne—of which there are just 500 bottles—is only vat treated, its fermentation at 16° to 18°C. There is no lees stirring, and it is bottled, the malo done, in June.

There is a pleasing elegance within his wines, as if he has eschewed the full-on, somewhat overcorpulent style that newcomers to this *appellation*'s wines have favoured. The classic St-Péray showed a true local feel in 2003, mixing dried fruits with a mineral tang on the finish. A wine of finesse, it was one of the few that could double as an aperitif wine that year.

The Prestige showed good depth and promising structure in 2003 and 2001, the length in both wines sound. It parades an overt fullness, by design. It is a wine that should become a leading light in years to come, providing Stéphane does not seek too much scale in it.

There is one low-key wine here, a rosé *vin de pays de l'Ardèche* L'Argonier made from his young St-Joseph and Cornas Syrah vines.

ST-PÉRAY CLASSIC

2003 ★ ★ ★ ★
2002 ★ ★

ST-PÉRAY CUVÉE PRESTIGE

2003 ★ ★ (★)
2002 ★
2001 ★ ★

Export 30 per cent (1) Great Britain, (2) Belgium, (3) Canada

LES VINS DE VIENNE

Bas Seyssuel 38200 Seyssuel +33(0)474 850452

See also Condrieu, Cornas, Côte-Rôtie, Crozes-Hermitage, Hermitage, St-Joseph.
The trio of Yves Cuilleron, Pierre Gaillard, and François Villard moved into St-Péray in order to complete their northern Rhône portfolio. "We are all keen on a relaunch," states Yves Cuilleron, best known for his rich, unctuous Condrieus. "We started with about 5,500 bottles of the 1999, buying the crop from two people and vinifying it in the modern way we like."

The classic wine is pure Marsanne and is 40 per cent oak, 60 per cent vat fermented and raised. The oak portion receives *bâtonnage*, or lees stirring. There are 7,000 bottles.

The main wine, Les Bialères, formerly 90 per cent Marsanne, 10 per cent Roussanne, has moved to a 40 per cent Roussanne content. It is made from crop bought from the southern, Toulaud sector, where the wines are inclined to be full. This is vinified and raised in one-third new oak, two-thirds oak one to two years old. It is left on its lees, with stirring until bottling over a year after the harvest.

"While the Marsanne fruit expression is good at St-Péray, we are after more Roussanne in the mix, so have raised this from 10 to 40 per cent. We consider this to be proper table wine,

not an aperitif, so it can go well with fish in rich sauces," comments Yves Cuilleron.

There are 3,000 bottles of this high-priced wine. It is aimed at the French restaurant trade and the export market, notably the United States and Japan, plus France.

The Bialères mixes buttery and mineral textures, with overtly ripe crop used to enhance the fatness. Because of the oaking, there are some standard exotic fruit aromas—pineapple, plus orange marmalade—in evidence.

ST-PÉRAY LES BIALÈRES

2002 ★ ★ (★)
2000 ★ ★
1999 ★ ★

ALAIN VOGE

4 Impasse de l'Equerre 07130 Cornas +33(0)475 403204

See also Cornas.
The busy Alain Voge is best known for his reliable and authentic Cornas. But with over five hectares of Marsanne, his is also one of the prominent private domaines at St-Péray. He makes two still wines, both oaked, and has dropped his vat-only wine "because I want to concentrate on working with the combination of Marsanne and oak."

His vineyards have grown up with him—now at least 40 years old. They are also in prime locations: *La Côte, Les Plantiers,* and *Hongrie,* the last near Chaboud. *La Côte* (1930s) has a full south exposure and finer-than-usual soil—some chalk and decomposed granite on top of a clay subsoil. His vines on *Les Plantiers* (1960s) are high up, where there is largely decomposed granite, right on the limit between Cornas and St-Péray, facing south-southeast. *Hongrie* (1930s) is made up of fine clay, with a little limestone in it. Behind the village, its vineyards face south-southeast.

Of his three sites, his favourite is *La Côte*: "It gives wines that age well, with a lot of matter in them, plus some minerality," he states. "I consider them to be fresh and also notable for their length."

Alain was early into wood fermentation—since the mid-1980s—with an experimental move towards American oak casks as well. He has now dropped them, stating that "their active effect didn't last more than three years, about half that of the French oak casks."

His Cuvée Boisée is fermented half in new, half in two-year-old casks, and raised with lees stirring until bottling in June, the malo done. There appears to be more conflict than necessary in this wine, and it is one whose best, most integrated moment is hard to predict—it's certainly worth waiting at least four years. The deep-seated fullness of the 2003 raised its standard.

The Fleur de Crussol is a little different, its preparation appealing to Alain's restless quest to experiment. It is taken from *La Côte*; 10 to 20 per cent is fermented in vat and is encouraged to complete its malolactic fermentation by being held at 20° to 22°C; this is then added in with the oak wine, half of which is new, and the lees are stirred until the end of March, when the outside temperature becomes too much for it to continue usefully. The wine is then raised for another year until bottling 18 months after the harvest.

Fleur de Crussol is promising and, in a very good vintage like 2001, has enough core juice to handle the oak. The mix of fleshy matter with a good potent kick results in an accomplished, surprisingly pretty wine that can live for eight to 12 years. Rather like the Tunnel Prestige wine, this is one to remember for the years to come.

Alain has always made more still than sparkling St-Péray, and continues to reduce the latter, now only 10 per cent of his white. It is vinified in his Cornas cellars, but by law the *tirage*, or taking on of the bubbles, must be done at St-Péray. Maybe that explains why he is now the only Cornas grower making sparkling St-Péray nowadays. He says its buyers are all French.

Of his still wine 15 to 20 per cent is exported, mainly to the United States, Great Britain, and Denmark.

ST-PÉRAY CUVÉE BOISÉE

2003 ★★
2002 ★
2001 ★
2000 ★

ST-PÉRAY FLEUR DE CRUSSOL

2002 ★★
2001 ★★★
2000 ★★

ST-PÉRAY VINTAGES

Earlier exceptional vintages: 1962, 1961, 1957, 1955

1964 Excellent.

1965 Poor.

1966 Good.

1967 Excellent.

1968 Mediocre.

1969 Excellent. Fruity and aromatic wines.

1970 Mediocre. The crop was very large and the wines unbalanced.

1971 Excellent. Very well balanced wines.

1972 Very good. Extra acidity helped the wines.

1973 Good. Better for the sparkling wines than the still wines.

1974 Fair. A vintage that varied from grower to grower.

1975 Fair. A tiny harvest, best suited for sparkling wine.

1976 Very good. Full wines. The excellent Clape could run to 2005.

1977 Mediocre.

1978 Very good.

1979 Good, especially for the sparkling wines.

1980 Quite good. A large crop; medium-weight wines.

1981 Fair. Better for the sparkling wines.

1982 Fair. Lack of freshness a problem.

1983 Good. Solid wines.

1984 Fair. Rot a problem. Better for the sparkling wines.

1985 Good, better still wines than sparklers. Low acidity.

1986 Quite good. A large crop.

1987 Quite good. The largest crop of the last 30 years.

1988 Good. Good matter and balance in the wines.

1989 Very good. Firm wines, due to the drought.

★★ Dom Fauterie

1990 Good. Full, rounded wines, sometimes low in acidity.

★★ A. Clape, J. Lionnet

1991 Excellent. Great balance—ripe wines that lived well. Drink.

★★★★★ J-L & F. Thiers

★★ J. Lionnet

1992 Fair. After three dry years, June–July rains brought mildew. Then came August hail, so growers like J. Lionnet made under 15 hl/ha, A. Clape none at all. Early-drinking wines.

★ B. Gripa

1993 Quite good. After a quite fine August, the grapes were ripe by the first week of September, before the 10 September–onward rains. Drink them up.

1994 Good. The wines held sound depth, with enough acidity to live for 10 to 12 years.

★★ J. Lionnet

1995 Good. The year was dry but never very hot after late July. Bouts of rain at harvest time. Full wines, with some elegance.

★ A. Clape

1996 Very good, a typical rainy year when the whites outdo the local reds. The weather brought freshness and long life to the wines. Ripening came with a late August–September run of fine weather. There is a good mineral tang in the wines. They can live for 12-plus years.

★★★ B. Gripa

1997 Fair to good. Fat, plump wines lacking the usual amount of mineral cut. There were nice floral, honeysuckle-style bouquets when young. The wines were pleasant but could finish short. The best managed some freshness and were nicely persistent on the finish. Drink them up.

★★ Cave de Tain Les Nobles Rives, Voge Mélodie William

1998 Good. A tiny crop of only 1,493 hl, against 2,560 hl in 1997 and 2,730 hl in 1999. Frost was the main problem.

The style is mixed. Bouquets on the oaked wines can show exotic fruit aromas—pineapple, tropical fruits. The traditional wines were tight and chewy when young. Others hold some *gras* on the palate, then narrow down to a tangy ending. Overall, the wines contain a fair amount of extract. Some are a bit short.

★★ Chaboud Marsanne

★ Cave de Tain Les Nobles Rives, A. Clape, B. Gripa, J. Lionnet, Voge Cuvée Boisée

1999 Very good. Usually later harvesters like Lionnet picked from an early 18 September. Quantity and quality were good.

The wines are full and often buttery right through the palate. Aromas are well defined, with good mineral aspects and length. A year for the noninterventionists—nature did the job very well. These juicy wines will live well—up to 10 years.

★★★ Chapoutier, J. Lionnet, J-L & F. Thiers

★★ Chaboud Assemblage, Delas, Dom Fauterie, Vins de Vienne Bialères

★ A. Clape, P. Jaboulet

2000 Quite good. The vintage was made late on, after an indifferent June and July, which lacked sunshine. August was very hot, with not a lot of rain. The crop was ripe, and acidity levels were low.

The aromas are gently buttered, with a typical, quite full lime tart aspect on the palate and some pebbly endings. Textures are fat, and these splendid wines will mostly be good to drink by around 2006–07.

The regular cuvées are markedly softer than the obvious oaked versions, which can move along fine, provided the oak use has not been clumsy.

★★ A. Clape, Delas, B. Gripa regular/Figuiers, J. Lionnet, J-L & F. Thiers, Voge Fleur de Crussol

★ Chapoutier, P. Jaboulet, Vins de Vienne Bialères, Voge Cuvée Boisée

2001 Very good. A year when the late summer decided the outcome, and one where growers were not under pressure to harvest at speed. A good vintage for the Roussanne, with clear acidities in the wines.

"I find the wines a lot richer than the 2000s," commented Jean-Louis Thiers; "they have more balance—it's a classic year for graceful wines that can age for at least 10 years."

The wines possess a very good core, and the mature Marsanne vines lend them a full breadth of flavour. Bernard Gripa spoke of their finesse and sound length. They are chewy and well constructed and certainly represent good value for money. The only real risk with age is whether the wines will round out or remain angular, as some have been in their youth. Given their usually clear, pretty fruit and clean finishes, I would back them to run on to a multilayered middle age. They are well worth laying down.

★★★ Chapoutier, A. Clape, Colombo Belle de Mai, G. Darona, Dom Fauterie, B. Gripa Figuiers, J. Lemenicier Traditionelle, J. Lionnet, J-L & F. Thiers, Voge Fleur de Crussol

★★ Chaboud Roussanne/Marsanne/ Assemblage/Boisée, B. Gripa,

P. Jaboulet, J. Lemenicier Boisée, Dom du Tunnel Prestige

★ Cave de Tain Nobles Rives, Delas, Voge Cuvée Boisée

2002 Fair. A rot-affected vintage thanks to the poor summer and the late rain. It's uneven because some growers picked too soon and compensated by chaptalising their wines, while the wise ones waited up until 10 September. The latter have produced wines that are restrained and hold gentle fruit.

The rot advanced from mid-August on, which meant throwing away a lot of grapes. "The key this year was to drop a lot of crop, and then harvest late," stated Sylvain Bernard; "the degree came good if you waited." Jean-Louis Thiers agreed, and added that by waiting, "it was possible to achieve Marsanne of 13° without difficulty." There was a lot of rain at the end of August, which returned around 20 September, so harvesting had to be completed in a narrow time span.

The wines have some body, but several lack true core and can be propped up by the chaptalisation or by clumsy cellar work involving extraction and oak. The best are quite expressive, with some freshness and style, and likely to drink well in their second phase, around 2006 on. Textures are often soft, with a mild plumpness.

★★★ Cave de Tain

★★(★) Vins de Vienne Bialères

★★ Clape, G. Darona classic/ Jardin des Faures, Dom Fauterie (varies to nil), B. Gripa Figuiers, P. Jaboulet, J. Lemenicier Cuvée Boisée, Tardieu-Laurent, J-L & F. Thiers, Dom du Tunnel, Voge Fleur de Crussol

★ Chaboud Roussanne, Chapoutier, Dom du Tunnel Prestige, J. Lionnet, Voge Cuvée Boisée

2003 Good to very good. Crop for the sparkling wine was picked from 15 August; the still-wine harvest started a week earlier than usual, 1 September. Growers like J. Lionnet (40 per cent) and Darona (55 per cent) lost a lot of crop due to April frost and two hailstorms four days apart in the first week of August. Sylvain Bernard lost 80 per cent: "We were hit on 13 and 24 July from two directions, but please note the remaining 20 per cent is fantastic!"

The clay soil areas naturally handled the drought best, and some of the wines have higher-than-ever alcohol levels, around 14.5°. "It's the first year I've ever had such rich St-Péray," commented Jean Lionnet. "I've no reference point for wine like this."

The Marsanne, often grown in clay, resisted the drought better than the Roussanne, but there are two problems—low acidity levels, which encouraged some growers to bottle earlier than usual, and rather heated, overly firm textures, the result of the brewing of the grapes in the vineyards. At its best, the Marsanne influence is stronger than usual, and its dominance gives the wines every chance of ticking over and living off their power for eight to 10 years.

The best are full, concentrated wines that will always do well with food rather than taken as an aperitif. Aromas can be more floral than usual, and on the palate of some Marsannes, there is a more honeyed flavour than is the custom. The wines will show well around 2006–07.

★ ★ ★ ★   B. Gripa classic/Figuiers, Dom du Tunnel

★ ★ ★   Les Champs Libres, Chapoutier, Clape, J-L & F. Thiers

★ ★ (★)   Dom du Tunnel Prestige

★ ★   Chaboud Marsanne, J. Lionnet, Voge Cuvée Boisée

★   Dom Fauterie

2004 Very good. The year followed the regional pattern of dry weather, and some stress for the vines until mid-August. There was some incidence of oïdium between June and August, but this year frost and hail did not feature. Ten to 15 millimetres (about half an inch) of rain fell in early August, then in midmonth there were three storms of about 30 to 50 mm (1.2–2 inches) each. This set the vines off on the final stage of their cycle, with dry weather and drying wind helping to ward off rot. The crop was healthy when harvested in the second half of September, with Chaboud reporting his still wine grapes as holding 12° to 12.5°. "There was no need to be in a hurry to harvest," reported Auguste Clape, whose domaine brought in crop at almost 14°.

The wines have aromas that are fresh and interesting. The fruit is direct and clean, and there is a typical sprinkling of minerality towards the finish. The wines will show well early on, and can run for six to eight years.

9

Regional Wines and *Vins de Pays*

CÔTES DU RHÔNE BRÉZÈME

"If I hadn't got the Guigal business going, I would have bought the hillside of Brézème," was what the founder Étienne Guigal said about the choice ahead of him when still working on the Vidal-Fleury payroll. To this day, this remains a mystery vineyard, its small size keeping it confidential.

A little over 10 miles south of Valence lies this final spur to the northern Rhône. Brézème is a gentle hillside and plateau on the east side of the Rhône, at a point where the valley is very broad. It is a land of fruit, sunflowers, and maize, the old N7 road winding through it, fronted by forgotten buildings daubed in old advertisements.

It is an old vineyard that has experienced ups and downs over the last 200 years. In 1781 it was recorded under the name "Coteaux du Livron," the nearby town, and more detail was provided in a work of 1805 that specifically cited the hill of Brézème, which, "although small, produced wines recognised for their finesse and quality" (Yann Stéphan, *Recherches Historiques sur le Vignoble de Brézème*).

The main site was called *Piquet*, supported by a château, and a Syrah-based red wine.

Phylloxera knocked out the vineyard, and with fruit and cereal production easily manageable around on the open lands, the vine did not reappear in any scale. Before the First World War, the vineyard was still at one-third of its prephylloxera size.

Wine was a sideline here, although in 1937 *appellation* Côtes du Rhône status was granted, applying to a notional area of 58 hectares. One reference to this epoch survives, with an Haut Brézème *blanc* 1937 called "Flower Hill Cuvée d'Or" sold to Britain, bottled by one Paul Rigaud.

The reality was that there were hardly any producers, but the seeds of a revival were laid when Jean-Marie Lombard's father came to work here in 1941. His main activity was fruit, but son Jean-Marie took over a farm in 1972 that included one-quarter of a hectare of Côtes du Rhône Syrah vines. At the time, there was one other grower with three-quarters of a hectare, which had been the status quo since the 1950s.

"We grew mainly peaches then—it's more apricots now," he states; "I decided to replant the vineyard in 1973–74 and see what could be done. I sold the crop to the Co-opérative at Loriol-sur-Drôme. The real encouragement to

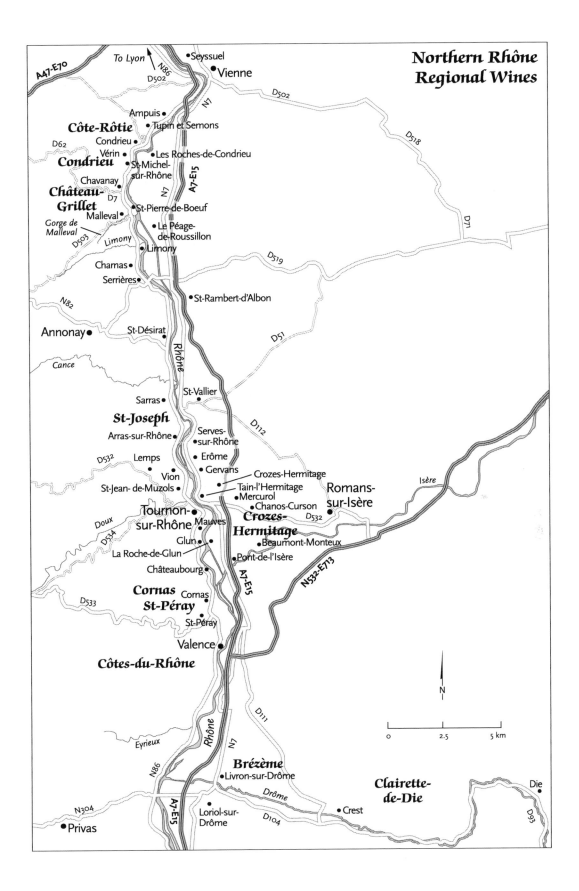

Northern Rhône Regional Wines

A47-E70

To Lyon
N86
D502
• Seyssuel
N7
• Vienne
D502
D518

• Ampuis
• Tupin et Semons

Côte-Rôtie
D62
• Condrieu
• Vérin • Les Roches-de-Condrieu
Condrieu
N7
• St-Michel-sur-Rhône
A7-E15
• Chavanay
D7
Château-Grillet
D71
• Malleval • St-Pierre-de-Boeuf
Gorge de Malleval
• Le Péage-de-Roussillon
D503
Limony
• Limony
• Charnas
D519
• Serrières
N82
• St-Rambert-d'Albon

Annonay •
• St-Désirat
D51
Cance

Rhône

• Sarras
• St-Vallier
St-Joseph
D112
• Arras-sur-Rhône
• Serves-sur-Rhône
D532
• Lemps
• Erôme
• Vion
• Gervans
• St-Jean- de-Muzols
Crozes-Hermitage
Isère
• Tain-l'Hermitage
• Mercurol
Romans-sur-Isère
Doux
Tournon-sur-Rhône
• Mauves
• Chanos-Curson
D532
D534
Crozes-Hermitage
• Glun
• Beaumont-Monteux
La Roche-de-Glun
• Pont-de-l'Isère
N532-E713
• Châteaubourg
A7-E15
Cornas
• Cornas
St-Péray
D533
• St-Péray
• **Valence**

Côtes-du-Rhône

N
D111
Rhône
N7
Eyrieux
N86
Brézème
• Livron-sur-Drôme
A7-E15
Drôme
Clairette-de-Die
• Die
N304
• Loriol-sur-Drôme
D104
• Crest
D93
• **Privas**

0   2.5   5 km

extend the vineyard came in 1979–80 when Gérard Chave from Hermitage came along with Michel Chabran, the restaurateur. They found the wine good, and said I should vinify it myself. That's what I did, starting in 1981. M. Chave gave me advice, as did Pierre Gonon of St-Joseph, while I took a wine course at the Suze-la-Rousse School."

M. Lombard was the first man to make forward moves here, and as word spread, some other growers outside the Loriol Co-opérative started up. There are now 26 hectares, planted mostly with Syrah and a little Marsanne and Viognier for the white Brézème. M. Lombard himself grows 4.5 hectares of Syrah and 0.90 ha of white vines, 80 per cent Marsanne and 20 per cent Viognier.

There are two soils; on the plateau of *Piquet* facing the open Rhône valley, at a level of around 145 metres, there are pale-brown alluvial stones on a red clay-iron subsoil. "The soil is quite rich and has more clay than near the Isère River and Crozes further north, where there is more gravel," says M. Lombard. This is where his 30-year-old vines grow.

The other area involves the Drôme River valley more than the Rhône. These are steeper slopes of marl-limestone, with quite deep subsoil that possesses more clay than on the plateau—"good soil for finesse in the whites," says M. Lombard. The slopes face full south, and are about 300 metres from the River Drôme. Unlike the *Piquet* vineyards, these are naturally sheltered from the prevailing north wind. Plantation density here for M. Lombard is 0.90 by 1.0 metre, as opposed to the wire-trained 2.5 metre by 1 metre of the more workable plateau, where M. Lombard turns the soil.

There are now six independent growers, and three cultivators who send their crop to the Loriol Co-opérative. Total production runs at around 1,000 hl of red and under 100 hl of white wine. "We consider ourselves at the bottom of the northern Rhône here," is M. Lombard's statement on the Syrah and its suitability. "The Grenache doesn't work well here—some

of the Co-opérateurs planted it, but it doesn't ripen well every year."

Brézème Côtes du Rhône *rouge* is a meaty, robust wine, its tannins pretty forceful. It carries an earthy appeal that makes it suitable drinking with casserole food and, when older—five or six years or more—game. M. Lombard counsels grilled beef and lamb when the wine is young.

The white expresses the almond, slightly bitter side of the Marsanne and is sound, the mix with Viognier lighting up the midpalate richness. There is also a pure Roussanne produced by the *négociant* Éric Texier.

Some of the growers also make *vin de pays de la Drôme* from varieties like Merlot and Syrah.

JEAN-MARIE LOMBARD
26250 Livron-sur-Drôme +33(0)475 616490

M. Lombard largely destalks his Syrah, and for part of the old vines' crop performs daily pumping-overs and cap punching. He relies only on natural yeasts. The classic red vinification lasts 12 to 15 days, the Vieilles Vignes 18 days in concrete vats.

The classic Grand Chêne, named after the old oak tree in his first vineyard, receives eight to 10 months in five-to-seven-year-old casks. The Vieilles Vignes Eugène de Monicault (7,000 bottles), made from the Syrah planted in 1974, is aged for a year in three-to-five-year-old casks. The wines are not fined, but are lightly filtered.

The white Brézème, 80 per cent Marsanne (1989), 20 per cent Viognier (1989, 1995), is also sold as Côtes du Rhône. M. Lombard is happy to pick the Marsanne quite late, when it may carry 13° or more. After a cool decantation at 12°C, the juice is fermented in two-year-old casks and receives a lees stirring. It is bottled in April, the malo completed.

BRÉZÈME CUVÉE DU GRAND CHÊNE ROUGE
2003 ★(★)

BRÉZÈME CUVÉE EUGÈNE DE MONICAULT ROUGE
2001 ★★

BRÉZÈME BLANC

2003 ★★

Export 10 per cent (1) Great Britain

ÉRIC TEXIER

Bel Air 69380 Charnay +33 (0)472 542618

See also Condrieu, Hermitage, St-Joseph.
Éric Texier is a Bordelais who was seduced by
the east of France. His studies were at Lyon,
where he met his wife, Laurence, and where he
discovered wine.

His subject was engineering, but from 1993
he pursued wine studies on the side, working
with Jean-Marie Guffens in the Mâconnais,
before finally making wine his only business in
1999, when he was 36 years old. His first vinification was in 1996, and the first wine was produced in 1998.

The wine is vinified at Brézème and raised at
his cellars in the Beaujolais from February
onwards. There are two reds, both cask raised.
The classic is raised in casks over three years
old; the Vieilles Vignes, called "Domaine de Pergault" since 2003, receives 13 months in one-to-
two-year-old casks.

Unusually, the white Brézème is pure Roussanne—cask fermented, it is bottled in the
spring. "The Roussanne vineyard is fascinating," observes M. Texier; "with just the one
grower in the 1950s, everything was very arti-
sanal. He used *sélection massale* and hand grafted
all his young vines, and I'm sure there's a mix of
other varieties in with the Roussanne. Contacts
in those days here were more with the Isère
than the Rhône valley region, and it's probable
that there are Savoyard vines present, too." The
Roussanne plot averages perhaps 40 years
in age.

The Roussanne is fermented in 33 to 50 per
cent new oak, the difference in one-to-two-year-
old casks. It is bottled 12 to 14 months after the
harvest, having remained on its lees until then.
"But I don't stir the lees in the very ripe, big
years, says M. Texier; "I'm seeking the mineral,
sometimes salty side of the Roussanne, not a

very overripe style of wine." The oak presence
on this Roussanne can be marked, which bring
into play tropical fruit aromas and spiced white
fruits.

The standard of his Brézèmes is sound. The
cask sample of the Domaine de Pergault 2003
was hearty, a ripe fruit wine with earthy textures, best to drink from 2006.

In the northern Rhône, M. Texier also offers
red and white St-Joseph, a red Crozes-Hermitage, red and white Hermitage, Côte-Rôtie,
and two Condrieus.

Export 60 per cent (1) USA, (2) Japan,
(3) Canada

Other Producers

YVES MENGIN
12 rue Basse du Verger 26270 Loriol-sur-Drôme
+33(0)475 856001

DOMAINE DE LA ROLIÈRE
Château de la Rolière 26250 Livron-sur-Drôme
+33(0)475 616004

VIGNOBLE BREYSEME
Les Bérangères 26400 Allex +33(0)475 626667

CHÂTILLON-EN-DIOIS

This has always been an *appellation* that makes
me feel uneasy about the whole system, whereby
local influence contrived to promote an inferior
region to full *appellation* status. The wine-producing region of Châtillon-en-Diois is very
restricted, with vineyards covering no more than
60 hectares, a slight fall since the early 1990s. It
is centred on 13 *communes* and hamlets to the
south and east of Die, and most of the wine—
red, white, and rosé—is made by the Cave
Co-opérative of Die.

In 1974 Châtillon-en-Diois was promoted
from VDQS (Vin Délimité de Qualité Superi-
eure) status to full *appellation contrôlée*. As a

result the red and rosé wines have to be up to three-quarters composed of the Gamay Noir grape, with a maximum of one-quarter coming from the Syrah and Pinot Noir grape varieties. The white wines also bear a Burgundian slant and must be made from the Aligoté and Chardonnay grapes, of which around 10 hectares have been planted.

The principal vine-growing communities are Châtillon-en-Diois, Menglon, St-Roman, and Laval d'Aix. All are in the beautiful, wild, mountainous countryside that follows the river Drôme as it runs south of Die and on to the most southerly wine-producing village, Poyols, which is 19 kilometres (12 miles) from Die. The soils are gravelly, with some limestone, and the vineyards high up, at 600 to 750 metres, meaning that good ripening is not guaranteed.

Every year a total of about 240,000 litres of wine is made, two-thirds red, one-third white. Just two private domaines, Cornillon and Maupas, stand outside the Co-opérative. The wines undergo a brief vinification, with a rapid fermentation and bottling early in the new year. Unfortunately, the mainstream wines are all thoroughly nondescript, the red in particular failing to live up to its noble Gamay-Syrah-Pinot "breeding." Often very pale, weak, and watery, it possesses little intrinsic charm or character; it merely remains a point of amazement that such a wine can have been considered worthy, on its own, of qualifying for the highest accolade in French viticulture—full *appellation* status.

CLAIRETTE DE DIE

About 65 kilometres (40 miles) southeast of Valence, the old town of Die nestles easily into the first Alpine mountain ranges. Beside it, the river Drôme runs on a steady course down towards the Rhône, and the green, poplar-lined Drôme Valley exactly traces the 1,390 hectares of vineyards of Clairette de Die, along with its fellow *appellations* the Crémant-de-Die and Coteaux-de-Die.

These extend for 56 kilometres (35 miles) on either bank, all the way from Aouste, three kilometres (two miles) east of Crest, up to Luc-en-Diois, 19 kilometres (12 miles) southeast of Die. Aouste stands at 160 metres, Luc around 550 metres. The vineyard area has risen from 1,200 hectares in the early 1990s.

As the vineyards go east, the countryside becomes steadily more Alpine, and after Crest is truly spectacular on a fine day. The land rises all the while, and little chalets that stand away from the sleepy villages are dwarfed by the high mountains looming over them. Sudden patches of luscious, dark-green grass are cropped by grazing goats, and at the foot of the hillsides tight little clumps of pine trees add extra colour to the vivid scene. The hills acquire a magical, mysterious hue, and the fresh air livens even a jaded soul.

Wine has probably been made in the region of Die for almost 2,000 years, since there was a lengthy reference to a local wine in Chapter 9 of Pliny's *Natural History* (c. AD 77). Here Pliny criticized the 13 known varieties of sweet wine then found in Greece and the Roman Empire, some of them, he said, being products of art and not of Nature, while others were guilty of being given mixtures devised to make them simulate honey. One, known as honey wine, even received salt and honey in its must, thereby producing a very rough flavour.

The star wine for Pliny was the natural form of "Aigleucos," or sweet wine then being made by the Vocontii people. "In order to make it," Pliny wrote, "they keep the grape hanging on the tree for a considerable time, taking care to twist the stalk." When Pliny was writing, the capital town of the Vocontii was called Dea Augusta; today it is Die.

The wine Pliny referred to is sparkling today but is still made by natural methods, with no addition of any substance or liquid to give it its bubbles. It goes by the title of Clairette de Die "Tradition" or "Méthode Dioise Ancestrale." Officially given *appellation* status in 1942, it is made from partly fermented must that when bottled in early December, must contain at least

55 gm of fermentable sugar per litre. At that stage its specific gravity is around 1030 to 1035.

After a minimum of four months in bottle, during which it continues to ferment and so acquires its bubbles, there must be at least 35 gm of residual sugar present. The 10-week process of turning the bottles, or *remuage*, is now done by hand in *pupitres*, or wooden holders, by very few growers—the domaines J-C Raspail at Saillans and Raymond Bec at Aurel, notably. Otherwise machines are used. The Tradition is then filtered, given a cork, and put on sale. It is a low-degree wine—only 7.5 to 8. Tradition forms around 75 per cent of all the bottled wine at Clairette de Die.

Meanwhile another sparkling wine has been made since the early 1960s, along formal Champagne lines with the addition of a liqueur for the in-bottle fermentation; this sells as Clairette de Die Brut. Unlike the Tradition, which is made from at least 75 per cent Muscat, plus Clairette, grapes, the Brut comes solely from the low-scented Clairette grape and has less individual style about it. It must be cellared for at least nine months in bottle after the addition of the liqueur, and is sold as a clean, dry wine. What is called the Method of Transfer is used prior to its release on sale—the bottles are not turned and disgorged, but are instead emptied, filtered to remove the particles, and then refilled—one quick action only.

The third style is the Crémant de Die, whereby sparkling wine is made from a still-wine base; the second fermentation is done in the bottle with the addition of a *liqueur de tirage* and Champagne yeasts at some date after 1 January, following the harvest. Introduced in 1993, the Crémant is another vehicle for the Clairette, with by law a minimum of 55 per cent demanded, the rest composed of at least 10 per cent Aligoté and 5 to 10 per cent Muscat.

In reality the Clairette content runs at 75 to 80 per cent. The Crémant has to be cellared for at least a year before release, its residual sugar level set at a maximum of 15 gm per litre. Some producers make vat- and cask-raised Crémants, the cask ageing lasting around six months in young or partly new oak, followed by storage in bottle of three or four years. The storage is thought to encourage a gain in finesse and aroma for the Clairette.

There is a little still dry white wine of quite reasonable quality, made from the Clairette. Now termed "Coteaux de Die," this was Die's main wine until 1926, when the first sparkling wine experiments took place. This effectively forms the base wine for the Crémant, with little bottled on its own. It is regarded as an aperitif or hors d'oeuvre wine.

Growers also work with Chardonnay in places, and this provides a *vin de pays de la Drôme* that is very respectable in the hands of domaines like J-C Raspail.

Because the wine region is so long, as it traces the wandering route of the Drôme River, the composition of the vineyards is very varied. The Tradition wines from different ends of the *appellation* can also vary very widely in character. The most common soil elements are limestone and clay, while the rock soil base becomes progressively harder the nearer one is to Die and the high Alps.

This seems to suit the Muscat more than the Clairette, but in recent years it has been the latter whose plantation has increased. This is because it is a hardier vine than the Muscat, and because the more neutral-tasting Brut wine is easier to sell than the Tradition. The Muscat used at Die is the *blanc, petits grains* variety, which is also found at Beaumes-de-Venise and which gives the Tradition its strong, flowery bouquet.

Vineyard elevation varies as well along the route of the *appellation*. Saillans in the west stands at around 270 metres, the next village of Vercheny is at 350 metres, and Die itself is at 415 metres. Some of the highest vineyards are beyond Die, at St-Roman and Aix-en-Diois, over 600 metres, with a ripening date usually about two weeks behind Saillans. These villages are regarded by some as being inappropriate for good-quality Die, with good grape maturity one year in five. Obviously a vintage like 2003 was successful, while the 2004 vintage was welcomed by growers because of its good balance, a late-September flourish allowing an extended ripening season.

Around the esteemed *commune* of Saillans, the soil is varied enough to suit the making of different wines. The deep clay-chalk areas suit the Muscat. The clay played a leading, helpful role in the high heat of 2003, for instance. On the half slopes, the soil is stony—very small white stones mixed in with sand and just a little clay. Erosion is an issue after heavy rain due to soil slippage, and drainage is swift. The cooler, lighter stony soil suits the Clairette, which always ripens behind the Muscat; this late start to its year means that frost is not a main threat to it.

Downstream from Saillans there is more schist, that is considered suitable for the Muscat, while upstream, towards villages like Barsac and Aurel, there is marl or chalky clay. Aurel and Barsac share the same flank of a hill at around 400 metres, the latter's vineyards turned more northwesterly, so receiving the setting sun.

Near the Drôme River can be found alluvial stones, the river having traced a path a little south of today's course. North of the river, at Vercheny and Sainte-Croix, there are areas of *grès*, or small stones, as the altitude climbs. Vercheny is a well-regarded *commune*, seen by some as the core of the *appellation*, with southeast-facing clay-chalk hillsides.

Harvesting commences in late September and can continue nearly into November. The region is cooler than the Rhône Valley, with rain often arriving from the Ardèche to the west but stopping around Crest.

Legislation on the Tradition has been tightened to ensure that it is a primarily Muscat wine; in the past, the two largest houses of the Cave Co-opérative of Die and Buffardel Frères were using only half and one-quarter Muscat, respectively, and the wine's character was being neutered. It was left to small domaines to persist with the three-quarters Muscat recipe.

The difference in style between the Tradition and the Brut is startling. The Brut is usually paler and much less scented and fully flavoured; because of this it is simpler to drink than the Tradition, and a well-chilled bottle can disappear very rapidly on a warm summer's afternoon.

The Tradition is the more interesting wine, however. It is often called locally "Demi-Sec," and this description gives some idea of its basic style. Slightly lime-yellow coloured, it is a wine of appealing richness and roundness. Aromas are broad, with lavender and spice elements. Fruit flavours resemble pears, apricots, or gooseberries; a good bottle has a long, just very partly sweet aftertaste. It is not a quaffing wine like the Brut, but a glass or two is ideal as the introduction to a good meal. One or two family domaines also make pure Muscat Tradition as well as the three-quarters–Muscat edition.

In serving the wine, growers recommend that the Tradition be poured at 2° to 4°C, with care not to let the glasses be too warm. The Crémant can be served nearer 4° to 6°C as an aperitif or with patisserie. The Tradition is considered good with *foie gras*, and of course is the King of Wines for Desserts, a wide variety suitable, except for dark, rich chocolate. *Pain brioche* is also put forward by growers.

Production of Clairette de Die has increased steadily over the years to over 10.5 million bottles, and one of the main reasons for this is the impetus given to the region by one of its two Cave Co-opératives, the ambitious Cave de Die. Founded in 1951, this has a well-organized international sales network, a factor that has encouraged farmers to plant more vines. The second Co-opérative is that of the Union des Jeunes Viticulteurs Récoltants at Vercheny. In all there are 37 private domaines.

The second-largest producer at Die for some years was Buffardel Frères. This has disappeared following its purchase by the enormous Cellier des Dauphins in the southern Rhône at Tulette. Another grouping, although a much looser organization than the Co-opérative, is CUMA, which consists of about 20 small farmer-*vignerons* who created a mutual grouping in 1967 to share the equipment needed for *dégorgement* on the Crémant.

SELECTED DOMAINES

DOMAINE ACHARD-VINCENT
Le Village 26150 Sainte-Croix +33(0)475 212073

This is a good 11-hectare domaine run by Jean-Pierre Achard, and has been organic since 1978.

CAROD FRÈRES
D93 26340 Vercheny +33(0)475 217377

Many of the growers sell their wine to the *négociant* trade, and the second-largest producer these days is Carod Frères, who have over 40 hectares of vine that are worked organically. Based at Vercheny, their wines are fair.

CAVE DE DIE
avenue de la Clairette 26150 Die +33(0)475 223031

Like many Co-opératives, the Cave de Die has set aside a flagship 18-hectare vineyard for special cultivation—in this case, organic. The Cave's commercial name is "Jaillance," and includes the ownership of a Crémant de Bordeaux. Die Crémant and Tradition wines are produced.

DOMAINE DIDIER CORNILLON
26410 St-Roman +33(0)475 218179

Another important private domaine is that of Didier Cornillon, who works 15 hectares at St-Roman. He also works with red and white Châtillon-en-Diois, the former in three versions —pure Syrah, pure Gamay, and a Pinot Noir, Syrah, and Gamay mix. His wines are reliable.

DOMAINE JACQUES FAURE
D93 26340 Vercheny +33(0)475 217222

A 23-hectare domaine, with sound Tradition.

DOMAINE DES MUTTES
Le Village 26340 Aurel +33(0)475 217181

A third generation producer, Raymond Bec works seven hectares at Aurel. His vineyards stand at 400 metres, and he has a high proportion of Muscat—4 ha, with 3 ha of Clairette.

His Tradition is 80 per cent Muscat, 20 per cent Clairette, and his Cuvée Alexandra is pure Muscat, vinified as a Tradition as well. There is also a Crémant.

DOMAINE ALAIN POULET
Quartier La Chapelle 26150 Pontaix +33(0)475 217280

This is a well-regarded domaine, with consistent wines. M. Poulet is fourth generation, and works 10 hectares of Muscat and five hectares of Clairette on the clay-chalk hillsides above Pontaix. A Tradition and a Crémant are produced, the former composed of 80 per cent Muscat, 20 per cent Clairette. It is a wine with nutty flavours and fair grip on the palate.

DOMAINE JEAN-CLAUDE RASPAIL
Route de Die 26340 Saillans +33(0)475 215599

One of the leading family domaines is that of Jean-Claude Raspail at Saillans. Like several of the growers at Die, he worked in a Champagne house, that of de Castellane, to gain experience and looks back on "40 years of *remuage!*"

His organic Domaine de la Mûre covers 15 hectares, including one hectare of Chardonnay planted in 1990. His oldest Muscat dates from the 1950s, and he makes the full range of wines, including a pure Muscat Tradition. His go-ahead son Frédéric and daughter-in-law Anouck work with him, with practices largely time-honoured: half the vineyard is composed of *sélection massale* vines, half is clones, and harvesting is done by hand, unlike most domaines these days.

With Jean-Claude having hit 60 in 2004, Frédéric is more and more in the limelight. His schooling included studies in Champagne and work at the House of Bollinger, and investment in new cellar equipment indicates the long view being taken here. The wines are very sound, with highlights the appealing *fut de chêne Brut*, which shows well after four to seven years, and an appealing Chardonnay *vin de pays* that receives six months in cask. The Tradition is a rich, pretty wine.

UNION DES JEUNES VITICULTEURS RÉCOLTANTS
route de Die 26340 Vercheny +33(0)475 217088

In existence since the 1970s, the name carries a degree of dry mirth since some of the founders have retired. It groups eight associates who cover different tasks from vineyard care to sales, and their 62 hectares are centred on the prime sites of Vercheny. Eighty per cent is Muscat (oldest 55 years, average under 20 years), and 20 per cent Clairette (average 25 years).

The Tradition never receives a vintage, always being a mix of the previous two years. It is often a ★ to ★★ wine, and achieves the group's stated policy of "balance and rich aromas of the Muscat with the finesse and vivacity of the Clairette."

DOMAINE JEAN-CLAUDE VINCENT
26150 Barsac +33(0)475 217143

Sound quality.

VIN DE PAYS

The northern Rhône's best-known *vin de pays* category is the Collines Rhodaniennes, with able growers at Côte-Rôtie producing this from a mix of young Côte-Rôtie vines and from Syrah outside the *appellation* zone. It also applies to the recent vineyard at Seyssuel, north of Vienne.

With an allowance of up to 85 hl/ha in yield, and a minimum degree of 10.5 for the reds, these are not usually intended to be wines of structure and poise. However, in the hands of the Bonnefond brothers, Patrick Jasmin and Stéphane Ogier, they are well fruited and capable of living and developing over six to eight years. The whites are often Viognier, with an allowance of 90 hl/ha in yield and minimum degree of 10.

There are other *vins de pays* that can be called after the name of their *département* of origin, bringing in the *vin de pays de la Drôme, Isère*, and *Ardèche*. There is also a thriving "Coteaux de l'Ardèche" category from the hills along the west bank of the Rhône.

CHASSE-SUR-RHÔNE

M. CHAPOUTIER
18 ave Dr Paul Durand 26600 Tain l'Hermitage
+33(0)475 082865

The Chapoutier version of the Seyssuel experiment, involving the recreation of vineyards north of Côte-Rôtie, is at Chasse-sur-Rhône. This is one mile north of Seyssuel on the same east bank of the Rhône.

After clearing, planting started in 2003 and 2004—2.5 hectares of Syrah, including 2 to 3 per cent Viognier, with a further half hectare to come. The soil is typical of this spot—schist—and the slope faces south-southwest at a height of 80 to 100 metres. The vines lie further from the Rhône than those at Seyssuel, around half a kilometre.

In 2004 the producers of these northern *vins de pays des Collines Rhodaniennes* formed the Terra de Viena association—the first union to promote and defend the Syrah and Viognier wines from these old hillsides.

SEYSSUEL

The revived vineyards of Seyssuel, north of Côte-Rôtie, represent an old epoch, when the east bank of the Rhône also grew Syrah at this level of the river. Their hillsides had lain uncultivated for some decades until a trio of local growers got together to relaunch them. Yves Cuilleron, best known for his full-bodied Condrieu, is one of them. The other two are the lively, flamboyant François Villard—also best known for Condrieu—and the more reserved, grounded Pierre Gaillard—his reputation founded around good Condrieu, St-Joseph, and Côte-Rôtie.

"Every time I drove up to Lyon, I saw this slope and thought it would be a good place for a vineyard," recalls Yves. The hillsides were overgrown with acacias and oaks and brush, but Yves mentioned it to François Villard one day as they drove north past it. As the crow flies, the hill is under four miles away from the northern vineyards of Côte-Rôtie, but by land there is a sweeping curve in the Rhône to negotiate at

Vienne, as the river runs first southeast, then southwest as it heads south.

Pierre Gaillard had also read about this old vineyard, perhaps the one that produced the *vinum picatum*, or pitch wine, of Vienne in Roman times—written of by Pliny, among others. Vienne's seven hills were a draw for the Romans, and it was a very important centre for them.

In 1995 the trio went to inspect the site and discovered that it extended to over 100 hectares. "We recuperated 25 hectares," states Yves, "dealing with six people for that. Not everyone wanted to sell, so we started by renting, and now own three hectares."

The first vines were planted in 1996, a Syrah vineyard suited to the stony schist found in the northern part of Côte-Rôtie on sites like *La Landonne*. One hectare of Viognier was planted in 1998 on soil deeper than the schist—there are outcrops of clay and also sand in the higher reaches. The incline runs at 50° on the full slopes, so the vines are stake-trained there, wire-trained lower down. The schist congregates around the mid- to lower slopes, with mica and quartz mixed in. The hard rock lies around 80 cm (32 in.) below the topsoil.

By 2004 the vineyard ran to 11 hectares planted—10 Syrah, one Viognier. The first red wine, the Sotanum (pure Syrah), was made in 1998, the first white, Taburnum (Viognier) in 2000. They are both *vins de pays des Collines Rhodaniennes*.

The location reflects the geological shifts of some millions of years ago. "The hill is at the same altitude as Côte-Rôtie; in effect the Rhône drove between the two hills," comments Yves. Ripening is assured in this microclimate. Barbary figs grow, as well as a protected flower called the Gagée du Rocher, more often found in the south; lavender appears in sudden patches. The hill faces south-southwest.

It is an arid, dry spot, but the freshness is noticeable compared to standing at river level at Côte-Rôtie. Two hillsides stand either side of the Rhône here, and their funnel channels the wind. Clear skies and clean air are common,

but there is more often a south than a north wind. "This compacts the grapes and is important to help us achieve the extreme ripeness that is our policy," states Denis Chorot, the manager. As a result, the Syrah is not picked much before early October. The Viognier is also left until early to mid-October to secure a level of around 40 per cent botrytis that is deemed desirable.

Around the rather dishevelled old warehouse that is used for the cellars, the country has the air of mixed cultivation—pine trees, vegetables, ponies in a field—and doesn't necessarily lead thoughts to the vine. The vineyard stands behind the old château of the Bishops of Vienne, which was abandoned in the sixteenth century; its legacy is a series of walls that add a break against the wind.

"One in three days is windy here—you can see white horses on the river's water," comments Serge Mathias, the head of the vineyard. "The narrowness of the valley here is what accelerates the wind—once you go south of Vienne, the valley is four or five times broader and disperses the wind more."

It's said that before phylloxera, there were 200 hectares of vineyards at Seyssuel. Subsequently, the vineyard never regained enough momentum to consider an attempt at *appellation* status, and in the 1950s and 1960s, was largely planted with hybrid vines that supplied the *bistrots* of Vienne. When hybrids were outlawed, the few local growers took out their vines and turned the land over to cherry and almond trees.

The hill rises to around 250 metres, but the nights are quite warm, with frost less of an issue than on the other bank of the river, further south. The bottom of the vineyard stands right above the railway line and the autoroute south. The air is filled with the firm noise of the cars, punctuated by the occasional throb of barges taking their loads south.

Seven of the best-quality clones were chosen by the Vins de Vienne team for the Syrah, as well as some Sérine taken from old vines at Côte-Rôtie. Density runs from 6,000 to 8,000 plants a hectare. Grass has been planted across one-quarter of the area to limit erosion and to cut the vigour of the vines.

Seyssuel Domaines

STÉPHANE OGIER
3 chemin du Bac 69420 Ampuis +33(0)475 561075

This keen young grower from Côte-Rôtie planted 0.6 hectare of Syrah in 2002 on a site just under the château called *Le Vieux Château*. He is looking to make keeping wines, encouraged by the schist soil that he knows from his home vineyard.

By 2004 a total of 0.8 ha was planted, with production running around 2,000 bottles. Cask raising is for 18 to 24 months, one-third of the oak new.

ANTHONY PARET
Place de l'Eglise 42520 Saint-Pierre-de-Boeuf +33(0)474 871209

The son of Alain Paret, well known for his Condrieu and his links with actor Gérard Depardieu, Anthony Paret planted 2.5 hectares near the ruined château in 1999. The vineyard is composed of 90 per cent Sérine—the old *massale* vinestock of the Syrah—and 10 per cent Viognier.

Called "Serinaë," the first wine appeared in 2002. It is raised in a mix of 600- and 225-litre new casks for 14 to 16 months. About 8,000 bottles are produced.

LES VIGNOBLES DE SEYSSUEL
Pangon 07340 Limony +33(0)475 340288

This was the second grouping to move into Seyssuel, spearheaded by the busy Louis Chèze, best known for his St-Joseph and his Condrieu. Louis got together with three neighbours, notably the cousins Laurent and Pascal Marthouret and his own brother-in-law. Louis is friendly with the Vins de Vienne trio and was tempted to join in on the project.

The first planting in 2001 was 1.3 hectares. The slope vineyards are south of the ruined château, and the total plantation, a mix of clone and *massale* Syrah, has reached six hectares, with the first wine vinified chez Louis in 2003.

LES VINS DE VIENNE
Bas Seyssuel 38200 Seyssuel +33(0)474 850452

The Cuilleron-Gaillard-Villard trio make 25,000 bottles of all-Syrah Sotanum, a figure that will rise to 40,000 when all the planted 11 hectares are in production. It is 20 to 50 per cent destemmed, cooled for a week at 10°C, and then fermented for eight to 10 days in steel. Vinification runs over four weeks, and raising lasts 17 to 18 months in new-oak casks. Because there is only one racking in that period, there can be some reductive smells (stinky ones) that can be allayed by decanting the wine.

There has been no fining or filtration since 2000. A curiosity appears: the floral elements that can be found on the bouquet reflect more the granite than the schist areas of Côte-Rôtie—the opposite of what one would anticipate. The labels bear the Roman numerals for the vintage, so 2000 is MM.

Early signs are that this is an attractive wine, founded on elegance. As the vineyard matures, it can only gain in depth and complexity.

After a cold decantation, the Viognier juice for the Taburnum juice is vinified in new casks and receives a 19-month raising; the lees are stirred once a week for the first nine months, then once every six weeks for the rest of the *élevage*. Around 5,000 bottles are made.

The trio also set up their merchant business, Les Vins de Vienne, on their Seyssuel premises. This deals in all the *appellations* of the northern Rhône. All the white wines are produced from the purchase of crop, and the reds are a mix of purchased grapes and young wine. Southern Rhône wines like Châteauneuf-du-Pape, Gigondas, Vacqueyras, and Côtes du Rhône also feature.

VIN DE PAYS DES COLLINES RHODANIENNES SOTANUM

2003 (CASK) ★★ Tight bouquet, black fruits/herbs. Firm, cooked fruit, chewy tannins, has *gras*. Length OK. Can become stylish. 2011–13.

2002 (CASKS) ★ Gentle bouquet, some dark fruit. Upright, clear-cut fruit on palate. More on fruit than content. Esp 2005–07.

2001 ★★ Floral effects on nose, suave black fruit, some depth. Refined texture, decent black fruit, lasts quietly and well. Some final tar, licorice. Oak touch on end. 2010–13.

2000 ★★ Very ripe, almost rotting fruit, black olives, some reduction on nose. Gentle, delicate flavour, quietly rounded. Lacks flesh in midpalate. Oak aspects on finish. Has character. 2010–12.

1998 ★ Soaking black fruit, after four years, shows animal/second phase on bouquet. Oily attack, cooked red fruits. Funky wine, but tendency to dry from the oak. Licorice finale.

VIN DE PAYS DES COLLINES RHODANIENNES TABURNUM

2002 ★ Some exotic fruit aromas, rich underlay. Midweight palate, a quiet year. No great richness. Just about fair.

2001 ★★ Overt orange marmalade/mandarin, brown sugar bouquet. Stewed pear flavour, quince, peach fruit on finish, with licorice. Has some interesting nuances. 20 per cent botrytis.

2000 ★ Yellow *robe*; exotic, pineapple oak/vanilla bouquet. Quite rich texture (10 per cent botrytis). Overt, modern style. Lacks depth towards finish. Nice enough, just a bit heavy.

Selected Vin de Pays Domaines

Growers who make sensibly priced and sound quality *vins de pays* include:

BAROU, EMMANUEL, AT ST-JOSEPH His Syrah Cuvée des Vernes is raised for a year in four-to-five-year-old casks. Also a sound Viognier.

DOMAINE LA BATELLERIE AT CROZES-HERMITAGE A charming red *vin de pays des Collines Rho-daniennes*, 60 per cent Syrah, 40 per cent Gamay

BECHERAS, ÉTIENNE, AT ST-JOSEPH A hearty Viognier

BONNEFOND, PATRICK AND CHRISTOPHE, AT CÔTE-RÔTIE Their Syrah *vin de pays des Collines Rho-daniennes* receives a year in two-to-three-year-old casks.

CHAMBEYRON, BERNARD, AT CÔTE-RÔTIE AND CONDRIEU A vat-only Viognier *des Collines Rho-daniennes* is worth seeking out.

DOMAINE DU CHÂTEAU VIEUX AT ST-JOSEPH Very good value Syrah *vin de pays de la Drôme*, especially the cask-raised Vieille Vigne from older vines

DOMAINE DU CHÊNE AT ST-JOSEPH A good Syrah

CUILLERON, YVES, AT CONDRIEU, CÔTE-RÔTIE, AND ST-JOSEPH Yves' touch with whites is excellent, as witnessed by his very good Viognier *des Collines Rhodaniennes*. Also a good Marsanne.

DELAS Sell a good Viognier *vin de pays de la Drôme* from time to time

DURAND, JOËL AND ERIC, AT ST-JOSEPH AND COR-NAS Their good Syrah *vin de pays de l'Ardèche* is made when they have young Cornas or St-Joseph vines.

FINON, PIERRE, AT ST-JOSEPH Sound Viognier and Syrah, good Marsanne from the *Collines Rhodaniennes*

GÉRIN, JEAN-MICHEL, AT CÔTE-RÔTIE His Syrah is a mix of any young Côte-Rôtie vines with Syrah aged between three and 50 years growing outside the *appellation*. It is aged for a year in young oak.

THE JAMET BROTHERS AT CÔTE-RÔTIE Make a very good Syrah *des Collines Rhodaniennes*—a mix of 1970s Syrah from the plateau near their cellars and young Côte-Rôte vine fruit when the latter is available

JAMET, PASCAL, AT ST-JOSEPH He picks his Viognier in mid- to late October, with some botrytis; the wine is rich and pleasant.

JASMIN, PATRICK, AT CÔTE-RÔTIE His delightful Syrah is from young vine fruit.

MARSANNE, JEAN-CLAUDE, AT ST-JOSEPH Uncluttered, agreeable Syrah

DOMAINE MORTIER AT ST-JOSEPH A peppery Syrah that can live for around five years

OGIER, STÉPHANE, AT CÔTE-RÔTIE His La Rosine is from Semons and receives 14 months in young to two-year-old oak.

DOMAINE DES REMIZIÈRES AT CROZES-HERMITAGE Produces a sound Viognier that can either be nonvintage or carry a specific year.

DOMAINE ROMANEAUX-DESTEZET AT ST-JOSEPH An interesting *vin de pays de l'Ardèche* Roussanne-Viognier mix, cask fermented

CAVE DE TAIN AT HERMITAGE An agreeable, early-bottled Marsanne

DOMAINE GEORGES VERNAY AT CONDRIEU Especially a very accomplished Viognier called *Pied de Samson*

VILLARD, FRANÇOIS, AT CONDRIEU AND ST-JOSEPH Ever tinkering with new ideas, François Villard produced a special 2003 Syrah called "Grande grue glacée en 2003," a very respectable wine that mixed richness with some sound grip.

Appendix One

Appellation Contrôlée Laws

	BASE YIELD (HL/HA)	BUFFER YIELD (HL/HA)	MINIMUM (MAXIMUM) DEGREE	
Château-Grillet White wine only allowed	37	41	11	
Condrieu White wine only allowed	37	41	11	
Cornas Red wine only allowed	40	46	10.5	(13.5)
Côte-Rôtie Red wine only allowed	40	46	10	
Crozes-Hermitage Red and white wines allowed	45[*]	50	10	
Hermitage Red and white wines allowed	40	46	10.5 11 14	(reds) (whites) (*vin de paille*)
St-Joseph Red and white wines allowed	40	46	10	
St-Péray Sparkling and still white wines only allowed	45	52	10 9	(still) (sparkling)

[*]Up from 40 hl/ha in early 1990s

NOTE: 1 hectolitre (hl) per hectare (ha) = approximately 54 bottles per acre. The base yield, or *rendement de base*, can be exceeded on demand from growers if the crop has been particularly abundant (and, one hopes, of decent uniform quality). The percentage allowed is negotiable, but the table lists the usual buffer, or top, quantity in a full year like 2004. It is called the *rendement butoir*.

Appendix Two

*Total Area (in hectares) under Vine Cultivation,
1971–2005 (selected years)*

	1971	1973	1982	1989	1991	1995	2000	2003	2004	2005
Château- Grillet	1.7	2.7*	3		3.8	3.8	3.8	3.8	3.8	3.8
Condrieu	12	12	14	40	55	93	105	113	117	124
Cornas	53	75	67	65	74	89	91	101	104	102
Côte-Rôtie	70	72	102	135	154	192	205	217	225	230
Crozes- Hermitage	454	550	903	1,050	1,006	1,128	1,252	1,325	1,325	1,311
Hermitage	123	123	123	125	117	117	135	131	131	135
St-Joseph	97	122	245	540	606	796	922	975	989	1,005
St-Péray	56	56	48	65	62	52	55	64	61	52

*1977

Appendix Three

Declaration of the Crop, 1970–2004 (hectolitres)

	1970	1971	1972	1973	1974	1975	1976	1977	1978
Château- Grillet	65	47	28	84	87	40	87	63	29
Condrieu	138	142	66	206	122	105	176	115	96
Cornas	1,787	1,022	1,145	2,029	1,586	810	1,424	1,354	1,551
Côte-Rôtie	2,355	1,562	1,428	2,927	1,831	1,468	2,132	2,108	3,077
Crozes- Hermitage	19,542	13,203	19,768	27,997	21,044	17,748	20,014	17,584	27,106
Hermitage	5,576	3,128	3,356	4,108	3,859	2,022	3,304	3,159	3,136
St-Joseph	3,145	1,821	1,962	4,093	4,310	2,188	4,684	3,812	5,726
St-Péray	1,453	1,458	1,183	1,447	1,716	880	1,447	1,646	1,061

	1979	1980	1981	1982	1983	1984	1985	1986	1987
Château- Grillet	97	116	75	91	137	144	53	91	97
Condrieu	298	363	310	390	426	622	449	894	822
Cornas	1,854	1,894	1,718	1,979	1,799	1,699	1,731	2,858	2,615
Côte-Rôtie	4,128	3,378	4,185	4,661	4,729	3,516	2,631	3,803	4,092
Crozes- Hermitage	34,387	40,783	33,541	36,166	29,965	38,222	39,509	41,161	40,026
Hermitage	4,895	4,582	4,093	4,712	4,636	3,999	4,340	4,340	6,180
St-Joseph	8,492	7,836	10,272	10,607	17,321	12,411	13,542	17,531	18,303
St-Péray	1,423	1,981	2,053	2,325	2,307	2,003	1,810	2,789	3,167

continued

	1988	1989	1990	1991	1992	1993	1994	1995	1996
Château-Grillet	57	78	158	111	136	88	108	71	124
Condrieu	688	1,183	1,711	1,517	2,309	2,003	2,483	2,175	3,669
Cornas	2,420	3,082	3,059	2,907	2,284	3,092	2,956	2,581	3,451
Côte-Rôtie	4,984	6,952	4,461	6,300	6,284	7,037	7,713	6,795	8,539
Crozes-Hermitage	44,290	51,148	49,517	47,971	36,448	34,478	43,758	43,103	50,257
Hermitage	5,010	5,373	5,361	5,525	3,775	4,369	4,064	3,635	4,418
St-Joseph	17,613	22,203	22,833	24,792	21,755	25,425	27,581	25,681	31,693
St-Péray	2,097	2,626	2,784	1,818	1,659	2,693	2,246	1,897	2,029

	1997	1998	1999	2000	2001	2002	2003	2004	2005
Château-Grillet	131	93	147	124	110	78	24	90	91
Condrieu	3,868	2,482	4,131	4,111	4,169	3,575	2,788	4,700	4,395
Cornas	3,435	2,761	4,029	4,008	3,999	3,213	2,375	3,823	3,529
Côte-Rôtie	8,304	6,920	7,115	8,625	8,746	7,070	4,984	9,549	8,420
Crozes-Hermitage	58,944	56,566	60,782	61,897	61,666	54,672	39,110	61,023	60,679
Hermitage	4,680	4,767	5,857	5,670	5,581	4,229	3,637	4,783	4,295
St-Joseph	32,722	23,246	34,499	37,920	36,993	30,633	23,061	37,343	35,961
St-Péray	2,560	1,493	2,730	2,556	2,558	1,975	1,644	2,501	1,682

Appendix Four

Rhône Valley Exports

Year	VOLUME (HECTOLITRES)	VALUE IN FF MILLIONS	VALUE IN € MILLIONS
1965	122,278	34.09	4.87
1968	170,204	46.31	6.62
1969	185,380	55.26	7.89
1970	191,416	73.62	10.52
1971	231,029	89.41	12.77
1972	271,897	123.06	17.58
1973	352,256	169.57	24.22
1974	364,598	60.65	22.95
1975	418,025	71.48	24.50
1976	368,637	98.16	28.31
1977	374,907	254.76	36.39
1978	392,685	313.47	44.78
1979	451,804	54.04	50.58
1980	516,282	77.27	53.90
1981	602,365	462.04	66.01
1982	541,900	53.91	79.13
1983	584,293	90.69	84.38
1984	599,134	61.16	94.45
1985	605,186	37.25	105.32
1986	667,403	03.19	114.74

Year	VOLUME (HECTOLITRES)	VALUE IN FF MILLIONS	VALUE IN € MILLIONS
1987	685,086	856.92	122.42
1988	669,749	889.42	127.06
1989	673,465	938.72	134.10
1990	619,776	940.52	134.36
1991	632,512	947.28	135.33
1992	652,862	992.07	141.72
1993	398,578	529.13	75.59
1994	550,964	814.36	116.33
1995	624,129	1,013.68	144.81
1996	777,293		
1997	904,950		232.87
1998	982,323		263.85
1999	992,494		272.71
2000	1,064,185		313.43
2001	1,023,618		325.76
2002	994,922		342.91
2003	886,223		312.91
2004	783,128		265.38
2005	761,723		261.92

Appendix Five

Rhône Exports by Country (hectolitres)

	UK	BELGIUM, LUXEMBOURG	NETHERLANDS	GERMANY	DENMARK	SWEDEN, FINLAND, NORWAY, ICELAND	SWITZERLAND	USA	CANADA	JAPAN	SOUTH-EAST ASIA
1951	1,738	4,445	391	6,620		29	11,573	957			
1952	1,390	2,993	674	7,553			9,663				
1959	1,999	8,508	1,591	18,962	1,150	1,422	18,841	4,540	292	71	
1961	2,141	10,749	2,114	16,749	2,833	2,909	26,375	6,639	550	40	
1962	2,077	10,658	1,744	19,269			30,731				
1966	7,550	19,319	4,223	19,534	4,191	5,257	50,071	12,852	1,127	59	
1971	14,613	28,304	7,111	25,398	10,736	5,802	93,027	22,825	3,827	419	
1972	18,585	36,628	14,409	25,057			97,767				
1976	24,213	49,685	26,409	31,365	22,748	17,187	137,974	24,049	9,734	906	
1981	55,043	104,351	61,327	68,235	36,781	20,192	177,303	24,005	21,965	1,458	
1985	82,953	76,224	75,832	66,749	25,150	12,515	153,583	32,264	37,517	3,478	

Year										
1986	95,614	87,626	94,779	79,755	20,464	15,631	163,437	26,204	33,564	5,423	
1987	99,485	91,957	95,887	87,483	25,614	16,137	162,882	23,094	32,325	4,933	
1988	111,048	92,805	93,345	92,115	23,499	14,435	137,247	23,651	26,484	8,291	
1989	109,021	90,546	89,212	81,455	17,018	14,147	158,891	22,794	34,314	7,416	
1990	108,459	85,854	81,172	83,175	12,192	11,591	137,585	22,833	26,290	6,429	
1991	117,216	92,266	94,072	83,834	12,632	8,677	133,052	19,159	23,811	4,979	
1992	120,235	101,182	100,500	78,207	13,015	7,234	127,013	28,148	29,589	6,040	
1993	44,675	54,941	66,716	51,623	27,086	6,977	75,765	18,759	17,137	4,346	
1994	79,365	93,982	79,858	50,841	14,594	8,069	124,687	26,618	20,167	6,389	
1995	104,003	102,922	97,570	66,784	12,021	4,649	129,578	27,352	25,139	10,375	
1996	129,287	137,175	129,262	88,032	18,261	16,573	141,245	40,236	28,767	12,547	
1997	175,210	151,170	134,748	103,637	22,591	15,544	149,897	46,892	28,332	25,427	5,415
1998	180,393	176,944	160,105	102,023	36,349	21,390	133,175	44,896	31,915	54,808	
1999	190,518	198,657	141,160	111,349	41,612		136,843	52,907	32,145	24,971	
2000	203,755	191,798	144,385	116,727	55,867		127,054	81,433	46,018	30,307	
2001	222,491	154,075	126,272	100,258	52,552	33,765	115,246	82,762	49,260	31,172	2,857
2002	221,871	153,598	132,647	83,208	53,692	23,154	111,421	88,224	32,396	28,384	2,489
2003	194,705	146,630	103,847	75,338	55,173	12,154	105,376	73,527	47,022	23,261	2,110
2004	177,376	127,529	91,697	62,308	44,691	10,547	102,155	62,098	41,362	20,290	2,454
2005	199,093	119,393	77,356	57,832	49,375		84,079	65,553	33,456	21,687	

Appendix Six

Weather Records for Crozes-Hermitage 1972–2001

	JAN.	FEB.	MAR.	APRIL	MAY	JUNE	JULY	AUG.	SEPT.	OCT.	NOV.	DEC.	YEAR AVERAGE
Temperature*													
Maximum	6.7	8.7	12.9	15.6	20.8	24.2	27.5	27.2	22.7	17.1	10.6	7.3	16.8
Average	3.5	4.9	8.1	10.3	15	18.2	21.1	20.8	17.0	12.5	7.0	4.3	11.9
Minimum	0.3	1.1	3.2	5.1	9.3	12.3	14.6	14.3	11.1	7.9	3.3	1.3	7.0
Rainfall													
Monthly average	51.3	46.0	59.7	77.0	82.2	66.7	54.5	60.2	106.6	112.1	73.1	51.5	840.8
Days above 1 mm	8.0	7.5	7.7	9.1	9.6	8.2	5.4	5.8	7.1	9.3	8.1	7.8	93.6
Days above 10 mm	1.3	1.1	1.7	2.5	2.5	2.0	1.9	2.0	2.8	3.3	2.0	1.6	24.8

*Frost Dec.–Feb. average 57 days, 1972–2001

NOTE: The Marsaz weather station is five miles northeast of the village of Crozes-Hermitage, at 160 metres. Displayed are the average monthly temperatures and rainfall totals recorded at the station for the years 1972–2001. Temperatures in degrees centigrade, rainfall in millimetres. 20 degrees centigrade = 68 degrees Fahrenheit; 25.4 mm = 1 inch.
Source: Gaudriot study of the Ilôts Vitrines du Crozes-Hermitage, Feb. 2003.

Appendix Seven

Calendar of Wine Fairs

JANUARY

AROUND 20 JAN.

Ampuis—the Marché aux Vins, or Fair of the Wines of Côte-Rôtie, with other northern Rhône wines present as well. Lasts four days, two of them for the public, the others for wine trade. The weekend chosen is always that of Saint-Vincent, patron saint of *vignerons*.

Contact: +33(0)474 561820

FEBRUARY

AROUND 26 FEB.

Tain l'Hermitage—the Marché aux Vins, or public Fair of the Wines of Hermitage, with other northern Rhône wines present as well. There are celebrations in the town; this is a communal event. Always the last weekend of February.

Contact: +33(0)475 080681

MARCH

AROUND 20 MARCH

All along the Rhône Valley—Découvertes en Vallée du Rhône. This is a five-day moving tour of the northern and southern Rhône areas with tasting halls in each *appellation*. Held every two years—2005, 2007, 2009—the northern section lasts two days, the first covering Condrieu and Côte-Rôtie, the second the remaining *appellations*. It is aimed at wine trade professionals.

Contact: +33(0)490 272400

APRIL/MAY

EARLY APRIL OR MAY

Crozes-Hermitage—De Caves en Caves, a weekend when 25 domaines open their doors for visitors to try the wines and talk to the growers.

Contact: +33(0)475 079150

SEPTEMBER

AROUND 5 SEPT.

St-Péray—the Marché aux Vins de la Vallée du Rhône, a veritable spectacle of street processions and conviviality, with other northern Rhône wines present. A very full weekend—strong stamina recommended. Open to all.

Contact: +33(0)475 082865

AROUND 5 SEPT.

The Fête de la Clairette de Die et les Terres Gourmands. In the pretty eastern Drôme area of Clairette de Die, this event on the first weekend of September includes local products like olives and truffles from nearby villages. Open to all.

Contact: Syndicat des AoCs de Die, BP 4, 26340 Vercheny or +33(0)475 215599

DECEMBER

Cornas—Marché aux Vins de Cornas, or public Fair of the Wines of Cornas. It includes other northern Rhône wines, and is a popular Ardèche event. Always the first weekend of December.

Contact: +33(0)475 403364

Chavanay—Marché aux Vins de Chavanay, or public Fair of the Wines of Chavanay. It includes other northern Rhône wines. The two weekend days are for public visitors, and the Monday is for wine trade. Always the second weekend of December.

Contact: +33(0)474 872474

Appendix Eight

Wine Stores Stocking Northern Rhône Wines

Antic Wine 18 rue du Boeuf, 69005 Lyon
+33 (0)478 370896
1,800 wines listed, the zany Georges dos Santos (aka The Flying Sommelier) at the helm. 250 Rhônes, including several Côte-Rôties.

La Bouteillerie 41-43 Route Nationale 86, BP 27, 69420 Condrieu
+33(0)474 598496
Owned by Philippe Gérin and the ebullient Olivier Leteinturier, this displays a very sound cross section of prominent names in the northern Rhône, with a decent exposure to the southern Rhône as well.

Cave Malleval 11 rue Emile Zola, 69002 Lyon
+33 (0)478 420207
A classic wine store, near the Place Bellecour; 2,500 wines, 600 Rhônes

La Cave de Pic 2 place Aristide Briand, 26000 Valence
+33 (0)475 441667
Run by Anne-Sophie Pic of the famous restaurant family, this offers a selection of 500 Rhône wines. Conducts tastings with growers present.

Le Cercle des Vignerons 98 Boulevard des Allées, 69420 Ampuis
+33 (0)474 567229
Richard Dommerc was for some years the manager of Domaine de Bonserine at Côte-Rôtie. He is well informed and sells the wines from very small producers as well as some of the classics. There is a simple *bistrot* as well.

Compagnie de l'Hermitage 7 place du Taurobole, 26600 Tain l'Hermitage
+33(0)475 081970
A fixture at Hermitage for 20 years, Le Grec—Georges Lelektsoglou—sells the most luxurious bottles of good Rhône, north and south, as well as a sprinkling of midsized domaines. Prices can be high, but the wines are available.

Espace Vins Foch 65 ave Foch, 69006 Lyon
+33 (0)478 894461
800 wines listed

Paris Friand 7 avenue P. Sémard, 26000 Valence
+33 (0)475 440676
400 wines listed, with a Rhône emphasis

Les Terrasses du Rhône rue Joseph Péala, 26600 Tain l'Hermitage
+33(0)475 084056
Run with great enthusiasm by Fabien Louis, this is a veritable one-man show. If no one turns up, he goes home. If people stay late, he stays late. Has tasted and visited widely, good for small domaines. Simple food. Hangout of especially younger growers.

Les Vins du Rhône No. 75 RN86, 42410 Chavanay
+33(0)474 482133
Marc Jurdit runs this shop that is on the N86 at Chavanay, next to the Restaurant Alain Charles.

Vinum 26 place Jean-Jaurès, 26100 Romans-sur-Isère
+33(0)475 729036
150 different wines, including top northern and southern Rhônes

GLOSSARY

APPELLATION D'ORIGINE CONTRÔLÉE The certificate of authenticity attached to wines of a high quality: such wines must conform to strict rules on grape varieties, yields, and alcohol levels in order to merit the status. The word *appellation* by itself refers to a specific vineyard area—e.g., Côte-Rôtie, St-Joseph.

ARZELLE Local term used at Condrieu and southern Côte-Rôtie hamlets of Tupin and Semons for the sanded granite topsoil of the hillside vineyards.

BAN DES VENDANGES Public proclamation of the start of the harvest.

BARRIQUE The Bordeaux name for their small ageing casks of 225 litres.

BÂTONNAGE Stirring of the wine's lees after fermentation. A Burgundian technique used there to increase the richness of the wine, activating the particles at the bottom of a cask.

BENEAU A conical grape harvest holder, made either of wood or, more commonly, plastic, that is carried on the back.

BIGOT A special hoe used in the northern Rhône vineyards.

BIODYNAMIC The extension of organic farming whereby applications of composts and even ground horn are applied to the soil to nourish its minerals and to foster the health of the vines. A lunar calendar is followed, set in place by Rudolph Steiner's follower Maria Thun. The prevailing tone is of thoughtful respect and active nurturing of the balance between land, sun, and solar system.

BISE The local term in the northern Rhône for the prevailing north wind.

BONBONNE A large glass jug, stoppered with a flat, wide cork, used for holding bulk drinking wine. An average capacity is 10 to 15 litres.

BOULES The steel balls that are used in the target game of PÉTANQUE; also the name of the game itself.

CAVISTE A cellar worker.

CÉPAGE A grape variety—Syrah or Marsanne, for instance.

CHAI A standing cellar, above ground.

CHALAIS A dried-stone terrace.

CHAPEAU The top of fermenting grapes, mainly skins and pips, and bits of stalk if included.

CHAPTALISATION The addition of prescribed sugar at fermentation to boost alcohol levels. Rarely required, except in rainy years like 2002. Growers can add the equivalent of 1.5° alcohol, for instance. Chaptalised wines can carry a discernible "sweetness" that stands outside the fruit impact on the palate.

CLAIE A straw or cane mat. Often used in making VIN DE PAILLE.

CLIMAT A named section within a vineyard. The noble title for the best sites.

CLONE A reproduction of a vine variety geared towards control of a particular deficiency or weakness. The early clones of the 1970s sought to increase yields, and so counteract poor fruit formation or COULURE, for instance. The blights of perishing Syrah and the esca mushroom today have notably hit clones planted in the late 1980s.

CONFIT Crystallised fruit; close to *confiture*, the word for jam. Found in low-acidity vintages like 1997, or when the red grapes have been deliberately picked late. Can be a texture aimed by growers at drinkers with a sweet tooth.

CÔTE Slope.

COTEAU Hillside; *demi-coteau* is a gentle incline, *pied de coteau* is a much-used euphemism for flat ground.

COULURE Malformation of the fruit at the time of flowering, often in late May. The vine's bunches remain partially formed.

CRU Growth, as in a grower's best wine.

CUVE A vat

CUVÉE After *assemblage*, or the assembly of different vats, a final integrated wine. *Tête de cuvée* represents the very best wine that a grower makes in any one year.

DÉLESTAGE A technique to aereate and invigorate a fermenting vat; around two-thirds of the vat is drained off to another vat and a few hours later is poured back over the cap of the first vat. Used for colour and material extraction.

DEMI-MUID A cask of 550 to 600 litres. The oak-wine interaction is gentler than that in a 228-litre cask.

DÉROGATION The right to sell, under the full *appellation contrôlée* label, wine that is in excess of the statutory quantity allowed.

EAU-DE-VIE Distilled alcohol spirit. *Eau-de-vie de marc* refers to the spirit taken from the distilled grape MARC left over after fermentation.

ÉGRAPPAGE Destalking of the grapes prior to fermentation.

ÉLEVAGE Cask or vat raising of the young wine after its fermentation.

ÉRAFLAGE Destemming or destalking of the grapes before fermentation.

FINING To clarify a wine, egg white or a solution called bentonite can be added to draw out loose particles. This is practised much less today than in the past.

FOUDRE A large barrel—running into sizes such as 3,000 litres or more—used for raising and maturing wine.

FOULAGE Crushing of grapes before fermentation.

FÛT Term for a cask—as in *vieilli en fûts de chêne* (aged in oak casks) found on some labels, where the grower vaunts the oak influence on his or her wine.

GALET A stone. Often used to refer to small stones.

GARRIGUE The hill and plateau scrubland in southern France that is home to herbs, crickets, and dry, often stony soil. A spring or summer walk quickly assails the senses with the mixed fragrant aromas and scents of these parched outcrops.

GÉNÉRIQUE Generic, or the wine of the most basic quality in a grower's lineup. Interchangeable with, and more nobly expressed by, the term *classique*, for the simple wine of an estate.

GIBIER Game, as in birds and beasts.

GNEISS Metamorphic rock like granite that contains quartz, white mica, and feldspars. As it weathers, its colour lightens.

GORE Term used to denote rotted granite that has broken down from its hard rock texture. Sanded particles can be present.

GOÛT DE TERROIR Literally, earthy taste. It really means a profound, very "thick" flavour in a wine that is thought to be drawn from the soil composition of its vineyards.

GRAIN A single grape.

GRANITE The dark-brown rock that weathers and breaks down over time. It is quartz and feldspar rich but poor in iron and magnesium. A tough rock, it can be used for walls and houses and even cities like Aberdeen in Scotland.

GRÈS Sandstone.

INAO Institut National des Appellations d'Origine. The state-sponsored body that manages the *appellation* system in France.

INOX Stainless steel.

KAOLIN White clay, especially that found at Crozes-Hermitage. Also used to make earthenware or pizza ovens.

LEES The leftovers after fermentation, particles that include yeasts and that can be stirred to activate and enrich the wine.

LIEU-DIT A specific site name within the vineyards of an *appellation*—*Bessards* or *Méal* at Hermitage, for instance. The term used by the mapmakers, although the word CLIMAT is more noble and poetic.

LIQUEUR DE TIRAGE A blend of sugar and yeasts, which is added to wine at the moment it is bottled to encourage a further fermentation.

LOESS Loose, sandy-silty soil—dusty and compact when piled up. Known as "dead soil" by growers, and often selected for Marsanne rather than Syrah. The CLIMAT known as *L'Hermite* at Hermitage contains loess areas high up.

MAISON DU VIN A wine house. The term often indicates an owner of vineyards who doubles as a merchant in other wines.

MAITRE DE CHAI A cellar master.

MALOLACTIC FERMENTATION The transformation of the wine's malic acid into lactic acid, after the primary, alcoholic fermentation. In a vintage like 2003, the malic acid levels were low due to the extreme ripeness, and the malos took place early and quickly.

MARC The crushed leftovers of the pulp after it has been pressed. It is composed mainly of skins, pips, and stalks and is often distilled to produce grape-flavoured spirit.

MASSALE Selection of vines through taking cuttings from current healthy plants. The old, traditional way of propagation, before the advent of clones.

MÉTHODE CHAMPENOISE Wine that is made sparkling through the application of the pure champagne-making process.

MÉTIER Profession or craft.

MICRO-OXYGENATION A technique to accelerate the softening of a wine through exposure to air. It also eliminates the need to rack or transfer the wine from one cask to another, and is used to avoid the stinkiness of Syrah known as REDUCTION.

MILDEW Fungal pest that affects the vine, often early in the growing cycle after poor weather. Related to OÏDIUM.

MORAINE The debris carried down and deposited by a shifting glacier—likely to be light soil and stones.

MUID An old term for a Rhône Valley barrel of 675 litres' capacity. Also used in Burgundy.

MUTAGE The addition of alcohol spirit to a wine, so the latter is fortified.

NATURE A still wine.

NÉGOCIANT A wine merchant. The Rhône tradition has been for *négociants* like Chapoutier, Guigal, and Paul Jaboulet Aîné to own vineyards as well as to buy grapes and wine from external sources.

NÉGOCIANT-ÉLEVEUR A merchant who buys grapes and/or wine. The wine is raised in his or her cellars to mature until ready for sale.

OÏDIUM Powdery form of MILDEW. The Roussanne vine is especially susceptible.

OUILLAGE The topping up of a cask following the evaporation of its wine.

PARCELLE A plot of vineyard—often small in the northern Rhône due to the split between children from inheritance. This can mean growers moving between 25 *parcelles* when their holding is under 10 hectares.

PASSERILLAGE Grapes used for sweet wines when they have started to dry and become low in juice and rich in sugar. Not to be confused with botrytis grapes, where rot is present.

PÉPIN A grape pip.

PÉTANQUE The very popular French game of bowls, played with small metal balls.

PHENOLS The word for the tannic elements and their maturity in a wine. It refers to stalks, skins, and stems. They often lag the sugar in the ripening cycle, and since the 1980s, growers have become much more aware of this aspect of the vineyard process.

PHYLLOXERA The bug that destroyed most of the French vineyards in the 1870s. Vineyards were ripped out or flooded in attempts to overcome it, until the solution of grafting on to disease-resistant American rootstock was found.

PICHET A short wooden stump used for immersing the CHAPEAU during fermentation.

PIÈCE A cask of 228 litres' (Burgundy size, most common in the Rhône) or 225 litres' (Bordeaux size) capacity. It serves to age the wine.

PIGEAGE The immersion of the cap, or CHAPEAU, of skins and pips in the juice during a vat's fermentation. Increasingly done by machine rather than manually.

PORTEUR A carrier of the harvest.

POUDINGUE A local word, especially used at Hermitage, for the clods of earth and stones stuck together and found on sites like *La Croix*. It is an alluvial stone-clay–sandstone mix.

POURRITURE Rotting of the grapes.

PRIMEUR A short-lived wine that is made by an abbreviated vinification process. It is released for sale in the middle of November, and also passes under the name *vin nouveau*. Wine sales *en primeur* refer to the trading of the wine before it has been bottled.

PROPRIÉTAIRE-NÉGOCIANT A vineyard owner who supplements his or her wine holding by buying other people's grapes or wine.

PROPRIÉTAIRE-RÉCOLTANT A vineyard owner who makes nothing but his own wine.

PUPITRE A wooden holder in which bottles of wine made by the MÉTHODE CHAMPENOISE accumulate their deposit around the neck of the bottle.

QUARTIER A section of a vineyard.

RACKING The transfer of wine during its raising from one cask to another. Done to freshen the wine.

RAISIN ENTIER A whole, uncrushed grape. A term used when the grapes are not crushed before fermentation.

RAPÉ The discard, or rejected portion, of the grape harvest. Such overripe or underripe grapes can be made into a wine of the same name, subject to a special tasting.

REDUCTION The stinky, farmyard, or stewed fruit gums smell that afflicts the Syrah and other varieties like the Tannat if the wine is not exposed to oxygen during its vinification and raising. Solved by RACKING.

REMONTAGE The pumping of the bottom of a vat of wine over the top, or CHAPEAU, during its fermentation. This helps to keep the *chapeau* cool and aids colour extraction.

REMUAGE The "turning" of bottles of sparkling wine made by the traditional champagne method. It acts to lodge any deposits in the neck of the bottle.

ROBE The general appearance of a wine; not only its colour but also its lustre or brilliance.

ROOTSTOCK The underground part of the vine that, after the phylloxera attack in the 1870s, became usually sourced from America. This is grafted on to the vine variety.

SAIGNÉE The bleeding off of early juice from a vat to allow the colour to intensify.

SCHIST A layered, recrystallised rock that is grey or sometimes blue tinged. It is crisp and breakable, and can be referred to as shale. It is high in mica content, both black and white. Talc is derived from schist.

SOMMELIER (SOMMELIÈRE) A wine waiter (waitress).

SOUS-BOIS A tasting term describing an advanced stage in the evolution of the bouquet of Syrah wines. Literally, like damp leaves in an autumn forest, or the slightly rotting smell when lifting up a long-untouched piece of wood.

SYNDICAT DES VIGNERONS A Wine Growers Union.

TERROIR The French word for the place, microclimate, air, sky, and natural influences on a vineyard. Nothing to do with winemaking that uses tricks or additives, nor is it to do with the narrow definition of a grape variety.

TONNEAU A wine barrel of no specific dimension.

TONNELIER A cooper.

TRIAGE A qualitative sorting of the grape harvest.

VENDANGE(S) The grape harvest. The word is used in both singular and plural form.

VENDANGEUR A grape picker.

VIEILLES VIGNES Literally, Old Vines. Definitions vary, but this should be a wine made from the grower's oldest plantings, at least 30 years old. At Hermitage and Cornas, the tradition has long been for plots of 60 years and upwards.

VIGNERON (VIGNERONNE) A wine grower.

VIN DE GARDE A long-lived wine, one suitable for laying down.

VIN DÉLIMITÉ DE QUALITÉ SUPÉRIEURE Literally, a delimited wine of superior quality. This is the category below APPELLATION CONTRÔLÉE, and the winemaking rulings, although similar in form, are accordingly less demanding.

VIN DE MÉDECINE A "booster" wine used to fill out a weak wine. Hermitage served this purpose for Bordeaux for many decades before PHYLLOXERA.

VIN DE PAILLE Literally, "straw wine." It is a white wine made from grapes that are left to dry out completely before fermentation. The Marsanne variety at Hermitage is well suited to this.

VIN DE PAYS The regional wine quality where the vine variety can be named on the label. Permitted yields are much higher than they are for the full *appellation* wines. The most popular and successful one in the northern Rhône is the *vin de pays des Collines Rho-*

daniennes, from the slopes and high ground above Côte-Rôtie and St-Joseph.

VIN DE TABLE Table wine—a wine that bears no particular name and, often, no particular quality.

VIN DE TOUS LES JOURS An everyday drinking wine

VIN MOUSSEUX Sparkling wine.

VIN ORDINAIRE Ordinary wine, like *vin de table*, the most basic category of wine that exists in France.

VOLATILE ACIDITY The acidity that accrues if wine is too exposed to air during its preparation; mainly acetic acid. The wine is on the way to vinegar if there is too much, but all the best wines of history have contained some. In excess, gives a sickly, flat taste to the wine.

VRAC Goods that are transported in bulk. In the wine world the term refers to wines that have not been bottled before they are moved around. *Vrac* sales are a way for a grower to get early cash flow after the harvest.

INDEX

Page numbers in italic refer to figures and maps.

INTERIOR DESIGN: Victoria Kuskowski
CARTOGRAPHER: Hayden Foell
COMPOSITION: Michael Bass Associates
TEXT: 9/13 Scala, Scala Caps
DISPLAY: Scala Sans, Scala Sans Caps